Rα

CRITICAL SURVEY

OF

LONG FICTION

CRITICAL SURVEY

OF

LONG FICTION

Second Revised Edition

Volume 1

Chinua Achebe - Karel Čapek

Editor, Second Revised Edition
Carl Rollyson
Baruch College, City University of New York

Editor, First Edition, English and Foreign Language Series
Frank N. Magill

SALEM PRESS, INC.
Pasadena, California   Hackensack, New Jersey

Managing Editor: Christina J. Moose
Research Supervisor: Jeffry Jensen
Acquisitions Editor: Mark Rehn
Photograph Editor: Karrie Hyatt
Manuscript Editors: Lauren M. D'Andrea, Doug Long
Research Assistant: Jun Ohnuki
Production Editor: Cynthia Beres
Layout: William Zimmerman
Graphics: Yasmine Cordoba

Some of the essays in this work, which have been updated, originally appeared in the following Salem Press publications: *Critical Survey of Long Fiction, English Language Series, Revised Edition* (1991), *Critical Survey of Long Fiction, Foreign Language Series* (1984).

Library of Congress Cataloging-in-Publication Data

Critical survey of long fiction / editor, Carl Rollyson ; editor, English and foreign language series, Frank N. Magill.—2nd rev. ed.

p. cm.

"The current reference work both updates and substantially adds to the previous editions of the Critical survey from which it is partially drawn: the Critical survey of long fiction. English language series, revised edition (1991) and the Critical survey of long fiction. Foreign language series (1984)"—Publisher's note.

Includes bibliographical references and index.

ISBN 0-89356-883-X (v. 1 : alk. paper) — ISBN 0-89356-882-1 (set : alk. paper)

1. Fiction—History and criticism. 2. Fiction—Bio-bibliography—Dictionaries. I. Rollyson, Carl E. (Carl Edmund) II. Magill, Frank Northen, 1907-1997.

PN3451.C75 2000
809.3—dc21   00-020195

First Printing

PRINTED IN THE UNITED STATES OF AMERICA

CONTENTS

PUBLISHER'S NOTE

The *Critical Survey of Long Fiction, Second Revised Edition*, follows in the Magill tradition of Critical Survey series, providing in-depth overviews of major authors in one of the major literary genres: long fiction (the novel, novella, and related long forms).

Consisting of eight volumes covering 463 world authors and 53 major areas of study, the current reference work both updates and substantially adds to the previous editions of the *Critical Survey* from which it is partially drawn: the *Critical Survey of Long Fiction, English Language Series, Revised Edition* (1991) and the *Critical Survey of Long Fiction, Foreign Language Series* (1984). First, the current *Second Revised Edition* combines the most important and most often studied authors from both of the older sets: Of the 332 English-language authors in the 1991 revised edition, 298 have been retained, the remainder weeded because they are rarely or no longer taught; of the original 182 foreign-language authors in the 1984 foreign-language series, 103 were selected for inclusion in this *Second Revised Edition*; and of the combined 401 author essays, fully 138 have been substantially updated. To these have been added 62 new author essays, covering figures previously omitted or who, over the past decade, have earned their place in classroom discussion—from such classic authors as Louisa May Alcott, Isaac Asimov, and Alan Paton to established contemporary voices such as Rudolfo A. Anaya, Bebe Moore Campbell, Barbara Kingsolver, Michael Ondaatje, Leslie Marmon Silko, and Tom Wolfe.

Librarians and their patrons often wonder what a publisher means by "updating"—especially relevant to a compilation of essays many of which concern writers who are still actively contributing to their body of work. All parts of the essays were scrutinized: The authors' latest books and other publications were added to the front-matter and back-matter listings of their works; new translations were added to listings for foreign-language authors; and deceased authors' listings were re-checked for accuracy as well as currency. Having identified 263 of the original articles as not in need of substantial updating (most of these authors died long ago), Salem's editors and researchers nevertheless reviewed all listings for these authors, and Editor Carl Rollyson carefully reviewed these authors' annotated bibliographies, weeding out superseded citations and adding previously overlooked, new, and important entries for students who are seeking secondary sources for further study. In addition, those 138 author essays deemed in need of updating by academic experts received similar and even fuller attention: Each section of text was reviewed to ensure that, for example, major awards were added to "Achievements"; that new biographical details were incorporated into "Biography" for still-living authors; and that the "Analysis" examined one or more recently published works of long fiction. The bibliographies of these articles were also updated.

The first seven volumes of the resulting *Second Revised Edition*, therefore, contain 463 essays on novelists likely to be studied in most high school and undergraduate classrooms in the English-speaking world. They are arranged alphabetically by author's last name. The basic format of these articles remains the same as in the previous edition of the *Critical Survey*: Beginning with full data on dates and places of birth and death, ready-reference top matter includes a list of the author's "Principal Long Fiction" (original title, original date of publication, English title-in-translation, and English translation date). The brief overview of "Other Literary Forms" places the author in a larger literary context: The fact that Samuel Beckett was equally well known as a dramatist, for example, or that Ann Beattie is also a major voice in the short form, is noted here. Two longer sections, "Achievements" and "Biography," follow. The former summarizes the author's innovations and contributions to literature, as well as noting any major honors and awards. The latter rehearses the basic life events, from birth and upbringing to death (or the present day, for authors still living).

The meat of the author essays will be found in the section headed "Analysis," in which the author's work *in the long fiction form* is described and examined in terms of its themes, typical concerns, characters, motifs, and the like. Subsections within this major portion of the text are headed plainly with the titles of works that receive special or prolonged attention. It is here that students will learn, for example, that William Melvin Kelley's novels are sufficiently interrelated to be called sagas, as well as other general information about the writer's novelistic production. In the subsections that follow, students will find description and analysis of selected important novels—learning, for example, that Kelley's *A Different Drummer* (1962), set in the Civil Rights era, bases its narrative in the fundamental issues of race relations in the United States.

The final section of each of the author essays, "Bibliography" lists both classic and up-to-date resources deemed most useful to students approaching the writer's work for the first time. Candidates for inclusion in the Bibliography include biographies, literary surveys, monographs, and other book-length secondary works geared to a student or general audience; occasionally, however, journal articles, interviews, or chapters in books are also included—particularly where book-length works are less likely to be widely available (as for very contemporary novelists such as Paul Auster). As previously mentioned, each of the older essays' bibliographies was reviewed and updated; the 62 newly written author essays contain bibliographies that are up to date by virtue of having been generated within a few months of publication.

Volume 8 has been devoted to a set of 53 surveys of long fiction, arranged in four sections: Long Fiction in History (chronological overviews), World Long Fiction (covering major regions of the world), North American Long Fiction (covering various groups and genres in the United States and Canada), and Genre Overviews (addressing prominent ongoing subgenres, from the detective novel to feminist fiction). These lengthy essays include not only updated versions of the original 29 essays from the *English Language Series* and the *Foreign Language Se-*

ries but also 24 entirely new essays to round out the set. Hence, for example, the old "Long Fiction in Antiquity" has been revised thoroughly and now appears as "Long Fiction in the Ancient Greco-Roman World," while "Origins and Development of the Novel, Since 1890" has been revised and updated as "Origins and Development of the Novel, 1890-1980" and a new essay, "Contemporary Long Fiction," has been added to review trends in the postwar world. "Postcolonial Long Fiction" also examines recent trends in a contemporary global community where issues of diversity and cultural conflict are increasingly expressed, and addressed, through fiction. Similarly, to the plate of updated essays covering parts of the world—from "African Long Fiction" and "Chinese Long Fiction" through "Spanish Long Fiction"— have been added several previously neglected, including "The Australian Novel," "Irish Long Fiction," and "The Middle Eastern Novel." North America has experienced a blossoming of interest in the long-fiction form as practiced by African Americans, Asian Americans, Canadians, Caribbeans, Jewish Americans, Latinos, Native Americans, immigrants, and Southerners—all of whom are represented in discrete essays here, for the first time. Finally, to the standard subgenre overviews, from the epistolary novel to the science-fiction novel, we have added several new essays to fill gaps and address major new areas of study, "Experimental Long Fiction," "Feminist Long Fiction," "Gay and Lesbian Long Fiction," "The Horror Novel," and "Self-Reflexive Long Fiction" among them.

Volume 8 ends with several tools for further research and better access to the wealth of information contained in the *Second Revised Edition*: An updated "Glossary of Literary Terms" defines basic literary concepts. The "Chronological List of Authors" organizes the 463 novelists covered in these volumes into a time line by year of birth, allowing students to identify contemporaries quickly. The "Geographical List of Authors" will give those looking for all Russians covered in these pages (for example) quick access to those authors. A "Categorized List of Authors" organizes each author under subgenre and subject matter headings. Finally, the Subject Index lists all titles, authors, and literary movements or terms that receive substantial discussion in these volumes.

Wherever possible, the original contributors of these essays were invited to update their work; we are equally indebted to the fine talents of the many academicians who took on the task of updating, or writing new material, for the book. Their names are listed in the "Contributors" section that follows. Finally, we are indebted to Professor Carl Rollyson of Baruch College, City University of New York for his care and counsel in the development of the table of contents for the *Second Revised Edition.*

CONTRIBUTORS TO THE *SECOND REVISED EDITION*

Carl Rollyson, Editor
Baruch College, City University of New York

McCrea Adams
Independent Scholar

Michael Adams
CUNY Graduate Center

Patrick Adcock
Henderson State University

Daniel Altamiranda
Universidad de Buenos Aires

Heather Russell Andrade
Barry University

Andrew J. Angyal
Elon College

Gerald S. Argetsinger
Rochester Institute of Technology

Karen L. Arnold
Montpelier Cultural Arts Center

Patricia Kennedy Bankhead
University of South Carolina

Thomas Banks
Ohio Northern University

Carl L. Bankston III
University of Southwestern Louisiana

James Barbour
Independent Scholar

Paula C. Barnes
Hampton University

David Barratt
Independent Scholar

Alvin K. Benson
Brigham Young University

Jacquelyn Benton
Metropolitan State College of Denver

Cynthia A. Bily
Adrian College

Margaret Boe Birns
New York University

Nicholas Birns
New School University

Mary A. Blackmon
Hardin-Simmons University

B. Diane Blackwood
Independent Scholar

Steve D. Boilard
Independent Scholar

Bernadette Lynn Bosky
Independent Scholar

Jay Boyer
Arizona State University

Virginia Brackett
Independent Scholar

Mary Hanford Bruce
Monmouth College

Faith Hickman Brynie
Independent Scholar

Susan Butterworth
Independent Scholar

Edmund J. Campion
University of Tennessee

Thomas Cassidy
South Carolina State University

Nancy E. Castro
Baruch College, CUNY

Allan Chavkin
Southwest Texas State University

Robin Payne Cohen
Southwest Texas State University

David W. Cole
*University of Wisconsin Center-
Baraboo*

David Conde
Metropolitan State College of Denver

Julian Connolly
University of Virginia

Richard Hauer Costa
Texas A&M University

David Cowart
University of South Carolina

Marsha Daigle-Williamson
Spring Arbor College

Clark Davis
Northeast Louisiana University

M. Casey Diana
*University of Illinois at Urbana-
Champaign*

Margaret A. Dodson
Independent Scholar

Stefan Dziemianowicz
Independent Scholar

Anita M. Eckhardt
Independent Scholar

Grace Farrell
Butler University

Cristina Farronato
University of California, San Diego

T. A. Fishman
Purdue University

Tom Frazier
Cumberland College

Kelly Fuller
Claremont Graduate University

Joe B. Fulton
Dalton State College

Ann D. Garbett
Averett College

Keith Garebian
Independent Scholar

Marshall Bruce Gentry
University of Indianapolis

Craig Gilbert
Portland State University

Lucy Golsan
Independent Scholar

Charles A. Gramlich
Xavier University of Louisiana

Jeffrey Greer
Western Michigan University

L. M. Grow
Broward Community College

Richard A. Spurgeon Hall
Methodist College

Betsy P. Harfst
Kishwaukee College

June Harris
University of Arizona - Sierra Vista

Stephen M. Hart
University College London

Peter B. Heller
Manhattan College

Cynthia Packard Hill
University of Massachusetts at Amherst

Arthur D. Hlavaty
Independent Scholar

Nika Hoffman
Crossroads School for Arts & Sciences

William Hoffman
Independent Scholar

John R. Holmes
Franciscan University of Steubenville

Gregory D. Horn
Southwest Virginia Community College

Pierre L. Horn
Wright State University

E. D. Huntley
Appalachian State University

Julie Husband
SUNY, Buffalo

Harland W. Jones III
University of South Carolina

Theresa M. Kanoza
Lincoln Land Community College

Steven G. Kellman
University of Texas at San Antonio

Grove Koger
Boise Public Library

Margaret Krausse
Linfield College

Ralph L. Langenheim Jr.
University of Illinois - Urbana

Eugene Larson
Pierce College

William Laskowski
Jamestown College

Linda Ledford-Miller
University of Scranton

Christine Levecq
University of Liege

Leon Lewis
Appalachian State University

R. C. Lutz
University of the Pacific

Janet McCann
Texas A&M University

Joanne McCarthy
Tacoma Community College

Gina Macdonald
Loyola University

Richard D. McGhee
Arkansas State University

Edythe M. McGovern
West Los Angeles College

Joseph McLaren
Hofstra University

David W. Madden
California State University, Sacramento

Mary E. Mahony
Wayne County Community College

Daryl F. Mallett
Independent Scholar

John L. Marsden
Indiana University of Pennsylvania

Charles E. May
California State University, Long Beach

Laurence W. Mazzeno
Alvernia College

Patrick Meanor
SUNY-College at Oneonta

Jaime Armin Mejía
Southwest Texas State University

Vasa D. Mihailovich
University of North Carolina

P. Andrew Miller
Northern Kentucky University

Kathleen N. Monahan
Saint Peter's College

Robert A. Morace
Daemen College

Roark Mulligan
Christopher Newport University

Daniel P. Murphy
Hanover College

John M. Muste
Ohio State University

William Nelles
*University of Massachusetts-
    Dartmouth*

Allan Nelson
Caldwell College

Elizabeth R. Nelson
Saint Peter's College

John Nizalowski
Mesa State College

Jim O'Loughlin
Penn State Erie - The Behrend College

Bruce Olsen
Austin Peay State University

James Norman O'Neill
Bryant College

Lisa Paddock
Independent Scholar

Robert J. Paradowski
Rochester Institute of Technology

David B. Parsell
Furman University

Marion Petrillo
Bloomsburg University

Mary Ellen Pitts
Rhodes College

Andrew B. Preslar
Lamar University at Orange

Victoria Price
Lamar University

Maureen J. Puffer-Rothenberg
Valdosta State University

Rosemary M. Canfield Reisman
Charleston Southern University

Martha E. Rhynes
*Oklahoma East Central State
    University*

J. Thomas Rimer
University of Pittsburgh

Carl Rollyson
Baruch College, CUNY

Paul Rosefeldt
Delgado Community College

Robert L. Ross
University of Texas at Austin

Sabah A. Salih
Bloomsburg University

Beverly Schneller
Millersville University

Chenliang Sheng
Northern Kentucky University

Nancy E. Sherrod
Armstrong Atlantic State University

Anne W. Sienkewicz
Independent Scholar

Thomas J. Sienkewicz
Monmouth College

Charles L. P. Silet
Iowa State University

Nirmala Singh
University of Michigan

Genevieve Slomski
Independent Scholar

Marjorie Smelstor
University of Wisconsin - Eau Claire

Gilbert Smith
North Carolina State University

Rebecca G. Smith
Barton College

Roger Smith
Independent Scholar

Traci S. Smrcka
Hardin-Simmons University

Jean M. Snook
Memorial University of Newfoundland

George Soule
Carleton College

Brian Stableford
Independent Scholar

Isabel Bonnyman Stanley
East Tennessee State University

Joshua Stein
University of California, Riverside

Karen F. Stein
University of Rhode Island

Judith L. Steininger
Milwaukee School of Engineering

J. David Stevens
Seton Hall University

Gerald H. Strauss
Bloomsburg University

Geralyn Strecker
Ball State University

Trey Strecker
Ball State University

Philip A. Tapley
Louisiana College

Judith K. Taylor
Northern Kentucky University

Christine D. Tomei
Columbia University

Richard Tuerk
Texas A&M University - Commerce

Scott D. Vander Ploeg
Madisonville Community College

Dennis Vannatta
University of Arkansas at Little Rock

Steven C. Walker
Brigham Young University

Jaquelyn W. Walsh
McNeese State University

Gary P. Walton
Northern Kentucky University

Qun Wang
California State University-Monterey Bay

Gladys J. Washington
Texas Southern University

Dennis L. Weeks
University of Great Falls

John T. West III
Grambling State University

Gary Westfahl
University of California, Riverside

James Whitlark
Texas Tech University

Albert Wilhelm
Tennessee Technological University

Thomas Willard
University of Arizona

Donna Glee Williams
The North Carolina Center for the Advancement of Teaching

Tyrone Williams
Xavier University

Judith Barton Williamson
Sauk Valley Community College

James A. Winders
Appalachian State University

Michael Witkoski
Independent Scholar

Gay Annette Zieger
Santa Fe Community College

CONTRIBUTORS TO THE *CRITICAL SURVEY OF LONG FICTION, ENGLISH LANGUAGE SERIES, REVISED EDITION* AND THE *CRITICAL SURVEY OF LONG FICTION, FOREIGN LANGUAGE SERIES*

Michael Adams
Timothy Dow Adams
Patrick Adcock
S. Krishnamoorthy Aithal
Terry L. Andrews
Andrew J. Angyal
Stanley Archer
Edwin T. Arnold III
Marilyn Arnold
Bryan Aubrey
Linda C. Badley
Jane L. Ball
Lowell A. Bangerter
Thomas Banks
Stanisław Barańczak
Dan Barnett
Carol M. Barnum
David Barratt

Jean-Pierre Barricelli
Fiora A. Bassanese
Joseph F. Battaglia
Robert Becker
Kirk H. Beetz
Kate Begnal
Todd K. Bender
Richard P. Benton
Frank Bergmann
Randi Birn
András Boros-Kazai
Frederick Bowers
Harold Branam
Anne Kelsch Breznau
J. R. Broadus
Joseph Bruchac
Carl Brucker
Domenic Bruni

Mitzi M. Brunsdale
Hallman B. Bryant
Paul Budra
C. F. Burgess
Suzan K. Burks
Jean-Pierre Cap
Karen Carmean
John Carpenter
Leonard Casper
Edgar L. Chapman
Allan Chavkin
John R. Clark
Samuel Coale
John L. Cobbs
Richard N. Coe
Steven E. Colburn
John J. Conlon
Deborah Core

David Cowart
Carol I. Croxton
Diane D'Amico
Reed Way Dasenbrock
J. Madison Davis
Mary E. Davis
Frank Day
Paul J. deGategno
Bill Delaney
Joan DelFattore
Lloyd N. Dendinger
A. A. DeVitis
Richard H. Dillman
Lillian Doherty
Henry J. Donaghy
David C. Dougherty
Virginia A. Duck
David B. Eakin
Roberto González Echevarría
Grace Eckley
Wilton Eckley
Bruce L. Edwards, Jr.
Robert P. Ellis
Ann Willardson Engar
Thomas L. Erskine
Howard Faulkner
William L. Felker
Richard A. Fine
Bruce E. Fleming
Robert J. Forman
Margot K. Frank
Howard Fraser
June M. Frazer
Kenneth Friedenreich
Miriam Fuchs
Robert L. Gale
Honora Rankine Galloway
Kristine Ottesen Garrigan
James R. Giles
L. H. Goldman
Dennis Goldsberry
Peter W. Graham
John R. Griffin
Stephen I. Gurney
Franz P. Haberl

Angela Hague
Jay L. Halio
David Mike Hamilton
Todd C. Hanlin
Terry L. Hansen
Klaus Hanson
John P. Harrington
Melanie Hawthorne
William J. Heim
Terry Heller
Greig E. Henderson
Erwin Hester
Jane Hill
James L. Hodge
Watson Holloway
Linda Howe
Helen Mundy Hudson
Edward W. Huffstetler
Mary Anne Hutchinson
Archibald E. Irwin
Abdul R. JanMohamed
Clarence O. Johnson
Betty H. Jones
Jane Anderson Jones
Feroza Jussawalla
Lothar Kahn
Deborah Kaplan
Irma M. Kashuba
Anna B. Katona
Catherine Kenney
Sue L. Kimball
Anne Mills King
James Reynolds Kinzey
John V. Knapp
Paula Kopacz
Sarah B. Kovel
Lawrence F. Laban
Brooks Landon
Eugene Larson
Donald F. Larsson
Norman Lavers
Penelope A. LeFew
Avril S. Lewis
Ward B. Lewis
Henry J. Lindborg

Naomi Lindstrom
Robert Emmet Long
Michael Lowenstein
Philip A. Luther
James J. Lynch
Tim Lyons
Barbara A. McCaskill
Andrew Macdonald
Gina Macdonald
James C. MacDonald
Fred B. McEwen
Dennis Q. McInerny
David W. Madden
Bryant Mangum
Lois A. Marchino
Patricia Marks
Paul Marx
Charles E. May
Richard A. Mazzara
Laurence W. Mazzeno
Jeremy T. Medina
Jean-Pierre Metereau
Siegfried Mews
N. J. Meyerhofer
Jennifer Michaels
Vasa D. Mihailovich
George Mihaychuk
Joseph R. Millichap
Kathleen Mills
Mark Minor
Sally Mitchell
Robert A. Morace
Carole Moses
C. Lynn Munro
Carol J. Murphy
Earl Paulus Murphy
Brian Murray
John M. Muste
William Nelles
F. William Nelson
Stella A. Nesanovich
Martha Nochimson
George O'Brien
Robert M. Otten
Cóilín Owens

Donald Palumbo
Robert J. Paradowski
Makarand Paranjape
John G. Parks
David B. Parsell
Carole Deering Paul
William Peden
William E. Pemberton
Genaro J. Pérez
Janet Pérez
Robert C. Petersen
Peter Petro
Alice Hall Petry
Linda Schelbitzki Pickle
Janet Polansky
Karen Priest
Charles H. Pullen
Philippe Radley
Victor J. Ramraj
K. Bhaskara Rao
Paul Reichardt
Edward C. Reilly
Rosemary M. Canfield Reisman
Helene M. Kastinger Riley
Michael Ritterson
Samuel J. Rogal
Deborah D. Rogers
Carl Rollyson
Joseph Rosenblum
Sven H. Rossel
Victor Anthony Rudowski
Murray Sachs

David Sadkin
Jan St. Martin
Arthur M. Saltzman
Dale Salwak
John K. Saunders
Thomas C. Schunk
Lucy M. Schwartz
Kenneth Seib
Joan Corey Semonella
Lynne P. Shackelford
Vasant A. Shahane
Walter Shear
Frank W. Shelton
John C. Shields
T. A. Shippey
Jack Shreve
R. Baird Shuman
William L. Siemens
Anne W. Sienkewicz
Thomas J. Sienkewicz
Charles L. P. Silet
Linda Simon
Jan Sjåvik
Gilbert Smith
Katherine Snipes
Philip H. Solomon
Sherry G. Southard
Sharon Spencer
Brian Stableford
Sonja G. Stary
William B. Stone
W. J. Stuckey

Mary Ellen Stumpf
Stan Sulkes
Eileen Tarcay
Thomas J. Taylor
Victor Terras
Christopher J. Thaiss
Gary Topping
Charles Trainor
Linda F. Tunick
Kim Vivian
Hans Wagener
Nancy Walker
Ronald G. Walker
John Michael Walsh
Bernice Larson Webb
Judith Weise
Steven Weisenburger
Craig Werner
Dexter Westrum
David Allen White
Bruce Wiebe
Roger E. Wiehe
Raymond L. Williams
James A. Winders
Chester L. Wolford
Philip Woodard
Jennifer L. Wyatt
Sanroku Yoshida
Michele Wender Zak
Harry Zohn
Leon Zolbrod

CRITICAL SURVEY
OF
LONG FICTION

A

CHINUA ACHEBE

Born: Ogidi, Nigeria; November 16, 1930

PRINCIPAL LONG FICTION
Things Fall Apart, 1958
No Longer at Ease, 1960
Arrow of God, 1964
A Man of the People, 1966
Anthills of the Savannah, 1987

OTHER LITERARY FORMS

The short stories of Chinua Achebe, written over a period of twenty years, were first published in England by Heinemann under the title *Girls at War* (1972), though most of them had already appeared in various periodicals and in a Nigerian publication, *The Sacrificial Egg and Other Short Stories* (1962). Achebe's poems, most of them written during the Biafran crisis (1967-1970), came out soon after the war as *Beware: Soul Brother and Other Poems* (1971), and a year later in an enlarged edition. Doubleday then published this Heinemann collection in America as *Christmas in Biafra and Other Poems* (1973). Additional poems and an essay by Achebe were combined with photographs by Robert Lyons in a full-color coffee-table book, *Another Africa* (1998), an overview of the beauty and complexity of modern Africa. Achebe has gathered together various autobiographical, political, literary, and cultural essays under the intriguingly optimist title, *Morning Yet on Creation Day* (1975), published by both Doubleday and Heinemann. In 1983, Heinemann published his short book, *The Trouble with Nigeria*, challenging his contemporaries to overcome their growing resignation. *Hopes and Impediments* (Doubleday, 1988) brings together some fifteen essays, mainly on literature and the writer's role and covering a twenty-three-year period, some of them previously pub-lished, including five from *Morning Yet on Creation Day*. Achebe has also written the children's stories *Chike and the River* (1966) and, jointly with John Iroaganachi, *How the Leopard Got His Claws* (1972). Achebe helped edit a collection of short stories, *African Short Stories* (1985).

ACHIEVEMENTS

From the beginning of his literary career, with the publication of *Things Fall Apart*, Achebe recognized and accepted his role as that of spokesman for black Africa. The primary function of that role was to reinterpret the African past from an African's point of view. This he successfully does in *Things Fall Apart* and *Arrow of God*, which correct the imperialist myth of African primitivism and savagery by re-creating the Igbo culture of the Eastern Region of Nigeria, its daily routines, its rituals, its customs, and especially its people dealing with one another in a highly civilized fashion within a complex society. The reinterpretation necessitated, as well, a look at the invading culture; Achebe tilted the balance in the Africans' favor by depicting individuals in the British administration as prejudiced, imperceptive, unnecessarily bu-

(Rocon/Engu, Nigeria)

1

reaucratic, and emotionally impotent. Since his main subject was the African crisis, he did not go to great pains to explore the private lives of the British or to mollify the British public. He needed to show that white civilization and white people were not intrinsically superior, and to restore to the African a respect for his own culture and his own person.

Achebe did not conceive his role as that of a mere propagandist, however, as any reader of the novels would acknowledge. His interpretation paid due respect to Western civilization and seriously criticized aspects of his own. In spite of certain fictional shortcuts—which some critics regard as crucial flaws—Achebe's attempt was to arrive at an objective appraisal of the conflict between Africa and the West. In fact, the central focus of his three other novels—*No Longer at Ease*, *A Man of the People*, and *Anthills of the Savannah*—set in contemporary times, is on the failure of Africans to meet challenges in the modern world. Of these, the first two are satirical attacks, the third a subtle blend of irony, compassion, and traditional wisdom, and a sane perspective on the chaotic Nigerian scene.

Achebe's importance as a spokesman for and to his own people has drawn criticism from some Western readers who are more interested in the quality of a novel than in its social function. Achebe has had several angry words to say to such aesthetically minded critics. His defense is that literature is a human and humane endeavor, not primarily a formal one. Still, one can easily defend his novels on aesthetic grounds, even arguing, as Charles Larson has done, that Achebe is actually an innovative writer who has transformed the novel to suit the African setting. Certainly, the most remarkable thing that Achebe has done, especially in *Things Fall Apart* and *Arrow of God*, is to transform the English language itself into an African idiom. Bernth Lindfors and others have demonstrated the skill with which Achebe uses imagery, allusions, figures of speech, proverbs, sentence patterns, standard English, and various forms of substandard English to capture a particular historical moment as well as the African mentality, but just as important to unify the novels around major motifs and themes. Achebe has not written mere social documents or so-

cial manifestos, but creditable works of literature that can stand the test of critical analysis; his contribution to the African world goes far beyond his five novels, but they are his major literary achievement.

As a consequence of his eight-year achievement as a novelist, Achebe was named chairman of the Society of Nigerian Authors and became a Member of Council at the University of Lagos. He also received the New Statesman Award for his third novel, *Arrow of God*. Among other honors were a Rockefeller Travel Fellowship to East and Central Africa (1960) and a United Nations Educational, Scientific, and Cultural Organization (UNESCO) Travel Fellowship to the United States and Brazil (1963). In 1989 Achebe was elected the first president of the Nigerian chapter of the International Association of Poets, Playwrights, Editors, Essayists, and Novelists (PEN), although he was living in the United States at the time.

Some twenty American, European, and African institutions, including Dartmouth College, Stanford University, the Open University of Great Britain, and the University of Port Harcourt in Nigeria, have granted him honorary degrees. He holds the influential position of founding editor of the African Writers Series, which, more than any other publisher, is responsible for the worldwide recognition of literary talent from Africa. The London *Times* included Achebe among its 1993 list of one thousand "Makers of the Twentieth Century." In 1996 he was awarded the Campion Award, sponsored by the Catholic Book Club to honor a "Christian person of letters" who combines faith and literary talent. *Things Fall Apart* has been translated into more than forty-five languages and has sold millions of copies, making it the most widely read and influential African novel ever written.

BIOGRAPHY

Chinua Achebe was born on November 16, 1930, in Ogidi, in the Eastern Region of Nigeria. He gives some details about his family and his early life in an essay, "Named for Victoria, Queen of England" (1973, in *Morning Yet on Creation Day*). His parents, Isaiah and Janet Achebe, were both Christian, his father an evangelist and church teacher. His maternal grandfather, like Okonkwo in *Things Fall Apart*, was a wealthy and distinguished community leader. He was not Christian but exercised tolerance when Achebe was converted. Achebe was baptized Albert Chinualumogu after Queen Victoria's consort, but dropped the Albert while at his university, evidently as a reaction against the British and his Christian heritage. He explains, however, that he was never really torn between the two cultures. There was none of the agony that is often found in African writers such as Cheikh Hamidou Kane. Achebe enjoyed the rituals of both religions. He did come to wonder if the apostates were not the Christians rather than the pagans, but he cites advantages brought in by Christianity: education, certain humane reforms, paid jobs. There seems to have been a pragmatic and tolerant strain in Achebe from the beginning.

For his secondary education, Achebe attended Government College, Umuahia (1944-1947), and he received his B.A. degree from University College, Ibadan, in 1953. During the next twelve years he worked for the Nigerian Broadcasting Corporation, first as producer in Lagos (1954-1958), then as controller in Enugu (1959-1961), and finally as Director of External Broadcasting in Lagos (1961-1966). In 1961, he married Christiana Chinwe Okoli, and they had two sons and two daughters. Also during these years Achebe wrote his first four novels, beginning with his most famous, *Things Fall Apart*, in 1958, and ending with *A Man of the People* in 1966. Achebe explains his novelistic career as the result of a revolution in his thinking during the nationalist movement after World War II. He decided that foreigners really could not tell the Nigerian story adequately. Joyce Cary's *Mister Johnson* (1939) was a prime example of this failure. Achebe regarded *Things Fall Apart* as an atonement for his apostasy, a ritual return to his homeland.

By 1966 Achebe was a distinguished member of the international literary community. In 1967, however, his career was interrupted by the outbreak of the war in Biafra, Achebe's Igbo homeland in the Eastern Region of Nigeria. It came to be essentially a civil war. Achebe joined the Biafran Ministry of Information and played a diplomatic role in raising money for the Biafran cause. Bound as he was by emotional ties and personal commitment to his country's fate, Achebe had no time to write novels. All he could manage were short poems, which were published a year after the war was over (1971).

Achebe's career after the war was taken up primarily by the academic world. In 1972, he was a Senior Research Fellow at the Institute of African Studies at the University of Nigeria in Nsukka. From 1972 to 1975, he was a professor at the University of Massachusetts at Amherst, and in 1975-1976 at the University of Connecticut. He then became professor at the University of Nigeria, Nsukka, and ten years later was again at the University of Massachusetts. Three of his publications during that time were a collection of short stories, *Girls at War*, written over a period of years going back to his university days; a collection of essays, *Morning Yet on Creation Day*, which give his views on a number of issues from the Biafran War to the problems of African literature in the Western world; and a book-length essay on the Nigerian situation, *The Trouble with Nigeria*. When it seemed that Achebe had left his career as a novelist behind him, twenty-one years after *A Man of the People*, he produced the carefully crafted *Anthills of the Savannah*, bringing up to date the apparently futile attempts to end the vicious cycles of corruption and coups in Nigeria.

In March, 1990, while en route to the airport in Lagos, Nigeria, Achebe was involved in a serious car accident and suffered a spinal injury that left him confined to a wheelchair. After nearly six months of recovery in various hospitals, he accepted an endowed professorship at Bard College in New York. For the next several years he turned his energies increasingly to the academic world, teaching, editing, and writing political and critical nonfiction.

ANALYSIS

Chinua Achebe is probably the best-known and, at the same time, the most representative African novelist. He may very well have written the first African novel of real literary merit—such at least is the opinion of Charles Larson—and he deals with what one can call the classic issue that preoccupies his fellow novelists, the clash between the indigenous cultures of black Africa and a white, European civilization. He avoids the emotionally charged subject of slavery and concentrates his attention on the political and cultural confrontation. His five novels offer, in a sense, a paradigm of it. He begins in *Things Fall Apart* with the first incursion of the British into the Igbo region of what became the Eastern Region of Nigeria, and his subsequent novels trace (with some gaps) the spread of British influence into the 1950's, and beyond that into the post-independence period of the 1960's. The one period he slights, as he himself admits, is the generation in transition from traditional village life to the new Westernized Africa. He had difficulty imagining the psychological conflict of the man caught between two cultures. There is no example in Achebe of Cheikh Hamidou Kane's "ambiguous adventure." He does, however, share with Kane and with most other African novelists the idea that his function as a writer is a social one.

Achebe insists repeatedly on this social function in response to Western critics who tend to give priority to aesthetic values. He seems to suggest, in fact, that the communal responsibility and the communal tie are more fundamental than artistic merit for any writer, but certainly for the African writer and for himself personally at the present stage in African affairs. He describes himself specifically as a teacher. His purpose is to dispel the colonial myth of the primitive African and to establish a true image of the people and their culture. This message is intended, to some extent, for a Western audience, but especially for the Africans themselves, since they have come to believe the myth and have internalized the feeling of inferiority: Achebe's aim is to help them regain their self-respect, recognize the beauty of their own cultural past, and deal capably with the dilemmas of contemporary society.

It is important, however, that Achebe is not fulfilling this role as an outsider. He returns to the traditional Igbo concept of the master craftsman and to the *Mbare* ceremony to explain the functional role of art in traditional society. He insists that creativity itself derives from a spiritual bond, the inspiration of a shared past and a shared destiny with a particular

people: The alienated writer such as Ayi Kwei Armah cannot be in tune with himself and is therefore likely to be imitative rather than truly creative. It would appear, then, that Achebe values originality and freshness in the management of literary form, but considers these attributes dependent on the sensitivity of the writer to his native setting.

Whereas Achebe's motivation in writing may be the restoration of pride in the African world, his theme, or rather the specific advice that he offers, albeit indirectly, is much more pragmatic. He does not advocate a return to the past or a rejection of Western culture. Like other African writers he decries the destructive consequences of colonial rule: alienation, frustration, and a loss of cohesiveness and a clear code of behavior. He recognizes as well, however, certain undesirable customs and superstitions that the foreign challenge exposed. His practical advice is to learn to cope with a changing world. He teaches the necessity of compromise: a loyalty to traditional wisdom and values, if not to tribal politics and outmoded customs, along with a suspicion of Western materialism but an openness to Western thought. He notes that in some cases the two cultures are not so far apart: Igbo republicanism goes even beyond the British-American concept of democracy, a view that the Ghanaian novelist, Armah, has developed as well. Unlike the Negritude writers of francophone Africa, Achebe, in his attempt to reinterpret the African past, does not paint an idyllic picture. He regrets the loss of mystery surrounding that past, but chooses knowledge, because he considers judgment, clarity of vision, and tolerance—virtues that he locates in his traditional society—to be the way out of the present confusion and corruption.

This key idea of tolerance pervades Achebe's work. One of his favorite stories (Yoruba, not Igbo) illustrates the danger in dogmatism. The god Echu, who represents fate or confusion, mischievously decides to provoke a quarrel between two farmers who live on either side of a road. He paints himself black on one side and white on the other, then walks up the road between the two farmers. The ensuing argument is whether the stranger is black or white. When he walks back down the road, each farmer tries to outdo the other in apologizing for his mistake. Achebe's most pervasive vehicle for this idea of tolerance, however, is in the concept of the *chi*, which is central to Igbo cosmology. Achebe interprets it as the ultimate expression of individualism, the basic worth and independence of every person. Politically it means the rejection of any authoritarian rule. Morally it means the responsibility of every person for his or her own fate. The *chi* is his other self, his spiritual identity responsible for his birth and his future. Thus, while one's *chi* defines his uniqueness, it also defines his limitations. As Achebe frequently notes in his novels, no one can defeat his own *chi*, and the acceptance of one's limitations is the beginning of tolerance.

It is the social purpose, this "message" of tolerance in Achebe's novels, that dictates the form. His plots tend to be analytic, static, or "situational," as Larson argues, rather than dynamic. Instead of narrative movement, there is juxtaposition of past and present, of the traditional and the modern. Achebe achieves balance through comparison and contrast. He uses exposition more than drama. His main characters tend to be representational. Their conflicts are the crucial ones of the society. The protagonists of the two novels set in the past, *Things Fall Apart* and *Arrow of God*, are strong men who lack wisdom, practical sense, an ability to accept change, and a tolerance for opposing views. The protagonists of *No Longer at Ease* and *A Man of the People* are weak and vacillating. They accept change but are blinded by vanity and have no satisfactory code of conduct to resist the unreasonable pressures of traditional ties or the corruption and attractions of the new age. The two male protagonists of *Anthills of the Savannah*, also hindered by vanity, prove inadequate idealists in a power-hungry environment and wake up too late to their lack of control over events. An even more predominant feature of the five novels is their style. Achebe makes the necessary compromise and writes in English, a foreign tongue, but manipulates it to capture the flavor of the native Igbo expression. He does this through dialect, idiom, and figurative language, and through proverbs that reflect traditional Igbo wisdom, comment ironically on the inadequacies of the characters, and state the central theme.

Thus Achebe manages, through the authorial voice, to establish a steady control over every novel. To some extent one senses the voice in the proverbs. They represent the assessment of the elders in the clan, yet the wisdom of the proverb is itself sometimes called into question, and the reader is invited to make the judgment. In general, it is Achebe's juxtaposing of character, incident, proverb, and tone that creates the total assessment. Against this background voice one measures the pride, vanity, or prejudice of the individuals who, caught in the stressful times of colonial or postcolonial Nigeria, fail to respond adequately. The voice does not judge or condemn; it describes. It reminds the Nigerian of the danger of self-deception. It also recognizes the danger of failing to communicate with others. Achebe keeps ever in mind the tale (found in numerous versions all over Africa) of humankind whose message to Chukwa (the Supreme Deity) requesting immortality is distorted by the messenger and thus fails in its purpose. The voice he adopts to avoid the distortion is one of self-knowledge, practical sense, pragmatism, and detachment, but also of faith, conviction, and humor. The voice is, in a sense, the message itself, moderating the confrontation between Africa and the West.

THINGS FALL APART

Significantly, Achebe takes the title of his first novel, *Things Fall Apart*, from W. B. Yeats's 1920 apocalyptic poem "The Second Coming," which prophesies the end of the present era and the entrance on the world's stage of another that is radically different. *Things Fall Apart* treats the early moments of that transition in an Igbo village. For those people the intrusion of the British is as revolutionary as the coming of a second Messiah, Yeats's terrible "rough beast." To some extent, Achebe creates a mythic village whose history stretches back to a legendary past. Chapters are devoted to the daily routines of the people, their family life, their customs, games, and rituals, their ancient wisdom, their social order, and legal practices. Achebe remains a realist, however, as he identifies also certain flaws in the customs and in the people. Superstition leads them to unnecessary cruelties. The protagonist, Okonkwo, reflects a basic conflict within the society. He is, on the one hand, a respected member of the society who has risen through hard work to a position of wealth and authority. He conscientiously accepts the responsibilities that the elders lay on him. At the same time, he is such an individualist that his behavior runs counter to the spirit of traditional wisdom. His shame over his father's weak character provokes him to be excessive in proving his own manhood. There is a defensiveness and uncertainty behind his outward assertiveness. It is true that the clan has its mechanisms to reprimand and punish the Okonkwos for their errant behavior. Nevertheless, even before the British influence begins to disturb the region, the cohesiveness of the clan is already in question.

One particular chink in Okonkwo's armor, which identifies a weakness also in the clan as it faces the foreign threat, is his inflexibility, his inability to adapt or to accept human limitations. Since he, in his youth, overcame adversity (familial disadvantages, natural forces such as drought and excessive rains, challenges of strength as a wrestler), he comes to believe that he has the individual strength to resist all challenges to his personal ambition. He cannot accept the presence of forces beyond his control, including the forces of his own personal destiny. It is this and the other aspects of Okonkwo's character that Achebe develops in the first section of the novel against the background of the tribe to which he belongs. Part 1 ends with the symbolic act of Okonkwo's accidentally killing a young man during a funeral ceremony. Like death, the act is beyond his control and unexplainable, yet it is punishable. The elders exile him for seven years to the village of his mother's family. This separation from his village is itself symbolic, since in a way Okonkwo has never belonged to it. While he is away, the village changes. With the coming of the missionaries, traditional religious practices begin to lose their sanction, their absoluteness. In part 3, Okonkwo returns from exile but finds that his exile continues. Nothing is as it was. Open hostility exists between the new religion and the traditional one. The British government has begun to take over authority from the elders. The novel ends with Okonkwo's irrational killing of a messenger from the British District Officer and with his sub-

sequent suicide. Okonkwo rightly assumes, it would seem, that no authority now exists to judge him: The old sanctions are dead, and he refuses to accept the new ones. He must be his own judge.

There is, however, if not a judge, a voice of reason and compassion, detached from the action but controlling its effects, that assures Okonkwo of a fair hearing. The voice is heard in the proverbs, warning Okonkwo not to challenge his own *chi* (his own spiritual identity and destiny), even though another proverb insists that if he says yes his *chi* will say yes too. It is heard in the decisions of the elders, the complaints of the wives, and the rebellion of Okonkwo's own son, Noye, who turns to Christianity in defiance against his father's unreasonableness. It is found in the tragic sense of life of Okonkwo's uncle, Uchendu, who advises this man in exile to bear his punishment stoically, for his sufferings are mild in comparison to those of many others. Achebe locates his voice in one particular character, Obierika, Okonkwo's closest friend and a man of thought rather than, like his friend, a man of action. In the important eighth chapter, Achebe measures his protagonist against this man of moderation, reflection, and humor, who can observe the white invader with tolerance, his own society's laws with skepticism, and, at the end of the novel, his dead friend with respect and compassion. Achebe's voice can even be seen in the ironically insensitive judgment of the District Commissioner as the novel closes. As superficial and uninformed as that voice might be in itself, Achebe recognizes that the voice nevertheless exists, is therefore real, and must be acknowledged. The final view of Okonkwo and of the village that he both reflects and rejects is a composite of all these voices. It is the composite also of Okonkwo's own complex and unpredictable behavior, and of his fate which is the result of his own reckless acts and of forces that he does not comprehend. Amid the growing chaos one senses still the stable influence of the calm authorial voice, controlling and balancing everything.

No Longer at Ease

From the early 1900's of *Things Fall Apart*, Achebe turns in his second novel, *No Longer at Ease*, to the mid-1950's just before independence. The protagonist, Obi Okonkwo, grandson of the tragic victim who lashed out against British insolence, resembles to some extent his grandfather in his inadequacy to deal with the pressures of his society, but has far different loyalties. The novel begins after things have already fallen apart; Nigeria is between societies. Obi no longer belongs to the old society. His father is the rebellious son of Okonkwo who left home for the Christian church and was educated in mission schools. Obi received a similar education and was selected by his community to study in England. This financial and personal obligation to Umuoria plagues Obi throughout the novel, for after his Western education he no longer shares the old customs and the old sense of loyalty. He considers himself an independent young man of the city, with a Western concept of government and administration. After his return from England he receives a civil service job and has visions of reforming the bureaucracy. The story is thus about the practical difficulties (it is not really a psychological study) of an ordinary individual separating himself cleanly from the past while adapting to the glitter and temptations of the new. Obi faces two particular problems. He has chosen to marry a woman, Clara, who belongs to a family considered taboo by the traditional community. He attempts to resist family and community pressure, but eventually succumbs. Meanwhile, Clara has become pregnant and must go through a costly and embarrassing abortion. Obi essentially abandons his responsibility toward her in his weak, halfhearted respect for his family's wishes. He likewise fails at his job, as he resists self-righteously various bribes until his financial situation and morals finally collapse. Unfortunately, he is as clumsy here as in his personal relations. He is arrested and sentenced to prison.

As in his first novel, Achebe's subject is the individual (and the society) inadequate to the changing times. His main concern is again a balanced appraisal of Nigerian society at a crucial stage in its recent history, because the greatest danger, as Achebe himself observes, is self-deception. He presents a careful selection of characters whose vanity, prejudice, or misplaced values allow them only a partial view of reality. Obi is, of course, the main example. He leaves his home village as a hero, is one of the few Nigerians to receive a foreign education, and, as a civil servant and proud possessor of a car, is a member of the elite. His vanity blinds him to such an extent that he cannot assess his proper relationship to his family, to Clara, or to his social role. His father, caught between his Christian faith and tribal customs, cannot allow Obi his independence. Mr. Green, Obi's British superior at the office, is trapped by stereotypical prejudices against Africans. There is no one individual such as Obierika within the novel to provide a reasonable interpretation of events.

One nevertheless feels the constant presence of Achebe as he balances these various voices against one another. Achebe also assures perspective by maintaining a detached tone through irony, wit, and humor. The narrator possesses the maturity and the wisdom that the characters lack. This novel also shows Achebe experimenting with structure as a means of expressing the authorial voice. The novel opens (like Leo Tolstoy's *The Death of Ivan Ilych*, 1886) with the final act, the trial and judgment of Obi for accepting a bribe. Achebe thus invites the reader to take a critical view of Obi from the very beginning. There is no question of getting romantically involved in his young life and career. This distancing continues in the first three chapters as Achebe juxtaposes present and past, scenes of reality and scenes of expectation. The real Lagos is juxtaposed directly against the idyllic one in Obi's mind. A picture of the later, strained relationship between Obi and Clara precedes the romantic scenes after they meet on board ship returning from England. Through this kind of plotting by juxtaposition, Achebe turns what might have been a melodramatic story of young love, abortion, betrayal, and corruption into a realistic commentary on Nigerian society in transition. In *Things Fall Apart* he rejects a paradisal view of the African past; in *No Longer at Ease* he warns against selfish, irresponsible, and naïve expectations in the present.

ARROW OF GOD

In his third novel, *Arrow of God*, Achebe returns to the past, taking up the era of British colonization a few years after the events of *Things Fall Apart*. The old society is still intact, but the Christian religion and the British administration are more firmly entrenched than before. Achebe again tries to re-create the former Igbo environment, with an even more elaborate account of the daily life, the customs, and the rituals, and with the scattering throughout of traditional idioms and proverbs. The foreigners, too, receive more detailed attention, though even the two main personalities, Winterbottom and Clarke, hardly achieve more than stereotyped status. Rather than work them late into the story, this time Achebe runs the two opposing forces alongside each other almost from the very beginning in order to emphasize the British presence. Now it is the political, not the religious, power that is in the foreground, suggesting historically the second stage of foreign conquest, but the Church also takes full advantage of local political and religious controversy to increase its control over the people. Achebe continues to be realistic in his treatment of traditional society. It is not an idyllic Eden corrupted by satanic foreign power. In spite of the attractive pictures of local customs, the six villages of Umuaro are divided and belligerent, and, in two instances at least, it is ironically the British government or the Christian church that ensures peace and continuity in the communal life. By this stage in the colonization, of course, it is difficult (and Achebe does not try) to untangle the causes of internal disorder among the Igbo.

Like Okonkwo, the protagonist in *Arrow of God* is representative of the social disorder. In him Achebe represents the confidence in traditional roles and beliefs challenged not only by the new British worldview, but also by forces within. Personal pride, egotism, and intolerance sometimes obscure his obligation to the welfare of the community. Whereas Okonkwo is one among several wealthy members of the clan, Ezeulu occupies a key position as the priest of Ulu, chief god of the six villages. Thus the central cohesive force in the society is localized in this one man. In another way, too, Ezeulu differs from Okonkwo. Whereas Okonkwo stubbornly resists the new Western culture, Ezeulu makes such gestures of accommodation that his clan actually accuses him of being the white man's friend. Instead of disowning

his son for adopting Christianity, he sends Oduche to the mission school to be his spy in the Western camp. Ezeulu's personality, however, is complex, as are his motives. Accommodation is his pragmatic way of preserving the clan and his own power. When the opportunity arises for him to become the political representative of his people to the British government, he refuses out of a sense of loyalty to his local god. This complexity is, however, contradictory and confusing, thus reflecting again the transitional state of affairs during the early colonial period. Ezeulu does not always seem to know what his motives are as he jockeys for power with Winterbottom and with the priest Idemili. In trying to save the community he sets up himself and his god as the sole sources of wisdom. As priest—and thus considered half man and half spirit—he may, as Achebe seems to suggest, confuse his sacred role with his human vanity.

It is in the midst of this confusion that Achebe again questions the existence of absolutes and advises tolerance. The central concept of the *chi* reappears. Does it say yes if humanity says yes? If so, humankind controls its own destiny. If not, it is severely limited. In any case, the concept itself suggests duality rather than absoluteness. Even Ezeulu, while challenging the new power, advises his son, Oduche, that one "must dance the dance prevalent in his time." Chapter 16, in which this statement appears, contains the key thematic passages. In it one of Ezeulu's wives tells her children a traditional tale about a people's relation with the spirit world. It turns upon the importance of character—the proper attitude one must have toward oneself and toward the gods. A boy accidentally leaves his flute in the field where he and his family had been farming. He persuades his parents to let him return to fetch it. An encounter with the spirits, during which he demonstrates his good manners, temperance, and reverence, leads to material reward. The envious senior wife in the family sends her son on a similar mission, but his rudeness and greed lead only to the visitation of evils on human society. The intended message is obvious, but the implied one, in the context of this novel, is that traditional values appear to be childhood fancies in the face of contemporary realities.

At the end of the chapter, Ezeulu puts those realities into focus. He describes himself as an arrow of god, whose very defense of religious forms threatens the survival of his religion, but he goes on to suggest the (for him) terrifying speculation that Oduche, his Christian son, and also Christianity and the whites themselves, are arrows of god. At the end of his career, Ezeulu is opening his mind to a wide range of possibilities. This tolerance, however, is double-edged, for as Achebe seems to suggest, humanity must be not only receptive to unfamiliar conceptions, but also tough enough to "tolerate" the pain of ambiguity and alienation. Ezeulu is too old and too exhausted to endure that pain. The final blow is his son's death while performing a ritual dance. Ezeulu interprets it as a sign that Ulu has deserted him.

Indeed, the voice in *Arrow of God* is even more ambiguous than that in the first two novels. There is no Obierika to correct Ezeulu's aberrations. Akueke, his friend and adviser, is not a sure guide to the truth. Achebe works through dialogue even more than in *Things Fall Apart*, and the debates between these two men do not lead to a clear answer. Akueke cannot decipher the priest's motives or anticipate his actions. Ezeulu, as a strange compound of spirit and man, is to him "unknowable." Nor does Achebe make the task any easier for the reader. Ezeulu does not seem to understand his own motives. He considers himself under the spiritual influence of his god. His sudden, final decision not to seek a reconciliation with his people he imagines as the voice of Ulu. He thus sacrifices himself and his people (as well as the god himself) to the will of the god. Achebe remains silent on the issue of whether the voice is the god's or Ezeulu's. One can only speculate that since the society created the god in the first place (or so the legend went), it could also destroy him.

A MAN OF THE PEOPLE

Like *No Longer at Ease*, Achebe's fourth novel, *A Man of the People*, seems rather lightweight in comparison with the two historical novels. It takes place not in Nigeria but in an imaginary African country, a few years after independence. Achebe seems to be playing with some of the popular situations in contemporary African literature, as though he were paro-

dying them. The main character, Odili, has relationships with three different women: Elsie, a friend from the university who functions as a sort of mistress, but who remains a shadowy figure in the background; Jean, a white American with whom he has a brief sexual relationship; and Edna, a beautiful and innocent young woman with whom he "falls in love" in a rather conventional Western sense. There is also the typical estrangement of the university-educated son from his traditionally oriented father. Achebe contrives a somewhat romantic reconciliation during the last third of the novel. Finally, while all of Achebe's novels are essentially political, this one pits two candidates for public office against each other, with all the paraphernalia of personal grudges, dirty tricks, campaign rhetoric, and even a military coup at the end that ironically makes the election meaningless. (In fact, it was already meaningless because the incumbent, Nanga, had arranged that Odili's name not be officially registered.) Furthermore, the contest is a stock romantic confrontation between the idealism of youth and the corrupt opportunism of an older generation. While the story might at first glance appear to be a melodramatic rendering of the romantic world of love and politics, it so exaggerates situations that one must assume Achebe is writing rather in the comic mode.

Along with this choice of mode, Achebe also creates a more conventional plot line. The rising action deals with the first meeting after sixteen years between Odili, a grammer school teacher, and Nanga, the "man of the people," Odili's former teacher, local representative to Parliament, and Minister of Culture. In spite of his skepticism toward national politics, Odili succumbs to Nanga's charm and accepts an invitation to stay at his home in the city. The turning point comes when Odili's girl friend, Elsie, shamelessly spends the night with Nanga. Odili sees this as a betrayal by Elsie, even though he himself feels no special commitment to her. More important, Odili feels betrayed and humiliated by Nanga, who does not take such incidents with women at all seriously. His vanity touched by this rather trivial incident, Odili suddenly reactivates his conscience over political corruption and vows to seek revenge. The attack is twofold: to steal Edna, Nanga's young fiancée, who is to be his second wife, and to defeat Nanga in the next elections. Odili's motives are obviously suspect. The rest of the novel recounts his gradual initiation into love and politics. The revenge motive drops as the relationship with Edna becomes serious. The political campaign fails, and Odili ends up in the hospital after a pointless attempt to spy on one of Nanga's campaign rallies. Again, it is tempting to treat this as a conventional initiation story, except that Odili's experiences do not really cure him of his romantic notions of love and politics.

For the first time, Achebe elects to use the first-person point of view: Odili tells his own story. This may be the reason that the balancing of effects through juxtaposition of scenes and characters does not operate as in the earlier works. The tone is obviously affected as well: Odili is vain and pompous, blind to his own flaws while critical of others. Hence, Achebe has to manipulate a subjective narrative to express the objective authorial voice, as Mark Twain does in *The Adventures of Huckleberry Finn* (1884) or (to use an African example) Mongo Beti in *Le Pauvre Christ de Bomba* (1956; *The Poor Christ of Bomba*). The primary means is through Odili's own partial vision. Odili frequently makes criticisms of contemporary politics that appear to be just, and therefore do represent the judgment of Achebe as well. At the same time, Odili's affected tone invites criticism and provides Achebe with an occasion to satirize the self-deception of the young intellectuals whom Odili represents. Achebe also expresses himself through the plot, in which he parodies romantic perceptions of the contemporary world. In addition, he continues to include proverbs in the mouths of provincial characters as guides to moral evaluation.

Achebe emphasizes one proverb in particular to describe the political corruption in which Nanga participates. After a local merchant, Josiah, steals a blind beggar's stick to make his customers (according to a figurative twist of reasoning) blindly purchase whatever he sells, the public reacts indignantly with the proverb: "He has taken away enough for the owner to notice." Unlike Achebe's narrator in the first three novels, Odili cannot allow the proverb to

do its own work. He must, as an academic, analyze it and proudly expand on its meaning. He had done this before when he became the "hero" of Jean's party as the resident expert on African behavior and African art. He may very well be correct about the political implications of the proverb, that the people (the owners of the country) are now being blatantly robbed by the politicians, but he fails to identify emotionally with the local situation. Nor is he objective enough to admit fully to himself his own immoral, hypocritical behavior, which he has maintained throughout the novel. He is an egotist, more enchanted with his own cleverness than concerned about the society he has pretended to serve. In like manner, at the close of the story Odili turns the real death of his political colleague, Max, into a romantic fantasy of the ideal sacrifice. Totally pessimistic about the reliability of the people, he returns once again to the proverb to illustrate their fickle behavior as the melodramatic villains: They always return the Josiahs to power. Achebe may to some extent share Odili's view of the public and the national leadership it chooses, but he is skeptical of the Odilis as well; and hence he positions the reader outside both the political structure and Odili as an observer of the society. Achebe, then, even in this first-person narrative did not abandon his authorial voice, nor the role of social spokesman that he had maintained in all his other novels.

ANTHILLS OF THE SAVANNAH

Achebe's fifth novel, *Anthills of the Savannah*, written twenty-one years after his fourth, shares some of its interests. Achebe once again makes the situation political and the setting contemporary. As in *A Man of the People*, the country, Kangan, is fictitious (though the resemblance to Nigeria is again hardly disguised), but somewhat later in the independence period, perhaps in the 1970's or the early 1980's. Also, once again, the main actors in the drama knew one another under different circumstances in the past. Whereas the former relationship between Nanga and Odili was teacher and student, the three male protagonists of *Anthills of the Savannah* are of the same generation and first knew one another as fellow students at Lord Lugard College when they were thirteen years old. The novel deals with their lives during twenty-seven years, including their experiences in England at the University of London, their adventures in love, and their choice of careers. These years are shown only through flashbacks, however, for the focus is on a two-week period in the present, on the edge of a political crisis, when they are forty years old.

Achebe does not present his narrative in a straight chronological line; not only are there flashbacks, but even during the two-week present he recounts, or has his characters recount, events out of chronological order—a technique Achebe used in his other novels as well to control reader response. The events of this two-week period begin, as the novel does, on a Thursday morning as Sam, now His Excellency, President of Kangan, presides over his weekly cabinet meeting. Sam had decided long before, following the advice of his headmaster at Lord Luggard, to choose the army over a medical career because it would turn him into a "gentleman." His choice proved to be a good one when, after a military coup two years earlier, he was named president of the new government. A fellow student at Lord Luggard, Christopher Oriko, became his minister of information. Chris used his influence over Sam to name five of the twelve cabinet members and to appoint another old school friend, Ikem Osodi, editor of the *National Gazette*. The political conflict in the novel focuses on these three men, though Sam as a character remains largely in the background. The relationship between Chris and Sam has become increasingly strained over the two-year period, as Sam has expanded his drive for status into an ambition to be president for life with total authority. He is now highly suspicious of Chris and has appointed the tough, ruthless Major Johnson Ossai as his chief of staff and head of intelligence. Chris, meanwhile, as he himself admits in the opening chapter, has become an amused spectator and recorder of events, almost indifferent to the official drama before him. Such an attitude has also driven a wedge between him and Ikem, who, as a crusading journalist, has continued to attack government incompetence and to represent and fight for the hapless public, while Chris has counseled patience and diplomacy in dealing with Sam.

The inciting force on this Thursday is a delegation from Abazon—the northern province of Kangan devastated, like Nigeria's own northern regions, by drought—that has come to the capital city of Bassa to seek relief. Ikem has only recently written an editorial, his allegorical Hymn to the Sun that dries up the savannah, accusing the president (the sun) of responsibility and promoting the delegation's cause. Sam at first feels threatened by the loud demonstrations outside his office, but when he learns that the delegation consists of only six elders and that the rest of the demonstrators are Bassa locals, he decides to use the situation to rid himself of his old school buddies and to entrench himself in power surrounded by loyal henchmen such as Ossai. Chris and Ikem do not realize what is going on behind the scenes—nor does the reader—until events get beyond their control. Within hours, Sam has Ikem arrested and murdered (though the official version is shot while resisting arrest for plotting "regicide"), the Abazon delegation put in prison, and Chris declared an accomplice of both. Chris himself has managed to escape, hiding out with friends and sympathizers and eventually in disguise traveling by bus past roadblocks to the Abazon province. There he learns that a military coup has toppled Sam from his throne and that Sam has mysteriously disappeared. Ironically, at this very moment, in the midst of riotous celebration at a roadblock, Chris is shot by a police sergeant while trying to prevent him from abducting and raping a girl. The novel leaves no hope that the next regime will offer Kangan any better leadership.

The men in this modern African state consistently fail to bring the persistent political incompetence under control. Sam is a variation on the Nanga type, the amoral, self-serving servant of power who does not foresee the consequences of his ruthless treatment of others. This naïveté of the tyrant is matched by the naïve idealism of the moral crusader, Ikem, and the naïve detachment of the philosophical observer, Chris. While most of the novel is an omniscient third-person narrative, with Achebe providing a clear, balanced perspective, five of the first seven chapters are told in first person, with Chris and Ikem being two of the three narrators. Inside their minds, the reader sees a false self-confidence that Achebe eventually parleys into a chauvinism, apparently characteristic of the African male. For the first time in his novels, Achebe takes up the feminist theme, stating flatly that women need to be a major part of the solution to Africa's woes. Sam, as perceived by the third character-narrator, Beatrice, Chris's fiancée, treats women as sex objects, as he invites Beatrice to a dinner party at his lake retreat, assuming that she will be honored to serve her president. The two male protagonists, Ikem and Chris, innocent carriers of long-held assumptions, treat the women they love too lightly, and neither understands until only days before their deaths the wisdom and spiritual power of Beatrice, the central female character in the novel.

In fact, Beatrice herself seems only half aware of her strength until the crisis in Kangan puts it to the test. In chapters 6 and 7, which she narrates, she reveals the change that takes place in her. Chapter 6 is her account of the visit to Sam's retreat, where her defensiveness and vanity obscure her actual superiority over the other guests, including a young American female reporter who uses her sexuality to gain access to Sam. Beatrice sees herself, rather vaingloriously at this point, as a sacrificial shield to protect Sam—a symbol for her of the African leader—from the white temptress. Still, she rebuffs Sam's sexual advances, and he, insulted and humiliated, sends her home in ignominy. Beatrice sees dimly, however, the role that she must play. In chapter 7, she receives help from Ikem, who visits her for the last time before his death. With her help he has made a great discovery, for she had long accused him of male chauvinism, and he reads to her the "love letter" that she has inspired. It is a feminist recantation of his chauvinism, a rejection of the two traditional images of women, both found in biblical and in African sources: the woman as scapegoat, the cause of evil and men's suffering, and the woman idealized as the mother of the male god, called upon to save the world when men fail. His final word on the insight she had given him, however, is that the women themselves must decide their role; men cannot know. Beatrice tells this story of Ikem's last visit in her journal, written months after Ikem has died. Only

then is she able to put the pieces of the tragedy together in her mind.

Chris, too, begins to see a special power in Beatrice during the weeks of crisis. She becomes for him a priestess of sexual and spiritual resources who could, as a prophetess, tell the future. Indeed, it is Beatrice (a literary allusion to Dante's Beatrice which is only one of several whimsical allusions in the novel) who warns Chris and Ikem that they must mend their relationship, that tragedy is in store not only for them but also for Sam. They do not take her seriously enough, however, as they soon discover. Yet Achebe does not allow the elevation of Beatrice into the traditional Igbo role of half-woman, half-spirit (the Chielo of *Things Fall Apart*, as Beatrice herself notes), to be the work of the characters alone. In chapter 8, Achebe himself, as omniscient narrator, recounts the Igbo legend of the sun-god who sent his daughter to earth as a harbinger of peace. This legend suggests that henceforth women must stand as mediators between men and their desires, but this too is not Achebe's final word on the subject. As Ikem says in his confession to Beatrice in chapter 7, "all certitude must now be suspect."

In the last chapter, Achebe tries to bring together his thoughts on women and numerous other themes throughout the novel. The scene is Beatrice's flat and the time is nine months after the tragedy. Those present are a family of friends, including among others Elewa, Ikem's fiancée; Agatha, Beatrice's housekeeper; and Abdul Medani, the army captain who secretly helped Chris escape from Bassa. The occasion is the naming ceremony for Elewa and Ikem's twenty-eight-day-old daughter. The women, along with the men present, are trying to put their lives and, symbolically, the lives of their countrymen in order. Beatrice fears, however, that they are all fated pawns of "an alienated history." They acknowledge the value of people and the living ideas that they leave behind, the importance of humor and the need to laugh at oneself, the "unbearable beauty" even of death, and the community of all religions that can dance the same dance. They learn that women can perform tasks usually reserved for men; since Ikem is not present, Beatrice, the priestess, names the child:

Amaechina, the path of Ikem, a boy's name for a baby girl. Elewa's uncle, a male representative of traditional thinking, arrives to preside over the naming but instead pays homage to the young people in the room. "That is how to handle this world," he says, "give the girl a boy's name," make her "the daughter of all of us."

It is important not to take oneself too seriously. Sam, Ikem, and Chris forgot, as Beatrice had to remind them, that their story is not "the story of this country," that "our story is only one of twenty million stories." That reminder may be the main message in *Anthills of the Savannah*, that the other millions of people are not ants caught in a drought, retreating from the sun into their holes, but people with their own stories. As the elder in the Abazon delegation reminds Ikem, the story is the nation's most valued treasure, the storyteller possessed by Agwu, the god of healers and the source of truth. Beatrice, like Ikem and Chris, is a writer, a teller of stories. Uchendu, in *Things Fall Apart*, warns that all stories are true; this fifth novel, itself full of proverbs, stories, legends, and political allegory of the sun shining on the anthills of the savannah, is an ambitious exposé and a compassionate vision of the future.

Thomas Banks, updated by Cynthia A. Bily

OTHER MAJOR WORKS

SHORT FICTION: *The Sacrificial Egg and Other Stories*, 1962; *Girls at War*, 1972.

POETRY: *Beware: Soul Brother and Other Poems*, 1971, 1972; *Christmas in Biafra and Other Poems*, 1973.

NONFICTION: *Morning Yet on Creation Day*, 1975; *The Trouble with Nigeria*, 1983; *Hopes and Impediments*, 1988; *Conversations with Chinua Achebe*, 1997 (Bernth Lindfors, editor); *Another Africa*, 1998 (with Robert Lyons).

CHILDREN'S LITERATURE: *Chike and the River*, 1966; *How the Leopard Got His Claws*, 1972 (with John Iroaganachi); *The Flute*, 1977; *The Drum*, 1977.

EDITED TEXTS: *Don't Let Him Die: An Anthology of Memorial Poems for Christopher Okigbo, 1932-1967*, 1978 (with Dubem Okafor); *Aka Weta: An Anthology of Ibo Poetry*, 1978; *African Short Stories*, 1985 (with C. L. Innes); *Beyond Hunger in Africa*, 1990 (with others).

BIBLIOGRAPHY

Ezenwa-Ohaeto. *Chinua Achebe: A Biography*. Bloomington: Indiana University Press, 1997. A full-length biography of Achebe, this book benefits from its author's insights as a former student of Achebe, a native of Nigeria, and a speaker of Igbo. Ezenwa-Ohaeto examines Achebe's life and literary contributions and places them within their social, historical, and cultural contexts. Written with the cooperation of Achebe and his family, the book includes several rare and revealing photographs.

Innes, C. L. *Chinua Achebe*. Cambridge, England: Cambridge University Press, 1990. In this first title in the Cambridge Studies in African and Caribbean Literature series, Innes gives a detailed analysis of each of Achebe's novels, showing how Achebe adapted what he found in Western fiction to create a new literary form—the Africanized novel. Innes also includes a chapter on the critical and political writings, demonstrating how the Nigerian Civil War changed Achebe's politics and his fiction.

Innes, C. L., and Bernth Lindfors, eds. *Critical Perspectives on Chinua Achebe*. D.C.: Three Continents Press, 1978. This collection of essays by twenty different critics offers a comprehensive overview of Achebe's work. Contains a brief introduction to Achebe's life and background, five general assessments of his fiction, commentaries on his first four novels and his poetry, and an extensive bibliography.

Iyasere, Solomon O., ed. *Understanding "Things Fall Apart": Selected Essays and Criticism*. Troy, N.Y.: Whitston, 1998. Nine essays demonstrate the breadth of approaches taken by recent critics: They include a reading of Okonkwo as a tragic hero, a discussion of the rhythm of the novel's prose as it echoes African oral tradition, and a discussion of how Achebe successfully transformed the colonizers' language to tell the story of the colonized.

Muoneke, Romanus Okey. *Art, Rebellion, and Redemption: A Reading of the Novels of Chinua Achebe*. New York: Peter Lang, 1994. Muoneke examines Achebe's role as a public chronicler of Nigeria's social, economic, and political problems, as a way of exploring the larger issues of the writer's redemptive role in society. Argues that Achebe's novels challenge colonialism and negritude, two forces that have distorted the African image.

Wren, Robert M. *Achebe's World: The Historical and Cultural Context of the Novels*. D.C.: Three Continents Press, 1980. The purpose of this seemingly authoritative and well-documented presentation is to clarify what might be confusing to a reader not familiar with the Nigerian context. Offers comforting evidence that Achebe's fiction (his first four novels) is an essentially truthful and reliable guide to the historical Nigeria. Includes an extensive glossary of terms and a helpful bibliography.

RICHARD ADAMS

Born: Newbury, England; May 9, 1920

PRINCIPAL LONG FICTION

Watership Down, 1972
Shardik, 1974
The Plague Dogs, 1977
The Girl in a Swing, 1980
Maia, 1984
Traveller, 1988

OTHER LITERARY FORMS

Richard Adams has written two collections of short fiction, one of which, *Tales from Watership Down* (1996), is in part a sequel to his most famous novel. His other works include several illustrated children's books in verse; an illustrated series of nature guides; an account of a journey to Antarctica, *Voyage Through the Antarctic* (1982), cowritten with Ronald M. Lockley, the author of the factual basis for *Watership Down*; and an autobiography covering the first part of his life through his demobilization after World War II, *The Day Gone By* (1990).

ACHIEVEMENTS

Called by English writer A. N. Wilson "the best adventure-story-writer alive," Richard Adams is most famous for taking the talking-animal story out of the genre of children's literature and informing it with mature concerns and interests, as in his first great success, *Watership Down*, which won the Carnegie Award and the *Guardian* award for children's fiction in 1972. He continued this transformation in *The Plague Dogs* and *Traveller*. Adams also made his mark in fantasy literature; his imaginary kingdom of Bekla is the backdrop for *Shardik* and *Maia*, novels whose main concerns, slavery and warfare, definitely remove them from the realm of children's literature. He also wrote a less successful full-length ghost story, *The Girl in the Swing*.

BIOGRAPHY

The youngest of three children, Richard Adams spent an idyllic childhood ("the happiest [days] of my life") growing up on the outskirts of Newbury, England. His father, a local doctor, transmitted his knowledge of and love for the flora and fauna of the region to his son, whose later devotion to animal welfare was also inspired by Hugh Lofting's Dr. Dolittle books. Adams's father also instilled in his son a lifelong interest in storytelling, which Adams later honed in bedtime tales told to roommates at prep school. Other important influences included the Uncle Remus stories of Joel Chandler Harris, *Uncle Tom's Cabin* (1852) by Harriet Beecher Stowe, *The Three Mulla-Mulgars* (1910) by Walter de la Mare, and the silent Rin-Tin-Tin films. All would later echo in his fiction.

While his time at prep school was often unpleasant, Adams thoroughly enjoyed his public school experience at Bradfield. The school put on a yearly play in its open-air theater, often a classical Greek drama, and Adams called the theater the place where he was "more consistently happy than anywhere else." Bradfield also encouraged his love of literature, the Greek and Roman classics, and history, the subject in which Adams won a scholarship to Worcester College, Oxford, in 1938. Adams was grateful to Oxford for its acceptance of what he calls one's "fantasy potential."

Adams's Oxford years were interrupted, like those of so many others, by World War II. Adams chose to serve in the Royal Army Service Corps (RASC), which is mainly concerned with transport and communication duties, but later he volunteered for the airborne arm of the RASC and served in the Middle East and in Singapore. On his return to England, Adams was shocked to learn how many of his Oxford companions had died during the war.

After demobilization, Adams soon met Elizabeth Acland, whom he would later marry and with whom he would have two daughters. In 1948 he joined the British Civil Service, but he never abandoned his love for storytelling. *Watership Down* began, like many other "children's" classics, as a story initially told by the author to his children (in this case to entertain them on a long car trip); two years after its publication, Adams was able to retire from the Civil Service and write full-time at his various homes in the south of England.

ANALYSIS

In each of his novels, Richard Adams adopts a different individual narrative voice: easygoing and colloquial in *Watership Down* and *Maia*, stately and epic in *Shardik*, ironic and densely allusive in *The Plague Dogs*, and the very different first-person voices in *The Girl in a Swing* and *Traveller*. On the surface, Adams's natural gift as a storyteller is his strongest talent. Yet his novels deserve to be read more for his habitual concerns: a love for "the surface of the earth," as George Orwell called it, as manifested in the English countryside and the creatures who inhabit it; a hatred for the cruelties that human beings inflict on the other inhabitants of this world, as well as on themselves; and an acute awareness of the transitory nature of existence and the evanescence of friendship and love.

(Nordisk Pressefoto/Archive Photos)

WATERSHIP DOWN

Watership Down burst on the literary scene in 1972, as unlikely a success as J. R. R. Tolkien's *The Lord of the Rings* (1955) had been two decades earlier. Its plot and character seemed those of a children's book: A group of rabbits leave their threatened burrow and make a dangerous journey to find a new home, as well as enough new rabbits to ensure its continuation. Yet in its length and often violent action it certainly went beyond the boundaries of a children's work, and it succeeded with many adults. It even led to some shameless imitations, such as William Horwood's mole epic, *Duncton Wood* (1980), but none had the imagination and freshness of the original.

As Tolkien did with the hobbits, Adams made his exotic characters familiar by giving them an easily identifiable demotic speech. Hazel, Bigwig, and the others speak much like what the originals they are modeled on must have sounded like: Adams's companions in the 205th company of the RASC during World War II. (Hazel, according to Adams, is his commanding officer, John Gifford, and Bigwig is Paddy Kavanagh, who was killed in battle.) The rabbits, like their soldier counterparts, are believable everyday heroes. Their persistence in the face of daunting odds, their relatively unflappable demeanor as they are introduced into new and dangerous surroundings, their ingenuity in overcoming their difficulties—all recall the best qualities of those soldiers in the war.

The familiar speech is also reproduced in the novel's narrative voice, which is often that of a good oral storyteller; as Adams said, "A true folk-tale teller is usually rather colloquial." This informality helps to disguise the classical underpinnings of the work, the main one of which is Vergil's *Aeneid* (c. 29-19 B.C.E.). There are also echoes of Xenophon's *Anabasis* (fourth century B.C.E.) and Homer's *Iliad* and *Odyssey* (both c. 800 B.C.E.), with Hazel as a more trustworthy Odysseus, and Bigwig a less belligerent Achilles. These archetypal characters and plot devices are also supported by the scientific accuracy of the details of the rabbits' lives, which Adams culled from *The Private Life of the Rabbit* by R. M. Lockley (1964). Familiar yet exotic characters, an epic story, and verisimilitude of milieu contribute to the lasting and deserved appeal of *Watership Down*. (*Tales from Watership Down*, in its latter half a sequel to the novel, also serves as an answer to those who accused the original of, among other charges, sexism.)

SHARDIK

Adams's next novel, *Shardik*, disappointed many of his readers, for while on the surface, like *Watership Down*, a fantasy, it was far removed from the first novel in setting, characters, and plot. Adams constructs the mythical land of Bekla, whose precarious peace is shattered by the emergence of a great bear, which is taken by many to be the avatar of the god Shardik. After a short rule by the bear's chief follower, Kelderek, the bear escapes, and Kelderek must learn the real meaning of the irruption of Shardik into the lives of so many people. For much of the book, the characters are unlikable, the setting is foreign without being exotic, and the plot seems to be nothing but one violent incident after another. The narration is also different from that in *Watership Down*, in

this case, much more stately and epic in tone, with self-consciously Homeric similes interrupting the narrative flow.

Yet, in the end *Shardik* is satisfying, once the reader grasps the greater themes of the novel. Shardik's reign has allowed slavery to flourish once again in Bekla, and only by suffering and death can Shardik and Kelderek redeem themselves and society. Adams's own horror at slavery, both literary and real, echoes in the plot: The evil slaver Genshed is consciously modeled on Stowe's great villain in *Uncle Tom's Cabin*, Simon Legree, and the mutilated beggar boys seen by Adams from a troop train in India are reproduced in some Beklan slaves. Adams's own hatred of war causes the first half of the book almost to be antiepic in its drive: The religious war it depicts is nasty, brutish, and long. Once the arc of the plot is evident, *Shardik* can be seen as an epic indictment of the horrors of epic war.

THE PLAGUE DOGS

The Plague Dogs is the most tendentious of Adams's novels. The title characters are trying to escape from a laboratory in England's Lake Country, where they have been subjected to cruel and unnecessary experiments. Although seemingly a return to the mode of his greatest success, the grown-up animal novel, it is much more a satire filled with savage indignation at the lengths to which humans will use and abuse other species, a satire which gains effect from Adams's experience working in government bureaucracies. Like *Shardik*, it is an investigation of cruelty, this time toward what the novel calls "animal slaves": "It's a bad world for the helpless," as one of its characters says. Once again Adams adopts a new narrative voice, particularly in the sections concerning humans, this one arch and packed with literary allusions. The novel is not totally one-sided, the case being made near the end for useful animal medical experimentation. Yet again it is in his animal portrayals that Adams best succeeds, particularly those of the dog Snitter, whose nonsense language, caused by a brain operation, echoes that of dramatist William Shakespeare's fools, and of the wild fox, whose feral otherness seems to be an answer to criticisms of Adams's cozy rabbits.

THE GIRL IN A SWING

Adams's next two novels are major departures, explorations of the themes of sexuality and love, subjects he only tangentially touched on previously. *The Girl in a Swing* is nominally a ghost story, but more a depiction of the obsessive love that the hero, Alan Desland, feels for Käthe, a German girl whom he meets in Copenhagen and swiftly marries, not knowing that she is trying to escape a ghost from her past. There are echoes of Emily Brontë's *Wuthering Heights* (1847)—Käthe as Cathy Earnshaw—but Alan is no Heathcliff, and while Adams's depictions of local scenery remain one of his strengths—much of the locale is again borrowed from Adams's childhood—the end of the novel is more deflationary than chilling. Adams said that ghosts in English horror writer M. R. James's short stories are knowingly artificial, but the one in *Girl in a Swing* is unfortunately no less an *umbra ex machina*, a ghost from the machine.

MAIA

Maia returns to the fantasy world of Bekla which Adams created in *Shardik* to tell the story of the eponymous heroine who undergoes a transformation from literal sex slave to country matron, all described at sometimes tedious length, in more than twelve hundred pages. Adams's narrative style here is more familiar than that in *Shardik*, his similes shorter, homelier, and less epic. However, the reproduction of the girl's countrified speech becomes irritating, and anachronisms such as discussions of infection and primitive vaccination are annoying. The plot is basic: Girl meets boy; girl loses boy; girl gets boy. However, the girl does not even meet the boy until almost halfway through the novel, making for difficult reading. The underlying theme is much the same as *Shardik*'s, as the good side attempts to eradicate slavery in the Beklan empire, but this time the scenes of sadism that Adams describes become extremely uncomfortable. In *Shardik* such scenes had a moral point, but here their purpose seems cloudier: We know these characters are villains, so several scenes explicitly depicting their villainy are uncalled for. On the positive side, Adams once again depicts actions that undercut fantasy epic conventions: Maia's most heroic actions are undertaken to prevent, and not to further, violence and warfare. Yet at the end, when Maia has become a contented country wife and mother, the reader wonders how this matron grew out of the girl who, some nine hundred pages earlier, had realized she possessed "an exceptional erotic attitude" and proceeded to use and enjoy it.

TRAVELLER

Traveller is basically the story of the Civil War seen through the eyes and told by the voice of Confederate general Robert E. Lee's famous horse. In this novel, Adams plays to all his strengths, including a new narrative voice, this one a modification of Joel Chandler Harris's in the Uncle Remus stories; a singular, believable animal persona through which the action is described; and a depiction of his favorite themes: hatred of war, admiration for those who must suffer through it, and sorrow over the ephemerality of comrades and friendship. The bravery of Lee's Army of Northern Virginia is, as Adams elsewhere said, a reflection of Adams's own pride in the gallantry of the British 1st Airborne Division in the battle of Arnhem. Lee is Adams's quintessential hero because he treats both animals and people with dignity and respect. Traveller, like satirist Jonathan Swift's Houyhnhnms (*Gulliver's Travels*, 1726), is aghast at humankind's capacity for cruelty, but he is not keen enough (or anachronistic enough) to see the cruelty that slavery commits. Traveller is, as another horse calls him, "thick": At Gettysburg, he thinks Pickett's charge succeeds, and at Appomattox, he thinks the Federals have surrendered to "Marse Robert." However, he gets the basic truth right: "Horses [are] for ever saying goodbye." It was the lesson Adams learned when he returned to Oxford after the war to learn of his friends' deaths, and it is the grave lesson that has informed his best fiction.

William Laskowski

OTHER MAJOR WORKS

SHORT FICTION: *The Unbroken Web: Stories and Fables*, 1980 (originally *The Iron Wolf and Other Stories*); *Tales from Watership Down*, 1996.

NONFICTION: *Nature Through the Seasons*, 1975 (with Max Hooper); *Nature Day and Night*, 1978 (with Hooper); *Voyage Through the Antarctic*, 1982 (with Ronald M. Lockley); *A Nature Diary*, 1985; *The Day Gone By*, 1990.

CHILDREN'S LITERATURE: *The Tyger Voyage*, 1976; *The Adventures of and Brave Deeds of the Ship's Cat on the Spanish Maine: Together with the Most Lamentable Losse of the Alcestis and Triumphant Firing of the Port of Chagres*, 1977; *The Legend of Te Tuna*, 1982; *The Bureaucats*, 1985.

EDITED TEXT: *Sinister and Supernatural Stories*, 1978.

BIBLIOGRAPHY

Bridgman, Joan. "The Significance of Myth in *Watership Down*." *Journal of the Fantastic in the Arts* 6, no. 1 (1993): 7-24. Demonstrates the influence of Walter de la Mare's *The Three Mulla-Mulgars* on the novel.

Chapman, Edgar. "The Shaman as Hero and Spiritual Leader: Richard Adams' Mythmaking in *Watership Down* and *Shardik*." *Mythlore* 5 (August, 1978): 7-11. Solid treatment of *Shardik* and myth; less reliable on *Watership Down*.

Kitchell, Kenneth. "The Shrinking of the Epic Hero: From Homer to Richard Adams's *Watership Down*." *Classical and Modern Literature* 7 (Fall, 1986): 13-30. Convincing argument that Adams's novel is a modern epic.

Meyer, Charles. "The Power of Myth and Rabbit Survival in Richard Adams' *Watership Down*." *Journal of the Fantastic in the Arts* 3, no. 4 (1994): 139-150. Shows the connections between the novel and R. M. Lockley's *The Private Life of the Rabbit*.

Miltner, Robert. "*Watership Down*: A Genre Study." *Journal of the Fantastic in the Arts* 6, no. 1 (1993): 63-70. Traces the various literary genres to which the novel belongs.

JAMES AGEE

Born: Knoxville, Tennessee; November 27, 1909
Died: New York, New York; May 16, 1955

PRINCIPAL LONG FICTION

The Morning Watch, 1951
A Death in the Family, 1957

OTHER LITERARY FORMS

James Agee's earliest published book, *Permit Me Voyage* (1934), was a collection of poems, his second a nonfiction account of Alabama sharecroppers in the Depression. He and photographer Walker Evans lived with their subjects for eight weeks in 1936 on a *Fortune* magazine assignment, with a number of critics hailing the resulting book, *Let Us Now Praise Famous Men* (1941), as Agee's masterpiece. From 1941 through 1948, Agee wrote film reviews and feature articles for *Time* and *The Nation*; thereafter, he worked on film scripts in Hollywood, his most notable screenplay being his 1952 adaptation of C. S. Forester's novel *The African Queen* (1935). He also wrote an esteemed television script on Abraham Lincoln for the *Omnibus* series in 1952. *Letters of James Agee to Father Flye* (1962) contains his thirty-year correspondence with an Episcopalian priest who had been his teacher.

ACHIEVEMENTS

The prestigious Yale Series of Younger Poets sponsored Agee's first book, Archibald MacLeish contributing its introduction. Agee went on to gain an unusual degree of literary fame for a man who published only three books, two of them slim ones, in his lifetime. Sometimes accused of wasting his talent on magazine and film "hack" work, Agee lavished the same painstaking attention on film reviews as on his carefully crafted books. His film work was highly prized by director John Huston, and their collaboration on *The African Queen* resulted in a film classic. His greatest fame developed posthumously, however, when his novel *A Death in the Family* won a 1958 Pulitzer Prize. Three years later, Tad Mosel's dramatization of the novel, *All the Way Home* (1960), earned another Pulitzer. The continued popularity of Agee's work attests his vast human sympathy, his unusual lyrical gift, and his ability to evoke the tension and tenderness of family life in both fiction and nonfiction.

BIOGRAPHY

Born in Knoxville, Tennessee, on November 27, 1909, James Rufus Agee was the son of Hugh James Agee, from a Tennessee mountain family, and Laura Whitman Tyler, the well-educated and highly religious daughter of a businessman. His father sang mountain ballads to him, while his mother passed on to him her love of drama and music. Hugh Agee's death in an automobile accident in the spring of 1916 profoundly influenced young Rufus, as he was called in the family.

Agee received a first-rate education at St. Andrew's School, near Sewanee, Tennessee, where he developed a lifelong friendship with Father James Harold Flye; at Phillips Exeter Academy, Exeter, New Hampshire; and at Harvard College, where in his senior year he edited the *Harvard Advocate*. Upon his graduation in 1932, he went immediately to work for *Fortune* and later its sister publication, *Time*. Over a sixteen-year period, he did a variety of staff work, reviewing, and feature stories while living in the New York metropolitan area.

From 1950 on, Agee spent considerable time in California working mostly with John Huston, but his health deteriorated. Highly disciplined as a writer, Agee exerted less successful control over his living habits, with chronic insomnia and alcohol contributing to a succession of heart attacks beginning early in 1951. Agee was married three times and had a son by his second wife and three more children by his third, Mia Fritsch, who survived him. He succumbed to a fatal heart attack in a New York taxicab on May 16, 1955, at the age of forty-five.

ANALYSIS

Neither James Agee's novella *The Morning Watch* nor his novel *A Death in the Family* offers much in the way of plot. The former covers a few hours of a boy's Good Friday morning at an Episcopalian boys' school, the latter a few days encompassing the death and funeral of a young husband and father. His fiction develops a remarkable lyric intensity, however, and dramatizes with sensitivity the consciousness of children. He presents the minutiae of life as experienced by his characters at times of maximum awareness

(Library of Congress)

and thereby lifts them out of the category of mere realistic detail into the realm of spiritual discovery.

Even a cursory glance at the facts of Agee's life reveals how autobiographically based his fiction is. There is no reason to doubt that St. Andrew's, where he spent the years from ten to sixteen, supplies the framework for *The Morning Watch*, or that Agee's own family, seen at the time of Hugh Agee's fatal accident, furnishes the building blocks of the more ambitious *A Death in the Family*. At the same time, Agee permitted himself artistic freedom in selecting, altering, and arranging the facts of raw experience. It is clear that his literary appropriation of his childhood owes much to reflection and interpretation in the light of maturity.

Agee was a writer who stayed close to home in his work. His fiction displays no trace of the two-thirds of his life spent mainly in New England, New York, and California. As is so often the case with Southern writers, Agee's work is imbued with a sense of his origins, of folk traditions viewed in their own right and in competition with the emerging urban culture. The South, with its insistence on the primacy of personal and familial relationships, was in his bones. In keeping to his earliest and most vividly felt years, Agee created a convincing context in which experiences of universal significance can unfold.

THE MORNING WATCH

At the beginning of *The Morning Watch*, a preadolescent boy and several of his classmates are awakened in the wee hours of Good Friday morning to spend their assigned time in an overnight vigil in the school chapel as part of the Maundy Thursday-Good Friday devotions. Anyone who has experienced a period of religious scrupulosity in childhood will respond to Agee's presentation of Richard. While his friends fumble and curse in the darkness, Richard prepares for adoration. Once in the chapel before the veiled monstrance, he strives to pray worthily despite the inevitable distractions of potentially sinful thoughts, the dangers of spiritual pride, and the torture of the hard kneeling board. Richard wonders whether he can make a virtue of his discomfort: To what extent is it proper for him to suffer along with the crucified Savior? Agee brings Richard intensely alive and conveys the power and the puzzlement of mighty spiritual claims at this stage of life.

The narrative also develops from the start Richard's sense of his relationships with the other boys, most of whom, he realizes, lack his delicate spiritual antennae. After the stint in the chapel is over, he and two classmates do not return to the dormitory as expected but decide on an early morning swim. Their adventure is presented in a heavily symbolic way. Richard dives into deep water at their swimming hole, stays down so long that his friends begin to worry, and emerges before his lungs give out. The boys torture and kill a snake, with Richard (who, like Agee himself, cannot bear to kill) finishing off the job. He debates in his mind whether the snake is poisonous and whether to wash the slime from his hand, deciding finally in the negative. He carries back to the school a locust shell he has found on the way. The snake, which seemingly cannot be killed, suggests both ineradicable evil and, in its victimization, Christ; the locust shell, which he holds next to his heart, seems to represent suffering in a purer form. Richard's dive into the water and subsequent resurfacing obviously symbolize his own "death" and "resurrection" in this Christian Holy Week.

Some critics have noted the influence of James Joyce on this novella. Certainly Richard resembles in certain ways the young protagonists of some of Joyce's *Dubliners* (1914) stories as well as Stephen Dedalus in *A Portrait of the Artist as a Young Man* (1916). Attracted by religious mysteries and artifacts, Richard wishes to appropriate them for his own purposes. He senses the conflict of religion with the world, evinces distaste for the practices of the latter, and hopes to fashion a life that blends the best of both. While Richard's appropriation of religious rite and doctrine is less consciously the artist's than is that of Stephen Dedalus, the reader senses that his individualistic spirituality will inevitably bring him into a Joycean conflict with conservative religious practice.

A DEATH IN THE FAMILY

Since *The Morning Watch*, despite its provocatively ambiguous conflict between the world and the spirit, is somewhat labored and precious, and since Agee's short stories were few and insignificant, his reputation as an important American novelist rests primarily on one book which he did not quite complete before his early death, *A Death in the Family*. As he left it, the story begins at the supper table of the Follet household in Knoxville, Tennessee, in about 1915, and ends just after Jay Follet's funeral on the third day following. Agee had written a short descriptive essay, "Knoxville: Summer 1915" (which makes an appropriate preface to the novel), and six additional sections, which together make up about one-fifth the length of the narrative.

Although all the six scenes (as they will be termed here) pertain to times prior to that of the main story, it remains unclear where Agee intended to place them, or whether he would have used stream-of-consciousness flashbacks, a story-within-a-story technique, or perhaps another method suggested by his cinematic experience to incorporate them. Surely he intended to use them, for they illuminate and enrich the death story despite the absence of any formal linkage among them or collectively to the narrative. The editorial decision to print three of them after each of the first two parts of the three-part narrative seems as logical as any other way under the circumstances.

The novel has no single protagonist. Jay Follet, strong, tall, and taciturn, is described most specifically, at one point being compared to President Abraham Lincoln, though apparently more handsome. Last seen alive one-third of the way through the narrative, he appears in five of the six scenes and remains the main object of the other characters' thoughts in the last two parts of the narrative. At various stages, each important family member reflects on him: his wife Mary, son Rufus, brother Ralph, Mary's parents, Joel and Catherine, Mary's aunt Hannah and her brother Andrew, and even Jay's and Mary's three-year-old daughter, also named Catherine. Agee employs Rufus and Mary as a focus most frequently. No point of view outside the family circle intrudes, and, except on two occasions when the six-year-old Rufus interacts with neighborhood children outside, attention is focused on family members exclusively. Throughout the novel, Agee juxtaposes the tensions and tendernesses of domestic life. The reader is constantly made to feel not only how much the family members love one another but also how abrasive they can be. Recognizing that a family does not succeed automatically, Agee portrays a continual struggle against external divisive pressures and selfishness within.

Jay and Mary's marriage has withstood a number of strains. First of all, their origins differ greatly. Mary's people are the citified, well-educated Lynches; the Follets are Tennessee mountain folk. The couple's ability to harmonize their differences is exemplified in the second of the six scenes. Rufus notes that when singing together, his father interprets music flexibly, "like a darky," while his mother sings true and clear but according to the book. Rufus particularly admires his father's sense of rhythm. Sometimes, the boy observes, his mother tries to sing Jay's way and he hers, but they soon give up and return to what is natural.

Jay's father, who indirectly causes Jay's death, is one point of difference. Mary's antipathy to him is

known to all the Follets, but even Jay realizes that his likable father is weak of character. When Jay's brother calls and informs him that their father is very ill, Jay wastes no time in preparing to go to him, despite his suspicion that the unreliable Ralph has greatly exaggerated the danger. It is on his return trip, after learning that his father is all right, that a mechanical defect in Jay's car causes the crash that kills him instantly.

Jay's drinking problem, a Follet weakness, has also distressed his wife, and Jay has vowed to kill himself if he ever gets drunk again. In one of the scenes, Rufus, aware that whiskey is a sore point between his parents, accompanies his father when he stops at a tavern, and it appears that he has overcome his habit of excess, but his reputation has spread. Both the man who finds Jay's body and the children who later taunt Rufus on the street corner attribute his accident to drunken driving, and Mary has to fight off the temptation to consider the possibility.

Religion is another divisive issue. Jay does not appear to be a denominational Christian, while Mary is, like Agee's own mother, a fervent Episcopalian. The men on both sides of the family are either skeptics or thoroughgoing unbelievers. A devotee of Thomas Hardy's fiction, Mary's father, Joel, has little use for piety or what he calls "churchiness." Although he originally disapproved of Mary's marriage to Jay, he has come to terms with Jay, whom he views as a counterweight to Mary's religiosity. Mary's brother Andrew carries on open warfare with the Christian God. When he first hears of Jay's accident, Mary senses that he is mentally rehearsing a speech about the folly of belief in a benevolent deity. Even young Rufus is a budding skeptic. Told that God has let his father "go to sleep," he ferrets out the details and concludes that the concussion he has heard about, "not God," has put his father to sleep. When he hears that his father will wake up at the Final Judgment, he wonders what good that is. The women accept the inscrutable as God's will, but the men take an agnostic stance and fear the influence of the church. Father Jackson, the most unpleasant person in the novel, ministers to Mary in her bereavement. Rufus quickly decides that the priest's power is malevolent and that, were his real father present, the false father would not be allowed into his home.

Some hours after the confirmation of Jay's death, Mary feels his presence in the room, and though Andrew and Joel will not concede any kind of spiritual visitation, they acknowledge that they too felt "something." Later, Andrew tells Rufus of an event he considers "miraculous": the settling of a butterfly on Jay's coffin in the grave and the creature's subsequent flight, high into the sunlight. The men's unbelief, then, is not positivistic; they recognize the possibility of a realm beyond the natural order, but they bitterly oppose the certified spiritual agent, Father Jackson, as too self-assured and quick to condemn.

To counter the estrangements brought on by cultural and religious conflicts in the family, reconciliations dot the narrative. Rufus senses periodic estrangements from his father and then joyful feelings of unity. Jay frequently feels lonely, even homesick. Crossing the river between Knoxville and his old home, he feels restored. To go home is impracticable, bound up with a vanished childhood. In one of the scenes, the family visits Rufus's great-great-grandmother. It is a long, winding journey into the hills and into the past. It is apparent that none of the younger generations of Follets has gone to see the old woman in a long time. Rufus, who has never been there, comes home in a way impossible to his father. The old woman, more than one hundred years old, barely acknowledges any of her numerous offspring, but she clasps Rufus, the fifth-generation descendant, who is joyful to her. On other occasions, Jay, by imaginative identification with Rufus, can feel as if he is his "own self" again.

Mary also feels alternate waves of friendship with, and estrangement from, her father. He, in turn, has a wife with whom communication is difficult because of her deafness. When Catherine cannot hear her husband, she seldom asks him to repeat himself, as if fearful of exasperating him. In this way, she is insulated from his unbelief. Although they talk little, they communicate by gestures and physical closeness. Agee shows him taking her elbow to help her over a curb and carefully steering her up the street toward their home. Rufus and his father are usually silent on their walks; they communicate by sitting together on a favorite rock and watching passersby.

Much of the talk following Jay's death is irritable and nerve-shattering. Andrew dwells thoughtlessly on the one-chance-in-a-million nature of Jay's accident, for which his father rebukes him. Mary begs Andrew to have mercy and then hysterically begs his forgiveness, upon which her aunt censures her for unwarranted humility. Both Mary and Andrew are enduring crises, however, and are hardly responsible for what they say. She is resisting the temptation to despair of God's mercy; he is trying to come to terms with a possibly meaningless universe. Andrew communicates best with services; throughout the hours of distress, he is unfailingly helpful.

The truest communication exists between Jay and Mary. When he is not silent, he can be sullen or wrathful. As he prepares to set forth on his journey to his father's, Mary dreads the "fury and profanity" she can expect if, for example, the car will not start, but this sometimes harsh husband stops in the bedroom to recompose their bed so it will look comfortable and inviting when she returns to it. She disapproves of his drinking strong coffee, but she makes it very strong on this occasion because she knows he will appreciate it. By dozens of such unobtrusive deeds, Jay and Mary express their love, which prevails over the numerous adverse circumstances and personal weaknesses that threaten it.

Long before he began work on *A Death in the Family*, Agee expressed his intention to base a literary work on his father's death. The eventual novel is thus deeply meditated and very personal. At the same time, it attains universality by means of its painstaking precision. In the Follets can be seen any family that has striven to harmonize potentially divisive differences or has answered courageously a sudden tragedy. As in loving families generally, the tensions do not disappear. At the end, Andrew, for the first time in his life, invites Rufus to walk with him. Sensing the negative feelings in his uncle, Rufus nevertheless is afraid to ask him about them. Walking home with this man who can never replicate his father but who will fill as much of the void as possible,

Rufus comes to terms with his father's death in the silence that in Agee's fiction communicates beyond the power of words. In this reconstruction of his own most momentous childhood experience, Agee portrays the most difficult reconciliation of all.

Robert P. Ellis

OTHER MAJOR WORKS

SHORT FICTION: "A Mother's Tale," 1952; *Four Early Stories by James Agee*, 1964; *The Collected Short Prose of James Agee*, 1968.

SCREENPLAYS: *The Red Badge of Courage*, 1951 (based on Stephen Crane's novel); *The African Queen*, 1952 (based on C. S. Forester's novel); *The Bride Comes to Yellow Sky*, 1952 (based on Crane's short story); *Noa Noa*, 1953; *White Mane*, 1953; *Green Magic*, 1955; *The Night of the Hunter*, 1955; *Agee on Film: Five Film Scripts*, 1960.

POETRY: *Permit Me Voyage*, 1934; *The Collected Poems of James Agee*, 1968.

NONFICTION: *Let Us Now Praise Famous Men*, 1941; *Agee on Film: Reviews and Comments*, 1958; *Letters of James Agee to Father Flye*, 1962.

BIBLIOGRAPHY

Barson, Alfred. *A Way of Seeing: A Critical Study of James Agee*. Amherst: University of Massachusetts Press, 1972. A revisionist view of Agee, whose earliest critics thought that the writer's talents were dissipated by his diverse interests, causing him not to produce enough quality material, but who judged him to have been improving and focusing his skills at the time of his death. Barson inverts this thesis, stating that Agee's finished work should not be so slighted, and that his powers were declining when he died. Contains notes and an index. Should not be confused with *A Way of Seeing: Photographs of New York* (New York: Viking Press, 1965), a collection of photographs by Helen Levitt with an essay by Agee.

Bergeen, Laurence. *James Agee: A Life*. New York: E. P. Dutton, 1984. The definitive biography of Agee, based on interviews with those who knew him and examinations of his papers. Also contains illustrations, notes, a bibliography of Agee's writings, a bibliography of works about him, and an index.

Hersey, John. Introduction to *Let Us Now Praise Famous Men*. Boston: Houghton Mifflin, 1988. A long and thorough appraisal by one of Agee's contemporaries who practiced much the same blend of reportage and literary interpretation that distinguishes Agee's best work.

Kramer, Victor A. *James Agee*. Boston: Twayne, 1975. This short introduction to the life and works of Agee is a good book for the beginning researcher. Besides providing a biography of the writer and a careful discussion of all of his major works, Kramer also includes a chronology of Agee's life, an annotated bibliography, and an index.

Lofaro, Michael, ed. *James Agee: Reconsiderations*. Knoxville: University of Tennessee Press, 1992. Contains an Agee chronology; a brief biography; essays on *Let Us Now Praise Famous Men*, on *A Death in the Family*, and on Agee's journalism; and a bibliography of secondary sources. Several essays argue for ranking Agee higher as a literary figure than previous critics have allowed.

Madden, David, ed. *Remembering James Agee*. 2d ed. Baton Rouge: Louisiana State University Press, 1997. An excellent collection of memories about and assessments of Agee by his friends and coworkers, including Walker Evans, Dwight Macdonald, Father James Harold Flye, John Huston, and Agee's wife, Mia Agee. Also includes illustrations and a detailed chronology of Agee's life.

Spiegel, Alan. *James Agee and the Legend of Himself: A Critical Study*. Columbia: University of Missouri Press, 1998. This analysis of Agee's work includes bibliographical references and an index.

CONRAD AIKEN

Born: Savannah, Georgia; August 5, 1889
Died: Savannah, Georgia; August 17, 1973

Principal long fiction

Blue Voyage, 1927
Great Circle, 1933
King Coffin, 1935
A Heart for the Gods of Mexico, 1939
Conversation: Or, Pilgrim's Progress, 1940
The Collected Novels of Conrad Aiken, 1964

Other literary forms

Conrad Aiken was one of the most prolific of modern American writers, publishing more than forty separate volumes of poetry, novels, plays, short stories, and criticism. Aiken published five collections of stories, culminating in the *Collected Short Stories of Conrad Aiken* (1966). He is the author of *Mr. Arcularis* (1957), a play based on an adaptation by Diana Hamilton of his short story of the same title. His nonfictional writing includes introductions to *Two Wessex Tales by Thomas Hardy* (1919) and *Selected Poems of Emily Dickinson* (1924), as well as a lifetime of reviews, originally published in such leading journals as *The New Republic, Poetry, The Dial, The Nation*, and *The New Yorker*, and collected in *A Reviewer's ABC: Collected Criticism of Conrad Aiken from 1916 to the Present* (1958). An earlier critical work was *Skepticisms: Notes on Contemporary Poetry* (1919). His most famous nonfictional work, and one of his most lasting contributions to American literature, is his third-person autobiography, *Ushant: An Essay* (1952). He published twenty-nine collections of poetry; the best of his early poems were collected in *Selected Poems* (1929), while the best of his total poetic output can be found in *Collected Poems* (1953, 1970). In addition, Aiken served as editor for numerous anthologies of poetry, including *A Comprehensive Anthology of American Poetry* (1929, 1944), and was a contributing editor of *The Dial* from 1917 to 1918. Finally, under the pseudonym Samuel Jeake, Jr., Aiken was a London correspondent for *The New Yorker* from 1934 to 1936.

Achievements

Aiken's literary reputation is based on his poetry, for which he received the Pulitzer Prize in 1930, the National Book Award in 1954, and the Bollingen

(Library of Congress)

Prize in 1956. Despite these major awards, his reputation seems fixed among the most major of minor poets, a position that virtually all of his critics agree is too low. Of his fiction, the short stories "Silent Snow, Secret Snow" and "Mr. Arcularis" are often anthologized and discussed, though few of his others are ever mentioned. His reputation as a novelist is even more tenuous; none of his novels is now in print, and few critical articles about them have been published. When his first novel, *Blue Voyage*, appeared, its initial reputation as an experimental novel and its personal revelations about Aiken's interior life brought the book some notoriety. Subsequent critical opinion, however, has treated *Blue Voyage* as an inferior version of James Joyce's *A Portrait of the Artist as a Young Man* (1916) or *Ulysses* (1922). *Great Circle*, Aiken's second novel, was praised by literary critics as a psychological case study and was admired by neurologist Sigmund Freud himself for its Freudian overtones. Aiken's last three novels received little praise or attention. *A Heart for the Gods of Mexico* was not even published in America until

the collected edition of his novels appeared. Aiken himself considered *King Coffin* a failure; he admits in *Ushant* that his last novels were unsuccessful and says that he does not mind his relative obscurity, but in a letter to his friend Malcolm Cowley, he wrote "Might I also suggest for your list of Neglected Books a novel by c. aiken called *Great Circle*, of which the royalty report, to hand this morning, chronicles a sale of 26 copies in its second half year?" Later critics, like Aiken's contemporaries, saw the major value of his novels in their experimental nature, their Freudian images, and their amplification of the themes of Aiken's poetry.

BIOGRAPHY

Conrad Potter Aiken was born in Savannah, Georgia, on August 5, 1889. Both of his parents were New Englanders. His mother, Anna Potter Aiken, was the daughter of William James Potter, minister of the Unitarian First Congregational Society of New Bedford, Massachusetts, and a friend of poet Ralph Waldo Emerson. His father, William Ford Aiken, was a physician educated at Harvard. The central event of his childhood—and in fact of his whole life—took place in 1900 when, as an eleven-and-a-half-year-old boy, he discovered the dead bodies of his parents. Aiken's father had killed his mother with a revolver and then shot himself. This event remained forever embedded in his psyche. As Aiken writes in *Ushant*, "He had tiptoed into the dark room, where the two bodies lay motionless, and apart, and, finding them dead, found himself possessed of them forever."

Following this crucial event, Aiken's two brothers were separated from him, and he spent the remainder of his childhood living with a great-great-aunt in New Bedford. He attended the Middlesex School in Concord and, in 1907, entered Harvard University during the same period as T. S. Eliot, John Reed, Walter Lippmann, e. e. cummings, and Robert Benchley. At college, Aiken was president of the Harvard *Advocate*, a frequent contributor to the Harvard *Monthly*, and a leader among his classmates in literary discussions, but he also established a pattern which was to hold true throughout his life—he was always a loner, following neither particular schools

of criticism nor prevailing literary styles. Placed on probation for poor class attendance as a senior, Aiken left Harvard in protest and spent half a year in Europe, thus establishing another constant pattern: For the remainder of his life he made frequent trips to Europe, living as often abroad as at home until World War II, after which he lived in New England, primarily in Brewster, Massachusetts.

Following his return to Harvard, Aiken was graduated in 1912 and immediately began writing poems for his first collection, *Earth Triumphant and Other Tales in Verse* (1914). For the rest of his life, Aiken supported himself solely by his writing, except for a brief stint as an English tutor at Harvard in 1927. He married three times, divorcing his first wife, Jessie McDonald, after eighteen years of marriage and the rearing of three children; his second wife, Clarice Lorenz, he divorced after seven years. He remained married to his third wife, Mary Hoover, from 1937 until his death from a heart attack on August 17, 1973, in Savannah, Georgia, the city of his birth, to which he had returned to complete the great circle of his life.

For most of his career, Aiken simultaneously worked on his poetry, fiction, and criticism. From 1925 to 1935, he alternated short-story collections with novels. In 1939 and 1940, he published his last two novels, *A Heart for the Gods of Mexico* and *Conversation*, thereafter concentrating on poetry and criticism. During the 1920's and 1930's, Aiken was involved with such American expatriates as T. S. Eliot, Ezra Pound, and Malcolm Lowry, yet he was always deliberately apart from the center of artistic circles, choosing, for example, to live in London and Brewster rather than Paris and New York. The best source of information about Aiken's relation with other writers is *Ushant*, in which Eliot, Pound, and Lowry appear as the Tsetse, Rabbi Ben Ezra, and Hambo.

ANALYSIS

The central event in Conrad Aiken's personal life—the murder-suicide of his parents—was also the central event of his artistic life, for all of his literary work is in some way aimed at coming to terms with the childhood tragedy. In *Ushant*, Aiken says of his parents that "he was irrevocably dedicated to a life-long—if need be—search for an equivalent to it all, in terms of his own life, or work; and an equivalent that those two angelic people would have thought acceptable." The search for understanding of his personal tragedy motivated Aiken to try to understand the universal tragedy of modern man, what Joseph Warren Beach called "moral terror," the basic question of good and evil in the human heart that American writers have been struggling with since the advent of American letters.

Aiken's search for a way to maintain equilibrium in the face of his contradictory love for his parents and his revulsion for their deaths lies outside of theological or conventional ethical questions; his search centered on his own consciousness, on himself. The major subject of each of his five novels is a search for self, an interior exploration—often expressed metaphorically as a circular journey. *Blue Voyage* and *Great Circle* focus on psychological understanding in which the protagonist attempts to get back to himself by a circular analysis of his past. *King Coffin* is a psychological horror story of a madman's decision to murder a complete stranger, a decision that eventually leads the protagonist around full circle until he kills himself. *A Heart for the Gods of Mexico* presents a literal journey—a train trip from Boston to Mexico—in which the narrator attempts to reconcile the beauty and strangeness of the changing landscape with the impending death of his woman companion. Finally, *Conversation* describes the circular arguments in a lover's quarrel which eventually runs its course, returning to its starting place.

In each novel, Aiken's chief character is trying to complete what in plane geometry is called a great circle of a sphere, a circle whose plane passes through the center of the sphere. For Aiken's protagonists, the circle is a descent into their pasts and the sphere is the shape of their lives. Because of this self-analysis, each novel is introspective and confessional. Taken together, the novels chart a series of points on Aiken's great circle, a graphic display of his search for understanding his own life. Each novel is based, in varying degrees, on autobiographical details from his life, and each is discussed in *Ushant*, where

Aiken says "the artificer, in the very act of displaying himself in the new shape of the artifact, must remain wholly neutral to that part of himself which is his subject—which is to say, his all."

Aiken's attempt to get to the bottom of or to the other side of his parents' deaths led him on a series of physical voyages between America and Europe and on a series of literary voyages between poetry and fiction, which he called in his 1958 poem "The Crystal," "The westward pour of the worlds and the westward pour of the mind." In both his life and his art he speaks of a constant tension between two opposing forces: a desire for artistic expression, for bringing art to bear on the chaos of human existence which was in constant confrontation with what Frederick Hoffman calls "the shock of reality, which continually challenges the creative spirit and, in moments of terror or violence, may even severely dislocate it." Although the shortest distance between two points may be a straight line, when those points are located within these opposing spheres, then the shortest arc between the comfort of art and the moral terror of reality becomes the great circle that Aiken so thoroughly and so gracefully traced in his novels.

BLUE VOYAGE

Writing in 1952 about his first novel *Blue Voyage* (which in *Ushant* he calls, half-ironically, *Purple Passage*), Aiken said it was "a compromise in which the voice of Joyce had been too audible." This Joycean comparison refers to the hero of the novel, William Demarest, who has booked a second-class passage aboard a steamship en route to England, ostensibly to search for his lost love Cynthia, but actually to search within himself for an explanation of his feelings about Cynthia and about himself as a writer. Demarest clearly resembles Aiken, both in autobiographical detail (when Demarest's parents die he is sent as a boy to live in New Bedford) and in critical reputation (Demarest names as his literary weakness the inability to present a "theme energetically and simply" instead of dressing it "in tissue upon tissue of proviso and aspect . . . from a hundred angles"). The novel is also Joycean in style, for when Demarest discovers that Cynthia is actually on board the ship, he returns to his stateroom and launches himself into a lengthy regression which Jay Martin in his *Conrad Aiken: A Life of His Art* (1962) calls a "preconscious monologue." This regression is filled with allusions to self-crucifixion, bizarre sexual dreams, fragments of popular songs, bits of English poetry, extended lists of numbers, noises, and a constant repetition of the capitalized word MISERY, all accompanied by the incessant throbbing of the ship's engines.

Jay Martin sees *Blue Voyage* as an attempt at combining the confessional and the aesthetic novel, and like *A Portrait of the Artist as a Young Man*, Aiken's first novel includes discussions of its hero's theories about art and literature with Aiken's Cranley/Lynch figure, a man named Silverstein, who acts as Demarest's psychoanalyst. *Blue Voyage* tries to go beyond Joyce's early work in terms of experimentation, for in the sixth chapter, Aiken presents a lyrical out-of-body experience in which the main characters of the novel perform a hallucinatory ritualistic parody of the Crucifixion which results in Cynthia's being metamorphosed into a Gothic stained-glass window. The book ends with a series of undelivered letters from Demarest to Cynthia that alternate between intense self-loathing and a passionate attempt to explain the letter writer to his lost love, to himself, and, by extension, to explain Aiken to his readers. As Demarest says in his second letter, "It is precisely the sort of thing I am always trying to do in my writing—to present my unhappy reader with a wide-ranged chaos—of actions and reactions, thoughts, memories and feelings—in the vain hope that at the end he will see that the whole thing represents only *one moment, one feeling, one person*."

GREAT CIRCLE

In his autobiography, Aiken's second novel, *Great Circle*, appears as *Dead Reckoning*, a punning title that encompasses the major themes of the novel: navigation along the great circle as a metaphor for exploration of the psyche of a man whose world, like the author's, turns over with the horrifying discovery of his parents' betrayal by sudden death. *Great Circle* opens with its protagonist, Andrew Cather, on board a train to Cambridge, where he will surprise his wife in the act of adultery, an act that was forewarned both by a friend and by signs the protagonist has refused

to see. Andrew Cather, who is often called "One-eye Cather" because of an ambiguously explained injury to one eye, is not able to stop the marital infidelity he knows is coming, any more than the Cyclops in Homer's epic can avoid Odysseus's prophesied appearance.

Cather's discovery leads him to Aiken's familiar dilemma: how to maintain balance in the face of moral terror. Cather's initial response is to avoid the terror by avoiding consciousness of it, at first by maintaining a false air of melodrama about the situation and then by repeatedly drinking himself into a stupor. The combination of drunkenness and estrangement from his wife, whose adultery was consummated with Cather's best friend, causes him to fall into the lengthy reverie about his childhood which constitutes all of chapter 2, the most successfully sustained section in all of Aiken's prose fiction. This section is a sensually lyrical evocation of the summer in Cather's childhood in Duxbury, Massachusetts, during which he first felt the strangeness of his father's absence and his mother's attachment to his Uncle David. The chapter is Joycean in style and Faulknerian in content, full of lyrical passages that call up ocean and shore. Like Maisie from Henry James's *What Maisie Knew* or William Faulkner's Quentin Compson from *The Sound and the Fury*, the young Andy Cather slowly comes to awareness about the sexuality of the adults who move around him. Reading a letter from his father to his mother, Andy Cather realizes imperfectly that his mother is having an affair with his uncle. The chapter ends with Andy's terrible discovery of the bodies of his mother and her lover, drowned during a storm. Speaking of this chapter, Jay Martin says, "Aiken intends it to be real, an exact and complete account of his experience insofar as it entered the consciousness of the boy."

The third chapter of *Great Circle* consists of a nightlong amateur psychoanalysis session in which Cather speaks an exhaustive monologue in an attempt at talking through his marital problems in the present, the horror of his childhood discovery, and the interconnection between the two events. Realizing that he unconsciously associates the physical intimacies of marriage with the discovery of his mother, dead in his uncle's embrace, Cather makes an actual trip to Duxbury, thus confronting and completing the great circle voyage through his past and his psyche. Aiken's novel reflects Henry David Thoreau's argument at the conclusion of *Walden* (1854) that "Our voyaging is only great-circle sailing," for the horrible scene from his protagonist's childhood is, of course, suggestive of Aiken's own childhood tragedy. The image of circularity echoes throughout the novel, from the title to the description of Cather "hurrying from point to point on the earth's surface, describing his swift little arc" to the later statement that he is running "round in mad circles, like a beheaded hen." Later, Cather says to himself about the origin of his problems, "It is your own little worm-curve; the twist that is your own life; the small spiral of light that answers to the name of Andrew Cather." The entire second chapter is enclosed within outsized parentheses, suggestive of the great-circle, and in one of his childhood revelations, Cather remembers an old riddle— "Rats live on no evil star," a palindrome that "spells the same thing backward"—which reminds the reader that Andrew Cather's initials backward are Conrad Aiken's, and that Cather's attempt at rescuing his marriage through a series of therapeutic returns to his childhood is also Aiken's attempt at resolving his own problems by writing about them in novels.

KING COFFIN

Aiken's third novel, *King Coffin*, is the only one he leaves out of *Ushant*, probably because he considered it to be a major failure, unredeemable by subsequent analysis. Although most critics refer to *King Coffin* as a major failure, if they mention it at all, Aiken's best critic, Jay Martin, argues that the author meant *King Coffin* as a parody of a psychological novel, playing "lightly with a serious psychological subject while still retaining a real sense of its dignity and importance." The subject of the novel is an insane plan conceived half in jest by Jasper Ammen (a name suggestive of E. A. Robinson's *King Jasper*, 1936) to demonstrate his innate superiority by murdering an ordinary person chosen at random—a person Ammen comes to call "a specimen man" or "the anonymous one." The motive for the murder is the achievement of a perfectly pure relationship, in

Ammen's simplification of Nietzschian/Emersonian ideas, between the superior man and the ordinary one. Initially, Ammen claims he has chosen his victim and is studying the dailiness of his life as background for a novel about "pure" murder, a novel he plans to call *King Coffin*.

As the actual novel progresses, Ammen begins to think of Jones, his intended victim, as "one-who-wants-to-be-killed." This short novel ends with Ammen's too-close identification with his victim; seeing that Jones's wife's newly born baby has died, Ammen decides that the perfect ending to his plan would be his own murder, thereby bringing the novel full circle: The random victim has unconsciously caused Ammen to kill himself. Although Jay Martin sees *King Coffin* as its protagonist's "attempt to recognize and resolve his own strangeness, to realize his ego completely by fully understanding its complexity," most critics have seen the book as a competent murder-mystery at best, clearly the least successful of Aiken's novels. Because Jasper Ammen is labeled a psychotic at the start of the novel, the rationalizations he uses for his bizarre plan never become compelling; they are neither the ravings of a madman nor the thoughts of a superior human. Instead they fall somewhere in between. *King Coffin* is considerably shorter than Aiken's previous novels and interesting mainly for its conception: Aiken creates a psychopathic killer who pretends to write the book that Aiken actually writes, just as the narrator of *Ushant*, a character Aiken calls only D., discusses his attempt at writing the very autobiography in which one reads his discussion.

A HEART FOR THE GODS OF MEXICO

Aiken's penultimate novel, *A Heart for the Gods of Mexico*, returns to the author's now-familiar themes. The story tells of a lengthy train trip from Boston to Mexico by day coach, taken by a woman who knows she is soon to die of heart failure; her fiancé, who is unaware of her condition; and her friend, who is half in love with her. Noni, the young woman who is soon to die, puzzles over her upcoming death in a manner that recalls *King Coffin*: "It seems so ridiculously random . . . it's *that* that's so puzzling." Unlike the psychopathic protaganist of that novel, however, the young woman is a sympathetic character. She and her friend are constantly struggling with such questions as whether the subterfuge is ethical, whether the trip is hastening her inevitable death, and whether the startling tropical beauty of Mexico should make them forget the impending death or revel in it.

Both critics and its author have described *A Heart for the Gods of Mexico* as a curious failure; the novel contains brilliant landscape scenes, strong and affecting portrayals of character, particularly Noni's, and a passionate depiction of the traveler's meeting in Cuernavaca with Hambo, Aiken's name for Malcolm Lowry, the author of *Under the Volcano* (1947). Unlike *Blue Voyage* and *Great Circle*, however, this book lacks form. The trip is too long in getting started, and too much local color is presented along the way. *A Heart for the Gods of Mexico* is the shortest of Aiken's novels. The book offers no flashbacks, no self-analysis, no sense of any concentric structure except for the shape imposed on the novel by the narrative of the trip itself, Noni's "great-circle to Mexico" upon which she takes her "heart as an offering to the bloodstained altar of the plumed serpent."

CONVERSATION

Aiken's last novel, *Conversation*, records the bitterly circular quarrel of Timothy and Enid Kane, whose marital argument, like the one in *Great Circle*, is (on the surface, at least) about infidelity, this time on the part of the male. In some ways, the novel deals with feminism; Enid Kane wants to live in an urban environment while her husband, a painter, wants to live in the country on Cape Cod rather than remain in the city painting commissioned portraits. Timothy sees the journey to the country as a chance to get back in touch with his natural artistic creativity; his wife sees the move as "all that nonsense of yours about plain living and high thinking, about living the natural and honest life of our Pilgrim ancestors, and being independent—but it's no good for a woman." While Enid is wrong in thus belittling her husband's desire to paint freely, Timothy is also wrong in hiding the fact that the move is partly to get away from his in-town affair. The bucolic escape turns into a series of get-togethers with bohemian Greenwich Village artists and poets, such as Karl Roth, who represents

the poet Maxwell Bodenheim. Enid Kane's reference to the pilgrims suggests one of the connections between this portrait of the artist as a young married man, the novel's subtitle, and the excerpts from *A Journal of the Pilgrims at Plymouth* (1962) that head each chapter of the novel. Like the early visitors to Massachusetts, Timothy Kane wants to recapture a spirit of freedom so that he can overcome the sterility he has felt, both in his art and in his life, since the birth of his daughter. Although his daughter's birth represents the highest womanly creative act in his wife's mind, and although his daughter's freshly imaginative outlook on nature is exactly the kind of artistic rebirth Timothy is looking for, he comes to see during the course of the long, circuitous argument that his repressed anxieties about the physical details of his daughter's birth are the cause of his inability to hold a conversation with his wife. Like Andrew Cather, who is disgusted by the "filthy intimacies" of marriage, Timothy Kane finds the effect of childbirth, what his friend calls "that butcher-shop and meaty reality," to be "something for which love's young dream hadn't at all been prepared. A loss of belief."

The argument in *Conversation* continues along Aiken's familiar circular path, until, like a snake with its tail in its mouth, it comes back to where it began and resolves itself with the reunion of the Kanes and a decision to have a son; however, since no one can predict the sex of an unborn child before conception, it is clear that this resolution will likely lead the couple back onto another loop of their argument. In the middle of his last novel, Aiken presents a scene in which Kane is comparing his idea of marriage while still engaged with his vision after his child's birth. Using the metaphors of poetry and prose, Kane gives Conrad Aiken's final critical assessment of the relationship between his own work in the two genres: "The poetry had been too pure a poetry, its further implications (of all that the body, and passion, could exact, or time and diurnal intimacy dishevel and destroy) had been too little understood; and when the prose followed, it had inevitably seemed only too ingrainedly prosaic."

This assessment is accurate. Despite their relative

merits, Aiken's five novels would probably not be read today were it not for the poetic reputation of their author. In his autobiography, Aiken says of his parents' deaths that "he was to discover, while at Harvard, that the staining sense of guilt and shame had been mysteriously exorcised, as no longer there," but clearly some degree of both guilt and shame must have remained throughout the author's life, despite the therapy gained from writing these five novels.

Timothy Dow Adams

OTHER MAJOR WORKS

SHORT FICTION: _Bring! Bring! and Other Stories_, 1925; _Costumes by Eros_, 1928; _Among the Lost People_, 1934; _Short Stories_, 1950; _Collected Short Stories_, 1960; _Collected Short Stories of Conrad Aiken_, 1966.

PLAYS: _Mr. Arcularis: A Play_, pb. 1957 (first pr. as _Fear No More_, 1946).

POETRY: _Earth Triumphant and Other Tales in Verse_, 1914; _Turns and Movies and Other Tales in Verse_, 1916; _The Jig of Forslin_, 1916; _Nocturne of Remembered Spring and Other Poems_, 1917; _The Charnel Rose_, 1918; _Senlin: A Biography and Other Poems_, 1918; _The House of Dust_, 1920; _Punch: The Immortal Liar_, 1921; _Priapus and the Pool_, 1922; _The Pilgrimage of Festus_, 1923; _Changing Mind_, 1925; _Priapus and the Pool and Other Poems_, 1925; _Prelude_, 1929; _Selected Poems_, 1929; _John Deth: A Metaphysical Legend, and Other Poems_, 1930; _Gehenna_, 1930; _The Coming Forth by Day of Osiris Jones_, 1931; _Preludes for Memnon_, 1931; _And in the Hanging Gardens_, 1933; _Landscape West of Eden_, 1934; _Time in the Rock: Preludes to Definition_, 1936; _And in the Human Heart_, 1940; _Brownstone Eclogues and Other Poems_, 1942; _The Soldier: A Poem by Conrad Aiken_, 1944; _The Kid_, 1947; _Skylight One: Fifteen Poems_, 1949; _The Divine Pilgrim_, 1949; _Wake II_, 1952; _Collected Poems_, 1953, 1970; _A Letter from Li Po and Other Poems_, 1955; _The Fluteplayer_, 1956; _Sheepfold Hill: Fifteen Poems_, 1958; _Selected Poems_, 1961; _The Morning Song of Lord Zero_, 1963; _A Seizure of Limericks_, 1964; _Cats and Bats and Things with Wings: Poems_, 1965; _The_

Clerk's Journal, 1971; _A Little Who's Zoo of Mild Animals_, 1977.

NONFICTION: _Skepticisms: Notes on Contemporary Poetry_, 1919; _Ushant: An Essay_, 1952; _A Reviewer's ABC: Collected Criticism of Conrad Aiken from 1916 to the Present_, 1958; _Selected Letters of Conrad Aiken_, 1978.

EDITED TEXTS: _A Comprehensive Anthology of American Poetry_, 1929, 1944; _Twentieth Century American Poetry_, 1944.

BIBLIOGRAPHY

Butscher, Edward. _Conrad Aiken: Poet of White Horse Vale_. Athens: University of Georgia Press, 1988. A definitive biography, this lengthy, well-illustrated book relies heavily on psychological theory, mostly Freudian, and primary sources to trace Aiken's life. The bibliography is extremely helpful, including not only the standard items but also Aiken's edited anthologies and his critical essays, and a list of relevant psychological texts and studies.

Denney, Reuel. _Conrad Aiken_. Minneapolis: University of Minnesota Press, 1964. An early, short volume, which covers both Aiken's prose and his poetry, though the latter, especially in the case of _Senlin: A Biography and Other Poems_, receives more attention. Looks briefly at the novels and the short story "Silent Snow, Secret Snow," but is more interested in Aiken's experimental prose narrative, _Ushant: An Essay_. Includes a selected bibliography.

Hoffman, Frederick. _Conrad Aiken_. New York: Twayne, 1962. A useful volume on Aiken, offering a succinct reading, through a Freudian approach, of Aiken's prose and poetry, which Hoffman believes is Aiken's most significant literary contribution. Includes a chronology of Aiken's life, a bibliography of his work, and an annotated bibliography of the books and articles written about him.

Marten, Harry. _The Art of Knowing: The Poetry and Prose of Conrad Aiken_. Columbia: University of Missouri Press, 1988. Marten applies his knowledge of Aiken's life to his poetry and prose, which receive equal treatment in this critical study.

Senlin: A Biography and Other Poems is at the center of Aiken's life and work, and the focus is on the narrative voice in the poems. The explications of poems are short because many are discussed. Includes a bibliography.

Seigal, Catharine. *The Fictive World of Conrad Aiken: A Celebration of Consciousness.* De Kalb: Northern Illinois University Press, 1993. Chapters on the Freudian foundation of Aiken's fiction, on his New England roots, and on *Blue Voyage*, *Great Circle*, *King Coffin*, *A Heart for the Gods of Mexico*, and *Conversation*. Concluding chapters on Aiken's autobiography, *Ushant*, and an overview of his fiction. Includes notes, selected bibliography, and index.

LOUISA MAY ALCOTT

Born: Germantown, Pennsylvania; November 29, 1832

Died: Boston, Massachusetts; March 6, 1888

(Library of Congress)

PRINCIPAL LONG FICTION

Moods, 1864 (revised 1881)

Little Women, 1868

Little Women, Part 2, 1869 (also known as *Good Wives*, 1953)

An Old-Fashioned Girl, 1870

Little Men, 1871

Work: A Story of Experience, 1873

Eight Cousins, 1875

Rose in Bloom, 1876

A Modern Mephistopheles, 1877

Under the Lilacs, 1878

Jack and Jill, 1880

Jo's Boys, 1886

OTHER LITERARY FORMS

In addition to her novels, Louisa May Alcott authored a collection of fairy tales, *Flower Fables* (1854); several short-story collections, notably *Aunt Jo's Scrap-Bag* (1872-1882, 6 volumes), *A Garland for Girls* (1887), and *Lulu's Library* (1895); a nonfiction work, *Hospital Sketches* (1863); a collection of plays, *Comic Tragedies Written by "Jo and Meg" and Acted by the "Little Women"* (1893); a few poems; and some articles and reviews for major periodicals. Surviving letters and journal entries were edited and published in 1889 by Ednah D. Cheney.

ACHIEVEMENTS

Louisa May Alcott first gained the recognition of a popular audience and then acceptance by the critics as a serious writer, becoming a giant in the subgenre of adolescent girls' novels and the family story. She was unique in having moral lessons exemplified by her characters' actions, thus avoiding the sermonizing of her contemporaries. Her heroes and heroines are flawed humans often trying to overcome their weaknesses. Much of the time, Alcott managed to avoid making her novels a vehicle to promote social or political issues, which was a fairly common practice of the day. She was a master of character development, and, despite adverse scholarly criticism and changing literary tastes among readers, her novels endure for what they offer in timeless values: the importance of a strong family life and honest, hard work.

BIOGRAPHY

Louisa May Alcott was the second daughter of Abby May and Amos Bronson Alcott, a leader in the Transcendentalist movement headed by Ralph Waldo Emerson. When it became evident that Bronson Alcott would not be a reliable provider for the family, Louisa perceived it as her mission in life to support the family. The death of her younger sister and the marriage of her older sister were traumatic experiences, and partly to fill the void left by their absence, partly to seek some purpose in life and to participate in the Civil War in the only way open to women, Alcott became an army nurse in Washington, D.C. After six weeks, she contracted typhoid fever, from which she never fully recovered, due to the effects of mercury poisoning from her medication. These experiences are recorded in *Hospital Sketches*, the work which would establish her as a serious writer.

Alcott had also begun writing gothic thrillers, which brought in money for the family but did not enhance her literary reputation. Her first novel appeared in 1864. In 1865, Alcott toured Europe, and soon after her return, she became editor of the children's magazine *Merry's Museum*. About that time, the editor Thomas Niles urged Alcott to write a novel for girls, resulting in *Little Women*, an overnight success. After her father suffered a stroke in 1882, Alcott moved him to Boston, and she continued to try to write. Sensing by this time that she would not regain her health, she adopted her nephew, John Sewell Pratt, who would become heir to her royalties and manage her affairs after her death. Louisa May Alcott died on March 6, 1888, two days after the death of her father. The two are buried in the Sleepy Hollow Cemetery, Concord, Massachusetts.

ANALYSIS

Versatility characterizes the canon of Louisa May Alcott, which includes children's literature, adult novels, gothic thrillers, autobiography, short stories, poetry, and drama. While Alcott's works for children may be distinguished from those of other writers of children's stories in some important ways, they nonetheless fit into the broader context of American literature of the time. What set Alcott's children's novels apart from the rest was her careful avoidance of the overt didacticism and sermonizing that characterized many others. A code of proper behavior is implicit, but it is detected in situations in the novels rather than showcased by authorial intrusion. In the juvenile novels, excepting the March family works, Alcott wrote less from her own experiences, and she was more prone to rewrite earlier works. The most enduring of Alcott's collection are the girls' novels and the family stories, which continue to be read because of the vitality of the characters—how they deal with life situations and challenges with humor, even fun—and the way Alcott uses detail to present simple, honest lives. Although criticism of Alcott's work in the late twentieth century found the children's novels to be overly sentimental, readers of the day enjoyed them.

The works for adults portray a less simplistic view of life than do the children's stories. Readers meet people with boring, unhappy, or even sordid lives, lives that would not be deemed suitable for those works which earned Alcott the epithet "children's friend." Alcott's skill in building character, in using dialogue, and in exploring social issues of the day is evident.

MOODS

Moods, Alcott's first and favorite novel, was published in 1864. Having been advised to cut its length by about half, Alcott submitted a text predictably unsatisfactory both to her and to her critics. Some twenty years later, a new edition was published with some deletions and the restoration of former chapters. The basic story remained the same: The heroine, Sylvia Yule, is dominated by mood swings. Governed more by feelings than by reason, she is prone to making misguided judgments in love. She loves Adam Warwick, a model of strength, intellect, and manliness, but she learns, too late, that he uses others to serve his own purposes and then shuns them. After Adam leaves Sylvia, his best friend, Geoffrey Moor, becomes a true friend to Sylvia, but he mistakes the friendship for love. He is totally unlike Adam Warwick: slight of build, sweet, and tranquil. Sylvia decides to marry him because he is a "safe" choice, not because she loves him. When Sylvia finally confesses to Geoffrey her love for Adam, Geoffrey leaves for one year to see if his absence will help her learn to love him. The plan works, but on his way back to claim her love, Adam, Geoffrey's traveling companion, is drowned. Though saddened, Sylvia and Geoffrey are reunited, wiser and more cognizant of the value of their mutual love. In the 1864 edition of the book, Sylvia develops tuberculosis, and when Geoffrey returns, he nurses her through her terminal illness, before she dies in his arms. In the 1881 edition, in which Sylvia falls ill but recovers and accepts Geoffrey's love, Alcott focuses more clearly on the theme of moods rather than of marriage, and plot and characterization are more even.

LITTLE WOMEN

Although Louisa May Alcott was already an established author upon the publication of *Little Women*, it was that novel which brought her an enduring reputation. The novel was written quickly; the original manuscript was completed in six weeks. Because the public clamored for a sequel revealing how the sisters married, Alcott obliged with *Little Women, Part 2* (later published as *Good Wives*) one year later. The two were subsequently published as a single novel. *Little Women* is based on the fictionalized life of the Alcott sisters at their house in Concord. The plot is episodic, devoting at least one chapter to each sister. The overall theme is the sisters' quest to face the challenges of life and to overcome those "burdens" so that they may develop into "little women." The chief burden of Meg, the eldest, is vanity. Jo, like her mother, has a temper which she must learn to control if she is to become a "little woman." Beth, thirteen, is already so nearly perfect that her burden is simply to overcome her shyness. Amy is the proverbial spoiled baby in the family, and she must try to overcome her impracticality and thoughtlessness. When the sisters are not sharing intimacies and producing dramatic productions for entertainment, they interact with the next-door neighbors, Mr. Lawrence

and his orphaned grandson Laurie. Laurie is wealthy in material things but longs to have family; he often enjoys the March girls' activities vicariously, from a window. Mrs. March, affectionately called Marmee, is a central character in the novel. The girls know that they can confide in their mother about anything, and at any time. She is strong, wise, and loving, clearly the anchor of the family. Mr. March is a clergyman who has gone to serve in the Civil War and so is absent during the course of the novel. The story ends with the engagement of Meg, the eldest sister; with Jo's decision to become a writer and to leave her tomboyish childhood for a mature relationship; and with Amy's betrothal to Laurie. Beth, tragically, dies of a terminal illness. *Little Women* was an overnight success, and the public eagerly awaited the sequel, provided in *Little Women, Part 2*.

LITTLE WOMEN, PART 2

The sequel to *Little Women* was released in January of 1869. *Little Women, Part 2* begins with Meg's wedding day; she settles into a conventional marriage in which her husband is the breadwinner and she is the docile, dependent wife. They have two children, Daisy and Demi-John. For a time, Alcott allows Jo to be happy being single and to enjoy her liberty. After she has married Amy off to Laurie in another conventional romantic marriage, she bows to the wishes of her readers and has Jo marry Professor Bhaer, the kindly older man about whom Jo became serious in *Little Women*. Jo is able to maintain a degree of freedom and to pursue intellectual interests in a way that conventional marriages of the day would not have allowed. Together, they operate the Plumfield School, whose pedagogy parallels the philosophy of Alcott's father in his Temple School; thus, the success of Plumfield is a tribute to Bronson Alcott.

AN OLD-FASHIONED GIRL

Alcott's 1870 novel, *An Old-Fashioned Girl*, was not as commercially successful as were the March family books. The theme of this book is that wealth in itself does not bring happiness. Polly Milton pays an extended visit to her wealthy friend Fanny Shaw, only to realize that this very "new-fashioned" family is not much of a family at all: Brother Tom is left uncared for by everyone except his grandmother, who is also ignored by the rest of the family; Maud, the six-year-old sister, is a petty, ill-tempered child. The father gives himself wholly to his work; the mother neglects the household largely because of a self-proclaimed invalidism. Fanny herself is lazy and shallow. Polly Milton's family, on the other hand, though poor, is noble. The Reverend Milton is a country parson who provides for his family's needs and has a loving and happy family. Mrs. Milton, like Marmee of *Little Women*, is a wise and caring confidante who dresses Polly appropriately for her age and who teaches respect and charity by word and deed. She is an able seamstress and cook; she operates the household economically and within their means. Polly helps improve the Shaw family, and she returns unspoiled to her loving family. She becomes a music teacher so that she can send her brother to college. Polly is not perfect, however; her flaw is vanity. As a working woman without a fashionable wardrobe, she does not enjoy full social acceptance.

Polly seeks proper marriages for the Shaw children. A reversal of financial circumstances in the Shaw family forces Fanny to learn from the Miltons how to make do with little, but it is a blessing because both Tom and Fanny become better people. By the end of the novel, marriages have been planned for all except Maud, who remains a happy spinster.

Little Men

Little Men, published in 1871, employs the episodic technique of earlier novels to continue the story that *Little Women* began. The focus is on Professor and Jo March Bhaer and their students at Plumfield. Jo has a son Rob and a lovable baby boy, Teddy; Daisy and Demi, Meg's twins, are now old enough to be students at the school, as is Bess, Laurie and Amy's daughter. Professor Bhaer's nephews, Emil and Franz, are senior students. Other students include the stock characters Stuffy Cole, Dolly Pettingill, Jack Ford, Billy Ward, and Dick Brown. Four other students are more fully developed: Tommy Bangs, an arsonist; Nat Blake, who loves music and tells lies; Nan, who wanted to be a boy and becomes a physician; and Dan Kean, a troublemaker who threatens to upset the reputation the Bhaers have gained for success in reforming wayward students. The children are

rarely seen in the classroom, carrying out Bronson Alcott's Temple School principle of cultivating healthy bodies and spirits as well as developing the intellect. Corporal punishment of students is not practiced, and the school is coeducational. Under the guidance of the long-suffering Professor Bhaer and the now-motherly Jo, the school is like a magnet that draws its former charges back to its stable shelter.

Work

Some critics consider *Work* to be Alcott's most successful novel for adults. Christie Devon, an orphan, leaves home to seek independence. She goes through a number of jobs quickly—a chapter is given to each one, in episodic fashion—before she meets Rachel, a "fallen" woman whom she befriends. When Rachel's past is discovered, she is fired from her job, as is Christie for remaining her friend. Christie becomes increasingly poor, hungry, lonely, and depressed, to the point of contemplating suicide. Rachel comes along in time and takes Christie to a washerwoman who introduces her to the Reverend Thomas Power. He arranges for Christie to live with the widow Sterling and her son David, a florist. Christie tries to make David heroic, which he is not, but in time they are married, just before David goes off to war. He is killed, and Christie goes to live with David's family and has a child. Rachel turns out to be David's sister-in-law. The novel focuses on the loneliness and frustration of women in situations such as these. Like Alcott, they find salvation in hard work, and though financial recompense is paltry, it is not deemed beneath their dignity. More than in her other novels, Alcott realistically portrays relationships between men and women.

Eight Cousins

Alcott published *Eight Cousins* in 1875. She does not resort to the episodic technique of earlier novels as she focuses clearly on the character Rose Campbell, also the heroine of the sequel to *Eight Cousins*, *Rose in Bloom*. A ward of her Uncle Alex, the orphaned heiress Rose comes to live with her relatives. Her six aunts all have strong opinions about Rose's education, but her schooling merely crams Rose full of useless facts; she is not really educated. Finally, Uncle Alex takes over her education and provides her with "freedom, rest, and care," echoing Bronson Alcott's educational philosophy. Rose is in frequent contact with her seven male cousins, to whom she becomes a confidante. She submits to Uncle Alex's wholesome regimen, but she has her ears pierced despite his disapproval, and she admires what is fashionable even though she chooses the outfits her uncle suggests. The central theme of the novel is a woman's education. It prescribes physical exercise, housework, and mastery of some kind of trade. It allows courses that were nontraditional for women at the time the novel appeared and rests on practical experience rather than reading of books, although reading is respected. While the novel clearly has in mind a treatment of various social issues, it succeeds nevertheless because of Alcott's development of the children and the humor with which she views the foibles of the adult characters.

A MODERN MEPHISTOPHELES

In 1876, Alcott's publisher requested a novel to be published anonymously in the No Name series of works by popular writers. She chose a manuscript written ten years earlier that had been deemed sensational. A revised version enabled Alcott to write in the gothic mode without compromising her reputation as a children's writer. Furthermore, she had been impressed with Johann Wolfgang von Goethe's *Faust* (1808, 1833), and the parallels to Goethe's masterpiece are obvious. Just when Felix Canaris, a rejected but aspiring poet, is contemplating suicide, Jasper Helwyze comes along, rescues Felix, and befriends him, promising to make him successful. Within a year, Felix has indeed succeeded. He falls in love with Olivia, a former love who had rejected Jasper, but Gladys, an orphan protégé of Olivia, also falls in love with Felix.

Completely under Jasper's influence, Felix is forced to marry Gladys instead of Olivia. Jasper harasses the young couple in various ways. As they look forward to life with a child, Jasper forces Felix to reveal his secret to Gladys: He has no real talent— Jasper has been writing the successful poetry. Gladys does not reject Felix, but after going into premature labor, she and the baby both die. Before her death, she implores Felix and Jasper to forgive each other.

Thus, Felix is freed from his bondage to Jasper and goes on to live a worthwhile life; Jasper has a stroke. Alcott's novel is not simply a rewritten *Faust*; a dominant theme in the novel is the power of women, both wives and mothers, to save men from themselves, an idea of high interest to the readers of the day. There is a great deal of foreshadowing, partly because of its parallels to *Faust*. Alcott explores the darker side of human nature in a way that she could not, or would not, do in her works for children.

JACK AND JILL

Jack and Jill's episodic plot may be explained by the fact that it was first serialized in the *St. Nicholas* magazine in 1879 and 1880, although several of Alcott's other novels also employed this technique. Alcott called it a "village story," and Harmony Village is her fictionalized Concord. Jack and Frank are modeled after Anna Alcott's sons, and Ed is based on Ellsworth Devens, a Concord friend. Jack and Jill are recovering from a serious sliding accident, and the novel concerns the way the other Harmony Village children are inspired by the near tragedy to improve their ways, both physically and morally. Like Beth of *Little Women*, Ed is almost too good to be true, foreshadowing his early death. This novel, like *Little Men*, is an educational novel.

JO'S BOYS

In 1886, Alcott brought closure to the March family novels with a final story portraying the changes that have occurred within the previous ten years. Mr. Lawrence, the kind next-door neighbor of *Little Women*, endows a college next door to the Plumfield School of *Little Women, Part 2* and *Little Men*. Mrs. Meg notes the absence of the beloved Marmee, Beth, and her late husband John. Readers learn that Demi has gone into the publishing business; Daisy is a "little woman" who marries Nat Blake, and Nan becomes a doctor. Nat completes his musical education in Germany; Emil becomes a ship's officer who takes charge of a lifeboat when the captain becomes ill; Dan, who decided to seek his fortune in the West, kills a man in self-defense when a crooked card game goes sour. It is remembering and upholding the honor of Plumfield that guides these young men. The one character who cannot return to the inner circle of the

March family is the "bad boy," Dan Kean. He does come back to Plumfield after he is wounded while working with Native Americans in the West, but he is not allowed to marry Beth, the daughter of Amy March and Laurie Laurence. Feminism is the main focus of the novel; all of the young women succeed in careers that were denied the title characters in *Little Women*.

Victoria Price

OTHER MAJOR WORKS

SHORT FICTION: *Flower Fables*, 1854; *On Picket Duty and Other Tales*, 1864; *Morning-Glories, and Other Stories*, 1867; *Aunt Jo's Scrap-Bag*, 1872-1882 (6 volumes); *Silver Pitchers: And Independence, a Centennial Love Story*, 1876; *Spinning-Wheel Stories*, 1884; *A Garland for Girls*, 1887; *Lulu's Library*, 1895.

PLAY: *Comic Tragedies written by "Jo and Meg" and Acted by the "Little Women,"* 1893.

NONFICTION: *Hospital Sketches*, 1863; *Life Letters, and Journals*, 1889 (Ednah D. Cheney, editor); *The Journals of Louisa May Alcott*, 1989 (Joel Myerson and Daniel Shealy, editors).

BIBLIOGRAPHY

Delamar, Gloria T. *Louisa May Alcott and "Little Women."* London: McFarland, 1990. Unlike other Alcott biographers, Delamar includes reviews and critical analyses of Alcott's work, ratings given to *Little Women*, her showing in polls, and her commemoration with a postage stamp.

Elbert, Sarah. *A Hunger for Home*. Philadelphia: Temple University Press, 1984. Elbert analyzes the dynamics between Louisa and the other family members and places the Alcotts' lifestyle and frequent upheaval in context. Alcott's "hunger for home" is rooted in her never having had a permanent domestic environment.

Showalter, Elaine. *Sister's Choice: Traditions and Change in American Women's Writing*. Oxford, England: Clarendon Press, 1991. Chapter 3 discusses the wide variance in feminist critical reception of Alcott's *Little Women*: Some feel that bowing to pressures of the time kept her from ful- filling her literary promise; others see the novel as an excellent study of the dilemma of a literary woman writing in that age.

Stern, Madeleine B. *Louisa May Alcott*. Norman: University of Oklahoma Press, 1950. Considered the standard biography of Alcott, it provides a readable account of the author's life and an excellent bibliography.

_____. *Louisa May Alcott: From Blood and Thunder to Hearth and Home*. Boston: Northeastern University Press, 1998. In evaluating Alcott's literary reputation, Stern concludes that the author was more than just the "children's friend."

NELSON ALGREN
Nelson Ahlgren Abraham

Born: Detroit, Michigan; March 28, 1909
Died: Sag Harbor, New York; May 9, 1981

PRINCIPAL LONG FICTION

Somebody in Boots, 1935
Never Come Morning, 1942
The Man with the Golden Arm, 1949
A Walk on the Wild Side, 1956
The Devil's Stocking, 1983

OTHER LITERARY FORMS

Although Nelson Algren is known primarily as a novelist, some critics believe that the short story, because it does not make the structural demands the novel does, was a more appropriate genre for him, and his *The Neon Wilderness* (1947) has been acclaimed one of the best collections of short stories published in the 1940's. *Chicago: City on the Make* (1951) is a prose poem which has been variously described as a social document and a love poem to the city that serves as the center of Algren's fictional world. Similar nonfiction writings include *Who Lost an American?* (1963), a self-described "guide to the seamier sides" of several cities, including Chicago, and *Notes from a Sea Diary: Hemingway All the Way*

(1965); both books combine travel writing and personal essays. What little poetry Algren wrote that is not included in his novels (*The Man with the Golden Arm*, for example, concludes with a poem of the same name which Algren terms an "epitaph") is included in *The Last Carousel* (1973), along with some unpublished stories and sketches. He also collaborated with H. E. F. Donohue on the book *Conversations with Nelson Algren* (1964), a series of interviews. *Nelson Algren's Own Book of Lonesome Monsters* (1962), an anthology to which he contributed a preface

(Library of Congress)

and the concluding story, sounds Algren's recurring theme: Human beings are always alone.

ACHIEVEMENTS

While Algren's first novel, *Somebody in Boots*, failed commercially, it drew the attention of serious literary critics, who were even more impressed by his second novel, *Never Come Morning*, which won for Algren in 1947 one thousand dollars from the American Academy of Arts and Letters. Also in 1947, he received a grant from the Newberry Library to assist him in the writing of *The Man with the Golden Arm*, which subsequently received the National Book Award in 1950. Since many of the stories in *The Neon Wilderness* had previously appeared in the O. Henry Memorial collections or in *Best American Short Stories*, Algren's stature as a first-class writer of fiction was assured by 1950. Because his fictional world, for the most part, was Chicago, Algren is frequently linked with James T. Farrell and Richard Wright, who belong to what some critics have termed the "Chicago School." While he denied any literary indebtedness to Farrell and Wright, Algren admitted that his work was influenced by Carl Sandburg, partly because Algren's prose tends to the poetic, so much so that he was termed by the famous literary

historian Malcolm Cowley "the poet of the Chicago slums."

Maxwell Geismar termed Algren a "neo-naturalist" with roots in the American realistic tradition of Stephen Crane, Theodore Dreiser, and Ernest Hemingway (Algren acknowledged his debt to Hemingway, who in return hailed Algren as, after William Faulkner, among America's first writers). Unfortunately, critics, including Geismar, have also found many of the excesses of naturalism—melodrama, romanticism, oversimplification of characters and motives, and "over-writing"—in Algren's work, which has also been assailed for its formlessness. What Algren lacks in style and form, however, he more than compensates for in rich detail and insightful observations about what George Bluestone has called the "world's derelicts," those unfortunates who had largely been ignored, even by those writers who were ostensibly concerned with the "lumpen proletariat." In fact, so preoccupied is he with the victims of the American Dream, those losers customarily associated with the Depression, that one seldom encounters the other America in his fiction. Consequently, some readers have found his work dated, and while *The Man with the Golden Arm* and *A Walk on the Wild Side* were both filmed (in 1955 and 1962, respectively), thereby testifying to Algren's popularity, his critical standing declined. Yet from 1945 to 1960, he was among America's most acclaimed writers because of his focus and his vision, both of which were compatible with post-World War II America.

BIOGRAPHY

Nelson Ahlgren Abraham was born in Detroit, Michigan, on March 28, 1909, to second-generation Chicagoans, who moved back to Chicago when Algren was three years old. From 1912 until 1928, Algren absorbed the Chicago environment that was to become the center of his fictional world. After receiving his journalism degree from the University of Illinois in 1931, he began traveling across the Southwest, working at odd jobs (door-to-door coffee salesman in New Orleans, migrant worker, co-operator of a gasoline station in Texas, and carnival worker) and gathering the raw material that he later transformed into his fiction, particularly *A Walk on the Wild Side*. After serving time for stealing a typewriter (an oddly appropriate theft for a writer), he returned to Chicago, where he continued his "research" on the Division Street milieu and began to write short stories, poems, and his first novel, *Somebody in Boots*, a Depression tale about the Southwest that became, after extensive revision, *A Walk on the Wild Side*.

After World War II—he served three years in the Army—Algren legally shortened his name, returned again to Chicago, and within five years enjoyed a reputation as one of America's finest fiction writers. *The Man with the Golden Arm* received the National Book Award, and several stories were also recognized for their excellence. It was during this period that Algren had his now-famous affair with French novelist and philosopher Simone de Beauvoir. *A Walk on the Wild Side* and its subsequent filming, as well as the cinematic adaptation of *The Man with the Golden Arm*, brought Algren to the height of his popularity during the 1950's and 1960's, but aside from some travel books and his last novel, his writing career essentially ended in 1956. In his later years, he taught creative writing, before spending his last years on *The Devil's Stocking*, a thinly veiled fictional treatment of the trial and imprisonment of Reuben

"Hurricane" Carter, a middleweight boxer. The "novel" did little to restore Algren's literary reputation.

ANALYSIS

Whether the setting is Chicago or New Orleans, Nelson Algren's characters live, dream, and die in an environment alien to most Americans, many of whom have achieved the financial success and spiritual failure endemic to the American Dream. His characters are, at their best, losers in the quest for success; at their worst, they are spectators, not even participants, in that competitive battle. While his protagonists do aspire to escape from their environments, to assume new identities, and to attain that American Dream, they are so stunted by their backgrounds and so crippled with their own guilt that their efforts are doomed from the start and their inevitable fate often involves the punishment that their guilt-ridden souls have unconsciously sought. In *Never Come Morning*, Bruno cannot escape his guilt for allowing Steffi to be raped by his gang and almost welcomes his punishment for the murder of another man; in *The Man with the Golden Arm*, Frankie Machine cannot escape his guilt for the accident that incapacitates his wife and so can end his drug addiction only by hanging himself; in *A Walk on the Wild Side*, Dove cannot escape his guilt for having raped Terasina, to whom he returns after having been blinded in a fight. In all three novels, the guilt that the man experiences from having abused a woman leads to a self-destructive impulse that negates his attempt to escape from his environment and produces the punishment he seeks.

NEVER COME MORNING

Although it is not his first published novel (*Somebody in Boots*, a commercial failure that Algren revised and reissued as *A Walk on the Wild Side*, was his first published novel), *Never Come Morning* is Algren's first major novel. As the chronicle of a young man's passage from boyhood to manhood, *Never Come Morning* is another, albeit more cynical, American initiation novel, in which Bruno Bicek's initiation leads to his death. Like many young men, Bruno dreams of escaping from the ghetto through professional sports, either boxing or baseball ("Lefty" Bicek is a pitcher), but Algren quickly indicates, through similar chapter headings, that Bruno shares a "problem" with Casey Benkowski, his idol, whose defeat in the ring foreshadows Bruno's eventual defeat in life. Bruno's dreams are illusory, the product of the media: He reads *Kayo* magazine, sees pictures of boxers on matchbook covers, and watches Jimmy Cagney films. His dream of becoming a "modern Kitchel," a former Polish-American boxing champion, reflects his desire to become someone else, to define his success in terms of other people, not himself. To become a successful man, he seeks status as the president and treasurer of the Warriors, his street gang, but his allegiance to the gang reflects his childish dependence on the group, not his adult leadership of it. His "other-directedness" also affects his relationship with Steffi, whom he seduces partly in order to gain status from the Warriors, who subsequently assert their own sexual rights to her. Rather than defend her and reveal the very "softness" that wins the readers' respect, he yields to the Warriors, thereby forsaking independence and manhood and incurring the guilt that eventually destroys him.

Like most of Algren's women, Steffi has a supporting role and exists primarily in terms of the male protagonist. She is the agent by which he comes of age sexually, acquires his spiritual guilt, eventually becomes an independent man, and finally, since she has alienated the informant Bonifacy, is doomed. Despite being the victim of a gang rape, Steffi retains her capacity for love and forgiveness, limited as that is, and becomes the stereotyped "whore with the heart of gold" whose love enables the "hero," antiheroic as he is, to overcome the odds. Her passivity is reflected symbolically through Algren's description of the fly without wings in Steffi's room: After he "seduces" her, Bruno destroys the fly. Later, when Bruno wins a Kewpie doll and subsequently and unthinkingly destroys it, Algren ties the fate of the doll, an appropriate symbol, to Steffi, who is won and destroyed by Bruno. Steffi's fate seems even crueler than Bruno's, since he will "escape" in death but Steffi will remain trapped with the other prostitutes who endure at "Mama" Tomek's brothel.

Before he is incarcerated, Bruno does mature through a series of tests that prove his manhood. Although he cannot articulate his love and desire for forgiveness, he does come to understand that love is compatible with manhood. When he arranges a fight for himself with Honeyboy Tucker, he acts independently; when he overcomes Fireball Kodadek and Tiger Pultoric, Bonifacy's thugs, he overcomes his fear of physical mutilation (Fireball's knife) and of his idol and father figure (Pultoric is the former champion). Before he can "be his own man," Bruno must overcome his childish dependence and hero worship. Bruno's subsequent victory over Tucker makes his earlier symbolic victory official and gives him the identity he seeks as a promising "contender," but that identity is destroyed when he is arrested only minutes later and sent to jail.

Images of imprisonment pervade the novel, which is concerned with the institutions that house inmates. When Bruno first serves time, Algren digresses to describe prison life, just as he does when he recounts Steffi's life at the brothel, where she is no less a prisoner. While she is there, she dreams of a "great stone penitentiary" and of the "vault" that is the barber's room. The prison and the brothel are appropriate institutions for a city which Algren compares to a madhouse. (Algren also sees the prostitutes as inmates of an insane asylum.) There is no escape for Steffi or Bruno, just as there is no real morning in this somber tale of darkness and night. Algren's Chicago is America in microcosm: As madhouse, prison, and brothel, it is an insane, entrapped world where people "sell out," thereby prostituting themselves.

THE MAN WITH THE GOLDEN ARM

In *The Man with the Golden Arm*, also set in Polish-American Chicago, Algren reiterates many of the themes, images, and character types that exist in *Never Come Morning*. Although the novel's controversial theme of drug addiction has received much attention, Algren is not concerned with drug addiction per se, but with the forces, external and internal, that lead to the addictive, dependent personalities that render people unable to cope with their environments or escape from them. Once again, Algren's characters are life's losers, "the luckless living soon to become the luckless dead," the "wary and the seeking, the strayed, the frayed, the happy and the hapless, the lost, the luckless, the lucky and the doomed" who become the "disinherited," those who emerge "from the wrong side of its [America's] billboards." The "hunted who also hope" in *Never Come Morning* become the "pursued" in *The Man with the Golden Arm*, which also relies on naturalistic metaphors comparing people and animals.

Since the characters are themselves victims of a system that excludes them, it seems ironic that they should experience guilt, but Algren's protagonist, Frankie Machine, is trapped by the guilt he feels at having been responsible for the car accident that has paralyzed Sophie, his wife. (Since Sophie has induced the paralysis—there is nothing physically wrong with her—his guilt is even more ironic.) Sophie uses Frankie's guilt to "hook" (a word suggesting addiction) him, punish him, and contribute to their self-destructive mutual dependence. Algren describes Frankie's guilt as "slow and cancerous" and even has Louie, the pusher, attribute drug addiction to the desire for self-punishment. Frankie, the "pursued," is not alone in his guilt, for Algren portrays Record Head Bednar, the "pursuer," as also afflicted by a consuming guilt. As the agent of "justice," he feels "of all men most alone, of all men most guilty of all the lusts he had ever condemned in others." Bednar, who is hardly without sin, must nevertheless "cast the first stone."

Sin and guilt permeate this novel, which belabors religious imagery, particularly that concerning the crucifixion. The controlling metaphor in the novel is Sophie's "luminous crucifix," which she uses to enslave Frankie. Sophie states, "My cross is this chair. I'm settin' on *my* cross. . . . I'm *nailed* to mine." When her friend Violet suggests that she is driving in her own "nails," Sophie evades the issue because her "crucifixion," while voluntary, is not selfless but selfish. Algren observes the parallels between Sophie and Christ—both have been betrayed and bleed for the sins of others—but Sophie lacks love. In another parody of the crucifixion, Sparrow protests to Bednar, "You're nailin' me to the cross, Captain"; Bednar responds, "What the hell you think they're

[the politicians] doin' to me?" Although they have enough religious teaching to mouth biblical allusions, Algren's characters use Christianity only as popular culture, as a source, like advertising and films, of reference to their own ego-centered worlds. Although Algren suggests that "God had forgotten His own," at least in Frankie's case, it is at least equally true that, as Sophie confesses, she and Frankie have forgotten God. Sophie's pathetic, self-centered musing about God having gone somewhere and keeping His distance indicate that He has no place in the world of Division Street. Surely Algren's allusion to the gamblers' God, who watches Sparrow's "fall," reflects the post-Christian modern world.

In Algren's naturalistic world, the characters are seen as caged animals waiting to be slaughtered. At the beginning of the novel, Frankie, who waits for justice from Bednar, watches a roach drowning in a bucket and is tempted to help it, but the roach dies before he intercedes, just as Frankie dies without anyone interceding for him. Algren's metaphor for the trapped Sophie is equally flattering. When she hears the mousetrap in the closet snap shut, "she felt it close as if it had shut within herself, hard and fast forever." Even Molly Novotny, who resembles Steffi in being a "fallen woman" and agent of redemption, is depicted as living in a "nest." In fact, Algren uses the animal imagery to suggest Frankie's impending fate. When Frankie is apprehended for stealing irons, Algren uses "over-fed hens" and "bosomy biddies" to describe the saleswomen and then has Frankie glimpse "a butcher holding a broken-necked rooster." Since Frankie finally hangs himself, the glimpse is ironically prophetic. Frankie's addiction is also expressed in animal terms: Frankie has a "monkey on his back," and while he temporarily rids himself of the monkey, permanent escape is impossible. The two caged monkeys at the Kitten Klub shriek insults at the patrons and serve as the metaphor incarnate for Frankie's addiction.

Frankie's addiction is also expressed in terms of an army buddy also addicted to morphine, Private McGantic, whose "presence" is akin to the monkey's. By the end of the novel Frankie has "become" Private

McGantic: Frankie calls himself "Private Nowhere," suggesting both the identification and the lack of direction. "Private McGantic" is, however, only one of Frankie's identities; the novel recounts his futile attempt to become someone other than Frankie Machine (the assumed name reflects his lost humanity), the Dealer. He wants Molly to call him the "Drummer," not the "Dealer," but he never becomes a professional musician, and part of his tragedy is that he does not know who he is: "Who am I anyway, Solly?" The answer Solly (Sparrow) gives, "Be yourself," is a meaningless cliché, an example of circular reasoning because Frankie does not know what his "self" is. The official inquest into the death of Francis Majcinek (Frankie's "real" name) establishes nothing of consequence (his addiction is not even alluded to) except that he is the "deceased," one of the "luckless dead" Algren mentions earlier in the novel. Even his fictional life is not "real": It is a "comic strip" from birth to death.

A WALK ON THE WILD SIDE

A Walk on the Wild Side, Algren's fourth novel, is a reworking of *Somebody in Boots*, published some twenty years earlier. As a result, although it resembles the other two in its characters, loose structure, and imagery, it also looks back to an earlier time, the Depression, and its setting is New Orleans rather than Chicago. Once again, Algren focuses on prison inmates, whose "kangaroo court" justice is superior to the justice they receive "outside," and on prostitutes, who also "serve their time" and are compared to caged birds (the brothel is an "aviary"). Despite their situation and their pasts, they are "innocent children" in their naïveté and illusions, and one of them is the means by which the hero is redeemed. Other notable characters include the freaks and the cripples who frequent Dockerty's "Dollhouse" and who are the physical counterparts of the emotional cripples in the novel. Achilles Schmidt, legless former circus strongman, is the exception, for he has found psychological strength through the accident that should have "crippled" him. It is only when Dove Linkhorn, the protagonist, is blinded and therefore "crippled" by Schmidt that he rids himself of the illusions that have weakened him.

A parody of the Horatio Alger myth of the American Dream, *A Walk on the Wild Side* concerns an ambitious young man who "wants to make something of himself" and leaves the farm to find fame and fortune in the city. Dove's journey is "educational," in terms of the reading instruction he receives and the culture he acquires, as well as the "lessons" he learns about capitalism and life in general. At the beginning of the novel, Dove is an "innocent," as his name suggests, but that "innocence" is not sexual—he rapes Terasina, the Earth Mother who is also his first "mentor"—but experiential, in that he believes in the "Ladder of Success" with "unlimited opportunities" for "ambitious young men." Algren offers Dove a naturalistic parable of capitalism, particularly on the tenuous nature of life at the top. The headless terrapin in the fish market struggles to the top by using its superior strength in "wading contentedly over mothers and orphans," but its reign as King of the Turtles is short-lived, and it has literally and symbolically "lost its head." Algren adds that Dove does not know that "there was also room for one more on the bottom." Before he reaches the bottom, Dove becomes a salesman, the epitome of the enterprising capitalist; the coffee scam and the phony beauty-parlor certificate racket, while illegal, are also seen as integral parts of capitalism.

Before he achieves his greatest success as a "salesman" of sex, Dove works, appropriately, in a condom manufacturing plant, which also sells sex. In his role as "Big Stingaree" in Finnerty's brothel, he is paid to perform an art which involves the "deflowering" of "virgins," who are played by prostitutes. In effect, the brothel, the primary setting in the novel, also serves as the symbolic center since Algren presents a society that has sold itself, has "prostituted" itself to survive. Ironically, the real prostitutes in the brothel are morally superior to the "prostitutes" in mainstream American society, the "Do-Right Daddies," the powerful people who crusade against sin but also sin within the laws they create.

Hallie Breedlove, a prostitute, "sins," but she is capable of love and compassion, first with Schmidt and then with Dove, with whom she leaves the brothel. The "escape" is futile, however, for her subsequent pregnancy, in the light of her black "blood," threatens their future, and she believes that she can have her child only if she returns to her past, the mulatto village where she was born. Dove lacks her insight and in his attempt to find her is jailed, released, and then loses his sight in a battle with Schmidt. Metaphorically, however, in searching for her, he finds himself, and in losing his vision, he gains insight. Having learned that the "loser's side of the street" is superior to the "winners'," Dove abandons his quest for success and returns to his Texas hometown to be reconciled to Terasina. Unlike Bruno and Frankie, Dove not only survives but also resolves to deal constructively with the guilt caused by his sin against his woman.

THE DEVIL'S STOCKING

Algren's last novel, *The Devil's Stocking*, is not so much a novel as a fictional treatment of Reuben Carter's trial and imprisonment. What began as an *Esquire* assignment, covering a boxer's murder trial, grew to "novel" proportions, probably because of the boxing and the trial, both of which appear in his other novels. The Algren characters—prostitutes, gamblers, police officers, and petty crooks—reappear in the novel about Carter, renamed Ruby Calhoun for fictive purposes. Because of its geographical and chronological distance from his earlier novels, as well as its blending of fact and fiction, it is not among the works for which Algren will be remembered.

Despite the qualified optimism of *A Walk on the Wild Side*, Algren's novels tend to paint a negative image of capitalistic American society with its nightmarish American Dream. Chicago and New Orleans become microcosms of America, a country marked by images of madness, imprisonment, and prostitution. In that world, virtue, such as it is, resides on the "loser's side of the street," in the prisons and the brothels. Constricted by their backgrounds, Algren's male protagonists typically strive to escape and assume a new identity, sin against a woman (thereby incurring guilt that compounds their problems), serve time in prison (presented as a place of refuge), and pursue a self-destructive course that leads inevitably to death or mutilation.

Thomas L. Erskine

OTHER MAJOR WORKS

SHORT FICTION: *The Neon Wilderness*, 1947; *The Last Carousel*, 1973 (also includes sketches and poems).

NONFICTION: *Chicago: City on the Make*, 1951; *Who Lost an American?*, 1963; *Conversations with Nelson Algren*, 1964; *Notes from a Sea Diary: Hemingway All the Way*, 1965.

EDITED TEXT: *Nelson Algren's Own Book of Lonesome Monsters*, 1962.

BIBLIOGRAPHY

Cox, Martha Heasley, and Wayne Chatterton. *Nelson Algren*. Boston: Twayne, 1975. This well-executed critical biography traces the development of Algren's major works, with a section on Symbolism and an overall assessment for each. The concluding chapter refers to Algren as both poet—he continued to write poetry that echoed his fictional themes—and prophet—in his fictional approach to social consciousness. A chronology, notes, and a bibliography are included.

Donohue, H. E. F., with Nelson Algren. *Conversations with Nelson Algren*. New York: Hill & Wang, 1964. A book of interviews (from 1962 and 1963). Effectively covers Algren's family background, experiences as a wanderer during the Depression, and notions of the writer's role in relation to society.

Drew, Bettina. *Nelson Algren: A Life on the Wild Side*. New York: Putnam, 1989. This biography of Algren includes twenty-five pages of bibliographical references.

Giles, James R. *Confronting the Horror: The Novels of Nelson Algren*. Kent, Ohio: Kent State University Press, 1989. Giles attempts to resuscitate Algren's reputation by emphasizing his existentialism and de-emphasizing his naturalism. This short book traces Algren's literary antecedents and discusses his influence on such latter-day naturalists as Hubert Selby, Jr., and John Rechy.

Pitts, Mary Ellen. "Algren's El: Internalized Machine and Displaced Nature." *South Atlantic Review* 52 (November, 1987): 61-74. Focuses on Chicago's elevated railway as a symbol of entrapment in the inner city in Algren's major works; the prisonlike bars of the El's framework symbolize the circumscription of the characters' lives and echo the "danger" of technology—the enclosing of the human mind that occurs when technology is unquestioned. Details from Algren's fiction are thoroughly explored.

ISABEL ALLENDE

Born: Lima, Peru; August 2, 1942

PRINCIPAL LONG FICTION

La casa de los espíritus, 1982 (*The House of the Spirits*, 1985)

De amor y de sombra, 1984 (*Of Love and Shadows*, 1987)

Eva Luna, 1987 (English translation, 1988)

El plan infinito, 1991 (*The Infinite Plan*, 1993)

Hija de la fortuna, 1999 (*Daughter of Fortune*, 1999)

OTHER LITERARY FORMS

Isabel Allende was a journalist before she turned to fiction, and she has published widely in many forms. Besides news and feature articles, Allende has written fiction for children, including *La gorda de porcelana* (1984); humor pieces, including the essay collection *Civilice asu troglodita: Los impertinentes de Isabel Allende* (1974); short stories, such as *Cuentos de Eva Luna* (1990; *The Stories of Eva Luna*, 1991); and many essays, television scripts, and film documentaries. She has also written a book-length memoir of her daughter's illness and death, which includes excursions into her own life, *Paula* (1994). Her book *Afrodita: Cuentos, recetas, y otros afrodisiacos* (1997; *Aphrodite: A Memoir of the Senses*, 1997) is unclassifiable by genre, being a mingling of erotic recipes, stories, old wives' tales, and advice about food and sex. Some of Allende's work blurs the boundaries between novel and creative nonfiction. The real people and events of her own and her country's past figure largely in her fiction writing, and "magical" elements, such as telepathy and clairvoyance, sometimes appear in her nonfiction.

ACHIEVEMENTS

Isabel Allende's books have been translated into more than twenty-seven languages and have been best-sellers in Europe, Latin America, and Australia, as well as the United States. A few of the dozens of awards and honors she has won include Chile's Best Novel of the Year award in 1983 for *The House of the Spirits*, France's Grand Prix d'Evasion in 1984, Mexico's Best Novel award in 1985 for *Of Love and Shadows*, a German Author of the Year prize in 1986, and an American Critic's Choice Award in 1996. Her work has been celebrated by major honors in more than a dozen countries, the range of these awards reflecting her mixed popular and scholarly audience.

(Reuters/Gustau Nacarino/Archive Photos)

She has also been awarded numerous honorary degrees from institutions including Bates College, Dominican College, New York State University, and Florida Atlantic University. Her version of Magical Realism has greatly influenced a new generation of experimental writers.

BIOGRAPHY

Isabel Allende was born in Lima, Peru, and moved to Chile when she was three years old; she comes from a major Chilean political family and identifies herself as a Chilean. Her childhood was spent with her maternal grandparents in Santiago, Chile, following the divorce of her parents. She represents her grandparents as Esteban and Clara Trueba in her best-known novel, *The House of the Spirits*. Educated partly in England and Europe, Allende returned to Chile in her early twenties to become a journalist and to involve herself in feminism and political causes. She spent the years 1964 through 1974 writing articles and editing journals; she also worked on television shows and film documentaries. Early experiences before the 1973 military coup in Chile, which changed her life, included editing *Paula* magazine and interviewing for television stations.

Allende was married to engineer Miguel Frias in 1962 and was divorced from him in 1987; her two children, Paula and Nicholas, were born of this union. Her daughter Paula's illness and death, the major tragedy of Allende's adult life, are recounted in the memoir *Paula*. In 1988 Allende married William Gordon.

The daughter of a cousin of Chilean president Salvador Allende, Isabel Allende was always preoccupied with Chilean history and politics, particularly the events leading to her uncle's death during a military coup in 1973 which overthrew Allende's socialist government and led to military commander Augusto Pinochet's dictatorship. Chile's internal problems have always been a major factor in her works. Allende at first attempted to help the forces attempting to overthrow the new regime, but she was forced to escape with her family to Venezuela in 1974. Following her exile, she lived in various parts of the world and taught in a number of institutions, including in the United States at the University of Virginia, Barnard College, and the University of California at Berkeley.

ANALYSIS

Isabel Allende's work is at the forefront of the Magical Realism movement. Magical Realism is, in essence, the putting together of realistic events with fantastic details in a narrative that is written as if it were factual. Although it is practiced worldwide, Magical Realism is associated mostly with Latin American writers such as Gabriel García Márquez, whose novel *Cien años de soledad* (1967; *One Hundred Years of Solitude*, 1970) is perhaps the prototypical Magical Realist novel. Magical Realism equates intuitive knowledge with factual knowledge, so that readers' definition of reality is challenged and they are able to understand the importance of all the types of knowledge. Allende adds another dimension to Magical Realism, because she often uses it to examine women's issues and problems in Latin American society. Critic Patricia Hart asked, "Has [Allende] by her politics, her commitment to women's issues, her liberal, liberated female characters, and even her gender forged a new category that we might call magical feminism?" It seems clear from her works that she is not merely another Magical Realist writer. Her magical elements tend to define a concept of the feminine that equates it with fruition, generation, and the spiritual and allows hope for the future through womankind. Thus the green hair of Clara in *The House of the Spirits* may be seen as a complicated symbol suggesting intuition, passion, feminine nature, and growth.

Allende's novels are many layered, which may account for their tremendous popularity worldwide and their translation into so many languages. They each contain a striking narrative, with elements of the surreal woven into the story so flawlessly that readers are forced to accept the fantastic premises (such as women being born with green hair, levitating, or reading minds) as though these were ordinary physical facts. The narrative builds up lively suspense, and the intriguing plots and unusual, yet somehow believable, characters contribute to the appeal. Allende uses her startling symbolism to define the male and female realms of power and influence and to show how women manage to achieve power even in societies that greatly repress them. Allende also makes use of the political narrative, which may not be fully understandable to readers unfamiliar with Latin American history. However, the representation of history is also woven into the narrative fabric, so readers do not feel their lack of knowledge; rather, they learn without effort. Allende is that rarity, a popular novelist whose work has literary complexity and merits rereading.

THE HOUSE OF THE SPIRITS

The House of the Spirits, Allende's first novel, remains her most widely read book. It is based on the events of her childhood and on the Chilean political situation that resulted in the death of her cousin Salvador Allende. It tells the story of three generations of women, from the traditionally feminine Clara, based in part on Allende's own grandmother, to Blanca, her daughter, who appears to conform to the family's expectations, to Alba, Clara's grandchild and the revolutionary who barely holds onto her life. Despite their differences, the three women—whose names mean "clear" (Clara) or "white" (Blanca and Alba)—have deep unconscious bonds that help them survive overwhelming odds. These bonds include the inheritance of extrasensory perception, which, most vivid in the child Clara and in her beautiful doomed sister Rosa, begins the story. The women could be seen as simply swept along in the masculine-dominated course of events, but they are not: Although their actions and motivations are markedly different from the men's, and although their actions are circumscribed by custom, the women play an important role. The climax of the story, the bloody confrontation between the aristocrats and the socialist government of Chile, is an account of the actual military coup which resulted in Salvador Allende's death and Isabel Allende's exile from Chile.

The novel traces the lives of the women and their men, three generations of masculine pride and feminine intuition, of bloodshed and love. The frame story involves the healing of wounds between the granddaughter Alba and her dying grandfather, Este-

ban Trueba, whose unyielding pride has caused much grief for many. This healing is facilitated by the reading of grandmother Clara's diaries, which help Alba to understand her grandfather and her family's and country's history.

Sex roles are clearly defined in the story: the men from the old tradition associated with conquering and controlling, the women left to a kitchen role and keeping their values and hopes alive through their intuitions and their spiritual communication. As the society becomes more modern, these gender definitions change somewhat, but they are never eliminated. The change gives rise to hope that new politics may bring about a new understanding between the sexes, which will allow more freedom to both.

OF LOVE AND SHADOWS

Of Love and Shadows is less a Magical Realist novel than *The House of the Spirits*. It is based on a real event, the finding of fifteen bodies in a secret grave in the Chilean countryside. This novel also uses the paranormal in a factual way, but the "miracles" are marginal to the story of love and death in a world that mirrors dictator Pinochet's.

The story has a fairy-tale beginning, describing the switching of two identically named babies. One baby grows into an epileptic seer whose disappearance will be investigated by Irene Beltran and Francisco Leal, the daughter of a wealthy family and the son of a Spanish Civil War exile. These two work together as reporter and photographer to unravel a mystery. Several members of the *sindicato agrícola*, a farmers' organization set up during the brief agrarian reform, have mysteriously vanished. When Evangelina Ranquileo, an adolescent mystic, publicly accuses Juan de Dios Ramírez of the crime, she disappears too. Irene and Francisco work toward the foregone conclusion: discovery of massive political corruption and murder.

The "shadows" of the title refer to this sinister event; the "love" of the title refers to the affair between Irene and Francisco, after Irene leaves her less intellectual soldier lover for Francisco. Widely read in the wake of *The House of the Spirits*, this novel is less popular with scholars, partly because its political message and its love story are less neatly woven together than in *The House of the Spirits*, partly because the magical and realistic elements of the story do not form the seamless unity of the earlier novel. Nevertheless, the persuasive political message and the ebullient, passionate love story make the novel memorable reading, and while Allende's characteristic magical elements are less highlighted than previously, they are present with their symbolic force.

EVA LUNA

In *Eva Luna* Magical Realism reasserts itself, in a book that is as complex and as playful about serious concerns as *The House of the Spirits*. Eva Luna, the narrator, tells the story of her life, which includes the stories of countless other lives. The line is thin between Eva's made-up world ("I describe life as I would like it to be") and the real world from which she draws her stories. Eva is a hapless child born of a servant girl's desire to comfort a South American Indian dying of a snakebite. However, the painful and odd things that happen to her do not leave her embittered; rather, she becomes open to others' experiences and empathizes with them. As critic Alan Ryan commented, "For Eva Luna, everything that happens in life is a conjunction of countless stories already in progress and, at the same time, the starting point for others not yet told. . . . Stories, for her, transform life." When a character tells Eve of the sad death of his sister, Eva invents another story: 'All right, she died, but not the way you say. Let's find a happy ending for her.' And so it is. . . .''

Latin American political events are present in this novel too, but they are not so well known as those in *The House of the Spirits*, nor are the political messages so clearly underscored as those in *Of Love and Shadows*. The casual or uninformed reader may miss them. Some critics found the story sentimental because of the improbable happy ending and the irrepressible good nature of the main character, despite some Candide-like misfortunes. Other critics balked at the number of stories left open-ended, situations never resolved. Still, the structure of the novel represents the incoherent tangle of lives. This novel blurs the real and surreal and provides a constant challenge to linear thinking.

Janet McCann

OTHER MAJOR WORKS

NONFICTION: *Civilice a su troglodita: Los impertinentes de Isabel Allende*, 1974; *Paula*, 1994 (English translation, 1995).

SHORT FICTION: *Cuentos de Eva Luna*, 1990 (*The Stories of Eva Luna*, 1991).

CHILDREN'S LITERATURE: *La gorda de porcelana*, 1984.

MISCELLANEOUS: *Afrodita: Cuentos, recetas, y otros afrodisiacos*, 1997 (*Aphrodite: A Memoir of the Senses*, 1997).

BIBLIOGRAPHY

Allende, Isabel. "Writing as an Act of Hope." In *Paths of Resistance: The Art and Craft of the Political Novel*, edited by William Zinsser. Boston: Houghton Mifflin, 1989. Allende gives insight into her use of politics in her novels and stories.

Hart, Patricia. *Narrative Magic in the Fiction of Isabel Allende*. Cranbury, N.J.: Associated University Presses, 1989. This book gives a clear and lucid discussion of Allende's fiction, especially those elements of it identifiable as Magical Realism. Unfortunately, there are no translations for the Spanish quotations, but this is an extremely useful book.

Marketta, Laurila. "Isabel Allende and the Discourse of Exile." In *International Women's Writing, New Landscapes of Identity*, edited by Anne E. Brown and Marjanne E. Gooze. Westport, Conn.: Greenwood Press, 1995. This book is helpful, both for Marketta's analysis of Allende's use of the language of exile and for other Allende materials in the collection.

Rodden, John. *Conversations with Isabel Allende*. Austin: University of Texas Press, 1999. This series of interviews provides new autobiographical material in addition to answering most questions general readers may have about Allende's work.

Roof, Maria. "Maryse Conde and Isabel Allende: Family Saga Novels." *World Literature Today* 70, no. 2 (Spring, 1996): 410-416. Looks at *The House of the Spirits* and another novel in the context of the generational novel.

_____. "W. E. B. Du Bois, Isabel Allende, and the Empowerment of Third World Women." *CLA Journal* 39, no. 4 (June, 1996): 401-416. A good source for readers interested in the feminist elements in Allende.

JORGE AMADO

Born: Near Ilhéus, Bahia, Brazil; August 10, 1912

PRINCIPAL LONG FICTION

O país do carnaval, 1931
Cacáu, 1933
Suor, 1934
Jubiabá, 1935
Mar morto, 1936
Capitães da areia, 1937 (*Captains of the Sand*, 1988)
Terras do sem fim, 1942 (*The Violent Land*, 1945)
São Jorge dos Ilhéus, 1944 (*The Golden Harvest*, 1992)
Seara vermelha, 1946
Os subterrâneos da liberdade, 1954 (includes *Agonia da noite*, 1961; *A luz no túnel*, 1963; and *Os ásperos tempos*, 1963)
Gabriela, cravo e canela, 1958 (*Gabriela, Clove and Cinnamon*, 1962)
Os velhos marinheiros, 1961 (includes *A morte e a morte de Quincas Berro D'Agua* [*The Two Deaths of Quincas Wateryell*, 1965] and *A completa verdade sôbre as discutidas aventuras do Comandante Vasco Moscoso de Aragão, capitão de longo curso* [*Home Is the Sailor*, 1964])
Os pastores da noite, 1964 (*Shepherds of the Night*, 1967)
Dona Flor e seus dois maridos, 1966 (*Dona Flor and Her Two Husbands*, 1969)
Tenda dos milagres, 1969 (*Tent of Miracles*, 1971)
Tereza Batista cansada de guerra, 1972 (*Tereza Batista: Home from the Wars*, 1975)
Tiêta do Agreste, 1977 (*Tieta, the Goat Girl*, 1979)

Farda Fardão, camisola de dormir, 1979 (*Pen, Sword, Camisole*, 1985)
Tocaia Grande: A face obscura, 1984 (*Showdown*, 1988)
O sumiço da santa: Uma história de feitiçaria, 1988 (*The War of the Saints*, 1993)

OTHER LITERARY FORMS

Although known primarily for his long fiction, the prolific Jorge Amado has also written much nonfiction, including journalism and several books. His nonfiction indicates his interests even more obviously than does his fiction, as translation of the following titles shows: *Guia das ruas e dos misterios da cidade do Salvador* (1945; guide to the streets and mysteries of Salvador), *Homens e coisas do Partido Comunista* (1946; men and facts of the Communist Party), *União Soviética e democracias populares* (1951; the Soviet Union and popular democracies), and *Bahia boa terra Bahia* (1967; Bahia, sweet land

(Bernard Gotfryd/Archive Photos)

Bahia). Also pertinent here are two biographies of Brazilians, *ABC de Castro Alves* (1941), about a Romantic nineteenth century abolitionist poet known as "the poet of the slaves," and *Vida de Luíz Carlos Prestes* (1942), featuring a twentieth century revolutionary and Marxist hero. Efforts in other genres include a collection of prose poems, *A estrada do mar* (1938); a play, *O amor de Castro Alves* (1947; also as *O amor do soldado*); and various film scenarios.

ACHIEVEMENTS

During the first stage of his career, in the 1930's, Amado was frequently criticized for writing propagandistic novels, for allowing his left-wing politics to take precedence over his novelistic art. Though Amado proudly admitted such a priority, part of the explanation for his early awkwardness is that he was only beginning to learn his art. Of his novels of the 1930's, the most notable is *Jubiabá*. Although Amado's early novels are his least read, with many still untranslated into English, they do establish his credentials as a writer of the people and help account for his 1951 Stalin International Peace Prize.

With *The Violent Land*, Amado's first acknowledged masterpiece, his politics became less overt. Samuel Putnam, Amado's early translator into English, maintained that Amado succumbed to the repressive censorship of the Getúlio Vargas dictatorship in Brazil, but, if so, argues Fred P. Ellison, the ironic result was more effective art. Part of the explanation again seems to be that Amado's art simply matured in *The Violent Land*, that he developed from thesis novels to a fuller version of reality.

Gabriela, Clove and Cinnamon, Amado's next masterpiece, marked another shift in his career—adoption of a humorous stance. The entertaining novels of this period represent the height of Amado's art. Other comic masterpieces include *Dona Flor and Her Two Husbands* and the volume *Os velhos marinheiros*, which contains two novels translated as *The Two Deaths of Quincas Wateryell* and *Home Is the Sailor*.

With *Tereza Batista*, *Tieta, the Goat Girl*, and his later novels, Amado's art became hackneyed, as he indulged in shallow (and wordy) repetition of previ-ously successful formulas, such as centering his novel on a sexy woman. The effect of his formulaic prose is magnified in translation, wherein Amado's famed lyricism is mostly lost, but even in the original Portuguese, Amado has been prone to repeat himself from novel to novel and even within the same novel.

Despite his limitations, Amado is an immensely popular writer, the best-known Brazilian novelist in his country and in the world. His work has been translated into more than fifty languages and has gained mass circulation via radio and film. Amado always had a good eye for popularity, even in the early days when proletarian novels were in vogue. Perhaps his popularity explains why he has been a perennial candidate for the Nobel Prize in Literature.

BIOGRAPHY

A *Nordestino* (a person from the Brazilian northeast), Jorge Amado writes about the people and places he has experienced at first hand: the cacao plantations and seacoast towns of his native state of Bahia. Son of João Amado de Faria and Eulália Leal Amado, he was born August 10, 1912, on his father's cacao plantation near Ilhéus. When he was old enough to work, Amado spent his summers working in the cacao groves with other Bahian laborers. These early experiences among Brazil's impoverished provided an invaluable learning experience for Amado and a foundation for much of his writing.

It was a turbulent and violent period, as documented in *The Violent Land*, where Amado depicts himself as a fascinated child observing a much publicized murder trial. He attended primary school in Ilhéus; his headmistress, Dona Guilhermina, appears briefly in *Gabriela, Clove and Cinnamon*, where her reputation for severity is "legendary." Amado went on to secondary school in Salvador, first at the strict Jesuit Colégio Antánio Vieira (from which he ran away) and then at the progressive Ginásio Ipiranga. He attended law school at the Federal University of Rio de Janeiro, receiving his degree in 1935.

Appreciating Amado's penchant for social realism requires an understanding of the sociopolitical climate in which he first began to write. Following a global economic crisis that shattered the coffee industry and forced masses of Brazilians into poverty, Brazil's 1930 presidential election was also turbulent. When the liberal challenger Getúlio Vargas met with apparent defeat, he led an armed rebellion against the state and gained control of civilian and military institutions, disbanded the congress, and issued a decree of absolute power for his government. Initially, the overthrow of the old order produced a renaissance of sorts among Brazil's writers. Vargas publicly advocated achievement and reform, and writers were quick to adopt this spirit of social renewal. The new literature of Brazil revealed the squalor of its lower classes and offered solutions for a nation needing change.

While a student at the Ginásio Ipiranga, Amado began writing for newspapers and magazines and joined the Academia dos Rebeldes (academy of rebels), a Bohemian group of writers and artists. Similar activities continued in Rio de Janeiro, where Amado published his first novel when he was nineteen. By that time, he was already attracted to leftist politics, and his second novel, *Cacáu*, branded subversive, landed him briefly in jail. Thus began a whole series of clashes with censors, detentions and imprisonments (1935-1936, 1938), and exiles (1936-1937, 1941-1943, 1948-1952).

In 1945, Amado married Zélia Gettai of São Paulo; they would have two children, João Jorge and Paloma. Also in 1945, after the military overthrew the Vargas dictatorship, Amado, running on the Communist Party ticket, was elected Federal Deputy of the Brazilian Parliament and helped draft a new constitution. His political career ended in 1948 after the Communist Party was outlawed and Amado was forced into exile.

During his exiles, Amado traveled through the rest of South America, Mexico, the United States, Western and Eastern Europe, and Asia, living perhaps for the longest periods in Mexico, Argentina, Uruguay, Paris, Czechoslovakia, and Poland.

After 1952, as Amado's worldwide popularity increased, conditions improved for him in Brazil. From 1956 to 1959, he edited *Para todos*, a prominent cultural periodical in Rio de Janeiro. In 1961, he was ap-

pointed to the Literary Committee of the Conselho Nacional de Cultura and elected to the Academia Brazileira de Letras. In 1962 Amado traveled to Cuba and Mexico shortly after the death of his father, and in 1963 he and his family returned to Salvador to live.

After traveling to Europe and North America, Amado was a writer-in-residence at Pennsylvania State University in 1971. During the 1990's Amado spent much of his time in Paris and London, after his Salvador home began attracting hordes of tourists. He was back in Brazil in 1996 to undergo heart surgery.

ANALYSIS

Some critics are made uneasy by the coexistence in Jorge Amado of Marxist commitment and the Bahian version of *far niente* or "Let the good times roll." Amado's duality was evidenced by his popularity on both sides of the former Iron Curtain, by the unlikely conjunction of his early propagandistic novels and his later spate of sexy best-sellers. Yet there is more consistency in Amado's career than first appears. As Amado himself maintained, his sympathies throughout his writing have been with the working class and the poor. In part, Amado's metamorphoses indicate his strategy: He had to present his case in the face of disinterest, opposition, and censorship. After all, if sex and humor could be used to sell toothpaste and automobiles, then they could be used to sell Marxist views. Amado also answered the question of what to do while one waits for the revolution: One has a good time and invites the rich to a party. Indeed, in Amado's easygoing Marxism, revolution might not even be necessary, since modern society seems to be evolving on its own toward a humane civilization free of want, repression, and prejudices.

The duality in Amado's outlook is reflected in his depiction of the working-class poor. On the one hand, they are ground down by hunger and serfdom, yet, paradoxically, they are also heroic. As a class they are heroic because it is mainly with their blood, sweat, and tears that civilization has been built. The working-class poor also furnish most of Amado's individual heroes and heroines. In the early novels, heroic proletarians abound, the most notable being the black António Balduíno, who becomes a labor leader in *Jubiabá*. Later examples are the mulatto beauties Gabriela and Tieta, who subvert the bourgeois social order with their sexual freedom; the Syrian immigrant Nacib Saad, who has to choose between Gabriela and bourgeois macho respectability, might also be included here. In general, the Bahian poor, with their urge to enjoy life, best exemplify Amado's ideal of humane civilization, whereas the repressed bourgeoisie are driven by greed, puritanism, snobbery, and other demons. The bourgeoisie rule, but when they want a good time they have to go to the Bahian poor. Through the interaction of these two classes, Amado shows the evolution of society taking place.

THE VIOLENT LAND

The most primitive stage of social organization is represented in *The Violent Land*, set in early twentieth century Bahia. Although Bahia has been at least sparsely settled for centuries, frontier conditions reminiscent of the Wild West still prevail in the novel. The main enemy is the dark rain forest, the Sequeiro Grande, full of fearsome animals and imagined goblins presided over by an old witch doctor who delivers his Voodoo curse. The jungle constantly threatens to reclaim the cacao plantations carved from it, a threat symbolized by the cries of frogs being swallowed by snakes in a pond next to a plantation house. The darkness lurking in the hearts of men and women—ignorance, lawlessness, amorality, and greed—also threatens. To bring order out of this impending chaos and drive the wedge of conquest deeper into the jungle requires a few strongman types; therefore, the resulting social order is a feudal plantation system presided over by the strongmen-owners, such as Sinhô and Juca Badaró and Colonel Horacio da Silveira.

The defects of this feudal strongman system, however, are immediately apparent. Only the strongmen (the "colonels") and their close henchmen benefit substantially; the workers live on a subsistence level, laboring long hours daily and completely subject to the will of the strongmen. The social order achieved at such high cost is minimal: The only law is the whim of the strongmen. Corrupted by their power, the strongmen corrupt their followers; this moral morass is symbolized by the sticky cacao ooze which clings to the hands and feet of the workers, who can rise in the order only by becoming assassins for their bosses (a description which also gives some notion of how the social order is enforced). The only ideal is a macho code of personal courage (which, however, is flexible enough to allow bullying and bushwhacking; beating women is also considered acceptable). Most of the women serve as cooks or prostitutes, though Ana Badaró impresses everyone with her ability to shoot as straight as any man.

Paradoxically, the strongman social order is very weak. Dependent on the head man, it waits for his orders before anything gets done, and then it is limited by his vision. The system's fragility is demonstrated most clearly when the strongmen clash, as happens in *The Violent Land*. The principle of survival of the fittest returns: In the cacao war between Colonel Horacio and the Badarós, the Badarós are decimated and their plantation burned to the ground.

Amado thus shows the feudal strongman system to be only one step beyond the jungle, a primitive stage which belongs to a civilized country's past. As long as it stays in the past, it can be celebrated, and *The Violent Land* thus possesses epic qualities: a grand design, sweeping action, a lyric prose style that breaks out into ballads. The colorful characters tend toward the mockheroic-gamblers, whores, assassins, adulterers, colonels. Above all, Amado has an epic theme, the struggle and sacrifice required to achieve progress: He never tires of saying that the land was fertilized by human blood, mainly the blood of workers. To lose what has been achieved at such great cost would be a betrayal.

GABRIELA, CLOVE AND CINNAMON

Gabriela, Clove and Cinnamon shows the next step up for society, the transition from a feudal order to a crude form of democracy. The novel is set in Ilhéus in 1925-1926, during a boom period for the cacao industry. Significantly, material change, especially the growth of cities, has preceded political change. Representing the old feudal order is the octogenarian Colonel Ramiro Bastos, in addition to a clutch of other colonels, some sporting scars of the cacao wars. Representing the new order is the cacao exporter Mundinho Falcão, who gathers a following of town dignitaries and a few enlightened colonels. Ruling by decree, Colonel Ramiro Bastos stands in the way of further progress—schools, roads, sewers, and especially a port which will accommodate large ships. Throughout the novel, the political campaign between Colonel Ramiro Bastos and Mundinho Falcão heats up. Colonel Ramiro's followers propose to bring back the old-style violence, but their plans fizzle when the old man dies. Ultimately the issues are settled peacefully, by an honest election, itself an innovation for the region.

Significantly, the agent of change, Mundinho Falcão, is not a native of the region but the youngest son of a rich and politically prominent Rio de Janeiro family. Another, humbler agent of change is also an outsider: the Syrian Nacib Saad, owner of the Vesuvius Bar. The novel's other main line of action concerns Nacib's love for the beautiful backlander Gabriela, a mulatto whom he hires as cook at a migrant labor pool called the Slave Market. When Gabriela proves to be as good in bed as she is in the kitchen ("color of cinnamon, smell of clove"), Nacib marries her. A flower of the people, generous and loving, Gabriela seems an ideal woman, but the marriage is a mistake, like the caged bird Nacib gives her as a present. Free and easy as a bird, Gabriela cannot stomach the middle-class restrictions of marriage in Ilhéus.

When Nacib finds Gabriela in bed with the town Romeo, he is faced with a dilemma: The old macho code decrees that he must kill her and her lover, but the easygoing Nacib, however heartbroken, is no killer. The solution is another triumph for civilization in the region: Nacib and Gabriela's marriage is declared legally void, and, after a period of separation, they go back to living and loving together. The triumph is underlined when a cacao colonel who had killed his wife and her lover is sent to prison—the first such conviction in Ilhéan history.

These cases and others are discussed nonstop in the homes, businesses, and taverns of Ilhéus, especially in the Vesuvius Bar. Amado's characters do like to talk, and they tell all. As Amado notes here

and elsewhere, the main entertainment in small-town Bahia is gossip. Obviously the Ilhéans are well entertained, as are Amado's readers: In *Gabriela, Clove and Cinnamon*, a masterpiece of plotting, character, and theme, gossip is raised to a fine art.

THE TWO DEATHS OF QUINCAS WATERYELL

A smaller masterpiece is *The Two Deaths of Quincas Wateryell*. Here, in a funny, fantastic little story that verges on allegory, Amado attacks middle-class pretensions and restrictions head-on. His hero is Joaquim Soares da Cunha, an exemplary family man and bureaucrat who, at the age of fifty, retires from the State Rent Board and inexplicably leaves his home and family to become a bum, roaming the slummy Salvador waterfront in the company of drunks and whores. In his new identity, Joaquim Soares da Cunha becomes Quincas Wateryell, named after the outraged scream he lets out when he drinks a glass of water thinking it is white rum. After ten years, Quincas's convivial life of drinking, whoring, and gambling catches up with him: When the novella opens, he lies dead on a rancid flophouse bed, his big toe sticking out of a hole in his dirty sock. Still, there is a smile on the corpse's face.

As his relatives gather to give Quincas a "decent" burial, his reason for running away from home becomes clear. His straitlaced family, scandalized and mortified all of those years, is finally relieved by his death. In particular, his smug daughter Vanda determines to put the domestic screws to Quincas in death, just as her "saintly" mother did in life. That is, she symbolically dresses him up and has the undertaker make him up as Joaquim Soares da Cunha. Nothing, however, can be done about his immoral smile, which Vanda thinks is mocking her. Indeed, she thinks she hears the corpse whistle and call her "Viper!" Her efforts to reclaim Quincas for respectability are defeated when four of his buddies appear at the wake. Left alone with the corpse, they revive it with rum and take it for a last night on the town, including a fight in a bar and a visit to Quincas's mistress. The drunken party ends up out at sea in a fishing boat, from which the corpse "leaps" to its death in the cleansing waters—a proper end for an old salt like Quincas.

DONA FLOR AND HER TWO HUSBANDS

After *Gabriela, Clove and Cinnamon*, *Dona Flor and Her Two Husbands* is perhaps the best known of Amado's novels. *Dona Flor and Her Two Husbands* is the story of a young lower-middle-class cooking teacher named Florípedes Paiva. The story is set in the Salvador, Bahia, of the 1920's and 1930's. Florípedes's marriage to the promiscuous and gambling Vadinho Guimarães is suddenly terminated by his premature death. Flor is devastated, despite his exploitation and abuse of her, because he was the source of her greatest pleasure, with a zest for life and passionate lovemaking.

Despite serious misgivings, Flor accepts the marriage proposal of a respectable but dull local pharmacist, Dr. Teodoro Madureira. Yet her newly found security and respectability are not able to satisfy her needs. In response to Flor's emotional and sexual vulnerability, Vadinho reappears as a ghost, overcomes her defenses, and regains his place in her marriage bed. Soon, however, he begins to disappear as the result of a Bahian Candomblé ritual that Flor had earlier ordered in an effort to halt his illicit advances. It is only through Flor's personal intercession that the decision of the gods is later reversed, thus allowing her to enjoy the best of both Vadinho and Teodoro.

To critics, it appeared strange that such a politically engaged author should publish an apparently frivolous work just two years after the imposition of a brutal military dictatorship. Consequently, some critics viewed the two husbands, diametrically opposed to each other, as metaphors for two contradictory political forces in Brazil: the leftist populism of the 1950's and early 1960's versus the opposing military and technocratic forces. The heroine's magical solution, which granted her the best of both her husbands, could be read as a statement about the problems of and answers for the Brazilian people. On one level, no one narrow sociopolitical philosophy is, in Amado's opinion, capable of meeting the country's needs, whether it be populist and democratic in nature or technocratic and military, whether it is oriented to the values and demands of the working classes or to those of the bourgeoisie. Only by combining both of these forces can an effective society be achieved. Brazil, like Flor, is otherwise left vulnerable, unsatisfied, and incomplete.

TIETA, THE GOAT GIRL

A similar attack on bourgeois values informs *Tieta, the Goat Girl*, an example of Amado's later work. *Tieta, the Goat Girl*, however, is neither little nor a masterpiece. The wordy, rambling story runs on interminably (672 pages in the English translation), as silly as it is raunchy. The first half or so details the 1966 return of a "prodigal daughter," Tieta "the goat girl," to her poor hometown of Agreste on the Bahian seacoast. Twenty-six years before, her father beat her and drove her from home for giving away sexual favors. Now, supposedly the widow of a rich São Paulo industrialist, the beautiful and generous Tieta is enfolded in the bosom of her family, and the dazzled town declares her a saint. The joke is that Saint Tieta became rich by learning to sell her sexual favors, eventually becoming madam of the fanciest whorehouse in Brazil. When this joke wears thin, Amado tries, in the book's last half, to whip up reader enthusiasm for an ecological battle: A polluting titanium dioxide factory wants to move into town and spoil the beaches and fishing.

Despite the novel's sophomoric plot and characters, *Tieta, the Goat Girl* is still entertaining. Amado's unrestrained style is not merely wordy; it has a veritably Rabelaisian range and exuberance. Consistent with his uninhibited style is Amado's satiric attack on bourgeois hypocrisy and greed, including recent extremes manifested in the consumer society and destructive industries. Amado's attack reaches its literal and symbolic climax in Tieta's seduction of her nephew Ricardo, a seventeen-year-old seminarian. Saint Tieta, the expert, teaches Ricardo a new life-affirming religion, as Ricardo is assured by the liberation theologian Frei Thimóteo, a Franciscan friar. Other characters representing this religion in the novel are a group of hippies who visit the fabulous beach of Mangue Seco and a group of fishing families who have always lived there.

Coming from another direction, but deriving its inspiration from Marx as well as Jesus, liberation theology is not too far away from Amado's own easygoing Marxism. The appearance of liberation theology in recent decades supports Amado's view that modern society—at least in Brazil—is evolving toward a humane civilization free of want, repression, and prejudice. Both liberation theology and Amado represent the frustration and optimism of Brazil—and the new combinations of thought emanating from that vital land.

THE WAR OF THE SAINTS

In *The War of the Saints*, Amado creates a tale of Magical Realism that reverberates with the sights, sounds, smells, and tastes of a carnival. The novel opens with the description of a statue of Saint Barbara of the Thunder, famed for her eternal beauty and miraculous powers. The statue has just been transported from the altar of a provincial church across the Bay of All Saints to Bahia for an exhibition of religious art. Soon after the ship docks, the statue takes life and disappears into the crowd. The icon is transformed into the living African deity Saint Barbara Yansan. The novel recounts the magical events of the next forty-eight hours. If the mulatto culture of this part of Brazil, which is based on the mixture of Roman Catholicism and West African animism, is the underlying subject of the novel, it is clear that the author's sympathy lies nearly entirely with the latter religion. Candomblé, an African Brazilian religious ceremony partly of Yoruban origin, is the book's true protagonist and winner in the cultural struggle depicted in the novel.

Saint Barbara Yansan has come to rescue Manela, a young girl who is in love with a taxi driver named Miro, from the puritanical clutches of her devoutly Catholic aunt, Adalgisa. Being a goddess, Saint Barbara naturally succeeds. Along the way, she permits her humble servant, the author, to create a riotously satiric epic that pokes fun at critics and professors, Marxists and fascists, generals and judges, priests, politicians, and policemen—in short, anyone with any power in Brazil. Concurrently, however, Amado paints a loving portrait of Bahia's powerless, particularly artists, poets, musicians, lovers, and the priests and priestesses of Candomblé. The book is a consummate celebration of life amid misery, and it is unabashedly triumphant.

Harold Branam, updated by Genevieve Slomski

OTHER MAJOR WORKS

PLAY: *O amor de Castro Alves*, pb. 1947 (also as *O amor do soldado*).

POETRY: *A estrada do mar*, 1938.

NONFICTION: *ABC de Castro Alves*, 1941 (biography); *Vida de Luíz Carlos Prestes*, 1942; *O cavaleiro da esperança*, 1945 (biography); *Bahia de todos os santos*, 1945 (travel sketch); *Guia das ruas e dos misterios da cidade do Salvador*, 1945; *Homens e coisas do Partido Comunista*, 1946; *O mundo da paz*, 1951 (travel sketch); *União Soviética e democracias populares*, 1951; *Bahia boa terra Bahia*, 1967; *Bahia*, 1971 (English translation, 1971); *O menino grapiúna*, 1981; *Navega ção de Cabotagem*, 1992.

CHILDREN'S LITERATURE: *O gato malhado e a andorinha sinhá: Uma historia de amor*, 1976 (*The Swallow and the Tom Cat: A Love Story*, 1982).

BIBLIOGRAPHY

Brookshaw, David. *Race and Color in Brazilian Literature*. Metuchen, N.J.: Scarecrow Press, 1986. Detects racial stereotyping and prejudice in the characterization of blacks in *Jubiabá*, *Gabriela, Clove and Cinnamon*, and *Tent of Miracles*. Includes bibliography.

Chamberlain, Bobby J. *Jorge Amado*. Boston: Twayne, 1990. Provides excellent and detailed analysis of Amado's later works of fiction. Discusses Amado as a writer, social critic, and politician and places Amado's works in social, political, and historical context. Concluding chapter discusses the author's contradictory status as a man of letters and a literary hack. Contains biographical information, chronology, and bibliography.

Lowe, Elizabeth. *The City in Brazilian Literature*. Rutherford, N.J.: Fairleigh Dickinson University Press, 1982. Characterizes Amado's depiction of Salvador, Bahia, as "picturesque exoticism," and his portrayal of urban poor as "carnivalization." Contains bibliography.

Patai, Daphne. *Myth and Ideology in Contemporary Brazilian Fiction*. Rutherford, N.J.: Fairleigh Dickinson University Press, 1983. Chapter 5 is a critique of *Tereza Batista*, which Patai feels undercuts itself ideologically. She criticizes Amado for his use of the supernatural, for his use of humor, which she feels trivializes social injustice, and for what she regards as his patronizing view of the poor. In her view, Amado's work blurs the distinction between history and fiction. Includes bibliography.

Pescatello, Ann. "The Brazileira: Images and Realities in the Writings of Machado de Assis and Jorge Amado." In *Female and Male in Latin America: Essays*, edited by Ann Pescatello. Pittsburgh, Pa.: University of Pittsburgh Press, 1973. Compares and contrasts female characters in several of Amado's major novels with those of Machado de Assis. Detects a preoccupation with race and class in both writers' female characterizations. Includes bibliography.

KINGSLEY AMIS

Born: London, England; April 16, 1922
Died: London, England; October 22, 1995

PRINCIPAL LONG FICTION

Lucky Jim, 1954
That Uncertain Feeling, 1955
I Like It Here, 1958
Take a Girl Like You, 1960
One Fat Englishman, 1963
The Egyptologists, 1965 (with Robert Conquest)
The Anti-Death League, 1966
Colonel Sun: A James Bond Adventure, 1968 (as Robert Markham)
I Want It Now, 1968
The Green Man, 1969
Girl, 20, 1971
The Riverside Villas Murder, 1973
Ending Up, 1974
The Crime of the Century, 1975 (serial), 1987 (book)
The Alteration, 1976
Jake's Thing, 1978
Russian Hide-and-Seek, 1980

Stanley and the Women, 1984
The Old Devils, 1986
Difficulties with Girls, 1988
The Crime of the Century, 1988
The Folks That Live on the Hill, 1990
The Russian Girl, 1992
You Can't Do Both, 1994
The Biographer's Moustache, 1995

OTHER LITERARY FORMS

Kingsley Amis is best known as a novelist, but readers have turned often to his other writings for the insight they give into the man and his fiction. Many of the themes which are explored in depth in his novels are expressed indirectly in the peripheral works. He published several collections of short stories, entitled *My Enemy's Enemy* (1962), *Collected Short Stories* (1980), and *Mr. Barrett's Secret and Other Stories* (1993). *Dear Illusion*, a novella, was published in 1972 in a limited edition of five hundred copies. His collections of poetry include: *Bright November* (1947), *A Frame of Mind* (1953), *A Case of Samples: Poems, 1946-1956* (1956), *The Evans Country* (1962), *A Look Round the Estate: Poems, 1957-1967* (1967), and *Collected Poems: 1944-1979* (1979). Amis published his opinionated *Memoirs* in 1991. His criticism covers an extremely wide range; in addition to studies of figures as diverse as Jane Austen and Rudyard Kipling, he published one of the first significant critical books on science fiction, *New Maps of Hell: A Survey of Science Fiction* (1960), a work that has done much to encourage academic study of the genre and to win recognition for many gifted writers. *The James Bond Dossier* (1965), *Lucky Jim's Politics* (1968), several volumes of collected science fiction, edited with Robert Conquest and entitled *Spectrum: A Science Fiction Anthology* (1961-1965), and *The King's English: A Guide to Modern Usage* (1997) offer further evidence of the extraordinary range of his work.

ACHIEVEMENTS

Almost from the beginning of his career, Amis enjoyed the attention of numerous commentators. Because his works have been filled with innovations, surprises, and variations in techniques and themes, it is not surprising that critics and reviewers alike found it difficult to make a definitive statement about his achievements. The range of his work is extraordinary: fiction, poetry, reviews, criticism, humor, science fiction, and biography. Of all of his writings, however, his achievement depends most upon his novels.

Amis's early novels are considered by many critics to be "angry" novels of protest against the contemporary social, political, and economic scene in Britain. The themes include: resentment of a rigid class stratification; rejection of formal institutional ties; discouragement with the economic insecurity and low status of those without money; loathing of pretentiousness in any form; and disenchantment with the past. Because many of Amis's contemporaries, including John Wain, John Osborne, John Braine, and Alan Sillitoe, seemed to express similar concerns, and because many came from working or lower-middle-class backgrounds, went to Oxford or Cambridge Universities, and taught for a time at a provincial university, journalists soon spoke of them as belonging to a literary movement. The "Angry Young Men," as their fictional heroes were called, were educated men who did not want to be gentlemen. Kenneth Allsop called them "a new, rootless, faithless, classless class" lacking in manners and morals; W. Somerset Maugham called them "mean, malicious and envious . . . scum" and warned that these men would some day rule England. Some critics even confused the characters with the writers themselves. Amis's Jim Dixon (in *Lucky Jim*) was appalled by the tediousness and falseness of academic life; therefore, Dixon was interpreted as a symbol of antiintellectualism. Dixon taught at a provincial university; therefore, he became a symbol of contempt for Cambridge and Oxford. Amis himself taught at a provincial university (Swansea); therefore, he and Dixon became one and the same in the minds of many critics. Like all literary generalizations, however, this one was soon inadequate. The most that can be said is that through Amis's early heroes there seemed to sound clearly those notes of disillusionment that were to become dominant in much of the literature of the 1950's.

(© Washington Post; reprinted by permission of the D.C. Public Library)

Because it seems so artless, critics have also found Amis's fiction difficult to discuss. His straightforward plotting, gift for characterization, and ability to tell a good story, they say, are resistant to the modern techniques of literary criticism. Because Amis lacks the obscurity, complexity, and technical virtuosity of James Joyce or William Faulkner, these critics suggest that he is not to be valued as highly. In many of the early reviews, Amis is described as essentially a comic novelist, an entertainer, or an amiable satirist not unlike P. G. Wodehouse, the Marx Brothers, or Henry Fielding. Furthermore, his interest in mysteries, ghost stories, James Bond thrillers, and science fiction confirms for these critics the view that Amis is a writer lacking serious intent.

Looking beyond the social commentary and entertainment found in Amis's work, other critics find a distinct relationship between Amis's novels and the "new sincerity" of the so-called Movement poets of the 1950's and later. These poets (including Amis himself, Philip Larkin, John Wain, and D. J. Enright, all of whom also wrote fiction) saw their work as an alternative to the symbolic and allusive poetry of T. S. Eliot and his followers. In a movement away from allusion, obscurity, and excesses of style, the Movement poets encouraged precision, lucidity, and craftsmanship. They concentrated on honesty of thought and feeling to emphasize what A. L. Rowse calls a "businesslike intention to communicate with the reader." Amis's deceptively simple novels have been written with the same criteria he imposed on his poetry; one cannot read Amis with a measure suitable only to Joyce or Faulkner. Rather, his intellectual and literary ancestors antedate the great modernist writers, and the resultant shape is that of a nineteenth century man of letters. His novels may be appreciated for their commonsense approach. He writes clearly. He avoids extremes or excessive stylistic experimentation. He is witty, satirical, and often didactic.

Amis's novels after 1980 added a new phase to his career. One of the universal themes that most engaged Amis is the relation between men and women, both in and out of marriage. After 1980, he moved away from the broad scope of a society plagued by trouble to examine instead the troubles plaguing one of that society's most fundamental institutions—relationships—and the conflicts, misunderstandings, and drastically different responses of men and women to the world. Most of his characters suffer blighted marriages. Often they seem intelligent but dazed, as if there were something they had lost but cannot quite remember. Something has indeed been lost, and loss is at the heart of all of Amis's novels, so that he is, as novelist Malcolm Bradbury calls him, "one of our most disturbing contemporary novelists, an explorer of historical pain." From the beginning of his canon, Amis focused upon the absence of something significant in modern life: a basis, a framework, a structure for living, such as the old institutions like religion or marriage once provided. Having pushed that loss in societal terms to its absolute extreme in the previous novels, Amis subsequently studied it in personal terms, within the fundamental social unit. In *The Old Devils*, for example (for which he won the 1986 Booker Fiction Prize), his characters will not regain

the old, secure sense of meaning that their lives once held, and Amis does not pretend that they will. What success they manage to attain is always partial. What, in the absence of an informing faith or an all-consuming family life, could provide purpose for living? More simply, how is one to be useful? This is the problem that haunts Amis's characters, and it is a question, underlying all of his novels, that came to the forefront near the end of his life.

In looking back over Amis's career, critics have found a consistent moral judgment quite visible beneath the social commentary, entertainment, and traditional techniques that Amis employs. Beginning in a world filled with verbal jokes, masquerades, and incidents, Amis's view of life grew increasingly pessimistic until he arrived at a fearfully grim vision of a nightmare world filled with hostility, violence, sexual abuse, and self-destruction. Critics, therefore, view Amis most significantly as a moralist, concerned with the ethical life in difficult times. Amis's response to such conditions was to use his great powers of observation and mimicry both to illuminate the changes in postwar British society and to suggest various ways of understanding and possibly coping with those changes. For all these reasons, one can assert that Amis has achieved a major reputation in contemporary English fiction, and, as is so often the case today, his is an achievement that does not depend upon any single work. It is rather the totality of his work with which readers should reckon.

Biography

Kingsley William Amis was born in London on April 16, 1922. His father, William Robert, was an office clerk with Coleman's Mustard and fully expected his only child to enter commerce. His son's intention, however, was to be a writer—a poet, really—though it was not until the publication of his rollicking and irreverent first novel, *Lucky Jim*, in 1954, that Amis achieved his goal.

By Amis's own account, he had been writing since he was a child. Writing became for him a means of coming to terms with certain fears. As a boy he suffered from the routine terrors of childhood—fear of the dark, fear of the future, fear of other children, fear of his parents' disapproval—but as he grew older the subjects of his fears changed. He was a complicated individual; depression alternated with laughter, and an inner loneliness counterbalanced his social charm. Typically, one fear involves his health. Like many of his characters, one of his strongest fears was and continues to be the fear of loneliness. "Being the only person in the house is something I wouldn't like at all," he said, years later. "I would develop anxiety. By this I mean more than just a rational dislike of being alone and wanting company but something which means, for me, becoming very depressed and tense. I've always been terribly subject to tension. I worry a lot."

Kingsley Amis as an author and his characters themselves often seem to be running scared, playing out their lives while always looking over their shoulders, afraid that the truth of life's meaninglessness will catch up to them. Amis admitted that writing fiction encourages the illusion that there is some sense in life. "There isn't," he said, "but if that's all you thought, you'd go mad." In his fiction, if not in life, he was able to pretend that there is a pattern in events and that the suffering of his characters can be justified, or explained, or atoned for, or made all right. Such power to conjure up meaning where it otherwise may not exist brings with it the "wonderful feeling of being Lord of Creation."

Long before Amis was to experience this power, he was merely a schoolboy at St. Hilda's local fee-paying school. At St. Hilda's he learned French from Miss Crampton and he also developed a crush on his English teacher, Miss Barr, "a tall, Eton-crowned figure of improbable eloquence." It is in these inauspicious surroundings, he said, humorously, that perhaps "we can date my first education into the glories of our literature." Perhaps because of Miss Barr but more probably because of his temperament and interests, he developed a fascination for anything to do with writing—pens, paper, erasers.

His interest may have been piqued at St. Hilda's but his first literary efforts occurred at Norbury College. There he was exposed to the vast entertainment that the days held for a British public school boy in the 1930's: Under the tutelage of his teachers, he be-

gan to write stories and poems. His first published work of fiction, a three-hundred-word adventure story called "The Sacred Rhino of Uganda," appeared in the school magazine. In the fall of 1934, he entered the "really splendid" City of London School—a day school of seven hundred boys, overlooking the Thames by Blackfriars Bridge. Amis read much during this period. He specialized in the classics until he was sixteen, then switched to English, but later would wish that he had been more interested in scripture and divinity at the time and had been touched by the wings of faith, a wish that his fiction would ultimately demonstrate. He also read French. Early artistic delights included watercolors, Dadaism, and architecture. He especially loved to read poetry, and with his keen mind and quick sensibilities he could take in a considerable amount of material quickly.

In the prewar year of 1939, while he was in the sixth form, Amis and many of his school chums were suddenly surprised to find themselves being sent to Marlborough College in Wiltshire as evacuees; there he spent the next five terms. He found himself in the small country town of Marlborough, one of the most undisturbed countrysides remaining in the southwest of England. There, in vivid contrast to the suburbia he knew in Clapham, Amis was initiated into the beauties and mysteries of nature, and for the rest of his life he would carry images of Marlborough with him and re-create them in his fictional country scenes.

Amis's first novel, *The Legacy*, written while he attended St. John's College at the University of Oxford (1941-1942, 1945-1947), was rejected by fourteen publishers. Eventually Amis abandoned it altogether, having come to regard it as boring, unfunny, and derivative. Although his studies at Oxford were interrupted by the war, Amis persisted, earning his B.A. (with honors) and M.A. degrees in English.

Several factors influenced Amis's development into a writer whose stories and style are unique. His comic proclivities were encouraged by his father—a man with "a talent for physical clowning and mimicry." Amis described himself as "undersized, law-abiding, timid," a child able to make himself popular by charm or clowning, who found that at school he could achieve much by exploiting his inherited powers of mimicry. His school friends testified to Amis's capacity for making people laugh. Philip Larkin's description of their first meeting (1941), in the 1963 introduction to his own novel, *Jill*, suggests that it was Amis's "genius for imaginative mimicry" that attracted him: "For the first time I felt myself in the presence of a talent greater than my own." John Wain has also recalled how, in the "literary group" to which both of them belonged, Amis was a "superb mimic" who relished differences of character and idiom.

This period of "intensive joke swapping," as Larkin called it, continued when Amis entered the army in 1942. He became an officer, served in the Royal Signals, and landed in Normandy in June, 1944. After service in France, Belgium, and West Germany, he was demobilized in October, 1945. This period was to provide material for such stories as "My Enemy's Enemy," "Court of Inquiry," and "I Spy Strangers," but its immediate effect was to open his eyes to the world, to all sorts of strange people and strange ways of behaving.

Amis's status as an only child also contributed to his development as a writer, for he found himself looking at an early age for "self-entertainment." He satisfied this need by reading adventure stories, science fiction, and boys' comics. During these years, too, Amis became interested in horror tales. He recalled seeing the Boris Karloff version of *Frankenstein* (1931) and *The Mummy* (1932) and the Fredric March version of *Dr. Jekyll and Mr. Hyde* (1932). After that time, Amis was interested in what might be called the minor genres on grounds of wonder, excitement, and "a liking for the strange, the possibly horrific." Amis became aware that the detective story, various tales of horror or terror, and the science-fiction story provided vehicles for both social satire and investigation of human nature in a way not accessible to the mainstream novelist.

Along with his natural comic gifts, his interest in genre fiction, and his war experiences, Amis's development was influenced by his early exposure to an English tradition that has resisted the modernist innovations so influential in America and on the Continent at the time. His dislike for experimental prose may be traced in part to the influence of one of his tutors at Oxford, the Anglo-Saxon scholar Gavin Bone, and to his readings of certain eighteenth century novelists whose ability to bring immense variety and plentitude to their work without reverting to obscurity or stylistic excess appealed to the young Amis.

Amis attributed his personal standards of morality both to his readings in Charles Dickens, Henry Fielding, and Samuel Richardson and to the training in standard Protestant virtues he received while growing up at home. Both of his parents were Baptists, but in protest against their own forceful religious indoctrination, their visits to church became less and less frequent as they grew older. Any reader of Amis's works soon becomes aware that there is in his writings a clear repudiation of traditional Christian belief. Nevertheless, from his parents he received certain central moral convictions which crystallized a personal philosophy of life and art. Hard work, conscientiousness, obedience, loyalty, frugality, patience—these lessons and others were put forward and later found their way into his novels, all of which emphasize the necessity of good works and of trying to live a moral life in the natural—as opposed to the supernatural—world.

Despite these convictions, however, Amis was not able to live his private life impeccably—as he himself would ultimately testify. His long-standing marriage to Hilary ("Hilly") Bardwell, which produced a daughter and two sons, including novelist Martin Amis, was marred by frequent infidelities and was ultimately destroyed by his romantic involvement with fellow novelist Elizabeth Jane Howard. Amis and Hilly were divorced in 1965. Amis's subsequent marriage to Howard was not happy, however, and the two separated in 1980. Misogynistic novels such as *Jake's Thing* and *Stanley and the Women* mirror his dissatisfaction with his relationship with Howard in particular and with relations between the sexes in general.

The sunnier aspect of Amis's final novels—especially *The Old Devils* and *The Folks That Live on the Hill*—owes its character to Amis's reconcilement (of sorts) with his first wife. In 1981 Amis, Hilly, and her third husband, Alistair Boyd (Lord Kilmarnock), set up housekeeping together. The arrangement was to last until Amis's death in late 1995. During this final period Amis was to win Britain's highest literary award, the Booker Prize, for *The Old Devils*. His unusual domestic arrangements are described in detail in Eric Jacobs's *Kingsley Amis: A Biography* (1995). Amis's final novel, *The Biographer's Moustache*, reflected his somewhat uneasy feelings over having his biography written. According to Jacobs, Amis remained a writer until his death in 1995. During his last illness he was busy compiling notes about hospital routines to be incorporated into yet another novel.

ANALYSIS

Kingsley Amis's fiction is characterized by a recurring preoccupation with certain themes and concepts, with certain basic human experiences, attitudes, and perceptions. These persistent themes are treated with enormous variety, however, particularly in Amis's novels which draw on the conventions of genre fiction—the mystery, the spy thriller, the ghost story, and so on. Of the twenty novels Amis has published, his development as a seriocomic novelist is especially apparent in *Lucky Jim*, *Take a Girl Like You*, *The Anti-Death League*, *The Green Man*, *The Old Devils*, *The Folks That Live on the Hill*, and *The Russian Girl*, his most substantial and complex works, each of which is representative of a specific stage in his career. All these novels are set in contemporary England. Drawing upon a variety of traditional techniques of good storytelling—good and bad characters, simple irony, straightforward plot structure, clear point of view—they restate, in a variety of ways, the traditional pattern of tragedy: A man, divided and complex, vulnerable both to the world and to himself, is forced to make choices that will determine his destiny. Built into this situation is the probability that he will bring down suffering on his head and injure others in the process.

In *Lucky Jim*, for example, Amis establishes a comic acceptance of many of life's injustices in the academic world. The novel is distinguished by clearcut cases of right and wrong, a simple irony, and

knockabout farce. Because he has neither the courage nor the economic security to protest openly, the hero lives a highly comic secret life of protest consisting of practical jokes and rude faces, all directed against the hypocrisy and pseudointellectualism of certain members of the British establishment. While only hinted at in *Lucky Jim*, Amis's moral seriousness becomes increasingly evident beginning with *Take a Girl Like You*. Whereas in *Lucky Jim* the values are "hidden" beneath a comic narrative, gradually the comedy is submerged beneath a more serious treatment. Thus, *Take a Girl Like You* is a turning point for Amis in a number of ways: The characterization is more complex, the moral problems are more intense, and the point of view is not limited to one central character. Distinguished also by a better balance between the comic and the serious, the novel is more pessimistic than its predecessors, less given to horseplay and high spirits.

In later novels such as *The Anti-Death League* and *The Green Man*, Amis continues to see life more darkly, shifting to an increasingly metaphysical, even theological concern. Contemporary England is viewed as a wasteland of the spirit, and his characters try vainly to cope with a precarious world filled with madness and hysteria, a world in which love and religion have become distorted and vulgarized. Threatened with death and ugly accidents by a malicious God, Amis's characters feel powerless to change, and in an attempt to regain control of their lives, act immorally. Amis's ultimate vision is one in which all of the traditional certainties—faith, love, loyalty, responsibility, decency—have lost their power to comfort and sustain. Humanity is left groping in the dark of a nightmare world. In the later *The Old Devils*, Amis's study of a Wales and a Welshness that have slipped out of reach forever clearly shows a culmination of his increasing damnation of Western society, portrayed through the microcosm of human relationships. The final picture is one of the aimlessness of old age, the meaninglessness of much of life itself.

LUCKY JIM

In *Lucky Jim*, a bumbling, somewhat conscientious hero stumbles across the social and cultural landscape of contemporary British academic life, faces a number of crises of conscience, makes fun of the world and of himself, and eventually returns to the love of a sensible, realistic girl. This is the traditional comic course followed by Amis's first three novels, of which *Lucky Jim* is the outstanding example. Beneath the horseplay and high spirits, however, Amis rhetorically manipulates the reader's moral judgment so that he leaves the novel sympathetic to the hero's point of view. By triumphing over an unrewarding job, a pretentious family, and a predatory female colleague, Dixon becomes the first in a long line of Amis's heroes who stand for common sense and decency; for the belief that life is to be made happy now; for the notion that "nice things are nicer than nasty things."

To develop his moral concern, Amis divides his characters into two archetypal groups reminiscent of the fantasy tale: the generally praiseworthy figures, the ones who gain the greatest share of the reader's sympathy; and the "evil" characters, those who obstruct the good characters. Jim Dixon (the put-upon young man), Gore-Urquhart (his benefactor or savior), and Christine Callaghan (the decent girl to whom Dixon turns) are among the former, distinguished by genuineness, sincerity, and a lack of pretense. Among the latter are Professor Welch (Dixon's principal tormentor), his son, Bertrand (the defeated boaster), and the neurotic Margaret Peele (the thwarted "witch"), all of whom disguise their motives and present a false appearance.

One example should be enough to demonstrate Amis's technique—the introduction to the seedy, absentminded historian, Professor Welch. In the opening chapter, Amis establishes an ironic discrepancy between what Welch seems to be (a scholar discussing history) and what he is in reality (a "vaudeville character" lecturing on the differences between flute and recorder). Although he tries to appear a cultured, sensitive intellecual, all of the images point to a charlatan leading a boring, selfish life. His desk is "misleadingly littered." Once he is found standing, "surprisingly enough," in front of the college library's new-books shelf. Succeeding physical description undercuts his role-playing: He resembles

"an old boxer," "an African savage," "a broken robot." What is more, his speech and gestures are mechanized by cliché and affectation. Professing to worship "integrated village-type community life" and to oppose anything mechanical, he is himself a virtual automaton, and becomes more so as the novel progresses. Although Amis does not term Welch a ridiculous phony, the inference is inescapable.

Central to the novel's theme is Dixon's secret life of protest. Although he hates the Welch family, for economic reasons he dares not rebel openly. Therefore, he resorts to a comic fantasy world to express rage or loathing toward certain imbecilities of the Welch set. His rude faces and clever pranks serve a therapeutic function—a means by which Dixon can safely release his exasperations. At other times, however, Dixon becomes more aggressive: He fantasizes stuffing Welch down the lavatory or beating him about the head and shoulders with a bottle until he reveals why he gave a French name to his son.

In Amis's later novels, when the heroes' moral problems become more intense, even life-threatening, such aggressive acts become more frequent and less controlled. In this early novel, however, what the reader remembers best are the comic moments. Dixon is less an angry young man than a funny, bumbling, confused individual for whom a joke makes life bearable. There are, of course, other ways in which to react to an unjust world. One can flail at it, as does John Osborne's Jimmy Porter (*Look Back in Anger*, 1956). One can try to escape from it, as will Patrick Standish in *Take a Girl Like You*, or one can try to adapt to it. Like Charles Lumley's rebellion against middle-class values in John Wain's *Hurry on Down* (1953), Dixon's rebellion against the affectations of academia ends with an adjustment to the society and with a partial acceptance of its values. By remaining in the system, he can at least try to effect change.

Take a Girl Like You

Ostensibly another example of the familiar story of initiation, Amis's fourth novel, *Take a Girl Like You*, contains subtleties and ironies which set it apart from *Lucky Jim*. The characterization, the balance between the comic and the serious, and the emphasis on sexual behavior and the pursuit of pleasure blend to make this novel a significant step forward in Amis's development as a novelist.

The plot of this disturbing moral comedy is built around a variety of motifs: the travelogue and the innocent-abroad story, the theme of love-in-conflict-with-love, and the country-mouse story of an innocent girl visiting the big city for the first time. Jenny Bunn, from whose point of view more than half of the novel is narrated, is the conventional, innocent young woman who has not been touched by deep experience in worldly matters. Like Jim Dixon, she finds herself in an unfamiliar setting, confronting people who treat her as a stranger with strange ideas. Out of a simpleminded zeal for the virtues of love and marriage, she becomes the victim of a plausible, nasty man.

Jenny carries out several artistic functions in the story. She is chiefly prominent as the perceptive observer of events close to her. Again like Dixon, she is able to detect fraud and incongruities from a considerable distance. When Patrick Standish first appears, for example, she understands that his look at her means he is "getting ideas about her." Amis draws a considerable fund of humor from Jenny's assumed naïveté. His chief device is the old but appropriate one of naïve comment, innocently uttered but tipped with truth. Jenny, a young girl living in a restrictive environment and ostensibly deferential toward the attitudes and opinions of the adults who compose that environment, yet also guided by her own instinctive reactions, may be expected to misinterpret a great deal of what she observes and feels. The reader follows her as she is excited, puzzled, and disturbed by Patrick's money-mad and pleasure-mad world—a world without fixed rules of conduct. Many of the "sex scenes" between them are built upon verbal jokes, comic maneuvers, digressions, and irrelevancies, all of which give life to the conventional narrative with which Amis is working.

Patrick Standish is the antithesis of the good, moral, somewhat passive Jenny. Like the masterful, selfish Bertrand Welch, he is a womanizer and a conscious hypocrite who condemns himself with every word he utters. In spite of Patrick's intolerable be-

havior and almost crippling faults, Amis maintains some degree of sympathy for him by granting him more than a surface treatment. In the earlier novels, the villains are seen from a distance through the heroes' eyes. In *Take a Girl Like You*, however, an interior view of the villain's thoughts, frustrations, and fears allows the reader some measure of understanding. Many scenes are rhetorically designed to emphasize Patrick's isolation and helplessness. Fears of impotence, cancer, and death haunt him. He seeks escape from these fears by turning to sex, drink, and practical jokes, but this behavior leads only to further boredom, unsatisfied longing, and ill health.

Also contributing to the somber tone of the novel are secondary characters such as Dick Thompson, Seaman Jackson, and Graham MacClintoch. Jackson equates marriage with "'legalised bloody prostitution.'" MacClintoch complains that, for the unattractive, there is no charity in sex. Jenny's ideals are further diminished when she attends a party with these men. The conversation anticipates the emotional barrenness of later novels, in which love is dead and in its place are found endless games. Characters speak of love, marriage, and virtue in the same tone as they would speak of a cricket game or a new set of teeth.

With *Take a Girl Like You*, Amis leaves behind the hilarity and high spirits on which his reputation was founded, in order to give expression to the note of hostility and cruelty hinted at in *Lucky Jim*. Drifting steadily from bewilderment to disillusionment, Jenny and Patrick signal the beginning of a new phase in Amis's moral vision. Life is more complex, more precarious, less jovial. The simple romantic fantasy solution at the end of *Lucky Jim* is not possible here.

THE ANTI-DEATH LEAGUE

The Anti-Death League represents for Amis yet another extension in philosophy and technique. The conventions of the spy-thriller provide the necessary framework for a story within which Amis presents, from multiple viewpoints, a world view that is more pessimistic than that of any of his previous novels. A preoccupation with fear and evil, an explicit religious frame of reference, and a juxtaposition of pain and laughter, cruelty and tenderness all go to create a sense of imminent calamity reminiscent of George

Orwell's *Nineteen Eighty-Four* (1949). No longer does Amis's world allow carefree, uncomplicated figures of fun to move about, relying upon good luck and practical jokes to see them through their difficulties. Life has become an absurd game, and the players are suffering, often lonely and tragic individuals, caught in hopeless situations with little chance for winning the good life, free from anxieties, guilts, and doubts.

As the controlling image, the threat of death is introduced early in the novel in the form of an airplane shadow covering the principal characters. Related to this scene is an elaborate metaphor drawn from the language of pathology, astronomy, botany, and thermonuclear war. Part 1 of the three-part structure is entitled "The Edge of a Node"—referring to Operation Apollo, an elaborate project designed to destroy the Red Chinese with a horrible plague. As the narrative progresses, the characters are brought to the edge or dead center of the node.

Related to this preoccupation with death is the sexual unhappiness of the characters. Jim Dixon's romps with Margaret are farcical and at times rather sad. Patrick Standish's pursuit and conquest of Jenny Bunn are disgusting and somewhat tragic. In *The Anti-Death League*, the characters' pursuit of love and sex leads only to unhappiness and even danger. Two disastrous marriages and several unhappy affairs have brought Catherine Casement to the brink of madness. An unfaithful husband and a possessive lover have caused Luzy Hazell to avoid any emotional involvement whatsoever. A desire to get away from love impels Max Hunter, an alcoholic and unabashed homosexual, to join the army.

Along with the inversion of love, Amis dramatizes an inversion of religion. In place of a benevolent, supreme being, Amis has substituted a malevolent God whose malicious jokes lead to death and tragic accidents. In protest, Will Ayscue, the army chaplain, declares war on Christianity as the embodiment of the most vicious lies ever told. Max Hunter writes a poem against God ("To a Baby Born Without Limbs"), organizes the Anti-Death League, and demolishes the local priory. James Churchill cites Max Hunter's alcoholism, the death of a courier, and

Catherine's cancer as reasons for retreating from a world gone bad. While, in the preceding novels, laughter helps the heroes cope with specific injustices, in *The Anti-Death League*, laughter only intensifies the horror, the pain. Sometimes Amis shifts abruptly from laughter to pain to intensify the pain. A lighthearted moment with Hunter in the hospital is followed by a depressing scene between Catherine and Dr. Best. News of Catherine's cancer is juxtaposed with Dr. Best's highly comic hide-and-seek game.

Hysteria, depression, boredom: These are some of the moods in the army camp, bespeaking a malaise and a loss of hope from which neither sex nor religion nor drink offers any escape. Although the reader both condemns and laughs at the characters' foibles, he feels a personal involvement with them because he sees the suffering through the sufferers' eyes. Alone, trying to regain control of their lives, they act irresponsibly and immorally. Only Moti Naidu—like Gore-Urquhart, a moral voice in the novel—speaks truth in spite of the other characters' tragic mistakes. His recommendations that they aspire to common sense, fidelity, prudence, and rationality, however, go unheeded.

THE GREEN MAN

Although *The Green Man* offers the same preoccupation with God, death, and evil as *The Anti-Death League*, the novel is different from its predecessor in both feeling and technique. The work is, to begin with, a mixture of social satire, moral fable, comic tale, and ghost story. Evil appears in the figure of Dr. Thomas Underhill—a seventeenth century "wizard" who has raped young girls, created obscene visions, murdered his enemies, and now invades the twentieth century in pursuit of the narrator's thirteen-year-old daughter. God also enters in the person of "a young, well-dressed, sort of after-shave lotion kind of man," neither omnipotent nor benevolent. For him, life is like a chess game whose rules he is tempted to break. A seduction, an orgy, an exorcism, and a monster are other features of this profoundly serious examination of dreaded death and all of its meaningless horror.

The novel is narrated retrospectively from the point of view of Maurice Allington. Like Patrick

Standish and James Churchill, he spends most of his time escaping, or trying to escape, from himself—and for good reason. Death for him is a fearful mystery. Questions of ultimate justice and human destiny have been jarred loose of any religious or philosophical certainties. He suffers from "jactitations" (twitching of the limbs) as well as unpleasant and lengthy "hypnagogic hallucinations." What is more, problems with self extend to problems with his family and friends: He is unable to get along well with his wife or daughter, and his friends express doubts about his sanity. In fact, the only certainty Maurice has is that as he gets older, consciousness becomes more painful.

To dramatize Maurice's troubled mind, Amis also employs supernatural machinery as an integral part of the narrative. The windowpane through which Maurice sees Underhill becomes a metaphor for the great divide between the known, seen world of reality and the unknown, hence fearful world of the supernatural. Dr. Underhill, a *Doppelgänger*, reflects Maurice's own true nature in his selfish, insensitive manipulation of women for sexual ends. Also, Underhill's appearances provide Maurice with an opportunity to ennoble himself. In his pursuit and eventual destruction of both Underhill and the green monster, Maurice gains self-knowledge—something few of Amis's characters ever experience. He realizes his own potential for wickedness, accepts the limitations of life, and comes to an appreciation of what death has to offer as an escape from earthbound existence. For the first time in his life, Maurice recognizes and responds to the loving competence of his daughter, who looks after him when his wife leaves.

On one level, this elaborately created story is a superbly entertaining, fantastic tale. On another level, it is a powerful and moving parable of the limitations and disappointments of the human condition. Unlike *Lucky Jim* and *Take a Girl Like You*, both of which are rooted in the real world and are guided by the laws of nature, *The Green Man*—and to some extent *The Anti-Death League*—employs fantastic and surreal elements. Ravens, specters, vague midnight terrors, all associated with guilt and despair, provide fitting emblems for Maurice's self-absorbed condition.

THE OLD DEVILS

The Old Devils is not an easy book to read, but it is an almost irresistibly easy book to reread. It is one of Amis's densest novels, its many different characters and their stories diverging, interweaving, and dovetailing with a striking precision that requires the utmost concentration of the reader. The novel has no central hero-narrator; each of the major characters claims his (or her) own share of reader attention. Though their talks and thoughts wander from topic to topic casually, appearing aimless and undirected, actually the inner workings of the characters are carefully regulated, as are the descriptive comments by the omniscient narrator, to support, define, develop, and ultimately embody the novel's themes.

In terms of narrative, the story itself is painted in muted tones. Alun Weaver has chosen to retire from his successful television career in London as a kind of "professional Welshman" and third-rate poet and return after thirty years with his beautiful wife, Rhiannon, to South Wales. The novel explores, over a span of a few months, the effect of this return on their circle of old friends from university days. The old devils—a group of Welsh married couples all in their sixties and seventies—include Malcolm Cellan-Davies, an unsung local writer, and his wife, Gwen; Peter Thomas, a chemical engineer, and his wife, Muriel; Charlie Norris, the proprietor of a restaurant, and his wife, Sophie; Percy and Dorothy Morgan; and Garth Pumphrey, a former veterinarian who with his wife, Angharad, now attends to business at a local pub. Of the five couples, the first three have never left their home town or accomplished anything very remarkable; their lives have passed them by. They are old now, retired from their professions, and do little else but drink heavily, a device Amis has often used to lower his characters' defenses and reveal their true emotional states. As Sophie says of her husband, "I never realised how much he drank till the night he came home sober. A revelation, it was."

The physical ill health the cronies worry about extends to the spiritual health of their marriages. With the exception of Rhiannon, her daughter Rosemary, and a few minor characters, the women in this novel not only are plain, hard, sharp, critical, or cross but also lack any reasonable relation with their husbands that would make significant communication possible. Only Alun and Rhiannon, married for thirty-four years, seem still to have an appetite for life and love as well as drink, and most of their misunderstandings lead only to teasing, not to disaster. Their arrival, however, arouses conflict among their old friends. "You know," says Muriel early in the novel, "I don't think that news about the Weavers is good news for anyone." The conflict comes in part because their return revives memories of various youthful liaisons and indiscretions, and also because the egotistical Alun immediately sets out to re-woo the three women with whom he had affairs in the old days.

Yet *The Old Devils* is about more than an aging present; it is also very much about the past and its impingements upon everyone. Many of the characters in *The Old Devils* are carrying scars from bitterness and regret because of something that happened in their lives long ago, something they hide carefully from the world, but on which their conscious attention is fixed. Past choices weigh heavily on all of them. These memories, like the memories of the aging characters in earlier novels, touch various notes, some sweet, some sour, some true, and others a bit off pitch. Indeed, these old devils are bedeviled by worries and fears of all kinds that deepen their uncertainty about life and increase their preoccupation with the past. Amis points out that one of the reasons old people make so many journeys into the past is to satisfy themselves that it is still there. When that, too, is gone, what is left? In this novel, what remains is only the sense of lost happiness not to be regained, only the awareness of the failure of love, only the present and its temporary consolations of drink, companionship, music, and any other diversions they might create, only a blind groping toward some insubstantial future. Neither human nor spiritual comfort bolsters their sagging lives and flagging souls; Malcolm speaks for all the characters, and probably for Amis himself, when he responds to a question about believing in God: "It's very hard to answer that. In a way I suppose I do. I certainly hate to see it all disappearing."

As in earlier novels, Amis finds in the everyday concerns of his ordinary folk a larger symbolic meaning, which carries beyond the characters to indict a whole country. By the end of the novel, one character after another has uncompromisingly attacked television, the media, abstract art, trendy pub decor, rude teenagers, children, shoppers, rock music, Arab ownership of shops and pubs, and anything that smacks of arty or folksy Welshness. The point, says Malcolm, sadly, is that Wales is following the trends from England and has found a way of destroying the country, "not by poverty but by prosperity." The decline and the decay, he says, are not the real problem. "We've faced that before and we've always come through." What he abominates is the specious affluence. "It's not the rubble I deplore," he says, "it's the vile crop that has sprung from it." Both extremes—decay and affluence—are suggested by the homes the characters occupy, and unhappiness characterizes either extreme. Amis's awareness of rooms, of houses, and of what they reveal about their inhabitants is a critical commonplace. Here, in each instance, the description of a character's personal environment is a means of rendering his or her appalled and irritated perception of the world.

Amis's characterization in *The Old Devils*, however, goes beyond a study of that final form of human deterioration. Rather, the novel examines an often debilitating process of moral and spiritual decay, a lessening of these people as human beings as life goes on and their hopes have dimmed along with their physical and mental powers. Perhaps Rhiannon, the most well-rounded of Amis's female characters in the novel, has kept her spiritual core more intact than any of the old devils. Without a doubt she holds a certain moral superiority over her husband in a way that is reminiscent of Jenny Bunn (in *Take a Girl Like You*), and the differences in husband and wife are played against each other. Rhiannon emerges as the voice of common sense in the novel, serene and utterly down-to-earth; Alun is condemned, by his actions and words, as a shallow, worldly, selfish man. In the end, he meets death, while Rhiannon survives and, in fact, looks ahead to future happiness. The two are unreconciled at Alun's death, no mention is made of her mourning, no homage is paid to his memory, and at the end of the novel she turns to Peter, her lover of forty years before. She finally forgives him for his long-ago abandonment, and the two begin to look forward to spending their last years together.

That event is one of two at the end of the novel that vitiate its undertone of pain, despair, and anxiety. The other positive event is the wedding of Rosemary, the Weavers' daughter, to William, the son of Peter and Muriel, suggesting the replacing of the older generation by the new, which in one sense is heralded by the author as a sign of progress and fulfillment. The reader feels that they will go on to live somewhat happy, placid lives. Despite the overriding negativism in the novel, there is some possibility of redemption. In *The Old Devils*, Amis pictures two relatively attractive people who show promise of living and working together peacefully, using their energy to make a new world instead of destroying an existing one.

THE FOLKS THAT LIVE ON THE HILL

The Folks That Live on the Hill appeared only four years after *The Old Devils*, and while the two share certain similarities—especially the deployment of a wide, even panoramic, cast of characters—the latter novel exhibits a greater degree of acceptance of humankind's foibles. This attitude is displayed in particular by the novel's protagonist, Harry Caldecote, a retired librarian who cannot help caring about—and caring for—other people. These include a widowed sister who keeps house for him in the London suburb of Shepherd's Hill, a niece by marriage whose alcoholism is reaching catastrophic proportions, and a brother whose mediocre poetry Harry nevertheless shepherds toward publication. Providing a kind of running commentary on the novel's hapless characters are two immigrant brothers, a pair of bemused outsiders who see the follies of the "folks" all too clearly. When offered an attractive job in the United States, Harry chooses to remain where he is, partly through inertia but largely because he knows he is needed where he is. Yet Harry is recognizably an Amis character, and a distinctly male one at that. Twice-married and twice-divorced, he is largely intolerant of women, other classes, and their annoying patterns of speech.

THE RUSSIAN GIRL

The Russian Girl encapsulates many of Amis's perennial motifs and patterns, yet the gentler note sounded in *The Folks That Live on the Hill* remains. The novel's protagonist is Richard Vaisey, an opinionated professor of Russian literature and language, who is fighting to maintain the integrity of his subject in the face of academic progress. (It seems that Richard's considerable knowledge of his subject "dates" him.) Richard's wife Cordelia is perhaps the most harpy-like of all Amis's female characters, a rich, sexually attractive but wholly villainous creation noted for her absurd but attention-getting accent. The "girl" of the title is Anna Danilova, a visiting Russian poet who becomes involved with Richard. Their affair propels Richard from his comfortable, sheltered existence into a life of possibility.

Saving the novel's plot from a certain predictability is the fact that Anna, like Harry's brother Freddie in *The Folks That Live on the Hill*, is not a good poet. (To drive the point home, Amis reproduces an embarrassingly poor poem Anna has written in loving tribute to Richard.) This is a situation that Richard understands, yet ultimately chooses to accept. In turn, Anna senses Richard's true opinion of her work and accepts it as well. Although not his final novel, *The Russian Girl* represents in many ways the culmination of Amis's fictional career. More sharply focused than many of its predecessors, it forces its protagonist through very difficult moral and intellectual choices. Anna too achieves a kind of dignity because of, not despite, her very lack of talent and emerges as one of Amis's most gratifyingly complex female characters.

In retrospect, it is clear that Kingsley Amis is a moralist as well as a humorist. The early novels exhibit a richly comic sense and a considerable penetration into character, particularly in its eccentric forms. With *Take a Girl Like You*, Amis begins to produce work of more serious design. He gives much deeper and more complex pictures of disturbing and distorted people, and a more sympathetic insight into the lot of his wasted or burnt-out characters. In all of his novels, he fulfills most effectively the novelist's basic task of telling a good story. In his best novels— *Lucky Jim, Take a Girl Like You, The Anti-Death*

League, The Green Man, The Old Devils, The Folks That Live on the Hill, and *The Russian Girl*—Amis tries to understand the truth about different kinds of human suffering, then passes it on to the reader without distortion, without sentimentality, without evasion, and without oversimplification. His work is based on a steadying common sense.

Dale Salwak, updated by Grove Koger

OTHER MAJOR WORKS

SHORT FICTION: *My Enemy's Enemy*, 1962; *Collected Short Stories*, 1980; *We Are All Guilty*, 1991; *Mr. Barrett's Secret and Other Stories*, 1993.

POETRY: *Bright November*, 1947; *A Frame of Mind*, 1953; *A Case of Samples: Poems, 1946-1956*, 1956; *The Evans Country*, 1962; *A Look Round the Estate: Poems, 1957-1967*, 1967; *Collected Poems: 1944-1979*, 1979.

NONFICTION: *New Maps of Hell: A Survey of Science Fiction*, 1960; *The James Bond Dossier*, 1965 (with Ian Fleming); *What Became of Jane Austen? and Other Questions*, 1970; *On Drink*, 1972; *Tennyson*, 1973; *Kipling and His World*, 1975; *An Arts Policy?*, 1979; *Everyday Drinking*, 1983; *How's Your Glass?*, 1984; *Memoirs*, 1991; *The King's English: A Guide to Modern Usage*, 1997.

EDITED TEXTS: *Spectrum: A Science Fiction Anthology*, 1961, 1962, 1963, 1964, 1965 (with Robert Conquest); *Harold's Years: Impressions from the "New Statesman" and the "Spectator,"* 1977; *The Faber Popular Reciter*, 1978; *The New Oxford Book of Light Verse*, 1978; *The Golden Age of Science Fiction*, 1981; *The Great British Songbook*, 1986 (with James Cochrane); *The Amis Anthology*, 1988; *The Pleasure of Poetry: From His "Daily Mirror" Column*, 1990; *The Amis Story Anthology: A Personal Choice of Short Stories*, 1992.

BIBLIOGRAPHY

Bradbury, Malcolm. *No, Not Bloomsbury*. London: Deutsch, 1987. Bradbury devotes a chapter to the comic fiction through *The Old Devils*, charting Amis's course from anger to bitterness. Bradbury notes Amis's moral seriousness, honesty, and humor. Includes a chronology and an index.

Bradford, Richard. *Kingsley Amis*. London: Arnold, 1989. This key study shows how Amis confounds customary distinctions between "popular" and "literary" fiction. Bradford argues that it is time to readjust the criteria for judging literary worth. Includes secondary bibliography and index.

Fussell, Paul. *The Anti-Egotist: Kingsley Amis, Man of Letters*. New York: Oxford University Press, 1994. An appreciation of Amis's versatile talents and accomplishments by a personal friend.

Gardner, Philip. *Kingsley Amis*. Boston: Twayne, 1981. This first full-length study of Amis's life and career treats his novels (through *Jake's Thing*) and nonfiction, paying particular attention to the recurrence of certain themes and character types, to his modes of comedy, and to the relationship between his life and fiction. Supplemented by a chronology, notes, selected primary and annotated secondary bibliographies, and an index.

Jacobs, Eric. *Kingsley Amis: A Biography*. New York: St. Martin's Press, 1998. A readable, sometimes painfully candid biography written with Amis's full cooperation. Includes photographs, notes, a primary bibliography, and an index. This American edition includes material that did not appear in the first (British) edition of 1995.

Laskowski, William. *Kingsley Amis*. New York: Twayne, 1998. Laskowski stresses Amis's overall accomplishment as a man of letters, divides his output into letters, genre fiction, and mainstream novels, and devotes equal consideration to each category. Published soon after Amis's death, this volume surpasses the coverage of Gardner's study (above), but does not replace it. Supplementary material is updated but otherwise similar.

McDermott, John. *Kingsley Amis: An English Moralist*. Basingstoke, England: Macmillan, 1989. This first British book-length study of Amis's work seeks to show that the novels are serious as well as funny, that they are distinctively English, and that they offer a wide range of approaches to significant aspects of human behavior. Includes substantial primary and secondary bibliographies and an index.

Mosley, Merritt. *Understanding Kingsley Amis*. Columbia: University of South Carolina Press, 1993. A short survey stressing Amis's accomplishments as a professional man of letters. Includes an annotated secondary bibliography and an index.

Salwak, Dale, ed. *Kingsley Amis: In Life and Letters.* New York: St. Martin's Press, 1990. Brings together the impressions, reminiscences, and judgments of twenty of Amis's friends and readers. The essays cover Amis's novels and poetry, his interest in science fiction, his tenures at various colleges and universities, his style, his changing social and moral attitudes, and his personality. Includes primary and secondary bibliographies, an index, and photographs.

MARTIN AMIS

Born: Oxford, England; August 25, 1949

PRINCIPAL LONG FICTION

The Rachel Papers, 1973
Dead Babies, 1975 (also known as *Dark Secrets*, 1977)
Success, 1978
Other People: A Mystery Story, 1981
Money: A Suicide Note, 1984
London Fields, 1989
Time's Arrow: Or, The Nature of the Offence, 1991
The Information, 1995
Night Train, 1997

OTHER LITERARY FORMS

Invasion of the Space Invaders (1982), a history of video games; *The Moronic Inferno: And Other Visits to America* (1986), a collection of journalistic pieces on America; and *Einstein's Monsters* (1987), a collection of short stories reflecting life in the shadow of nuclear weapons; *Visiting Mrs. Nabokov and Other Excursions* (1993), essays on literature, politics, sports, and popular culture; and *Heavy Water and Other Stories* (1998), another collection of short stories, are among Amis's other works.

ACHIEVEMENTS

Martin Amis has been a force on the modern literary scene since his first novel, *The Rachel Papers*, won the Somerset Maugham Award for 1974. Critical and popular acclaim accompanied his sixth novel, *London Fields*, which was a best-seller on both sides of the Atlantic. Amis has a powerfully comic and satiric vision of the ills of contemporary society, which he caricatures in a way that has reminded many reviewers of Charles Dickens. Amis spares his reader little in his depiction of low-life characters in all their physical grossness and emotional aridity. The emptiness and corruption inherent in a materialistic culture are recurring themes of his work. Yet in spite of the often-sordid subject matter, Amis's novels are illuminated by their stylistic exuberance and ingenuity. More than one critic has remarked on the American flavor of his work, and he is regularly compared to Tom Wolfe and Saul Bellow.

BIOGRAPHY

The son of the novelist Kingsley Amis, Martin Amis spent his early years in Swansea, in south Wales, where his father held a teaching position at Swansea University. The family spent a year in Princeton, New Jersey, in 1959, and then moved to Cambridge, England. Amis's parents were divorced when Amis was twelve, and this had a disruptive effect on his schooling: He attended a total of fourteen schools in six years. As a teenager he had a brief acting career, appearing in the film *A High Wind in Jamaica* (1965). In 1968 he entered Exeter College, Oxford, and graduated in 1971 with first-class honors in English. He immediately became editorial assistant for *The Times Literary Supplement* and began writing his first novel, *The Rachel Papers*. In 1975 Amis became assistant literary editor of the *New Statesman*, and his second novel, *Dead Babies*, was published in the same year.

In 1980, when Amis was a writer and reviewer for the London newspaper *The Observer*, he reported his discovery that the American writer Jacob Epstein had plagiarized as many as fifty passages from *The Rachel Papers* for his own novel *Wild Oats* (1979). The accusation created a storm in the literary world. Epstein quickly conceded that he had indeed copied passages from Amis's novel and others into a notebook which he had then inadvertently used for his own novel. Thirteen deletions were made for the second American edition of Epstein's book, but Amis was infuriated because he thought that the revisions were not sufficiently extensive.

Martin Amis married Antonia Phillips, an American professor of aesthetics, in 1984, and they had two sons, Louis and Jacob. The controversy that has often accompanied Amis's writings spilled over into his private life from 1994 to 1996. First, he left his wife for American writer Isabel Fonseca. Then Amis fired his agent, Pat Kavanagh, when Kavanagh was unable to obtain a large advance from his publisher, Jonathan Cape, for his next novel, *The Information*. His new agent, the American Andrew Wylie, eventually made a deal with HarperCollins, and the whole proceedings were reported in the British press with an intensity rarely given literary figures such as Amis. The controversy was compounded by the report that Amis spent part of his new earnings for extensive dental work in the United States. In 1996 it was revealed that he was the father of a twenty-year-old daughter from a 1975 affair. In 1999 he agreed to write three books and a screenplay for the multimedia company Talk Miramax.

ANALYSIS

Martin Amis remarked in an interview that he wrote about "low events in a high style," and this comment gives a clue to the paradox his work embodies. Although the content of his novels is frequently sordid and nihilistic—dictated by the depressing absence in his characters of traditional cultural values—Amis's rich, ornate, and continually inventive style lifts the novels to a level from which they give delight. "I would certainly sacrifice any psychological or realistic truth for a phrase, for a paragraph that has a spin on it," Amis has commented. The result is that Amis's novels, in spite of the fact that they are often uproariously hilarious, do not make easy or quick reading. Indeed, Kingsley Amis has remarked that he is unable to get through his son's novels because of their ornate style, which he attributes to the influence of Vladimir Nabokov.

THE RACHEL PAPERS

Amis's first novel, *The Rachel Papers*, set the tone for most of his subsequent work, although his later novels, beginning with *Money*, have exhibited greater depth and range, as the force of his satire—his immense comic hyperbole—has steadily increased. Furthermore, one senses a sharp moral awareness in *Money* and *London Fields*, although Amis chooses not to offer any solutions to the individual and social ills he identifies so acutely.

The Rachel Papers is a lively but fairly innocuous satire about the turbulent adolescence of Charles Highway, the first-person narrator. Highway is a rather obnoxious young man, a self-absorbed intellectual studying for his Oxford examinations and aspiring to become a literary critic. The action takes place the evening before Highway's twentieth birthday and is filled out by extensive flashbacks. A substantial portion of Highway's intellectual and physical energy is devoted to getting his girlfriend Rachel into bed and to writing in his diary detailed descriptions of everything that happens when he succeeds. Amis's hilarious and seemingly infinitely inventive wordplay is never more effectively displayed than when Highway is describing his sexual adventures.

DEAD BABIES

Dead Babies, which chronicles the weekend debaucheries of a group of nine privileged young people, is considerably less successful than Amis's first novel, and Amis has since declared his own dislike for it. The theme seems to be a warning about what happens when traditional values (the dead babies of the title) are discarded. For the most part, however, the characters are too repulsive, and their indulgence in drugs, sex, alcohol, and violence too excessive, for the reader to care much about their fate.

SUCCESS

In *Success*, Amis chronicles a year in the lives of two contrasting characters. The handsome and conceited Gregory comes from an aristocratic family and appears to have all the worldly success anyone could want. He shares a flat in London with his foster brother Terry, who from every perspective is Gregory's opposite. Terry comes from the slums, he is physically unattractive and has low self-esteem, and he is stuck in a boring job which he is afraid of losing. The two characters take turns narrating the same events, which they naturally interpret very differently. As the year progresses, there is a change. Gregory is gradually forced to admit that his success is little more than an illusion. He has been fooling himself most of the time, and realization of his true ineptitude and childlike vulnerability causes him to go to pieces. Meanwhile, Terry's grim persistence finally pays off: He makes money, loses his self-hatred, and finally acquires a respectable girlfriend. For all of his crudity and loutishness, he is more in tune with the tough spirit of the times, in which traditional values are no longer seen to be of any value, and those who in theory represent them (like Gregory) have become effete.

Success is a clear indication of Amis's pessimism about life in London in the 1970's. Frequently employing extremely coarse language, the novel depicts some of the least attractive sides of human nature, and although this grimness is relieved (as in almost all Amis's books) by some ribald humor, on the whole *Success* is a depressing and superficial book. Indeed, it had to wait nine years after publication in Great Britain before an American publisher would take it on.

OTHER PEOPLE

In Amis's fourth novel, *Other People: A Mystery Story*, he appears to have been trying to write something with more philosophical and existential depth than the satires that came before. This time the protagonist is a young woman, who suffers from total amnesia. Released from hospital, she wanders alone through alien city streets, viewing other people as a separate species and virtually unable to distinguish between animate and inanimate things. Taking the name Mary Lamb, she experiences life in complete innocence, having to relearn everything that being alive involves: not only who she is but also the purpose of everyday things such as shoes and money. She mixes with a range of people from drunks and down-and-outs to upper-class degenerates, at the same time edging closer to a discovery of her real identity. It transpires that her real name is Amy Hide and that everyone thinks that she was killed after being brutally attacked by a man. Adding to the surreal

atmosphere of the novel is a mysterious character called Prince, whom Mary/Amy keeps encountering. Prince seems to fulfill many roles: He is a policeman, perhaps also the man who attacked her, and a kind of tutelary spirit, an awakener, under whose guidance she discovers her own identity.

Other People was written according to what is known in Great Britain as the Martian school of poetry, a point of view in which no knowledge about human life and society is assumed. This technique is intended to allow the most mundane things to be examined in a fresh light. Although Amis achieves some success in this area, the novel is spoiled by excessive obscurity. The novelist has simply not left enough clues to his intention, and the reader is left to grasp at bits of a puzzle without being able to construct an intelligible whole. Realizing that few people had grasped his meaning, Amis explained in an interview what his intention had been:

> Why should we expect death to be any less complicated than life? Nothing about life suggests that death will just be a silence. Life is very witty and cruel and pointed, and let us suppose that death is like that too. The novel is the girl's death, and her death is a sort of witty parody of her life.

This may not be of much help to readers who are especially puzzled by the novel's concluding pages. Perhaps the most rewarding parts of the novel are Amis's depictions of the characters Mary encounters; their physical and mental deformities are captured with merciless wit.

MONEY

In *Money: A Suicide Note*, Amis continued to devote attention to what he undoubtedly depicts best: people who have been deformed, who have failed to reach their full human growth, by the shallow materialism of the age. Yet the scope of *Money* is far wider and more impressive than anything Amis had produced before: Not only is it much longer, but it also fairly rocks with vulgar energy. Clearly, Amis has finished his writing apprenticeship and is moving into top gear.

The protagonist is John Self, a wealthy, early-middle-aged maker of television commercials who is visiting New York to direct what he hopes will be his first big motion picture. Yet the project runs into every difficulty imaginable, and after a series of humiliating experiences Self ends up back in London with nothing. The problem with Self is that although he is wealthy, he is uneducated and lacks all culture. He lives at a fast pace but spends his money and his time entirely on worthless things—junk food, alcohol, pornography, television. Satisfying pleasures continually elude him. Amis himself has commented on Self: "The world of culture is there as a sort of taunting presence in his life, and he wants it but he doesn't know how to get it, and all his responses are being blunted by living in the money world."

LONDON FIELDS

Amis's attack on the "money world" continues in *London Fields*, although Amis's finest novel is far more than that. It is at once a comic murder-mystery and a wonderfully rich and varied evocation of the decline of civilization at the end of the millennium. Many of the comic scenes are worthy of Charles Dickens, and the plot is acted out against a cosmic, apocalyptic background, as the planet itself seems to be on the brink of disintegration.

Set in post-Thatcherite London in 1999, the plot centers on three main characters. The first is the antiheroine Nicola Six. Nicola has a gift for seeing the future, and she has a premonition that on her next birthday, which happens to be her thirty-fifth, she will be murdered by one of two men she meets at a London pub called the Black Cross. She sets out to avenge herself in advance by using her sexual power to entice them and draw them to ruin. Nicola is a temptress of the first magnitude, and Amis employs comic hyperbole (as he does throughout the novel) to describe her: "Family men abandoned sick children to wait in the rain outside her flat. Semi-literate builders and bankers sent her sonnet sequences."

The second character, the possible murderer, is Keith Talent. Talent is probably Amis's finest creation, a larger-than-life character who might have stepped out of the pages of Dickens. He is a petty criminal, compulsive adulterer, wife-beater, and darts fanatic. He makes a living by cheating people, whether it be by selling fake perfume, running an outrageously expensive taxi service, or doing botched household repair jobs. He earns more money than the prime minister but never has any, because he loses it each day at the betting shop. Keith is not totally bad but wishes that he were: He regards his redeeming qualities as his tragic flaw. Obsessed with darts and television (which for him is the real world), his driving ambition is to reach the televised finals of an interpub darts competition. The miracle of the novel is that Amis has succeeded, as with John Self in *Money*, in making such a pathetic character almost likable.

The second possible murderer is Guy Clinch. Clinch is quite different from Keith Talent. He is a rich, upper-class innocent "who wanted for nothing and lacked everything." One of the things he lacks is a peaceful home life, after his wife, Hope, gives birth to Marmaduke, a ferocious infant who almost from birth is capable of acts of quite stunning malice and violence. (The only nurses who can cope with him are those who have been fired from lunatic asylums.) Once more the comedy is irresistible.

The convoluted plot, with its surprise ending, is narrated by a terminally ill American writer named Samson Young, who is in London on a house swap with the famous writer Mark Asprey. That the absent Asprey's initials are the same as those of Martin Amis is perhaps no coincidence. Young is in a sense the author's proxy, since he is himself gathering the material and writing the story of *London Fields* for an American publisher. To make matters even more subtle, a character named Martin Amis also makes an appearance in the novel, just as there had been a Martin Amis character in *Money*. Deconstructing his own fictions in this manner, Amis reminds the reader that in the manipulative world he depicts, he himself is the chief manipulator, but his own novel is only one fiction in a world of fictions.

The setting of *London Fields* is integral to the plot. The London of the near "future" (which 1999 was at the time of the novel's publication in 1989) possesses an oppressive, almost Blakean apocalyptic atmosphere. Not only has urban prosperity evaporated—parts of the city have sunk back into squalor—but the natural environment is in rapid decay also. Everyone is talking about the weather, but it is no longer simply small talk. Weather patterns are violently unstable; the sun seems to hang perpetually low in the sky, and rumors of impending cosmic catastrophe abound. The threat of a nuclear holocaust remains. When Nicola Six was a child, she invented two imaginary companions and called them Enola Gay and Little Boy. Enola Gay is the name of the airplane that dropped the first atom bomb, nicknamed Little Boy, on Hiroshima in 1945. Yet Samson Young, the narrator, calls nuclear weapons "dinosaurs" when compared to the environmental disasters that now threaten the earth. Eventually Young refers to the situation simply as "The Crisis," a term that also well describes the human world that Amis ruthlessly exposes, in which love, decency, and genuine feeling have been superseded by violence, greed, and lust. Microcosm and macrocosm are joined in a kind of horrible, frenzied dance of death. The world of *London Fields*, in which people and planet hurtle helplessly toward disaster, is where all Amis's fiction has been leading.

TIME'S ARROW

Time's Arrow is an unusual departure for Amis. Not only does this most contemporary of writers deal with the past, but he also does so with a less realistic and more overtly moralistic approach than in his other novels. A Nazi doctor's life is told in reverse order from his death in the United States to his birth in Germany, though his true identity is not apparent until more than half of the way through the narrative. While many of Amis's narrators may not be completely reliable, the narrator of *Time's Arrow* is relatively innocent. The physician's reverse life is told by his alter ego, who stands outside the action until finally merging with the protagonist near the end.

Time's Arrow also deals with the question of identity in the twentieth century, as Tod Friendly progresses from an elderly, rather anonymous man into a Massachusetts physician; into another physician, this time in New York City, named John Young; into an exile in Portugal named Hamilton de Souza; into his true identity as Odilo Unverdorben, a concentration-camp doctor and protégé of the ominous Auschwitz monster he calls Uncle Pepi. In telling Friendly's in-

creasingly complicated tale, Amis tries to encompass much of the history of the twentieth century, with particular attention to the Vietnam War era and the Cold War.

By telling the story backward, Amis also explores such themes as the banality of human communication, exemplified by conversations appearing with the sentences in reverse order: answers coming before questions. Amis gets considerable comic mileage out of the horrifying images of such acts as eating and excreting depicted backward. In this ironic, perverse universe, suffering brings about joy. The narrator, one of several Amis *Doppelgänger*s, is alternately irritated and disgusted by Friendly's behavior, particularly his crude treatment of his longtime American lover, Irene. The narrator also professes his affection for and admiration of Jews before finally admitting that he and Unverdorben are one, a highly ironic means of accepting responsibility for one's actions.

Many critics have dismissed *Time's Arrow* as a narrative stunt. In an afterword, Amis acknowledges that other writers have also employed reverse narratives, mentioning the famous account of a bomb traveling backward to its origins underground in *Slaughterhouse-Five* (1969) by Kurt Vonnegut, Jr., as a particular influence. *Time's Arrow* is most notable for presenting less subtly Amis's moral concerns, which have often been compared to those of Saul Bellow.

THE INFORMATION

With *The Information*, Amis returns to more typical themes. Two writers, best friends, are contrasted by their success, fame, and sex lives. Richard Tull, author of two little-read novels, edits *The Little Magazine*, a minor literary journal, serves as director of a vanity press, and writes reviews of biographies of minor writers. Gwyn Barry, on the other hand, has published a best-seller and is a major media figure. Married, with twin sons, Richard lusts after Lady Demeter, Gwyn's glamorous wife. Richard is not jealous of Gwyn's success so much as resentful that Gwyn's book is so universally beloved when it is completely without literary merit, an assessment with which both their wives agree. All of Richard's plans for revenge backfire, including hiring Steve Cousins, a mysterious criminal known as "Scozzy," to assault Gwyn.

In addition to addressing his usual topics—sex, violence, greed, and chaos—Amis presents a satirical view of literary infighting and pretensions. Richard creates primarily because of his need for love and attention. He perceives the world as an artist would, but he is unable to transform his vision into accessible literature: When editors read his latest effort, they become ill. Only the psychotic Scozzy seems to understand what he is trying to say. Richard cannot give up writing, however, because then he would be left with nothing but the tedium of everyday life. Gwyn is equally ridiculous. Obsessed by his fame, he reads newspaper and magazine articles about all subjects in hopes of seeing his name. The two writers are like a comic pair of mismatched twins.

The Information is also a typical Amis work in that it is highly self-conscious. The narrator who explains the warped workings of Scozzy's mind makes occasional appearances, first as "I," then as "M. A.," and finally as "Mart," yet another of Amis's cameo roles in his fiction. The narrator seems, as when he tries to explain that he cannot control Scozzy, to call attention to the artifice of the novel and to force the reader, as a willing participant in this satire, to share responsibility for the world's chaos.

Although some feminists have reservations about Amis's work (and it is true that most of his male characters treat their women with contempt), he is a formidable and critically acclaimed writer, certainly one of the most accomplished of the generation of English writers who came of age in the 1970's. Few others could have attempted a work on the scale of *London Fields*. Together with Salman Rushdie, Julian Barnes, and Peter Ackroyd—in their different ways—Amis has broken through the neat, middle-class boundaries of much contemporary English fiction and reached out toward a fiction that is more challenging and comprehensive in its scope.

Bryan Aubrey, updated by Michael Adams

Other major works

NONFICTION: *Invasion of the Space Invaders*, 1982; *The Moronic Inferno: And Other Visits to America*, 1986; *Visiting Mrs. Nabokov and Other Excursions*, 1993.

SHORT FICTION: *Einstein's Monsters*, 1987; *Heavy Water and Other Stories*, 1998.

Bibliography

Alexander, Victoria N. "Martin Amis: Between the Influences of Bellow and Nabokov." *Antioch Review* 52 (Fall, 1994): 580-590. Traces the influence of Saul Bellow and Vladimir Nabokov on Amis, showing how Amis's style represents a hybrid of Bellow's passion and Nabokov's coolness. Like his mentors, Amis is concerned with the decline of Western civilization.

Diedrick, James. *Understanding Martin Amis*. Columbia: University of South Carolina Press, 1995. The first book-length study of Amis examines his works through *The Information*. Argues that Amis's bad-boy image results from his challenging the genteel tradition dominating contemporary British fiction.

Finney, Brian. "Narrative and Narrated Homicides in Martin Amis's *Other People* and *London Fields*." *Critique* 37 (Fall, 1995): 3-15. Argues that in these two novels, by using manipulative, self-conscious narrators who victimize the other characters, Amis forces his readers to recognize how the characters are immersed both in and outside of the action.

Marowski, Daniel G., ed. *Contemporary Literary Criticism*. Vol. 38. Detroit, Mich.: Gale Research, 1986. Includes a summary of Amis's work and achievements up to *Money*, as well as extensive extracts from reviews of *Dead Babies, Success, Other People*, and *Money*, from both Great Britain and the United States. Volume 4 (1975) and volume 9 (1978) in the same series also have sections on Amis.

Moyle, David. "Beyond the Black Hole: The Emergence of Science Fiction Themes in the Recent Work of Martin Amis." *Extrapolation* 36 (Winter, 1995): 305-315. Shows how Amis adapts traditional science-fiction themes, such as time travel, concern about the end of the world, and a Doctor Frankenstein-like lack of regard for conventional morality, in *Time's Arrow* and *London Fields*.

Stout, Mira. "Martin Amis: Down London's Mean Streets." *The New York Times Magazine*, February 4, 1990, 32. A lively feature article, in which Amis, prodded by Stout, discusses a range of topics, including *London Fields*, his interest in the environment, his early life and career, his relationship with his father, the state of the novel as a form, the Thatcher government, middle age, and his daily work routine.

RUDOLFO A. ANAYA

Born: Pastura, New Mexico; October 30, 1937

PRINCIPAL LONG FICTION
Bless Me, Ultima, 1972
Heart of Aztlán, 1976
Tortuga, 1979
The Legend of La Llorona, 1984
Alburquerque, 1992
Zia Summer, 1995
Jalamanta, 1996
Rio Grande Fall, 1996

OTHER LITERARY FORMS
In addition to his novels, Rudolfo Anaya has written short stories, children's literature, essays, plays, and poetry. His early short stories are collected in *The Silence of the Llano* (1982). *The Farolitos of Christmas*, first published in 1987, is a children's short story; it was published again as an illustrated edition in 1995. Anaya's essay output is largely a result of his many lectures offered around the United States. An important exception, however, is *A Chicano in China* (1986), which is a daily account of a visit to China in 1984. *The Anaya Reader* (1995) is a collection of short stories, essays, a poem, and plays, including *Who Killed Don José?* (pr. 1987).

ACHIEVEMENTS
Rudolfo Anaya became one of the foremost Chicano novelists of the twentieth century. He came to the forefront of the literary field as the Chicano movement of the late 1960's began to strengthen its vision in the early 1970's. His first novel, *Bless Me, Ultima*, won the Premio Quinto Sol literary award in 1972. The recognition of his work brought him into the center of an important discussion on the issues of the history, culture, and identity of the Chicano. Anaya answered the challenge of his new role as a force in the evolution of Chicano letters by publishing *Heart of Aztlán*, a novel that represents a search for the Chicano soul in the barrios of Albuquerque, New Mexico. Aztlán, the legendary homeland of the Aztecs and the term used as a symbol of unity during the Chicano movement, is a key term in Chicano history. With *Heart of Aztlán* the term also becomes important in literature.

Alburquerque won the International Association of Poets, Playwrights, Editors, Essayists, and Novelists (PEN) Center West Award for fiction. Anaya's work in children's literature has also been recognized nationally. The 1995 illustrated edition of *The*

(Michael Mouchette)

73

Farolitos of Christmas, a warm tale of family love and a traditional Christmas, received the Southwest Texas State University Tomás Rivera Mexican American Children's Book Award.

BIOGRAPHY

Rudolfo Anaya was born in the little town of Pastura in eastern New Mexico. His family moved to Santa Rosa, New Mexico, while he was still a child. His experience during those early years in the countryside served as the material for his first novel, *Bless Me, Ultima*. Later, Anaya's family moved to Albuquerque, where he attended high school. *Heart of Aztlán* takes Albuquerque as its setting. As a sophomore in high school, the author experienced a serious spinal injury in a swimming accident. The pain and suffering caused by this injury are reflected in *Tortuga*, his third novel, which uses the ordeal of pain as part of the hero's search for universal understanding.

Anaya attended the University of New Mexico as an undergraduate and graduate student, eventually earning master's degrees in both literature and counseling. It was at the university that he began to write. His poetry and early novels dealt with major questions about his own existence, beliefs, and identity. He ended that phase of his life by burning all of the manuscripts of his work. After college he took a teaching job and was married; his wife was a great source of encouragement and an excellent editor.

Anaya began writing *Bless Me, Ultima* in the 1960's. He struggled with the work until, in one of his creative moments, Ultima appeared to him in a vision. She became the strongest character of the novel, as well as the spiritual mentor for both the protagonist and the novelist. Finding a publisher was not easy. After dozens of rejection letters from major publishers, Anaya turned to Quinto Sol Publications, a small Chicano press in Berkeley, California. The publishers not only accepted the work for publication but also awarded to him the Premio Quinto Sol for writing the best Chicano novel published in 1972. Anaya went on to become an internationally known storyteller and writer, as well as a mentor to young and old seeking to practice the craft of writing. He also became a committed advocate of Chicano self-definition and a major voice in the process of bringing cultures together for mutual enrichment.

ANALYSIS

Anaya's works project a Magical Realism that blends contemporary life with the hidden manifestations of humanity and cultural identity. In his books, the principal characters struggle with the sometimes contradictory notions of Chicano identity tied both to an Aztec and Spanish past and to the English-speaking world of the present. Most of Anaya's developed characters are influenced by that duality. The struggle caused by these contesting notions elevates the Chicano human condition to that of every person. Anaya's first three novels, *Bless Me, Ultima*, *Heart of Aztlán*, and *Tortuga*, best exemplify these themes and characterizations.

BLESS ME, ULTIMA

Bless Me, Ultima is Anaya's first novel of a trilogy, which also includes *Heart of Aztlán* and *Tortuga*. *Bless Me, Ultima* is a psychological and magical portrait of a child's quest for identity. In this classic work, Antonio, the protagonist, is subjected to competing realities which he must master in order to grow up. These realities are interwoven with symbolic characters and places, the most powerful of which are Ultima, a *curandera* (healer) who evokes the timeless past of a pre-Columbian world, and a golden carp that swims the river waters of the supernatural and offers a redeeming future.

Antonio is born in Pastura, a very small village on the eastern New Mexican plain. Later his family moves to a village across the river from the small town of Guadalupe, where Antonio spends his childhood. His father is a cattleman, and his mother is from a farming family. They represent the initial manifestation of the divided world into which Antonio is born and a challenge he must resolve in order to find himself. Antonio's father wants him to become a horseman of the plain, like his ancestors before him. His mother wants Antonio to become a priest to a farming community, which is the honored tradition. The parents' wishes are symptoms of a deeper spiritual challenge facing Antonio, involving his Catholic beliefs and those associated with the magical world of the pre-Columbian past. Ultima, the *curandera* and a creature of both worlds, is a magical character who guides Antonio through the ordeal of understanding and dealing with these challenges. She is there to supervise his birth; she comes to stay with the family in Guadalupe when Antonio is seven. On several occasions, Antonio is a witness to her power in life-and-death battles.

Antonio's adventure takes him beyond the divided world of the farmer and the horseman and beyond the Catholic ritual and its depictions of good and evil. With Ultima's help, he is able to bridge these opposites and channel them into a new cosmic vision of nature, represented by the river, which stands in the middle of his two worlds, and the golden carp, which points to a new spiritual covenant. The novel ends with the killing of Ultima's owl by one of her enemies. Because the owl carries her spiritual presence, Ultima dies as well. However, her work is completed before her death: Antonio can now choose his own destiny.

HEART OF AZTLÁN

Heart of Aztlán, Anaya's second novel of the trilogy, is, like *Bless Me, Ultima*, a psychological and magical portrait of a quest for Chicano identity and empowerment. It is the story of the Chávez family, who leave the country to search for a better life in the city, only to discover that their destiny lies in a past believed abandoned and lost. The story focuses on two characters, Clemente Chávez, the father, and Jason, one of the sons. Jason best depicts the adjustments the family has to make to everyday life in the city. However, it is Clemente who undergoes a magical rebirth, which brings to the community a new awareness of its destiny and a new will to fight for its birthright.

The novel begins with the Chávez family selling the last of their land and leaving the small town of Guadalupe for a new life in Albuquerque. They go to live in Barelas, a barrio on the west side of the city where many other immigrants reside. The Chávezes soon learn, as the other people of the barrio have discovered, that their lives do not belong to them. They are controlled by industrial interests, represented by the railroad and a union that has compromised the

workers. They are manipulated by politicians through Mannie García, "el super," who delivers the community vote.

In Barelas, Clemente also begins to lose the battle for control of his household, especially his daughters, who have no regard for his insistence on the tradition of respect and obedience to the head of the family. The situation worsens when Clemente loses his job in the railroad yard during a futile strike. He becomes an alcoholic, and in his despair he attempts suicide. Crespín, a magical character who represents eternal wisdom, comes to his aid and shows him the way to a new life. With Crespín's help, Clemente solves the riddle of a magical stone in the possession of "la India," a sorceress who symbolically guards the entryway to the heart of Aztlán, the source of empowerment for the Chicano.

Clemente's rebirth takes the form of a journey to the magical mountain lake that is at the center of Aztlán and of Chicano being. Reborn, Clemente returns to his community to lead the movement for social and economic justice in a redeeming and unifying struggle for life and for the destiny of a people. The novel ends with Clemente taking a hammer to the Santa Fe water tower in the railroad yard, a symbol of industrial might, before coming home to lead a powerful march on his former employers.

TORTUGA

Tortuga, the third novel of the trilogy, is a tale of a journey to self-realization and supernatural awareness. In the story, Benjie Chávez, the protagonist, undergoes a symbolic rebirth in order to take the place of Crespín, the keeper of Chicano wisdom, who upon his death will pass his position to Benjie. At the end of *Heart of Aztlán*, Benjie was wounded by his brother Jason's rival, fell from the railyard water tower, and was paralyzed. He was transported to the Crippled Children and Orphans Hospital in the south for rehabilitation. His entry into the hospital was also a symbolic entry into a world of supernatural transformation.

The hospital sits at the foot of a mountain called Tortuga (which means turtle), from which flow mineral springs with healing waters. Benjie is also given the name Tortuga after he is fitted with a body cast that makes him look like a turtle. What follows is a painful ordeal, both physically and psychologically, as the protagonist is exposed to every kind of human suffering and deformity that can possibly afflict children. Not even this, however, prepares him for the visit to the ward of the "vegetables," the immobile children who cannot breathe without the help of an iron lung. There Tortuga meets Salomón, also a vegetable, but one with supernatural insight into the human condition. Salomón enters Tortuga's psyche and guides him on the path to spiritual renewal.

Salomón compares Tortuga's challenge with the terrible ordeal newly born turtles undergo as they dash to the sea. Most of them do not survive, because other creatures lie in wait to devour them. Tortuga must endure the turtle's dash in order to arrive at his true destiny, which is called "the path of the sun." Tortuga experiences a near-death ordeal, which includes a climactic moment when Danny, an important character, pushes him into a swimming pool, where he would have drowned if others had not rushed to his aid. Tortuga survives his symbolic turtle dash to the sea. The vegetables are not so lucky; one night Danny succeeds in turning off the power to their ward. With the iron lungs turned off, they all die. The end of novel and Tortuga's rehabilitation also bring the news that Crespín, the magical helper of Tortuga's neighborhood, has died. The news of Crespín's death arrives along with his blue guitar, a symbol of universal knowledge, which is now Benjie's.

The trilogy that ends with this novel, along with Anaya's literary production as a whole, reflects a search for the meaning of existence as expressed in Chicano life. This search is often a journey that takes the protagonists into the past and the present and into the physical and mythical landscapes of the urban and rural worlds of the Southwest, revealing the relationship of these worlds to the social and political power structure of mainstream America.

David Conde

OTHER MAJOR WORKS

SHORT FICTION: *The Silence of the Llano*, 1982.

PLAYS: *Who Killed Don José?*, pr. 1987; *Billy the Kid*, pb. 1995.

NONFICTION: *A Chicano in China*, 1986.

CHILDREN'S LITERATURE: *The Farolitos of Christmas*, 1987, 1995 (illustrated edition).

MISCELLANEOUS: *The Anaya Reader*, 1995.

BIBLIOGRAPHY

Dick, Bruce, and Silvio Sirias, eds. *Conversations with Rudolfo Anaya*. Jackson: University of Mississippi Press, 1998. For students and general readers, this book is designed to present Anaya's point of view and philosophy. Includes index.

González-T, César A., ed. *Rudolfo A. Anaya: Focus on Criticism*. La Jolla, Calif.: Lalo Press, 1990. Mainly for specialists. The author is an eminent scholar and critic of Anaya. Contains select bibliography and index.

Martínez, Julio, and Francisco A. Lomelí. *Chicano Literature: A Readers' Guide*. New York: Greenwood Press, 1985. A good starting point for determining Anaya's place in Chicano literature. Includes biographical essays on Anaya and other Chicano authors.

Tatum, Charles M. *Chicano Literature*. Boston: Twayne, 1982. Provides an excellent perspective of the evolution of Chicano literature, especially in the 1970's, when Anaya came into prominence. Includes summaries of his works.

Vasallo, Paul, ed. *The Magic of Words: Rudolfo Anaya and His Writings*. Albuquerque: University of New Mexico Press, 1982. Provides an excellent reading and discussion of Anaya's early literary work.

SHERWOOD ANDERSON

Born: Camden, Ohio; September 13, 1876
Died: Colón, Panama Canal Zone; March 8, 1941

PRINCIPAL LONG FICTION

Windy McPherson's Son, 1916
Marching Men, 1917
Winesburg, Ohio, 1919

Poor White, 1920
Many Marriages, 1923
Dark Laughter, 1925
Beyond Desire, 1932
Kit Brandon, 1936

OTHER LITERARY FORMS

In addition to *Winesburg, Ohio*, which some critics regard as a collection of loosely related short stories, Sherwood Anderson produced three volumes of short stories: *The Triumph of the Egg* (1921); *Horses and Men* (1923); and *Death in the Woods and Other Stories* (1933). He published two books of prose poems, *Mid-American Chants* (1918) and *A New Testament* (1927). *Plays: Winesburg and Others* was published in 1937. Anderson's autobiographical writings, among his most interesting prose works, include *A Story Teller's Story* (1924), *Tar: A Midwest Childhood* (1926), and the posthumously published *Sherwood Anderson's Memoirs* (1942). All three are such a mixture of fact and fiction that they are sometimes listed as fiction rather than autobiography. Anderson also brought out in book form several volumes of journalistic pieces, many of which had appeared originally in his newspapers: *Sherwood Anderson's Notebook* (1926), *Perhaps Women* (1931), *No Swank* (1934), *Puzzled America* (1935), and *Home Town* (1940). *The Modern Writer* (1925) is a collection of lectures.

ACHIEVEMENTS

Anderson was not a greatly gifted novelist; in fact, it might be argued that he was not by nature a novelist at all. He was a brilliant and original writer of tales. His early reputation, which brought him the homage of writers such as James Joyce, Ford Madox Ford, Gertrude Stein, Ernest Hemingway, and F. Scott Fitzgerald, was established by the stories published in *Winesburg, Ohio*, *The Triumph of the Egg*, and *Horses and Men*. Anderson had published two novels before *Winesburg, Ohio* and was to publish five more afterward, but none of these achieved the critical success of his short pieces.

Anderson's difficulties with the novel are understandable when one sees that his great gift was for

(Library of Congress)

rendering moments of intense consciousness—"epiphanies," as James Joyce called them—for which the short story or the tale is the perfect vehicle. The novel form requires a more objective sense of a world outside the individual consciousness as well as the ability to move characters through change and development and to deal to some extent with the effect of character on character. The best parts of Anderson's novels are those scenes in which he deals, as in the short stories, with a minor character trapped by his own eccentric nature in a hostile world.

Another serious limitation to Anderson's talent as a novelist was his inclination to preach, to see himself as a prophet and reformer and to make sweeping generalizations that are as embarrassing as they are inartistic. Even in *Poor White*, probably his best novel, his characters run to types and become, finally, representative figures in a social allegory. In his worst novels, the characters are caricatures whose absurdity is not perceived by their author. Anderson's style, which could at times work brilliantly, became excessively mannered, a kind of self-parody, which was a sure sign that he had lost his grip on the talent that had produced his best and earlier work.

Winesburg, Ohio is without doubt Anderson's great achievement. It is a collection of tales striving to become a novel; indeed, most critics regard it as a novel, a new form of the novel, which, though perhaps first suggested by Edgar Lee Master's *Spoon River Anthology* (1915), took on its own expressive form and became the model for later works such as Hemingway's *In Our Time* (1924) and William Faulkner's *The Unvanquished* (1938). A few of the Winesburg stories, such as "Godliness," are marred by a tendency to generalization, but on the whole they assume the coherence and solidity of such masterpieces as Mark Twain's *The Adventures of Huckleberry Finn* (1884) and Stephen Crane's *The Red Badge of Courage* (1895), which bristle with implications not only about the life of their times but also about the present. If Anderson had published only *Winesburg, Ohio*, he would be remembered and ranked as an important minor American novelist.

BIOGRAPHY

Sherwood Anderson was born September 13, 1876, in Camden, Ohio, to Irwin and Emma Anderson. When he was eight years old, his family moved to Clyde, Ohio, where Anderson spent his most impressionable years. In later life, Anderson remembered Clyde as an ideal place for a boy to grow up; it became a symbol of the lost innocence of an earlier America. Many of his best stories have a fictionalized Clyde as their setting, and his memory of it shaped his vision of the American past and became a measure of the inadequacies of the industrialized, increasingly mechanized America of city apartments and bloodless sophistication.

Anderson's family was poor. Irwin Anderson, a harness maker, was thrown out of work by industrialization and periods of economic instability. Thus he was forced to work at various odd jobs, such as house painter and paper hanger. Anderson's mother took in washing, while Sherwood and his brother did odd jobs to help support the family. In his autobiographical accounts of growing up, *A Story Teller's Story*, *Tar*, and *Memoirs*, Anderson expresses his humiliation at his impoverished childhood and his resentment toward his father for the inability to support his family. Anderson was particularly bitter about the hardship inflicted on his mother, to whom he was deeply attached. He held his father accountable for his mother's early death, and in *Windy McPherson's Son* one may see in the portrait of the father Anderson's view of his own father as a braggart and a fool whose drunkenness and irresponsibility caused the death of his wife. In time, Anderson's attitude toward his father softened; he came to see that his own gifts as a storyteller were derived from his father, who was a gifted yarn spinner. Even more important in Anderson's development as a writer was the sympathy awakened in him by his father's failures. A braggart and a liar, Irwin Anderson nevertheless had romantic aspirations to shine in the eyes of the world; his pathetic attempts to amount to something made him grotesque by the standards of the world. An underlying tenderness for his father grew stronger as Sherwood Anderson grew older, enabling him to sympathize with those people in life who become the victims of the wrong kinds of dreams and aspirations. The portrayal of the narrator's father in "The Egg" is one example of Anderson's eventual compassion for such individuals.

Anderson's young manhood, however, was marked by a rejection of his father and a worship of progress and business success. He eagerly embraced the current version of the American Dream as exemplified in the Horatio Alger stories: the poor boy who becomes rich. Anderson's own career followed that pattern with remarkable fidelity. He took any odd job that would pay, whether it was selling papers or running errands, and earned himself the nickname "Jobby." After a brief stint in the army during the Spanish-American War and a year at the Wittenburg Academy completing his high school education, Anderson started in advertising in Chicago and moved up the financial ladder from one position to the next until he became the owner of a paint factory in Elyria, Ohio, the success of which depended upon his skill in writing advertising letters about his barn paint.

Anderson's personal life also developed in a traditional way. In 1904 he married a young woman from a middle-class family, had three children, and associated with the "best" people in Elyria. Around 1911, however, contradictory impulses at work in Anderson precipitated a breakdown. He worked hard at the paint factory and at night spent increasing amounts of time in an attic room writing fiction. The strain eventually took its toll, aided by the pressures of conflicting values: Anderson wanted business and financial success, yet, deep down, he believed in something very different. One day, without warning, he walked out of his paint factory and was later found wandering about the streets in Cleveland, dazed and unable to give his name and address. After a short stay in the hospital, Anderson returned to Elyria, closed out his affairs, and moved to Chicago.

Anderson later told the story of his departure from the paint factory and each time he told it, the details were different. Whatever the exact truth, the important fact appears to be that his breakdown was the result of serious strain between the kind of life he was leading and the kind of life something in him was urging him to live. Rex Burbank in *Sherwood Anderson* (1964) remarks that the breakdown was moral as well as psychological; it might be called spiritual as well, for it had to do with feelings too vague to be attached to questions of right and wrong. Anderson, in his best work, was something of a mystic, a "Corn Belt mystic" one detractor called him, and his mystical sense was to be the principal source of his gift as a fiction writer, as well as his chief liability as a novelist.

Anderson's life after he left the paint factory in Elyria was a mixture of successes and failures. He wandered from Chicago to New York to New Orleans and finally to Marion, Virginia, in 1927, where he built a house and became the publisher of two local newspapers. His first marriage had ended in divorce shortly after he moved to Chicago; he married three more times, his last to Eleanor Copenhaver, a Virginian. Anderson's financial status was always somewhat precarious. His reputation had been established early among Eastern intellectuals who were attracted to what they saw as Anderson's primitivism, a quality he learned to cultivate. Except for *Dark Laughter*, however, which was something of a best-seller, none of his books was very successful financially, and he

was forced to lecture and to do journalistic writing. His most serious problem, though, was the waning of his creative powers and his inability after 1923 to equal any of his earlier successes. During his later years, before his final and happiest marriage, Anderson often was close to a breakdown.

During his years in Virginia and under the influence of his fourth wife, Anderson increasingly became interested in social problems. He visited factories, wrote about labor strife, and lent his name to liberal causes. His deepest commitment, however, was not to politics but to his own somewhat vague ideal of brotherhood, which he continued to espouse. In 1941, while on a goodwill tour to South America for the State Department, he died of peritonitis.

ANALYSIS

All novelists are to some extent autobiographical, but Sherwood Anderson is more so than most; indeed, all of Anderson's novels seem to arise out of the one great moment of his life, when he walked out of the paint factory and left behind the prosperous middle-class life of Elyria. In his imagination, his defection from material success took on great significance and became not only the common paradigm for his protagonists but also the basis for his message to the modern world. Industrialization and mechanization, money making, advertising, rising in the world, respectability—all of which Anderson himself had hankered after or had sought to encourage in others—became in his fiction the target of criticism. This is not to accuse him of insincerity, but only to point out the extent of his revulsion and the way in which he made his own personal experience into a mythological history of his region and even of the modern world. Anderson's heroes invariably renounce materialism and economic individualism and their attendant social and moral conventions and seek a more spiritual, more vital existence.

WINDY MCPHERSON'S SON

Anderson's first published novel, *Windy McPherson's Son*, though set in Caxton, Iowa, is clearly based on Anderson's boyhood in Clyde, Ohio, and his later years in Elyria and Chicago. Sam McPherson is a fictionalized version of "Jobby" Anderson, with his talent for money-making schemes; his father, like Anderson's own, is a braggart and liar who frequently disgraces his hardworking wife and ambitious son in front of the townspeople of Caxton. After his mother's death, Sam leaves Caxton and takes his talent for money making to Chicago, where in effect he takes over management of an arms manufacturing plant. Sam becomes rich and marries the boss's daughter, but, instead of finding satisfaction in his wealth and position, he discovers that he is dissatisfied with business success and his childless marriage. He walks out of the business, abandons his wife, and wanders through the country attempting to find meaning in existence. After discovering that "American men and women have not learned to be clean and noble and natural, like their forests and their wide, clean plains," Sam returns to his wife Sue, bringing with him three children he has adopted. Out of some sense of responsibility, he allows himself to be led back into the darkened house from which he had fled, a curious and unsatisfactory "happy" ending.

MARCHING MEN

Marching Men, Anderson's second novel, repeats the same basic pattern: success, revolt, search, revelation, elevation—but in a less convincing way. The setting is Coal Creek, a Pennsylvania mining town. The hero is Beaut McGregor, who rebels against the miners' passive acceptance of their squalid existence and escapes to Chicago, where he becomes rich. McGregor continues to despise the miners of Coal Creek until he returns for his mother's funeral; then, he has an awakening, a sudden illumination that gives him a spiritual insight that alters his existence. He sees the miners as men marching "up out of the smoke," and that insight and the marching metaphor become the inspiration for McGregor's transformation. Back in Chicago, he becomes the leader of a new movement called the "marching men," an organization as vague and diffuse as its aim: to find "the secret of order in the midst of disorder," in order that "the thresh of feet should come finally to sing a great song, carrying the message of a powerful brotherhood into the ears and brains of the marchers." A great march takes place in Chicago on Labor Day, and though the marching of the men makes its power

felt when the day is over, it is clear that the movement, whatever its temporary success, has no future. The marchers disperse in roving gangs, and an "aristocratic" opponent of the movement muses on its success and failure, wondering whether in deliberately turning away from the success of business and embracing the ultimate failure of the marching men, Beaut McGregor did not achieve a higher form of success.

Though a failure as a novel, *Marching Men* is interesting as Anderson's attempt to give expression to his own kind of achievement and as a place to experiment with concepts successfully handled later in *Winesburg, Ohio*. Anderson had given up success in the business world for a precarious career as a writer; he saw himself as a prophet preaching ideals of brotherhood that had nothing to do with political movements or social programs, but that expressed a mystical yearning for order and unity. The metaphor of the marching men was intended to express this vague ideal. The quest for order and brotherhood was a theme to which Anderson was to return in his next novel, *Winesburg, Ohio*, where he found the form best suited to its expression. The format of *Marching Men*, with its lack of convincing motivation and realistic development, exposed the inadequacy of Anderson's marching metaphor for sustaining a full-length realistic novel.

WINESBURG, OHIO

Winesburg, Ohio is Anderson's masterpiece, a collection of interrelated stories which are less like chapters than like the sections of a long poem; within these pieces, however, there is what might be called a submerged novel, the story of George Willard's growth and maturation. Willard appears in many of the stories, sometimes as a main character, but often as an observer or listener to the tales of other characters. There is the story of Alice Hindeman, who refuses to elope with Ned Curry because she does not want to burden him and eventually runs naked out into the rain. There is also Wing Biddlebaum in "Hands" and Elmer Cowley of "Queer," who desperately try to be normal but only succeed in being stranger than ever. There is the Reverend Curtis Hartman, who spies through a chink in his study window the naked figure of Kate Swift and ends by having a spiritual insight: Christ manifest in the body of a naked woman. These minor characters raise an important critical question: What bearing have they on the submerged *Bildungsroman*?

In five stories, beginning with "Nobody Knows" and ending with "Sophistication" and including "The Thinker," "An Awakening," and "The Teacher," George Willard moves from a lustful relationship with Louise Trunion to a feeling of respectful communion with Helen White, discovering the ultimate reverence for life which Anderson describes as the only thing that makes life possible in the modern world. The discovery was one Anderson himself had made in the early years of his newfound freedom in Chicago, following his escape from the paint factory. In "An Awakening," the pivotal story in the submerged novel, George is made to undergo a mystical experience in which he feels himself in tune with a powerful force swinging through the universe; at the same time, he feels that all of the men and women of his town are his brothers and sisters and wishes to call them out and take them by the hand, including, presumably, the so-called grotesques of the other stories.

The precise relationship of these other stories to those that constitute the growth and maturation of George Willard is a matter of continual critical conjecture, for *Winesburg, Ohio* is the kind of book that does not give up its meanings easily, partly because the kind of meaning the book has can only be suggested, but also because Anderson's way of suggesting is so indirect, at times even vatic. Anderson was possibly influenced by the French post-Impressionist painters such as Paul Cézanne and Paul Gauguin, whose works he had seen in Chicago, and his interest in rendering subjective states indirectly might well parallel theirs. Whether such influences were in fact exerted is arguable. What is clear, however, is that Anderson was by temperament an oral storyteller and that he depended upon tone, colloquial language, and folk psychology rather than the more formal structures of the novelist. In *Winesburg, Ohio* he was also a poet, working by suggestion and indirection, a method that produces intellectual and narrative gaps

which the reader is obliged to cross under his or her own power.

One of the chief critical issues of *Winesburg, Ohio* is the nature of Anderson's characters. In an introductory story, "The Book of the Grotesque" (an early title for the novel), Anderson supplied a definition of a grotesque as one who took a single idea and attempted to live by it, but such a definition, while it can be applied to some characters such as Doctor Parcival of "The Philosopher," hardly fits others at all. In an introduction to the Viking edition of *Winesburg, Ohio* (1960), Malcolm Cowley suggested that the problem of the Winesburg characters was an inability to communicate with one another. Jarvis Thurston's article in *Accent* (1956), "Anderson and 'Winesburg': Mysticism and Craft," offers a more compelling view; the Winesburg characters, Thurston says, are all spiritual questers, and their often violent behavior is symptomatic, not of their inability to communicate, but of a blockage of the spiritual quest. Only George Willard succeeds in that quest, when he undergoes, in "An Awakening," a transcendent experience. Burbank, however, in *Sherwood Anderson*, emphasizes the difference between Willard and the other characters of *Winesburg, Ohio* in this way: They are all "arrested" in a state of loneliness and social isolation. George, on the other hand, because he has heard the stories of the grotesques and has absorbed their lives, has managed to break out of a meaningless existence into a meaningful one. Burbank calls George "an artist of life."

Whatever view one takes of Anderson's characters, it is clear that no simple explanation will suffice, especially not the old writer's, though some critics think of him as Anderson's spokesman. Indeed, the prospect of a single idea summarizing and explaining all of the characters seems ironic in the light of the old writer's assertion that such simplemindedness produces grotesques. *Winesburg, Ohio* has its own kind of unity, but it has its own kind of complexity as well. It is a book of contradictory impulses that stands conventional judgment on its head; at times it is funny and often at the same time profoundly sad. It is a book in praise of the emotions, but, at the same time, it is aware of the dangers of emotional excess.

Winesburg, Ohio was well received by reviewers and even had a moderate financial success. It also confirmed, in the minds of Eastern critics such as Van Wyck Brooks and Waldo Frank, Anderson's authentic American genius. He was seen as part of that native American tradition that came down through Abraham Lincoln, Walt Whitman, and Mark Twain, expressing the essential nature of American life, its strengths, its weaknesses, and its conflicts.

Winesburg, Ohio has not been without its detractors. From a certain point of view, the antics of a character such as Alice Hindeman dashing naked into the rain are ridiculous, and Anderson's style at times slips into the mode of the fancy writer of slick fiction; even his mysticism can be ridiculed if one sees it as Lionel Trilling does in *The Liberal Imagination* (1950) as a form picking a quarrel with respectable society. Despite its faults, however, *Winesburg, Ohio* still lives—vital, intriguing, moving. It remains a modern American classic, expressing in its eccentric way a certain quality of American life that is all but inexpressible.

POOR WHITE

Anderson's next novel was to be a more traditional sort of work with a hero and a heroine and a "happy" ending that included the requisite embrace, though the hero and the embrace were anything but popularly traditional. Hugh McVey, the protagonist of *Poor White*, is the son of a tramp, born on the muddy banks of the Mississippi and content to live there in a dreamy, sensual existence until taken up by a New England woman who does her best to civilize him. Hugh is tall and lanky, rather like Lincoln in appearance if more like Huck Finn in temperament. When Sarah Shepard, the New England woman, leaves Missouri, Hugh goes east to the town of Bidwell, Ohio, where he becomes the town's telegrapher, and then, out of boredom, begins inventing laborsaving machinery. Being naïve and something of a social outcast, Hugh is unaware of the changes his inventions make in Bidwell. He thinks he is making life easier for the laborers, but opportunists in the town get hold of Hugh's inventions; the factories they bring into being exploit both Hugh and the farm laborers, who, without work in the fields, have swarmed into the new factories, slaving long hours for low pay. Inadvertently, Hugh has succeeded in corrupting the lives of the very people he had set out to help.

Clearly, the story of Hugh's "rise" from a dreamy loafer into a rich inventor and the changes that take place in Bidwell from a sleepy farm community into a bustling factory town are meant to tell the story of mid-America's transformation from a primitive, frontier society of hardworking, God-fearing people to an urban society that differentiates between the rich and the poor, the exploiters and the exploited, the slick new city types and the country-bred factory hands. It is meant to be a pathetic story. In welcoming industry and mechanization—and for the best of reasons—America has managed to stamp out and stifle the older, more primitive but vital life of the frontier. Hugh's "love" affair is less clearly and convincingly done. He marries, is separated from, and then reunited with the daughter of the rich farmer who exploits him. This part of the novel attempts to make a statement, presumably, about emotional life in the new industrial period, but it seems contrived and mechanical compared with the chapters dealing with Hugh's rise.

Poor White, then, is not an entirely successful novel. There are too many flat statements and not enough scenes; the character of Hugh McVey—part Lincoln, part Finn, part Henry Ford—seems at times too mechanical. Still, *Poor White* has its moments; it is an ambitious attempt to deal fictionally with the changes in American life which Anderson himself had experienced in his journey from poor boy to businessman to writer. It is by common assent his best novel after *Winesburg, Ohio*.

MANY MARRIAGES and DARK LAUGHTER

After *Poor White*, Anderson's career as a novelist seriously declined. He continued to write and to publish novels: *Many Marriages* in 1923, and in 1925, *Dark Laughter*, which became a best-seller. Both novels, however, betray what Anderson himself condemned in other writers: the tendency to oversimplify the psychological complexities of human nature. Both novels are anti-Puritan tracts, attacking sexual repression, which writers and popular critics of the day singled out as the source of so much modern unhappiness. In *Many Marriages*, John Webster, a washing-machine manufacturer who has found true sexual fulfillment with his secretary, decides to liberate his militantly virginal daughter by appearing naked before her and lecturing her and her mother on the need to free their sexual impulses. *Dark Laughter* retells the story of Anderson's escape from the paint factory by inventing an improbable hero who gives up his career as a journalist and goes back to the town in which he grew up. There he becomes the gardener and then the lover of the factory owner's wife, an experience meant to suggest the interrelation of physical and spiritual love.

Both *Many Marriages* and *Dark Laughter* suffer from Anderson's inability to think through the implications of his theme and to dramatize it effectively with developed characters and situations. The same limitations are reflected in his last two published novels, *Beyond Desire*, a novel about labor unions and strikes, which is badly confused and poorly written, and *Kit Brandon*, the story of a young woman who is the daughter-in-law of a bootlegger. The weaknesses of these last four novels show that Anderson's talent was not essentially novelistic. His real strengths lay in rendering an insight or an illumination and in bodying forth, often in a sudden and shocking way, an unexplained and unexplainable revelation: Wash Williams smashing his respectable mother-in-law with a chair, or the Reverend Curtis Hartman rushing out into the night to tell George Willard that he had seen Christ manifest in the body of a naked woman. Both of these scenes are from *Winesburg, Ohio*, a book that by its structure did not oblige Anderson to develop or explain his grotesque characters and their sudden and violent gestures. In *Many Marriages* and *Dark Laughter*, scenes of nakedness and sexual awakening are made ridiculous by Anderson's attempt to explain and develop what is better left evocative.

After his death in 1941, Anderson was praised by writers such as Thomas Wolfe and William Faulkner for the contribution he had made to their development and to the development of modern American fiction. Though he was limited and deeply flawed as a novelist, he ranks with Mark Twain, Stephen Crane, and

Ernest Hemingway as an important influence in the development of American prose style, and he deserves to be remembered as the author of *Winesburg, Ohio* and a number of hauntingly evocative short stories.

W. J. Stuckey

OTHER MAJOR WORKS

SHORT FICTION: *The Triumph of the Egg*, 1921; *Horses and Men*, 1923; *Death in the Woods and Other Stories*, 1933; *The Sherwood Anderson Reader*, 1947.

PLAYS: *Plays: Winesburg and Others*, pb. 1937.

POETRY: *Mid-American Chants*, 1918; *A New Testament*, 1927.

NONFICTION: *A Story Teller's Story*, 1924; *The Modern Writer*, 1925; *Tar: A Midwest Childhood*, 1926; *Sherwood Anderson's Notebook*, 1926; *Hello Towns!*, 1929; *Perhaps Women*, 1931; *No Swank*, 1934; *Puzzled America*, 1935; *Home Town*, 1940; *Sherwood Anderson's Memoirs*, 1942; *The Letters of Sherwood Anderson*, 1953; *Sherwood Anderson: Selected Letters*, 1984; *Letters to Bab: Sherwood Anderson to Marietta D. Finley, 1916-1933*, 1985.

BIBLIOGRAPHY

Anderson, David D., ed. *Sherwood Anderson: Dimensions of His Literary Art*. East Lansing: Michigan State University Press, 1976. A 141-page collection of critical essays treating Anderson's fiction from several perspectives, including his theories of fiction, his approach to desire, and the isolation of his characters.

Papinchak, Robert Allan. *Sherwood Anderson: A Study of the Short Fiction*. New York: Twayne, 1992. Part 1 discusses Anderson's contribution to the American short story, his first stories, and his masterpiece, *Winesburg, Ohio*. Part 2 includes Anderson's own statements about story writing, including excerpts from *A Story Teller's Story* and *The Modern Writer*. Part 3 includes five essays by different critics on Anderson's short fiction. Contains a chronology and bibliography.

Rideout, Walter B., ed. *Sherwood Anderson: A Collection of Critical Essays*. Englewood Cliffs, N.J.: Prentice-Hall, 1974. Treats Anderson from a variety of perspectives: as prophet, storyteller, and maker of American myths.

Small, Judy Jo. *A Reader's Guide to the Short Stories of Sherwood Anderson*. New York: G. K. Hall, 1994. Provides commentary on every story in *Winesburg, Ohio*, *The Triumph of the Egg*, *Horses and Men*, and *Death in the Woods*. Small summarizes the interpretations of other critics and supplies historical and biographical background, accounts of how the stories were written, the period in which they were published, and their reception. Ideally suited for students and general readers.

Townsend, Kim. *Sherwood Anderson*. Boston: Houghton Mifflin, 1987. This critical biography traces Anderson's life and the development of his fiction (370 pages).

White, Ray Lewis, ed. *The Achievement of Sherwood Anderson: Essays in Criticism*. Chapel Hill: University of North Carolina Press, 1966. This collection of essays treats an important variety of subjects, including isolation, Freudianism, and socialism in Anderson's texts, as well as his development as an artist.

Ivo Andrić

Born: Dolac, Yugoslavia; October 10, 1892
Died: Belgrade, Yugoslavia; March 13, 1975

Principal long fiction

Travnička hronika, 1945 (*Bosnian Story*, 1958, better known as *Bosnian Chronicle*)
Na Drini ćuprija, 1945 (*The Bridge on the Drina*, 1959)
Gospodjica, 1945 (*The Woman from Sarajevo*, 1965)
Prokleta avlija, 1954 (novella; *Devil's Yard*, 1962)

Other literary forms

Ivo Andrić began his writing career with two volumes of poems in 1918 and 1920 and continued to publish poetry in magazines throughout his life. During the 1920's and 1930's, he published several volumes of short stories and brought out a fourth volume in 1948. His essay "Conversations with Goya" (1934) sets out his creed as a writer and a humanist. Between 1945 and his death in 1975, he also published essays on various philosophical, aesthetic, and literary subjects. A selection of his short stories from all periods of his career, *The Pasha's Concubine and Other Tales*, was published in English in 1968.

Achievements

Ivo Andrić is undoubtedly best known in the English-speaking world as the author of what has been called one of the great novels of the twentieth century, *The Bridge on the Drina*. Primarily for this novel, and for two others about life in his native Bosnia published at the same time, he won the Nobel Prize in Literature in 1961. Until this "Bosnian Trilogy" brought him considerable fame, he had not been widely known outside his own country. His reputation has gone through three distinct phases. From 1918 to 1941, Andrić came to be recognized, primarily in Yugoslavia, as that nation's leading writer of short stories and as one of its better poets and essayists. The second phase, from 1941 to 1961, established his fame as a writer of novels and novellas, culminating in his winning the Nobel Prize. In this period, especially in the 1950's, he gained his first wide readership throughout the Western Hemisphere. Finally, in the period from the Nobel Prize onward, he gained worldwide recognition, with his novels and short stories translated into more than thirty languages and many paperback reprints.

Andrić is one of a very few Nobel Prize winners whose work continues to be admired equally by professional critics and the general public. As a novelist, he has been praised especially for his vivid and lifelike characterizations, for his ability to relate individual dilemmas to larger social forces, and for "the epic force with which he has depicted themes and human destinies drawn from the history of his country," in the words of the Nobel Prize Committee. It was Andrić's fame which first drew the attention of the rest of the world to the high quality of Yugoslav literature in general.

BIOGRAPHY

Ivo Andrić's family origins embody that ethnic, religious, and cultural diversity of modern Yugoslavia which has always been one of the underlying subjects of his fiction. He was born in the tiny hamlet of Dolac in Bosnia (then a province of the Austro-Hungarian Empire and now in Yugoslavia) on October 10, 1892. His father, a Serb of the Orthodox faith, was a poor coppersmith; his mother was a Croat and a Roman Catholic. When Ivo was an infant, his father died, and his mother took him to live with her parents in Visegrad, where he played on the bridge erected by the Turks which was later to be the location and subject of his greatest novel. A brilliant student, he had translated some of Walt Whitman's poetry into Serbo-Croatian by the time he was nineteen. His education, however, was interrupted by his political activities. As a youth he had joined Young Bosnia, an organization dedicated to creating an independent nation for the South Slavs. When another member of the organization assassinated the Archduke Franz Ferdinand in 1914 (the event that precipitated World War I), Andrić was arrested and imprisoned for three years.

Andrić always said that his imprisonment forced him to mature rapidly, both as a writer and as a human being. He read extensively, especially the Danish philosopher Søren Kierkegaard, whose work gave substance to Andrić's already developing pessimism. Released from prison in 1917, he began to publish poetry written in prison, joined the editorial staff of a literary journal, and resumed his academic career. During the next six years, Andrić studied languages, philosophy, and history at universities in Poland, Austria, and Yugoslavia, earning a Ph.D. in history from the University of Graz, Austria, in 1923. His thesis, a study of Bosnian spiritual and intellectual life during four centuries of Turkish rule, provided a solid underpinning of historical knowledge for his later novels and stories of Bosnian life. That same year, Andrić, then thirty-one, joined the diplomatic corps of the new kingdom of Serbs, Croats, and Slovenes, a country roughly equivalent to contemporary Yugoslavia, created out of the ruins of the Austro-Hungarian and Ottoman empires after World

(The Nobel Foundation)

War I. He was to serve in a variety of posts in Rome, Madrid, Budapest, Geneva, Trieste, Graz, and Bucharest over the next eighteen years, rising to be the Yugoslav ambassador to Germany from 1939 to 1941.

Andrić had published his first piece of fiction, the long story "Voyage of Ali Djerzelez," in 1920 while still in the university, but his diplomatic career allowed little time for sustained writing. He did manage to write and publish three volumes of short stories—in 1924, 1931, and 1936—but had to postpone writing several novels for which he had developed sketches and done considerable research. His diplomatic career ended, and his years as a novelist began, with the Nazi invasion of Yugoslavia in April of 1941. Arriving in Belgrade just ahead of the first German bombers, Andrić placed himself under voluntary house arrest in his apartment. There he spent the remainder of the war, enduring the destruction and writing novels and short stories. He refused to flee the city in the periodic bombardment and panic because, he said later, "I had nothing to save but my life and it was beneath human dignity to run for that." The three novels he wrote at that time all deal with the suffering and endurance of his native Bosnia at various times in its history.

With the end of the war in 1945, Andrić quickly published *Bosnian Chronicle, The Bridge on the Drina*, and *The Woman from Sarajevo*, as well as a volume of translations from Italian. Yugoslavia had become a Communist Federated Republic under Marshal Tito. Andrić joined the Communist Party, served as president of the Yugoslav Writers' Union, and in subsequent years sat as a representative for Bosnia in the Yugoslav Parliament. Throughout the 1940's and 1950's, he continued to write prolifically, publishing four novellas, a number of short stories, philosophical and travel essays, and critical studies of key figures in Western art, including Petrarch and Francisco Goya. He won many awards in Yugoslavia for his writing, and, in 1961, he was awarded the Nobel Prize for Literature. Advancing age and the burdens of fame slowed Andrić's output after that time. A bachelor for most of his life, he married Milica Babic, a well-known painter and theatrical designer, in 1959. He died in Belgrade at the age of eighty-two on March 13, 1975.

Analysis

Ivo Andrić's native Bosnia, the setting for almost all of his fiction, functions as a microcosm of human life. It is for his characters a land of fear, hatred, and unrelenting harshness. To all who enter it, mere survival becomes a victory. Its effect on outsiders especially is one of confusion, panic, and sometimes even insanity. Bosnia's strategic location in southern Europe has given it a peculiar character which Andrić exploits fully in his novels. In ancient times, it formed a border between Eastern and Western empires, and later between Roman Catholic and Eastern Orthodox forms of Christianity and culture. In the sixteenth century, it became an outpost of the Ottoman Empire, which was Turkish and Muslim. All of these religions, in addition to Judaism, existed in uneasy juxtaposition in Bosnia, with periodic outbursts of religious, ethnic, and political violence between various religious and ethnic groups. Subject to constant nationalistic upheaval, foreign conquest, and the crude violence of Turkish rule, Bosnian history is for Andrić the epitome of the dangers, sufferings, and uncertainties of human life. All people live in a kind of prison as they struggle against one another and against their own fears and insecurities. Undoubtedly, certain facts of Andrić's life help to explain his views. He spent both world wars in confinement, able to write yet unable to act in other ways. His efforts to keep Yugoslavia out of World War II failed, showing him his powerlessness as a diplomat to change the course of history. Finally, the literary heritage of Bosnia that Andrić knew so thoroughly offers several important writers and cultural figures with similar views of human life.

Andrić's fiction is concerned not only with the unpredictability of human life but also with his characters' attempts to understand their place in history, to escape their fears, and to find some measure of constancy and hope. He presents his characters against a background of the inexorable flow of time and its cumulative effect on future generations. His concept of history is not one of discrete periods of time, but rather of the constant change that is to him the basic fact of human existence. His characters fail whenever they attempt to relive time rather than to understand its flow, when they concentrate on mere memory of the past rather than on its meaning for the future. In an essay, he stated: "Only ignorant and unreasonable men can maintain that the past is dead and by an impenetrable wall forever separated from the present. The truth is rather that all that man once thought and did is invisibly woven into that which we today think, feel, and do."

Andrić has been praised most often for the masterful character portrayals in his novels. His main characters are usually figures of lesser importance: priests, consuls, wealthy local farmers, petty bureaucrats, and small merchants; yet they are chosen by Andrić for detailed treatment because on them the whole weight of the injustices, cruelties, and irrationalities of life tend to fall most heavily. As he says of his protagonist in *Bosnian Chronicle:* "He is one of those men who are predestined victims of great historic changes, because they neither know how to stand with these changes, as forceful and exceptional individuals do, nor how to come to terms with them, as the great mass of people manage to do." His other characters are drawn with equal skill. It has been said that there is no such thing as a flat character in an Andrić novel. This pattern results from the fact that he explores carefully the background of every person whom he introduces, however briefly each appears. As a result, the reader knows all the characters intimately, yet the narrative flow is never unnecessarily interrupted in order to impart this information. It is a technique which serves Andrić's thematic purposes as well, for it embeds his characters more deeply in the stream of time. The plots of his novels develop out of this careful delineation of his characters' past. The meaning of their lives is the product of that confluence of personal and national history of which all humans are made yet which relatively few novelists have portrayed as successfully as has Andrić.

BOSNIAN CHRONICLE

Although Andrić's first three novels were published simultaneously in 1945, *Bosnian Chronicle* was the first to be written after he returned to Belgrade in 1941. He began writing, he says, because

> it was a way of surviving. I remembered the moments in history when certain peoples seemed to lose out. I thought of Serbia and Bosnia blacked out in the Turkish tide of the sixteenth century. The odds against one were so monstrous . . . even hope was an aspect of despair. . . . I pulled the past around me like an oxygen tent.

The act of writing under these conditions, he goes on, was "like drawing up a testament." *Bosnian Chronicle* is set in the town of Travnik during the height of Napoleon's power, from 1806 to 1814. Its main characters are the consuls and viziers who represent the various governments having an interest in Bosnia. The Turkish vizier is there because his Empire "owns" Bosnia; the French consul because the French are trying to extend their power inland from the coast; the Austrian consul because the Austrians

fear French power as a threat to their own. The protagonist of the novel is the French consul, Jean Daville, and the plot grows out of his efforts as a European to comprehend the strange mixture of Eastern and Western cultures that is Bosnia. He is alternately bewildered, frustrated, and horrified at the barbarity of Turkish rule, the ignorance of the peasantry, and the endless intrigues of the contending powers represented in Travnik. Daville's ideals, formed during the French Revolution, are slowly being eroded and betrayed in this outpost of the Empire; he comes to see that he is merely a pawn in a game of international politics played without principle or mercy.

Daville has trouble working with his friends as well as with his enemies. He and his assistant, Desfosses, a generation apart in age, epitomize the opposite approaches that Westerners take toward the Orient. Daville follows the "classical" strategy: He emphasizes order and form, tradition, pessimism about sudden change, and a refusal to take local culture seriously. Desfosses, on the other hand, follows the "Romantic" attitude: He approaches problems with optimism, energy, impatience with tradition, and a great respect for local culture. The several Turkish viziers with whom the French consul must deal present him with complex moral and political dilemmas. The first one, Husref Mehmed Pasha, poisons an emissary from the Sultan who has come to order the Husref Pasha's removal. Daville is shocked but can see no ready way to deal with the situation or even to reveal it to anyone. The second vizier, Ibrahim Halimi Pasha, is, like Daville, incurably pessimistic but even more violent than Husref Pasha. Just when Daville believes he has found someone with whom he can solve diplomatic problems rationally, Ibrahim Pasha gives Daville a present of a sack full of ears and noses purportedly severed from the heads of rebellious Serbs but actually taken from Bosnian peasants massacred at a religious festival. Ibrahim Pasha also shoots one of his own army captains merely because the Austrians ask him to do so. Daville must acknowledge that "morbid circumstances, blind chance, caprice and base instincts" are simply taken for granted in Bosnia. A mindless anarchy seems to pervade everything when the bazaar riots against some captured Serbs, brutally torturing and executing some of them in the town square. The third vizier to appear in Travnik, Silikhtar Ali Pasha, makes no pretense of using anything but unbridled terror as his main instrument of policy.

One of Andrić's most common themes is the various ways human beings attempt either to live with or to escape from the dismal conditions of human life. Desfosses and the Austrian consul's wife try to escape through sexual desire, but their efforts are frustrated by chance, and, in the wife's case, by extreme instability. Cologna, physician at the Austrian consulate, converts to Islam to save his wife during the bazaar riots but is found dead the next morning at the base of a cliff. Daville himself attempts to bring order to his life through an epic he is writing about Alexander the Great; he never finishes it because, the narrator implies, he has no roots in this culture and therefore no way to nourish his creativity. Only Daville's happy family life keeps him from losing his reason as the years pass. As he nears the end of his tenure in Travnik (Napoleon has been defeated in Russia and will soon abdicate), he concludes that there is really no such thing as progress in human affairs:

> In reality all roads led one around in a circle. . . . The only things that changed were the men and the generation who travelled the path, forever deluded. . . . One simply went on. The long trek had no point or value, save those we might learn to discover within ourselves along the way. There were no roads, no destinations. One just travelled on. . . . spent oneself, and grew weary.

Even though the reader undoubtedly must take Daville as a "chorus" character reflecting Andrić's own views, Daville does not have the last word in the novel. The work begins and ends not with Europeans but with native Bosnians in the small coffeehouses as they assess the import of the events in their region. The narrator shows that, ultimately, the Bosnian people will survive these various foreign occupations, their character having been tested in these trials of the body and spirit. As one of them says to Daville while the latter prepares to leave Bosnia forever:

"But we remain, we remember, we keep a tally of all we've been through, of how we have defended and preserved ourselves, and we pass on these dearly bought experiences from father to son." The stream of history carries away much good along with the bad, but their cumulative knowledge has formed the bedrock of the Bosnian character, and they will survive.

The fact that Andrić did not write his first novel until he had had more than twenty years' experience with successful short stories meant that *Bosnian Chronicle* emerged as an unusually mature work. One of its weaknesses, however, is the characterization of its protagonist, Jean Daville. Even though the story is narrated from his point of view, he is never as fully developed or as believable as most of the other characters in the novel. The plot also suffers from being too episodic, lacking the sense of direction which a journey, for example, can give an episodic plot. Nevertheless, *Bosnian Chronicle* remains an impressive work, showing Andrić's extraordinary descriptive powers and his great gift for developing a memorable group of characters.

THE BRIDGE ON THE DRINA

Nowhere in Andrić's fiction is the handling of the great flow of history more impressive than in his second novel, *The Bridge on the Drina*. It is a marvelous condensation of four centuries of Bosnian culture, as acted out in the town of Visegrad and on its bridge across the Drina, linking Bosnia and Serbia, East and West. In its structure, this novel, too, is episodic, a fact that Andrić emphasizes by labeling it a "chronicle." Yet its plot is more successful than that of *Bosnian Chronicle* because the episodes, though they cover many years, are unified by the novel's two great symbols, the bridge and the river. In addition, the author wisely devotes about half of the novel to the fifty-odd years before the destruction of the bridge at the beginning of World War I, the years in which all that the bridge represents is most severely tested.

The bridge originated in the early sixteenth century in the dreams of the Grand Vizier of the Ottoman Empire, Mehmed Pasha. As a young peasant growing up in the nearby Bosnian village of Sokolovici, he had witnessed the horror of children being ferried across the Drina as blood sacrifices for the Empire. Later, though he was to serve three sultans for more than sixty years and win battles on three continents, he would still remember his boyhood home by ordering a bridge across the Drina at Visegrad as a way of exorcising his memory of the ferry of death. Ironically, in the first of many arbitrary deaths in the novel, Mehmed Pasha himself is assassinated shortly after the bridge is completed.

The Bridge on the Drina, like all of Andrić's fiction, is filled with memorable characters. Early in the novel there is Abidaga, the ruthless supervisor of construction of the bridge. He catches a young Bosnian attempting to sabotage the project and has him impaled alive on a huge stake, in what is undoubtedly one of the most horrifying scenes in Western literature. There is Fata Avdagina, the ravishingly beautiful merchant's daughter on her way to a wedding with a man she does not want to marry. There is Alihodja Mutevelic, the Muslim merchant and cleric whose fate in the last half of the novel personifies that of the bridge and of the Ottoman Empire: He dies gasping on the hill above the town, old and worn out, as the bridge just below him is destroyed by the opening salvos of the war. He cannot believe that a work made centuries ago for the love of God can be destroyed by man. There is Salko Corkan, the one-eyed vagabond who, drunk one night, dares to attempt what no one has done before: to walk the ice-covered parapet of the bridge. He succeeds and becomes in later generations part of the folklore of the town. There is Milan Glasicanin, a wealthy young man who cannot stop gambling. One night on the bridge, he meets a mysterious stranger who, in a game of chance, takes him for everything he has. Andrić had a great interest in and respect for the folklore of Bosnia. His merging of history and folklore in *The Bridge on the Drina* is one of the novel's most impressive characteristics.

The symbolic function of the bridge and the river is obvious enough, verging on cliché, yet in Andrić's hands, these obvious symbols become profoundly suggestive of what is ephemeral and what is permanent in human life. The river represents, above all,

the ceaseless flow of time and history which continually threatens to obliterate all evidence of human effort. The bridge is many things. It is permanence and therefore the opposite of the river: "Its life, though mortal in itself, resembled eternity, for its end could not be perceived." It is the perfect blend of beauty and utility, encouraging and symbolizing the possibilities of endurance: Life is wasted, and life endures. It is a symbol of man's great and lasting works, of his finest impulses as expressed in the words of its builder: "the love of God." Like all great works of art, though it is not completely safe from the ravages of time, it remains for generations and centuries to inspire humankind, to provide comfort and constancy in an uncertain universe. The bridge says to human beings that they need not become paralyzed by fear and by change. In this novel, as in Andrić's other fiction, no one can escape the fear and uncertainty that is the human lot, but the bridge enables the reader to perceive those aspects of life in their true proportions. In the end, the people will endure, because the bridge sustains their vision as well as their commerce.

THE WOMAN FROM SARAJEVO

Ivo Andrić's achievement in the novels written during World War II is all the more remarkable in that the three works he produced are so different in purpose, plot, and setting. In *The Woman from Sarajevo*, instead of the vast canvas of four centuries of history or the political intrigues of diplomats, he concentrates on one ordinary person: a moneylender, Raika Radakovich. "Miss," as she is universally known, lives an outwardly uneventful life, dying old and alone in a Belgrade apartment in 1935. Yet Miss Raika becomes for Andrić an example of how human beings often attempt, unsuccessfully, to fend off the dangers and uncertainties of life. His exploration of the development of her personality from childhood to old age is one of the masterpieces of characterization in world literature.

Miss Raika can deal with life only through an extreme miserliness. For her, thrift is something almost spiritual in character. Her miserliness originates in her youth, when the father whom she idolizes loses everything and dies a pauper. On his deathbed, he tells her she must suppress all love of luxury, "for the habit of thrift should be ruthless, like life itself." Thereafter, as a young woman in Sarajevo, she becomes an extremely shrewd manager of her money, relishing the power that having money to lend gives her over the lives of other people. Money enables her, she believes, to avoid the desperation and unhappiness which she perceives in the eyes of those who come to her to borrow. If through thrift and careful lending she can become a millionaire, only then will she be able to atone for her father's death. She vows never to make his mistakes, such as feeling compassion for or generosity toward another human being. If one has no emotional ties to anyone, then one is not obligated to be compassionate.

The outbreak of World War I seriously threatens her financial situation. Surrounded by people who feel intensely the great social and political changes then taking place in Bosnia and in Eastern Europe, she searches desperately for someone with whom she can have a strictly "business" relationship, but there is no one except the memory of her dead father. Shunned by the town as a "parasite," abandoned by her advisers (who are ruined by the war), unable to lend money at interest, she leaves Sarajevo in 1919 and moves to Belgrade. There, among relatives whom she detests, she resumes her career. In one of the most revealing episodes in the novel, she repeatedly loans money to a charming young man despite clear evidence of his irresponsibility. The narrator makes the point that because her miserliness never allowed her to develop either knowledge of others or self-knowledge, she cannot prevent herself from making the same mistake again and again. Her last years are increasingly lonely, as money turns out not to be the proof against unhappiness that she had imagined. More and more fearful of robbery, she bars doors and windows to guard her gold. In the powerful last scene of the novel, Miss Raika dies of a heart attack brought on by her irrational fear that every sound she hears is that of a thief breaking in to steal her money.

In this novel, like his others with a much vaster canvas, Andrić's strength is to be able to relate the life of Miss Raika to the historical currents of her time and place. The acid test for Andrić's characters is always how well they can adapt to the constant change and uncertainty that is human life and human history. Miss Raika fails not simply because hoarding money is somehow "wrong" but because, in being a miser, she fails to understand either her own life or the lives of others. There is perhaps also a hint that Miss Raika fails because she represents the decay of the capitalist ethic, which can think of no other response when its values are challenged but to hoard what it has left. More tightly plotted than *Bosnian Chronicle* or *The Bridge on the Drina*, *The Woman from Sarajevo* is, in its structure and in the characterization of its protagonist, Andrić's most successful novel.

THE VIZIER'S ELEPHANT

In answer to an interviewer's question, Andrić stated that he thought the novella form more congenial to the Yugoslav temperament than the full-length novel. *The Vizier's Elephant*, one of three novellas which Andrić wrote in the first few years after the war, is based on a kind of folktale which circulated unrecorded in Bosnia during the nineteenth century. The story takes place in Travnik in 1820 (in the same location as, and only a few years later than, *Bosnian Chronicle*). A new vizier, Sayid Ali Jelaludin Pasha, proves to be unusually cruel even for a Turkish imperial official. The Ottoman Empire is decaying in its outlying regions, so the Sultan has sent a man known for his viciousness to conquer the anarchic Bosnian nobility. The new vizier has a two-year-old pet elephant which in its rambunctiousness destroys the town market, frightens people away, and in general causes havoc in the town. The vizier's retinue makes things worse by punishing anyone who dares to object to the elephant's behavior. Finally, the merchants decide they must act. One of their number, Alyo, volunteers to go see the dreaded vizier about the problem. He is too frightened to go into the palace, so instead he fabricates a story about his "visit," claiming that he has told the vizier that the people of the town love the elephant so much, they wish to have more elephants. Finally, the merchants make repeated attempts to poison the beast—attempts which never succeed—until the vizier himself commits suicide when he learns he is to be replaced because his cruelties have only created more, not less, anarchy.

As always, Andrić tells an interesting story. However, *The Vizier's Elephant* is perhaps his least successful novella, especially in its halting attempts to attach a larger significance to the eccentricities of its characters. The narrator does encourage the reader to view the elephant as a symbol of the Empire: Causing constant fear and apprehension, behaving in a mindless, destructive way, the elephant is ungainly and out of place in a changing world. Andrić, however, never commits himself completely to this or any other narrative approach. The vizier and Alyo never emerge as more than stereotypes, and Alyo's motives especially are too often left unexplained. The reader tends not to be as affected by the anguish of human existence as he usually is in an Andrić story; the comic effects of the elephant's behavior are not developed enough to make the humor dominant, yet these same comic effects dilute the force of the tragedy that lies behind the vizier's cruelties.

ANIKA'S TIMES

Anika's Times, a novella also published in 1948, is more complex and satisfying than *The Vizier's Elephant*. It is set in the village of Dobrun in two different time periods. The first part concerns Father Vuyadin Porubovich, the Orthodox parish priest, and takes place in the 1870's. After the death of his wife, who died in childbirth, Father Vuyadin gradually loses his grip on reality. He comes to feel enormous disgust for the people whose spiritual needs it is his job to satisfy. His behavior becomes erratic, and he refuses to speak to anyone. Finally, no longer able to stand the strain of his own hypocrisy, he seizes his rifle and fires at some peasants visible from his window. He then flees into the night but is later captured and confined to an insane asylum. How, the narrator asks, is one to explain the priest's behavior?

The narrator's "answer" to this question takes the reader back to the times of Vuyadin's grandparents. The story at this point concerns a beautiful young woman named Anika, her feebleminded brother, Lale, and the various men who cannot resist Anika's charms. She first has an affair with a young man named Mihailo. They break up, and Mihailo takes up with a married woman whose husband he unintentionally helps the wife to murder. Though returning to Anika in the hope of forgetting his guilt, Mihailo cannot hold her, and she develops into the classic "evil woman," inflaming men and causing them to act like fools. She takes up with Yaksha Porubovich, who will become the grandfather of Father Vuyadin. This is too much for Yaksha's father, who calls the police to have Anika arrested. Hedo Salko, the chief of police in Visegrad, is reluctant to carry out the order. He believes that no problem is ever solved: "Evil, misfortune and unrest are constant and eternal and . . . nothing concerning them can be changed." On the other hand, he says, "every single problem will somehow be resolved and settled, for nothing in this world is lasting or eternal: The neighbours will make peace, the murderer will either surrender himself or else flee into another district. . . ." Since Salko will not act, the Mayor intervenes, but Anika seduces the Mayor.

Anika's tangled *amours* now begin to trap her. When she visits a religious festival in Dobrun, huge mobs surround her, and Yaksha's father attempts to shoot her from the same window from which his great-grandson Vuyadin will try to kill the peasants seventy years later. The family steps in, however, and Yaksha's father can only curse Anika from his darkened room. Yaksha himself attempts to kill the Mayor in a fit of jealousy, but he fails and flees into the hills. It is here that Andrić shows his supreme skill at managing the climax of a narrative involving many characters. Mihailo reappears, still haunted by the murder of the husband eight years before and convinced that the husband's death foretold his own. No longer able to distinguish Anika from the married woman he had also loved, he goes to her house intending to kill her, but he finds that someone else has already done it and fled. No one is arrested, though it appears that Lale may have been the killer. Yaksha is reconciled with his father, but his father predicts that Anika will poison the town for a century.

Andrić's handling of theme and atmosphere in *Anika's Times* is similar to that in many stories of the American writer Nathaniel Hawthorne. Like Hawthorne, Andrić in this novella is concerned with the ways in which "the sins of the fathers are visited on the sons." He is able to suggest in subtle and complex ways how behavior patterns in the village are constantly changing yet remain fundamentally the same. A number of his characters, even those, such as Salko, who appear only briefly, come vividly alive. Andrić knows how mysterious human behavior can be, how ambiguous and tentative explanations of it must often remain.

ZEKO

The longest of the three novellas published in 1948, *Zeko* is Andrić's only piece of long fiction concerned with the World War II period in Yugoslav history. It is the story of a meek little man, Isidore Katanich, nicknamed "Zeko" (meaning "Bunny"), who in the course of his various tribulations comes to understand the meaning of his own and his country's life during the years of depression and war. The other main character besides Zeko is his domineering wife, Margarita—nicknamed "Cobra." She is full of aggressive energy, constantly twitching, with "greedy, mistrustful, deadly eyes." Her occupation is managing the apartment building which she and Zeko own. They have a son, Mihailo, a handsome, egocentric, and entirely shiftless young man without moral values, who has been nicknamed "Tiger." Since he and his mother take sides constantly against Zeko, it is an uneven match: Cobra and Tiger versus Bunny.

There are signs in the book that Andrić intends Zeko's life to parallel and therefore to comment upon the development of the Yugoslav people during the twentieth century. Though not strictly speaking an allegory, *Zeko* shows through its protagonist the developing national consciousness and desire for freedom of the South Slavs. Zeko had been a gifted artist, but he lost confidence in himself and went to law school at the time of the Austrian annexation of Bosnia in 1908. When the 1912 Balkan War begins, Zeko joins the army but suffers continually from typhus and is finally forced to return home. He marries Margarita, but World War I intervenes. He returns home in 1919 to find his wife a horrible shrew. He hears rumors that Mihailo was fathered by someone else while he was away at war, but he cannot establish the truth or falsehood of the rumor. "Everything around him was

changed, turbulent, shattered . . . this was a time of fatigue and of the acceptance of half-truths." As the years go on, Zeko is increasingly desperate to find a way out of his marriage (his years with Margarita corresponding to the years of the "marriage" of the Serbs, Croats, and Slovenes in the Kingdom of Yugoslavia—that is, 1919 to 1941).

Zeko finds several forms of escape. He associates more and more with his sister-in-law and her family, and he discovers the subculture of those who live on and by the Sava River. Their lives are uncertain and dangerous—what the narrator calls "the true life of most people." Zeko does manage to find true peace and acceptance among these "strenuous, unsettled lives, full of uncertainty, where efforts invested in work were out of proportion to the rewards." The members of his sister-in-law's family become Communists, and symbolically, as it were, Zeko gravitates increasingly toward their values, away from the greed and selfishness of his capitalistic wife and son. Zeko becomes, then, a true man of the people and, in embracing their fate and their future, finds meaning for his own life.

With the coming of Adolf Hitler's invasion, Cobra and Tiger, because of their fear and lack of self-knowledge, do not have the inner resources necessary to withstand the despair of war. Zeko, however, does: Becoming more aware of the need for meaningful action, he is less tempted to hide from conflict, as he had done on the river: "The most important thing was to do away, once and for all, with a barren and undignified life, and to walk and live like a man." Like Yugoslavia itself, Zeko learns the value of independence. He finally joins the Partisans (Tito's anti-Nazi guerrilla organization), while his wife and son, finding it difficult to orient themselves amid the suffering of war, flee Belgrade and disappear. On Zeko's first mission against the Germans, he is caught in an ambush and, attempting to flee, drowns in the Sava River. Yet Zeko's death is not a defeat, for, like his country, he was finally learning how to live with dignity; like his country, he had finally decided what creed he would follow.

One of the chief virtues of *Zeko* is that Andrić allows the parallels between Zeko and Yugoslavia to resonate within the story without ever forcing them on the reader. The other main characters have a vividness which prevents them from fading into stereotypes. The gradual awakening of Zeko's consciousness is portrayed with much of the same skill that Andrić had shown in the characterization of Miss Raika in *The Woman from Sarajevo*.

DEVIL'S YARD

If each of Andrić's novels and novellas has important images representing the dangers and uncertainties characteristic of human life, in his last novella, *Devil's Yard*, such an image for the human condition comes to dominate everything in the story: "Devil's Yard," the notorious prison in Istanbul under the Ottoman Empire. One can be thrown into this prison on suspicion of almost anything, on the principle that it is easier to release a man who has been proved innocent than to track down one who has been proved guilty. The inmates are mostly the weak, the poor, the desperate of society. In Devil's Yard (and in roughly the first half of the novella), the dominant character is the warden, Karadjos. His name means "shadow show," and he will appear anywhere in the prison without warning, trying to trick or frighten a confession out of a prisoner. He is overweight, horribly ugly, with a powerful, piercing eye. His governing principle is that, because everyone is guilty of something, everyone who ends up in Devil's Yard belongs there, whether guilty or not of the particular crime with which he is charged.

In *Devil's Yard*, the prison is a metaphor for human life, with Karadjos as its "god," or fate. He is inscrutable, unpredictable, and tyrannical. In addition to the constant fear felt by the inmates, there is the constant mingling of truth, half-truth, and falsehood which, according to Andrić, is a basic characteristic of human existence. Karadjos fosters this climate of rumor and suspicion with an endless series of threats, cajolery, incredible jokes, and surprise remarks. The prisoners "complained about him the way one complains about one's life and curses one's destiny. Their own damnation had involved them with him. Therefore, despite their fear and hate, they had grown to be one with him and it would have been hard for them to imagine life without him."

Andrić's *Devil's Yard* is his only piece of long fiction told as a story within a story (in fact, it includes several stories within stories). This technique, which he handles with great ease, seems meant to reinforce the notion that in life itself there are layers of truths, half-truths, and falsehoods among which one must try to distinguish. The outermost frame-story concerns a young monk: He is helping sort through the effects of another monk named Brother Petar, who has recently died. As the young monk does so, he recalls Brother Petar's story of having once been held for several months in Devil's Yard while on a visit to Istanbul. The next frame is that of Brother Petar narrating his stay in the prison. While there, he meets a young, educated Turk, Djamil Effendi. The story of Djamil's life is actually narrated by a depressed, apprehensive, and talkative Jew from Smyrna, named Haim. This Haim has "a passion for narrating and explaining everything, for exposing all the errors and follies of mankind." The story he tells of Djamil's life, though at times incredible, has a ring of truth about it simply because its teller has such a passion for the truth, or at least for detail.

It seems that Djamil has studied the history of the Turkish Empire to the point where he has begun to imagine himself one of its ill-fated sultans—Djem Sultan, who in the late fifteenth century was bested in a struggle for the throne by his brother. When Djamil himself returns to the prison yard after several days' interrogation, he tells Petar the story of Djem Sultan. Djamil's story of Djem Sultan is the innermost tale in this intricately narrated novella. He has been confined in Devil's Yard because his complete identification with Djem Sultan bears an uncomfortably close resemblance to the life of the current sultan, whose own throne is threatened by his own brother. Thus Djamil seems to illustrate the danger of people accepting too completely the accounts of their own history and therefore the meaning of their lives as embodied in that history. Djamil finally disappears, and the very mystery of his fate—is he free? was he murdered? confined in a hospital for the insane?—only underlines the confusion that passes for human knowledge.

As his imprisonment drags on, apparently for no

reason except the arbitrary will of some higher authority, Brother Petar realizes that he is becoming irrational. He cannot find anyone whose talk seems sane. The brutal Karadjos has dominated the first half of the novella, and Djamil Effendi, equally irrational, has dominated the second half. Under their influence, Brother Petar could not have retained his own sanity had he remained in prison much longer. Like most of Andrič's protagonists, Brother Petar has had to spend all of his energy simply to escape madness and despair. When the first narrator, the young monk, resumes his own frame-tale at the end of *Devil's Yard*, he is forced out of his reverie by the "dull clang of metal objects thrown on the pile" of Petar's earthly possessions. This is a "reality" which the reader views in a far different light from that of his earlier impression.

There is no use pretending that Andrič is an optimist about the human condition. His impressive accomplishments in the novel and the novella hinge on other things: an impeccable style; a depth of insight into human motivation almost unmatched in Western literature; a profound sympathy for the sufferings of his characters; vivid dramatization of the ethnic character of his province, built up over the centuries against oppression and civil war; and perhaps most important, an ability to turn local history into universal symbols, so that readers knowing nothing of Bosnia can see in his fiction the common lot of humankind.

Mark Minor

OTHER MAJOR WORKS

SHORT FICTION: *Pripovetke*, 1924, 1931, 1936; *Nove pripovetke*, 1948; *Priča o vezirovom slonu*, 1948 (*The Vizier's Elephant: Three Novellas*, 1962; includes *Pričo o vezirovom slonu* [*The Vizier's Elephant*], *Anikina vremena* [*Anika's Times*], and *Zeko* [English translation]); *Odabrane pripovetke*, 1954, 1956; *Panorama*, 1958; *The Pasha's Concubine and Other Tales*, 1968.

POETRY: *Ex Ponto*, 1918; *Nemiri*, 1920; *Šta sanjam i šta mi se dogadja*, 1976.

NONFICTION: *Zapisi o Goji*, 1961.

MISCELLANEOUS: *Sabrana dela*, 1963.

BIBLIOGRAPHY

Goy, E. D. "The Work of Ivo Andrič." *The Slavonic and East European Review* 41 (1963): 301-326. A useful overview and introduction to Andrič's writing.

Hawkesworth, Celia. *Ivo Andrič: Bridge Between East and West*. London: Atholone Press, 1984. A comprehensive introduction to Andrič's work, including verse, short stories, novels, essays, and other prose. Includes notes on the pronunciation of Serbo-Croatian names, notes, and a bibliography.

Kadič, Ante. *Contemporary Serbian Literature*. The Hague: Mouton, 1964. See the discussion of Andrič in chapter 2, "Between the Wars (1918-1941)." Includes an index of names and notes, but no bibliography.

Mukerji, Vanita Singh. *Ivo Andrič: A Critical Biography*. Jefferson, N.C.: McFarland, 1990. Often cited along with Hawkesworth as providing the best biographical and critical introduction to Andrič.

Pribič, Nikola. "Ivo Andrič and His Historical Novel *The Bridge on the Drina*." *Florida State University Papers* 3 (1969): 77-80. A short but helpful study of Andrič's masterpiece.

Vucinich, Wayne S., ed. *Ivo Andrič Revisited: The Bridge Still Stands*. Berkeley: University of California Press, 1995. Essays on Andrič and his times, his short stories, his view of Yugoslavia and of history, Bosnian identity in his work, his handling of grief and shame, women, the folk tradition, and narrative voice. Includes notes and index but no bibliography. Vucinich's introduction is the place to begin a study of Andrič's role in the history of Yugoslavia and of its literary traditions.

AYI KWEI ARMAH

Born: Sekondi-Takoradi, Ghana; 1939

PRINCIPAL LONG FICTION

The Beautyful Ones Are Not Yet Born, 1968
Fragments, 1969

Why Are We So Blest?, 1972
Two Thousand Seasons, 1973
The Healers, 1978
Osiris Rising, 1995

OTHER LITERARY FORMS

Although Ayi Kwei Armah is primarily a novelist, he has written and published in other forms as well. Among his short stories, "Yaw Manu's Charm" has appeared in *The Atlantic Monthly* (1968) and "The Offal Kind" in *Harper's* (1969). His poem "Aftermath" is included in *Messages: Poems from Ghana* (1970). Armah has also worked as a translator for *Jeune Afrique* and the Algerian-based *Révolution Africaine*. His polemical essay "African Socialism: Utopian or Scientific?," appeared in *Présence Africaine* (1967).

ACHIEVEMENTS

Though Armah has become Ghana's best-known writer on the international scene, he would probably prefer to measure his achievement by the reception of his African audience. He has been vulnerable to suspicion and resentment both in Africa and abroad. Not only has he been in exile from his own nation, choosing to live in other African countries, in Paris, and in the United States, but he has also attacked virulently the corruption and materialism of his country's elite and has absolutely condemned the white race (whether European or Arab) for its perverted mentality and for its past and present role in the destruction of African culture. There is an abrasive quality about Armah's early novels—their oppressive naturalism, their sadomasochistic sexuality, their melodramatic casting of blame—that demands more than mere tolerance on the part of his audience. These novels require the reader to go beyond the vehicle to the attitude and the argument that it reveals. A reasonably careful reading will get beyond this abrasiveness and may even dispel the suspicion and resentment, because Armah's real achievement lies in his making the novel not a simple outlet for his venom, but a functional instrument in the African cause. Armah is one of the few truly experimental African novelists. He takes a Western literary form and shapes it into a voice for the African in the modern world.

In his first novel, *The Beautyful Ones Are Not Yet Born*, he turns naturalism and romantic irony into a symbolic, existential statement. In the next two novels, he experiments with narration through multiple points of view. In all three cases, his purpose is to explore the isolation of the individual African in his transformed society. It is evident that Armah is searching for a voice. In his later novels the voice is that of the traditional historian and storyteller of the tribe. The Western concept of point of view merges with the oral tradition, and fictional realism merges with history, legend, and myth. In *Osiris Rising*, his sixth novel, Armah returns to the realism of his earliest work but imbues this with a new symbolic undercurrent based on the Osiris and Isis myth cycle, one of Africa's earliest foundational stories. Armah does not engage in experimentation for its own sake: technique and form are in the service of the larger human concern, the preservation of a culture and the fulfillment of his role within it.

BIOGRAPHY

Ayi Kwei Armah was born in 1939, in the seaport town of Sekondi-Takoradi in western Ghana. Unlike the unnamed protagonist of his first novel, Armah was able to attend mission schools and Achimota College, near the capital city of Accra, and he then received scholarships to continue his education in America. Like the "man" in *The Beautyful Ones Are Not Yet Born*, however, his early life was dramatically influenced by the effects of colonial rule. During World War II, the British sent Ghanaians to fight in Burma and on other battlefields; the postwar period was marked by economic crises, social unrest and strikes, the rise of political parties, and the achieving of independence.

Armah did not experience directly the events after independence. In 1959, he received a scholarship to attend Groton School in Massachusetts. He went on to Harvard, where he was graduated summa cum laude in sociology. In 1963, he visited Algeria and worked as translator for the *Révolution Africaine*. He saw firsthand what was happening in African countries after independence: a continuation of the old policies, of African subservience, and of poverty. The novel *Why Are We So Blest?* appears to be a distillation of Armah's experiences during these years.

During his brief return to Ghana in 1966, Armah attempted to apply his American education and his talents as a writer in various ways. He was a research fellow at the university, a journalist, a teacher of English, and a television scriptwriter. His second novel, *Fragments*, appears to be a spiritual biography of this frustrated attempt to adapt himself again to his society. In 1967, Armah was again in the United States, attending Columbia University on a writing fellowship, and then in Paris as editor-translator for the news magazine *Jeune Afrique*. In 1968, he taught at the University of Massachusetts and published his first novel, *The Beautyful Ones Are Not Yet Born*, which traces the Ghanaian experience from World War II to the overthrow of Kwame Nkrumah in 1966 but concentrates on the corruption in Ghanaian society around the time of the coup.

Armah continued to teach at universities in diverse locales, both in Africa and abroad. He held academic appointments at the Teachers' College in Dar es Salaam, Tanzania; the University of Lesotho; the University of Wisconsin at Madison; and in Nigeria. Armah settled in Popenguine, Senegal. In the mid-1990's he and some friends formed a cooperative printing and publishing company dedicated to the promotion of the local African book industry.

ANALYSIS

Ayi Kwei Armah's novels have provoked conflicting reactions. On one hand, one can argue that Armah is essentially Western, not African. He is certainly not African in the manner of the Nigerian novelist Chinua Achebe. While Achebe's works are to some degree "social documents," Armah moves rapidly from social realism to a symbolic level, even within his first novel. His succeeding novels move away from external detail toward the inner life and the idealism of legend and myth. Achebe is a realist, Armah a romantic. Achebe maintains an objective stance in his analysis of the colonial and postcolonial eras in Nigeria. Armah's voice is strident and polemical. Whereas Achebe is likely to make the society it-

self as important a "character" as the individual protagonist, Armah, in his early works at least, focuses on the individual consciousness.

Armah's novels thus bear the obvious marks of contemporary European and American fiction. His protagonists are alienated antiheroes who deserve sympathy and who are essentially correct in their moral attitudes, but who are ineffectual misfits. The society itself is clearly wrong but defeats the individual moral person through sheer force of numbers, viewing such protagonists as mad or criminal. In fact, this society is the typical twentieth century wasteland, whether it is in Ghana, northern Africa, or the United States. Armah's Ghanaians resemble black Americans trying to be white in order to participate fully in the technological age. Finally, the protagonist within this society resembles, and often in fact is, the isolated artist—a typical Western figure, not at all African.

One can easily argue that if these are not incidental features, they are at least sketched into a larger picture that identifies Armah with an essentially African sensibility. Judging from his first five novels and not emphasizing simply the early works, one could conclude that Armah is an African writing for Africans. For him, the identity of the African artist is inseparable from the society that he serves. He would not want to be judged according to the Western criterion of art for its own sake, or by Western standards of what makes a satisfactory novel. He tries to make his novels functional within an African context. His primary stress is on the individual African sensibility isolated from his society. His novels are a search not so much for private redemption as for communal salvation, and in this respect he reflects an essentially African rather than Western mentality. He is a philosophical novelist: realism is in the service of, or sacrificed to, an idea. He is a social critic searching for a philosophical and historical framework. His protagonists are social failures but heroes in the cause of the greater Africa. His ultimate purpose is pan-African in scope, and his experimentation with technique and form, even though the source may be Western, is a search for the appropriate voice to further the end of common understanding.

Though the novels individually could not be called

Bildungsromane, together they appear, in retrospect, to trace the individual protagonist from confusion and frustration to a sense of wholeness and communal belonging. The "man" in *The Beautyful Ones Are Not Yet Born* cannot be sure of his own identity or his moral values because he receives no reinforcement from his society, while Densu in the fifth novel, *The Healers*, rejects his immediate society and joins a small outcast community that understands the larger African tradition.

Armah has some interesting things to say sociologically as well. Like most contemporary African novelists, he deals with the traumatic experience of colonialism, the rapid change from traditional to modern society, the effects of the slave trade and of Western influence in general, the difficulties of adapting to the technological age, the political corruption immediately after independence, and the cultural vacuum. His novels move from the narrow confines of one Ghanaian city in *The Beautyful Ones Are Not Yet Born* to the larger international scene of America, Europe, and North Africa, in order to show at first hand those forces that helped create the filth and artificiality surrounding his protagonist. In *Two Thousand Seasons* and *The Healers*, Armah leaves the 1960's to give a picture of African society in the distant and recent past. In general, he argues that foreign exploitation has perverted the traditional communal values, which are, if anything, superior to the ones that have replaced them. What seems to concern Armah particularly, however, are the psychological implications of this displacement. The protagonists of the second two novels are mentally disturbed and require professional therapy or convalescence. Juana of *Fragments* is a psychologist, and the outcast priests of *Two Thousand Seasons* and *The Healers* are practitioners of traditional therapies. The essential problem that Armah identifies is the impotence and extreme depression of the sensitive individual rejected by the westernized African society. In addition, Armah explores the nightmares and dreams of his frustrated protagonists, and in his novels seeks an answer to frustration through the revival of racial consciousness in myth and legend. The ultimate purpose of his novels is therapeutic.

THE BEAUTYFUL ONES ARE NOT YET BORN

If the central issue in Armah's novels is the relationship between the individual and his community, then *The Beautyful Ones Are Not Yet Born* is a depressing omen. The main character, the center of consciousness, has no name—not so much because he represents all men or even because he represents the man of integrity, though these are possible readings, but because he is anonymous. Society does not recognize his existence. He is an outcast because he attempts to hold on to moral values while the rest of society has succumbed to bribery, corruption, and materialism. This isolation is total. Even his own family urges him to advance himself for their benefit within the corrupt system. The isolation, however, extends beyond family and community. Even in this first novel, Armah introduces the historical context. The "man" is trapped within the present. He has no sense of belonging to a Ghanaian or to an African tradition. He cannot identify the source of his integrity or of his moral judgment. Hence, he resides in a historical void which makes him question the very values that give him sustenance. Honesty seems unnatural, cruel, obstinate, even criminal and insane.

The story evolves at a specific time in the contemporary history of Ghana. Though Armah does not give dates, it is clear that the early episodes (chapters 1-12) take place late in Kwame Nkrumah's reign, in the mid-1960's. The final three chapters deal with the hours just after Nkrumah's fall in February, 1966. The "man" is a controller for the railroad, a husband, and the father of two children. Armah describes in naturalistic detail a day in the man's life, his journey to and from work, the oppressiveness of the physical surroundings, the boring, insignificant responsibilities of his job, and the return home to an unsympathetic and accusing wife. The only dramatic event in these first chapters is the man's rejection of a bribe. To seek relief and reassurance, he pays a visit to his former teacher, who shares his moral awareness and can explain to some extent the origin of the present malaise, but who has withdrawn from society. The teacher has no family and hence no compelling responsibility. He refuses to participate in the corruption but also declines to fight it. All he can do for the man is understand his situation. He is, nevertheless, the first of a series of figures in the five novels who represent the wisdom of a way of life that Ghana no longer knows. Within this realistic and cynical first novel it is not surprising that the teacher lacks the confidence and the vision necessary to save the man or his society. In spite of this, Armah leaves no doubt as to the importance of the teacher and his philosophical appraisal of contemporary Ghana. He places the visit at the very center of the novel. From this point, the man must accept total isolation. He cannot lean on his elder and former guide: he must find his own solution.

The problem that faces the man in the final third of the novel involves him in the corruption of an old classmate who is a minister under Nkrumah. His wife and mother-in-law agree to participate in the illegal purchase of a fishing boat, which is primarily for the benefit of Minister Koomsan. When the man refuses complicity, he becomes even more of an outcast within the family. His wife constantly measures him against the successful Koomsan, who has surrounded himself with the things of modern civilization. The last three chapters, however, reverse the situation. Nkrumah falls. Koomsan, a pitifully frightened victim of the coup, comes to the man for aid. The two escape from the house just as the authorities arrive, and the man leads him to the fishing boat and to exile. The man himself swims back to shore and to his family. Though he has involved himself in the corruption he despises, the act of saving Koomsan must be seen as a heroic and humane gesture. The man's wife, at least, now recognizes his courage and his worth. The novel thus moves from almost total submergence in the repulsive details of daily life to a romantic but ironic act of heroism, whose ultimate significance is nevertheless left ambiguous.

Armah is already suggesting the larger movement from realism to myth in the figurative and even symbolic dimension of the narrative. What first strikes the reader's attention, in fact overwhelms him, is the vivid and disgusting insistence on the filth, the excrement, and the vomit that one touches and breathes in the city. Yet this physical reality is at the same time the political and moral corruption that the society discharges as it continues to pursue and consume the "things" of Western technology. Koomsan's escape through the latrine is symbolically a wallowing in his own excrement. A second symbol special to this novel is the chichidodo bird, which despises excrement but subsists on the worms that the excrement nourishes: the man, as much as he may try to remain free of taint, is implicated in the social guilt. Finally, Armah uses a third image, the stream, that recurs in all the other novels. He seems to identify water in a traditional way as a purifying agent. During one of his walks, the man notices, in an otherwise muddy stream, a perfectly clear current which seems to have no source. He associates it with a gleam of light—his own moral awareness—a clarity of vision that he cannot trace to any source. He sets this clarity against the brightness of new things imported from the West, but it is not strong enough or permanent enough to give him hope. In spite of his heroism, his baptismal dip in the ocean, and his "rebirth," he still must recognize at the end that "the beautyful ones are not yet born."

FRAGMENTS

In *Fragments*, Armah continues the exploration of the individual and his obligation to both family and community. The scene again takes place in the later 1960's, but the situations are considerably changed. Baako Onipa (the hero now has a name, which means "Only Person") is a "been-to," a member of the educated elite who has spent five years studying in the United States. In this respect, he resembles Armah himself, an American-educated intellectual who must have had similar difficulties readjusting to Ghanaian society. Like Armah, Baako is a writer searching for a role within his newly independent nation. No longer is the protagonist buried in lower-class poverty. His education gives him access to prominent men in the community and to the "things" of modern technology. He thus has the means to satisfy the expectations of his family, especially his mother. He resembles the man, however, in his inability to sacrifice his personal integrity in order to take advantage of his opportunities. In a sense, his situation is even more critical than that of the man. He is a highly sensitive artist. Whereas the man has perceived the "madness" of his obstinacy, Baako has already experienced insanity in America and is on the edge of it again throughout this novel, the title of which, *Fragments*, is thus particularly appropriate.

The story does not follow a clear chronological path, because Armah has chosen to present it through three centers of consciousness. The emphasis is thus not on the exterior world but, much more obviously than in *The Beautyful Ones Are Not Yet Born*, on the psychological responses to the world of the two main characters, Baako and Juana, a Puerto Rican psychologist who becomes Baako's confidant, and of Baako's grandmother, Naana, who represents the traditional wisdom of the people. The novel opens with Naana recalling Baako's ritual departure five years before and her anticipation of his cyclical return. Baako does return, unannounced, however, to avoid the inevitable ritual ceremony. He dreads to face his family because he brings no gifts and because he knows that he will be unable to fulfill his mother's expectations. His mother expects what the man's wife expected in *The Beautyful Ones Are Not Yet Born*, money and the comforts of the modern age. Baako, in his rebellion against this imitation of Western values, goes to his former teacher, Ocran, for advice. Ocran has himself chosen to pursue his profession as an artist in solitude, because he sees no possibility for useful work within the contemporary Ghanaian society. Against Ocran's advice, the less experienced Baako has decided to make the attempt by turning his talents as novelist to a more public role as a television scriptwriter. He hopes to transform popular Ghanaian myths into scripts for television, and in general to raise the consciousness of the people by introducing them to the true traditions of Ghana. The authorities, preferring to use the television screen as an instrument of propaganda, reject this proposal as dangerous. Baako goes back to the privacy of the writing table and, thus isolated, gradually loses his mind. His family places him in an asylum, from which he is about to be rescued by Juana as the novel closes.

The threat of insanity, in fact, has plagued Baako from the very beginning. He goes to Juana for help early in the novel. She becomes his lover and, along

with Ocran, his spiritual guide. The novel thus ends as does *The Beautyful Ones Are Not Yet Born*, ambiguously—but with a note of hope, and with the nucleus of a new community, two Ghanaians and the outsider, Juana, who represents not the evils of white society, but the sensitivities of a minority. Furthermore, Ocran seems to offer a temporary compromise between the two extremes that have driven Baako to insanity, a compromise that Armah develops in the later novels. Whereas society and family demand that Baako yield to their values, and Baako, while recognizing his inherent need for identity within the community, must maintain his integrity, Ocran proposes a kind of synthesis: Baako cannot expect to achieve his goal immediately. He must submit to a temporary isolation from the present society and work for the larger community of the future. Naana reinforces this view as her commentary closes the novel with a picture of contemporary Ghana in fragments. This novel thus has raised the argument to a more philosophical level than that of *The Beautyful Ones Are Not Yet Born* by using four different characters who reflect on the problem of the perceptive individual within a materialistic society.

In other ways, too, Armah moves away from the naturalism of his first novel. Even the naturalistic scenes, such as the killing of the "mad" dog, are obviously symbolic of something beyond themselves. Just as Juana observes a crowd of soldiers who close in on a dog that they only suspect to be mad, so she watches the community and the family judge and incarcerate Baako for his "insane" ideas. The novel also incorporates ritualistic and religious elements. Naana contrasts the unifying role of traditional ritual with the fragmentation of the present. The mother appeals to an itinerant, spiritualist preacher to aid her in praying for Baako's return. Baako and Juana discuss the similarities between Catholicism and animism, as opposed to the isolating force of Protestantism. Baako is concerned in particular with myth: he contrasts his overseas experience with the traditional hero's departure and triumphal return to save the community. He and Juana repeat the myth of Mame Water, who rises from the sea periodically to meet her lover and give him special powers, but at the same time leaves him with an excruciating sense of isolation. The water itself, like the stream from *The Beautyful Ones Are Not Yet Born*, flows into *Fragments*. Baako pictures himself swimming upstream against a cataract; water still seems to be a purifying force and the stream itself the natural flow of history.

WHY ARE WE SO BLEST?

In retrospect, *Why Are We So Blest?* appears to be a transition between Armah's first two novels and the mythical ones to follow. It continues the trend away from realistic description toward a study of multiple consciousness, a philosophical reflection, a larger international context, and an emphasis on personal relationships. The time of the novel, however, remains the same, the mid-to-late 1960's, as does the central premise: the individual isolated from his community and hence from his own identity. Again, Armah seems to be drawing from his own experience, this time as a student in an American university, and from the guilt feelings that inevitably arise in one who is given special treatment while his country suffers from the very hands that feed him. In a sense, the Ghanaian character, Modin, is Baako receiving the education that is so useless to him upon his return, though Armah has a far different fate for this avatar. The other major African character, Solo, shares with Modin a situation that Armah has not created in the first two novels. They both remain abroad, completely detached from their societies, Modin as a student and would-be revolutionary, Solo as a disillusioned revolutionary in exile. Solo, the dispassionate observer, finds in Modin a reincarnation (with variations) of his own past fascination with revolution and with a Western woman. This third major character is Aimée Reitsch, a white American coed of German ancestry, whose perverted fascination with Africa and with Modin precipitates his destruction.

The narrative in *Why Are We So Blest?* resembles that of *Fragments* in that it, too, has three centers of consciousness. The two principal actors in the drama, Modin and Aimée, have kept journals about their experiences, which Aimée leaves with Solo after Modin's death. Solo thus functions as editor, providing personal information and commentary and arranging the journal entries to reconstruct the story of their

lives and his encounter with them in northern Africa. He opens the novel with an account of his own life before he met them and fills out this autobiography at intervals throughout the book. He is a reviewer of books eking out an existence in the fictional town of Laccryville (Algiers) and making occasional visits to the headquarters of a revolutionary organization which he once wished to join.

The story of Modin and Aimée, as Solo reconstructs it, goes back to Modin's days as a scholarship student in African Studies at Harvard. Immediately after arriving, he receives a warning from Naita, the black secretary of his sponsor, that he must not trust those who have brought him to America. They actually consider him their property. Modin eventually realizes that she is right about the white race in general being the black man's destroyer, but makes the mistake of considering Aimée an exception. He leaves for Africa with her to join the revolutionary organization in Laccryville. Its leaders are suspicious of Aimée and hence reject them both. Solo meets them and would like to do something to save Modin, but realizes that he is doomed. Modin and Aimée take off on a futile hitchhiking journey across the Sahara, only to be picked up by white male racists who sexually abuse them and leave Modin to die. Aimée returns to her middle-class life in America and Solo is left frustrated in his isolation. It would seem, however, that Solo as author has finally found his voice, and is fulfilling a useful function after all in this "book" that he is offering to the public. That is, Solo has discovered the role that Armah himself has chosen.

In this respect, *Why Are We So Blest?* looks forward to the positive and hopeful tone of the next three novels. What the "man" and Baako lacked, Solo has discovered. In other ways, too, this novel looks forward. The stream as a motif reappears, but it is no longer muddy as in *The Beautyful Ones Are Not Yet Born*, and the swimmer is no longer fighting against the current. Instead, Solo is observing its continuous flow and waiting for a place to enter and become a part of it. Madness, obsession, and psychological tension continue to be significant motifs, but while *Fragments* ends with Baako in an asylum, this novel opens with Solo's overcoming a bout of mental depression by committing himself to a month's convalescence in a hospital. His return to health accompanies a transformation in his view of society, the nature of revolution, and the role of militants. By this third novel, also, Armah has transformed the African female figure into a kind of soulmate. Naita possesses sexual purity, a natural grace, and a wisdom that could have been Modin's salvation. She attains an almost mythical dimension. The most significant symbol in the novel, in fact, is sexuality. Through it, Armah exposes the selfish aggressiveness of the white female and the cruel fascism of the white male. The novel announces with violent acerbity a thesis that appears for the first time in Armah's fiction, the essential animosity between black and white. It bears the sure stamp of the Black Muslim movement that must have deeply affected him in America. The white race becomes identified as the destroyer, the enemy. The African has lost his identity because the white race has taken away the tradition and the community that gave him meaning.

TWO THOUSAND SEASONS

In *Two Thousand Seasons*, Armah prophesies a more fruitful course. He makes a leap of faith in his narrative style and, more important, in his promise of an answer to the frustrated heroes of the first three novels. This novel has no hero, unless it be the community itself. No isolated personality is trapped within his own consciousness. The narrator, as character, is the ubiquitous member of every generation who knows the true history of the tribe. He is the "griot," the tribal historian, the wise man, the poet. He is a member of the select few whose task it is to maintain the spiritual coherence of the group. The story he tells is the group's chronicle. Thus Armah, as author, effaces himself by adopting the traditional and anonymous role of historian—a significantly symbolic act since Armah must recognize that he too finds his identity only if he merges with the community.

The chronicle begins a thousand years (two thousand seasons) ago, when the Akan tribe, probably intended to represent the black race, living in peace, harmony, and "reciprocity" on the edge of the desert, succumbs to the "predators" of the north, the Arab/Muslim civilization of North Africa. The narrator describes the destruction of the social order and the enslavement of the people. It is here that the community first loses its cohesiveness. A small nucleus of people, particularly women of the tribe, initiate and lead a revolt, and then a migration away from the desert toward the south. The eventual destination is present-day Ghana, but the people arrive only to find another threat from the sea. The Europeans have begun their exploitation of the continent. The last half of the novel concentrates on the disintegration of the tribe as the forces from without create division within. The narrator focuses on one particular period, when one generation of youths undergoing initiation escapes into the forest and organizes a resistance movement. A seer named Isanusi leads them and trains them in the "Way," the traditional values of the tribe. Their king, Koranche, subsequently persuades them to return, deceives them, and sells them into slavery. They are able to escape from the slave ship and make their way back to the forest retreat, bringing with them new recruits. These guerrilla warriors, the "beautyful ones," operate against the oppressive authorities who have betrayed the tribal traditions.

Armah has thus solved the essential problem facing the protagonists of the early novels. He has achieved the synthesis adumbrated by Ocran in *Fragments*. Though it may be impossible to join and serve the particular society in Ghana today, it is possible to participate spiritually in the larger society and in the genuine traditions of the people. This solution certainly explains the mythical and romantic mode of this novel in contrast to the naturalism or realism at the base of the first three. No longer caught within the contemporary world of the 1960's, the initiates of *Two Thousand Seasons* belong to an ancient tradition. A mythical pattern controls the novel. The tribe begins in Eden, falls from grace, and moves toward the cyclical return. It is this confidence in the future and in the total pattern of life that separates this novel from its predecessors. The racism of *Why Are We So Blest?* becomes a struggle for cultural identity on a panoramic scale. The whites, whether Muslim or Christian, are the enemy. Their culture is oppressive and destructive to blacks. They represent class divisions and hierarchical structures. The African "way" is reciprocity, equality, and a sharing of responsibility and power. Armah is obviously dealing in romantic terms. He is also trying to find his own *modus vivendi*: a justification of his "exile" and a role within the larger pattern of his nation's fate.

THE HEALERS

Armah called *The Healers* a historical novel. It is, to be sure, based on particular events in the 1870's during the Second Asante War, and Armah's purpose—as in the previous novels, especially *Two Thousand Seasons*—is to offer an interpretation of Ghanaian (African) society and to reevaluate African history. His method, however, is not so much historical as romantic and mythical. The story is a mixture of fact and fiction, and the characters and events conform to an idea of the essential African mentality and the future of the African continent. It thus continues the optimistic chronicle of the previous novel. The storyteller is again the "anonymous" griot. The tale begins as an epic, *in medias res*. It proceeds immediately to narrate the initiation of nine Asante boys into manhood. Densu is obviously a young man of heroic proportions. He refuses to engage in the wrestling contest because the competition required violates the spirit of cooperation that he values. He nevertheless demonstrates his superior strength and grace in this and other games, while finally refusing to win to avoid being named the next chief in the tribe. He resists this temptation held out by Ababio, the evil adviser who remains Densu's nemesis throughout the novel. Densu's ambition is to join the spiritual ones, the "priests" or "healers" who live as outcasts in the forest and who preserve the values of the community which are being perverted by ambitious men such as Ababio. Before he can realize this goal, however, he must not only convince Damfo, the chief healer, and his spiritual guide, that he can truly sacrifice the things of common life, but also overcome Ababio's scheme to condemn him falsely for murder, and to engage in the war against the British as General Nkwanta's aid. The novel ends melodramatically with the betrayal and defeat of the Asante army, the last-minute acquittal of Densu at the murder trial, and the various African tribes dancing on the beach, ironically brought together by the invading British.

Armah thus suggests a future pan-African unity. For the present, however—if the events of the 1870's offer a paradigm for the contemporary situation—the solution to the sociological and psychological problems facing Ghanaians is much the same as that proposed in *Two Thousand Seasons*. The perceptive individual who works for a solution must not expect an immediate communal identity. Again, Armah clarifies the choices available through romantic simplification. In *Two Thousand Seasons*, the proponents of the Way face a challenge from the white predators and destroyers and from the zombies among their own people. In *The Healers*, the choice is between competition and manipulation on the one hand, and cooperation and inspiration on the other. Densu chooses to leave his tribe because he knows that the leaders and the people are not ready for the essential virtues of the true community. Instead, he is initiated by Damfo into the community of healers. Damfo, in his dealings with other people, never resorts to manipulation or even persuasion, but rather relies on spiritual understanding and respect. This is presented as the only way to establish a genuine community.

In this fifth novel, Armah seems to be consciously drawing in all the threads from his early works. The "beautyful ones," it would seem, are born, but they reside outside the society itself, preparing for the future. Unlike the "man," they fully accept the pain of nonconformity. The healer, Damfo, fulfills the tasks that frustrate the teacher, Ocran, Juana, Naana, and Solo. In his conversations with Densu, he employs a method of instruction that is both Socratic and therapeutic. The philosophical and psychological conflicts that plague the early heroes thus find their resolutions in the spiritual communication and intimate friendship between priest and initiate. Nightmares become dreams of self-discovery. Body, mind, and spirit achieve harmony in Densu. He sees the chaos of the present within the perspectives of history. He is also at home in the natural world. The stream that flows as a minor motif through the other novels is a significant part of the setting in *The Healers*. Densu wins the swimming contest not by competing but by becoming at one with the natural element. He later escapes arrest by holding on to roots at the bottom of the stream and breathing through a hollowed-out cane. Even later, he and Damfo master the stream in a long journey against the current. Finally, in this river of life Densu contemplates his own image and purpose. Clearly, Armah creates a hero in *The Healers* who has found his place in the stream of history, a hero who gives meaning to Armah's own chosen role in his community.

OSIRIS RISING

Osiris Rising, Armah's sixth novel—and his first in seventeen years—represents a further evolution of his perspective along this axis. The old themes are once again in evidence: pan-African unity, historical consciousness, intellectual nonconformity, and disgust with the corrupt African leadership. The Osiris and Isis myth alluded to in the title provides an important symbolic background for this otherwise realistic text. As a genuinely African myth of origin, the Osiris legend mirrors a major theme of the novel, which explicitly deals with the need for Africa to put its own culture at the center of its historical consciousness. The magnificence of ancient Egypt then serves as the perfect and natural locus for this shift.

The novel tells the story of Ast, a young African American Egyptologist who feels displaced in America and thus "goes home" to Africa in search of her roots and a sense of belonging. She is also following Asar, her college lover who has returned to his homeland in Africa to fight against the injustices of the postindependence puppet regimes. Significantly, the country to which she travels (and where the rest of the novel takes place) is never named directly. Armah's pan-Africanism makes him more interested in the symbolic aspects of the story than in its relevance to any single national entity. In Africa, Ast comes across another acquaintance from her university days, Asar's longtime rival and countryman Seth, who has risen in the corrupt administration to become Chief of Security for the entire nation. The action of the novel revolves largely around Ast's and Asar's grassroots political organizing on the campus where they both teach, set against the insipid political machinations of Seth, who sees Asar in particular as a threat to his way of life. Ultimately, Seth appears to "win" at the close of the novel as Asar's body is literally blown into fragments by the guns of Seth's death squad.

When considered alongside the informing Osiris myth, however, Seth's victory is exposed as transitory and futile against the greater advances for which Asar's teaching has set the stage. The myth tells of Osiris and his sister and wife Isis, who ruled Egypt as king and queen. Their brother Seth murdered Osiris and scattered fragments of the body across Egypt, which historically accounted for the spread of the Osiris cult. Isis then raised their son Horus to manhood, at which time he avenged his father's murder by deposing Seth and assuming power as king of the living. Osiris, reassembled by Isis, became lord of the underworld. With this in mind, an allegorical reading of the novel becomes clear: Asar, who has clearly stated throughout the novel that his death would be an insignificant obstacle for the widespread communal movement for African unity, is the martyr Osiris, and the rising alluded to in the title suggests that indeed the movement will yet prevail. Likewise, that Ast is pregnant with Asar's child would seem to prophesy the child's ultimate defeat of Seth and victory for the representatives of African justice.

Thomas Banks, updated by Harland W. Jones III

OTHER MAJOR WORKS

SHORT FICTION: "Yaw Manu's Charm," in *The Atlantic*, 1968; "The Offal Kind," in *Harper's*, 1969.

POETRY: "Aftermath," in *Messages: Poems from Ghana*, 1970.

NONFICTION: "African Socialism: Utopian or Scientific?," in *Présence Africaine*, 1967.

BIBLIOGRAPHY

Fraser, Robert. *The Novels of Ayi Kwei Armah: A Study in Polemical Fiction*. London: Heinemann, 1980. An excellent place for the general reader to start. The first chapter provides the context of liberation and resistance informing Armah's work and is followed by five chapters on individual novels. Conclusion, bibliography, and index.

Lazarus, Neil. *Resistance in Postcolonial African Fiction*. New Haven, Conn.: Yale University Press, 1990. Full-length study that focuses on the politics and ideology of Armah's first three novels.

A cogently argued critique of early postcolonial nationalisms.

Ogede, Ode. *Ayi Kwei Armah: Radical Iconoclast.* London: Heinemann, 1999. Full-length study of Armah's entire oeuvre, from one of the most prolific Armah scholars. Focuses on the juxtapositions of "imaginary" worlds with the "actual." Part of the Studies in African Literature series.

Palmer, Eustace. "Negritude Rediscovered: A Reading of the Recent Novels of Armah, Ngugi, and Soyinka." *The International Fiction Review* 8 (1981): 1-11. This discussion of the concept of negritude pays particular attention to three works: Wole Soyinka's *Season of Anomy*, James Ngugi's *Petals of Blood*, and Armah's *Two Thousand Seasons*. Notes.

Research in African Literatures 18 (Summer, 1987). A special issue on Ayi Kwei Armah including three articles, a bibliography of studies in African literature at a Nigerian university, and seventeen book reviews. Notes on contributors.

Wright, Derek. *Ayi Kwei Armah's Africa: The Sources of His Fiction.* London: Hans Zell, 1989. Traces the African background of Armah's fiction, particularly the early novels, and provides a broad cultural and anthropological context. Useful for the student and reader already familiar with Armah's work and seeking more specialized analysis. Chapter notes, bibliography, and index.

_____. *Critical Perspectives on Ayi Kwei Armah.* Boulder, Colo.: Three Continents Press, 1992. Wide-ranging collection of twenty-two essays on Armah's early career. Includes four general essays and seven on *The Beautyful Ones Are Not Yet Born*, with the rest evenly distributed among the other four early novels. Extensive and valuable bibliography and notes on contributors.

Sholem Asch

Born: Kutno, Poland; November 1, 1880
Died: London, England; July 10, 1957

Principal long fiction

Dos Shtetl, 1905 (*The Little Town*, 1907)
Amerike, 1911 (*America*, 1918)
Motke Ganev, 1917 (*Mottke the Thief*, 1917)
Onkl Mozes, 1918 (*Uncle Moses*, 1920)
Kiddush Hashem, 1920 (English translation, 1926)
Toyt Urteyl, 1926 (*Judge Not*, 1938)
Khayim Lederers Tsurikkumen, 1927 (*Chaim Lederer's Return*, 1938)
Farn Mabul, 1927-1932 (*Three Cities*, 1933)
Der Tilim Yid, 1934 (*Salvation*, 1934)
Three Novels, 1938 (includes *Uncle Moses*, *Judge Not*, and *Chaim Lederer's Return*)
Der Man fun Notseres, 1943 (*The Nazarene*, 1939)
The Apostle, 1943
Ist River, 1946 (*East River*, 1946)
Mary, 1949
Moses, 1951
Der Novi, 1955 (*The Prophet*, 1955)

Other literary forms

Although Sholem Asch is remembered chiefly as a novelist, much of his early work consists of dramas. When *Der Got fun Nekome* (1907; *The God of Vengeance*, 1918) was performed on Yiddish stages in Russia and Poland, Max Reinhardt, who understood Yiddish, decided to produce it at the Deutsche Theater. This was the first time that a Yiddish work had appeared in the international literature. This play, in which a brothel owner purchases a Torah to place in his daughter's room, hoping it will protect her from the impurities in the apartment below, was widely condemned as sacrilegious. Many other dramas followed, including adaptations of such novels as *Mottke the Thief*, which enjoyed considerable success on Yiddish stages.

Asch also published *From Many Countries: The Collected Stories of Sholem Asch* (1958) and other collections of short fiction, as well as an autobiographical essay, *What I Believe* (1941), in which he reacted to criticism levied against him by the Jewish community.

ACHIEVEMENTS

Until 1950, Asch was indisputably the best-known, most translated, most successful Yiddish writer. More than anyone before him, he managed to inject the Yiddish word into world culture, making the world aware of a major literature that had been unjustly ignored. This broader world sometimes seemed more kindly disposed to him than the segment of his Jewish readers who objected to his delineation of the seamier aspects of Jewish life in some works and to his sympathetic treatment of Christianity in others. The bulk of his Jewish readers remained faithful and recognized in him a lover of the poor and weak, a God-seeker, a gentle soul keenly aware that man did not live

(Library of Congress)

by bread alone. In spite of his high regard for Christianity, Asch remained faithful to Jewish life and tradition, acutely aware of the anti-Semitism all around him. While his characters accept this intolerance as a fact of life, Asch himself could not always assume the same stance. He returned a medal awarded to him by the Polish government when he realized that the policies of that government permitted a heightened anti-Jewish feeling.

A student of the revered I. L. Peretz, whose influence he acknowledged as late as 1951, Asch went beyond the teachings of this master and dealt with topics that Yiddish literature had theretofore avoided. His work marks an abandonment of the rational ways that the Jewish enlightenment had made obligatory for Jewish writers. Like Isaac Bashevis Singer, who replaced him as *the* Yiddish writer on the world stage, Asch was attracted to folkloristic and irrational elements. Because of the diversity of his oeuvre, critics have found it difficult to classify Asch. There is the Romantic who idealized the life of simple Jews and insisted on the primacy of tradition and faith in faith; there is the naturalist who brilliantly depicted the milieus of thieves, jugglers, and prostitutes; there is the didactic moralist who strove to teach the mean-

ing of the good life. There is even a hint of the publicist who fought Hitlerite anti-Semitism by underscoring the basic nobility of Jewish existence and demonstrating the common bonds uniting Judaism and Christianity. This very multiplicity suggests Asch's enduring appeal.

BIOGRAPHY

The tenth child of a pious and prosperous Hasid, Sholem Asch underwent an early formal education in Hebrew language and literature, especially the Bible. His progress indicated sufficient promise for his father to entertain hopes for him in a rabbinic career. In his mid-teens, Asch came upon his first secular book and became "enlightened." He found employment as a "scribe," writing letters for the illiterate, which likely gave him unique insights into the human psyche. At the same time, he was teaching himself German, Russian, and Polish and reading whatever books by major writers became available to him.

At the age of sixteen, Asch visited Peretz, whose stories he had admired, and requested that the master comment on his own efforts, which he was then writing in Hebrew. Peretz liked what he read but urged the youngster to change to Yiddish. Asch's first story,

"Moshele," appeared in *Der Jud* in late 1900. A collection of Hebrew stories published in 1902 was followed in 1903 by another in Yiddish. (His writing then, as later, was colored by the dark and dingy places in which he had lived and the hunger he had suffered and which he was never to forget.) Asch married Mathilda Shapiro, the daughter of a teacher and minor poet. In 1904, he serialized his "poem in prose" *The Little Town* in *Der Freint*; in 1905, it was published as a book that quickly established him at the forefront of Yiddish writers.

Asch visited Palestine in 1907 and the United States in 1909. He was awed by biblical sites in Palestine and the evidence of Jewish and Christian events. In America, the landscapes impressed him, but he was repelled by the sweatshops, the tenements, and the quality of the life he observed.

In the ten years preceding World War I, Asch completed ten plays. He lived mostly in France but was forced to leave upon the outbreak of the conflict. Besides *Mottke the Thief*, his wartime writing, emanating mostly from New York, included *Uncle Moses*, a novel of immigrants in their initial years in New York.

After the war, Asch revisited Eastern Europe as the representative of a Jewish relief agency. He was horrified by the slaughter of Jews at the hands of Cossacks and White Russians. What he saw reminded him of a seventeenth century Ukrainian slaughterer of Jews whose soldier-peasants terrorized the countryside. The result was the first of his historical novels, *Kiddush Hashem* (sanctification of the name).

In the words of Sol Liptzin, Asch in the postwar years continued "glorifying Jewish deeds of brotherly love and quiet heroism." Before Adolf Hitler rose to power, Asch believed that contrasting such quiet deeds of Jews with the crude Hitlerite reliance on force would be his way of fighting the Nazi menace. *Salvation*, written in 1932, was the most spiritual novel he wrote, and he was embittered by its poor reception.

Asch's spiritual orientation, accompanied by the desire to strengthen the Jewish position, led to novels on Jesus (*The Nazarene*), Paul (*The Apostle*), and

Mary (*Mary*). These works alienated his Jewish readers, who feared a case of apostasy at a time when Hitler was decimating European Jewry. *The Nazarene* was published in English before a Yiddish publisher would touch it. The controversy continued for nearly a decade. The resilience of European Jews and the establishment of a Jewish state tore Asch out of his isolation and prompted him to turn to *Moses*, which he had begun long before and had laid aside in favor of his Christian novels.

In 1954, having lived in the United States and France, Asch settled permanently in Israel, where, in 1955, he wrote *The Prophet*. As the chronicler of a world that had disappeared, Asch became again an object of admiration—a condition that his insatiable ego demanded. In 1957, he suffered a mild stroke. While in London for an operation, he died before surgery could be performed.

ANALYSIS

Nearly all of Sholem Asch's works are related, in a broad sense, to some religious concern. His many themes are clearly intertwined: the simple, traditional life of the Jew; saintliness in the quest for God and service to man; the ugliness of poverty but the distinct possibility of meaningful beauty even in poverty; the emptiness of a purely material existence; the Jewish roots of Christianity and the need to close the gap between the two faiths. In fact, faith in both its meanings—trust in God and different institutionalized ways of reaching Him—is a thread running through all of Asch's works, but especially his later works.

THE LITTLE TOWN

Even in his first major work, *The Little Town*, Asch had romanticized the inwardness of Jewish life in the shtetl, a different approach from the ridicule usually heaped upon the backward enclaves in literature. Asch perceived nobility and charm in the poverty-ridden, filth-infested shtetl.

Similarly, he dealt with spiritual and sacrifical heroism before dealing with it directly in *Kiddush Hashem*. Living far out in the Padolian steppe, a Jewish innkeeper, Mendel, dreams of the day when other Jews will join him in the town and enable him to build a synagogue and lead a Jewish existence. Mendel eventually overcomes the threats of the local priest, and a small but flourishing Jewish community comes into being. Mendel and the congregation are dangerously sandwiched between the machinations of the Catholic priest and the Greek Orthodox priest. The former is intent upon humbling the latter. What better means of debasing his rival than to force him to go to the Jew Mendel to obtain the key to his own church? In his frustration, the Orthodox priest threatens Mendel: Sooner or later "the little brothers" will come to liberate the peasants from the Polish lords and the filthy Jews.

The "little brothers" eventually come, under the leadership of Bogdan Chmelnitzky, and lay waste not only to Mendel's but also to every Jewish community far and wide. Mendel's attachment to his synagogue is such that he refuses to leave, but the rabbi reminds him that the synagogue is only stone, while a human life is a human life. Mendel's Jews flee, joining the stream of refugees; they put up a heroic fight with virtually no weapons. They are finally conquered through the betrayal of the Polish lords, who are only too willing to sacrifice their Jewish allies in the mistaken belief that they can thereby save themselves.

Through Mendel and his family, which includes a learned son and his beautiful wife, Asch depicts the simplicity and piety of Jewish life and the Jews' willingness to live and die for "the sanctification of the name." Jews are offered a chance to save their lives by bowing before the Cross, but they will bow only before their one and only God. All resist the easy way out, sacrificially preferring to suffer cruelty, death, and martyrdom. Although the body may be destroyed, the will and spirit are indestructible. Asch only implies that the Jews' imperishable faith in God has ensured their survival in the past and will ensure it in the future.

Charles Madison has stated that "Asch's compassionate brooding gives the tragic tale the poignant quality of imaginative truth." This critic has also distinguished between two forms of martyrdom—Mendel's, which is not a pure martyrdom in that it is wholly passive, and his daughter-in-law's, which is active: She persuades the Cossack captor who loves her that he should shoot her, on the pretense that no bullet can hurt her.

KIDDUSH HASHEM

Kiddush Hashem is perhaps Asch's only novel in which religious motifs and Jewish historical destiny, especially the Jews' suffering for their survival as a group, fuse successfully. The structure of the novel, on the other hand, is awkward, which prevents it from becoming the masterpiece it might have been.

MOTTKE THE THIEF

If *The Little Town* and *Kiddush Hashem* are, to use Sol Liptzin's words, in a Sabbath mood, *Mottke the Thief* is decidedly workaday. Asch abandons the idealized Jews of earlier works to offer such sad human specimens as Blind Layb and Red Slatke, Mottke's parents. Layb is a vicious, irresponsible father whose only guidance to his child is the lash, which he uses freely and cruelly. Not only is Jewish life imperfect in *Mottke the Thief*, in spite of some obedience to forms and tradition, but also it exists on the lowest levels of humanity. Asch shows an exceptional virtuosity in this novel. The first half combines picaresque with gargantuan, larger-than-life features; the second half is Zolaesque in its depressing naturalism. The abused Mottke, first open enough to seek affection even from a curious dog, is transformed into a callous pimp and murderer, a development that calls for considerable skill, which Asch demonstrates in good measure.

His earlier work might have given rise to the impression that there was something do-goodish in Asch, that his feet were not firmly planted on the ground. With the creation of Mottke, this impression was swept aside. From the moment Mottke joins a group of vaudevillians, uses and abuses them, seduces or is seduced by Mary, the rope dancer, and competes with the treacherous Kanarik, he becomes a character apart from any that Asch had previously created. The erstwhile thief's descent into total depravity continues. With Mary's help, he kills Kanarik, assumes Kanarik's identity, and acquires his own small staff of prostitutes. Yet the Mottke who had once enjoyed something of a Jewish upbringing, however atypical, is not wholly dead. He is fatally attracted to a decent girl, and his love generates decent impulses that have long been submerged. The desire for chastity, piety, and living in the love of and reverence for God, however, has been resurrected too late. Perhaps Mottke's conversion, which comes to naught, is not the most persuasive part of the book; in any case, Mottke is betrayed by the sweet girl he loves. Yet even in the novel's variety of depressing settings, Asch still emerges as a man with a profound faith in faith.

SALVATION

Salvation, a story of the saintly Jekhiel and his quest for God and ways of serving man, is more in the mainstream of Asch's fiction than is *Mottke the Thief*. It is probably the most purely "spiritual" of Asch's novels—a term he himself used to describe it—and he attributed its relative failure with the reading public to the refusal of the modern world to address spiritual questions.

Jekhiel's father was a Hasid who left his wife and younger son to join his rabbi in study. Jekhiel was a deep disappointment to him, for, unlike Jekhiel's older brother, Jekhiel has failed to grasp the subtleties of the Talmud. Jekhiel, oppressed by a sense of failure, helps his mother eke out a bare living in the marketplace. She dies, and the youngster serves as tutor to an innkeeper's children, to whom he teaches the elements of the Hebrew language. Jekhiel is heartened one day by a wise stranger, who tells him that knowing the Psalms, with their simple yet warm teachings, is every bit as important in the sight of God as the subtle shadings of talmudic disputation. Soon Jekhiel is known as the "Psalm-Jew" (which was, indeed, the original Yiddish title of the novel).

In this first half of *Salvation*, Asch poses several questions, to which his answers are clear. He is not enamored of the father, who puts study—however strong an ethic in Jewish tradition—ahead of his familial obligations; Asch does not place learning the Talmud above simpler aspects of the Jewish obligation to ponder the ways of God. A cold, rational approach to religion attracts him less than a warmer, human, perhaps less rational mode.

Jekhiel, without wishing it, develops a following of his own, becoming the rabbi of the Psalms, simple and humble. He is also known for miracles, for which, however, he claims no credit. On one occa-

sion, Jekhiel, under great pressure, commits God to giving a child to a hitherto barren woman. A girl is born. When Jekhiel's wife dies shortly thereafter, the pious rabbi sees it as a sign from Heaven. He leaves home and, in the manner of ascetic saints of all faiths, roams the countryside in rags. He is finally recognized and forced to return.

The years pass, and the girl whose birth he had promised has grown to maturity and fallen in love with a strapping young Polish soldier. They plan to marry. In preparation for her conversion to Catholicism, she enters a convent. There is consternation in the girl's family. Torn by conflicting pressures, the girl jumps to her death. Jekhiel, who had fought the conversion, is troubled for the second time: Has he overstepped proper bounds again? Was not human life and the search for God more precious than the particular way of reaching Him: the Jewish or the Christian?

Asch's implied tolerance of intermarriage again brought him into conflict with his Jewish readers. *Salvation* paved the way for a work that would nearly lead to a rupture with these readers: the story of Jesus of Nazareth, whose emphases within Judaism were not that different from those of Jekhiel the Psalm-Jew.

THE NAZARENE

The problem of Christian anti-Semitism is omnipresent in the oeuvre of Sholem Asch. Considering the author's vision of Jesus, an extension of his characterization of Jekhiel, it is not surprising that Asch often felt bitter about the crimes against Jews committed in the name of the saintly Nazarene. Throughout *The Nazarene*, Asch has his Rabbi Jeshua repeat that he has not come to destroy the Law but to fulfill it. Jeshua observes all but one or two of the ritual commandments, but it is his failure to observe those that his wealthy detractors use against him. Asch's Jesus is learned in the Torah; the character appears to be depicted in the tradition of the great teacher Hillel; he is a man of infinite wisdom and compassion. If, in spite of its strengths, *The Nazarene* fails to satisfy completely, that failure must be attributed to the nature of the subject. Jeshua as man, as self-revealed Messiah, and as Son of Man (interpreted to mean the

Son of God) is a difficult fusion to achieve. Asch is as successful as any novelist who has ever attempted it or, for that matter, biographers and interpreters. There are times, however, when Jeshua, ever mysterious—now very human, now very enigmatic, even furtive—suggests ever so slightly the religious charlatan. Yet this was far from Asch's intent and has not been the impression of all readers.

Jeshua's teachings are within the frame of Jewish tradition, but as he himself says, the fulfillment of that tradition requires new interpretations and emphases. The occasional impressions of hucksterism are held only by the more cynical modern reader, reacting to Jesus' refusal to answer questions directly, to speak in parables only, to select carefully his moments of healing and revealing, to satisfy the doubts of the most searching and spiritually avid of his disciples and admirers. Rabbi Jeshua has a talent for the grand gesture and for the attention-getting phrase or figure of speech, but this image is not one created by Asch; it is, rather, inherent in the subject matter, which he derives entirely from New Testament sources. There are few famous sayings of Jesus that are not quoted, and the endless quotations, although necessary, at times slow the pace of the narrative. Asch underscores the innovations of the teachings of Jesus: compassion for the poor, the sick, the neglected; the emphasis on the spirit, not the forms, of observance; the primacy of faith; a piety that adds to fervor of the divine humility and an all-encompassing pity; and an involvement in the affairs of man. Jesus attacks privilege, be it hereditary or earned. The task of involving oneself in the suffering of others must be never-ending; it must lead to the more fortunate assisting those who are suffering. Rabbi Jeshua's leniency toward the sinner, reassurance of the untutored and ignorant, and forebearance vis-à-vis those who have disappointed him all contribute to making him an innovative teacher and preacher. In the end, Jeshua dies, like so many of Asch's noble characters, for the sanctification of the name.

Asch was attracted to the story of Jesus on an early trip to Palestine, but he did not turn to writing it until decades later, when the need for closer Jewish-Christian ties seemed to him highly desirable. The device he finally employed for telling it was ingenious: A half-demented anti-Semitic Polish scholar, imagining that he was Pontius Pilate's right-hand man, relates the first third of the novel. Judas Ischariot, Jesus' most learned disciple, whom Asch rehabilitates in the novel, tells the next third in the form of a diary. The final third, recounted by a Jewish disciple of Nicodemus, a rabbi sympathetic to Jeshua, reports on the political and religious evasions within the Sanhedrin and Pilate's desire to rid himself of the troublemaking revolutionary.

Again, Asch displays his mastery of painting different milieus. The messianic craving among lowly and wealthy Jews, the Roman cynicism toward this strangest of peoples, the Jews, the doings in the Temple, the political rivalries between priests and scholars, the evocation of historical figures, the atmosphere of Jesus' preaching and reception in Galilee—all come alive in Asch's prose. If Rabbi Jeshua is only partly convincing, it is because his dual status as man and Messiah may well elude even the most skillful of writers.

EAST RIVER

Set on New York's East Side, another radically different milieu, *East River* is hardly one of Asch's better novels. The writing, even the syntax, appears a bit sloppy, and the work bears the marks of haste. The novel does, however, pull together many of Asch's most typical themes and interests: the poor sorely tried, and not by poverty alone; one son given to learning, the other to practical pursuits; traditional Jewish religious learning transformed into secular equivalents; anti-Semitism and the need for Jewish-Christian dialogue; the spirit of a religion versus its mere forms. Intermarriage, which unleashed a minor religious war between contending religious leaders in *Salvation*, is treated here with sympathy and understanding. To be sure, Moshe Wolf, symbol of the old life, cannot reconcile himself to his wealthy son's intermarriage, but neither can he accept—in spite of, or because of, his own poverty—this son's exploitation of Jewish and Christian workers. Moshe Wolf, a near-saint, accepts with love and understanding the burdens imposed on him by God: his beloved older son's crippling polio, this son's failure to use his dazzling intelligence to study Scripture, applying it instead to secular ideas, which often frighten the traditional Jew in him. Wolf's wife, Deborah, thoroughly Americanized, has more understanding for the tycoon son than for the "cripple." For her, the former has succeeded; the latter, with his superfluous learning, is useless.

The Catholic girl who originally loved the cripple but then married the tycoon is treated sympathetically and is ultimately accepted by Moshe Wolf as a God-loving, God-seeking human being. Mary breaks with her pathologically anti-Semitic failure of a father and leads her husband back to the ways of decency and righteousness. Mary's relationships with her father and husband are not credible and detract seriously from any power the novel might have. Yet for whatever it is worth, Mary convinces her husband not to live only for himself or even his immediate family, but to enlist himself in the war against poverty, injustice, and cruelty. The old lesson is repeated here in less subtle form: Man does not live by bread, or money, alone.

Asch's daring in tackling milieus that cannot have been close to him is admirable: a grocery store, Tammany Hall, sweatshops, synagogue politics, Jewish-Irish relations, the garment industry. It is interesting to speculate what this book would have been like at the height of Asch's literary power. A courageous failure, it testifies to the profoundly ecumenical spirit of his fiction.

Lothar Kahn

OTHER MAJOR WORKS

SHORT FICTION: *From Many Countries: The Collected Stories of Sholem Asch*, 1958.

PLAYS: *Tsurikgekumen*, pr. 1904; *Der Got fun Nekome*, pr. 1907 (*The God of Vengeance*, 1918).

NONFICTION: *What I Believe*, 1941; *One Destiny: An Epistle to the Christians*, 1945.

BIBLIOGRAPHY

Brodwin, Stanley. "History and Martyrological Tragedy: The Jewish Experience in Sholem Asch and Andre Schwartz." *Twentieth Century Literature* 40 (1994): 72-91. An excellent comparative analysis.

Fischthal, Hannah Berliner. "Christianity as a Consistent Area of Investigation of Sholem Asch's Works Prior to *The Nazarene*." *Yiddish* 9 (1994): 58-76. Compare with Lieberman.

Landis, Joseph C. "Peretz, Asch, and the God of Vengeance." *Yiddish*, 1995, 5-17. An article that situates Asch carefully in the tradition of Yiddish literature.

Lieberman, Herman. *The Christianity of Sholem Asch*. New York: Philosophical Library, 1953. An early but still valuable study.

Liptzin, Sol. *The Flowering of Yiddish Literature*. New York: Thomas Yoseloff, 1963. Contains a well-informed chapter on Asch.

_____. *A History of Yiddish Literature*. Middle Village, N.Y.: Jonathan David, 1972. Another good introduction to Asch.

Morgentaler, Goldie. "The Foreskin of the Heart: Ecumenism in Sholem Asch's Christian Trilogy." *Prooftexts: A Journal of Jewish Literary History* 8 (1988): 219-244. Compare with Fischthal.

Siegel, Ben. *The Controversial Sholem Asch: An Introduction to His Fiction*. Bowling Green, Ohio: Bowling Green State University Press, 1976. Often cited as the best biographical and critical introduction. Includes a chronology and detailed index.

Slochower, Harry. *No Voice Is Wholly Lost: Writers and Thinkers in War and Peace*. New York: Creative Age Press, 1945. Contains "Franz Werfel and Sholem Asch: The Yearning for Status." Another good comparative analysis to be read in conjunction with Brodwin.

ISAAC ASIMOV

Born: Petrovichi, Russia; January 2, 1920
Died: New York, New York; April 6, 1992

PRINCIPAL LONG FICTION

Pebble in the Sky, 1950
Foundation, 1951

The Stars Like Dust, 1951

The Currents of Space, 1952

Foundation and Empire, 1952

Second Foundation, 1953

The Caves of Steel, 1954

The End of Eternity, 1955

The Naked Sun, 1957

The Death-Dealers, 1958 (also known as *A Whiff of Death*)

Fantastic Voyage, 1966

The Gods Themselves, 1972

Murder at the ABA: A Puzzle in Four Days and Sixty Scenes, 1976

Foundation's Edge, 1982

The Robots of Dawn, 1983

Robots and Empire, 1985

Foundation and Earth, 1985

Fantastic Voyage II: Destination Brain, 1987

Prelude to Foundation, 1988

Azazel, 1988

Robot Dreams, 1989

Nemesis, 1989

Robot Visions, 1990

Nightfall, 1991 (with Robert Silverberg)

The Ugly Little Boy (with Silverberg), 1992

Forward the Foundation, 1993

The Positronic Man, 1993 (with Silverberg)

(Library of Congress)

OTHER LITERARY FORMS

Isaac Asimov was an unusually prolific author with more than five hundred published books in his bibliography, including fiction, autobiographies, edited anthologies of fiction, and nonfiction works ranging in subject from the Bible to science, history, and humor; only the most famous, "principal" novels are listed above. Asimov also wrote regular articles on science and literature and lent his name to a science-fiction magazine for which he wrote a monthly article. He wrote three autobiographies. *In Memory Yet Green* (1979) covers his life from 1920 to 1954. *In Joy Still Felt* (1980) continues from 1954 to 1974, and *I, Asimov: A Memoir* (1994) spans his life in more anecdotal form. *Yours, Isaac Asimov* (1995) is a posthumous collection of excerpts from letters written by Asimov and edited by his brother Stanley.

ACHIEVEMENTS

Isaac Asimov was widely known as one of "the big three" science-fiction writers, the other two being Robert Heinlein and Arthur C. Clarke. In addition to obtaining a doctorate in biochemistry from Columbia University, Asimov was awarded fourteen honorary doctoral degrees from various universities. He won seven Hugo Awards (for achievements in science fiction) in various categories. He was awarded the Nebula Award (awarded by the Science Fiction Writers of America) in 1972 for *The Gods Themselves* and again in 1977 for the novelette "The Bicentennial Man" (later expanded by Robert Silverberg to *The Positronic Man*). Ten years later, in 1987, Asimov received the Nebula Grand Master Award, the eighth to be given. All seven of the previous awards had been given to science-fiction authors who were still living and had begun publication before Asimov. Earlier, the American Chemical Society had given him the

James T. Grady Award in 1965, and he had received the Westinghouse Science Writing Award in 1967. Asimov wrote on a huge number of subjects, and he has at least one book numbered in each of the ten Dewey Decimal Library System's major classifications.

BIOGRAPHY

Isaac Asimov immigrated to the United States with his Russian Jewish parents when he was three years old; they settled in Brooklyn, New York. Encountering early science-fiction magazines at his father's candy store, where he began working when his mother was pregnant with his brother, led him to follow dual careers as a scientist and author. Asimov was the oldest of three children; he had a sister, Marcia, and a brother, Stanley. He considered himself an American and never learned to speak Russian, although in later life he studied Hebrew and Yiddish. He started at Columbia University at age fifteen. By age eighteen, he sold his first story to the magazine *Amazing Stories*. He had been writing a regular column for his high school newspaper prior to that.

Graduating from Columbia with a B.S. in chemistry in 1939, he applied to all five New York City medical schools and was turned down. He was also rejected for the master's program at Columbia but convinced the department to accept him on probation. He earned his master's degree in chemistry in 1941. His doctoral program was interrupted by his service in World War II as a junior chemist at the Philadelphia Naval Yard from 1942 through 1945. He worked there with fellow science-fiction writer Robert Heinlein. Asimov earned his doctorate in biochemistry in 1948.

After graduation, Asimov worked for a year as a researcher at Columbia, then became an instructor at Boston University School of Medicine. He was granted tenure there in 1955, but he gave up his duties to write full-time, while retaining his title. The university promoted him to the rank of full professor in 1979. Asimov married Gertrude Blugerman in July of 1942. They had two children, a son named David and a daughter named Robyn Joan. They were divorced on November 16, 1973, and Asimov mar-

ried Janet Opal Jeppson fifteen days later. They had no children, but they wrote the Norby robot children's books together.

Asimov was afraid of heights and flew in airplanes only twice in his life. On the other hand, he enjoyed closed-in places, and he thought that the city he describes in his book *The Caves of Steel* would be a very appealing place to live. Asimov was not religious but was proud of his Jewish ethnic heritage. Asimov enjoyed public speaking almost as much as he enjoyed writing and had an exuberant personality.

ANALYSIS

Isaac Asimov was especially known for his ability to explain complicated scientific concepts clearly. Although his writing reputation was based on his science fiction, his nonfiction writings are useful reference works on the many subjects he covered. His goal was not only to entertain but also to inform.

Asimov's novels are primarily science fiction, and of these almost half, fourteen novels, are tied together at some point with part of the Foundation series. Early in his writing career Asimov established four series of stories: the Empire series, consisting of three novels and collections of short stories; the Foundation series, consisting of seven novels, with more that Asimov outlined to be finished by other authors; the Robot series, consisting of four novels and collections of short stories; and the Lucky Starr series, a collection of six juveniles not related to the Foundation series. Asimov borrowed heavily from history, specifically the history of the Roman Empire, to create his plot lines for the Foundation books. Of all his novels, *The Gods Themselves*, a Hugo and Nebula Award winner, was Asimov's favorite.

THE EMPIRE SERIES

The Empire series consists of three novels, *Pebble in the Sky*, *The Stars Like Dust*, and *The Currents of Space*. Later Foundation series books attempt to tie these three into that series. Asimov's first published novel, *Pebble in the Sky*, is the best of these. The writing is not Asimov's most polished, but the hero, Joseph Schwartz, provides an interesting middle-aged counterpoint to Bel Arvardan, a younger man of action coping with a postapocalyptic, radioactive Earth.

THE FOUNDATION SERIES

The Foundation series began as a trilogy. The first three Foundation books, known for some time as the Foundation trilogy, were written in the 1950's and took much of their plot line from the history of the Roman Empire. Because of the length of the trilogy, it is rarely taught in schools, but the first two of the three books, *Foundation* and *Foundation and Empire*, are examples of Asimov's fiction at its best.

The hero of these novels is Hari Seldon, a mathematician who invents the discipline of psychohistory. Using psychohistory, Seldon is able to predict the coming fall of the Empire and to help set up the Foundation in order to help humankind move more quickly through the coming "dark ages" that will be caused by the collapse of the Empire. Psychohistory is unable to predict individual mutations and events in human history, however, so Seldon's Foundation is unable to predict the rise to power of the Mule, a mutant of superior intelligence. Asimov's introduction of the concept of psychohistory, a science that could predict the future course of humankind, has inspired many history, psychology, sociology, and economics majors, and was significant in the creation of an actual psychohistory major at some colleges and universities.

By the third book, *Second Foundation*, Asimov was tired of the Foundation story and came up with two alternate endings that he hoped would let him be free of it. In the first, the Mule discovers the secret second Foundation and destroys it, thereby ending Seldon's plan. Asimov's editor talked him out of this ending, so he wrote another, in which the Second Foundation triumphs. Seldon's plan is restored to course and nothing of interest happens again to the human species—thus freeing Asimov from the need to write further Foundation novels. Time and financial incentives eventually overcame Asimov's boredom with the Foundation trilogy, and thirty years later, in the 1980's and 1990's, he began filling in the gaps around the original stories with four other novels. He went on to produce *Foundation's Edge*, *Foundation and Earth*, *Prelude to Foundation*, and *Forward the Foundation*. None has quite the same magic as the first two Foundation novels.

THE ROBOT SERIES

The ideas introduced by Asimov in the Robot series are perhaps his most famous. Asimov's robots are human in form and have "positronic" brains. In the late 1980's and 1990's, the television program and films of *Star Trek: The Next Generation* contributed to public awareness of this concept through the character of the android Data, who, like Asimov's robots, has a positronic brain. Asimov also invented the three Laws of Robotics, which he tended not to let other people use. His invention of mechanical creatures with built-in ethical systems is used freely, however, and from that standpoint Data is an Asimovian robot. The concept of a tool designed for safety in the form of a robot was new to science-fiction writing when Asimov introduced it, and it stood in sharp contrast to the usual mechanical men of science-fiction pulp magazines, which tended to be dangerous and run amok.

There are exciting ideas and parts in each of the four Robot novels, *The Caves of Steel*, *The Naked Sun*, *The Robots of Dawn*, and *Robots and Empire*. *The Caves of Steel* is a good place to start. The character R. Daneel Olivaw is introduced in this novel and appears in six additional novels. The "R." stands for robot. This particular novel is also notable for its blending of two genres, science fiction and mystery. Additionally, the title describes Asimov's solution to an overcrowded Earth, an incredible complex of multilayered mega-cities covering the entire planet.

THE LUCKY STARR SERIES

Because he was intentionally writing juvenile novels of the Lucky Starr series for a hoped-for television series and was afraid that they would affect his reputation as a serious science-fiction writer, Asimov originally published them under the pseudonym Paul French. In these novels, David Starr and his friend Bigman Jones travel around the solar system in a spaceship. Asimov adapted Western stereotypes to create these plots, but he used his amazing ability to explain science to create plot devices and solutions based on science.

THE GODS THEMSELVES

The Gods Themselves is one of Asimov's best novels and one of the few unrelated to any others. Yet to single it out as a "stand-alone" novel would imply that the books of his series are dependent upon one another, which is not true. *The Gods Themselves* is one of the few Asimov novels dealing with aliens.

The Gods Themselves (the title is taken from a quote by German dramatist Friedrich Schiller, "Against stupidity the gods themselves contend in vain") is actually a series of three interrelated stories treating stupidity and responses to it. Humans exchange energy with aliens in a parallel universe with the Inter-Universe Electron Pump. When one human realizes the pump will eventually cause the sun to explode, he works to warn others, but nobody listens. Meanwhile, in the parallel universe, one of the "paramen" also attempts to shut down the pump. Although neither succeeds due to stupidity on the part of their peers, the problem eventually is solved by others, and the human universe is saved.

FANTASTIC VOYAGE and FANTASTIC VOYAGE II

Fantastic Voyage was contracted as a novelization of the 1966 film of the same name. However, because of the rapidity of Asimov's writing and the slow pace of filmmaking, the book actually appeared before the film. In the novel Asimov attempted to explain and justify some of the scientific impossibilities and inaccuracies of the film but never succeeded to his own satisfaction. *Fantastic Voyage II: Destination Brain* was in many ways a second attempt at rectifying the science of the first.

NOVELETTES

As a publishing ploy, it was arranged that Robert Silverberg expand three of Asimov's best and most famous novelettes, "Nightfall," "The Bicentennial Man" (which became *The Positronic Man*), and "The Ugly Little Boy," into full novels. Although Silverberg is an excellent and literary writer, his style and Asimov's do not blend particularly well. Given the opportunity, readers should begin by reading the original award-winning work. "Nightfall" in particular has won worldwide aclaim and is the most mentioned and remembered of Asimov's stories. Its premise concerns what happens to the psyches of a people who live in a world that only experiences total darkness once every two thousand years.

B. Diane Blackwood

OTHER MAJOR WORKS

SHORT FICTION: *I, Robot*, 1950; *The Martian Way*, 1955; *Earth Is Room Enough*, 1957; *Nine Tomorrows*, 1959; *The Rest of the Robots*, 1964; *Asimov's Mysteries*, 1968; *Nightfall and Other Stories*, 1969; *The Early Asimov*, 1972; *Tales of the Black Widowers*, 1974; *Buy Jupiter and Other Stories*, 1975; *More Tales of the Black Widowers*, 1976; *The Bicentennial Man and Other Stories*, 1976; *Good Taste*, 1977; *The Key Word and Other Mysteries*, 1977; *Casebook of the Black Widowers*, 1980; *The Winds of Change and Other Stories*, 1983; *The Union Club Mysteries*, 1983; *Computer Crimes and Capers*, 1983; *Banquets of the Black Widowers*, 1984; *The Disappearing Man and Other Mysteries*, 1985; *Alternate Asimovs*, 1986; *Isaac Asimov: The Complete Stories*, 1990.

NONFICTION: *The Chemicals of Life: Enzymes, Vitamins, Hormones*, 1954; *Inside the Atom*, 1956; *The World of Carbon*, 1958; *The World of Nitrogen*, 1958; *Words of Science and the History Behind Them*, 1959; *Realm of Numbers*, 1959; *The Intelligent Man's Guide to Science*, 1960; *The Wellsprings of Life*, 1960; *Life and Energy*, 1962; *The Search for the Elements*, 1962; *The Genetic Code*, 1963; *The Human Body: Its Structures and Operation*, 1964; *The Human Brain: Its Capacities and Functions*, 1964; *A Short History of Biology*, 1964; *Asimov's Biographical Encyclopedia of Science and Technology*, 1964; *Planets for Man*, 1964 (with Stephen H. Dole); *The Greeks: A Great Adventure*, 1965; *A Short History of Chemistry*, 1965; *The New Intelligent Man's Guide to Science*, 1965; *The Neutrino: Ghost Particle of the Atom*, 1966; *The Roman Republic*, 1966; *Understanding Physics*, 1966; *The Genetic Effects of Radiation*, 1966; *The Universe: From Flat Earth to Quasar*, 1966; *The Roman Empire*, 1967; *The Egyptians*, 1967; *Asimov's Guide to the Bible*, 1968-1969 (2 volumes); *The Dark Ages*, 1968; *Science, Numbers, and I*, 1968; *The Shaping of England*, 1969; *Asimov's Guide to Shakespeare*, 1970 (2 volumes); *Constantinople: The Forgotten Empire*, 1970; *Electricity and Man*, 1972; *The Shaping of France*, 1972; *Worlds Within Worlds: The Story of Nuclear Energy*, 1972; *The Shaping of North America from Earliest Times to*

1763, 1973; *Today, Tomorrow, and . . .* , 1973; *Before the Golden Age*, 1974 (autobiography); *Earth: Our Crowded Spaceship*, 1974; *Our World in Space*, 1974; *The Birth of the United States, 1763-1816*, 1974; *Our Federal Union: The United States from 1816 to 1865*, 1975; *Science Past—Science Future*, 1975; *The Collapsing Universe*, 1977; *The Golden Door: The United States from 1865 to 1918*, 1977; *A Choice of Catastrophes: The Disasters That Threaten Our World*, 1979; *Extraterrestrial Civilizations*, 1979; *In Memory Yet Green: The Autobiography of Isaac Asimov, 1920-1954*, 1979; *The Annotated "Gulliver's Travels,"* 1980; *Asimov on Science Fiction*, 1980; *In Joy Still Felt: The Autobiography of Isaac Asimov, 1954-1978*, 1980; *Visions of the Universe*, 1981; *Exploring the Earth and the Cosmos: The Growth and Future of Human Knowledge*, 1982; *The Roving Mind*, 1983; *The History of Physics*, 1984; *The Edge of Tomorrow*, 1985; *Robots: Machines in Man's Image*, 1985 (with Karen A. Frenkel); *Asimov's Guide to Halley's Comet*, 1985; *Exploding Suns*, 1985; *The Dangers of Intelligence and Other Science Essays*, 1986; *Beginnings: The Story of Origins—of Mankind, Life, the Earth, the Universe*, 1987; *Past, Present, and Future*, 1987; *Asimov's Annotated Gilbert and Sullivan*, 1988; *The Relativity of Wrong*, 1988; *Asimov on Science*, 1989; *Asimov's Chronology of Science and Discovery*, 1989; *Asimov's Galaxy*, 1989; *Frontiers*, 1990; *Asimov's Chronology of the World: The History of the World from the Big Bang to Modern Times*, 1991; *Atom: Journey Across the Subatomic Cosmos*, 1991; *Yours, Isaac Asimov: A Lifetime of Letters*, 1995 (Stanley Asimov, editor).

CHILDREN'S LITERATURE: *David Starr: Space Ranger*, 1952; *Lucky Starr and the Pirates of the Asteroids*, 1953; *Lucky Starr and the Oceans of Venus*, 1954; *Lucky Starr and the Big Sun of Mercury*, 1956; *Lucky Starr and the Moons of Jupiter*, 1957; *Lucky Starr and the Rings of Saturn*, 1958.

BIBLIOGRAPHY

Asimov, Isaac. *I, Asimov: A Memoir.* New York: Doubleday, 1994. Spans his entire life in more introspective and anecdotal form.

_____. *In Memory Yet Green: The Autobiography of Isaac Asimov, 1920-1954.* New York: Doubleday, 1979. Asimov's autobiographies are the three best sources about the life and times of this author. Covers Asimov's life through 1954.

_____. *In Joy Still Felt: The Autobiography of Isaac Asimov, 1954-1978.* Garden City, N.Y.: Doubleday, 1980. Continues from 1954 to 1974 and provides vignettes of the publishing world and other science-fiction authors.

Goble, Neil. *Asimov Analyzed.* Baltimore: Mirage, 1972. An academic examination of the author's style as well as his motivations for writing his major works.

Gunn, James. *Isaac Asimov: The Foundations of Science Fiction.* Rev. ed. Metuchen, N.J.: Scarecrow Press, 1996. Gunn teaches, writes, and critiques science fiction. He has produced several excellent textbooks and teaching anthologies of science fiction. His analysis of Asimov is insightful.

Hassler, Donald M. *Isaac Asimov.* Mercer Island, Wash.: Starmont House, 1991. Difficult to find since Starmont House was bought by Borgo Press, but Hassler brings some unusual perspectives to the study of Asimov's work.

Patrouch, Joseph F., Jr. *The Science Fiction of Isaac Asimov.* Garden City, N.Y.: Doubleday, 1974. A strong analysis of Asimov's literary style by a critic well versed in the science-fiction genre.

Touponce, William F. *Isaac Asimov.* Boston: Twayne, 1991. Good overview of Asimov's life and works. Contains index and bibliography.

White, Michael. *Asimov: The Unauthorised Life.* London: Millennium, 1994. An unauthorized biography published after Asimov's death. Includes bibliographic references.

MIGUEL ÁNGEL ASTURIAS

Born: Guatemala City, Guatemala; October 19, 1899
Died: Madrid, Spain; June 9, 1974

PRINCIPAL LONG FICTION

El Señor Presidente, 1946 (*The President*, 1963)

Hombres de maíz, 1949 (*Men of Maize*, 1975)

Viento fuerte, 1950 (*The Cyclone*, 1967; better known as *Strong Wind*)

El papa verde, 1954 (*The Green Pope*, 1971)

Los ojos de los enterrados, 1960 (*The Eyes of the Interred*, 1973)

El alhajadito, 1961 (*The Bejeweled Boy*, 1971)

Mulata de tal, 1963 (*Mulata*, 1967)

Maladrón, 1969

OTHER LITERARY FORMS

Although known primarily as a novelist, Miguel Ángel Asturias produced work in a variety of literary forms, including several volumes of short stories, a few plays, and two substantial collections of verse. In addition, Asturias published a number of sociological and journalistic works.

Most of Asturias's works, regardless of genre, are interrelated in one way or another. The short stories collected in *Week-end en Guatemala* (1956), for example, are an integral part of the political and artistic statement of the novels of the Banana Trilogy (*Strong Wind, The Green Pope*, and *The Eyes of the Interred*). Similarly, the play *Soluna* (1955; sun-moon) provides a helpful introduction to the novels *Men of Maize* and *Mulata* and presents an overview of primitive magic lacking in the novels. The complementarity between individual works has led many critics to regard Asturias's oeuvre as a unified whole and to analyze it on that basis.

ACHIEVEMENTS

The works of Miguel Ángel Asturias are the expression of a mind intensely engaged with the essence of America. A virtuoso in the use of language and a master of many genres, Asturias focused his craft on a great variety of issues and themes. Two of these concerns had special importance for him, and a majority of his published works can be identified as explorations of those topics. His achievements were identical with his interests: the combination of Mayan cosmology with an aesthetic technique often called Magical Realism for the purpose of making a unique interpretation of modern Indian and mestizo reality, and a blend of social protest and art which attacked dictatorship and imperialism through the forum of world literature.

Asturias's concerns ran parallel with those of his generation. With the passing of Romanticism and *Modernismo* in the first decades of the twentieth century, Latin American writers began to seek inspiration in native rather than European themes. Realistic and naturalistic traditions in the novel developed into an original "literature of the land" which sought to portray a distinctively American experience. Peasants, supposedly in harmony with their surroundings but exploited by other elements of society, increasingly became

(Archive Photos)

the subjects of important works of fiction. The American landscape in art and literature changed from the idealized, idyllic paradise it had often been in nineteenth century fiction and poetry to an unforgiving wilderness.

Asturias's literary use of Indian myth was the most elaborate application of Native American lore in the history of Central American letters and represented a total break with European themes. The main works of his Mayan Cycle, *Leyendas de Guatemala* (1930), *Men of Maize*, and *Mulata*, present a kaleidoscopic view of Indo-America, redefining it with an often startling freedom of interpretation and with a philosophy of the novel which respects few traditional preconceptions about plot.

The political fiction of Asturias is equally innovative and American. *The President*, possibly the most significant and accomplished novel ever published by a Guatemalan author, along with *Week-end en Guatemala* (1956) and the books of his Banana Trilogy, form a literary parallel with Guatemala's liberal revolution of 1946 to 1953, confronting the misuse of economic, military, and political power. Asturias strengthened the role of literature in national life by including in his fiction, as part of its legitimate function, inquiry into the forces that control Guatemala. He was rewarded in 1967 with the Nobel Prize in Literature.

BIOGRAPHY

The son of a magistrate and a schoolteacher, Miguel Ángel Asturias belonged to Ladino (non-Indian) upper-middle-class society. When he was about six years old, the family moved to a farm of his paternal grandparents in Baja Verapaz. The move to the country was caused by his father's political difficulties with the dictator of Guatemala, Manuel Estrada Cabrera, and the family's three-year retreat away from the city was significant in Asturias's development, introducing him to the effects of dictatorship as well as to the countryside and its people.

When the political crisis was over, Asturias's family returned to Guatemala City, and Asturias began his studies at the Instituto Nacional de Varones (National Men's Institute) in 1912. Although student unrest crystallized into isolated protests against Estrada Cabrera between 1910 and 1920, Asturias was generally apolitical during his early school years. He participated in one disorder, a window-breaking spree with political overtones, but otherwise he refrained from attacks on the dictatorship until the formation of the Unionist Party in 1919. He signed a student manifesto against the government in August of that year, his first public stand against Estrada Cabrera.

After the Unionist victory, Asturias became a leader in the reform movement. He and his friends founded a popular university dedicated to educating the lower classes, with the ultimate goal of bringing the country into the twentieth century. Asturias's concerns were expressed in the dissertation he wrote for his law degree, but he was not able to find a local outlet for his social conscience after graduation because political pressures made necessary his departure from the country.

He traveled to England and then to France. In Paris, he studied anthropology at the Sorbonne, under Professor George Raynaud, and, with the help of another student, translated the Mayan documents *Popol Vuh* (c. 1550) and *Annals of the Cakchiquels* (sixteenth century) from Raynaud's French versions into Spanish. This apprenticeship to Indian literature and tradition had a profound effect on Asturias and deeply influenced his literary production. His first book, *Leyendas de Guatemala*, was the direct result of his work in Paris.

In 1933, Asturias returned to Guatemala, where he managed his radio news program *El diario del aire*. He began his political career as a deputy to the National Congress in 1942, and, after the fall of Jorge Ubico in 1944, he was made cultural attaché to Mexico. It was there that he arranged to have his first novel, *The President*, published privately. In 1947, he was named cultural attaché to Buenos Aires, a position he held for six years. That period was one of intense literary activity during which he wrote two volumes of his Banana Trilogy as well as *Men of Maize*.

In June of 1954, Colonel Castillo Armas, with a small army and American support, invaded Guatemala and toppled the Arbenz government, of which Asturias was a firm supporter. Castillo Armas deprived Asturias of his citizenship, and the author took refuge in South America. He stayed for a time with poet Pablo Neruda in Chile, where he completed *Week-end en Guatemala*, a series of stories condemning the military intervention of 1954 and describing the causes and effects of the coup. Throughout his exile, Asturias wrote steadily and continued to publish. The avant-garde play *Soluna* appeared in 1955, and another play, *La audiencia de los confines* (border court), in 1957. The final volume of the Banana Trilogy appeared in 1960; subsequently, *The Bejeweled Boy* and *Mulata*, his most elaborate and complex fictions, complemented the nonpolitical cycle of his works. In 1966, he was awarded the Lenin Peace Prize in recognition of the anti-imperialist thrust of his oeuvre, and, on his birthday in 1967, he received the Nobel Prize in Literature. Asturias's diplomatic career resumed with a change of government in Guatemala, and he was ambassador to France from 1966 to 1970. He continued to live and write in Europe until his death in Madrid on June 9, 1974.

ANALYSIS

The writers who formed Guatemala's Generation of '20—which included Miguel Ángel Asturias—were typical of numerous Latin American intellectuals of the early twentieth century who questioned the values of the past and the relevance of European traditions. The authors of that group were disheartened over the failures of Western civilization in World War I and had lost confidence in what had always been considered foreign superiority. Feeling that they had nowhere to turn except to themselves, Asturias and his contemporaries began to study factors which distinguished their peoples from the French and the Spanish.

The cultural pendulum swung away from the escapism of preceding decades toward a confrontation with the essence of America. Central American history was reappraised, and that revision of ideas was disseminated through the free popular university which Asturias helped to found. In attempting to come to terms with Guatemalan reality, Asturias and others also became aware of the importance of the Central American Indians, who formed the excluded, oppressed majority in that nation's society. Not only was it believed that no truly nationalistic philosophy or literature could evolve until all aspects of the racial issue were considered, but it was also believed that any progress was impossible until the problem of the Indian had been resolved. Literary clubs and magazines were formed to express progressive Guatemalan aesthetics and to encourage the creation of a national folklore. Journals such as *Ensayos, Cultura, Tiempos nuevos*, and *Claridad*, which flourished briefly in the 1920's and on many of which Asturias collaborated, created a distinctive literary environment. Although Asturias left Guatemala shortly after his graduation from San Carlos and spent much of his life in Europe or South America, the formative issues of the Generation of '20, the concerns with authenticity and social reform, were his persistent literary obsessions.

Asturias's interests went far beyond political protest and literary re-creation of the Mayan spirit, but his most significant vision of Central America can be found in the books of those two cycles. Most of his later works do not fit easily into the two principal types of fiction—political and Mayan—already discussed. *The Bejeweled Boy*, for example, which explores the inner world of a child, is interesting from a psychological and technical point of view, but it does not create the kind of thematic drama which characterizes his earlier writings. His other plays, fiction, and poetry, as well as the previously unpublished material being published posthumously from the Fons Asturias in Paris, add depth and complexity to a body of writing which has yet to be fully viewed and understood. It is possible that, as additional works are published, critics will find more meaningful interpretations of his earlier books and redefine the borders of the "cycles."

By the time Asturias died in 1974, the political dreams of Guatemala's Generation of '20 had not come true. The new Guatemala which might have replaced that of Estrada Cabrera and Ubico fell to Castillo Armas and another series of strongmen. In literature, however, Asturias and his contemporaries such as Flavio Herrera, David Vela, and Rafael Arévalo Martínez brought their country into the mainstream of Latin American letters. Writer Epaminondas Quintana has remarked that the award of the Nobel Prize to his friend Asturias amounted to worldwide recognition not only of the writer himself but also of his generation and its ideals. To many Guatemalans, this is a significant part of Asturias's achievement.

LEYENDAS DE GUATEMALA

The heart of Asturias's Guatemalan perspective was the acceptance of Mayan theology as an intellectual superstructure for his art, and the effects of his study and translation of the *Popul Vuh* and the *Annals of the Cakchiquels* are clearly visible in his first collection of tales, *Leyendas de Guatemala*. Written between 1923 and 1928, the tales reflect a non-Western worldview of the Mayan documents on which Asturias was working at the time. These "legends" foreshadow the techniques that he employed in his Mayan Cycle—notably a surrealistic presentation of scenes that blends everyday reality with bizarre fantasy to create a Magical Realism. The lyricism of the author's language, his fondness for elaborate wordplay and Guatemalan puns, combined with his exposition of an Indian worldview and his use of an exotic tropical setting, produced the radical transformation of national aesthetics sought by the Generation of '20. In French translation, with a preface by Paul Valéry, *Leyendas de Guatemala* won the Prix Sylla Monsegur.

MEN OF MAIZE

Men of Maize, which appeared nineteen years after *Leyendas de Guatemala*, is a much longer and more complex vision of the Guatemalan people and landscape. Asturias's inspiration for the novel was, again, traditional Indian texts. There is no clearly defined plot in this second work of the Mayan Cycle; rather, Asturias presents a series of events and a gallery of characters united by themes that reflect a Mayan frame of reference. In the first part of the novel, Indians violently object to the commercial growing of corn, a crop which they consider sacred. Troops are sent to rescue the growers, and the military commander, Colonel Godoy, succeeds in quieting the revolt by having its leader poisoned. Subsequently, a curse is put on Godoy and his accomplices, all of whom die within seven years. The second section of the novel is concerned with María Tecún, a child of one of the unfortunate conspirators, who leaves her beggar husband, Goyo Yic. The latter spends most of his life looking for María; he does not find her until the final pages of the book. The third part of *Men of Maize* is the story of Nicho Aquino, an Indian mail carrier who also loses his wife; his search for her is fruitful in that, although he finds that she has been killed accidentally, he meets a mysterious seer, Seven Year Stag, who teaches him the lost wisdom of the race.

Asturias was criticized by a number of prominent Latin American scholars for the seemingly unrelated events of the novel's separate sections; however, themes such as metamorphosis and *nahualismo* (a belief that people have alter egos in certain plants or animals) give *Men of Maize* unity on a level other than plot.

SOLUNA

Open to widely divergent interpretations, *Men of Maize* can be less than satisfying to the uninitiated. It is of some use, however, to compare this novel with other major pieces of the Mayan Cycle, *Soluna* and *Mulata*. The former concerns the personal crisis of Mauro, the owner of a country estate, whose wife, Ninica, has just left him. Mauro consults Soluna, a shaman, who gives him a mask to help him solve the problem. When Mauro falls asleep, the mask on his lap, he dreams an elaborate dream in which Ninica finally returns. When he wakes up, he finds that his wife's train has derailed, and she, having reassessed her relationship with her husband, has come back to stay. From the dreamlike action of the play and the unlikely details of its plot emerges the story of a modern, Westernized Guatemalan who, in the midst of a deep trauma, finds consolation in superstition. There is a similarity between Mauro's search for a resolution of his crisis in the irrational and Nicho Aquino's experience in which Seven Year Stag plays such an important role in *Men of Maize*.

MULATA

Mulata is a surrealistic tale about Yumi, an Indian peasant who sells his wife to Tazol, the corn husk spirit, in order to achieve wealth and fulfillment.

Yumi's near-fatal mistake is lusting after an apparently sensuous *mulata* (a mulatto woman) who, in fact, is hardly sexual and proves to have supernatural powers. After a series of strange adventures, Yumi succeeds in regaining his wife, who assists him in trying to avoid the vengeance of the *mulata*. Here, as in *Leyendas de Guatemala, Soluna,* and *Men of Maize,* it is perhaps easier to take all the grotesque, extraordinary episodes at face value, accepting them for what they are in themselves, like a series of painted scenes, rather than trying to find logical connections between events. Indeed, it is possible to argue that Asturias had no intention of making each individual portion of these works relate to other sections and that, collectively, the scenes convey the nonrational cosmos and the dense theological texture of the Indian mentality better than could any logical, consecutive narrative.

THE PRESIDENT

In the Political Cycle of his fiction, Asturias turns away from the totally Indian universe which dominates the Mayan Cycle and concentrates instead on ruthless dictatorship and unscrupulous imperialism in Central America. The shift of theme is accompanied by a change in structure and style. The political novels and stories have more recognizable and traditional plotting than *Men of Maize* and *Mulata,* although Asturias never abandons his lyrical, surrealistic style.

The President is one of Asturias's most polished works. This first novel is a carefully constructed critique of the dictatorship of Estrada Cabrera, and it vividly evokes the climate of fear and repression which permeated Guatemalan life in the early decades of the twentieth century. The novel's main character is Miguel Cara de Ángel, the president's right-hand man. He is told to kill General Canales, who has lost favor with the dictator; Cara de Ángel, however, takes pity on Canales and his daughter, Camila, and helps them to escape. The general dies before he has the chance to start his own revolution, and Camila, rejected by the rest of her family for fear of reprisal by the president, is saved by Cara de Ángel, who falls in love with her. As she hides from government spies in the back room of a tavern, she

becomes ill with pneumonia. On the advice of an occultist, Cara de Ángel marries her "because only love can stand up to death." After her recovery, they consummate the marriage, and Camila becomes pregnant. Cara de Ángel is soon arrested, jailed, and never heard from again, and Camila gives birth to their son, Miguelito, whose name means "little Miguel."

Throughout the development of the plot, there is less political propaganda than vivid description of the brutal abuse of power. Asturias allows the actions of the president to speak for themselves. The book's message is enhanced by the fact that Camila and Cara de Ángel are not political characters. The former is an innocent victim of her father's unpopularity with the dictator, but she is not necessarily of the innocent masses; nor is Cara de Ángel a revolutionary hero who fights injustice. He is human and flawed, and his break with the president is caused by indiscretion, not by ideology. His actions toward Camila are motivated by love, not by his desire to save his people from the tyrant.

The President is one of the most successful and moving protests against dictatorship in the history of modern fiction. In addition, its craftsmanship contributed to making it one of the few Latin American novels published before 1950 to reach more than a local audience. *The President* also played no small role in elevating Asturias from the status of a talented Guatemalan author in exile to recipient of the Nobel Prize in Literature.

THE BANANA TRILOGY

Between the publication of *Men of Maize* and *Mulata,* Asturias was preoccupied with four works of fiction that complement the position taken in *The President.* The three novels of his Banana Trilogy, *Strong Wind, The Green Pope,* and *The Eyes of the Interred,* as well as the collection of stories *Week-end en Guatemala* are among the strongest statements in Central American literary history against the presence of the United States in that region. Far more polemical and political in tone than *The President,* these works provide a sensitive analysis of the problems associated with colonialism: economic exploitation of people and natural resources, the corruption of government officials who betray their nation to foreign interests, and military intervention.

STRONG WIND

The trilogy documents the history of the United Fruit Company and portrays both North Americans and Guatemalans whose lives are dominated by the company. *Strong Wind* provides a broad panorama of the extent of the United Fruit Company's influence as well as an introduction to the people who have been victimized by the fruit monopoly. An intensely drawn tropical environment, prominent in all of Asturias's fiction, is the setting for the story of Lester Mead, a planter and member of the corporation. Mead lives and works incognito in the midst of the exploited Guatemalans in order to bring about change from within the system. His struggles form the principal line of action around which Asturias depicts the extensive corruption brought about by the United Fruit Company.

THE GREEN POPE

The Green Pope, which appeared four years later, follows a similar pattern of presenting history and characterization with a clearly political purpose. The first part of the novel concentrates on a detailed accounting of the United Fruit Company's development in the country, while the second continues the train of events from *Strong Wind*. *The Green Pope* is essentially the saga of George Maker Thompson, another North American, who, in alliance with the Lucero family, eventually becomes the major stockholder in the company and its president. As in *Strong Wind*, the machinations of the United Fruit Company are exposed and severely criticized.

THE EYES OF THE INTERRED

The final work of the trilogy, *The Eyes of the Interred*, finished while Asturias was in exile, completes the dream of reform begun in the other works and traces the efforts of Octavio Sansor to form a union and establish worker control over the company. Although he first plans a revolution and a violent end to dictatorship and foreign economic control, Sansor ultimately chooses nonviolence, and his victory is the organization of the workers' syndicate, a general strike, the resignation of the president, and company concessions to the union.

William L. Felker

OTHER MAJOR WORKS

SHORT FICTION: *Leyendas de Guatemala*, 1930; *Week-end en Guatemala*, 1956; *El espejo de Lida Sal*, 1967; *Novelas y cuentos de juventud*, 1971; *Viernes de dolores*, 1972.

PLAYS: *Soluna*, pb. 1955; *Teatro: Chantaje, Dique Seco, Soluna, La audiencia de los confines*, pb. 1964.

POETRY: *Sien de alondra*, 1949; *Bolívar*, 1955; *Clarivigilia primaveral*, 1965.

NONFICTION: *Sociología guatemalteca: El problema social del indio*, 1923 (*Guatemalan Sociology*, 1977); *La arquitectura de la vida nueva*, 1928; *Rumania: Su nueva imagen*, 1964 (essays); *Latinoamérica y otros ensayos*, 1968 (essays); *Tres de cuatro soles*, 1977.

MISCELLANEOUS: *Obras completas*, 1967 (3 volumes).

BIBLIOGRAPHY

Callan, Richard. *Miguel Ángel Asturias*. New York: Twayne, 1970. An introductory study with a chapter of biography and a separate chapter discussing each of Asturias's major novels. Includes a chronology, notes, and an annotated bibliography.

Gonzalez Echevarria, Roberto. *Myth and Archive: A Theory of Latin American Narrative*. Cambridge, England: Cambridge University Press, 1990. A very helpful volume in coming to terms with Asturias's unusual narratives.

Harss, Luis, and Barbara Dohmann. *Into the Mainstream*. New York: Harpers, 1967. Includes an interview with Asturias covering the major features of his thought and fictional work.

Himmelblau, Jack. "Love, Self and Cosmos in the Early Works of Miguel Ángel Asturias." *Kentucky Romance Quarterly* 18 (1971). Should be read in conjunction with Prieto.

Perez, Galo Rene. "Miguel Ángel Asturias." *Americas*, January, 1968, 1-5. A searching examination of *El Señor Presidente* as a commentary on the novelist's society.

Prieto, Rene. *Miguel Ángel Asturias's Archaeology of Return*. Cambridge, England: Cambridge University Press, 1993. The best available study in English of the novelist's body of work. Prieto discusses both the stories and the novels, taking up issues of their unifying principles, idiom, and eroticism. See Prieto's measured introduction, in which he carefully analyzes Asturias's reputation and identifies his most important work. Includes very detailed notes and bibliography.

West, Anthony. Review of *El Señor Presidente*, by Miguel Ángel Asturias. *The New Yorker*, March 28, 1964. Often cited as one of the best interpretations of the novel.

MARGARET ATWOOD

Born: Ottawa, Ontario, Canada; November 18, 1939

PRINCIPAL LONG FICTION

The Edible Woman, 1969
Surfacing, 1972
Lady Oracle, 1976
Life Before Man, 1979
Bodily Harm, 1981
The Handmaid's Tale, 1985
Cat's Eye, 1988
The Robber Bride, 1993
Alias Grace, 1996

OTHER LITERARY FORMS

A skillful and prolific writer, Margaret Atwood has published many volumes of poetry. *Double Persephone* (1961), *The Animals in That Country* (1968), *The Journals of Susanna Moodie* (1970), *Procedures for Underground* (1970), *Power Politics* (1971), *You Are Happy* (1974), *Selected Poems* (1976), *Two-Headed Poems* (1978), *True Stories* (1981), *Interlunar* (1984), and *Selected Poems II* (1987) have enjoyed a wide and enthusiastic readership, especially in Canada. During the 1960's, Atwood published in limited editions poems and broadsides illustrated by Charles Pachter: *The Circle Game* (1964), *Kaleidoscopes Baroque: A Poem* (1965), *Speeches for Dr. Frankenstein* (1966), *Expeditions* (1966), and *What Was in the Garden* (1969).

Atwood has also written and illustrated books for children, including *Up in the Tree* (1978) and *Anna's Pet* (1980). Her volumes of short stories, a collection of short fiction and prose poems (*Murder in the Dark*, 1983), a volume of criticism (*Survival: A Thematic Guide to Canadian Literature*, 1972), and a collection of literary essays (*Second Words*, 1982) further demonstrate Atwood's wide-ranging talent. In 1982, Atwood coedited the revised *Oxford Book of Canadian Poetry*. She has also written articles and critical reviews too numerous to list. She has contributed prose and poetry to literary journals such as *Acta Victoriana* and *Canadian Forum*, and her teleplays have been aired by the Canadian Broadcasting Corporation.

ACHIEVEMENTS

Early in her career, Atwood's work was recognized for its distinction. This is particularly true of her poetry, which has earned her numerous awards, including the E. J. Pratt Medal in 1961; the President's Medal from the University of Western Ontario in 1965; and the Governor-General's Award, Canada's highest literary honor, for *The Circle Game* in 1966. Twenty years later, Atwood again won this prize for *The Handmaid's Tale*. Atwood won first prize from the Canadian Centennial Commission Poetry Competition in 1967, and won a prize for poetry from the Union League Civic and Arts Foundation in 1969. Honorary doctorates were conferred by Trent University and Queen's University. Additional prizes included the Bess Hoskins Prize for poetry (1974), the City of Toronto Award (1977), the Canadian Bookseller's Association Award (1977), the St. Lawrence Award for Fiction (1978), the Canada Council Molson Prize (1980), and the Radcliffe Medal (1980).

BIOGRAPHY

Margaret Atwood was born in Ottawa, Ontario, Canada, on November 18, 1939, the second of Carl Edmund and Margaret Killam Atwood's three children. At the age of six months, she was backpacked into the Quebec wilderness, where her father, an entomologist, pursued his special interests in bees, spruce budworms, and forest tent caterpillars. Throughout her childhood, Atwood's family spent several months of the year in the bush of Quebec and northern Ontario. She did not attend school full-time until she was twelve.

Though often interrupted, Atwood's education seems to have been more than adequate. She was encouraged by her parents to read and write at an early age, and her creative efforts started at five, when she wrote stories, poems, and plays. Her serious composition, however, did not begin until she was sixteen.

In 1961, Atwood earned her B.A. in the English honors program from the University of Toronto, where she studied with poets Jay Macpherson and Margaret Avison. Her M.A. from Radcliffe followed in 1962. Continuing graduate work at Harvard in 1963, Atwood interrupted her studies before reentering the program for two more years in 1965. While she found graduate studies interesting, Atwood's energies were largely directed toward her creative efforts. To her, the Ph.D. program was chiefly a means of support while she wrote. Before writing her doctoral thesis, Atwood left Harvard.

Returning to Canada in 1967, Atwood accepted a position at Sir George Williams University in Montreal. By this time, her poetry was gaining recognition. With the publication of *The Edible Woman* and the sale of its film rights, Atwood was able to concentrate more fully on writing, though she taught at York University and was writer-in-residence at the University of Toronto. In 1973, Atwood divorced her American husband of five years, James Polk. After the publication of *Surfacing*, she was able to support herself through her creative efforts. Atwood moved to a farm near Alliston, Ontario, with Canadian novelist Graeme Gibson. A daughter, Eleanor Jess Atwood Gibson, was born in 1979. In 1980, Atwood's family returned to Toronto, where Atwood and Gibson became active in the Canadian Writers' Union,

(© Washington Post; reprinted by permission of the D.C. Public Library)

Amnesty International, and the International Association of Poets, Playwrights, Editors, Essayists, and Novelists (PEN).

ANALYSIS

For Margaret Atwood, an unabashed Canadian, literature became a means to cultural and personal self-awareness. "To know ourselves," she writes in *Survival*, "we must know our own literature; to know ourselves accurately, we need to know it as part of literature as a whole." Thus, when she defines Canadian literary concerns, she relates her own as well, for Atwood's fiction grows out of this tradition. In her opinion, Canada's central reality is the act of survival: Canadian life and culture are decisively shaped by the demands of a harsh environment. Closely related to this defining act of survival, in Atwood's view, is the Canadian search for territorial identity—or, as literary theorist Northrop Frye put it, "Where is here?"

Atwood's heroines invariably discover themselves to be emotional refugees, strangers in a territory they can accurately label but one in which they are unable to feel at home. Not only are they alienated from their environment, but also they are alienated from language itself; for them, communication becomes a decoding process. To a great degree, their feelings of estrangement extend from a culture that, having reduced everything to products, threatens to consume them. Women are particularly singled out as products, items to be decorated and sold as commodities, though men are threatened as well. Indeed, Canadian identity as a whole is in danger of being engulfed by an acquisitive American culture, though Atwood's "Americans" symbolize exploitation and often turn out to be Canadian nationals.

Reflective of their time and place, Atwood's characters are appropriately ambivalent. Dead or dying traditions prevent their return to a past, a past most have rejected. Their present is ephemeral at best, and their future inconceivable. Emotionally maimed, her heroines plumb their conscious and unconscious impressions, searching for a return to feeling, a means of identification with the present.

Atwood often couches their struggle in terms of a journey, which serves as a controlling metaphor for inner explorations: The unnamed heroine of *Surfacing* returns to the wilderness of Quebec, Lesje Green of *Life Before Man* wanders through imagined Mesozoic jungles, Rennie Wilford of *Bodily Harm* flies to the insurgent islands of Ste. Agathe and St. Antoine. By setting contemporary culture in relief, these primitive sites define the difference between nature and culture and allow Atwood's heroines to gain new perspectives on their own realities. They can see people and places in relation to each other, not as isolated entities. Ultimately, however, this resolves little, for Atwood's novels end on a tenuous note. Although her heroines come to terms with themselves, they remain estranged.

Supporting her characters' ambivalence is Atwood's versatile narrative technique. Her astringent prose reflects their emotional numbness; its ironic restraint reveals their wariness. Frequent contradictions suggest not only the complexity of her characters but also the antagonistic times they must survive. By skillful juxtaposition of past and present through the use of flashbacks, Atwood evokes compelling fictional landscapes which ironically comment on the untenable state of modern men and women. Still,

there remains some hope, for her characters survive with increased understanding of their world. Despite everything, life does go on.

SURFACING

The first of Atwood's novels to arouse critical praise and commentary, *Surfacing* explores new facets of the *Bildungsroman*. What might have been a conventional novel of self-discovery develops into a resonant search for self-recovery imbued with mythic overtones and made accessible through Atwood's skillful use of symbol and ritual. At the same time, Atwood undercuts the romantic literary conventions on which *Surfacing* is built by exposing the myth of ultimate self-realization as a plausible conclusion. To accept the heroine's final emergence as an end in itself is to misread this suggestively ironic novel.

The unnamed heroine of *Surfacing*, accompanied by her lover Joe and a married couple named David and Anna, returns to the Canadian wilderness where she was reared in hopes of locating her missing father. His sudden disappearance has recalled her from a city life marked by personal and professional failures which have left her emotionally anesthetized. While her external search goes forward, the heroine conducts a more important internal investigation to locate missing "gifts" from both parents. Through these, she hopes to rediscover her lost ability to feel. In order to succeed, however, she will need to expose the fiction of her life.

At the outset of her narrative, the heroine warns her readers that she has led a double life when she recalls Anna's question, "Do you have a twin?" She denies having one, for she apparently believes the elaborate fiction she has created, a story involving a spurious marriage, divorce, and abandonment of her child. As additional protection, the heroine has distanced herself from everyone. She refers to her family as "they," "as if they were somebody else's family." Her relationship with Joe is notable for its coolness, and she has only known Anna, described as her best friend, for two months.

By surrounding herself with friends whose occupation of making a film significantly entitled *Random Samples* reveals their rootlessness, the heroine seeks to escape the consequences of her actions. Indeed, she describes herself both as a commercial artist, indicating her sense of having sold out, and as an escape artist. Reluctantly approaching the past she sought to escape, the heroine feels as if she is in foreign territory.

That she feels alienated by the location of her past is not surprising, for she is an outsider in a number of telling ways: of English descent in French territory; a non-Catholic, indeed nonreligious person among the devout; a woman in a man's world. Her French is so halting that she could be mistaken for an American, representing yet another form of alienation, displacement by foreigners. Most of all, she is a stranger to herself. Rather than focusing on her self-alienation, she is consumed by the American usurpation of Canada, its wanton rape of virgin wilderness, in order to avoid a more personal loss of innocence.

Canada's victimization by Americans reflects the heroine's victimization by men. Having been subjected to the concept that "with a paper bag over their head they're all the same," the protagonist is perceived as either contemptible or threatening. Her artistic skills are denigrated by a culture in which no "important" artists have been women. Even her modest commercial success is treated as a personal assault by Joe, who has an "unvoiced claim to superior artistic skills." By telling herself that the wilderness can never recover from abuse, the protagonist denies her own recovery. Although she feels helpless at the beginning of the novel, she soon rediscovers her own capabilities, and as these are increasingly tested, she proves to be a powerful survivor. Thus, the wilderness, a self-reflection, provides the key to self-discovery.

Perhaps the most important lesson the heroine learns is that the wilderness is not innocent. Her encounter with and response to a senselessly slaughtered heron evoke a sense of complicity, leading her to reflect on similar collusion in her brother's animal experiments when they were children. Finding her refuge in childhood innocence blocked, the heroine goes forward with her search. Once again, nature provides information, for in discovering her father's body trapped under water, she finally recognizes her aborted child, her complicity in its death by yielding

to her lover's demands. On a broader scale, she acknowledges death as a part of life and reclaims her participation in the life-process by conceiving a child by Joe.

In a ceremony evocative of primitive fertility rites, she seduces her lover. Then, assured of her pregnancy, she undergoes a systematic purgation in order to penetrate to the very core of reality. During this process, the protagonist discovers her parents' gifts—her father's sense of sight and her mother's gift of life. With body and mind reunited, she takes an oath in which she refuses to be a victim. Whole, she feels free to reenter her own time, no longer either victim or stranger.

Atwood's procedure for bringing her heroine to this state of consciousness is remarkable for its intricacy. Though she distrusts language, the protagonist proceeds to tell her story by describing what she sees. Since she has lost her ability to feel, much of this description seems to be objective—until the reader realizes just how unreliable her impressions can be. Contradictions abound, creating enormous uncertainty as intentional and unintentional irony collide, lies converge, and opinion stated as fact proves to be false. Given this burden of complexity, any simple conclusion to *Surfacing* is out of the question. Clearly, Atwood hints at a temporary union with Joe, but this is far from resolving the heroine's dilemma. Outer reality, after all, has not altered. Thus, Atwood's open-ended conclusion is both appropriate and plausible, for to resolve all difficulties would be to give in to the very romantic conventions which her fiction subverts.

LIFE BEFORE MAN

Coming after the gothic comedy of *Lady Oracle*, *Life Before Man* seems especially stark. Nevertheless, its similarity with all of Atwood's novels is apparent. A penetrating examination of contemporary relationships, it peels away protective layers of deceptions, stripping the main characters until their fallible selves are presented with relentless accuracy. Lesje Green and Elizabeth and Nate Schoenhof are adrift in a collapsing culture in which they struggle to survive. As she focuses on each character, Atwood reveals unrecognized facets of the others.

In this novel, wilderness and culture converge in the Royal Ontario Museum, where Lesje works as a paleontologist and Elizabeth works in public relations. There is little need for the bush country of Quebec, since culture is something of a jungle itself. Unlike the Mesozoic, however, the present anticipates its own extinction because of abundant evidence: pollution, separatist movements, political upheaval, lost traditions, disintegrating families. Humanity is in danger of drowning in its own waste. Whatever predictability life held in the past seems completely absent; even holidays are meaningless. Still, the novel is fascinated with the past, with the behavior of animals, both human and prehistoric, and with the perpetuation of memory, particularly as it records the history of families.

As in *Surfacing*, a violent death precipitates emotional withdrawal. Most affected is Elizabeth Schoenhof, whose lover Chris has blown off his head as a final gesture of defiance, the ultimate form of escape. His act destroys Elizabeth's sense of security, which resides both in her home and in her ability to manipulate or predict the actions of others. A supreme manipulator, Elizabeth attempts to make everyone act as reasonably as she. Not surprisingly, Elizabeth has at least two selves speaking different languages, genteel chic and street argot, and what passes for "civilized" behavior is merely an escape from honest confrontation with such basic human emotions as love, grief, rejection, and anger. In fact, all of the novel's characters prefer escape to self-realization, and while they pay lip service to social decorum, they quietly rebel.

Their rebellious emotions are reflected in the larger world, a political world aflame with separatist zeal. René Lévesque, with whom Nate identifies, is gaining momentum for the separation of Quebec and the reestablishment of French as the major language, threatening to displace the English. Indeed, the world seems to be coming apart as international, national, and personal moves toward separation define this novel's movement. As a solution, however, separation fails to satisfy the characters' need to escape, for no matter how far they run, all carry the baggage of their past.

Elizabeth in particular has survived a loveless past, including abandonment by both parents, the painful death of her alcoholic mother, her sister's mental breakdown and drowning, and her Auntie Muriel's puritanical upbringing. All of this has turned Elizabeth into a determined survivor. Beneath her polished exterior is a street fighter from the slums, a primitive. Indeed, Elizabeth recognizes an important part of herself in Chris. Nate and Lesje share a different kind of past, where love created as much tension as affection. Lesje's Jewish and Ukrainian grandmothers treated her as disputed territory, speaking to her in languages she could not understand and driving her to seek refuge in her fantasy world of Lesjeland.

Feeling like a refugee in treacherous territory, each character attempts to build a new, stable world, notwithstanding the continual impingement of the old, messy one. Nate, having forsaken his mother's futile idealistic causes to save the world, falls in love with Lesje, whom he envisions as an exotic subtropical island free from rules. For a time, Elizabeth inhabits a clean expanse of space somewhere between her bed and the ceiling, and Lesje explores prehistoric terrain, wishing for a return to innocence. When these fantasies diminish in power, the characters find substitutes, challenging the reader to reexamine the novel's possibilities.

Despite its bleak tone, its grimy picture of a deteriorating culture, its feeling of estrangement and futility, its rejection of simplistic resolutions, *Life Before Man* is not without hope. Each character emerges at the end of this novel with something he or she has desired. Nate has Lesje, now pregnant with his child—a child who, in turn, confirms Lesje's commitment to life by displacing her preoccupation with death. Having exorcised the evil spirits of her past, Elizabeth experiences a return of direct emotion.

There is, however, a distinct possibility that the apparent resolution is as ambivalent as that of *Surfacing*. What appears to be a completely objective third-person point of view, presiding over chapters neatly cataloged by name and date, sometimes shifts to first-person, an unreliable first-person at that. Through her revolving characters, their identification with one another, and their multiple role-reversals, Atwood creates contradictory, problematic, and deceptive human characters who defy neat categorization. Taken separately, Nate, Elizabeth, and Lesje can easily be misinterpreted; taken as a whole, they assume an even more complex meaning, reflecting not only their own biased viewpoints but also the reader's. Atwood's ability to capture such shifting realities of character and place is one of her chief artistic distinctions.

BODILY HARM

Rather like the narrator of *Surfacing*, Rennie Wilford in *Bodily Harm* has abandoned her past, the stifling world of Griswold, Ontario, to achieve modest success as a freelance journalist. To Rennie, Griswold represents values of duty, self-sacrifice, and decency found comic by contemporary standards. It is a place where women are narrowly confined to assigned roles which make them little better than servants. Rennie much prefers city life, with its emphasis on mobility and trends such as slave-girl bracelets and pornographic art. In fact, Rennie has become an expert on just such trends, so adept that she can either describe or fabricate one with equal facility. Having learned to look only at surfaces, Rennie has difficulty accepting the reality of her cancerous breast, which *looks* so healthy.

Her cancer serves as the controlling metaphor in the novel, spreading from diseased personal relationships to a political eruption on St. Antoine. Indeed, the world seems shot through with moral cancer. The symptoms are manifest: Honesty is a liability, friends are "contacts," lovers are rapists, pharmacists are drug pushers, and no one wants to hear about issues. What should be healthy forms of human commerce have gone out of control, mirroring the rioting cells in Rennie's breast. When confronted by yet another manifestation of this malaise, a would-be murderer who leaves a coil of rope on her bed, Rennie finds a fast escape route by landing a magazine assignment on St. Antoine.

Her hopes of being a tourist, exempt from participation and responsibility, are short-lived as she is drawn into a political intrigue more life-threatening than her cancer. Before reaching St. Antoine, she learns of its coming election, ignoring Dr. Minnow's allusions to political corruption and makeshift operations. What puzzles her most about their conversation is his reference to the "sweet Canadians." Is he being ironic or not, she wonders. Her superficial observations of island life reveal little, though plenty of evidence points to a violent eruption. Rennie seems more concerned about avoiding sunburn and arrest for drug possession than she is about the abundant poverty and casual violence. Her blindness allows her to become a gun-runner, duped by Lora Lucas, a resilient survivor of many injurious experiences, and Paul, the local connection for drugs and guns, who initiates Rennie into genuine, albeit unwilling, massive involvement.

As a physical link to life, Paul's sexual attention is important to Rennie, who appreciates the value of his touch. His hands call forth the "missing" hands of her grandmother, her doctor's hands, and Lora's bitten hands, hands which deny or offer help. Paul's "aid" to the warring political factions, like Canada's donation of canned hams and Rennie's assistance, is highly questionable, and the results are the reverse of what was planned. Trying to escape from his botched plan, Rennie is brought to confront her own guilt.

Again, Atwood uses flight as a route to self-discovery and deprivation as a source of spiritual nourishment. In Rennie's case, however, these are externally imposed. In her underground cell, with only Lora as company, Rennie ultimately sees and understands the violent disease consuming the world, a disease growing out of a human need to express superiority in a variety of ways and at great spiritual expense. Rennie becomes "afraid of men because men are frightening." Equally important, she understands that there is no difference between *here* and *there*. Finally, she knows that she is not exempt: "Nobody is exempt from anything."

If she survives this ordeal, Rennie plans to change her life, becoming a reporter who will tell what truly happened. Once again, though, Atwood leaves this resolution open to questions. Rennie is often mistaken about what she sees and frequently misinterprets events. Her entire story may well be a prison journal, an account of how she arrived there. When projecting her emergence from prison, she uses the future tense. For Atwood's purposes, this is of relative unimportance, since Rennie has been restored in a way she never anticipated. In the end, stroking Lora's battered hand, Rennie finally embodies the best of Griswold with a clear vision of what lies beneath the surface of human reality.

The Handmaid's Tale

In *The Handmaid's Tale*, Atwood's fiction turns from the realistic to the speculative, though she merely takes the political bent of the 1980's to its logical—and chilling—conclusion. Awash in a swill of pollution, promiscuity, pornography, and venereal disease, late twentieth century America erupts into political and religious battles. Rising from the ashes is the Republic of Gilead, a theocracy so conservative in its reactionary bent that women are channeled into roles as Daughters, Wives, Marthas (maids), Econowives, and Handmaids (mistresses).

The narrator, Offred (referring to her status as a possession *of* her master), is among the first group of Handmaids, fertile women assigned to high-ranking government officials. Weaving between her past and present in flat, almost emotionless prose, Offred draws a terrifyingly real picture of a culture retreating to fundamentalist values in the name of stability. At first, her prose seems to be accurate, a report from an observer. Deeper in the story, readers come to understand that Offred is numb from all that has changed in her life. Besides, she does not trust anyone, least of all herself. Still, as a survivor, she determines to stay alive, even if that means taking risks.

Her loss of freedom and identity create new hungers in Offred: curiosity about the world, a subversive desire for power, a longing for feeling, a need to take risks. In many ways, *The Handmaid's Tale* is a novel about what loss creates. Gilead, in fact, is created partially in response to men's loss of feeling, according to Fred, Offred's Commander. Yet Offred takes little comfort in his assurance that feeling has returned.

As she knows, feeling is ephemeral, often unstable, impossible to gauge. Perhaps this is why her characterization of others in the novel seems remote. While Offred observes gestures, facial movements,

and voice tone, she can only guess at intent. Implicit in the simplest statement may be an important message. Thus, Offred decodes all kinds of communication, beginning with the Latin inscription she finds scratched in her wardrobe: "Nolite te bastardes carborundorum." Even this injunction, however, which becomes her motto, is a corruption. Though desperate for communication, Offred cautiously obscures her own message. Her struggle to understand reflects Atwood's familiar theme of the inability to truly understand another person, another situation.

By having Offred acknowledge the impossibility of accurately decoding messages, Atwood calls attention to the narrative itself. Another interesting fictional element is the narrative's remove in time. Offred tells her story in the present, except when she refers to her life before becoming a Handmaid. Ironically, readers learn that not only is she telling her story after events, but her narrative has been reconstructed and presented to an audience at a still greater temporal remove. All of this increases the equivocal quality of the novel and its rich ambiguity.

While Atwood demands attention, she provides direction in prefatory quotations. Most revealing is her quotation from Jonathan Swift's "A Modest Proposal." Like Swift's satire, Atwood's skates on the surface of reality, often snagging on familiar actions and only slightly exaggerating some attitudes, especially those commonly held about women. Perennial issues of a woman's place, the value of her work, and her true role in society, are at the center of this novel.

Cat's Eye

These concerns appear again in *Cat's Eye*, but in a more subdued form. In subject and theme, *Cat's Eye* is an artistic retrospective. Elaine Risley, a middle-aged painter, is called to Toronto to prepare for her first artistic retrospective. Risley takes the occasion to come to terms with the dimensions of self in time, which she perceives as a "series of transparencies, one laid on top of another." Her return to Toronto, where she grew up, gives her an opportunity to look through the layers of people and events from her present position on the curve of time. This perspective, often ironic and tenuous, allows Risley to accept herself, including her foibles.

Cat's Eye takes full advantage of Atwood's visual style as it reiterates the importance of perspective in relation to change. The novel's art theme emphasizes interpretation while simultaneously satirizing the kind of inflated yet highly subjective criticism published for public consumption. Atwood's most personal novel to date, *Cat's Eye* tackles the physics of life and art and arrives at Atwood's least ambiguous conclusion. Returning to her family in Vancouver, Risley notes that the starlight she sees is only a reflection. Still, she concludes, "it's enough to see by."

THE ROBBER BRIDE

In *The Robber Bride* communication as a decoding process occurs both figuratively and literally, as one of the four protagonists, the historian Antonia (Tony) Fremont, seeks to discover the underlying meaning of the past. In her own storytelling she sometimes uses a reverse code, transforming herself into her imagined heroine Ynot Tnomerf. In fact, each of the women in the novel has renamed herself to gain distance from past traumas: Karen becomes Charis to cast out the memory of sexual abuse; Tony hopes to escape the "raw sexes war" that characterized her family; Roz Grunwald becomes Rosalind Greenwood as her family climbed the social ladder. Although cast in comic form, the novel explores issues of identity, reality versus fiction, and women's friendship. The three friends meet for lunch and reminisce about their betrayal at the hands of Zenia, a mysterious femme fatale who seduced Tony's and Roz's husbands and Charis's lover. Zenia has multiple stories about her origins, all dramatic but plausible. By preying on their fears and hopes, she ensnares her victims. Speaking about the novel, Atwood has remarked that Zenia is the equivalent of the fiction writer, a liar, a trickster who creates stories to captivate her audience.

ALIAS GRACE

Alias Grace is a historical novel based on the character of Grace Marks, a nineteenth century Irish immigrant to Canada accused of being an accomplice in the murder of her employer and his housekeeper-mistress. The novel combines gothic elements, social commentary, and conventions of nineteenth century fiction to tell its story. Spinning out several parallel courtship plots, the novel elucidates the implications of class and gender: Servant women were often the victims of wealthy employers or their bachelor sons. Grace's friend Mary Whitney dies of a botched abortion when she becomes pregnant.

The story is told through letters and narration by Grace and Dr. Simon Jordan, a young physician who has been employed by Grace's supporters to discover the truth of the murder. Dr. Jordan is a foil to Grace: As her fortunes rise, his fall. Hoping to win a pardon from her prison sentence, the shrewd Grace narrates her life story in great detail but claims she cannot clearly remember the events surrounding the murder. Dr. Jordan hopes to restore her faulty memory and to learn the facts of the case. However, in an ironic twist of plot he becomes embroiled in a shabby romantic liaison and, to avoid the consequences, flees Canada in haste. He is injured while serving as a physician in the American Civil War and loses his recent memory. Grace is released from prison, given a job as a housekeeper, and marries her employer. Dr. Jordan remains in the care of his mother and the woman she has chosen to be her son's wife. At the end of the novel all the plot threads are conveniently tied together as in the conventional nineteenth century novel, but at the heart of the story Grace herself remains a mystery.

Atwood's own vision is as informed and humane as that of any contemporary novelist. Challenging her readers to form their own judgments, she combines the complexity of the best modern fiction into the moral rigor of the great nineteenth century novelists. Atwood's resonant symbols, her ironic reversals, and her example challenges readers and writers alike to confront the most difficult and important issues of the contemporary world.

Karen Carmean, updated by Karen F. Stein

OTHER MAJOR WORKS

SHORT FICTION: *Dancing Girls*, 1977; *Bluebeard's Egg*, 1983; *Murder in the Dark*, 1983; *Wilderness Tips*, 1991.

POETRY: *Double Persephone*, 1961; *The Circle Game*, 1964; *Talismans for Children*, 1965; *Kaleidoscopes Baroque: A Poem*, 1965; *Speeches for Dr. Frankenstein*, 1966; *Expeditions*, 1966; *The Animals in That Country*, 1968; *What Was in the Garden*, 1969; *The Journals of Susanna Moodie*, 1970; *Procedures for Underground*, 1970; *Power Politics*, 1971; *You Are Happy*, 1974; *Selected Poems*, 1976; *Two-Headed Poems*, 1978; *True Stories*, 1981; *Snake Poems*, 1983; *Interlunar*, 1984; *Selected Poems II*, 1987; *Poems 1965-1975*, 1991; *Poems 1976-1989*, 1992; *Morning in the Burned House*, 1995.

NONFICTION: *Survival: A Thematic Guide to Canadian Literature*, 1972; *Second Words: Selected Critical Prose*, 1982; *Margaret Atwood: Conversations*, 1990; *Good Bones*, 1992.

CHILDREN'S LITERATURE: *Up in the Tree*, 1978; *Anna's Pet*, 1980 (with Joyce Barkhouse); *Princess Prunella and the Purple Peanut*, 1995 (with Maryann Kowalski).

EDITED TEXT: *The New Oxford Book of Canadian Verse in English*, 1982.

BIBLIOGRAPHY

Hite, Molly. *The Other Side of the Story: Structures and Strategies of Contemporary Feminist Narrative*. Ithaca, N.Y.: Cornell University Press, 1989. Feminist criticism on the writing of Atwood, Alice Walker, and Jean Rhys. The chapter on Atwood presents an insightful commentary on her novel *Lady Oracle* with reference to other criticism available on this novel. Discusses the novel's gothic elements, the use of satire, and its political implications.

Howells, Coral Ann. *Margaret Atwood*. London: Macmillan, 1996. Studies primarily the novels and *Wilderness Tips*. Treats shifts of emphasis in Atwood's treatment of politics over time.

McCombs, Judith, ed. *Critical Essays on Margaret Atwood*. Boston: G. K. Hall, 1988. Reprints reviews and critical studies of the novels and poetry. Introductory biographic essay reviews the reception of Atwood's works.

Rosenberg, Jerome H. *Margaret Atwood*. Boston: Twayne, 1984. A full-length study on Atwood with emphasis on critical commentary, although Rosenberg presents a capsule biography of Atwood's earlier years. In addition to an analysis of Atwood's five novels up until 1983, also discusses her nonfiction and critical studies, such as *Survival*, and her poetry. Includes a chronology and a useful selected bibliography.

Sullivan, Rosemary. *The Red Shoes: Margaret Atwood, Starting Out*. Toronto: Harper Flamingo, 1998. A biography focusing on Atwood's early life until the end of the 1970's. Attempts to answer the question of how Atwood became a writer and to describe the unfolding of her career.

York, Lorraine M., ed. *Various Atwoods*. Concord, Ontario: Anansi, 1995. Critical essays chiefly on the later poetry and fiction.

LOUIS AUCHINCLOSS

Born: Lawrence, New York; September 27, 1917

PRINCIPAL LONG FICTION

The Indifferent Children, 1947 (as Andrew Lee)
Sybil, 1951
A Law for the Lion, 1953
The Great World and Timothy Colt, 1956
Venus in Sparta, 1958
Pursuit of the Prodigal, 1959
The House of Five Talents, 1960
Portrait in Brownstone, 1962
The Rector of Justin, 1964
The Embezzler, 1966
A World of Profit, 1968
I Come as a Thief, 1972
The Partners, 1974
The Dark Lady, 1977
The Country Cousin, 1978
The House of the Prophet, 1980
The Cat and the King, 1981
Watchfires, 1982
Exit Lady Masham, 1983
The Book Class, 1984
Honorable Men, 1985
Diary of a Yuppie, 1986
The Golden Calves, 1988
Fellow Passengers, 1989

The Lady of Situations, 1990
Three Lives, 1993 (novellas)
Tales of Yesteryear, 1994
The Education of Oscar Fairfax, 1995

OTHER LITERARY FORMS

While best known as a novelist, Louis Auchincloss became a prolific and successful writer in a variety of other literary forms. Among his strongest collections of short fiction are *The Romantic Egoists* (1954), *Powers of Attorney* (1963), and *Tales of Manhattan* (1967), each of which presents stories linked by narration, characters, or theme in such a way as to resemble a novel. An accomplished critic, Auchincloss published studies of a wide range of writers, from William Shakespeare to Edith Wharton; among his best-known critical works are *Reflections of a Jacobite* (1961) and *Reading Henry James* (1975). *Life, Law, and Letters: Essays and Sketches* (1978) consists chiefly of essays on literary subjects, while the autobiographical memoir *A Writer's Capital* (1974) provides valuable insight into the formation of Auchincloss's outlook. Finally, Auchincloss published several heavily illustrated biographies and works of nonfiction intended for a general readership; among these works are *Richelieu* (1972), *Persons of Consequence: Queen Victoria and Her Circle* (1979), *False Dawn: Women in the Age of the Sun King* (1984), *The Vanderbilt Era: Profiles of a Gilded Age* (1989), and *The Roman Empire of Corneille and Racine* (1996).

ACHIEVEMENTS

During the 1950's, Auchincloss emerged as a strong social satirist and novelist of manners, rivaling in his best work the accomplishments of John Phillips Marquand and John O'Hara. Unlike those writers, however, Auchincloss was clearly an "insider" by birth and breeding, belonging without reservation to the social class and power structure that he so convincingly portrayed. With the waning of the tradition represented by figures such as Marquand and O'Hara, Auchincloss stands nearly alone as an American novelist of manners, unrivaled in his analysis of social and political power.

(Jerry Bauer)

Freely acknowledging his debt to Henry James and Edith Wharton as well as to Marcel Proust and the Duc de Saint-Simon, Auchincloss transforms the stuff of success into high art, providing his readers with convincing glimpses behind the scenes of society and politics where top-level decisions are often made for the most personal and trivial of reasons. As a rule, his featured characters are credible and well developed, if often unsympathetic; Auchincloss's apparent aim is to describe what he has seen, even at the risk of alienating readers who care so little about his characters as not to wonder what will become of them. At the same time, Auchincloss's characteristic mode of expression leaves him open to accusations that he is an "elitist" writer, featuring characters who are almost without exception white, Anglo-Saxon, and Protestant. Such accusations, however, do little to undermine the basic premise that emerges from the body of Auchincloss's work: For good or for ill, the people of whom he writes are those whose decisions and behavior have determined the shape of the American body politic.

Biography

Louis Stanton Auchincloss was born September 27, 1917, in Lawrence, New York, a village on Long Island where his parents owned a vacation house. Their permanent residence was New York City's upper East Side, where Auchincloss spent his entire life except for his years of education and military service. His parents, Joseph and Priscilla Auchincloss, were related to many prominent families in New York City society. Auchincloss attended the Bovee School for Boys and graduated from the prestigious Groton School, where his English teacher, Malcolm Strachan, fostered his literary interests. He entered Yale University in 1935 with plans to become a writer, only to withdraw several months short of graduation in 1939 after his initial efforts at publication had been rejected. Deciding instead to pursue a career in law, he received his degree from the University of Virginia in 1941 and worked briefly for the firm of Sullivan and Cromwell in New York before joining the Navy.

During World War II Auchincloss served in Naval Intelligence in the Panama Canal Zone and as a gunnery officer on landing ship tanks off the coast of France. Later he was commanding officer on similar craft in the Pacific Ocean. Returning to Sullivan and Cromwell after World War II, Auchincloss again tried his hand at creative writing, this time with demonstrable success. His first novel, *The Indifferent Children*, incorporated some of his experiences in the Navy and used an upper-class military officer as its protagonist, but it was published under the pseudonym Andrew Lee. Auchincloss's parents disapproved of the novel because they thought it might diminish his social standing and harm his legal career.

In 1951, Auchincloss withdrew from the practice of law and devoted himself to writing full-time, only to decide after some three years that law and literature were indeed compatible, even symbiotic, and that the writer's life excluding all other pursuits was a bore. During this period he also had intensive psychotherapy. In 1954, he returned to the practice of law with the Manhattan firm of Hawkins, Delafield, and Wood, of which he became a partner in 1958. The previous year, he had married the former Adele

Lawrence, to whom he dedicated several of his publications. Three children were born to them: John Winthrop Auchincloss in 1958, Blake Leay Auchincloss in 1960, and Andrew Sloane Auchincloss in 1963. Auchincloss retired from Hawkins, Delafield, and Wood in 1986.

In the 1960's Auchincloss achieved critical acclaim, but during the next decade he experienced persistent doubts about his creative ability and his reputation as a writer. After several years in which he wrote mainly nonfiction, he became more productive and began to explore new forms. After 1980 he wrote historical fantasies such as *Exit Lady Masham* and stories that are more decidedly comic, such as those in *Narcissa and Other Fables*.

In addition to his work as writer and lawyer, Auchincloss was active in civic and cultural affairs. He served as president of the Museum of the City of New York and was a member of the advisory board of *Dictionary of Literary Biography*. He also became a life fellow of the Pierpont Morgan Library.

Analysis

For a writer with a full-time professional career, Louis Auchincloss proved astoundingly prolific, producing nearly one book of fiction or nonfiction each year from the 1950's through the 1990's. Like that of many highly prolific writers, the quality of his work is decidedly uneven. At his best, however, Auchincloss meets and surpasses the standard set by J. P. Marquand and John O'Hara for twentieth century American social satire, displaying a resonant erudition that somehow eluded the two older writers even in their brightest moments. Even in the best of his novels, the results of Auchincloss's erudition are sometimes too conspicuous for the reader's comfort, but they can easily be overlooked in favor of the authenticity displayed by characters portrayed in convincing situations.

Auchincloss's reputation as a major writer rests primarily on novels written during the 1960's, a time somewhat past the vogue of social satire in the United States but coinciding neatly with the author's full maturity: The worst of his mistakes were behind him, and he had not yet experienced the temptation to repeat himself. *Pursuit of the Prodigal*, published in

1959, shows Auchincloss approaching the height of his powers, yet not quite free of his earlier mode as he portrays the tribulations of a "maverick" lawyer who is uncomfortable with the conventions into which he was born. Set in the immediate postwar years, *Pursuit of a Prodigal*, despite the distinct insider's voice, shows a clear indebtedness to Marquand's *Point of No Return*, published a decade earlier. The following year, however, Auchincloss broke new and enviable ground with *The House of Five Talents*, ostensibly the memoirs, composed in 1948, of the septuagenarian Miss Gussie Millinder, heiress to and survivor of an impressive nineteenth century New York fortune. The author's demonstrated skill at characterization and narration served clear notice of his new, mature promise, soon to be fulfilled with *Portrait in Brownstone*, *The Rector of Justin*, and *The Embezzler*, any one of which would suffice to confirm Auchincloss's reputation as the successor to O'Hara and Marquand as a master observer of American society and a superior stylist.

It is hardly surprising that Auchincloss achieved his greatest success with books narrated by the characters themselves, frequently by two or more characters in successive sections of one novel. Although his early novels and certain of his short stories bear witness to his control of third-person narration, Auchincloss is doubtless at his best when assuming the voice and persona of a featured character, striking a thoroughly convincing tone of vocabulary, style, and reflection. At times, his narrators are authentically unreliable without, however, approaching the virtuoso performances sought and achieved by Marquand in such works as *The Late George Apley* (1937) or *H. M. Pulham, Esq.* (1941). Unlike Marquand, Auchincloss seeks less to ridicule his characters than to represent them true to life, allowing readers to draw their own conclusions. It is to Auchincloss's credit that he can credibly assume such diverse personae as those of Miss Gussie Millinder and the three main characters of *The Embezzler*, as well as the slightly fussy schoolmaster who narrates *The Rector of Justin*.

Given the fact that Auchincloss has chosen to serve as a chronicler of his generation and those immediately preceding, it stands to reason that a num-

ber of his featured characters are drawn rather closely upon recognizable models—perhaps too closely in *The House of the Prophet*, rather less so in *The Embezzler* and *The Rector of Justin*. Such a practice has both its benefits and its pitfalls. At his best, Auchincloss meets and surpasses the aims of the finest historical fiction, showing rounded characters where the record presents only flatness. On other occasions, however, his presentation is so sparse as to require the readers' knowledge of the facts behind the fiction. This is not to say, however, that any of Auchincloss's novels are simple *romans à clef*; in each case, Auchincloss is careful to discover and point a message that goes far deeper than a simple recitation of documented facts.

Together with the highest minded of his characters, Auchincloss exhibits and values a strong sense of moral and ethical responsibility; unlike certain of his predecessors and erstwhile competitors in the genre, he never indulges in sensationalism or exposé for its own sake. Even when scandal invades the lives of his characters, as often it must, there is no perceptible intent to scandalize or titillate readers. Indeed, given the Proustian atmosphere that reigns in many of Auchincloss's novels, readers often wait in vain for the comic catharsis, however slow to build, with which Marcel Proust frequently rewards his readers' patience. Still, it must be noted that Auchincloss presents all but the meanest of his characters with considerable indulgence, providing a human warmth that is totally lacking in the work of such satirists as Sinclair Lewis and often absent in the more bitter works of O'Hara and Marquand.

A New Yorker by proclivity as well as by birth, Auchincloss remains, above all, a New York novelist; his characters spend most of their time in the metropolis, leaving it only for such traditional wateringplaces as Newport and Bar Harbor or for higher civic duty in Washington, D.C. The author's sense of place serves to illustrate and to explain the dominant role traditionally played by New Yorkers in the shaping of American society.

THE HOUSE OF FIVE TALENTS

In the first work of his "mature" period, *The House of Five Talents*, Auchincloss undertakes a personal record of upper-level Manhattan society through the still-perceptive eyes of one Augusta Millinder, age seventy-five, whose immigrant grandfather, Julius Millinder, founded one of the less conspicuous but more durable of the major New York fortunes. The Millinders had, by the time of Augusta's birth in 1873, established a position of quiet dominance, based upon diversified investments. The world in which Augusta and her more attractive elder sister Cora grew to maturity was thus one of easy movement and understated privilege, pursued frequently aboard yachts and in private railroad cars. As a memoirist, Augusta remains securely inside the closed world that she describes, yet she is privileged to have a gift for shrewd observation.

As the second and less attractive of two daughters, "Gussie" Millinder learned at an early age to view male admiration with a jaundiced eye. Indeed, the only man to whom she ever became engaged had proposed several years earlier to her vacuous sister Cora, who subsequently married a French prince. Although it seems likely that Lancey Bell, a rising young architect, has proposed to Gussie in good faith, she remains so skeptical that she breaks the engagement, having developed such inner resources that she no longer believes marriage to be necessary or desirable. In fact, the marriages in and around Gussie's family do little to encourage her faith in that institution. Soon after ending her engagement, Gussie becomes a reluctant participant in the dismantling of her own parents' marriage and household. Her father, aged sixty, has become enamored of a former actress half his age and wishes to marry her, supported in his folly by Gussie's older brother Willie and sister-in-law Julia.

Although the divorce and remarriage eventually take place as planned, Gussie has discovered in the meantime her own increasingly formidable talent for high-minded meddling. She has also begun to explore the extent of a freedom uniquely available to rich and well-read spinsters. Although dissuaded from attending college in her youth, she has taken enough courses at Columbia during her early adulthood to qualify her for part-time teaching in a private school. Later, around the age of forty, she becomes

deeply involved in volunteer work. By 1948, when she at last addresses herself to her memoirs, she has led a life both independent and fulfilling, but not without its disappointments.

Appropriately, Gussie's greatest disappointments have less to do with spinsterhood than with her various relatives, many of whom seem to have a singular talent for ruining their lives, at least when measured by Gussie's demanding but forgiving standards. Gussie's personal favorite appears to have been her nephew Lydig, a versatile and talented former army flight instructor who tries his hand at various pursuits successfully but without commitment, only to seek fulfillment in a life of adventure. Having taken up mountain-climbing, he dies in an avalanche around the age of thirty, a year before the stock market crash of 1929.

The changes wrought by the Depression and its consequences upon the Millinders are recorded with a sympathetic but dispassionate eye by Gussie, whose own personal fortune is sufficiently great to sustain major loss without requiring more than minimal changes in her privileged lifestyle. Among the few things she is obliged to forfeit is her private railroad car, while the chauffeured limousine remains. To the others, Gussie remains a rock of stability in a river of change, able to avert disaster with a well-placed loan (or gift) and a bit of timely meddling. At seventy-five, however, she admits that her interventions have not always been the right ones, much as they may have seemed so at the time. Several marriages remain broken beyond all possible repair and certain of her cousins face congressional investigation for their leftist sympathies.

Self-aware, yet not too much so for credibility, Gussie Millinder remains one of Auchincloss's most engaging narrators and one of his most satisfying creations, combining in her large and slightly outrageous person the best qualities of observer and participant in the action that she records.

PORTRAIT IN BROWNSTONE

Auchincloss's next novel, *Portrait in Brownstone*, attempts a broader picture of New York society. While fulfilling much of the promise held forth by *The House of Five Talents*, it falls short of its predecessor in tightness of construction, in part because of a multiplicity of narrative voices and viewpoints. Each chapter is presented from the viewpoint of a particular character, and while certain characters speak for themselves, others do not, presumably because their self-awareness is so limited as to require the author's third-person intervention.

The principal character of *Portrait in Brownstone*, although never a viewpoint character, is one Derrick Hartley, a minister's son from New England whose Harvard education and contacts facilitate his rapid rise within the presumably closed world of New York high finance. In the hands of O'Hara or Marquand, such a character as Derrick would emerge as a perceptive outsider with just a hint of the romantic hero; Auchincloss, however, presents Derrick as a thoroughgoing professional and opportunist, quick to impose his own stamp upon the closed world that almost did not allow him within its confines. He is also quick to enjoy and exploit the attentions of two female cousins, nieces of the employer whom he will eventually replace.

Set principally in the period during and surrounding World War I, *Portrait in Brownstone* underlines the contrast between "old money" and well-bred industry. Derrick, although polished and considerably less of an arriviste than certain of Auchincloss's later protagonists, has a talent for making money that renders him conspicuous among the Denison descendants, for whom the presence of money has obviated the need for making it.

After a brief and disastrous infatuation with the treacherous and ultimately unhappy Geraldine, Derrick returns his attentions to the younger, somewhat plainer cousin, Ida Trask, who had been his first love. Although disabused of her earlier illusions, Ida agrees to marry Derrick and soon bears him two children, a daughter and then a son. Ida, as a main viewpoint character, narrates much of the novel's action, developing considerably as a character in proportion to a growing awareness of her own innate strengths; Ida is a survivor, a resourceful, intelligent woman who, born in a later time, might well have rivaled her own husband's success. In any case, she is the only woman in the novel who could possibly handle the strains of marriage to a hard-driving businessman such as Derrick, whose strongest attentions and affections are reserved for his work. Like Gussie Millinder, Ida has developed character and intelligence in the absence of great beauty. Unlike Gussie, however, she is willing and able to function competently within the demands of marriage and parenthood. Because of her intelligence and understanding, her marriage to Derrick survives a number of shocks, including their daughter's marital problems and a late-blooming affair between Derrick and Geraldine.

Minor character that she may be, it is Ida's cousin Geraldine whose life and eventual suicide polarize the action of the novel. Although it is Ida who should resent Geraldine and not the other way around, Geraldine continues to envy Ida's relatively stable marriage and often genuine happiness. As Ida observes, "She remained to the end the little girl who had come down with a bright face and bright flowing hair to find in her Christmas stocking a switch and a book of sermons while mine was crammed with packages that I dared not open." Childless despite several marriages, resentful of Derrick's mechanical approach to lovemaking during their brief affair, Geraldine begins drinking heavily to dull the pain of bright promise unfulfilled.

Among the other characters portrayed in some detail are the Hartleys' two children, born shortly before World War I. Dorcas, who has inherited her father's temperament but little of his discipline, seeks a career of her own in publishing that is cut short by her marriage to a rebellious young editor who accepts the Hartley's largesse while professing to scorn its source. Eventually, Dorcas enters into a second marriage with one Mark Jesmond, an associate of Derrick who, during an earlier career as a lawyer, had handled the details of her divorce from the editor. Dorcas at last finds fulfillment of sorts in assisting Mark in efforts to "depose" her father from headship of his firm, much as Derrick himself had done years earlier to Ida's uncle Linnaeus Tremain. Dorcas's brother Hugo, meanwhile, is beginning to enter adulthood at the age of thirty-five, thanks mainly to his mother's direct intervention in the choice of his wife and career: Ida, it seems, has begun to assert herself as a matriarch.

Although marred by loose construction and a multiplicity of viewpoints, *Portrait in Brownstone* is notable for the keenness of its observation and the presentation of several memorable scenes. In any case, Auchincloss's readers did not have long to wait before the publication of *The Rector of Justin*, considered by several critics to be the finest of his novels.

THE RECTOR OF JUSTIN

Despite the fact that it shares with *Portrait in Brownstone* the potential pitfalls of loose construction and multiple viewpoints, *The Rector of Justin* is considerably more successful both as novel and as document. Auchincloss manages to broaden the appeal of the novel through his choice of subject matter, focusing upon the concept and execution of the American preparatory school. In analyzing the life and career of one Francis Prescott, founder of "Justin Martyr, an Episcopal boys' boarding school thirty miles west of Boston," Auchincloss provides through various viewpoint characters a thoughtful examination of a powerful American institution.

The main narrator of *The Rector of Justin* is Brian Aspinwall, whose arrival at Justin coincides with the outbreak of World War II in Europe. Brian has recently returned to the United States after several years of study at Oxford, where doctors have diagnosed a heart murmur that renders him unfit for service in the British Army. Unsure as yet of his vocation to become an Episcopal priest, Brian welcomes the prospect of teaching at Justin as an opportunity to test his suitability for the priesthood as well as for teaching, another possibility. Drawn gradually deeper into the affairs of the school and its founder-headmaster, Brian records his observations and experiences in a journal that forms the backbone of the book. Later, as the idea of recording the school's history begins to take form in his mind, he includes the testimony—both oral and written—of Dr. Prescott's family, friends, and former students. The result is thus more unified and better organized than *Portrait in Brownstone*, despite the old-maidish Brian's obvious limitations both as narrator and as observer.

By the time of Brian's arrival, Francis Prescott is nearly eighty years of age and long overdue for retirement; as both founder and headmaster, however,

he is such an institution that no one has given serious thought to replacing him. Brian vacillates between admiration and harsh criticism for the old man and his "muscular Christianity." To Brian's incredulity, the aging Prescott remains unfailingly democratic in pronouncements both public and private, seemingly unaware of the fact that he and his school have helped to perpetuate an American class system that Prescott personally deplores. This basic irony continues to animate the novel, providing as it does the subject matter for Brian's continuing research.

Early in the novel, Brian learns that Prescott, as a young man, took pains to examine at close range the British public-school system preparatory to founding a boarding school of his own; at no point does Prescott or anyone near him appear to have considered the difference between British aristocracy and American democracy. In fact, many of the questions raised in Brian's mind are left hanging, at least for readers, calling attention to the anomalous role of private education in America. Prescott, for his part, continues to deny the existence of an American ruling class even when faced with evidence to the contrary from his own alumni rolls.

Brian's continuing research gradually uncovers a wealth of conflicting evidence concerning Prescott's accomplishment. It is clear in any case that the realization of Prescott's lifelong dream has been achieved only at great personal cost. Brian finds the darker side of Justin's history in both a document penned by the long-dead son of the school's charter trustee, on whose behalf Prescott's efforts failed miserably, and in the spoken recollections of Prescott's youngest daughter, ironically named Cordelia. When Brian meets her, Cordelia is in her middle forties, an unreconstructed Greenwich Village bohemian with nymphomaniacal tendencies that, on one occasion, send Brian fleeing for his life. Prescott, it seems, did much to ruin not only her early first marriage but also a later liaison with a mortally wounded veteran of World War I. Cordelia ascribes much of her unhappiness to the fact that both men, as "old boys" of Justin Martyr, perceived a higher obligation to her father than to herself.

Ending with Prescott's death in retirement at age eighty-six, *The Rector of Justin* concludes much as it began, undecided as to the ultimate value of Prescott's achievement. Brian, however, has made a decision; now a fully ordained priest, he continues as a member of the faculty at Justin Martyr.

Together with *The House of Five Talents*, *The Rector of Justin* stands as one of Auchincloss's more impressive accomplishments; in few of his other novels are the interdependent questions of privilege and responsibility discussed with such thoughtfulness or candor. If the book has a major weakness it is that the characters, especially Prescott himself, are often stretched so flat as to strain the readers' belief; even then, it is possible to accept flatness in the case of a character who adamantly refuses to admit life's ambiguities.

THE EMBEZZLER

Published two years after *The Rector of Justin*, *The Embezzler* builds on the author's known strengths to provide a strong social satire in the tradition of O'Hara and Marquand, yet it transcends the accomplishments of both authors with its spareness and authority. Recalling in its essentials one of the subplots in *The House of Five Talents*, wherein Gussie Millinder reluctantly covers the defalcations of a distant relative threatened with exposure, *The Embezzler* credibly re-creates the heyday of high finance in America before, during, and after the crash of 1929.

The title character and initial narrator of *The Embezzler* is Guy Prime, writing in 1960 to set straight the record of his notoriety some twenty-five years earlier. His antagonist and eventual successor as narrator is Reginald (Rex) Geer, an erstwhile friend and associate since college days. The gathering tension between the two men, reflected in the conflict between their recollections of the same events, provides the novel with its major human interest. Throughout the novel, it is up to readers to weigh conflicting testimony and to form their own considered judgments.

Grandson of a former Episcopal bishop of New York, Guy Prime has grown up less rich than other of Auchincloss's main characters. His breeding and Harvard education, however, qualify him to function competently at the upper reaches of Manhattan's financial establishment. His classmate Rex Geer, like

Derrick Hartley the son of a rural New England parson, is perhaps even better suited than Guy to the "art" of making money. Rex is not, however, a social climber; to interpret him as such, as a number of the characters do, is to oversimplify a personality of multiple and often conflicting motivations. Guy, for his part, is hardly less complex, an essentially humane man whose interactions with his fellow mortals are inevitably compounded by a flair for the dramatic and a tendency toward hero-worship.

From the start, the friendship of Guy Prime and Rex Geer is complicated by their interlocking relationships with women whom neither man quite understands. The first of these is Guy's wealthy cousin Alix Prime, a doll-like heiress with whom Rex falls suddenly and disastrously in love, quite to his own consternation. Although ambitious and industrious, Rex is immune to the blandishments of inherited wealth and quite undone by the common opinion that he covets Alix for her money. The second woman is Guy's wife Angelica, reared mainly in Europe by her expatriate mother. An affair in middle life between Rex and Angelica permanently alters the lives of all three characters, serving at least in part as Guy's justification for his ventures into thievery. To Guy's way of thinking, the affair between his wife and his best friend suffices to suspend his belief in permanent values; the fact remains, however, that Guy has already begun to borrow large sums of money from Rex to cover high-risk stock market activities. With the increase of risk, Guy "simply" begins to pledge the value of securities that have been left in trust with his firm.

Later testimony supplied by Rex (and by Angelica herself in a short concluding chapter) casts serious doubt upon some of the assertions made by Guy in the brief memoir that has been discovered following his death in 1962. Even so, there are few hard-and-fast answers to the questions that remain in the readers' mind. Auchincloss does not make any serious attempt to justify the plainly unethical conduct of his principal character; what he seeks, rather, is a credible re-creation of a significant moment in recent American history, leading immediately to the extensive financial reforms implemented by the administration of Franklin D. Roosevelt. To a far greater degree than in his earlier novels, Auchincloss presents characters caught and portrayed in all their understandably human ambiguity. Despite its limited scope and relative brevity, *The Embezzler* may well be the tightest and finest of Auchincloss's novels to date.

THE HOUSE OF THE PROPHET

A prophet, according to Scripture, is not without honor save in his own house. In *The House of the Prophet*, Auchincloss, drawing from that proverb, has fashioned a novel based loosely on the life of the prominent political journalist Walter Lippmann. The novel's protagonist, Felix Leitner, a respected attorney, widely read pundit, and adviser to presidents, emerges diminished from the examination of his life undertaken by Roger Cutter, an erstwhile assistant and aspiring biographer. A variety of lesser narrative voices, including those of Leitner's two former wives, do their best to show the private truth behind the public image.

As in many of his later efforts, Auchincloss in *The House of the Prophet* returns with diminished success to a number of conventions and devices that have served him well in the past: The basic format of the novel, including the fussy, would-be "historian," owes much to *The Rector of Justin*, while Leitner, speaking occasionally in his own voice, recalls both Rex Geer and Guy Prime of *The Embezzler*. Although the action and characters are both credible and engrossing, *The House of the Prophet* gives the disturbing impression of a novel that one has already read, in which only the names and certain of the circumstances have been changed.

In its weakest moments, *The House of the Prophet* borders upon self-parody. Roger Cutter, the "main" narrator whose memories and intentions form the backbone of the novel, often comes across as Brian Aspinwall in caricature: Rendered impotent for life by a diabetic crisis sustained in early adulthood, Roger is (even more obviously than the old-maidish Brian) cast in the role of house eunuch, free to observe and record the master's movements while remaining immune to any possible entanglement with the numerous female characters. Only in its documentary interest and its plausible interpretations of

recent American history does *The House of the Prophet* bear serious comparison with the strongest of the author's earlier novels.

Viewed purely as a "political" novel, *The House of the Prophet* is a creditable example of the genre, showing that Auchincloss, when he chooses, can examine politics with the same shrewd powers of observation that he customarily applies to business and the law. As Leitner the pundit grows increasingly conservative with the onset of old age, his changing opinions are attributed less to the ossification of his mind than to the necessary tension between the "prophet" and his changing times. Toward the end of his life, for example, Leitner prepares a brilliant but outrageous column suggesting that America, through the forced resignation of Richard Nixon, "is engaging in one of the most ancient of tribal rituals: the burial of the fisher king." Roger Cutter, appalled by the likely consequences should such opinions be allowed to appear in print under Leitner's respected byline, acts quickly and effectively to have the column suppressed. Leitner's intelligence, however touched by senility, remains as keen and sensitive as ever; he has simply outlived his own time.

HONORABLE MEN

Political controversy provoked by the Vietnam War is an important issue in *Honorable Men*, but this novel remains primarily a treatment of personal and family crises. Spanning four decades (the 1930's through the 1960's), the book displays the troubled lives of Chip Benedict and his wife Alida. Sections of the novel focusing on Chip use third-person narration, but Alida's sections use first-person and thereby elicit more sympathy.

As a young woman, Alida Struthers dabbles in adolescent rebellion but eventually re-creates herself as the most famous debutante in America. By this means she escapes the genteel poverty into which her family has fallen and marries the rich and handsome Chip.

Chip is the only male descendant in a New England family who has become wealthy from manufacturing glass, a commodity as fragile as many relationships in the novel. Born with great privileges but also burdened by family expectations, Chip displays both self-righteous hypocrisy and guilt at his own inadequacies. He continually searches for Puritanical moral certainty as a buttress against his own less honorable impulses. As his name implies, he can scarcely define himself except as a chip off the family block. In a key episode that echoes the novel's title, Chip forces his best friend to resign from law school for presumably violating the honor code. Chip's action shows that he can adhere rigidly to the rules but has no larger faith that might give real meaning to the code of honor.

Chip's actions always appear good, but eventually his active support of the Vietnam War shatters his family. Alida leaves him, his daughter becomes an antiwar activist, and his son goes to Sweden to escape the draft. In an ending that some readers may find too facile, Chip finally receives assurance of his mother's unqualified love and apparently finds happiness by marrying his adoring secretary.

THE EDUCATION OF OSCAR FAIRFAX

In *The Education of Oscar Fairfax* Auchincloss revisits much of the territory explored in *Honorable Men* and other novels. Spanning seventy years, the narrative takes Oscar through a New England boys' school, on to Yale University, and eventually to a partnership in the Wall Street law firm founded by his grandfather. The chapters are loosely linked, but each episode provides an opportunity for Oscar's further enlightenment.

At St. Augustine's School, for example, he learns the possible dangers of close male relationships and saves a senior master from damaging accusations. At Yale he regretfully acknowledges the limits of his own literary talents but heartily condemns the ruthless tactics of a more brilliant classmate. As a wealthy and successful lawyer, Oscar repeatedly ponders the appropriate use of his power—in influencing the opinion of a Supreme Court justice regarding New Deal legislation, in introducing an idealistic young man from Maine into his own jaded social and professional realm, in meddling with his son's rigorous ethics. Early in the novel Oscar's future wife accuses him of caring more for art than for people. Throughout the book, however, Oscar is a keen observer of all those around him. In keeping his

eyes open and exercising subtle power, he also manages to change the lives of many for the better.

David B. Parsell, updated by Albert Wilhelm

OTHER MAJOR WORKS

SHORT FICTION: *The Injustice Collectors*, 1950; *The Romantic Egoists*, 1954; *Powers of Attorney*, 1963; *Tales of Manhattan*, 1967; *Second Chance*, 1970; *The Winthrop Covenant*, 1976; *Narcissa and Other Fables*, 1983; *The Book Class*, 1984; *Skinny Island: More Tales of Manhattan*, 1987; *Fellow Passengers: A Novel in Portraits*, 1989; *False Gods*, 1992 (fables); *The Collected Stories of Louis Auchincloss*, 1994; *The Atonement and Other Stories*, 1997; *The Anniversary and Other Stories*, 1999.

NONFICTION: *Reflections of a Jacobite*, 1961; *Pioneers and Caretakers: A Study of Nine American Women Novelists*, 1965; *Motiveless Malignity*, 1969; *Edith Wharton: A Woman in Her Time*, 1971; *Richelieu*, 1972; *A Writer's Capital*, 1974; *Reading Henry James*, 1975; *Life, Law and Letters: Essays and Sketches*, 1979; *Persons of Consequence: Queen Victoria and Her Circle*, 1979; *False Dawn: Women in the Age of the Sun King*, 1984; *The Vanderbilt Era: Profiles of a Gilded Age*, 1989; *J. P. Morgan: The Financier as Collector*, 1990; *Love Without Wings: Some Friendships in Literature and Politics*, 1991; *The Style's the Man: Reflections on Proust, Fitzgerald, Wharton, Vidal, and Others*, 1994; *The Man Behind the Book: Literary Profiles*, 1996; *La Gloire: The Roman Empire of Corneille and Racine*, 1996; *Woodrow Wilson*, 2000.

BIBLIOGRAPHY

Bryer, Jackson R. *Louis Auchincloss and His Critics.* Boston: G. K. Hall, 1977. A comprehensive, annotated bibliography of works by and about Auchincloss from 1931 to 1976. The first secondary sourcebook dealing exclusively with Auchincloss and his work, it remains authoritative in its record of his developing reputation as a writer.

Dahl, Christopher C. *Louis Auchincloss.* New York: Frederick Ungar, 1986. The first book-length study of Auchincloss's work, examining his novels and stories in chronological order and offering a balanced view of his accomplishments. Of special interest is the investigation of the boundaries between fiction and fact, which explores possible historical antecedents for characters and plot in *The Embezzler, The House of the Prophet*, and *The Rector of Justin*.

Milne, Gordon. *The Sense of Society*. Rutherford, N.J.: Fairleigh Dickinson University Press, 1977. This overview of the American novel of manners devotes a chapter to Auchincloss, stressing his characterizations and prose style.

Parsell, David B. *Louis Auchincloss*. Boston: Twayne, 1988. Begins with a summary of Auchincloss's views on the novels of J. P. Marquand and John O'Hara and proceeds to locate Auchincloss within the "novel of manners" tradition, with particular attention paid to recurrent themes. In his "thesis" chapter, Parsell attempts to reconstruct Auchincloss's fictional universe, showing its relation to recent American political and social history.

Piket, Vincent. *Louis Auchincloss: The Growth of a Novelist*. New York: St. Martin's Press, 1991. Piket incorporates criticism and interpretation of Auchincloss's novels into his study. Includes bibliographical references and index.

Tuttleton, James W. *The Novel of Manners in America*. Chapel Hill: University of North Carolina Press, 1972. The first academic critic to discuss Auchincloss, Tuttleton deals with his work at length in his penultimate chapter, focusing on *The House of Five Talents* and *Portrait in Brownstone*, concluding that, in the main, Auchincloss's other novels deal less with manners than with "character."

JANE AUSTEN

Born: Steventon, England; December 16, 1775
Died: Winchester, England; July 18, 1817

PRINCIPAL LONG FICTION
Sense and Sensibility, 1811
Pride and Prejudice, 1813
Mansfield Park, 1814
Emma, 1815
Northanger Abbey, 1818
Persuasion, 1818
Sanditon, 1871 (fragment)
The Watsons, 1871 (fragment)

OTHER LITERARY FORMS

In addition to writing novels, Jane Austen was the author of various short juvenile pieces, most of them literary burlesques mocking the conventions of the eighteenth century novel. Her other works are *Lady Susan*, a story told in letters and written c. 1805; *The Watsons*, a fragment of a novel written about the same time; and *Sanditon*, another fragmentary novel begun in 1817 (all appended by J. E. Austen-Leigh to his 1871 *Memoir of Jane Austen*). All these pieces appear in *Minor Works* (Vol. 6 of the *Oxford Illustrated Jane Austen*, 1954, R. W. Chapman, editor). Jane Austen's surviving letters have also been edited and published by Chapman.

ACHIEVEMENTS

Austen, who published her novels anonymously, was not a writer famous in her time, nor did she wish to be. From the first, though, her novels written in and largely for her own family circle, gained the notice and esteem of a wider audience. Among her early admirers were the Prince Regent and the foremost novelist of the day, Sir Walter Scott, who deprecated his own aptitude for the "big Bow-Wow" and praised her as possessing a "talent for describing the involvements and feelings and characters of ordinary life which is to me the most wonderful I ever met with." Since the days of Scott's somewhat prescient praise, her reputation has steadily grown. The critical consensus now places Jane Austen in what F. R. Leavis has termed the "Great Tradition" of the English novel. Her talent was the first to forge, from the eighteenth century novel of external incident and internal sensibility, an art form that fully and faithfully presented a vision of real life in a particular segment of the real world. Austen's particular excellences—the elegant economy of her prose, the strength and delicacy of her judgment and moral discrimination,

(Library of Congress)

On the rector's retirement in 1801, Austen moved with her parents and Cassandra to Bath. After the Reverend George Austen's death in 1804, the women continued to live for some time in that city. In 1806, the Austens moved to Southampton, where they shared a house with Captain Francis Austen, Jane's older brother, and his wife. In 1808, Edward Austen (who subsequently adopted the surname Knight from the relations whose two estates he inherited) provided his mother and sisters with a permanent residence, Chawton Cottage, in the Hampshire village of the same name. At this house, Austen was to revise her manuscripts that became *Sense and Sensibility, Pride and Prejudice*, and *Northanger Abbey* and to write *Mansfield Park, Emma*, and *Persuasion*. In 1817, it became evident that she was ill with a serious complaint whose symptoms seem to have been those of Addison's disease. To be near medical help, she and Cassandra moved to lodgings in Winchester in May, 1817. Austen died there less than two months later.

ANALYSIS

Jane Austen's novels—her "bits of ivory," as she modestly and perhaps half-playfully termed them—are unrivaled for their success in combining two sorts of excellence that all too seldom coexist. Meticulously conscious of her artistry (as, for example, is Henry James), Austen is also unremittingly attentive to the realities of ordinary human existence (as is, among others, Anthony Trollope). From the first, her works unite subtlety and common sense, good humor and acute moral judgment, charm and conciseness, deftly marshaled incident and carefully rounded character.

Austen's detractors have spoken of her as a "limited" novelist, one who, writing in an age of great men and important events, portrays small towns and petty concerns, who knows (or reveals) nothing of masculine occupations and ideas, and who reduces the range of feminine thought and deed to matrimonial scheming and social pleasantry. Though one merit of the first-rate novelist is the way his or her talent transmutes all it touches and thereby creates a distinctive and consistent world, it is true that the set-

the subtlety of her wit, the imaginative vividness of her character drawing—have been emulated but not surpassed by subsequent writers.

BIOGRAPHY

Jane Austen's life contained little in the way of outward event. Born in 1775, she was the seventh of eight children. Her father, the Reverend George Austen, was a scholarly clergyman, the rector of Steventon in rural Hampshire, England. Mrs. Austen shared her husband's intelligence and intellectual interests, and the home they provided for their children was a happy and comfortable one, replete with the pleasures of country life, genteel society, perpetual reading, and lively discussion of ideas serious and frivolous. Jane Austen, who never married, was devoted throughout her life to her brothers and their families, but her closest relationship was with her older sister Cassandra, who likewise remained unmarried and whom Austen relied upon as her chief critic, cherished as a confidante, and admired as the ideal of feminine virtue.

tings, characters, events, and ideas of Austen's novels are more than usually homogeneous. Her tales, like her own life, are set in country villages and at rural seats, from which the denizens venture forth to watering places or travel to London. True, her characters tend to be members of her own order, that prosperous and courteous segment of the middle class called the gentry. Unlike her novel-writing peers, Austen introduced few aristocrats into the pages of her novels, and the lower ranks, though glimpsed from time to time, are never brought forward. The happenings of her novels would not have been newsworthy in her day. She depicts society at leisure rather than on the march, and in portraying pleasures her literary preference is modest: Architectural improvement involves the remodeling of a parsonage rather than the construction of Carlton House Terrace and Regent's Park; a ball is a gathering of country neighbors dancing to a harpsichord, not a crush at Almack's or the Duchess of Richmond's glittering fête on the eve of Waterloo.

These limitations are the self-drawn boundaries of a strong mind rather than the innate restrictions of a weak or parochial one. Austen was in a position to know a broad band of social classes, from the local lord of the manor to the retired laborer subsisting on the charity of the parish. Some aspects of life that she did not herself experience she could learn about firsthand without leaving the family circle. Her brothers could tell her of the university, the navy in the age of Horatio Nelson, or the world of finance and fashion in Regency London. Her cousin (and later sister-in-law) Eliza, who had lost her first husband, the Comte de Feuillide, to the guillotine, could tell her of Paris during the last days of the old regime. In focusing on the manners and morals of rural middle-class English life, particularly on the ordering dance of matrimony that gives shape to society and situation to young ladies, Austen emphasizes rather than evades reality. The microcosm she depicts is convincing because she understands, though seldom explicitly assesses, its connections to the larger order. Her characters have clear social positions but are not just social types; the genius of such comic creations as Mrs. Bennet, Mr. Woodhouse, and Miss Bates is that each

is a sparkling refinement on a quality or set of qualities existing at all times and on all levels. A proof of Austen's power (no one questions her polish) is that she succeeds in making whole communities live in the reader's imagination with little recourse to the stock device of the mere novelist of manners: descriptive detail. If a sparely drawn likeness is to convince, every line must count. The artist must understand what is omitted as well as what is supplied.

The six novels that constitute the Austen canon did not evolve in a straightforward way. Austen was, memoirs relate, as mistrustful of her judgment as she was rapid in her composition. In the case of *Pride and Prejudice*, for example, readers can be grateful that when the Reverend George Austen's letter offering the book's first incarnation, *First Impressions* (1797), to a publisher met with a negative reply, she was content to put the book aside for more than a decade. *Sense and Sensibility* was likewise a revision of a much earlier work. If Austen was notably nonchalant about the process of getting her literary progeny into print, one publisher with whom she had dealings was yet more dilatory. In 1803, Austen had completed *Northanger Abbey* (then entitled *Susan*) and, through her brother Henry's agency, had sold it to Crosby and Sons for ten pounds. Having acquired the manuscript, the publisher did not think fit to make use of it, and in December, 1816, Henry Austen repurchased the novel. He made known the author's identity, so family tradition has it, only after closing the deal. For these various reasons the chronology of Austen's novels can be set in different ways. Here, they will be discussed in order of their dates of publication.

SENSE AND SENSIBILITY

Sense and Sensibility, Austen's first published novel, evolved from *Elinor and Marianne*, an epistolary work completed between 1795 and 1797. The novel is generally considered her weakest, largely because, as Walton Litz convincingly argues, it strives but fails to resolve "that struggle between inherited form and fresh experience which so often marks the transitional works of a great artist." The "inherited form" of which Litz speaks is the eighteenth century antithetical pattern suggested in the novel's title. According to this formula, opposing qualities of temperament or mind are presented in characters (generally female, often sisters) who despite their great differences are sincerely attached to one another.

In *Sense and Sensibility*, the antithetical characters are Elinor and Marianne Dashwood, the respective embodiments of cool, collected sense and prodigal, exquisite sensibility. In the company of their mother and younger sister, these lovely young ladies have, on the death of their father and the succession to his estate of their half-brother, retired in very modest circumstances to a small house in Devonshire. There the imprudent Marianne meets and melts for Willoughby, a fashionable gentleman as charming as he is unscrupulous. Having engaged the rash girl's affections, Willoughby proceeds to trifle with them by bolting for London. When chance once again brings the Dashwood sisters into Willoughby's circle, his manner toward Marianne is greatly altered. On hearing of his engagement to an heiress, the representative of sensibility swoons, weeps, and exhibits her grief to the utmost.

Meanwhile, the reasonable Elinor has been equally unlucky in love, though she bears her disappointment quite differently. Before the family's move to Devonshire, Elinor had met and come to cherish fond feelings for her sister-in-law's brother Edward Ferrars, a rather tame fellow (at least in comparison with Willoughby) who returns her regard—but with a measure of unease. It soon becomes known that Ferrars's reluctance to press his suit with Elinor stems from an early and injudicious secret engagement he had contracted with shrewd, base Lucy Steele. Elinor high-mindedly conceals her knowledge of the engagement and her feelings on the matter. Mrs. Ferrars, however, is a lady of less impressive self-control; she furiously disinherits her elder son in favor of his younger brother, whom Lucy then proceeds to ensnare. Thus Edward, free and provided with a small church living that will suffice to support a sensible sort of wife, can marry Elinor. Marianne—perhaps because she has finally exhausted her fancies and discovered her latent reason, perhaps because her creator is determined to punish the sensibility that throughout the novel has been so much more attrac-

tive than Elinor's prudence—is also provided with a husband: the rich Colonel Brandon, who has long loved her but whom, on account of his flannel waistcoats and his advanced age of five-and-thirty, she has heretofore reckoned beyond the pale.

The great flaw of *Sense and Sensibility* is that the polarities presented in the persons of Elinor and Marianne are too genuinely antithetical to be plausible or dynamic portraits of human beings. Elinor has strong feelings, securely managed though they may be, and Marianne has some rational powers to supplement her overactive imagination and emotions, but the young ladies do not often show themselves to be more than mere embodiments of sense and sensibility. In her second published novel, *Pride and Prejudice*, Austen makes defter use of two sisters whose values are the same but whose minds and hearts function differently. This book, a complete revision of *First Impressions*, the youthful effort that had, in 1797, been offered to and summarily rejected by the publisher Cadell, is, as numerous critics have observed, a paragon of "classic" literature in which the conventions and traditions of the eighteenth century novel come to full flowering yet are freshened and transformed by Austen's distinctive genius.

PRIDE AND PREJUDICE

The title *Pride and Prejudice*, with its balanced alliterative abstractions, might suggest a second experiment in schematic psychology, and indeed the book does show some resemblances to *Sense and Sensibility*. Here again, as has been suggested, the reader encounters a pair of sisters, the elder (Jane Bennet) serene, the younger (Elizabeth) volatile. Unlike the Dashwoods, however, these ladies both demonstrate deep feelings and perceptive minds. The qualities alluded to in the title refer not to a contrast between sisters but to double defects shared by Elizabeth and Fitzwilliam Darcy, a wealthy and well-born young man she meets when his easygoing friend Charles Bingley leases Netherfield, the estate next to the Bennets' Longbourn. If so rich and vital a comic masterpiece could be reduced to a formula, it might be appropriate to say that the main thread of *Pride and Prejudice* involves the twin correction of these faults. As Darcy learns to moderate his tradition-based view of society and to recognize individual excellence (such as Elizabeth's, Jane's, and their Aunt and Uncle Gardiner's) in ranks below his own, Elizabeth becomes less dogmatic in her judgments, and in particular more aware of the real merits of Darcy, whom she initially dismisses as a haughty, unfeeling aristocrat.

The growing accord of Elizabeth and Darcy is one of the most perfectly satisfying courtships in English literature. Their persons, minds, tastes, and even phrases convince the reader that they are two people truly made for each other; their union confers fitness on the world around them. Lionel Trilling has observed that, because of this principal match, *Pride and Prejudice* "permits us to conceive of morality as style." Elizabeth and Darcy's slow-growing love may be *Pride and Prejudice*'s ideal alliance, but it is far from being the only one, and a host of finely drawn characters surround the heroine and hero. In Jane Bennet and Charles Bingley, whose early mutual attraction is temporarily suspended by Darcy and the Bingley sisters (who deplore, not without some cause, the vulgarity of the amiable Jane's family), Austen presents a less sparkling but eminently pleasing and well-matched pair. William Collins, the half-pompous, half-obsequious, totally asinine cousin who, because of an entail, will inherit Longbourn and displace the Bennet females after Mr. Bennet's demise, aspires to marry Elizabeth, but, when rejected, gains the hand of her plain and practical friend Charlotte Lucas. Aware of her suitor's absurdities, Charlotte is nevertheless alive to the advantages of the situation he can offer. Her calculated decision to marry gives a graver ring to the irony of the novel's famous opening sentence: "It is a truth universally acknowledged, that a single man in possession of a good fortune, must be in want of a wife." The last of the matches made in *Pride and Prejudice* is yet more precariously based. A lively, charming, and amoral young officer, George Wickham, son of the former steward of Pemberley, Darcy's estate, and source of many of Elizabeth's prejudices against that scrupulous gentleman, first fascinates Elizabeth, then elopes with her youngest sister, mindless, frivolous Lydia. Only through Darcy's personal and financial

intervention is Wickham persuaded to marry the ill-bred girl, who never properly understands her disgrace—a folly she shares with her mother. Mrs. Bennet, a woman deficient in good humor and good sense, is—along with her cynical, capricious husband, the ponderous Collins, and the tyrannical Lady Catherine De Bourgh—one of the great comic creations of literature. Most of these characters could have seemed odious if sketched by another pen, but so brilliant is the sunny intelligence playing over the world of *Pride and Prejudice* that even fools are golden.

MANSFIELD PARK

Mansfield Park, begun in 1811 and finished in 1813, is the first of Austen's novels to be a complete product of her maturity. The longest, most didactic, least ironic of her books, it is the one critics generally have the most trouble reconciling with their prevailing ideas of the author. Although *Mansfield Park* was composed more or less at one stretch, its conception coincided with the final revisions of *Pride and Prejudice*. Indeed, the critics who offer the most satisfying studies of *Mansfield Park* tend to see it not as a piece of authorial bad faith or self-suppression, a temporary anomaly, but as what Walton Litz calls a "counter-truth" to its immediate predecessor.

Pleased with and proud of *Pride and Prejudice*, Austen nevertheless recorded her impression of its being "rather too light, and bright, and sparkling"— in need of shade. That darkness she found wanting is supplied in *Mansfield Park*, which offers, as Trilling observes in his well-known essay on the novel, the antithesis to *Pride and Prejudice*'s generous, humorous, spirited social vision. *Mansfield Park*, Trilling argues, condemns rather than forgives: "its praise is not for social freedom but for social stasis. It takes full notice of spiritedness, vivacity, celerity, and lightness, only to reject them as having nothing to do with virtue and happiness, as being, indeed, deterrents to the good life."

Most of the action of *Mansfield Park* is set within the little world comprising the estate of that name, a country place resembling in large measure Godmersham, Edward Austen Knight's estate in Kent; but for her heroine and some interludes in which she figures,

Austen dips into a milieu she has not previously frequented in her novels—the socially and financially precarious lower fringe of the middle class. Fanny Price, a frail, serious, modest girl, is one of nine children belonging to and inadequately supported by a feckless officer of marines and his lazy, self-centered wife. Mrs. Price's meddling sister, the widowed Mrs. Norris, arranges for Fanny to be reared in "poor relation" status at Mansfield Park, the seat of kindly but crusty Sir Thomas Bertram and his languid lady, the third of the sisters. At first awed by the splendor of her surroundings, the gruffness of the baronet, and the elegance, vigor, and high spirits of the young Bertrams—Tom, Edmund, Maria, and Julia—Fanny eventually wins a valued place in the household. During Sir Thomas's absence to visit his property in Antigua, evidence of Fanny's moral fineness, and the various degrees in which her cousins fall short of her excellence, is presented through a device that proves to be one of Austen's most brilliant triumphs of plotting. Visiting the rectory at Mansfield are the younger brother and sister of the rector's wife, Henry and Mary Crawford, witty, worldly, and wealthy. At Mary's proposal, amateur theatricals are introduced to Mansfield Park, and in the process of this diversion the moral pollution of London's Great World begins to corrupt the bracing country air.

Just how the staging of a play—even though it be *Lovers' Vows*, a sloppy piece of romantic bathos, adultery rendered sympathetic—can be morally reprehensible is a bit unclear for most twentieth century readers, especially those who realize that the Austens themselves reveled in theatricals at home. The problem as Austen here presents it lies in the possible consequences of role-playing: coming to feel the emotions and attitudes one presents on the stage or, worse yet, expressing rather than suppressing genuine but socially unacceptable feelings in the guise of mere acting. In the course of the theatricals, where Fanny, who will not act, is relegated to the role of spectator and moral chorus, Maria Bertram, engaged to a bovine local heir, vies with her sister in striving to fascinate Henry Crawford, who in turn is all too ready to charm them. Mary Crawford, though it is "her way" to find eldest sons most agreeable, has the

good taste to be attracted to Edmund, the second son, who plans to enter the Church. Mary's vivacity, as evidenced by the theatricals, easily wins his heart.

Time passes and poor Fanny, who since childhood has adored her cousin Edmund, unintentionally interests Henry Crawford. Determined to gain the affections of this rare young woman who is indifferent to his charms, Crawford ends by succumbing to hers. He proposes. Fanny's unworldly refusal provokes the anger of her uncle. Then, while Fanny, still in disgrace with the baronet, is away from Mansfield Park and visiting her family at Portsmouth, the debacle of which *Lovers' Vows* was a harbinger comes about. The *homme fatal* Henry, at a loss for a woman to make love to, trains his charms on his old flirt Maria, now Mrs. Rushworth. She runs away with him; her sister, not to be outdone in bad behavior, elopes with an unsatisfactory suitor. Mary Crawford's moral coarseness becomes evident in her casual dismissal of these catastrophes. Edmund, now a clergyman, finds solace, then love, with the cousin whose sterling character shines brightly for him now that Mary's glitter has tarnished. Fanny gains all she could hope for in at last attaining the heart and hand of her clerical kinsman.

Emma

Austen's next novel, *Emma*, might be thought of as harmonizing the two voices heard in *Pride and Prejudice* and *Mansfield Park*. For this book, Austen claimed to be creating "a heroine whom no one but myself will much like," an "imaginist" whose circumstances and qualities of mind make her the self-crowned queen of her country neighborhood. Austen was not entirely serious or accurate: Emma certainly has her partisans. Even those readers who do not like her tend to find her fascinating, for she is a spirited, imaginative, healthy young woman who, like Mary Crawford, has potential to do considerable harm to the fabric of society but on whom, like Elizabeth Bennet, her creator generously bestows life's greatest blessing: union with a man whose virtues, talents, and assets are the best complement for her own.

Emma's eventual marriage to Mr. Knightley of Donwell Abbey is the ultimate expression of one of

Austen's key assumptions, that marriage is a young woman's supreme act of self-definition. Unlike any other Austen heroine, Emma has no pressing need to marry. As the opening sentence of the book implies, Emma's situation makes her acceptance or rejection of a suitor an act of unencumbered will: "Emma Woodhouse, handsome, clever, and rich, with a comfortable home and happy disposition, seemed to unite some of the best blessings of existence; and had lived nearly twenty-one years in the world with very little to distress or vex her."

Free though circumstance allows her to be, Emma has not been encouraged by her lot in life to acquire the discipline and self-knowledge that, augmenting her innate intelligence and taste, would help her to choose wisely. Brought up by a doting valetudinarian of a father and a perceptive but permissive governess, Emma has been encouraged to think too highly of herself. Far from vain about her beauty, Emma has—as Mr. Knightley, the only person who ventures to criticize her, observes—complete yet unfounded faith in her ability to judge people's characters and arrange their lives. The course of *Emma* is Miss Woodhouse's education in judgment, a process achieved through repeated mistakes and humiliations.

As the novel opens, the young mistress of Hartfield is at loose ends. Her beloved governess has just married Mr. Weston, of the neighboring property, Randalls. To fill the newly made gap in her life, Emma takes notice of Harriet Smith, a pretty, dim "natural daughter of somebody," and a parlor-boarder at the local school. Determined to settle her protégée into the sort of life she deems suitable, Emma detaches Harriet from Robert Martin, a young farmer who has proposed to her, and embarks upon a campaign to conquer for Harriet the heart of Mr. Elton, Highbury's unmarried clergyman. Elton's attentiveness and excessive flattery convince Emma of her plan's success but at the same time show the reader what Emma is aghast to learn at the end of book 1: that Elton scorns the nobody and has designs upon the heiress herself.

With the arrival of three new personages in Highbury, book 2 widens Emma's opportunities for misconception. The first newcomer is Jane Fairfax, an elegant and accomplished connection of the Bates family and a girl whose prospective fate, the "governess trade," shows how unreliable the situations of well-bred young ladies without fortunes or husbands tend to be. Next to arrive is the suave Mr. Frank Churchill, Mr. Weston's grown son, who has been adopted by wealthy relations of his mother and who has been long remiss in paying a visit to Highbury. Finally, Mr. Elton brings home a bride, the former Augusta Hawkins of Bristol, a pretentious and impertinent creature possessed of an independent fortune, a well-married sister, and a boundless fund of self-congratulation. Emma mistakenly flatters herself that the dashing Frank Churchill is in love with her, and then settles on him as a husband for Harriet; she suspects the reserved Miss Fairfax, whose cultivation she rightly perceives as a reproach to her own untrained talents, of a clandestine relationship with a married man. She despises Mrs. Elton, as would any person of sense, but fails to see that the vulgar woman's offensiveness is an exaggerated version of her own officiousness and snobbery.

Thus, the potential consequences of Emma's misplaced faith in her judgment intensify, and the evidence of her fallibility mounts. Thoroughly embarrassed to learn that Frank Churchill, to whom she has retailed all her hypotheses regarding Jane Fairfax, has long been secretly engaged to that woman, Emma suffers the deathblow to her smug self-esteem when Harriet announces that the gentleman whose feelings she hopes to have aroused is not, as Emma supposes, Churchill but the squire of Donwell. Emma's moment of truth is devastating and complete, its importance marked by one of Jane Austen's rare uses of figurative language: "It darted through her, with the speed of an arrow, that Mr. Knightley must marry no one but herself!" Perhaps the greatest evidence of Emma's being a favorite of fortune is that Mr. Knightley feels the same as she does on this matter. Chastened by her series of bad judgments, paired with a gentleman who for years has loved and respected her enough to correct her and whom she can love and respect in turn, Emma participates in the minuet of marriage with which Austen concludes the book, the other couples so united being Miss Fairfax and Mr. Churchill and Harriet Smith (ductile enough to form four attachments in a year) and Robert Martin (stalwart enough to persist in his original feeling).

Emma Woodhouse's gradual education, which parallels the reader's growing awareness of what a menace to the social order her circumstances, abilities, and weaknesses combine to make her, is one of Austen's finest pieces of plotting. The depiction of character is likewise superb. Among a gallery of memorable and distinctive characters are Mr. Woodhouse; Miss Bates, the stream-of-consciousness talker who inadvertently provokes Emma's famous rudeness on Box Hill; and the wonderfully detestable Mrs. Elton, with her self-contradictions and her fractured Italian, her endless allusions to Selina, Mr. Suckling, Maple Grove, and the *barouche landau*. Life at Hartfield, Donwell, and Highbury is portrayed with complexity and economy. Every word, expression, opinion, and activity—whether sketching a portrait, selecting a dancing partner, or planning a strawberry-picking party—becomes a gesture of self-revelation. *Emma* demonstrates how, in Austen's hands, the novel of manners can become a statement of moral philosophy.

NORTHANGER ABBEY

Northanger Abbey was published in a four-volume unit with *Persuasion* in 1818, after Austen's death, but the manuscript had been completed much earlier, in 1803. Austen wrote a preface for *Northanger Abbey* but did not do the sort of revising that had transformed *Elinor and Marianne* and *First Impressions* into *Sense and Sensibility* and *Pride and Prejudice*. The published form of *Northanger Abbey* can therefore be seen as the earliest of the six novels. It is also, with the possible exception of *Sense and Sensibility*, the most "literary." *Northanger Abbey*, like some of Austen's juvenile burlesques, confronts the conventions of the gothic novel or tale of terror. The incidents of her novel have been shown to parallel, with ironic difference, the principal lines of gothic romance, particularly as practiced by Ann Radcliffe, whose most famous works, *The Romance of the Forest* (1791) and *The Mysteries of Udolpho* (1794), had appeared several years before Jane Austen had begun work on her burlesque.

Like *Emma, Northanger Abbey* is centrally concerned with tracing the growth of a young woman's mind and the cultivation of her judgment. In this less sophisticated work, however, the author accomplishes her goal through a rather schematic contrast. As an enthusiastic reader of tales of terror, Catherine Morland has gothic expectations of life despite a background most unsuitable for a heroine. Like the gothic heroines she admires, Catherine commences adventuring early in the novel. She is not, however, shipped to Venice or Dalmatia, but taken to Bath for a six-week stay. Her hosts are serenely amiable English folk, her pastimes the ordinary round of spa pleasures; the young man whose acquaintance she makes, Henry Tilney, is a witty clergyman rather than a misanthropic monk or dissolute rake. Toward this delightful, if far from gothic, young man, Catherine's feelings are early inclined. In turn, he, his sister, and even his father, the haughty, imperious General Tilney, are favorably disposed toward her. With the highest expectations, Catherine sets out to accompany them to their seat, the Abbey of the novel's title (which, like that of *Persuasion*, was selected not by the author but by Henry Austen, who handled the posthumous publication).

At Northanger, Catherine's education in the difference between literature and life continues. Despite its monastic origins, the Abbey proves a comfortable and well-maintained dwelling. When Catherine, like one of Radcliffe's protagonists, finds a mysterious document in a chest and spends a restless night wondering what lurid tale it might chronicle, she is again disappointed: "If the evidence of her sight might be trusted she held a washing-bill in her hand." Although Catherine's experience does not confirm the truth of Radcliffe's sensational horrors, it does not prove the world a straightforward, safe, cozy place. Catherine has already seen something of falseness and selfish vulgarity in the persons of Isabella Thorpe and her brother John, acquaintances formed at Bath. At Northanger, she learns that, though the General may not be the wife-murderer she has fancied him, he is quite as cruel as she could imagine. On learning that Catherine is not the great heiress he has mistakenly supposed her to be, the furious general packs her off in disgrace and discomfort in a public coach.

With this proof that the world of fact can prove as treacherous as that of fiction, Catherine returns sadder and wiser to the bosom of her family. She has not long to droop, though, for Henry Tilney, on hearing of his father's bad behavior, hurries after her and makes Catherine the proposal which he has long felt inclined to offer and which his father has until recently promoted. The approval of Catherine's parents is immediate, and the General is not overlong in coming to countenance the match. "To begin perfect happiness at the respective ages of twenty-six and eighteen is to do pretty well," observes the facetious narrator, striking a literary pose even in the novel's last sentence, "and . . . I leave it to be settled by whomsoever it may concern, whether the tendency of this work be altogether to recommend parental tyranny, or reward filial disobedience."

PERSUASION

Persuasion, many readers believe, signals Austen's literary move out of the eighteenth century and into the nineteenth. This novel, quite different from those that preceded it, draws not upon the tradition of the novelists of the 1790's but on that of the lionized poets of the new century's second decade, Sir Walter Scott and Lord Byron. For the first time, Austen clearly seems the child of her time, susceptible to the charms of natural rather than improved landscapes, fields, and sea cliffs rather than gardens and shrubberies. The wistful, melancholy beauty of autumn that pervades the book is likewise romantic. The gaiety, vitality, and sparkling wit of *Pride and Prejudice* and *Emma* are muted. The stable social order represented by the great estate in *Mansfield Park* has become fluid in *Persuasion:* here the principal country house, Kellynch Hall, must be let because the indigenous family cannot afford to inhabit it.

Most important, *Persuasion*'s heroine is unique in Jane Austen's gallery. Anne Elliott, uprooted from her ancestral home, spiritually isolated from her selfish and small-minded father and sisters, separated from the man she loves by a long-standing estrangement, is every bit as "alienated" as such later nineteenth century heroines as Esther Summerson, Jane

Eyre, and Becky Sharp. Anne's story is very much the product of Austen's middle age. At twenty-seven, she is the only Austen heroine to be past her first youth. Furthermore, she is in no need of education. Her one great mistake—overriding the impulse of her heart and yielding to the persuasion of her friend Lady Russell in rejecting the proposal of Frederick Wentworth, a sanguine young naval officer with his fortune still to make and his character to prove—is some eight years in the past, and she clearly recognizes it for the error it was.

Persuasion is the story of how Anne and Frederick (now the eminent Captain) Wentworth rekindle the embers of their love. Chance throws them together when the vain, foolish Sir Walter Elliott, obliged to economize or rent his estate, resolves to move his household to Bath, where he can cut a fine figure at less cost, and leases Kellynch to Admiral and Mrs. Croft, who turn out to be the brother-in-law and sister of Captain Wentworth. Initially cool to his former love—or rather, able to see the diminution of her beauty because he is unable to forgive her rejection—the Captain flirts with the Musgrove girls; they are sisters to the husband of Anne's younger sister Mary and blooming belles with the youth and vigor Anne lacks. The old appreciation of Anne's merits, her clear insight, kindness, highmindedness, and modesty, soon reasserts itself, but not before fate and the Captain's impetuosity have all but forced another engagement upon him. Being "jumped down" from the Cobb at Lyme Regis, Louisa Musgrove misses his arms and falls unconscious on the pavement. Obliged by honor to declare himself hers if she should wish it, Wentworth is finally spared this self-sacrifice when the susceptible young lady and the sensitive Captain Benwick fall in love. Having discovered the intensity of his devotion to Anne by being on the point of having to abjure it, Wentworth hurries to Bath, there to declare his attachment in what is surely the most powerful engagement scene in the Austen canon.

Though the story of *Persuasion* belongs to Anne Elliott and Frederick Wentworth, Austen's skill at evoking characters is everywhere noticeable. As Elizabeth Jenkins observes, all of the supporting characters present different facets of the love theme.

The heartless marital calculations of Mr. Elliott, Elizabeth Elliott, and Mrs. Clay, the domestic comforts of the senior Musgroves and the Crofts, and the half-fractious, half-amiable ménage of Charles and Mary Musgrove all permit the reader more clearly to discern how rare and true is the love Anne Elliott and her captain have come so close to losing. The mature, deeply grateful commitment they are able to make to each other is, if not the most charming, surely the most profound in the Austen world.

Peter W. Graham

OTHER MAJOR WORKS

SHORT FICTION: *Minor Works*, 1954 (volume 6 of the *Oxford Illustrated Jane Austen*; R. W. Chapman, editor).

NONFICTION: *Jane Austen's Letters to Her Sister Cassandra and Others*, 1952 (R. W. Chapman, editor).

BIBLIOGRAPHY

Bush, Douglas. *Jane Austen*. New York: Macmillan, 1975. Addressed to students and general readers, this survey by an eminent scholar provides a straightforward introduction to Austen's work. Overviews of Austen's England, her life, and her early writings set the stage for chapter-length discussions of her six novels; two unfinished works, *The Watsons* and *Sanditon*, also receive a chapter each.

Copeland, Edward, and Juliet McMaster, eds. *The Cambridge Companion to Jane Austen*. Cambridge, England: Cambridge University Press, 1997. This collection of thirteen new essays on Austen is divided between those concerning her own world and those that address modern critical discourse, such as Claudia L. Johnson's "Austen Cults and Cultures." While some essays focus on Austen's novels, others deal with broad issues such as class consciousness, religion, and domestic economy. This excellent overview includes a chronology and concludes with an assessment of late twentieth century developments in Austen scholarship.

Grey, J. David, ed. *The Jane Austen Companion*. New York: Macmillan, 1986. An encyclopedic guide to Austen's life and works. Among the topics covered are "Characterization in Jane Austen," "Chronology of Composition," and "Editions and Publishing History." There are brief essays on "Dancing, Balls, and Assemblies," "Dress and Fashion," "Post/Mail," and many other aspects of everyday life in Austen's time. Each essay includes a bibliography. An indispensable resource.

Hardy, Barbara. *A Reading of Jane Austen*. New York: New York University Press, 1976. A thematic approach to Austen's fiction (Hardy does not discuss Austen's juvenilia or her fragmentary works). In the first chapter, "The Flexible Medium," Hardy argues that while Austen was not, on the surface, a radical innovator, she nevertheless transformed the genre in which she worked: "Indeed she may be said to have created the modern novel." Two later chapters provide a valuable study of Austen's handling of narrative point of view and of "telling and listening" in her novels. Lacks an index.

Lane, Maggie. *Jane Austen's England*. New York: St. Martin's Press, 1986. This fascinating book is full of illustrations which give Austen's readers a look at the world of her novels. Arranged chronologically, taking the reader to the places Austen would have gone, usually through contemporary paintings. The text is useful; the first chapter, "The England of Jane Austen's Time," gives a good basic summary of social conditions around the beginning of the nineteenth century. Includes references to the novels; for example, Lane quotes the Box Hill episode from *Emma* and provides a painting of Box Hill. Also includes a map, a short bibliography, and an index.

Mooneyham, Laura G. *Romance, Language, and Education in Jane Austen's Novels*. New York: St. Martin's Press, 1986. Covers all six of Austen's complete novels, theorizing that a relationship exists among language, education, and romance. Asserts that the romance between heroine and hero is in itself educational for the heroine because romance offers the opportunity for open communication. This approach is provocative and useful, especially because it emphasizes Austen's own preoccupations. Each chapter discusses a separate novel, which may be useful for the study of one of Austen's works.

Myer, Valerie Grosvenor. *Jane Austen: Obstinate Heart*. New York: Arcade Publishing, 1997. This biography of Jane Austen emphasizes her self-consciousness, born of an inferior social position and constant money worries. Still, she would refuse the proposal of a wealthy suitor because, as Myer states, Austen's "obstinate heart" would only allow her to marry for love.

Nokes, David. *Jane Austen: A Life*. New York: Farrar, Straus and Giroux, 1997. Nokes attempts to uncover a more authentic Jane Austen than the saintly, censored image that her family presented to the public after her early death. His method is novelistic, in that he attempts, as much as possible, to present Austen's life from her own perspective.

Sulloway, Alison. *Jane Austen and the Province of Womanhood*. Philadelphia: University of Pennsylvania Press, 1989. Attempts to place Austen into a framework of "women-centered" authors from the tract-writers Mary Astell, Mary Wollstonecraft Godwin, and Catharine Macaulay, to novelists Fanny Burney, Maria Edgeworth, and Charlotte Smith. Counters early views of Austen as a conservative woman upholding the status quo in her novels. Suggests that Austen was a moderate feminist who sought reforms for women rather than outright revolution. Instead of reading Austen's novels separately, Sulloway focuses on themes which she calls "provinces": the ballroom (dancing and marriage), the drawing room (debate), the garden (reconciliation). A valuable book which is thought-provoking and not overly theoretical.

Tomalin, Claire. *Jane Austen: A Life*. New York: Knopf, 1998. This compelling account of Austen's life is exceedingly well written and, like Nokes's biography, attempts to tell the story from the subject's own perspective. Proceeding in chronological order, the book concludes with a postscript on the fates of Austen's family members and two interesting appendixes: a note of Austen's final illness and an excerpt from the diary of Austen's niece, Fanny.

PAUL AUSTER

Born: Newark, New Jersey; February 3, 1947

PRINCIPAL LONG FICTION

City of Glass, 1985
Ghosts, 1986
The Locked Room, 1986
In the Country of Last Things, 1987
Moon Palace, 1989
The Music of Chance, 1990
Leviathan, 1992
Mr. Vertigo, 1994
The New York Trilogy, 1994 (includes *City of Glass*, *Ghosts*, and *The Locked Room*)
Timbuktu, 1999

OTHER LITERARY FORMS

As a young man, Paul Auster distinguished himself in the literary forms of translation and poetry. His well-received translations of French poets Stéphane Mallarmé, Jacques Dupin, and André du Bouchet led to his editing a bilingual anthology titled *The Random House Book of Twentieth-Century French Poetry*, published in 1982. Beginning in 1974, his own poetry was published in reviews and by small presses. The poetry collections *Disappearances: Selected Poems* (1988) and *Ground Work: Selected Poems and Essays, 1970-1979* (1990) were published after Auster made a name for himself in fiction. The nonfiction prose collection *The Art of Hunger and Other Essays* and the memoir *The Invention of Solitude* were originally published in 1982, and a later memoir, *Hand to Mouth: A Chronicle of Early Failure*, appeared in 1997, after the publication of eight novels. Scriptwriting is another genre for which Auster is noted. Auster wrote the screenplays for the films *Smoke* (1995), *Blue in the Face* (1995), which he also codirected, and *Lulu on the Bridge* (1998).

ACHIEVEMENTS

City of Glass was nominated for an Edgar Award for best mystery novel in 1986, and *The Locked*

Room was nominated for a *Boston Globe* Literary Press Award for fiction in 1990. Auster received the Chevalier de l'Ordre des Arts et des Lettres in 1993, and he won the French Prix Medicis Étranger for foreign literature that year, for *Leviathan*.

BIOGRAPHY

Paul Auster grew up in the suburbs of Newark, New Jersey. He benefited early from the influence of an uncle who was a skilled translator and who encouraged his nephew's developing interest in writing and literature. In the summer between high school and college, Auster traveled to Europe. He returned to the United States to attend Columbia University. In 1966, he began a relationship with Lydia Davis, who attended Barnard College and also became a writer of considerable distinction. In 1967, Auster went to Paris for Columbia's Junior Year Abroad. He supported himself during his college years with a variety of freelance jobs, including translation and interpretation. In June, 1969, Auster graduated from Columbia with a B.A. in English and comparative literature, and he received his M.A. in the literature of the Renaissance the following year. Auster returned to Paris in 1971 and lived in France until 1974.

Back in New York in late 1974, Auster and Davis were married. They worked on translations, and Auster began to publish poetry, reviews, and essays. In 1977, their son Daniel was born. By 1979, his marriage had ended. He continued to work on poetry and translation, but by 1980 he had begun work on *The Invention of Solitude* and other work in prose.

In 1981, Auster met and married Siri Hustvedt. A fertile time in his writing career began, and during the 1980's he published *The Random House Book of Twentieth-Century French Poetry*, *The Art of Hunger*, and

more translations. The three novels of *The New York Trilogy*, as well as *In the Country of Lost Things* and *Moon Palace*, received good reviews. In addition, he took a position as a lecturer at Princeton University, and his daughter Sophie was born.

Auster's next novel, *The Music of Chance*, published in 1990, attracted the attention of the motion-picture industry. The film version was released in 1993. At the same time, Auster's story "Auggie Wren's Christmas Story" appeared in *The New York Times*, and director Wayne Wang became interested in turning the story into a film. Auster's script became the film *Smoke*, which was followed shortly by the companion piece *Blue in the Face*. By the time the two films were released in 1995, Auster had published two more novels, *Leviathan* and *Mr. Vertigo*. In 1997, the memoir *Hand to Mouth* was released. Auster was a member of the jury for the 1997 Cannes Film Festival; in 1998, the film *Lulu on the Bridge* appeared.

ANALYSIS

Paul Auster is best known as a postmodernist writer. Postmodernism is an elusive academic term,

(AP Photo/Mark Lennihan)

applied to unconventional twentieth century fiction that in style and theme investigates the methods of fiction. Beneath a deceptively simple fictional form—the detective novel, science fiction, the picaresque story—lies intellectually stimulating, thematically complex interplay between reader and author as well as protagonist and writer. Auster's fiction is accessible on the surface level, yet the subtext is worthy of the term "experimental." The appeal of postmodern fiction is intellectual; readers are forced to think about the writer's allusions, use of unexpected devices, and breaking of the rules of conventional fiction.

Auster's work reflects the spiritual and artistic atmosphere of the postmodern era. The three short novels collected as *The New York Trilogy* (*City of Glass*, *Ghosts*, and *The Locked Room*) are Auster's most often discussed. The use of the detective-story form to introduce themes of isolation and the crisis of the individual is taken as a prime example of postmodern literature, writing which may use traditional forms in ironic or displaced ways. Characteristic of postmodernist stories, the protagonists of Auster novels do not reach a solution. Many of his heroes disappear, die a mysterious death, or lose all of their personal possessions.

Throughout his long fiction, Auster is critically admired for his diversity of form, his intelligence, the agility of his prose, and the complexity of his structure and themes. His writing appeals to a mass audience as well as to literary scholars; his fiction has a cult following among students. He is known for the variety of genres that he works in: poetry, memoirs, essays, and screenplays. The later novels are less discussed because it became increasingly difficult to label his works. Much of Auster's work is characterized by its examination of language. Even his detectives focus on the fitting word, the description, the act of writing down. There is an interplay of language among Auster's books, as names, places, and patterns reappear. Finally, odd coincidences pervade the novels.

THE NEW YORK TRILOGY

Auster's most discussed work of fiction is *The New York Trilogy*, composed of the three short novels

City of Glass, *Ghosts*, and *The Locked Room*. The three novels share a common style, theme, and New York setting. Auster intentionally blurs the distinction between reality and text, placing himself as a character in the first novel. This postmodern device raises questions of identity that resonate throughout the series. Auster takes the convention of mistaken identity and develops it into a metaphor for contemporary urban life.

The first novel, *City of Glass*, opens as a standard detective novel. Quinn, a detective novelist, receives a telephone call intended for a detective named Paul Auster. Quinn decides to take on Auster's identity and accept the case. The job is to tail a madman named Stillman who has been recently released from a mental institution. Once a promising linguist, Stillman had been committed for isolating his son in a locked room for nine years to try to re-create the primitive language of Adam and Eve. Now that Stillman has been released, the son's life is in danger.

The novel subtly shifts from a standard detective story to an existential quest for identity. It moves into the realm of serious literature as it explores themes of the degeneration of language, the shifting of identity, and the struggle to remain sane in the anonymity of the metropolis. Each detail is significant. Coincidences abound, particularly coincidences involving names. Quinn the watcher becomes as seedy and degenerate as Stillman the quarry. True to its postmodern identity, and typical of Auster's work, the novel is not actually resolved. Questions remain unanswered; characters simply disappear.

Ghosts, the second novel of the trilogy, explores many of the same questions of identity and blurred distinctions between watcher and prey, detective and client, but on a more abstract plane. A client named White hires a detective named Blue to follow a man named Black. The three characters merge into one as Blue passes years watching Black writing a book in a room across the street, while Blue records his observations and mails them weekly to White.

Clearly the novel is meant to be a metaphor, and after carefully paying attention to details and clues, as is necessary in a mystery story, the reader is left with the question, What does it all mean? As in the first novel, the detective hired to watch merges into the watched. However, in this novel neither the reader nor the protagonist knows why the detective is watching his subject.

The final volume in the trilogy, *The Locked Room*, is the least abstract but the richest and most accessible of the three. The narrator is summoned by the wife of his old friend Fanshawe, who has disappeared and is presumed dead. Fanshawe, a brilliant writer, has left behind a closet full of manuscripts and instructions for his friend to have them published. The narrator moves into Fanshawe's life, marrying his wife and publishing his work. He almost succumbs to believing the rumors that he is actually Fanshawe, or at least the creator of the works, until he receives a communication from the real Fanshawe. The plot becomes suspenseful and dangerous, as the narrator follows Fanshawe to the brink of annihilation. He so identifies with Fanshawe that he nearly joins him in his dark night of the soul. Lines between truth and fiction are dramatically blurred in a deeply satisfying conclusion to the trilogy.

IN THE COUNTRY OF LAST THINGS

In the Country of Last Things also uses an established genre, this time science fiction, for Auster's postmodernist ends. This novel shares stylistic and thematic concerns with *The New York Trilogy*. The heroine, Anna Blume, travels to a large metropolis on another continent in search of her missing brother. She discovers a city in chaos, a hellish apocalypse, a futuristic nightmare of doom.

At first the reader believes this is a dystopian novel of the future in the tradition of Aldous Huxley's *Brave New World* (1932) or George Orwell's *Nineteen Eighty-Four* (1949). Yet soon the reader realizes that this world represents the ethical, spiritual, and cultural chaos of the urban jungle of the present. Auster concludes that, without art and creativity, life is bleak.

MOON PALACE

The novels following *In the Country of Last Things* cannot be so easily categorized by genre. Looser in structure, *Moon Palace* is sometimes referred to as a picaresque novel, as it follows its young hero's adventures on a journey in search of his lost

father. This novel employs some of the familiar motifs of the *Bildungsroman*: the struggling orphan, the lost father, the search for self, the journey as initiation into manhood. Yet the writer-narrator seems unconcerned with creating a realistic or believable plot; in fact, he himself does not seem to believe what he has written. The writer violates realistic conventions intentionally to investigate other functions of the novel. Plot and character are secondary to structure, the relationship between reader and writer, and the act of reading.

THE MUSIC OF CHANCE

The Music of Chance is another accessible story that can be enjoyed on many levels. It begins as protagonist Jim Nashe takes to the road in search of himself. When his money runs out, he joins a young gambler, Pozzi, in a poker game against two eccentric lottery winners. When Jim and Pozzi fall into debt, they are forced to build a stone wall for the eccentrics as payment.

Critics have faulted the novel for weakness of plot and character, yet once again these "faults" seem to be intentional. The novel gives Auster the opportunity to explore some of his favorite themes: the roles of coincidence and random chance, the consequences of solitude, the limitations of language and free will. Character and plot are deliberately unconvincing, calling attention to the author's other literary aims. Beneath a conventional exterior, Auster's fiction is disturbing, intellectually challenging, and structurally experimental.

LEVIATHAN

Leviathan, published in 1992, is a complex novel in the looser style Auster had adopted with *Moon Palace* three years earlier. The themes of the book are secrets, multiple selves, and connections. The novel's form is unconventional; the climax of the story, the death by explosion of the New York writer Benjamin Sachs, is unveiled on the first page. Another writer, Peter Aaron, becomes obsessed with writing the story of his friend's life, not unlike the narrator's obsession with Fanshawe in *The Locked Room*. Aaron uncovers a world of secrets, multiple and exchanged identities, and previously unknown connections between characters.

MR. VERTIGO

Auster's eighth novel, *Mr. Vertigo*, tells the story of Walt, an orphaned street urchin who is taught to levitate by a mystical showman. On the verge of fame and fortune, Walt loses his gift and travels around America, ending up in Chicago in the world of gangsters. Walt writes the story of his childhood and youth from the reflective point of view of an old man. *Mr. Vertigo* can be read as an American adventure story of the glory, frustration, and loss of the American Dream. Some critics consider this the weakest of Auster's novels, flawed by Walt's dialogue of bad puns and smart answers. Yet others find it delightfully entertaining and at times lyrical. Certainly Walt's dialogue expresses Auster's preoccupation with words and language, and *Mr. Vertigo* is another exploration of one of Auster's favorite themes, the crisis of the individual.

Susan Butterworth

OTHER MAJOR WORKS

SCREENPLAYS: *"Smoke" and "Blue in the Face": Two Screenplays*, 1995; *Lulu on the Bridge*, 1998.

POETRY: *Disappearances: Selected Poems*, 1988; *Ground Work: Selected Poems and Essays, 1970-1979*, 1990.

NONFICTION: *The Art of Hunger and Other Essays*, 1982 (also as *The Art of Hunger: Essays, Prefaces, Interviews*, 1991); *The Invention of Solitude*, 1982, 1988; *Hand to Mouth: A Chronicle of Early Failure*, 1997.

TRANSLATIONS: *The Notebooks of Joseph Joubert: A Selection*, 1983; *A Tomb for Anatole* (of Stéphane Mallarmé's poetry), 1983.

EDITED TEXT: *The Random House Book of Twentieth-Century French Poetry*, 1982.

BIBLIOGRAPHY

Barone, Dennis, ed. *Beyond the Red Notebook: Essays on Paul Auster*. Philadelphia: University of Pennsylvania Press, 1995. This collection of critical essays on Auster's poetry and prose is a major source on Auster. It collects several essays previously published in periodicals and includes a detailed bibliography of works by and about Paul Auster.

_____, ed. "Paul Auster/Danilo Kis Issue." *The Review of Contemporary Fiction* 14, no. 1 (Spring, 1994): 7-96. Includes essays by Dennis Barone, Charles Baxter, Sven Birkerts, Paul Bray, Mary Ann Caws, Robert Creeley, Alan Gurganus, Gerald Howard, Mark Irwin, Barry Lewis, Mark Osteen, Mark Rudman, Chris Tysh, Katherine Washburn, Steven Weisenburger, and Curtis White.

Birkerts, Sven. *American Energies: Essays on Fiction*. New York: William Morrow, 1992. Includes a chapter on *Moon Palace*.

Bradbury, Malcolm. *The Modern American Novel: New Edition*. New York: Viking, 1993. Includes a chapter on *The New York Trilogy*.

Drenttel, William, comp. and ed. *Paul Auster: A Comprehensive Bibliographic Checklist of Published Works, 1968-1994*. New York: W. Drenttel in association with Delos Press, 1994. An exhaustive bibliography of Auster's works.

MARIANO AZUELA

Born: Lagos de Moreno, Mexico; January 1, 1873
Died: Mexico City, Mexico; March 1, 1952

PRINCIPAL LONG FICTION

María Luisa, 1907
Los fracasados, 1908
Mala yerba, 1909 (*Marcela: A Mexican Love Story*, 1932)
Andrés Pérez, maderista, 1911
Sin amor, 1912
Los de abajo, 1916, rev. 1920 (*The Underdogs: A Novel of the Mexican Revolution*, 1929; new trans. 1963)
Los caciques, 1917 (*The Bosses*, 1956)
Las moscas, 1918 (*The Flies*, 1956)
Domitilo quiere ser diputado, 1918
Las tribulaciones de una familia decente, 1918 (*The Trials of a Respectable Family*, 1963)
La malhora, 1923

El desquite, 1925
La luciérnaga, 1932 (*The Firefly*, 1979)
Precursores, 1935
El camarada Pantoja, 1937
San Gabriel de Valdivias, comunidad indígena, 1938
Regina Landa, 1939
Avanzada, 1940
Nueva burguesía, 1941
La marchanta, 1944
La mujer domada, 1946
Sendas perdidas, 1949
La maldición, 1955
Esa sangre, 1956
Two Novels of Mexico, 1956
Two Novels of the Mexican Revolution, 1963
Three Novels, 1979

OTHER LITERARY FORMS

Apart from his long fiction, Azuela also tried his hand at theater and biography. He wrote three plays, *Los de abajo*, a dramatization of the novel of the same name which had its premiere in 1929; *Del Llano Hermanos, S. en C.*, based on *Los caciques* and staged in 1936; and *El búho en la noche*, based on *El desquite*, which never reached the stage. He also wrote biographies: *Pedro Moreno, el insurgente* (1932) and *El padre Don Agustín Rivera* (1942). All these works are now available in volume 3 of Mariano Azuela's complete works, put out by the Fondo de Cultura Económica in Mexico City in 1960. Some of Azuela's novels have made their way to the big screen, but it was only the film version of *Los de abajo* (1940), directed by Chano Ureta, with musical accompaniment by Silvestre Revuelta and camera work by Gabriel Figueroa, which met with any real acclaim.

ACHIEVEMENTS

Azuela's masterpiece, *The Underdogs*, is a very important work on the Mexican Revolution. Though largely unrecognized by the literary establishment in his early years, Azuela was showered with literary honors in later life. He was awarded the Premio de Letras by the Ateneo Nacional de Ciencias y Artes in

1940, and he became a member of the Seminario de Cultura Mexicana and of the Academia de la Lengua in 1942. He was one of the founding members of the Colegio Nuevo in 1943.

BIOGRAPHY

Mariano Azuela was born into a provincial, middle-class family in Mexico; his father owned a local grocery store in Lagos de Moreno, a town in eastern Jalisco. In 1887 he went to Guadalajara to study for the priesthood but left the seminary two years later, deciding instead to pursue a medical career. He qualified as a doctor at the University of Guadalajara in 1889; during his student days he also read much nineteenth century literature, which influenced the fiction he later wrote. In 1900 he married Carmen Rivera, with whom he had ten children.

Azuela was a supporter of Francisco Madero, who eventually dislodged President Porfirio Díaz in the national elections held in 1912, and Azuela was rewarded with the post of *jefe político* (political chief) in Lagos. Madero, however, was not to remain in power for long (he was murdered and succeeded by his own minister of war, Victoriano Huerta, in 1914) and, given that Azuela supported Madero, it is no wonder that he saw the ensuing events of the Mexican Revolution (with the rapid successions and deaths of leaders Venustiano Carranza, Álvaro Obregón, and Emiliano Zapata) as a process of mindless carnage. He witnessed military action in 1914-1915 while working as a surgeon in the army of Julián Medina, then of revolutionary Pancho Villa.

After the latter's northern division was routed, Azuela crossed the U.S. border in 1915 and took refuge in El Paso, Texas, where he completed the text which would make him famous. *The Underdogs* was published in a local Spanish-language newspaper in El Paso, *El Paso del Norte*, in twenty-three weekly installments from October to November (for which Azuela was paid ten dollars per week). Azuela brought out a revised, expanded version of the novel at his own expense in Mexico City in 1920 and, quite by chance, it caught the attention of the reading public in 1924, bringing him instant fame. As a result Azuela was able to exchange his stethoscope for the pen, and he remained a writer until the end of his life. Some of his later works, such as *The Trials of a Respectable Family* and *The Firefly*, gave him some notoriety, but it was *The Underdogs* which earned him fame in Mexico and abroad. Azuela died on March 1, 1952, and, in keeping with a writer of his stature, was buried in the Rotunda of Illustrious Men in Mexico City.

ANALYSIS

In the first few decades of the twentieth century the novel in Latin America focused on two interrelated themes: the struggles over political space (that is, the identity of the nation) and over geographical space (namely, national territory). Though Azuela's fiction, like that of his contemporaries, concentrated on the struggle for political and geographical space (specifically in the context of the Mexican Revolution), it had the advantage of offering something entirely new to contemporary readers. Azuela was one of the first writers in Latin America to introduce two of the techniques of cinematography into the novel, namely the description of the appearance of things as if the camera were simply rolling, and the use of the cinematic "cross-cut" from one scene to the next as a means of echoing the chaos of war. It is noteworthy that, of the twenty-four novels Azuela wrote, nearly two-thirds of them either name a particular individual in the title (such as María Luisa) or refer to groups of individuals (such as "los de abajo," the underdogs), which suggests that the Mexican writer was interested in how individuals function within society, that is, the interplay between individual and collective psychology.

THE UNDERDOGS

Azuela's detractors have argued that *The Underdogs* presents the events of the Mexican Revolution from too provincial a perspective. They also charge its author with failing to understand (or reveal) the ideological causes of the Revolution. It is true that the Revolution as depicted in this novel is largely confined to Jalisco, Aguascalientes, and Zacatecas (these were the areas in which Azuela had witnessed the events), and that the characters in Azuela's version of the drama seem strikingly ignorant of the

larger picture. The decisive battles of the Mexican Revolution, for example, occur "offstage" in Azuela's novel; Demetrio and his followers, for example, only find out about the Battle of Celaya, which occurred in the spring of 1915 and in which Villa was decisively defeated by Obregón, when they question some soldiers they suspect of being deserters. None of the various political manifestos which shaped the course of the Revolution are even mentioned by the characters in the book. Pancracio manages to mispronounce Carranza's name, calling him Carranzo, while Valderrama expresses lack of interest in either Villa, Obregón, or Carranza; they are simply meaningless names to him.

The geographical limitations of the novel are the judicious restraints of a seasoned artist rather than those of a timid one. Azuela pointed out, for example, in a speech given on January 26, 1950, when he was awarded the Premio Nacional de Ciencias y Artes, that he saw his role as one of describing rather than explaining events: "As a novelist I have tended to describe our evils and point them out; it is the task of others to find a solution for them." Indeed, in this novel Azuela homes in on the dangers involved in an idealized version of reality. The intellectual who accompanies Macías's army, Luis Cervantes, for instance, describes the Revolution as a time when the underdogs will finally be rewarded, but his views are greeted scornfully by his companions, and, indeed, he finally reveals himself to be a smooth-talking opportunist when he escapes to the United States to avoid danger.

Cervantes's name, given the obvious allusion to the Spanish author of the literary masterpiece *Don Quixote de la Mancha* (1605, 1615), Miguel de Cervantes, is also meant to signal his lack of pragmatism. Even Solís, whom a number of critics have seen as a projection of Azuela himself, offers a pessimistic view of the Revolution: He refers to the "psychology" of the Mexican people as "summed up" by two words: "robbery and murder." These insights seem borne out by the various events described in the novel, involving violence, vengeance, rape, and pillage. Life is cheap; one soldier boasts how he killed a man because he gave him some currency printed by the enemy Huerta, and another plays sadistically with one of his prisoners, threatening to kill him and then postpone the event until the following day. Culture is systematically destroyed: A typewriter is smashed on the rocks, and Dante's literary masterpiece, *The Divine Comedy* (c. 1320), is torn to shreds. The ending of the novel seems to lend credence to the notion that the Revolution is presented as a vicious circle, as we are left with an image of Macías fighting against impossible odds in exactly the same place that he started. Despite its pessimism, however, *The Underdogs* is unequalled in its vivid re-creation of the daily events of the Revolution, its fast-moving narrative pace which cross-cuts from scene to scene, and its racy, colloquial style.

THE TRIALS OF A RESPECTABLE FAMILY

This novel portrays the events that took place in Mexico City in 1916 and 1917 during the administration of President Venustiano Carranza, known in the novel ironically as "el primer Jefe" (the number-one boss). The Vázquez Prados, an upper-middle-class family from Zapatecas, take refuge in Mexico City in order to escape the ravages of the Revolution. In the capital, however, the family is overwhelmed by the massive social upheaval created by the war, for it is a world in which cynical opportunists, such as General Covarrubias, use crime as a means of achieving high office. The novel has some compelling scenes, such as the brutality of soldiers' treatment of the civilian population in downtown Mexico City described by Lulú and César, which ensure the novel's place in the Azuela canon as a valuable social document. Procopio, the patriarch of the family, is presented sympathetically; he loses his fortune but comes to terms with his fate when he finds a job as an office employee, a situation he would never have accepted in Zacatecas. The two main themes of this work are the betrayal of the Revolution and the virtue of honest work.

THE FIREFLY

This novel, claimed by some scholars to be Azuela's best, is a psychological as well as a social-protest novel. It portrays three major characters: Dionisio, his wife Conchita ("the firefly"), and his brother José María. Like *The Trials of a Respectable*

Family, the plot centers on the disastrous decision made by a family to move from the provinces to Mexico City. Dionisio moves his family from Cienguilla in search of a better life, to which end he intends to use Conchita's inheritance of fifteen thousand pesos, a considerable sum in those days. However, once in the capital, Dionisio is robbed by an assortment of unscrupulous businessmen and crooks, and he turns to drink in order to drown his sorrows. While driving a bus under the influence of alcohol, he loses control of the vehicle and is involved in a collision in which many of the passengers are killed. To make matters worse, his daughter is murdered in a brothel frequented by high-ranking politicians, his son dies of tuberculosis, and his miserly brother refuses to lift a finger to save him from financial ruin.

All is not lost, however, since his wife, Conchita, like a firefly beating back the darkness of sin, returns to Mexico City to save him. The novel uses a number of innovative techniques; most notably, it has a fragmented, nonchronological structure, cutting unexpectedly from one scene to the next, which is an appropriate vehicle with which to express Dionisio's gradual descent into alcoholism. Just as striking, the novel uses the device of indirect interior monologue, whereby the unarticulated and highly subjective thoughts of the three main chracters are expressed in third-person prose. A highly experimental novel, *The Firefly* manages to draw vivid, well-rounded characters who capture the reader's imagination.

Stephen M. Hart

OTHER MAJOR WORKS

SHORT FICTION: *María Luisa y otros cuentos*, 1937.

PLAYS: *Los de abajo*, pr. 1929; *Del Llano Hermanos, S. en C.*, pr. 1936; *El buho en la noche*, pb. 1938.

NONFICTION: *Pedro Moreno, el insurgente*, 1933 (serial), 1935 (book); *El padre Don Agustín Rivera*, 1942; *Cien años de novela mexicana*, 1947; *Páginas autobiográficas*, 1974.

MISCELLANEOUS: *Mariano Azuela: Obras completas*, 1958-1960 (Alí Chumacero, editor); *Epistolario y archivo*, 1969.

BIBLIOGRAPHY

Griffin, Clive. *Azuela: Los de abajo*. London: Grant and Cutler, 1993. An excellent study of Azuela's masterpiece, with separate chapters on the historical backdrop to the Revolution, realism, characterization, and structure.

Herbst, Gerhard R. *Mexican Society as Seen by Mariano Azuela*. New York: Ediciones ABRA, 1977. Studies eight of Azuela's novels and deduces his vision of Mexican society. Shows that although Azuela became embittered once Villa, whom he supported, was defeated, he nevertheless maintained a faith in the man of the street.

Leal, Luis. *Mariano Azuela*. New York: Twayne, 1971. An excellent overview of Azuela's work by a writer with great insight into Azuela as a person and as a writer.

Martínez, Eliud. *The Art of Mariano Azuela: Modernism in "La malhora," "El desquite," "La Luciérnaga."* Pittsburgh: Latin American Literary Review, 1980. A competent study of Azuela's lesser-known novels. Particularly good is the chapter on *The Firefly*, which analyses the novel chapter by chapter and shows how Azuela uses avant-garde techniques in order to enhance his message. Argues that *The Firefly* is Azuela's best novel.

Robe, Stanley L. *Azuela and the Mexican Underdogs*. Berkeley: University of California Press, 1979. Compares the first version of *The Underdogs* when serialized in 1915 with its definitive version published in 1920. Also provides a detailed picture of the two years of political unrest, 1914 and 1915, in which this novel is set.

Sommers, Joseph. *After the Storm: Landmarks of the Modern Mexican Novel*. Albuquerque: University of New Mexico Press, 1968. The section on *The Underdogs* was the first to argue convincingly that Azuela focuses so much in his novel on the carnage and immediacy of the Mexican Revolution that he does not understand (or indeed reveal) its causes.

B

JAMES BALDWIN

Born: New York, New York; August 2, 1924
Died: St. Paul de Vence, France; November 30, 1987

PRINCIPAL LONG FICTION

Go Tell It on the Mountain, 1953
Giovanni's Room, 1956
Another Country, 1962
Tell Me How Long the Train's Been Gone, 1968
If Beale Street Could Talk, 1974
Just Above My Head, 1979

OTHER LITERARY FORMS

Before he published his first novel, James Baldwin had established a reputation as a talented essayist and reviewer. Many of his early pieces, later collected in *Notes of a Native Son* (1955) and *Nobody Knows My Name: More Notes of a Native Son* (1961), have become classics; his essays on Richard Wright, especially "Everybody's Protest Novel" (1949) and "Many Thousands Gone" (1951), occupy a central position in the development of "universalist" African American thought during the 1950's. Culminating in *The Fire Next Time* (1963), an extended meditation on the relationship of race, religion, and the individual experience in America, Baldwin's early prose demands a reexamination and redefinition of received social and cultural premises. His collections of essays *No Name in the Street* (1971) and *The Devil Finds Work* (1976) reflected a more militant stance and were received less favorably than Baldwin's universalist statements. *The Evidence of Things Not Seen* (1985) is a book-length essay on the Atlanta child-murders, while *The Price of the Ticket: Collected Nonfiction 1948-1985* (1985) includes all of Baldwin's essay collections as well as a number of previously uncollected pieces. Less formal and intricate, though in some cases more ex-

plicit, reflections of Baldwin's beliefs can be found in *A Rap on Race* (1971), an extended discussion with anthropologist Margaret Mead, and *A Dialogue* (1975), a conversation with poet Nikki Giovanni.

Baldwin also wrote children's fiction (*Little Man, Little Man*, 1975), the text for a photographic essay (*Nothing Personal*, 1964, with Richard Avedon), an unfilmed scenario (*One Day, When I Was Lost: A Scenario Based on "The Autobiography of Malcolm X,"* 1972), drama, and short stories. Most critics prefer Baldwin's first play, *The Amen Corner* (produced 1954), to *Blues for Mister Charlie* (1964) despite the latter's four-month Broadway run. Although he published little short fiction after the collection *Going to Meet the Man* (1965), Baldwin was an acknowledged master of the novella form. "Sonny's Blues" (1957), the story of the relationship of a jazz musician to his "respectable" narrator-brother, anticipates many of the themes of Baldwin's later novels and is widely recognized as one of the great American novellas.

ACHIEVEMENTS

Baldwin's public role as a major African American racial spokesman of the 1950's and 1960's guar-

(AP Photo)

antees his place in American cultural history. Though not undeserved, this reputation more frequently obscures than clarifies the nature of his literary achievement, which involves his relationship to African American culture, existential philosophy, and the moral tradition of the world novel. To be sure, Baldwin's progression from an individualistic, universalist stance through active involvement with the integrationist Civil Rights movement to an increasing sympathy with militant Pan-Africanist thought parallels the general development of African American thought between the early 1950's and the mid-1970's. Indeed, his novels frequently mirror both Baldwin's personal philosophy and its social context. Some, most notably *Another Country*, attained a high degree of public visibility when published, leading to a widely accepted vision of Baldwin as a topical writer. To consider Baldwin primarily as a racial spokesman, however, imposes a stereotype which distorts many of his most penetrating insights and underestimates his status as a literary craftsman.

More accurate, though ultimately as limited, is the view of Baldwin primarily as an exemplar of the African American presence in the "mainstream" of the American tradition. Grouped with Ralph Ellison as a major "post-Wright" black novelist, Baldwin represents, in this view, the generation which rejected "protest literature" in favor of "universal" themes. Strangely at odds with the view of Baldwin as racial spokesman, this view emphasizes the craftsmanship of Baldwin's early novels and his treatment of "mainstream" themes such as religious hypocrisy, father-son tensions, and sexual identity. Ironically, many younger African American novelists accept this general view of Baldwin's accomplishment, viewing his mastery of Jamesian techniques and his involvement with continental literary culture as an indication of alienation from his racial identity. Recasting political activist Eldridge Cleaver's political attack on Baldwin in aesthetic terms, the African American writer Ishmael Reed dismisses Baldwin as a great "white" novelist. A grain of truth lies in Reed's assertion; Baldwin rarely created new forms. Rather, he infused a variety of Euro-American forms, derived from Wright and William Faulkner as well as from

Henry James, with the rhythms and imagery of the African American oral tradition.

Like the folk preacher whose voice he frequently assumed in secular contexts, Baldwin combined moral insight with an uncompromising sense of the concrete realities of his community, whether defined in terms of family, lovers, race, or nation. This indicates the deepest level of Baldwin's literary achievement; whatever his immediate political focus or fictional form, he possessed an insight into moral psychology shared by only a handful of novelists. Inasmuch as the specific circumstances of this psychology involve American racial relations, this insight aligns Baldwin with Wright, Faulkner, Mark Twain, and Harriet Beecher Stowe. Inasmuch as his insight involves the symbolic alienation of the individual, it places him with American romantics such as Nathaniel Hawthorne and European existentialists such as Albert Camus. Since his insight recognizes the complex pressure exerted by social mechanisms on individual consciousness, it reveals affinities with James Joyce, George Eliot, and Ellison. As a writer who combined elements of all of these traditions with the voice of the anonymous African American preacher, Baldwin cannot be reduced to accommodate the terms of any one of them. Refusing to lie about the reality of pain, he provided realistic images of the moral life possible in the inhospitable world that encompasses the streets of Harlem and the submerged recesses of the mind.

BIOGRAPHY

James Baldwin once dismissed his childhood as "the usual bleak fantasy." Nevertheless, the major concerns of his fiction consistently reflect the social context of his family life in Harlem during the Depression. The dominant figure of Baldwin's childhood was clearly that of his stepfather, David Baldwin, who worked as a manual laborer and preached in a storefront church. Clearly the model for Gabriel Grimes in *Go Tell It on the Mountain*, David Baldwin had moved from New Orleans to New York City, where he married Baldwin's mother, Emma Berdis. The oldest of what was to be a group of nine children in the household, James assumed a great deal of the responsibility for the care of his half-brothers and sisters. Insulated somewhat from the brutality of Harlem street life by his domestic duties, Baldwin, as he describes in *The Fire Next Time*, sought refuge in the Church. Undergoing a conversion experience, similar to that of John in *Go Tell It on the Mountain*, at age fourteen in 1938, Baldwin preached as a youth minister for the next several years. At the same time, he began to read, immersing himself in works such as *Uncle Tom's Cabin* (1852) and the novels of Charles Dickens. Both at his Harlem junior high school, where the African American poet Countée Cullen was one of his teachers, and at his predominantly white Bronx high school, Baldwin contributed to student literary publications. The combination of family tension, economic hardship, and religious vocation provides the focus of much of Baldwin's greatest writing, most notably *Go Tell It on the Mountain*, *The Fire Next Time*, and *Just Above My Head*.

If Baldwin's experience during the 1930's provided his material, his life from 1942 to 1948 shaped his characteristic approach to that material. After he was graduated from high school in 1942, Baldwin worked for a year as a manual laborer in New Jersey, an experience which increased both his understanding of his stepfather and his insight into America's economic and racial systems. Moving to Greenwich Village in 1943, Baldwin worked during the day and wrote at night for the next five years; his first national reviews and essays appeared in 1946. The major event of the Village years, however, was Baldwin's meeting with Richard Wright in the winter 1944-1945. Wright's interest helped Baldwin secure first a Eugene F. Saxton Memorial Award and then a Rosenwald Fellowship, enabling him to move to Paris in 1948.

After his arrival in France, Baldwin experienced more of the poverty which had shaped his childhood. Simultaneously, he developed a larger perspective on the psychocultural context conditioning his experience, feeling at once a greater sense of freedom and a larger sense of the global structure of racism, particularly as reflected in the French treatment of North Africans. In addition, he formed many of the personal

and literary friendships which contributed to his later public prominence. Baldwin's well-publicized literary feud with Wright, who viewed the younger writer's criticism of *Native Son* (1940) as a form of personal betrayal, helped establish Baldwin as a major presence in African American letters. Although Baldwin's first novel, *Go Tell It on the Mountain*, was well received critically, it was not so financially successful that he could devote his full time to creative writing. As a result, Baldwin continued to travel widely, frequently on journalistic assignments, while writing *Giovanni's Room*, which is set in France and involves no black characters.

Returning to the United States as a journalist covering the Civil Rights movement, Baldwin made his first trip to the American South in 1957. The essays and reports describing that physical and psychological journey propelled Baldwin to the position of public prominence which he maintained for more than a decade. During the height of the movement, Baldwin lectured widely and was present at major events such as the March on Washington and the voter registration drive in Selma, Alabama. In addition, he met with most of the major African American activists of the period, including Martin Luther King, Jr., Elijah Muhammad, James Meredith, and Medgar Evers. Attorney General Robert Kennedy requested that Baldwin bring together the most influential voices in the black community, and, even though the resulting meeting accomplished little, the request testifies to Baldwin's image as a focal point of African American opinion. In addition to this political activity, Baldwin formed personal and literary relationships—frequently tempestuous ones—with numerous white writers, including William Styron and Norman Mailer. A surge in literary popularity, reflected in the presence of *Another Country* and *The Fire Next Time* on the best-seller lists throughout most of 1962 and 1963, accompanied Baldwin's political success and freed him from financial insecurity for the first time. He traveled extensively throughout the decade, and his visits to Puerto Rico and Africa were to have a major influence on his subsequent political thought.

Partly because of Baldwin's involvement with prominent whites and partly because of the sympathy for homosexuals evinced in his writing, several black militants, most notably Eldridge Cleaver, attacked Baldwin's position as "black spokesman" beginning in the late 1960's. As a result, nationalist spokesmen such as Amiri Baraka and Bobby Seale gradually eclipsed Baldwin in the public literary and political spotlights. Nevertheless, Baldwin, himself sympathetic to many of the militant positions, continued his involvement with public issues, such as the fate of the Wilmington, North Carolina, prisoners, which he addressed in an open letter to Jimmy Carter shortly after Carter's election to the presidency. In his later years, though he returned periodically to the South, Baldwin lived for much of the time in France and Turkey. It was in St. Paul de Vence, France, that he died, on November 30, 1987.

ANALYSIS

Uncompromising in his demand for personal and social integrity, James Baldwin from the beginning of his career charged the individual with full responsibility for his or her moral identity. Both in his early individualistic novels and in his later political fiction, he insisted on the inadequacy of received definitions as the basis for self-knowledge or social action. Echoing the existentialist principle "existence precedes essence," he intimated the underlying consistency of his vision in the introductory essay in *Notes of a Native Son*: "I think all theories are suspect, that the finest principles may have to be modified, or may even be pulverized by the demands of life, and that one must find, therefore, one's own moral center and move through the world hoping that this center will guide one aright." This insistence on the moral center and movement in the world cautions against associating Baldwin with the atheistic or solipsistic currents of existential thought. Never denying the possibility of transcendent moral power—which he frequently imaged as the power of love—he simply insisted that human conceptions must remain flexible enough to allow for the honest perception of experience. Fully recognizing the reality of existential pain and despair, Baldwin invoked honesty and self-acceptance as the necessary supports for the love capable of generating individual

communication and at least the groundwork for political action.

Baldwin's social vision, reflecting his experience in a racist culture, acknowledges the forces militating against self-knowledge and moral responsibility. Each of his novels portrays a series of evasive and simplifying definitions built into religious, economic, and educational institutions. These definitions, which emphasize the separation of self and other, control the immediate contexts of individual experience. As a result, they frequently seem to constitute "human nature," to embody the inevitable limits of experience. While sympathizing with the difficulty of separating the self from context without simultaneously denying experience, Baldwin insists that acquiescing to the definitions inevitably results in self-hatred and social immorality. The individual incapable of accepting his or her existential complexity flees to the illusion of certainty provided by the institutions which assume responsibility for directing moral decisions. This cycle of institutional pressure encouraging existential evasion ensuring further institutional corruption recurs in each of Baldwin's novels. On both personal and social levels, the drive to deny the reality of the other—racial, sexual, or economic—generates nothing save destruction. Derived from the streets of Harlem rather than from Scripture, Baldwin's response echoes Christ's admonition to "love thy neighbor as thyself." The derivation is vital; in Baldwin's novels, those who extract the message from the Bible rather than from their lives frequently aggravate the pain that makes evading reality seem attractive.

The immediate focus of Baldwin's attention gradually shifted from consciousness to context, creating the illusion of a change in his basic concerns. While he always worked in the realistic tradition of the novel, his choice of specific forms paralleled this shift in thematic focus, though again his later work indicates an underlying unity in his fiction. His first novel, *Go Tell It on the Mountain*, employs a tightly focused Jamesian form to explore the developing awareness of the adolescent protagonist John Grimes, who is not yet aware of the evasive definitions conditioning his experience. After a second

Jamesian novel, *Giovanni's Room*, Baldwin adapted the relatively unstructured Dreiserian mode in *Another Country* and *Tell Me How Long the Train's Been Gone*. Characters such as Rufus Scott and Vivaldo Moore in *Another Country* continue to struggle for individual awareness, but Baldwin's new narrative stance emphasizes the impact of the limiting definitions on a wide range of particular social circumstances. Attempting to balance the presentation of consciousness and context, Baldwin's last two novels, *If Beale Street Could Talk* and *Just Above My Head*, synthesize the earlier technical approaches. Returning to the immediate focus on the individual consciousness in these first-person narratives, Baldwin creates protagonists capable of articulating their own social perceptions. Consciousness and context merge as Baldwin's narrators share their insights and, more important, their processes with their fellow sufferers.

These insights implicitly endorse William Blake's vision of morality as a movement from innocence through experience to a higher innocence. Beginning with an unaware innocence, individuals inevitably enter the deadening and murderous world of experience, the world of the limiting definitions. Those who attempt to deny the world and remain children perish alongside those who cynically submit to the cruelty of the context for imagined personal benefit. Only those who plunge into experience, recognize its cruelty, and resolve to forge an aware innocence can hope to survive morally. Specifically, Baldwin urges families to pass on a sense of the higher innocence to their children by refusing to simplify the truth of experience. This painful honesty makes possible the commitment to love despite the inevitability of pain and isolation. It provides the only hope, however desperate, for individual or social rejuvenation. To a large extent, Baldwin's career developed in accord with the Blakean pattern. John Grimes begins his passage from innocence to experience in *Go Tell It on the Mountain*; Rufus Scott and Vivaldo Moore, among others, struggle to survive experience in *Another Country*, which intimates the need for higher innocence. Baldwin's last two novels portray the entire process, focusing on the attempt first to

find and then to pass on the higher innocence. *Just Above My Head*, with its middle-aged narrator and his teenage children, clearly represents a more highly developed and realistic stage of the vision than *If Beale Street Could Talk*, with its teenage mother-narrator and her newborn infant.

GO TELL IT ON THE MOUNTAIN

Go Tell It on the Mountain centers on the religious conversion and family relationships of John Grimes, whose experience parallels that of Baldwin during his youth. Although he believes himself to be the natural son of Gabriel Grimes, a preacher who, like Baldwin's stepfather, moved to New York after growing up in the South, John is actually the son of Gabriel's wife, Elizabeth, and her lover, Richard, who committed suicide prior to John's birth. Growing up under the influence of his hypocritical and tyrannical stepfather, John alternately attempts to please and transcend him. Gabriel expends most of his emotional energy on his openly rebellious son Roy, whose immersion in the violent life of the Harlem streets contrasts sharply with John's involvement with the "Temple of the Fire Baptized," the storefront church where his conversion takes place. To the extent that Baldwin organizes *Go Tell It on the Mountain* around John's attempt to come to terms with these pressures, the novel appears to have a highly individualistic focus.

The overall structure of the novel, however, dictates that John's experience be viewed in a larger context. Of the three major sections of *Go Tell It on the Mountain*, the first, "The Seventh Day," and the third, "The Threshing Floor," focus directly on John. The long middle section, "The Prayers of the Saints," a Faulknerian exploration of history, traces the origins of John's struggle to the experience of his elders, devoting individual chapters to Elizabeth, Gabriel, and Gabriel's sister Florence. Together the prayers portray the Great Migration of African Americans from South to North, from rural to urban settings. Far from bringing true freedom, the movement results in a new indirect type of oppression. As Elizabeth recognizes: "There was not, after all, a great difference between the world of the North and that of the South which she had fled; there was only this difference:

the North promised more. And this similarity: what it promised it did not give, and what it gave, at length and grudgingly with one hand, it took back with the other." Even in his most individualistic phase, Baldwin is aware of the power of institutional pressures. The origins of John's particular struggle against the limiting definitions go back to their impact on both Elizabeth and Gabriel.

Elizabeth's relationship with John's true father, at least in its early stages, appears to offer hope for at least a limited freedom from external definition. Highly intelligent and self-aware, Richard struggles to transcend the limitations imposed on black aspiration through a rigorous program of self-education, which he shares with Elizabeth. Despite his intelligence and determination, however, Richard maintains a naïve innocence concerning the possibility of self-definition in a society based on racist assumptions. Only when arrested on suspicion of a robbery he had nothing to do with does he recognize that his context defines him simply as another "nigger." Unable to reconcile this imposed definition with his drive for social transcendence, he despairs and commits suicide. This act, in turn, destroys Elizabeth's chance for obtaining a greater degree of freedom. She is not, however, simply a victim. Fearing that Richard will be unable to cope with the responsibility of a family, she fails to tell him of her pregnancy. Far from protecting him, this evasion contributes to his destruction by allowing Richard to view his situation as purely personal. Elizabeth's own choice, conditioned by the social refusal to confront reality, combines with the racist legal system to circumscribe her possibilities. Forced to care for her infant son, she marries Gabriel, thus establishing the basic terms for John's subsequent struggle.

Seen in relation to John in "The Seventh Day," Gabriel appears to be one of the most despicable hypocrites in American literature. Seen in relation to his own history in "The Prayers of the Saints," however, he appears victimized by the institutional context of his youth. In turn, he victimizes his family by attempting to force them into narrowly defined roles. The roots of Gabriel's character lie in the "temple-street" dichotomy of his southern childhood. Encour-

aged by his religious mother to deny his sensuality, Gabriel undergoes a conversion experience and immerses himself in the role of preacher. As a result, he enters into a loveless asexual marriage with his mother's friend Deborah, herself a victim of the racist psychology—enforced by blacks and whites—which condemns *her* after she has been brutally raped by a group of whites. Eventually, Gabriel's repressed street self breaks out and he fathers a son by the sensual Esther. Again attempting to deny his sensuality, Gabriel refuses to acknowledge this son, Royal. Like John's half-brother Roy, the first Royal immerses himself in the street life which Gabriel denies; he dies in a Chicago barroom brawl. Gabriel fears that Roy will share Royal's fate, but his attempt to crush his second son's street self merely strengthens the resulting rebellion. Faced with the guilt of Royal's death and the sense of impending doom concerning Roy, Gabriel retreats into a solipsism which makes a mockery of his Christian vocation. Far from providing a context for moral responsibility, the Church—both in the South and in the North—simply replaces the original innocence of religious fervor with a cynical vision of religion as a source of the power needed to destroy the innocence of others.

Against this backdrop, John's conversion raises a basic question which will recur in slightly different circumstances in each of Baldwin's novels: Can an individual hope to break the cycle of evasion which has shaped his personal and social context? In John's case, the problem takes on added dimensions, since he remains ignorant of many of the events shaping his life, including those involving his own birth. By framing the prayers with John's conversion, Baldwin stresses the connection between past and present, but the connection can be perceived as either oppressive or liberating. The complex irony of "The Threshing Floor" section allows informed readings of John's conversion as either a surrender to evasion or as a movement toward existential responsibility. Focusing primarily on John's internal experience as he lies transfixed on the church floor, "The Threshing Floor" revolves around a dialogue between an "ironic voice" which challenges John to return to the street and the part of John which seeks traditional salvation. Throughout John's vision, the narrative voice shifts point of view in accord with John's developing perception. As John accepts the perceptions implied by his vision, the ironic voice shifts its attention to yet deeper levels of ambiguity. To the extent that John resolves these ambiguities by embracing the Temple, his experience seems to increase the risk that he will follow Gabriel's destructive example.

Several image patterns, however, indicate that John may be moving nearer to a recognition of his actual complexity. Chief among these are those involving the curse of Ham, the rejection of the father, and the acceptance of apparent opposites. From the beginning of the vision, the ironic voice ridicules John for accepting the curse of Ham, which condemns him both as son and as "nigger." Manipulating John's sense of guilt for having indulged his street self by masturbating, the ironic voice insists that John's very existence "proves" Gabriel's own sexual weakness. If Gabriel condemns John, he condemns himself in the process. As a result, John comes to view himself as the "devil's son" and repudiates his subservience before his "father." Without this essentially negative, and ultimately socially derived, definition of himself, John finds himself in an existential void where "there was no speech or language, and there was no love."

Forced to reconstruct his identity, John progresses from this sense of isolation to a vision of the dispossessed with whom he shares his agony and his humanity. John's vision of the multitude whose collective voice merges with his own suggests suffering as the essential human experience, one obliterating both the safety and the isolation of imposed definitions. Significantly, this vision leads John to Jesus the Son rather than God the Father, marking an implicit rejection of Gabriel's Old Testament vengeance in favor of the New Testament commitment to an all-encompassing love. The son metamorphoses from symbol of limitation to symbol of liberation. Near the end of his vision, John explicitly rejects the separation of opposites—street and temple, white and black—encouraged by his social context: "The light and the darkness had kissed each other, and were married now, forever, in the life and the vision of John's

soul." Returning to his immediate environment from the depths of his mind, John responds not to the call of Gabriel but to that of Elisha, a slightly older member of the congregation with whom he has previously engaged in a sexually suggestive wrestling match reminiscent of that in D. H. Lawrence's *Women in Love* (1920). John's salvation, then, may bring him closer to an acceptance of his own sensuality, to a definition of himself encompassing both temple and street. Baldwin ends the novel with the emergence of the newly "saved" John onto the streets of Harlem. His fate hinges on his ability to move ahead to the higher innocence suggested by his vision of the dispossessed rather than submitting to the experiences which have destroyed and deformed the majority of the saints.

ANOTHER COUNTRY

Another Country, Baldwin's greatest popular success, analyzes the effects of deforming pressure and experience on a wide range of characters, black and white, male and female, homosexual and heterosexual. To accommodate these diverse consciousnesses, Baldwin employs the sprawling form usually associated with political rather than psychological fiction, emphasizing the diverse forms of innocence and experience in American society. The three major sections of *Another Country*, "Easy Rider," "Any Day Now," and "Toward Bethlehem," progress generally from despair to renewed hope, but no single consciousness or plot line provides a frame similar to that of *Go Tell It on the Mountain*. Rather, the novel's structural coherence derives from the moral concerns present in each of the various plots.

Casting a Melvillean shadow over the novel is the black jazz musician Rufus Scott, who is destroyed by an agonizing affair with Leona, a white southerner recently arrived in New York at the time she meets him. Unable to forge the innocence necessary for love in a context which repudiates the relationship at every turn, Rufus destroys Leona psychologically. After a period of physical and psychological destitution, he kills himself by jumping off a bridge. His sister Ida, an aspiring singer, and his friend Vivaldo Moore, an aspiring white writer, meet during the last days of Rufus's life and fall in love as they console each other over his death. Struggling to overcome the racial and sexual definitions which destroyed Rufus, they seek a higher innocence capable of countering Ida's sense of the world as a "whorehouse." In contrast to Ida and Vivaldo's struggle, the relationship of white actor Eric Jones and his French lover Yves seems Edenic. Although Baldwin portrays Eric's internal struggle for a firm sense of his sexual identity, their shared innocence at times seems to exist almost entirely outside the context of the pressures that destroyed Rufus. The final major characters, Richard and Cass Silenski, represent the cost of the American Dream. After Richard "makes it" as a popular novelist, their personal relationship decays, precipitating Cass's affair with Eric. Their tentative reunion after Richard discovers the affair makes it clear that material success provides no shortcut to moral responsibility.

Baldwin examines each character and relationship in the context of the institutional pressures discouraging individual responsibility. His portrait of Rufus, the major accomplishment of *Another Country*, testifies to a moral insight and a raw artistic power resembling that of Wright and Émile Zola. Forgoing the formal control and emotional restraint of his earlier novels, Baldwin opens *Another Country* with the image of Rufus who "had fallen so low, that he scarcely had the energy to be angry." Both an exceptional case and a representative figure, Rufus embodies the seething anger and hopeless isolation rendering Baldwin's United States a landscape of nightmare. Seeing his own situation as unbearable, Rufus meditates on the fate of a city tormented by an agony like his own: "He remembered to what excesses, into what traps and nightmares, his loneliness had driven him; and he wondered where such a violent emptiness might drive an entire city." Forcing readers to recognize the social implications of Rufus's situation, Baldwin emphasizes that his specific situation originates in his own moral failure with Leona. Where Gabriel Grimes remained insulated from his immorality by arrogance and pride, Rufus feels the full extent of his self-enforced damnation. Ironically and belatedly, his destitution clarifies his sense of the extent of his past acceptance of the social definitions which destroy him.

Wandering the streets of Manhattan, Rufus feels himself beyond human contact. Desperately in need of love, he believes his past actions render him unfit for even minimal compassion. His abuse of Leona, who as a white woman represents both the "other" and the source of the most obvious social definitions circumscribing his life as a black male, accounts for his original estrangement from family and friends, who find his viciousness uncharacteristic. All, including Rufus, fail to understand soon enough that his abuse of Leona represents both a rebellion against and an acceptance of the role dictated by racial and sexual definitions. Separated from the psychological source of his art—jazz inevitably rejects the substructure of Euro-American definitions of reality—Rufus falls ever further into a paranoia which receives ample reinforcement from the racist context. Largely by his own choice, he withdraws almost entirely from both his black and white acquaintances. Once on the street following Leona's breakdown, he begins to recognize not only his immediate but also his long-term acceptance of destructive definitions. Thinking back on a brief homosexual affair with Eric to which he submitted out of pity rather than love, Rufus regrets having treated his friend with contempt. Having rejected the "other" in Eric and Leona, Rufus realizes he has rejected a part of himself. He consigns himself to the ranks of the damned, casting himself beyond human love with his plunge off the bridge.

While not absolving Rufus of responsibility for his actions, Baldwin treats him with profound sympathy, in part because of his honesty and in part because of the enormous power of the social institutions which define him as the "other." Throughout *Another Country*, Baldwin emphasizes that white heterosexual males possess the power of definition, although their power destroys them as surely as it does their victims. Television producer Steve Ellis, a moral cripple embodying the basic values of the American economic system, nearly destroys Ida and Vivaldo's relationship by encouraging Ida to accept a cynical definition of herself as a sexual commodity. Vivaldo, too, participates in the cynicism when he visits the Harlem prostitutes, indirectly perpetuating the definitions which reduce black people to sexual objects, and thus implicating himself in Rufus's death. In fact, every major character with the exception of Eric bears partial responsibility for Rufus's destruction, since each at times accepts the definitions generating the cycle of rejection and denial. The constituting irony, however, stems from the fact that only those most actively struggling for moral integrity recognize their culpability. Vivaldo, who attempts to reach out to Rufus earlier on the night of his suicide, feels more guilt than Richard, who simply dismisses Rufus as a common "nigger" after his mistreatment of Leona.

This unflinching portrayal of moral failure, especially on the part of well-meaning liberals, provides the thematic center of *Another Country*. Baldwin concludes the novel with the image of Yves's reunion with Eric, who is apparently on the verge of professional success with a starring role in a film of a Fyodor Dostoevski novel. This combination of personal and financial success seems more an assertion of naïve hope than a compelling part of the surrounding fictional world. The majority of the narrative lines imply the impossibility of simple dissociation from institutional pressure. Ultimately, the intensity of Rufus's pain and the intricacy of Ida and Vivaldo's struggle overshadow Eric and Yves's questionable innocence. As Ida tells Vivaldo, "Our being together doesn't change the world." The attempt to overcome the cynicism of this perception leads to a recognition that meaningful love demands total acceptance. Ida's later question, "How can you say you loved Rufus when there was so much about him you didn't want to know?" could easily provide the epitaph for the entire society in *Another Country*.

JUST ABOVE MY HEAD

In *Just Above My Head*, Baldwin creates a narrator, Hall Montana, capable of articulating the psychological subtleties of *Go Tell It on the Mountain*, the social insights of *Another Country*, and the political anger of *Tell Me How Long the Train's Been Gone*. Like other observer-participants in American literature, such as Nick Carraway in *The Great Gatsby* (1925) and Jack Burden in *All the King's Men* (1946), Hall tells both his own story and that of a more publicly prominent figure, in this case his

brother Arthur, a gospel singer who dies two years prior to the start of the novel. Significantly, *Just Above My Head* also reconsiders Baldwin's own artistic history, echoing countless motifs from his earlier writings. Though not precisely a self-reflexive text, *Just Above My Head* takes on added richness when juxtaposed with Baldwin's treatment of religious concerns in *Go Tell It on the Mountain*; the homosexuality theme in *Giovanni's Room*; the relationship between brothers and the musical setting in "Sonny's Blues"; racial politics in *Blues for Mister Charlie* and *Tell Me How Long the Train's Been Gone*; the Nation of Islam in *The Fire Next Time* and *No Name in the Street*; and, most important, the intermingled family love and world politics in *If Beale Street Could Talk*. Baldwin's reconsideration of his own history, which is at once private like Hall's and public like Arthur's, emphasizes the necessity of a continual reexamination of the nature of both self and context in order to reach the higher innocence.

Similarly, Hall's resolve to understand the social and existential meaning of Arthur's experience originates in his desire to answer honestly his children's questions concerning their uncle. Refusing to protect their original innocence—an attempt he knows would fail—Hall seeks both to free himself from the despair of experience and to discover a mature innocence he can pass on to the younger generation. Tracing the roots of Arthur's despair to pressures originating in numerous limiting definitions and failures of courage, Hall summarizes his, and Baldwin's, social insight:

> The attempt, more the necessity, to excavate a history, to find out the truth about oneself! is motivated by the need to have the power to force others to recognize your presence, your right to be here. The disputed passage will remain disputed so long as you do not have the authority of the right-of-way. . . . Power clears the passage, swiftly: but the paradox, here, is that power, rooted in history, is also, the mockery and the repudiation of history. The power to define the other seals one's definition of oneself.

Recognizing that the only hope for meaningful moral freedom lies in repudiating the power of definition, Hall concludes: "Our history is each other. That is our only guide. One thing is absolutely certain: one can repudiate, or despise, no one's history without repudiating and despising one's own."

Although Baldwin recognizes the extent to which the definitions and repudiations remain entrenched in institutional structures, his portrayal of Hall's courage and honesty offers at least some hope for moral integrity as a base for social action. If an individual such as Hall can counteract the pressures militating against personal responsibility, he or she may be able to exert a positive influence on relatively small social groups such as families and churches, which in turn may affect the larger social context. Nevertheless, Baldwin refuses to encourage simplistic optimism. Rather than focusing narrowly on Hall's individual process, he emphasizes the aspects of the context which render that success atypical. Although Hall begins with his immediate context, his excavation involves the Korean War, the Civil Rights movement, the rise of Malcolm X, and the role of advertising in American culture. Hall's relation with his family and close friends provides a Jamesian frame for the Dreiserian events of the novel, somewhat as John's conversion frames the historical "Prayers of the Saints" in *Go Tell It on the Mountain*. *Just Above My Head*, however, leaves no ambiguity concerning the individual's ability to free himself or herself from history. Only a conscious decision to accept the pain and guilt of the past promises any real hope for love, for the higher innocence. Similarly, Baldwin reiterates that, while the desire for safety is understandable, all safety is illusion. Pain inevitably returns, and, while the support of friends and lovers may help, only a self-image based on existential acceptance rather than repudiation makes survival possible.

Arthur's death, occupying a thematic and emotional position similar to Rufus's in *Another Country*, provides the point of departure for Hall's excavation. A gifted gospel singer as a teenager, Arthur rises to stardom as the "emperor of soul." Despite his success, however, he never frees himself from doubts concerning his own identity or feels secure with the experience of love. Even though his parents offer him a firm base of love and acceptance, Arthur feels a deep sense of emotional isolation even as a child, a sense reinforced by his observations of life in Harlem and, later, in the South. Though he accepts his own homosexuality with relatively little anxiety, his society refuses the freedom necessary for the development of a truly satisfying emotional life. The Edenic innocence of Eric and Yves clearly fails to provide a sufficient response to the institutional context of *Just Above My Head*.

Arthur's childhood experiences provide clear warnings against the attempt to maintain innocence through simplistic self-definition. Julia Miller, like John in *Go Tell It on the Mountain*, undergoes a salvation experience and embarks on a career as a child evangelist. Encouraged by her parents, friends of the Montanas who rely on their daughter for economic support, she assumes a sanctimonious attitude which she uses to manipulate her elders. Arthur's parents deplore the indulgence of Julia, unambiguously rejecting the idea that her religious vocation lifts her beyond the "naughty" street side of her personality. Ultimately, and in great pain, Julia confronts this truth. After her mother's death, she discovers that her father, Joel, views her primarily as an economic and sexual object. His desire to exploit her earning potential even when she says she has lost her vocation reflects his underlying contempt for the spirit. This contempt leads to an incestuous rape which destroys Julia's remaining innocence and drives her to a life as a prostitute in New Orleans. Eventually, Julia recovers from this brutalization, but her example provides a clear warning to Arthur against confusing his vocation as a gospel singer with a trancendence of human fallibility.

The experiences of the members of Arthur's first gospel group, the Trumpets of Zion, reveal how institutions infringe even on those not actively committed to simplifying definitions. At one extreme, the social definitions establish a context which accepts and encourages murder—symbolic and real—of the other. Peanut, a member of the Trumpets and later Arthur's companion on the road, vanishes into the Alabama night following a civil rights rally, presumably murdered by whites seeking to enforce the definition of blacks as "niggers." Equally devastating though less direct is the operation of the context on Red, another member of the Trumpets, who turns to drugs in an attempt to relieve the pain of the Harlem streets. Even Hall finds himself an unwilling accomplice to the imposition of social definitions when he is drafted and sent to Korea. Powerless to alter the institutional structure, Hall recognizes, and tells Arthur, that the American military spreads not freedom but repudiation in the Third World. Hall's subsequent employment by an advertising agency involves him in another aspect of the same oppressive system. Viewed as an anomaly by his employers, as an atypical high-class "nigger," Hall nevertheless participates in the creation of images designed to simplify reality for economic gain, which will be used to strengthen the oppressive system. The juxtaposition of Julia's false innocence with the destructive experiences of Peanut, Red, and Hall protects Arthur against the urge to dismiss any aspect of his awareness. A large part of his power as a singer derives from his recognition of the reality of both street and temple, expressed in his ability to communicate sexual pain in gospel songs and spiritual aspiration in the blues.

Arthur, then, appears ideally prepared for the responsible exercise of existential freedom. His failure even to survive underscores the destructive power of the corrupt institutional context. The roots of Arthur's doom lie in his homosexual relationship with Crunch, the final member of the Trumpets. Highly desirable physically, Crunch feels locked into a definition of himself as a sexual object prior to his involvement with Arthur. In its early stages, Arthur and Crunch's love, like that of Yves and Eric in *Another Country*, seems an idyllic retreat, a spot of innocence in the chaos of experience. The retreat, however, proves temporary, in part because Crunch cannot free himself from the urge for self-simplification and in part because of the continuing presence of the outside world. Uneasy with his sexual identity, Crunch becomes involved with Julia when he discovers the extent of her father's abuse. Arthur recognizes that Crunch is not abandoning him by reacting to Julia's pain and accepts the relationship. Granted sufficient time for adjustment, Arthur and Crunch seem capable of confronting their experience and forging a

higher innocence as the basis for a lasting love. The time does not exist. Crunch is drafted and sent to Korea. Separated from Arthur's reassurance and tormented by self-doubt, Crunch never fully accepts his sexuality. After his return to Harlem, he and Arthur gradually lose contact.

The repeated losses—of Peanut, Red, and Crunch—create a sense of isolation which Arthur never overcomes. The expectation of loss periodically overpowers his determination to communicate, the determination which makes him a great singer. Even during periods of real joy, with his French lover Guy in Paris or with Julia's brother Jimmy, who is both his pianist and his lover, Arthur suffers acute emotional pain. Attempting to survive by rededicating himself to communication, to his artistic excavation of history, Arthur drives himself past the limits of physical and psychological endurance. He dies in the basement bathroom of a London pub after a lover's quarrel, clearly only temporary, with Jimmy. By concluding Arthur's life with an image of isolation, Baldwin emphasizes the power of the limiting definitions to destroy even the most existentially courageous individual.

Arthur's death, however, marks not only a conclusion but also the beginning of Hall's quest for the higher innocence, which he, along with his wife Ruth, Julia, and Jimmy, can pass on to the younger generation. This higher innocence involves both individual and social elements, ultimately demanding the mutual support of individuals willing to pursue excavation of their own histories. This support expresses itself in the call and response dynamic, a basic element of African American oral culture which Arthur employs in his interaction with audiences while singing. As Baldwin re-creates the traditional form, the interaction begins with the call of a leader who expresses his own emotional experience through the vehicle of a traditional song which provides a communal context for the emotion. If the community recognizes and shares the experience evoked by the call, it responds with another traditional phrase which provides the sense of understanding and acceptance that enables the leader to go on. Implicitly the process enables both individual and community to define themselves in opposition to dominant social forces. If the experience of isolation is shared, it is no longer the same type of isolation which brought Rufus to his death. In *Just Above My Head*, the call and response rests on a rigorous excavation requiring individual silence, courage, and honesty expressed through social presence, acceptance, and love. Expressed in the interactions between Arthur and his audiences, between Hall and his children, between Baldwin and his readers, this call and response provides a realistic image of the higher innocence possible in opposition to the murderous social definitions.

As in John's vision in *Go Tell It on the Mountain* and Rufus's self-examination in *Another Country*, the process begins in silence, which throughout Baldwin's novels offers the potential for either alienation or communication. The alienating silence coincides thematically with institutional noise—mechanical, social, political. The majority of Americans, Baldwin insists, prefer distracting and ultimately meaningless sounds to the silence which allows self-recognition. Only individuals sharing Arthur's willingness to remove himself from the noise can hope to hear their own voices and transform the silence into music. Every moment of true communication in *Just Above My Head* begins in a moment of silence which effectively rejects the clamor of imposed definitions. The courage needed for the acceptance of silence prepares the way for the honest excavation of history which must precede any meaningful social interaction. The excavation remains a burden, however, without that interaction. No purely individual effort can alter the overwhelming sense of isolation imposed by social definitions. The individual stage of the process merely heightens the need for acceptance, presence, and love. Arthur sounds the call amid the noise; he cannot provide the response. Perhaps, Baldwin indicates, no one, not even Jimmy, can provide a response capable of soothing the feeling of isolation emanating from early experiences. Nevertheless, the attempt is vital. Julia recognizes both the necessity and the limitation of presence when she tells Hall of her relationship with Jimmy: "I don't know enough to change him,

or to save him. But I know enough to be there. I *must* be there."

If presence—being there—is to provide even momentary relief, it must be accompanied by the honest acceptance underlying love. Refusing to limit his acceptance, Hall answers his son Tony's questions concerning Arthur's sexuality with complete honesty. Understanding fully that his acceptance of Arthur entails an acceptance of the similar complexity in himself and in Tony, Hall surrenders his voice to Jimmy's, imaginatively participating in a love which repudiates social definition, which rises up out of the silence beyond the noise. Implicitly, Hall offers both Tony and his daughter Odessa the assurance of presence, of acceptance, of love. They need not fear rejection if they have the courage to accept their full humanity. The assurance cannot guarantee freedom, or even survival. It can, and does, intimate the form of mature innocence in the world described by the composite voice of Baldwin, Jimmy, and Hall, a world that "doesn't have any morality. Look at the world. What the world calls morality is nothing but the dream of safety. That's how the world gets to be so fucking moral. The only way to know that you are safe is to see somebody else in danger—otherwise you can't be sure you're safe."

Against this vicious safety, a safety which necessitates limiting definitions imposed on others, Baldwin proposes a responsibility based on risk. Only by responding to the call sounding from Arthur, from Jimmy and Hall, from Baldwin, can people find freedom. The call, ultimately, emanates not only from the individual but also from the community to which he or she calls. It provides a focus for repudiation of the crushing definitions. Hall, using Jimmy's voice, describes the call: "The man who tells the story isn't *making up* a story. He's listening to us, and can only give back, to us, what he hears: from us." The responsibility lies with everyone.

Craig Werner

OTHER MAJOR WORKS

SHORT FICTION: *Going to Meet the Man*, 1965.

PLAYS: *The Amen Corner*, pr. 1954; *Blues for Mister Charlie*, pr., pb. 1964; *One Day, When I Was*

Lost: A Scenario Based on "The Autobiography of Malcolm X," pb. 1972; *A Deed from the King of Spain*, pr. 1974.

POETRY: *Jimmy's Blues: Selected Poems*, 1983.

NONFICTION: *Notes of a Native Son*, 1955; *Nobody Knows My Name: More Notes of a Native Son*, 1961; *The Fire Next Time*, 1963; *Nothing Personal*, 1964 (with Richard Avedon); *No Name in the Street*, 1971; *A Rap on Race*, 1971 (with Margaret Mead); *A Dialogue*, 1975 (with Nikki Giovanni); *The Devil Finds Work*, 1976; *The Evidence of Things Not Seen*, 1985; *The Price of the Ticket*, 1985; *Conversations with James Baldwin*, 1989.

CHILDREN'S LITERATURE: *Little Man, Little Man*, 1975.

BIBLIOGRAPHY

Campbell, James. *Talking at the Gates: A Life of James Baldwin*. New York: Viking, 1991. A good narrative biography, with detailed notes and bibliography.

Kinnamon, Keneth, ed. *James Baldwin*. Englewood Cliffs, N.J.: Prentice-Hall, 1974. A part of the Twentieth Century Views series, this collection contains some important appraisals of Baldwin's work and career by Langston Hughes, Eldridge Cleaver, and Sherley Anne Williams, among others.

Macebuh, Stanley. *James Baldwin: A Critical Study*. New York: Third Press, 1973. A good presentation of the social and historical background of Baldwin's work.

Standley, Fred L., and Nancy V. Burt, eds. *Critical Essays on James Baldwin*. Boston: G. K. Hall, 1988. A collection of contemporary reviews and essays covering Baldwin's entire career.

Sylvander, Carolyn Wedin. *James Baldwin*. New York: Frederick Ungar, 1980. A study that examines in particular the links between Baldwin's works and his life.

Troupe, Quincy, ed. *James Baldwin: The Legacy*. New York: Simon and Schuster, 1989. Equally divided between memoirs of the writer and discussions of his work. Includes a very useful bibliography.

Weatherby, W. J. *James Baldwin: Artist on Fire*. New York: Donald I. Fine, 1989. An important biography written by one of Baldwin's friends. Weatherby is, at times, too close to his subject to be objective.

J. G. BALLARD

Born: Shanghai, China; November 15, 1930

PRINCIPAL LONG FICTION
The Wind from Nowhere, 1962
The Drowned World, 1962
The Drought, 1964 (later published as *The Burning World*)
The Crystal World, 1966
Crash, 1973

(CORBIS/David Reed)

Concrete Island, 1974
High Rise, 1975
The Unlimited Dream Company, 1979
Hello America, 1981
Empire of the Sun, 1984
The Day of Creation, 1987
Running Wild, 1988 (novella)
The Kindness of Women, 1991
Rushing to Paradise, 1994
Cocaine Nights, 1996

OTHER LITERARY FORMS

J. G. Ballard has been a prolific short-story writer; there are more than twenty collections of his stories, though some are recombinations of stories in earlier collections, and the American and British collections constitute two series in which the same stories are combined in different ways. He has written occasional essays on imaginative fiction, and also on surrealist painting—he contributed an introduction to a collection of work by Salvador Dalí. Many of these essays are collected in *A User's Guide to the Millennium: Essays and Reviews* (1996). The best of his short fiction is to be found in two retrospective collections: *Chronopolis and Other Stories* (1971) and *The Best Short Stories of J. G. Ballard* (1978).

ACHIEVEMENTS

Ballard is one of a handful of writers who, after establishing early reputations as science-fiction writers, subsequently achieved a kind of "transcendence" of their genre origins to be accepted by a wider public. This transcendence was completed by the success of *Empire of the Sun*, which was short-listed for the Booker Prize and won the Guardian Prize before being boosted to best-seller status by a film produced by Steven Spielberg. In 1997, maverick director David Cronenberg turned Ballard's cult classic *Crash* into an equally disturbing *film noir*, which quickly found a dedicated audience. For a time in the early 1960's, Ballard seemed to constitute a one-man avant-garde in British science fiction, and his influence was considerable enough for him to become established as the leading figure in the movement which came to be associated with the magazine *New*

Worlds under the editorship of Michael Moorcock. His interest in science-fiction themes was always of a special kind; he is essentially a literary surrealist who finds the near future a convenient imaginative space. His primary concern is the effect of environment—both "natural" and synthetic—upon the psyche, and he has therefore found it appropriate to write about gross environmental changes and about the decay and dereliction of the artificial environment; these interests distance him markedly from other modern science-fiction writers and have helped him to become a writer *sui generis*.

BIOGRAPHY

James Graham Ballard was born and reared in Shanghai, China, where his father—originally an industrial chemist—was involved in the management of the Far East branch of a firm of textile manufacturers. The Sino-Japanese war had begun, and Shanghai was effectively a war zone by the time Ballard was seven years old; all of his early life was affected by the ever-nearness of war. After Japan's entry into World War II and its invasion of Shanghai, Ballard was interned in a prisoner-of-war camp. This was in the summer of 1942, when he was eleven; he was there for more than three years.

Ballard has said that his experience of the internment camp was "not unpleasant"—it was simply a fact of life which, as a child, he accepted. Children were not generally mistreated by the guards, and the adults made sure that the children were adequately fed, even at their own expense. He has observed that his parents must have found the regime extremely harsh. Although his family was among the fortunate few who avoided malaria, his sister nearly died of a form of dysentery.

After his release, Ballard went to England in 1946. His family stayed in the Far East for a while, and his father did not return until 1950, when he was driven out of China by the Communist victory. Ballard has recalled that after spending his early years in "Americanized" Shanghai, England seemed very strange and foreign. He went to Leys' School in Cambridge for a while, then went to King's College, Cambridge, to study medicine. His ultimate aim at this time was to become a psychiatrist. At Cambridge he began writing, initially intending to maintain the activity as a hobby while he was qualifying. In fact, though, he dropped out of his course after two years and subsequently went to London University to read English. The university seems to have found him unsuitable for such a course, and he left after his first year.

He then embarked upon a series of short-term jobs, including working for an advertising agency and selling encyclopedias. Eventually, to end this aimless drifting, he enlisted in the Royal Air Force and was sent for training to Moosejaw, Saskatchewan, Canada. He was not suited to the air force either, but while in Canada he began reading magazine science fiction, and while waiting for his discharge back in England he wrote his first science-fiction story, "Passport to Eternity" (it was not published for some years). Shortly after this, in 1955, he married and worked in public libraries in order to support his family.

In 1956, Ballard began submitting short stories to Ted Carnell, editor of the British magazines *New Worlds* and *Science Fantasy*. Carnell was not only enthusiastic about Ballard's work but also helpful in finding Ballard a new job working on a trade journal. Eventually, Ballard became assistant editor of *Chemistry and Industry*, a job which he held for four years. He moved in 1960 to the small Thames-side town of Shepperton, where he would make his permanent home. By this time he had three children and was struggling to find time to devote to his writing. During a two-week annual holiday he managed to write *The Wind from Nowhere*, whose publication in America represented something of a breakthrough for him—the same publisher began to issue a series of short-story collections, and the income from these books allowed him to become a full-time writer. His wife died in 1964, when his youngest child was only five years old. As a result, he began to combine his career as a writer with the exacting pressures of being a single parent. The fame that followed the success of *Empire of the Sun* seems not to have disturbed his lifestyle at all.

For a reader curious about Ballard's life upon his move from China to England, his 1991 novel, *The Kindness of Women*, offers an enticing mix of autobiography and imagination. While real-life events are covered and include details such as Ballard's car crash, his subsequent exhibition of crashed cars at an avant-garde gallery in London, and his experimentation with hallucinogenic drugs in the 1970's, the novel should not be mistaken for a genuine autobiography. Composite characters and imagined or greatly exaggerated events abound, and most real-life characters are given new names, with the prominent exception of the protagonist, called Jim Ballard.

Unlike this novel's character, J. G. Ballard seems to have spent a lot of his creative energy on his imaginative writing. In addition to producing a steady output of original novels and short stories, Ballard has also been an active writer of essays and book reviews, which have made his a familiar voice in British literary circles.

ANALYSIS

J. G. Ballard's first seven novels can be easily sorted into two groups. The first four are novels of worldwide disaster, while the next three are stories of cruelty and alienation set in the concrete wilderness of contemporary urban society. All of his novels are, however, linked by a concern with the disintegration of civilization on a global or local scale.

Ballard's early disaster stories follow a well-established tradition in British imaginative fiction. British science-fiction writers from H. G. Wells to John Wyndham always seem to have been fascinated by the notion of the fragility and vulnerability of the human empire, and have produced many careful and clinical descriptions of its fall. The earlier works in this tradition are didactic tales, insisting on the vanity of human wishes and reveling in the idea that when the crunch comes, only the tough will survive. Ballard, in contrast, is quite unconcerned with drawing morals—his disaster stories are not at all social Darwinist parables. His main concern is with the psychological readjustments which the characters are forced to make when faced with the disintegration of their world: He sees the problem of catastrophic change largely in terms of adaptation.

In one of his earliest essays on science fiction—a "guest editorial" which he contributed to *New Worlds* in 1962—Ballard committed the heresy of declaring that H. G. Wells was "a disastrous influence on the subsequent course of science fiction." He suggested that the vocabulary of ideas to which science-fiction writers and readers had become accustomed should be thrown overboard, and with them its customary narrative forms and conventional plots. It was time, he said, to turn to the exploration of inner space rather than outer space, and to realize that "the only truly alien planet is Earth." He offered his opinion that Salvador Dalí might be the most pertinent source of inspiration for modern writers of science fiction. The rhetorical flourishes which fill this essay caution readers against taking it all *too* seriously, but in the main this is the prospectus which Ballard has tried to follow. He has practiced what he preached, shaking off the legacy of H. G. Wells, dedicating himself to the exploration of inner space and the development of new metaphysical (particularly metapsychological) systems, and steering well clear of the old plots and narrative formulas. In so doing, he made himself one of the most original writers of his generation; such novels as *Empire of the Sun* and *The Day of Creation* do indeed demonstrate the essential alienness of the planet on which we live.

The Wind from Nowhere

In *The Wind from Nowhere*, which is considerably inferior to the three other disaster novels, a slowly accelerating wind plucks the human-made world apart. No one can stand firm against this active rebellion of nature—neither the American armed forces nor the immensely rich industrialist Hardoon, who seeks to secrete himself within a gigantic concrete pyramid, which the wind eventually topples into an abyss. *The Wind from Nowhere* has a whole series of protagonists and shows the catastrophe from several viewpoints. This was one of the well-tried methods of retailing disaster stories, but it was unsuited to Ballard's particular ambitions, and in the other novels of this early quartet he employed single protagonists as focal points—almost as measuring devices to analyze in depth the significance of parallel physical and psychological changes.

The Drowned World

In *The Drowned World*, Earth's surface temperature has risen and is still gradually rising. Water released by the melting of the ice caps has inundated much of the land, and dense tropical jungle has spread rapidly through what were once the temperate zones, rendering them all but uninhabitable. Ballard suggests that the world is undergoing a kind of retrogression to the environment of the Triassic period. The novel's protagonist is Robert Kerans, a biologist monitoring the changes from a research station in partly submerged London.

The psychological effects of the transfiguration first manifest themselves as dreams in which Kerans sees "himself" (no longer human) wandering a primitive world dominated by a huge, fierce sun. These dreams, he concludes, are a kind of memory retained within the cellular heritage of humankind, now called forth again by the appropriate stimulus. Their promise is that they will free the nervous system from the domination of the recently evolved brain, whose appropriate environment is gone, and restore the harmony of primeval proto-consciousness and archaic environment. Kerans watches other people trying to adapt in their various ways to the circumstances in which they find themselves, but he sees the essential meaninglessness of their strategies. He accepts the pull of destiny and treks south, submitting to the psychic metamorphosis that strips away his humanity until he becomes "a second Adam searching for the forgotten paradises of the reborn sun."

The Drowned World was sufficiently original and sophisticated to be incomprehensible to most of the aficionados of genre science fiction, who did not understand what Ballard was about or why. A minority, however, recognized its significance and its import; its reputation is now firmly established as one of the major works of its period.

The Drought

In *The Drought* (later published as *The Burning World*), the pattern of physical change is reversed: Earth becomes a vast desert because a pollutant molecular film has formed on the surface of the world's oceans, inhibiting evaporation. The landscape is gradually transformed, the concrete city-deserts becoming surrounded by seas of hot sand instead of arable land, while the seashore retreats to expose new deserts of crystalline salt. The soil dies and civilization shrivels, fires reducing forests and buildings alike to white ash. Ransom, the protagonist, is one of the last stubborn few who are reluctant to join the exodus to the retreating sea. From his houseboat he watches the river dwindle away, draining the dregs of the social and natural order. He lives surrounded by relics of an extinguished past, bereft of purpose and no longer capable of emotional response.

Eventually, Ransom and his surviving neighbors are driven to seek refuge in the "dune limbo" of the new seashore and take their places in a new social order dominated by the need to extract fresh water from the reluctant sea. Here, he finds, people are simply marking time and fighting a hopeless rear-guard action. In the final section of the story, he goes inland again to see what has become of the city and its last few inhabitants. They, mad and monstrous, have found a new way of life, hideous but somehow appropriate to the universal aridity—which is an aridity of the soul as well as of the land.

THE CRYSTAL WORLD

In *The Crystal World*, certain areas of the Earth's surface are subjected to a strange process of crystallization as some mysterious substance is precipitated out of the ether. This is a more localized and less destructive catastrophe than those in *The Drowned World* and *The Drought*, but the implication is that it will continue until the world is consumed. The initially affected area is in Africa, where the novel is set. The central character is Dr. Sanders, the assistant director of a leper colony, who is at first horrified when he finds his mistress and some of his patients joyfully accepting the process of cystallization within the flesh of their own bodies. Eventually, of course, he comes to realize that no other destiny is appropriate to the new circumstances. What is happening is that time and space are somehow being reduced, so that they are supersaturated with matter. Enclaves from which time itself has "evaporated" are therefore being formed—fragments of eternity where living things, though they cannot continue to live, also cannot die, but undergo instead a complete exis-

tential transubstantiation. Here, metaphors developed in *The Drought* are literalized with the aid of a wonderfully gaudy invention.

The transformation of the world in *The Crystal World* is a kind of beautification, and it is much easier for the reader to sympathize with Sanders's acceptance of its dictates than with Kerans's capitulation to the demands of his dreams. For this reason, the novel has been more popular within the science-fiction community than either of its predecessors. It is, however, largely a recapitulation of the same theme, which does not really gain from its association with the lush romanticism that occasionally surfaces in Ballard's work—most noticeably in the short stories set in the imaginary American west-coast artists' colony Vermilion Sands, a beach resort populated by decadent eccentrics and the flotsam of bygone starcults who surround themselves with florid artificial environments.

CRASH

Seven years elapsed between publication of *The Crystal World* and the appearance of *Crash*. Although Ballard published numerous retrospective collections in the interim, his one major project was a collection of what he called "condensed novels"—a series of verbal collages featuring surreal combinations of images encapsulating what Ballard saw as the contemporary zeitgeist. In the world portrayed in these collages, there is a great deal of violence and perverted sexual arousal. Ubiquitous Ballardian images recur regularly: dead birds, junked space hardware, derelict buildings. Mixed in with these are secular icons: the suicide of entertainer Marilyn Monroe, the assassination of President John F. Kennedy, and other personalities whose fates could be seen as symbolic of the era in decline.

The theme of *Crash* is already well developed in the condensed novels (collected in the United Kingdom under the title *The Atrocity Exhibition*, 1969, and in the United States under the title *Love and Napalm: Export U.S.A.*). Cars, within the novel, are seen as symbols of power, speed, and sexuality—a commonplace psychoanalytic observation, to which Ballard adds the surprising further representation of the car crash as a kind of orgasm. The protagonist of the novel, who is called Ballard, finds his first car crash, despite all the pain and attendant anxiety, to be an initiation into a new way of being, whereby he is forced to reformulate his social relationships and his sense of purpose. Ballard apparently decided to write the book while considering the reactions of members of the public to an exhibition of crashed cars which he held at the New Arts Laboratory in London.

Although it is mundane by comparison with his previous novels—it is certainly not science fiction—*Crash* is by no means a realistic novel. Its subject matter is trauma and the private fantasization of alarming but ordinary events. The hero, at one point, does bear witness to a transformation of the world, but it is a purely subjective one while he is under the influence of a hallucinogen. He sees the landscapes of the city transformed, woven into a new metaphysics by the attribution of a new context of significance derived from his perverted fascination with cars and expressway architecture.

CONCRETE ISLAND

The two novels which followed *Crash* retain and extrapolate many of its themes. *Concrete Island* and *High Rise* are both robinsonades whose characters become Crusoes in the very heart of modern civilization, cast away within sight and earshot of the metropolitan hordes but no less isolated for their proximity. In *Concrete Island*, a man is trapped on a traffic island in the middle of a complex freeway intersection, unable to reach the side of the road because the stream of cars is never-ending. Like Crusoe, he sets out to make the best of his situation, using whatever resources—material and social—he finds at hand. He adapts so well, in the end, that he refuses the opportunity to leave when it finally arrives.

HIGH RISE

The high-rise apartment block which gives *High Rise* its title is intended to be a haven for the well-to-do middle class, a comfortable microcosm to which they can escape from the stressful outside world of work and anxiety. It is, perhaps, *too* well insulated from the world at large; it becomes a private empire where freedom from stress gives birth to a violent anarchy and a decay into savagery. If *Concrete Island* is spiritually akin to Daniel Defoe's *Robinson*

Crusoe (1719), then *High Rise* is akin to William Golding's *Lord of the Flies* (1954), though it is all the more shocking in translocating the decline into barbarism of Golding's novel from a remote island to suburbia, and in attributing the decline to adults who are well aware of what is happening rather than to children whose innocence provides a ready excuse. As always, Ballard's interest is in the psychological readjustments made by his chief characters, and the way in which the whole process proves to be ultimately cathartic.

A major theme in the condensed novels, which extends into the three novels of the second group, is what Ballard refers to as the "death of affect"—a sterilization of the emotions and attendant moral anesthesia, which he considers to be a significant contemporary trend induced by contemporary lifestyles. The greatest positive achievement of the characters in these novels is a special kind of ataraxia—a calm of mind rather different from the one Plato held up as an ideal, which allows one to live alongside all manner of horrors without being unusually moved to fear or pity.

THE UNLIMITED DREAM COMPANY

Another gap, though not such a long one, separates *High Rise* from *The Unlimited Dream Company*, a messianic fantasy of the redemption of Shepperton from suburban mundanity. Its protagonist, Blake, crashes a stolen aircraft into the Thames River at Shepperton. Though his dead body remains trapped in the cockpit, he finds himself miraculously preserved on the bank. At first he cannot accept his true state, but several unsuccessful attempts to leave the town and a series of visions combine to convince him that he has a specially privileged role to play: He must teach the people to fly, so that they can transcend their earthly existence to achieve a mystical union with the vegetable and mineral worlds, dissolving themselves into eternity as the chief characters did in *The Crystal World*. Though the name of the central character is significant, the book also appears to be closely allied with the paintings of another artist: the eccentric Stanley Spencer, who lived in another Thames-side town (Cookham) and delighted in locating within its mundane urban scenery images of biblical and transcendental significance.

The kind of redemption featured in *The Unlimited Dream Company* is as ambivalent as the kinds of adaptation featured in earlier novels, and its promise does not carry the same wild optimism that similar motifs are made to carry in most science-fiction and fantasy novels. It is perhaps best to view *The Unlimited Dream Company* as one more novel of adaptation, but one which reverses the pattern of the earlier works. Here, it is not Blake who must adapt to changes in the external world, but Shepperton which must adapt to him—and he, too, must adapt to his own godlike status. Blake is himself the "catastrophe" which visits Shepperton, the absolute at large within it whose immanence cannot be ignored or resisted. If the novel seems to the reader to be upbeat rather than downbeat, that is mainly the consequence of a change of viewpoint—and had the readers who thought *The Drowned World* downbeat been willing to accept such a change, they might have been able to find that novel equally uplifting.

HELLO AMERICA

Although *The Unlimited Dream Company* does not represent such a dramatic change of pattern as first appearances suggest, *Hello America* is certainly, for Ballard, a break with his own tradition. There is little in the novel that seems new in thematic terms, although it recalls his short stories much more than previous novels, but there is nevertheless a sense in which it represents a radical departure. The plot concerns the "rediscovery" in the twenty-second century of a largely abandoned America by an oddly assorted expedition from Europe. What they find are the shattered relics of a whole series of American mythologies. The central character, Wayne, dreams of resurrecting America and its dream, restoring the mythology of technological optimism and glamorous consumerism to operational status. He cannot do so, of course, but there is a consistent note of ironic nostalgia in his hopeless ambition. What is remarkable about the book is that it is a confection, an offhand entertainment to be enjoyed but not taken seriously. From Ballard the novelist, this is totally unexpected, though his short fiction has frequently shown him to be a witty writer, and a master of the ironic aside.

EMPIRE OF THE SUN

This change of direction proved, not unexpectedly, to be a purely temporary matter—a kind of brief holiday from more serious concerns. *Empire of the Sun* recovered all the mesmeric intensity of Ballard's earlier work, adding an extra turn of the screw by relating it to historically momentous events through which the author had actually lived. Although the book's young protagonist is named Jim and is the same age as Ballard was when he was interned by the Japanese, *Empire of the Sun* is—like *Crash* before it—by no means autobiographical in any strict sense. Jim's adventures are as exaggerated as the fictional Ballard's were, but the purpose of the exaggeration is here perfectly clear: What seems from an objective point of view to be a horrible and unmitigated catastrophe is to Jim simply part of the developing pattern of life, to which he must adapt himself, and which he takes aboard more or less innocently. From his point of view, given that the internment camp *is* the world, and not (as it is from the point of view of the adult internees) an intolerable interruption of the world, it is the behavior of the British prisoners which seems unreasonable and hostile, while the Japanese guards are the champions of order. The world does not begin to end for Jim until the war comes toward its close and the orderliness of camp life breaks down; that which others see as a source of hope and a possibility of redemption from their living hell is for Jim something else entirely, to which he reacts in characteristically idiosyncratic fashion. The frightful irony of all this is, as usual, overlaid and disguised by a straight-faced matter-of-factness which forbids the reader to cling to the conventional verities enshrined in an older, inherited attitude toward the war with Japan.

THE DAY OF CREATION

The Day of Creation returns to the Africa of *The Crystal World*, this time disrupted by the seemingly miraculous appearance of a new river whose "discoverer," Dr. Mallory of the World Health Organization, hopes that it may restore edenic life to territory spoiled for millennia by drought and ceaseless petty wars. Mallory's odyssey along the river upon which he bestows his own name might be seen as an inversion of Marlow's journey in Joseph Conrad's *Heart of Darkness* (1902), in which the mysteriously silent girl Noon is the hopeful counterpart of the soul-sick Kurtz; but the redemption promised by the river is a temporary illusion, and Noon herself may only be a figment of Mallory's imagination.

RUNNING WILD

The novella *Running Wild*, thinly disguised as a mass-murder mystery in which the entire adult population of a small town is massacred, is another playfully ironic piece, though rather less gaudy than *Hello America*—appropriately, in view of its setting, which is a cozy suburban landscape of the Home Counties; it is a long short story rather than a short novel, but it carries forward the argument of *High Rise* as well as brief black comedies such as "The Intensive Care Unit."

THE KINDNESS OF WOMEN

The Kindness of Women revisits Ballard's semiautobiographical subject matter, which he introduced with *Empire of the Sun*. The novel opens amid the Japanese invasion of Shanghai in 1937, an event Ballard himself witnessed as a boy. His protagonist's carefree adolescence is literally shattered by a bomb blast, when the Japanese air raid surprises a boy, again named Jim Ballard, as he strolls down the middle of Shanghai's amusement quarters. Moving from 1937 directly to Jim's arrival in post-World War II Great Britain, *The Kindness of Women* accompanies its protagonist to way stations modeled after significant events in the author's life, mixing imagination and autobiographical material. While *The Kindness of Women* covers terrain familiar to readers of Ballard's work, it nevertheless manages to shed fresh light on the author's recurring obsessions, themes, and symbols, such as the ubiquitous instances of downed aircraft, drained swimming pools, and concrete flyovers encircling Heathrow airport.

RUSHING TO PARADISE

Ballard's next novel, *Rushing to Paradise*, has been marketed as a satire on the follies of the environmentalist movement, but it is a more complicated text than that. Antihero Dr. Barbara Rafferty is on a quest to establish a South Sea sanctuary for the albatross on an island wrested from the French government. The novel suggests that this is really a private attempt to build a murderous playground to live out psychosexual needs of her own. This boldly unconventional idea is obviously linked to Ballard's familiar suggestion of the dominance of the psychological over the material. The novel's invention of new psychological disorders and obsessions, and its iconoclastic depiction of an environmentalist physician who develops into a quasi commandant presiding over a disused airfield and ruined camera towers, clearly gives *Rushing to Paradise* the surrealist streak common to Ballard's fiction.

Perhaps not surprisingly, *Rushing to Paradise* largely failed to connect with a larger audience. Even though the novel's premise of renewed French nuclear testing in the South Seas uncannily anticipated the real-life development of such tests in the mid-1990's and thus predicted the future, something rarely accomplished by traditional science-fiction texts, many readers apparently did not forgive Ballard his choice of an environmentalist woman as the novel's surreal centerpiece. Ballard's idiosyncratic characters, who had alienated science-fiction fans when *The Drowned World* was published, managed again to distance his work from readers unwilling to engage the author on his own unique artistic grounds.

COCAINE NIGHTS

Cocaine Nights, however, won great critical acclaim from British reviewers, who hailed the novel as Ballard's masterpiece for its fusion of surrealism and detective story. Ostensibly, *Cocaine Nights* tells of Charles Prentice's quest to exonerate his brother Frank, who is held in a Spanish jail and charged with a murder to which he has confessed. Utterly unconvinced that his brother has killed a wealthy family at a posh resort on the coast of southern Spain and believing his confession absurd, Charles tries to find the real culprit. His investigation quickly draws him into the orbit of Bobby Crawford, a rogue tennis instructor and self-appointed leader of a group of thrill-seeking English who fight terminal boredom by committing highly imaginative crimes and outrageous acts of vandalism.

With its emerging thesis that only the existence of crime can energize the somnolent resort community of terminally exhausted upper-middle-class retirees,

Ballard's novel flies again in the face of the common-sense reader used to realistic fiction. Like his best work before, *Cocaine Nights* entices by its outrageously absurd proposal of the criminal as benefactor to humanity, and it confirms Ballard's position as one of England's most imaginative, original, and creative novelists.

Brian Stableford, updated by R. C. Lutz

OTHER MAJOR WORKS

SHORT FICTION: *The Voices of Time*, 1962; *Billenium*, 1962; *The Four-Dimensional Nightmare*, 1963; *Passport to Eternity*, 1963; *The Terminal Beach*, 1964; *The Impossible Man*, 1966; *The Disaster Area*, 1967; *The Overloaded Man*, 1967; *The Atrocity Exhibition*, 1969 (also known as *Love and Napalm: Export U.S.A.*); *Vermilion Sands*, 1971; *Chronopolis and Other Stories*, 1971; *The Best Short Stories of J. G. Ballard*, 1978; *Myths of the Near Future*, 1982; *Memories of the Space Age*, 1988; *War Fever*, 1990.

NONFICTION: *A User's Guide to the Millennium: Essays and Reviews*, 1996.

BIBLIOGRAPHY

Jones, Mark. "J. G. Ballard: Neurographer." In *Impossibility Fiction*, edited by Derek Littlewood. Amsterdam: Rodopi Press, 1996. Jones sees Ballard's fiction as characterized by the recurring theme of the author's description of the human mind as a kind of geographic landscape. Praises Ballard for his radical, surrealist descriptions of a new relationship between mind and reality.

Luckhurst, Roger. *"The Angle Between Two Walls": The Fiction of J. G. Ballard*. New York: St. Martin's Press, 1997. Most comprehensive study of Ballard's work. Thorough discussion and analysis of his fiction. Well-researched and extremely informative.

_____. "Petition, Repetition, and 'Autobiography': J. G. Ballard's *Empire of the Sun* and *The Kindness of Women*." *Contemporary Literature* 35, no. 4 (Winter, 1994): 688-708. Useful study of the historical veracity of Ballard's two novels. Luckhurst tries to discover methods and thematic and aesthetic strategies that have organized and informed Ballard's fictional work along with his autobiographical source material.

Pringle, David. *Earth Is the Alien Planet: J. G. Ballard's Four-Dimensional Nightmare*. San Bernardino, Calif.: Borgo Press, 1979. A monograph in Borgo's Milford series, featuring a biographical sketch and an excellent analysis of Ballard's work, by a critic who has followed the author's career very closely.

Re-Search: J. G. Ballard. San Francisco: Re-Search, 1983. A special issue of a periodical publication devoted to Ballard and his works, including an interview, critical articles, and some unusual items by Ballard; it views Ballard as an avant-garde literary figure rather than a science-fiction writer.

Stableford, Brian. "J. G. Ballard." In *Science Fiction Writers*, edited by E. F. Bleiler. New York: Charles Scribner's Sons, 1982. A competent overview of the author's work.

HONORÉ DE BALZAC

Born: Tours, France; May 20, 1799
Died: Paris, France; August 18, 1850

PRINCIPAL LONG FICTION

La Comédie humaine, 1829-1848 (17 volumes; *The Comedy of Human Life*, 1885-1893, 1896 [40 volumes]; also as *The Human Comedy*, 1895-1896, 1911 [53 volumes], includes all titles listed below)

Les Chouans, 1829 (*The Chouans*)

Physiologie du mariage, 1829 (*The Physiology of Marriage*)

Gobseck, 1830 (English translation)

La Maison du chat-qui-pelote, 1830, 1869 (*At the Sign of the Cat and Racket*)

Le Chef-d'œuvre inconnu, 1831 (*The Unknown Masterpiece*)

La Peau de chagrin, 1831 (*The Wild Ass's Skin*; also as *The Fatal Skin*)

(Library of Congress)

Melmoth réconcilié, 1835 (*Melmoth Converted*)
Le Père Goriot, 1834-1835 (*Daddy Goriot*, 1860;
    also as *Père Goriot*)
Le Lys dans la vallée, 1836 (*The Lily in the Valley*)
*Histoire de la grandeur et de la décadence de
    César Birotteau*, 1837 (*History of the Grandeur
    and Downfall of César Birotteau*, 1860; also as
    César Birotteau)
Illusions perdues, 1837-1843 (*Lost Illusions*)
Splendeurs et misères des courtisanes, 1838-1847,
    1869 (*The Splendors and Miseries of Courte-
    sans*; includes *Comment aiment les filles*, 1838,
    1844 [*The Way That Girls Love*]; *À combien
    l'amour revient aux viellards*, 1844 [*How Much
    Love Costs Old Men*]; *Où mènent les mauvais
    chemins*, 1846 [*The End of Bad Roads*]; *La
    Dernière incarnation de Vautrin*, 1847 [*The
    Last Incarnation of Vautrin*])
Pierrette, 1840 (English translation)
Le Curé de village, 1841 (*The Country Parson*)
Mémoires de deux jeunes mariées, 1842 (*The Two
    Young Brides*)
Une Ténébreuse Affaire, 1842 (*The Gondreville
    Mystery*)
Ursule Mirouët, 1842 (English translation)
La Cousine Bette, 1846 (*Cousin Bette*)
Le Cousin Pons, 1847 (*Cousin Pons*, 1880)

Sarrasine, 1831 (English translation)
Le Curé de Tours, 1832 (*The Vicar of Tours*)
Louis Lambert, 1832 (English translation)
Maître Cornélius, 1832 (English translation)
La Femme de trente ans, 1832-1842 (includes
    Premières fautes, 1832, 1842; *Souffrances
    inconnues*, 1834-1835; *À trente ans*, 1832,
    1842; *Le Doigt de Dieu*, 1832, 1834-1835,
    1842; *Les Deux Rencontres*, 1832, 1834-1835,
    1842; *La Vieillesse d'une mère coupable*, 1832,
    1842)
Eugénie Grandet, 1833 (English translation, 1859)
La Recherche de l'absolu, 1834 (*Balthazar: Or,
    Science and Love*, 1859; also as *The Quest of
    the Absolute*)
Histoire des treize, 1834-1835 (*History of the Thir-
    teen*; also as *The Thirteen*; includes *Ferragus,
    chef des dévorants*, 1834 [*Ferragus, Chief of the
    Devorants*; also as *The Mystery of the Rue
    Solymane*]; *La Duchesse de Langeais*, 1834
    [*The Duchesse de Langeais*]; *La Fille aus yeux
    d'or*, 1834-1835 [*The Girl with the Golden
    Eyes*])

OTHER LITERARY FORMS

In addition to his fiction, Honoré de Balzac wrote
several plays, including *Cromwell* (1925; written
1819-1820), *Vautrin* (1840; English translation, 1901),
and *Le Faiseur*, also known as *Mercadet* (first performed in 1849; English translation, 1901), but he
was not a playwright and generally devoted time to
the theater only when he felt that there was a good
profit to be made with little effort. Likewise, many of
the articles and essays that Balzac wrote between
1825 and 1834, published in such journals as *Le
Voleur*, *La Mode*, *La Caricature*, *La Silhouette*, and
La Revue de Paris, were composed in order to acquire ready money. Balzac's letters to the Polish baroness Evelina Hanska, to his family, and to Madame
Zulma Carraud were published after the novelist's
death.

ACHIEVEMENTS

The Human Comedy, Balzac's masterwork, is one of the greatest literary achievements of all time. It contains many novels beyond those listed above, the bulk of which were written between 1830 and 1847. Before 1829, Balzac wrote under various pseudonyms—notably "Lord R'Hoone" and "Horace de Saint Aubin"—and frequently composed novels in collaboration with other writers. These twenty or so early volumes, which include *Sténie: Ou, Les Erreurs philosophiques* (1936; Sténie: or, philosophical errors), *Falturne* (1950), *Le Centenaire: Ou, Les Deux Beringheld* (1822; *The Centenarian: Or, The Two Beringhelds*, 1976), and *La Dernière Fée* (1823; the last fairy), were later renounced by Balzac, and rightly so, for they were written in haste and were obvious attempts to exploit the current taste for gothic melodrama and romantic adventures.

BIOGRAPHY

Honoré Balzac was born in Tours, France, on May 20, 1799, of bourgeois parents. He was to acquire the predicate of nobility—the name by which he is known today—when, in 1831, in tribute to his official commitment to embark upon the writing of *The Human Comedy*, he dubbed himself Honoré *de* Balzac. This change of name is symptomatic of Balzac's lifelong craving to be an aristocrat and to enjoy the deep respect and the want-for-nothing lifestyle which accompanied that status.

The eldest of four children, Balzac was treated very coldly by his parents, who entrusted him to the care of a wet nurse for four years, then sent him to board with a family of strangers for two years, and finally had him attend for seven years a boarding school in Vendôme. Balzac's childhood years were loveless and painful, which probably encouraged him to turn inward toward dreams and fantasies. By 1816, Balzac had finished his studies in Vendôme, albeit with far less than a brilliant record, and was sent off to Paris to study jurisprudence, his mother ordering him to "shape up" and work very hard. At the age of twenty, however, Balzac declared to his family his surprising intention to become a writer, not a lawyer. When his parents skeptically agreed to his wishes,

Balzac was permitted to live in Paris for two years, where he was set up in a poorly furnished apartment and was given a deliberately insufficient allowance, which was intended to demonstrate to this wayward son the harsh economic facts of life.

Between 1819 and 1829, Balzac was forced to earn a living from writing, a situation that led him to compromise his literary genius for money; when this endeavor proved inadequate, he was not too proud to undertake other occupations. In an effort to ensure his freedom to write, Balzac became a bookseller, then a printer, then a journalist. All of these enterprises, however, ultimately failed. His most notorious business venture occurred in 1838, when he speculated on Sardinian silver mines. Everything Balzac tried to do as a businessman only drove him deeper into debt, a state of affairs that he often transposed to the realm of his fiction; yet even when Balzac was at the mercy of creditors and in danger of being arrested, he remained, at bottom, optimistic. His new novel would rescue him, at least temporarily, from financial embarrassment, or his current business venture would surely make him wealthy, or, best of all, an aristocratic lady—and there was nearly always a prospect—would soon become his wife and give him not only her love but also her fortune. Nearly all of the women who mattered to Balzac were, in fact, noble, from Madame Laure de Berny, who sacrificed both her morals and her money to help the budding genius to survive, to Madame Evelina Hanska, the Polish baroness who began by writing anonymous letters of admiration to the well-known author and eventually, after her husband's death and her daughter's marriage, consented to become Balzac's wife.

It is an irony which suitably parallels that of the fictional world portrayed in *The Human Comedy* that Balzac's marriage to this woman of his dreams occurred only five months before his death. Balzac died from what one may term outright exhaustion on August 18, 1850.

ANALYSIS: THE HUMAN COMEDY

At the age of thirty, Balzac resolved to become a great French writer. At first, he believed that he could accomplish this goal by emulating the Scottish writer Sir Walter Scott, whose historical novels were highly esteemed in France during the first half of the nineteenth century. Like Scott, Balzac would be a historian of social, psychological, and political life. Later, however, as Balzac explains in his preface to *The Human Comedy*, this idea was modified. Balzac finally saw his true and original role to be that of "the secretary of society" rather than that of a social historian; that is, instead of bringing the past to life, as Scott had done, Balzac chose to transcribe the life around him into fiction. In many ways, the author of *The Human Comedy* is faithful to this role, drawing a picture of French society at all levels from roughly 1815 until the end of his writing career in 1848. In his novels, Balzac reveals the driving passions and needs of a wide range of individuals in various social positions: noblemen and aristocratic ladies; politicians, bankers, businessmen, and moneylenders; scientists, doctors, and priests; lawyers, policemen, and criminals; musicians, painters, sculptors, and writers. This picture of society delineates not only ambitious members of the bourgeoisie and proud aristocrats but also the environments in which they live and work, including the luxurious, exhilarating, and cutthroat life of Paris and the comparatively dull and inactive existence of small provincial French towns. The two thousand characters whom Balzac depicts in *The Human Comedy* are not, however, mere social types. On the contrary, Balzac's protagonists are, in general, strongly individualistic, some of them to the point of eccentricity.

Each novel of *The Human Comedy* contains a single story that may be read and appreciated for itself; at the same time, each story is linked to the whole. A protagonist encountered in one novel might very well appear again, like an old acquaintance, within the context of another novel and possibly a very different plot. The small number of characters who travel from one novel to another give unity to Balzac's works and at the same time convey the impression that the fictional world described in *The Human Comedy* is alive and infinite in scope.

With regard to tone, Balzac's plots embrace a wide range of attitudes: tragically sad or comically ironic, highly idealistic, fantastic, or romantic. The novelist, however, is judged to have excelled particularly as a realist in his candid portrayal of the tremendous will to power of human nature and of the influence of money upon social behavior.

In Balzac's works, many of the characteristic impulses of the nineteenth century coincided and reinforced one another. Balzac's legendary energy, his enormous, hubristic ambition, his tireless interest in the world, and his sheer appetite for experience—all these elements worked together to produce a massive tapestry of an entire society, unmatched in scope and detail before or since the author's time.

There are three themes in Honoré de Balzac's fiction that can be seen as reflections of the novelist's personality. First, there is the theme of madness or monomania; second, the large role given to money; and third, the recurrent search of Balzac's characters for love and success. The madmen of *The Human Comedy* include some of Balzac's most original and memorable characters. These figures are generally obsessed by an idea which they try to make into a reality and for which they sacrifice everything. Although the individual obsessions of these protagonists vary, Frenhofer, the painter in *The Unknown Masterpiece*, Grandet, the miser in *Eugénie Grandet*, and Claes, the scientist in *The Quest of the Absolute*, are nevertheless shadows of Balzac, the author, who expresses through them his own obsession: the painstaking composition of *The Human Comedy*. Balzac wrote for hours, weeks, and months on end to prove his genius to the world. Everything was sacrificed for his literary task, including a comfortable lodging, clothes, and the most insignificant of worldly amusements.

The monomaniacs of Balzac's creation are particularly interesting figures. They are intelligent and possess glorious ideas, which, if they initially seem eccentric, at the same time denote genius. Their bold determination to accomplish all they have set out to do is, however, admirable only to a point. Balzac always shows that the obsessions of his monomaniacs dehumanize them. When, for example, Claes in *The Quest of the Absolute* sacrifices the sustenance of his family in order to continue financing his experiments, Balzac pushes his protagonist's passion to an extreme. The manias of Balzac's characters slowly annihilate everything around them until, in the end, these figures appear so blinded by their passion that they are completely enslaved by it. The tragic depiction of Balzac's monomaniacs is undoubtedly one of the cornerstones of *The Human Comedy*. These characters, who first command one's admiration, then appeal to one's sympathy, and finally elicit one's scorn, cause one to ponder with Balzac the force of human thought and willpower. Moreover, by means of his monomaniacs, Balzac expresses his own obsession and his fear of it.

Another important theme of *The Human Comedy* is money, which, in Balzac's fictional world, dominates all other values. In a sense, Balzac's attitude toward money is ambivalent. On one hand, he often shows nostalgia for the neoclassic age, when, under the monarchy, a member of the nobility was assured a life of ease and intellectual grandeur. On the other hand, however, Balzac accepts and objectively portrays the bourgeois society of his day. It is a society whose wheels are oiled by money, but many of Balzac's heroes feel optimistically that, by means of their intelligence, they can succeed in conquering the cycle. Apparently, Balzac himself believed that the appearance of money was enough to command respect and receive social acceptance. Sometimes when his characters wear expensive-looking clothes and ride about in fancy carriages, they are, in fact, engaged in a carefully calculated masquerade to fool society by using its own superficial code against it. Of course, some of Balzac's protagonists succeed in this way, but most of them fail—paralleling the novelist's career, in which successes were few and financial failures many. Balzac's most pointed criticism of the role of money in society is not, however, that it is the entry ticket to social success. In such novels as *Père Goriot* and *Eugénie Grandet*, Balzac portrays money in its most diabolical role, as a corrupter of the noblest of human feelings, love.

Balzac depicts two kinds of love in his novels. Ideal love is the quest of many protagonists of *The Human Comedy*, who suffer in its absence and fail to realize its glorious promise. Desirable women in Balzac's fiction are often much older than their aspiring lovers, leading biographers to speculate about Balzac's own mother's indifference toward him and about the novelist's first amorous adventure with Madame de Berny, who—when Balzac met her at the age of twenty-two—was twenty-two years older than he. Aristocratic and maternal women such as Madame de Mortsauf in *The Lily in the Valley* represent a supreme love the likes of which cannot be matched. The very ideal quality of this love, however, is perhaps what leads to its impossibility. Although Balzac's characters glimpse the perfect love object time and time again, the latter generally remains out of reach because of societal or financial constraints. In contrast, love, as Balzac portrays it in his fictional society, is a dangerous counterfeit. Coquettish females of *The Human Comedy*, such as Antoinette de Langeais in *The Duchess de Langeais* (a part of *The Thirteen*), provoke innocent gentlemen to fall in love with them only to cultivate their own egos. For the boldest male protagonists of *The Human Comedy*, love is like money, something to be used to advance oneself in society. Rastignac in *Père Goriot* and Raphaël de Valentin in *The Wild Ass's Skin*, for example, make the calculated decision to fall in love, one with a wealthy banker's wife and the other with an aristocratic lady. Family love and devotion are also shams, falling into insignificance when confronted by personal ambition and money.

THE WILD ASS'S SKIN

Balzac classified the novels of *The Human Comedy* into three large areas: "Studies of Social Manners," "Philosophical Studies," and "Analytical Studies." *The Wild Ass's Skin*, published in 1831, was placed into the category "Philosophical Studies," probably because of its fantastic theme, the possession of a magic skin. Like many of Balzac's best novels, however, *The Wild Ass's Skin* is actually a mixture of cold reality and fantastic illusion. The hero of the novel, Raphaël de Valentin, a downtrodden genius whom society persistently ignores, is clearly a figure with whom the novelist could identify. Balzac's protagonist has written a philosophical treatise entitled "Théorie de la volonté" ("Theory of the Will"), a work whose exact contents are never revealed but whose significance for Balzac and for *The Human Comedy* is evident. Like his hero, Valentin, Balzac is engaged in an analysis of man's will. Valentin may appear to be more theoretical than the novelist, but both Balzac and his protagonist find the power of ideas at work in the mind to be a fascinating and dangerous study. One suspects that Valentin is actually an image of Balzac's own projected success as well as the foreboding prototype of his failure.

The destiny of Raphaël de Valentin follows a curve from failure to success and back to failure again. At the beginning of the book, he thinks seriously about committing suicide for two reasons. First, he has suffered very deeply in his love for a beautiful but heartless coquette named Foedora. Second, Valentin is destitute. Even though his "Theory" has finally been completed—a lifework that ought to be acknowledged as striking proof of his genius—societal acclaim is still denied him. When Balzac later explains in his epilogue to the novel that Foedora is actually a symbol of society, one understands that her indifference to Valentin includes not only a condemnation of a would-be lover but also a cruel underestimation of his intelligence, the hero's very *raison d'être*. The initial tragedy of Valentin is realistically portrayed as a battle between a sensitive romantic young man and Parisian society.

In the next phase of Valentin's destiny, however, one sees an abrupt transformation which at first appears to project Balzac's hero to the heights of success. Valentin acquires from a mysterious antiquarian a wild ass's skin. Because, as in a fairy tale, the magic skin grants its owner's every wish, Valentin need no longer be poor. Indeed, it is society's turn to court him! Now the Parisian society that Valentin previously hoped to please is depicted as thoroughly repulsive and morally corrupt. As a sign of Valentin's rejection of it, one of his wishes is that he may forget Foedora, the novel's symbol of society. One may find in Valentin's change of attitude toward society the novelist's own admission to himself that what he ultimately seeks—general recognition of his genius as a writer—simply does not exist in a world ruled by personal vanity and money. Now that Foedora has been forgotten, she is replaced in Valentin's heart by

Pauline, a poor, innocent young girl who has always shown him true love and devotion.

This "happy ending" is short-lived, however. In the final phase of Valentin's destiny, Balzac returns to the philosophical theme of man's will. The wild ass's skin that Valentin possesses is not a blessing after all, but a curse. After each wish that it grants to its owner, the skin shrinks in dimension, its dwindling size quickly becoming a horrifying picture of the diminishing length of Valentin's life.

It is interesting to correlate this tragic depiction of Balzac's hero with the situation of the novelist himself. When Balzac wrote *The Wild Ass's Skin* in 1831, he was already aware that his enormous writing task would take him away from the world of reality and cause him to become a more firmly established inhabitant of his fictional world. After the protagonist of *The Wild Ass's Skin* has unmasked society, he attempts to withdraw from it. Perhaps, pen in hand, wearing his monk's cloak, Balzac, too, may have thought that he could escape to the fictional realm of his imagination. Eventually, however, reality always intervened and subjugated the writer to its practical demands. Hence, Balzac gives that part of himself which repudiates money and all those who worship it a kind of allowance analogous to money. Valentin must make fewer and fewer wishes and finally tries not to express any desires at all, simply in order to continue living.

In this complex novel, Balzac transposes into fiction his own misery, his maddening drive to succeed, his dreams and love for life, while giving the reader a survey of the themes that will permeate many novels of *The Human Comedy*: money, unrealized love, the drive to succeed, and madness.

THE VICAR OF TOURS

Balzac finished writing *The Vicar of Tours* in April, 1832. In this short novel, Balzac, like Gustave Flaubert in his famous short story "Un Coeur simple" ("A Simple Heart"), relates a story that superficially seems unworthy of mention. Balzac's hero, Birotteau, like Flaubert's heroine, Félicité, is rather simpleminded and lives an uneventful life. True to the nature of Balzac's most memorable heroes, however, Birotteau is quite different from Félicité in that, despite his lack of intelligence, he is ambitious. Furthermore, he is naïvely happy. Balzac alternately pities and ridicules his provincial priest, whose passion it is to possess the beautiful apartment of his colleague, Chapeloud. While pointing out that a desire for material wealth is not seemly for a priest, Balzac ironically pardons his hero, who is, after all, only human and whose ambition, as ambitions go, can only be termed petty.

When Birotteau's ambition is fulfilled upon the death of Chapeloud, the apartment becomes the subject of a war of wills, involving not only Birotteau's spinster landlady, Mademoiselle Gamard, but eventually the whole town of Tours. Indeed, a political career in the highest echelons of the French government and the important advancement of a priest within the Catholic Church both end up having, in some way, a relationship to what begins as Birotteau's "insignificant" passion.

In some ways, Birotteau is the opposite of the typical Balzacian monomaniac. Happy to let everything be handled by his friends and incapable of understanding what is going on, he watches the battle rage around him. Birotteau would not purposely hurt a fly, and he does not have an inkling of why he is being attacked.

As in many novels of *The Human Comedy*, an important turn in the plot of *The Vicar of Tours* hinges upon a legal document, in this case the apartment lease. Balzac's years as a law student often served him well, and he used his knowledge of the law in composing many of his plots. Essentially missing from this novel is one of Balzac's major themes, money. Nevertheless, the vanity of the characters in *The Vicar of Tours* and their drive for personal success and power are keenly developed subjects of satire and, at the same time, very realistic studies of human psychology and social behavior. Balzac classed *The Vicar of Tours* under the heading "Scenes of Provincial Life," a subcategory of "Studies of Social Manners"—where the largest number of novels in *The Human Comedy* can be found.

LOUIS LAMBERT

Approximately three months after completing *The Vicar of Tours*, in July, 1832, Balzac finished *Louis Lambert*. This novel was eventually included with *The Wild Ass's Skin* and eighteen other novels in the category "Philosophical Studies," but its relationship to Balzac's "Studies of Social Manners" is strengthened through the device of recurring characters. One of the minor figures of *The Vicar of Tours* is an old woman, Mademoiselle Salomon de Villenoix, who befriends Birotteau and shows him a great deal of compassion. In *Louis Lambert*, the same woman plays a more important role, as Balzac describes Mademoiselle de Villenoix in her youth, when she was the ideal love object of Louis Lambert, the principal character of the novel.

The parallels between *The Wild Ass's Skin* and *Louis Lambert* are quite interesting. Like Raphaël de Valentin, Louis Lambert is a genius who composes a philosophical work on the will; the title of his work, "Traité de la volonté" ("Treatise on the Will"), is virtually identical with Valentin's. Valentin and Lambert succeed in finding an ideal woman whose name is Pauline: Pauline de Villenoix in *Louis Lambert* and Pauline de Witschnau in *The Wild Ass's Skin*. Finally, the tragedy of both genius-heroes lies in the fact that they go mad. The Paulines of the two novels react to the inexplicable madness of the men they love by devoting themselves totally to them, somewhat like nurses or angels of mercy.

The similarities between *Louis Lambert* and *The Wild Ass's Skin* give one a fairly clear idea of what must have been Balzac's attitude toward himself. The novelist instills in his heroes two great passions that are undoubtedly reflections of his own drives: to become a recognized genius and to be loved. In these two novels, Balzac appears to demonstrate his belief that love and genius cannot coexist and that when one attempts to blend them, they annihilate each other. In this sense, the madness that overcomes Balzac's protagonists represents a double failure. Both Lambert and Valentin fall short of attaining ideal love and also fail to develop the potential of their genius.

It is nevertheless true that Balzac shows the passions of Louis Lambert for love and for recognition of his genius somewhat differently from the way he portrays these passions in his earlier novel. In *Louis*

Lambert, the novelist seems to indicate a preference for one of the two goals when he emphasizes Lambert's genius. From the beginning of the novel, Lambert is seen through the eyes of an admiring narrator who relates in retrospect the bitter experiences of school days shared with Balzac's genius-hero. In detailing these experiences, Balzac transposes into fiction many of his own memories of the lonely years spent as a boarder at the Collège de Vendôme. Both the narrator and Lambert are neglected by their parents, ostracized by their peers, punished by their teachers, and forbidden—as in a prison—to enjoy even the slightest amusement. The narrator admits to being inferior to Lambert, whose genius he sensed when they were in school together and whose insights, although they now can be only half-remembered, had the power of truth.

At the end of the novel, Balzac intensifies sympathy for the plight of his genius-hero gone mad by reproducing a series of philosophical fragments which, because they are written down by Lambert's loving companion, Pauline, are only sketchy transcriptions of his actual thoughts. It is not important that these fragments appear puzzling and in some cases absurd: Like the incomplete recollections of the narrator, they are powerfully evocative *because* they are fragmentary, tantalizingly so, suggestive of what the world lost with the genius of Louis Lambert.

EUGÉNIE GRANDET

Before the publication of *Eugénie Grandet* in 1833, Balzac had continued to experiment in his novels with the theme of madness. In addition to *Louis Lambert*, Balzac had written other "Philosophical Studies" between 1830 and 1832 which expand on this theme, including *The Unknown Masterpiece* and *Maître Cornélius*. In *The Unknown Masterpiece*, Balzac portrayed a painter, Frenhofer, whose madness manifests itself in his increasing inability to transpose the idealized feminine figure he imagines to a canvas. The hero of *Maître Cornélius* suffers from an insidious malady. When he sleepwalks, his unconscious self steals the money which, in reality, he is supposed to guard.

In *Eugénie Grandet*, however, the theme of madness reaches a turning point. Balzac's protagonist,

Old Grandet, like Maître Cornélius, is a miser, but what distinguishes him from the latter is that his mania does not indicate total sickness or madness. Grandet's passion does not seem to debilitate him in any way. On the contrary, it is his *raison d'être* and is willfully and, one may even say, intellectually directed. Grandet, one of the most fascinating characters of *The Human Comedy*, is a full-blown monomaniac. What makes him so interesting is that he is not one-dimensional. Although Grandet's obsessive drive for money remains constant throughout the novel, he is not always seen in the same light. In relations with his wife, his cook, his small-town neighbors, and especially his daughter, Eugénie, Grandet sparks off a variety of reactions to his miserly behavior. At times, he is admired and feared for his sharp intelligence. At other times, he is condemned for his lack of understanding and unyielding ruthlessness.

Yet manifestations of Grandet's monomania do not, by themselves, dominate the novel. Rather, Grandet's avarice competes for importance with another, complementary plot: the awakening of Grandet's daughter to love. Indeed, in *Eugénie Grandet*, the three subjects which have been identified as key themes in Balzac's fiction—madness, money, and the search for love—converge. Grandet's obsession with money comes into conflict with Eugénie's equally strong impulse to love. While her father's nature is to hoard money even if it means that his family must be destitute, Eugénie finds in giving away all of her money to her beloved cousin, Charles, a supreme expression of love.

Balzac pits his young heroine against other adversaries as well: provincial opportunism, social morality, and Charles's ambitions. Using his innocent and naïve heroine as a foil, Balzac reveals the crass motives of provincial society, contrasting Eugénie's exceptional, giving nature with the self-interest of others who, like Eugénie's father, are motivated primarily by money. Balzac placed *Eugénie Grandet* into the subcategory of *The Human Comedy* entitled "Scenes of Provincial Life."

PÈRE GORIOT

Published in 1835, *Père Goriot*, given its Parisian locale, could easily have been placed into the category of *The Human Comedy* called "Scenes of Parisian Life." Balzac finally classified it, however, among his "Scenes of Private Life," which is an equally suitable designation for the novel. *Père Goriot* is a pivotal novel of *The Human Comedy* in several ways. First, with respect to Balzac's trademark, the use of recurring characters, nearly all the characters in this novel, whether their roles are large or small, can be found somewhere else in Balzac's opus, with the exception of Goriot himself. Some characters were already seen in works published before 1835; others would be developed in subsequent novels. Eugène de Rastignac, the young hero of *Père Goriot*, for example, appeared briefly as a friend of Raphaël de Valentin in *The Wild Ass's Skin*. Similarly, Goriot's older daughter, Anasthasie, was already portrayed in a short novel, *Gobseck*, published in 1830. The criminal Jacques Collin, alias Vautrin, who makes his debut in *Père Goriot*, would be given prominent roles in such later works as *Lost Illusions* and *The Splendors and Miseries of Courtesans*.

Balzac successfully interweaves three different plots in *Père Goriot*, their relationship being that the principal protagonists of all three live in the same Parisian boardinghouse, La Maison Vauquer. Eugène de Rastignac is an innocent provincial young man, new to Parisian manners but eager to learn. In a sense, Rastignac takes up the same crusade as did Raphël de Valentin in *The Wild Ass's Skin*, in that he directs all of his efforts toward "conquering" society—which means that, like Valentin, he strives to earn social acceptance and esteem. One notes, however, that Balzac does not make Rastignac a writer, like Valentin. Rather, shadowing another part of Balzac's own past, the young hero of *Père Goriot* is a poor law student.

Old Goriot himself is another inhabitant of La Maison Vauquer. He is a Balzacian monomaniac, a hero whose "madness" is self-willed and consciously directed. Goriot is not, however, another copy of Balzac's miser, Grandet; rather, Balzac opposes these two figures. Goriot is not a miser; he does not hoard money. On the contrary, he spends it on his two daughters, Anasthasie and Delphine. Whereas Grandet causes his family to live like paupers in order to

continue amassing money, Goriot willingly strips himself of his means of sustenance in order to continue giving money to his daughters. Balzac's intent in portraying Goriot may have been to examine the power of money in a situation which contrasts directly with that of his miser, Grandet. Certainly, Balzac never found a more intense formula for tragedy than when he created his monomaniac Goriot, who attempts to link money and love.

The third major plot of *Père Goriot* centers upon another inhabitant of La Maison Vauquer, Vautrin, who—unbeknown to the other boarders of Madame Vauquer's establishment—is an escaped convict wanted by the police. Vautrin's view of society is in absolute opposition to that of Rastignac; whereas the young man attempts to court social favor, Vautrin denounces everything to do with the social order, calling it a *bourbier*, or mudhole. Intelligent and cynical, Vautrin advocates a different sort of social conquest, namely, bold defiance and outright rebellion.

Unlike most of the preceding novels in *The Human Comedy, Père Goriot* is a novel with multiple heroes and multiple plots. Balzac offers the reader a fresco of social manners through characters who represent very different classes of society, from the aristocrat and the bourgeois to the criminal *révolté*. Balzac's technique of portraying his protagonists from various contrasting angles—seen in *The Vicar of Tours* and in *Eugénie Grandet*—is used much more extensively in *Père Goriot*. Goriot, Goriot's daughters, Rastignac, Vautrin, and other characters as well are alternately judged to be admirable, honest, and powerful, and to be imperfect, deceitful, and helpless. Goriot, in particular, is delineated by means of a kaleidoscope of contrary impressions. He loves his daughters, but he also hates them. His love is fatherly and not so fatherly. He is both self-sacrificing and self-interested. In death, he curses his daughters and pardons them in the same breath. Clearly, in *Père Goriot*, Balzac reached maturity as a novelist.

COUSIN BETTE

Cousin Bette was published rather late in Balzac's career, in 1846, and was placed, along with a complementary work entitled *Cousin Pons*, among the "Scenes of Parisian Life." In the ten years between the publication of *Père Goriot* and that of *Cousin Bette*, Balzac wrote approximately forty-five other novels, many of which continued to develop the three major themes in his fiction—madness, money, and the search for love and success.

It is interesting to see all three themes once again interwoven in *Cousin Bette*, albeit in a strikingly different manner. In one of the novel's subplots, a new type of monomania is depicted in Baron Hulot d'Evry, who is driven repeatedly to commit adultery although it is an embarrassment to himself, his wife, and his family. Balzac hints at Hulot's hidden motivation when he describes his protagonist's wife, Adeline, as a martyr figure, a religious zealot, and a model of propriety.

Elisabeth Fischer—called "Cousin Bette"—is aware that the Hulot family, headed by Adeline, receives her only out of family duty and that, as a poor relation, she is neither loved nor esteemed by them. Even though she realizes that the apparent good fortune and happiness of the Hulot family are a carefully contrived sham, Bette is jealous of her cousin Adeline for having always been prettier, wealthier, and more successful than she. Cousin Bette's vengeance against the Hulot family, which is the principal plot of the novel, incorporates all three of the major themes of Balzac's fiction. Because Cousin Bette has no money, no success, and no love, her maddened drive for vengeance is unleashed. Her desire for revenge becomes a mania, and she is soon driven to the point where there is absolutely no limit to what she will do to ruin her cousin's life, including finding new females to entice both the Baron and Adeline's proposed son-in-law, Steinbock.

As though to intensify the diabolical power of Cousin Bette, Balzac adds to it the equally unscrupulous machinations of his heroine's pretty neighbor, Valérie Marneffe. Valérie helps Bette carry out her revenge against the Hulot family, and Bette, in return, aids her neighbor in an enterprise to extract money from her many male admirers. Valérie, a beautiful and ambitious middle-class woman, discovers that she can find financial success by seducing men and making them pay for her love. It is interesting that when Valérie is given the chance to run away to South America with an exotic Brazilian nobleman who loves her sincerely, she refuses in order to continue the business of her lucrative and ego-building seductions. In *Cousin Bette*, the possibility of an ideal love, like that glimpsed in earlier novels such as *The Wild Ass's Skin* and *Louis Lambert*, is seen as utterly impossible.

In *Cousin Bette*, Balzac makes a mockery not only of love but also of monomania. Through a gross exaggeration, this eccentric passion no longer characterizes a single figure of the novel, as in *Eugénie Grandet* or *Père Goriot*. Rather, no fewer than three characters of the novel can be called monomaniacs: Cousin Bette, Valérie Marneffe, and Baron Hulot. It is true, however, that the two females are far more developed than Hulot. These two female protagonists, as they strengthen and complement each other, offer a hyperbolic image of monomania, parodying one of the trademarks of Balzac's fiction. By means of this parody, Balzac plainly shows that he has dissociated himself from his characters' plight. Perhaps he was able to satirize monomania because his career as a novelist was unquestionably successful, and he was beginning to receive some of the recognition he had always sought. Nevertheless, his own "mania" persisted: Until he simply became too sick to write, he continued to work on yet another novel in *The Human Comedy*, with ten more volumes projected and endless bills to pay.

Sonja G. Stary

OTHER MAJOR WORKS

SHORT FICTION: *Les Contes drolatiques*, 1832-1837 (*Droll Stories*, 1874, 1891).

PLAYS: *Vautrin*, pr., pb. 1840 (English translation, 1901); *La Marâtre*, pr., pb. 1848 (*The Stepmother*, 1901, 1958); *Le Faiseur*, pr. 1849 (also as *Mercadet*; English translation, 1901); *The Dramatic Works*, pb. 1901 (2 volumes; includes *Vautrin*, *The Stepmother*, *Mercadet*, *Quinola's Resources*, and *Pamela Giraud*); *Cromwell*, pb. 1925 (wr. 1819-1820).

NONFICTION: *Correspondance*, 1819-1850, 1876 (*The Correspondence*, 1878); *Lettres à l'étrangère*, 1899-1950; *Letters to Madame Hanska*, 1900 (translation of volume 1 of *Lettres à l'étrangère*).

BIBLIOGRAPHY

Beizer, Janet L. *Family Plots: Balzac's Narrative Generations*. New Haven, Conn.: Yale University Press, 1986. A careful study of the family and other hierarchies in Balzac's novels. Beizer argues that the structure of the family itself is an ordering principle of the fiction. Beizer's introduction clearly situates her in the tradition of Balzac criticism while making clear how her book differs from earlier studies.

Festa-McCormick, Diana. *Honoré de Balzac*. Boston: Twayne, 1979. A good introductory study, including chapters on Balzac as the author of *The Human Comedy*, on his philosophical novels, his productive years, his treatment of women, his fame, and his posterity. Separate chapters are devoted to his most important novels. Chronology, notes, and annotated bibliography make this a particularly useful volume.

Kanes, Martin. *Balzac's Comedy of Words*. Princeton, N.J.: Princeton University Press, 1975. Divided into sections on approaches and theories, problems of narration, and essential texts. This sophisticated study is for advanced students. Includes bibliography.

_____, ed. *Critical Essays on Honoré de Balzac*. Boston: G. K. Hall, 1990. Divided into sections on literary vignettes and essays (1837-1949) and critical essays (subsections covering periods from 1850 to 1990). Includes detailed introduction, bibliography, and index.

Marceau, Felicien. *Balzac and His World*. Westport, Conn.: Greenwood Press, 1976. A reprint and translation of earlier editions in French and English (1955 and 1966, respectively). Divided into sections on Balzac's characters and themes. Includes a useful index to the characters of *The Human Comedy*.

Maurois, André. *Prometheus: The Life of Balzac*. New York: Harper & Row, 1965. A lively biography of nineteenth century literary figures, this book provides a well-informed, dramatized introduction both to Balzac's life and his times.

Prendergast, Christopher. *Balzac: Fiction and Melodrama*. New York: Holmes and Meier, 1978. Chapters on Balzac's use of melodrama, his relationship with the reading public, and his handling of chance and reality, connection and totality, antithesis and ambiguity, surface and depth, the pastoral, and type and transgression. Includes notes and bibliography.

Robb, Graham. *Balzac*. New York: Norton, 1994. The best scholarly biography, with several appendices on Balzac's handling of money, his career after 1850, and the titles in *The Human Comedy* in order of their dates of composition. Includes notes, bibliography, index of characters, and index of works.

Zweig, Stefan. *Balzac*. New York: Viking, 1946. A popular biography similar to Maurois's and still valuable as an introduction to the man and the writer. Includes a very useful chronology, but the bibliography is out of date.

TONI CADE BAMBARA

Born: New York, New York; March 25, 1939
Died: Philadelphia, Pennsylvania; December 9, 1995

PRINCIPAL LONG FICTION
The Salt Eaters, 1980
Those Bones Are Not My Child, 1999

OTHER LITERARY FORMS

Toni Cade Bambara is best known for her short stories, which appear frequently in anthologies. She has also received recognition as a novelist, essayist, journalist, editor, and screenwriter, as well as a social activist and community leader. Her stories depict the daily lives of ordinary people who live in the black neighborhoods of Brooklyn, Harlem, and sections of New York City and the rural South. Although she wrote in other genres, her short stories established her reputation. In *Gorilla, My Love* (1972), a collection of fifteen stories, Bambara focuses on the love of friends and neighborhood as she portrays the positive side of black family life and stresses the strengths of the African American community. These fast-paced stories, characterized by her use of the black dialect of the street, are full of humorous exchanges and verbal banter. *The Sea Birds Are Still Alive* (1977) is a collection of short stories that reflect Bambara's concern with people from other cultures; the title story focuses on the plight of Vietnamese refugees at the end of the Vietnam War. *Deep Sightings and Rescue Missions*, a collection of Bambara's writings, most of which never appeared before in print, was published posthumously in 1996.

ACHIEVEMENTS

Bambara received the Peter Pauper Press Award in Journalism from the *Long Island Star* in 1958, the John Golden Award for Fiction from Queens College in 1959, and the Theater of Black Experience Award in 1969. She was also the recipient of the George Washington Carver Distinguished African American Lecturer Award from Simpson College, Ebony's Achievement in the Arts Award, and the American Book Award, for *The Salt Eaters*, in 1981. *The Bombing of Osage Avenue* won the Best Documentary of 1986 Award from the Pennsylvania Association of Broadcasters and the Documentary Award from the National Black Programming Consortium in 1986.

As an editor of anthologies of the writings of African Americans, Bambara introduced thousands of college students to the works of these writers. She was a founder of the Southern Collective of African American Writers and played a major role in the 1984 Conference on Black Literature and the Arts at Emory University.

During the last fourteen years of her life, Bambara devoted her energies to the film industry, writing screenplays.

BIOGRAPHY

Miltona Mirkin Cade was born in New York on March 25, 1939, to Helen Brent Henderson Cade. She grew up in Harlem, Bedford-Stuyvesant, and Queens, where she lived with her mother and brother, Walter. She credited her mother with "cultivating her creative spirit and instilling in her a sense of independence and self-sufficiency." In 1970, after finding the

(Joyce Middler)

name Bambara written in a sketchbook in her grandmother's trunk, she legally changed her surname to Bambara. She received a B.A. in theater arts and English literature from Queens College in 1959, and that same year her first short story, "Sweet Town," was published in *Vendome* magazine. After studying in Italy and Paris, she earned a master's degree in American literature at City College of New York and completed additional studies in linguistics at New York University and the New School for Social Research. She was a social worker for the Harlem Welfare Center and director of recreation in the psychiatric division of Metro Hospital in New York City. She taught in the Search for Education, Elevation, Knowledge (SEEK) program at City College.

In 1970, under the name of Toni Cade, she published *The Black Woman: An Anthology*, a collection of essays, short fiction, poetry, and letters exploring the experiences of black women, with emphasis on their involvement with the Civil Rights movement and the women's movement. In 1971 she edited *Tales and Stories for Black Folks*, a collection of writings from students in her composition class, along with the work of well-known authors.

As an assistant professor at Livingston College at Rutgers University from 1969 to 1974, Bambara was active in black student organizations and arts groups. She was a visiting professor in Afro-American Studies at Emory University and an instructor in the School of Social Work at Atlanta University. In 1973 on a visit to Cuba, Bambara met with the Federation of Cuban Women, and in 1975 she traveled to Vietnam. These experiences served to broaden Bambara's view of the importance of community involvement and political action and provided subject matter for stories in *The Sea Birds Are Still Alive*.

Bambara and her daughter, Karma, lived in Atlanta from 1974 to 1986, during which time Bambara continued to be active in community political and artistic organizations, hosting potluck dinners in her home and organizing writers and artists in the community. In 1986 Bambara moved to Philadelphia, where she continued her active participation in the community and worked on *The Bombing of Osage Avenue*, a 1986 documentary on the bombing of a house where a group of black nationalists lived. She also worked on a film about African American writer Zora Neale Hurston.

Bambara was known as a writer, civil rights activist, teacher, and supporter of the arts. Her work represents her dedication to the African American community and her desire to portray the ordinary lives of the people who live in those communities. As a lecturer and teacher she worked to raise the consciousness of other African Americans and to encourage a sense of pride in their heritage. Bambara died in a suburb of Philadelphia on December 9, 1995, of cancer.

ANALYSIS

Toni Cade Bambara's work reflects her experiences with political action committees and her belief in the necessity for social responsibility. The political activism of the 1960's and 1970's provides the subject matter for her work, as she explores the conse-

quences of the Civil Rights movement and the divisions in the African American community. In describing this community, Bambara portrays the individual characters with affection and humor.

THE SALT EATERS

Set in the 1970's, Bambara's novel *The Salt Eaters* focuses on the effects of the Civil Rights movement on the inhabitants of the small town of Claybourne, Georgia. The plot centers on the attempted suicide of its main character, Velma Henry, a community activist who has tried to kill herself by slitting her wrists and sticking her head in an oven. The other major character is Minnie Ransom, a conjure woman who uses her healing powers to restore Velma to health. Minor characters include Fred Holt, the bus driver; Obie, Velma's husband; and Dr. Julius Meadows. These members of the African American community are suffering from the fragmentation and alienation that have occurred in the wake of the Civil Rights movement. Velma was so filled with rage that she sought death as an answer to her pain. The novel traces Velma's journey from despair to mental and spiritual health. Bambara's own experiences with political activism provide her with the background for the events of the novel.

Throughout the novel, Bambara stresses the importance of choice. In the opening line of the novel, Minnie Ransom asks Velma, "Are you sure, sweetheart, that you want to be well?" Freedom of choice requires acceptance of responsibility. If Velma is to heal herself, she must make a conscious choice of health over despair. Characters in the novel are seen in relationship to the larger community. Godmother Sophie M'Dear reminds Velma that her life is not solely her own, but that she has a connection and obligation to her family and community. Other characters are reminded of their responsibility to others. When Buster gets Nadeen pregnant, her uncle Thurston arrives with a gun, ordering Buster to attend parenting classes. Doc Serge tells Buster that abortion is not a private choice but a choice that involves the whole community. The characters echo Bambara's belief that membership in a community entails responsibilities to that community.

For most of the novel Velma sits on a stool in a

hospital, suffering from depression, overwhelming fatigue, and a mental collapse. She remains immobile and seemingly frozen as scenes from the past and present play in her mind in no particular order. Other characters seem to whirl past Velma and blend into one another, reflecting the problems that have brought Velma to this hospital room. Bambara shows that these problems are a result of alienation from the community. Because of his light skin, education, and profession, Dr. Julius Meadows has lost touch with his roots. Through a chance encounter with two young black men, Julius begins his journey back to the black community. Reflecting on the encounter, Julius feels that "whatever happened, he wasn't stumbling aimlessly around the streets anymore, at loose ends, alone." Meadows's journey back into the black community parallels Velma's journey to health. Alienation from the community had brought Velma to the brink of destruction, and realignment with the community heals her. Velma's journey is similar to the spiritual journey of Tayo, the Native American protagonist in Leslie Marmon Silko's *Ceremony* (1977). The horrors Tayo experienced as a prisoner of the Japanese during World War II and the sense of alienation he experiences when he returns to his Laguna reservation have nearly destroyed his will to survive. Through immersion in the Native American culture, traditions, beliefs, and stories, Tayo finds his way back to health. As Tayo and Velma embrace their cultural heritages, they begin to heal.

The predominant image in the novel is the vision of the mud mothers painting the walls of their cave. This recurring vision haunts Velma until she sees the cave as a symbol of cultural history and identity. Other characters reflect on the responsibility of the older generation to educate and nurture the children of the community. If the children are forgetting the values of the community, it is because the elders have failed in their responsibility to instill community values in the young.

Bambara believes that to keep traditions alive, every generation has to be nurtured and educated, has to be taught the old stories. At times the novel seems to be a catalog of African American cultural history, which includes African tribal customs and rituals,

slave ships, and names of famous leaders. In the early part of the novel, Ruby, one of the most politically active characters, laments the loss of leaders and causes: "Malcolm gone, King gone, Fanni Lou gone, Angela quiet, the movement splintered, enclaves unconnected." Near the end of the novel, Velma realizes how much she has learned from the leaders and influences that are part of her background, "Douglass, Tubman, the slave narratives, the songs, the fables, Delaney, Ida Wells, Blyden, DuBois, Garvey, the singers, her parents, Malcolm, Coltrane."

Bambara enriches the novel with background from folk legends and literary works. At times she merely mentions a name, such as Shine, the famous African American trickster, or the legendary Stagolee, who killed a man for his hat. Fred's friend Porter, borrowing a term from Ralph Ellison's novel *Invisible Man* (1952), explains his feelings about being black: "They call the Black man the Invisible Man. . . . Our natures are unknowable, unseeable to them." The following lines show how Bambara packs cultural, historical, and political history into one sentence: "Several hotheads, angry they had been asleep in the Sixties or too young to participate, had been galvanized by the arrival in their midst of the legless vet who used to career around Claybourne fast and loose on a hot garage dolly."

In contrast to the positive images, Bambara shows the negative side of society in describing the "boymen" who hang around women in grocery stores begging for money in a ritual she calls "market theater." In another scene, Ruby complains about the way women have had to carry the burden of improving society, "taking on . . . drugs, prisons, alcohol, the schools, rape, battered women, abused children," while the men make no contribution to the organization.

One of the most distinctive aspects of Bambara's style is her use of black dialect with its colorful vocabulary, playful banter, and unique phrasing and speech patterns. At times the rhythm and rhyme of phrases give a musical quality to the prose: "Cause the stars said and the energy belts led and the cards read and the cowries spread." At other times Bambara describes the atmosphere in musical terms:

"the raga reggae bumpidity bing zing was pouring out all over Fred Holt" and "the music drifted out over the trees . . . maqaam now blending with the bebop of Minnie Ransom's tapes."

The major theme of the novel is that identification with one's cultural history can be liberating and empowering. In *The Salt Eaters*, loss of cultural identity has brought despair. Bambara provides flashbacks to the civil rights struggles of the 1960's and the legacy of slavery. As they struggle for political power, African Americans must remember the past and maintain their best traditions. As Velma begins to heal she thinks that she knows "how to build resistance, make the journey to the center of the circle . . . stay centered in the best of her people's traditions."

Judith Barton Williamson

OTHER MAJOR WORKS

SHORT FICTION: *Gorilla, My Love*, 1972; *The Sea Birds Are Still Alive: Collected Stories*, 1977; *Raymond's Run: Stories for Young Adults*, 1989.

DOCUMENTARY: *The Bombing of Osage Avenue*, 1986.

EDITED TEXTS: *The Black Woman: An Anthology*, 1970; *Tales and Stories for Black Folks*, 1971; *Southern Exposure* 3, 1976 (periodical; Bambara edited vol. 3).

MISCELLANEOUS: "What Is It I Think I'm Doing Anyhow," *The Writer on Her Work*, 1981 (Janet Sternburg, editor); *Deep Sightings and Rescue Missions: Fiction, Essays, and Conversations*, 1996.

BIBLIOGRAPHY

Alwes, Derek. "The Burden of Liberty: Choice in Toni Morrison's *Jazz* and Toni Cade Bambara's *The Salt Eaters*." *African American Review* 30, no. 3 (Fall, 1996): 353-365. In comparing the works of Toni Morrison and Bambara, Alwes argues that while Morrison wants readers to participate in a choice, Bambara wants them to choose to participate. Bambara's message is that happiness is possible if people refuse to forget the past and continue to participate in the struggle.

Butler-Evans, Elliott. *Race, Gender, and Desire: Narrative Strategies in the Fiction of Toni Cade Bambara, Toni Morrison, and Alice Walker*. Philadelphia: Temple University Press, 1989. This book focuses on the political and social views of the three African American authors. Includes an index and bibliography.

Collins, Janelle. "Generating Power: Fission, Fusion, and Post-Modern Politics in Bambara's *The Salt Eaters*." *Melus* 21, no. 2 (Summer, 1996): 35-47. Collins argues that Bambara's nationalist and feminist positions inform the text of the novel as she advocates political and social change.

Evans, Mari, ed. *Black Women Writers (1950-1980): A Critical Evaluation*. Garden City, N.Y.: Anchor Press/Doubleday, 1984. In the essay "Salvation Is the Issue," Bambara says that the elements of her own work that she deems most important are laughter, use of language, sense of community, and celebration.

Tate, Claudia, ed. *Black Women Writers at Work*. New York: Continuum, 1983. Tate interviews fourteen African American women writers about social and political issues as well as aspects of their personal lives. In Bambara's interview, she says that she works to "applaud the tradition of struggle in our community" as she focuses on the "ordinary folks on the block."

JOHN BANVILLE

Born: Wexford, Ireland; December 8, 1945

PRINCIPAL LONG FICTION

Nightspawn, 1971
Birchwood, 1973
Doctor Copernicus, 1976
Kepler, 1981
The Newton Letter, 1982 (novella)
Mefisto, 1986
The Book of Evidence, 1989
Ghosts, 1993
Athena, 1995
The Untouchable, 1997

OTHER LITERARY FORMS

John Banville's first published book was a collection of short stories, *Long Lankin* (1970, revised 1984), and he has written a small amount of uncollected short fiction. He has also collaborated in writing television adaptations of *The Newton Letter* and *Birchwood*.

ACHIEVEMENTS

Banville is one of the most original and successful Irish novelists of his generation. His work has received numerous awards, including the prestigious James Tait Black Memorial Prize, the American-Irish Foundation Award, and the GPA Prize. Reviewers have treated each new work with increasing respect for its ambition, verbal felicity, and individuality, and for such a comparatively young writer, Banville has inspired a sizable amount of critical commentary. The development of his career coincides with a period of restlessness and experimentation in Irish fiction. Not the least significant of Banville's achievements is that he has availed himself of the artistic example of such postwar masters of fiction as Jorge Luis Borges, Gabriel García Márquez, and Italo Calvino. By admitting such influences, as well as those of the great Irish modernists James Joyce and Samuel Beckett, John Banville's fiction has embodied a new range of options for the Irish novel and has provided an international dimension to an often provincial literary culture.

BIOGRAPHY

John Banville was born in Wexford, the seat of Ireland's southeasternmost county, on December 8, 1945. He was educated locally, first at the Christian Brothers School and, on the secondary level, at St. Peter's College. After school, he worked for Aer Lingus, the Irish airline. Subsequently, he worked in England for the post office, and briefly, for a London publisher. Returning to Ireland, he worked as a subeditor for *The Irish Press*, a national daily. The recipient of numerous awards, he also spent a semester in the International Writing Program at the University of Iowa. He made his home in Dublin with his wife and two sons and became literary editor of the *Irish Times*.

ANALYSIS

Banville's subject matter and methods of artistic execution form the basis of his reputation for originality. In the context of contemporary fiction, he is notable for his commitment, for his felicity of phrase, and for his relationship to an important fictional genre, the historical novel. He has communicated, both by his artistic strategies and by his choice of material, some of the main questions faced by contemporary fiction—communicated them perhaps too conspicuously and with an ease and self-possession uncharacteristic of many contemporary writers. Some readers may find that this author's manner is paradoxically at odds with his central themes.

John Banville's short stories, his novella *The Newton Letter*, and his novels constitute a remarkably unified and consistent body of work. From the outset of his career, he has shown immense artistic self-possession and an equally assured possession of his themes. Over the years, his style, while not remaining constant, has undergone comparatively little change. It is therefore possible to speak of Banville in terms of a completeness and typicality which most novelists of his age are still in the process of discovering.

The unity and integrity that are the most striking features of Banville's career and oeuvre become more striking still by virtue of being so thematically important in his work. Fascination with the spectacle of the mind in the act of creation is a major concern of this author, and his career may be described in terms of an increasingly deliberate and far-reaching series of attempts to articulate this subject. This preoccupation has given his work a range, ambition, and commitment to large concepts which are extremely rare in modern Irish fiction, and only slightly less rare in contemporary fiction generally.

In addition, the manner in which Banville elaborates his interest in humanity's creative dimension commands more critical attention than it has received. For example, his fiction is suffused with hints suggesting links between artistic strategies, scientific inquiry, and historical actuality. From these, it is possible to detect a rudimentary, though sustained, critique of traditional epistemological procedures. To complement this critique, the typical Banville protagonist either discovers unsuspected modes of perception or believes that he has no other choice but to set out deliberately to discover them.

Together with the intellectual commitment implicit in such concerns, Banville's work possesses a typically complete and essentially unchanging aesthetic apparatus through which ideas and fiction's critique may be perceived. Since it is central to Banville's artistic vision that fiction's critique of conceptual thinking be considered inevitable and unavoidable, his novels' aesthetic apparatus is largely premised on techniques of doubleness, repetition, echoes, and mirrors. Protagonists often have problematical brothers or missing twins. Personal experience finds its counterpart in historical events. The result is a paradox: The duplicitous character of experience, which renders humanity's possession of its existence so frail and tentative, impels people, precisely because of that very frailty, to anchor themselves in the presumed security of defined abstractions.

NIGHTSPAWN

Despite the presence of these thematic concerns throughout Banville's output, and despite the fact that his treatment of them has always been marked more by an ironic playfulness than by earnest sermonizing, his first two works of fiction are somewhat callow. In particular, *Nightspawn*, the story of an Irish writer's adventures in Greece on the eve of the Colonel's coup, treats the material with a kind of relentless playfulness which is both tiresome in itself and in questionable taste. Despite the author's admitted—though not uncritical—affection for this novel, and despite its containing in embryonic form the concerns which beset all of his work, *Nightspawn*, as perhaps its title suggests, is an example of a young writer allowing his wonderfully fertile imagination to run to baroque lengths.

BIRCHWOOD

It is more appropriate, therefore, to begin a detailed consideration of John Banville's fiction with his second novel, *Birchwood*. Like *Nightspawn*, this novel is written in the first person—arguably Banville's preferred narrative mode. In *Birchwood*, Gabriel Godkin, the protagonist, tells in retrospect the story of his dark heritage and his efforts to escape it.

Again, as in *Nightspawn*, much of the material has baroque potential, which the novel's middle section, depicting Gabriel's adventures with the circus of a certain Prospero, accentuates rather than dispels.

The circus escapade shines in the novel like a good deed in an evil world. While Gabriel is within the protected ring of the circus troupe he seems to be essentially immune from the troubles of his past and from the state of famine and unrest which consumes the country through which the circus travels. Thanks to Prospero, he is islanded and becalmed in the surrounding tempest. Yet even under such conditions of childish play, the world is not a safe place. Adult imperfections continually intrude. Crimes are committed in the name of love; futile and obsessive hostilities break out. Innocent Gabriel flees the disintegrating circle—it seems appropriate to think of the circus in etymological terms, since circle and ring possess strong connotations of unity and completeness.

Gabriel forsakes the circus in a state of rather paranoid distress and finds himself, still more distressingly, to have come full circle back to where he started. Now, however, he finds himself compelled to face his origins, which lie in the house of doom which gives this novel its title. The first part of the novel gives the history of the Godkin family. Like the circus sequence, this opening section of *Birchwood* owes more to imagination than it does to actuality. Many readers will be reminded of both Edgar Allan Poe and William Faulkner by Banville's combination of brooding atmosphere and theme of cultural decay upon which this section is premised. Banville's farcical tone, however, without prejudicing young Gabriel's sensitivity, prevents the heavy-handedness and extravagance to which the gothic nature of his material is in danger of giving rise. The seriousness with which the elder Godkins take their insecurities is rendered laughable by the incompetence which ensues from their transparent intensity.

Yet Gabriel, for all of his alienation from his heritage's inadequacies, finds it impossible to do other than to confront them. In a novel which satirically articulates the cultural shibboleth of bad blood, Gabriel feels compelled to carry out an act of blood which will purge his house of the usurper. The usurper in question is Gabriel's twin brother, Michael. The novel ends with Gabriel in sole possession of Birchwood.

This turn of events, however, does not mean that Gabriel is able, or intends, to restore the house to its former glory, a glory in which he never participated. As a writer, his objective seems to be to reclaim the house as it really was, rather than imagine it as something other, something which imaginative treatment would make easier to assimilate. In this objective, students of Irish literature may see a critique of the lofty status often accorded the Big House in the poetry of William Butler Yeats. An appreciation of John Banville's fiction does not require that he be seen as a defacer of the cultural icons of a previous generation. Nevertheless, the status of the Big House in *Birchwood*, coupled with themes of survival, inheritance, and artistic expression, offers a sense of the oblique manner in which this author regards his own cultural heritage, while at the same time situating his regard in the wider, more generic contexts of such concerns as individuality, history, the role of the artist, and the nature of the real.

Given the significant, if problematical, status of the Big House in modern Irish literature (Big House being the generic name given to the imposing mansions of the socially dominant, landowning Anglo-Irish class), the degree to which *Birchwood* avoids a specific historical context is noteworthy. There are a sufficient number of clues (the famine and unrest mentioned earlier, the frequent mention of "rebels" in the first part of the novel) to suggest that the locale is Ireland. Yet a larger historical context is obviated by the obsessive, and more psychologically archetypal, quality of Gabriel's sense of his personal history. The result is a novel which is ultimately too reflexive, private, and inward looking to be entirely satisfactory.

DOCTOR COPERNICUS

It may be that the author himself reached the same conclusion, since in his next two novels, *Doctor Copernicus* and *Kepler*, a specific and detailed sense of history is an important dimension of events. *Doctor Copernicus* inaugurates Banville's most important and ambitious project, and the one on which his international reputation will probably be based. This project consists of four books dealing with the nature of the creative personality, conceived of in terms of the scientific imagination. A subtitle for the series might be *The Scientist as Artist*, meaning that Banville considers that which Copernicus, Kepler, and Isaac Newton (subject of *The Newton Letter*) accomplished in the field of scientific inquiry to be comparable to what an artist might produce. The series concludes with *Mefisto*, which both crystallizes and challenges the assumptions of its predecessors. The most fundamental link between the four books is chronological, *Mefisto* being set in contemporary Ireland. Although there are other more sophisticated connections between each of the four, each may also be read independently.

Doctor Copernicus is a fictionalized biography of the astronomer who revolutionized humanity's sense of its place in the order of creation. The biography is presented in such a way as to dramatize the crucial tensions between Copernicus and the history of his time. Beginning with the astronomer's unhappy childhood, the novel details the essentially flawed, anticlimactic, unfulfilling (and unfulfillable) nature of human existence as Copernicus experiences it. The protagonist's character is conceived in terms of his inability to give himself fully to the world of men and women and affairs, whether the affairs are those of state or of the heart.

Sojourning in Italy as a young man, Copernicus has a homosexual affair which temporarily makes him happy. Yet he lacks the self-confidence and will to believe in his happiness and rejects it in an attack of spleen and confusion. Later in his career, he is required to take a political role, negotiating with Lutheran enemies of the Catholic Church, and administering Church properties. Although he discharges his obligations in a responsible manner, it is perfectly clear that, given the choice between being a man of his time or being a student of the stars in their eternal courses, Copernicus prefers the latter isolated, impersonal service. The imperfections of the world—not only in the aggregate, demonstrated by the machinations of history, but also intimately, embodied by the astronomer's syphilitic brother, Andreas—prove emotionally insupportable, philosophically unjustifiable, and morally anesthetizing. Finding no basis for unity and completeness in the sorry state of mortal man, Copernicus takes the not particularly logical, but impressively imaginative, step of considering the heavens.

The astronomer's declared intention in pursuing this line of inquiry is not to bring about the revolution which history commemorates in his name. On the contrary, Copernicus sees his pursuits as conservative, intended to assert a model of order, design, and harmony where it cannot be said for certain one exists. Copernicus's efforts are fueled by his will and spirit, and the intensity of his commitment should not be underestimated because his results are stated in mathematical terms. What his conclusions provide is the fiction of order, a fiction posited on the conceit of mathematics being essentially a rhetoric—a product of mind, not an offspring of matter. Indeed, as Copernicus's career in the world of things and people suggests, his fiction elicits worldlings' assent all the more urgently for being necessarily untrue.

KEPLER

Banville's approach as a biographer in *Doctor Copernicus* is strictly chronological, which gives the novel both scope and a sense of the inevitability of the protagonist's development. Copernicus's integrity, continually challenged, is nourished by the inevitable nature of his spiritual needs and tendencies; in *Kepler*, the approach is fundamentally the same.

Instead of providing a chronology of Kepler's life, however, Banville concentrates on the astronomer's productive years, using flashbacks to illuminate and enlarge aspects of the protagonist's character, as the need arises. This approach shifts the narrative emphasis from the protagonist's temperament, as it was in *Doctor Copernicus*, to the protagonist's working conditions. The effect of this modulation in authorial standpoint is to give historical circumstances greater prominence than previously, and thus provide, from an aesthetic perspective, an image of humankind in the world which reverses that provided in *Doctor Copernicus*. Kepler is far more life-loving (which Banville communicates as far more capable of love) than his predecessor. He is far more attuned to the eddies and quicksands of the historical forces of his

time, consciously aligning himself with one set of forces rather than another, instead of disdainfully and brokenheartedly attempting to rise above them, as Copernicus tries to do.

Kepler's astronomy, therefore, is presented as, in his own eyes, the opposite of Copernicus's model of conservation. Much of Kepler's achievement, in fact, is based on his critique of the predecessor's findings. In addition, Kepler's generally worldly disposition leads him to develop practical applications of astronomical researches. Yet, when most successful in his own eyes, constructing his geometrical model of planetary harmony, he is unwittingly failing. His model is adequate to his own need of it but is not, by virtue of that adequacy, foolproof. The reader is given a strong sense that Kepler's discoveries, or rather the model which his discoveries serve, introduces as many errors as it corrects in Copernicus's model. In Copernicus's case, the model is the necessary transmutation of sorrow; in Kepler's case, it is the necessary transmutation of joy. Despite fate's cruel blows, Kepler asserts that the world should be considered part of a harmoniously integrated system. Because of fate's cruel blows, Copernicus asserts the same theory.

It would be invidious to conclude that one of these heroic figures suffers more than the others. Banville is at pains, as the dramatic structure of *Kepler* demonstrates, to point out that the astronomer's faith in the world proves to be as destructively alienating as Copernicus's skepticism. The spectacle—which concludes the novel—of this great scientific visionary spending his time and energy attempting to bring his debtors to book is a painfully ludicrous commentary on the all too understandable vanity of human wishes, as well as a cogent expression of Banville's own perspective on his material.

THE NEWTON LETTER

In the novella *The Newton Letter* Banville changes his approach, without quite changing his theme, returning once more to an ironic treatment of the Big House theme. Here the scenario is not biography, but failed biography. The protagonist is not the great scientist, but the apparently less than great modern writer attempting to recapture the scientist's life. This short work gives an inverted picture of the procedures which seemed natural in the two earlier works in the series. The presupposition of expository coherence leading to insight and comprehension which was crucial, however unspoken, to the fictionalized biographies has, in *The Newton Letter*, become a subject open to criticism—open, like the procedures of Copernicus and Kepler, to the charge of fiction.

In addition, the fictional biographer (the protagonist of *The Newton Letter*) is failing to complete his work because of Newton's failure to pursue his researches. By this means, the interrelationship between fiction and reality, and the possibility that these terms interchangeably reflect dual perspectives on immutable phenomena, is brought yet more clearly to the forefront of Banville's concerns.

Indeed, as in the case of the earlier novels of the series, life keeps interrupting the Newton biographer. The country house to which he has retreated in order to complete his work, while not possessing the menace and uncertainty of Birchwood, distracts and ultimately ensnares him, so that he is forced to choose between the demands of completeness (his work) and the obligations of incompleteness (his life). The biographer's failed project becomes a synonym for his mortal destiny.

MEFISTO

Banville's rejection of the biographical approach to the life of the mind is completed in the final volume of the series, *Mefisto*, in which the protagonist, a mathematician named Gabriel Swan, writes his own story. With this formal development, the procedure of both *Doctor Copernicus* and *Kepler* is completely inverted, and the value of the project both from a biographical and from a scientific point of view is most rigorously challenged. One reason it is possible to make such a claim is that *Mefisto* reaches back beyond its three predecessors to *Birchwood*, to which it bears some strong resemblances.

The most obvious novelty of *Mefisto*, however, is that it does not deal with a historical twentieth century scientist. Most of Banville's readers were not prepared for this development, which is a tribute to Banville's own conception of his project's integrity. It is unlikely, however, that the question of integrity is the only one at issue here. On one hand, this development is typical of the sly and slapstick humor which pervades Banville's work. On the other hand, the fictitiousness of *Mefisto*'s protagonist is an obvious expression of the status of failure in Banville's oeuvre, the failure from which the artist is obliged to begin, and which his work, by attempting to mask or redeem it, merely makes more obvious. In addition, given that *Mefisto* has a historical context about which it is possible to say much, and that it is a novel which brings to an end a series of works in which historical events were given a prominent and influential place, it must be considered provocative and instructive that *Mefisto* eschews explicit information of a historical nature.

Mefisto is a novel of missing parts. It lacks a sense of specific sense of time and space, though the alert reader will find part 1 of the novel set in a market town in provincial Ireland and part 2 in an Irish city which is presumably Dublin. The hero, Gabriel (a name which, in a novelist as self-conscious as Banville, must be an echo of the protagonist of *Birchwood*, particularly since in part 1 there is a dilapidated, Birchwood-like house), is a mathematician of genius, but it is difficult to deduce what his branch of mathematics is.

It is Gabriel's misfortune to believe that there can be a redemptive function in his symbols and abstractions. He mistakenly believes that, because of the light he finds shining in the purity of math, he can rescue damsels in distress—in genuine distress, like the drug-besotted Adele in part 2. This belief is cultivated by the jauntily cynical and amoral Felix, who fills the role of Mephistopheles, Gabriel's dark angel. There is enough twinning and doubling in the novel to suggest that Felix may also be Gabriel's stillborn twin brother. Events prove both the hopelessness and inevitability of Gabriel's outlook. First, Gabriel is severely burned, the potential fate, no doubt, of all who make Mephistophelian contact. Second, he is brokenhearted by his failure to rescue Adele. Yet the end of the novel finds him rededicating himself to his vision of mathematics, to the rhetoric of perfection and security which it symbolizes.

The combination of failure and rededication on which *Mefisto* ends is an illuminating gloss on one of

John Banville's most crucial themes. Echoing a pronouncement of Samuel Beckett, he believes that the artist necessarily has failure for his theme and that his work articulates that theme's pressing reality. On the other hand, Banville is still romantic enough to conceive of his theme in terms of world-changing, concept-forming figures. Thus, his work is also preoccupied with the meaning of success, which in turn is linked to ideas of progress, clarity, precision, and enlightenment. Failure is relativized by success, and success by failure. The sense of doubleness and unity suggested by such a conclusion is typical of Banville's outlook.

THE BOOK OF EVIDENCE

Binary interplay is very much to the fore in Banville's most commercially successful novel, *The Book of Evidence*. This work takes the form of a first-person account, while he is awaiting trial, of a vertiginous fall from grace undertaken by a lapsed mathematician, Freddie Montgomery. In financial straits, Freddy decided to steal a painting, and in order to do so murdered an innocent bystander, a servant. No good comes of these actions, unless it is to reveal to the scapegrace protagonist the necessity that his nature acknowledge limits, and that the limits are those enjoined by the existence of others. As Freddy perceives, his failure to imagine the lives of others leads him into reckless disregard of those lives. His crime is this failure. Through the comprehensiveness and comprehension of his narrative, Freddy arrives at a perspective on his actions which he had previously lacked, having been hitherto driven to act by cupidity, fear, and callowness.

In a reflexive turn typical of Banville, Freddy's book becomes more substantial than his life. For all its narrative discontinuities, the story remains a simple one, reminiscent of a ballad, providing *The Book of Evidence* with an unlikely kinship to *Long Lankin*, whose stories are premised on a ballad. This formal association also suggests *The Book of Evidence*'s indebtedness to two classics of jail literature, both by Oscar Wilde: *De Profundis* (1905; a first-person attempt at vindication) and *The Ballad of Reading Gaol* (1898; with its refrain, "For each man kills the thing he loves," which is clearly the case of Freddy

and the stolen painting). Such objective possibilities of order counterpoint Freddy's subjective flouting of law—not merely the law of the land, which is held at such a distance in *The Book of Evidence* as to seem beside the point, but laws more fundamentally pertaining to the viability of the project of being human, with its obligations to others, obligations which in the distorted form of financial indebtedness to hoodlums motivate Freddy's murderous actions. While conceptually and stylistically *The Book of Evidence* is at least the equal of Banville's earlier attainments, it also articulates much more decisively than does *Mefisto* the author's sense of contemporary social reality, and its uniformly favorable critical reception suggests that it is the work that will earn for Banville the wider readership that his originality, commitment to large questions, and aesthetic poise deserve.

ATHENA

Athena completes the trilogy begun with *The Book of Evidence* and continued with the ethereal *Ghosts*. Each novel centers on Freddie, here referred to only as Morrow, and once again Banville sets the action in another decaying house, portentously located on Rue Street. Morrow's criminal past reasserts itself as he falls in with Morden, a enigmatic figure who commissions the protagonist to catalog and evaluate eight Flemish paintings. The narrative is then punctuated by detailed descriptions of seven of these paintings, each of which is a fraud.

As he becomes more enmeshed in Morden's machinations, he enters a hypnotic and masochistic relationship with another mysterious figure, a woman known only as A. Gradually the mystery evaporates—Morden and A. are siblings working for Da, their father—and Morrow is little more than a useful and available tool. Like Banville's earlier novels, *Athena* is driven by the self-conscious ruminations of the principal character, and like those other protagonists, Morrow is obsessed with the gulf between chaotic, shoddy reality and the perfection of art and the imagination. He longs for order, the model of which he finds in art, but his actions lead repeatedly to more frustration and havoc. The novel positively brims with allusions to other paintings and novels, and thus the self-conscious and ironic practices of early novels are maintained. Along with *The Newton Letter*, *Athena* arguably ranks among Banville's best novels for its inventiveness and epistemological probity.

THE UNTOUCHABLE

In his work *The Untouchable*, Banville returns to the historical concerns that characterize so many of his earlier works. Here, Victor Maskell, narrator, art scholar, and ex-spy, is a thinly disguised version of Anthony Blunt, the British traitor who joined a spy ring while a student at Cambridge University in the 1930's. The novel is set in the 1970's, when Blunt was exposed, but again another subjective narrator shuttles back and forth through time in a mélange of history and personal reflection. The story takes the reader through Maskell's boyhood, years at Cambridge, and years during World War II, when his involvement with the Russians deepens in spite of his skepticism of their social project.

Like Morrow, Maskell is dedicated to art and ascends to the influential position of Keeper of the Royal Pictures, confessing that art is the only thing of any importance or stability in his life. Art in fact become a lens through which he views and evaluates himself, whereby he is alternately creator and created, forever suspended on his own perfect Grecian urn. However, the single painting around which he has organized his life and which he purchased as a young man, French classical artist Nicolas Poussin's *The Death of Seneca*, may be a forgery, thus making his whole life a fraud. Like earlier Banville characters, Maskell is a searcher, seeking a fixed sense of identity which is forever out of reach. Once again, the subjective narrator is a self-betrayed figure, one whose most clever deceptions and stratagems rebound disastrously upon him; once again readers encounter a profoundly lonely, alienated character.

George O'Brien, updated by David W. Madden

OTHER MAJOR WORKS

SHORT FICTION: *Long Lankin*, 1970, revised 1984.
PLAY: *The Broken Jug*, pb. 1994 (after Heinrich von Kleist).
SCREENPLAYS: *Reflections*, 1984; *Birchwood*, 1986.
TELEPLAY: *Seaview*, 1994.

BIBLIOGRAPHY

Deane, Seamus. "'Be Assured I Am Inventing': The Fiction of John Banville." In *The Irish Novel in Our Time*, edited by Patrick Rafroidi and Maurice Harmon. Lille, France: Publications de l'Université de Lille, 1975. Excellent discussion of Banville's first three works of fiction by Ireland's leading contemporary critic. Particularly insightful on the reflexive elements in *Long Lankin*, *Nightspawn*, and *Birchwood*, this article concludes with a challenging critique of the cultural significance of Banville's work.

D'Haen, Theo. "Irish Regionalism, Magic Realism, and Postmodernism." In *International Aspects of Irish Literature*, edited by Toshi Furomoto et al. Gerrards Cross, England: Smythe, 1996. Compares Banville's *Birchwood* and Desmond Hogan's *A Curious Street* to demonstrate the postmodern and Magical Realist qualities of each. Such features express the marginality of Ireland and of the Irish to Europe's dominant beliefs in Banville's fiction.

Imhof, Rudiger. *John Banville: A Critical Introduction*. Dublin, Ireland: Wolfhound Press, 1989. An early study of Banville's works, up to and including *Mefisto*. Complete with an intellectual guide to Banville's fictional preoccupations as well as a full bibliography.

Irish University Review 11 (Spring, 1981). "A John Banville Special Number." A comprehensive survey of Banville's career, consisting of a number of critical overviews, a bibliography, a wide-ranging interview, and the transcript of a talk given by him at the University of Iowa's Writers' Workshop—one of Banville's rare formal statements on fiction and authorship.

Jackson, Tony E. "Science, Art, and the Shipwreck of Knowledge: The Novels of John Banville." *Contemporary Literature* 38, no. 8 (1997): 510-533. Examines Banville's postmodern sensibility in five novels. Basing his argument on Friedrich Nietzsche's theories about the indeterminacy of truth, Jackson demonstrates that scientific truths in Banville's novels can never explain everything, and that art fills the gaps for which history and science cannot account.

McIlroy, Brian. "Pattern in Chaos: John Banville's Scientific Art." *Colby Quarterly* 31, no. 1 (1995): 1050-5873. Concentrating on *Doctor Copernicus*, *Kepler*, *The Newton Letter*, and *Mefisto*, the essay shows how Banville illustrates the similarities between scientific and artistic methods of thinking and discovery. It further shows the ways in which history, politics, religion, and sex influence scientific inquiry and art.

McMinn, Jo. "An Exalted Naming: The Poetical Fiction of John Banville." *Canadian Journal of Irish Studies* 14 (July, 1988): 17-27. Deals with the various senses in which poetry enters into Banville's fiction, including treatment of his poetic allusions, his attainments as a prose stylist, and the visionary dimension of his work.

O'Brien, George. "John Banville: Portraits of the Artist." In *New Irish Writing*, edited by James D. Brophy and Eamon Grennan. Boston: Twayne, 1989. Concentrating on Banville's science tetralogy, this article appraises the cult of creativity upon which *Doctor Copernicus*, *Kepler*, *The Newton Letter*, and *Mefisto* are premised and which they recuperate. The article mainly dwells on Banville's protagonists but also assesses in passing Banville's preoccupation with the creative act in his earlier works.

"Q. & A. with John Banville." *Irish Literary Supplement* (Spring, 1987): 13. A rare interview with the media-shy author.

JULIAN BARNES
Dan Kavanagh

Born: Leicester, England; January 19, 1946

PRINCIPAL LONG FICTION
Metroland, 1980
Duffy, 1980 (as Dan Kavanagh)
Fiddle City, 1981 (as Kavanagh)
Before She Met Me, 1982
Flaubert's Parrot, 1984

Putting the Boot In, 1985 (as Kavanagh)
Staring at the Sun, 1986
Going to the Dogs, 1987 (as Kavanagh)
A History of the World in 10½ Chapters, 1989
Talking It Over, 1991
The Porcupine, 1992 (novella)
England, England, 1998

OTHER LITERARY FORMS

Julian Barnes has served as a journalist and columnist for several British newspapers and magazines. He has also published numerous essays and book reviews.

ACHIEVEMENTS

Barnes is one of a number of British writers born after World War II who gravitated toward London and its literary scene. Reacting to the certainties and assumptions of the previous generation, they have often resorted to irony and comedy in viewing the contemporary world. Some have experimented with the form of the traditional novel. Barnes's early novels were narrative and chronological in approach, but his fifth book, *Flaubert's Parrot*, combined fact and fiction, novel and history, biography and literary criticism. For that work he was nominated for Great Britain's most prestigious literary award, the Booker Prize, and was awarded the Geoffrey Faber Memorial Prize. He has also won literary prizes in Italy and France, and he received the E. M. Forster Award from the American Academy of Arts and Letters. In *Staring at the Sun* and *A History of the World in 10½ Chapters*, Barnes continued his exploration of the novel and its form.

BIOGRAPHY

Born in the English Midlands city of Leicester just after World War II to parents who were French teachers, Julian Patrick Barnes studied French at Magdalen College, Oxford, from which he was graduated with honors in 1968 with a degree in modern languages. After leaving Oxford, his abiding interest in words and language led him to a position as a lexicographer for the *Oxford English Dictionary Supplement*. In 1972 Barnes became a freelance writer, preferring that parlous profession to the law. During the 1970's and 1980's, he wrote reviews for *The Times Literary Supplement* and was contributing editor to the *New Review*, assistant literary editor of *New Statesman*, and deputy literary editor of the *Sunday Times* of London. For a decade he served as a television critic, most notably for the London *Observer*, where his comments were witty, irreverent, and provocative.

Influenced by the French writer Gustave Flaubert, particularly his concern for form, style, and objectivity, Barnes's serious novels continued to exhibit his fascination with language and literary experiments, in contrast with the more traditional narrative approach and narrow subject matter of many twentieth century English novelists. Under the pseudonym Dan Kavanagh, Barnes also published a number of detective novels.

(AP/Wide World Photos)

By the 1990's Barnes had become one of Britain's leading literary figures. His literary reviews appeared in many of the leading publications in both his own country and the United States. He also wrote brilliant journalistic pieces on various topics—political, social, and literary—some of them appearing in *The New Yorker*. Many of these essays were collected and published in *Letters from London* (1995). His long-standing fascination with France was revealed in his collection of short stories *Cross Channel* (1996), a series of tales about English men and women and their experiences of living and working in France.

In the mid-1990's Barnes accepted a one-year teaching position at The Johns Hopkins University, in part, he said, to increase his knowledge of American society, the United States being second only to France among Barnes's foreign fascinations. After a several-year novelistic hiatus, in 1998 he published *England, England*, which was widely reviewed and was short-listed for the Booker Prize, Britain's premier literary award, evidence that Barnes continued to be recognized as one of the most interesting novelists writing in English.

ANALYSIS

In all of his works Barnes has pursued several ideas: Human beings question, even though there can be no absolute answers; humanity pursues its obsessions, often resulting in failure. Yet his novels have at the same time evolved in form and approach—the earliest are more traditional and conventional, the latter more experimental. Barnes's wit and irony, his use of history, literary criticism, myth, and fable, his melding of imagination and intellect, and his continuing risk in exploring new forms and methods make him one of the most significant English novelists of his generation.

METROLAND

Barnes's first novel, *Metroland*, is orthodox in technique and approach; divided into three parts, it is a variation on the traditional *Bildungsroman*, or coming-of-age novel. In part 1, the narrator, Christopher Lloyd, and his close friend, Toni, grow up in 1963 in a north London suburb on the Metropolitan rail line (thus the title), pursuing the perennial adolescent dream of rebellion against parents, school, the middle class, and the establishment in general. Convinced of the superiority of French culture and consciously seeking answers to what they believe to be the larger questions of life, they choose to cultivate art, literature, and music in order to astound what they see as the bourgeoisie and its petty concerns.

Part 2, five years later, finds Christopher a student in Paris, the epitome of artistic bohemianism, particularly when compared to Metroland. It is 1968, and French students are demonstrating and rioting in the streets for social and political causes. None of this touches Christopher: He is more concerned about his personal self-discovery than about changing or challenging the wider world.

Nine years later, in part 3, set in 1977, Christopher is back in Metroland, married to Marion, an Englishwoman of his own class, with a child, a mortgaged suburban house, and a nine-to-five job. Toni, still a rebel, chides Christopher for selling out to the enemy. Ironically, however, Christopher is contented with life in Metroland. He consciously examines and questions his present circumstances but accepts their rewards and satisfactions. Questioning and irony are continuing themes in all Barnes's novels, as is the absence of significant character development except for the leading figure. Toni, Christopher's French girlfriend Annick, and Marion, his English wife, are not much more than supporting figures. Relationships are explored through Christopher's narration alone, and Christopher finds himself, his questions, and his life of most concern and interest to him.

BEFORE SHE MET ME

Before She Met Me is also a story of an individual's attempt to relate to and understand his personal world. Graham Hendrick, a forty-year-old professor of history, has recently remarried. Now beginning a new life, happy with Ann, his new wife, and outwardly contented, both personally and professionally, Hendrick seems to be an older variation of Christopher and his self-satisfied middle-class existence. As in his first novel, Barnes has included a bohemian writer, Jack Lupton, as a foil for Hendrick's respectable conformity. Before they were married,

Ann acted in several minor films, and after viewing one of them, Hendrick, the historian, begins to search out his wife's past. At first his quest seems based on simple curiosity; soon, however, Ann's history begins to take over Hendrick's present life. Losing his professional objectivity as a historian, succumbing to jealousy, compulsively immersing himself in Ann's past, blurring the distinction between the real Ann and her image on the screen, Hendrick becomes completely obsessed. Seeing the present as a world without causes, Hendrick finds his crusade in the past, and that crusade is no longer public but private. Bordering on the melodramatic, *Before She Met Me* is the story of the downward spiral of an individual who can no longer distinguish fantasy from reality. Did the love affairs Ann had on the screen replicate her private life off camera? Were her love affairs in the past continuing in the present?

Barnes poses the question, not only for Hendrick, caught up in his obsession, but also for the reader: What is reality, and can one discover the truth? Like *Metroland*, this novel has many comic and witty moments but ultimately ends tragically. Ann and Lupton had an affair that has since ended, but Hendrick, in his obsessive quest, falsely concludes that it continues; he murders Lupton and then, in Ann's presence, he takes his own life. Although told in the third person, *Before She Met Me* centers on the plight of a single figure questioning his world. Hendrick and his compulsions dominate the novel: His first wife, their child, Ann, and Lupton are figures perceived through his persona.

FLAUBERT'S PARROT

With his third novel published under his own name, *Flaubert's Parrot*, Barnes received considerable praise as a significant writer of fiction, less parochial in form and technique than most English novelists of his time. His first book published in the United States, *Flaubert's Parrot* was the recipient of numerous prizes. It too is a novel of questions and obsessions, which unite the past and present. Yet in its collage of literary techniques, it is not a traditional narrative novel, including as it does fiction, biography, history, and literary criticism. As in his earlier works, here Barnes focuses upon a single individual,

Geoffrey Braithwaite, an English medical doctor in his sixties, a widower, with a long-standing interest in the French writer Gustave Flaubert. Barnes also has been a student of French and admirer of Flaubert, and early in *Metroland* Christopher reads a work by Flaubert; several critics have examined the possible relationships between the fictional figures, Braithwaite, Christopher, Hendrick, and the author.

Told in the first person, *Flaubert's Parrot* examines Braithwaite's attempt to discover which of two different stuffed parrots on exhibit in competing Flaubert museums is the one that sat on Flaubert's desk when he wrote his short story "Un Cœur simple" ("A Simple Heart"). In the story, an old servant, Félicité, is left after fifty years of service with only a parrot as a companion. When the parrot dies, Félicité has it stuffed. As her health fails, she confuses the parrot with the Holy Ghost, traditionally represented as a dove. On her deathbed she believes that she sees a giant parrot above her head. Braithwaite's quest to determine the real parrot allows him, and Barnes, to pursue with wit and irony numerous aspects of Flaubert's biography; his published works, including *Madame Bovary* (1857); his ideas for works he did not write; his travels; his use of animals in his writings; and his lovers. The novel includes chronologies, a dictionary, and an examination paper.

Yet the work is not concerned only with Braithwaite's interest in Flaubert's past and the two surviving stuffed parrots. As the doctor pursues Flaubert and his parrot, he also begins to reveal his own history. Braithwaite's wife had been frequently unfaithful to him, as Emma Bovary was to her husband Charles, and she had eventually committed suicide. As Braithwaite explores the relationship between Flaubert and his fiction, seeking to know which is the real parrot, he also attempts to understand the realities of his own life and his connection with the fictional Charles Bovary. He becomes obsessive about discovering the truth of the parrots, but he is also obsessive about discovering his own truth. The difficulty, however, is that truth and reality are always elusive, and the discovery of a number of small realities does not result in the illumination of absolute truth. In the course of his discussions, Braithwaite muses upon the incompetence even of specialists in ferreting out the truth; he criticizes a prominent Flaubertain scholar, whom he accuses of pronouncing French badly, of mistakenly identifying a portrait as Flaubert, and of being unable to specify the color of Emma Bovary's eyes.

Flaubert's parrot, too, is seen as a symbol of this dichotomy of fact and fiction. The parrot can utter human sounds, but only by mimicking what it hears; still, there is the appearance of understanding, regardless of whether it exists. Is a writer, such as Flaubert, merely a parrot, writing down human sounds and observing human life without understanding or interpretation? At the end of Braithwaite's search for the real stuffed parrot used by Flaubert while writing his short story, the doctor discovers that dozens of stuffed parrots exist which Flaubert could have borrowed and placed upon his desk. Thus Braithwaite's has been one of many quests with no resolutions, questions without final answers.

STARING AT THE SUN

Staring at the Sun, Barnes's fourth novel published under his own name, exhibits a stronger narrative line than *Flaubert's Parrot*, but as in the story of Braithwaite, narrative here is not the primary concern of the author; questions remain paramount. The central figure is a lower-middle-class woman, Jean Serjeant, significantly unlike earlier Barnes protagonists because she is naïve and unsophisticated, lacking any intellectual pretensions. The tone of Barnes's portrayal of Jean contrasts sharply with the wit and irony featured throughout *Flaubert's Parrot*. Yet even Jean asks questions, such as what happened to the sandwiches Charles Lindbergh did not eat when he flew over the Atlantic Ocean in 1927, and why the mink is so tenacious of life (a statement from a print that hung in her bedroom when she was a child). Those questions have no answers, and Jean muses that questions that do have answers are not real questions.

The novel begins in 1941, with a prologue set during World War II. Sergeant-pilot Prosser is flying back across the Channel to his English base from France, just before dawn. The sun rises from the waves on the eastern horizon, captivating Prosser's attention. Shortly after, he reduces his altitude when he sees the smoke from a steamship far below. As he flies at the lower altitude, the sun comes up again from the sea into his view, and for the second time in a single morning he watches the sun's ascent. He calls this event an ordinary miracle, but he never forgets it. Neither does Jean, after Prosser relates it to her a few months later while temporarily billeted in her parents' home. Prosser soon disappears from Jean's life but not from her memories: He kills himself, she later discovers, by flying directly into the sun. She marries Michael, a policeman who has no time for or interest in questions.

After twenty years of marriage, at the age of forty, Jean becomes pregnant for the first time. She leaves Michael in order to discover what she calls a more difficult, first-rate life; she is more on a quest for self than seeking an escape from her unsatisfactory husband. When her son, Gregory, is old enough to be left alone, Jean begins to travel widely, often by airplane. She pursues her own Seven Wonders of the World. While visiting Arizona's Grand Canyon, she observes an airplane flying below the canyon's rim. At first it seems to her to be against nature, but she concludes instead that it is against reason: Nature provides the miracles, such as the Grand Canyon and the double rising of the sun. As the novel proceeds, Jean becomes more like Barnes's other figures and less like her naïve and unsophisticated young self.

Gregory also parallels Barnes's earlier intellectual characters and their questions that can yield no conclusive answers. Afraid of death but contemplating suicide, he meditates upon God and His existence. He posits fourteen possible answers, but no final truth. The last part of the novel is set in the future, a world of intrusive and obtrusive computers. All the world's knowledge has been incorporated into the General Purposes Computer (GPC), open to everyone. Yet it cannot answer why minks are so tenacious of life. A special informational program, TAT (The Absolute Truth), is added to the GPC, but when Gregory asks TAT whether it believes in God, the computer answers that his question is not a real question, and when he asks why it is not a real question, TAT again responds that Gregory's second question

is also not a real question. Only "real" questions, it appears, can be answered by computers. In what she believes will be the last incident in her long life, in 2021, Jean, at the age of ninety-nine, accompanied by Gregory, makes a final flight, observing the sun this time as it sets in the west rather than rising in the east, as it had done twice during Prosser's "ordinary miracle" so many years before.

A HISTORY OF THE WORLD IN 10½ CHAPTERS

In *A History of the World in 10½ Chapters*, Barnes continued his experimentation in form and style. Unlike his earlier novels, this one has no central character. Instead, the reader is presented with a number of chapters or stories, ostensibly historical, which are loosely connected by several common themes. The first tale or fable is a revisionist account of the story of Noah and the ark. Narrated by a woodworm, the story portrays Noah as a drunk, humanity as badly flawed, and God and His plan as leaving much to be desired. Human beings fare equally poorly in the other chapters, and the ark returns in later stories: A nineteenth century English woman searches for the ark on Mount Ararat; a twentieth century American astronaut, also seeking the ark, finds a skeleton that he identifies as Noah's but that is really the bones of the woman explorer; another chapter discusses the ark in the form of the raft of the *Medusa*, painted by Théodore Géricault.

In this novel Barnes raises the question of how one turns disaster into art, or how one turns life into art. In a half chapter, or "Parenthesis," he discusses history and love: "History isn't what happened. History is just what historians tell us. . . . The history of the world? Just voices echoing in the dark, images that burn for a few centuries and then fade; stories, old stories that sometimes seem to overlap; strange links, impertinent connections." Barnes connects love to truth, but truth, objective truth, can never be found. Still, Sisyphus-like, one must constantly toil to find it. So it is with love: "We must believe in it, or we're lost." *A History of the World in 10½ Chapters* does not always succeed: The stories do not always successfully relate to one another, and the tone at times fails to achieve the ironic brilliance of *Flaubert's Parrot*.

TALKING IT OVER

Talking It Over is superficially a less ambitious novel than *A History of the World in 10½ Chapters*. The novel features three characters: Stuart, a decent, dull banker; his wife, Gillian; and Stuart's old friend, Oliver, a flashy, "cultured" language instructor who falls in love with Gillian, who eventually leaves Stuart for Oliver. The characters are somewhat predictable, as is the eventual outcome, but Barnes's technique reveals the same events narrated by all three characters, who speak directly in monologues to the reader. Considered something of a minor work by critics, the novel again shows considerable verbal felicity, and in spite of the seeming predictability of the plot and the ordinariness of the characters, by the end the reader comes to appreciate their quirks and foibles.

ENGLAND, ENGLAND

It was several years before Barnes's next full-length novel appeared, in 1998, with *England, England*. In the interim he had written a novella, *The Porcupine*, set in an Eastern European country in the aftermath of the fall of Communism. In it Barnes notes how difficult it is to escape from the past, from history, and from its illusions and delusions, and he asks what one will escape to—to what new illusions and imaginings. *England, England* is also a meditation on history. A serious novel with a comedic and satirical core, it features Sir Jack Pitman, a larger-than-life, egocentric businessman who builds a historical Disneyland-style theme park on the Isle of Wight, off England's southern coast. Here tourists can enjoy and experience all of England's past and present at the same place, from the real king and queen, who have moved from the real England to "England, England," to a new Buckingham Palace, a half-sized Big Ben, cricket matches, William Shakespeare's wife Anne Hathaway's cottage, Stonehenge, poet William Wordsworth's daffodils, and every other event or place that in popular belief represents the English past. In time, this new England—"England, England"—becomes more successful, economically and in all other ways, than the country that inspired it.

Parallel to Pitman's story is that of Martha Cochrane, a leading member of his staff who briefly replaces him after discovering Pitman's unusual sexual proclivities. She, too, has had a difficult relationship with history, realizing that even personal reminiscences, like broader history, lack objective reality, and that even memories are constructs. The past becomes, perhaps, what we want it to be, or what we fear it was. Eventually, in old age, Cochrane escapes the present, returning to the former England, which itself has retreated into a largely preindustrial, rural past and is now called Anglia. The question becomes, can history go backward? Is Cochrane's Anglia any more authentic than Pitman's theme park; was old England itself ever more "real" than Pitman's "England, England," or was it too just an assembly of illusions and delusions?

Eugene Larson

OTHER MAJOR WORKS

SHORT FICTION: *Cross Channel*, 1996.
NONFICTION: *Letters from London*, 1995 (essays).

BIBLIOGRAPHY

Carey, John. "Land of Make-Believe." *The Sunday [London] Times*, August 23, 1998, p. 1. Carey, a leading British academic and a literary critic, discusses *England, England* as an unusual combination of the comic and the serious, a philosophical novel which posits important questions about reality.

Hulbert, Ann. "The Meaning of Meaning." *The New Republic* 196 (May 11, 1987): 37-39. Reviewing *Staring at the Sun*, Hulbert notes Barnes's continuing interest in the relationship between life and art; she comments on the differences in tone and technique between that novel and his earlier works, particularly *Flaubert's Parrot*.

Jenkins, Mitch. "Novel Escape." *The [London] Times Magazine*, January 13, 1996, p. 18. An interview with Barnes and a wide-ranging discussion of his life and works.

Kermode, Frank. "Obsessed with Obsession." *The New York Review of Books* 32 (April 25, 1985): 15. Kermode, an English literary critic, in his favorable review of *Flaubert's Parrot*, discusses some of the social and literary background of the younger generation of English novelists.

Locke, Richard. "Flood of Forms." *The New Republic* 201 (December 4, 1989): 40-43. Locke, a professor of comparative literature, places Barnes's interest in form and style in the context of modern literature, beginning with Flaubert. He summarizes all the novels, focusing particularly upon *A History of the World in 10½ Chapters*.

Lodge, David. "The Home Front." *The New York Review of Books* 34 (May 7, 1987): 21. Lodge is an English novelist, of the same generation as Barnes but generally less experimental in form. He finds *Staring at the Sun* less successful than *Flaubert's Parrot* and argues that Barnes attempted to incorporate too many elements into the former work.

Moseley, Merritt. *Understanding Julian Barnes*. Columbia: University of South Carolina Press, 1997. One of the volumes in the Understanding Contemporary British Literature series. Moseley finds Barnes to be one of the most intriguing and significant of modern British authors.

(Teturo Maruyama)

JOHN BARTH

Born: Cambridge, Maryland; May 27, 1930

PRINCIPAL LONG FICTION
The Floating Opera, 1956
The End of the Road, 1958
The Sot-Weed Factor, 1960
Giles Goat-Boy: Or, The Revised New Syllabus, 1966
Chimera, 1972
Letters, 1979
Sabbatical: A Romance, 1982
The Tidewater Tales: A Novel, 1987
The Last Voyage of Somebody the Sailor, 1991
Once upon a Time: A Floating Opera, 1994

OTHER LITERARY FORMS

While John Barth's novels have ensured his eminence among contemporary American writers, his short fictions have been no less influential or controversial. In addition his novels, he published a collection of shorter works, *Lost in the Funhouse* (1968), the technical involutions of which plumb the nature of narrative itself and disrupt conventional relationships between teller and tale. Barth also wrote two essays of particular significance. In "The Literature of Exhaustion," he discusses those writers whose suspicion that certain forms of literature have become obsolete is incorporated both thematically and technically in the fictions they produce. He highlights the successes of Jorge Luis Borges, Vladimir Nabokov, and Samuel Beckett in the face of apparent artistic impasse; they acknowledge and push beyond the boundaries staked out by their literary predecessors and employ a potentially stifling sense of "ultimacy" in the creation of new work, so that their forms become metaphors for their aesthetic concerns. "The Literature of Replenishment" seeks to correct any misreading of the former essay as a complaint that contemporary writers have little left to accomplish save the parody of conventions which they arrived upon too late to benefit from themselves. Barth's method is to define and legitimize postmodernism by placing its most interesting practitioners—he singles out Italo Calvino and Gabriel García Márquez for praise—in a direct line of succession which may be traced through the great modernists of the first half of the twentieth century back to eighteenth century novelist Laurence Sterne and sixteenth century writer Miguel de Cervantes. "The Literature of Replenishment" makes clear that Barth is not averse to admitting realistic elements into his fictional worlds, provided they do not constrain the imagination. Both of these essays are collected in _The Friday Book: Essays and Other Nonfiction_ (1984). _The Friday Book_ and its companion volume, _Further Fridays_ (1995), also contain many essays dealing with Barth's affection for and interest in his native state of Maryland.

ACHIEVEMENTS

Perhaps Barth's method is a mark of a growing receptivity among readers and critics to formally venturesome fiction; perhaps it is merely a result of the writer's inevitable passage from unexpected new voice to mature artist. Whatever the case, Barth infiltrated the literary establishment with relative ease, with no perceptible compromise. He became America's foremost existential novelist, but his approach to the rather somber question of the arbitrariness of moral values and the absence of intrinsic meaning has always been richly overlaid with humor that is at times intricate and esoteric and often expansive and full of delight in its own verbal virtuosity. He has shown a career-long obsession with mythology, with how classical tales may be reconstituted in and provide resonance for contemporary fiction, and with how the novel may continue to respond to the age-old and seemingly insatiable need for the coherent pleasures of narrative.

Barth still has his detractors, whose accusations typically focus on his tendency to overwork his jokes

(a condemnation which often attends _Giles Goat-Boy_) or to surrender to vulgar effects (as in his revisionist history of John Smith's encounter with Pocahontas in _The Sot-Weed Factor_). Nevertheless, few would dispute Barth's stature as the most widely appreciated postmodernist, a designation which he embraces despite its connotation of self-absorption and unreadability. He won the National Book Award in 1973 for _Chimera_.

BIOGRAPHY

John Barth was born John Simmons Barth on May 27, 1930, in Cambridge, Maryland, the contemporary and historical environs of which have provided the setting for much of his writing. He attended Cambridge High School, after which he accommodated his passion for jazz and the drums with a brief stay at the Juilliard School of Music. His unspectacular showing there led him to enroll at The Johns Hopkins University, a move made possible when he won a scholarship he forgot he had applied for. He achieved the highest grade point average in the College of Arts and Sciences upon receiving the B.A. in 1951.

To pay off tuition debts and support his wife (Harriet Anne Strickland, whom he had married in 1950), Barth took a job in the Classics Library, where he first became absorbed in the Asian tale-cycles which would later inform the style and content of his own fiction. During this period came his first publications in student literary magazines, including one story, "Lilith and the Lion," whose appearance in _The Hopkins Review_ when Barth was twenty may rightly be considered his first professional work. His master's project was _The Shirt of Nessus_, a novel based on a love triangle including a father and son and populated by rapists, murderers, bootleggers, and lunatics; Barth confesses it a miscarriage, and he says it now rests in the Dorchester marshes on Chesapeake Bay.

Having received his M.A. in the spring of 1952, he began studying for a Ph.D. in the aesthetics of literature while tutoring and teaching freshman composition courses, until the cost of supporting both his family (his third child was born in January, 1954) and his education compelled him to teach full-time. He took a position at Pennsylvania State University in 1953; his experience with freshman composition there would eventually find its way into *The End of the Road*. (He did not earn his doctorate until 1969, from the University of Maryland.) While at Penn State, Barth began a series of one hundred stories, in the bawdy manner of Giovanni Boccaccio's *The Decameron* (1348-1353), detailing the history of Dorchester County. He abandoned the project within a year, but fifty of the proposed hundred stories were completed; a handful were published separately and others later were incorporated into *The Sot-Weed Factor*.

Barth advanced from instructor to associate professor at Penn State, where he taught until 1965, and it was during this twelve-year period that he established his reputation. In the fall of 1954, Barth found a photograph of an old showboat; borrowing something of the conversational style of Laurence Sterne's *Tristram Shandy* (1759-1767) and some plot devices from *Don Casmurro* (1900), by the Brazilian novelist Joachim Maria Machado de Assis, he began *The Floating Opera* in January, 1955. It was completed in three months, but several publishers rejected it, and Appleton-Century-Crofts demanded many revisions before publishing it in 1956. By the fall of 1955, however, Barth was already at work on *The End of the Road*. Like *The Floating Opera*, with which it is often associated as a philosophical companion-piece, it was finished in three months. It was ultimately published by Doubleday in 1958.

The Floating Opera was nominated for a National Book Award, which it failed to win; neither the book nor its successor sold well. Barth was denied a Guggenheim grant in 1958, but his school's research fund did manage $250 to send him to Maryland to gather information for his next project. He had expected *The Sot-Weed Factor* to be another three-month venture, but that mammoth refurbishing of the eighteenth century picaresque turned out to be nearly three years in the writing. That novel, too, met with relative public indifference, but it later became his first major critical success when it was released in paperback in 1964.

Giles Goat-Boy was begun in 1960, and it would be six years from inception to publication. In 1965, Barth left Penn State for a full professorship at the State University of New York in Buffalo. *Giles Goat-Boy* introduced Barth to the best-seller lists in 1966, but he was already at work on *Lost in the Funhouse*, a brain-teasing, technically probing collection of multimedia pieces which came out in 1968, for which Barth received his second unsuccessful nomination for a National Book Award.

His next book did earn that elusive honor, however; *Chimera*, Barth's most direct confrontation of ancient narrative in the form of three metafictions, won the National Book Award in 1973. In that same year, Barth changed locale once more, accepting a post at his alma mater, Johns Hopkins. It was not until 1979 that his next book, *Letters*, was published. Instead of creating a new form, Barth decided, as he had done in *The Sot-Weed Factor*, to resuscitate a traditional one: in this case, the epistolary novel. *Letters* plumbs the author's personal literary history as well, for its principal correspondents are characters from Barth's earlier novels.

Whether the familiar hybrid of writer-teacher nourishes or diminishes creativity will not be decided on the basis of one man's example, but Barth has found the academic atmosphere to be not only hospitable to his talents but also generous as an occasion and setting for his fiction: Two of his novels are set specifically in college communities, and the theme of education—be it in a school, under the auspices of a spiritual adviser, or in the shifting, multifarious outside world of affairs—has been repeatedly highlighted in Barth's work. In 1970, Barth married Shelley Rosenberg, a former student of his at Penn State whom he reencountered after some years. Shelley Barth, a high school literature teacher, is often alluded to in the various heroines in Barth's later works, many of which feature an enriching second marriage that helps frame the novel's story. From the 1970's onward, Barth taught writing at The Johns Hopkins University. In August, 1979, he bought a weekend and summer residence on Langford Creek in Dorchester County, Maryland, where he did most of his writing. As with his fictional protagonists, traveling, especially sailing, became one of his favorite avocations. In 1992, he formally retired from teaching at Johns Hopkins. Barth was, however, named professor emeritus there and would occasionally teach writing seminars.

ANALYSIS

The literary historian and the literary technician meet in the novels and attitudes of John Barth. His eagerness to affirm the artificiality of the art he creates enables him to strip-mine the whole range of narrative that precedes his career for usable personalities and devices; similarly, by beginning with the premise of literature as a self-evident sham, he greatly enlarges the field of possibility within his own fictions, so that outrageous plot contrivances, protean characters (or characters who are essentially banners emblazoned with ruling philosophies), and verbal acrobatics all become acceptable. Barth's general solution for handling the fracture between art and reality is not to heal it, but rather to heighten his readers' awareness of it. This is why, despite his penchant for intellectual confrontation and long interludes of debate in his novels, Barth most often looks to humor—jokes and pranks, parody, and stylistic trickery—to make the philosophy palatable.

Barth meticulously reconstructs the fabric and feel of allegory (*Giles Goat-Boy*) or of the *Künstlerroman* (*The Sot-Weed Factor*), then minimizes the appropriateness of such patterns in the contemporary world by vigorously mocking them. He takes on formidable intellectual questions—the impossibility of knowing external reality, the unavailability of intrinsic values, the fragility of the self in an incurably relativistic universe—but chooses to do so in, to borrow one of his own most durable metaphors, a funhouse atmosphere. In fact, in Barth's fiction, abstract discussion is consistently revealed as a dubious alternative to passionate participation in life. Given the ambiguous state of the self, exposure to the world could be fatal if not for the strategy of fashioning and choosing from among a variety of masks which afford the beleaguered self a sense of definition and a schedule of valid responses to whatever situations the world presents. The willful choosing of masks is Barth's main

theme; it suggests that the alternative to despair in the face of universal chaos and indifference is the responsibility to exercise one's freedom, much as an artist exercises his creative faculties in writing and editing tales that satisfy him. In this sense, Barth's heroes are artists of the self, who view the elasticity of character as a challenge to their mythmaking abilities, and who treat their private lives as fictions which are amenable to infinite revision.

THE FLOATING OPERA

"Good heavens," complains Todd Andrews in *The Floating Opera*, "how does one write a novel! I mean, how can anybody stick to the story, if he's at all sensitive to the significance of things?" The doubts and false starts which frustrate the progress of this protagonist's Inquiry—a hodgepodge of papers contained in peach baskets in his hotel room, for which, life being on so tenuous a lease from eternity, he pays rent on a daily basis—reflect those which potentially stymie Barth himself, were he not to make them part of his subject. Like his narrator/alter ego in *The Floating Opera*, Barth contends with the problem of making art out of nihilism. In Andrews's hands, that problem takes the shape of a book-long (and, he confesses, lifelong) obsession with how, and whether, to live. There is little of traditional suspense to propel the narrative; after all, this is an examination of a decision *not* to commit suicide, so that Andrews's private undertaking of Hamlet's well-known question has led him to accept life, at least provisionally and despite its absence of intrinsic values.

The quality of life is described by the title of the novel and symbolized by the barge show—part vaudeville, part minstrel show—which flashes in and out of view as it moves along the river. No other image in literature so effectively captures the idea of Heraclitean flux: The "performance" is never the same for any two spectators, nor can one resume watching it at the same place in the show as when it last passed by. Furthermore, the nature of this floating phenomenon is operatic: sentimental, bizarre, wildly melodramatic, and often simply laughable. The players are amateurish, and they are best appreciated by an unrefined audience who are not bothered by the gaps in their understanding or by the unevenness of the performance. Andrews entertains the notion of building a showboat that has a perpetual play going on, and the novel itself is the alternative result; like the floating extravaganza, it is "chock-full of curiosities" and considers every possible taste: games, violence, flights of fancy and philosophy, legal and sexual intrigue, war and death, artwork and excrement. The implication here, as emphasized by T. Wallace Whittaker's rendition of William Shakespeare (one of the more delicate turns on the bill, to please the ladies), is that not only are all people players on a stage, but also they are apparently purposeless, scriptless players at that.

There is something of the floating opera in the stylistic range of the novel as well. Todd Andrews is a monologist in the comic, voluble tradition of Tristram Shandy. In fact, both men write autobiographical inquiries into the strangeness of the human condition which digress and associate so frequently that they are destined to become life works; both are artists racing to create against death, although Andrews is as likely to be felled by rational suicide as by his heart murmur; and both combine intellectual pursuits with technical "entertainments" (which include, in Barth's novel, repeated paragraphs, a double column of narrative "options," and a reproduction of the handbill announcing the schedule of events in "Adam's Original and Unparalleled Ocean-Going Floating Opera").

Motivation sets these two narrators apart, however, for if Tristram is compelled by life's delights, Andrews is alienated by its absurdity. Andrews is engaged in a search for purpose; his life hangs in the balance. His Inquiry began as an attempt to come to terms with his father's suicide in 1930, an event too complex to chalk up to an escape from debts incurred after the stock-market crash. It then absorbed a letter to his father which, with the obsessive diligence of Franz Kafka in a similar enterprise, Andrews had begun in 1920 and continued to redraft even after his father's death. The Inquiry continued to blossom until, by the time the novel opens in 1954, it is autobiography, journal, and religious/philosophical treatise all in one, and it floats by at the moment of focus on the decision (made on one of two days in June,

1937), after a failed effort, not to commit suicide. (Todd Andrews admonishes readers not to confuse his name with its meaning of "death" in German; his name, which misspells the German word, is more aptly read as "almost death.")

Given the kinds of experience he relates, his final acceptance of life is rather surprising. His father's suicide is but one of a series of incidents which suggest that life may not be worth the salvaging effort. Sexuality, for example, is represented by his wonder at the ridiculousness of the act when, at age seventeen, he spies himself in a mirror in the midst of intercourse, and later, when his five-year affair with Jane Mack is revealed to have been directed by her husband, Harrison. Andrews's most profound confrontation with his own self, during World War I, reveals him to be "a shocked, drooling animal in a mudhole." When an enemy soldier stumbles upon him, they share their terror, then silent communion and friendship . . . and then Andrews stabs him to death. All actions are equally pointless; all commitments are arbitrary; all attempts to solve human incomprehension are laughable.

From rake to saint to cynic, Andrews endures without much joy as an expert lawyer, although he does admit to a certain detached interest in the law's arbitrary intricacies, epitomized in the search for the legitimate will among the seventeen left to posterity by Harrison Mack, Sr., which, when found, decides the fate of more than one hundred pickle jars brimming with his excrement. Andrews is actually comfortable enough living in the Dorset Hotel among a collection of society's aged castoffs, until a casual reference by his mistress to his clubbed hands initiates a kind of Sartrean nausea at the utter physical fact of himself; his growing detestation of that mortal coil, coupled with an absolute conviction that all value is artificially imposed, leads him to the brink of suicide, in the form of a scheme to blow up the opera boat (which, in the restored 1967 edition of the novel, would include hundreds of spectators, with the Macks and Jeannine, their—or possibly Andrews's—daughter among them).

What stays him is the revelation that, if all values are arbitrary, suicide is not less arbitrary; furthermore, even arbitrary values may offer a way to live. This uneasy treaty with a relativistic universe is Andrews's provisional conclusion to the Inquiry, for the suicide does not come off. Some accident—a psychological shudder, an instinct beyond the intellect's dominion, or a spasm of sentimental concern for the little girl who had suffered a sudden convulsion—disrupts the plan, so the novel's philosophical journey concludes in the anticlimax promised by the narrator at the outset. If Barth frustrates some readers by forsaking the questions he has so fastidiously prepared them for, they must understand that the willingness to handle the sublime and the ridiculous alike with a shrug of good humor is part of the point: In the end, even nihilism is shown to be yet one more posture, one more mask.

THE END OF THE ROAD

In his next novel, *The End of the Road*, Barth's speculations on the nature and necessity of masks becomes more formulaic, although with somewhat bleaker results for his hero. Jake Horner—the name is borrowed from William Wycherley's sly seducer in *The Country Wife* (1673)—suffers from "cosmopsis," a disease of hyperconsciousness: the awareness that one choice is no more inherently valid or attractive than another. When a nameless black doctor materializes near a bench at Pennsylvania Station, he discovers Jake as hopelessly rooted to the spot as the statuette Jake keeps of the tortured Laocoön. The doctor recognizes his paralysis and initiates a program of therapy which forces his patient into action. He explains that no matter how arbitrary the system of "choosing" which he advocates may appear, "Choosing is existence: to the extent that you don't choose, you don't exist." All of Jake's subsequent activities—the plot of the novel—represent his execution of the doctor's precepts.

At the outset, Jake's quest is meticulously prescribed *for* him. He is advised to begin with simple, disciplined choices between well-defined alternatives; should he happen to get "stuck" again beyond his mentor's reach, he is to choose artificially according to Sinistrality, Antecedence, and Alphabetical Priority. He is made to worship the hard facts of an almanac and to travel in straight lines to scheduled locations; because it is a monument to fixity, he is to devote himself to teaching of prescriptive grammar at Wicomico State Teachers College. In short, Jake is to undergo Mythotherapy: the regular assignment of roles to the befuddled ego in order to facilitate participation in the world.

Once Jake's quest is complicated by relationships which overextend the narrative "masks" behind which he operates, that neatly contrived therapy proves insufficient. Joe and Rennie Morgan, characters analogous to Harrison and Jane Mack in *The Floating Opera*, confuse his roles: Joe is a strident god whose rational self-control and mechanical theorizing make him his wife's mentor and Jake's intimidator; Rennie's sexuality and mixture of admiration and helplessness toward her husband are provocative, but she involves Jake in a script he cannot handle. His "road" grows tortuous and overwhelming, as his strictly plotted career is diverted into adulterous liaisons and philosophical tournaments, deceit and death. The profundity of his relapse into irresponsibility is much greater this time, however, for he is not the only one victimized by it. By failing to control his roles at critical times, he becomes the instrument of Rennie's death: Rennie will not lie to ensure a safe operation, and Jake's frantic role-playing in order to secure an abortion ends in a grisly death at the hands of Jake's doctor. The reality of Rennie's bleeding on the table is one which, unlike his callous affair with the lonely Peggy Rankin, Jake cannot manipulate or evade; it is the end of the road for him as a free agent in the world. Because he apparently requires further training in order to function successfully, he escapes with the doctor to a new site of the Remobilization Farm.

Of course, Jake's intellectual adversary fares little better under the pressure of real events. Joe Morgan personifies Todd Andrews's supposition that an arbitrary value could be transformed into the "subjective equivalent of an absolute" which might then provide the coherent way of life so crucial to a man who deifies the intellect. Both Jake and Joe begin from the premise of relativism, which explains their mutual attraction, but while Jake tends to succumb to "weatherlessness" (a numbness incurred by the randomness of events and the loss of an essential I), Joe is smug about the rational system he and his wife abide by. That self-assurance sanctions Rennie's being exposed to Jake's influence and provokes Jake to undermine him. When Joe is revealed as something less than pure mind and standards (Jake and Rennie spy him through a window masturbating, grunting, picking his nose), the god loses his authenticity, and the affair merely emphasizes Joe's fall from eminence. Rennie does bring her guilt to Joe, but he returns her to Jake to reenact the betrayal until she can account for it rationally. In the same way, Joe refuses to face up to the fact of Rennie's death, which was indirectly engineered by his experimental obsession, and proves himself to be far more comfortable in handling abstract ideas than in facing up to the welter of uncertainties beyond his field of expertise.

The road's end serves as a final blessing to Jake; the conclusion of the novel is not the completion of a quest but a relief from it. Since the turbulence of the world of affairs has proved unmanageable, he capitulates and numbly offers his "weatherless" self up to the auspices of the doctor, the price for performing Rennie's abortion. Jake retreats into submission after a disastrous initiation into the world.

THE SOT-WEED FACTOR

In his next two novels, Barth grants his philosophical preoccupations the panoramic expansiveness and formal openness of a Henry Fielding or François Rabelais, as if seeking epic dimension for what might well be considered in his first novels to be merely the idiosyncrasies of constipated personalities. *The Sot-Weed Factor* features a riotously inventive plot and a cast of characters including poets and prostitutes, lords and brigands, landowners and Indians, merchants and thieves, but the triumph of the novel is in its authentic language and texture: For some eight hundred pages, Barth's novel impersonates one of those sprawling eighteenth century picaresque English novels, complete with protracted authorial intrusions, outrageous coincidences, dizzying turns of plot, and a relish for lewd humor.

Barth borrows a satirical poem on colonial America by Ebenezer Cooke (1708) for the foundation of his novel and resuscitates Cooke himself to be his hero. Barth's Eben Cooke is a timid, awkward fellow, who, unlike Andrews and Horner, maintains a steadfast virginity—sexual, social, and political—in a world teeming with sin and subterfuge. His steadfast adherence to a chosen mask—that of poet laureate of Maryland—with its requisite responsibilities keeps him on course. Until he happens upon that identity, Eben is overwhelmed by "the beauty of the possible," so much so that he cannot choose among careers; a broad education shared with his twin sister, Anna, at the hands of the ubiquitous Henry Burlingame, serves to increase his wonder rather than to specify a direction, so that readers discover him as a young man who haunts the London taverns, somewhat ill at ease among more raucous peers. He cannot muster an identity reliable enough to survive the pressure of alternatives.

What could have become a lifelong "cosmopsic" stagnation is interrupted by an encounter with a whore, Joan Toast; instead of having sex, Eben chooses to defend his innocence, for he sees in it a symbolic manifestation of his ultimate role. He exalts the deliciously earthy Joan into a bodiless goddess of verse; it is this indifference to reality that will enable him to survive, if not to transcend, the subversive and often grotesque facts of the New World, and the astounding contrasts between the poet's rhapsodizing and the world's stubborn brutishness provide much of the novel's ironic humor.

That confrontation with the New World is set into motion by Eben's father, who, when advised of his son's failure to lead a useful life in London, commands him to set off for his tobacco (sot-weed) estate in Maryland. Armed with a sense of his true calling, Eben wins from Lord Baltimore an agreement to write the "Marylandiad," a verse epic glorifying the province he knows nothing about, and is granted the laureateship in writing. The balance of *The Sot-Weed Factor* is a prolonged trial of Eben's confidence: His initiation into political intrigue and worldly corruption lays siege to his high-flown illusions about humankind. The people he meets are rapacious victimizers, ravaged victims, or crass simpletons, and Eben's promised land, his Malden estate, turns out to be an opium den and brothel. One illusion after another is stripped away, until the poet's tribute to Maryland is metamorphosed into the bitter satire on the deformities of America and Americans found in the poem by the historical Cooke.

Eben would not survive the conspiracies and uglinesses of reality were it not for the tutelage and example of Henry Burlingame. Whereas Eben labors to maintain one role—his "true" self—after years of aimlessness, Burlingame accepts and celebrates a series of roles, for he argues that, in a world of "plots, cabals, murthers, and machinations," an elastic personality will prove most useful. Therefore, he ducks in and out of the novel unpredictably, assuming a variety of guises (including that of John Coode, Baltimore's devilish enemy, Lord Baltimore himself, and even Eben Cooke) as the situation demands. Eben's discussions with his mentor, although they do not cause him to forsake his belief in the essential truth of man's perfectibility and of his own career, do instruct him in how to dissemble when necessary, as exemplified during the voyage to America, when an exchange of roles with his servant, Bertram, proves expedient. In a sense, *The Sot-Weed Factor* boils down to the contrast and the tentative accommodations made between the ideal and the real, or between innocence and experience, as represented by the virgin-poet, who is linked to a past (his father) and to a future (his commission), and by the orphaned jack-of-all-trades, who embraces adventures and lovers with equal vivacity.

The Sot-Weed Factor insists on no conclusive resolution between these attitudes; as is Barth's custom throughout his fiction, the struggles between theoretical absolutes must end in compromise. If Eben's first problem is to rouse himself out of languor, his second is to realize the inadequacy of a single, unalterable role. Accordingly, Eben repudiates his sexual abstinence in order to wed the diseased, opium-addicted Joan Toast—his ruined Beatrice, who has followed him secretly to America—and so accepts a contract between the ideal and the actual. Similarly, Burlingame can only win and impregnate his beloved Anna after he completes his search for his family roots, which is to say, after he locates a stable identity. The novel ends in good comic fashion: Lovers

are finally united; plot confusions are sorted out. Significantly, however, Barth adds twists to these conventions, thereby tempering the comic resolution: Joan dies in childbirth, and Burlingame disappears without trace. Barth replicates the eighteenth century picaresque novel only to parody it; he seduces readers into traditional expectations only to undermine them.

For many readers, the most satisfying passages in *The Sot-Weed Factor* are not the philosophical or the literary exercises but rather the bawdy set pieces, the comic inventories and the imaginative diaries; nor should any discussion of this novel neglect to mention the war of name-calling between whores, or the "revisionist" rendition of Captain Smith's sexual assault on the otherwise impregnable Pocahontas. Barth has written of his enjoyment of Tobias Smollett's *Roderick Random* (1748) for its "nonsignificant surfaces," and in such glittering surfaces lie the charm of *The Sot-Weed Factor* as well. Fiction invades history and finds in its incongruities and intricacies of plot, character, and motivation a compatible form. Of all the deceptions perpetrated in the novel, perhaps none is so insidious as that of American history itself—the ultimate ruse of civilization, an imperfect concealment of savagery and selfishness. To remain innocent of the nature of history is irresponsible; Eben Cooke's practiced detachment, as implied by his virginity, is morally unacceptable. This lesson enables him to mature both artistically and ethically, and to dedicate himself to the world of which he claims to be poet laureate.

GILES GOAT-BOY

Following immediately upon his satire of the historical past is Barth's satire of the future—a computer narrative. The novel-long analogy ruling *Giles Goat-Boy* transforms the universe into a university; this Newest Testament portrays a world divided (between East and West Campus) and waiting for the Grand Tutor, the Savior of the academic system, to protect Studentdom from the satanic Dean o' Flunks.

Barth provides Giles, an amalgam of worldwide messiah-heroes, as the updated instrument of human destiny. Giles (Grand-Tutorial Ideal, Laboratory Eugenical Specimen) is the child of the prodigious

WESCAC computer and a virgin, who later appears as Lady Creamhair. Raised as a goat (Billy Bocksfuss) by an apostate scientist-mentor, Max Spielman, he eventually leaves the herd to join humanity as a preacher of the Revised New Syllabus on the West Campus of New Tammany College. The novel traces his attempts to verify and institute his claim to be Grand Tutor. Such a task entails a loss of innocence comparable in kind (although far more extensive in its implications for humanity) to those undertaken by his predecessors in Barth's canon. In *Giles Goat-Boy*, the initiation into complexity assumes a mythical overlay, as the hero passes from his exotic birth to his revelation of purpose in the womb of WESCAC (in whose mechanical interior he and Anastasia, a student who serves as Female Principle, come together) to a series of "assignments" through which he must prove his worth to his role as lawgiver and deposer of the false prophet, Harold Bray, and finally, to his sacrificial death for the sake of humankind.

Giles's career invokes Lord Raglan's systematic program for the stages of the hero's life, yet readers are irresistibly drawn to make correlations between the novel's allegorical personalities and events, and counterparts in journalistic reality. East and West Campus are barely fictional versions of Russia and the United States, with the H-bomb, in the form of WESCAC, the source of their power struggle. John F. Kennedy, Nikita Khrushchev, Joseph McCarthy, Albert Einstein, and other contemporary world figures populate the novel, as do such ancient luminaries as Moses, Socrates, and Christ Himself (Enos Enoch, accompanied by Twelve Trustees). These textures give *Giles Goat-Boy* the authority of sociopolitical history, but as is the case in *The Sot-Weed Factor*, Barth's penchant for discovering his own artifice casts a thick shadow of unreliability over the proceedings. For example, readers must share in the doubts over Giles's legitimacy, both filial and messianic: Not only do many people fail to accept his Grand Tutorhood (he predicts betrayal by the masses, who will drive him out on a rusty bicycle to his death on Founder's Hill), but also he himself is never completely certain that his words have not been programmed into him by WESCAC. The document

itself—the pages before the readers—brought to "J. B." by Giles's son, is framed by disclaimers, editorial commentaries, footnotes, and postscripts, so that, finally, the "true text" is indistinguishable from the apocrypha. Moreover, Barth's liberal infusion of verse, puns, allusions, and stylistic entertainments strains the heroic conventions, which he has assembled from a great variety of literary and mythic sources. In short, the quality of revelation as espoused by Gilesianism is consistently affected by the doubt and self-effacement implied in the structure of the narrative.

Despite Barth's typical supply of structural equivocations, *Giles Goat-Boy* is his most ambitious attempt to recognize correspondences between factual and fictional accounts, between politics and mythology, between public and personal history. If the hero's quest leads him into a world of complexity, there is at least, by virtue of these correspondences, the promise of insight. Under Burlingame's direction in *The Sot-Weed Factor*, readers learn that the human personality, correctly apprehended, is a compendium of various, even contradictory, selves; in *Giles Goat-Boy*, this lesson is applied to the whole history of human learning and progress. Only when Giles accepts the all-encompassing nature of truth—PASS ALL and FAIL ALL are inextricably connected, not separable opposites but parts of a mystical oneness—does he mature into effectiveness. His passage through experience will include failure, but failure will guarantee growth, itself evidence of passage. Giles is a condenser in whom worldly paradoxes and dichotomies—knowledge and instinct, asceticism and responsibility, Spielman and Eirkopf, West and East Campus, and all other mutually resistive characters and systems of thought—manage a kind of synthesis. Keeping in mind that Giles's story originates from a fundamental willingness to accept his humanity over his "goathood," one comes to appreciate that, although the novel is a satirical fantasy, it is inspired by the same receptivity to experience and the same optimistic energy in the face of desperate circumstances that are exalted by the tradition of quest literature.

The image of Giles and Anastasia united in WESCAC is the philosophical center of the novel; at this climactic moment, flesh is integrated with spirit, animal with human, and scientific hardware with "meaty tubes," all in the service of the improvement of the race. The gospel of *Giles Goat-Boy* is that the very impulse to enter the labyrinth is an affirmation, however unlikely the hero's chances against the beasts and devils (such as Stoker, the gloomy custodian of the power station) who reside within. Giles's victory is a transcendence of categories, a faith in the unity of the universe, and that revelation is enough to overcome the lack of appreciation by the undergraduates. No obstacle or imposture of the dozens which antagonize the hero obscures the meeting of goat-boy with computer; the circuitry of myth remains intact, even in this age of broken atoms.

LETTERS

"When my mythoplastic razors were sharply honed, it was unparalleled sport to lay about with them, to have at reality." So proclaimed Jake Horner in *The End of the Road* while praising articulation as his nearest equivalent to a personal absolute. The narrative impulse is the principal source of faith for Barth's array of protagonists, insofar as faith is possible in an undeniably relativistic environment. In *Letters*, he allows those characters a fuller opportunity to engage in an authorial perspective. *Letters* solidifies Barth's associations with Modernists such as James Joyce and Samuel Beckett; here Barth takes license not only with established literary forms—specifically, the epistolary novel—but also with his private literary past, as he nonchalantly pays visits and respects to old fictional personalities. Because *Letters*, by its very form, intensifies one's awareness of the novel as a fabricated document (and, for that matter, of characters as collections of sentences), it is Barth's most transparently metafictional work; as the novel's subtitle unabashedly declares, this is "an old time epistolary novel by seven fictitious drolls and dreamers each of which imagines himself actual." *Letters* breaks down into seven parts, one for each letter of the title, and covers seven months of letter-writing. Place the first letter of each of the eighty-eight epistles in *Letters* on a calendar so that it corresponds with its date of composition, and the title of the novel will appear; like *Ulysses* (1922), *Let-*

ters testifies to the diligence, if not to the overindulgence, of the craftsman.

Among these letter-writers are a group recycled from previous works as well as two figures, Germaine Pitt (Lady Amherst) and the Author, newly created for this book. In spite of Barth's assertions to the contrary, an appreciation of these characters is rather heavily dependent on a familiarity with their pre-*Letters* biographies: Todd Andrews emerges from *The Floating Opera* as an elderly lawyer who writes to his dead father and is drawn to incest while enjoying one last cruise on Chesapeake Bay; Jacob Horner remains at the Remobilization Farm to which he had resigned himself at the conclusion of *The End of the Road*, and where his latest Information Therapy demands that he write to himself in an elaborate reconstitution of the past; Ambrose Mensch, the now-mature artist out of "Lost in the Funhouse," directs his correspondences to the anonymous "Yours Truly" whose message he found in a bottle years earlier, and constructs his life, including an affair with Germaine Pitt, in accordance with Lord Raglan's prescription for the hero. Readers also meet descendants of previous creations: Andrew Burlingame Cook VI busily attempts to shape the nation's destiny in a Second American Revolution, and Jerome Bonaparte Bray, a mad rival to Barth himself who may be a gigantic insect, seeks to program a computer-assisted novel, *Numbers*, to compete with the authority of the one that treated him so shabbily.

The third level of writers in *Letters* includes the two who have no prior existence in Barth's works: Germaine Pitt, a colorful widow who had been the friend of James Joyce, H. G. Wells, Aldous Huxley, and other literary notables, anxiously campaigns as Acting Provost to ensure the prestige of her college against the administrative dilutions and hucksterism of one John Schott; the Author enters the novel as Pitt's own alternative candidate for an honorary doctorate (which Schott proposes to give to the dubious activist, State Laureate A. B. Cook VI), and he writes to everyone else in the vicinity of *Letters*.

The most consistent theme tying the letters and authors together is the conflict between restriction and freedom. The setting is the volatile America of the 1960's, when sexual, moral, political, and even academic norms underwent the most serious reevaluation in American history. Obviously, Barth's creative history is the most evident aspect of this theme, and the repetitions and echoes among his novels and within *Letters* seduce readers into joining his search for pattern in the flux of human affairs. The ambiguous nature of history itself has also been one of his most durable themes—one recalls a chapter in *The Sot-Weed Factor* which examined the question of whether history is "a Progress, a Drama, a Retrogression, a Cycle, an Undulation, a Vortex, a Right- or Left-Handed Spiral, a Mere Continuum, or What Have You"—and the suggestion here is that any sort of orthodoxy can be revealed, especially in times of social crisis, as fictional. Student protests against the establishment are replicated in the antagonism between characters and an established text; the societal disruptions in the novel disrupt and contaminate the narrative.

A. B. Cook VI, one of the novel's seven correspondents, is the descendant of Ebenezer Cooke in *The Sot-Weed Factor*. Taking his cue from his ancestor, he is involved in the political intrigues of his own time, but he also attempts to rewrite history, providing alternative versions of storied events in the American past. The history of the Cook family is an antiestablishment one, filled with various attempts to launch "The Second American Revolution." This involves both rolling back the original American Revolution (for instance, during the War of 1812 the Cooks are on the British side) and extending it by making America more democratic. The Cooks, for instance, frequently ally with Native American peoples.

In contrast to Cook's historical vision stands the aesthetic one of Ambrose Mensch. Mensch is the prototypical modern artist, as presented in modern novels by writers such as James Joyce and Thomas Mann. His goal in life is to mold his own experience into a finished object, remote from the contingencies of time and place. Barth recognizes that both Cook's and Mensch's visions are partial. To bring together the two polarities, his instrument is Germaine Pitt, Lady Amherst, who serves in many ways as the muse of the book. Germaine reconciles art and history and

shows the way for the novel, and life itself, to have a productive future.

In contrast to Samuel Richardson's definitive use of the epistolary form, *Letters* is populated by characters who are more than vaguely aware of their unreality, and therefore of the need to bargain with Barth for personal status and support. When the Author intrudes as a character, no convention is above suspicion; although he describes himself as turning away from the "fabulous irreal" toward "a détente with the realistic tradition," if this novel is the result, it is a severely qualified détente, indeed. Perhaps the structural "confusion" of the novel explains the smugness of Reg Prinz, an avant-garde filmmaker who wants to create a version of all of Barth's books in a medium which he feels to be superior and more up-to-date. What had been a playful interest in the relationships between creative media in *Lost in the Funhouse* has escalated in *Letters* into a battle for aesthetic dominance between the word-hating Prinz and the word-mongering Barth. (That Prinz is a prisoner of the novel, of course, enables Barth to sway the outcome of this battle, at least temporarily.)

Letters, like history itself, concludes in blood and ambiguity; one suspects that Barth means to undergo a catharsis of the books and characters that have obsessed him and that continue to infiltrate his creative consciousness. It is testimony to Barth's ability to elicit admiration for his craft that readers do not leave *Letters*—or, for that matter, most of his fictions—with a sense of defeat. The keynote of his literary career is exuberance; if nihilism and existential gloom have been his thematic preoccupations, their potentially numbing effects are undercut by Barth's cleverness, his stylistic ingenuity, and his campaign for the rewards of narrative.

SABBATICAL

Barth's *Sabbatical* continues to bend philosophy into escapade. Subtitled "A Romance," *Sabbatical* is rather a postmodernization of romance: All the well-established Barthian formal intrigues, ruminative digressions, plot coincidences (the married pair of main characters, in the same vein as *The Sot-Weed Factor*, are both twins), and other examples of literary self-consciousness complicate the vacation cruise of Fenwick Scott Key Turner, a former CIA agent and a contemporary novelist, and his wife, Susan, herself an established academic and critic. The nine-month sea journey—a frequent theme for Barth—leads to the birth of the novel itself, in whose plot the narrating "parents" seek clues to some conspiratorial Agency "plot" against them. (Fenwick has written an exposé that makes his "life as voyage" a perilous journey indeed—even when on sabbatical.) So the creative couple prepare, nurture, take pride in, and exhaustively analyze their verbal offspring, while the real world blows into their story from the shore in another dizzying mixture of fact and fiction.

Yet, as readers have come to expect from Barth, the imagination is exalted above and beyond its moorings in the "real world," all the while calling attention to its own altitude. As Fenwick declares to his loving coauthor: "I won't have our story be unadulterated realism. Reality is wonderful; reality is dreadful; reality is what it is." The intensity, the scope, and the truth of reality are more appropriately the province of experimental technique.

THE TIDEWATER TALES

The Tidewater Tales: A Novel is closely related to *Sabbatical*. Fenwick Scott Key Turner reappears in the guise of Franklin Key Talbott, and Carmen B. Seckler has become the main character Peter Sagamore's mother-in-law, Carla B. Silver. Following the theme of twins in *Sabbatical*, Peter's wife, Katherine, is eight and a half months pregnant with twins. In fact, much of the plot consists of Peter and Katherine sailing around in their sloop *Story* while waiting for Katherine to come to term.

The sloop's name is an obvious reference to both Peter's and Katherine's (and Barth's) profession. Peter is a writer, and Katherine is an oral history expert—a storyteller. The intricate narratives become a line of stories within stories, as Barth concentrates on capturing all of reality within his fictive form.

THE LAST VOYAGE OF SOMEBODY THE SAILOR

The Last Voyage of Somebody the Sailor is a retelling of the Arabic short-story cycle *The Arabian Nights' Entertainments* (c. fifteenth century), with an interesting difference. Whereas traditionally the Arabian Nights stories have been valued as exotic fanta-

sies wholly divergent from conventional modern realism, Barth demonstrates that what is usually considered realism can often also be considered fantastic. When Somebody (also known as Simon Behler), a modern-day sailor whose biography parallels Barth's own to some degree, arrives in medieval Baghdad, his stories of American boyhood, sexual awakening, and marital trouble are seen as amazing and weird by his Arabian audience, for whom the "marvelous" is all too familiar. Though this novel may lack the psychological depth of some of Barth's earlier works, such as *The End of the Road*, it does attempt a serious moral critique. Somebody's Arabian equivalent is the renowned sailor Sindbad, who initially appears to be a hero but whose avarice and cruelty are soon found out and duly punished. Somebody marries the beautiful princess Yasmin, with whom he has a happy relationship (though readers are perpetually reminded that it is a fictional one). Somebody's better adjusted, more humane kind of heroism is eventually celebrated by the Arabian Nights society, and thus the novel becomes an even happier version of Mark Twain's time-travel novel *A Connecticut Yankee in King Arthur's Court* (1889).

ONCE UPON A TIME

Once upon a Time is a hybrid of fiction and autobiography. Barth gives readers a bare-bones account of his life and career, sometimes fleshed out with extended anecdotes. Interspersed with this, however, are scenes of voyages to the Caribbean and back, as well as meditations on the nature of storytelling itself. The strongest fictional element of the book is a totally invented character, Jay Scribner. Scribner serves as Barth's alter ego in the book. He is a more outwardly vigorous and outspoken figure who bounces off the character of the author. Scribner at once comments upon and frames Barth's own sensibility. As the book proceeds on its jaunty course, Barth appends footnotes of what is going on, politically and otherwise, in the "real" world. The gently made point of the narrative is that autobiography is as much a fiction as fiction itself. What is real and what is imaginary (especially in the life and mind of a novelist) are always intertwining and cannot definitively be separated from each other. Nor would readers in search of truly enlightening entertainment want such a thing to occur.

　　Arthur M. Saltzman, updated by Nicholas Birns

OTHER MAJOR WORKS

　　SHORT FICTION: *Lost in the Funhouse*, 1968; *On with the Story*, 1996.

　　NONFICTION: *The Friday Book: Essays and Other Nonfiction*, 1984; *Further Fridays: Essays, Lectures, and Other Nonfiction*, 1995.

BIBLIOGRAPHY

Bowen, Zack R. *A Reader's Guide to John Barth.* Westport, Conn.: Greenwood Press, 1994. A good introduction to Barth's works, this study includes bibliographical references and an index.

Harris, Charles B. *Passionate Virtuosity: The Fiction of John Barth.* Urbana: University of Illinois Press, 1983. A study of Barth's first seven books—a deliberate cutoff, as Harris believes that *Letters* marked the end of a certain phase in Barth's development as a writer. Included are copious and detailed notes to each chapter as well as a bibliography of works about Barth and an index.

Morrell, David. *John Barth: An Introduction.* University Park: Pennsylvania State University Press, 1976. Morrell provides biographical information in addition to criticism of Barth's work. Although the bibliographical lists are somewhat dated, they are very detailed. Also includes an index.

Schulz, Max F. *The Muses of John Barth: Tradition and Metafiction from "Lost in the Funhouse" to "The Tidewater Tales."* Baltimore: The Johns Hopkins University Press, 1990. Schulz believes that Barth is one of the great modern novelists in the tradition of John Updike. Discusses the place of Barth's canon in Western literature and provides in-depth literary criticism. The annotations for each chapter are helpful in directing readers for further research. Includes an index.

Waldmeir, Joseph J., ed. *Critical Essays on John Barth.* Boston: G. K. Hall, 1980. Includes general discussions about Barth's work in addition to pieces on individual novels. Contains an index, as well as references and notes for each essay.

Walkiewicz, E. P. *John Barth.* Boston: Twayne, 1986. Provides biographical information, a chronology of important personal and professional events in Barth's life, and criticism of Barth's work, but only a brief mention of *The Tidewater Tales.* Includes notes, references, primary and secondary bibliographies, and an index.

DONALD BARTHELME

Born: Philadelphia, Pennsylvania; April 7, 1931
Died: Houston, Texas; July 23, 1989

PRINCIPAL LONG FICTION

Snow White, 1967
The Dead Father, 1975
Paradise, 1986
The King, 1990

OTHER LITERARY FORMS

　　Donald Barthelme became known first as a short-story writer, perhaps because the third of his long works appeared only three years before his death, and the fourth was posthumous. For some commentators, as a result, Barthelme's name is still primarily associated with short stories—the more so because even his long fiction tends to be composed of the same fragments as his short. Barthelme was also the author of a children's book entitled *The Slightly Irregular Fire Engine: Or, The Hithering Thithering Djinn* (1971).

ACHIEVEMENTS

　　Barthelme was one of the great innovators in fictional techniques of the post-World War II era of American literature. Drawing on the technical discoveries of the Anglo-American modernist authors (including T. S. Eliot, Gertrude Stein, James Joyce, and Samuel Beckett), he developed a type of fiction that was largely structured on principles other than plot and character, the building blocks of nineteenth century "realistic" fiction. His fragmentary, collage-like splicing of historical and literary references expresses a certain world-weariness as well as a sense that history does not advance. Nevertheless, the irony expressed by this style softens a bit in the later works.

In addition to winning the National Book Award for his children's book in 1972, Barthelme was the recipient of a Guggenheim Fellowship (1966) and of the PEN/Faulkner Award for Fiction for *Sixty Stories* (1981), one of the two collections of selected stories to appear during his lifetime.

BIOGRAPHY

Donald Barthelme was born in Philadelphia, where his parents were students at the University of Pennsylvania. A few years later, the family moved to Houston, where his father became a professor of architecture at the University of Houston. In high school, Barthelme wrote for both the school newspaper and the school literary magazine. In 1949, he en-

(Bill Wittliff)

tered the University of Houston, majoring in journalism. During his sophomore year (1950-1951), he was the editor of the college newspaper, the *Cougar*. During this year he also worked as a reporter for the *Houston Post*.

In 1953, Barthelme was drafted into the U.S. Army, arriving in Korea the day the truce was signed, at which point he became the editor of an army newspaper. Upon his return to the United States, he once again became a reporter for the *Houston Post* and returned to the University of Houston, where he worked as a speechwriter for the university president and attended classes in philosophy. Although he attended classes as late as 1957, he ultimately left without taking a degree. When he was thirty, he became the director of Houston's Contemporary Arts Museum.

In 1962, Barthelme moved to New York to become the managing editor of the arts and literature magazine *Location*. His first published story appeared in 1961; his first story for *The New Yorker* appeared in 1963. After that time, most of his works appeared first in this magazine, and eventually Barthelme's name became almost a synonym for an ironic, fragmentary style that characterized its pages in the late 1960's and early 1970's.

Barthelme taught for brief periods at Boston University, the State University of New York at Buffalo, and the College of the City of New York, at the last of which he was Distinguished Visiting Professor of English from 1974 to 1975. He was married twice. His only child was a daughter, Anne Katharine, born in 1964 to his first wife, Birgit. It was for Anne that he wrote *The Slightly Irregular Fire Engine*. At the time of his death from cancer on July 23, 1989, he was survived by his second wife, Marion.

ANALYSIS

For the reader new to Donald Barthelme, the most productive way to approach his works is in terms of what they are not: looking at what they avoid doing, what they refuse to do, and what they suggest is not worth doing. Nineteenth century literature, and indeed most popular ("best-selling") literature of the twentieth century, is principally structured according to the two elements of plot and character. These

Barthelme studiously avoids, especially in his earlier works, offering instead a collage of fragments whose coherence is usually only cumulative, rather than progressive. Some readers may find the early works emotionally cold as a result, given that their unity is to be found in the realm of the intellect rather than in that of feeling.

This style has resulted in the frequent classification of Barthelme as a "postmodernist" author, one of a generation of American writers who came to international prominence in the late 1960's and 1970's and who include Thomas Pynchon, John Barth, John Hawkes, William H. Gass, Ishmael Reed, and Kurt Vonnegut, Jr. This label indicates, among other things, that Barthelme's most immediate predecessors are the modernist authors of the early years of the century, such as T. S. Eliot, James Joyce, and Franz Kafka. Yet critics have split regarding whether Barthelme is doing fundamentally the same things as the earlier modernist authors or whether his works represent a significant development of their method.

Barthelme clearly diverges from the modernists in that he seems to lack their belief in the power of art to change the world; his most characteristic stance is ironic, self-deprecating, and anarchistic. Since this ironic posture is productive more of silence than of talk, or at best produces parodic talk, it is not surprising that Barthelme began his career with shorter pieces rather than longer. Nor does it seem coincidental that the novels *Paradise* and *The King* were produced in the last years of his life, by which point his short stories had become slightly less frenetic in pace.

SNOW WHITE

Barthelme's longer works seem to divide naturally into two pairs. The earlier two are dense reworkings of (respectively) a fairy tale and a myth. The second pair are more leisurely, the one involving autobiographical elements, the other making a social point. Barthelme's first longer work, *Snow White*, is reasonably easy to follow, largely by virtue of the clarity with which the author indicates to the reader at all points what it is that he is doing—or rather, what he is avoiding, namely the fairy tale evoked by the work's title. Every reader knows the characters of

this fairy tale; in fact, all of them have their equivalents in the characters of Barthelme's version, along with several others unaccounted for in the original. In Barthelme's version of the story, Snow White is twenty-two, lives with seven men with whom she regularly has unsatisfying sex in the shower, and seems to have confused herself with Rapunzel from another fairy story, as she continually sits at her window with her hair hanging out. Her dwarfs have modern names such as Bill (the leader), Clem, Edward, and Dan, and they suffer from a series of ailments, of which the most important seems to be that Bill no longer wishes to be touched. During the day the seven men work in a Chinese baby-food factory.

The closest thing this retelling of the myth has to a prince is a man named Paul, who does not seem to want to fulfill his role of prince. Avoiding Snow White, he spends time in a monastery in Nevada, goes to Spain, and joins the Thelemite order of monks. Ultimately he ends up near Snow White, but only as a Peeping Tom, armed with binoculars, in a bunker before her house. Barthelme's version of the wicked queen is named Jane; she writes poison-pen letters and ultimately makes Snow White a poisoned drink. Paul drinks it instead, and he dies.

The underlying point of the contrast generated by these modernized versions of the fairy-tale characters is clearly that which was the point of Joyce's version of *Ulysses* (1922), namely that there are no more heroes today. This in fact is the crux of the personality problems both of Paul, who does not want to act like a prince though he is one, and Snow White, who is unsure about the nature of her role as Snow White: She continues to long for a prince but at the same time feels it necessary to undertake the writing of a lengthy (pornographic) poem that constitutes her attempt to "find herself."

THE DEAD FATHER

The Dead Father, Barthelme's second long work, may be seen in formal terms as the author's overt homage to the fictions of the Anglo-American modernists, most notably Stein, Joyce, and Beckett. Certain of its sections appear to be direct appropriations of the formal innovations of Joyce's *Ulysses*. The result is a complex overlayering of techniques that seems as much about literary history as about any more objective subject matter. The text presupposed by this novel is that of the Greek story of Oedipus, and of Sigmund Freud's treatment of it. Freud's version insists on the potentially lethal effects of an overbearing father and suggests that sons must symbolically kill their fathers to attain independence. Without an understanding of the association of father with threat, the plot of this novel can make little sense.

Nineteen men are pulling the Dead Father—who in fact is not really dead until the end, and perhaps not even then—across the countryside by a cable. The Father is huge, like Joyce's Humphrey C. Earwicker from *Finnegans Wake* (1939), covering a great expanse of countryside. There are four children, named Thomas, Edmund, Emma, and Julie, who accompany the Father on his journey to his grave. Along the way his children cut off his leg and his testicles and demand his sword. This does not stop the Dead Father's sexual desires; one of the objectionable aspects of the old man is clearly the fact that he has not ceased to function as a male. An encounter with a tribe known as the Wends, who explain that they have dispensed with fathers entirely, develops the background situation.

The plot is discernible only in flashes through the dense thicket of fragmentary conversations and monologues. The narration of the journey is constantly being interrupted by textual digressions. One of the most developed of these is a thirty-page "Manual for Sons" that the children find and that is reprinted in its entirety in the text. The complexity of this work is undeniable. It differs from *Snow White* in that the underlying mood does not seem to be that of alienation: The power of the Father is too great. Yet it may be that the use of so many modernist techniques splits the technical veneer of the book too deeply from the deeper emotional issues it raises.

PARADISE

Barthelme's third long work, *Paradise*, comes the closest of the four to being a traditional novel. It is set in a recognizable place and time (Philadelphia and New York in the last quarter of the century) and uses the author's standard plot fragmentation to ex-

press the state of mind of its protagonist, an architect named Simon, who is going through a sort of midlife crisis. Simon has taken in three women, with whom he sleeps in turn; this arrangement solves none of his problems, which have to do with his previous marriage, his child by that marriage, his other affairs, and the drying up of his architectural inspiration. A number of chapters are set in the form of questions and answers, presumably between Simon and his analyst.

In this work Barthelme draws on his knowledge of the Philadelphia architectural scene (especially the works of Louis Kahn) and seems to be expressing some of his own reactions to aging in the personality of the protagonist. This is certainly the easiest of the four novels for most readers to like.

THE KING

Barthelme's final long work, *The King*, once again returns to a literary prototype, this time the Arthurian romances. Like the characters in *Snow White*, Barthelme's Arthur, Guinevere, Lancelot, and knights are twentieth century characters; unlike the earlier ones, they are particular public personages, identified with the King and Queen of England during World War II. (At the same time, their language and exploits situate them in the Celtic legends, or at least the Renaissance retelling of these by Sir Thomas Malory.) Barthelme is exploiting his usual anachronistic confusion of times here, yet his purpose in this work seems not to be merely that of comedy. While readers can be distanced from the categories of "friends" and "enemies" that the characters use in their aspect as figures in Arthurian romance, it is more difficult to be this distanced from a conflict still as much a part of contemporary culture as World War II. Barthelme's point seems to be that carnage is carnage and war is war, and that from the point of view of a future generation even twentieth century people's moral certainty regarding this more recent conflict will seem as irrelevant and incomprehensible as that of Arthur and his knights.

Though Barthelme never abandons his concern with form over the course of his four novels, it seems clear that the second pair deals with issues that the average educated reader may find more accessible than those treated in the first two. Moving from the textual ironies of the first and second to the more measured plotting of the third and fourth, Barthelme's novels show signs of a gradual emotional warming process for which many readers may be thankful.

Bruce E. Fleming

OTHER MAJOR WORKS

SHORT FICTION: *Come Back, Dr. Caligari*, 1964; *Unspeakable Practices, Unnatural Acts*, 1968; *City Life*, 1970; *Sadness*, 1972; *Amateurs*, 1976; *Great Days*, 1979; *Sixty Stories*, 1981; *Overnight to Many Distant Cities*, 1983; *Forty Stories*, 1987.

NONFICTION: *Guilty Pleasures*, 1974.

CHILDREN'S LITERATURE: *The Slightly Irregular Fire Engine: Or, The Hithering Thithering Djinn*, 1971.

BIBLIOGRAPHY

Gordon, Lois. *Donald Barthelme*. Boston: Twayne, 1981. The most accessible and complete overview of Barthelme's fiction up to 1981. Its 223 pages begin with a biographical sketch and, besides analyses of the first two novels and most of the short-story collections, include a selected bibliography.

Klinkowitz, Jerome. "Donald Barthelme." In *The New Fiction: Interviews with Innovative American Writers*, edited by Joe David Bellamy. Urbana: University of Illinois Press, 1974. One of the most informative, standard sources for biographical information regarding Barthelme's life.

_____. *Donald Barthelme*. Durham, N.C.: Duke University Press, 1991. Klinkowitz writes about all of Barthelme's major novels, but he argues for the "centrality" of *The Dead Father*. Includes a useful bibliography.

Patteson, Richard F., ed. *Critical Essays on Donald Barthelme*. New York: G. K. Hall, 1992. Part of the Critical Essays on American Literature series, this collection includes bibliographical references and an index.

Stengel, Wayne B. *The Shape of Art in the Short Stories of Donald Barthelme*. Baton Rouge: Louisiana State University Press, 1985. This longer (227-page) scholarly work is a readable consideration of Barthelme's short stories, examined under typal rubrics. Despite the lack of overt consideration of the novels, the work is useful in situating the longer works in their larger context.

Trachtenberg, Stanley. *Understanding Donald Barthelme*. Columbia: University of South Carolina Press, 1990. A basic guide to Barthelme's body of work, including brief discussions of his biography and major work. Includes an excellent annotated bibliography.

ANN BEATTIE

Born: Washington, D.C.; September 8, 1947

PRINCIPAL LONG FICTION

Chilly Scenes of Winter, 1976
Falling in Place, 1980
Love Always, 1985
Picturing Will, 1989
Another You, 1995
My Life, Starring Dara Falcon, 1997

OTHER LITERARY FORMS

Beattie has published numerous short stories, including those anthologized in *Distortions* (1976) and a children's book entitled *Goblin Tales* (1975).

ACHIEVEMENTS

Hailed by many as the spokesperson for her generation, Beattie won numerous awards for her novels and short stories focusing on vapid, upper-middle-class characters. Along with several scholastic honors, Beattie also received a literary award from the American Academy and Institute of Arts and Letters and a Distinguished Alumnae award from American University, both in 1980. A member of the International Association of Poets, Playwrights, Editors, Essayists, and Novelists (PEN) and of the Authors Guild, in 1992 she was elected to the American Academy and Institute of Arts and Letters.

(Benjamin Ford)

BIOGRAPHY

The daughter of an administrator in the U.S. Department of Health, Education, and Welfare, James A. Beattie, and Charlotte (née Crosby) Beattie, Ann Beattie was born in Washington, D.C., in 1947 and grew up in its suburbs. As a child, she was encouraged to paint, read, and write. An avid scholar, she enrolled at American University in Washington, D.C., in 1966 and received her B.A. only three years later, in 1969. During this short tenure, she edited the university literary journal and was chosen by *Mademoiselle* magazine to be a guest editor in 1968. After her graduation, Beattie entered the M.A. program at the University of Connecticut as a graduate assistant to study eighteenth century literature. She received her degree in 1970 and began to work toward a doctorate; however, she quickly became frustrated and turned to

writing short stories. It was then that—encouraged by her mentor, John O'Hara—she submitted several stories to small-press literary journals. After initial, moderate success with these publications, she finally had "A Platonic Relationship" published by *The New Yorker* in 1974. Later that same year, *The New Yorker* printed two more Beattie short stories, a signal of her arrival in the literary world.

At this, Beattie quit the university to concentrate on her writing. After that, she served on the faculties of several universities as a writing instructor. In 1972 she married David Gates, a fellow University of Connecticut student; they were divorced in 1980. In 1985, a mutual friend introduced Beattie to the painter Lincoln Perry, a visiting professor at the University of Virginia, where Beattie had taught several years before. They were married in 1988. After several years in Charlottesville, they moved to Maine.

ANALYSIS

Although Beattie's work has often been criticized as pointless and depressing, there is a method to her seeming madness. The stories and novels are not a mix of ennui and untapped angst but rather detailed examinations of the lives of several apparently different—but uniquely similar—people. Not one specific character is repeated in any story, but some, like the Vietnam veteran, appear in different versions and perform different functions, as plot catalysts, for example. At the same time, all Beattie's characters share the same vague feelings of discontent and lack of fulfillment, the knowledge that something is missing in their lives.

CHILLY SCENES OF WINTER

Initially, a Beattie character may seem feisty and self-assured, even defensive about his or her lack of enthusiasm. In Beattie's first novel, *Chilly Scenes of Winter*, one player remarks, "[Y]ou could be happy, too, Sam, if you hadn't had your eyes opened in the 60's." The promise of a better life that was given to these characters has been transmogrified into unhappiness and loneliness without relief. Beattie's novels are, accordingly, laced with irony.

Yet it is the acknowledgment of this transgression through the use of irony that provides a saving grace for the stories and novels. The main character of *Chilly Scenes of Winter* is granted all that he wishes; in the end, however, all that he wants is to escape his gratification. Charles, the protagonist, is in love with Laura, a married woman. His desire for her eventually dominates his life, so that he is unable to function without that desire or—as he would believe—without her.

Charles's obsession with Laura colors his relationship with his own family: his mother, Clara; her second husband, Pete; and Charles's sister, Susan. Even though his sister has accepted Pete, Charles refuses to acknowledge him as a replacement for their father, a man whose good qualities are magnified by the virtue of his death. Charles regards Pete as both a loser and a catalyst for Clara's chronic hypochondria. He claims that Pete refuses to accept life as it is and, instead, continues to make excuses for Clara's instability. The irony is that what Charles so clearly perceives as Pete's faults are really his own. Charles cannot—or will not—admit that he, too, fantasizes about the woman he loves and constructs absurd ideas about her that are founded on nothing but his own imagination. Charles will never be able to have a normal life with Laura, just as Pete will never be able to have one with Clara.

There is also the thought, which runs throughout the novel, that marriage itself is not a desirable norm. Sam, Clara's friend, comments, "It's nuts to get married," and indeed none of the relationships in *Chilly Scenes of Winter* seems to bode well for the participants. Pete and Clara's marriage is tainted by her mental illness, Jim and Laura's seems emptied by their lack of interest, and Charles and Laura's relationship is adulterous (and thus unable to be acknowledged).

The lack of sanction for Charles's love is typical of his whole existence. Nothing in his life lives up to his expectations, so he wanders pathetically, searching for both the ideal and the unreal. He is terrified of discovering a truth in his miserable existence, and this fear prevents him from completing his quest for love and a meaningful life. Charles is consumed by the thought that he will develop an "inoperable melanoma," even though there is no indication that he will; it is merely a phrase he has overheard in a hospital room. After Laura leaves Jim, Charles refuses to contact her; he will only drive past her house, hoping for a signal that will never be given.

FALLING IN PLACE

In contrast to this world where the characters are forced to wander endlessly, searching for a direction, the players in *Falling in Place* are given a very clear signal when a significant event occurs. The story opens with John Knapp, his estranged wife Louise, their children Mary and John Joel, and John's mistress Nina. During the week, John lives with his mother, ostensibly to be close to his job in New York City but really to be far away from Louise and the children and closer to Nina. Naturally, this situation affects his children, and they become bitter and distanced not only from their father but also from their mother. Instead of swimming in a maelstrom of their own emotions, however, the characters in *Falling in Place* actually reach out to others and are influenced by them. John Joel's deviant friend Parker brings the action of the novel to a head: He provides John Joel with a handgun, and the latter proceeds to shoot his sister Mary in the side. When asked why he shot her, John Joel explains to his father, "She was a bitch."

Perhaps this phrase succinctly sums up Beattie's child characters in the story. Instead of behaving like real children, their circumstances force them to become miniature adults, faced with adult problems and desires. John Joel has an eating disorder, his friend Parker smokes a pack of cigarettes a day, and cold Mary dreams of sacrificing her virginity to singer Peter Frampton. They are a sad band of children, imitating the worst habits of their adult counterparts in the worst possible way. John Joel mouths adult words and defines his teenage sister in adult terms.

Finally, John and Louise divorce, freeing themselves and their children to pursue meaningful existences. None however, really believes that he or she will be able to attain this. At one point, John complains to Mary, "Don't you think I might already realize that my existence is a little silly?" Mary replies, "[T]hat's what *Vanity Fair* is like. Things just fall into place." John wonders if his daughter's advocacy of predestination seals her fate or if she simply cannot, or will not, try to imagine a future over which she has any control. Mary is not, however, the only member of her family who refuses to admit to a future. After Nina and John finally unite, Nina begs him to consider her wants: "Acres of land. Children. A big house. Try to *realize* what you love." John only replies, "You're what I want."

John, then, refuses to realize, to make real, his existence with Nina and any sort of happiness they might have. He and his fellow characters are moderately pleased with their ties to the past and present; one boasts of a once-removed acquaintance with singer Linda Ronstadt. No one, however, will consider the effect of his or her present actions on the future. No one wants to be responsible for shaping a future; all merely accept whatever happens as a logical consequence of an illogical life.

Love Always

In contrast, the characters in *Love Always* begin by rejoicing that they are "beating the system." Hildon and his ex-student friends run a slick journal named *Country Daze*, the success of which, Hildon maintains, is "proof positive that the whole country is coked-out." Because America, or at least the readership of *Country Daze*, has gone to rack and ruin, Hildon and associates decide that their behavior does not have to measure up to any modern-day standards. Hildon continues his long-standing affair with coworker and advice columnist Lucy, despite his marriage. Lucy's fourteen-year-old niece, Nicole, is taking a brief vacation with her aunt from her role as a teenage junkie on a popular soap opera.

Nicole is yet another of Beattie's adult children, as are John Joel and Mary in *Falling in Place*. She serves as a foil for the adults in her world who are childishly hiding from the responsibilities and terrors of the outside world in a world of their own devising. Nicole's aunt, Lucy, writes under the name Cindi Coeur. Ironically, she does not wear her heart on her sleeve but rather flees from mature relationships. Lucy is equally unhappy about Nicole's adult behavior, but she does not know what to do about it.

Picturing Will

In the mid-1980's the direction of Beattie's fiction began to change. While there were still passive, directionless characters in her novels, there were also instances of redemption, primarily through a commitment to other human beings that no one in the earlier works seemed willing or able to make. There are still a great many characters in these novels who fail both themselves and others, however. In *Picturing Will*, for example, the needs of the five-year-old protagonist are ignored by both of his divorced parents. His mother Jody is more interested in becoming a famous photographer than in taking care of her son, and his shiftless father Wayne would rather drink and womanize than pay attention to Will. The real hero of the story is Jody's lover, and later her second husband, Mel Anthis. It is Mel who sacrifices his own literary ambitions in order to dedicate his life to child-rearing, thus ensuring that Will becomes the secure man and the loving husband and father we meet at the end of the novel.

Another You

In *Picturing Will*, Mel is introduced as a caring person, capable of loving a woman as difficult as Jody, and his affection for Will is believable. In the protagonist of *Another You*, however, a striking change in personality occurs, one which promises redemption. At the beginning of the book, Marshall Lockard seems much like the passive characters in Beattie's earlier novels, except that he is quite content with his purposeless life; in fact, Marshall has deliberately arranged his way of life. As an English professor at a small New Hampshire college, he can live vicariously through literary characters, and he has so well mastered the art of sarcasm that he can repel his students at will. Because his wife Sonja believes him too vulnerable to be subjected to any emotional stress, it is she, not Marshall, who goes to the nursing home to visit Marshall's stepmother, who reared him and loves him dearly. Although Sonja has become bored enough with this well-ordered existence to indulge in a little adultery with her employer, she does not mean for her husband to find out about it.

Despite all his precautions, however, Marshall is drawn into the untidy world. It all begins with a simple request from one of his students: She wants him to speak to someone on campus about her friend, who is claiming that she was assaulted by Marshall's colleague Jack MacCallum. Soon Marshall finds himself kissing the student and worrying about repercussions, explaining to the police why MacCallum was stabbed by his pregnant wife in the Lockard home, and dealing with his stepmother's death and his wife's infidelity, not to mention the two students' having fabricated their story and the supposed victim's turning out to be a narcotics agent. Marshall is so shaken by these heavy blows of reality that he decides to go to Key West, visit his older brother Gordon, and ask about some events in their childhood that have always haunted him. Although only Beattie's readers find out the truth, not Marshall, by simply confronting the issue Marshall gains new strength. Instead of becoming another drifter in Key West, he heads back to New Hampshire, cold weather, and real life, hopefully with Sonja.

MY LIFE, STARRING DARA FALCON

In Beattie's early works, the characters are often far more interested in the lives of celebrities, such as Janis Joplin and Lucille Ball, than in their own lives. After all, it is much less risky to invest in a tabloid than in another person. A similar kind of vicarious existence is the subject of *My Life, Starring Dara Falcon*. Here, however, the protagonist, Jean Warner, is so young and so malleable that this is obviously a coming-of-age novel. Beattie even reassures her readers of a happy ending by beginning her book two decades after most of its events and by showing the narrator as a happily married, mature woman who understands herself and others. Thus readers know from the outset that Jean did escape from her husband's large extended family, which smothered her rather than giving her the security she sought, from a rather dull husband who is ruled by his family, and, most important, from the manipulations of the Machiavellian Dara Falcon.

In both *My Life, Starring Dara Falcon* and *Another You*, the protagonists begin as passive creatures who live vicariously through others, but they can and do choose to change, first by coming to terms with their own identities, then by daring to care about oth-

ers. If in her early works Beattie showed what was wrong with the members of her generation, in her later works she offers hope to them and, indeed, to all of us.

Jennifer L. Wyatt,
updated by Rosemary M. Canfield Reisman

OTHER MAJOR WORKS

SHORT FICTION: *Distortions*, 1976; *Secrets and Surprises*, 1978; *Jacklighting*, 1981; *The Burning House*, 1982; *Where You'll Find Me and Other Stories*, 1986; *What Was Mine and Other Stories*, 1991; *Park City: New and Selected Stories*, 1998.

NONFICTION: *Alex Katz*, 1987.

CHILDREN'S LITERATURE: *Goblin Tales*, 1975; *Spectacle*, 1985.

BIBLIOGRAPHY

Beattie, Ann. "An Interview with Ann Beattie." Interview by Steven R. Centola. *Contemporary Literature* 31, no. 4 (1990): 405-422. While Beattie agrees with Centola that her works do reflect contemporary American society, she would prefer to be thought of not as a social historian but as someone who understands human nature. She responds to searching questions about structure, symbolism, point of view, and tone.

Lee, Don. "About Ann Beattie." *Ploughshares* 21, no. 2-3 (1995): 231-235. A good biographical and critical essay, based on an interview and including extensive quotations. Beattie points out that as she has matured, her novels have become more complex and therefore more time-consuming to produce. She describes her difficulties with *Another You*, which left her even more partial than before to short fiction.

Montresor, Jay Berman, ed. *The Critical Response to Ann Beattie*. Westport, Conn.: Greenwood Press, 1993. A collection of essays on subjects ranging from the author's use of imagery to gender definitions and parenting. Includes a 1992 interview conducted by the editor. Also contains bibliographical references and index.

Murphy, Christina. *Ann Beattie*. Boston: Twayne, 1986. Despite what may be deemed the prematurity of this biography (Beattie is still young and active in her field), this book is very useful for the researcher. In addition to a chronology, notes, a selected bibliography, and an index, the discussion examines Beattie's works from *Distortions* to *Love Always* in a thorough and painstaking manner. The last chapter is devoted to an overview of Beattie's career as a "neorealist," one of a new group of authors.

Stein, Lorin. "Fiction in Review." *Yale Review* 85, no. 4 (1997): 156-165. After an excellent summary of Beattie's early fiction, the writer proceeds to analyze *My Life, Starring Dara Falcon*, which he thinks has been underrated by critics. It is suggested that the central theme of betrayal in this novel may derive not from antipathy toward men, which is not evident in Beattie's previous works, but from a new realization by the author's generation that their promised liberation has itself proved to be a betrayal.

Wyatt, David. "Ann Beattie." *The Southern Review* 28, no. 1 (1992): 145-159. Presents evidence that in the mid-1980's there was a marked alteration in Beattie's fiction. Instead of withdrawing from life and its dangers, her characters chose to care about other people and to commit themselves to creativity. A perceptive and convincing analysis.

SIMONE DE BEAUVOIR

Born: Paris, France; January 9, 1908
Died: Paris, France; April 14, 1986

PRINCIPAL LONG FICTION

L'Invitée, 1943 (*She Came to Stay*, 1949)
Le Sang des autres, 1945 (*The Blood of Others*, 1948)
Tous les hommes sont mortels, 1946 (*All Men Are Mortal*, 1955)
Les Mandarins, 1954 (*The Mandarins*, 1956)
Les Belles Images, 1966 (English translation, 1968)

OTHER LITERARY FORMS

Simone de Beauvoir is best known for her social and political philosophy, especially her contributions to feminism. Foremost among her nonfiction works is her four-volume autobiography, *Mémoires d'une jeune fille rangée* (1958; *Memoirs of a Dutiful Daughter*, 1959), *La Force de l'âge* (1960; *The Prime of Life*, 1962), *La Force des choses* (1963; *Force of Circumstance*, 1964), and *Tout compte fait* (1972; *All Said and Done*, 1974). Equally important is her monumental sociological study on women, *Le Deuxième Sexe* (1949; *The Second Sex*, 1953). Two other sociological works follow *The Second Sex*, the first on China, *La Longue Marche* (1957; *The Long March*, 1958), and the second on the aged, *La Vieillesse* (1970; *The Coming of Age*, 1972). *Les Bouches inutiles* (1945), her only play, was not translated into English. She also published two collections of short stories, *La Femme rompue* (1967; *The Woman Destroyed*, 1968) and *Quand prime le spirituel* (1979; *When Things of the Spirit Come First: Five Early Tales*, 1982). Her most important philosophical essays include *Pyrrhus et Cinéas* (1944), *Pour une morale de l'ambiguïté* (1947; *The Ethics of Ambiguity*, 1948), *L'Existentialisme et la sagesse des nations* (1948), and *Privilèges* (1955; partial translation, "Must We Burn Sade?," 1953). A number of other essays appeared in newspapers and journals. She also wrote a chronicle of her travels in the United States, *L'Amérique au jour le jour* (1948; *America Day by Day*, 1953); a powerful account of her mother's illness and death, *Une Mort très douce* (1964; *A Very Easy Death*, 1966); and a tribute to Jean-Paul Sartre, *La Cérémonie des adieux* (1981; *Adieux: A Farewell to Sartre*, 1984).

ACHIEVEMENTS

De Beauvoir was a presence in French intellectual life during the second half of the twentieth century. She is one of the foremost examples of existentialist *engagement* and its most respected moral voice; the breadth of her writing alone secures de Beauvoir a prominent position in twentieth century letters. Her novels, especially *She Came to Stay, The Blood of Others,* and *The Mandarins* (for which she won the

Prix Goncourt in 1954), pose some of the central philosophical and ethical questions of our time, exploring the problems of social morality, political commitment, and human responsibility. Along with her autobiography, her novels chronicle the time before and after World War II and the experiences that made her one of the most influential writers of the twentieth century.

De Beauvoir wrote numerous articles for *Les Temps modernes*, a periodical founded and directed by Sartre, and she was a member of its editorial board. In 1973, she became the editor of the journal's feminist column. *The Second Sex*, her carefully documented study of the situation of women, became one of the major theoretical texts of the women's movement. Always an activist for women's rights and social justice, she demonstrated against France's restrictive abortion laws and signed the *Manifeste des 343*, a document listing women who admitted having had abortions. She was president of Choisir (1971) and of the Ligue des Droits des Femmes (1974), an organization fighting sex discrimination. De Beauvoir was also one of the founders of the feminist journal *Questions féministes*. Her indictment of social injustice is evidenced by *The Coming of Age*, her defense of a free press (the Maoist underground newspaper *La Cause du Peuple*), and her political actions.

(Archive Photos)

BIOGRAPHY

Simone de Beauvoir was born in Paris on January 9, 1908. Her father, Georges de Beauvoir, came from a wealthy family and was a lawyer by profession. A religious skeptic, he was openly contemptuous of the bourgeoisie and encouraged his daughter in intellectual pursuits. In contrast, her mother, Françoise, came from a provincial town, received her education in convents, and was a devout Catholic. Under her mother's supervision, the young de Beauvoir was educated at a conservative Catholic school for girls, the Cours Désir.

In *Memoirs of a Dutiful Daughter*—which covers the years from 1908 to 1929—de Beauvoir describes her early piety, her subsequent disenchantment with

Catholicism, and the beginning of her rebellion against her middle-class background. Influenced by early readings of Louisa May Alcott and George Eliot, she decided at age fifteen that she wanted to be a writer. After leaving the Cours Désir, she pursued the study of literature at the Institut Catholique in Paris. In 1926, she attended the Sorbonne and studied philosophy, Greek, and philology. Three years later, after a year at the prestigious École Normale Supérieure, she passed the examination for the *agrégation de philosophie*, the highest academic degree conferred in France.

In 1929, de Beauvoir met the philosopher Jean-Paul Sartre and began an association with him that lasted until his death in April, 1980. The years from 1929 to 1944 are chronicled in the second volume of her autobiography, *The Prime of Life*. Having completed her academic degrees, she was assigned a series of teaching positions, first in Marseilles and later in Rouen and Paris. Her first novel, *She Came to Stay*, appeared in 1943; it established her as a writer, and she stopped teaching. During the war years, she became interested in political action. By the end of World War II, de Beauvoir and Sartre were labeled "existentialists," and their success and celebrity were assured. In 1947, de Beauvoir was invited on a lecture tour of the United States (described in *America Day by Day*) and began her four-year affair with American writer Nelson Algren.

During the postwar years, de Beauvoir became increasingly preoccupied with the problems of the intellectual in society, and she continued to examine the relationship between freedom and social commitment. In *Force of Circumstance* (which spans the years 1944 to 1962), the third volume of her autobiography, political events such as the Korean War and the Algerian crisis occupy progressively more space. She saw Sartre destroy his health to work on *Critique de la raison dialectique* (1960; *Critique of Dialectical Reason*, 1976) and became painfully aware of human mortality and solitude. Old age and death are themes that run through de Beauvoir's work from this period, such as *The Woman Destroyed, The Coming of Age*, and the last volume of her autobiography, *All Said and Done*. In spite of this, the general tone of *All Said and Done*—as well as of the frequent interviews she gave—is one of a woman content to have achieved her existentialist project before her death in 1986.

ANALYSIS

Simone de Beauvoir's novels are grounded in her training as a philosopher and in her sociological and feminist concerns. *She Came to Stay, The Blood of Others, All Men Are Mortal*, and *The Mandarins* all revolve around the questions of freedom and responsibility and try to define the proper relationship between the individual and society. Her characters search for authenticity as they attempt to shape the world around them. Their education is sentimental as well as intellectual and political. While most of her heroes accommodate themselves successfully to real-

ity, the same may not be said of her heroines. In the later novels, *The Mandarins* and *Les Belles Images*, her female characters, who are successful by worldly standards, suffer a series of psychological crises. As they undertake what the feminist critic Carol Christ has called "spiritual quests," they often face suicide and madness. The existentialist enterprise of *engagement*, or commitment with a view of defining the self through action, seems more possible for the men in her novels than for the women. In *Simone de Beauvoir on Woman* (1975), Jean Leighton has observed the absence of positive heroines in de Beauvoir's work: Woman seems condemned to passivity while man's fate is one of transcendence. Arguments from *The Second Sex* and from her philosophical essays echo in the novels. The tension between her philosophical ideas and their potential realization by the women characters is clearly visible in her fiction.

SHE CAME TO STAY

De Beauvoir's first novel, *She Came to Stay*, is an imaginative transposition of her relationship with Olga Kosakiewicz. In 1933, Beauvoir and Sartre had befriended Kosakiewicz, one of Beauvoir's students. They had attempted a *ménage à trois*; *She Came to Stay* is the story of its failure.

The heroine, Françoise Miquel, is a young writer who has lived with Pierre Labrousse, a talented actor and director, for eight years. They feel that their relationship is ideal since it allows them both a great deal of freedom. Françoise befriends Xavière, a young woman disenchanted with provincial life, and invites her to Paris, where she will help her find work. Once in Paris, Xavière makes demands on the couple and is openly contemptuous of their values. Pierre becomes obsessed with Xavière; Françoise, trying to rise above the jealousy and insecurity she feels, struggles to keep the trio together. Out of resentment, Françoise has an affaire with Gerbert, Xavière's suitor. The novel ends as Xavière recognizes Françoise's duplicity; Xavière has now become the critical Other. Unable to live in her presence, Françoise turns on the gas and murders her.

She Came to Stay is a meditation on the Hegelian problem of the existence of the Other. The novel plays out the psychological effects of jealousy and questions the extent to which coexistence is possible. Critics such as Hazel Barnes and Carol Ascher have noted the close ties between de Beauvoir's first novel and Sartre's *L'Être et le neant* (*Being and Nothingness*, 1956), published in the same year. Both texts deal with the central existentialist theme of letting others absorb one's freedom.

Despite Françoise's apparent independence, she needs Pierre to approve her actions and give them direction. Françoise's self-deception and the inauthenticity of her life anticipate de Beauvoir's analysis of *l'amoureuse*, the woman in love, in *The Second Sex*. Confronted with a rival, Françoise becomes aware that her self-assurance and detachment are illusory. Her growth as a character occurs as she sheds the unexamined rational premises she holds about herself and her relationship with Pierre. The gap between the intellect and the emotions continues to widen until it reaches a crisis in the murder of Xavière. Françoise is finally forced to confront her long-concealed hatred. In spite of the often stylized dialogue, *She Came to Stay* is a lucid, finely executed study of love and jealousy and one of de Beauvoir's finest novels.

THE BLOOD OF OTHERS

Although de Beauvoir was later to consider her second novel overly didactic, *The Blood of Others* is one of the best novels written on the French Resistance. The book opens with the thoughts of Jean Blomart as he keeps vigil over his mistress Hélène, who is dying from a wound received during a mission. The novel proceeds by flashback and alternates between the stories of Jean, a Resistance hero, and his companion Hélène. The son of a wealthy bourgeois family, Jean is plagued by feelings of guilt over his comfortable situation. He takes a job as a worker and tries to lead a life of uninvolvement. His attempted detachment is based on his belief that he can thus avoid contributing to the unhappiness of others. Passive at the outbreak of the war, he is finally drafted. Upon his return to Paris, he realizes that his detachment is actually a form of irresponsibility. He organizes a resistance group and becomes its leader. As he watches the dying Hélène, he questions whether he has the right to control the lives of his comrades. Although he is doomed to act in ignorance of the consequences of his decisions, he decides that he nevertheless has an obligation to act. The novel ends with Hélène's death and his renewed commitment to the Resistance.

If *The Blood of Others* is the story of Jean's *engagement*, it is also the story of Hélène's political awakening. Like him, she is politically indifferent until a young Jewish friend is in danger of deportation. She then turns to Jean and becomes an active member of his group. Of all de Beauvoir's women, Hélène is one who, in her political commitment, manages to define herself through her actions rather than through her emotional attachments.

The Blood of Others presages the discussion of individual freedom in *The Ethics of Ambiguity*. In both the novel and the philosophical essay, the problem of the Other is interfaced with the question of social responsibility. With its emphasis on the denial of freedom during the Occupation, the novel underscores the necessity of political action to ensure individual freedoms. The closed space of the love triangle in *She Came to Stay* is replaced by the larger obligations of the individual to a historical moment. *The Blood of Others* conveys the problematic quality of ethical decisions; as Robert Cottrell has noted in *Simone de Beauvoir* (1975), it evokes "the sense of being entrapped, of submitting to existence rather than fashioning it." Nevertheless, *The Blood of Others* is a more optimistic book than *She Came to Stay* in its portrayal of the individual working toward a larger social good.

ALL MEN ARE MORTAL

Individual actions are seen against a series of historical backdrops in *All Men Are Mortal*. The novel traces the life of Count Fosca, an Italian nobleman who is endowed with immortality. At the request of Régine, a successful young actress, he recounts his varied careers through seven centuries. A counselor to Maximilian of Germany and then to Charles V of Spain, he discovers the Mississippi, founds the first French university, and becomes an activist in the French Revolution. Like other existentialist heroes, Fosca paradoxically admits that only death gives life meaning. His goal of building an ideal, unified humanity remains unrealized as violence and useless destruction prevail.

Fosca's story is framed by that of Régine, who is embittered by her life and haunted by death. When she learns of Fosca's immortality, she thinks that she can transcend death by living forever in his memory. Like the women in love in the preceding novels, Régine depends on others to give her life meaning. The story ends with Régine's cry of despair as she understands the futility and vanity of human action.

All Men Are Mortal takes up the theme of the uncertain outcome of individual actions and gives it a more decidedly pessimistic turn. This theme is modified somewhat by the more optimistic section on the French Revolution. Here, Fosca follows the career of one of his descendants, Armand. Armand's zeal in fighting for the Republican cause leads Fosca to modify his skepticism about human progress and to take comfort in the solidarity he experiences with Armand and his friends.

Fosca's discovery of the rewards of comradeship is very similar to that of Jean Blomart. Although Fosca's individual actions are either undercut by the presence of others or lost in history, actions taken by the group seem to have a more powerful impact on reality. Like *The Blood of Others*, *All Men Are Mortal* predicts de Beauvoir's later Marxist sympathies and reflects her growing politicization. Both Jean and Fosca tend to break with the solipsistic tendencies of the characters in *She Came to Stay* and move in the direction of greater social commitment. The context of the action in *All Men Are Mortal* is wider than in the preceding novels from a narrative and political point of view. It is perhaps its vast historical scope that makes *All Men Are Mortal* the least satisfying of de Beauvoir's novels. Philosophical speculations on love, history, and death dominate the narrative; the characters are lifeless and seem caught in a series of historical still lifes.

THE MANDARINS

The Mandarins, de Beauvoir's finest novel, covers the period from 1944 to the early 1950's and focuses on the relationship between political commitment and literature. The narrative voice shifts between Henri Perron, a novelist, journalist, and Resistance hero, and Anne Dubreuilh, a respected psychiatrist and the wife of Robert Dubreuilh, a prominent writer.

Robert, initiated into political activism during his years in the Resistance, believes that literature must now take second place to political concerns. He engages himself wholeheartedly in founding the S.R.L., an independent leftist political party. The problems that Robert confronts as a political figure point to the painful reality of making decisions that are not always satisfactory. He draws Henri into politics by convincing him that his newspaper, *L'Espoir*, should be the voice of the S.R.L. When they receive news of Soviet labor camps, they try to decide if they should publish it. Knowing that they will play into Gaullist hands and alienate the Communists to whom they are sympathetic, they reluctantly decide to print the story.

For Henri, questions of political commitment after the war are more problematic. He would like *L'Espoir* to remain apolitical and is nostalgic for the prewar years when literature and politics appeared to be mutually exclusive interests. Henri tries to act in good faith, but because of his sensitivity to others, he often opts for the less idealistically pure solution. He is reluctant to break with Paule, his mistress of ten years, and he protects acquaintances who were German collaborators because he fears that, like Paule, they could not survive without his help. Throughout the novel, he is torn between politics and a desire to return to literature. He gradually faces the impossibility of "pure" literature. At the end of the novel, having lost *L'Espoir*, he and Robert decide to found a new journal of the Left.

The questions that de Beauvoir examines through Robert and Henri have a striking immediacy that captures the problem of the intellectual in the modern world. Much of the action in *The Mandarins* is a fictionalized account of her experiences as a member of the intellectual Left during the postwar years. Critics have sought to identify Sartre with Robert, Albert Camus with Henri, and de Beauvoir herself with Anne. In *Simone de Beauvoir and the Limits of Commitment* (1981), Anne Whitmarsh notes that there is much of Sartre's experiences with the Rassemblement Démocratique Révolutionnaire in Robert's ties with the S.R.L. and that some of the early problems facing *Les Temps modernes* are reflected in the debates on the political role of *L'Espoir*.

The problems faced by the male characters are less pressing for Anne. Married to a man twenty years older, she seems out of touch with herself and her surroundings. Her work as a psychiatrist fails fully to occupy her, and her relationship with her unhappy daughter, Nadine, gives Anne little satisfaction. Encouraged by Robert, she accepts an invitation to lecture in the United States. In Chicago, she experiences an emotional awakening when she falls in love with Lewis Brogan, an up-and-coming writer. Her visits to Brogan are described in a highly lyric style full of images of country life and nature. The physical and affective aspects of her life with Brogan form an effective counterpoint to the intellectual character of her relationship with her husband. The shifting loyalties she experiences for both men give Anne's narrative a schizophrenic quality.

Back in Paris, Anne tries to help Paule, who has suffered a nervous breakdown. Paule rarely leaves her apartment and is unable to function without Henri. Anne sends her to a psychiatrist, who "cures" her by having her forget the past. Like Françoise and Régine, Paule represents the temptation of living through others. In Paule's case, however, the dependence reaches an existential crisis from which she never fully recovers. Paule's illness is mirrored in Anne as the psychiatrist herself plunges into a long depression. When Brogan ends their relationship, she contemplates suicide. Thinking of the pain her death would cause Robert and Nadine, she decides to live. Despite this decision, Anne's alienation from her family and indeed from her own being is more acute than ever.

Anne's emotional awakening and Paule's mental breakdown leave them both as only marginal participants in life. Neither woman achieves the transcendence that characterizes the lives of her male counterpart. As Robert and Henri accommodate themselves to political realities, they become more integrated into society. The female quest for self-knowledge acts as a negative counterpoint to the male quest. The final scene is not unlike a collage in which the two parts of the composition are radically divided. The enthusiasm of Henri and Robert as they search for an appropriate title for their journal is juxtaposed to Anne's stillness; she sits off to the side, withdrawn, and hopes that her life may still contain some happiness.

LES BELLES IMAGES

Les Belles Images is one of de Beauvoir's most technically innovative novels. Laurence, the main character, is a young woman who writes slogans for a French advertising agency. She is married to a successful young architect and has two daughters. Catherine, her eldest daughter, is beginning to question social values. Laurence comes from the same mold as de Beauvoir's other heroines. She is, for all appearances, a confident young woman. Like them, her façade of well-being dissolves to reveal an individual profoundly alienated from herself and her society. *Les Belles Images* is the story of Laurence's progressive withdrawal from society. Her interior journey ends in a mental and physical breakdown.

The novel is set in Paris during the 1960's. Some friends have gathered at the fashionable home of Dominique, Laurence's mother. Laurence, uninterested in the group, leafs through a number of magazines containing the *belles images*, or beautiful pictures, she is paid to create. The dialogue among the guests is filtered through Laurence, who then adds her own reflections. The conversations are trite and filled with clichés; like the slogans Laurence invents, they conceal the real problems of war, poverty, and unhappiness. The discrepancy between the advertisements and the things they represent precipitates Laurence's budding consciousness of herself as yet another *belle image*. Laurence's perception of the inauthenticity of her own life and of the lives of the people around her results in illness. Having already suffered a nervous breakdown five years before, she becomes anorexic and unable to relate to the artificial world around her.

Through her daughter Catherine, she faces her unresolved feelings toward her childhood. She recalls the lack of emotional contact with her mother in a series of flashbacks in which she appears dressed as a child in a publicity snapshot. At the insistence of Laurence's husband, Catherine has been sent to a psychiatrist because she is overly sensitive to social injustices. Laurence sees the treatment that Catherine receives as an attempt to integrate her daughter into the artificial bourgeois world. At the novel's end, Laurence emerges from her illness to save her daughter from a fate similar to hers. Like other de Beauvoir heroines, Laurence chooses her illness as a means of escaping certain destructive social myths. Her breakdown, rather than the result of an original flaw discovered within herself, is an indication of the failure of society as a whole. Against the inauthentic world of the other characters, Laurence's illness appears as a victory and an occasion for emotional growth. Much like Anne in *The Mandarins*, Laurence is a voice from the outside who sees the social games and reveals them for what they are.

All of de Beauvoir's novels examine the relationship between the self and the Other that is at the heart of existentialist philosophy. In her early novels, *She Came to Stay, The Blood of Others*, and *All Men Are Mortal*, there is often an explicit existentialist premise underlying the action. In her later works, *The Mandarins* and *Les Belles Images*, the philosophical message, although still present, is clearly subordinated to the narrative. De Beauvoir's conclusions in *The Second Sex* appear to have led her to a closer examination of the lives of her female characters. Her later fiction adds another dimension to the quests for authenticity that mark her early production. For her heroes, the quest usually ends in some type of existentialist commitment; for her heroines, the quest seems to involve a withdrawal from harmful social myths. If at times the quests border on madness or isolation, they do so without losing their striking immediacy or their profound sense of reality. Like other great twentieth century quests, de Beauvoir's novels chart a journey into the heart of contemporary alienation.

Carole Deering Paul

OTHER MAJOR WORKS

SHORT FICTION: *La Femme rompue*, 1967 (*The Woman Destroyed*, 1968); *Quand prime le spirituel*,

1979 (*When Things of the Spirit Come First: Five Early Tales*, 1982).

PLAY: *Les Bouches inutiles*, pb. 1945.

NONFICTION: *Pyrrhus et Cinéas*, 1944; *Pour une morale de l'ambiguïté*, 1947 (*The Ethics of Ambiguity*, 1948); *L'Amérique au jour le jour*, 1948 (travel sketch; *America Day by Day*, 1953); *L'Existialisme et la sagesse des nations*, 1948; *Le Deuxième Sexe*, 1949 (*The Second Sex*, 1953); *Privilèges*, 1955 (partial translation, "Must We Burn Sade?," 1953); *La Longue Marche*, 1957 (travel sketch; *The Long March*, 1958); *Mémoires d'une jeune fille rangée*, 1958 (4 volumes; *Memoirs of a Dutiful Daughter*, 1959); *La Force de l'âge*, 1960 (memoir; *The Prime of Life*, 1962); *La Force des choses*, 1963 (memoir; *Force of Circumstance*, 1964); *Une Mort très douce*, 1964 (*A Very Easy Death*, 1966); *La Vieillesse*, 1970 (*The Coming of Age*, 1972); *Tout compte fait*, 1972 (memoir; *All Said and Done*, 1974); *La Cérémonie des adieux*, 1981 (*Adieux: A Farewell to Sartre*, 1984).

BIBLIOGRAPHY

Ascher, Carol. *Simone de Beauvoir: A Life of Freedom*. Boston: Beacon Press, 1981. The first biography, still useful, although written without de Beauvoir's cooperation. Chapters on friendships, lovers, political commitments, early fiction, *The Mandarins, The Second Sex*, death, freedom, and wholeness. Includes notes and chronology.

Bair, Deirdre. *Simone de Beauvoir*. New York: Putnam's, 1990. The most scholarly and comprehensive biography of de Beauvoir written with her cooperation, although completed after her death.

Bieber, Konrad. *Simone de Beauvoir*. Boston: Twayne, 1979. Contains only one chapter on the fiction; the rest of the book pertains to de Beauvoir's essays, memoirs, and other autobiographical writing. Includes chronology and annotated bibliography.

Brown, Catherine Savage. *Simone de Beauvoir Revisited*. Boston: G. K. Hall, 1991. Chapters on de Beauvoir's biography, her role as a female writer, her early fiction and drama, her later fiction, her philosophical and political studies, and her memoirs. Brown aims at a focused study, criticizing late twentieth century emphasis on anecdotal reports and biography.

Evans, Mary. *Simone de Beauvoir: A Feminist Mandarin*. New York: Tavistock, 1985. Although devoted mainly to nonfiction, this study does explore the autobiographical roots of de Beauvoir's novels.

Fallaize, Elizabeth. *The Novels of Simone de Beauvoir*. New York: Routledge, 1988. Separate chapters on *She Came to Stay, The Blood of Others, All Men Are Mortal, The Mandarins*, and *Les Belles Images*. Also discusses the short-story cycles. Includes introduction, biographical notes, and bibliography.

Francis, Claude, and Fernande Gontier. *Simone de Beauvoir: A Life, a Love Story*. New York: St. Martin's Press, 1979. A lively, well-documented biography for general readers, less comprehensive than Bair.

Fulbrook, Kate, and Edward Fulbrook. *Simone de Beauvoir and Jean-Paul Sartre: The Remaking of a Twentieth-Century Legend*. New York: Basic Books, 1994. Revises previous readings of the relationship, relying on new documents (letters and memoirs) that show how the two fashioned their legend. Extensive discussion of *She Came to Stay*.

Leighton, Jean. *Simone de Beauvoir on Woman*. Teaneck, N.J.: Fairleigh Dickinson University Press, 1975. Chapters on *She Came to Stay* and *The Mandarins*. Other chapters focus on nonfiction and de Beauvoir's relationship with women's liberation.

Simon, Margaret A., ed. *Feminist Interpretations of Simone de Beauvoir*. University Park: Pennsylvania State University Press, 1995. Several essays on *The Second Sex*, de Beauvoir's relationship with Sartre, *The Mandarins*, and her views on the Algerian war. Bibliography and index.

Whitmarsh, Anne. *Simone de Beauvoir and the Limits of Commitment*. Cambridge, England: Cambridge University Press, 1981. Contains succinct discussions of the long fiction, including a section summarizing de Beauvoir's fictional works. Biographical notes and bibliography add to this volume's usefulness.

SAMUEL BECKETT

Born: Foxrock, Ireland; April 13, 1906
Died: Paris, France; December 22, 1989

PRINCIPAL LONG FICTION
Murphy, 1938
Molloy, 1951 (English translation, 1955)
Malone meurt, 1951 (*Malone Dies*, 1956)
L'Innommable, 1953 (*The Unnamable*, 1958)
Watt, 1953
Comment c'est, 1961 (*How It Is*, 1964)
Mercier et Camier, 1970 (*Mercier and Camier*, 1974)
Le Dépeupleur, 1971 (*The Lost Ones*, 1972)
Company, 1980
Mal vu mal dit, 1981 (*Ill Seen Ill Said*, 1981)
Worstward Ho, 1983

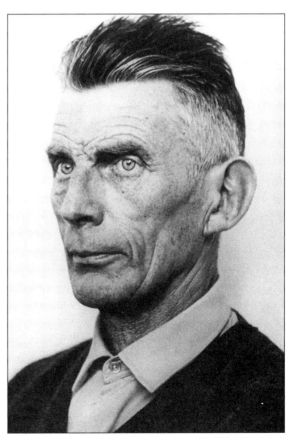

(The Nobel Foundation)

OTHER LITERARY FORMS

Samuel Beckett produced work in every literary genre. His first book, published in 1931, was the critical study *Proust*, and during the next fifteen years, Beckett published a number of essays and book reviews that have yet to be collected in book form. After struggling with an unpublished play entitled *Eleuthéria* in the late 1940's, he began publication of the series of plays that are as important as his novels to his present literary reputation. These include, notably, *En attendant Godot* (1952; *Waiting for Godot*, 1954), *Fin de partie* (1957; *Endgame*, 1958), *Krapp's Last Tape* (1958), *Happy Days* (1961), and many short pieces for the stage, including mimes. In addition to these works for the stage, he wrote scripts for television, such as *Eh Joe* (1966); scripts for radio, such as *All That Fall* (1968); and one film script, titled *Film* (1965). Most, but not all, of his many short stories are gathered in various collections, including *More Pricks than Kicks* (1934), *Nouvelles et textes pour rien* (1955; *Stories and Texts for Nothing*, 1967), *No's Knife: Collected Shorter Prose 1947-1966* (1967), *First Love and Other Shorts* (1974), and *Pour finir encore et autres foirades* (1976; *Fizzles*, 1976). Beckett's poetry, most of it written early in his career for periodical publication, has been made available in *Poems in English* (1961) and *Collected Poems in English and French* (1977). Many of the various collections of his short pieces mix works of different literary genres, and Richard Seaver has edited a general sampling of Beckett works of all sorts in an anthology entitled *I Can't Go On, I'll Go On: A Selection from Samuel Beckett's Work* (1976).

ACHIEVEMENTS

Beckett did not begin to write his most important works until he was forty years of age, and he had to wait some time beyond that for widespread recognition of his literary achievements. By the time he received the Nobel Prize in Literature in 1969, however, he had established a solid reputation as one of the most important and demanding authors of plays and novels in the twentieth century.

In the 1930's, when he began to write, Beckett seemed destined for the sort of footnote fame that has overtaken most of his English and Irish literary companions of that decade. His work appeared to be highly derivative of the avant-garde coterie associated with *Transition* magazine and especially of the novels of James Joyce, who as an elder Irish expatriate in Paris befriended and encouraged the young Beckett. By the time that he was forty years old and trying to salvage a literary career disrupted by World War II, Beckett's anonymity was such that his own French translation of his first novel *Murphy* had sold exactly six copies. At the same time he presented his skeptical Paris publisher with another manuscript.

Nevertheless, it was at that time—the late 1940's—that Beckett blossomed as a writer. He withdrew into a voluntary solitude he himself referred to as "the siege in the room," began to compose his works in French rather than in English, and shed many of the mannerisms of his earlier work. The immediate result was the trilogy of novels that constitutes his most important achievement in prose fiction: *Molloy, Malone Dies*, and *The Unnamable*. This period also produced *Waiting for Godot*, and it was this play that first brought Beckett fame. *Waiting for Godot*, considered a formative influence on the Theater of the Absurd, stimulated the first serious critical treatments of Beckett's work. Although Beckett himself attached more importance to his novels than to his plays, it was not until the 1960's that critics went beyond his plays and began to bring his prose works under close scrutiny. Then, as now, most criticism of Beckett's fiction focused on the trilogy and the austere prose fiction in French that followed it.

In the years since then, Beckett's novels have risen in critical estimation from essentially eccentric if interesting experiments to exemplars of self-referential "postmodern" fiction commonly cited by literary theorists. Disagreements about the nature of particular works and skepticism about the bulk of commentary generated by very brief prose fragments have also inevitably accompanied this rather sudden enshrinement of a difficult and extremely idiosyncratic body of work. However, even the most antagonistic later analyses of Beckett's novels grant them a position of importance and influence in the development of prose fiction since World War II, and they also accept

Samuel Beckett's stature as one of the most important novelists since his friend and Irish compatriot James Joyce.

BIOGRAPHY

Samuel Barclay Beckett was born in Foxrock, a modestly affluent suburb of Dublin, Ireland. He gave Good Friday, April 13, 1906, as his birthdate, but some convincing contrary evidence suggests that this particular day may have been chosen more for its significance than for its accuracy. His parents, William and Mary (May) Jones Roe, belonged to the Protestant middle class known as Anglo-Irish in Ireland. Beckett's childhood, in contrast to the unpleasant imagery of many of his novels, was a relatively cheery one of genteel entertainment at the family home, Cooldrinagh, private education at Portora Royal School in County Fermanagh, and greater success on the cricket green than in the classroom.

Beckett matriculated to Trinity College, Dublin, in 1923, and there he developed his first literary interests. He completed a curriculum in romance languages at Trinity, and this led to an appointment as lecturer at the École Normale Supérieure in Paris after graduation in 1927. In Paris, Beckett began to associate with the bohemian intellectual circles of French, English, and American writers for which the city was then famous. Beckett returned to Dublin for a brief time in 1930 for graduate work and a teaching position at Trinity, but within a few months, he returned to the Continent for travel throughout Germany and France and an extended reunion with his friends in Paris, including James Joyce. His first works of fiction, the stories in *More Pricks than Kicks* and the novel *Murphy*, are set in Dublin and its environs, but their intellectual preoccupations and bohemian antagonism toward middle-class complacency derive more from the environment of Paris than that of Ireland.

At the outbreak of World War II, Beckett was a permanent resident of Paris. As an Irish citizen, he could have returned home, but instead, he took refuge in the French countryside from the Occupation of Paris. There, he assisted the Resistance and began to write the novel *Watt*, which marks a movement toward the style of his major fiction in its strangely dislocated senses of time and place. After the war, Beckett was decorated with the Croix de Guerre for his assistance to the French underground, and this award is generally cited as evidence of an essential humanism underlying the frequently misanthropic tenor of his novels. All evidence suggests, however, that the experience of the war increased Beckett's antagonism toward social affiliations and his skepticism about humanistic values.

Beckett returned to Paris after the war, and from 1946 to 1950, he retired into the "siege in the room," his most fertile period in a long literary career. By the time *Waiting for Godot* established his reputation, he had already developed the reclusive lifestyle which he maintained in his years of fame, despite persistent media attention. He was married to longtime companion Suzanne Deschevaux-Dumesnil in secrecy in London in 1961, and he refused to attend the award ceremony for his Nobel Prize in Literature in 1969. He died in Paris on December 22, 1989.

ANALYSIS

It was a matter of some pleasure to Samuel Beckett that his work resists explication. His most important novels and plays are artfully constructed contemplations on their own form rather than commentaries on the familiar world of causal relationships and social contingencies. His most important novels abandon progressive narrative for the more difficult and subtle suggestiveness of haunting images, deliberate enigmas, and complexly ironic epigrams.

Although Beckett's work defies criticism, the author issued critical statements and congenially submitted to interviews with critics, managing to transform both sorts of critical occasions into intellectual performances as provocative, and occasionally as humorous, as his fiction. Two particular comments by Beckett, out of many stimulating ones, may serve as instructive introductions to the body of his prose works. In his first published book, *Proust*, Beckett wrote that artistic creation is essentially an excavatory process, comparable to an attempt to reach an ideal, impossibly minuscule, core of an onion.

Beckett's novels relentlessly pursue this sort of process, stripping away layers of assumptions about the self and the world, peeling away conventional modes of thought to reach a pure essence of existence free of the inevitably distorting effects of intellect, logical structure, and analytical order. This image of the onion is a rich one because it communicates the sense in Beckett's work that this excavatory process is unending, that disposal of each mode of thought reveals yet another, even more resistant habit of mind. Beckett himself often spoke of his novels as a series, and it is this progressive penetration through one form of thought to another that marks the stages in the series.

Thirty years after *Proust*, Beckett submitted to an unusually provocative interview with Tom Driver that was published in Columbia University Forum in the summer of 1961. In this interview, he dwelled specifically on form. After contrasting the orderly form of most art to the intransigently chaotic nature of existence, he said: "The Form and the chaos remain separate. The latter is not reduced to the former. . . . [T]o find a form that accommodates the mess, that is the task of the artist now." Beckett's novels reveal three stages in this attempt to discover a literary form that will accommodate the chaotic nature of existence. In the first stage, represented by *Murphy* and *Watt*, the process is a destructive one of ridiculing literary convention by parody and satire to suggest an as yet undiscovered alternative form of expression. In the second stage, represented by the trilogy, the attempt to give voice to that alternative takes the form of the disordered and at times deliberately incoherent monologues of individual narrators. In the third stage, represented by *How It Is* and the subsequent short prose pieces, the process takes the form of presenting metaphorical worlds that accommodate their own chaos.

This last stage, especially, is marked by the unpleasant emphasis on miserable degradation and the recurring private images that have given Beckett an undeserved reputation for misanthropy and deliberate obscurity. These charges are effectively rebutted by his own stated sense of "the task of the artist now." Beckett's works do not provide relaxing reading experiences. They are designed to disorient, to dislocate, and to thwart intellectual complacency. The formidable difficulties they present to the reader, however, are essential records of the intellectual ambience of advanced mid-twentieth century thought.

MURPHY

Beckett's earliest fiction, the stories in *More Pricks than Kicks*, described the passive resistance to social conformity and death under anesthesia of a protagonist named Belacqua (an allusion to Dante). Beckett's first novel, *Murphy*, presents the same resistance and senseless death in the story of Murphy, given the most common surname in Ireland. Murphy is the first of numerous Beckett protagonists who seek to relinquish all ties to their environment and their compulsion to make sense of it. The centerpiece of *Murphy* is an analysis of the discrete zones of his mind in the sixth chapter. The third and last of these zones is a darkness of selflessness in which mind itself is obviated. It is this zone beyond consciousness that most Beckett protagonists seek; it is their failure to reach it that creates the tension in most of Beckett's fiction.

Murphy is surrounded by representatives of two frames of reference that prevent his withdrawal from the world. The first is nationality, represented here by character types such as the drunken Irish poet Austin Ticklepenny and monuments to national ideals such as the statue of Cuchulain in the Dublin General Post Office. The second frame of reference is erudition, represented here by a plethora of arcane references to astronomy, astrology, philosophy, and mathematics. Assaulted by these adjuncts of identity, Murphy remains unable to disengage himself fully from the world, to withdraw completely into the third zone of his mind.

The problem that Beckett confronts in *Murphy* is central to all of his novels: to define consciousness in a novel without the usual novelistic apparatus of recognizable environment, nationality, and psychology. The novel only approaches such a definition in the chapter on Murphy's mind and in the image of an eerily withdrawn character named Mr. Endon. Elsewhere, Beckett is able to suggest an alternative only by destructive means: by heaping scorn on things

Irish, by deflating intellectual pretensions, and by parodying novelistic conventions. These forms of ridicule make *Murphy* Beckett's most humorous and accessible novel. The same reliance on ridicule, however, ensures that *Murphy* remains derivative of the very forms of thought and literature it intends to challenge.

WATT

Although it was not published until 1953, after *Molloy* and *Malone Dies, Watt* was written a decade earlier and properly belongs among Beckett's early novels. It is a transitional work, written in English, in which one can observe intimations of the central concerns of the trilogy of novels written in French.

Like Murphy, Watt is an alienated vagabond seeking succor from the complexities of existence. In the opening and closing sections of this four-part novel, Watt's world is a recognizably Irish one populated with middle-class characters with small social pretensions. In the central two sections, however, Watt works as a servant on the surreal country estate of a Mr. Knott. *Watt* most resembles Beckett's later fiction in these central sections. In them, Watt ineffectually attempts to master simpler and simpler problems without the benefit of reliable contingencies of cause and effect or even the assurance of a reliable system of language. The structure of the novel is ultimately dislocated by the gradual revelation that the four parts are not in fact presented in chronological order and that they have been narrated by a character named Sam rather than by an omniscient narrator. Sam's account proves unreliable in particulars, thus completing the process by which the novel undermines any illusion of certainty concerning the interaction of the characters Watt ("What?") and Knott ("Not!").

Watt, like *Murphy*, relies on satire of literary precedents and disruption of novelistic conventions. There are allusions in the novel to the work of W. B. Yeats and James Joyce and to the poet Æ (George William Russell), to cite only the Irish precedents. The great disruption of novelistic conventions is effected by "Addenda" of unincorporated material at the end of the text and by pedantic annotations throughout the novel. Nevertheless, *Watt* does look

ahead to *Molloy* in its central sections, dominated by episodic problems such as the removal of Knott's slops and the attempt of the wretched Lynch family to have the ages of its living members total exactly one thousand. The full emergence of this sort of episodic narrative in Beckett's fiction, however, seems to have required the focus of attention on language itself (rather than on literary conventions). That was one important effect of his decision to begin to compose novels in French rather than English.

MERCIER AND CAMIER

Mercier and Camier, although published in 1970, was written in French in 1946, soon after Beckett returned to Paris at the end of the war. Like *Watt*, it is best placed among Beckett's works by date of composition rather than publication. Written at the outset of the "siege in the room" that produced Beckett's major novels, it illuminates the process by which the style of the trilogy emerged from concentration on elements of composition rather than on the social concerns that dominate most conventional novels.

Mercier and Camier is an account of an aimless journey by two decrepit characters out of and back into a city that resembles Dublin. A witness-narrator announces his presence in the opening sentence but remains otherwise inconspicuous. The descriptions of the two characters' generally enigmatic encounters with others, however, are periodically interrupted by subtly disported tabular synopses that call attention to the arbitrary features of the narrator's accounts. The novel is thus a shrewdly self-conscious narrative performance, with the emphasis falling on the telling rather than on the meaning of the tale.

The belated publication of *Mercier and Camier* was a welcome event because it represents what must have seemed to Beckett an unsatisfactory attempt to open the novel form to accommodate the "mess" he finds dominant in the world. His composition of the novel in French produced a spare prose style and calculated use of language that would prove essential to his later fiction. Like *Watt*, however, the novel retained a peripheral witness-narrator; this may have been one of the sources of Beckett's dissatisfaction with the novel, for immediately after it, he shifted to the monologue essential to the trilogy that followed.

Beckett's major accomplishment in prose fiction is the trilogy of novels begun with *Molloy*, written in French in 1947 and 1948. All three are narrative monologues, all seek to explain origins, and all expose various forms of self-knowledge as delusions. Thus, they approach that ideal core of the onion in their quest for explanations, and they assert the governing "mess" of incoherence, which continues to resist artificial, if comforting, intellectual fabrications.

MOLLOY

In structure, *Molloy*, translated into English by Beckett in collaboration with Patrick Bowles, is the most complex work in the trilogy. The first part of the novel is the narrative of the derelict Molloy, who discovers himself in his mother's room and attempts unsuccessfully to reconstruct his arrival there. The second part is the narrative of the Catholic and bourgeois detective Jacques Moran, who has been commissioned by an authority named Youdi to write a report on Molloy. As Moran's report proceeds, he gradually begins to resemble Molloy. His narrative ends with the composition of the sentence with which it began, now exposed as pure falsehood.

Molloy and Moran are counterparts whose narratives expose the alternative fallacies, respectively, of inward and outward ways of organizing experience. Molloy's self-involved preoccupations, such as his chronic flatulence, function as counterparts of Moran's more social preoccupations, such as Catholic liturgy and his profession. Both are left in unresolved confrontation with the likelihood that the ways they have attempted to make sense of their origins and present circumstances are pure sham. The special brilliance of *Molloy* is the manner in which this confrontation is brought about by the terms of each narrator's monologue. The prose style of the novel is dominated by hilarious deflations of momentary pretensions, ironic undercutting of reassuring truisms, and criticism of its own assertions. It is in this manner that *Molloy* manages to admit the "mess" Beckett seeks to accommodate in the novel form: Its compelling and humorous narratives effectively expose the limits rather than the fruits of self-knowledge.

MALONE DIES

Malone Dies is the purest of the narrative performances of Beckett's storytellers. In it, a bedridden man awaits death in his room and tells stories to pass the time. His environment is limited to the room, the view from a window, and a meager inventory of possessions he periodically recounts with inconsistent results. Beyond these, he is limited to the world of his stories about a boy named Sapo, an old man named MacMann, an employee in an insane asylum named Lemuel, and others. All are apparently fictions based on different periods in Malone's own life. At the end of the novel, his narrative simply degenerates and ends inconclusively in brief phrases that may suggest death itself or simply the end of his willingness to pursue the stories further.

It is essential to the novel that Malone criticize his own stories, revise them, abandon them, and rehearse them once again. His predicament is that he knows the stories to be false in many respects, but he has no alternative approach to the truth of his own origins. Like Beckett, Malone is a compulsive composer of fictions who is perpetually dissatisfied with them. As a result, *Malone Dies* is one of the most completely self-critical and self-involved novels in the twentieth century stream of metafictions, or novels about the nature of the novel. It demonstrates, with bitter humor and relentless self-examination, the limits of fiction, the pleasure of fiction, and the lack of an acceptable substitute for fiction.

THE UNNAMABLE

In *The Unnamable*, Beckett pursues the preoccupations of *Molloy* and *Malone Dies* to an extreme that puts formidable difficulties before even the most devoted reader of the modern novel. In *Molloy*, the focus was on two long narrative accounts; in *Malone Dies*, it narrowed to concentrate on briefer stories; and in *The Unnamable*, it shrinks further to probe the limits of language itself, of words and names. As the title suggests, these smaller units of literary discourse prove to be just as false and unreliable as those longer literary units had in Beckett's previous two novels. In *The Unnamable*, there is no character in the ordinary sense of the term. Instead, there are only bursts of language, at first organized into paragraphs, then only into continuous sentences, and finally into pages of a single sentence broken only by commas.

The premise of the novel is that a paralyzed and apparently androgynous creature suspended in a jar outside a Paris restaurant speaks of himself and versions of himself labeled with temporary names such as Mahood and Worm. As he speaks, however, he is diverted from the content of his speech by disgust with its elements, its words. The names of Murphy, Molloy, and Malone are all evoked with complete disgust at the complacent acceptance of language inherent in the creation of such literary characters. *The Unnamable* thus attempts to challenge assumptions of literary discourse by diverting attention from plot and character to phrase and word. It is tortuous reading because it calls into question the means by which any reading process proceeds.

The preoccupation with speaking in the novel leads naturally to a corollary preoccupation with silence, and *The Unnamable* ends with a paradoxical assertion of the equal impossibility of either ending or continuing. At this point, Beckett had exhausted the means by which he attempted to admit the "mess" into the form of the novels in his trilogy. He managed to proceed, to extend the series of his novels, by exploring the richness of metaphorical and generally horrific environments like that of the unnamable one suspended, weeping, in his jar.

How It Is

Beckett's critics commonly refer to the series of prose fictions begun with *How It Is* as "post-trilogy prose." The term is useful because it draws a distinction between the methods of Beckett's works as well as their chronology. Even in the midst of the incoherence of *The Unnamable*, there were references to the familiar world, such as the fact that the narrator was located in Paris. In *How It Is* and the works that followed, however, the environment is an entirely metaphorical and distinctly surreal one. Without reference to a familiar world, these works are governed by an interior system of recurrent images and memories. *How It Is* marks the beginning of this final stage in the series of Beckett's works, and so its French title *Comment c'est* is an appropriate phonetic pun meaning both "how it is" and *commencer*, or "to begin."

In *How It Is*, the speaker, named Bom, is a creature crawling in darkness through endless mire, dragging with him a sack of canned provisions, and torturing and being tortured by other creatures with their indispensable can openers. His narrative takes the form of brief, unpunctuated fragments separated by spaces on the page. Each fragment is of a length that can be spoken aloud, as they ideally should be, and the style may be in part a product of Beckett's experience in the production of plays. There is a second character named Pim, against whom the narrator tends to define his own status. The novel, which many prefer to term a prose poem, is thus broken into three parts: before Pim, with Pim, and after Pim.

The Bom and Pim interaction is an excruciating account of misery in a netherworld of darkness and slime. It is related entirely in retrospect, however, and the changing relationships of domination and subordination are less important than the manner in which the language of the fragments creates its own system of repetitions and alterations of phrases. *How It Is* dramatizes, in fact, how it *was* for Bom, and in place of clear references to the familiar world, it offers a verbal model for the mechanics of memory. This remains a consistent, if extraordinarily complex, extension of Beckett's attempt to accommodate the "mess" of chaos in the novel form. Its extremely calculated prose creates a sense of the consistent, but inexplicable and ultimately uninformative, impingement of the past on the present.

THE LOST ONES

The Lost Ones is a representative example of Beckett's prose fiction immediately following *How It Is*. He composed many brief prose pieces in this period, abandoned most of them, and resurrected them for publication at the urging of enthusiastic friends. Most are published in collections of his short works. *The Lost Ones*, however, is a more sustained narrative performance (sixty-three pages in the American edition). It was abandoned in an incomplete form in 1966 but retrieved and supplemented with an effective conclusion in 1970. It has also gained greater attention than most of Beckett's works from this period because of an innovative stage adaptation by the Mabou Mines Company in New York City in 1973.

The Lost Ones is unique among Beckett's works because it focuses on a group rather than an individual. In fifteen unnumbered passages of prose, it describes the workings of a huge cylinder populated by male and female figures who maneuver throughout its various areas by means of ladders. The prose style is remarkably understated in comparison to the painful, if metaphorical, imagery of *How It Is*, and the primary action is the continual reorganization of this closed set of persons according to an entropic process of diminishing energies. Mathematical computation, a motif in many of Beckett's novels, is a primary feature in *The Lost Ones*. As language had in so many of Beckett's earlier novels, numerical calculations prove an inadequate means of organizing experience in this work, and the crucial final paragraph added in 1970 is a fatalistic exposure of the worthlessness of these computations as indications of the past, present, or future of this surreal environment. As in many of Beckett's later prose pieces, the metaphorical environment created by the prose is open to many interpretive referents. The text is subtly allusive—the French title, for example, evokes Lamartine—and the viability of literature as an effective indication of past, present, or future is among the possible subjects of this spare and immensely suggestive text.

COMPANY

Excepting *The Lost Ones* and other aborted works, nearly twenty years elapsed between the writing of *How It Is* and the next of Beckett's prose fictions to approach the novel in form if not in length. *Company* ended this relative silence, during which Beckett produced a variety of works in other genres. Like *How It Is* and the intervening works, *Company* presents a generally metaphorical environment and a consistent emphasis on the workings of memory. Unlike Beckett's other late works, however, it was composed in English and apparently generated out of contemplation of distinctly autobiographical images.

Company is a narrative by a figure immobilized on his back in darkness. Despite this surreal premise, it dwells on images of a familiar, suggestively Irish environment marked by features such as Connolly's store and the Ballyogan Road. It thus combines the astringency of Beckett's "post-trilogy prose" with the references to an identifiable world common in the trilogy. It is, however, far from a regression from ex-

perimental form or an abandonment of the attempt to accommodate the "mess" in a novel. Instead, it represents the fruit of Beckett's years of careful manipulation of a spare prose style in his second language. Like *How It Is, Company* concentrates on the inexplicable workings of memory. Unlike *How It Is*, the novel does so in a passive and restrained mixture of nostalgic and ironic images free of the vulgar and painful hostility of that earlier novel. In less flamboyant ways than Beckett's earlier works, *Company* also manages to underscore its own nature as an artificial, literary construction. Its governing metaphor of "company" manages to encompass both the memories surrounding the narrator and the meeting of author and reader of a literary text.

ILL SEEN ILL SAID

Company was followed by *Ill Seen Ill Said*, a series of paragraphs consisting primarily of sentence fragments. They describe a woman and her attempt to capture the details of her environment. The devotion to detail is such that vocabulary, rather than image, tends to capture attention, frequently because of intentional neologisms, interior rhymes, and sporadic echoes. It is more an evocation of a mood than a plotted novel, one that reveals the author, having rid himself of complacent use of language in earlier works, as a prose stylist with marked affinities to a poet. *Ill Seen Ill Said*, despite the disparagement of voice in its title, marks the emergence in Beckett's works of a devotion to pure sensation unmodulated by systems of logic or desire. It is in this respect that *Ill Seen Ill Said* is a necessary and inevitable extension of "the task of the artist now" addressed in a long series of novels. Rather than suggesting an alternative literary expression by destructive irony or subverting complacency by incoherent monologue, it attempts to present consciousness free of artificial order in a distinctly lyrical form of prose fiction.

In an early essay on the Irish poet Denis Devlin published in *Transition* in 1938, Beckett offered this dictum: "Art has always been this—pure interrogation, rhetorical question less the rhetoric." Like so many of his statements on other writers, this has a special relevance to Beckett's own literary career. Over a period of a half century, he produced fictions that relentlessly question assumptions of intellectual and literary order. He did so with a single-minded devotion to what he took to be "the task of the artist now" and so compiled an oeuvre that is unique in the twentieth century in its concentration on a central purpose and in its literary expression of the great philosophical preoccupations of its time. Beckett's work has been discussed by critics in reference to other innovative thinkers of the century as disparate as Albert Einstein, Sigmund Freud, and Jean-Paul Sartre. In addition to fueling the literary debates of his time, his work may be said to have created, in part, contemporary literary theories such as structuralism and deconstruction. Despite their formidable difficulties, then, Beckett's novels have an indisputable importance to anyone seriously interested in the intellectual climate of the twentieth century.

John P. Harrington

OTHER MAJOR WORKS

SHORT FICTION: *More Pricks than Kicks*, 1934; *Nouvelles et textes pour rien*, 1955 (*Stories and Texts for Nothing*, 1967); *No's Knife: Collected Shorter Prose, 1947-1966*, 1967; *First Love and Other Shorts*, 1974; *Pour finir encore et autres foirades*, 1976 (*Fizzles*, 1976).

PLAYS: *En attendant Godot*, pb. 1952 (*Waiting for Godot*, 1954); *Fin de partie: Suivi de Acte sans paroles*, pr., pb. 1957 (music by John Beckett; *Endgame: A Play in One Act, Followed by Act Without Words: A Mime for One Player*, 1958); *All That Fall*, pr., pb. 1957; *Krapp's Last Tape*, pr., pb. 1958; *Act Without Words II*, pr., pb. 1960 (one-act mime); *Happy Days*, pr., pb. 1961; *Play*, pr., pb. 1963 (English translation, 1964); *Come and Go: Dramaticule*, pr., pb. 1965 (one scene; English translation, 1967); *That Time*, pr., pb. 1976; *Footfalls*, pr., pb. 1976; *Ends and Odds*, pb. 1976; *A Piece of Monologue*, pr. 1979; *Rockaby*, pr., pb. 1981; *Ohio Impromptu*, pr. 1981; *Catastrophe*, pr. 1982; *Company*, pr. 1983; *Collected Shorter Plays*, pb. 1984.

SCREENPLAY: *Film*, pr. 1965.

TELEPLAYS: *Eh Joe*, 1966 (*Dis Joe*, 1967); *Not I*, 1972; *Tryst*, 1976; *Shades*, 1977; *Quad*, 1981.

RADIO PLAYS: *Embers*, pr., pb. 1959; *Words and Music*, 1962 (music by John Beckett); *Cascando*, 1963 (music by Marcel Mihalovici); *All That Fall*, 1968.

POETRY: *Whoroscope*, 1930; *Echo's Bones and Other Precipitates*, 1935; *Poems in English*, 1961; *Collected Poems in English and French*, 1977.

NONFICTION: *Proust*, 1931.

TRANSLATION: *An Anthology of Mexican Poetry*, 1958 (Octavio Paz, editor).

MISCELLANEOUS: *I Can't Go On, I'll Go On: A Selection from Samuel Beckett's Work*, 1976 (Richard Seaver, editor).

BIBLIOGRAPHY

Brienza, Susan D. *Samuel Beckett's New Worlds: Style in Metafiction*. Norman: University of Oklahoma Press, 1987. A study of twelve of Beckett's works of fiction written since 1958. Brienza compares the French versions of the works to the English versions to obtain clues to the meaning of Beckett's impenetrable prose. A book for advanced students of Beckett, yet written in a highly readable style.

Davis, Robin J., and Lance S. Butler, eds. *Make Sense Who May: Essays on Samuel Beckett's Later Works*. New York: Barnes & Noble Books, 1988. Contains fifteen essays culled from "Samuel Beckett at Eighty," a conference held in August, 1986, at Stirling University. The essays look at Beckett's work in the 1970's and 1980's in terms of poststructuralism and deconstruction. For advanced students.

Ellman, Richard. *Four Dubliners: Wilde, Yeats, Joyce, and Beckett*. New York: George Braziller, 1988. Examines the Irish roots in Beckett's plays and novels and their subsequent influence on Irish writing. A lively and interesting study of four Irish writers, suitable for all students.

Hill, Leslie. *Beckett's Fiction*. Cambridge, England: Cambridge University Press, 1990. In his preface, Hill briefly characterizes previous criticism and finds it reductive. Chapters on the trilogy, duality, repetition, fables of genealogy, experiment, and failure. Includes notes and bibliography.

Knowlson, James. *Damned to Fame: The Life of Samuel Beckett*. New York: Simon and Schuster, 1996. A comprehensive biography with much new material, detailed notes, and bibliography.

APHRA BEHN

Born: England; July (?), 1640
Died: London, England; April 16, 1689

PRINCIPAL LONG FICTION

Love Letters Between a Nobleman and His Sister, 1683-1687 (3 volumes)
Agnes de Castro, 1688
The Fair Jilt: Or, The History of Prince Tarquin and Miranda, 1688
Oroonoko: Or, The History of the Royal Slave, 1688
The History of the Nun: Or, The Fair Vow-Breaker, 1689
The Lucky Mistake, 1689
The Nun: Or, The Perjured Beauty, 1697
The Adventure of the Black Lady, 1698
The Wandering Beauty, 1698

OTHER LITERARY FORMS

As a truly professional writer, perhaps the first British female to have written for profit, Aphra Behn moved easily through the various literary genres and forms. Her plays include *The Forced Marriage: Or, The Jealous Bridegroom* (1670); *The Amorous Prince: Or, The Curious Husband* (1671); *The Dutch Lover* (1673); *The Town Fop: Or, Sir Timothy Tawdry* (1676); *Abdelazar: Or, the Moor's Revenge* (1676); *The Rover: Or, The Banished Cavaliers*, I, II (1677, 1681); *Sir Patient Fancy* (1678); *The Roundheads: Or, The Good Old Cause* (1681); *The City Heiress: Or, Sir Timothy Treat-All* (1682); *The Lucky Chance: Or, An Alderman's Bargain* (1686); *The Emperor of the Moon* (1687); *The Widow Ranter: Or, The History of Bacon of Virginia* (1689); and *The Younger Brother: Or, The Amorous Jilt* (1696).

Although she enjoyed only mild success as a poet, her verse was probably no better or worse than that of a large number of second-rank versifiers of the Restoration. Behn's best poetry can be found in the song "Love in fantastic triumph sate" (1677), from her tragedy of *Abdelazar*, and in a metrical "Paraphrase on Oenone to Paris" for Jacob Tonson's volume of Ovid's *Epistles* (1680). The remainder of her verse includes a long, amorous allegory, *A Voyage to the Isle of Love* (1684); an adaptation of Bernard de Fontenelle's epic which she entitled *A Discovery of New Worlds* (1688); and two occasional pieces: "A Pindarick on the Death of Charles II" (1685) and "A Congratulatory Poem to Her Most Sacred Majesty" (1688).

ACHIEVEMENTS

Behn's achievement as a novelist should be measured principally in terms of the modest gains made by that form in England during the seventeenth century. Prior to *Oroonoko*, the English novel lingered in the shadows of the theater. Thus, the small reading

(Library of Congress)

public contented itself with works such as John Lyly's *Euphues, the Anatomy of Wit* (1579), Sir Philip Sidney's *Arcadia* (1590), Thomas Lodge's *Rosalynde* (1590), Thomas Nashe's *The Unfortunate Traveler: Or, The Life of Jack Wilton* (1594), and Thomas Deloney's *Jack of Newbury* (1597)—all long, episodic stories, sprinkled with overly dramatic characterization and improbable plot structures. In *Oroonoko*, however, Behn advanced the novel to the point where her more skilled successors in the eighteenth century could begin to shape it into an independent, recognizable form.

Behn possessed the natural gifts of the storyteller, and her narrative art can easily stand beside that of her male contemporaries. A frankly commercial writer, she simply had no time, in pursuit of pleasure and the pen, to find a place in her narratives for intellectual substance. Nevertheless, she told a story as few others could, and the force of her own personality contributed both reality and a sense of immediacy to the still inchoate form of seventeenth century British fiction.

BIOGRAPHY

The details of Aphra Behn's birth are not known. The parish register of the Sts. Gregory and Martin Church, Wye, England, contains an entry stating that Ayfara Amis, daughter of John and Amy Amis, was baptized on July 10, 1640. Apparently, John Johnson, related to Lord Francis Willoughby of Parham, adopted the girl, although no one seems to know exactly when. Ayfara Amis accompanied her stepparents on a journey to Suriname (later Dutch Guiana) in 1658, Willoughby having appointed Johnson to serve as deputy governor of his extensive holdings there. Unfortunately, the new deputy died on the voyage; his widow and children proceeded to Suriname and took up residence at St. John's, one of Lord Willoughby's plantations. Exactly how long they remained is not clear, but certainly the details surrounding the time spent at St. John's form the background for *Oroonoko*.

Biographers have established the summer of 1663 as the most probable date of Behn's return to England. At any rate, by 1665 Behn was again in London and married to a wealthy merchant of Dutch ex-

traction, who may well have had connections in, or at least around, the court of Charles II. In 1665 came the Great Plague and the death of Behn's husband; the latter proved the more disastrous for her, specifically because (again for unknown reasons) the Dutch merchant left nothing of substance for her—nothing, that is, except his court connections. Charles II, in the midst of the first of his wars against Holland, hired Aphra Behn as a secret government agent to spy upon the Dutch, for which purpose she proceeded to Antwerp. There she contacted another British agent, William Scott, from whom she obtained various pieces of military information, which she forwarded to London. Although she received little credit for her work, and even less money, Behn did conceive of the pseudonym Astrea, the name under which she published most of her poetry. The entire adventure into espionage proved a dismal failure for her; she even had to borrow money and pawn her valuables to pay her debts and obtain passage back to England. Once home, early in 1667, she found no relief from her desperate financial situation. Her debtors threatened prison, and the government refused any payment for her services. Prison followed, although the time and the exact length of her term remain unknown. Some of Behn's biographers speculate that she was aided in her release by John Hale (d. 1692)—a lawyer of Gray's Inn, a wit, an intellectual, a known homosexual, the principal subject of and reason for Behn's sonnets, and the man with whom she carried on a long romance. When she did gain her release, she determined to dedicate the rest of her life to writing and to pleasure, to trust to her own devices rather than to rely upon others who could not be trusted.

Behn launched her career as a dramatist in late December, 1670, at the new Duke's Theatre in Little Lincoln's Inn Fields, London. Her tragicomedy *The Forced Marriage* ran for six nights and included in the cast the nineteen-year-old Thomas Otway (1652-1685), the playwright-to-be only recently arrived from Oxford. Because of the length of the run, Behn, as was the practice, received the entire profit from the third performance, which meant that she could begin to function as an independent artist. She followed her first effort in the spring of 1671 with a comedy, *The*

Amorous Prince, again at the Duke's; another comedy, *The Dutch Lover*, came to Drury Lane in February, 1673, and by the time of her anonymous comedy *The Rover*, in 1677, her reputation was secure. She mixed easily with the literati of her day, such as Thomas Killigrew, Edward Ravenscroft, the earl of Rochester, Edmund Waller, and the poet laureate John Dryden, who published her rough translations from Ovid in 1683. With her reputation came offers for witty prologues and epilogues for others' plays, as well as what she wanted more than anything—money. A confrontation with the earl of Shaftesbury and the newly emerged Whigs during the religious-political controversies of 1678, when she offended Charles II's opponents in a satirical prologue to an anonymous play, *Romulus and Hersilia*, brought her once again to the edge of financial hardship, as she was forced to abandon drama for the next five years.

Fortunately, Behn could fall back upon her abilities as a writer of popular fiction and occasional verse, although those forms were not as profitable as the London stage. Her series *Love Letters Between a Nobleman and His Sister* (1683-1687) and *Poems upon Several Occasions* (1684) were well received, but the meager financial returns from such projects could not keep pace with her personal expenses. When she did return to the stage in 1686 with her comedy *The Lucky Chance*, she met with only moderate success and some public abuse. *The Emperor of the Moon*, produced the following season, fared somewhat better, although by then the London audience had lost its stomach for a female playwright—and a Tory, at that. She continued to write fiction and verse, but sickness and the death of her friend Edmund Waller, both in October, 1688, discouraged her. Five days after the coronation of William III and Mary, on April 16, 1689, Behn died. She had risen high enough to merit burial in Westminster Abbey; John Hoyle provided the fitting epitaph: "Here lies proof that wit can never be/ Defense enough against mortality."

ANALYSIS

In the early twentieth century, Vita Sackville-West, in trying to estimate Aphra Behn's contribution to English fiction, asked "what has she left behind her that is of any real value?" Sackville-West bemoaned Behn's failure in her fiction to reflect fully London life, London characters, London scenes; attention to exotic themes, settings, and characters merely debased and wasted her narrative gifts. Such a judgment, while plausible, fails to consider Behn's fiction in its historical and biographical context. Her tales abound with German princes, Spanish princesses, Portuguese kings, French counts, West Indian slaves, and various orders of bishops, priests, and nuns, yet, Behn's *real* world was itself highly artificial, even fantastic: the intrigue of the Stuart court, the ribaldry of the London stage, the gossip of the drawing room, the masquerade, and the card parlor. Behn, in her *real* world, took in the same scenes as did John Dryden, Samuel Pepys, and the earl of Rochester. Thus, to assert that her fiction neglects her actual experience in favor of fantastic and faraway window dressing may be too hasty a conclusion.

In *Agnes de Castro*, Behn lets loose various powers of love, with the result that her heroines' passions affect the fortunes of their lovers. Thus, Miranda (*The Fair Jilt*) reflects the raving, hypocritical enchantress whose very beauty drives her lovers mad; Ardelia (*The Nun*) plays the capricious lover, whose passion carries her through a series of men, as well as a nunnery; and Agnes de Castro presents a slight variation from the preceding, in that the titled character is a product of circumstance: She is loved by the husband of her mistress.

Another primary theme in Behn's work is the often discussed noble savage that has traditionally been assigned to *Oroonoko*, as has the subordinate issue of antislavery in that same novel. In 1975, Professor George Guffey suggested a withdrawal from the feminist-biographical positions (those from which the noble savage/antislavery ideals spring) and a movement toward "a hitherto unperceived level of political allusion." Guffey did not label *Oroonoko* a political allegory but did suggest that readers should look more closely at events in England between 1678 and 1688. Guffey maintains that the novelist deplores not the slavery of a black, noble savage but the bondage of a *royal prince*—again a reference to the political climate of the times. The interesting aspect of Guffey's analysis is that his approach lends substance to Behn's principal novel and to her overall reputation as a literary artist, and it parries the complaint that she failed to echo the sound and the sense of her own age.

In 1678, Sir Roger L'Estrange (1616-1704) published *Five Love Letters from a Nun to a Cavalier*, a translation of some fictional correspondence by the minor French writer Guilleraques. Behn used the work as a model for at least three of her prose pieces—*Love Letters Between a Nobleman and His Sister, The History of the Nun*, and *The Nun*. For the latter two, the novelist took advantage, at least on the surface, of the current religious and political controversies and set forth the usual claims to truth.

THE HISTORY OF THE NUN

There may be some validity to the claim that *The History of the Nun* exists as one of the earliest examinations by a novelist into the psychology of crime and guilt. The events, at the outset, proceed reasonably enough but become less believable, and, by the novel's conclusion, the events appear to be exceedingly unreal. Despite this difficulty, the novel does have some value. Behn demonstrates her ability to develop thoroughly the key aspects of the weaknesses and the resultant sufferings of the heroine, Isabella. Behn immediately exposes the concept that "Mother Church" can take care of a girl's problems, can easily eradicate the desires of the world from her heart and mind, can readily transform a passionate maiden into a true, devoted sister of the faith. In addition, despite her wickedness, Isabella is still very much a human being worthy of the reader's understanding. At every step, the girl pays something for what she does; with each violation against the Church and each crime of passion, she falls deeper into the darkness of her own guilt. What she does, and how, is certainly contrived; how she reacts to her misdeeds reflects accurately the guilty conscience of a believable human being.

THE NUN

The second "Nun" novel, not published until 1697, certainly leads the reader through a more complicated plot entanglement than the 1688 story, but it contains none of the virtue exhibited in the earlier work. The interesting aspect of *The Nun*'s plot is that Behn kills the heroine, Ardelia, first; only afterward do the principal rivals, Don Sebastian and Don Henriques, kill each other in a fight. The interest, however, is only fleeting, for those events do not occur until the end of the novel. All that remains of the bloody situation is Elvira, Don Sebastian's unfaithful sister. After weeping and calling for help, she is seized with a violent fever (in the final paragraph) and dies within twenty-four hours. Certainly, Behn's ingenuity in this piece demands some recognition, if for no other reason than her adeptness, according to James Sutherland, at "moving the pieces around the board."

AGNES DE CASTRO

Because of the relative sanity of its plot, in contrast to the two previous tragedies, *Agnes de Castro* comes close to what Behn's feminist supporters expect of her. In other words, in this piece, pure evil or a series of tragic events cannot be blamed entirely on love or upon reckless female passion. Although Don Pedro genuinely loves his wife's maid-of-honor, Agnes, she, out of loyalty to her mistress, refuses to yield to his passion. Such action encourages the other characters to exhibit equal degrees of virtue. Constantia, Don Pedro's wife, seems to understand that the power of Agnes's charms, although innocent enough, is no match for her husband's frailty of heart over reason. Thus, she resents neither her husband nor her maid; in fact, she is willing to tolerate the presence of Agnes to keep her husband happy.

The novel, however, does not exist as a monument to reason. Something must always arise, either in politics or romance, to disrupt reasonable people's attempts at harmony. In the novel, a vengeful woman lies to Constantia and plants the rumor in her mind that Agnes and Don Pedro are plotting against her. Such a report breaks Constantia's trust in her husband and her maid, and the honest lady dies of a broken heart. The novel, however, remains believable, for Behn simply emphasizes the frailty of honor and trust in a world dominated by intrigue and pure hatred. Given the political and religious climates of the decade, the setting and the plot of *Agnes de Castro* are indeed flimsy façades for the court and coffee-house of seventeenth century London.

THE FAIR JILT

Although in *The Fair Jilt*, Behn continued to develop the conflict between love and reason, the novel has attracted critical attention because of its allusions to the writer's own experiences. Again, she lays claim to authenticity by maintaining that she witnessed parts of the events and heard the rest from sources close to the action and the characters. In addition, the events occur in Antwerp, the very city to which the novelist had been assigned for the performance of her spying activities for Charles II's ministers.

From the outset of the novel, Behn establishes the wickedness of Miranda, who uses her beauty to enchant the unsuspecting and even tempts the weak into commiting murder. Obviously, had Behn allowed her major character to succeed in her evil ways, nothing would have been gained from the novel. What results is the triumph of the hero's innate goodness; as weak as he is, he has endured. His loyalty and devotion have outlasted and, to a certain extent, conquered Miranda's wickedness.

OROONOKO

Behn's literary reputation today rests almost totally upon a single work, *Oroonoko*. The novel succeeds as her most realistic work, principally because she recounts the specifics of Suriname with considerable detail and force. Behn installs her hero amid the splendor of a tropical setting, a Natural Man, a pure savage untouched by the vices of Christian Europe, unaware of the white man's inherent baseness and falsehood.

In lashing out at the weaknesses of her society, Behn does not forget about one of her major concerns—love. Thus, Oroonoko loves the beautiful Imoinda, a child of his own race, but the prince's grandfather demands her for his own harem. Afterward, the monarch sells the girl into slavery, and she finds herself in Suriname—where Oroonoko is brought following his kidnapping. The prince embarks upon a term of virtuous and powerful adventures in the name of freedom for himself and Imoinda, but his captors deceive him. Thereupon, he leads a slave revolt, only to be captured by the white

scoundrels and tortured. Rather than see Imoinda suffer dishonor at the hands of the ruthless white planters and government officers, Oroonoko manages to kill her himself. At the end, he calmly smokes his pipe—a habit learned from the Europeans—as his captors dismember his body and toss the pieces into the fire.

The final judgment upon Behn's fiction may still remain to be formulated. Evaluations of her work have tended to extremes. Some critics assert that her novels, even *Oroonoko*, had no significant influence on the development of the English novel, while others argue that her limited attempts at realism may well have influenced Daniel Defoe, Samuel Richardson, Henry Fielding, and others to begin to mold the ostensibly factual narrative into the novel as the twentieth century recognizes it. From Behn came the background against which fictional plots could go forward and fictional characters could function. Her problem, which her successors managed to surmount, was the inability (or refusal) to make her characters and events as real as their fictional environment. That fault (if it was a fault) lay with the tendencies and the demands of the age, not with the writer. Indeed, it is hardly a failure for a dramatist and a novelist to have given to her audience exactly what they wanted. To have done less would have meant an even quicker exit from fame and an even more obscure niche in the literary history of her time.

Samuel J. Rogal

OTHER MAJOR WORKS

PLAYS: *The Forced Marriage: Or, The Jealous Bridegroom*, pr. 1670; *The Amorous Prince: Or, The Curious Husband*, pr., pb. 1671; *The Dutch Lover*, pr., pb. 1673; *Abdelazer: Or, The Moor's Revenge*, pr. 1676; *The Town Fop: Or, Sir Timothy Tawdry*, pr. 1676; *The Rover: Or, The Banished Cavaliers, Part I*, pr., pb. 1677, *Part II*, pr., pb. 1681; *Sir Patient Fancy*, pr., pb. 1678; *The Feigned Courtesans: Or, A Night's Intrigue*, pr., pb. 1679; *The Young King: Or, The Mistake*, pr. 1679; *The Roundheads: Or, The Good Old Cause*, pr. 1681; *The City Heiress: Or, Sir Timothy Treat-All*, pr., pb. 1682; *The Lucky Chance: Or, An Alderman's Bargain*, pr. 1686; *The Emperor of the*

Moon, pr., pb. 1687; *The Widow Ranter: Or, The History of Bacon of Virginia*, pr. 1689; *The Younger Brother: Or, The Amorous Jilt*, pr., pb. 1696.

POETRY: *Poems upon Several Occasions, with a Voyage to the Island of Love*, 1684 (including adaptation of Abbé Paul Tallemant's *Le Voyage de l'isle d'amour*); *Miscellany: Being a Collection of Poems by Several Hands*, 1685 (includes works by others).

TRANSLATIONS: *Aesop's Fables*, 1687 (with Francis Barlow); *Of Trees*, 1689 (of book 6 of Abraham Cowley's *Sex libri plantarum*).

MISCELLANEOUS: *La Montre: Or, The Lover's Watch*, 1686 (prose and poetry); *The Case for the Watch*, 1686 (prose and poetry); *Lycidus: Or, The Lover in Fashion*, 1688 (prose and poetry; includes works by others); *The Lady's Looking-Glass, to Dress Herself By: Or, The Art of Charming*, 1697 (prose and poetry); *The Works of Aphra Behn*, 1915, 1967 (6 volumes; Montague Summers, editor).

BIBLIOGRAPHY

Goreau, Angeline. *Reconstructing Aphra: A Social Biography of Aphra Behn*. New York: Dial Press, 1980. Draws on Behn's own writings as well as contemporary comments about her, re-creating the life of the first professional female writer. Like Virginia Woolf, Behn is praised for providing a model for later women who took up the pen. The thirty-seven illustrations contribute to the reconstruction of the age. Little discussion of the fiction and later plays.

Guffey, George. "Aphra Behn's *Oroonoko*: Occasion and Accomplishment." In *Two English Novelists: Aphra Behn and Anthony Trollope: Papers Read at a Clark Library Seminar, May 11, 1974*. Los Angeles: Clark Library, 1975. Argues that *Oroonoko* is not an attack on slavery or a celebration of the natural man but rather a defense of James II, who is the model for the hero, as Suriname is made to resemble England.

Link, Frederick M. *Aphra Behn*. New York: Twayne, 1968. After a brief account of Behn's life, this book provides a critical survey of her works, devoting about half to her drama. Concludes with a survey of Behn's reputation since her death and includes a useful annotated bibliography of criticism.

O'Donnell, Mary Ann. *Aphra Behn: An Annotated Bibliography of Primary and Secondary Sources*. New York: Garland, 1986. After a detailed description of more than one hundred primary works, O'Donnell annotates 661 books, articles, essays, and dissertations written about Behn after 1666. These works are listed chronologically. Indexed.

Sackville-West, Vita. *Aphra Behn: The Incomparable Astrea*. New York: Viking Press, 1928. Sackville-West admires the woman more than the writing, though she finds the lyrics praiseworthy. Sympathetic and well written.

Todd, Janet, ed. *Aphra Behn Studies*. Cambridge, England: Cambridge University Press, 1996. Part 1 concentrates on Behn's plays, part 2 on her poetry, part 3 on her fiction, and part 4 on her biography. Includes an introduction outlining Behn's career and the essays in the volume and an index.

_____. *The Secret Life of Aphra Behn*. New Brunswick, N.J.: Rutgers University Press, 1996. The introduction summarizes efforts to study Behn's work and life, her place in literature, her ability to write in all the genres (except the sermon), and the biographer's efforts to overcome the paucity of biographical facts. In addition to a long, speculative narrative, Todd includes a bibliography of works written before 1800 and a bibliography of work published after 1800.

Woodcock, George. *The Incomparable Aphra*. London: Boardman, 1948. Behn is not only a good writer but also "a revolutionary influence on the social life and literature of her age."

SAUL BELLOW

Born: Lachine, Quebec, Canada; June 10, 1915

PRINCIPAL LONG FICTION
Dangling Man, 1944
The Victim, 1947

(AP/Wide World Photos/Elise Amendola)

The Adventures of Augie March, 1953
Seize the Day, 1956
Henderson the Rain King, 1959
Herzog, 1964
Mr. Sammler's Planet, 1970
Humboldt's Gift, 1975
The Dean's December, 1982
More Die of Heartbreak, 1987
A Theft, 1989
The Bellarosa Connection, 1989
The Actual, 1997 (novella)
Ravelstein, 2000

OTHER LITERARY FORMS

In addition to his many novels, Saul Bellow has published short stories, plays, and a variety of nonfiction. His stories have appeared in *The New Yorker*, *Commentary*, *Partisan Review*, *Hudson Review*, *Esquire*, and other periodicals, and he has published two collections of short stories, *Mosby's Memoirs and Other Stories* (1968) and *Him with His Foot in His Mouth and Other Stories* (1984; includes short novels). His full-length play *The Last Analysis* was produced for a short run on Broadway in 1964, while three one-act plays, *Orange Soufflé*, *A Wen*, and *Out*

from Under, were staged in 1966 in America and Europe. Another one-act play, *The Wrecker*, was published, though not staged, in 1954. Throughout his career, Bellow has written numerous articles on a variety of topics. In 1976, he published an account of his trip to Israel, *To Jerusalem and Back: A Personal Account*.

ACHIEVEMENTS

Often described as America's best contemporary novelist, Bellow earned enormous critical praise and a wide readership as well. He was awarded the Nobel Prize in Literature in 1976. His popularity is, perhaps, surprising, because his novels do not contain the usual ingredients one expects to find in best-selling fiction—suspense, heroic figures, and graphic sex and violence. In fact, his novels are difficult ones that wrestle with perplexing questions, sometimes drawing from esoteric sources such as the anthroposophy of Rudolf Steiner and the psychology of Wilhelm Reich. One of America's most erudite novelists, Bellow often alludes to the work of philosophers, psychologists, poets, anthropologists, and other writers in his fiction. He once stated that the modern movelist should not be afraid to introduce complex ideas into his work. He finds nothing admirable about the anti-intellectualism of many modern writers and believes that most of them have failed to confront the important moral and philosophical problems of the modern age. Opposed to the glib pessimism and the "complaint" of the dominant tradition of modern literature, Bellow struggled for affirmation at a time when such a possibility was seen by many writers as merely an object of ridicule.

In contrast to many American writers, who produced their best work when they were young and then wrote mediocre or poor fiction as they grew older, Bellow is known for the consistent high quality of his work. Moreover, his fiction reveals an immense versatility. In his work, one finds highly structured Flaubertian form as well as picaresque narrative, naturalistic realism as well as romance.

Bellow earned a reputation as a master of narrative voice and perspective, a great comic writer (perhaps the best in America since Mark Twain), and a fine craftsman whose remarkable control of the language allows him to move easily from the highly formal to the colloquial. Most important, his novels illuminate the dark areas of the psyche and possess immense emotional power. Bellow once complained that many contemporary authors and critics are obsessed with symbolism and hidden meanings. A literary work becomes an abstraction for them, and they contrive to evade the emotional power inherent in literature. Bellow's novels do not suffer from abstraction; they deal concretely with passion, death, love, and other fundamental concerns, evoking the whole range of human emotions for his readers.

BIOGRAPHY

Saul Bellow was born in Lachine, Quebec, Canada, on June 10, 1915, the youngest of four children. Two years before, his parents, Abraham and Liza (Gordon) Bellow, had immigrated to Canada from St. Petersburg, Russia. The family lived in a very poor section of Montreal, where Bellow learned Yiddish, Hebrew, French, and English. In 1923 Bellow was diagnosed with tuberculosis and spent half a year in Montreal's Royal Victoria Hospital. When he was nine, the family moved to Chicago, where they lived in the tenements of Humboldt Park.

In 1933, after graduating from Tuley High School on the Northwest Side, he entered the University of Chicago. Two years later he transferred to Northwestern University, where he received a bachelor's degree with honors in sociology and anthropology. In 1937, he entered the University of Wisconsin at Madison to study anthropology but left school in December to marry Anita Goshkin and to become a writer. He was employed briefly with the Works Progress Administration Writers' Project and then led a bohemian life, supporting himself with teaching and odd jobs. During World War II, he served in the merchant marine and published his first novel, *Dangling Man*.

After publishing his second novel, *The Victim*, he was awarded a Guggenheim Fellowship in 1948, which enabled him to travel to Europe and work on

The Adventures of Augie March, parts of which he published in various periodicals before publishing the novel in 1953. This third novel won the National Book Award for Fiction in 1953 and established Bellow as one of America's most promising novelists.

After his return from Europe in 1950, he spent a large part of the next decade in New York City and Dutchess County, New York, teaching and writing before moving back to Chicago to publish *Herzog*. While *Seize the Day* and *Henderson the Rain King* did not receive the critical attention they deserved, *Herzog* was an enormous critical and financial success, even becoming a best-seller for forty-two weeks and selling 142,000 copies, making Bellow wealthy for the first time in his life. *Herzog*, which prompted several thousand readers to send letters to the author pouring out their souls, is not only Bellow's masterpiece but also the most autobiographical of his novels. The impetus for the novel was the breakup of his second marriage, to Sondra Tschacbasov, because of her affair with his best friend, the writer Jack Ludwig. Although the novel reveals all of the important episodes of Bellow's life up to the time of the writing of *Herzog*, the primary focus of the novel is on the triangle of Herzog (Bellow), an academic suffering from writer's block, his beautiful and strong-willed wife Madeleine (Sondra), and the flamboyant charlatan Valentine Gersbach (Jack Ludwig). The shameless Gersbach pretends to be Herzog's best friend and even provides marital counseling for the despondent husband while cuckolding him.

The next two novels, *Mr. Sammler's Planet* and *Humboldt's Gift*, helped increase his reputation but also created some controversy. *Mr. Sammler's Planet* was critical of the excesses of the late 1960's, and some complained that Bellow had become a reactionary. Although Bellow opposed the Vietnam War, he found it difficult to identify with the "counterculture." *Humboldt's Gift* disturbed some critics, who complained that Bellow's interest in the ideas of Austrian social philosopher Rudolf Steiner indicated that he was becoming an escapist; it was a mistaken assumption. An ardent supporter of Israel, Bellow traveled to that country in 1975 and published an account of his journey, *To Jerusalem and Back*. In 1976 he was awarded the Nobel Prize in Literature. Winning the Nobel Prize did not result in a loss of Bellow's creativity, and he published important books in the 1980's and 1990's which challenge conventional thinking on political, aesthetic, and philosophical matters.

Bellow was married five times and had three sons by his first three wives. After living in Chicago for many years, he moved to Massachusetts in 1994, where he became a professor of literature at Boston University.

ANALYSIS

Saul Bellow's mature fiction can be considered as a conscious challenge to modernism, the dominant literary tradition of the age. For Bellow, modernism is a "victim literature" because it depicts an alienated individual who is conquered by his environment. According to him, this "wasteland" tradition originated in the middle of the nineteenth century with the birth of French realism and culminates in the work of Samuel Beckett and other nihilistic contemporary writers. This victim literature reveals a horror of life and considers humanist values useless in a bleak, irrational world. Modernism assumes that the notion of the individual self which underlies the great tradition of the novel is an outmoded concept, and that modern civilization is doomed.

DANGLING MAN

Bellow's first two novels owe a large debt to the wasteland modernism that he would explicitly reject in the late 1940's. *Dangling Man* is an existentialist diary that owes much to Fyodor Dostoevski's *Notes from the Underground* (1864). The demoralized protagonist Joseph is left "dangling" as he waits to be drafted during World War II. A moral casualty of war, he has no sense of purpose and feels weary of a life that seems boring, trivial, and cruel. Excessively self-conscious and critical of those around him, he spends most of his time alone, writing in his journal. He can no longer continue his past work, writing biographical essays on philosophers of the Enlightenment. Although he is alienated, he does realize that he should not make a doctrine out of this feeling. The conclusion of the novel reveals Joseph's ultimate fail-

ure to transcend his "victimization"; he is drafted and greets his imminent regimentation enthusiastically.

THE VICTIM

Bellow's next novel, *The Victim*, also depicts a passive protagonist who is unable to overcome his victimization. As Bellow has admitted, the novel is partially modeled on Dostoevski's *The Eternal Husband* (1870) and uses the technique of the *Doppelgänger* as Dostoevski did in *The Double* (1846). Bellow's novel presents the psychological struggle between Asa Leventhal, a Jew, and Kirby Allbee, his Gentile "double." A derelict without a job, Allbee suggests that Leventhal is responsible for his grim fate. Leventhal ponders the problem of his guilt and responsibility and tries to rid himself of his persecuting double. Despite his efforts to assert himself, he is still "dangling" at the end of the book—still a victim of forces that, he believes, are beyond his control.

THE ADVENTURES OF AUGIE MARCH

After his second novel, Bellow became disenchanted with the depressive temperament and the excessive emphasis on form of modernist literature. His first two novels had been written according to "repressive" Flaubertian formal standards; they were melancholy, rigidly structured, restrained in language, and detached and objective in tone. Rebelling against these constricting standards, Bellow threw off the yoke of modernism when he began to write his third novel. The theme, style, and tone of *The Adventures of Augie March* are very different from his earlier novels, for here one finds an open-ended picaresque narrative with flamboyant language and an exuberant hero who seeks to affirm life and the possibility of freedom. While the environment has a profound influence upon Joseph and Asa Leventhal, Augie refuses to allow it to determine his fate. During the course of many adventures, a multitude of Machiavellians seek to impose their versions of reality upon the good-natured Augie, but he escapes from them, refusing to commit himself.

With his third novel, then, Bellow deliberately rejected the modernist outlook and aesthetic. The problem was to find an alternative to modernism without resorting to glib optimism. It seems that he found an alternative in two older literary traditions—in nineteenth century English Romantic humanism and in a comedy that he considers typically Jewish. Unlike the modernists, who denigrate the concept of the individual, Bellow believes in the potential of the self and its powerful imagination that can redeem ordinary existence and affirm the value of freedom, love, joy, and hope.

While comedy in Bellow is a complex matter, its primary function seems to be to undercut the dejection that threatens his heroes. The comic allows Bellow's protagonists to cope with the grim facts of existence; it enables them to avoid despair and gain a balanced view of their problematical situation. Comedy, the spirit of reason, allows them to laugh away their irrational anxieties. Often Bellow seems to encourage his worst anxieties in order to bring them out into the open so that he can dispose of them by comic ridicule.

SEIZE THE DAY

If *The Adventures of Augie March* presents Bellow's alternative to a "literature of victimization," his subsequent novels can be regarded as probing, exploratory studies in spiritual survival in a hostile environment.

Seize the Day is a much more somber novel than *The Adventures of Augie March*. Bellow felt that his liberation from Flaubertain formalism had gone too far, and that he must use more restraint in his fourth novel. He realized that Augie was too effusive and too naïve. The protagonist of *Seize the Day* is similar to the protagonists of the first two novels, but while Tommy Wilhelm is a "victim," Bellow's attitude toward him is different from his attitude toward Joseph and Asa Leventhal. In his fourth novel, Bellow sought to show the spiritual rebirth of such a "victim."

The short novel, divided into seven parts, presents the day of reckoning in the life of a forty-four-year-old ex-salesman of children's furniture whose past consists of a series of blunders. Living in the Hotel Gloriana (which is also the residence of his wealthy father, Dr. Adler), Wilhelm feels that he is in a desperate situation. He is unemployed and unable to obtain money from his unsympathetic father. He gives his last seven hundred dollars to be invested for him by the mysterious psychologist Dr. Tamkin, a man

who has become not only his surrogate father and financial adviser but also his instructor in spiritual and philosophical matters. Furthermore, Wilhelm's wife, Margaret, from whom he is separated, is harassing him for money. Depressed and confused by the memories of his failures in the past and absorbed by his problems in the present, Wilhelm needs love and compassion. Dr. Adler, Dr. Tamkin, and Margaret all fail him.

Seize the Day is a harsh indictment of a money-obsessed society, where a father is unable to love a son who is unsuccessful. Tamkin's speech on the two souls, no doubt the most important passage in the novel, helps clarify Bellow's social criticism. The psychologist argues that there is a war between man's "pretender soul," his social self, and his "real soul." When the pretender soul parasitically dominates its host, as is common in modern society, one becomes murderous. If one is true to the real soul, however, and casts off the false pretender soul, one can learn to love and "seize the day."

Bellow shows that all of the characters in the novel are products of an exploitative, materialistic society—all are dominated by their pretender souls. Dr. Adler has fought his way up the economic ladder to success. Revered by the residents of the Hotel Gloriana, he is full of self-love. He desires to spend his remaining years in peace and refuses to acknowledge his paternal obligation to his desperate son. Wilhelm's appeals for money are actually pleas for some sign of paternal concern. He provokes his father, trying to disturb the polite barrier of aloofness that the old man has constructed to prevent any kind of real communication between father and son. While Wilhelm is a difficult son for a father to cherish, Dr. Adler is a cold-hearted man who has no real affection for his son, or for anyone else except for himself. When, at the end of the novel, Wilhelm begs him for some kind of sympathy, the hard-boiled Adler brutally rejects him, revealing his hatred for his "soft" son.

Dr. Adler's failure as a father results in Wilhelm's turning to the strange psychologist Dr. Tamkin. Down on his luck, Tamkin is a confidence man hoping to make easy money. He is another one of Bellow's eccentric fast talkers, full of fantastic stories and philosophical and psychological insights. Wilhelm is attracted to him not only because he is a father figure who promises to save him from his dire financial crisis but also because he is one man in a cynical society who speaks of spiritual matters. The direct result of Tamkin's advice is the loss of Wilhelm's money, but while the doctor is a phony whose flamboyant personality enables him to dupe the naïve ex-salesman, he does indirectly allow Wilhelm to obtain a kind of salvation.

Wilhelm is the only character in the novel who is able to forsake his pretender soul. He is a product of society as the other characters are, but he is different from them in his instinctive distaste for the inveterate cynicism at the heart of society. Accepting society's definition of success, he considers himself a failure. He suffers immensely and constantly ponders his life and his errors in the past. Yet while he can at times degenerate into a buffoon indulging in self-pity and hostility, he is also attracted to the idealism that Tamkin occasionally expounds.

A significant moment occurs near the end of the novel when Wilhelm suddenly feels a sense of brotherhood with his fellow travelers in the New York subway. For once he has transcended his self-absorption, though he is immediately skeptical of this intuitive moment. At the very end of the novel, there is another heightened moment in which he does make the breakthrough foreshadowed in the subway scene. Having lost all of his money, he pursues into a funeral home a man who resembles Tamkin. Suddenly he finds himself confronting a corpse, and he begins to weep uncontrollably. His weeping is not merely out of self-pity, as some have suggested, but for humankind. Understanding that death and suffering are an inextricable part of the human condition, he feels humility and is able to overcome his excessive self-absorption. He is finally able to cast off his pretender soul. The work concludes with a powerful affirmation and suggests an alternative to the spiritual death of a materialistic, predatory society.

HENDERSON THE RAIN KING

Bellow's next novel, *Henderson the Rain King*, is the first fully realized work of his maturity. It is Bellow's first novel of which one can say that no other

writer could have conceived it, much less written it. Although it has some characteristics of the picaresque, the fable, and the realistic novel, *Henderson the Rain King* assumes the most widely used form for longer works during the English romantic era—the quest-romance. The tone of the novel is somewhat different from that typically heard in the quest-romance, however; it is exuberant and comic, and the book is full of wit, parody, farce, and ironic juxtapositions.

The novel might be seen as Bellow's version of Joseph Conrad's *Heart of Darkness* (1902). Like Conrad's Marlow, Eugene Henderson recalls his journey into the heart of Africa and his bizarre adventures there, which culminate in his meeting with a Kurtz-like instructor who has a profound influence upon him. While Kurtz reveals to Marlow man's potential for degradation, Dahfu conveys to Henderson man's promise of nobility. With its allusions to William Wordsworth, Samuel Taylor Coleridge, Percy Bysshe Shelley, and William Blake, the novel affirms the possibility of the individual's regeneration by the power of the human imagination; it is a trenchant rejection of Conrad's pessimism.

The novel can be divided into three basic parts: Chapters 1-4 depict Henderson's alienation; chapters 5-9 present his journey to the African tribe of the Arnewi; and chapters 10-22 portray his journey to the African tribe of the Wariri and his spiritual regeneration.

The first section presents Henderson's discursive recollections of his life before he set out for Africa, in which he attempts to reveal the reasons for the journey. While these chapters provide a plethora of information about him, he is never able to articulate the reasons for his "quest," as he calls it. Bellow is suggesting in this section that there are no clear-cut reasons for the African journey. Henderson leaves his wife and family for the African wilderness because of his dissatisfaction with his meaningless existence. A millionaire with tremendous energy but no scope for it, Henderson has spent most of his life suffering or making others suffer. Middle-aged, anxious about his mortality, and unable to satisfy the strident inner voice of "I want, I want," he leaves for Africa, hoping to burst "the spirit's sleep," as he phrases it, echoing Shelley's *The Revolt of Islam* (1818).

With his loyal guide Romilayu, he first visits the Arnewi tribe. These people are "children of light" who represent a healthy existence; they are gentle, peaceful, and innocent. Queen Willatale, who rules the tribe, informs Henderson that man wants to live—"grun-tu-molani." It is an important message for Henderson, but he soon demonstrates that he is unable to follow Willatale's wisdom. Desiring to help the tribe, whose water supply has been infested by frogs, he decides to kill the creatures. His bomb is too powerful and destroys the cistern as well as the frogs. Henderson has violated the code of the Arnewi, who abhor violence and have love for all living creatures.

After Henderson leaves the Arnewi, he visits the Wariri, "the children of darkness," who are violent and hostile, reminiscent of the predatory society of Bellow's earlier novels. He does meet one extraordinary individual, however, and establishes a friendship with him. King Dahfu is a noble man who completes Henderson's education begun with the Arnewi. He perceptively observes that Henderson's basic problem is his avoidance of death: He is an "avoider." Dahfu helps him by persuading him to go down into a lion's den to overcome his anxiety over mortality. Dahfu believes, too, that Henderson can absorb qualities of the lion and slough off his porcine characteristics.

Dahfu is another one of Bellow's eccentric teachers who speaks both wisdom and nonsense. His greatest importance for Henderson is that he embodies the nobility of man, who can by the power of his imagination achieve spiritual regeneration. At the end of the novel, Henderson finally bursts the spirit's sleep and leaves Africa for America. He has a sense of purpose and can love others. He plans to become a physician and will return home to his wife.

HERZOG

Herzog is by most accounts Bellow's best and most difficult novel. It is a retrospective meditation by a middle-aged professor who seeks to understand the reasons for his disastrous past. A complex discursive work, pervaded by sardonic humor, it defies tra-

ditional labeling but owes a debt to the novel of ideas, the psychological novel, the epistolary novel, and the romantic meditative lyric. *Herzog* is a meditative work in which the protagonist compulsively remembers and evaluates his past, striving to avoid complete mental breakdown. There are reminiscences within reminiscences, and the story of Moses Herzog's life is related in fragments. Bellow's method enables the reader to see how Herzog's imagination recollects and assembles the fragments of the past into a meaningful pattern.

Distraught over his recent divorce from his second wife, Madeleine, Herzog has become obsessed with writing letters to everyone connected with that event as well as to important thinkers, living and dead, who concern him. He associates his domestic crisis with the cultural crisis of Western civilization, and therefore he ponders the ethics of Friedrich Nietzsche as well as those of his psychiatrist, Dr. Edvig. His letter-writing is both a symptom of his psychological disintegration and an attempt to meditate upon and make sense of suffering and death.

At his home in the Berkshires, Herzog recalls and meditates upon the events of his recent past; the five-day period of time that he recalls reveals the severity of his psychological deterioration. His mistress Ramona believes that a cure for his nervous state can be found in her Lawrentian sexual passion, but he considers her "ideology" to be mere hedonism; impulsively, he decides to flee from her to Martha's Vineyard, where he has friends. After arriving there, the unstable professor leaves almost immediately and returns to New York. The next evening he has dinner with Ramona and spends the night with her, waking in the middle of the night to write another letter. The following morning he visits a courtroom while waiting for a meeting with his lawyer to discuss a lawsuit against Madeleine. Hearing a brutal child-abuse and murder case causes the distraught professor to associate Madeleine and her lover with the brutal child-murderers; he flies to Chicago to murder them. As he spies upon them, he realizes his assumption is absurd and abandons his plan. The next morning he takes his young daughter Junie for an outing but has a car accident and is arrested by the police for carrying a gun.

He confronts an angry Madeleine at the police station and manages to control his own temper. Later, he is released and returns to his run-down home in the Berkshires, and the novel ends where it began.

Interspersed within these recollections of the immediate past are memories of the more distant past. By piecing these together, one learns the sad story of Herzog's domestic life. Feeling a vague dissatisfaction, the successful professor divorced his first wife Daisy, a sensible midwestern woman, and began affairs with a good-natured Japanese woman, Sono, and the beautiful, bad-tempered Madeleine. After marrying Madeleine, Herzog purchased a house in the Berkshires, where he intended to complete his important book on the Romantics. Soon they returned to Chicago, however, where both saw a psychiatrist, and Madeleine suddenly announced that she wanted a divorce. The shocked Herzog traveled to Europe to recuperate, only to return to Chicago to learn that Madeleine had been having an affair with his best friend and confidant the whole time their marriage had been deteriorating.

Herzog's grim past—his disastrous marriages and the other sad events of his life that he also recalls—becomes emblematic of the pernicious influence of cultural nihilism. Herzog is devoted to basic humanist values but wonders if he must, as the ubiquitous "reality-instructors" insist, become another mass man devoted to a brutal "realism" in the Hobbesian jungle of modern society. His antipathy for the wastelanders' cynicism is strong, but he knows his past idealism has been too naïve. Repeatedly, the "reality instructors" strive to teach ("punish") Herzog with lessons of the "real"—and the "real" is always brutal and cruel. Sandor Himmelstein, Herzog's lawyer and friend, proudly announces that all people are "whores." It is an accurate description not only of Himmelstein but also of his fellow reality instructors. Their cynical view is pervasive in modern society, in which people play roles, sell themselves, and seduce and exploit others for their own selfish ends.

The turning point of the novel is Herzog's revelation in the courtroom episode. Intellectually, he has always known about evil and suffering, but emotionally he has remained innocent. His hearing of the case in which a mother mistreats and murders her son while her lover apathetically watches is too much for him to bear; here is a monstrous evil that cannot be subsumed by any intellectual scheme. In a devastating moment the professor is forced to realize that his idealism is foolish.

At the end of the novel, Herzog has achieved a new consciousness. He recognizes that he has been selfish and excessively absorbed in intellectual abstractions. A prisoner of his private intellectual life, he has cut himself off from ordinary humanity and everyday existence. He sees that his naïve idealism and the wastelanders' cruel "realism" are both escapist and therefore unacceptable attitudes; they allow the individual to evade reality by wearing masks of naïve idealism or self-serving cynicism. The exhausted Herzog decides to abandon his compulsive letter-writing and to stop pondering his past. The threat of madness has passed, and he is on the road to recovery.

MR. SAMMLER'S PLANET

Mr. Sammler's Planet is a meditative novel of sardonic humor and caustic wit. The "action" of the novel centers upon the protagonist's recollection of a brief period of time in the recent past, though there are recollections of a more distant past, too. Once again the mental state of the protagonist is Bellow's main concern. Like Herzog, Artur Sammler has abandoned a scholarly project because he finds rational explanations dissatisfying; they are unable to justify suffering and death. The septuagenarian Sammler is yet another of Bellow's survivors, a lonely humanist in a society populated by brutal "realists."

This seventh novel, however, is not merely a repetition of Bellow's previous works. Sammler is detached and basically unemotional, yet he reveals a mystical bent largely absent in Bellow's other protaganists. He is drawn to the works of Meister Eckhart and other thirteenth century German mystics. While he does not literally believe in their ideas, he finds reading their works soothing. His religious inclination is a recent phenomenon.

Sammler had been reared in a wealthy, secular Jewish family in Krakow. As an adult, he became a haughty, cosmopolitan intellectual, useless to everyone, as he readily admits. On a visit to Poland in 1939, when the Germans suddenly attacked, he, his wife, and others were captured and ordered to dig their own graves as the Nazis waited to murder them. Although his wife was killed in the mass execution, miraculously he escaped by crawling out of his own grave. After the war ended, Sammler and his daughter Shula were rescued from a displaced persons camp by a kind nephew, Dr. Elya Gruner, who became their patron.

The experience of the Holocaust destroyed what little religious inclination Sammler possessed, but in his old age he has become concerned with his spiritual state. Unfortunately, it is difficult to pursue spiritual interests in a materialistic society hostile to them. The basic conflict in the novel is between Sammler's need to ponder the basic questions of existence—a need accentuated by the dying of the noble Gruner—and the distractions of contemporary society. In the primary action of the novel, Sammler's main intention is to visit the dying Gruner, who finds Sammler a source of great comfort. Several "accidents" distract Sammler from his goal, and on the day of his nephew's death, he arrives too late.

The "accidents" which encumber Sammler reveal clearly the "degraded clowning" of contemporary society. Sammler is threatened by a black pickpocket who corners the old man and then exposes himself. In the middle of a lecture he is shouted down by a radical student who says that Sammler is sexually defective. His daughter Shula steals a manuscript from an Indian scholar, and Sammler must waste precious time to recover it. Even Gruner's self-centered children, who have little compassion for their dying father, distract Sammler by their thoughtless actions.

Opposed to Gruner, who is part of the "old system" which esteems the family, the expression of emotion, and the traditional humanist values, is the contemporary generation, a kind of "circus" characterized by role-playing, hedonism, amorality, self-centeredness, and atrophy of feeling. Despite its flaws, Bellow sympathizes with the "old system." The novel concludes after Sammler, despite the objections of the hospital staff, goes into the postmortem room and says a prayer for Gruner's soul.

HUMBOLDT'S GIFT

As in Bellow's previous novels, the tension and the humor of *Humboldt's Gift* have their origin in the protagonist's attempt to free himself from the distractions of contemporary society and pursue the needs of his soul. The protagonist Charlie Citrine strives to define for himself the function of the artist in contemporary America. He tries to come to terms with the failure and premature death of his one-time mentor, Von Humboldt Fleisher, who had the potential to be America's greatest modern poet but achieved very little. Charlie wonders if the romantic poet can survive in a materialistic society; he wonders, too, if he can overcome his fear of the grave and exercise his imagination. A writer who has squandered his talent, Charlie has intimations of terror of the grave and intimations of immortality. He spends much time reading the anthroposophical works of Rudolf Steiner; although he is skeptical of some of Steiner's more esoteric teachings, he is sympathetic to the spiritual world view of anthroposophy, even finding the notion of reincarnation quite persuasive.

The primary nemesis of Charlie's spiritual life is Ronald Cantabile, a small-time criminal. Renata, Charlie's voluptuous mistress, Denise, his ex-wife, and Pierre Thaxter, a confidence man, are also major distractions. When Charlie, on the advice of a friend, refuses to pay Cantabile the money he owes him from a poker game, the criminal harasses him. In fact, the proud, psychopathic Cantabile refuses to leave Charlie alone even after he agrees to pay him the money. He continually humiliates Charlie and even tries to involve him in a plot to murder the troublesome Denise.

Denise, Renata, and Thaxter also distract Charlie from pondering the fate of Humboldt and meditating upon fundamental metaphysical questions. Hoping Charlie will return to her, Denise refuses to settle her support suit and continues to demand more money. When Charlie is forced to put up a two-hundred-thousand-dollar bond, he is financially ruined, and the loss of his money results in the loss of the voluptuous Renata, who decides to marry a wealthy undertaker. A third disillusioning experience involves Thaxter, who has apparently conned Charlie. Charlie had invested a small fortune in a new journal, *The Ark*, which was supposed to restore the authority of art and culture in the United States. Thaxter, the editor of *The Ark*, never puts out the first issue and has, it appears, stolen the money. His confidence game symbolizes America's lack of respect for art and culture, impractical subjects in a practical, technological society.

Charlie does, however, overcome these "distractions." Humboldt's posthumously delivered letter, accompanied by an original film sketch (his "gift") and a scenario that the two had written at Princeton years before, provides the genesis for Charlie's salvation. The original film idea and the scenario of their Princeton years enable Charlie to attain financial security, but more important, Humboldt's letter provides the impetus for Charlie's decision at the end of the novel to repudiate his past empty life and to pursue the life of the imagination. Humboldt's ideas, bolstered by the poetry of Blake, Wordsworth, and John Keats, enable Charlie to avoid the fate of the self-destructive artist. He decides to live in Europe and meditate upon the fundamental questions—in short, to take up a different kind of life.

When, at the end of the novel, Charlie gives Humboldt and the poet's mother a proper burial, Bellow suggests that Charlie's imagination is ready to exert itself and wake him from his self-centered boredom and death-in-life. The final scene of the novel promises Charlie's spiritual regeneration.

THE DEAN'S DECEMBER

Bellow's 1982 novel, *The Dean's December*, is "a tale of two cities," Chicago and Bucharest, in which the protagonist, a dean at an unnamed college in Chicago, ponders private and public problems. Albert Corde experiences at first hand the rigid penitentiary society of the Communist East as well as the anarchic society of the non-Communist West, which seems on the verge of disintegration. The novel is a protest against the dehumanization of the individual. The East has enslaved its population, while the West has "written off" its doomed "Underclass." Like *Humboldt's Gift*, this novel can be seen as a kind of retrospective crisis meditation in which the protagonist attempts to come to terms with an immensely

complex and threatening "multiverse," as Augie March calls it.

The complicated plot defies a succinct summary, but one can outline the basic situation. The dean and his wife, Minna, arrive in Rumania to visit her dying mother. Corde tries to help his despairing wife, who is unable to reconcile herself to the grim reality of her mother's death. He also ponders the controversy that he has provoked in Chicago. The dean has published two articles in *Harper's* in which he comments upon the political and social problems of the city. The articles outrage the powerful members of Chicago society, and the administration of his college disapproves of the controversy that the dean has provoked. Moreover, Corde creates another controversy when he pressures the police to solve the murder of a white graduate student, Rickie Lester. A sensational trial, a media "circus," is the result of the dean's search for justice.

While more than any other novel by Bellow, *The Dean's December* is concerned with contemporary public issues, especially the vile conditions of the inner city, it is also concerned with the spiritual state of the individual. In fact, Bellow suggests that there is a connection between the spiritual malady of the individual and the spiritual anarchy of society. The novel is a protest against not only people's lack of political freedom but also the spiritual enslavement that is the result of their inability to see clearly and to experience reality. Corde implies that this inability to experience reality is largely a product of "seeing" the world with a kind of reductive journalism completely lacking in imagination. Disgusted with contemporary journalism which provides only substitutes for reality, Corde intends to incorporate "poetry" into writing. The novel suggests that in Corde's kind of poetic vision there is hope for the spiritual rebirth of the individual and society.

MORE DIE OF HEARTBREAK

Three years after the publication of his collection *Him with His Foot in His Mouth and Other Stories* (1984), Bellow published *More Die of Heartbreak*. This comic novel does not have a highly structured plot but might be best described as an elaborate monologue from the overstimulated mind of the bachelor narrator, Kenneth Trachtenberg. Kenneth, an expert in Russian history and culture, is preoccupied with his uncle, Benn Crader, a renowned botanist. The only important "action" in the novel revolves around the attempt of Dr. Layamon, his daughter Matilda, and her fiancé Benn Crader to "extort" money from Benn's relative, Harold Vilitzer, a political racketeer in bad health. Years before, Vilitzer had cheated the Crader family in a real estate deal. The greedy Dr. Layamon sees his daughter's marriage to Benn as a marvelous opportunity to acquire a fortune if Benn will agree to pressure Vilitzer for the money the corrupt politician stole from the Crader family. Although he wants to please his beautiful fiancée and her father, Benn is not enthusiastic about the plan. As the narrator suggests, Benn is a man who should be in search of "higher meanings." At the end of the novel, Benn flees from the Layamons to the North Pole to carry out his research. The implication is that now he will be able to pursue his neglected aesthetic and metaphysical goals.

A THEFT

After being rejected by two periodicals because it was "too long," the short novel *A Theft* was published in 1989 as a paperback original. Like so many of Bellow's works, the plot of this 109-page novel is subordinate to Bellow's interest in character. Just as *Seize the Day* might be considered an intimate psychological exploration of Wilhelm, *A Theft* is a detailed exploration of the soul of the heroine. Clara Velde was brought up on old-time religion but has led a disorganized life, including disappointing love affairs, suicide attempts, and four marriages. Her fourth marriage is not successful, and she is actually in love with "an old flame," Ithiel Regler, a Henry Kissinger-like high-powered adviser to statesmen. For Clara, transcendent love between her and Ithiel is symbolized by an emerald ring that he gave her years ago. When this ring is stolen, Clara finds herself in a troubling search for it and experiences a kind of spiritual quest as well. She feels a special sense of kinship with her self-possessed au pair girl, Gina. In its epiphanylike quality, the conclusion of the novel is reminiscent of *Seize the Day*.

THE BELLAROSA CONNECTION

Another paperback original, the short novel *The Bellarosa Connection* is narrated by the wealthy founder of the Mnemosyne Institute in Philadelphia. The institute instructs businesspersons and others in the use of memory. The narrator, a retired widower, focuses his immense powers of recollection on two relatives who haunt him—Harry and Sorella Fonstein. Harry narrowly escaped the Nazi death camps, thanks to the Broadway producer Billy Rose, who made use of his gangster connections in Italy to help Fonstein and others escape to freedom. Billy Rose's generosity is particularly noteworthy, the narrator implies, because the Broadway producer has a sleazy reputation.

In the United States, Harry marries the intelligent, capable Sorella and becomes successful but is frustrated by Rose's repulsing Harry's repeated attempts to meet him and express his gratitude. The central scene of the novel is the dramatic encounter between Sorella and Billy Rose, in which the determined woman attempts to coerce the stubborn producer into meeting her husband by threatening to reveal sordid details of Rose's private life. Despite Sorella's "blackmail," Rose refuses to meet Harry.

As in "The Old System," Bellow in this short novel is pondering how the assimilation of Jews into American life can corrupt not only their values but also their souls. Sorella reflects: "The Jews could survive everything that Europe threw at them. I mean the lucky remnant. But now comes the next test—America." Apparently the United States proves "too much" for at least some of them.

THE ACTUAL

The novella *The Actual* is narrated by Harry Trellman, an introspective man in his sixties who grew up in a lower-middle-class Jewish neighborhood in Chicago. His father was a simple carpenter; his mother's family was wealthy. Harry was put in an orphanage despite the fact that both his parents were alive because his hypochondriacal mother did not have the time to care for him; she spent much time abroad and in the United States at various sanitariums looking for a cure for her disease of the joints. The bills for sojourns abroad and at home were paid by the mother's family; her brothers were successful sausage manufacturers who could pay for the cures she took at Bad Nauheim or Hot Springs, Arkansas.

After the Korean War, the government sent Harry to study Chinese at a "special school." He spent a number of years in the Far East, the final two in Burma, where he made business connections, and then returned to Chicago, where he had "unfinished emotional business." Although the precise source of Harry's income is not clear, apparently he is well off. Semiretired and without financial concerns, Harry is nevertheless far from being content. For more than four decades he has loved Amy Wustrin, whom he first knew in high school. When Harry returned to Chicago after his Far East sojourn, he and Amy met again. Despite for Harry a momentous sexual encounter in which he kissed Amy "under the breast and inside the thigh," the relationship did not progress. After divorcing her first husband, she married Jay Wustrin, Harry's best friend in high school. Both Jay and Amy did not pay much heed to their marriage vows, and the result was a bitter divorce which culminated in Jay's playing tapes in divorce court of Amy's adulterous lovemaking in which one could hear her orgasmic cries. None of this disheartening history dampened Harry's ardent love for Amy.

Harry and Amy are brought together by the ninety-two-year-old billionaire Sigmund Adletsky, for whom Amy is working as an interior decorator and Harry as adviser in his "brain trust." Harry accompanies Amy in her emotionally arduous task of exhuming Jay's body from his cemetery plot next to the grave of Amy's mother so that Amy can bury her father there. (A practical joker with nihilistic proclivities, Jay had purchased the plot from Amy's father.) In the grave scene which concludes the novel, the withdrawn intellectual Harry takes decisive action by confessing his love for Amy and asking her to marry him. This scene is reminiscent of the conclusion to *Humboldt's Gift*, when the protagonist in the cemetery achieves an epiphany and the work ends with the implication that the protagonist, keenly aware of mortality and the death-in-life of his past existence, will be spiritually reborn.

Allan Chavkin

OTHER MAJOR WORKS

SHORT FICTION: *Mosby's Memoirs and Other Stories*, 1968; *Him with His Foot in His Mouth and Other Stories*, 1984; *Something to Remember Me By: Three Tales*, 1991.

PLAYS: *The Wrecker*, pb. 1954; *The Last Analysis*, pr. 1964; *Under the Weather*, pr. 1966 (also known as *The Bellow Plays*; includes *Out from Under*, *A Wen*, and *Orange Soufflé*).

NONFICTION: *To Jerusalem and Back: A Personal Account*, 1976; *It All Adds Up: From the Dim Past to the Uncertain Future*, 1994.

ANTHOLOGY: *Great Jewish Short Stories*, 1963.

BIBLIOGRAPHY

Bigler, Walter. *Figures of Madness in Saul Bellow's Longer Fiction*. Bern, Switzerland: Peter Lang, 1998. This study examines the psychological makeup of Bellow's characters. Includes bibliographical references.

Cronin, Gloria L., and L. H. Goldman. *Saul Bellow in the 1980's: A Collection of Critical Essays*. East Lansing: Michigan State University Press, 1989. This excellent collection of essays contains both general essays on Bellow's canon and specialized essays on individual works. The general essays consider such topics as Bellow's sense of history, his attitude toward Judaism, women in his novels, his allegiance to the English Romantic tradition, his criticism of the university and American culture, and his interest in character as a subject of his books. Includes notes, an index, and an introduction.

Fuchs, Daniel. *Saul Bellow: Vision and Revision*. Durham, N.C.: Duke University Press, 1984. Makes extensive use of Bellow's vast collection of unpublished manuscripts, including his unpublished letters. Fuchs shows the reader how a novel evolves through a number of drafts as Bellow in the process of revision discovers what he wants to say. In the first part, Fuchs analyzes Bellow's literary and cultural milieus, with particular attention to the "modern tradition" and to the "example of Dostoevski." In the second part, he examines specific works from *The Adventures of Augie*

March to *Humboldt's Gift*. Includes detailed discussions of Bellow's play *The Last Analysis* and some of his short stories, as well as a brief discussion of *The Dean's December*. Index.

Goldman, Liela, ed. *Saul Bellow Journal*, 1982-   . Praised in *American Literary Scholarship: An Annual*, this journal is published twice annually and includes articles on Bellow's work and life, book reviews, and a useful annotated critical bibliography.

Hollahan, Eugene, ed. *Saul Bellow and the Struggle at the Center*. New York: AMS Press, 1996. Part of the Georgia State Literary Studies series, this volume includes bibliographical references and an index.

Kiernan, Robert. *Saul Bellow*. New York: Continuum, 1988. This lucidly written book contains chapters on Bellow's fiction, from *Dangling Man* to *More Die of Heartbreak*. Kiernan also presents an introductory chapter on Bellow's life and career. Although Kiernan does not discuss Bellow's drama, he does examine the stories and short novels in the writer's two collections. Includes a chronology; a useful, detailed bibliography of works by and about Bellow; an index; and notes.

ARNOLD BENNETT

Born: Shelton, near Hanley, England; May 27, 1867
Died: London, England; March 27, 1931

PRINCIPAL LONG FICTION

A Man from the North, 1898
Anna of the Five Towns, 1902
The Grand Babylon Hotel, 1902 (pb. in U.S. as *T. Racksole and Daughter*)
The Gates of Wrath, 1903
Leonora, 1903
A Great Man, 1904
Teresa of Watling Street, 1904
Sacred and Profane Love, 1905 (pb. in U.S. as *The Book of Carlotta*)

Hugo, 1906
Whom God Hath Joined, 1906
The Sinews of War, 1906 (with Eden Phillpotts; pb. in U.S. as *Doubloons*)
The Ghost, 1907
The City of Pleasure, 1907
The Statue, 1908 (with Phillpotts)
Buried Alive, 1908
The Old Wives' Tale, 1908
The Glimpse, 1909
Helen with the High Hand, 1910
Clayhanger, 1910
The Card, 1911 (pb. in U.S. as *Denry the Audacious*)
Hilda Lessways, 1911
The Regent, 1913 (pb. in U.S. as *The Old Adam*)
The Price of Love, 1914
These Twain, 1915
The Lion's Share, 1916
The Pretty Lady, 1918
The Roll-Call, 1918
Lilian, 1922
Mr. Prohack, 1922
Riceyman Steps, 1923
Elsie and the Child, 1924
Lord Raingo, 1926
The Strange Vanguard, 1928 (pb. in U.S. as *The Vanguard*, 1927)
Accident, 1928
Piccadilly, 1929
Imperial Palace, 1930
Venus Rising from the Sea, 1931

OTHER LITERARY FORMS

Besides fifteen major novels, Arnold Bennett published thirty-three other novels generally considered potboilers by his critics. Some of them Bennett himself regarded as serious works; others he variously called "fantasias," "frolics," "melodramas," or "adventures." His total published work exceeds eighty volumes, including eight collections of short stories, sixteen plays, six collections of essays, eight volumes of literary criticism, three volumes of letters, six travelogues, and volumes of autobiography, journals, and reviews, as well as miscellaneous short arti-

cles, introductions, pamphlets, "pocket philosophies," and a few poems. Much of his journal has
never been published. Bennett collaborated in the
production of five films and operas, three of which
were adapted from his plays and novels. Four of his
plays and novels were adapted for film by other
screenwriters, and two of his novels were adapted for
the stage.

ACHIEVEMENTS

Although Arnold Bennett won only one major literary award, the James Tait Black Memorial Prize for
Riceyman Steps, his contribution to the history of the
novel exceeds that accomplishment. Bennett's early
novels played an important role in the transition from
the Victorian to the modern novel. A somewhat
younger contemporary of Thomas Hardy, Henry
James, and Joseph Conrad, he helped to displace the
"loose, baggy" Victorian novel and to develop the realistic movement in England. With fine detail he
portrayed the industrial Five Towns, his fictional version of the six towns of pottery manufacturing in

(Library of Congress)

Staffordshire County. His early career was strongly
influenced by the aestheticism in form and language
found in works by Gustave Flaubert, Guy de
Maupassant, and Ivan Turgenev, and he admired the
naturalism of Honoré de Balzac, Émile Zola, and
Edmond and Jules de Goncourt. Later, however, he
rejected what he called the "crudities and . . . morsels
of available misery" of naturalism, and, while retaining an interest in form and beauty, he came to feel
that aesthetics alone is an empty literary goal and that
the novelist must combine "divine compassion," be-
lievability, and the creation of character with the "artistic shapely presentation of truth" and the discovery
of "beauty, which is always hidden." With these aims
in mind, he chose as the subject of his best works that
which is beautiful and remarkable about the lives of
unremarkable, middle-class people. Although his novels rarely sold well enough to earn his living, his best
novels were highly regarded by critics and fellow authors. He carried on a correspondence of mutual encouragement and criticism with Conrad and H. G.
Wells; some of these letters have been published.

Conrad, a master of style, wrote: "I am . . .
fascinated by your expression, by the ease of
your realization, the force and delicacy of
your phrases." Despite their acclaim for
Bennett's best work, however, even his admirers regretted his propensity to write potboilers
for money.

Because of the volume of his work, Bennett is remembered today as a novelist, but in
his lifetime his income derived from his
equally prodigious output of plays and journalism; his "pocket philosophies" and critical
reviews also won him an enormous public
prestige. During the 1920's he was virtually
the arbiter of literary taste, a reviewer who
could make or break a book's sales or a newcomer's career. He was among the first to
praise the literary merits of such controversial
newcomers as D. H. Lawrence, T. S. Eliot,
William Faulkner, Virginia Woolf, and James
Joyce. Bennett regarded himself less a novelist than a professional writer who should be
able to, and did, undertake any genre with

competence and craftsmanship. (The exception was poetry; he never wrote poetry to meet his own standards.) His reputation suffered in the latter part of his career for those very qualities, which too often fell short of genius and inspiration. He did reach the level of greatness occasionally, however, and his literary reputation is firmly established with the inclusion of *The Old Wives' Tale* in most lists of the great English novels.

BIOGRAPHY

Enoch Arnold Bennett was born on May 27, 1867, in Shelton, Staffordshire County, England, near the six towns that constitute the Potteries region in central England, the scene of much of Bennett's early work. His father, Enoch Bennett, was successively a potter, a draper, a pawnbroker, and eventually, through hard work and study, a solicitor. Bennett attended the local schools, where he passed the examination for Cambridge University. He did not attend college, however, because his autocratic father kept him at home as clerk in the solicitor's office.

As a means of escape from the grime and provincialism of the Potteries district, Bennett began writing for the *Staffordshire Sentinel* and studying shorthand. The latter skill enabled him to become a clerk with a London law firm in 1888. In London, he set about seriously to learn to write. He moved to Chelsea in 1891 to live with the Frederick Marriott family, in whose household he was introduced to the larger world of the arts. His first work published in London was a prizewinning parody for a competition in *Tit-Bits* in 1893; this work was followed by a short story in *The Yellow Book* and, in 1898, his first novel, *A Man from the North*. He became the assistant editor and later the editor of the magazine *Woman*, writing reviews pseudonymously as "Barbara," a gossip and advice column as "Marjorie," and short stories as "Sal Volatile." It is generally thought that this experience provided a good background for female characterization. As he became better known as a journalist, Bennett began writing reviews for *The Academy* and giving private lessons in journalism. His journalistic income allowed him in 1900 to establish a home at Trinity Hall Farm, Hockliffe, in Bedfordshire. He

brought his family to Hockliffe after his father had been disabled by the softening of the brain which eventually killed him. Bennett wrote prodigiously there, producing not only his admired *Anna of the Five Towns* but also popular potboilers and journalism, including the anonymous "Savoir-Faire Papers" and "Novelist's Log-Book" series for *T. P.'s Weekly*. This production financed some long-desired travel and a move to Paris in 1903.

Bennett lived in France for eight years, some of the busiest and happiest of his life. Shortly after his arrival, he observed a fat, fussy woman who inspired the thought that "she has been young and slim once," a thought that lingered in his mind for five years and inspired his masterwork, *The Old Wives' Tale*. Meanwhile, he continued writing for newspapers and magazines, including the first of his series "Books and Persons," written under the nom de plume "Jacob Tonson" for *The New Age*. Between 1903 and 1907 he also wrote ten novels. In 1907, he married Marguerite Soulié, an aspiring actress who had worked as his part-time secretary. From the beginning of the marriage, it was evident that the two were incompatible, but she did provide him with an atmosphere conducive to his undertaking the novel which had germinated for so long and which he felt beforehand would be a masterpiece. He determined that *The Old Wives' Tale* should "do one better than" Guy de Maupassant's *Une Vie* (1883), and his careful crafting of the book was recognized by critics, who immediately acclaimed it as a modern classic. Before moving back to England in 1913, he wrote six more novels, three of which are among his best: *Clayhanger, The Card*, and *Hilda Lessways*. In 1911, he traveled in the United States, where his books were selling well and were highly respected. After the tour, he moved to the country estate Comarques at Thorpe-le-Soken, Essex, where he had access to the harbor for a yacht, his means of gaining what relaxation he could.

The yacht was important to Bennett, because he had suffered since youth from a variety of ailments, mostly resulting from his high-strung temperament. He had a serious stammer or speech paralysis, which exhausted him in speaking; compulsive personal habits; and a liver ailment and chronic enteritis which restricted his diet and caused great discomfort when he ate incautiously. As he grew older, he suffered increasingly from excruciating neuralgia, headaches, and insomnia, almost without relief near the end of his life. Except for the yacht, his recreation was to write; he probably wrote his light works as a relief from the tension of the serious novels, yet he demanded good style from himself even for them. His craftsmanship was conscious and intense, and his drive to produce great quantity while still maintaining quality undoubtedly sapped his strength, both physically and psychologically, and contributed to his death at the age of sixty-three.

Bennett's physical maladies were probably exacerbated by World War I and the collapse of his marriage. Although he continued his usual pace of writing during the war—five more novels between 1914 and 1919—much of his energy was spent in patriotic activities ranging from entertaining soldiers to frontline journalism. From May 9, 1918, until the end of the war, he served as volunteer director of British propaganda in France. He refused knighthood for his services. After the war, he tried to restore his depleted finances by writing plays, which had been more remunerative than novels, but the later ones were unsuccessful. In 1921, he and Marguerite separated. He gave her a settlement so generous that for the rest of his life he was under pressure to publish and sell his writing. Contemporary critics believed that these years of low-novel production marked the end of his creativity.

Bennett surprised his critics, however, with *Riceyman Steps*, which was critically acclaimed and was awarded the James Tait Black Memorial Prize, Bennett's only literary award. This was followed by *Lord Raingo* and *Imperial Palace*, as well as six less distinguished novels and one unfinished at his death. This creative resurgence may have resulted in part from his relationship with Dorothy Cheston, who bore his only child, Virginia, in 1926. His journalistic career had never waned, and in the 1920's he continued his "Books and Persons" series in the *Evening Standard*, with a prestige that influenced the reading public and allowed him to promote the careers of

many young authors. Bennett's health was steadily deteriorating, however, and in 1931 he died in his Chiltern Court flat from typhoid fever.

ANALYSIS

As a self-designated professional author, Arnold Bennett not only wrote an extraordinary quantity in a great variety of genres but also created a broad range of themes and characters. A common approach or theme is difficult to detect in a corpus of forty-eight novels, which include fantasy, realism, romance, naturalism, satire, symbolism, comedy, tragedy, melodrama, Freudian psychology, allegory, economics, regionalism, cosmopolitanism, politics, medicine, and war. Nevertheless, in spite of this diversity, Bennett is generally esteemed for his realistic novels, which are considered his serious work. In most, if not all, of these fifteen novels, certain related themes recur, rising from his youthful experiences of growing up in Burslem under the domination of his father. His desire to escape the intellectual, aesthetic, and spiritual stultification of his Burslem environment led to a cluster of themes related to escape: rebellion against the ties of the home conflicting with love for one's roots, aspiration versus complacence and philistinism, fear of failure to escape and fear of failure after escape, and the problem of coping with success if it comes. Another cluster of themes relates to his conflict with his father and the shock of his father's debilitating illness and death: the generation gap, emotional repression by dominating parents, the cyclical influence of parents on their children, a soul parent who vies in influence with the natural parent, degeneration and illness, the pathos of decrepitude in old age, and awe at the purpose or purposelessness of life.

A MAN FROM THE NORTH

A Man from the North, Bennett's first novel, includes the themes of aspiration, emotional repression, the soul parent, illness and death, and failure after escape. It is the story of Richard Larch, an aspiring writer from the Potteries, who goes to London to experience the greater intellectual and moral freedom of a cosmopolis. There he meets his soul father, Mr. Aked, a journalist and failed novelist who introduces Larch to the drama—the "tragedy"—of ordinary lives. Aked, however, is an unsuccessful guide; he dies. Larch is also unable to succeed; he eventually marries a woman he does not love and settles down to the sort of life Aked had described. It is the story of what Bennett himself might have been if he had not succeeded after leaving Burslem.

ANNA OF THE FIVE TOWNS

Anna of the Five Towns, on the other hand, is the story of the failure to escape. Anna is repressed by her overbearing and miserly father; under the influence of her soul mother, Mrs. Sutton, she learns to aspire to a few amenities, such as new clothes for her wedding, but these aspirations come too late to change her life significantly. Accepting the values of the community rather than escaping them, she marries Henry Mynors, her more prosperous suitor, rather than Willie Price, the man she loves in her own way. While the themes of these books are similar, they differ in that Anna stays and copes with her environment with some success. She does not escape Bursley (Bennett's fictional name for Burslem), but she escapes her father's control and improves her perceptions of beauty and human relationships to some degree. The books also differ in that *A Man from the North* presents an unrelentingly grim memory of Burslem. Later, however, Bennett read George Moore's *A Mummer's Wife* (1884), and its section on Burslem showed him that "beauty, which is always hidden," could be found in the lives of its people and in art expressing those lives. Thus, Bennett returned to the locale for *Anna of the Five Towns*, and although the portrayal is still grim, Anna's life has tragic beauty. Anna rebels against the ties of home, but she also has some love for her roots there, in the person of Willie Price.

THE OLD WIVES' TALE

Between *Anna of the Five Towns* and *The Old Wives' Tale*, Bennett wrote eleven minor novels, some of which were serious and some not, but all taught him something that contributed to the greatness of *The Old Wives' Tale*. Several of them were light comedies, and in writing these Bennett developed the assured comic touch which marks even his serious novels. Three of them were Five Towns nov-

els about female characters from various segments of Bursley society; in these he developed those skills in characterizing women which were so admired in his finest novels. These skills were honed in France, where Bennett learned a great deal about the literary presentation of sex. During these years, Bennett said, he learned more about life than he had ever known before.

When Bennett was ready to write his masterpiece, *The Old Wives' Tale*, he had reached full artistic maturity and was at the height of his literary power. He had published one critically acclaimed novel and several others that had allowed him to improve his characterization, especially of women, to temper his realism with humor, and to perfect his themes in various plots. His dislike of Burslem's grime and provincialism had been balanced by compassion for its inhabitants and awareness of what beauty and aspiration could be found there. His personal involvement in the town had been modified by experience in London and Paris, so that he could be objective about the sources of his material. This balance of technique and emotion is reflected in the structure of *The Old Wives' Tale*. The novel counterpoints the lives of two sisters, Constance and Sophia Baines, the first of whom stays in Bursley, while the second leaves but later returns. Their stories parallel not only each other but also those of preceding and succeeding generations. In fact, the first section of the book is subtitled "Mrs. Baines" (the mother).

In section one, *The Old Wives' Tale* takes up in mid-career one generation's old wife, with a husband so ill that the wife is running his draper's business and rearing two young daughters. As the girls grow up, Mrs. Baines finds them increasingly hard to handle. During a town festival in which an elephant has to be executed for killing a spectator, Mr. Baines dies. Shortly afterward, Sophia elopes with Gerald Scales, a traveling salesman, and Constance marries Samuel Povey, the former shop assistant, whom Mrs. Baines considers "beneath" her. When Samuel and Constance take over the business, introducing progressive marketing methods, Mrs. Baines retires to live with her elder sister, and dies there. The story of Mrs. Baines, then, is the end of the life of a woman who "was young and slim once," although she is not depicted so and that part of her life is understood only by later comparison with the stories of her daughters.

The cycle of Mrs. Baines continues with Constance, who represents the person who stays in Bursley, held by the roots of the past. As Mrs. Baines's successor, Constance marries a husband whose aspiration is to improve, not to leave, Bursley, and they run the business with a combination of youthful progressiveness and family tradition. Constance and Samuel have a son, Cyril. After a scandal in which Samuel's cousin is executed for murdering his alcoholic wife, Samuel dies. Constance continues the business for a while, unresponsive to further progressive business practices, and spoils her son until he becomes hard for her to manage. She is finally forced to retire from business by changes in the business structure of Bursley, and Cyril escapes from her and Bursley to London to study art. As a result, Constance comes to depend emotionally on Cyril's cousin, Dick.

Sophia, the rebel against Bursley, finds a soul mother in the schoolteacher, who introduces her to a world of wider intellectual aspiration. In her eagerness to experience more than Bursley offers, however, she elopes with a salesman, who represents sophistication and romance to her. They go to France, where they squander their money and slip into mutual disillusionment and recrimination. After observing the public execution of the murderer of a courtesan, Sophia becomes ill and is abandoned by Gerald. She eventually acquires a boardinghouse in Paris, where she supports several dependents and survives the siege of Paris through single-minded hoarding and hard work. She becomes a reclusive fixture on her street, much like Constance on her square in Bursley. When she becomes ill and the business becomes hard for her to manage, she sells it and returns to Bursley to grow old and die.

Each daughter's life recapitulates Mrs. Baines's in certain respects. Each marries, loses a husband, succors children or other dependents, runs a business, gradually loses control over her life (the change marked in each case by a symbolic execution), loses

health and strength, and retires to die as a burdensome old woman like the one Bennett saw in the Paris restaurant. Further, although they are not women, the two Povey young men, Cyril and his cousin Dick, recapitulate the early years of Sophia and Constance: Cyril, the rebel who leaves Bursley but does not succeed; and Dick, the stay-at-home progressive idealist. At the end, Dick is engaged to marry a slim, young counterpart to Constance, who will no doubt carry on the cycle. The thematic repetitions are not so obvious as they appear here, of course; the variations of individual character allow the reader a sense of more difference than similarity.

The variations also mark a further step in Bennett's use of his themes. Constance and Sophia are not so warped by Bursley as was Anna in *Anna of the Five Towns*; in fact, Sophia, who escapes, is warped more than Constance, who stays. Both have strength derived from their roots, and while neither can be said to escape or to achieve happiness or grace in living, both transcend Bursley more successfully than other townspeople. The theme of their decrepitude in old age is a separate one, also used in other novels, but not related to the escape and success themes. The Baineses are grouped in other Five Towns stories with those who succeed on Bursley's terms. Beginning in 1906 in *Whom God Hath Joined*, in the collection of short stories *The Matador of the Five Towns* (1912), and in *The Old Wives' Tale*, there is a growing emphasis upon those members of Burslem society who have some education, culture, and sophistication. Perhaps Bennett had been reassured by his personal success that his childhood in Burslem could be accepted.

CLAYHANGER

Whether it is true that Bennett had come to accept his past, it is certainly true that his next serious book, *Clayhanger*, was his most nearly autobiographical. After the completion of the trilogy of which *Clayhanger* was the first volume, Bennett turned from the Five Towns to London as the setting for his novels. The Clayhanger trilogy is the story of a man who at first is defeated in his desire to escape Bursley. Having been defeated, however, he learns from his soul father to rise above Bursley's philistinism. Over the years, he breaks one after another of his bonds to Bursley until he has succeeded in escaping intellectually, and, eventually, he completely abandons the Five Towns.

Much of this story occurs in the third volume of the trilogy, *These Twain*. *Clayhanger* itself is the story of the generational conflict between Edwin Clayhanger and his father Darius. The conflict is similar to the one between Anna and her father in *Anna of the Five Towns* and between Sophia and Mrs. Baines in *The Old Wives' Tale*, but in *Clayhanger* it is much more intense and more acutely observed. Edwin is sensitively introduced in the first two chapters; he has within him "a flame . . . like an altar-fire," a passion "to exhaust himself in doing his best." He is rebelling against his father, whose highest aspiration for his son is to have him take over his printing business. The advancement of the theme in *Clayhanger* over its treatment in the earlier novels is that the generational conflict is presented sympathetically on both sides. In chapters 3 and 4, Darius is portrayed as sensitively as Edwin has been previously. In an intensely moving chapter, his childhood of promise, stifled at seven years by poverty and abusive child labor, is described. Because Darius as a "man of nine" was unable to "keep the family," they were sent to the poorhouse. They were rescued from this degradation by Darius's Sunday school teacher (his soul father), who had recognized Darius's promise and who secured Darius a decent job as a printer's devil. This background of deprivation and emotional sterility prevents Darius from expressing his softer emotions, such as his love for Edwin; his total dedication to the business which he built and by which he supports his family is thoroughly empathetic to the reader. It is no wonder that he can conceive nothing nobler for Edwin than to carry on this decent business. Because Darius can never discuss these traumatic childhood experiences, Edwin never understands him any more than Darius understands Edwin.

In his desire to hold onto his son and keep him in the family business, Darius simply ignores and overrides Edwin's inchoate talent for architecture. Later, he uses Edwin's financial dependence to squelch his desire to marry Hilda Lessways, whom Edwin has met through the architect Osmond Orgreave. Although Edwin resents his father's domination, he cannot openly rebel; he feels inadequate before his father's dominance, and he looks forward to the day when he will have his vengeance. This day comes when Darius becomes ill with softening of the brain, the same ailment that killed Bennett's own father. The progression of the illness and Edwin's emotions of triumph, irritation, and compassion are exquisitely detailed. Even after Darius's death, however, Edwin is not free from his father's presence, for he becomes increasingly like his father, learning to take pride in the business and to tyrannize over his sisters and Hilda, with whom he is reconciled at the end of the book. *Clayhanger* thus concludes with the apparent defeat of aspiration by the cycle of parental influence.

HILDA LESSWAYS

The hope of eventual success has been raised, however, by the death of Darius, that primary symbol of Bursley repression, and the return of Hilda, the symbol of aspiration. In *Hilda Lessways*, the second book of the trilogy, Bennett picks up her parallel story of generational conflict with her mother and cultural conflict with Turnhill, another of the Five Towns. Hilda's story is far less compelling than Edwin's, though, and adds little to the plot development. More important, its structure repeats what Bennett did successfully in *The Old Wives' Tale*: It contrasts two efforts to cope with Bursley, which provide for a double perspective on the problem, and then brings them together for the denouement made possible by that combined perspective. The double perspective also allows Bennett to maintain his characteristic objectivity and touch of humor.

THESE TWAIN

These Twain was the last Five Towns novel; it presents the marriage of Edwin and Hilda. Through a series of adjustments and small victories, the two are able to achieve a social success in the Five Towns, which allows them to wean themselves emotionally from the Potteries and leave forever. The *Clayhanger* trilogy thus deals with escape and success, rather than some aspect of failure as in the earlier novels.

In changing his fictional settings from Bursley to London or the Continent, Bennett also extended his themes from success or failure in escaping poverty and provincialism to success or failure in handling the accomplished escape. Perhaps that is another reason, besides the ones usually offered, for Bennett's long period of low productivity and substandard potboilers from 1915 to 1922. Between *Anna of the Five Towns* and *The Old Wives' Tale*, one should remember, there had been a similar period of low-quality work during which Bennett perfected skills that made the Five Towns novels great. Similarly, in his postwar characters Audrey Moze, George Cannon, G. J. Hoape, Lilian Share, and Mr. Prohack, Bennett experimented with stories of people who must cope with financial or social responsibilities for which they may have been poorly prepared. Also in these stories he experimented more boldly with varieties of sexual relationships: in *The Lion's Share*, implied lesbianism; in *The Pretty Lady*, prostitution; in *Lilian*, a mistress. Furthermore, although these next qualities do not show up clearly in the low-quality work of this period, the use of symbols and psychological insight must have been developing in Bennett's mind. These qualities emerge rather suddenly and very effectively in the novels beginning with *Riceyman Steps*. They may account for some of the high acclaim which that novel received after the period of reorientation, but the adapted themes were perfected by 1923, as well.

RICEYMAN STEPS

The themes in *Riceyman Steps* are variations on those of the Five Towns novels, not departures which might seem necessary to a metropolitan setting. The decayed and grimy industrial area of Clerkenwell is in many respects Bursley resituated in London. Henry Earlforward, the miser, represents Bursley's industrial materialism. Henry, like Edwin Clayhanger, has succeeded in that environment; he has a well-respected bookstore that offers him financial self-sufficiency. Unlike Edwin, however, Henry's complacent rootedness to Clerkenwell progressively cuts him off from grace, beauty, then love, and finally even life. His wife, Violet, also has financial security, but because she fears the loss of her success, she has become almost as miserly as he. Both are described as sensual; Henry's rich red lips are mentioned sev-

eral times, and Violet, formerly a widow, wears red flowers in her hat. Money, however, is the chief object of their eroticism. Henry's miserliness is his passion, and he gives Violet her own safe as a wedding gift. Violet becomes "liquid with acquiescence" after seeing the hoarded disorder of his house, and she urges him to bed after he has shown her the gold coins in his private safe. The passion for money soon overrides the related passion of human love. Henry especially, and Violet in acquiescence, lock doors more tightly about themselves to protect their treasures until each is figuratively shut into a private, iron-walled safe. Starving emotionally and intellectually in their isolation, they finally starve themselves physically as well, rather than spend money for adequate food. Here, aspiration gone awry, the fear of failure and the inability to cope with success become literally debilitating diseases. Violet dies of a tumor and malnutrition and Henry of cancer. After death, they are scarcely missed, the ultimate symbols of the stultification which Bennett's characters strive with varying success to escape.

FINAL YEARS

After *Riceyman Steps*, the next few novels—*Lord Raingo, Accident*, and *Imperial Palace*—continue the themes of coping with success, and the protagonists are given increasing ability to handle it. Much as Clayhanger finally overcomes the problems of escape, Evelyn Orcham in *Imperial Palace* is the culminating figure in the second cluster of themes. Ironically, Bennett died shortly after he had resolved the problems underlying the themes of his serious novels.

All of Bennett's serious works are firmly rooted in the realistic tradition (although he used more symbolism than has generally been recognized), and he excelled in the presentation of detail that makes his themes and characters credible. In the late years of his career, he was criticized by Virginia Woolf for portraying people's surroundings, rather than the people themselves, and forcing his readers to do his imagining for him, even though he believed that character creating was one of the three most important functions of a novel. Woolf's criticism was sound enough to seriously damage Bennett's standing as a major novelist, and it has been the keystone of critical opinion ever since. Yet, a sense of environmental impact has always been accepted as an important means of characterization in realistic literature. Woolf's criticism says as much about changing styles in literature as it does about the merits of Bennett's fiction. More important, it was a criticism aimed at Bennett's total canon, since his potboilers had not yet died of their natural ailments when Woolf wrote. Sophia and Constance Baines, Edwin and Darius Clayhanger, and Henry Earlforward are finely articulated, memorable characters. It is, after all, for his best work that any artist is remembered. Bennett's sense of place, characters, and universality of themes combine to make his finest novels memorable; *The Old Wives' Tale* is sufficient to secure Bennett's stature as one of the outstanding novelists of his era.

Carol I. Croxton

OTHER MAJOR WORKS

SHORT FICTION: *The Loot of Cities*, 1905; *Tales of the Five Towns*, 1905; *The Grim Smile of the Five Towns*, 1907; *The Matador of the Five Towns*, 1912; *The Woman Who Stole Everything*, 1927; *Selected Tales*, 1928; *The Night Visitor*, 1931.

PLAYS: *Polite Farces*, pb. 1899; *Cupid and Commonsense*, pr. 1908; *What the Public Wants*, pr., pb. 1909; *The Honeymoon: A Comedy in Three Acts*, pr., pb. 1911; *Milestones: A Play in Three Acts*, pr., pb. 1912 (with Edward Knoblock); *The Great Adventure: A Play of Fantasia in Four Sets*, pr. 1912; *The Title*, pr., pb. 1918; *Judith*, pr., pb. 1919; *Sacred and Profane Love*, pr., pb. 1919; *Body and Soul*, pr., pb. 1922; *The Love Match*, pr., pb. 1922; *Don Juan*, pb. 1923; *London Life*, pr., pb. 1924 (with Knoblock); *Flora*, pr. 1927; *Mr. Prohack*, pr., pb. 1927 (with Knoblock); *The Return Journey*, pr., pb. 1928.

NONFICTION: *Journalism for Women*, 1898; *Fame and Fiction*, 1901; *The Truth About an Author*, 1903; *How to Become an Author*, 1903; *Things That Interested Me*, 1906; *Things Which Have Interested Me*, 1907, 1908; *Books and Persons: Being Comments on a Past Epoch*, 1908-1911; *Literary Taste*, 1909; *Those United States*, 1912 (pb. in U.S. as *Your United States*); *Paris Nights*, 1913; *From the Log of the Velsa*, 1914; *The Author's Craft*, 1914; *Over There*, 1915; *Things That Have Interested Me*, 1921, 1923, 1926; *Selected Essays*, 1926; *Mediterranean Scenes*, 1928; *The Savour of Life*, 1928; *The Journals of Arnold Bennett*, 1929, 1930, 1932-1933.

BIBLIOGRAPHY

Batchelor, John. *The Edwardian Novelists*. New York: St. Martin's Press, 1982. After quoting Virginia Woolf's reservations about Bennett's fiction, Batchelor goes on to compare the two novelists, especially in terms of their treatment of women as being socially conditioned. In addition to discussing *Clayhanger*, *A Man from the North*, *Anna of the Five Towns*, and *The Old Wives' Tale*, Batchelor examines Bennett's acclaimed short story "The Death of Simon Fuge."

Drabble, Margaret. *Arnold Bennett*. New York: Alfred A. Knopf, 1974. Drawing from Bennett's *Journals* and letters, this biography focuses on Bennett's background, childhood, and environment, which she ties to his literary works. Profusely illustrated, containing an excellent index (the entry under Bennett provides a capsule summary of his life) and a bibliography of Bennett's work.

Lucas, John. *Arnold Bennett: A Study of His Fiction*. London: Methuen, 1974. After a brief review of Bennett criticism, Lucas examines Bennett's fiction, devoting lengthy treatments to his major novels which are discussed in terms of character and plot. Ardently defends Bennett's realism, which is regarded as equal to that of D. H. Lawrence. This impressionistic study lacks documentation, except for copious quotations from Bennett's work.

Roby, Kinley. *A Writer at War: Arnold Bennett, 1914-1918*. Baton Rouge: Louisiana State University Press, 1972. Although primarily biographical, this book also offers valuable insights into Bennett's work during and after World War I. Defends Bennett's post-1914 work, contending that it was influenced by Bennett's exhaustion of his Five Towns material, by his steadily deteriorating relationship with his wife, Marguerite, and by the war itself. Contains works cited and an excellent index.

Squillace, Robert. *Modernism, Modernity, and Arnold Bennett*. Lewisburg, Pa.: Bucknell University Press, 1997. Squillace argues that Bennett saw more clearly than his contemporary novelists the emergence of the modern era, which transformed a male-dominated society to one open to all people regardless of class or gender. Very detailed notes and a bibliography acknowledge the work of the best scholars.

Wright, Walter F. *Arnold Bennett: Romantic Realist*. Lincoln: University of Nebraska Press, 1971. Sees Bennett as vacillating between the two extremes of Romanticism and realism and describes his novels as mildly experimental.

THOMAS BERGER

Born: Cincinnati, Ohio; July 20, 1924

PRINCIPAL LONG FICTION

Crazy in Berlin, 1958
Reinhart in Love, 1962
Little Big Man, 1964
Killing Time, 1967
Vital Parts, 1970
Regiment of Women, 1973
Sneaky People, 1975
Who Is Teddy Villanova?, 1977
Arthur Rex, 1978
Neighbors, 1980
Reinhart's Women, 1981
The Feud, 1983
Nowhere, 1985
Being Invisible, 1987
The Houseguest, 1988
Changing the Past, 1989
Orrie's Story, 1990
Meeting Evil, 1992
Robert Crews, 1995
Suspects, 1996
The Return of Little Big Man, 1999

OTHER LITERARY FORMS

Thomas Berger has published numerous articles, reviews, and short stories in magazines such as the *Saturday Evening Post*, *Esquire*, *Harper's*, and *Playboy*. He has written three plays, all unpublished, but one of which, *Other People*, was staged in 1970 at the Berkshire Theatre Festival in Massachusetts.

ACHIEVEMENTS

Berger is one of America's most productive, most respected, and most challenging literary figures. His novels, including the highly acclaimed *Little Big Man* and critically and popularly successful works such as *Who Is Teddy Villanova?* and *Neighbors*, seem sure to earn for him a lasting place in American letters. His Reinhart series is one of the most singular and significant accomplishments of postwar American literature, forming as it does both a sociological epic and an index to the changing face of the American novel in the second half of the twentieth century. Acknowledged as a masterful prose stylist, Berger writes novels that are aggressively intelligent without being ostentatiously "difficult," works that are often hilariously funny without losing their serious bite.

In 1970, Richard Schickel correctly identified Berger as "one of the most radical sensibilities now writing in America" and bemoaned the fact that Berger had not received the recognition he deserved. More than a decade later, Thomas R. Edwards intensified this complaint with the charge that the failure to read and discuss Berger's work was no less than "a national disgrace." Edwards, however, was writing on the front page of *The New York Times Book Review*, and his praise for *Neighbors* was flanked by an interview with Berger, conducted by Schickel. In short, the recognition and acclaim that so long eluded Berger's writing seemed to be catching up with his career, and a growing number of doctoral dissertations and scholarly articles indicate that his work is being studied as well as applauded. Reviewing *Neighbors* for the *Chicago Tribune*, Frederick Busch may have best summed up Berger's stature as a novelist when he said: "This is a novel by Thomas Berger, and everything he writes should be read and considered."

BIOGRAPHY

Thomas Louis Berger was born in Cincinnati, Ohio, on July 20, 1924, and grew up in the nearby suburban community of Lockland. Disenchanted after a short bout with college, Berger enlisted in the Army, serving from 1943 to 1946, his experiences giving him some of the background for his first novel, *Crazy in Berlin.*

After the war, he returned to college, receiving his B.A. at the University of Cincinnati in 1948. He continued his studies as a graduate student in English at Columbia (1950-1951), where he completed course work for an M.A., and he began a thesis on George Orwell, never completing it. Instead, Berger turned his attention to the writers' workshop at the New School for Social Research. In that workshop, under the aegis of Charles Glicksberg, Berger began to write short stories. "I produced one story a week for three months, most of them melancholy in tone, maudlin in spirit, and simple of mind," he recounts, "Hemingway then being my model." Berger dismisses his short fiction, explaining "the marathon is my event, and not the hundred-yard dash." Despite this assessment, Berger's short fiction has appeared in magazines ranging from the *Saturday Evening Post* to *Harper's*, *Esquire*, *Playboy*, and *North American Review.*

From 1948 through 1951, Berger supported his writing by working as a librarian at the Rand School of Social Science. Between 1951 and 1952, he was a staff member of *The New York Times Index*, and the following year he was a copy editor for *Popular Science Monthly.* In 1956 Berger and his wife toured western Europe, including France, Italy, Austria, and Germany. Revisiting the scene of his army experience in Germany allowed him the emotional distance to abandon his work in progress and to begin and complete his first published novel, *Crazy in Berlin.* Until 1964 and the publication of his third novel, *Little Big Man*, Berger had to supplement the income from his fiction with freelance editing. From 1971 to 1973, Berger wrote a characteristically idiosyncratic film column for *Esquire*, managing to discuss almost everything *but* major motion pictures of the day.

In 1950, Berger married Jeanne Redpath, an artist he met at the New School. He has moved about, living, among other places, in London and on an island in Maine. In 1981-1982, Berger was a visiting lecturer at Yale, and in 1986 he was given an honorary doctor of letters degree by Long Island University.

ANALYSIS

The dust-jacket blurb written by Thomas Berger for *Who Is Teddy Villanova?* reviews the general scheme of his career, pointing out that each of his novels "celebrates another classic genre of fiction: the western [*Little Big Man*], the childhood memoir [*Sneaky People*], the anatomical romance [*Regiment of Women*], the true-crime documentary [*Killing Time*], and the Reinhart books [*Crazy in Berlin*, *Reinhart in Love*, and *Vital Parts*] together form a sociological epic." *Who Is Teddy Villanova?* extended this pattern to the classic American hard-boiled detective story, *Arthur Rex* extended it to Arthurian romance, *Neighbors* traces its lineage most directly to Franz Kafka, and *Reinhart's Women* continues the Reinhart series. In similar fashion, *The Feud* offers Dreiserian slice-of-life naturalism, *Nowhere* celebrates the utopian fantasy, *Being Invisible* acknowledges its precursors in the invisibility narratives of both H. G. Wells and Ralph Ellison, and with *Orrie's Story*, Berger "reinvents" the Greek tragedy of the Oresteia. The mistaken notion that these "celebrations" of classic novel forms are really parodies has dogged Berger's career, but unlike parody, his novels start from rather than aim toward literary traditions; he achieves a testing and broadening of possibilities rather than a burlesquing of limitations. If anything, his celebrations serve as kinds of *deparodisations*, twisting genres already self-conscious to the point of parody in ways that radically defamiliarize them. The variety of Berger's novels, a range with no equal in contemporary American literature, underlines the precision of his craft while distracting readers from the steadiness and the seriousness of his purpose.

Most critics have failed to consider that Berger's manipulations of novel forms are ultimately self-exploring and reflexive literary experiments. He tries to make of each novel an "independent existence," an alternative verbal reality he hopes the reader will approach "without the luggage of received ideas, a priori assumptions, sociopolitical axes to grind, or feeble moralities in search of support." This verbal world both owes its existence to a number of traditional and arbitrary literary conventions of representation and seeks to remind the reader that the working of those conventions is of interest and significance in itself—not only as a means to the representation of reality.

Failing to appreciate the independent existence of Berger's fictional worlds, reviewers have misread *Little Big Man* as an indictment of American abuse of Native Americans, *Regiment of Women* as a polemic for or against the women's movement, *Neighbors* as a critique of suburban life, and so on. Such a topical approach to these novels ignores the possibility that Berger's real theme is language, and that underlying the manically different surfaces of his novels is a constant preoccupation with the ways in which problems of human existence stem from the confusion of language with reality. Again and again, Berger's novels find new ways to suggest that the structures and institutions that order and give meaning to existence are much less important than the ways in which one talks about them, and that the ways one talks about those organizing beliefs inevitably have been designed by someone to influence and/or manipulate someone else's perception and judgment. His ex-wife spells this out for Reinhart when she chides: "It ought to begin to occur to you that life is just a collection of stories from all points of self-interest."

Accordingly, the lives of Berger's characters are affected more by words than by actions. Victimized by definitions that exclude or threaten them, by rhetoric that makes them lose sight of physical facts, and by language designed more to preclude than to encourage clear thinking, his characters are enslaved by language. For this reason, the plot of a Berger novel typically chronicles the efforts of the protagonist to free himself from someone else's verbal version of reality. In this way, Jack Crabb in *Little Big Man* bounces back and forth not only between white and plains Indian cultures, but also between competing codes of conduct designed to legitimize all manner of cruelty. Berger shows how Jack's greatest problems

are actually matters of definition, as he inevitably finds himself defined as white when the situation is controlled by Native Americans and as Native American when the situation is controlled by whites. All of Berger's novels explore the processes of victimization, as each Berger protagonist struggles, whether consciously or unconsciously, to free himself from the inexorable tendency to think of himself as a victim of outrages and impositions, both humorously small and tragically large.

While Berger refuses to subscribe to any single codified philosophy, whether romantic, existential, or absurd, his characters do live in worlds that seem to operate largely on Nietzschean principles. As Frederick Turner has observed, Berger's moral stance is consistently "beyond sentimentality, beyond classic American liberalism," concerning itself with fundamentals rather than with surfaces. Like philosopher Friedrich Nietzsche, Berger assumes that "there are higher problems than the problems of pleasure and pain and sympathy," though few of his characters would subscribe to this view—their pleasure, their pain, and their sympathy being of paramount importance to them.

Those characters are a string of outrageously impossible but compellingly plausible individuals who seem, in Berger's words, to be "persistent liars" and "monsters of one persuasion or another." Berger is uniformly fond of these "monsters," and his characters can never be branded as "good" or "evil," since all are as appealing in their often bizarre excesses as they are sadly humorous in their deficiencies. Most important, all of Berger's characters *do their best*. They may trick, abuse, and betray one another, but in a world where understanding seems full of drawbacks and the irresponsible consistently victimize those who feel obligations, they are finally no more nor less than normal. In the courtroom of his novels, Berger refuses to become either judge or advocate, choosing instead to establish a dialectic of wildly opposing viewpoints. He explains that his job is to maintain these characters in equilibrium, a concern of "art and not politics or sociology."

No analysis of Berger's novels would be complete without mentioning the delights of his prose style.

Berger is one of a handful of American writers, contemporary or otherwise, for whom the sentence is an event in itself. His style challenges the reader with precise but often elaborate or serpentine sentences, reflecting his conviction that "the sentence is the cell beyond which the life of the book cannot be traced, a novel being a structure of such cells: most must be vital or the body is dead." What sentence vitality means to Berger can be seen in the way he elaborates the commonplace metaphor of the "ham-fisted" punch in *Who Is Teddy Villanova?*:

> He had struck me on the forehead, that helmet of protective bone, an impractical stroke even for such stout fingers as his, had he not turned his hand on edge and presented to my skull the resilient karate blade that swells out between the base of the smallest digit and the wrist: in his case, the size and consistency of the fleshy side of a loin of pork.

This marvelous punch knocks out Russell Wren, Berger's private-eye narrator, who comes to with the equally meticulous and mannered realization: "My loafers were in a position just ahead of his coal-barge brogans, a yard from where I slumped; meanwhile, my feet, twisted on their edges and crushed under the crease between thigh and buttock, were only stockinged: he had knocked me out of my shoes!" Leonard Michaels described this style as "one of the great pleasures of the book . . . educated, complicated, graceful, silly, destructive in spirit," and his comment applies to all of Berger's novels. Noting that he looks for himself through the English language, Berger states that for him language is "a morality and a politics and a religion."

CRAZY IN BERLIN

In Berger's first novel, *Crazy in Berlin*, the twenty-one-year-old Carlo Reinhart, a United States Army medic in occupied Berlin, struggles to reconcile the conflicting claims of Nazism, Judaism, Communism, and Americanism, and his own German heritage—all overshadowed by the more fundamental concepts of friendship, victimization, and survival. This first of the Reinhart novels also features the points of view of a manic series of contradictory characters, including an American intelligence officer who is an idealistic Communist, a Russian officer who wants to become a capitalist, and a cynical ex-Nazi now working as a Russian agent.

REINHART IN LOVE

In the second Reinhart novel, *Reinhart in Love*, Berger's bumbling protagonist is discharged from the army, in which he had been happy, and returns to civilian life, which he finds singularly disastrous. His comic misadventures are guided by Claude Humbold, a wonderfully devious real-estate agent/con man for whom Reinhart reluctantly works, by the enterprising and calculating Genevieve Raven, whom he is tricked into marrying, and by Splendor Mainwaring, his black friend whose special talent is getting Reinhart into impossible situations.

LITTLE BIG MAN

Had Berger never written anything but *Little Big Man*, he would have earned a respected place in American literary history. This story of Jack Crabb's life in both the Cheyenne and white cultures of the historical as well as the dime-novel Old West has been called variously "the best novel about the West," "a Barthian western," and "a seminal event in what must now seem the most significant cultural and literary trend of the last decade—the attempt on many fronts to develop structures, styles, ways of thinking that are beyond any version of ethnocentricism." The story has been transcribed ostensibly from the tape-recorded reminiscences of "the late Jack Crabb—frontiersman, American Indian scout, gunfighter, buffalo hunter, adopted Cheyenne—in his final days upon this earth." That Jack's final days come 111 years after his first, and that he also claims to have been the sole white survivor of the Battle of the Little Bighorn, raises obvious questions about the truth of his account. Furthermore, Jack's narrative comes to the reader through the patently unreliable editorship of "Ralph Fielding Snell," a fatuous, gullible, self-professed "man of letters" who also happens to mention that he has suffered three or four nervous breakdowns in the past few years. Against these reflexive, metafictional devices, Berger balances the disarming realism of Jack Crabb's narration, its tone resonating with the wondering honesty and credibility of Huck Finn.

Frederick Turner has noted that part of the real power of this narration is derived from Jack's coming "to understand both myth and history as radically human constructs." What Turner means by "radically human constructs" can be understood from the way in which *Little Big Man* combines very different rhetorics or "codes" for talking about the Old West. Indeed, Jack's narrative consists of excerpts from and imitations of actual histories of the West, autobiographies, dime novels, Native American studies, and other codes that are mixed together in unpredictable combinations. This jumbling of codes and vocabularies (for example, Jack may mingle the crassest of frontier expressions with terms such as "colloquy," "circumferentially," "hitherto," or "tumult") exposes the perceptual biases of the "official" codes which have been developed for talking about the Old West—whether by Zane Grey, Francis Parkman, or L. A. Hoebel (an expert on Cheyenne culture). Jack begins to realize that even when his situation seems to be defined by bullets or arrows, the real conflict lies in the clash between the often antithetical ways in which he must think of himself, whether he is to define himself and act according to Cheyenne terms, cavalry terms, capitalist terms, journalistic terms, and so on.

Accordingly, the panorama of Jack's adventures, ranging from his adoption by the Cheyenne to his gunfight with Wild Bill Hickok to his being the only white survivor of Custer's Last Stand, is shadowed by the panorama of his changing narrative styles: Not only does Berger pack every classic Western theme into the novel, but he also fills it with subtly varied "codes" that make it—like all of his novels—at least in part an exploration of the workings of language. The genius of this novel is that its metafictional devices are so well woven into the fabric of Jack's fascinating story that they have eluded all but a handful of readers, reviewers, and scholars. By any standards, *Little Big Man* is a masterpiece, one of the most delightful novels ever written.

KILLING TIME

Killing Time is a kind of reflexive, even self-destructive murder mystery. Based in part on accounts by Frederic Wertham in *The Show of Violence* (1949)

and Quentin Reynolds in *Courtroom* (1950) of an actual sensational murder case in 1937, *Killing Time* tells the story of Joseph Detweiler, "an awfully nice guy" who is also a psychopathic murderer. The novel opens with the discovery that someone has murdered three people in an apartment. The plot seems to be developing into a routine murder mystery or police procedural as the investigative machinery goes into action, but the murderer, Joe Detweiler, turns himself in even before police suspicions about him crystallize. The balance of the novel, therefore, focuses on Detweiler's conversations with the police and his lawyer. Berger's book declines, however, to become a courtroom drama and proceeds instead through a variety of conventions from the detective story and the psychological thriller, to the courtroom drama and other well-codified genres.

Although Joe is a multiple murderer and is quite mad, all other personalities in *Killing Time* lack character in comparison. Joe is the criminal, but he alone among the policemen, lawyers, and judges truly believes in law and justice. His philosophy is bizarre, but Joe manages to change the perspectives of all those who know him. What really separates Joe from those around him is his profound mistrust of language. He sees actions as truth, while language is just "talking about talk."

To a significant extent, Berger is "talking about talk" in *Killing Time*, just as he is exploring the nature of language and the nature of fiction, for this is a supremely reflexive novel. The book is full of fictions within its larger fictional frame; all the characters apart from Joe are cast as conscious and unconscious makers of fiction. For example, Joe's lawyer derives his greatest satisfaction from "a favorable verdict returned by a jury who knew it had been hoaxed," and he explains to Joe that in the courtroom, "reality is what the jury believes." By presenting character after character whose verbal deceptions and artistry are obviously analogous to the techniques of the novelist (one character even becomes a novelist), and by putting his characters in situations analogous to that of the reader of a novel, Berger reminds his reader that the novel is just as much a hoax as any of those created by its characters. As Berger most bluntly states in the front of the book: "A novel is a construction of language and otherwise a lie."

VITAL PARTS

Vital Parts, the third Reinhart novel, picks up the adventures of its protagonist in the 1960's, as the forty-four-year-old Reinhart rapidly adds to the list of windmills with which he has unsuccessfully tilted. Bob Sweet, a flashy boyhood acquaintance, replaces Claude Humbold as his business mentor, luring him into his most dubious venture to date: a cryonics foundation for freezing the dead. His tough-minded wife, Genevieve, and his surly hippie son, Blaine, both despise him, while Winona, his fat, unhappy, sweetly innocent daughter worships him. Caught in a cultural crossfire, Reinhart threatens to succumb to the pressures and perversities of modern life.

REGIMENT OF WOMEN

Berger's next novel, *Regiment of Women*, managed to offend reviewers and readers on both sides of the women's movement. A dystopian novel set in America in the year 2047, the book presents a society in which traditional male and female roles have been completely reversed. Not only do women control the corporate, artistic, legal, and military machinery of this society, but also they sexually dominate it, strapping dildos over their pants to assault men. In such an inverted society, to be "manly" is to wear dresses and makeup, to hold only powerless jobs, to have silicone breast implants, and to be emotionally incapable of rational thought or significant action. To be "effeminate" is to bind breasts, to wear false beards, to dress in pants and suits, to be rough, physical, aggressive, and to have a reduced life expectancy caused by stress.

Berger's protagonist in this future world is a twenty-nine-year-old insecurity riddled male secretary named Georgie Cornell. An unlikely sequence of events lands him first in prison, arrested for wearing women's clothing (slacks, shirt, tie, and coat) and incorrectly suspected of being a men's liberation agent. Driven to discover accidentally that he is stronger than his female captors, Georgie escapes and is promptly appropriated as an agent/hero by the men's liberation underground. For the rest of the novel, Georgie struggles to discover his "natural" identity, a process which forces him to cast off received idea after received idea, discarding sexual generalizations to forge a particular definition of self. He is joined in this "rebellion" by a female FBI agent so demented that she wants only to be "masculine"—to wear dresses and makeup, to be gentle and sensitive.

Despite its topical focus, *Regiment of Women* is fundamentally concerned not with sexual roles but with the more basic problem of the hypostatizing power of language. From start to finish, the novel reminds the reader that Georgie's reality has been almost completely gloved by language, and in so doing, also calls attention both to the way language operates in the reader's reality and to the ways in which a novelist manipulates language to create an independent "reality." At the bottom of this concern with language and rhetoric lies Berger's belief that victimization in any realm starts as a linguistic phenomenon in which the generalizations and attendant rhetoric of some self-interest part company with the particulars of immediate experience. Accordingly, *Regiment of Women* is a book much more concerned with the discovery of true individuality and freedom and with the workings of language than with sexual politics.

SNEAKY PEOPLE

Berger's seventh novel, *Sneaky People*, is easily his most gentle (although much of its action concerns plans for a murder). *Sneaky People* reveals Berger's ear for the American vernacular as it chronicles the coming of age of a young boy, Ralph Sandifer, in a dreamy small-town world where nothing is as bucolic as it seems. Ralph's father owns a used-car lot and plans to have one of his employees murder Ralph's mother. The drab, mousy-seeming mother secretly writes and sells pornography of the must lurid sort. Indeed, this is a book which seems to say that it is "sneaky" acts which best reveal character, and it is a book that is itself something of a sneaky act, and continues Berger's obsession with the nature of language.

Berger has described *Sneaky People* as "my tribute to the American language of 1939—to be philologically precise, that of the lower-middle class in the eastern Middle West, on which I am an authority as on nothing else." The characters in this novel speak the vital, unleveled, pre-television American vernacular of the 1930's, and the prose style of *Sneaky People* is in a sense the real subject of the book, reflecting Berger's belief that "the possibilities for wit—and thus for life—decline with the homogenization of language."

WHO IS TEDDY VILLANOVA?

Berger's mastery of and play with prose style reaches its most exuberant high in *Who Is Teddy Villanova?*, which invokes the conventions of the hardboiled detective novel but also defies almost all of the expectations that attend those conventions. *Who Is Teddy Villanova?* gives evidence of Berger's great respect for the masters of this genre—Dashiell Hammett, Raymond Chandler, and Ross Macdonald—but it also adds a number of outlandish twists, most prominent among them being a first-person narrator who introduces himself with "Call me Russell Wren," and who tells his story "in a rococo style reminiscent by turns of Thomas De Quincey, Thomas Babington Macaulay, and Sir Thomas Malory." Wren is an ex-instructor of English more concerned with finding readers for the play he is writing than with finding out why a series of thugs and policemen brutalize him either in search of or in the name of a mysterious Teddy Villanova, about whom Wren knows absolutely nothing. The novel follows Wren through one misadventure after another as he pursues the elusive Villanova with Ahab's passion and some curiously "fishy" metaphors (a huge thug slips thorugh a doorway "as deftly as a perch fins among subaqueous rocks").

In truth, Wren does confuse his own small-fish situation with that of Herman Melville's great quest, and his confusion is symptomatic of a more profound problem: When faced with experience, Wren always tries to organize it in terms of the fictional worlds of literary and television private eyes. Like Ralph Fielding Snell in *Little Big Man*, another preposterous "man of letters," Wren perpetually falls victim to his own linguistic hypostatizations as he persistently confuses the literary life of fictional detectives with his own situation. A detective who questions him observes: "I suspect you are living the legend of the private eye, which I confess I had always believed mythical." Wren's narrative style is governed by his immersion in the literary myth of the private eye and his prose style is governed by his pseudointellectual background, producing such wonderfully incongruous lines as: "This wench is my ward . . . Toy with her fine foot if you like, but eschew her quivering thigh and the demesnes that there adjacent lie." The result is humorously self-conscious, almost forcing the reader to step back from the action of the novel and consider its implications for the act of reading and for language use itself.

ARTHUR REX

Its dust jacket announces that *Arthur Rex* is "Thomas Berger's salute to the Age of Chivalry from his own enmired situation in the Time of the Cad," and this novel has been prominently praised as "the Arthur story for our times." Berger brings to the Arthur legend both a profound respect for its mythic power and a modern perspective on the nature of its myth, as can be seen in a comment by Sir Gawaine, when, late in his life, he is asked if he does not long for the old days of action. Gawaine answers no, explaining:

> I am happy to have had them in my proper time, but of a life of adventure it can be said that there is no abiding satisfaction, for when one adventure is done, a knight liveth in expectation of another, and if the next come not soon enough he falleth in love, in the sort of love that is an adventure, for what he seeketh be the adventure and not the lovingness. And methinks this sequence is finally infantile, and beyond a certain age one can no longer be interested in games.

Berger's version of the Arthur legend in no way diminishes the glory of Arthur's attempt or the measure of his achievement, and it equally honors the stylistic achievement of Sir Thomas Malory's telling of the legend. Berger does devote greater attention to the cause of Arthur's final tragedy, which centers in his account on the erosion of the innocent belief that life can be governed by the simple principle of opposing good to evil. Complexity finally overwhelms Arthur: To Launcelot, he sadly admits that "evil doing hath got more subtle, perhaps even to the point at which it cannot properly be encountered with the sword." What Arthur does not realize is that strict adherence to a rigid code of conduct may create more problems than it solves, threaten order more than ensure it. Only too late do Arthur and some of his wiser knights begin to understand that the Code of Chivalry, like any inflexible system of abstract principles, comes into conflict with itself if pursued too blindly. In Berger's hands, Arthur's most anguishing discovery is not that he has been betrayed by his queen and his most trusted knight, but that his philosophy has been shallow, because "to the profound vision there is no virtue and no vice, and what is justice to one, is injustice to another."

Arthur recognizes the flaw in his great dream, but Berger makes it clear that Arthur's legend is not to be judged by the success or failure of that dream. The Lady of the Lake assures the dying Arthur that he could not have done better in his life than he did, and the ghost of Sir Gawaine offers to his king the Round Table's poignant epitaph: "We sought no easy victories, nor won any. And perhaps for that we will be remembered."

NEIGHBORS

Earl Keese, Berger's protagonist in *Neighbors*, is a quiet, reasonable, forty-nine-year-old suburbanite who tells people that his home sits "at the end of the road," because that phrase sounds less "dispiriting" than "dead end." In fact, his life has long since reached its apparent dead end, and it takes the arrival of mysterious and maddening new neighbors, Harry and Ramona, to confront Keese with a sequence of situations so outrageous that he can no longer maintain the hoax of his previously complacent life. Not only do Harry and Ramona (zany versions of Nietzsche's "free spirits") fail to observe the social amenities, but also they seem committed to deliberate provocation, pushing him to see how far he will go to avoid humiliation.

Their visits increasingly seem like motiveless assaults, as their comings and goings produce a series of off-balance events that gradually strip Keese of his easy social assumptions and habitual responses. As his bizarrely embarrassing experiences increasingly blur the line between comedy and nightmare, his re-

lations with all those around him begin to undergo subtle changes. He realizes that his life has grown so stale that Harry's and Ramona's aggravations may actually offer him a salvation of sorts—the chance to take control of and give style to his life. As Keese finally admits to Harry, "Every time I see you as a criminal, by another light you look like a kind of benefactor."

Madcap physical changes punctuate Berger's plot—entrances, exits, fights, a damaged car, a destroyed house—but for all its action, *Neighbors* might best be described as a series of functions of language: puns, platitudes, theories, definitions, excuses, accusations, rationalizations, promises, questions, threats—all acts performed with words. Keese knows better than to trust completely what he sees (he suffers from "outlandish illusions"), but he uncritically does believe his ears, consistently confusing rhetoric with reality, mistaking verbal maps for the territory of experience. In fact, *Neighbors* may offer the most verbal world Berger has created; like *Little Big Man*, it is a book in which language becomes the only operating reality. Vocabularies from law and ethics intertwine throughout the novel, and Berger does not fail to exploit the incongruities of the two lexicons. Terms having to do with guilt, justice, punishment, revenge, motive, confession, blame, crime, and accusation appear on virtually every page, resonating at once with the rhetoric of the courtroom and with that of Franz Kafka's *The Trial* (1925). Keese's "guilt" is not unlike that of Kafka's Joseph K., and the slapstick humor of this book records a deadly serious philosophical trial.

REINHART'S WOMEN

In *Reinhart's Women*, the now fifty-four-year-old Reinhart finally discovers something he can do well: cook. The novel finds Reinhart ten years after his divorce from Genevieve, living with and supported by his daughter, Winona, now a beautiful and successful fashion model. His son, Blaine, last seen as a surly radical in *Vital Parts*, now is a surly, snobbish, and successful stockbroker, unchanged in his disdain for his father. Having finally admitted that he is hopeless as a businessman, Reinhart has withdrawn from the world and contents himself with managing his daughter's household and with cooking "in a spirit of scientific inquiry." Actually, cooking has become for him an aesthetic philosophy, and for the first time in his life he does not "feel as if he were either charlatan or buffoon." "Food," Reinhart notes, "is kinder than people."

Long completely at the mercy of unmerciful women, particularly his mother and his ex-wife, Reinhart can now even take in stride the news that his daughter is having a lesbian affair with a successful older businesswoman. Age has taught him that "the best defense against any moral outrage is patience: wait a moment and something will change: the outrage, he who committed it, or, most often, oneself."

Winona's lover (a female version of the con men who have always directed Reinhart's forays into business) contrives to lure Reinhart back into the world, first as a supermarket product-demonstrator, then as a guest "chef" for a spot appearance on a local television show, and the novel closes with the strong prospect of his own show: "Chef Carlo Cooks." His apparent successes, however, are not confined to the kitchen, as Reinhart escapes the gentle and loving tyranny of his daughter, emerges unscathed from an encounter with his ex-wife, and begins a promising relationship with a young woman who seems in many ways a female version of himself—intelligent, considerate, awkward. In fact, Reinhart begins to gather around him a small band of kindred souls, hoping to buy and run a quaint small-town café. Once again, the lure of business proves irresistible for Reinhart, and once again the prospect of disaster cannot be discounted, but this time the odds seem more in Reinhart's favor. Jonathan Baumbach has summed up this most recent of the Reinhart books as "Berger's most graceful and modest book, a paean to kindness and artistry, a work of quiet dazzle."

Berger's first novel, *Crazy in Berlin*, started Reinhart, "a stumbling American Odysseus," on what Berger has termed "his long career of indestructibility." The subsequent novels in the series—*Reinhart in Love*, *Vital Parts*, and *Reinhart's Women*—follow Reinhart as he grows older and, ultimately, wiser. Said by one critic to be "a clowning knight errant, pure of heart—that is, a custodian of our conscience

and of our incongruities," Reinhart is an incurable idealist who really has no faith in idealism. Complexity, Reinhart's essence, is also his nemesis: He can always see both sides to every argument, feel responsibility for any injustice, and though he realizes that "true freedom is found only by being consistent with oneself," he has a very hard time figuring out how to do this, particularly in the novels before *Reinhart's Women*. Essentially, Reinhart seeks a consistent rationale for his unimpressive, awkward, but indomitable individuality. Combining the features of "a big bland baseball bat" with those of "an avatar of Job the beloved of a sadistic God," Reinhart can never shake the suspicion that he does not fit anywhere, but is nevertheless responsible for the general confusion that surrounds and usually engulfs him.

Reinhart is as ill-suited for despair, however, as he is for success. Although reminded by a successful aquaintance that he is "redundant in the logistics of life," he can never really be disillusioned, even though his dreams steadily fall prey to the practical opportunism of those around him. No match for a mother who can tell him, "if I ever thought you had truck with Filth, I'd slip you strychnine," or a shrewish wife whose advice to him is "if you're going to be an ass-kisser, then you ought to at least kiss the asses of winners," Reinhart can recognize the distinction between his secular search for a Holy Grail and the social meliorism that passes for idealism. Like all of Berger's characters, Reinhart never gives up: An indomitable toughness underlies his numerous weaknesses, and whatever the situation, he always muddles through, scarred but undaunted.

THE FEUD

In 1984, Berger almost gained the kind of critical recognition he has so long deserved as literary judges selected *The Feud* for the 1984 Pulitzer Prize—only to have their selection overruled in favor of William Kennedy's *Ironweed* (1983) by the Pulitzer administrative committee. What the vagaries and politics of literary prize determination should not obscure is the fact that Berger's twelfth novel (described by Berger as "my most modest work, a little memoir of the place and time of my youth" and "as a kind of Dreiserian slice of life") is a masterpiece of precision the posits its richly textured semblance of small-town life in 1930's America with a perfectly controlled minimum of exposition and a sense of quiet, timeless authority. In its narrowest sense, *The Feud* chronicles the sudden eruption and three-day playing out of an intense feud between two small-town families, the Beelers and the Bullards. Fueled by misunderstanding, misplaced pride, pathological insecurity, small-town xenophobia, self-serving interpretations of events, and the convergence of an incredible sequence of coincidences, this feud is finally remarkable for nothing quite so much as its representation of the way things actually happen in life. The action—both humorous and tragic—of this novel quickly reveals that the dynamics of feuding, quaint though the term may sound, is one of the received structures of human experience, a mold just waiting to be filled—whether by Montagues and Capulets, Hatfields and McCoys, or Beelers and Bullards.

ORRIE'S STORY

Orrie's Story, Berger's seventeenth novel, recreates much of the ambience of *The Feud* and *Sneaky People* but sets within that 1930's and 1940's small-town world the classic story of Orestes, son of Agamemnon and Clytemnestra, who, to avenge his father's murder by them, must kill both Clytemnestra and her lover Aegisthus. In the Oresteia of Aeschylus, a tragedy already recast in the Civil War era by Eugene O'Neill's *Mourning Becomes Electra* (1931), Berger has discovered another of the timeless stories of inescapable situations that have always informed and been reinterrogated by his writing. Matching the precision and control of *The Feud* and echoing its mastery of the American idiom, *Orrie's Story* may be Berger's best-written and most starkly powerful novel.

The Feud, *Being Invisible*, *The Houseguest*, and *Orrie's Story* all offer new twists to Berger's fascination with issues of discriminating "kickers" from "kickees," victims from victimizers, the disparate responses of humans confronted by the complexities of responsibility. And while *Nowhere*—which continues the misadventures of Russell Wren, protagonist of *Who Is Teddy Villanova?*, as he finds himself transported to the ironic utopia of a quirky kingdom

apparently modeled after American film musicals—raises issues usually larger than those facing the individual, it continues Berger's unsentimental confrontation with the essential insolubility of human problems. As Berger's protagonist in *Changing the Past* finally discovers after trying on and discarding a number of wishful alternative versions of his own past, "Life is taking your medicine."

ROBERT CREWS

For the main characters in *Robert Crews* and *Suspects*, that medicine of life, while bitter, offers the possibility of some kind of redemption. The former novel is Berger's reworking of Daniel Defoe's *Robinson Crusoe* (1719); however, Berger's eponymous hero is a far remove from Defoe's shipwrecked Christian incipient capitalist. Crews is an alcoholic parasite who is slowly drinking himself to death. Lost in some unidentified northern woods after a plane crash, with far fewer supplies than even Crusoe is provided with, Crews proves himself slowly and surely capable of surviving in what he calls "a state of nature." He saves not only himself but also his "Friday," a woman fleeing from an abusive husband. Although not quite as blameless as some others of Berger's "kickees," Crews is able at the end to approach what one critic calls the "esteem, apparent honor, and comradeship" which some Berger victim-protagonists attain. Crews's hold on them is precarious but, one at least hopes, lasting.

SUSPECTS

In *Suspects* Berger provides the reader with two bungling protagonists: Nick Moody, an alcoholic detective investigating a murder case, and Lloyd Howland, brother-in-law and uncle of the two victims. The novel itself takes the form of the small-town police procedural, as in books by Hillary Waugh and K. C. Constantine. In this case, though, Berger, instead of recasting or reworking the mode, deepens it, particularly in his presentation of character. Almost every character, major or minor, from the real culprit to a rookie police officer introduced near the end, is fleshed out and given three dimensions. Even so, Berger probes several characteristic concerns: the workings of fate, miscommunication between human beings, and the instability of language.

Lloyd finds himself a suspect because of a series of incongruous yet logical steps in a chain of circumstances, "an unbroken progress he was powerless to alter." He keeps losing jobs, primarily because he is a typical Berger "kickee." His victimization is caused by the misinterpretation of his actions by those around him: When he tries to return a box opener to his boss, he is perceived as wielding a threatening weapon. The main crime is the novel is also committed because the victim's actions are misconstrued by the murderer (although in this case, the error is much more willfully perverse). Both Lloyd and Nick Moody find themselves in their present circumstances because they cannot come up with an adequate definition for the word "love." This imprecision of definition in Lloyd's case makes him unable to have sex with someone with whom he is friends, and in Moody's case it leads to his broken marriages and strained relationship with his son. Yet at the end of the novel, it is Lloyd's reaching out to Moody that saves the detective from committing suicide. It is unsure whether Lloyd will make the police force or Moody will quit drinking, but at least a hint of redemption is offered.

Brooks Landon, updated by William Laskowski

OTHER MAJOR WORK

PLAY: *Other People*, pr. 1970.

BIBLIOGRAPHY

Landon, Brooks. *Thomas Berger*. Boston: Twayne, 1989. The first book-length study of Berger, this volume draws from the author's correspondence with Berger to support the thesis that the interpretation of Berger's novels *is* the study of his style. Beginning with a brief overview of Berger's career, Landon analyzes by conceptual grouping Berger's first fifteen novels, examining the considerable influence of Friedrich Nietzsche and affinities with Franz Kafka, Jorge Luis Borges, and Vladimir Nabokov.

Madden, David W. *Critical Essays on Thomas Berger*. New York: G. K. Hall, 1995. A solid collection that includes a valuable overview of Berger criticism by the editor, a lengthy interview with Berger, and the text of Berger's play *Other People*.

Malone, Michael. "Berger, Burlesque, and the Yearning for Comedy." *Studies in American Humor* 2 (Spring, 1983): 20-32. One of the most instructive essays in the two-volume *Studies in American Humor* special issue on Berger, this piece offers a persuasive analysis of Berger's complexity that also considers why his achievements have not been better celebrated. Malone claims that whatever the novel form, Berger writes comedy, as opposed to comic novels, bringing us "to confront our metaphysical (as opposed to our social) bewilderment."

Stypes, Aaron. "Thomas Berger and Sheer Incongruity." *South Dakota Review* 32 (Winter, 1994): 34-43. An interesting discussion of Berger's place in American literature and the sources of his comedy.

Wallace, Jon. "A Murderous Clarity: A Reading of Thomas Berger's *Killing Time*." *Philological Quarterly* 68 (Winter, 1989): 101-114. Superb analysis of the philosophical implications of Berger's use of sources in *Killing Time*. Wallace is one of the few critics to recognize the interpretive importance of Berger's style.

Wilde, Alan. "Acts of Definition: Or, Who Is Thomas Berger?" *Arizona Quarterly* 39 (Winter, 1983): 314-351. Perhaps the single most instructive essay on Berger's work, offering a phenomenology of Berger that astutely recognizes the inseparability for the author of the concepts of freedom and of self-definition. Wilde finds in Berger's novels, however, a "fear of otherness" that just as easily may be termed "fascination."

WENDELL BERRY

Born: Henry County, Kentucky; August 5, 1934

PRINCIPAL LONG FICTION

Nathan Coulter, 1960 (revised 1985)
A Place on Earth, 1967 (revised 1983)
The Memory of Old Jack, 1974

Remembering, 1988
A World Lost, 1996

OTHER LITERARY FORMS

Wendell Berry has published widely in most major genres—poetry, short fiction, and nonfiction prose (notably the essay), as well as long fiction. In addition to his novels and novellas, Berry is the author of several short-story collections and additional short stories about the Port William Membership. He has also published essay collections, nonfiction works, and many volumes of poetry.

ACHIEVEMENTS

The author of more than thirty books, Wendell Berry has been awarded many honorary degrees and writing awards, including the T. S. Eliot Award.

BIOGRAPHY

Wendell Berry was the eldest of four children born to a respected Kentucky family with deep farming roots in Henry County. His father was an attorney and one of the founders of the Burley Tobacco Growers Cooperative. Growing up during the 1930's in a tobacco-growing community, Berry always wanted to become a farmer. He attended the local New Castle Elementary School, though he was a reluctant student who would rather be outdoors wandering about the local countryside. As a teenager, he was particularly drawn to Curran's Camp, a fishing camp on the Kentucky River owned by his bachelor uncle.

Both Wendell and his brother John attended Millersburg Military Institute and the University of Kentucky in Lexington. Finding the university a welcome respite from the rigors of a military academy, Berry majored in English and began to take an interest in creative writing. He met his wife Tanya in Lexington, and they were married in 1957. A creative-writing fellowship brought Berry to Stanford University in 1958 to study with Wallace Stegner.

Returning from California in 1960, Berry and his family farmed for a year in Kentucky before Berry was awarded a Guggenheim Fellowship, which enabled the family to travel to Europe and live in Flor-

(Dan Carraco)

ence and the French Riviera while Berry worked on his second novel, *A Place on Earth*. An offer to direct the freshman writing program at the Bronx campus of New York University brought the family back to America in 1962, but Berry found urban life uncongenial, so they returned to Lexington when Berry accepted a teaching position at the University of Kentucky in 1964. He was still drawn to his childhood roots in Henry County, and, after a year, the Berrys were able to purchase some land in Port Royal and move to Lane's Landing Farm, which became their home. Berry continued to teach at the University of Kentucky until his retirement in the late 1990's, as well as write and farm.

ANALYSIS

Wendell Berry is perhaps the most prominent farming and agrarian writer in late-twentieth century America. Throughout his long and prolific career, virtually everything he has written has in some way either celebrated or advocated the values of traditional farming and rural life. As novelist Wallace Stegner noted, it it hard to decide in which genre Berry writes best. As one of Stegner's creative-writing students at Stanford, Berry shares affinities with other West Coast writers, such as Gary Snyder, Ken Kesey, and Ernest Gaines, but his vision is primarily that of a Kentucky regional writer and a southern agrarian. His novels and short stories recount the saga of the Port William Membership, a fictional rural Kentucky community of small tobacco farmers and their families. All of his fiction, except for *Remembering*, is set in the lower Kentucky River Valley, where Berry has spent most of his life. Much of his fiction evokes an elegiac sense of a rural community and a way of life gradually lost to the changing economics of the modern American consumer culture. Berry's pastoral, agrarian vision is not merely nostalgic, however, but is wed to a clear sense of environmental stewardship and responsibility to the land and to small-scale, local economics. His characters struggle to maintain community on all levels—social, economic, and environmental. Berry's fictional vision encompasses the unity of people, place, and the natural world.

More than anything else, Berry's novels are a continuous saga of a region—the Kentucky River Valley—and a rural way of life between the two world wars. His major character in these Port William Membership stories is the community itself, composed for the most part of decent, unassuming people trying to maintain their farming culture against the outside forces of war and economic and social change. Their major crop was burley tobacco, a demanding crop that bound families together in seasonal labor. World War II was the great watershed that marked the end of a self-sufficient rural economy and the agrarian lifestyle it nurtured. Young men were drawn off to war, leaving behind women, children, and the elderly to work the farms as best they could.

Berry's novels are largely the story of the decline and fall of this rural, agrarian culture and its impact on the Port William Membership. Hence, his tone is wistful and his themes are of recurring loss: elderly parents, sons killed in war, farms neglected or mismanaged, community and cultural continuity gone.

Berry's fictional world is populated mainly by three families—the Coulters, Catletts, and Beechams—with their quirks and eccentricities, along with other rural townfolk. His novels are often thinly plotted and episodic, with few major characters, relying on tone and description to convey the essence of the story. Berry's muted realism and lack of melodrama convey a sense of the ordinary pace of premechanized Kentucky rural life, although the absence of thematic conflict does not encourage strong character or plot development.

To some degree, these limitations are those of choice rather than ability, given the regional focus of Berry's fiction. The initial conflicts of pioneering and settlement of Kentucky were followed by the slow development of a rural culture based upon the cultivation of tobacco and livestock. The wilderness was gradually subdued by human effort, but the culture was careless and wasteful with natural resources. With so much land there for the taking, settlers saw no need to conserve the soil or prevent erosion.

A continual theme throughout Berry's novels is cultural and environmental conservatism—and the natural and cultural costs of failing to learn to conserve the land. He regrets the failure to create an enduring agrarian culture with strong local roots and a sense of history. Neither religion nor culture encouraged a sense of affection or respect for the land. His characters are warped by their harsh work ethic, their greed, their ignorance and indifference. Berry imposes his strong personal vision on his fictional world, blending storytelling with cultural history and a clear environmental philosophy. Berry's creative approach is to some degree recursive, returning to the same families in different episodes in successive novels.

NATHAN COULTER

Berry's first novel, *Nathan Coulter*, evolved from an early short story, "The Brothers," written during his undergraduate years at the University of Kentucky. First published in 1960, it was later revised and shortened for reissue in 1985. The initial sales were disappointing, although the novel received some favorable reviews. It was compared with other regional "tobacco novels," although it is really more of a coming-of-age story of two brothers, Nathan and

Tom Coulter, who are forced to deal with their father's harsh rejection of them after their mother's death. The revised version of *Nathan Coulter* eliminates the last three chapters and ends with Grandpa Coulter's death, providing greater focus and unity. Each of the five sections of the novel is built around a central episode in the lives of the brothers: their mother's death, after which they live with their grandparents; Tom's courtship, which separates him from his younger brother Nathan; the burning of their father's barn after it is struck by lightning; Tom's leaving home after a fight with his father; and the death of the boys' grandfather, old Dave Coulter, which brings Nathan to the verge of manhood. The novel is narrated in the first person by Nathan, the younger brother, encouraging the reader to empathize with him.

Berry's first novel presents a starkly realistic, unsentimental portrait of a boy's coming of age on a Kentucky tobacco farm before the age of mechanization. Berry presents a harsh, patriarchal world of unrelenting toil and obsessive work ethic among three generations who cannot get along because of their fierce pride and independence. Grandpa Coulter and his son Jarrat, the boys' father, are linked by their stubborn pride and irritability, which makes life miserable for those around them. Berry presents a hard, male world in which women are absent or subordinate—a Calvinistic world of work and self-deprivation. There is an implicit division between those who respect the land (and themselves) and those who abuse it or who are obsessively bound to it. Despite their constant labor, the lives of the Coulter men seem harsh and unattractive. The kind and unambitious Uncle Burley, Jarrat's brother, serves as a foil to Grandpa Dave and Jarrat and offers an alternative way of living in family and community.

A PLACE ON EARTH

Berry's second novel, *A Place on Earth*, was begun at Stanford in 1960 and published in 1967. The original version, as Berry admitted, was overwritten and needed to be revised and edited. Before it was reissued in 1983, Berry cut about a third of its length, reorganized the novel into five major sections, and added chapter titles.

A Place on Earth is the portrait of Port William, Berry's fictional community, toward the end of World War II, from late winter to fall, 1945. It is the story of a rural community's loss and atonement, through war, flood, and suicide, set against the natural rhythm of the seasons. The protagonist, Mat Feltner, learns that his son Virgil has been reported missing in action in Europe, and for the next six months, Mat, his wife Margaret, and their daughter-in-law Hannah struggle to accept their loss. Virgil's death is paralleled by the death of Annie Crop, a sharecropper's child swept away in a flood. Ernest Finley, Mat's cousin, a crippled war veteran and carpenter, takes his life when his infatuation for Ida Crop is gently rebuffed. The townsfolk of the Port William Membership learn to accept these deaths within the larger natural rhythm of the seasons and of rural life. Berry presents credible portraits of his rural characters—especially the older men, the village elders—Mat Feltner, Frank Lathrop, Jack Beechum, Burley Coulter, and Jayber Crow—who struggle to maintain their way of life, but the novel lacks strong dramatic or psychological conflict. Once again, Berry's major concern is the struggle by the older generation to maintain traditional farming practices in the face of war and loss. With the death of his son, Mat Feltner wonders who will farm and inherit his land. Jack Beechum also searches for a tenant to keep his farm from being sold off by his wealthy daughter and her banker husband. Work and love are the focal points of Berry's agrarian moral order: Characters are measured by their success or failure in farming and holding onto their land. The town's celebration of Japan's surrender marks the end of World War II and the beginning of the inevitable changes that peacetime will bring to the Port William Membership.

THE MEMORY OF OLD JACK

In Berry's third and best novel, *The Memory of Old Jack*, he turns to the story of Jack Beechum, who was introduced as an old man in *A Place on Earth*. Told retrospectively from the third-person point of view, it is the story of Jack's life and his attachment to his farm, with an unhappy marriage to Ruth Lightwood, who does not share his love of the land. Through the concentration on Jack's character and his conflicts, this novel gains a unity and focus absent in Berry's first two novels. Jack's story is told through his own recollections on a warm September day in 1952, as his friend Wheeler Catlett takes the ninety-two-year-old Jack from his boardinghouse in town out to his farm.

Jack's memories reach back to the end of the Civil War, when, after his parents' death, he was befriended by Ben Feltner, who taught him to farm. Jack's loveless marriage to Ruth Lightwood was the great regret of his life. Her desire for wealth and prestige forced him to overextend himself and almost lose his farm to debt. Cold and disapproving toward Jack, Ruth encourages their daughter Clara's disapproval of her father. Never having had a son, Jack turns to his lawyer, Wheeler, and to his young tenant farmer, Elton Penn, as spiritual heirs. In his will, Jack arranges with Wheeler to leave enough money for Elton to buy his farm, so that Clara and her husband cannot sell it. Jack's life unites love and work, but his love is for his farm, not his family.

REMEMBERING

Berry's next two works are about episodes in the life of Andy Catlett, farmer and son of Wheeler Catlett, a character who resembles Berry himself in some ways. *Remembering* recounts a crisis in Andy Catlett's life, during a lecture tour as an agricultural journalist, shortly after he loses his hand to a corn picker and becomes estranged from his wife and family. During a long night in a San Francisco hotel, he reexamines his life. As he remembers formative incidents from his childhood and the mentors who have influenced him, he regains his faith and purpose. Central to his conversion is a recollected interview with two farmers—an Amish man and a corporate farmer—whose contrasting values and scale of farming dramatize Berry's traditional agrarian philosophy. Andy returns home from his abortive trip to be reconciled with his wife and his sense of place as a traditional farmer.

A WORLD LOST

A World Lost, a more polished work, returns to Andy's childhood, during the summer of 1944, to recount the story of his uncle's murder and Andy's subsequent quest to understand the crime. It is a rich,

meditative work which traces a boy's attempts to comprehend the mysteries of the adult world. Andy's uncle Andrew is a rich and complex character, a heavy drinker and womanizer, a practical joker, and a storyteller, who compensates for his unhappy marriage and unfulfilling job as a salesman through his close relationship with his nephew. Young Andy does not fully understand the sexual aura that draws women to his uncle and results in his being shot over a jest he makes to Cap Harmon's daughter in a restaurant. Andy's determination to uncover the secret of his uncle's murder takes him on an odyssey from childhood to adulthood and results in some of Berry's best fictional writing.

Andrew J. Angyal

OTHER MAJOR WORKS

SHORT FICTION: *The Wild Birds*, 1986; *Fidelity*, 1992; *Watch with Me: And Six Other Stories of the Yet-Remembered Ptolemy Proudfoot and His Wife, Miss Minnie, nee Quinch*, 1994.

POETRY: *November Twenty-six, Nineteen Hundred Sixty-three*, 1963; *The Broken Ground*, 1964; *Openings*, 1968; *Findings*, 1969; *Farming: A Hand Book*, 1970; *The Country of Marriage*, 1973; *An Eastward Look*, 1974; *To What Listens*, 1975; *Horses*, 1975; *Sayings and Doings*, 1975; *The Kentucky River: Two Poems*, 1976; *There Is Singing Around Me*, 1976; *Three Memorial Poems*, 1976; *Clearing*, 1977; *The Gift of Gravity*, 1979; *A Part*, 1980; *The Wheel*, 1982; *Collected Poems: 1957-1982*, 1985; *Sabbaths*, 1987; *Traveling at Home*, 1989; *Sabbaths 1987-90*, 1992; *Entries*, 1994; *The Farm*, 1995; *A Timbered Choir: The Sabbath Poems, 1979-1997*, 1998; *The Selected Poems of Wendell Berry*, 1998.

NONFICTION: *The Long-Legged House*, 1969; *The Hidden Wound*, 1970; *The Unforeseen Wilderness*, 1971; *A Continuous Harmony*, 1972; *The Unsettling of America*, 1977; *The Gift of Good Land*, 1981; *Recollected Essays, 1965-1980*, 1981; *Standing by Words*, 1983; *Home Economics*, 1987; *Harlan Hubbard: Life and Work*, 1990; *What Are People For?*, 1990; *The Discovery of Kentucky*, 1991; *Standing on Earth*, 1991; *Sex, Economy, Freedom, and Community*, 1993; *Another Turn of the Crank*, 1995.

BIBLIOGRAPHY

Altherr, Thomas L. "The Country We Have Married: Wendell Berry and the Georgian Tradition of Agriculture." *Southern Studies* 1 (Summer, 1990): 105-115. An examination of the influence of Vergil's *Georgics* (c. 37-29 B.C.E.) on Berry's treatment of agriculture.

Angyal, Andrew J. *Wendell Berry*. New York: Twayne, 1995. A standard critical biography in the Twayne United States Authors series.

Freyfogle, Eric T. "The Dilemma of Wendell Berry." *University of Illinois Law Review* 2 (1994): 363-385. A detailed study of the moral implications of Berry's cultural criticism, especially in his fictional works.

Merchant, Paul, ed. *Wendell Berry*. Lewiston, Idaho: Confluence Press, 1991. Part of the American Authors series, this is a collection of critical essays and appreciations of Berry's work.

Nibbelink, Herman. "Thoreau and Wendell Berry: Bachelor and Husband of Nature." *South Atlantic Quarterly* 84 (1985): 127-140. Contrasts Henry David Thoreau's love of wilderness with Berry's preference for cultivated land in terms of the bachelor-husband metaphor.

Slovic, Scott. *Seeking Awareness in American Nature Writing*. Salt Lake City: University of Utah Press, 1992. A critical study of contemporary American nature writing, with a chapter on Berry.

HEINRICH BÖLL

Born: Cologne, Germany; December 21, 1917
Died: Merten, West Germany; July 16, 1985

PRINCIPAL LONG FICTION

Der Zug war pünktlich, 1949 (*The Train Was on Time*, 1956)

Wo warst du, Adam?, 1951 (*Adam, Where Art Thou?*, 1955)

Nicht nur zur Weihnachtszeit, 1952

Und sagte kein einziges Wort, 1953 (*Acquainted with the Night*, 1954)

Haus ohne Hüter, 1954 (*Tomorrow and Yesterday*, 1957)

Das Brot der frühen Jahre, 1955 (*The Bread of Our Early Years*, 1957)

Billard um halbzehn, 1959 (*Billiards at Half-Past Nine*, 1961)

Ansichten eines Clowns, 1963 (*The Clown*, 1965)

Ende einer Dienstfahrt, 1966 (*End of a Mission*, 1967)

Gruppenbild mit Dame, 1971 (*Group Portrait with Lady*, 1973)

Die verlorene Ehre der Katharina Blum: Oder, Wie Gewalt entstehen und wohin sie führen kann, 1974 (*The Lost Honor of Katharina Blum: Or, How Violence Develops and Where It Can Lead*, 1975)

Fürsorgliche Belagerung, 1979 (*The Safety Net*, 1982)

Der Vermächtnis, 1982 (*A Soldier's Legacy*, 1985)

Frauen vor Flusslandschaft, 1985 (*Women in a River Landscape*, 1988)

Der Engel Schwieg, 1992 (wr. 1950; *The Silent Angel*, 1994)

OTHER LITERARY FORMS

Although Böll is known chiefly for his novels and short stories, he also wrote plays, essays, and poems, and he was an active lecturer, critic, and translator. His essays on literature (which include discussions of Fyodor Dostoevski, Thomas Wolfe, François Mauriac, Mary McCarthy, and Aleksandr Solzhenitsyn) show his familiarity with European and American literature. In his essays on politics, Böll was an outspoken critic of trends in modern German society. Together with his wife, Böll translated works by Irish, English, and American authors into German, including works by John Synge, Brendan Behan, and J. D. Salinger. There is now a comprehensive ten-volume German edition of Böll's works. The first five volumes, published in 1977, contain novels and stories; the second five, published in 1978, contain radio plays, dramas, film texts, poems, essays, reviews, speeches, commentaries, and interviews.

ACHIEVEMENTS

Böll is probably the best-known twentieth century German writer in Germany and abroad. In Germany, his work is popular at all levels of society. His books have been widely translated into many languages. In the Soviet Union, Böll is the Western author most frequently published and read. Until 1951, however, he was virtually unknown. In that year, Gruppe 47 awarded him their prize for his story "Die schwarzen Schafe" ("The Black Sheep"). After that, Böll received many prizes, including the Nobel Prize in Literature in 1972. The Swedish Academy praised Böll for his broad perspective on his time and for his sensitive characterizations, acknowledging his contribution to the renewal of German literature after the Nazi era. In 1969, Böll was elected president of the West German P.E.N. Club, evidence of the respect that other writers had for him. He was elected president of the International P.E.N. Club in 1971, the first German to be so honored, and he served until May,

(The Nobel Foundation)

1974. In 1974, Böll received the Carl von Ossietzky Medal from the International League of Human Rights in recognition of his concern for human rights. He was made an honorary member of the American Academy of Art and Literature and of the American National Institute of Art and Literature in the same year. Böll's outspoken criticisms of social abuses he perceived in modern German society provoked widespread debate.

BIOGRAPHY

Heinrich Böll was born in Cologne, Germany, on December 21, 1917. On his father's side, his ancestors were ship carpenters who emigrated from England centuries before, Catholics fleeing from the persecutions of Henry VIII. On his mother's side, his ancestors were Catholic farmers and brewers. Böll's father was a cabinetmaker. In an autobiographical sketch of 1958 entitled "Über mich selbst" ("About Myself"), Böll describes the hunger, poverty, and unemployment in Germany during the inflationary years of the 1920's, topics which frequently recur in his works. He remembers the first money he received—a note for one billion marks with which he managed to buy a stick of candy. In an autobiographical sketch written in 1981, *Was soll aus dem Jungen bloss werden?* (*What's to Become of the Boy?*, 1984), Böll describes his childhood and youth during the Hitler years and his strong opposition to the Nazis. Whenever possible, he avoided participating in the Hitler Youth.

In an interview with the critic Horst Bienek in 1961, Böll said that he began to write when he was seventeen or eighteen. He wrote four, five, or perhaps six novels at this time, three of which were burned in Cologne during World War II. In the same interview, Böll acknowledged his debt to many writers, among them Karl May, Marcel Proust, Johann Peter Hebel, Dostoevski, Jack London, Ernest Hemingway, Albert Camus, Graham Greene, William Faulkner, Thomas Wolfe, Adalbert Stifter, Theodor Fontane, and Joseph Roth. When Böll left the *gymnasium* in 1937, he became an apprentice in the book trade in Bonn. In the winter of 1938, he was drafted into the labor service. He began to study German literature at the University of Cologne, but his studies were interrupted when he was called for military service in 1939. Although he was strongly opposed to the war, Böll had to serve as an infantryman in the German army for six years on the eastern and western fronts and was wounded four times. In 1942, he married Annemarie Cech, later a teacher of English. During the war, Böll deserted twice and was finally captured by the Americans. Böll draws on his firsthand experiences of the war in his early novels and stories. On his return from a prisoner-of-war camp in 1945, Böll worked briefly in the family carpentry shop until he found a job with the Cologne Bureau of Statistics. He also resumed his studies. After 1951, he earned his living as a writer. In the mid-1950's, Böll visited Ireland for the first time and liked it so much that he bought some property there. Thereafter he returned to reside in his native city of Cologne (often used as the setting of his novels) with his wife and three sons. He died in Merten, West Germany, on July 16, 1985.

ANALYSIS

Serious moral commitment is the essence of Heinrich Böll's writing. In an essay of 1952 entitled "Bekenntnis zur Trümmerliteratur" ("In Defense of Rubble Literature"), Böll praises Charles Dickens for the same commitment. Dickens wrote about the social abuses he saw in English schools, prisons, and poorhouses and, by depicting these abuses, helped to bring about change. Böll believed that literature can change society by making people more aware of the world in which they live. In his 1958 essay "Die Sprache als Hort der Freiheit" ("Language as the Stronghold of Freedom"), he says that words contain enough dynamite to destroy whole worlds. It is for this reason that dictatorships fear the printed word almost more than armed resistance. Böll's early works show the senseless destruction of the war and the hardships of the immediate postwar years in Germany, while his later works focus on contemporary German society. He had hoped that the experience of the Hitler years would change society for the better; instead, he saw the same opportunism, love of power, militarism, and greed that existed before the war. Besides having a strong sense of the moral and political

responsibility of the writer, Böll believed that the writer should be humane and compassionate. In his works, Böll's sympathy for his fellow human beings is always evident. He is especially sympathetic toward ordinary, unheroic people who are often victimized by a cruel society. These are the kind of people Böll chose for his protagonists. Böll's moral earnestness does not, however, preclude a sense of humor. His works are frequently humorous or satiric, although his satire is rarely vituperative.

ADAM, WHERE ART THOU?

In his interview with Horst Bienek, Böll said that his early novel *Adam, Where Art Thou?* was still one of his favorite works. It is the only one of Böll's novels that deals exclusively with World War II. In it, Böll draws extensively on his experiences as a soldier. The novel is structured episodically: The nine episodes are loosely connected by the figure of the soldier Feinhals, who is not, however, the protagonist. In some chapters, Feinhals plays only a peripheral role, and in two chapters he does not appear. Minor characters in one chapter become the central characters in another. As the name "Adam" in the title suggests, Böll's focus is on the suffering of man rather than on a specific individual. The novel is a strong denunciation of war, typical of Böll's attitude to war throughout his work. Böll depicts war as senseless, boring, and sordid. The action takes place mostly behind the lines, in military hospitals and hospital clearing stations, where Böll can bring the suffering caused by the war into sharper focus. Since the novel describes the retreat of the German army from the eastern front between 1944 and 1945, the loss of life is particularly senseless, because the outcome of the war is no longer in doubt. The individuals he depicts have no power to shape their own destinies but are hopelessly trapped in the war. In the tragic love affair between Feinhals and the Jewish-Catholic schoolteacher Ilona, Böll shows how the war disrupts personal relationships. This relationship has no chance to grow: Ilona is deported to a concentration camp where she is killed, and Feinhals is picked up by the military police and sent to the front.

At the beginning of the novel, Böll quotes from Antoine de Saint-Exupéry, who wrote that war is a disease, like typhoid. Even nature appears to be infected and hostile: The sun bathes everything in a bloody red or resembles a burning iron egg, about to wreak destruction like a shell or a grenade; melons rot like corpses in the fields. Chapter 3 depicts life in a military hospital and its evacuation as the Russians approach. Life for those working in the hospital is a dreary routine. In order to tolerate the daily boredom, Corporal Schneider has an elaborate ritual of drinking before he begins work. Böll also describes the turmoil of the retreat in this chapter. Even though the officers had known earlier about the retreat, they had not thought to tell the doctor, who had performed major surgery on two wounded soldiers that morning. Since moving these patients would cause their deaths, the doctor and Corporal Schneider choose to stay behind with them. Schneider goes out to meet the Russians, carrying a Red Cross flag. Ironically, he is not killed by the Russians but by a German shell, supposedly a dud, on which he accidentally treads. The explosion makes the Russians think they are being attacked, and they shell the hospital, killing the doctor and his two patients, before they realize that nobody is returning their fire. Despite the quiet heroism of the doctor and Schneider, the patients die.

In chapter 7, Böll depicts the concentration camp where Ilona is killed. It is the only time in Böll's works that a concentration camp appears. The commandant, Filskeit, is the epitome of what Hannah Arendt calls "the banality of evil." He is strict, industrious, ambitious, and reliable; does not drink, smoke, or consort with women; respects all authority; and has a firm belief in Nazi ideology. Although he does not like killing, he obediently carries out his orders, lacking any compassion or humaneness. He has a passionate love for music, especially for choral singing, yet instead of making him more human, his love of art has made him even more inhuman; in his treatise on the relationship between race and choir, he makes art serve Nazi ideology. His choral performances are technically perfect but completely sterile. When new prisoners are brought to the camp, Filskeit makes them sing for him; those who sing well escape the gas chamber for a while and sing in his choir. When Ilona is brought before him, she sings the All-Saints Litany. Ilona's love of music is contrasted with Filskeit's: Music for her expresses beauty, joy, and faith, not the technical perfection that Filskeit demands. Filskeit cannot endure the purity of Ilona's singing and the faith it reveals, and he brutally kills her.

The senselessness of war is particularly evident in the novel's last two episodes. In chapter 8, a bridge is blown up in a tiny village. German soldiers are sent to guard the area, but nothing ever happens, and the soldiers eat and drink and laze away the time. Finally, it is decided to rebuild the bridge. The engineer and his workers arrive and the bridge is rebuilt with model efficiency and speed; soon after it is completed, it is blown up again to halt the Russian advance. Chapter 9, which is rather melodramatic, shows Feinhals arriving home in his native village, which lies between the American and the German lines. He has survived the war and deserted the army. A vindictive German sergeant decides to shell the village to punish the inhabitants for their lack of patriotism (they are flying white flags). On the threshold of his home, Feinhals is hit by a shell and dies thinking "how absolutely senseless," a reflection of Böll's own attitude to the war.

BILLIARDS AT HALF-PAST NINE

Although Böll also denounces World War II and the Nazi era in *Billiards at Half-Past Nine*, he widens his scope to show a panorama of German history from 1907 to 1958. In his interview with Horst Bienek, Böll said that the novel was inspired by a historical event. In 1934, Hermann Göring had four young Communists beheaded in Cologne, the youngest of whom was only seventeen or eighteen—the same age as Böll when he started to write. This event gives rise in the novel to the story of Ferdi Progulske, who tries to assassinate the Nazi gymnastics teacher Wakiera with a homemade bomb and is beheaded for this deed. Another source of inspiration for the novel was the famous altarpiece by Jan and Hubert van Eyck, *Adoration of the Lamb*, a polyptych in the center of which is the Lamb of God, which Böll saw in Ghent.

The novel focuses on the lives of the Fähmel family, and the action takes place on one day, September 6, 1958, Heinrich Fähmel's eightieth birthday. Heinrich and Johanna Fähmel represent the older generation, which grew up in the Wilhelmine years and experienced World War I. Böll uses flashbacks in the form of recollections to depict the earlier lives of his characters. Heinrich Fähmel arrived in Cologne for the first time in 1907 and immediately began to build a role for himself as a successful architect. He won a commission to build Saint Anthony's Abbey, married Johanna Kilb, and became through his marriage a member of the patrician class. For fifty years he has played the same role, but eventually the role traps him. When he reminisces about his past life on his eightieth birthday, he realizes that he should not have followed the rules of the Establishment but should have protested against the Wilhelmine and Hitler governments. His wife, Johanna, did protest. During World War I, she criticized the Kaiser and German militarism; in World War II, she protested against the deportation of the Jews. In order to protect her, Heinrich had her committed to a mental institution in 1942. The sanatorium has been a refuge from reality for Johanna for sixteen years. When she leaves it to attend her husband's eightieth birthday party, she shoots at a minister because she thinks of him as the murderer of her grandchildren. She still sees the same militarism and love of power that she had criticized earlier. Her attempt to shoot the minister is a futile gesture of protest against the people in power.

Their son, Robert Fähmel, represents the generation that grew up under Hitler. He has withdrawn completely from life. Like his father, he is an architect, but he never spends more than an hour a day in his office and conducts all of his business by mail. Since the end of the war, Robert has been playing billiards each morning at the Prince Heinrich Hotel in an attempt to escape from modern society. While he plays billiards, he talks about his past life with the bellboy, Hugo, and listens to what Hugo tells him about his life. The reasons for this strange behavior gradually become apparent. During the Hitler years, Robert had protected his friend Schrella from being victimized by the Nazis Nettlinger and Wakiera; this led to his involvement in a group of people who re-

fused to partake of the "host of the beast." Among them he met Schrella's sister, Edith, who bore his child and whom he later married. Robert was part of the plot to kill the Nazi sadist Wakiera, for which the high school student Ferdi was arrested and beheaded. Schrella and Robert had to flee, and Robert escaped to Holland. He was allowed to return on the condition that he join the army when he finished his studies. In the army, Robert became a demolitions expert, the opposite of his profession as an architect, and in revenge destroyed buildings to protest the murder of innocent people during the war. At the end of the war, he destroyed the abbey that his father had built. When Schrella returns to Germany after twenty-three years of exile and attends Heinrich's party, he criticizes Robert for his withdrawal from society. Robert's decision to adopt Hugo, the bellboy, at the story's end shows that he has come to terms with his wasted life and intends to become involved again.

Böll employs a symbolic contrast between lambs and buffalo to characterize German society during the fifty-year span of the novel. The lambs are the good and innocent people such as Schrella, Edith (who is killed in the bombardments), and all the people who helped Robert while he was in exile and who were arrested and killed because of it. The lambs are those who keep their integrity and who are persecuted and killed by the buffalo. The majority of people in society are buffalo, people such as Nettlinger and Wakiera, who beat Robert and Schrella with barbed-wire whips, and Robert's brother Otto, who became a Nazi and would have denounced his own mother. These buffalo, who represent the martial spirit and the love of power, still exist in modern Germany. Hugo, for example, is persecuted because of his lamblike qualities.

The representatives of the modern generation are Robert's children, Joseph and Ruth, and Joseph's fiancée, Marianne. On his grandfather's eightieth birthday, Joseph, who is rebuilding Saint Anthony's Abbey, learns that his father was responsible for destroying it and wonders whether he should tell his grandfather. Heinrich, however, has already realized who has destroyed his masterpiece and is not upset, because he now realizes that people are more important than buildings. Finding out about his father's action makes Joseph think about his own life. The question of whether he will build or destroy is left open at the end.

The conclusion of the novel is both optimistic and pessimistic. The Fähmel family and the people associated with them—Schrella, Hugo, Marianne, and Robert's secretary Leonore—have been drawn close together. They form a tight circle of people who uphold idealism and humane values; they are an isolated circle of lambs in a world of buffalo. They cannot, however, change society and can preserve their values only by withdrawing from the world. Society on the whole has not changed for the better, Böll implies. Former Nazis such as Nettlinger are still in power, militarism still flourishes, and society is still inhumane: The buffalo are still in the majority and continue to persecute the lambs.

THE CLOWN

In *The Clown*, Böll's criticism of trends in modern German society becomes sharper. The protagonist, Hans Schnier, a twenty-seven-year-old clown who has just given a disastrous performance, is spending a lonely night in his apartment. The "action" of the novel is restricted to this single night, during which Hans telephones many of the people he knows, although (as in *Billiards at Half-Past Nine*) Böll uses extensive flashbacks in the form of recollections to relate Hans's past experiences. Some years earlier, Hans had fallen in love with Marie Derkum, a Catholic, left high school for her, and became a clown. To the annoyance of his wealthy family, Hans refused to adopt a middle-class profession. For five years, Hans was a successful clown, showing the absurdities of daily life in his act. He lived with Marie and traveled around with her. Marie then joined a group of progressive Catholics, after which their relationship deteriorated. Marie wanted Hans to marry her and sign papers promising to rear their children as Catholics. Although Hans refused at first, he eventually agreed. This, however, did not satisfy Marie: She accused him of agreeing to her demands merely to keep her rather than being convinced of the "justness of abstract principles of order." Marie left him and married Heribert Züpfner, one of the prominent Catholics in

the German Establishment. After this, Hans began to drink heavily, which ruined his clown act. In his apartment on the night covered in the novel, Hans makes a series of phone calls in a state of controlled desperation. He tries to win back Marie—with no success. The telephone is a symbol of his isolation, of the lack of real communication between people. At the end of the novel, Hans paints his face white and goes to the Bonn railway station to play his guitar and beg.

The group of progressive Catholics is the focus of Böll's criticism, causing Catholic groups in Germany to take offense. Böll is attacking not only Catholics, however, but also any group which values dogma more than individual human lives. The progressive Catholics in the group are narrow, self-sufficient, and hypocritical. Because they are tied to dogma, they lack all compassion and humaneness. During a gathering of this group, which Hans and Marie attend, the prominent Catholic Sommerwild tells about a Catholic writer who lived for a long time with a divorced woman. When he married her, an eminent church dignitary asked whether he could not have kept her as his concubine. All the Catholics laugh at this story. Hans is shocked by the cynical attitude toward human relationships that he finds in this group. He believes in the sanctity of relationships; the formality of a marriage license means nothing to him. He believes that his relationship with Marie is a marriage because of the commitment and love they have for each other. Like the progressive Catholics, Hans's brother Leo, who is studying to be a priest, places the letter of the law above human considerations. He will not leave the seminary to come to Hans's aid because it is against the rules.

Böll also attacks the ease with which people adapt to the prevailing ideology. One such example is Hans's mother. During the war, she was a racist and used such Nazi slogans as "our sacred German soil" (an ironic phrase, because the Schnier family makes its wealth from digging up the coal under the sacred German soil). In the last months of the war, she encouraged her daughter Henrietta to volunteer for antiaircraft duty, thereby causing her death. Hans's alienation from society began when his sister died. Now

Mrs. Schnier is president of the Executive Committee of the Societies for the Reconciliation of Racial Differences.

Despite her wealth, Mrs. Schnier is stingy. As a child, Hans was often hungry; one time Hans saw his mother go down to the storeroom to eat the food she would not give her children. Böll also gives examples of other born conformists. The fascist writer Schnitzler makes people believe that he was censored for his resistance to Hitler, which was not the case; he is now indispensable at the Foreign Office. Because the teacher Brühl never joined the Nazi Party (although his sympathies were with the Nazis), he now has the reputation of a man with a courageous political past and is a professor at a teacher training college. The ruthless Hitler Youth leader, Herbert Kalick, has recently been awarded a medal for his work in spreading democratic ideas among young people in Germany.

Böll also criticizes the greed and commercialism in West German society. Hans's father represents big business in Germany. Like Hans's mother, his father is also mean and refuses to help his son financially, and he is too concerned with prestige and respectability. Böll does not spare the German Democratic Republic: Hans was once invited to perform there, but when the Communists discovered that he wanted to perform "The Party Conference Elects Its Presidium" instead of anticapitalist skits, he had to leave on the next train.

The spontaneous and naïve Hans considers adapting to society and playing the role of the hypocrite but decides to keep his integrity: He refuses to compromise his ideals and adapt to social norms. Instead, he completely rejects German society; in his radical alienation from society he resembles Dostoevski's underground man, an indication of the impact that Dostoevski had on Böll's writing. Hans protests against the hypocrisy, sterile dogma, materialism, and opportunism of modern society. The clown, who as an outsider can be sharply critical of society, symbolizes Hans's protest. The conclusion of the novel is more pessimistic than that of *Billiards at Half-Past Nine*. Hans does not have a circle of friends and family—he is alone at the end, a beggar by choice.

GROUP PORTRAIT WITH LADY

Like *Billiards at Half-Past Nine, Group Portrait with Lady* shows a panorama of German history in the twentieth century. Böll's main focus in the novel is on the 1930's and 1940's, after which the focus shifts to the 1970's. The novel is made up of reports about Leni Pfeiffer, born Gruyten, a woman of forty-eight. The narrator, a character called the "author," gradually reconstructs Leni's life. He searches for material; interviews friends, relatives, and enemies of Leni; and comments on the reports. The many people he interviews form a cross section of German society, from millionaires to garbage workers, and through these interviews the reader is given a picture not only of Leni but also of the commentators themselves. The "author" is not objective, because he confesses that he loves Leni.

The novel highlights main events in Leni's life. She was born in Cologne in 1922. In 1938, she was dismissed from a Catholic high school and began to work in her father's engineering firm. During the war, her brother, Heinrich, and her cousin, Erhard, were shot by the Germans for trying to sell an antitank gun to the Danes, a futile act of protest against the Nazi regime. In 1941, Leni married Alois Pfeiffer, who was killed three days later. When her father was arrested in 1943 for illegal business dealings, Leni was left penniless and began making wreaths in a cemetery nursery. There she met Boris Lvovich Koltovsky, a Soviet prisoner of war, and they fell in love. During the heavy bombardments of the city in 1944, they met secretly in the underground vaults of the cemetery. In 1945, Leni gave birth to their son, Lev. When the Allies occupied the city, Boris was arrested on suspicion of being a German soldier. He was put to work in a French mine, where he died in an accident. Leni continued to work and look after her son.

Like most of Böll's protagonists, Leni is a naïve, innocent figure who refuses to conform to social norms. She is generous and compassionate to everyone and is perplexed by the evil in people. Leni has a healthy and natural attitude to sexuality, which Böll contrasts with society's hypocritical attitude toward the body. Because Leni maintains her integrity and refuses to conform, society persecutes her. After the war, in 1970, her neighbors hate her because she lets rooms cheaply to foreign workers and because she is expecting her Turkish lover's child. Whenever she ventures out of her apartment, her neighbors verbally abuse her, calling her a whore—some even would like to see her gassed, an indication that people are just as inhumane as they were during the Nazi era.

In this novel, Böll is sharply critical of racism. He satirizes the Nazi belief that the Slavs were subhuman. It is the Soviet prisoner Boris, with his knowledge of German literature, who ironically reminds the Germans of their humanistic tradition, perverted by the Nazis. The dummy company that Leni's father forms to swindle the government and avenge himself on the Nazis for killing his son reminds people of the great Russian literary tradition, because he names his fictitious workers after great Russian writers and characters in their works. The racism in Germany during the war years is still evident in modern German society; only the target of the racism has changed: Now the foreign workers are the deprived and misused members of society.

Böll's attack on greed, commercialism, and opportunism is particularly severe in this novel. Pelzer, the owner of the nursery where Leni worked, is an unscrupulous opportunist who profits from war. In World War I, he stole gold from the teeth of dead American soldiers. After the war, he joined the Communist Party for a time; when it became expedient, he joined the Nazi Party instead. When he was supposed to arrest prominent people, he let them go if they paid him. During World War II, he made money from wreaths, increasing his profit by reusing wreaths. Just before the Americans arrived in Cologne, he resigned from the Nazi Party and was thus allowed to stay in business. Pelzer is now very wealthy from his various business dealings. Böll does not, however, portray Pelzer entirely negatively: Pelzer's love of money stems from the poverty he endured as a youth. He also tried to protect Leni and Boris during the war. Hoyser, Leni's father's former head bookkeeper, has no redeeming qualities and is the epitome of crass commercialism. During the war,

Leni had allowed the Hoysers to live in her house rent-free. When she could not repay the money she had borrowed from Hoyser, he repossessed her house and immediately began charging her rent. At the end of the war, he made a profit by buying property cheaply from former Nazis, who in turn had stolen the property from Jews. Hoyser and his grandchildren decide at the end of the novel to evict Leni because she is letting rooms cheaply to foreigners. The Hoysers' lives revolve entirely around money, to the absolute exclusion of compassion.

As in his other novels, Böll is very critical of German society. Some hope, however, lies in the new generation, as represented here by Lev. He is in prison for crudely forging checks to try to get Leni's house back from the Hoysers. Lev is alienated from bourgeois society. At school, Lev was cruelly taunted for being illegitimate, and he purposely pretended to be stupid to show his contempt for the educational system (his true intelligence is evidenced by his fluent command of Russian and his sensitive understanding of German literature). As a child, Lev had a passion for cleanliness, and he is now a garbage worker; Böll's satiric message is that society needs to be cleansed. Lev has rejected middle-class society and values and has chosen to live as an outsider. Among the foreign garbage workers, he finds community and solidarity (the garbage workers cause a traffic jam with their trucks to prevent Leni's eviction). Hope also lies in the group of Leni's friends who work together to help her. As in *Billiards at Half-Past Nine*, however, the community of like-minded, idealistic people is helpless to change society: The members of the group can retain their integrity only on the fringes of society.

THE LOST HONOR OF KATHARINA BLUM and THE SAFETY NET

The Lost Honor of Katharina Blum: Or, How Violence Develops and Where It Can Lead and *The Safety Net* also focus on modern German social problems. In *The Lost Honor of Katharina Blum*, Böll shows how the media psychologically destroy an individual through sensationalistic and untruthful reporting. In addition to attacking irresponsible journalistic practices, Böll criticizes society for tolerating and indeed thriving on media spectacles. In *The Safety Net*, Böll deals with the problems of terrorism in a democratic society. His belief in the moral responsibility of the writer is as strong in these last works as it was in his earlier ones. Throughout his works, Böll is concerned with the individual who struggles to retain his integrity in a basically hostile world. The critic Marcel Reich-Ranicki sums up Boll's achievement succinctly in "Mehr als ein Dichter" ("More than a Poet"); he writes that without wanting to do so, Böll represents German literature of the twentieth century: He is a poet—more than a poet, because he speaks against all forms of tyranny in the world.

Jennifer Michaels

OTHER MAJOR WORKS

SHORT FICTION: *Wanderer, kommst du nach Spa . . .* , 1950 (*Traveller, If You Come to Spa*, 1956); *So ward Abend und Morgen*, 1955; *Unberechenbare Gäste*, 1956; *Doktor Murkes gesammeltes Schweigen und andere Satiren*, 1958; *Der Fahnhof von Zimpren*, 1959; *Erzählungen, Hörspiele, Aufsätze*, 1961; *Entfernung von der Truppe*, 1964 (*Absent Without Leave*, 1965); *Eighteen Stories*, 1966; *Children Are Civilians Too*, 1970; *Die Verwundung und andere frühe Erzählungen*, 1983 (*The Casualty*, 1986); *Veränderungen in Staech: Erzählungen, 1962-1980*, 1984; *The Stories of Heinrich Böll*, 1986.

PLAYS: *Ein Schluck Erde*, pb. 1962; *Aussatz*, pb. 1970.

SCREENPLAY: *Deutschland im Herbst*, 1978.

POETRY: *Gedichte*, 1972; *Gedichte mit Collagen von Klaus Staeck*, 1980.

NONFICTION: *Irisches Tagebuch*, 1957 (*Irish Journal*, 1967); *Brief an einen jungen Katholiken*, 1961; *Frankfurter Vorlesungen*, 1966; *Hierzulande*, 1967; *Aufsätze, Kritiken, Reden*, 1967; *Neue politische und literarische Schriften*, 1973; *Schwierigkeiten mit der Brüderlichkeit*, 1976; *Einmischung erwünscht*, 1977; *Missing Persons and Other Essays*, 1977; *Spuren der Zeitgenossenschaft*, 1980; *Gefahren von falschen Brüdern*, 1980; *Was soll aus dem Jungen bloss werden? Oder, Irgendwas mit Büchern*, 1981 (*What's to Become of the Boy? Or, Something to Do with Books*, 1984); *Vermintes Gelände*, 1982; *Bild, Bonn, Boenisch*, 1984.

MISCELLANEOUS: *Heinrich Böll Werke*, 1977-1979.

BIBLIOGRAPHY

Conard, Robert C. *Heinrich Böll*. Boston: Twayne, 1981. An excellent introductory study, with several chapters on his short fiction and novels, detailed notes, and bibliography.

_____. *Understanding Heinrich Böll*. Columbia: University of South Carolina Press, 1992. Includes a solid chapter of biography and chapters on the war stories, satires, and major novels. Very detailed notes and extensive, annotated bibliography.

Demetz, Peter. *Postwar German Literature*. New York: Pegasus, 1970. Contains an extensive section on Böll's fiction.

Ley, Ralph. "Compassion, Catholicism, and Communism: Reflections on Böll's *Gruppenbild mit Dame*." *University of Dayton Review* 10 (1973): 25-39. This article and Ziolkowki's are the best treatments in English of *Group Portrait with Lady*.

Reid, James Henderson. *Heinrich Böll: A German for His Time*. Oxford: Oswald Wolff, 1988. As the title indicates, a life-and-times approach to Böll's career. This is an excellent effort to situate Böll as a product of his culture.

_____. *Heinrich Böll: Withdrawal and Re-emergence*. Oxford: Oswald Wolff, 1973. An earlier but still valuable study of how Böll reacted to World War II and to postwar German history.

Ryan, Judith. *The Uncompleted Past: Postwar German Novels and the Third Reich*. Detroit, Mich.: Wayne State University Press, 1983. Contains one chapter on Böll.

Ziolkowski, Theodore. "Heinrich Böll: Conscience and Craft." *Books Abroad* 34 (1960): 213-222. A probing study of Böll's handling of moral and ethical issues.

_____. "The Author as *Advocatus Dei* in Heinrich Böll's *Group Portrait with Lady*." *University of Dayton Review* 12 (1976): 7-18. One of the best discussions of Böll's narrative methods.

ARNA BONTEMPS

Born: Alexandria, Louisiana; October 13, 1902
Died: Nashville, Tennessee; June 4, 1973

PRINCIPAL LONG FICTION
God Sends Sunday, 1931
Black Thunder, 1936
Drums at Dusk, 1939

OTHER LITERARY FORMS

Bontemps was a prolific author and editor. He wrote or cowrote many children's books, biographies, and histories. He edited or coedited more than a dozen works, including African American poetry anthologies, histories, slave narratives, and a folklore collection. His short stories were collected in *The Old South* (1973), and his poetry collection, *Personals*, appeared in 1963. He and Countée Cullen

(Library of Congress)

adapted Bontemps's novel *God Sends Sunday* for the New York stage in 1946 as *St. Louis Woman*. Bontemps's forty-two-year correspondence with writer Langston Hughes was published in 1980.

ACHIEVEMENTS

Bontemps's finely honed poems quietly reflect his lifelong Christian beliefs. After winning several prizes for his poems and short stories in the 1920's and 1930's, Bontemps was granted the first of two Rosenwald Fellowships in Creative Writing in 1939 (the other came in 1943). In 1949 and 1954 he received Guggenheim Fellowships for creative writing. He was given the Jane Addams Children's Book Award in 1956 for *The Story of the Negro* and was also runner-up for the Newbery Award. In 1969 he was appointed writer-in-residence at Fisk University, and in 1972 he was named honorary consultant to the Library of Congress in American cultural history. Beginning in the 1960's he was a popular national speaker, and he always offered encouragement to struggling black writers. He was loved and respected by his students, wherever he served as a teacher.

BIOGRAPHY

Arna Wendell Bontemps's parentage was Louisiana Creole. He was born in the front bedroom of his maternal grandfather's comfortable home at the corner of Ninth and Winn Streets in Alexandria, Louisiana. The house is still standing, though it has been moved, and is today the Arna Bontemps African American Museum. Bontemps's father, a skilled stonemason, bricklayer, and former trombonist with a New Orleans marching band, moved with his wife, children, and in-laws to California following a racial incident in Louisiana. The elder Bontemps also served as a Seventh-Day Adventist preacher after he abandoned Catholicism.

Bontemps's earliest childhood was spent happily in his grandparents' house in Alexandria. Later, in California, he recalled being greatly influenced by a great-uncle, Uncle Buddy, who came from Alexandria to stay with his relatives in California. Though Uncle Buddy was a down-at-the-heels alcoholic, he nevertheless represented, for young Bontemps, the essence of Louisiana culture, folklore, and history with his colorful stories and speech. Self-educated, intelligent, and articulate, Uncle Buddy was a good reader and storyteller and awakened in his grand-nephew a love of hearing and telling stories and of reading and reciting poetry. Most important, Uncle Buddy reminded young Bontemps of his Louisiana and southern roots, which were later to be a great literary storehouse for the budding author.

Bontemps's mother died when he was ten, and he and his sister went to live on his grandmother's farm near Los Angeles. Bontemps completed his secondary schooling at a private boarding school and his bachelor's degree at the University of the Pacific. In New York he joined the Harlem Renaissance, which was in full swing, and began a close, lifelong friendship with writer Langston Hughes.

Bontemps taught school in New York, married Alberta Jones when he was twenty-four, and subsequently fathered six children. In 1931 Bontemps and his family moved to Alabama, where he taught in a junior college and observed southern behavior and customs. In 1934 Bontemps and his family left Alabama because of a hostile racial climate following the trial of the Scottsboro Nine, black men who were unjustly convicted of raping two white women, and moved into his father's small house in California. There the author worked on his second novel, frequently writing outdoors with his small portable typewriter on a makeshift desk.

By 1943 he had moved to Chicago, where he earned a master's degree in library science. Accepting an appointment as full professor and head librarian at Fisk University in Nashville, he served there until the mid-1960's, when he accepted a professorship in history and literature at the University of Illinois at Chicago Circle. He also served as curator of the James Weldon Johnson Collection.

In 1969 he retired to work on his autobiography, which was unfinished at his death. In 1972 he published *The Harlem Renaissance Remembered* and returned to visit his birthplace in Louisiana. He died on June 4, 1973, and was honored at both Protestant and Catholic memorial services.

ANALYSIS

Though he lived and taught in many parts of America, Bontemps always identified with the South and set most of his fictional works there. Bontemps greatly valued his African American inheritance and tried to increase both racial pride and understanding through his many books about African American figures, life, and culture.

GOD SENDS SUNDAY

In God Sends Sunday, set in the 1890's, Bontemps depicts a diminutive black jockey, Little Augie, who lives on a Red River plantation in Louisiana with his older sister. Because he was born with a caul over his face, he is thought to be lucky. He discovers a talent for riding horses, which serves him well when he escapes to New Orleans on a steamboat and becomes a jockey. Augie grows rich, arrogant, and ostentatious. He falls in love with a beautiful young mulatto, Florence Desseau, but learns, to his sorrow, that she is the mistress of his rich white patron. Going to St. Louis to find a woman like Florence, Augie falls in with a crowd of prostitutes, gamblers, and "sugar daddies," one of whom he murders when the man bothers Augie's woman. Returning to New Orleans, Augie at last has Florence as his lover. However, she deserts him, taking his money and possessions. Augie's luck fades, and he declines rapidly into penury and alcoholism. In California, Augie commits another "passion murder" and escapes to Mexico.

The novel exhibits a remarkable *joie de vivre* among its black characters, but they are primarily caricatures within a melodramatic plot. Bontemps uses black dialect and folklore effectively, however, especially the blues, for which Augie has a great affection.

BLACK THUNDER

Bontemps's second novel, first published in 1936, was reissued in 1968 with a valuable introduction by Bontemps. In this essay, he describes finding a treasured store of slave narratives in the Fisk Library; he read the stories of slave insurrectionists Nat Turner, Denmark Vesey, and Gabriel Prosser. Bontemps identified Prosser as the slave-rebel-hero whose yearning for freedom most greatly resembled his own.

Black Thunder is generally acknowledged by readers and critics alike to be Bontemps's best novel; it has even been called the best African American historical novel. The French Revolution and the slave rebellion in Santo Domingo are a significant background; the story dramatizes an enslaved people's long-restrained desire for freedom. Bundy, an old black peasant, longs for the freedom that the legend of Haitian liberator Toussaint-Louverture has inspired in many slaves. When Bundy is viciously flogged to death, Gabriel Prosser, a strong young coachman, feels driven to seek freedom for himself and his people. This feeling is even held by already-freed slaves, such as Mingo, a leather worker, who plays a major role in the rebellion effort. The white Virginians, both patricians and common folk, hold Creuzot, a French painter, and Biddenhurst, a British lawyer, responsible for the slaves' disquiet. Moreover, the white population does not believe the slaves to be human; thus, they cannot understand why they would want freedom. The whites' interpretation of the Bible supports their racial beliefs.

Gabriel too is deeply religious, though not fanatical, and often echoes scripture, believing that God will free his people because Armageddon is at hand. He plans, with the assistance of free blacks, slaves, and a few sympathetic whites, to capture the arsenal at Richmond in order to seize the weapons and overpower the city. Unfortunately, a monsoonlike rainstorm on the night of the rebellion causes a delay in the insurrection. Bontemps's powers as a prose artist are especially strong as he describes, in haunting cadences, the revolt's defeat by nature's wrath. The slaves believe that it was ill luck and fateful weather that led to the revolt's collapse, though in actuality two elderly, spoiled house servants betrayed the cause. The collapse of the rebellion marks the climax of the story; what follows tells of the insurrectionists' capture and execution. Bontemps makes astute use of court records as he dramatizes Gabriel's trial.

Bontemps is in firmer control of his literary material in *Black Thunder* than in his other novels. All his characters—white planter-aristocrats, free blacks, and French zealots—are drawn with objectivity and restraint. Pro-freedom views are not praised at the expense of anti-freedom beliefs. Furthermore, Bontemps's characters, even minor ones, are richly complex. For example, Ben and Pharoah, the betrayers of the rebellion, evidence conflicting loyalties both to their aristocratic masters and to their African American brothers. In a memorable interior monologue, Ben condemns himself for the narcissism that made his own survival more important to him than that of his fellow slaves. His ironic curse is that he must live under the threat of a horrible revenge at the hands of his own people.

Bontemps's special achievement in *Black Thunder* is the skill with which he integrates Gabriel's revolt into the fabric of Virginian, and American, life by using a documentary style of exposition. While Virginia legislators debate further segregation of blacks as a way of dealing with race issues, quoted reports from Federalist newspapers oppose the liberal ideas of former president Thomas Jefferson and attribute Gabriel's revolt to his evil influence. These same newspapers support John Quincy Adams's presidential campaign.

Even more impressive is Bontemps's use of interior monologues and passages which present the point of view of several individual characters, Caucasian and African American. First- and third-person perspectives are blended in order to present both objective and subjective forces. Bontemps's careful synthesis of history and imagination helps him demonstrate the universal, age-old struggles of humankind to surmount barriers of race, class, and caste and gain equality, liberty, respect, and security. Because Bontemps allows Gabriel to maintain and even increase his integrity, he becomes a truly tragic figure for whom, at the end of the novel, "excellent is strength, the first for freedom of the blacks, . . . [he is] perplexed but unafraid, waiting for the dignity of death."

DRUMS AT DUSK

Drums at Dusk, like *Black Thunder*, is a historical novel in which Bontemps makes use of slave narratives and legal records to establish background for the black rebellion leading to Haiti's independence and Toussaint-Louverture's ascendancy. Bontemps centers the story around a young girl of French an-

cestry, Celeste Juvet, and Diron de Sautels, an aristocratic young Frenchman who claims membership in
Les Amis des Noirs, embraces enthusiastically the
ideas of writers of the French Revolution, and works
as an abolitionist. Celeste and her grandmother reside
on a large plantation where the owner's cousin,
Count Armand de Sacy, abuses ailing slaves and mistreats his mistresses, abandoning them at his uncle's.
De Sacy is deeply disliked, and when several slaves
foment an insurrection, the aristocrats are overturned
and rebel leaders successfully seize power.

Diron de Sautels's radical opinions influence
young blacks, and they fight with three other groups
for political control of Santo Domingo: rich aristocrats, poor whites, and free mulattos. *Drums at Dusk*
describes with melodramatic sensationalism the syb-
aritic lives of the wealthy and their sexual exploitation of light-skinned black women. Moreover, the
novel describes graphically the heinous conditions on
the slave ships and on many of the plantations. The
patricians' cruelty and abuse lead to a rapid spread of
liberal ideology and the rise of such leaders as
Toussaint-Louverture.

In spite of its faults, Bontemps's last novel, like
his second one, emphasizes the universal need and
desire for freedom, which he intimates is as necessary for the survival of human beings as water, air,
food, and shelter.

Philip A. Tapley

OTHER MAJOR WORKS

SHORT FICTION: *The Old South*, 1973.

PLAY: *St. Louis Woman*, pr. 1946 (with Countée
Cullen).

POETRY: *Personals*, 1963.

NONFICTION: *Father of the Blues*, 1941 (biography; with W. C. Handy); *They Seek a City*, 1945 (history; with Jack Conroy; revised as *Anyplace but
Here*, 1966); *One Hundred Years of Negro Freedom*,
1961 (history); *Free at Last: The Life of Frederick
Douglass*, 1971; *Arna Bontemps-Langston Hughes
Letters: 1925-1967*, 1980.

CHILDREN'S LITERATURE: *Popo and Fifina:
Children of Haiti* (with Langston Hughes), 1932; *You
Can't Pet a Possum*, 1934; *Sad-Faced Boy*, 1937; *The

Fast Sooner Hound, 1942 (with Conroy); *We Have
Tomorrow*, 1945; *Slappy Hooper: The Wonderful
Sign Painter*, 1946 (with Conroy); *The Story of the
Negro*, 1948; *Sam Patch*, 1951 (with Conroy); *Char-
iot in the Sky: A Story of the Jubilee Singers*, 1951;
The Story of George Washington Carver, 1954; *Lone-
some Boy*, 1955; *Frederick Douglass: Slave, Fighter,
Freeman*, 1959; *Famous Negro Athletes*, 1964; *Mr.
Kelso's Lion*, 1970; *Young Booker: Booker T. Wash-
ington's Early Days*, 1972; *The Pasteboard Bandit*,
1997 (with Hughes); *Bubber Goes to Heaven*, 1998.

EDITED TEXTS: *The Poetry of the Negro*, 1949 (revised 1971, with Hughes); *The Book of Negro Folklore*, 1958 (with Hughes); *American Negro Poetry*,
1963; *Great Slave Narratives*, 1969; *Hold Fast to
Dreams*, 1969; *The Harlem Renaissance Remembered*, 1972.

BIBLIOGRAPHY

Bone, Robert. *The Negro Novel in America*. New Haven: Yale University Press, 1965. Contains brief
but perceptive comments on Bontemps's two historical novels.

Davis, Mary Kemp. "Arna Bontemps' *Black Thunder*: The Creation of an Authoritative Text of 'Gabriel's Defeat.'" *Black American Literature Forum* 23, no. 1 (Spring, 1989): 17-36. Compares
Bontemps's novel with three previously published
versions of the Gabriel Prosser conspiracy.

Fleming, Robert E. *James Weldon Johnson and Arna
Wendell Bontemps: A Reference Guide*. Boston:
G. K. Hall, 1978. Contains a biography of
Bontemps, as well as indexes and bibliography.

Jones, Kirkland C. *Renaissance Man from Louisiana: A Biography of Arna Wendell Bontemps*.
Westport, Conn.: Greenwood Press, 1992. The
first full-scale biography of Bontemps. Treats the
author's life and career in detail, but only briefly
analyzes or evaluates the writings.

Reagan, Daniel. "Voices of Silence: The Representation of Orality in Arna Bontemps' *Black Thunder*." *Studies in American Fiction* 19 (Spring,
1991): 71-83. Examines the use of African American vernacular traditions in *Black Thunder* and
concludes that the novel's significant statements

of black cultural identity occur in the oral discourse that Bontemps portrays through figurative language.

Stone, Albert. "The Thirties and the Sixties: Arna Bontemps' *Black Thunder.*" In *The Return of Nat Turner: History, Literature, and Cultural Politics in Sixties America.* Athens: University of Georgia Press, 1992. Examines Bontemps's successful synthesis of history and his own imagination in *Black Thunder.*

Weil, Dorothy. "Folklore Motifs in Arna Bontemps' *Black Thunder.*" *Southern Folklore Quarterly* 25, no. 1 (March, 1971): 1-14. Analyzes Bontemps's authentic use of black folklore concerning death, spirits, portents, magic, and conjuring.

ELIZABETH BOWEN

Born: Dublin, Ireland; June 7, 1899
Died: London, England; February 22, 1973

PRINCIPAL LONG FICTION

The Hotel, 1927
The Last September, 1929
Friends and Relations, 1931
To the North, 1932
The House in Paris, 1935
The Death of the Heart, 1938
The Heat of the Day, 1949
A World of Love, 1955
The Little Girls, 1964
Eva Trout, 1968

OTHER LITERARY FORMS

The first seven of Elizabeth Bowen's novels were republished by Jonathan Cape in Cape Collected Editions between the years 1948 and 1954, when Cape also republished four of her short-story collections: *Joining Charles* (1929), *The Cat Jumps and Other Stories* (1934), *Look at All Those Roses* (1941), and *The Demon Lover* (1945). Other books of short stories are *Encounters* (1923), *Ann Lee's and Other*

Stories (1926), *Stories by Elizabeth Bowen* (1959), and *A Day in the Dark and Other Stories* (1965). *The Demon Lover* was published in New York under the title *Ivy Gripped the Steps and Other Stories* (1946) and, as the original title indicates, has supernatural content which scarcely appears in the novels. Bowen's nonfiction includes *Bowen's Court* (1942), a description of her family residence in Ireland; *Seven Winters* (1942), an autobiography; *English Novelists* (1946), a literary history; *Collected Impressions* (1950), essays; *The Shelbourne: A Center of Dublin Life for More than a Century* (1951), a work about the hotel in Dublin; *A Time in Rome* (1960), travel essays; and *Afterthought: Pieces About Writing* (1962), broadcasts and reviews. A play, coauthored with John Perry and entitled *Castle Anna*, was performed in London in March, 1948.

ACHIEVEMENTS

Considered a great lady by those who knew her, Bowen draws an appreciative audience from readers who understand English gentility—the calculated gesture and the controlled response. Bowen's support has come from intellectuals who recognize the values of the novel of manners and who liken her work to that of Jane Austen and Henry James. Her contemporaries and colleagues included members of the Bloomsbury Group and of Oxford University, where the classical scholar C. M. Bowra was a close friend. Many readers know Bowen best through her novel *The Death of the Heart* and her short stories, especially "The Demon Lover," "Joining Charles," and "Look at All Those Roses," which are frequently anthologized in college texts. Bowen was made a Commander of the British Empire in 1948, and she was awarded an honorary doctor of letters degree at Trinity College, Dublin, in 1949, and at Oxford University in 1957. She was made a Companion of Literature in 1965.

BIOGRAPHY

Although born in Ireland, Elizabeth Dorothea Cole Bowen came from a pro-British family who received land in County Cork as an award for fighting with Oliver Cromwell in 1649. The family built

Bowen's Court in 1776—what the Irish call a "big house"—as a Protestant stronghold against the mainly Catholic Irish and lived there as part of the Anglo-Irish ascendancy. Bowen was educated in England and spent some summers at Bowen's Court. Not until after the Irish Rising in 1916 did she come to realize the causes of the Irish struggle for independence; and in writing *Bowen's Court*, she admitted that her family "got their position and drew their power from a situation that shows an inherent wrong."

Her barrister father, when he was nineteen, had disobeyed forewarnings and carried home smallpox, which eventually killed his mother and rendered his father mad. Preoccupied with the desire for a son, the attempt to have one nearly killed his wife in 1904, and burdened with the debts of Bowen's Court, he suffered severe mental breakdowns in 1905 and 1906 and again in 1928. He was the cause of Elizabeth's removal to England, where, as an Irish outcast, her defense was to become excessively British. Living in a series of locations with her mother, she was kept uninformed of family circumstances; as an adult, her novels provided for her an outlet for her sense of guilt, the result of feeling responsible for the unexplained events around her. Her lack of roots was intensified with the death of her mother in 1912.

Bowen studied art, traveled in Europe, and worked as an air-raid warden in London during World War II. In 1923, she married Alan Charles Cameron, who was employed in the school system near Oxford, and they lived there for twelve years. She inherited Bowen's Court in 1928 when her father died, and in 1952, she and her husband returned there to live. Bowen's husband, however, died that year. She sold the home in 1960 and returned to Oxford.

Bowen's career as novelist spanned years of drastic change, 1927 to 1968, and, except for *The Last September*, she wrote about the present; her war experiences are reflected in the short-story collection *The Demon Lover* and in the novel *The Heat of the Day*. After 1935, she also wrote reviews and articles for *The New Statesman* and other publications, the Ministry of Information during World War II, and *The Tatler* (in the 1940's), and she helped edit the *London Magazine* in the late 1950's. Afflicted with a

(Library of Congress)

slight stammer, Bowen lectured infrequently but effectively; two of her BBC broadcasts, "left as they were spoken," may be read in *Afterthought*. After a visit to Ireland in 1973, she died in London, leaving an unfinished autobiographical work, *Pictures and Conversations* (1975).

ANALYSIS

Elizabeth Bowen had a special talent for writing the conversations of children around the age of nine, as she did in *The House in Paris*. Somewhat corresponding to her personal experience, her novels often present a homeless child (usually a girl), orphaned and shunted from one residence to another, or a child with one parent who dies and leaves the adolescent in the power of outwardly concerned but mainly selfish adults. Frequently, management by others prolongs the protagonist's state of innocence into the twenties, when the woman must begin to assert herself and learn to manage her own affairs. (At age twenty-four, for example, Eva Trout does not know how to boil water for tea.) On the other side of the relationship, the controlling adult is often a perfectly mannered woman of guile, wealthy enough to be idle and to fill the idleness with discreet exercise of power over others. The typical Bowen characters, then, are the child, the unwanted adolescent, the woman in her twenties in a prolonged state of adolescence, and the "terrible woman" of society. Young people, educated haphazardly but expensively, are culturally mature but aimless. Genteel adults, on the other hand, administer their own selfish standards of what constitutes an impertinence in another person; these judgments disguise Bowen's subtle criticism of the correct English.

Typical Bowen themes follow as "loss of innocence," "acceptance of the past," or "expanding consciousness." The pain and helplessness attendant upon these themes and the disguise of plentiful money make them unusual. Although she writes about the privileged class, three of her four common character types do not feel privileged. To handle her themes, Bowen frequently orders time and space by dividing the novels into three parts, with one part set ten years in the past and with a juxtaposition of at least two locations. The ten-year lapse provides a measure of the maturity gained, and the second location, by contrast, jars the consciousness into reevaluation of the earlier experience.

THE HOTEL

The fact that the Bowen women often have nothing to do is very obvious in *The Hotel*, set in Bordighera on the Italian Riviera, but, of greater interest, it is, like Ireland, another place of British occupancy. Guests' activities are confined to walking, talking, taking tea, and playing tennis. Mrs. Kerr is the managing wealthy woman who feeds on the attentions of her protégé, Sydney Warren, and then abandons Sydney when her son arrives. At age twenty-two, Sydney, for lack of better purpose, studies for a doctorate at home in England. Back in Italy, she gets engaged to a clergyman as a means of achieving an identity and popularity, but her better sense forces reconsideration, and she cancels the engagement and asserts her independence.

THE LAST SEPTEMBER

The Last September, set in 1920 when the hated British soldiers (the Black and Tans) were stationed in Ireland to quell rebellion, shows Sir Richard and Lady Myra Naylor entertaining with tennis parties at their big house. Like Bowen, who wrote in *Afterthought* that this novel was "nearest my heart," Lois Farquar is a summer visitor, aged nineteen, orphaned, asking herself what she should do. An older woman tells her that her art lacks talent. Almost engaged to a British soldier, Gerald Lesworth, she might have a career in marriage, but Lady Naylor, in the role of graceful-terrible woman, destroys the engagement in a brilliant heart-to-heart talk, in which she points out that he has no prospects.

As September closes the social season, Gerald Lesworth is killed in ambush, and as Lois—much more aware now and less innocent—prepares to depart for France, her home Danielstown is burned down, which signals her separation from the protected past.

TO THE NORTH

After *Friends and Relations*, Bowen entered the most fruitful part of her career. Her next four novels are generally considered to be her best work. *To the North* has rather obvious symbolism in a protagonist named Emmeline Summers whose lack of feeling makes her "icy." She runs a successful travel agency with the motto "Travel Dangerously" (altering "Live Dangerously" and "Travel Safe"); the motto reflects both her ability to understand intellectually the feelings of others through their experience and her orphan state in homelessness. Emmeline tries to compensate for her weaknesses by imposing dramatic opposites: Without a home of her own, she overvalues her home with her widowed sister-in-law, Cecilia Summers; frequently called an angel, she has a fatal attraction to the devil-like character Markie Linkwater. When Cecilia plans to remarry (breaking up the home), when Markie (bored with Emmeline) returns to his former mistress, and when Emmeline's travel business begins to fail rapidly because of her preoccupation with Markie, she smashes her car while driving Markie north; "traveling dangerously" at high speeds, she becomes the angel of death.

The cold of the North suggested by the novel's title also touches other characters. Lady Waters, who offers Emmeline weekends on her estate as a kind of second home, feeds mercilessly on the unhappiness of failed loves and gossip. Lady Waters tells Cecilia to speak to Emmeline about her affair with Markie and thereby initiates the fateful dinner party, which leads to the accident. Pauline, the niece of Cecilia's fiancé, is the orphaned adolescent character on the verge of becoming aware of and embarrassed by sex. Bowen describes Emmeline as the "stepchild of her uneasy century," a century in which planes and trains have damaged the stability and book knowledge of sexual research (indicated by the reading of Havelock Ellis), thereby freeing relationships but failing to engage the heart. The travel and the lack of warmth make the title a metaphor for the new century's existence. With her tenuous hold on home, love, and career, Emmeline commits suicide.

THE HOUSE IN PARIS

The House in Paris is set in three locations, which reflect different aspects of the protagonist, Karen Michaelis: England, the land of perfect society; Ireland, the land of awareness; and France, the land of passion and the dark past. Parts 1 and 3 take place in a single day in Paris; part 2 occurs ten years earlier, during four months when Karen was age twenty-three. The evils of the house in Paris become apparent in the flashback and can be appreciated only through recognition of the terrible woman who runs it, Mme Fisher, and the rootlessness of the foreign students who stay there. Among other students, Mme Fisher has had in her power Karen and her friend Naomi Fisher (Mme Fisher's daughter), and the young Max Ebhart, a Jew with no background. Ten years later, when Max wants to break his engagement with Naomi to marry another, Mme Fisher interferes, and he commits suicide.

The book begins and ends in a train station in Paris. In part 1, Leopold—age nine and the illegitimate child of Karen and Max Ebhart—and Henrietta Mountjoy—age eleven and the granddaughter of a friend of Mme Fisher—arrive on separate trains: Henrietta from England in the process of being shuttled to another relative, and Leopold from his adop-

tive parents in Italy to await a first acquaintance with his real mother. Leopold and Henrietta, meeting in the house in Paris, become symbolic of the possibility that, with Mme Fisher bedridden for ten years (since the suicide) and now dying, the future will be free of the mistakes of the past. Mme Fisher, in an interview with Leopold, tells him that the possibility of finding himself "like a young tree inside a tomb is to discover the power to crack the tomb and grow up to any height," something Max had failed to do.

Dark, egotistic, self-centered, and passionate like his father, Leopold constructs imaginatively a role for his unknown mother to play and then breaks into uncontrollable weeping when a telegram arrives canceling her visit. The mature and implacable Henrietta, orphaned like Leopold but accustomed to the vicissitudes of adult life, shows him how to crack out of the tomb of childhood. In part 3, quite unexpectedly, Ray Forrestier, who had given up diplomacy and taken up business to marry Karen in spite of her illegitimate child, urges a reunion with her son Leopold, takes matters into his own hands, and brings Leopold to Karen.

THE DEATH OF THE HEART

The three-part structure of Bowen's novels is most fully realized in *The Death of the Heart*; the parts are labeled "The World," "The Flesh," and "The Devil," and follow the seasons of winter, spring, and summer. The world of Windsor Terrace, the Quaynes' residence in London, is advanced and sterile. Portia enters into this world at age fifteen, an orphan and stepsister to the present Thomas Quayne. Thomas's wife Anna, who has miscarried twice and is childless, secretly reads Portia's diary and is indignant at the construction Portia puts on the household events. Portia sees much "dissimulation" at Windsor Terrace, where doing the "right" thing does not mean making a moral choice. As one of Bowen's radical innocents who has spent her youth in hotels and temporary locations, Portia says no one in this house knows why she was born. She has only one friend in this, her first home: the head-servant Matchett, who gives Portia some religious training. Of the three male friends who wait upon Anna—St. Quentin Martin, Eddie, and Major Brutt—Portia fastens on the affections of Eddie.

Spring, in part 2, brings a much-needed vacation for the Quaynes. Thomas and Anna sail for Capri, and Portia goes to stay with Anna's former governess at Seale-on-Sea. At the governess's home, dubbed Waikiki, Portia is nearly drowned in sensuality—the sights, smells, sounds, and feelings of a vulgar and mannerless household. Portia invites Eddie to spend a weekend with her at Seale-on-Sea, which further educates her in the ways of the flesh.

Portia's more open nature, on her return to London in part 3, is immediately apparent to Matchett, who says she had been "too quiet." The Devil's works are represented both obviously and subtly in this section, and they take many identities. St. Quentin, Anna, Eddie, even the unloving atmosphere of Windsor Terrace make up the Devil's advocacy. St. Quentin, a novelist, tells Portia that Anna has been reading her diary, a disloyalty and an invasion of privacy with which, after some contemplation, Portia decides she cannot live. Herein lies the death of her teenage heart, what Bowen calls a betrayal of her innocence, or a "mysterious landscape" that has perished.

Summer at Windsor Terrace brings maturity to Portia, as well as others: Anna must confront her own culpability, even her jealousy of Portia; St. Quentin, his betrayal of Anna's reading of the diary; Thomas, his neglect of his father and his father's memory. Even Matchett takes a terrified ride in the unfamiliar cab, setting out in the night to an unknown location to pick up Portia. They all share in the summer's maturation that Portia has brought to fruition.

William Shakespeare's Portia preferred mercy to justice, paralleling the Portia in this novel. Bowen's Portia observes everything with a "political seriousness." The scaffolding of this novel supports much allusion, metaphor, and drama—all artfully structured. The world, the flesh, and the Devil as medieval threats to saintliness are reinterpreted in this context; they become the locations of the heart that has been thrust outside Eden and comprise a necessary trinity, not of holiness but of wholeness. This novel earns critics' accord as Bowen's best.

THE HEAT OF THE DAY

In *The Death of the Heart*, ranked by many critics as a close second to *The Heat of the Day*, Bowen uses the war to purge the wasteland conditions that existed before and during the years from 1940 through 1945. Middle-class Robert Kelway has returned from Dunkirk (1940) with a limp that comes and goes according to the state of his emotions. At the individual level, it reflects the psychological crippling of his youth; at the national level, it is the culmination of the condition expressed by the person who says "Dunkirk was waiting there in us."

Upper-class Stella Rodney has retreated from the privileges of her past into a rented apartment and a war job. Having grown impassive with the century, divorced with a son (Roderick) in the army, she has taken Robert as her lover. She has become so impassive, in fact, that in 1942, a sinister and mysterious government spy named Harrison tells her that Robert has been passing information to the enemy, and she says and does nothing.

Critics have commented frequently on this novel's analogies to William Shakespeare's *Hamlet* (1600-1601), an obvious example being Holme Dene (Dane home), Robert Kelway's country home. Psychologically weak, Robert is ruled by his destructive mother, who also had stifled his father and planted the seeds of Robert's defection from English ways. While Stella visits Holme Dene and learns to understand Robert, her son visits a cousin who tells him that Stella did not divorce her husband, as was commonly thought, but rather was divorced by him while he was having an affair, although he died soon after the divorce. Roderick, however, has managed to survive Stella's homelessness with a positive and manly outlook and, when he inherits an estate in Ireland, finds that it will give him the foundation for a future.

EVA TROUT

In *Eva Trout*, the various autobiographical elements of Bowen's work come to life: Bowen's stammer in Eva's reticence, the tragic deaths of both parents, the transience and sporadic education, the delayed adolescence, the settings of hotels and train stations. Eva Trout lives with a former teacher, Iseult

Arbles, and her husband Eric while she waits for an inheritance. She turns twenty-four and receives the inheritance, which enables her to leave their home, where the marriage is unstable, to buy a home filled with used furniture. She also escapes the clutches of Constantine, her guardian who had been her father's male lover.

Eva discovers that a woman with money is suddenly pursued by "admirers," and Eric visits her in her new home. Eva subsequently lets Iseult think that Eric has fathered her child, whom she adopts in America. After eight years in American cities, where Eva seeks help for the deaf-mute child Jeremy, Eva and Jeremy return to England. From England, they flee to Paris, where a doctor and his wife begin successful training of Jeremy. Back in England, Eva attempts the next phase of reaching security and a normal life. She seeks a husband and persuades the son of Iseult's vicar to stage a wedding departure with her at Victoria Station. All her acquaintances are on hand to see the couple off, but Jeremy—brought from Paris for the occasion—playfully points a gun (he thought a toy) at Eva and shoots her. In the midst of revelry, on the eve of her happiness, Eva drops dead beside the train.

Eva Trout makes a poignant and haunting last heroine for the Bowen sequence and a final bitter statement on the elusiveness of security and happiness.

Grace Eckley

OTHER MAJOR WORKS

SHORT FICTION: *Encounters*, 1923; *Ann Lee's and Other Stories*, 1926; *Joining Charles*, 1929; *The Cat Jumps and Other Stories*, 1934; *Look at All Those Roses*, 1941; *The Demon Lover*, 1945 (pb. in U.S. as *Ivy Gripped the Steps and Other Stories*, 1946); *The Early Stories*, 1951; *Stories by Elizabeth Bowen*, 1959; *A Day in the Dark and Other Stories*, 1965; *Elizabeth Bowen's Irish Stories*, 1978; *The Collected Stories of Elizabeth Bowen*, 1980.

PLAY: *Castle Anna*, pr. 1948 (with John Perry).

NONFICTION: *Bowen's Court*, 1942; *Seven Winters*, 1942; *English Novelists*, 1946; *Collected Impressions*, 1950; *The Shelbourne: A Center of Dublin Life for More than a Century*, 1951; *A Time in Rome*,

1960; *Afterthought: Pieces About Writing*, 1962; *Pictures and Conversations*, 1975; *The Mulberry Tree: Writings of Elizabeth Bowen*, 1986.

CHILDREN'S LITERATURE: *The Good Tiger*, 1965.

BIBLIOGRAPHY

Austin, Allan. *Elizabeth Bowen*. Rev. ed. Boston: Twayne, 1989. Emphasizes Bowen's ability to depict locale, as in her account of World War II London in *The Heat of the Day*. Her characters worry and react to events more with emotion than with reason. Bowen presents these characters in a distinctive and urbane style. After a survey of Bowen's general traits as an author, Austin follows with a detailed account of the novels and some of the shorter fiction.

Craig, Patricia. *Elizabeth Bowen*. London: Penguin Books, 1986. Most useful for those wishing to read a shorter biography of Bowen than Glendinning's. Written in a vigorous style and included in the Lives of Modern Women series. Like Glendinning, Craig emphasizes Bowen's extensive circle of literary friends. The depiction of events in Bowen's life is good-humored and blunt.

Glendinning, Victoria. *Elizabeth Bowen*. New York: Alfred A. Knopf, 1978. The standard biography of Bowen. Portrays Bowen as someone with a dominant personality, charming but at times overwhelming. Gives full coverage to Bowen's Anglo-Irish background and her wide circle of Oxford friends. Her devotion to her husband, which did not preclude extramarital affairs, emerges as a leitmotif of Bowen's rather uneventful life. Gives a detailed account of the genesis of each of the major novels.

Jordan, Heather Bryant. *How Will the Heart Endure: Elizabeth Bowen and the Landscape of War*. Ann Arbor: University of Michigan Press, 1992. Explores Bowen's contradictory responses to two world wars, and her view of literary modernism and contemporary events. Treats Bowen as an Anglo-Irish novelist with a strong grounding in history, asserting that she must be read in the context of the events she fictionalized. Includes notes and bibliography.

Lassner, Phyllis. *Elizabeth Bowen: A Study of the Short Fiction*. New York: Twayne, 1991. Section 1 treats Bowen's comedies of sex, manners, and terror, as well as her studies of the female character. Section 2 contains excerpts from Bowen's prefaces and essays. Section 3 provides a sampling of Bowen critics. Includes chronology and bibliography.

Lee, Hermione. *Elizabeth Bowen: An Estimation*. New York: Barnes & Noble Books, 1981. The most detailed critical study of Bowen. Places her in a tradition of Anglo-Irish writers and ranks *The Death of the Heart* as worthy of the highest praise. Considers not only Bowen's novels but her short stories and nonfiction writing as well. Lee ranks a number of the short stories, such as "Summer Night" and "The Cat Jumps," as outstanding.

PAUL BOWLES

Born: New York, New York; December 30, 1910
Died: Tangiers, Morocco; November 18, 1999

PRINCIPAL LONG FICTION

The Sheltering Sky, 1949
Let It Come Down, 1952
The Spider's House, 1955
Up Above the World, 1966

OTHER LITERARY FORMS

Paul Bowles is probably critically appreciated best for his short fiction, even though he is also known for his novels. Famous as a translator especially of Moroccan fiction, he translated from Arabic, French, and Spanish and wrote poetry, travel literature, and even music, to which he devoted himself during the 1930's. His autobiography, *Without Stopping*, was well received when it was published in 1972.

ACHIEVEMENTS

Bowles has a unique place in American literature. As an exile, he shared with 1920's expatriate novelist

Gertrude Stein, among others, a distanced perspective on his native culture. Through his translations, he earned an international reputation as an author with a North African sensibility. His fiction reflects a world akin to that written about by existentialists Jean-Paul Sartre or Albert Camus, and indeed he has been described as America's foremost existentialist writer, a label more likely to restrict him to a time period than to characterize his fiction accurately. Although his nihilism does strike one as a bit recherché, it also has a modern application, reflecting as it does a dark vision of the world as contemporary as the times demand.

Bowles became a guru of sorts to the Beat generation, although Bowles's attraction for them was as much for his writings about drugs as for his generally pessimistic philosophy. Never an author of wide appeal, he has nevertheless had a loyal following among those interested in experimental and avant-garde writing, and his work has reflected a steady maturation, his 1982 experimental work *Points in Time* receiving praise from, among others, Tobias Wolfe, who wrote that the book was a completely original performance. Perhaps in the last analysis, Paul Bowles will be best remembered for his originality, his willingness to challenge definitions and the status quo in his fiction. With every work, he tried to forge new ground.

BIOGRAPHY

Paul Frederic Bowles spent most of his adult life living abroad, in permanent exile, mostly in Morocco, although for brief periods he also lived in France, Mexico, and South America. Admonished as a young man by his disapproving father that he could not expect merely to sit around and loaf as a writer when at home, Paul Bowles found places where he could sit and invite his soul.

He was born in the Jamaica section of New York City, the only child of a dentist and a mother who was a former schoolteacher. He was a precocious child and began writing at an early age. By the time he was in grade school, he had also begun composing music, a passion which occupied him more than did writing until after World War I. Immediately after

(Cherie Nutting)

high school, he attended very briefly the School of Design and Liberal Arts before enrolling in the fall of 1928 as a freshman at the University of Virginia, a choice made primarily because it was the school attended by Edgar Allan Poe. In March, he left the university and ran off to Paris, where he was already known as the writer whose poem "Spire Song" had been published in Eugène Jolas's little magazine *transition*. Bowles returned home the next fall and went to work for Dutton's bookstore while trying to write a novel in his spare time. In the spring, he returned to Virginia to complete his freshman year, at which point he ended forever his college career.

By 1929, Bowles had met and been encouraged by American composer Aaron Copland to pursue a career as a composer by returning to Paris to study with Nadia Boulanger, which he did in the spring of 1931. His second Paris sojourn began his literary life

when he met and became friends with Gertrude Stein, who took him under her ample wing and tutored him in writing. It was Stein's companion Alice Toklas who suggested that Bowles and Copland, who had joined him abroad, live someplace warm, and she suggested Morocco, to which the two composers moved in the late summer of 1931. It was the beginning of Bowles's love affair with North Africa and his life as a writer: From Tangiers Bowles sent Stein his first prose efforts and received back from her the encouragement to continue writing, although, as he admitted later, it was not until the 1940's, while watching his wife, Jane, compose her first novel, that he began to work seriously at the writer's trade.

From 1931 to 1933, Bowles traveled between Europe and North Africa, gathering the impressions that would later shape his first novel, *The Sheltering Sky*. In 1933 he moved to New York City, where he made a living writing music reviews for the *Herald Tribune* and composing theater music for works by Orson Welles, Lillian Hellman, Tennessee Williams, and others.

In 1938 Bowles married Jane Auer, and the couple moved to Mexico in 1940, where Jane Bowles wrote *Two Serious Ladies* (1943), the novel that inspired Paul Bowles to take his literary craft seriously, and where Paul composed his opera *The Wind Remains*, which premiered in New York in 1943. The opera's failure deepened Bowles's interest in pursuing fiction writing.

That same year the Bowleses moved back to New York. There, in 1947, Paul Bowles had an overpowering dream of Tangiers. The dream inspired him to begin *The Sheltering Sky* and prompted his return to North Africa, where he traveled for a year seeking material for the novel in progress. Jane joined him in 1948, and the two settled in Tangiers, where they would become the center of a lively artistic community that included writers William S. Burroughs and Brion Gysin and visitors Tennessee Williams and Truman Capote.

The Sheltering Sky was published in October of 1949, and by December it was on *The New York Times* best-seller list. That same month, Bowles plunged into his second novel, *Let It Come Down*.

Appearing in 1952, it did not receive the popular success or critical acclaim of his first novel, beginning a pattern which would persist throughout his literary career.

While working on novels, short stories, and poems, Bowles became interested in the tales of Moroccan oral storytellers, which he began to translate. By the 1960's, he was translating Moroccan writers as well.

Jane Bowles's declining literary career came to a close with her stroke in 1957. While she survived the illness, its debilitating effects stopped her writing and increased her problems with depression. By 1967 she had been committed to a psychiatric hospital in Spain, and she died in 1973. Reacting to Jane's death, Paul Bowles did little writing for nearly a decade, although he still actively translated. The 1982 critically acclaimed appearance of *Points in Time*, an avant-garde approach to history, marked Bowles's return to writing.

Public interest in Bowles increased dramatically with the 1990 release of Bernardo Bertolucci's film version of *The Sheltering Sky*, in which Bowles had a minor part, and with the 1995 Lincoln Center Paul Bowles celebration and symposium, which Bowles attended despite failing health. On November 18, 1999, Bowles died in Tangiers.

Analysis

Because of his small output of novels and because of his problematic relationship with American writing, Paul Bowles's reputation has yet to be firmly established. A writer who always attracted attention, and serious attention at that, he has not been accorded sufficient critical notice to measure his significance as a writer. To paraphrase Johannes Willem Bertens, one of his most perceptive critics, who has written on the critical response to Bowles's work, Bowles as a novelist can be classified in three categories: Romantic, existentialist, and nihilist. As a Romantic, Bowles saw the modern world in a disjunctive relationship with nature, and that vision pushed him to depict the march of Western progress in very pessimistic terms, which accounts for one of his most frequently recurring themes, namely, that of a sophis-

ticated Westerner confronting a less civilized and more primitive society in a quest of self-discovery. Such Romantic attitudes suggest the reasons for labeling Bowles as an existentialist. The search for an authentic life amid the self-doubts and the fragile, provisional nature of the civilized instincts, as Theodore Solotaroff describes it, places Bowles squarely within the existentialist tradition made more formal and philosophical by such writers as Camus and Sartre. The search for values in a world without God, a world with an ethical vacuum, suggests the third possible interpretation of Bowles's fiction, that of nihilism.

There are those critics, especially Chester E. Eisinger, who understand the novelist's universe as totally without hope, a region devoid of meaning and purpose and thereby representing a nihilistic philosophical position. This position is worked out through the clash between civilizations, or rather through the tension between civilization and the savage. Even Bowles himself remarked that life is absurd and the whole business of living hopeless, a conviction he would share with most of his central characters, thereby giving credence to any nihilistic interpretation of his fiction. Whichever position one takes, the central details of Bowles's novels remain the same: A Westerner, often an intellectual, searches through an Eastern, less civilized culture for meaning and direction, usually finding neither by the end of the book.

The Sheltering Sky

The Sheltering Sky is both Paul Bowles's first novel and his best-known novel. It is a book in which the author set forth those topics or themes which he would pursue throughout the rest of his fiction with almost obsessive tenacity. The story follows an American couple, Port and Kit Moresby, who have traveled to Morocco in search of themselves and to reinvigorate their marriage after years of indifference. The couple appear in Oran shortly after World War II and there experience a series of devastating events which eventually kill Port and destroy the mental stability of his wife, Kit.

Soon after their arrival, Port insists that they travel inland into the desert. Kit is opposed, so Port, accompanied by an Australian photographer and her son, depart, leaving Kit with Tunner, their American friend, who is to escort her on the night train later that day. Bored by the ride, Kit wanders into the fourth-class, or native, section of the train and passes a frightening night among the Arabs, later sleeping with Tunner. Meanwhile, Port has come to the realization that he desires a reconciliation with his wife. The novel follows this hapless pair as they progress farther and farther into the heart of the country, leaving civilization more distantly behind them. Port contracts typhoid and dies, leaving his wife alone to face the rigors of the desert. She is picked up by a passing caravan and made the sexual slave of the leaders of the group. She is both entranced and repulsed by the experience and is soon completely disoriented by her subjugation. Finally, she is rescued by a member of the American embassy only to disappear once again, this time for good, into the Casbah, or native quarter, in Oran.

The Sheltering Sky is considered Bowles's most uncompromisingly existential work and has been read by the critics along this line, with the fragile and provisional nature of civilized instincts being put to the test against the brutality and savagery of the primitive desert. Not only does Port test his febrile psyche against overwhelming powers of the North African terrain, but also he must face the fact that he harbors in himself no reserves, no hope—for it is all too late—of anything better. Unable to commit himself to his wife, or to anything else for that matter, Port is left with a void which, in the end, exacts a heavy price, leaving him utterly alone and unequipped to face the hostile environment. So, too, Kit is stripped of her defenses and forced back on herself, only to discover that she has no inner resolve either. In the end, these two civilized Americans lack the inner strength to combat the primitive forces, both within and without, which they encounter in their North African adventures.

The novel offers a convincing portrait of the disintegration of a couple of innocents thrust into a cruel environment for which they are totally unprepared. The writing in places is luminescent, the locale wonderfully realized—so much so that the novel's shortcomings pale by comparison, leaving a work, if flawed, at least magnificently so, and convincing in its portrait of nihilism in the modern world.

LET IT COME DOWN

Bowles's second novel, *Let It Come Down*, continues an existentialist quest by following Nelson Dyer, an American bank clerk, who throws over his job to join an old acquaintance who lives in Tangier and who offers Dyer a position in the travel agency he runs there. When he arrives, Dyer finds that his friend Jack Wilcox does not operate a successful agency and in fact seems to possess a mysterious source of income. As the story advances, Dyer's relationship with Wilcox takes on a Kafkaesque tone, as he is obviously not needed at the agency.

Out of money and in desperate need of a job, Dyer accepts an offer to help in a money scheme by transporting cash between a local bank and a shop. Realizing that he is being used for illegal purposes, Dyer takes the money he has been given and flees Tangier, only to discover that he is utterly helpless in a country where he neither speaks the language nor understands the customs. After he has killed his native guide, the novel concludes with Dyer alone and hunted in a foreign country but curiously pleased with his state of affairs as an isolated individual.

Once again, Bowles has thrust an upper-middle-class American into a North African environment and allowed him to become submerged in the native and alien culture. With his loss of identity, Dyer discovers something far more authentic about himself as he is systematically stripped of his civilized supports and is forced to fall back on what little reserves he possesses as an individual human being. This peeling away of the veneer of civilization reveals underneath an emptiness and void which leaves the protagonist, like Port Moresby, totally unprepared for the unfamiliar culture into which he is thrust. Under such pressure, he collapses and must seek refuge in internal strength, of which he possesses precious little. His plunge into an exotic culture, instead of rejuvenating him, debilitates his vigor, leaving him in a weakened if also enlightened condition.

As with other American writers, such as Edgar Allan Poe and Herman Melville, Bowles wrote of the exhaustion exacted by primitive cultures on the more civilized. It is a reversal of the romantic notion that cultured man, tired of his culture, can find rejuvenation through immersion in a more savage environment. Instead, like Joseph Conrad's heroes, Dyer finds only confusion and despair. At least, it may be argued, he discovers the truth, however unpalatable it might be, and the conclusion of the novel leaves him possessed of a dark actuality, if robbed of a comforting illusion.

THE SPIDER'S HOUSE

Bowles's next novel, *The Spider's House*, was set in 1954 against the political upheaval caused by the deposition of Morocco's hereditary ruler, Sultan Mohammed, by the colonial regime of the French. The fiction traces the tension caused by the collapse of the traditional way of life of the native inhabitants of the city of Fez through a fifteen-year-old boy, Amar, who, halfway through the novel, is befriended by John Stenham, an expatriate American writer, who has fallen in love with an American woman tourist named Lee Burroughs. By the conclusion of the novel, John leaves Fez with Lee, abandoning Amar to deal with the destruction of his way of life any way he can.

Although it is not a political novel, *The Spider's House* uses the tensions of the French colonial rule not only to highlight the theme of the disintegration of Muslim culture under the French but also to provide a backdrop against which to play out the drama of the on-again, off-again love affair between Lee and John. Amar is from a devout family but one which is not caught up in the political conflicts between the Istiqlal, the Nationalist party, with their use of terror, and the colonials. Both the French and the Nationalists are bent on stopping the ritual religious festival of *Aid el Kabir*, and Amar, who has been forbidden to leave the Medina where his family resides, gets caught outside the city's walls and is rescued by Lee and John, who have been observing the unfolding cycle of violence that is developing between the French and the Moroccans. John helps Amar return to his family through the city's walls, and Amar offers to take the couple to see the religious celebration in a village outside Fez. The Americans are fascinated by the exotic quality of the Arab life around them and agree to accompany Amar. The festival

turns out badly for them, however, when Lee is shocked and repulsed by the rituals of the feast. After a quarrel, Lee and John decide that they are beginning a love affair.

Meanwhile, Amar has received a large sum of money from Lee so that he can join the Nationalists in their fight against the French. Still apolitical, Amar again gets caught up in the action of the revolution and is manipulated by the Istiqlal, barely avoiding capture by the French. At the end of the novel, he wants to rejoin John and Lee but is rebuffed by the novelist, who is set on going off with his new lover. The fiction concludes when Amar is abandoned by his newly won friend into the political turmoil of a struggle he barely understands.

As the critics have pointed out, *The Spider's House* contains a nostalgia for a past which does not belong to either John Stenham or to Bowles, but it is a longing which is nevertheless keenly felt. It has also been described as a deeply religious book, one in which Bowles mourns for a lost religious belief no longer possible in Western civilization, with its emphasis on the rational and the scientific. Certainly, the book focuses on the consequences of destroying a traditional way of life and on a myopic colonialism which blunders along in an attempt to apply Western methods to a totally unsuitable situation. It is the story of all colonial experiences in which a foreign power tries to forge a new life for a people it only partially understands, which accentuates one of the main achievements of the book, the faithful rendering of the North African landscape with its traditions and cultures.

UP ABOVE THE WORLD

For his fourth novel, Bowles shifted his location to South America and his plot to that of the detective novel. Yet, although seen by many critics as a genre fiction of the whodunit variety, *Up Above the World* is a far cry from a run-of-the-mill thriller. It is, in fact, a deeply psychological study of the disintegration of another couple, Taylor and Day Slade, who, much in the same vein as the Moresbys, undergo a tragic transformation which ultimately destroys them.

The Slades arrive by ship in an unidentified South American country at the port town of Puerto Farol. A woman whom they had befriended on the ship is found dead in her hotel room—murdered, it is discovered later, at the behest of her son by a thug named Thorny. The son, Grover Soto, afraid that the Slades have been a witness to the killing, hunts down the couple, who have by now taken a train to the interior of the country. The Slades are finally subjected to the use of drugs and a variety of brainwashing techniques in order to erase the memory of Mrs. Rainmantle, the murdered woman, from their minds. While recuperating at the ranch of Grover Soto, Day sees some written instructions which were to have been destroyed, and in a moment of panic, Soto drugs and then kills Taylor. As the novel concludes, he is about to do the same with Day.

The novel is a psychological thriller much in the vein of Graham Greene's "entertainments," a lesser work not demanding the exertion either to read or to write that a more serious novel requires. Yet there are certain themes and characters which immediately label the book as one of Bowles's. The wandering Americans confronting themselves amid the exotic background of a less civilized and unknown world, their eventual disintegration as they experience an alien culture, and the search for meaning in what appears to be meaningless lives echo his earlier novels. Even the appearance of chance events, encounters onto which the critics have latched to tie the volume to the thriller genre, are also present in his earlier work. The big difference in *Up Above the World* is the novel's compactness. It is streamlined, and in that sense it provides a faster, perhaps more accessible read, but it is a novel no less interesting for all that.

The critics, especially Bertens, have been particularly hard on this book, largely because of its thriller status, which is unfair, since the novel goes beyond the requirements of mere genre fiction and into a netherworld of the truly black. In many ways, this book is Bowles's most pessimistic and most nihilistic, and, writing in the thriller vein, Bowles has made a contribution to the American fictional form most foreboding and dark, a form, in short, closest to his own hopeless vision.

Bowles's fiction will remain attractive both to the few who truly admire advanced writing and thinking

and to a general reading audience. It is unfortunate that Bowles's reputation as a writer's writer has limited the enjoyment of his work by the public, since he not only deserves a wider readership but also has much to offer the general reader. Too easily dismissed as the product of an expatriate writer and therefore of little interest to students of American literature, Bowles's work is nevertheless central to the American literary experience, dealing as it does with the protagonist facing the frontier on the edge of civilization, a position which recalls that of Melville's Ishmael, James Fenimore Cooper's Natty Bumppo, and even Mark Twain's Huck Finn. Finally, critics and the public alike need to read Bowles's fiction for its relevant encounters between modern humankind and an increasingly mechanistic and depersonalized world, a place truly of nihilism and despair.

Charles L. P. Silet, updated by John Nizalowski

OTHER MAJOR WORKS

SHORT FICTION: *The Delicate Prey*, 1950; *A Little Stone: Stories*, 1950; *The Hours After Noon*, 1959; *A Hundred Camels in the Courtyard*, 1962; *The Time of Friendship*, 1967; *Pages from Cold Point and Other Stories*, 1968; *Three Tales*, 1975; *Things Gone and Things Still Here*, 1977; *Collected Stories of Paul Bowles, 1939-1976*, 1979; *Midnight Mass*, 1981; *Unwelcome Words*, 1988; *A Distant Episode: The Selected Stories*, 1988; *A Thousand Days for Mokhtar, and Other Stories*, 1989.

POETRY: *Scenes*, 1968; *The Thicket of Spring: Poems, 1926-1969*, 1972; *Next to Nothing*, 1976; *Next to Nothing: Collected Poems, 1926-1977*, 1981.

NONFICTION: *Yallah*, 1957; *Their Heads Are Green and Their Hands Are Blue*, 1963; *Without Stopping*, 1972; *Points in Time*, 1982; *Days: Tangier Journal, 1987-1989*, 1991; *In Touch: The Letters of Paul Bowles*, 1994 (Jeffrey Miller, editor).

TRANSLATIONS: *The Lost Trail of the Sahara*, 1952 (of R. Frison-Roche's novel); *No Exit*, 1958 (of Jean-Paul Sartre's play); *A Life Full of Holes*, 1964 (of Driss ben Hamed Charhadi's autobiography); *Love with a Few Hairs*, 1967 (of Mohammed Mrabet's fiction); *The Lemon*, 1969 (of Mrabet's fiction); *M'Hashish*, 1969 (of Mrabet's fiction); *The Boy Who*

Set the Fire, 1974 (of Mrabet's fiction); *The Oblivion Seekers*, 1975 (of Isabelle Eberhardt's fiction); *Harmless Poisons, Blameless Sins*, 1976 (of Mrabet's fiction); *Look and Move On*, 1976 (of Mrabet's fiction); *The Big Mirror*, 1977 (of Mrabet's fiction); *The Beggar's Knife*, 1985 (of Rodrigo Rey Rosa's fiction); *Chocolate Creams and Dollars*, 1992 (of Mrabet's fiction).

MISCELLANEOUS: *Too Far from Home: The Selected Writings of Paul Bowles*, 1993.

BIBLIOGRAPHY

Caponi, Gina Dagel. *Paul Bowles*. New York: Twayne, 1998. Caponi is one of the finest critics of Bowles's work, and this book is an excellent introduction to Bowles and his writings. After a brief Bowles chronology and biography, Caponi explores the breadth of Bowles's canon through various critical lenses: existentialism, postcolonial literature, detective fiction, surrealism, extraordinary consciousness, travel writing, historical fiction, and late work.

_____. *Paul Bowles: Romantic Savage*. Carbondale: Southern Illinois University Press, 1994. Caponi's highly perceptive critical biography uniquely examines the links between Bowles's literary work, autobiographical writings, and musical compositions. Caponi also places Bowles in the matrix of history and geography, while focusing on Bowles's friendships with fellow creative artists, including Aaron Copland, Gertrude Stein, Virgil Thompson, and Jane Bowles.

Dillon, Millicent. *You Are Not I: A Portrait of Paul Bowles*. Berkeley: University of California Press, 1998. This unconventional biography weaves together rich descriptions of Dillon's interviews with Bowles, conventional biographical information, and passages from the works of Paul and Jane Bowles.

Green, Michelle. *The Dream at the End of the World: Paul Bowles and the Literary Renegades in Tangier*. New York: HarperCollins, 1991. Journalist Michelle Green's biography covers the period marked by Paul Bowles's arrival in Tangier in 1947 and Jane Bowles's departure to a Spanish psychiatric hospital in 1967. While focusing on the Bowleses' life and work, Green also depicts Tangier's social, artistic, and literary circles.

Hibbard, Allen. *Paul Bowles: A Study in Short Fiction*. New York: Twayne, 1993. Hibbard argues that Bowles's short stories are his best work and confirm his literary importance through their aesthetic excellence and cultural significance. Hibbard includes a chronological critique of Bowles's stories, excerpts from various interviews with Bowles, and key statements on Bowles's work by major critics and authors.

Lacey, R. Kevin, and Francis Poole, eds. *Mirrors on the Maghrib: Critical Reflections on Paul and Jane Bowles and Other American Writers in Morocco*. Delmar, N.Y.: Caravan Books, 1996. This collection of critical essays on the Bowleses and the Beats explores the relationship between the concept of otherness and Morocco. The book includes a number of essays by Moroccan critics, who provide a North African viewpoint on the strengths and weaknesses of Bowles's depiction of their homeland.

Patterson, Richard F. *A World Outside: The Fiction of Paul Bowles*. Austin: University of Texas Press, 1987. Instead of a reading guide, Patterson offers a way of reading Bowles. Gives critiques of Bowles's stories with little reference to his personal life. A thorough analysis of his novels and short stories within the context of architectural metaphor and a knowledgeable contribution to criticism on Bowles.

Pounds, Wayne. *Paul Bowles: The Inner Geography*. New York: Peter Lang, 1985. Within the context of the psychology of Sigmund Freud and R. D. Laing, Pounds seeks to define the divided self in Bowles's fiction and examines his relationship to Edgar Allan Poe. This scholarly study shows how Bowles's work diagnoses the ills of Western civilization. Contains a useful bibliography with extensive notes.

Stewart, Lawrence D. *Paul Bowles: The Illumination of North Africa*. Carbondale: Southern Illinois University Press, 1974. Stewart discusses the three novels and many of the stories that take place in North Africa and chronicles Bowles's travels in that region, providing a wealth of biographical information.

Voelker, Joseph. "Fish Traps and Purloined Letters: The Anthropology of Paul Bowles." *Critique: Studies in Modern Fiction* 17 (Fall, 1985): 25-36. Explores Bowles's travel writing, including his book *Their Heads Are Green and Their Hands Are Blue* and the novels *Let It Come Down* and *The Spider's House*. Voelker applauds Bowles's "supreme artistry" in the creation of his Muslim characters. Contains an interesting analysis of the protagonist in *Up Above the World*, who is both the "adept" and the victim.

Wagner, Linda. "Paul Bowles and the Characterization of Women." *Critique: Studies in Modern Fiction* 27 (Fall, 1985): 15-24. Declares Bowles to be more than a nihilistic existentialist or an imitator of Albert Camus. Examines Bowles's 1982 short montage fiction *Points in Time* for its departure from male-female relations to nature's effect on human beings. Also discusses his first novel, *The Sheltering Sky*, and his collection of stories, *The Delicate Prey*.

(Library of Congress)

The Seagull on the Step, 1955
Three Short Novels, 1958
Generation Without Farewell, 1960
The Underground Woman, 1975

KAY BOYLE

Born: St. Paul, Minnesota; February 19, 1902
Died: Mill Valley, California; December 27, 1992

PRINCIPAL LONG FICTION

Plagued by the Nightingale, 1931
Year Before Last, 1932
Gentlemen, I Address You Privately, 1933
My Next Bride, 1934
Death of a Man, 1936
Monday Night, 1938
Primer for Combat, 1942
Avalanche, 1944
A Frenchman Must Die, 1946
1939, 1948
His Human Majesty, 1949

OTHER LITERARY FORMS

Although she published many novels, Kay Boyle's principal recognition was for her shorter works. First published in the small magazines of the 1920's, her stories were collected in *Wedding Day and Other Stories* (1930) and *The First Lover and Other Stories* (1933). Active as an editor and critic on small magazines such as *Contempo* and on progressive political journals, she also translated such European writers as Joseph Delteil, Raymond Radiguet, and Marie-Louise Soupault. Two volumes of short stories, *The Smoking Mountain: Stories of Postwar Germany* (1951) and *Nothing Ever Breaks Except the Heart* (1966), reflect wartime and postwar Europe. Collected in *Fifty Stories* (1980), Boyle's short fiction would continue to appear in American periodicals.

Her poetry, also first published in small magazines, was collected in *A Glad Day* (1938) and *Collected Poems* (1962). *American Citizen Naturalized in Leadville, Colorado* (1944), based upon the experience of an Austrian refugee in the United States military, is dedicated to writer Carson McCullers, "whose husband is also overseas," and *Testament for My Students and Other Poems* (1970) concerns "that desperate year, 1968." *This Is Not a Letter and Other Poems* (1985) appeared fifteen years later.

As a European correspondent after World War II, Boyle wrote nonfiction prose of both journalistic and literary distinction, including her reportage of the war crimes trial of Heinrich Babb for *The New Yorker* and her essays on civil rights and the military establishment. Two memoirs, her edition of *The Autobiography of Emanuel Carnevali* (1967) and her chapters in Robert McAlmon's *Being Geniuses Together, 1920-1930* (1968), capture the literary underground of that period, while a subsequent collection, *The Long Walk at San Francisco State and Other Essays* (1970), reflects the antiwar movement of the 1960's. She also published three illustrated children's novels, *The Youngest Camel* (1939, 1959) and the Pinky novels.

ACHIEVEMENTS

The 1930's, declared her vintage period by critics, brought Boyle an O. Henry Prize for the title story of *The White Horses of Vienna and Other Stories* (1936), followed in 1941 by another for "Defeat," a story on the French collapse, which also appeared in *Primer for Combat*. Published widely in *Harper's*, *The New Yorker*, *Saturday Evening Post*, and *The Atlantic Monthly*, and collected in *Thirty Stories* (1946), Boyle won the praise of contemporaries as the "economical housewife of the short story technique."

BIOGRAPHY

The cross between Kay Boyle's midwestern roots and cosmopolitan experience produced the distinctive flavor of her work. Although born into an upper-class St. Paul family, Boyle spent her early years not in the Midwest but in the eastern United States, France, Austria, and Switzerland, and especially in the mountains, which become a symbol of human transcendence in her work. The active and involved nature of her childhood is expressed in her love of horses, riding, and skiing, and its aesthetic and creative aspect in the family custom of gathering sketches and stories into marbled covers for gift books. Katherine Evans Boyle, the "shining light" to whom Boyle dedicated her first works, provided an image of strength and purpose, introducing her daughter to the most avant-garde of European art and literature, as well as the most progressive of American populist politics. Her grandfather, Jesse Peyton Boyle, a dynamic, charismatic St. Paul businessman whom Boyle later called a "charming reactionary," was a model of the aggressive, compelling patriarch, in contrast to the more vulnerable and intuitive male figure typified by her father, Howard Peyton Boyle.

The next years saw Boyle return to the Midwest and then to the Greenwich Village literary and political circles which would provide her with friends and supporters. A series of financial reversals brought the family to Cincinnati, where Howard Boyle became established in the retail automotive business. After a brief stay at Shipley, Boyle studied violin at the Cincinnati Conservatory and architecture at Ohio Mechanics Institute, later calling hers "no education at all," saying that she had never been "properly through the eighth grade," and had instead pursued writing on her own, a training she advocated later for her students as well. Less than twenty years old, Boyle moved to New York, attended a few classes at Columbia, worked as a secretary, and met Greenwich Village literati of a progressive bent. In the space of her short stay, she worked for *Broom*, a journal of European and American experimentalism, and became acquainted with Harriet Monroe's *Poetry* magazine; with Lola Ridge, whose Gaelic ancestry she shared; and with William Carlos Williams, who became her friend and mentor. Described as a shy, timid ingenue, Boyle appears in Williams's memoirs attending Fourteenth Street parties with John Reed, Louise Bryant, Jean Toomer, Kenneth Burke, and Hart Crane.

The 1920's were another expatriate decade for Boyle. In 1921, she married Richard Brault, a French student whom she had met in Ohio, and she returned with him to his family's provincial seat. Williams recalls meeting a lonely and isolated Boyle in the vicinity of Le Havre, in which atmosphere her first two novels take place. When the marriage deteriorated and ended a few years later, Boyle remained in Paris and the Riviera, playing a central role in the literary underground of American exiles and the European avant-garde. Centered on the publication of small magazines, these groups brought Boyle together with Ernest Walsh, the effervescent poet, critic, and editor of *This Quarter*, the lover and compatriot whose death from lung injuries incurred as a pilot is recounted in *Year Before Last*.

The aesthetic of Boyle's group, represented by *Transition* magazine and Eugene Jolas, was eclectic, drawing on the work of Ernest Hemingway, James Joyce, Gertrude Stein, Ezra Pound, William Carlos Williams, and Carl Sandburg. Experimental, antirational, and antirealist, this loosely knit group ascribed to an informal creed known as Orphism, set down in the 1929 manifesto "the Revolution of the Word," signed by Boyle, Laurence Vail, Hart Crane, and others interested in representing a primarily interior reality in a rhythmic, "hallucinatory" style cognizant of current psychological and anthropological lore and inimical to standard realism and the genteel tradition. It was in this milieu that Boyle developed the lyrical subjectivism reflected in her early poems and stories, a quality she found in D. H. Lawrence and Arthur Rimbaud, Walt Whitman and Edgar Allan Poe, Stein and Joyce.

Following Walsh's death and the birth of her first child, Sharon, Boyle, out of money and dispirited, joined a communal art colony led by Raymond Duncan, Isadora's brother, whose personal charisma and exploitative idealism are reflected in a number of novelistic relationships in which one will is subsumed in another. Rescued from this amalgam of Jean Jacques Rousseau, Leo Tolstoy, and pseudo-anarchistic principles by Caresse and Harry Crosby, whose unconventional sun religion and Black Sun Press were underground institutions, Boyle spent her next years in the French and British settings, which are reflected in the novels of the period. In 1931, she

married the scholar and poet Laurence Vail, and in the following years she bore three more daughters, Apple-Joan, Kathe, and Clover.

Emerging aboveground in the late 1930's with a Simon and Schuster contract, Boyle published a major short-story collection, *The White Horses of Vienna*, which introduced the Lippizanner horses that became an important symbol in later works. Three highly praised short novels and two longer ones followed, including her own favorite, *Monday Night*, and she received a Guggenheim Fellowship to pursue the metaphor of aviation for human history. Before the fall of France in 1939, she wrote about the collapse of Europe's democracies before fascism. The war novels of that period are usually set in small French villages where an expatriated woman becomes involved in the political choices of various men, usually Austrians made nationless by the Anschluss. As the setting of her fiction moved from the interior to the external world, Boyle's style became more popular, often a journalistic diary, and more suited to the wider audiences of the *Saturday Evening Post* and the *Ladies Home Companion*. This development, decried by some critics, damaged her standing in literary circles in a way that it did not for an author such as Katherine Anne Porter, Boyle's friend, who kept her hackwork clearly separate from her artistic life. The conflict between resistance and collaboration addressed in her novels surfaced in Boyle's private life as well when Vail, whose sentiments are possibly expressed by several characters in *Primer for Combat*, disapproved of her efforts to secure visas for Jewish refugees, citing the "historical necessity" of fascism. Following their divorce, Boyle married Baron Joseph Von Franckenstein, an Austrian refugee whose experiences are reflected in *American Citizen Naturalized in Leadville, Colorado*, in *His Human Majesty*, and in the general situation of Austrian anti-fascists in the continental novels of the war period.

After the fall of France, the popular novels *Avalanche* and *A Frenchman Must Die* brought the Resistance experience to American audiences. Perhaps because of an establishment bias against best-sellers, against explicitly political intent, or, in some cases, against the notion of a woman writing about war and the "masculine side of the male character," as one critic stated, and surely because of their superficial and rather formulaic character, these novels received negative reviews from Diana Trilling, Edmund Wilson, and *The New Yorker*. Despite this criticism, Boyle continued to address the question of individual political choice in short novels such as *Decision*, set in post-Civil War Spain, and in *The Seagull on the Step*, which points out the growing inappropriateness of American occupation policy. After the war, Boyle's work became even more journalistic in her role as a European correspondent, chiefly in occupied Germany, where Von Franckenstein directed Amerika Dienst, an International Information Agency service, and Boyle reported on the war crimes trial of Heinrich Babb. She also commented upon European moral and political conditions in her short stories of the period, developing as she did so a vision of German and European history that she would use in later novels and in a planned nonfiction project. Like Thomas Mann, Ignazio Silone, and other anti-fascist intellectuals, Boyle addressed the vulnerabilities which continued to expose Western democracies to the totalitarian threat explored by Erich Fromm, Hannah Arendt, and many others.

Returning in 1953 to an America caught up in the events of McCarthyism, Boyle lost her job with *The New Yorker*, while Von Franckenstein, a war hero captured and tortured in Nazi Germany during his career with the OSS and an able civil servant, was removed from his state department post for his "questionable" loyalty in associating with Boyle, who was deemed a security risk. After frequent testimony by both before Internal Security committees, Von Franckenstein was reinstated in 1957. In 1958, the first American edition of *Three Short Novels*, including *The Crazy Hunter, The Bridegroom's Body*, and *Decision*, appeared, followed by *Generation Without Farewell*, Boyle's most ambitious postwar novel.

Following Von Franckenstein's death from cancer in 1963, Boyle continued her political commitment and her writing during the anti-Vietnam War movement, a cause in which her earlier analysis of French colonialism and European Fascism made her espe-

cially active. Supporting civil disobedience to military recruitment and induction and to weapons research and manufacture, she organized protest groups and petitions and traveled with one such group to Cambodia, where they brought the war there to media attention. The Christmas Eve of 1967, which Boyle spent in jail for her part in a sit-in at an Oakland induction center, is drawn upon in her novel *The Underground Woman*. As a teacher of creative writing at San Francisco State University, she courted dismissal to join the student protest. For her part in the protest, Boyle received a forty-five-day jail sentence, which was suspended until the following Easter. Because her prison time was spent with regular prisoners rather than with political protesters, Boyle became further convinced of the inequities of the social system. During her time in jail, she discovered that she had breast cancer, something she had long feared.

In June of 1968, Boyle published her version of Robert McAlmon's 1934 memoir, *Being Geniuses Together, 1920-1930*, hoping to introduce his writing to an American audience. She revised his work, adding alternate chapters presenting her own commentary and memories of the period. Boyle's writing was praised, but she also received criticism for romanticizing many incidents. During the same year, Boyle covered the trial of Huey Newton, the Black Panther leader who was accused of killing one policeman and injuring another. Boyle was an ardent supporter of the Black Panther Party, fully accepting their view that the police department was a racist institution, determined to eliminate black activists. *The Long Walk at San Francisco State and Other Essays* discusses her stands on social protest. During the 1970's, Boyle returned to writing poetry. She also developed an interest in the role of women in Ireland. The book she planned on these women never materialized, but she did publish a story about Ireland, "St. Stephen's Green," in *The Atlantic Monthly* in 1980. In 1978, she was inducted into the American Academy of Arts and Letters and received the San Francisco Art Commissions Award of Honor. Boyle retired from teaching in 1980, the year in which *Fifty Stories* appeared. This sparked renewed interest in her writing, and in

1982, *Three Short Novels* was reissued with an introduction by the Canadian writer Margaret Atwood. In 1986, she was given the *Los Angeles Times* award for her outstanding body of work. In 1992, Boyle became a supporter of the Bill Clinton presidential campaign. She died on December 27, 1992.

ANALYSIS

Perhaps more consistently and tenaciously than any other twentieth century American writer, Boyle sought to unite the personal and political, the past and present, the feminine and the masculine. Recognized in both the literary and the popular realms, her rich oeuvre unites the American and the European experience of twentieth century history.

Helpful though it may be as an outline, the conventional division of Boyle's achievement into an aesthetic period before 1939 and a polemical period after may obscure Boyle's constant focus upon the dialectic between subject and object. In the exploration of personal experience, her intense imaginative reconstruction posits the integration of conflicting aspects of the self, the struggle between self-abnegation and self-assertion, and the liberation of the individual from repressive aspects of personal or family relationships. Usually presented as a union of archetypally masculine and feminine characteristics in an individual or in a couple, often a pair of same-sex friends, Boyle's image of the completed self is one of growth beyond confining roles.

In her exploration of the self as a political creature, Boyle asserts the life-affirming potential of the individual and the community against destructive authoritarian or absolutist constructs, whether within the family or in the larger society. In her intense evocation of personal awakening to political morality, Boyle's synthesis reaches beyond the narrowly ideological to affirm the human search for tenderness in a landscape which, although distorted by repression, gives hope for regeneration. Like Thomas Mann, Ignazio Silone, and André Malraux, Boyle seeks to integrate the individual psyche into the larger social milieu, to make the self meaningful in history, exercising that responsibility which Mann called for when he said that had the German intellectual community remained

accountable, Nazism would have been prevented.

Using modernist techniques to refute contemporary nihilism, Boyle restores perspective to the confrontation between the individual sensibility and a complex, often hidden, social reality. Her decision to address a broad audience upon political as well as personal themes, sometimes seen as a "betrayal" of her talent, might more fully be understood as a commitment to the exercise of moral responsibility through literature. Exploring the need to unite discordant psychic and political elements and to assert the life-affirming, Boyle provides in her work a model of balanced wholeness in the larger as well as the smaller world.

PLAGUED BY THE NIGHTINGALE

Her first novel, *Plagued by the Nightingale*, which Hart Crane admired, introduced an expatriate American bride to her husband's family in their decaying French provincial seat. A crippling congenital disease afflicting all the family males, an emblem of general social decay, prevents the young husband, Nicole, from asserting independence, and requires the family to be always on the lookout to perpetuate itself. Bridget, the young wife, and Luc, a family friend whose energy and vivacity have earmarked him for marriage to one of Nicole's three sisters, are alternately drawn into and repelled by the patriarchal family's power to protect and engulf. By making the birth of an heir the condition upon which the young couple's inheritance depends, Nicole's father threatens to bring them entirely within the control of the patriarchal family. Freeing both herself and Nicole from the grasp of this decaying culture, Bridget chooses to bear a child not by Nicole, whose tainted genes would continue the cycle, but by Luc, a vigorous outsider whose health and vitality promise liberation and autonomy. Although ostensibly a narrative of personal life, this first novel becomes political in its exploration of the relationship between the self and the family, the will to immerse oneself in the group or to aspire to self-determination. The decaying and yet compelling power of the patriarchal family becomes a metaphor for Western culture itself in its paralyzing traditionalism and sacrifice of the individual to authority.

YEAR BEFORE LAST

Continuing this exploration of personal experience in search of security and selfhood, *Year Before Last* recounts Hannah's final year with her lover Martin, a poet and editor terminally ill with a lung disease. In the conflict between Martin's former lover Eve, who is his partner in the publication of the small magazine that is truly the group's creative life, and Hannah, self-sacrifice and self-assertion in pursuit of love and art are polarized. Eve, "strong and solitary" yet unfulfilled, and Hannah, vulnerable, nurturing, yet unaffirmed, both seek realization through Martin ("What are we but two empty women turning to him and sucking him dry for a taste of life?"), only to find it in themselves as they join in his care. They are complementary aspects of the self united to assert the primacy of love and art. In this resolution of two opposing sets of personal qualities, here presented as a bond between two women in support of a positive male, the self is empowered in the larger world of artistic creation.

MY NEXT BRIDE

This resolving dyad of two women appears in slightly different guise in *My Next Bride*, the final novel of this early self-exploratory group. Victoria, left emotionally and materially destitute, joins an art colony whose tunic-wearing, dancing anarchists are led by a charismatic, idealistic, but ultimately exploitive male, Sorrel, the reverse of the vital, creative male seen in Martin. Searching for security and idealism, Victoria falls instead into complete self-abnegation in a series of underworld trials, including prostitution and abortion, which represent total abandonment of selfhood and self-determination. She finally returns to herself with the support of two friends, one of whom becomes her lesbian lover and symbolizes the union of the submissive and the assertive, the passive and the active that appears in Boyle as an emblem of the healed psyche. Boyle's treatment of homosexual themes, especially her use of the homosexual couple as an image of the completed self, is remarkable for its freedom from negative stereotypes.

GENTLEMEN, I ADDRESS YOU PRIVATELY

In *Gentlemen, I Address You Privately*, Boyle breaks free from the reconstruction of her own experience to enter a totally imaginative landscape with a mythic quality never so markedly present before, a quality which comes to dominate the best of her later work. Here, the dyad is of two men, one a cleric cut off from experience in the contemplative heights of art and religion, the other a sailor plunged entirely into atavistic life at sea. Deserting cell and ship alike, they enter the human world, descending from Mont St. Michel (like all Boyle's mountains, a symbol of the transcendent and the ideal) to the muck of a squatter's hut, where they hide out as farmhands. In the common-law marriage of Quespelle, a brutal peasant who delights chiefly in killing rabbits, and Leonie, a madonnalike yet buddingly fertile female akin to William Faulkner's Lena Grove, the destructive and nurturing forces of the real world appear. This sharply polarized image of the human family, brutal masculinity and submissive femininity, proves too dualistic for reproduction and growth. A more positive figure of the male is posited in Munday, the gentle, intuitive aesthete who acts in defense of the old dog Quespelle intends to shoot, the bedraggled horse, the rabbits, and finally Leonie. Quespelle leaves for the city, and Munday is left with Leonie. The two have a "new taste for life," transformed by the love which "binds the two . . . together, hand and foot, and then sends [them] out, away from any other comfort"; Adam and Eve emerge from paradise to establish the human community in this Faulknerian affirmation of the self in opposition to both authoritarian families and absolute ideas.

CRAZY HUNTER

This liberation is again apparent in the better-known short novels, *Crazy Hunter* and *The Bridegroom's Body*, set in a Lawrentian English countryside where life must break free of repressive families and social structures. In *Crazy Hunter*, Nan must assert herself against the control of her mother, Mrs. Lombe, so she purchases a gelding against her mother's wishes but is disappointed when the horse suddenly goes blind. In condemning the horse to be shot, Mrs. Lombe becomes the authoritarian hunter whose presence is strong in Boyle's novels, her destructive power threatening both her husband Candy and Nan, who must assume her mother's strength without her repressiveness. Nan, in teaching the horse to jump at risk to her life, and Candy, putting his body between the veterinarian's pistol and the horse's flying hooves, establish the father's legitimate power and the daughter's liberation from the mother's control in defense of vital yet vulnerable life. The horse, which becomes for Boyle a symbol of this life force, retains its conventional identification with passion and strength while taking on more complex qualities of aspiration, idealism, and vulnerable beauty. Usually regarded as a primarily masculine symbol, the horse in Boyle is strongly associated with the gentle, intuitive male, or with the female, and particularly with emerging female sexuality.

THE BRIDEGROOM'S BODY

In *The Bridegroom's Body*, the repressive domination associated with the mother and confined to the immediate family in *Crazy Hunter* becomes patriarchal in its extension to the entire community in the country estate of the Glouries. A remote, rainy, brooding, and yet potentially fertile land, the estate is dominated by predatory hunters led by Lord Glourie, an insensitive, uncommunicative sportsman, an upper-class Quespelle, whose chief interests are hunting and drinking with other hunters. This predatory patriarchy is mirrored in the natural world by Old Hitches, chief of the swans, whose dominance is threatened by the Bridegroom, a young swan who has set up his nest in defiance of the patriarch and in assertion of a more gentle and intuitive male potency. Lady Glourie, an energetic, forceful woman in her tweeds and sturdy shoes, struggles to maintain life in an atmosphere completely lacking in spiritual and emotional fulfillment by caring for the sick sheep, the swan-master's pregnant wife, and the Bridegroom himself. An isolated figure made illegitimate and ineffective by the hunters, she longs for a female friend, hopes which rise only to be dashed when Miss Cafferty, the nurse called to care for the pregnant woman, proves not a comradely version of Lady Glourie, but rather her total opposite—young, conventionally attractive in her bright green dress, and seemingly vulnerable to male approval. Miss Cafferty eventually vindicates herself, however, imploring Lady Glourie to "see her own beauty," her

strength against the "butchers, murderers—men stalking every corner of the ground by day and night." This plea leaves Lady Glourie with the "chill" which Boyle expresses as the promise of regeneration, of union between the two versions of female strength which have as yet "no record, no sign, no history marked on them."

DEATH OF A MAN

Death of a Man, influenced by Boyle's own experiences in the Tyrol, is a love story set against the backdrop of the growing influence of the Nazi Party in Austria. Personal desires and needs are set against the uncontrollable influences of the political conflicts in Europe during the years prior to World War II. Like the short story "The White Horses of Vienna," the novel reflects the political unrest in Austria during the 1930's. Growing economic difficulties and dissatisfaction with the government led many Austrians to view favorably the political agenda of the Nazi party. In fact, the novel received several negative reviews for what many critics considered a sympathetic portrayal of the Nazis. Like many of her heroines, the main character, Pendennis, is an expatriate American who has no real roots in either her family or her country. She is bored by her husband, an Englishman whom she feels lacks passion and who is unable to provide her with the love and belonging she craves. Instead, she is fascinated by Dr. Procheska, a handsome man whose passion and compassion are matched by his strong political principles and devotion to the Nazi cause. Politics drives them apart since the Nazi leader in the area disapproves of this relationship, which distracts the doctor from his political commitment. Eventually the two come to realize that love should transcend politics; however, history overrules them. They end up in passing trains, Pendennis returning to Procheska's village to find him, Procheska fleeing to Italy as the Nazis are being arrested or driven out of Austria after one of their party members assassinates the head of government.

MONDAY NIGHT

Recognizing the destructive power of authoritarian personal and political ideologies in a more overtly public way, the psychological detective story *Monday Night* places the search of two American exiles, Wilt and Bernie, against a collapsing moral order in prewar Europe. They pursue the case of Monsieur Sylvestre, a chemist whose testimony holds such sway in the courts that he alone has convicted a series of young men of murder in several mysterious deaths by claiming to find traces of poisonous substances in the victims' "viscera." The Americans learn that Sylvestre himself has been the murderer; this "misanthropy too savage to be repudiated" is motivated by the fact that the young men, like the Bridegroom, affirm some kind of spontaneous and generous emotional life with their families, a life Sylvestre himself has repudiated by rejecting his lover and their young son and follows by expunging himself from his world. Against the backdrop of a brisk arms business carried on with both sides in the Spanish Civil War and instances of French chauvinism and contempt for foreign nationals and their own people in a series of fixed bicycle races, one French spokesman pleads for moral action against destructive totalitarianism ("It is you who could stop it if you, your country really cared"), for "everlasting and violent freedom" against the dead authoritarianism represented by Sylvestre. Expressing the terror of vulnerable humanity, Wilt, awakened to a moral apprehension, questions, "Is it possible that a madman whose passion it has been to toy with human life and with the honor and liberty of countless victims was put in a position of highest authority?"

DECISION

This individual moral awakening to larger choice underlies all the "war" novels of the 1940's. In an acclaimed short novel, *Decision*, a detached journalist is awakened to the modern hell of fascist Spain through her chance encounter with two young men, republicans under surveillance, executed for their part in a Madrid prison hunger strike. The human capacity for resistance, expressed by a republican flamenco singer with the phrase "you get up on stage and bellow your heart out," is found in an even more life-affirming form in women, whose "power of the weak," to use Elizabeth Janeway's term, means:

We, as women, have learned and forgotten more than they have ever set down in books . . . we are sustained

in our weakness by something they never even heard a whisper of . . . by a consecration to the very acts of hope, tenderness, love, whatever the name may be, which no man [that is, no fascist] has any share in.

In an awakening not narrowly political but moral in Hannah Arendt's sense, the narrator believes "at that instant . . . in each individual death, and the look of the sky as it must have been to them then, at the last trembling moment of defiance."

This apprehension of personal and political commitment exists in all the longer war novels. Set usually in mountain villages in the Savoy or the Tirol, where the ambiguity of the national identity makes choice necessary, these novels posit some encounter between an American woman exile and one or more men, often Austrian skiers, whose stateless position requires choice of a personal nationality. This interplay occurs in the context of the village and the larger nation, where alternating mendacity and heroism, resistance and collaboration, illustrate the consequences of such choices. In the short novel *1939*, Ferdl Eder's attempts to join the French army, frustrated by chauvinistic discrimination against foreigners, leaves him with no recourse but to accept the hated German passport; he leaves his American lover, who has herself abandoned a secure marriage to assert her choice.

PRIMER FOR COMBAT

Primer for Combat, the most involved of this group, expresses the need for what Phyl, the American woman, calls "participation . . . in the disaster. In humanity's disaster." Against a tapestry of characters in a French village during the first days of the occupation, in an introspective diary format, Boyle, in a manner reminiscent of Ignazio Silone and André Malraux, posits a complex relationship between fascism, colonialism, classism, and democracy and self-determination as they are internalized in personal commitment. Phyl is awakened from the moral torpor of her fascination with the Austrian Wolfgang, whose opportunistic collaboration she comes to recognize by contrast with Sepp Von Horneck, another Austrian, who, refusing to exchange liberation for reconstruction, escapes to join the Gaullist forces. Ultimately, Phyl's choice is not between men but between models of human action, acquiescence, or self-assertion. "I have found my own people," she says; "I have found my own side, and I shall not betray them." Fascism is located not within the political but within the personal realm, "not a national indication but an internal one." *Primer for Combat*, the best of the war novels, synthesizes the contradiction between the personal and the political.

HIS HUMAN MAJESTY

With *His Human Majesty*, Boyle abandons popular adventure and returns to serious literature. Although set during wartime, the novel's theme deals with individual sin and redemption. In 1943, Boyle began writing a series of short stories about the American ski troops who were training in Leadville, Colorado. The stories were never completed, and eventually she turned the material into a two-part novel focusing on universal human facts about honor, truth, and loyalty. The title is taken from William Blake's mythic poem about sin and redemption, "Jerusalem" (1804-1820). The main character, Fennington, a ski trooper, is the protagonist in both parts. In the first section, "Enemy Detail," he is portrayed as an aloof idealist. He avoids most of the others in his unit, finding them coarse and shallow. He occupies his time reading a one-hundred-year-old diary, written by Augusta Tabor, an early settler. His one friend, Pater, is a newspaper reporter who is married to a Hollywood star. When Fennington meets her, he falls in love, thereby betraying his friendship. Driven by guilt, he volunteers for a dangerous mission to rescue two stranded travelers, only to discover that they are Pater's wife and a German prisoner of war she was helping to escape. The rescue attempt proves too late, and Pater's wife dies. Fennington thus loses both his self-respect and the woman he loved.

"Main Drag," the second section, opens by describing the tensions and prejudices in camp. The flaws and weaknesses of the troopers and the townspeople are revealed. Eventually, Fennington meets the descendant of Augusta Tabor. When she receives word that her husband has been killed in the war, Fennington comforts her. The two kiss, discovering

that love provides the only hope for the future. Leadville becomes a microcosm exposing the evil and weaknesses of the larger society; however, acts of compassion and bravery can help to alleviate humanity's trials and sorrows. The novel ends stressing the need for commitment. For Boyle, individual redemption is found in love.

GENERATION WITHOUT FAREWELL

In two novels addressing the postwar period of occupation, *The Seagull on the Step* and *Generation Without Farewell*, Boyle's vision of the dialectic between the personal and the political becomes more fully a clash between the human and the totalitarian impulses in the heart and in history. In *Generation Without Farewell*, like *His Human Majesty* a study of the human response to authoritarianism, hunters stalk their prey in an occupied German village. Both Germans and Americans, led by the American Colonel Roberts, the universal authoritarian, hunt a wild boar believed hidden in the seemingly primeval forest surrounding the village. An expression of the people's will to survive and affirm the positive aspects of their nationality against the dead hand of their Nazi past, the boar is identified by an American observer, Seth Honerkamp, with an anti-fascist spirit and the great composers of the past. Jaeger, an anti-Nazi German searching for his roots in a past not distorted by fascism, sees in the hunt his people's historic tendency to create an "other" whose extermination becomes an obsession, destroying human liberty and ultimately the very source of the culture. The will to liberty breaks free, however, when Robert's wife Catherine and daughter Milly, both expressions of the reproductive and nurturing power contained in the Demeter-Persephone myth so pervasive in Boyle, join Jaeger and Christoph Horn. Horn is Milly's lover, whose identification with the Lippizanner horses in his care connects him with the most fertile and, at the same time, the most transcendent elements of the national spirit they represent. This identification is shared by Milly, whose pregnancy by Horn parallels the mare's pregnancy in a particularly female vision of the survival and continuity of the culture itself. Although the repressive qualities of both German and American authority unite in the hunt for the boar, an attempt to ship the horses to Brooklyn, and an epidemic of polio—the essentially American disease which fatally strikes Horn despite Jaeger and Honerkamp's efforts to secure an iron lung—Catherine joins Milly to protect the coming child, leaving a revitalized Jaeger and Honerkamp to continue their pursuit for the life-affirming aspects of both German and American culture.

THE UNDERGROUND WOMAN

The myth of the sorrowing mother in search of her daughter appears again in *The Underground Woman*. Against the background of the American antiwar movement, Athena Gregory's psychic restoration is connected to a vision of human transcendence expressed in a community of women. Athena, a university classics teacher, her husband lost to cancer and her daughter to a satanic cult, finds herself jailed during a sit-in at an induction center. Through a process of bonding not only with the other war protesters but also with the black, Hispanic, and poor white women there, she finds personal and political transformation in an intense female friendship with Calliope, another older woman whose intuitive, emotional nature balances Athena's own rational, analytical one. She also forms a friendship with a young woman musician, who replaces Athena's daughter Melanie, irrevocably lost to a cult serving Pete the Redeemer, an exploitative, charismatic leader who demands complete surrender of the will. Released from jail and from her mourning, Athena asserts her new self in a symbolic defense of all daughters when she successfully resists Pete's attempt to commandeer her home. In this affirmative vision of female power, Athena resolves the conflict between her two selves, the respectable, above-ground Athena sprung from Zeus's head and heir to his rationality, and the more emotional, intuitive "underground woman," as she joins Calliope to save the deer from the hunters and the Hispanic prostitute's children from the state. In this late novel, Kay Boyle's vision of personal and political self-affirmation advances the dialectic between subjective experience and objective reality which has marked her work from the beginning.

Janet Polansky, updated by Mary E. Mahony

OTHER MAJOR WORKS

SHORT FICTION: *Short Stories*, 1929; *Wedding Day and Other Stories*, 1930; *The First Lover and Other Stories*, 1933; *The White Horses of Vienna and Other Stories*, 1936; *The Crazy Hunter and Other Stories*, 1940; *Thirty Stories*, 1946; *The Smoking Mountain: Stories of Postwar Germany*, 1951; *Nothing Ever Breaks Except the Heart*, 1966; *Fifty Stories*, 1980; *Life Being the Best and Other Stories*, 1988.

POETRY: *A Glad Day*, 1938; *American Citizen Naturalized in Leadville, Colorado*, 1944; *Collected Poems*, 1962; *Testament for My Students and Other Poems*, 1970; *This Is Not a Letter and Other Poems*, 1985; *Collected Poems of Kay Boyle*, 1991.

NONFICTION: *Breaking the Silence: Why a Mother Tells Her Son About the Nazi Era*, 1962; *The Autobiography of Emanuel Carnevali*, 1967; *Being Geniuses Together, 1920-1930*, 1968 (with Robert McAlmon); *The Long Walk at San Francisco State and Other Essays*, 1970; *Enough of Dying! An Anthology of Peace Writings*, 1972; *Words That Must Somehow Be Said: The Selected Essays of Kay Boyle, 1927-1984*, 1985.

CHILDREN'S LITERATURE: *The Youngest Camel*, 1939, 1959; *Pinky, the Cat Who Liked to Sleep*, 1966; *Pinky in Persia*, 1968.

EDITED TEXT: *365 Days*, 1936 (with others).

BIBLIOGRAPHY

Ford, Hugh. *Four Lives in Paris*. San Francisco: North Point Press, 1987. Kay Boyle lived in Paris for nearly two decades; she is one of the four "expatriate" artists that Hugh selected for this study. Provides interesting background on Boyle, her beginnings as a writer, her involvement with the magazine *This Quarter*, and her writing "circle" in France.

Hollenberg, Donna. "Abortion and Identity Formation and the Expatriate Woman Writer: H. D. and Kay Boyle in the Twenties." *Twentieth Century Literature* 40 (Winter, 1994): 499-517. Discusses Boyle's emotional crises during the 1920's. Connects the theme of mother and daughter struggles with the conflict between the freedom of exile and the desire for home. Clear analysis of theme and character in *Plagued by the Nightingale*, *Year Before Last*, and *My Next Bride*.

Mellen, Joan. *Kay Boyle: Author of Herself*. New York: Farrar, Straus & Giroux, 1994. An extensive biography describing Boyle's life as a portrait of the twentieth century. Examines recurring themes throughout her fiction. An extremely helpful source.

Spanier, Sandra Whipple. *Kay Boyle: Artist and Activist*. Carbondale: Southern Illinois University Press, 1986. A valuable book-length study on Boyle, with emphasis on her commitment to activism, in both her writings and her life. Contains a wealth of biographical information, much of which was supplied by the author herself. The emphasis is on Boyle's life and work in the 1920's and early 1930's. Includes a bibliography.

Yalom, Marilyn. *Women Writers of the West Coast: Speaking of Their Lives and Careers*. Santa Barbara, Calif.: Capra Press, 1983. This volume grew out of a series of public dialogues with a handful of women authors. The entry on Boyle, however, came from an offstage conversation with photographer Margo Davis in March, 1982. Here Boyle recalls her involvement in the antiwar movement in the 1960's, about life in Paris, about being blacklisted in the 1950's, her writing, and the authors whom she admires. A source of valuable background information on Boyle.

(AP/Wide World Photos)

T. CORAGHESSAN BOYLE
Thomas John Boyle

Born: Peekskill, New York; 1948

PRINCIPAL LONG FICTION

Water Music, 1981
Budding Prospects: A Pastoral, 1984
World's End, 1987
East Is East, 1990
The Road to Wellville, 1993
The Tortilla Curtain, 1995
Riven Rock, 1998

OTHER LITERARY FORMS

T. Coraghessan Boyle published several collections of mostly satirical short stories that generally address the same themes seen in his longer fiction.

ACHIEVEMENTS

Boyle's novels have been praised for their originality, style, and comic energy. At a time when his contemporaries seem obsessed with the mundane details of everyday life—presented in a minimalist style—Boyle approaches fiction as an iconoclastic storyteller who embraces and borrows from the entire history of narrative literature, celebrating the profane, often-absurd complexities of human endeavors. His first collection of stories won the St. Lawrence Award for Short Fiction, *Water Music* received the Aga Khan Award, and the PEN/Faulkner Award for Fiction was given to *World's End*. Boyle also has been a recipient of the PEN short story award. Film director Alan Parker adapted *The Road to Wellville* for the screen in 1994, and several of Boyle's stories have been adapted for broadcast on cable television.

BIOGRAPHY

Born into a lower-middle-class family in Peekskill, New York, in 1948, Thomas John Boyle was a rebellious youth who played drums, sang in a rock-and-roll band, and drove fast cars. He did not get along with his father, a school-bus driver whose alcoholism killed him at fifty-four in 1972. Boyle's mother, a secretary, was also an alcoholic and died of liver failure. Assuming the name T. Coraghessan Boyle at the State University of New York at Potsdam, Boyle studied saxophone and clarinet until he realized that he lacked the necessary discipline for music and drifted into creative writing. After college, to avoid military service during the Vietnam War, he taught English for two years at Lakeland High School in Shrub Oak, New York, while increasing his use of drugs, including heroin.

In 1972, Boyle entered the creative writing program at the University of Iowa, where he studied under Vance Bourjaily, John Cheever, and John Irving. He also studied nineteenth century English literature and received a Ph.D. in 1977, with a short-story collection, later published as *Descent of Man* (1979), serving as his dissertation. He became head of the writing program at the University of Southern California and settled in Woodland Hills, a suburb of Los Angeles, with his wife, Karen Kvashay (whom he met when they were undergraduates), and their children, Kerrie, Milo, and Spencer.

ANALYSIS

T. Coraghessan Boyle's novels concern the misconceptions people of different sexes, races, nationalities, and backgrounds have about one another and the misunderstandings—some violent—that result. The clashes between Britons and Africans in *Water Music*, drug entrepreneurs and Northern California rednecks in *Budding Prospects*, Indians and Dutch settlers in New York in *World's End*, Americans and a half-American Japanese in *East Is East*, and privileged white Southern Californians and destitute illegal Mexican immigrants in *The Tortilla Curtain* all

allow Boyle to satirize the prejudices, eccentricities, and excesses of several cultures.

Boyle's ironic fiction is populated by a multitude of diverse characters, all convinced that theirs is the only possible way of perceiving and dealing with a complex, changing, often-hostile world. Boyle alternates the viewpoints of these protagonists to present events and issues from all possible sides and increase the irony of the situations. He writes both in a straightforward, economical style and in more ornate prose resembling that of such popular writers as John Barth and Thomas Pynchon. Far from being didactic, Boyle's serious fiction entertains through his masterful storytelling ability and through his control of his vivid style.

WATER MUSIC

Water Music alternates between the stories of Scottish explorer Mungo Park and London criminal Ned Rise until their destinies converge in Africa. Park (1771-1806), the first white man to see the Niger River, wrote a best-selling account of his adventures, *Travels in the Interior Districts of Africa* (1797), led a larger expedition into the interior of Africa, and drowned in the rapids of the Niger during an attack by natives. Boyle's fictionalized Park and the low-born Rise are used to contrast the levels of English society and attitudes toward the British Empire.

Park, a public hero, is less than heroic as imagined by Boyle. He thinks that he has had unique experiences because he is unable to recognize the humanity of the Africans he encounters. He selfishly ignores Ailie, his long-suffering fiancé and later devoted wife, thinking nothing of leaving her behind for years while he strives for glory. Park is less concerned with any benefits to humankind resulting from his expeditions than with mere adventure and fame. This need leads him to distort and romanticize his experiences in his writings. The irony of these exploits is that Park would be totally lost without the assistance of such nonwhites as Johnson, born Katunga Oyo. Sold into slavery in America, Johnson learns to read, wins his freedom, becomes a highly respected valet in London, and translates Henry Fielding's *Amelia* (1751) into Mandingo before returning to Africa. His earthy yet sophisticated realism strongly contrasts with Park's muddled idealism. Park's moral blindness suggests some of the causes of the collapse of the Empire.

Ned Rise, on the other hand, is a victim in the tradition of the picaros created by Fielding, Daniel Defoe, and Charles Dickens. (Dickens's mixture of colorful characterizations, humor, and moral outrage, as well as his use of odd names, seems to be a major influence on Boyle.) Rise is stolen from his mother at birth and forced to become a beggar when old enough. He has his right hand mutilated by a cleaver, is nearly drowned, is robbed, is wrongfully imprisoned and hanged—coming to life as he is about to be dissected—loses his true love, Fanny Brunch, is imprisoned again, and is shipped to Africa to become part of Park's fatal expedition. Park's Britain represents culture and privilege; Ned's stands for the poverty and depravity at the extreme other end of the social scale. Yet the ironically named Rise learns to survive.

In the tradition of such classics of the American picaresque novel as John Barth's *The Sot-Weed Factor* (1960) and Thomas Berger's *Little Big Man* (1964), *Water Music* is an enormously entertaining black comedy, a deliberately anachronistic, self-conscious narrative that frequently calls attention to its form and style. Boyle's delight in being a literary show-off, a tendency he has subdued as his career has progressed, led some of the novel's reviewers to dismiss it as a stunt, but *Water Music* quickly developed a cult following and has come to be seen as a clear announcement of the debut of an original, irreverent talent.

BUDDING PROSPECTS

Boyle presents another ill-conceived adventure, though on a much smaller scale, in *Budding Prospects: A Pastoral*. Its thirty-one-year-old protagonist, Felix Nasmyth, is a chronic failure given another shot at success by the mysterious Vogelsang, a Vietnam veteran and sociopath. With the assistance of Boyd Dowst, holder of a master's degree in botany from Yale University, Felix is to grow marijuana in rural Northern California. Vogelsang promises the desperate Felix that he will earn a half-million dollars from the enterprise.

Felix and his inept friends Phil and Gesh experience culture shock in isolated Willits, whose aggressively antagonistic citizens consider themselves morally superior to the rest of the decadent world. Obstacles to raising a productive marijuana crop include rain, fire, a hungry bear, a 320-pound alumnus of the state mental hospital's violent ward, and John Jerpbak, a menacing policeman who, like everyone in Willits, knows what Felix is doing. The comedy of *Budding Prospects* results from the dogged perseverance of Felix and friends in this doomed endeavor.

Beside his usual theme of individuals out of their element in a strange environment, Boyle offers a satire of the American free-enterprise system. As he interprets it, the system is motivated primarily by greed, with success coming less through intelligence or hard work than through luck. The dubious morality of Felix's project only adds to the irony. He and his friends want to get rich quickly and are honest only in admitting that they care about nothing but money. That they work harder to fail in an illegal business than they would to earn money honestly is yet another irony in a highly ironic tale. Felix's unreliable narration as he constantly compares himself to the pioneers who settled America adds comic hyperbole. Such humor keeps Boyle's examination of the materialistic side of the American Dream from being preachy.

WORLD'S END

Boyle returned to a larger canvas with *World's End*, his most ambitious and least comic novel, a consideration of America's self-destructive impulse. The Van Brunts, Dutch settlers in what is now northern Westchester County, New York, in the late seventeenth century, experience conflicts with a hostile nature and the voracious Van Warts, the patroons who own the land they farm. The lives of the Van Brunts become intertwined with those of the Kitchawanks, their Indian neighbors. The greedy machinations of the Van Warts lead to misery for the settlers and Indians and death for several of them.

Boyle alternates chapters about these characters with ones dealing with their twentieth century descendants, including Jeremy Mohonk, the last of the Kitchawanks, whose efforts to regain his birthright (stolen by the Van Warts) earn for him seventeen years in prison. Truman Van Brunt betrays his friends and relatives to save himself, just as one of the original Van Brunts had done. The protagonist of the twentieth century chapters is Walter Van Brunt, reared by communists after Truman runs away and his mother dies. In the late 1960's, Walter is torn between the countercultural life led by his friends and the wealth and social position of the Van Warts. After losing his wife when she finds him in bed with Mardi Van Wart and losing both his feet in separate motorcycle accidents, Walter tracks down his lost father in Barrow, Alaska, to discover that Truman has spent years researching his family's history to justify his actions. Walter returns home thoroughly disillusioned, and Jeremy Mohonk gains revenge against his enemies by impregnating the wife of the current Van Wart, ironically allowing the despised line to continue.

In *World's End*, Boyle shows how people of different races, sexes, and social and economic backgrounds exploit, betray, and fail one another. The characters either are desperate to control their destinies or consider themselves the victims of fates they are incapable of overcoming. Almost everyone is self-deluding, from the right-wing fanatic Dipe Van Wart in his pathetic attempts to resist change, to Walter, who sees himself as an alienated, existential antihero in the tradition of Meursault in Albert Camus's *L'Étranger* (1942; *The Stranger*, 1946). Walter thinks that his life will fall into place if he can understand his father, yet finding Truman leads only to confusion.

As Boyle rifles English literary traditions as part of his satire in *Water Music*, in *World's End* he draws upon the mythical views of America espoused by such writers as Washington Irving, James Fenimore Cooper, Nathaniel Hawthorne, Herman Melville, and William Faulkner. From the destruction of the virgin wilderness to the exploitation of the Indian to the curses inflicted upon several generations of characters to fatal obsession with the inexplicable, the novel is virtually a catalog of traditional American literary themes.

World's End represents a new maturity in Boyle as an artist. In it he eschews the too-easy irony and too-obvious satire that occasionally weaken his earlier fiction, while he confirms his skill at storytelling. Though *World's End* is a sprawling novel with more than one hundred characters, Boyle exerts masterful control over his complicated, overlapping plots, expecting his readers to share his joy in the manipulation of so many coincidences, parallels, and ironies.

East Is East

The inability of people of different backgrounds to understand one another is even more at the center of *East Is East* than of Boyle's other novels. Hiro Tanaka, a twenty-year-old cook on a Japanese ship, jumps overboard off the coast of Georgia. Hiro, another Boyle orphan, has never known his father, an American rock musician who loved and left Hiro's mother, an eventual suicide. Ostracized by Japanese society for being half American, Hiro longs to lose himself in the great melting pot but unfortunately washes ashore on isolated Tupelo Island, site of Thanatopsis House, an artists' colony.

After a series of confused encounters with the natives, Hiro finds refuge in the cottage of Ruth Dershowitz. A mediocre writer from California, Ruth is at Thanatopsis thanks to being the lover of Saxby Lights, son of Septima Lights, the colony's founder. Ruth pities the hungry, frightened fugitive from immigration authorities but also longs to incorporate Hiro into a short story with which she is having difficulty. Saxby finds out about Hiro, who is imprisoned, escapes to the Okefenokee Swamp, and is arrested again when near death.

Both the white and the black residents of Tupelo Island are frightened by their Japanese visitor, who is equally bewildered by them. Detlef Abercorn, the immigration official sent to find Hiro, is from Los Angeles and feels totally alienated in the South. An albino, he, like Hiro, has never truly fit in anywhere. Abercorn is assisted by Lewis Turco, a veteran of covert operations in Southeast Asia, who prides himself on being in control in any environment, but he is so paranoid that he creates nothing but chaos. No one in *East Is East* understands or trusts anyone else. The writers, painters, sculptors, and composers at Thanatopsis, who should be able to transcend the cultural differences that handicap the others, are instead so self-absorbed and crippled by petty jealousies that they are totally ineffective as human beings.

Hiro is another Boyle innocent destroyed by his inability to deal with the world's complexities and hostilities and by his own foolishness. Hiro has a system of beliefs—based on Japanese writer Yukio Mishima's theory of the samurai—to help guide him, but Mishima proves tragicomically ineffective in the Georgia swamps. Hiro trusts Ruth, to a degree, because he has no one else, and while she genuinely wants to help, her needs must come first. Ruth, the most fully developed female character in Boyle's novels, ironically finds success through being caught harboring an illegal immigrant, for she then lands a book contract to tell her story. The unscrupulousness of supposedly sensitive artists is as much the target of Boyle's satirical ire as are cultural differences.

THE ROAD TO WELLVILLE

Similar to each other in scheme and scope, *The Road to Wellville* and *Riven Rock* elaborate the wry appraisal of human nature and American values found in *Budding Prospects* and *East Is East* in period tales whose vivid historical tableaux call to mind Boyle's achievement in *Water Music* and *World's End*.

The Road to Wellville is a farcical examination of the career of Dr. John Harvey Kellogg, inventor of the corn flake and other "gastrically correct" natural foods. A devout vegetarian and zealous promoter of physical culture, Kellogg opens his Battle Creek Sanitarium to men and women at the beginning of the twentieth century, hoping to win them over to his vision of a healthier lifestyle through carefully restricted diets, vigorous exercise regimens, and crackpot medical interventions that include yogurt enemas and sinusoidal baths. Kellogg's "Temple of Health," as some deem it, is a magnet for celebrities, socialites, eccentrics, and connivers who represent a cross section of Boyle's America.

Among them is Eleanor Lightbody, an independent woman and self-proclaimed "Battle Freak" whose sense of liberation is tied to her willing embrace of Kellogg's instruction. Intelligent and principled, Eleanor is blind to the absurdity of Kellogg's methods and to the misery they cause her sickly hus-

band Will, who suffers the increasingly dangerous indignities of rehabilitation at the sanitarium out of love for his wife. Boyle interweaves the adventures of the Lightbodys with those of Charlie Ossining, a likable scalawag who has squandered the money given him by a patron to establish a competing health food company in Battle Creek. Ossining's inept efforts to duplicate Kellogg's products through cheap and eventually devious means offer a comic reflection on the underside of entrepreneurism and the free-enterprise system.

The book's most interesting character is George Kellogg, one of Dr. Kellogg's numerous adopted children and a symbol of the Kellogg method's failure. George spends most of the novel dissipated and disorderly, deliberately embarrassing his father to extort money from him. He embodies the tendency toward entropy that undermines the best-laid plans in all of Boyle's novels and the irrepressible primitive appetites that get the better of even the most sophisticated characters.

RIVEN ROCK

Boyle develops these character types and traits further in *Riven Rock*. Set at approximately the same time as *The Road to Wellville*, Riven Rock portrays another American captain of industry whose personal shortcomings reflect an inherent flaw in the human condition. Stanley McCormick, heir to the McCormick Reaper fortune, is afflicted with an apparently hereditary schizophrenia that manifests as sexual psychopathy. He spends most of the novel locked away at Riven Rock, a family retreat in Santa Barbara, deprived of the company of women—his wife included—because a mere glimpse of them provokes him to profane and lewd attacks. In flashbacks, Boyle portrays Stanley as a naïve and sensitive young man who has perhaps been driven mad by the pressure of family responsibilities, and almost certainly by the insensitivity of women in his life, including his domineering mother and his crusading wife.

As in his other panoramic novels, Boyle refracts the central conflicts and issues through the experiences of a number of characters. Chief among these is Stanley's wife, Katherine, a caring but ambitious woman who bears a striking resemblance in her attitudes to Eleanor Lightbody of *The Road to Wellville*. Educated and fiercely independent, Katherine is dedicated to Stanley's rehabilitation partly out of affection, but also as part of her selfish quest to have a child and know the fulfilled expression of her privilege and will. Edward O'Kane, Stanley's nurse and caretaker, complements Katherine. Sexually profligate and perpetually hostage to his lusts, he impregnates several women over the course of the novel, which leads to repeated comic complications with their families and his employer. In their own ways, Katherine and O'Kane embody the same appetites that govern Stanley. Boyle emphasizes this point through the efforts of Stanley's doctors to cure him by studying the insatiable sex drives of monkeys brought to the secluded estate. *Riven Rock* is possibly Boyle's most direct attempt to present the competing interests and compelling drives behind a culture and citizens as an expression of Darwinian biological imperatives.

The anger in Boyle's novels is tempered by the comedy. Even a relatively somber work such as *World's End* has moments of sublime silliness, as Dipe Van Wart fights middle-age depression by eating dirt from beneath his ancestral home—a fitting comic metaphor for his family's neuroticism and mindless consumption of the land. Boyle's fiction is also notable for the diversity of his style, which changes not only from novel to novel but also from chapter to chapter. He understands well how to play upon the natural rhythms of convoluted sentences and when to resort to the subtler joys of simpler ones, has a vocabulary rivaling Vladimir Nabokov's, and delights in parody. *East Is East* offers the mock Faulkner appropriate to a comic novel set in the South, but it avoids the overkill occasionally seen in Boyle's short stories and earlier novels. *The Road to Wellville* and *Riven Rock* are kaleidoscopic narratives in the style of Charles Dickens and William Makepeace Thackeray; their broad historical context accommodates their sweeping social satire. Most important is Boyle's ability to create believable, usually sympathetic, characters caught in absurd quests for truths they are incapable of understanding.

Michael Adams, updated by Stefan Dziemianowicz

OTHER MAJOR WORKS

SHORT FICTION: *Descent of Man*, 1979; *Greasy Lake and Other Stories*, 1985; *If the River Was Whiskey*, 1989; *The Collected Stories of T. Coraghessan Boyle*, 1993; *Without a Hero*, 1994; *T. C. Boyle Stories: The Collected Stories of T. Coraghessan Boyle*, 1998.

BIBLIOGRAPHY

Boyle, T. Coraghessan. Interview by William Brisick. *Publishers Weekly* 232 (October 9, 1987): 71-72. Boyle discusses the influence of growing up in the Hudson River Valley on the creation of *World's End*, his theory about using history in fiction, his difficult relationship with his father, and his dissatisfaction with the way his publishers have handled his books.

_____. "A Punk's Past Recaptured." Interview by Anthony DeCurtis. *Rolling Stone*, January 14, 1988, 54-57. In a revealing interview, Boyle talks about his drug use, the importance of understanding history, the influence of Washington Irving on *World's End*, and the autobiographical element in his fiction. He expresses the desire to be like Kurt Vonnegut, Jr., in showing that literature can be both serious and entertaining, and like John Updike in constantly changing his approach to fiction and improving as an artist.

Friend, Tad. "Rolling Boyle." *The New York Times Magazine*, December 9, 1990, 50, 64-68. A feature on Boyle's success and conscious courtship of notoriety, including appraisals of his writing by Russell Banks, Frank Conroy, George Plimpton, and other colleagues.

Pope, Dan. "A Different Kind of Post-Modernism." *Gettysburg Review* 3 (Autumn, 1990): 658-669. A discussion of Boyle's collection *If the River Was Whiskey*, along with a collection of short fiction by Rick DeMarinis and Paul West, as typifying the work of a new generation of writers who look beyond "the age of innocent realism."

Schenker, Daniel. "A Samurai in the South: Cross-Cultural Disaster in T. Coraghessan Boyle's *East Is East*." *The Southern Quarterly* 34 (Fall, 1995):

70-80. In-depth analysis of the cultural clashes and intransigence that inform the tragicomic vision of Boyle's novel.

Spencer, Russ. "The Jester Who Hath No King." *Book*, December, 1998-January, 1999, 38-43. Day-in-the-life type feature based on a visit to Boyle's home, with Boyle—described as "the Bacchus of American letters"—assessing his career and personal philosophies following the publication of *Riven Rock* and *T. C. Boyle Stories*.

Vaid, Krishna Baldev. "Franz Kafka Writes to T. Coraghessan Boyle." *Michigan Quarterly Review* 35 (Summer, 1996): 532-549. A fanciful attempt by one of Boyle's former professors, written in the manner of Franz Kafka's "Letter to His Father," to find parallels between themes and approaches in Kafka's and Boyle's fiction. Boyle appends the brief, comic "A Response to Kafka."

Walker, Michael. "Boyle's 'Greasy Lake' and the Moral Failure of Postmodernism." *Studies in Short Fiction* 31 (1994): 247-255. Using the title story of Boyle's second collection as a touchstone, the author criticizes Boyle for fiction in which characters fail to experience revelation and develop insight from their experiences. Written partly in response to Dan Pope's "A Different Kind of Post-Modernism."

(Thomas Victor)

A Graveyard for Lunatics: Another Tale of Two Cities, 1990
Green Shadows, White Whale, 1992

OTHER LITERARY FORMS

Ray Bradbury's principal literary form is the short story, and he published several important collections, including *Dark Carnival* (1947), *The Golden Apples of the Sun* (1953), and *I Sing the Body Electric!* (1969). A one-hundred-story collection, *The Stories of Ray Bradbury* (1980), seemed to sum up his life's work, but it was later followed by anthologies of new stories, *Quicker than the Eye* (1996) and *Driving Blind* (1997). In addition to his short stories and novels, he published in a wide variety of literary forms, from light verse and poetry to screenplays and dramas. A notable screenplay, which he wrote in collaboration with film director John Huston, is a 1956 adaptation of Herman Melville's *Moby Dick* (1851). A representative example of his poetry is *When Ele-*

RAY BRADBURY

Born: Waukegan, Illinois; August 22, 1920

PRINCIPAL LONG FICTION
The Martian Chronicles, 1950
The Illustrated Man, 1951
Fahrenheit 451, 1953
Dandelion Wine, 1957
Something Wicked This Way Comes, 1962
Death Is a Lonely Business, 1985

phants Last in the Dooryard Bloomed: Celebrations for Almost Any Day in the Year (1973) and of his plays is *The Pedestrian* (1966).

ACHIEVEMENTS

Although Bradbury became arguably the United States' best-known science-fiction writer, the majority of his work, which ranges from gothic horror to social criticism, centers on humanistic themes. Aficionados of the genre criticized his science-fiction stories for their scientific and technological inaccuracies, a criticism he shrugs off, stating that his dominating concerns are social, cultural, and intellectual issues, not scientific verisimilitude. His stories, which often explore the dehumanizing pressures of technocracies and the mesmerizing power of the imagination, are widely anthologized and translated into many foreign languages. His ascent from pulp magazines to literary respectability was intermittently recognized with several awards, including appearances in Martha Foley's annual best American short-story collections, two O. Henry prizes, the Benjamin Franklin Magazine Award, the National Institute of Arts and Letters Award, an Academy Award nomination, and a Golden Eagle Award for his screenplay *Icarus Montgolfier Wright* (1961). He was named a Nebula Grand Master and received the Bram Stoker Life Achievement Award as well as the Body of Work Award from the International Association of Poets, Playwrights, Editors, Essayists, and Novelists (PEN). His best works are wrenching indictments of the dangers of unrestrained scientific and technological progress, but his work also encourages the hope that humanity will deal creatively with the new worlds it seems driven to construct.

BIOGRAPHY

Ray Bradbury was born on August 22, 1920, in Waukegan, Illinois. His father, Leonard Spaulding Bradbury, whose distant ancestor Mary Bradbury was among those tried for witchcraft in Salem, was a lineman with the Waukegan Bureau of Power and Light; his mother, Esther Marie (née Moberg) Bradbury, emigrated as a child from Sweden. When he was three years old, his mother took him to his

first film, *The Hunchback of Notre Dame* (1923), and he was frightened and entranced by Lon Chaney in this film and, later, in *The Phantom of the Opera* (1925). As a child, Bradbury passed through a series of enthusiasms, from monsters to circuses to dinosaurs and eventually to the planet Mars. His development through childhood was aided by an older brother and by an aunt, Neva Bradbury, a costume designer, who introduced him to the theater and to the stories of Edgar Allan Poe.

In 1932, Bradbury's family moved to Arizona, where they had previously spent some time in the mid-1920's, largely because of his father's need to find work. In 1934 the family left behind both Arizona and Waukegan, settling in Los Angeles, which became Bradbury's permanent home. He attended Los Angeles High School and joined the Science Fiction Society (he had earlier begun reading Hugo Gernsback's *Amazing Stories*, which, he said, made him fall in love with the future). After graduation, Bradbury worked for several months in a theater group sponsored by the actress Laraine Day, and for several years he was a newsboy in downtown Los Angeles. He took these jobs to support his writing, an avocation that he hoped would soon become a vocation.

His poor eyesight prevented him from serving in the Army during World War II, which left him free to launch his writing career. During the early 1940's he began to publish his stories in such pulp magazines as *Weird Tales* and *Amazing Stories*, but by the late 1940's his work was appearing in such mass-market magazines as *Collier's*, *The Saturday Evening Post*, *The New Yorker*, *Harper's Magazine*, and *Mademoiselle*. Because these magazines paid well, he was able, on September 27, 1947, to marry Marguerite Susan McClure, a former English teacher at the University of California in Los Angeles. He continued, during the 1950's, to write for the pulp and mass-market magazines, and he routinely collected his stories for publication in books. In the mid-1950's he traveled to Ireland in connection with a screenplay of *Moby Dick* that he wrote with John Huston. Upon his return to the United States, Bradbury composed a large number of television scripts for such shows as *Alfred Hitchcock Presents*, *Suspense*, and *The Twi-*

light Zone. During the late 1950's and early 1960's, Bradbury's stories and novels focused mostly on his midwestern childhood—for example, *Dandelion Wine* and *Something Wicked This Way Comes*, the latter his favorite book.

During the 1960's and 1970's, Bradbury's output of fiction decreased, and his ideas found outlets in such forms as plays, poems, and essays. He also became involved in a number of projects, such as "A Journey Through United States History," the exhibit that occupied the upper floor of the United States Pavilion for the New York World's Fair in the mid-1960's. Because of this display's success, the Walt Disney organization hired him to help develop the themes for Spaceship Earth, an important part of Epcot Center at Disney World in Florida. Bradbury also helped design a twenty-first century city near Tokyo. He continued to diversify his activities in the 1980's and 1990's by collaborative and consultative work, and he also found time to return to his first love, the short story, and to write four novels. He collaborated with Jimmy Webb by composing lyrics for a musical version of *Dandelion Wine*, which was not successful, though critics praised the Bradbury novel that provided the inspiration for this production. These excursions into other fields were part of his expressed plan to work in "every writing medium," but his successes continued to be in the traditional forms of the novel and short story. He published two detective novels, *Death Is a Lonely Business* and *A Graveyard for Lunatics*, and a *roman à clef*, *Green Shadows, White Whale*. He also wrote a large number of short stories, some of them in his customary fields of science fiction, fantasy, and horror, but many dealing with extraordinary characters in ordinary life. These were collected in anthologies: *The Toynbee Convector* (1988), *Quicker than the Eye*, and *Driving Blind*.

ANALYSIS

Paradoxically, Bradbury's stories look both backward and forward. For him, each story is a way of discovering a self, and the self found in one story is different from the self found in another. Bradbury, like all human beings, is made of time, and human beings, like rivers, flow and change. Adapting the an-

cient Greek philosopher Heraclitus's famous statement that one cannot step into the same river twice, one could say that no person ever steps twice into the same self. Sometimes Bradbury discovered a self in the past, and sometimes, particularly in his science fiction, he discovered a self in the future. Several critics have pictured him as a frontiersman, ambivalently astride two worlds, who has alternately been attracted to an idealized past, timeless and nostalgic, and to a graphic future, chameleonic and threatening. This creative tension is present both in his own life and in the generation of Americans he liked to depict. It is also intimately connected with the genre—science fiction—with which he became so closely identified.

Bradbury has been called a Romantic, and his Romanticism often surfaces in the themes he investigates: the conflict between human vitality and spiritless mechanism, between the creative individual and the conforming group, between imagination and reason, between intuition and logic, between the innocence of childhood and the corruptions of adulthood, and between the shadow and light in every human soul. His stories make clear that, in all these conflicts, human beings, not machines, are at the center of his vision. An ambivalence about technology characterizes his life and work. For example, he never learned to drive, even while spending most of his life in Los Angeles, a city that has made the automobile not only an apparent necessity but also an object of worship. He also refused to use a computer, and he successfully avoided flying in an airplane for the first six decades of his life.

Each of these attitudes is rooted in some profoundly emotional experience; for example, he never learned to drive because, as a youth, he witnessed the horrible deaths of five people in an automobile accident. Because of his emphasis on basic human values against an uncritical embracing of technical progress, because of his affirmation of the human spirit against modern materialism, and because of his trust in the basic goodness of small-town life against the debilitating indifference of the cities, several critics have accused him of sentimentality and naïveté. Bradbury responded by saying that critics write from the head, whereas he writes from the heart.

The poetic style that he developed was admirably suited to the heartfelt themes that he explored in a cornucopia of highly imaginative stories. He cultivated this style through eclectic imitation and dogged determination. As an adolescent, he vowed to write several hundred words every day, for he believed that quantity would eventually lead to quality. Experience and the example of other writers would teach him what to leave out. According to Bradbury, his style was influenced by such writers as Charles Dickens, Mark Twain, Thomas Wolfe, and Ernest Hemingway. On another occasion, however, he stated that his style came as much from silent-film actor Charlie Chaplin as from Aldous Huxley, as much from Tom Swift as from George Orwell, as much from cowboy actor Tom Mix as from Bertrand Russell, and as much from Edgar Rice Burroughs as from C. S. Lewis. Bradbury was also influenced by such poets as Alexander Pope, Gerard Manley Hopkins, and Dylan Thomas, and such dramatists as William Shakespeare and George Bernard Shaw. Furthermore and surprisingly, such painters as El Greco and Tintoretto and such composers as Wolfgang Amadeus Mozart and Franz Joseph Haydn showed him how to add color and rhythm to his writing. According to him, all these influences—writers, poets, painters, and musicians—gloried in the joy of creating, and their works overflow with animal vigor and intellectual vitality. Their ardor and delight are contagious, and their honest response to the materials at hand calls forth a similar response in their readers, viewers, and listeners. This enchanting of the audience, similar to casting a magic spell, is what Bradbury attempted to do with his kaleidoscopic style: to transform colorful pieces of reality into a glittering picture that will emotionally intensify the lives of his readers.

Bradbury's writing is profoundly autobiographical, and childhood, adolescent, and adult experiences generated many of his stories. Graham Greene once said that there is always one moment in childhood when the door opens and lets the future in. Actually, for Bradbury, there were many such moments. He once said that everything he had ever done—all his activities, loves, and fears—were created by the primitive experiences of monsters and angels he had

when he was five years old. He also said, however, that the most important event in his childhood occurred when he was twelve years old, at a carnival, when the performance of a magician, Mr. Electrico, so energized his imagination that he began to write stories to communicate his fervid visions to others.

Numerous Bradbury stories, including several in his first collection, *Dark Carnival*, have as their provenance specific childhood events. For example, "The Small Assassin," which metamorphoses some of his childhood experiences and fears, tells of a newborn infant, terrified at finding himself thrust into a hostile world, taking revenge on his parents by first terrorizing, then murdering them. This story also reveals that Bradbury's view of childhood innocence is more complex than many critics realize, for, in Bradbury's view, beneath the façade of innocence lies a cauldron of sin—a dark vision of the human condition that some critics have called Calvinistic. Another tale, "The Lake," is based on Bradbury's experience as a seven-year-old, when his cousin nearly drowned in Lake Michigan. These and other early stories, which he published in such pulp magazines as *Weird Tales*, *Amazing Stories*, and *Astounding Science Fiction*, served as his apprenticeship, an opportunity to perfect his style, deepen his vision, and develop the themes on which he would play variations in his later, more accomplished short stories, novels, poems, and dramas.

One of these early themes that also haunted his later fiction is alienation. Bradbury himself experienced cultural alienation when he traveled to Mexico in 1945. Americans were then mostly Protestant, individualistic, and preoccupied with getting ahead. Mexicans, on the other hand, were mostly Catholic, communalistic, and preoccupied with death. On his trip to Guanajuato, northwest of Mexico City, Bradbury was both horrified and fascinated by the catacombs with their rows of propped-up mummified bodies. A story collected in *Dark Carnival*, "The Next in Line," grew out of this experience. In this story, a young American wife finds herself, after her traumatic ordeal in the Guanajuato crypts, alienated both from the strange Mexican society and from her own body, which she obsessively realizes is a potential mummy. Bradbury uses the metaphor of death to help the reader comprehend one reality, life, in terms of another, death. Metaphor thus becomes a medicine, a way of healing ourselves by envisioning ourselves into new modes of experiencing, learning, and surviving.

Despite his forays into long fiction, Bradbury's forte is the short story, and three major collections of his tales appeared in the 1980's and 1990's: *The Toynbee Convector, Quicker than the Eye*, and *Driving Blind*. Many of the later stories are either slightly camouflaged, grossly exaggerated, or an "absolutely accurate" detailing of events in the author's own life. Whatever the source of these stories, they are part of what Bradbury calls "the history of ideas." In the afterword to *Quicker than the Eye*, he confesses that he is not a writer of science fiction, fantasy, or Magical Realism; rather, he sees himself as a word magician who does not really "write these stories, *they* write *me*." He calculated that he had written close to five hundred stories, but he believed that "there must be at least 1,000 more . . . waiting to be discovered."

Several critics in the late 1980's and the 1990's detected a decline in the quality of Bradbury's later work, but the standard he set in the 1950's was very high. Because his work took so many different literary forms, and because, within each of these forms, his treatment of a potpourri of subjects was equally variegated, it is difficult to make neat generalizations about his oeuvre. The public has recognized him as the world's premier science-fiction writer, but only a third of his work has been in this genre. Certainly, his science-fiction stories have revealed that cultivated and craftsmanlike writing is possible in what was seen, before him, as a vulgar genre. Within the science-fiction community, however, a sharp difference of opinion exists about Bradbury's contributions. A sizable segment sees his work as reactionary, antitechnological, and anti-Utopian. As one of these critics put it, Bradbury is a science-fiction writer for people who do not really like science fiction. On the other hand, a large group, which includes a significant segment of the literary community (viewing him as one of their own), sees him as a humanist and a re-

gional writer. This group draws some good arguments from Bradbury's stories: For example, even when he writes about Mars, the planet symbolizes for him the geography—emotional and intellectual—of the American Midwest. In this sense, his regionalism is one of the mind and heart.

Actually, both sides of this debate can find evidence for their views in Bradbury's motley work. He can be both enthusiastic about a future transformed by technology and critical of the dangers posed by technocracies. Ultimately, for him, technology is a *human* creation, and it is therefore subject to the labyrinthine goods and evils of the human heart. Although his best work is deeply humanistic and includes a strong critique of unrestrained technology, he is no Luddite. It is true that the technological society has produced many problems—pollution, for example—but human beings love to solve problems; it is a defining characteristic of the species.

Those who see only Bradbury's critique of technology view him as a pessimistic writer. In the proper light, however, his work is really profoundly optimistic. His fiction may rest upon the gloomy foundation of the Fall, but, in traditional theology, the counterpart of the Fall is Redemption, and Bradbury believes that human beings will renew themselves, particularly in space, which he sees as modern humanity's religious quest. Space, then, is Bradbury's new wilderness, with an infinity of new challenges. In that inexhaustible wilderness, human beings will find themselves and be saved.

THE MARTIAN CHRONICLES

Although, at first glance, many of Bradbury's early stories seem notable for their great variety, he did deal, especially in his stories about Mars, with a set of conflicts that had a common theme, and so, when an editor suggested in 1949 that he compose a continuous narrative, he took advantage of the opportunity, since several of his stories about the colonization of Mars by Earthlings lent themselves to just such a treatment. Using the chronological frame of 1999 to 2026, Bradbury stitched these stories together with bridge passages that gave the book a semblance of unity (it also presented categorizers of his works with a problem: Some have listed the book as a novel, others as a short-story collection). Many critics have called *The Martian Chronicles* Bradbury's masterpiece, a magical and insightful account of the exploitation of a new frontier, Mars, by Earthlings whose personalities appear to have been nurtured in small midwestern American towns. By placing these normal human beings in an extraordinary setting, Bradbury was able to use the strange light of an alien world to illuminate the dark regions of human nature. The apparatus of conventional science fiction makes an appearance, including monsters and supermachines, but Bradbury's basic intent is to explore the conflicts that were troubling postwar America: imperialism, alienation, pollution, racism, and nuclear war. He therefore depicts not a comforting human progress but a disquieting cycle of rises and falls. He also sees the Martian environment, itself transformed by human ingenuity, transforming the settlers. Thus, his ultimate view seems optimistic: Humanity will, through creative adaptation, not only survive but thrive. In *The Martian Chronicles* Earthlings metamorphose into Martians, an action that serves as a Bradburian metaphor for the human condition, which is to be always in the process of becoming something else.

Even though scientists criticized *The Martian Chronicles* for its portrayal of Mars as a planet with a breathable atmosphere, water, and canals (known by astronomers in 1950 to be untrue), and even though science-fiction devotees found Bradbury's portrayal of Martian colonies implausible, the book was a triumphant success, largely, some have suggested, because of these "weaknesses." Bradbury's Mars mirrored the present and served as the stage upon which his eccentric characters—the misfits, opportunists, and romantics—could remake Mars in their own images (only to find themselves remade by Mars in the process). *The Martian Chronicles* has proved to be enduringly popular. It has passed through several editions, sold millions of copies, and been translated into more than thirty foreign languages.

THE ILLUSTRATED MAN

Another book of interlinked stories, *The Illustrated Man*, followed soon after the publication of *The Martian Chronicles*. In *The Illustrated Man* the device linking the stories together is the tattoos on the skin of one of the characters. Bradbury sets some of his stories on Mars, and a few bear some relation to the cycle of stories in *The Martian Chronicles*. By the early 1950's, Bradbury was a well-established writer, able to place his stories in both pulp and popular magazines and able to profit again when his collections of these stories were published as books. His fourth collection, *The Golden Apples of the Sun*, abandoned the frame narrative that he had been using and instead simply juxtaposed stories from a wide variety of genres—science fiction, fantasy, crime, and comedy.

FAHRENHEIT 451

During this most prolific period in Bradbury's literary life, he also published the book that would generate, along with *The Martian Chronicles*, his greatest success and influence. The story that came to be called *Fahrenheit 451* went through several transformations. In 1947 he had written a short story, "Bright Phoenix," in which the residents of a small town counter government book-burning edicts by memorizing the banned books. In 1951 he expanded this idea into a long story, "The Fireman," which appeared in *Galaxy Science Fiction*. A fire chief informed him that book paper first bursts into flame at 451 degrees Fahrenheit, which gave him the title for his novel-length story set in a future totalitarian state. Some critics interpreted this dystopian novel as an attack against McCarthyism, then at the height of its power, but the book also attacks the tyrannical domination of mass culture, especially in this culture's tendency to eschew complexity of thought and to embrace the simple sentiments of pressure groups. The central irony of the novel concerns firemen whose job is to set fires (burn books) rather than to put them out. Bradbury, a lifelong book lover, used his novel to show how important books are to freedom, morality, and the search for truth. His novel concludes with Montag, a fireman who has rejected his role as book burner, joining a community that strives to preserve books by memorizing them. Some critics have pointed out that this new society, where individuals abandon their identities to "become" the books they have memorized, inculcates a mass behavior as conformist as the one from which they and Montag have escaped, but Bradbury would respond that this new culture allows for a multiplicity of ideas and attitudes and thus provides the opportunity for human creativity to shape a hopeful legacy for the next generation.

DANDELION WINE

From the mid-1950's to the mid-1960's, Bradbury's writings tended to center on his midwestern childhood, without being camouflaged by a science-fiction or fantasy setting. His novel *Dandelion Wine* is a nostalgic account of a small Illinois town in the summer of 1928. Again, as in so much of his earlier work, his novel was composed of previously published stories, and the superficial unity he imposed on this material was not sufficiently coherent to satisfy several critics. Another similarity to his previous work was his theme of the twin attractions of the past and the future. The twelve-year-old hero finds himself between the secure, uncomplicated world of childhood and the frightening, complex world of adulthood. Despite the loneliness, disease, and death that seem to plague adults, the young man, like the colonists in *The Martian Chronicles*, must transform his past to create his future. Critics accused Bradbury of sentimentality in *Dandelion Wine*, pointing out how depressed and ugly Waukegan, Illinois (the model for Green Town), was at this time. Bradbury answered that he was telling his story from the viewpoint of the child, and factories, trains, pollution, and poverty are not ugly to children. Adults teach children what is ugly, and their judgments about ugliness are not always sound. For a child, as for Bradbury, Green Town was like William Butler Yeats's Byzantium, a vision of creativity and a dream for action.

SOMETHING WICKED THIS WAY COMES

Bradbury returned to some of these themes in another novel, *Something Wicked This Way Comes*, in which a father tries to save his son and his son's friend from the evil embodied in a mysterious traveling carnival. The friend, Jim Nightshade (a name indicative of the symbolic burden the characters in this novel must bear), is particularly susceptible to the carnival's temptations, since his shadow side is so powerful. The father ultimately achieves victory by using the power of laughter as his weapon; however,

the father also points out that human victories are never final and that each individual must constantly struggle never to permit the good that is in him or her to become a passive rather than an activating force. The potential for evil exists in every human being (a Christian idea, original sin, that surfaces in many of Bradbury's stories), and unless humans keep their goodness fit through creativity, evil will take over. For Bradbury, love is the best humanizing force that human beings possess.

Something Wicked This Way Comes marked a turning point in Bradbury's career. After this work failed to enhance his status as a significant American novelist, he turned increasingly to plays, poems, and essays. His turn to drama was essentially a return, since he had acted, as a boy, on the stage and on radio, and since he had written several plays when he was young (they were so bad that he vowed never to write plays again until he learned to write competently in other forms). Many of his plays are adaptations of his stories, and most of them have been staged in California, though a few have had productions Off-Broadway in New York. The majority of his plays have been published. His first collection, *The Anthem Sprinters and Other Antics*, appeared in 1963 (the "anthem sprinters" are Irishmen who flee from motion-picture theaters before the national anthem is played). Although his short-story writing diminished during the 1960's, it did not vanish, and in 1969 he published another collection, *I Sing the Body Electric!*, which was a miscellany of science-fiction and fantasy stories. Throughout his life, Bradbury has also been an avid reader of poetry. He often made use of poetic diction in his stories, but, as in the case of his playwriting, he refrained from publishing his poetry until late in his career, because he wanted it to be accomplished and stylistically refined. Heavily indebted to Gerard Manley Hopkins, Dylan Thomas, Walt Whitman, and others, his poetry has not had the success of his stories. Much of the poetry, whimsical in tone, can be categorized as light verse.

DEATH IS A LONELY BUSINESS

During the 1980's and 1990's, Bradbury's audacious approach to literary composition continued with his finding new twists on such old forms as short and long fiction, poetry, and plays, but he also found himself in such new roles as librettist for a musical and an opera. Though his poetry was collected as *The Complete Poems of Ray Bradbury* in 1982, this did not prevent him from publishing new volumes of poetry in the late 1980's and into the 1990's. In 1985 he published his first novel in twenty-three years, *Death Is a Lonely Business*, which also marked his entry into a new genre, the detective story, though its offbeat characters and elements of fantasy give it a distinctly Bradburian slant. Some reviewers considered the clash between the hard-boiled and the fantastic disconcerting and frustrating, but others found his re-creation of a bygone era in Southern California history appealing.

A GRAVEYARD FOR LUNATICS

His next novel, *A Graveyard for Lunatics: Another Tale of Two Cities*, used the same unnamed narrator and several other characters as *Death Is a Lonely Business*. The two cities of the subtitle are Venice and Hollywood, and the narrator, who is a young writer of stories for fantasy and detective magazines, has many adventures in the "graveyard" of Maximus Films, "the most successful studio in history," which also serves as a burial ground for the fantastic schemes of several eccentrics the narrator meets.

GREEN SHADOWS, WHITE WHALE

Green Shadows, White Whale represented Bradbury's fictionalization of the experiences he had more than forty years before, when he traveled to Ireland to write the screenplay for *Moby Dick* for director John Huston. He recounts entertaining incidents with a customs inspector, a priest, and the habitual denizens of an Irish pub, but Bradbury's exaggerated and barbed depiction of director Huston is what actually holds the book together.

Robert J. Paradowski

OTHER MAJOR WORKS

SHORT FICTION: *Dark Carnival*, 1947; *The Golden Apples of the Sun*, 1953; *The October Country*, 1955; *A Medicine for Melancholy*, 1959; *The Machineries of Joy*, 1964; *I Sing the Body Electric!*, 1969; *Long After Midnight*, 1976; *The Stories of Ray Bradbury*,

1980; *The Toynbee Convector*, 1988; *Quicker than the Eye*, 1996; *Driving Blind*, 1997.

PLAYS: *The Anthem Sprinters and Other Antics*, pb. 1963; *The World of Ray Bradbury: Three Fables of the Future*, pr. 1964; *The Day It Rained Forever*, pb. 1966; *The Pedestrian*, pb. 1966; *Dandelion Wine*, pr. 1967; *The Wonderful Ice Cream Suit and Other Plays*, pb. 1972; *Pillar of Fire and Other Plays for Today, Tomorrow, and Beyond Tomorrow*, pb. 1975; *That Ghost, That Bride of Time: Excerpts from a Play-in-Progress*, pb. 1976; *The Martian Chronicles*, pr. 1977; *Fahrenheit 451*, pr. 1979 (musical); *On Stage: A Chrestomathy of His Plays*, pb. 1991.

SCREENPLAYS: *It Came from Outer Space*, 1952 (with David Schwartz); *Moby Dick*, 1956 (with John Huston); *Icarus Montgolfier Wright*, 1961 (with George C. Johnson); *The Picasso Summer*, 1969 (with Ed Weinberger).

POETRY: *Old Ahab's Friend, and Friend to Noah, Speaks His Piece: A Celebration*, 1971; *When Elephants Last in the Dooryard Bloomed: Celebrations for Almost Any Day in the Year*, 1973; *Where Robot Mice and Robot Men Run Round in Robot Towns: New Poems, Both Light and Dark*, 1977; *Twin Hieroglyphs That Swim the River Dust*, 1978; *The Bike Repairman*, 1978; *The Haunted Computer and the Android Pope*, 1981; *The Complete Poems of Ray Bradbury*, 1982; *Death Has Lost Its Charm for Me*, 1987; *With Cat for Comforter*, 1997 (with Louise Max); *Dogs Think That Every Day Is Christmas*, 1997.

NONFICTION: *Zen in the Art of Writing: Essays on Creativity*, 1989; *Yestermorrow: Obvious Answers to Impossible Futures*, 1991.

CHILDREN'S LITERATURE: *Switch on the Night*, 1955; *R Is for Rocket*, 1962; *S Is for Space*, 1966; *The Halloween Tree*, 1972; *Fever Dream*, 1987; *Ahmed and the Oblivion Machines: A Fable*, 1998.

EDITED TEXTS: *Timeless Stories for Today and Tomorrow*, 1952; *The Circus of Dr. Lao and Other Improbable Stories*, 1956.

BIBLIOGRAPHY

Amis, Kingsley. *New Maps of Hell: A Survey of Science Fiction*. New York: Harcourt, Brace, 1960.

Known primarily as a novelist, Amis, a British writer, here tackled a genre that had been ignored by serious literary critics. Although the early history of science fiction was as much British as American, Amis discusses science fiction as a characteristically American product, and he praises Bradbury as one of America's most skilled writers, broader in range than any of his colleagues, a writer who has the courage to see life through his strongly held convictions.

Greenberg, Martin Henry, and Joseph D. Olander, eds. *Ray Bradbury.* New York: Taplinger, 1980. Part of the Writers of the Twenty-first Century series, this is an anthology of Bradbury criticism. Some of the articles defend Bradbury against the charge that he is not really a science-fiction writer but an opponent of science and technology; other articles defend him against the charge that he is a sentimentalist. Also includes an extensive Bradbury bibliography compiled by Marshall B. Tymn and an index.

Johnson, Wayne L. *Ray Bradbury.* New York: Frederick Ungar, 1980. After a brief chapter on Bradbury the writer, Johnson's work is organized thematically by such subjects as space travel, robots, and monsters. Sympathetic but not uncritical (Johnson believes that Bradbury's themes do not exhibit a development in emotional depth or rational complexity). With a short annotated bibliography.

McNelly, Willis E. "Ray Bradbury: Past, Present, and Future." In *Voices for the Future: Essays on Major Science Fiction Writers*, edited by Thomas D. Clareson. Vol. 1. Bowling Green, Ohio: Bowling Green University Popular Press, 1976. McNelly's article argues that Bradbury's themes place him in the mainstream of American life and letters. It should be read in conjunction with the article by A. James Stupple, "The Past, the Future, and Ray Bradbury," which sees Bradbury's work as sensitive to the complexities of the past, which can be simultaneously creative and destructive.

Mogen, David. *Ray Bradbury.* Boston: Twayne, 1986. This scholarly survey of Bradbury's career

analyzes the literary influences that formed his style and themes as well as the influences that shaped his reputation. Many references in the notes at the end of the book. Includes a bibliography and an index.

Nolan, William F., and Martin H. Greenberg, eds. *The Bradbury Chronicles: Stories in Honor of Ray Bradbury.* New York: NAL-Dutton, 1991. This anthology, published to commemorate the fiftieth anniversary of Bradbury's first published work, contains twenty-one stories by a distinguished group of science-fiction authors (along with a previously unpublished story by Bradbury). Though not a traditional book of scholarly articles, the stories do shed light on Bradbury's pervasive themes.

Slusser, George Edgar. *The Bradbury Chronicles.* San Bernardino, Calif.: Borgo Press, 1977. This booklet is part of a series, Popular Writers of Today. Intended for young students and general audiences, this brief work can treat only cursorily some of Bradbury's most important writings. Contains a bibliography.

Touponce, William F. *Naming the Unnameable: Ray Bradbury and the Fantastic After Freud.* Mercer Island, Wash.: Starmont House, 1997. Building on his earlier work (below) concerning Bradbury's creative fantasy and use of dream states (imaged reveries), Touponce finds the psychoanalytic ideas of Sigmund Freud and Carl Jung helpful in plumbing the effectiveness of much of Bradbury's work (though in a letter to the author, Bradbury himself denies any direct influence, since he has "read little Freud or Jung"). Nevertheless, Touponce believes that Bradbury has given us stories of a modern consciousness that often forgets its debt to the unconscious.

_____. *Ray Bradbury and the Poetics of Reverie: Fantasy, Science Fiction, and the Reader.* Ann Arbor: University of Michigan Research Press, 1984. This study, rooted in ideas developed by the French phenomenologist Gaston Bachelard, uses reverie (how the unconscious helps create new visions of the world) to make sense of Bradbury's fantasy and science-fiction literature.

Marion Zimmer Bradley

Born: Albany, New York; June 3, 1930
Died: Berkeley, California, September 25, 1999

Principal long fiction

The Door Through Space, 1961
The Planet Savers. The Sword of Aldones, 1962
The Bloody Sun, 1964
Star of Danger, 1965
The Winds of Darkover, 1970
The World Wreckers, 1971
Darkover Landfall, 1972
Hunters of the Red Moon, 1973 (with Paul Edwin Zimmer)
The Spell Sword, 1974
The Heritage of Hastur, 1975
The Shattered Chain, 1976
The Forbidden Tower, 1977
Two to Conquer, 1980
The House Between the Worlds, 1980
Sharra's Exile, 1981
Web of Light, 1983
The Mists of Avalon, 1983
Thendara House, 1983
The Firebrand, 1987
Renunciates of Darkover, 1991
Rediscovery: A Novel of Darkover, 1993
Towers of Darkover, 1993
The Forest House, 1993
Witchlight, 1996
Glenraven, 1996 (with Holly Lisle)
The Lady of Avalon, 1997

Other literary forms

Marion Zimmer Bradley wrote short fiction, though she is mostly known as a novelist. She published several collections of short stories and a few essays. Besides writing, Bradley made a name for herself as an editor. She founded *Marion Zimmer Bradley's Fantasy Magazine* in 1988. She also edited numerous anthologies, notably the Darkover anthologies and the Sword and Sorceress series.

Achievements

Bradley was one of the most prolific female science-fiction authors, with more than sixty novels to her name and others written under pseudonyms. Though she was nominated for both the Hugo and Nebula Awards, she never won either of science fiction's highest honors. However, her novels contributed to the growth of science fiction in numerous ways. Bradley pushed the boundaries of sexual taboos, especially on homosexuality, with her sympathetic homosexual characters. It could also be argued that she, like fellow fantasy writer Andre Norton, served as a role model for many women who wanted to write science fiction and fantasy. As an editor, Bradley published many authors' debut stories and helped other women writers become established in what had been traditionally a male-oriented field. She will always be known for creating one of the most enduring worlds and series in science fiction.

Biography

Marion Zimmer was born in Albany, New York, in 1930. As a teen, she was a science-fiction and fantasy fan. She made her first amateur sale to a fiction contest in *Fantastic/Amazing Stories* in 1949. That same year, she married Robert Alden Bradley. Her oldest son, David, was born in 1950. Bradley wrote during these early years, but only for fanzines and school magazines. Her first professional sale came in 1953 when she sold a short story to *Vortex Science Fiction*.

Bradley's first novel was published in 1961. In 1962, she published two novels together, including the first novel set on the planet Darkover. The Darkover novels eventually became her best-known works. She published several more novels in the 1960's, while going to college. Some of her work at this time was done under various pseudonyms, since she was earning her living by writing. She graduated from Hardin-Simmons University in Texas in 1964 with a B.A. From 1966 to 1967, she did graduate work at the University of California, Berkeley. During this time she and Robert Bradley divorced. Bradley then married Walter Breen. She had two children with Breen, Patrick and Moira.

During the 1970's, Bradley published an average of two books per year, usually a Darkover novel and another novel. The Darkover series generated fan groups specifically dedicated to that series. Also in the 1970's, Bradley became a pastoral counselor in California and began to study religion and counseling. Her writing career continued to flourish in the 1980's. In 1983, she published *The Mists of Avalon*, a best-seller. In 1980, she became an ordained priest of the Pre-Nicene Catholic Church and established the Centre for Nontraditional Religion. Religious themes also are demonstrated in her novels.

In the late 1980's, Bradley began editing her own magazine and the anthologies. She helped nurture up-and-coming writers, particularly female authors. In her magazine and the Sword and Sorceress anthologies, she made an effort to publish first-time authors. In 1990, Bradley divorced Breen. Her writing career continued, even with health problems. She was still editing her magazine and the anthologies until shortly before her death in 1999.

ANALYSIS

Bradley's early years fit the conventional mold of the science-fiction and fantasy genres in which she was publishing. However, as she matured as a writer, she explored nonconventional themes, particularly in the areas of religion and sexuality. She also moved away from hard science fiction into more traditional fantasy. Many of her characters possess psychic abilities or some sort of power that sets them apart from others. Most of the critical work on Bradley has been done on her as a woman writer and a writer of women characters and issues. She created memorable female characters, such as Morgaine from *The Mists of Avalon*, and female sisterhoods, such as the Free Amazons of Darkover. Though Bradley did not call herself a feminist, she was both criticized and applauded by those who have.

DARKOVER LANDFALL

Darkover Landfall is not the first book published about Darkover; however, it is the first book in chronological order of that series. *Darkover Landfall* details the origin of humans on the planet Darkover. A colonization ship, heading for another planet, crashes on the inhospitable planet. While trying to repair their ship, the crew and colonists are exposed to the Ghost Wind, a natural occurrence that spreads a psychoactive pollen over the crash party. The pollen activates latent psychic abilities, but, even more distressingly, it lowers sexual inhibitions. Various sexual unions occur among the survivors. Eventually, they realize that they will have to make their home on the world.

The plot is a fairly conventional one for a science-fiction novel. This book shows Bradley's interest in and use of psychic abilities in her novels. On a nonconventional level, the book, without giving details, explores alternate sexualities and alternate standards of marriage and partnerships. To ensure a broad gene pool, everyone must have children with different partners. What caused the biggest controversy for the novel, though, was the fact that Camilla Del Rey, the first officer, is forbidden to have an abortion when she wishes one. If it had not been for the crash, there would have been no problem with her choice, but since the colony knows fertility and infant survival rates will be low for the first several years, she is forced to have the child. This position, though defended in the world of the book, sparked controversy and ire among fans, feminists, and other writers. It was not until later books that Bradley changed their minds.

THE SHATTERED CHAIN

The Shattered Chain is another Darkover novel, but it differs from earlier works because it focuses on the Free Amazons, or Renunciates, of Darkover. Centuries after the crash of the starship, Darkover has become a planet with a harsh caste system and a mostly feudal political and economic system. Women have few or no rights in most of this society. The exception is the Free Amazons. The Free Amazons have renounced their allegiance and reliance on their former families and men. They renounce marriage. They swear an oath that they will give themselves to men and will have children only when they want to. They are often ridiculed by Darkoveran society. This novel in many ways answers the criticisms leveled at Bradley after the publication of *Darkover Landfall*. In this novel, the women are the protagonists and the capable characters.

The story is told in three sections, with twelve years separating part 1 from part 2. Parts 1 and 2 focus on rescues. In the first part, Rohanna Ardais, a telepathic noblewoman, hires the Free Amazons to rescue her abducted kinswoman because the men in her family have given up on her. Melora, Rohanna's cousin, is trapped in a Dry Town. In the Dry Towns, all women are chained, wearing the outward sign that they belong to the men. The Free Amazons rescue Melora and her daughter Jaelle so that Jaelle will not be chained. In part 2, Magda Lorne, a Terran sociologist, impersonates a Free Amazon to ransom her male friend, Peter Haldane, from a thief. She meets the grown Jaelle and her band and is forced to pledge the oath of the Amazons. She then realizes that she believes the oath. Part 3 focuses on the ramifications of Magda and Jaelle's oath.

While the first two parts carry most of the action for the story, it is the last section that reveals Bradley's themes. Throughout the section, the three female protagonists confront the choices they have made and the prices they have paid or will pay. Rohanna renounced her freedom of choice for security in marriage. Jaelle gained her freedom but renounced the ability to ever marry. Magda has to renounce her Terran allegiance to live as a Free Amazon. Bradley's point is that what is important is the choice—women should always have a choice in what they do. Rohanna did not have that choice and learns to live with it. Jaelle did have that choice but realizes it requires a price. She eventually chooses to live as a freemate with Peter Haldane. That she wants to give herself to a man is her choice as well.

There is a brief mention of the theme of fate in this novel, a theme Bradley explores in greater depth in later works. It seems to be pure chance that Magda meets Jaelle on her way to free Haldane. However, Lady Rohanna does not think it mere coincidence that Haldane looks exactly like Rohanna's son or that Magda meets Jaelle, the one person who could uncover her masquerade as a Free Amazon. Bradley suggests that there is a higher power at work. While feminists hated *Darkover Landfall*, many hailed *The Shattered Chain* as a feminist novel. Reviewer Joanna Russ, critical of the earlier work, later included *The Shattered Chain* in a listing of feminist utopias. The exploration of woman's choice continued in later Bradley works.

THE MISTS OF AVALON

While she will be known forever among the science-fiction community for creating Darkover, Bradley is known to a wider literary audience for *The Mists of Avalon*. It could be considered her magnum opus. An impressive length, it stayed on *The New York Times* best-seller list for months when it was published in 1983. It was her first and most successful crossover mainstream novel.

The themes Bradley explored in *The Shattered Chain* reappear in *The Mists of Avalon*. This is the story of the women of the Arthurian legend and their struggles with fate, religion, and the social strictures of that time. It deals with the matters of choice, or lack thereof. Though principally the story of Morgaine and Gwenhwyfar, attention is also given to Ingraine, the mother of Morgaine and Arthur; Viviane, the Lady of the Lake; Morguase, Morgaine's aunt and the mother of Gawaine; and Nimue, daughter of Lancelot and the nemesis of the Merlin, Kevin Harper. Through these women, Bradley reimagines the Arthurian legends into a woman's history and story.

Bradley reimagines the thematic conflict of the legend. In the book, the old ways of the Goddess religion are dying out to the encroachments of Christianity. The Lady of the Lake is the high priestess of the Goddess faith, with Avalon as her seat of power. The Merlin is the chosen messenger of the gods. Viviane, the Lady of the Lake, and Taliesin, the Merlin, plan to put Uther on the throne of Britain so that he can protect the people from both the Saxons and the Christians. They further arrange that Uther's son Arthur should be king of both Britain and Avalon. Their plans go awry when Gwenhwyfar turns out to be overly pious and converts Arthur into a Christian king.

Morgaine is raised on Avalon as priestess of the Goddess and vows to do Her will. However, when Viviane arranges for Arthur and Morgaine to participate in the ancient rites and have sexual intercourse, Morgaine feels betrayed and leaves Avalon. She joins

Arthur's court, though she never gives up her ways. She continually tries to make Arthur be true to his oath to Avalon. In Bradley's version of the legend, this is the source of the conflict between Arthur and Morgaine—the struggle of one religion over another. Mordred, the son of Arthur and Morgaine, is also incorporated into this struggle, as he has been raised in Avalon and sees himself as the one to return Britain to its old ways. To do so, he must remove his father. Morgaine never hates Arthur in this version; in fact, the siblings love each other. Morgaine has always been Arthur's first love.

The conflict between the religions spurs social conflict as well. Under the old ways, women had the choice of whom they would mate with or love. The priests bring patriarchy and the concept of adultery. Bradley makes it clear that few of these women have choices. Ingraine, at the age of fifteen, is given in marriage to the old Duke of Cornwall. Morgaine is given to Arthur in the rites. Gwenhwyfar is given to Arthur as part of a deal for horses. Arthur later arranges a marriage for Morgaine with the aged Uriens, king of North Wales. The women do what is expected of them, however much they internally question those rules. Besides having no social choices, Bradley suggests that the women have no choices at all. Viviane and Morgaine both have the Sight, a gift from the Goddess that gives them knowledge of the future. The implication is that everyone has a destiny to be carried out, and there is little that can be done to change that destiny.

The success of this novel may be attributed to many things. First, the Arthurian legend holds a certain mystique of its own, and Bradley captures that sense of awe in her own way. Second, Bradley manages to portray the conflict that many women feel with traditional Judeo-Christian religions. Bradley, through Gwenhwyfar, often mentions how priests teach that sin came into the world through a woman, and therefore all women are evil. Morgaine's character dismisses that notion with contempt, and even Gwenhwyfar seems to finally reject it, entering the embrace of the Goddess in the aspect of the Virgin Mary.

P. Andrew Miller

OTHER MAJOR WORKS

SHORT FICTION: *The Dark Intruder and Other Stories*, 1964; "A Sword of Chaos" and "The Lesson of the Inn," in *The Sword of Chaos*, 1981 (Bradley, editor); *The Best of Marion Zimmer Bradley*, 1985; *Sword and Sorceress: An Anthology of Heroic Fantasy*, 1985- (series; fifteen volumes as of 1998); *Lythande*, 1986.

NONFICTION: "Responsibilities and Temptations of Women Science Fiction Writers," in *Women Worldwalkers: New Dimensions of Science Fiction and Fantasy*, 1985 (Jane B. Weedman, editor).

EDITED WORK: *Snows of Darkover*, 1994.

CHILDREN'S LITERATURE: *The Brass Dragon*, 1970.

BIBLIOGRAPHY

Arbur, Rosemarie. *Marion Zimmer Bradley*. Mercer Island, Wash.: Starmont House, 1985. A great overall look at Bradley's work. Gives biographical and chronological overview of Bradley's writing as well as analysis of her books by type, such as Darkover, non-Darkover science fiction, and fantasy.

Hornum, Barbara. "Wife/Mother, Sorceress/Keeper, Amazon Renunciate: Status Ambivalence and Conflicting Roles." In *Women Worldwalkers: New Dimensions of Science Fiction and Fantasy*, edited by Jane B. Weedman. Lubbock: Texas Tech Press, 1985. Uses an anthropological approach to look at the women of Darkover and the Darkoveran society. Hornum argues that Bradley is exploring American social attitudes of a woman's place.

Russ, Joanna. "Recent Feminist Utopias." In *Future Females: A Critical Anthology*, edited by Marleen S. Barr. Bowling Green, Ohio: Bowling Green State University Popular Press, 1981. Critical article that draws comparisons among many feminist utopias, including *The Shattered Chain*.

Schwartz, Susan M. "Marion Zimmer Bradley's Ethic of Freedom." In *The Feminine Eye*, edited by Tom Staicar. New York: Frederick Ungar, 1982. Critical chapter on women in the Darkover novels, particularly *The Shattered Chain*. Schwartz examines Bradley's themes of choice and the price of choice.

Tober, Lee Ann. "Why Change the Arthur Story? Marion Zimmer Bradley's *The Mists of Avalon*."

Extrapolation 34, no. 2 (Summer, 1993): 147-157. Academic article that argues the feminist significance of Bradley's novel as an inversion of the male-centered Arthur legend.

RICHARD BRAUTIGAN

Born: Tacoma, Washington; January 30, 1935
Died: Bolinas, California; September, 1984

PRINCIPAL LONG FICTION

A Confederate General from Big Sur, 1964
Trout Fishing in America, 1967
In Watermelon Sugar, 1968
The Abortion: An Historical Romance, 1971
The Hawkline Monster: A Gothic Western, 1974
Willard and His Bowling Trophies: A Perverse Mystery, 1975
Sombrero Fallout: A Japanese Novel, 1976
Dreaming of Babylon: A Private Eye Novel 1942, 1977
The Tokyo-Montana Express, 1980
So the Wind Won't Blow It All Away, 1982

OTHER LITERARY FORMS

Richard Brautigan began his literary career as a poet. "I wrote poetry for seven years," he noted, "to learn how to write a sentence." Though a poet for many years, Brautigan maintained that his ambition was to write novels: "I figured I couldn't write a novel until I could write a sentence." Although most of Brautigan's later work was in novel form, he continued to publish poetry and also produced a collection of short stories (*Revenge of the Lawn: Stories 1962-1970*, 1971).

ACHIEVEMENTS

Short-story writer, novelist, and poet, Brautigan created a stream of works which resist simple categories—in fact, defy categorization altogether. Much of his popularity can be attributed to his peculiar style, his unconventional plots, simple language, and mar-

velous humor, which together provide a melancholy vision of American life and the elusive American Dream.

Much of Brautigan's work involves the search for simplicity—an expansion of the Emersonian search for pastoral America. Yet, the complacent rural life is no longer available in Brautigan's world: All the trout streams have been sold to the highest bidder, all the campgrounds are already filled, in fact overflowing; yet, the search must go on for new places where the imagination can still roam free—to a pastoral America where the individual can escape the suffocating din of technocracy.

Brautigan's work evolved into a new, unorthodox version of the American novel. His experimentation with language, structure, characterization, plot, and motif broke new ground. Because of this, many critics have been unable to characterize his work with ease. Unable to pinpoint his exact standing, they have dismissed him as a counterculture phenomenon, a faddish nonentity. Although Brautigan's oeuvre is indeed very uneven, his best work is genuinely original and ensures him a lasting place in American literature.

BIOGRAPHY

Richard Brautigan was born and reared in the Pacific Northwest. The son of Bernard F. Brautigan and Lula Mary Keho Brautigan, he spent his early years in Washington and Oregon. His literary career took hold when, in 1958, he moved to San Francisco and began writing poetry in the company of Lawrence Ferlinghetti, Robert Duncan, Philip Whalen, and Michael McClure. The company he kept led to his initial identification as a Beat poet, but Brautigan's unique and now well-known style defied the classification.

Resisting crass commercialism and the profits linked with corporate America, Brautigan's first books were published primarily for the benefit of his friends and acquaintances. Success finally forced him to allow a New York publication of his work in the 1960's, however, and Grove Press published his *A Confederate General from Big Sur*. Shortly after his change of allegiance from Four Seasons Foundation in San Francisco to Grove Press in New York, Brautigan was invited to become poet-in-residence at Pasadena's California Institute of Technology. Although he had never attended college, he accepted the invitation and spent the 1967 academic year at the prestigious school.

In 1957, Brautigan married Virginia Diorine Adler. They had one daughter, Ianthe, and later were divorced. In his later years, Brautigan divided his time among three places: Tokyo, San Francisco, and, when in retreat or fishing, a small town in Montana. He died in 1984, an apparent suicide.

ANALYSIS

Richard Brautigan's novels are generally characterized by the appearance of a first-person narrator (sometimes identified in the third person as Brautigan himself) who presents an autobiographical, oftentimes whimsical story. Brautigan's work employs simple, direct, short, and usually repetitive sentences. In his best work, he has an uncanny ability to create vibrant and compelling scenes from apparently banal subject matter. It is the voice of the "I," however, that carries the Brautigan novel, a voice that often unifies virtually plotless and quite heterogeneous materials.

A CONFEDERATE GENERAL FROM BIG SUR

Brautigan's first published novel, *A Confederate General from Big Sur*, is perhaps his funniest. A burlesque of American society long after the Civil War, the story is told by Jesse, a gentle, shy, withdrawn narrator (not unlike Brautigan himself) who meets Lee Mellon, a rebel, dropout, and activist living in San Francisco. Lee soon moves to Oakland, California, where he lives, rent-free, at the home of a committed mental patient. The story then moves to Big Sur, where Lee and Jesse live in a cabin, again owned by a mental patient. As Jesse and Lee figure out how to cope with life and no money, they find a fortune of six dollars and some loose change, get rip-roaring drunk in Monterey, and discover Elaine and a great deal of money. Johnston Wade, a crazed insurance man, arrives on the scene, informing everyone that he is fleeing from his wife and daughter (they want to commit him to a mental institution). He leaves as abruptly as he arrived, remembering an important business appointment he must keep. The book ends, as it must, without ending.

In *A Confederate General from Big Sur*, Brautigan is facing the question of how to cope with civilization. The flight from technology toward wilderness holds risks of its own. Brautigan offers no answers. Human life is not unlike that of the bugs sitting on the log Jesse has thrown into the fire. They sit there on the log, staring out at Jesse as the flames leap around them.

The theme of the novel is the ambition to control one's life and destiny. The ownership of the Big Sur log cabin by a mental patient and Johnston Wade's own mental aberrations only serve to illustrate the fleeting control all people have over their lives. Brautigan introduces Wade to burlesque the myth of American destiny. He is a parody, a ridiculous image of American business and technocracy: the self-made man running away from his wife and child who suddenly remembers an important business engagement.

IN WATERMELON SUGAR

Although not published until 1968, *In Watermelon Sugar* was written in 1964, during Brautigan's evolution from poet to novelist. The book reflects this evolutionary change, for in many ways it is more poetic than novelistic in its form. The story is that of

(Library of Congress)

a young man who lives in a small community after an unspecified cataclysm. In the first of the three parts of the book, the shy and gentle narrator tells the reader about himself and his friends. Their peaceful life was not always so, he explains, and he tells about iDEATH, a central gathering place which is more a state of mind than an actual physical location. In the second part of the novel, the narrator has a terrible dream of carnage and self-mutilation. The third part of the book begins with the narrator's awakening, strangely refreshed after the terrible dream. The gentle, leisurely pace of the first part then restores itself.

In Watermelon Sugar is like Aldous Huxley's *Brave New World* (1932): a utopian novel of the Garden of Eden, springing forth out of the chaos of today's world. It is his vision of the rustic good life in postindustrial society. From watermelons comes the juice that is made into sugar, the stuff of the lives and dreams of the people of iDEATH. By controlling their own lives, by creating their own order, the people of iDEATH recover society from chaos. The sense of order and recurrence is set in the very first line of the book, which both begins and ends "in watermelon sugar." That phrase is also used as the title of the first part of the book, as well as the title of the first chapter. Like a refrain, it sets a pattern and order in a world in which people live in harmony with nature and with their own lives.

THE ABORTION

Like several of Brautigan's books, *The Abortion: An Historical Romance* spent some time in the library of unpublished books that it describes, where dreams go (and can be found). The world of *The Abortion* is that of a public library in California: not an ordinary library, but one where losers bring their unpublishable books. Again Brautigan's narrator is a shy, introverted recluse—the librarian, unnamed because he is ordinary, like the people who bring their books to the library to have them shelved. Brautigan himself visits the library at one point in the novel to bring in *Moose*; he is tall and blond, with an anachronistic appearance, looking as if he would be more comfortable in another era. That circumstance is certainly the case with the narrator as well.

There is less action in *The Abortion* than in most of Brautigan's novels; the book plods along slowly, mimicking its central theme, which is that a series of short, tentative steps can lead one out of a personal and social labyrinth and toward the promise of a new life. Before the reader knows it, however, the librarian is out in the rain with a girl; she gets pregnant; and they journey to Tijuana so she can have an abortion. The girl is called Vida, and she represents life in the twentieth century. The librarian struggles with his inner self, afraid to move from the old ways, afraid to let go of his innocence. Brautigan contrasts him with his partner, Foster, a wild caveman who takes care of the books that have been moved from the library to dead storage in a cave. Foster is loud and outgoing—the opposite of the timid librarian—and he thinks of the library as an asylum.

With Vida, the librarian becomes embroiled in a quest for survival. Vida brings him out of the library into the world of change and conflict. He is frightened by it, but, step by tentative step, he confronts it.

The Abortion is a commentary on American culture. Brautigan draws a loose parallel between the library and American history: The librarian-narrator is the thirty-sixth caretaker of the library; at the time the book was written, there had been thirty-six presidents of the United States. The origins of the mysterious library go back into the American past as well, just as Brautigan himself appears as an anachronism from an earlier, easier time.

While Brautigan laments the times gone by and yearns for the "good old days" and the leisurely pace of the library, he also holds out hope for a fresh alternative. American culture has nearly been destroyed—the playboy beauty queen named Vida hates herself, and bombs and industrial technocracy threaten lives and deaden spirits. Strangely enough, by destroying life—by the abortion—one can begin anew, start a new life. The narrator and Vida share this hopefulness, which was widespread in the counterculture when *The Abortion* was published.

THE HAWKLINE MONSTER

With *The Hawkline Monster: A Gothic Western*, Brautigan began a series of novels which adapt the conventions of genre fiction in a quirky, unpredictable manner. Not strictly parodies, these hybrids sometimes achieve wonderful effects—odd, unsettling, comical—and sometimes fall flat. Combining the gothic novel, the Western, and a dash of romance, *The Hawkline Monster* is set in eastern Oregon during 1902 and centers on a magical Victorian house occupied by two equally baffling Victorian maidens with curious habits. The unreality of the situation does not affect the two unruffled Western heroes of the book, however, who methodically go about their task of killing the Hawkline Monster. The problem is not only to find the monster but also to discover what it is; the ice caves under the house complete the unreality of the situation. Brautigan moves lyrically from the mundane to the magical in this fusion of the real and the surreal.

TROUT FISHING IN AMERICA

Trout Fishing in America, Brautigan's most famous novel and his best, is a short, visionary inscape of the American nightmare. Brautigan has created a tragic symbol of what has happened to America: The trout streams are all gone, the campgrounds are full; escape to the American pastoral is no longer possible. Yet Brautigan assures his readers that all is not lost—there is still a place where they can find freedom. If all the land is being used and one cannot physically escape the city, then one must escape to the pastoral realm of one's imagination. Trout fishing, Brautigan insists, is thus a way of recapturing the simple while remaining aware of the complex.

Trout Fishing in America, like much of Brautigan's work (including his last novel, *So the Wind Won't Blow It All Away*), is autobiographical. The gentle, withdrawn narrator uses trout fishing as a central metaphor. A victim of the technological world, the narrator creates his own watery realm, complete with its own boundaries—a place where he can find solace from the technological stranglehold. His vision implies that all people have a fundamental right to the abundant richness and good life that America can provide but that are denied to many because the bankrupt ideas of the past still hold sway. Aware of the complexities of American life, Brautigan seems to be exhorting his readers to recapture the simple life, to escape the confinement of the city for the freedom of the wilderness. If that wilderness

in the actual sense is cut off and no longer accessible; if all the trout streams have been developed, disassembled, and sold; if the horizon is now not new but old and despoiled; if the parks are already overcrowded; if there is no other way, then one must escape through the imagination.

SO THE WIND WON'T BLOW IT ALL AWAY

In *So the Wind Won't Blow It All Away*, Brautigan gives readers a glimpse of what post-Trout-Fishing-in-America life has become. Billed as an "American tragedy," *So the Wind Won't Blow It All Away* focuses on the tragedy that America and American life have become: "dust . . . American . . . dust."

Written, as are most of his novels, in the first person, Brautigan's novel is the memoir of an anonymous boy reared in welfare-state poverty somewhere in the Pacific Northwest. Unloved but tolerated by his mother, the boy and his family go from town to town, meeting an odd assortment of minor characters. Although undeveloped, these characters serve to carry the novel's theme and serve as victims of the technocracy America has become. There is an old pensioner who lives in a packing-crate shack; adept at carpentry, the old man built a beautiful dock and boat and knows all the best fishing spots on the pond near his home, but he does not use his knowledge or equipment. A gas-station attendant who cares nothing about selling gas but likes to sell worms to fishermen also appears on the scene. There is a thirty-five-year-old alcoholic who traded ambition for beer; charged with the safety of the sawmill, the man dresses in finery (although readers are told that his appearances are not true-to-life), cares nothing about his job, and is continually encircled by boys who swoop like vultures to take his empty bottles back to the store for credit. Like America itself, the guard has brittle bones resembling dried-out weeds. Finally, Brautigan introduces a husband and wife who, each night, carry their living-room furniture to the pond, set it up, and fish all night.

Brautigan presents America as having come to the end of its greatness, like the end of a summer afternoon. The technological success that spurred the country to greatness has resulted in its downfall. The husband and wife have changed all their electrical lamps to kerosene and await the cool evening with its refreshing possibilities, but as they patiently fish in the wrong spot, America goes on, killing its imagination with the technology of mindless television.

So the Wind Won't Blow It All Away ends with the horrible climax of the death of a boy, shot by mistake in an orchard that has been left to die. With that end, however, is the beginning of a new life, for, though the orchard has been left alone to die, new fruit will grow. The novel recalls the message of *The Abortion*: The substitutions of the confinement of the city for the freedom of the wilderness, and of television for imagination, are choices people have. With this novel, Brautigan returned to the successful themes of his earliest novels, warning that to go on will result only in dust.

David Mike Hamilton

OTHER MAJOR WORKS

SHORT FICTION: *Revenge of the Lawn: Stories 1962-1970*, 1971.

POETRY: *The Return of the Rivers*, 1957; *The Galilee Hitch-Hiker*, 1958; *Lay the Marble Tea: Twenty-four Poems*, 1959; *The Octopus Frontier*, 1960; *All Watched over by Machines of Loving Grace*, 1967; *The Pill Versus the Springhill Mine Disaster*, 1968; *Please Plant This Book*, 1968; *Rommel Drives on Deep into Egypt*, 1970; *Loading Mercury with a Pitchfork*, 1976; *June 30th, June 30th*, 1978.

BIBLIOGRAPHY

Abbott, Keith. *Downstream from "Trout Fishing in America": A Memoir of Richard Brautigan*. Santa Barbara, Calif.: Capra Press, 1989. A personal account of Brautigan from a longtime friend. Some of the book is Abbott's own memoirs, but it also contains interesting anecdotes and insights into Brautigan's life and work. Chapter 8, "Shadows and Marble," presents critical commentary on Brautigan's novels, in particular *Trout Fishing in America*.

Bradbury, Malcolm. *The Modern American Novel*. Oxford, England: Oxford University Press, 1983. Chapter 7, "Postmoderns and Others: The 1960s and 1970s," cites Brautigan, placing him in the genre of writers who "celebrated the hippie youth spirit." Bradbury gives succinct but insightful critical commentary on Brautigan's novels. He sees Brautigan as much more than a hippie writer, whose spirit of "imaginative discovery" has spawned a number of literary successors.

Chenetier, Marc. *Richard Brautigan*. London: Methuen, 1983. Assesses Brautigan's writing in the context of the 1960's and traces the development of his art beyond the confines of a cult figure. An appreciative study that analyzes Brautigan in the light of his poetics.

Kaylor, Noel Harold, ed. *Creative and Critical Approaches to the Short Story*. Lewiston: The Edwin Mellen Press, 1997. See Farhat Iftekharuddin's essay, "The New Aesthetics in Brautigan's *Revenge of the Lawn: Stories 1962-1970*." Although this essay deals primarily with Brautigan's short stories, Iftekharuddin's discussion of literary innovation and his treatment of other Brautigan critics make this an important contribution to an understanding of the longer fiction as well.

Wanless, James, and Christine Kolodziej. "Richard Brautigan: A Working Checklist." *Critique: Studies in Modern Fiction* 16, no. 1 (1974): 41-52. A compilation of secondary material on Brautigan, complete through 1973. Lists novels (including their serial form), poetry, short stories, and uncollected pieces, as well as reviews and critical commentary on individual works. A valuable resource for the Brautigan scholar.

CHARLOTTE BRONTË

Born: Thornton, Yorkshire, England; April 21, 1816
Died: Haworth, Yorkshire, England; March 31, 1855

PRINCIPAL LONG FICTION

Jane Eyre, 1847
Shirley, 1849
Villette, 1853
The Professor, 1857

OTHER LITERARY FORMS

The nineteen poems which Charlotte Brontë selected to print with her sister Anne's work in *Poems by Currer, Ellis, and Acton Bell* (1846) were her only other works published during her lifetime. The juvenilia produced by the four Brontë children—Charlotte, Emily, Anne, and Branwell—between 1824 and 1839 are scattered in libraries and private collections. Some of Charlotte's contributions have been published in *The Twelve Adventurers and Other Stories* (1925), *Legends of Angria* (1933), *The Search After Happiness* (1969), *Five Novelettes* (1971), and *The Secret and Lily Hart* (1979). A fragment of a novel written during the last year of Brontë's life was published as *Emma* in *Cornhill Magazine* in 1860 and is often reprinted in editions of *The Professor*. *The Complete Poems of Charlotte Brontë* appeared in 1923. Other brief selections, fragments, and ephemera have been printed in *Transactions and Other Publications of the Brontë Society*. The nineteen-volume *Shakespeare Head Brontë* (1931-1938), edited by T. J. Wise and J. A. Symington, contains all of the novels, four volumes of life and letters, two volumes of miscellaneous writings, and two volumes of poems.

(Library of Congress)

ACHIEVEMENTS

Brontë brought to English fiction an intensely personal voice. Her books show the moral and emotional growth of a protagonist almost entirely by self-revelation. Her novels focus on individual self-fulfillment; they express the subjective interior world not only in thoughts, dreams, visions, and symbols but also by projecting inner states through external objects, secondary characters, places, events, and weather. Brontë's own experiences and emotions inform the narrative presence. "Perhaps no other writer of her time," wrote Margaret Oliphant in 1855, "has impressed her mark so clearly on contemporary literature, or drawn so many followers into her own peculiar path."

The personal voice, which blurs the distance between novelist, protagonist, and reader, accounts for much of the critical ambivalence toward Brontë's work. Generations of unsophisticated readers have identified with Jane Eyre; thousands of romances and modern gothics have used Brontë's situations and invited readers to step into the fantasy. Brontë's novels, however, are much more than simply the common reader's daydreams. They are rich enough to allow a variety of critical approaches. They have been studied in relation to traditions (gothic, provincial, realistic, Romantic); read for psychological, linguistic, Christian, social, economic, and personal interpretations; analyzed in terms of symbolism, imagery, metaphor, viewpoint, narrative distance, and prose style. Because the novels are so clearly wrought from the materials of their author's life, psychoanalytic and feminist criticism has proved rewarding. In Brontë's work, a woman author makes significant statements about issues central to women's lives. Most of her heroines are working women; each feels the pull of individual self-development against the wish for emotional fulfillment, the tension between sexual energies and social realities, the almost unresolvable conflict between love and independence.

BIOGRAPHY

Charlotte Brontë was the third of six children born within seven years to the Reverend Patrick Brontë and his wife Maria Branwell Brontë. Patrick Brontë was perpetual curate of Haworth, a bleak manufacturing town in Yorkshire. In 1821, when Charlotte Brontë was five years old, her mother died of cancer. Three years later, the four elder girls were sent to the Clergy Daughters' School at Cowan Bridge—the school which appears as Lowood in *Jane Eyre*. In the summer of 1825, the eldest two daughters, Maria and Elizabeth, died of tuberculosis. Charlotte and Emily were removed from the school and brought home. There were no educated middle-class families in Haworth to supply friends and companions. The Brontë children lived with a noncommunicative aunt, an elderly servant, and a father much preoccupied by his intellectual interests and his own griefs.

In their home and with only one another for company, the children had material for both educational and imaginative development. Patrick Brontë expected his children to read and to carry on adult conversations about politics. He subscribed to *Blackwood's Edinburgh Magazine*, where his children had access to political and economic essays, art criticism, and literary reviews. They had annuals with engravings of fine art; they taught themselves to draw by copying the pictures in minute detail. They were free to do reading that would not have been permitted by any school of the time—by the age of thirteen Charlotte Brontë was fully acquainted not only with John Milton and Sir Walter Scott but also with Robert Southey, William Cowper, and (most important) Lord Byron.

In 1826, Branwell was given a set of wooden soldiers which the four children used for characters in creative play. These soldiers gradually took on personal characteristics and acquired countries to rule. The countries needed cities, governments, ruling families, political intrigues, legends, and citizens with private lives, all of which the children happily invented. In 1829, when Charlotte Brontë was thirteen, she and the others began to write down materials from these fantasies, producing a collection of juvenilia that extended ultimately to hundreds of items: magazines, histories, maps, essays, tales, dramas, poems, news-

papers, wills, speeches, scrapbooks. This enormous creative production in adolescence gave concrete form to motifs that were later transformed into situations, characters, and concerns of Charlotte Brontë's mature work. It was also a workshop for literary technique; the young author explored prose style, experimented with viewpoint, and discovered how to control narrative voice. A single event, she learned, could be the basis for both a newspaper story and a romance, and the romance could be told by one of the protagonists or by a detached observer.

Because Patrick Brontë had no income beyond his salary, his daughters had to prepare to support themselves. In 1831, when she was almost fifteen, Charlotte Brontë went to Miss Wooler's School at Roe Head. After returning home for a time to tutor her sisters, she went back to Miss Wooler's as a teacher. Over the next several years, all three sisters held positions as governesses in private families. None, however, was happy as a governess; aside from the predictable difficulties caused by burdensome work and undisciplined children, they all suffered when separated from their shared emotional and creative life. A possible solution would have been to open their own school, but they needed some special qualification to attract pupils. Charlotte conceived a plan for going abroad to study languages. In 1842, she and Emily went to Brussels to the Pensionnat Héger. They returned in November because of their aunt's death, but in the following year Charlotte went back to Brussels alone to work as a pupil-teacher. An additional reason for her return to Brussels was that she desired to be near Professor Constantine Héger, but at the end of the year she left in misery after Héger's wife had realized (perhaps more clearly than did Charlotte herself) the romantic nature of the attraction.

In 1844, at the age of twenty-eight, Charlotte Brontë established herself permanently at Haworth. The prospectus for "The Misses Brontë's Establishment" was published, but no pupils applied. Branwell, dismissed in disgrace from his post as tutor, came home to drink, take opium, and disintegrate. Charlotte spent nearly two years in deep depression: Her yearning for love was unsatisfied, and she had repressed her creative impulse because she was afraid her fantasies were self-indulgent. Then, with the discovery that all three had written poetry, the sisters found a new aim in life. A joint volume of poems was published in May, 1846, though it sold only two copies. Each wrote a short novel; they offered the three together to publishers. Emily Brontë's *Wuthering Heights* (1847) and Anne Brontë's *Agnes Grey* (1847) were accepted. Charlotte Brontë's *The Professor* was refused, but one editor, George Smith, said he would like to see a three-volume novel written by its author. *Jane Eyre* was by that time almost finished; it was sent to Smith on August 24, 1847, and impressed him so much that he had it in print by the middle of October.

Jane Eyre was immediately successful, but there was barely any time for its author to enjoy her fame and accomplishment. Within a single year, her three companions in creation died: Branwell on September 24, 1848; Emily on December 19, 1848; and Anne on May 28, 1849. When Charlotte Brontë began work on *Shirley*, she met with her sisters in the evenings to exchange ideas, read aloud, and offer criticism. By the time she finished the manuscript, she was alone.

Charlotte Brontë's sense that she was plain, "undeveloped," and unlikely to be loved seems to have been partly the product of her own psychological condition. She had refused more than one proposal in her early twenties. In 1852 there was another, from Arthur Bell Nicholls, curate at Haworth. Patrick Brontë objected violently and dismissed his curate. Gradually, however, the objections were worn away. On June 29, 1854, Charlotte Brontë and the Reverend Nicholls were married and, after a brief honeymoon tour, took up residence in Haworth parsonage. After a few months of apparent content—which did not prevent her from beginning work on another novel— Charlotte Brontë died on March 31, 1855, at the age of thirty-eight; a severe cold made her too weak to survive the complications of early pregnancy.

ANALYSIS

The individualism and richness of Charlotte Brontë's work arise from the multiple ways in which her writing is personal: observation and introspec-

tion, rational analysis and spontaneous emotion, accurate mimesis and private symbolism. Tension and ambiguity grow from the intersections and conflicts among these levels of writing and, indeed, among the layers of the self.

Few writers of English prose have so successfully communicated the emotional texture of inner life while still constructing fictions with enough verisimilitude to appear realistic. Brontë startled the Victorians because her work was so little influenced by the books of her own era. Its literary forebears were the written corporate daydreams of her childhood and the romantic poets she read during the period when the fantasies took shape. Certain characters and situations which crystallized the emotional conflicts of early adolescence became necessary components of emotional satisfaction. The source of these fantasies was, to a degree, beyond control, occurring in the region the twentieth century has termed "the unconscious"; by writing them down from childhood on, Brontë learned to preserve and draw on relatively undisguised desires and ego conflicts in a way lost to most adults.

The power and reality of the inner life disturbed Brontë after she had passed through adolescence; she compared her creative urge to the action of opium and was afraid that she might become lost in her "infernal world." When she began to think of publication, she deliberately used material from her own experience and reported scenes and characters in verifiable detail. In this way, she hoped to subdue the exaggerated romanticism—and the overwrought writing—of the fantasy-fictions. "Details, situations which I do not understand and cannot personally inspect," she wrote to her publisher, "I would not for the world meddle with." Her drawing from life was so accurate that the curates and the Yorkes in *Shirley* were recognized at once by people who knew them, and Brontë lost the protection that her pseudonym had provided.

The years of practice in writing fiction that satisfied her own emotional needs gave Brontë the means to produce powerful psychological effects. She uses a variety of resources to make readers share the protagonist's subjective state. The truth of the outside world is only that truth which reflects the narrator's feelings and perceptions. All characters are aspects of the consciousness which creates them: Brontë uses splitting, doubling, and other fairy-tale devices; she replicates key situations; she carefully controls the narrative distance and the amount of information readers have at their disposal.

The unquietness which Brontë's readers often feel grows from the tension between direct emotional satisfactions (often apparently immature) on one hand and, on the other, mature and realistic conflicts in motive, reason, and sense of self. Read as a sequence, the four completed novels demonstrate both Brontë's development and the story of a woman's relationship to the world. Brontë's heroines find identity outside the enclosed family popularly supposed to circumscribe nineteenth century women. Isolation allows the heroines' self-development, but it impedes their romantic yearning to be lost in love.

THE PROFESSOR

At the beginning of *The Professor*, William Crimsworth is working as a clerk in a mill owned by his proud elder brother. He breaks away, goes to Brussels to teach English, survives a brief attraction to a seductive older woman, and then comes to love Frances Henri, an orphaned Anglo-Swiss lace-mender who had been his pupil.

Brontë's narrative devices supply shifting masks that both expose and evade the self. The epistolary opening keeps readers from identifying directly with Crimsworth but draws them into the novel as recipients of his revelations. The masculine persona, which Brontë used frequently in the juvenilia, gives her access to the literary mainstream and creates possibilities for action, attitude, and initiative that did not exist in models for female stories. The juvenile fantasies supply the feud between two brothers; the Belgian scenes and characters come from Brontë's own experiences. Although nominally male, Crimsworth is in an essentially female situation: disinherited, passive, timid. He has, furthermore, an exaggerated awareness and fear of the sexual overtones in human behavior.

Biographical details also go into the making of Frances Henri, the friendless older student working to pay for her lessons in the Belgian school. The poem that Frances writes is one Brontë had created out of her own yearning for Professor Héger. In *The Professor*, the dream can come true; the poem awakens the teacher's response.

Like the central figures in all Brontë novels, both Crimsworth and Frances enact a Cinderella plot. Each begins as an oppressed outcast and ends successful, confident, and satisfactorily placed in society. The details of Crimsworth's story work both symbolically and functionally. The imprisoning situations in the factory and the school reflect his perception of the world. At the same time, these situations are created by his own inner barriers. His bondage as a despised clerk is self-induced; he is an educated adult male who could move on at any time. In Belgium, he plods a treadmill of guilt because of Zoraïde Reuter's sexual manipulativeness—for which he is not responsible. His self-suppression is also seen through Yorke Hunsden, who appears whenever Crimsworth must express strong emotion. Hunsden voices anger and rebellion not permitted to the male/female narrator and becomes a voyeuristic alter ego to appreciate Frances and love.

The novel is weakest when it fails to integrate the biography, the emotion, and the ideas. True moral dilemmas are not developed. The heroine, seen through sympathetic male eyes, wins love for her writing, her pride, and her self-possession, and she continues to work even after she has a child. Brontë solves her chronic romantic dilemma (how can a strong woman love if woman's love is defined as willing subordination?) by letting Frances vibrate between two roles: She is the stately directress of the school by day, the little lace-mender by night.

JANE EYRE

In *Jane Eyre*, Brontë created a story that has the authority of myth. Everything which had deeply affected her was present in the book's emotional content. The traumatic experiences of maternal deprivation, the Clergy Daughters' School, and Maria's death create the events of Jane's early life. The book also taps universal feelings of rejection, victimization, and loneliness, making them permissible by displacement: The hateful children are cousins, not siblings; the bad adult an aunt, not a mother. Rochester's compelling power as a lover derives from neither literal nor literary sources—Rochester is the man Brontë had loved for twenty years, the duke of Zamorna who dominates the adolescent fantasies, exerting a power on both Jane and the reader that can hardly be explained by reason. Jane defied literary convention because she was poor, plain, and a heroine; she defied social convention by refusing to accept any external authority. Placed repeatedly in situations that exemplify male power, Jane resists and survives. At the end of the narrative, she is transformed from Cinderella to Prince Charming, becoming the heroine who cuts through the brambles to rescue the imprisoned sleeper. Identification is so immediate and so close that readers often fail to notice Brontë's control of distance, in particular the points of detachment when an older Jane comments on her younger self and the direct addresses from Jane to the reader that break the spell when emotions become too strong.

Place controls the book's structure. Events at Gateshead, Lowood, Thornfield, and Moor House determine Jane's development; a brief coda at Ferndean provides the resolution. Each of the four major sections contains a figure representing the sources of male power over women: John Reed (physical force and the patriarchal family), Reverend Brocklehurst (the social structures of class, education, and religion), Rochester (sexual attraction), and St. John Rivers (moral and spiritual authority). Jane protects herself at first by devious and indirect means—fainting, illness, flight—and then ultimately, in rejecting St. John Rivers, by direct confrontation. Compelled by circumstances to fend for herself, she comes—at first instinctively, later rationally—to rely on herself.

The book's emotional power grows from its total absorption in Jane's view of the world and from the images, symbols, and structures that convey multiple interwoven reverberations. The red room—which suggests violence, irrationality, enclosure, rebellion, rebirth, the bloody chamber of emerging womanhood—echoes throughout the book. The Bridewell charade, Jane's paintings, the buildings and terrain,

and a multitude of other details have both meaning and function. Characters double and split: Helen Burns (mind) and Bertha Mason (body) are aspects of Jane as well as actors in the plot. Recurring images of ice and fire suggest fatal coldness without and consuming fire within. Rochester's sexuality is the most threatening and ambiguous aspect of masculine power because of Jane's own complicity and her need for love. Her terrors and dreams accumulate as the marriage approaches; there are drowning images, abyss images, loss of consciousness. She refuses to become Rochester's mistress, finally, not because of the practical and moral dangers (which she does recognize) but because she fears her own willingness to make a god of him. She will not become dependent; she escapes to preserve her self.

As Jane takes her life into her own hands, she becomes less needy. After she has achieved independence by discovering a family and inheriting money, she is free to seek out Rochester. At the same time, he has become less omnipotent, perhaps a code for the destruction of patriarchal power. Thus, the marriage not only ends the romance and resolves the moral, emotional, and sexual conflicts but also supplies a satisfactory woman's fantasy of independence coupled with love.

SHIRLEY

For the book that would follow *Jane Eyre*, Brontë deliberately sought a new style and subject matter. *Shirley*, set in 1812, concerns two public issues still relevant in 1848—working-class riots and the condition of women. Brontë did historical research in newspaper files. She used a panoramic scene, included a variety of characters observed from life, and added touches of comedy. *Shirley* is told in the third person; the interest is divided between two heroines, neither of whom is a persona. Nevertheless, Brontë is strongly present in the narrative voice, which remains objective only in scenes of action. The authorial commentary, more strongly even than the events themselves, creates a tone of anger, rebellion, suffering, and doubt.

The novel is clearly plotted, although the mechanics are at times apparent. Brontë shifts focus among characters and uses reported conversations to violate the time sequence so that she can arrange events in the most effective dramatic order. Robert Moore, owner of a cloth mill, arouses the workers' wrath by introducing machinery. Caroline Helstone loves Robert but her affection is not reciprocated. Although Caroline has a comfortable home with her uncle the rector, she is almost fatally depressed by lack of love and occupation. Property-owner Shirley Keeldar discovers that having a man's name, position, and forthrightness gives her some power but fails to make her man's equal; she is simply more valuable as a matrimonial prize. Louis Moore, Shirley's former tutor, loves her silently because he lacks wealth and social position. Eventually Robert, humbled by Shirley's contempt and weakened by a workman's bullet, declares his love for Caroline, who has in the meantime discovered her mother and grown much stronger. Shirley's union with Louis is more ambivalent; she loves him because he is a master she can look up to, but she is seen on her wedding day as a pantheress pining for virginal freedom.

The primary source of women's tribulation is dependency. Caroline Helstone craves occupation to fill her time, make her financially independent, and give her life purpose. Women become psychologically dependent on men because they have so little else to think about. Brontë examines the lives of several old maids; they are individuals, not stereotypes, but they are all lonely. Shirley and Caroline dissect John Milton, search for female roots, and talk cozily about men's inadequacies. They cannot, however, speak honestly to each other about their romantic feelings. Caroline must hold to herself the deep pain of unrequited love.

Although *Shirley* deliberately moves beyond the isolated mythic world of *Jane Eyre* to put women's oppression in the context of a society rent by other power struggles (workers against employers, England against France, Church against Nonconformity), the individualistic ending only partially resolves the divisions. Brontë's narrative tone in the final passage is bleak and bitter. She reminds readers that *Shirley*'s events are history. Fieldhead Hollow is covered by mills and mill housing; magic is gone from the world.

VILLETTE

Villette is Brontë's most disciplined novel. Because *The Professor* had not been published, she was able to rework the Brussels experience without masks, as a story of loneliness and female deprivation, deliberately subduing the wish-fulfillment and making her uncompromising self-examination control form as well as feeling. Lucy Snowe is a woman without money, family, friends, or health. She is not, however, a sympathetic, friendly narrator like Jane Eyre. Her personality has the unattractiveness that realistically grows from deprivation; she has no social ease, no warmth, no mental quickness. Furthermore, her personality creates her pain, loneliness, and disengagement.

In the book's early sections, Lucy is not even the center of her narrative. She watches and judges instead of taking part; she tells other people's stories instead of her own. She is so self-disciplined that she appears to have neither feelings nor imagination, so restrained that she never reveals the facts about her family or the incidents of her youth that might explain to readers how and why she learned to suppress emotion, hope, and the desire for human contact. Despite—or perhaps because of—her anesthetized feeling and desperate shyness, Lucy Snowe drives herself to actions that might have been inconceivable for a woman more thoroughly socialized. Thrust into the world by the death of the elderly woman whose companion she had been, she goes alone to London, takes a ship for the Continent, gets a job as nursemaid, rises through her own efforts to teach in Madame Beck's school, and begins laying plans to open a school of her own.

The coincidental and melodramatic elements of the story gain authenticity because they grow from Lucy's inner life. When she is left alone in the school during vacation, her repressed need to be heard by someone drives her to enter the confessional of a Catholic church. Once the internal barrier is breached, she immediately meets the Bretton family. Realistically, she must have known they were in Villette; she knew that "Dr. John" was Graham Bretton, but she withheld that information from the reader both because of her habitual secretiveness and also because she did not really "know" the Brettons were accessible to her until she was able to admit her need to reach out for human sympathy. The characterization of Paul Emanuel gains richness and detail in such a manner that readers realize—before Lucy herself dares admit it—that she is interested in him. The phantom nun, at first a night terror of pure emotion, is revealed as a prankish disguise when Lucy is free to express feelings directly.

The novel's ending, however, is deliberately ambiguous, though not in event. (Only the most naïve readers dare accept Brontë's invitation to imagine that Paul Emanuel escapes drowning and to "picture union and a happy succeeding life.") The ambiguity grows from Lucy's earlier statement: "M. Emanuel was away for three years. Reader, they were the three happiest years of my life." In those years, Lucy Snowe prospered, became respected, expanded her school. Her happiness depends not on the presence of her beloved but rather on the knowledge that she is loved. With that knowledge, she becomes whole and independent. No longer telling others' stories, she speaks directly to the reader about her most private concerns. Only when her lover is absent, perhaps, can a woman treasure love and emotional satisfaction while yet retaining the freedom to be her own person.

Sally Mitchell

OTHER MAJOR WORKS

POETRY: *Poems by Currer, Ellis, and Acton Bell*, 1846 (with Emily and Anne Brontë); *The Complete Poems of Charlotte Brontë*, 1923.

CHILDREN'S LITERATURE: *The Twelve Adventurers and Other Stories*, 1925 (C. K. Shorter and C. W. Hatfield, editors); *Legends of Angria*, 1933 (Fannie E. Ratchford, compiler); *The Search After Happiness*, 1969; *Five Novelettes*, 1971 (Winifred Gérin, editor); *The Secret and Lily Hart*, 1979 (William Holtz, editor).

MISCELLANEOUS: *The Shakespeare Head Brontë*, 1931-1938 (19 volumes; T. J. Wise and J. A. Symington, editors).

BIBLIOGRAPHY

Barker, Juliet. *The Brontës*. New York: St. Martin's Press, 1995. This massive (more than one-thousand-page) study of the entire Brontë family sometimes overwhelms with detail, but it presents the most complete picture of one of English literature's most intriguing and productive families. Barker's analysis of the juvenilia, in particular, constitutes a major contribution to Brontë scholarship. Not surprisingly, she has more to say about Charlotte than about other members of the family, and she is honest in admitting that Emily remains an enigma.

Fraser, Rebecca. *The Brontës: Charlotte Brontë and Her Family*. New York: Crown, 1988. This thorough and engrossing biography of Charlotte Brontë and the Brontë family is carefully researched and annotated and offers a vividly written portrait of the Brontës and their world. Makes use of letters, published and unpublished manuscripts, and contemporary news sources to examine this complex literary family. Highly recommended.

Gaskell, Elizabeth C. *The Life of Charlotte Brontë*. 1857. Reprint. London: Penguin Books, 1975. Still an indispensable source for any student of Charlotte Brontë's life, Gaskell's biography offers the insights gained through her long friendship with Brontë. Herself a popular novelist of the time, Gaskell creates a memorable picture of Brontë as both a writer and a woman.

Gates, Barbara Timm. *Critical Essays on Charlotte Brontë*. Boston: G. K. Hall, 1990. The collection reprints some of the more provocative and salient evaluations of Charlotte Brontë's life and work, such as Adrienne Rich's "Jane Eyre: The Temptations of a Motherless Woman." The volume contains a set of five general essays grouped together under the rubric "Critical Perspectives on Brontë's Dualism," as well as eighteen devoted to Brontë's fiction.

Gordon, Lyndall. *Charlotte Brontë: A Passionate Life*. New York: W. W. Norton, 1994. Unlike Barker, Gordon had the blessing of the Brontë Society, which granted access to and permission to reproduce from its copious archives. Gordon makes good use of his materials, producing a readable account of Charlotte Brontë's life and literary output.

Lloyd Evans, Barbara, and Gareth Lloyd Evans. *The Scribner Companion to the Brontës*. New York: Charles Scribner's Sons, 1983. Provides an overview of the Brontë family as a whole. Includes the story of the Brontës' tragic history, sections on the young Brontës' juvenilia, discussions of Charlotte, Anne, and Emily's published works, and excerpts from criticisms written about those works at the time they were first published.

EMILY BRONTË

Born: Thornton, Yorkshire, England; July 30, 1818
Died: Haworth, Yorkshire, England; December 19, 1848

PRINCIPAL LONG FICTION

Wuthering Heights, 1847

OTHER LITERARY FORMS

Poems by Currer, Ellis, and Acton Bell (1846) contains poems by Charlotte, Emily, and Anne Brontë. Juvenilia and early prose works on the imaginary world of Gondal have all been lost.

ACHIEVEMENTS

Emily Brontë occupies a unique place in the annals of literature. Her reputation as a major novelist stands on the merits of one relatively short novel which was misunderstood and intensely disliked upon publication; yet no study of British fiction is complete without a discussion of *Wuthering Heights*. The names of its settings and characters, particularly Heathcliff, have become part of the heritage of Western culture, familiar even to those who have neither read the novel nor know anything about its author's life and career. Several film versions, the two most popular in 1939 and 1970, have helped perpetuate this familiarity.

The literary achievement of *Wuthering Heights* lies in its realistic portrayal of a specific place and time and in its examination of universal patterns of human behavior. Set in Yorkshire in the closing years of the eighteenth century, the novel delineates the quality of life in the remote moors of northern England and also reminds the reader of the growing pains of industrialization throughout the nation. In addition, more than any other novel of the period, *Wuthering Heights* presents in clear dialectic form the conflict between two opposing psychic forces, embodied in the settings of the Grange and the Heights and the people who inhabit them. Although modern readers often apply the theories of Sigmund Freud and Carl Jung to give names to these forces, Brontë illustrated their conflict long before psychologists pigeonholed them. *Wuthering Heights* is so true in its portrayal of human nature that it fits easily into many theoretical and critical molds, from the historical to the psychological. The novel may be most fully appreciated, however, as a study of the nature of human perception and its ultimate failure in understanding human behavior. This underlying theme, presented through the dialectic structure of human perception, unites many of the elements that are sometimes singled out or overemphasized in particular critical approaches to the novel.

Brontë's skill is not confined to representing the world and the human forces at work within her characters, great as that skill is. She has also created a complex narrative structure built upon a series of interlocking memories and perceptions, spanning three generations, and moving across several social classes. Told primarily from two often unreliable and sometimes ambiguous first-person points of view, the structure of the novel itself illustrates the limitations of human intelligence and imagination. Faced with choosing between Lockwood or Nelly Dean's interpretation of Heathcliff's life, the reader can only ponder that human perception never allows a full understanding of another soul.

BIOGRAPHY

Emily Jane Brontë was born at Thornton, in Bradford Parish, Yorkshire, on July 30, 1818, the fifth child of the Reverend Patrick and Maria Brontë. Patrick Brontë had been born in County Down, Ireland, one of ten children, on March 17, 1777. He was a schoolteacher and tutor before obtaining his B.A. from Cambridge in 1806, from where he was ordained to curacies, first in Essex and then in Hartshead, Yorkshire. He married Maria Branwell, of Penzance, in Hartshead on December 19, 1812, and in 1817, they moved to Thornton. The other children at the time of Emily's birth were Maria, Elizabeth, Charlotte, and Patrick Branwell; another daughter, Anne, was born two years later. Charlotte and Anne also became writers.

In early 1820, the family moved to Haworth, four miles from the village of Keighley, where the Reverend Brontë was perpetual curate until his death in 1861. Maria Brontë died on September 15, 1821, and about a year later, an elder sister, Elizabeth Branwell, moved in to take care of the children and household. She remained with them until her own death in 1842.

Life at Haworth was spartan but not unpleasant. There was a close and devoted relationship among the children, especially between Charlotte and Emily. Reading was a favorite pastime, and a wide range of books, including the novels of Sir Walter Scott and the poetry of William Wordsworth and Robert Southey, as well as the more predictable classics, was available to the children. Outdoor activities included many hours of wandering through the moors and woods. Their father wanted the children to be hardy and independent, intellectually and physically, indifferent to the passing fashions of the world.

Maria, Elizabeth, and Charlotte had already been sent away to a school for clergymen's daughters, at Cowan Bridge, when Emily joined them in November, 1824. Emily was not happy in this confined and rigid environment and longed for home. Two of the sisters, Elizabeth and Maria, became ill and were taken home to die during 1825; in June, Charlotte and Emily returned home as well.

From 1825 to 1830, the remaining Brontë children lived at Haworth with their father and Miss Branwell. In June, 1826, their father gave them a set of wooden soldiers, a seemingly insignificant gift that stimulated their imaginative and literary talents. The children devoted endless energy to creating an imaginary world for these soldiers. During these years, Charlotte and her brother Branwell created in

their minds and on paper the land of "Angria," while Emily and Anne were at work on "Gondal." Although all of these early prose works have been lost, some of Emily's poetry contains references to aspects of the Gondal-Angria creations.

In July, 1835, Emily again joined Charlotte, already a teacher, at the Roe Head school. She remained only three months, returning home in October. Three years later, she accepted a position as governess in a school in Halifax for about six months but returned to Haworth in December; Charlotte joined her there early in the following year. During 1839 and 1840, the sisters were planning to establish their own school at Haworth, but the plan was never carried through.

Charlotte left home again to serve as a governess in 1841, and in February, 1842, she and Emily went to Mme Héger's school in Brussels to study languages. They returned to Haworth in November because of Miss Branwell's death. Charlotte went back

(Library of Congress)

to Brussels to teach in 1843, but Emily never left Yorkshire again.

From August, 1845, the Brontë children were again united at Haworth. They did not have much contact with neighbors, whose educational level and intellectual interests were much inferior to theirs. They kept busy reading and writing, both fiction and poetry. *Wuthering Heights* was probably begun in October, 1845, and completed sometime in 1846, although it was not published until December, 1847, after the success of Charlotte's *Jane Eyre* (1847).

Meanwhile, the sisters published *Poems by Currer, Ellis, and Acton Bell* in May, 1846. Finding a press was very difficult, and the pseudonyms were chosen to avoid personal publicity and to create the fiction of male authorship, more readily acceptable to the general public. The reaction was predictable, as Charlotte reports: "Neither we nor our poems were at all wanted." The sisters were not discouraged, however, and they continued to seek publishers for their novels.

The first edition of *Wuthering Heights* was published in 1847 by T. C. Newby, with Anne's *Agnes Grey* as the third volume. It was a sloppy edition and contained many errors. The second edition, published in 1850, after the author's death, was "corrected" by Charlotte. The public reaction to *Wuthering Heights* was decidedly negative; readers were disturbed by the "wickedness" of the characters and the "implausibility" of the action. Until Charlotte herself corrected the misconception, readers assumed that *Wuthering Heights* was an inferior production by the author of *Jane Eyre*.

In October, 1848, Emily became seriously ill with a cough and cold. She suffered quietly and patiently, even refusing to see the doctor who had been called. She died of tuberculosis at Haworth on December 19, 1848. She was buried in the church alongside her mother, her sisters Maria and Elizabeth, and her brother Branwell.

These facts about Emily Brontë's life and death are known, but her character will always remain a mystery. Her early prose works have been lost, only three personal letters survive, and her poems give little insight into her own life. Most information about the Brontë family life and background comes from

Mrs. Elizabeth Gaskell's biography of Charlotte and the autobiographical comments on which she based her work. Charlotte comments that Emily was "not a person of demonstrative character" and that she was "stronger than a man, simpler than a child." She had a nature that "stood alone." The person behind this mystery is revealed only in a reading of *Wuthering Heights*.

ANALYSIS: WUTHERING HEIGHTS

Wuthering Heights is constructed around a series of dialectic motifs which interconnect and unify the elements of setting, character, and plot. An examination of these motifs will give the reader the clearest insight into the central meaning of the novel. Although *Wuthering Heights* is a "classic," as Frank Kermode points out in an essay, precisely because it is open to many different critical methods and conducive to many levels of interpretation, the novel grows from a coherent imaginative vision that underlies all the motifs. That vision demonstrates that all human perception is limited and failed. The fullest approach to Emily Brontë's novel is through the basic patterns that support this vision.

Wuthering Heights concerns the interactions of two families, the Earnshaws and Lintons, over three generations. The novel is set in the desolate moors of Yorkshire and covers the years from 1771 to 1803. The Earnshaws and Lintons are in harmony with their environment, but their lives are disrupted by an outsider and catalyst of change, the orphan Heathcliff. Heathcliff is, first of all, an emblem of the social problems of a nation entering the age of industrial expansion and urban growth. Although Brontë sets the action of the novel entirely within the locale familiar to her, she reminds the reader continually of the contrast between that world and the larger world outside.

Besides Heathcliff's background as a child of the streets and the description of urban Liverpool from which he is brought, there are other reminders that Yorkshire, long insulated from change and susceptible only to the forces of nature, is no longer as remote as it once was. The servant Joseph's religious cant, the class distinctions obvious in the treatment of

Nelly Dean as well as of Heathcliff, and Lockwood's pseudosophisticated urban values are all reminders that Wuthering Heights cannot remain as it has been, that religious, social, and economic change is rampant. Brontë clearly signifies in the courtship and marriage of young Cathy and Hareton that progress and enlightenment *will* come and the wilderness *will* be tamed. Heathcliff is both an embodiment of the force of this change and its victim. He brings about a change but cannot change himself. What he leaves behind, as Lockwood attests and the relationship of Cathy and Hareton verifies, is a new society, at peace with itself and its environment.

It is not necessary, however, to examine in depth the Victorian context of *Wuthering Heights* to sense the dialectic contrast of environments. Within the limited setting that the novel itself describes, society is divided between two opposing worlds: Wuthering Heights, ancestral home of the Earnshaws, and Thrushcross Grange, the Linton estate. Wuthering Heights is rustic and wild; it is open to the elements of nature and takes its name from "atmospheric tumult." The house is strong, built with narrow windows and jutting cornerstones, fortified to withstand the battering of external forces. It is identified with the outdoors and nature and with strong, "masculine" values. Its appearance, both inside and out, is wild, untamed, disordered, and hard. The Grange expresses a more civilized, controlled atmosphere. The house is neat and orderly, and there is always an abundance of light—to Brontë's mind, "feminine" values. It is not surprising that Lockwood is more comfortable at the Grange, since he takes pleasure in "feminine" behavior (gossip, vanity of appearance, adherence to social decorum, romantic self-delusion), while Heathcliff, entirely "masculine," is always out of place there.

Indeed, all of the characters reflect, to greater or lesser degrees, the masculine and feminine values of the places they inhabit. Hindley and Catherine Earnshaw are as wild and uncontrollable as the Heights: Catherine claims even to prefer her home to the pleasures of heaven. Edgar and Isabella Linton are as refined and civilized as the Grange. The marriage of Edgar and Catherine (as well as the marriage of Isabella and Heathcliff) is ill-fated from the start, not only because she does not love him, as her answers to Nelly Dean's catechism reveal, but also because each is so strongly associated with the values of his or her home that he or she lacks the opposing and necessary personality components. Catherine is too willful, wild, and strong; she expresses too much of the "masculine" side of her personality (the animus of Jungian psychology), while Edgar is weak and effeminate (the anima). They are unable to interact fully with each other because they are not complete individuals themselves. This lack leads to their failures to perceive each other's true needs.

Even Cathy's passionate cry for Heathcliff, "Nelly, I *am* Heathcliff," is less love for him as an individual than the deepest form of self-love. Cathy cannot exist without him, but a meaningful relationship is not possible, because Cathy sees Heathcliff only as a reflection of herself. Heathcliff, too, has denied an important aspect of his personality. Archetypally masculine, Heathcliff acts out only the aggressive, violent parts of himself.

The settings and the characters are patterned against each other, and explosions are the only possible results. Only Hareton and young Cathy, each of whom embodies the psychological characteristics of both Heights and Grange, can successfully sustain a mutual relationship.

This dialectic structure extends into the roles of the narrators as well. The story is reflected through the words of Nelly Dean—an inmate of both houses, a participant in the events of the narrative, and a confidante of the major characters—and Lockwood, an outsider who witnesses only the results of the characters' interactions. Nelly is a companion and servant in the Earnshaw and Linton households, and she shares many of the values and perceptions of the families. Lockwood, an urban sophisticate on retreat, misunderstands his own character as well as others'. His brief romantic "adventure" in Bath and his awkwardness when he arrives at the Heights (he thinks Cathy will fall in love with him; he mistakes the dead rabbits for puppies) exemplify his obtuseness. His perceptions are always to be questioned. Occasionally, however, even a denizen of the conventional world may gain a glimpse of the forces at work beneath the surface of reality. Lockwood's dream of the dead Cathy, which sets off his curiosity and Heathcliff's final plans, is a reminder that even the placid, normal world may be disrupted by the psychic violence of a willful personality.

The presentation of two family units and parallel brother-sister, husband-wife relationships in each also emphasizes the dialectic. That two such opposing modes of behavior could arise in the same environment prevents the reader from easy condemnation of either pair. The use of flashback for the major part of the narration—it begins *in medias res*—reminds the reader that he or she is seeing events out of their natural order, recounted by two individuals whose reliability must be questioned. The working out of the plot over three generations further suggests that no one group, much less one individual, can perceive the complexity of the human personality.

Taken together, the setting, plot, characters, and structure combine into a whole when they are seen as parts of the dialectic nature of existence. In a world where opposing forces are continually arrayed against each other in the environment, in society, in families, and in relationships, as well as within the individual, there can be no easy route to perception of another human soul. *Wuthering Heights* convincingly demonstrates the complexity of this dialectic and portrays the limitations of human perception.

Lawrence F. Laban

OTHER MAJOR WORKS

POETRY: *Poems by Currer, Ellis, and Acton Bell*, 1846 (with Charlotte and Anne Brontë); *The Complete Poems of Emily Jane Brontë*, 1941 (C. W. Hatfield, editor).

BIBLIOGRAPHY

Berg, Maggie. *"Wuthering Heights": The Writing in the Margin*. New York: Twayne, 1996. Part of the Twayne Masterworks series, this volume provides a good introduction to Emily Brontë's masterpiece. A chronology of her life and works is followed by a section devoted to the literary and social context of the novel and a reading emphasizing the importance of the novel's "marginal spaces," such as the diary that Catherine keeps in the blank spaces of books.

Bloom, Harold, ed. *Heathcliff*. New York: Chelsea House, 1993. Part of the Major Literary Characters series, *Heathcliff* collects in one volume some of the most salient evaluations of Emily Brontë's hero. All have appeared previously elsewhere, but such an anthology between two covers is useful. *Heathcliff* includes both excerpts from longer works—starting with a passage from one of Charlotte Brontë's letters—and nine full-length essays. Harold Bloom offers an interesting introduction regarding "The Analysis of Character," which provides a framework for readers attempting to come to terms with Emily Brontë's most memorable literary creation.

Frank, Katherine. *A Chainless Soul: A Life of Emily Bronte*. Boston: Houghton Mifflin, 1990. Frank's book attempts to strike a balance between the "purple heather school of Brontë biography" and later accounts that present Emily Brontë as a victim.

Fraser, Rebecca. *The Brontës: Charlotte Brontë and Her Family*. New York: Crown, 1988. Although Fraser's central focus is Brontë's sister, Charlotte, her intelligent and exhaustively researched book offers much valuable material on Emily as well. Its portrait of the Brontës as a family evokes a vivid picture of life in the remote Yorkshire parsonage and its effect in shaping Emily's own work.

Gaskell, Elizabeth C. *The Life of Charlotte Brontë*. 1857. Reprint. London: Penguin Books, 1975. Although the central focus is Charlotte Brontë, this invaluable book is a necessary part of any thorough study of Emily. Gaskell's friendship with Charlotte provides this biography with a unique and informative perspective on the Brontës and their lives.

Hewish, John. *Emily Brontë: A Critical and Biographical Study*. New York: St. Martin's Press, 1969. Part biography and part literary analysis, this study of Brontë places her within the context of her time and society, examining her life and the critical and public reception her work received.

Contains an extensive and exceptional bibliography of great use to any Brontë scholar.

Lloyd Evans, Barbara, and Gareth Lloyd Evans. *The Scribner Companion to the Brontës*. New York: Charles Scribner's Sons, 1983. Provides an overview of the Brontë family as a whole. Includes the story of the Brontës' tragic history, sections on the young Brontës' juvenilia, discussions of Charlotte, Anne, and Emily's published works, and excerpts from criticisms written about those works at the time they were first published.

Smith, Anne, ed. *The Art of Emily Brontë*. New York: Barnes & Noble Books, 1976. A collection of critical essays on Brontë's work, covering both her poetry and *Wuthering Heights*. Among the most interesting essays are Keith Sagar's comparison of Brontë and D. H. Lawrence, and Colin Wilson's thought-provoking comments on *Wuthering Heights*, which he views not as a great novel but as a "rough sketch for the masterpiece that should have followed."

(CORBIS/Christopher Cormack)

ANITA BROOKNER

Born: London, England; July 16, 1928

PRINCIPAL LONG FICTION

A Start in Life, 1981 (pb. in U.S. as *The Debut*, 1981)
Providence, 1982
Look at Me, 1983
Hotel du Lac, 1984
Family and Friends, 1985
The Misalliance, 1986
A Friend from England, 1987
Latecomers, 1988
Lewis Percy, 1989
Brief Lives, 1990
A Closed Eye, 1991
Fraud, 1992
A Family Romance, 1993 (pb. in U.S. as *Dolly*, 1993)

A Private View, 1994
Incidents in the Rue Laugier, 1995
Altered States, 1996
Visitors, 1997
Falling Slowly, 1998
Undue Influence, 1999

OTHER LITERARY FORMS

A distinguished historian of eighteenth and nineteenth century French art and culture, Anita Brookner wrote several books of nonfiction before she began to write novels. *Watteau* (1968) is an assessment of the early eighteenth century French artist Antoine Watteau. *The Genius of the Future, Studies in French Art Criticism: Diderot, Stendhal, Baudelaire, Zola, the Brothers Goncourt, Huysmans* (1971) is a collection of six essays on seven French writers; each writer is considered in the context of his time. The greatest space is given to Charles Baudelaire. *Greuze: The Rise and Fall of an Eighteenth-Century Phenomenon* (1972) is a study of the French painter Jean-Baptiste Greuze in a successful attempt to locate the back-

BROOKNER, ANITA

Critical Survey of Long Fiction

ground of a sentimental genre that is distinct from both rococo and classicism. *Jacques-Louis David* (1980), a biography of the foremost painter of the French revolutionary period, explores the relationship between David's life and work, places that work in the context of contemporary French painting, and details a career that spanned some of the most turbulent years in French history. *Soundings*, a collection of essays, was published in 1997. Brookner's translations include *Utrillo* (1960) and *The Fauves* (1962).

ACHIEVEMENTS

Brookner suddenly began to write fiction during her middle years, while still an active teacher and scholar. Although she continued her academic career, she quickly found equal success as a novelist. With the publication of several novels, she gained an international following and widespread critical acclaim. In 1984, Great Britain's prestigious Booker Prize for fiction was awarded to *Hotel du Lac*. Brookner was praised for her elegant and precise prose, her acute sense of irony, and her subtle insights into character and social behavior. Her witty explorations of manners and morals suggest to many a literary kinship to Jane Austen and Barbara Pym. While Brookner's somber, more complex moral vision disallows any sustained comparison to Pym, Austen and Brookner undeniably share a common concern for intelligent, subtle, clever heroines who seek to satisfy both private sensibility and public expectations.

To regard Brookner's novels as simply traditional novels of manners, however, is to misconstrue her art. Brookner's intentions greatly exceed this conventional genre; her achievements, indeed, take her far beyond it. Perhaps it is more useful to note the singularity of her contribution to British letters. Her highly developed pictorial sense; her baroque diction, with its balance of reason and passion; and her allusive, richly textured narratives, haunting in their resonances, reflect at every turn her extensive knowledge of the materials and motifs of eighteenth and nineteenth century paintings and literature.

Her works have been generously admired, but some dissenting voices have been raised. She is occasionally brought to task for fictive worlds too narrow

in scope and claustrophobic in their intensity, for overzealous, self-conscious, schematic fiction, and for excessive sentimentality that unfortunately evokes the pulp romance. Brookner's worlds, however, are invariably shaped toward significant moral revelations; technique rarely intrudes to the detriment of story; and her ability to maintain an ironic distance from her characters, one that allows her to reveal sentimentality, to make judgments dispassionately, is one of her greatest strengths as a writer.

BIOGRAPHY

Anita Brookner was born in London, England, on July 16, 1928, to Newsom and Maude Brookner. She was educated at James Allen's Girls' School; King's College, University of London; and received a Ph.D. in art history from the Courtauld Institute of Art in London in 1953. From 1959 to 1964, she was visiting lecturer at the University of Reading, Berkshire. In 1967-1968, she was Slade Professor at Cambridge University, the first woman to hold this position. From 1964 to 1988 she taught at the Courtauld Institute of Art, where she lectured on neoclassicism and the Romantic movement. She is a Fellow of New Hall of Cambridge University. In 1983, she became a fellow of the Royal Society of Literature, and in 1990 she was made a Commander, Order of the British Empire (CBE).

Brookner began her career as a novelist when she was more than fifty years old as an attempt, she hinted, to understand her own powerlessness after a grand passion went wrong. Between 1981 and 1997, she published a novel a year; *Hotel du Lac* won the prestigious Booker Prize. She has also written many articles, introductions, and reviews on art history and on both French and English literature. They have appeared in such publications as the *Burlington Magazine*, *The London Review of Books*, *The Times Literary Supplement*, *The Spectator*, *The Observer*, and *The Sunday Times*. Some of these pieces are collected in *Soundings*.

ANALYSIS

Anita Brookner established her reputation as a novelist with four books published in rapid succession between 1981 and 1984. Written in austerely elegant prose, each of these four novels follows essentially the same course. Each centers on a scholarly, sensitive, morally earnest young woman who leads an attenuated life. None of these heroines has intended a life so circumscribed. As their stories begin, they seek change, liberation from boredom and loneliness. They seek connection to a wider world. While these women are intelligent, endlessly introspective, and possessed of a saving ironic wit, they do not know how to get the things they most desire: the love of, and marriage to, a man of quality. With compassion, rue, and infinite good humor, Brookner makes it abundantly clear that these worthy women, these good daughters, good writers, and good scholars are unknowing adherents to a romantic ideal. Like the shopgirls and "ultrafeminine" women they gaze upon with such wonder and awe, these intellectually and morally superior women accept without question the cultural assumption that marriage is a woman's greatest good. Consistently undervaluing their own considerable talents and professional achievements, these heroines look to love and marriage as a way of joining the cosmic dance of a rational, well-ordered society. Their intense yearning for a transforming love shapes their individual plots; in each case, the conflict between what the romantic imagination wants and what it indeed does get impels these narratives forward. Brookner's concern is to illuminate the worthiness, the loneliness, the longing of these heroines for love and a more splendid life.

Before their stories can end, these women must abandon sentiment and accept their solitary state. Their triumph lies in their ability to confront their fall from romantic innocence and recognize it for what it is. These novels build inexorably toward an ending that is both startling and profoundly moving. While Brookner's heroines must struggle with sentimentality, Brookner herself does not. Her vision is bleak, unsparing. In telling their stories, she raises several other themes: The most notable of these are filial obligation, the "romantic" versus the "realistic" apprehension of life, truth and its relationship to self-knowledge, the determination of proper behavior in society, and the small pleasures that attend the trivia

of daily life. Brookner presents her major and minor themes against the background of fictive worlds so powerfully realized that her novels seem to be absorbed as much as read. These are novels of interior reality. Little that is overt happens; dramatic action rests in the consciousness of the heroine, who is always center stage.

THE DEBUT

Brookner's first novel, *The Debut*, lacks the richness and gradation of tone that marks her later fiction, but is nevertheless well crafted. Set against Honoré de Balzac's *Eugénie Grandet* (1833), *The Debut* tells the story of Ruth Weiss, a scrupulous, thoughtful scholar, who finds herself at forty with a life "ruined" by literature. A passionate reader from an early age, now a professor of literature specializing in Balzac, Ruth leads a narrow life alternating between teaching students and caring for an aging father. She blames the tradition of filial duty she found in literature for her mostly cheerless state.

Like Frances Hinton of *Look at Me* and Kitty Maule of *Providence*, Ruth began with expectations. In her youth, she once cast aside the burden of an oppressive heritage, one best symbolized by the deep silence and heavy, dark furniture in the mausoleum of a house she shared with her parents, and fled England for France. Ostensibly, her goal was to write a dissertation on vice and virtue; in actuality, it was as much to seek air and space and light. Although she at first endured a sense of displacement and exile, a condition that at one time or another afflicts many of Brookner's heroines, over time Ruth's transplant into foreign soil proved successful. Away from her charming, eccentric, but infinitely demanding parents, Ruth flourished. She acquired polish, sophistication, lovers. Yet even as she gloried in her new life, Ruth, like many of Brookner's other heroines, engaged in a constant internal debate over the question of how life is best lived. Does vice or virtue bring victory? She concluded that a life of conventional virtue can spell disaster for one's hopes; regretfully, Balzacian opportunism cannot be discounted. It is better to be a bad winner than a poor loser. Even though she observed that conventional morality tales were wrong, however, Ruth lamented the triumph of vice.

Suddenly called back to England because of what proves to be a final deterioration in her mother's fragile health, Ruth is forced to leave the comfortable, satisfying life she built for herself. Her spirited adventure over, Ruth is unable to extricate herself once more. At forty, the long and beautiful red hair indicative of her youthful potential for rebellion now compressed into a tight chignon, Dr. Ruth Weiss is a felon recaptured. She is tender with her father, gentle with her students, and expects little more from life. She is the first of Brookner's heroines who learns to renounce. Ruth's story is told retrospectively, in a way that recalls the French novel of meditation. The bold configurations of her story suggest the quality of a fable. The narrative also gains a necessary solidity and weight by the many allusions to Balzacian characters and texts. These allusions create a substructure of irony that continues to reverberate long after Ruth's story is complete.

PROVIDENCE

If Ruth is disheartened but finally resigned, Kitty Maule in *Providence*, Brookner's second novel, moves toward outright disillusionment. Kitty is also a professor of literature. Her interests lie in the Romantic movement; this novel, then, like the rest of Brookner's fiction, is filled with ideas, good talk, vigorous intellectual exchanges. Here, both Kitty's private musings and her running seminar on Benjamin Constant's *Adolphe* (1816) provide a context for the exploration of Romantic concerns. Brookner's use of Kitty as a teacher of the Romantic tradition is ultimately highly ironic, for Kitty cannot discern her own romanticism. Curiously, she has moments when she is almost able to see her romanticism for what it is. Yet in the end, she suppresses the would-be insights and retreats into her dreams and passionate longings. What Kitty longs for is love, marriage, and, perhaps, God. Her longing for God goes largely unrecognized; like her fellow Romantics, she requires a sign. Yet her longing for love, the love of one man in particular, is at the perceived center of her life.

The handsome, brilliant, but distant lover of the scholarly, sensitive woman in this novel is Maurice Bishop. Maurice, a professor of medieval history, is noted for his love of cathedrals and God. Well born,

rich, confident in the manner of those accustomed to deference, Maurice is everything that Kitty wants in life: He is the very cultural ideal of England itself. To be his wife is Kitty's hope of heaven; to capture him, she brings to bear all of her weapons at hand: subtle intelligence, grace of manners, enduring patience, and abiding love. That Kitty's love for Maurice has the fervor of a religious acolyte is suggested by his surname. Maurice may be in love with the idea of a religious absolute, but Kitty's religion is romantic love. All of her repressed romanticism is focused on this elegant, remote man.

Kitty's extreme dependence upon Maurice as the repository of her hopes and dreams stems in large part from her sense of cultural displacement. The child of a French mother and a British father, both dead in their youth, Kitty was born in England and brought up there by her immigrant French grandparents. Despite her British birth, however, Kitty never feels at home in England. In the face of concerted and varied efforts to "belong," she retains a sense of exile. Nor is she truly considered English by her colleagues and acquaintances. The product of her doting French grandparents, Kitty is unaware of her true cultural allegiance; ironically, it is the French heritage that dominates in her English setting. Her manners, clothes, and speech belie her English father. In Maurice, Kitty seeks an attachment that anchors, a place to be. Here and elsewhere in Brookner's fiction, the recurrent theme of the search for a home acquires the force and weight of myth. So powerfully realized is Kitty's intense desire for love, acceptance, and liberation from loneliness that it comes as a shock when Kitty, who is expecting Maurice's proposal of marriage, instead learns of his sudden engagement to a woman who shares his aristocratic background. The novel concludes with Kitty's realization that she had indeed lived in a haze of romantic expectation; the truth is, she has been first, last, and always an outsider.

In addition to the major theme of the passive, excellent, but self-deceived young woman in the service of an illusory ideal, Brookner presents in *Providence* themes which are relevant to all of her works. Maurice's betrayal of Kitty, for example, establishes a motif that recurs in later novels, while Brookner's superbly comic depiction of bored and boring academics, a staple in her fiction, reaches perhaps its finest statement here. If Balzacian allusions underlie *The Debut* and give it additional power, allusions to many French writers, but especially to Constant's *Adolphe* are used to provide ironic commentary on and foreshadowings of Kitty's fate. Most important, however, Kitty Maule herself is arguably the quintessential Brooknerian heroine. Like her fictional sisters, Ruth Weiss of *The Debut*, Frances Hinton of *Look at Me*, Edith Hope of *Hotel du Lac*, and Mimi Dorn of *Family and Friends*, Kitty waits patiently for her life to begin. She is blind to her own worth and discounts her singular achievements; longs for order, a place in a rational world; finds joy in the chores, duties, and routines of everyday life; is sensitive, compassionate, morally deserving. Finally, her final inevitable loss of a man morally her inferior leaves her stripped of all romantic illusions, a convert to reality.

LOOK AT ME

By her own admission a relentless observer, Frances Hinton, the heroine of *Look at Me*, Brookner's third novel, tells her own compelling story. To be sure, all of Brookner's heroines are detached observers, though probably none records and stores information so clinically as does Frances. All of Brookner's heroines suffer, yet perhaps none suffers more intensely than Frances. Like other Brooknerian heroines, Frances is virtuous, sensitive, bright, and in need of a more marvelous life. Like other Brooknerian heroines also, she does not know how to get the things she wants. Frozen into inaction, her intense melancholia is mirrored in the images of death and desolation that surround her. A medical librarian who catalogs prints and engravings of disease through the ages, Frances comments ironically on the scenes of madness, nightmare affliction, and death she must sort and mount. She lives in a tomb of a house where her mother has died; Brookner's use of Frances's house recalls her uses of houses elsewhere: They are symbols of oppressive traditions that constrain and weigh heavily upon those who inhabit them. For Frances, the world is somber, dark. The glittering, stylish couple who offer temporary access

to a dazzling social world prove cruelly false. In an act of betrayal so profound that Frances cannot but withdraw from the world she has long sought, the beautiful Nick and Alix Fraser hold Frances up to public ridicule. Her brief liberation from solitariness and the eternal prison of self ends abruptly. Always self-analytic, self-deprecatory, Frances sees her failure to find a place in the world as a failure of egotism or will. She observes that others advance through egotism, but she cannot mimic them. She decides to become a writer. Writing will allow her both to comment on life and to retreat from it.

As is usual in Brookner's works, the dramatic action is largely inner. Hers are novels of the interior; the terrain surveyed is that of the soul. Frances presents a commanding narrative voice as she sorts, gathers, and finally reassembles the fragments of her experience into a unified whole. In fullest voice, she provides useful insights into the processes of the creative, transforming imagination. From the detritus of her daily life she, as writer-at-work, will abstract significant form. If Brookner here provides a mirror of herself busy fashioning art from the materials of the ordinary, the details of eating or dressing or chatting that receive so much attention in her novels, she also repeats the characteristic fusion of the comic and the sad that lends such poignancy to her works. Further, the influence of the pictorial is reflected here as well; characters are often framed in an action, presented with a consciousness of scene or setting. Finally, Frances's long commentary on her experience that is the text of *Look at Me* again evokes the French novel of meditation, a literary form that subtly influences and pervades Brookner's fiction. Notably, as Frances begins to write on the last page of the novel, she is free of self-pity. Solitude may be her lot, but art will vindicate her. Art will represent the triumph of the unvanquished self.

HOTEL DU LAC

Edith Hope, the heroine of *Hotel du Lac*, Brookner's fourth novel and the winner of the 1984 Booker Prize, is also a writer. Edith writes pulp romances for a living. Yet until she learns better, she believes that romance is only her business, not her frame of mind. Brookner's fiction, however, reveals her tendency sometimes to use names to signal character traits or habits of thought. Such is the case here: Edith is indeed a romantic, although an unknowing one. Edith begins her stay at the Hotel du Lac in ignorance of her true nature; she leaves enlightened as to the deeper, more recessed aspects of her moral being.

It was not Edith's choice to leave England and travel to Switzerland, the setting of *Hotel du Lac*. Edith was sent away because of her severe breach of social decorum: She chose not to appear at her own wedding, thus profoundly humiliating a good man and eminently suitable husband. Her action was shocking to all, including Edith herself. Modest, unassuming, and usually anxious to please, Edith is in many ways a typical Brooknerian heroine. She, too, spends too much time alone, condemned to her own introspection. Her marriage would have broken that isolation. Edith's revolt and subsequent removal to Switzerland provide a context for the discussion of numerous moral and psychological questions. While Edith's story is always foremost, the novel itself alternates between first- and third-person narratives, with philosophical positions being argued, accepted, or dismissed. The central fact that emerges about Edith is her passionate love for a married man whom she only seldom sees. Like his fictional predecessors, Edith's David is exceedingly handsome, elegant, intelligent, and remote. For love of him, Edith jilted her dull but safe fiancé. At the Hotel du Lac, Edith's interactions with the other residents move her to a greater understanding of truth, self-knowledge, and the differences between romance and reality. Numerous other themes are present here as well, including that of "ultrafeminine" as opposed to "feminist" women. Edith understands these women as models of feminine response to feminine experience. In relative isolation at this Swiss hotel, she studies these models and rejects both. The will to power, the utility of egotism as a serviceable instrument in the world, a recurrent Brooknerian theme, also receives much discussion here.

What Edith eventually learns as she evaluates her exchanges and relationships with her fellow guests is accorded significant status by the mythological underpinnings of this novel. Inside the hotel, characters are both particular and types, acting out self-assigned roles in a grand comedy of manners. All the inhabitants exhibit a theatrical sense of themselves; they "present" themselves to this community consciously, deliberately. Such attention to the pictorial, personal presentation is a constant of Brookner's fiction. The details of clothes, manners, and mannerisms convey aspects of self and morality in Brookner's works as they do in the works of Henry James, to whom Brookner alludes in this novel. If inside the hotel the characters are on parade, making their statements with dress, or gesture, once outside the hotel, they are subsumed into the mythicized landscape. Gray mist, conveying a sense of menace and oppression, surrounds everything. Characters make journeys that are important only for their mythic impact. Much movement against this dreary landscape takes place as characters are directed toward crucial, definitive moral choices. The landscape helps Edith to perceive her dilemmas; she is finally able to reject a diabolical figure who offers marriage without love. He forces Edith to recognize her romanticism for what it is. At least in the end, however, when she returns to England and her married lover, Edith knows that she has chosen a cold and solitary path. Her self-determination represents a triumph for her and for this book. Edith is finally transformed by her successful journey to knowledge.

Having laid claim with her first four novels to a sharply defined fictional territory, Brookner has shown in subsequent books a willingness to extend her range. In *Latecomers*, for example, she centers her story for the first time on two male figures—close friends, both of whom were refugees brought from Germany to England as children during World War II. *Lewis Percy* features a single protagonist, again a man, in some ways the counterpart of Brookner's earlier heroines.

FAMILY AND FRIENDS

The book with which Brookner departed most radically from the pattern established in her first four novels was *Family and Friends*; perhaps because it violated readers' expectations, it was sharply criticized by some reviewers. Written in the historical present with virtually no dialogue, *Family and*

Friends is an extended meditation on the French tradition. It stems from the ruminations of a narrator who quickly disappears, makes only glancing reappearances, and is curiously never identified. Here, Brookner's concern is not with a particular heroine, but with the Dorn family, rich, most likely German immigrants who fled to England before the start of World War II. The war, when it comes, receives but scant attention; the novel focuses always on the small, interior world of the Dorn family. Little seems to exist outside the family and their immediate interests, sparking again charges of a work too narrow in range.

The lives of the Dorn family and their associates are followed over a period of time. Sofka, the gentle but strong matriarch of the family, is the moral center of the work. Widowed early in life, she rejects the idea of remarriage, directing her loving attentions to her family instead. Mimi and Betty are her two daughters. While Betty is selfish, willful, theatrical, tricking her family into giving her an independent life quite early, she is nevertheless the child Sofka secretly loves best. Sofka, beautiful and contained, admires her younger daughter's spirit. Mimi is virtuous, dreamy, passive, frozen into inertia in young womanhood when an early feeble attempt to reach out for love is unsuccessful. Mimi languishes for years afterward, until her mother urges her into marriage, and thereby respectability, with a gentle, good man who would normally be her social inferior. Also playing a significant part in the novel are Sofka's two sons: the sensitive, intelligent, responsible Alfred and his handsome, charming brother Frederick. Interestingly, it is Alfred's plight that mirrors the situation of the usual Brooknerian heroine. It is he who is trapped by filial obligation into a life he had not intended; it is he who suffers forever afterward from an unsatisfying search for love and a desire for a larger, more extended world. It is also he who ultimately becomes inured to long-established habits of insularity.

This, then, is the saga of a family whose interior lives and moral relations are acutely realized. Important themes here include familial relations, especially filial obligation; the search for a transcendent love; the need to venture, to dare, if one is to "win" in life. Structured around four wedding pictures, the novel impresses with its unity and intensity of tone; the pervasive, elegant irony; the discerning moral judgments; and the engrossing character portraits. Especially effective also is the novel's lament for the loss of youthful promise, energy, and innocence. The once-vibrant Betty, trapped in middle-aged stasis, is a case in point. Dominating this entire work is a rich narrative voice, stern, compassionate, and often sad. The Dorn family seems to exist in a twilight, dreamlike world outside time. Yet this world, while admittedly narrow, is nevertheless mesmerizing.

ALTERED STATES

Brookner writes novels in both the first and third person, and most of her novels center on women. *Altered States* represents a first: a novel told by a man, Alan Sherwood, in the first person. In *Hotel du Lac*, Brookner divides women into hares (happy winners in life's game) and tortoises (losers, for whom romance novels are written). In *Altered States*, Sherwood is a male tortoise; he is obsessed with a hare, the flashy and sexy Sarah Miller. As usual in Brookner, Alan the tortoise figure is a dull person, dutiful and bound to a parent. He is wheedled into marriage by another tortoise, Angela, and he is tortured by guilt after he betrays her and seemingly causes her death.

Altered States is different from other Brookner novels in other ways. Sarah is cruder, sexier, more selfish, and more anarchistic than any of Brookner's other hares; she embodies most of the seven deadly sins. Her lovemaking with Alan is more purely sexual than similar encounters elsewhere in Brookner. Alan, on the other hand, is not simply a tortoise; he *knows* he is a tortoise. He knows that he is dull and that he represents not just dullness but also civilized order. By the end of the novel, Alan not only learns about himself and the other people in his life, but he also has a small triumph over Sarah. He convinces her to step outside her character and perform a generous act.

VISITORS

In *Visitors*, the central character is once more a woman: Thea May, age seventy. She is perhaps Brookner's most inert and solitary tortoise—until a crisis makes her take a hare into her home. The hare is named Steve Best, a young friend of someone about to marry into Thea's late husband's family. The contrast could not be greater. Thea is a lonely, apprehensive, static old woman; Steve is a gregarious, wandering, confident young man. Her reaction to him is complicated. She responds to his presence and even coddles him, but at the same time she feels that her home has been violated, and she wishes he would leave.

Visitors is about understanding. Many characters, such as Thea's husband's self-centered family and the rude and charmless young people, understand each other hardly at all. They certainly do not understand Thea. However, as the novel proceeds, Thea displays a talent for understanding all of them and is even able to act on that understanding on a climactic occasion. As she is drawn out of her usual routine, Thea thinks more and more about her past. Since childhood she has harbored a secret fear of intruders—hares such as Steve and even her husband. By the end of the novel, Thea seems to come to terms with her anxieties. She acknowledges her affection for her husband's family and feels more receptive to daily joys.

Betty H. Jones, updated by George Soule

OTHER MAJOR WORKS

NONFICTION: *Watteau*, 1968; *The Genius of the Future, Studies in French Art Criticism: Diderot, Stendhal, Baudelaire, Zola, the Brothers Goncourt, Huysmans*, 1971; *Greuze: The Rise and Fall of an Eighteenth-Century Phenomenon*, 1972; *Jacques-Louis David*, 1980; *Soundings*, 1997.

TRANSLATIONS: *Utrillo*, 1960 (of Waldemar George's biography); *The Fauves*, 1962 (of Jean Paul Crespelle's book).

BIBLIOGRAPHY

Baxter, Gisèle Marieks. "Cultural Experiences and Identity in the Early Novels of Anita Brookner." *English* 42 (Summer, 1993): 125-139. Three central characters of early Brookner novels attempt (unsuccessfully) to find the formulas of literary romance in their lives. They aspire, not to the traditional aristocracy or even to the world of the gentry, but to the financially secure ideal of Prime Minister Margaret Thatcher's era.

Fisher-Wirth, Ann. "Hunger Art: The Novels of Anita Brookner." *Twentieth Century Literature* 41 (Spring, 1995): 1-15. At first glance, Brookner's heroines seem to be women trapped in a patriarchal world who accept their humiliation. A closer reading reveals that Brookner treats the universal human situation.

Haffenden, John. *Novelists in Interview*. London: Methuen, 1985. Includes a lively interview with Anita Brookner (pages 57-75) in which she discusses her novels, the ideas behind her writing, and the existential dilemmas of her characters. A substantial interview that provides a useful background to her works.

Hosmer, Robert E., Jr. "Paradigm and Passage: The Fiction of Anita Brookner." In *Contemporary British Women Writers: Narrative Strategies*. New York: St. Martin's Press, 1993. Brookner's central characters, like Brookner herself, are in the tradition of exile figures, from the Bible to contemporary times.

Sadler, Lynn Veach. *Anita Brookner*. Boston: Twayne, 1990. The first full-length study of Brookner's work, which discusses her first seven novels. Sadler compares Brookner to Barbara Pym and Margaret Drabble but also shows why Brookner has her own voice in feminist fiction. Analyzes Brookner's heroines and gives insight into the author's use of irony.

Skinner, John. *The Fictions of Anita Brookner: Illusions of Romance*. New York: St. Martin's Press, 1992. Skinner speculates on the close relationship of Brookner's novels to her life. He also discusses the novels in the light of contemporary narrative theory.

CHARLES BROCKDEN BROWN

Born: Philadelphia, Pennsylvania; January 17, 1771
Died: Philadelphia, Pennsylvania; February 22, 1810

PRINCIPAL LONG FICTION

Wieland: Or, The Transformation, 1798

Ormond: Or, The Secret Witness, 1799

Edgar Huntley: Or, Memoirs of a Sleep-Walker, 1799

Arthur Mervyn: Or, Memoirs of the Year 1793, Part I, 1799

Arthur Mervyn: Or, Memoirs of the Year 1793, Part II, 1800

Clara Howard: In a Series of Letters, 1801

Jane Talbot: A Novel, 1801

OTHER LITERARY FORMS

Charles Brockden Brown published two parts of a dialogue on the rights of women, *Alcuin*, in 1798; the last two sections appeared in William Dunlap's 1815 biography of Brown. Brown's later political and historical essays have not been collected but remain in their original magazine and pamphlet publications. Several fictional fragments appear in *Carwin, the Biloquist, and Other American Tales and Pieces* (1822) and in the Dunlap biography, notably the Carwin story and "Memoirs of Stephen Calvert." Several collected editions of his novels were published in the nineteenth century. Harry Warfel's edition of *The Rhapsodist and Other Uncollected Writings* (1943) completes the publication of most of Brown's literary works. Letters have appeared in scattered books and essays, but they are not yet collected. *Wieland and Memoirs of Carwin*, the first volume in the definitive edition of Brown's fiction under way at Kent State University Press, appeared in 1977.

ACHIEVEMENTS

The significant portion of Brown's literary career lasted little more than one year, from 1798 to 1800, during which he published the four novels for which he is best known: *Wieland, Ormond, Arthur Mervyn*, and *Edgar Huntly*. Though his career began with the essays comprising "The Rhapsodist" in 1789 and continued until his death, most of his other fiction, poetry, and prose is thought to be of minor importance.

Brown's literary reputation rests heavily on his historical position as one of the first significant American novelists. An English reviewer, quoted by Ber-

(Library of Congress)

nard Rosenthal in *Critical Essays on Charles Brockden Brown* (1981), wrote in 1824 that Brown "was the first writer of prose fiction of which America could boast." Brown's contemporaries recognized his abilities, and he received praise from William Godwin, John Keats, and Percy Bysshe Shelley. Though his American reputation remained unsteady, he was read by nineteenth century novelists such as James Fenimore Cooper, Edgar Allan Poe, and Herman Melville. In the twentieth and twenty-first centuries, scholars and advanced students of American culture have been his most frequent readers; they have rediscovered him in part because his concerns with identity and choice in a disordered world prefigure or initiate some of the major themes of American fiction.

Brown's four best-known novels begin the peculiarly American mutation of the gothic romance. There are similarities between his novels and the political gothic of Godwin and the sentimental gothic of Ann Radcliffe, but Brown's adaptations of gothic conventions for the exploration of human psychology, the analysis of the mind choosing under stress, and the representation of a truly incomprehensible world suggest that he may be an important bridge between the popular gothic tradition of eighteenth century England and the American gothic strain which is traceable through Poe, Melville, and Nathaniel Hawthorne to Henry James, William Faulkner, and such late twentieth century novelists as Joyce Carol Oates.

BIOGRAPHY

Born on January 17, 1771, Charles Brockden Brown was the fifth son of Elijah Brown and Mary Armitt Brown. Named after a relative who was a well-known Philadelphia official, Brown grew up in an intellectual Quaker family where the works of contemporary radicals such as Godwin and Mary Wollstonecraft were read, even though they were unacceptable by society's norms. Brown's health was never good; his parents tended to protect him from an active boy's life and to encourage his reading. When he was eleven, he began his formal education at the Friends' Latin School in Philadelphia under Robert Proud, a renowned teacher and scholar who later wrote *The History of Pennsylvania* (1797). Proud encouraged Brown to strengthen his constitution by taking walks in the country, similar to those Edgar Huntly takes with Sarsefield in *Edgar Huntly*. After five or six years in Latin School, Brown began the study of law under Alexander Willcocks (variously spelled), a prominent Philadelphia lawyer. Though he studied law for five or six years until 1792 or 1793, he never practiced. During Brown's years studying law, he taught himself French and increasingly leaned toward literary work. He became a member of the Belles Lettres Club, which met to discuss current literary and intellectual topics. In 1789, he published his first work, "The Rhapsodist," in the *Columbian Magazine*. In 1790, he met and became friends with Elihu Hubbard Smith of Litchfield, Connecticut, a medical student with literary interests. Smith encouraged Brown's literary aspirations, helping to draw him away from law. Brown's acquaintance with Smith brought him to New York City in 1794, where he came to know the members of the Friendly Club, a group of young New York intellectuals, one of whom was to be his first biographer, William Dunlap.

During this period, Brown wrote poetry, and by 1795 he had begun a novel. He began active publishing in 1798 in the Philadelphia *Weekly Magazine*. In the summer of 1798, when he was visiting Smith in New York, he published *Wieland*. Smith died during the yellow fever outbreak of that summer; Brown also became ill, but recovered. In 1799, Brown suddenly became an extremely busy writer. He published two novels and part of a third and also began *The Monthly Magazine and American Review*. In 1800, he published the second half of *Arthur Mervyn*, abandoned his magazine, and joined his brothers in business. After publishing his last two novels in 1801, he turned to political and historical writing. His 1803 pamphlet on the Louisiana Territory was widely read and provoked debate in Congress. In 1803, he began another magazine, *The Literary Magazine and American Register*, which lasted until 1806. His final magazine venture was *The American Register: Or, General Repository of History, Politics, and Science* (1807-1810). He was working on a geography publication when he died on February 22, 1810, of tuberculosis, a disease which had pursued him most of his life.

Brown's personal and intellectual life are known primarily through his writings. He married Elizabeth Linn on November 19, 1804, and his family eventually included three sons and a daughter. There is evidence that Brown entertained the liberal Quaker ideas of his parents, the Deism of Smith, and the ideas of the English radicals at various times. His dialogue on the rights of women, *Alcuin*, advocates sound education and political equality for women and, in the two posthumously published parts, even suggests a utopian state of absolute social equality between the sexes in which there would be no marriage. Though he entertained such radical ideas in his youth, Brown seems to have become more conservative with maturity, affirming in his later works the importance of both reason and religion in living a good life.

ANALYSIS

Charles Brockden Brown's aims in writing, aside from attempting to earn a living, are a matter of debate among critics. In his preface to *Edgar Huntly,* he makes the conventional claim of novelists of the time, that writing is "amusement to the fancy and instruction to the heart," but he also argues the importance as well as the richness of American materials:

> One merit the writer may at least claim:—that of calling forth the passions and engaging the sympathy of the reader by means hitherto unemployed by preceding authors. Puerile superstition and exploded manners, Gothic castles and chimeras, are the material usually employed for this end. The incidents of Indian hostility, the perils of the Western wilderness, are far more suitable; and for a native of America to overlook these would admit of no apology.

This statement suggests several elements of Brown's primary achievement, the development of gothic conventions for the purposes of exploring the human mind in moments of ethically significant decision. Such an achievement was important for its example to later American novelists.

AMERICAN GOTHIC

Brown's novels are like William Godwin's in their use of radical contemporary thought; they are like Ann Radcliffe's in that they continue the tradition of the rationalized gothic. Brown, however, proves in some ways to be less radical than Godwin, and his fictional worlds differ greatly from Radcliffe's. Brown brings into his novels current intellectual debates about education, psychology and reason, epistemology, ethics, and religion. Characters who hold typical attitudes find themselves in situations which thoroughly test their beliefs. The novels do not seem especially didactic; they are rather more like Radcliffe's romances in form. A central character or group undergoes a crisis which tests education and belief. Brown's novels tend to be developmental, but the world he presents is so ambiguous and disorderly that the reader is rarely certain that a character's growth really fits him or her better for living.

This ambiguity is only one of the differences which make Brown appear, in retrospect at least, to be an Americanizer of the gothic. In one sense, his American settings are of little significance, since they are rather simple equivalents of the castle grounds and wildernesses of an Otranto or Udolpho; on the other hand, these settings are recognizable and much more familiar to an American reader. Rather than emphasizing the exoticism of the gothic, Brown increases the immediacy of his tales by using an American setting. He also increases the immediacy and the intensity of his stories by setting them close to his readers in time. Even though his novels are usually told in retrospect by the kinds of first-person narrators who would come to dominate great American fiction, the narratives frequently lapse into the present tense at crises, the narrators becoming transfixed by the renewed contemplation of past terrors. Brown avoids the supernatural; even though his novels are filled with the inexplicable, they do not feature the physical acts of supernatural beings. For example, Clara Wieland dreams prophetic dreams which prove accurate, but the apparently supernatural voices which waking people hear are hallucinatory or are merely the work of Carwin, the ventriloquist. All of these devices for reducing the distance between reader and text contribute to the success of his fast-paced if sometimes overcomplicated plots, but they also reveal Brown's movement away from Radcliffe's rationalized gothic toward the kind of realism that would come to dominate American fiction in the next century.

Perhaps Brown's most significant contribution to the Americanization of the gothic romance is his representation of the human mind as inadequate to its world. Even the best minds in his works fall victim to internal and external assaults, and people avoid or fall into disaster seemingly by chance. In Radcliffe's fictional world, Providence actively promotes poetic justice; if the hero or heroine persists in rational Christian virtue and holds to his or her faith that the world is ultimately orderly, then weaknesses and error, villains and accidents will be overcome and justice will prevail. In Brown, there are no such guarantees. At the end of *Wieland,* Clara, the narrator, reflects: "If Wieland had framed juster notions of moral duty, and of the divine attributes; or if I had been gifted with ordinary equanimity or foresight, the double-tongued deceiver would have been baffled and repelled." Clara's moralizing is, in fact, useless, even to herself. She was not so "gifted"; therefore, she could never have escaped the catastrophes which befell her. Furthermore, she persists in seeing Carwin, the "double-tongued deceiver," as a devil who ruined her brother, even though Carwin is no more than a peculiarly gifted and not very moral human being. Clara is able to moralize in this way only because, for the time being, disasters do not threaten her. Placed once again in the situation in which she completed the first portion of her narrative, she would again reject all human comfort and wish for death. Brown's fictional worlds defy human comprehension and make ethical actions excessively problematic.

This apparent irony in *Wieland* illustrates a final significant development in Brown's adaptation of the gothic romance. Though it is difficult, given his sometimes clumsy work, to be certain of what he intends, Brown seems to have experimented with point of view in ways which foreshadow later works. *Arthur Mervyn*, written in two parts, seems a deliberate experiment in multiple points of view. Donald Ringe points out that while the first part, told primarily from Mervyn's point of view, emphasizes Mervyn's naïve victimization by a sophisticated villain, the second part, told from a more objective point of view, suggests that Mervyn may unconsciously be a moral chameleon and confidence man. This shifting of point of view to capture complexity or create irony reappears in the works of many major American novelists, notably in Herman Melville's "Benito Cereno" and in William Faulkner.

By focusing on the mind dealing with crises in an ambiguous world, making his stories more immediate, and manipulating point of view for ironic effect, Brown helps to transform popular gothic conventions into tools for the more deeply psychological American gothic fiction which would follow.

WIELAND

Clara Wieland, the heroine of *Wieland*, is a bridge between the gothic heroine of Radcliffe and a line of American gothic victims stretching from Edgar Allan Poe's narrators in his tales of terror through Henry James's governess in *The Turn of the Screw* (1898) to Faulkner's Temple Drake and beyond. Her life is

idyllic until she reaches her early twenties, when she encounters a series of catastrophes which, it appears, will greatly alter her benign view of life. When her disasters are three years behind her and she has married the man she loves, Clara returns to her view that the world is reasonably orderly and that careful virtue will pull one through all difficulties.

The novel opens with an account of the Wieland family curse on the father's side. Clara's father, an orphaned child of a German nobleman cast off by his family because of a rebellious marriage, grows up apprenticed to an English merchant. Deprived of family love and feeling an emptiness in his spiritual isolation, he finds meaning when he chances upon a book of a radical Protestant sect. In consequence, he develops an asocial and paranoid personal faith which converts his emptiness into an obligation. He takes upon himself certain duties which will make him worthy of the god he has created. These attitudes dominate his life and lead eventually to his "spontaneous combustion" in his private temple on the estate he has developed in America. The spiritual and psychological causes of this disaster arise in part from his guilt at failing to carry out some command of his personal deity, perhaps the successful conversion of American Indians to Christianity, the project which brought him to America. Clara's uncle presents this "scientific" explanation of her father's death and, much later in the novel, tells a story indicating that such religious madness has also occurred on her mother's side of the family. Religious madness is the familial curse which falls upon Clara's immediate family: Theodore Wieland, her brother; his wife, Catharine; their children and a ward; and Catharine's brother, Pleyel, whom Clara comes to love.

The madness strikes Theodore Wieland; he believes he hears the voice of God commanding him to sacrifice his family if he is to be granted a vision of God. He succeeds in killing all except Pleyel and Clara. The first half of the novel leads up to his crimes, and the second half deals primarily with Clara's discoveries about herself and the world as she learns more details about the murders. Clara's ability to deal with this catastrophe is greatly complicated by events that prove to be essentially unrelated to it, but which coincide with it. In these events, the central agent is Carwin.

Carwin is a ventriloquist whose background is explained in a separate short fragment "Memoirs of Carwin the Biloquist." Because ventriloquism is an art virtually unknown in Clara's world, Carwin seems monstrous to her. As he explains to Clara near the end of the novel, he has been lurking about the Wieland estate, and his life has touched on theirs in several ways. He has used his art to avoid being detected in his solitary night explorations of the grounds. The apparently supernatural voices he has created may have contributed to the unsettling of Theodore Wieland, but Wieland's own account during his trial indicates other more powerful causes of his madness. Much more dangerous to Clara has been Carwin's affair with her housekeeper, Judith, for by this means he has come to see Clara as a flower of human virtue and intellect. He is tempted to test her by creating the illusion that murderers are killing Judith in Clara's bedroom closet. This experiment miscarries, leading Clara to think she is the proposed victim. He later uses a "supernatural" voice which accidentally coincides with one of her prophetic dreams; though his purpose is to frighten her away from the place of his meetings with Judith, Carwin confirms Clara's fears and superstitions. He pries into her private diary and concocts an elaborate lie about his intention to rape her when he is caught. Out of envy and spite and because he is able, Carwin deceives Pleyel into thinking that Clara has surrendered her honor to him.

Throughout these deceptions, Carwin also fosters in Clara the superstition that a supernatural being is watching over and protecting her by warning her of dangers. Carwin's acts are essentially pranks; he never intends as much harm as actually occurs when his actions become threads in a complex net of causality. The worst consequence of his pranks is that Pleyel is convinced that Clara has become depraved just at the moment when she hopes that he will propose marriage, and this consequence occurs because Carwin overestimates Pleyel's intelligence. Pleyel's accusation of Clara is quite serious for her because it culminates the series of dark events which Clara perceives as engulfing her happy life. Carwin's scattered acts have convinced her that rapists and murderers lurk in every dark corner and that she is the center of some impersonal struggle between forces of good and evil. Pleyel's accusation also immediately precedes her brother's murders. These two crises nearly destroy Clara's reason and deprive her of the will to live.

The attack on Clara's mind is, in fact, the central action of the novel. All the gothic shocks come to focus on her perception of herself. They strip her of layers of identity until she is reduced to a mere consciousness of her own integrity, a consciousness which is then challenged when she comes to understand the nature of her brother's insanity. When all the props of her identity have been shaken, she wishes for death. Tracing her progress toward the wish for death reveals the central thematic elements of the novel.

The attack on Clara's mind is generated from poles represented by her brother and Pleyel. Wieland crumbles from within, and Pleyel is deceived by external appearances. Each falls prey to the weakness to which he is most susceptible. Clara's more stable mind is caught in the midst of these extremes. Theodore Wieland has the family temperament, the tendency to brood in isolation over his spiritual state and over "last things." Pleyel is the gay and optimistic rationalist, skeptical of all religious ideas, especially any belief in modern supernatural agencies. While Wieland trusts his inner voice above all, Pleyel places absolute faith in his senses. Both are certain of their powers to interpret their experience accurately, and both are wrong on all counts. Wieland sees what he wants to see, and Pleyel's senses are easily deceived, especially by the skillful Carwin. Wieland interprets his visions as divine revelations even though they command murder, and Pleyel believes Clara is polluted even though such a belief is inconsistent with his lifelong knowledge of her.

Clara's sense of identity first suffers when her idyllic world begins to slip away. Her world becomes a place of unseen and unaccountable danger. As her anxiety increases, she finds herself unable to reason about her situation. Brown shows this disintegration in one of his more famous scenes, when Clara comes to believe there is someone in her closet, yet persists in trying to enter it even though she has heard the murderers there and even after her protecting voice has warned her away. Critics take various attitudes toward this scene, which prolongs the reader's wait to learn who is in the closet in order to follow minutely Clara's thoughts and reactions. Brown creates suspense which some critics have judged overwrought, but his main purpose is clearly the close analysis of a strong mind coming apart under great pressure. Even though Pleyel's mistakes emphasize the inadequacy of individual rationality to the complexity of the world, that faculty remains the isolated person's only means of active defense. As Clara's rationality disintegrates, her helplessness increases.

Seeing her world divide into a war between good and evil in which her reason fails to help her, Clara's anxiety develops into paranoia. After Carwin tells how he intended to rape her, she begins to see him as a supernatural agent of Satan. When Pleyel accuses her of self-transforming wickedness with Carwin, Clara loses her social identity. Unable to change Pleyel's mind, she can only see recent events as a devilish plot against her happiness. Just when she thinks she is about to complete her identity in marriage, she is denied the opportunity. When she loses the rest of her family as a result of Wieland's insanity, she loses the last supporting prop of her identity, leaving only her faith in herself, her consciousness of her own innocence, and her belief that the satanic Carwin has caused all of her catastrophes.

Two more events deprive Clara of these remaining certainties. She learns that Wieland, rather than Carwin, whom she has suspected, was the murderer, and when she understands Wieland's motives, she loses confidence in her perceptions of herself, for should she be similarly transformed, she would be unable to resist. In fact, she sees herself, prostrate and wishing for death, as already transformed: "Was I not likewise transformed from rational and human into a creature of nameless and fearful attributes?" In this state, she understands her brother's certainty of his own rectitude. She cannot know herself. When she finally meets Carwin and hears how trivial and without malice his acts have been, she is unable to

believe him, unable to give up her belief that she is the victim of a supernatural agency. Like Wieland, whom she meets for the last time on the same evening she talks with Carwin, she insists that divinity stands behind her disasters; the paranoid Wielands stand at the head of the line of American monomaniacs of whom Melville's Ahab is the greatest example. Deprived of her ordered world, Clara asserts against it an order which gives her reason, at least, to die. Wieland himself commits suicide when Carwin convinces him he has listened to the wrong voice.

Criticism has been rightly skeptical of the apparent clumsiness of the last chapter, Clara's continuation of the narration three years after Wieland's suicide. That chapter tidies up what had appeared earlier to be a subplot involving the Wielands' ward, Louisa Conway, and it also puts together a conventional happy ending. The recovered Clara marries Pleyel after he resolves several complications, including learning the truth about Clara and losing his first wife. Though it remains difficult to determine what Brown intended, it is unlikely that a writer of Brown's intelligence, deeply interested in the twistings of human thought, could be unaware that Clara's final statement is a manifest tissue of illusion. No attainable human virtue could have saved her or Wieland from the web of events in which they became enmeshed. That she persists in magnifying Carwin's responsibility shows that she fails to appreciate the complexity of human events even as Carwin himself has failed. That the Conway/Stuart family disasters of the last chapter recapitulate her own emphasizes Clara's failure to appreciate fully the incomprehensibility of her world.

Brown apparently intended in the final chapter to underline the illusory quality of social normality. When life moves as it usually does, it appears to be orderly, and one's ideas of order, because they are not seriously challenged, seem to prevail and become a source of comfort and security. That these ideas of order all break down when seriously challenged leads Clara to the wisdom of despair: "The most perfect being must owe his exemption from vice to the absence of temptation. No human virtue is secure from degeneracy." Such wisdom is not, however, of much use under normal conditions and is of no use at all in a crisis. Perhaps more useful is Clara's reflection as she looks back from the perspective of three years, her idea that one's perceptions and interpretations, because of their imperfection, must be tested over time and compared with those of other observers. The Wieland family curse and Pleyel's errors might be moderated if each character relied less on his or her unaided perceptions and interpretations. In the midst of chaos, however, this maxim may be no more helpful than any other; Clara, for example, violently resists the sympathy of friends who might help to restore the order of her mind.

Though not a great novel, *Wieland* is both intrinsically interesting and worthy of study for the degree to which it foreshadows developments of considerable importance in the American novel. By subjecting Clara to a completely disordered world and by taking her through a loss of identity, Brown prepares the way for greater American gothic protagonists from Captain Ahab to Thomas Sutpen.

EDGAR HUNTLY

Edgar Huntly appears at first to be a clumsily episodic adventure novel, but the more closely one looks at it, the more interesting and troubling it becomes. The protagonist-narrator, Edgar Huntly, writes a long letter to his betrothed, Mary Waldegrave, recounting a series of adventures in which he has participated. This letter is followed by two short ones from Huntly to his benefactor, Sarsefield, and one final short letter from Sarsefield to Huntly. The last letter suggests some of the ways in which the apparent clumsiness becomes troubling. Midway through the novel, Edgar learns that he will probably be unable to marry his fiancée, for her inheritance from her recently murdered brother seems not really to belong to her. Later, it appears that the return of Edgar's recently well-married friend, Sarsefield, once again puts him in a position to marry, but Sarsefield's last letter raises doubts about this event which remain unresolved. The reader never learns whether Edgar and Mary are united. The purpose of Sarsefield's letter is to chastise Edgar.

Edgar's main project in the novel becomes to cure the mad Clithero, who mistakenly believes he has been responsible for the death of Sarsefield's wife, formerly Mrs. Lorimer. By the end of his adventures, Edgar understands the degree to which Clithero is mistaken about events and believes that when Clithero learns the truth, he will be cured. To Edgar's surprise, when Clithero learns the truth, he apparently sets out to really kill his benefactress, Mrs. Sarsefield. Edgar writes his two letters to Sarsefield to warn of Clithero's impending appearance and sends them directly to Sarsefield, knowing that his wife may well see them first. She does see the second letter, and collapses and miscarries as a result. Sarsefield chastises Edgar for misdirecting the letters, even though Sarsefield knew full well from the first letter that the second was on its way to the same address. While, on the one hand, Edgar's error seems comically trivial, especially in comparison with the misguided benevolence which drives him to meddle with Clithero, on the other hand, the consequences are quite serious, serious enough to make one question why Edgar *and* Sarsefield are so stupid about their handling of the letters. The reader is left wondering what to make of Edgar and Sarsefield; does either of them know what he is doing?

The novel seems intended in part as a demonstration that one is rarely if ever aware of what he or she is doing. Paul Witherington, in *Narrative Techniques in the Novels of Charles Brockden Brown* (1967), notes that the novel takes the form of a quest which never quite succeeds, a story of initiation in which repeated initiations fail to take place. Edgar returns to his home shortly after the murder of his closest friend, Waldegrave, in order to solve the crime and bring the murderer to justice. When he sees Clithero, the mysterious servant of a neighbor, sleepwalking at the murder scene, he suspects Clithero of the murder. When he confronts Clithero, Edgar learns the story of his past. In Ireland, Clithero rose out of obscurity to become the favorite servant of Mrs. Lorimer. His virtue eventually led to Mrs. Lorimer's allowing an engagement between Clithero and her beloved niece. This story of virtue rewarded turned sour when, in self-defense, Clithero killed Mrs. Lorimer's blackguard twin brother. Mrs. Lorimer believed her life to be mysteriously entwined with her brother's and was convinced that she would die when he did. Clithero believed her and was convinced that by killing the father of his bride-to-be he had also killed his benefactress. In a mad refinement of benevolence, he determined to stab her in order to spare her the pain of dying from the news of her brother's death. Failing with the sword, he resorted to the word, telling her what had happened. Upon her collapse, he took flight, ignorant of the actual consequences of his act. Mrs. Lorimer did not die; she married Sarsefield and they went to America. Though Clithero's guilt seems unconnected with the murder of Waldegrave, except that the event has renewed Clithero's anguish over what he believes to be his crime, Edgar still suspects him. Furthermore, Clithero's story has stimulated Edgar's benevolence.

Edgar becomes determined to help Clithero, for even if he is Waldegrave's murderer, he has suffered enough. Clithero retires to the wilderness of Norwalk to die after telling his story to Edgar, but Edgar pursues him there to save him. After three trips filled with wilderness adventures, Edgar receives a series of shocks. He meets the man who is probably the real owner of Mary's inheritance and loses his hope for a speedy marriage. Fatigued from his adventures in the wilderness and frustrated in his efforts to benefit Clithero, perhaps guilty about prying into Clithero's life and certainly guilty about his handling of Waldegrave's letters, he begins to sleepwalk. His sleepwalking mirrors Clithero's in several ways, most notably in that he also hides a treasure, Waldegrave's letters, without being aware of what he is doing. After a second episode of sleepwalking, he finds himself at the bottom of a pit in a cave with no memory of how he arrived there; this is the second apparent diversion from his quest for Waldegrave's murderer.

Edgar takes three days to return to civilization, moving through a fairly clear death and rebirth pattern which parallels the movement from savagery to civilization. His adventures—drinking panther blood, rescuing a maiden, fighting Native Americans, losing and finding himself in rough terrain, nearly killing his friends, and successfully evading his own rescue while narrowly escaping death several times—are filled with weird mistakes and rather abstract humor.

For example, he is amazed at his physical endurance. When he finds himself within a half-day's walk of home, he determines, despite his three days of privation, to make the walk in six hours. Six hours later, he has not yet even gained the necessary road, and, though he knows where he is, he is effectively no closer to home than when he started out. Though he has endured the physical trials, he has not progressed.

Of his earlier explorations of the wilderness, Edgar says, "My rambles were productive of incessant novelty, though they always terminated in the prospects of limits that could not be overleaped." This physical nature of the wilderness is indicative of the moral nature of human life, which proves so complex that while people believe they can see to the next step of their actions, they find continually that they have seen incorrectly. Edgar repeatedly finds himself doing what he never thought he could do and failing at what he believes he can easily accomplish. The complexities of his wilderness experience are beyond the reach of this brief essay, but they seem to lead toward the deeper consideration of questions Edgar raises after hearing Clithero's story:

> If consequences arise that cannot be foreseen, shall we find no refuge in the persuasion of our rectitude and of human frailty? Shall we deem ourselves criminal because we do not enjoy the attributes of Deity? Because our power and our knowledge are confined by impassable boundaries?

In order for Edgar to be initiated and to achieve his quest, he needs to come to a just appreciation of his own limits. Although he can see Clithero's limitations quite clearly, Edgar fails to see his own, even after he learns that he has been sleepwalking, that he has been largely mistaken about the events surrounding the Indian raid, that he has mistaken his friends for enemies, and that he has made many other errors which might have caused his own death. Even after he learns that an American Indian killed Waldegrave and that his efforts with Clithero have been largely irrelevant, he persists in his ignorant attempt to cure the madman, only to precipitate new disasters. Edgar does not know himself and cannot measure the consequences of his simplest actions, yet he persists in meddling with another equally complex soul which he understands even less. Before Clithero tells Edgar his story, he says, "You boast of the beneficence of your intentions. You set yourself to do me benefit. What are the effects of your misguided zeal and random efforts? They have brought my life to a miserable close." This statement proves prophetic, for prior to each confrontation with Edgar, Clithero has determined to try to live out his life as best he can; each of Edgar's attempts to help drives Clithero toward the suicide that he finally commits.

Insofar as Edgar's quest is to avenge his friend's murder, he succeeds quite by accident. Insofar as his quest is for ethical maturity, he fails miserably, but no one else in the novel succeeds either. If a measure of moral maturity is the ability to moderate one's passions for the benefit of others, no one is mature. The virtuous Mrs. Lorimer cannot behave rationally toward her villainous brother, and her suffering derives ultimately from that failure. Clithero will murder out of misguided benevolence. Sarsefield, a physician, will let Clithero die of wounds received from American Indians because he believes that to Clithero, "Consciousness itself is the malady, the pest, of which he only is cured who ceases to think." Even though Edgar must assent to this statement, concluding that "Disastrous and humiliating is the state of man! By his own hands is constructed the mass of misery and error in which his steps are forever involved," he still wishes to correct some of Clithero's mistakes. In doing so, he provokes Clithero's suicide. No character understands himself or herself, his or her limitations, or his or her actions thoroughly; in the case of each of these characters, benevolence issues in murder, direct or indirect. One of the novel's many ironies is that among Edgar, Sarsefield, and Clithero, only Clithero is never morally responsible for a death other than his own.

In *Edgar Huntly*, as in *Wieland*, the stage of human action is beyond human comprehension. In *Wieland*, although there is no sanctuary for the virtuous, virtue remains valuable at least as a source of illusions of order, but in *Edgar Huntly* positive virtue becomes criminal because of inevitable human error.

The phenomenon of sleepwalking and the motif of ignorance of self encourage the reader to consider those darker motives that may be hidden from the consciousness of the characters. Edgar must indeed affirm that people are criminal because they have not the attributes of Deity.

Wieland and *Edgar Huntly* are good examples of Brown's interests and complexity of fiction. His wedding of serious philosophical issues with forms of the popular gothic novel accounts for his distinctive role in the development of the American novel and his continuing interest for students of American culture.

Terry Heller

OTHER MAJOR WORKS

SHORT FICTION: *Carwin, the Biloquist, and Other American Tales and Pieces*, 1822; *The Rhapsodist and Other Uncollected Writings*, 1943.

NONFICTION: *Alcuin: A Dialogue*, 1798.

BIBLIOGRAPHY

Christopherson, Bill. *The Apparition in the Glass: Charles Brockden Brown's American Gothic.* Athens: University of Georgia Press, 1993. See chapter 2 for a good discussion of the American romance. Separate chapters are devoted to each of Brown's novels. Includes detailed notes but no bibliography.

Clark, David L. *Charles Brockden Brown: Pioneer Voice of America.* Durham, N.C.: Duke University Press, 1952. Still the most complete book on Brown, this study combines biography, criticism, and liberal quotations from Brown's papers. Some of Brown's letters were published here for the first time.

Grabo, Norman S. *The Coincidental Art of Charles Brockden Brown.* Chapel Hill: University of North Carolina Press, 1981. A scholarly yet easy-to-read analysis of Brown's major fiction, with a focus on the psychology of the characters and what they reveal about Brown's own mind.

Hinds, Elizabeth Jane Wall. *Private Property: Charles Brockden Brown's Gendered Economics of Virtue.* Newark: University of Delaware Press, 1997. Contains chapters on economics and gender in the 1790's and separate chapters on each of Brown's major novels. Includes detailed notes and bibliography.

Ringe, Donald A. *Charles Brockden Brown.* New York: Twayne, 1966. Though brief and written to a strict format, this book contains some of the most helpful criticism of Brown's works to be found. The biographical portion is necessarily brief, but each of Brown's novels is discussed in the main portion of the book. Includes a chronology of Brown's life and writings and an annotated bibliography.

Rosenthal, Bernard, ed. *Critical Essays on Charles Brockden Brown.* Boston: G. K. Hall, 1981. A valuable collection of original essays by various scholars, this volume opens with a summary of criticism on Brown up to 1980. The first section contains a good selection of early reviews; the second section, containing contemporary articles, includes essays on Brown's lesser-known novels as well as major works.

RITA MAE BROWN

Born: Hanover, Pennsylvania; November 28, 1944

PRINCIPAL LONG FICTION
Rubyfruit Jungle, 1973
In Her Day, 1976
Six of One, 1978
Southern Discomfort, 1982
Sudden Death, 1983
High Hearts, 1986
Bingo, 1988
Wish You Were Here, 1990 (with Sneaky Pie Brown)
Rest in Pieces, 1992 (with Sneaky Pie Brown)
Venus Envy, 1993
Dolley: A Novel of Dolley Madison in Love and War, 1994
Murder at Monticello: Or, Old Sins, 1994 (with Sneaky Pie Brown)

Pay Dirt: Or, Adventures at Ash Lawn, 1995 (with Sneaky Pie Brown)
Murder, She Meowed: Or, Death at Montpelier, 1996 (with Sneaky Pie Brown)
Riding Shotgun, 1996
Cat on the Scent, 1999 (with Sneaky Pie Brown)
Loose Lips, 1999
Outfoxed, 2000

OTHER LITERARY FORMS

Rita Mae Brown is a versatile writer. Besides her novels, many of which she says she wrote with her cat, Sneaky Pie Brown, she wrote an autobiography, *Rita Will: Memoir of a Literary Rabble-Rouser* (1997); a collection of political articles, *A Plain Brown Rapper* (1976); and books of poetry, *The Hand That Cradles the Rock* (1971) and *Songs to a Handsome Woman* (1973). Brown wrote an introduction to *The Troll Garden* (1905) by Willa Cather and has had works published in *Vogue* magazine. In 1982, she produced a screenplay, *The Slumber Party Massacre,* and a teleplay, *I Love Liberty.*

ACHIEVEMENTS

Brown was a member of the Literature Panel for the National Endowment for the Arts from 1978 to 1982, and she received the National Endowment for the Arts fiction grant in 1978. In 1982 *I Love Liberty* was nominated for an Emmy Award for Best Variety Show, and it received the Writers Guild of America Award for Best Variety Show on Television. Brown was named a Literary Lion by the New York Public Library in 1987. She is a member of the International Academy of Poets and the International Association of Poets, Playwrights, Editors, Essayists, and Novelists (PEN) Club. Wilson College awarded an honorary doctorate in humanities to Brown in 1992.

BIOGRAPHY

Rita Mae Brown was born in Hanover, Pennsylvania, on November 28, 1944, to Juliann Young, a single mother. Within two weeks, Young gave Rita Mae up for adoption to Ralph and Julia Ellen Brown, Young's half cousin. Brown began school in Pennsylvania, then moved with her family to Fort Lauderdale, Florida, in 1955. She enrolled at the University of Florida in Gainesville in 1962. In 1964, she was dismissed from the university for being a lesbian. She returned to Fort Lauderdale and attended Broward Junior College, where she earned an A.A. in 1965. Following her graduation, Brown relocated, earning a B.A. in English and classics from New York University in 1968, a degree in cinematography from the New York School of Visual Arts that same year, and a Ph.D. in English and political science in 1976 from the Institute for Policy Studies in Washington, D.C.

Brown began her writing career with *Rubyfruit Jungle* in 1973 and continued to write in a variety of styles, including nonfiction, poetry, and screenplays. She settled in Charlottesville, Virginia.

ANALYSIS

Critics of Rita Mae Brown often write that she is too radical and too argumentative in her works. However, she is dealing with a problem of acceptance that has been the plight of many minor writers. In point of fact, Brown is no more defensive about her sexuality than are many other homosexual writers, such as Allen Ginsberg in his poetic statement *Howl* (1956).

What sets Brown's work apart is that she does not disguise her prolesbian stance and does not become an apologist, as did some writers before her. Brown's work is feminist and has put off some conservative readers. However, one must remember that Brown began writing in the early 1970's and was influenced by the National Organization for Women (NOW, an organization that asked her to leave because of her political views), the women's liberation movement, the protests against the Vietnam War, and most important, her own sense of freedom upon coming to New York City, where she could lead an open lesbian life.

RUBYFRUIT JUNGLE

Brown's novels draw upon her own life; most of her work is clearly autobiographical. In her autobiography, *Rita Will*, Brown writes that when *Rubyfruit Jungle* was released, she received hate mail and threats on her life from the conservative wing of the feminist movement. Brown's book is radical and upsetting.

Rubyfruit Jungle is a coming-of-age novel for pro-

Rita Mae Brown and Sneaky Pie Brown (Mark Homan)

tagonist Molly Bolt; it is also a direct statement of Brown's own coming of age. It describes the early life of Bolt, an adopted daughter of a poor family living in Coffee Hollow, Pennsylvania. Brown traces Molly's life from Coffee Hollow to Florida to New York City and takes Molly from a naïve young girl of seven to a mature, worldly-wise woman in her midtwenties. Molly Bolt's life story is exactly Rita Mae Brown's. In most cases, Brown presents all of the characters as merely renamed family members and friends from childhood through her time in New York. During the course of the novel, the reader sees Molly defy local authority figures of every kind: parents, educators, family members, employers, and lovers. In this respect, Molly has been described by at least one critic as similar to Huckleberry Finn in his rebellion against authority. Like Mark Twain's, Brown's style employs folk humor and observations about the world. Unlike Twain, however, Brown does not rely upon dialect or local color, though Brown's style is in the vein of other southern American writers, such as

Flannery O'Connor, Eudora Welty, and Alice Walker, who have a sharp eye for idiosyncratic behavior.

Molly moves to Florida, as did Brown. While there, Molly becomes aware of her lesbianism, falls in love with her college roommate at the University of Florida, and is expelled for this love, just as Brown was expelled from the university for her own lesbian lifestyle. Molly leaves Florida and arrives in New York City, where she establishes herself in the homosexual community of Greenwich Village. Here Molly finds a menial job, puts herself through school, and meets a beautiful woman who becomes her lover. From this point on, the novel concentrates on Molly's life as a lesbian.

When Molly left for New York, she was estranged from her mother. Only when she returns to Florida to film her mother as a final project for her degree does Molly really understand that the choices she has made have helped her to develop as an individual who can face the reality of her world. Breaking away from the homogeneity of family, friends, and society has been a difficult ordeal for Molly; however, it is something she had to do in order to grow.

In Her Day

In Her Day, which treats the difficulties and divisions within the women's movement of the 1970's, was Brown's second novel. The focus is on Carole, an art historian at New York University (NYU); LaVerne and Adele, women in their forties who are friends of Carole; Bon and Creampuff, a couple who are friends of the first three women; and a young woman named Ilse, a waitress in a feminist café where all the women dine one night. Ilse is attracted to Carole, and the two begin a relationship. The novel details the age conflict between Carole and Ilse and the even greater conflicting political views of the two women. Eventually, a radical newspaper exposes Carole as a lesbian to her misogynist chairman at NYU, and when she suffers at his hands she realizes that perhaps she is too conservative. In the meantime, Ilse's moderate views are influenced by Carole, and she begins to become more conservative. Although the women are unable to reach a common ground that will support their unstable relationship, the novel does illustrate a sense of compromise, which is clearly a nod from

Brown to the feminist movement that disowned her when she was young and living in New York.

This novel is weaker than the first: Brown tries too hard to be humorous, and her humor is too dark and crude for the novel. Also, *In Her Day* is somewhat harsh and offputting, with its diatribes against heterosexuals and society in general.

Venus Envy

Venus Envy, another autobiographical novel, revolves around Mary Frazier Armstrong, owner of a successful art gallery in Charlottesville, Virginia. The heroine, known as Frazier to her family and friends, is hospitalized with what is thought to be a terminal cancer. In a drug-induced state, Frazier writes letters to all the people who are important to her, including her mother, father, alcoholic brother, lover, business partner, and two gay male friends. In these letters, Frazier sums up her relationship with each recipient and then informs each one that she is a lesbian. The next time the doctor visits the hospitalized Frazier, he tells her he has made a mistake, and she will not die. The rest of the novel portrays Frazier dealing with the consequences of her letters.

With *Venus Envy*, Brown reclaims her stature as a writer who is able to use humor, in this case derived from the plot, to bring across her point that people should be accepted as they are and should be allowed to lead their own lives. The novel redeems Brown as a radical of the 1960's and 1970's. While *Rubyfruit Jungle* is clearly her best work, *Venus Envy* shows that by eliminating the strident tone of *In Her Day*, Brown could recapture her unique style and voice.

Dennis L. Weeks

Other major works

SCREENPLAY: *The Slumber Party Massacre*, 1982.

TELEPLAY: *I Love Liberty*, 1982.

POETRY: *The Hand That Cradles the Rock*, 1971; *Songs to a Handsome Woman*, 1973.

NONFICTION: *A Plain Brown Rapper*, 1976; *Starting from Scratch: A Different Kind of Writer's Manual*, 1988; *Rita Will: Memoir of a Literary Rabble-Rouser*, 1997.

TRANSLATION: *Hrotsvitha: Six Medieval Latin Plays*, 1971.

BIBLIOGRAPHY

Decure, Nicole. "The Feat of Telling It Like It Is: Concealment Tactics in Rita Mae Brown's Fiction." *Women's Studies International Forum* 17, no. 4 (July/August, 1994): 425-433. Treats Brown's condemnation of women's tendencies to conceal socially unpopular practices, such as lesbianism.

Ward, Carol Marie. *Rita Mae Brown*. New York: Twayne, 1993. A good introduction to Brown's life and works.

JOHN BUCHAN

Born: Perth, Scotland; August 26, 1875
Died: Montreal, Canada; February 11, 1940

PRINCIPAL LONG FICTION

Sir Quixote of the Moors, Being Some Account of an Episode in the Life of the Sieur de Rohaine, 1895
John Burnet of Barns, 1898
A Lost Lady of Old Years, 1899
The Half-Hearted, 1900
Prester John, 1910 (pb. in U.S. as *The Great Diamond Pipe*)
Salute to Adventurers, 1915
The Thirty-nine Steps, 1915
The Power-House, 1916
Greenmantle, 1916
Mr. Standfast, 1919
Huntingtower, 1922
Midwinter: Certain Travellers in Old England, 1923
The Three Hostages, 1924
John Macnab, 1925
The Dancing Floor, 1926
Witch Wood, 1927
The Courts of the Morning, 1929
Castle Gay, 1930
The Blanket of the Dark, 1931
A Prince of the Captivity, 1933
The Free Fishers, 1934

The House of the Four Winds, 1935
The Island of Sheep, 1936 (pb. in U.S. as *The Man from the Norlands*)
Sick Heart River, 1941 (pb. in U.S. as *Mountain Meadow*)

OTHER LITERARY FORMS

Although John Buchan is remembered chiefly for his novels, more than half of his published work is in the form of nonfiction prose. He wrote numerous biographies and works of history, and he published speeches and lectures, educational books for children, and countless articles, essays, pamphlets, notes, and reviews. Late in his life, he produced an autobiographical work, and after his death his widow edited and published two collections of selections from his works.

Buchan's fictional works include not only novels but also a story for children, *The Magic Walking-Stick* (1932), and several collections of short stories.

(CORBIS/Hulton-Deutsch Collection)

Some of the settings and situations in these stories later appeared in slightly altered form in Buchan's novels, and several of the stories in the later collections make use of characters from the novels, including Richard Hannay, Sandy Arbuthnot, and Sir Edward Leithen. Two of Buchan's volumes of short stories, *The Path of the King* (1921) and *The Gap in the Curtain* (1932), connect independent episodes and are bound together by a narrative frame; as a result, these works are sometimes listed as novels, although the individual episodes are actually quite distinct from one another.

In addition to his prose works, Buchan published a number of poems and edited three volumes of verse. He also edited several works of nonfiction, including Francis Bacon's *Essays and Apothegms of Francis Lord Bacon* (1597, edited in 1894) and Izaak Walton's *The Compleat Angler: Or, The Contemplative Man's Recreation* (1653, edited in 1901).

ACHIEVEMENTS

While he was still an undergraduate at Oxford University, Buchan received two major prizes for writing: the Stanhope Historical Essay Prize for an essay on Sir Walter Ralegh (1897) and the Newdigate Prize for Poetry for *The Pilgrim Fathers* (1898). He was graduated in 1899 with a first-class honors degree, and shortly thereafter he was appointed private secretary to the High Commissioner for South Africa (1901-1903). This was the first of many prestigious posts that Buchan filled: He was a conservative member of Parliament for the Scottish universities (1927-1935), president of the Scottish History Society (1929-1933), Lord High Commissioner to the general assembly of the Church of Scotland (1933, 1934), chancellor of the University of Edinburgh (1937-1940), and governor-general of Canada (1935-1940). In 1935, in recognition of his accomplishments and of his new post as governor-general, he was created Baron Tweedsmuir of Elsfield.

In part because of his political prominence and his reputation as a historian and in part because of his achievements as a novelist, Buchan received honorary doctorates from Oxford, Harvard, Yale, Columbia, McGill, and McMaster Universities and from the Universities of Glasgow, St. Andrews, Edinburgh, Toronto, Manitoba, and British Columbia. He also became an honorary fellow of Brasenose College, Oxford.

Although Buchan was clearly not a full-time writer of fiction, his achievements as a novelist include some degree of critical success and a great deal of commercial popularity, particularly during the period between World War I and the 1960's. His novels appealed to a wide and varied audience, including students, laborers, clergy, academics, members of various professions, and such celebrities as A. J. Balfour, Stanley Baldwin, Clement Atlee, Ezra Pound, C. S. Lewis, J. B. Priestley, King George V, and Czar Nicholas II. Although they have declined in popularity in the United States since the early 1960's, Buchan's novels continue to sell moderately well in Great Britain, and they have been translated into a number of foreign languages, including French, German, Spanish, Dutch, Danish, Czech, Swedish, and Arabic.

BIOGRAPHY

John Buchan was born in Perth, Scotland, on August 26, 1875. He spent his early childhood near the Firth of Forth, an area to which he often returned for holidays and which served as the setting for a great deal of his fiction. His father was a minister of the Free Church of Scotland; his mother was the daughter of a sheep farmer. From both of his parents, but particularly from his strong-minded mother, Buchan learned to value endurance, hard work, and, above all, perseverance, and he placed such emphasis on these qualities in his novels that many readers have come to regard this emphasis as the hallmark of his work.

When Buchan was thirteen, his father was called to the John Knox Free Church in Glasgow. There Buchan attended Hutcheson's Grammar School and, later, the University of Glasgow, whose faculty then included such scholars as Lord Kelvin, A. C. Bradley, George Ramsay, and Gilbert Murray; the latter became one of Buchan's closest friends. At the end of his third year at the University of Glasgow, Buchan won a Junior Hulme Scholarship to Oxford

University, and in the autumn of 1895, he began his studies there at Brasenose College.

Because his scholarship was not sufficient to meet all of his expenses, Buchan earned extra money by reading manuscripts for the publishing firm of John Lane; among the manuscripts that he recommended for publication was Arnold Bennett's first novel, *A Man from the North* (1898). Buchan also became a regular reviewer for several publications and continued to work steadily on his own novels and nonfiction prose. In 1898, he had the distinction of being listed in *Who's Who*: He had at that time six books in print, two in press, and three in progress, and he had published innumerable articles, essays, and reviews. He was also an active member of several prestigious Oxford and London clubs and organizations, notably the Oxford Union, of which he was librarian and later president. In 1899, he sat for his final examinations and earned a first-class honors degree; one year later, having "eaten his dinners" and passed the examination, he was called to the bar.

During the two years following his graduation, Buchan wrote leading articles for *The Spectator*, worked as a barrister, and continued to write both fiction and nonfiction. In 1901, he accepted the post of political private secretary to Lord Milner, who was then High Commissioner for South Africa. During the two years he spent in that country, Buchan became familiar with the practical administrative aspects of political situations which he had discussed on a more theoretical level in his essays for *The Spectator*. He also acquired background material for several of his novels, notably *Prester John*.

When he returned to London in 1903, Buchan resumed his legal work at the bar and his literary work on *The Spectator*. In 1906, he became second assistant editor of *The Spectator*, and, in 1907, he accepted the position of chief literary adviser to the publishing firm of Thomas Nelson. He also continued to extend the circle of acquaintances that he had begun to form at Oxford, and he became one of the best-known and most promising young men in London society and politics.

Buchan was greatly attracted to a young lady whom he met at a London dinner party, and on July 15, 1907, he and Susan Grosvenor were married at St. George's, Hanover Square. Their first child, Alice, was born one year later, followed by John (1911), William (1916), and Alastair (1918). Until the outbreak of World War I, the Buchans lived comfortably in London while John Buchan continued to write fiction, legal opinions, and essays and articles for such publications as *The Spectator* and *The Times Literary Supplement*.

Shortly after World War I began, Buchan, who had been asked to write a continuing history of the war for Nelson's and who also acted as correspondent for *The Times*, visited a number of French battlefields as a noncombatant. In 1916, he returned to France as a temporary lieutenant-colonel, acting as press officer and propagandist for the foreign office and working for Field Marshal Lord Douglas Haig as official historian. In February, 1917, he was appointed director of information, in charge of publicity and propaganda. In the midst of all of his war-related activities, between 1914 and 1918, he wrote three of his most popular novels: *The Thirty-nine Steps*, *Greenmantle*, and *Mr. Standfast*.

When World War I ended, Buchan purchased Elsfield, a country house near Oxford, and settled down to a routine of writing, working at Nelson's, and entertaining his numerous friends, including T. E. Lawrence, Robert Graves, W. P. Ker, Gilbert Murray, and A. L. Rowse. In 1919, he became a director of the Reuters news agency, and four years later he became deputy chairman. Buchan's peaceful routine at Elsfield, however, ended in the spring of 1927, when he was elected to Parliament as the member for the Scottish universities, a position he held until 1935. He became as active a member of London society during his term in Parliament as he had been as a younger man, and he became increasingly well known and influential in political circles. He was appointed Lord High Commissioner to the general assembly of the Church of Scotland in 1933 and again in 1934, and in 1935 he was appointed to a much more important post: governor-general of the Dominion of Canada. In recognition of his accomplishments and of his new position, he was created a baron; he chose as his title Lord Tweedsmuir of Elsfield.

Buchan's tenure of office as governor-general (1935-1940) coincided with the growing tension in Europe which eventually led to World War II, and, because his post was largely a ceremonial one, he had to be extremely cautious in his statements and in his behavior. Among the delicate diplomatic situations that he handled well were the visits of President Franklin Delano Roosevelt and of King George VI and Queen Elizabeth to Canada; his greatest error in diplomacy occurred when he made a speech in which he suggested that Canada's defense policy was inadequate. Despite occasional lapses of this type, however, Buchan was a successful governor-general, in part because he made a point of visiting not only such cultural centers as Montreal and Quebec but also more remote places such as Medicine Hat, Regina, Saskatoon, and Edmonton. In addition to enhancing his popularity as governor-general, these trips provided background material for his last novel, *Sick Heart River*.

As the end of his five-year term of office approached, Buchan was asked to allow himself to be nominated for another term. He refused because of his steadily declining health and his plans to leave Canada at the end of 1940. On February 6, 1940, however, he suffered a cerebral hemorrhage and, falling, struck his head; five days later he died. He left an autobiographical work, a novel, a children's history of Canada, a volume of essays, and a volume of lectures, all of which were published posthumously, as well as an unfinished novel and two chapters of a nonfiction work; these chapters appear at the end of the autobiography.

ANALYSIS

Despite his manifold activities, John Buchan is remembered primarily as a writer of implausible but exciting adventure fiction with overtones of the nineteenth century romance. Most of his novels fall into the general category of thrillers, but a few, such as *Salute to Adventurers, Midwinter, Witch Wood*, and *The Blanket of the Dark*, are more accurately classified as historical romances. Despite some variations in form and emphasis, however, all of Buchan's novels share certain features which contribute to the characteristic flavor of his fiction; these include melodramatic sequences, unusually effective descriptions of landscape and atmosphere, frequent references to such qualities as endurance and perseverance, and exciting but comparatively nonviolent action.

The melodramatic quality of Buchan's fiction arises from a number of sources, including his admiration for the highly melodramatic thrillers of E. Phillips Oppenheim and his own overdeveloped sense of the theatrical. Although Buchan was seldom original in his choice of melodramatic elements, he made good use of them in enhancing the suspense and excitement of his novels. For example, *Prester John, Greenmantle, The Three Hostages, The Dancing Floor*, and *Witch Wood* owe a great deal of their atmosphere and effect to indistinctly defined and therefore singularly mysterious antique rituals and ceremonies, including pagan sacrifice and devil worship. Other novels, including *Huntingtower, Midwinter*, and *The House of the Four Winds*, feature royalty in distress and simple but noble-hearted adventurers who risk their lives for "the cause." Buchan also made frequent use of such staple elements of melodramatic fiction as secret societies, talismans and tokens, fairylike heroines (milky-skinned and graceful), exotic villainesses (brunette and slinky), and characters who bear a Burden of Secret Sorrow.

As these examples suggest, Buchan did not hesitate to employ many of the clichés of the thriller and romance genres. Moreover, his work is not only derivative, but also repetitive, containing numerous examples of devices which he found successful and therefore used repeatedly. For example, in addition to the novels that make use of some form of magic and those that deal with royalty and adventurers, he wrote five novels in which foiling the villain depends upon decoding a cipher, six in which one of the villains tries to mesmerize the protagonist, and eleven in which one of the villains passes for a time as an irreproachable member of society. In addition to reusing successful plot devices, Buchan had the irritating habit of repeating certain favorite words, including "eldritch," "dislimn," "totem," and "frowst."

Buchan's tendency to repeat himself is not surprising in view of the speed with which he wrote. In the period between 1915 and 1936, he produced twenty-one volumes of fiction and almost thirty volumes of nonfiction. Despite his hasty writing, his repetitiveness, and his overuse of clichés, however, Buchan was by no means a mere hack. He wrote disciplined, polished, occasionally elegant prose, seldom stooping to sensationalism and describing even the most exciting or dramatic scenes in a clear narrative style that was seldom equaled in the thriller fiction of that period. More important, like Sir Walter Scott and Robert Louis Stevenson, whose work Buchan greatly admired, he was not only acutely sensitive to local color and atmosphere but also gifted in expressing that sensitivity in his fiction. He was particularly adept at making use of settings with which he was familiar: Many of his novels, including *The Thirty-nine Steps, John Macnab*, and *Witch Wood*, are set in the Scottish countryside where Buchan grew up and to which he often returned; *Prester John* is set in South Africa, where Buchan served as Lord Milner's secretary; several novels, including *The Power House* and *The Three Hostages*, contain scenes in the parts of London that he frequented during the years before World War I and during his term in Parliament; and most of the action in *Sick Heart River* takes place in the far north of Canada, which he visited during his term as governor-general.

Buchan's depiction of these familiar settings and of the atmospheres associated with them is both denotative and connotative, and this combination, which is responsible for a great deal of the power and charm of his books, does much to raise his work above the level of run-of-the-mill adventure fiction. The denotative quality of Buchan's descriptions stems from his talent in selecting the salient features of a landscape and producing vividly lifelike verbal pictures of them in disciplined and concise prose. The connotative quality results from his ability to imbue the landscape with an atmosphere that is so vivid that it might almost be called a personality and to derive from the landscape a mood or even a moral valence that complements the action of the novel. In *Witch Wood*, for example, the open and innocent Scottish countryside is marred by a black wood, which is not only an appropriate setting for the devil-

ish rites that take place in it, but also the novel implies the cause of them in some obscure manner.

In a number of Buchan's novels, the complementary relationship between the setting and the action reaches the level of allegory when the protagonist and in some cases other characters undertake a long and arduous journey through a landscape that includes steep hills, swamps or difficult waters, natural pitfalls, and traps designed by enemies who often pose as friends. The difficulties that arise in the course of this journey provide opportunities for the exciting chase scenes and the suspenseful action that are essential to adventure literature, but they also do more: As characters overcome each of the obstacles presented by the landscape through which they move, they acquire or display appropriate qualities of soul that redeem them or confirm them in their morality and status. This allegorical use of landscape, which is clearly based on one of Buchan's favorite books, John Bunyan's *The Pilgrim's Progress* (1678), serves as the central plot device in almost all of his best-known novels, including *The Thirty-nine Steps, The Power-House, Greenmantle, Mr. Standfast, Midwinter*, and *Sick Heart River*.

The most important effect of Buchan's repeated use of landscape as an allegory is the stress that this technique enables him to place upon the redeeming quality of certain types of behavior. In order to overcome the obstacles that beset them, the characters in his novels must display courage, endurance, and, above all, perseverance in hard work despite fatigue, setbacks, and apparently hopeless delays. These qualities are so central to his novels that all of his major characters are defined and evaluated in terms of them. Some characters already possess these attributes before the action begins and are finally triumphant because they successfully apply to a particular set of circumstances the qualities they had already developed and, in some cases, displayed in earlier adventures; other characters develop these attributes as the action progresses.

The protagonist with predeveloped virtues is a character type common to almost all adventure literature, and, in most cases, Buchan's treatment of it is not particularly memorable. In the novels that center around Sir Edward Leithen, however, Buchan handles the theme quite effectively, showing that even someone who spends a great deal of time at a desk can possess the courage, endurance, and perseverance of a true hero. Further, in addition to these basic qualities, Buchan endows Leithen with a degree of sensitivity that allows him to absorb and to respond to the influences of various landscapes, thus deriving from his adventures not only the satisfaction of accomplishing his external objective, but also increased insight, depth of soul, and spiritual regeneration. This theme is consistent and progressive in the Leithen novels, so that in the last one, *Sick Heart River*, Leithen's renewal of soul, resulting from his responsiveness to the influences of the environment, is carried almost to the point of apotheosis.

In addition to characters such as Leithen, who clearly possess the qualities necessary for success, Buchan's novels include a number of lesser characters who, as the action progresses, display or attain unexpected greatness of soul through unaccustomed exertion and suffering. Buchan was generally successful in dealing with such characters, in part because of the surprising liberality of his attitude toward character types who would, in most of the other adventure literature of that period, have no redeeming—or even redeemable—qualities whatsoever. Because his initial description of these characters is unusually balanced, their conversion in the course of participating in the adventure is far more convincing than it otherwise would have been.

One such character, found in Buchan's thriller, *Mr. Standfast*, is a World War I conscientious objector named Launcelot Wake who first appears as a hot-eyed, sallow young man ridiculing everything that is held sacred by the protagonist, Brigadier-General Richard Hannay. Nevertheless, Hannay, and through him the reader, finds it impossible to dislike Wake, who is strong-willed, intelligent, and sincere in his beliefs. As he willingly accompanies Hannay on a difficult and dangerous climb through an Alpine pass, voluntarily exposing himself to enemy fire on the front lines and finally receiving his death wound, Wake gradually achieves dignity, self-respect, and spiritual regeneration—yet he remains, to the end of

the novel, a staunch pacifist who resolutely refuses to take up arms. No other major thriller-writer of Buchan's generation would have had the tolerance or the breadth of mind to make a demi-hero of a recusant conscientious objector, particularly in a novel written in the middle of World War I while its author was on active service as a lieutenant-colonel in the British army.

As Buchan's sympathetic depiction of Launcelot Wake suggests, his overall point of view was far from the bellicose and sometimes fascist attitude associated with writers such as "Sapper," Edgar Wallace, and Gerard Fairlie, whose protagonists unhesitatingly inflict physical injury and even death upon villains whom they encounter. Buchan's protagonists seldom administer any form of punishment, and if the villains die at all, it is usually the result of an accident or, more rarely, at the hands of a minor character in the story. In *Greenmantle*, for example, the exotically beautiful villainess is accidentally killed by artillery fire; in *Mr. Standfast*, a German spy is killed by German fire in the trenches; in *The Three Hostages*, the arch-villain falls to his death despite Hannay's efforts to save him; in *Midwinter*, one traitor is placed on parole in consideration of his wife's feelings and another is sent into exile; in *Witch Wood*, the principal warlock is beset by his own demons and dies in his madness. Buchan never dwelt upon or glorified any form of bloodshed, and some of his novels involve no violence at all, stressing instead imaginative if occasionally melodramatic situations, suspenseful action, and seemingly insurmountable challenges to the strength and determination of the characters.

THE HANNAY NOVELS

Although all of his novels share certain common features, in some cases Buchan made use of one of his three major series protagonists, each of whom imbues the novels in which he appears with his distinctive flavor. By far the most popular of these is Richard Hannay, who is the central figure in *The Thirty-nine Steps, Greenmantle, Mr. Standfast*, and *The Three Hostages* and appears in *The Courts of the Morning* and *The Island of Sheep*. Hannay is by far the most typical thriller hero whom Buchan created:

Physically strong and morally intrepid, he is always ready for a bracing climb in the Scottish hills or a brisk run across the moors, usually dodging at least two sets of pursuers and an occasional dog. Becomingly modest regarding his own accomplishments and courage, Hannay generously admires the greatness—albeit perverted greatness—of his foes. Although several villains, including the old man with the hooded eyes in *The Thirty-nine Steps*, Hilda von Einem in *Greenmantle*, and most notably, Dominic Medina in *The Three Hostages*, try to hypnotize Hannay, he is protected by his solid common sense and by a strong will fortified by frequent cold baths. He is also more sportsmanlike than practical; for example, when he finally gets a clear shot at the highly elusive and dangerous villain of *Mr. Standfast*, he allows him to escape yet again because firing at him under those conditions seems "like potting at a sitting rabbit." On the other hand, Hannay is far from being one of the mindless anti-intellectuals who infest early twentieth century thriller literature. In *Mr. Standfast*, for example, he willingly undertakes a course of reading in the English classics, and throughout the series most of his attitudes and reflections are, if not profound, at least reasonably intelligent.

Although Hannay is by no means a mere beefy dolt, many of the opinions expressed in the course of his first-person narration reflect the prejudices common to his generation and social class, and these include racial and ethnic attitudes which many readers find offensive. Since most of the slighting references to blacks, Germans, Italians, Russians, and Jews that appear in Buchan's work are concentrated in the Hannay stories, it is possible to argue, as several of Buchan's supporters have done, that Hannay's attitudes and language arise from his characterization rather than from the kind of prejudice on Buchan's part that is associated with such writers as "Sapper," Gerald Fairlie, and Dornford Yates. Buchan's partisans also point out that there are comparatively few such references even in the Hannay books, and that these are not nearly so virulent as similar references in the works of many of Buchan's contemporaries. Further, Buchan is known to have supported a number of Jewish causes; for example, in 1932 he

succeeded Josiah Wedgwood as chairman of a pro-Zionist parliamentary committee, and in 1934 he spoke at a demonstration organized by the Jewish National Fund.

Buchan's detractors, on the other hand, point to passages in his personal correspondence that are critical of various ethnic groups. They also maintain that his attitude toward blacks, formed in part during his experience in South Africa, was paternalistic and patronizing, and it is certainly true that even when he meant to express admiration for members of the black race, as he did in *Prester John*, his attitude and his choice of language were often unconsciously—and therefore all the more offensively—condescending. Perhaps the fairest conclusion that can be drawn from this controversy is that, although some of Buchan's racial and ethnic prejudices would be considered offensive today, the prejudices that he attributed to the fictional character of Richard Hannay are probably more extreme than his own. Further, by the standards of his age and class, he was commendably moderate in his use of racial and ethnic stereotypes.

T<small>HE</small> M<small>C</small>C<small>UNN</small> N<small>OVELS</small>

Buchan's second series protagonist was Dickson McCunn. The three McCunn novels are the most overtly, yet humorously, romantic of Buchan's thrillers: *Huntingtower* features an exiled Russian princess who is loved by a left-wing poet and rescued with the help of a group of Glasgow street urchins, and *Castle Gay* and *The House of the Four Winds* deal with the restoration of the rightful Prince of Evallonia with the help of the same urchins (now grown), a reluctant newspaper magnate, and a circus elephant. McCunn himself is a middle-aged, recently retired grocer who looks forward to "Seeing Life" and "Doing Noble Deeds." He dreams of becoming involved in pure Sir Walter Scott adventures, and, because of his dreams, he tends to view real-life people and situations through a rosy, romantic haze; for example, he reverences the rather weak and worldly Prince of Evallonia as the embodiment of all the qualities associated with the Bonnie Prince Charlie of legend. Nevertheless, McCunn is saved from being ridiculous by his solid common sense and essential decency and by Buchan's implication that, if what

McCunn sees is not precisely what *is*, it is at least what *should be*.

The dramatic, in some respects melodramatic, quality of the McCunn novels is blessedly undercut by the verbal and situational humor that is their hallmark. In *Huntingtower*, for example, Wee Jaikie, the street boy who later becomes the true protagonist of *Castle Gay* and *The House of the Four Winds*, helps to rescue a Romanov princess while singing garbled versions of Bolshevik hymns that he learned at a socialist Sunday School. Similarly, at one point in *The House of the Four Winds*, a friend of Jaikie who assists him in a series of swashbuckling episodes appears outside his second-story window mounted on an elephant named Aurunculeia and asks in German for a match. Through his handling of these humorously improbable situations, Buchan gently ridiculed the more preposterous aspects of an excessively romantic view of life, while retaining and even enhancing those qualities which he never ceased to admire, such as constancy, devotion, and faith.

THE LEITHEN NOVELS

Buchan's last series protagonist, Sir Edward Leithen, is featured in four novels: *The Power-House, John Macnab, The Dancing Floor,* and *Sick Heart River*. These are somewhat atypical adventure stories, largely because they are "about" not only a series of suspenseful activities, but also a group of central themes, including the thinness of civilization and the ethic of success. These themes are expressed through the first-person narration of Leithen, who is a far more sophisticated and reflective character than Richard Hannay, Buchan's other first-person series narrator.

In view of the legal and political background with which Buchan endowed Leithen, it is not surprising that he demonstrates an intense awareness of the thinness of the shell of civilization within which he and his contemporaries desire to believe themselves safe. This concept is explored from a number of perspectives within the series: For example, in *The Power-House*, which is the earliest Leithen novel and the closest to the traditional thriller mode, the expression of this theme centers around the imminence of violence and the vulnerability of ordinary individu-

als, while in the more recondite novel *The Dancing Floor*, the thinness of civilization is associated with the terrifying attractiveness of obscurely fearsome pre-Christian religious rites to whose power Leithen himself, in many respects the quintessential civilized man, nearly succumbs.

Buchan provided a balance for the sensibility that Leithen displays in his reflections upon the thinness of civilization by attributing to him not only a shrewd and practical legal mind, but also a respect for worldly success which is so marked that it borders upon careerism. Although this emphasis upon competitive success is by no means confined to the Leithen novels, it is most evident in them. Leithen himself is greatly in demand as a solicitor, is elected to Parliament, and eventually becomes solicitor-general, and more important, the novels which he narrates contain numerous approving references to persons who are not merely successful but unsurpassed in their fields. Nevertheless, a close reading of the Leithen novels shows that although worldly success is spoken of with respect, it is treated not as an end in itself, but as a testimony to the stamina, hard work, and perseverance of the individual who has attained it. If the Leithen novels abound in references to success, they also abound in references to exhaustion, and both types of references apply to the same individuals. Success in competition with others in one's field is, in the Leithen novels, simply an extension of the Bunyanesque ethic of hard work and perseverance which, in all of Buchan's fiction, leads to success in competition with villains and with natural forces. Further, in all of Buchan's novels, worldly success is second in importance to more basic values, such as courage, honor, and compassion. To Leithen and to Buchan's other major characters, success is admirable but it is emphatically not enough.

As the preceding discussion indicates, Buchan's novels are written in polished prose and include sensitive descriptions of settings which are incorporated into both the plots of the novels and the development of the characters. Further, his liberal attitudes not only redeem his work from jingoism, egregious racism, and gratuitous violence, but also contribute to the development of less stereotyped, more varied, and more complex characters than are usually found in adventure fiction. Buchan was not, however, a serious literary figure and never claimed to be. He wrote his novels quickly and in the midst of numerous distractions, seldom revised, and often made use of clichéd situations and of devices which he himself had used, in many cases repeatedly, in earlier stories. Further, although he did create some unusually good characters, he also created a large number of cardboard ones. His villains, in particular, are with few exceptions unsubstantial figures whose machinations are overshadowed to the point of eclipse by the journey and chase scenes that dominate and, in this respect, upset the balance of several of his novels. The structure of the novels is further weakened by the fact that, although the emphasis which Buchan places upon the moral order seldom becomes overtly didactic, it does provide an excuse for the use of a profusion of providential occurrences which are virtually indistinguishable from mere blatant coincidences. Despite their flaws, however, Buchan's novels are well-written and sensitive tales of adventure whose *raison d'être* is to provide salutary entertainment; that they usually succeed in doing so is no minor accomplishment.

Joan DelFattore

OTHER MAJOR WORKS

SHORT FICTION: *Grey Weather: Moorland Tales of My Own People*, 1899; *The Watcher by the Threshold and Other Tales*, 1902; *The Moon Endureth: Tales and Fancies*, 1912; *The Path of the King*, 1921; *The Runagates Club*, 1928; *The Gap in the Curtain*, 1932.

POETRY: *The Pilgrim Fathers: The Newdigate Prize Poem, 1898*, 1898; *Ordeal by Marriage: An Eclogue*, 1915; *Poems, Scots and English*, 1917, revised 1936; *The Poetry of Neil Munro*, 1931.

NONFICTION: *Scholar Gipsies*, 1896; *Sir Walter Raleigh*, 1897; *Brasenose College*, 1898; *The African Colony: Studies in the Reconstruction*, 1903; *The Law Relating to the Taxation of Foreign Income*, 1905; *A Lodge in the Wilderness*, 1906; *Some Eighteenth Century Byways and Other Essays*, 1908; *What the Home Bill Means*, 1912; *The Marquis of*

Montrose, 1913; *Andrew Jameson, Lord Ardwall*, 1913; *Britain's War by Land*, 1915; *The Achievements of France*, 1915; *Nelson's History of the War*, 1915-1919 (24 volumes); *The Battle of Jutland*, 1916; *The Battle of Somme, First Phase*, 1916; *The Future of the War*, 1916; *The Purpose of the War*, 1916; *The Battle of Somme, Second Phase*, 1917; *The Battle-Honours of Scotland, 1914-1918*, 1919; *The Island of Sheep*, 1919 (with Susan Buchan); *The History of South African Forces in France*, 1920; *Francis and Riversdale Grenfell: A Memoir*, 1920; *Miscellanies, Literary and Historical*, 1921 (2 volumes); *A Book of Escapes and Hurried Journeys*, 1922; *The Last Secrets: The Final Mysteries of Exploration*, 1923; *The Memory of Sir Walter Scott*, 1923; *Days to Remember: The British Empire in the Great War*, 1923 (with Henry Newbolt); *Lord Minto: A Memoir*, 1924; *Some Notes on Sir Walter Scott*, 1924; *The History of the Royal Scots Fusiliers, 1678-1918*, 1925; *The Man and the Book: Sir Walter Scott*, 1925; *Two Ordeals of Democracy*, 1925; *Homilies and Recreations*, 1926; *The Fifteenth Scottish Division, 1914-1919*, 1926 (with John Stewart); *To the Electors of the Scottish Universities*, 1927; *Montrose*, 1928; *The Cause and the Causal in History*, 1929; *What the Union of the Churches Means to Scotland*, 1929; *Montrose and Leadership*, 1930; *The Revision of Dogmas*, 1930; *The Kirk in Scotland, 1560-1929*, 1930 (with George Adam Smith); *Lord Rosebery, 1847-1930*, 1930; *The Novel and the Fairy Tale*, 1931; *Sir Walter Scott*, 1932; *Julius Caesar*, 1932; *Andrew Lang and the Border*, 1933; *The Margins of Life*, 1933; *The Massacre of Glencoe*, 1933; *Gordon at Khartoum*, 1934; *Oliver Cromwell*, 1934; *The Principles of Social Service*, 1934; *The Scottish Church and the Empire*, 1934; *The University, the Library, and the Common Weal*, 1934; *The King's Grace, 1910-1935*, 1935 (pb. in U.S. as *The People's King: George V*); *The Western Mind, an Address*, 1935; *A University's Bequest to Youth, an Address*, 1936; *Augustus*, 1937; *The Interpreter's House*, 1938; *Presbyterianism: Yesterday, Today, and Tomorrow*, 1938; *Canadian Occasions: Addresses by Lord Tweedsmuir*, 1940; *Comments and Characters*, 1940 (W. Forbes Gray, editor); *Memory Hold-the-Door*,

1940 (pb. in U.S. as *Pilgrim's Way: An Essay in Recollection*); *The Clearing House: A Survey of One Man's Mind*, 1946 (Lady Tweedsmuir, editor).

CHILDREN'S LITERATURE: *Sir Walter Raleigh*, 1911; *The Magic Walking-Stick*, 1932; *The Long Traverse*, 1941 (pb. in U.S. as *Lake of Gold*).

EDITED TEXTS: *Essays and Apothegms of Francis Lord Bacon*, 1894; *Musa Piscatrix*, 1896; *The Compleat Angler: Or, The Contemplative Man's Recreation*, 1901; *Great Hours in Sport*, 1921; *A History of English Literature*, 1923; *The Nations of Today: A New History of the World*, 1923-1924; *The Northern Muse*, 1924; *Modern Short Stories*, 1926; *The Teaching of History*, 1928-1930 (11 volumes).

BIBLIOGRAPHY

Buchan, Anna. *Unforgettable, Unforgotten*. London: Hodder & Stoughton, 1945. A personal look at Buchan's life by one of his sisters. Indexed and illustrated, it is especially good for his early life.

Buchan, William. *John Buchan: A Memoir*. Toronto: Griffen House, 1982. Written by his son, this very readable biography humanizes Buchan by concentrating on his personal, rather than public, life. Based on William's childhood memories, as well as his own expertise as a novelist, poet, and literary critic. Well indexed and contains a good bibliography.

Cawelti, John G., and Bruce A. Rosenberg. *The Spy Story*. Chicago: University of Chicago Press, 1987. Cawelti's essay, "The Joys of Buchaneering," argues that Buchan's Richard Hannay stories are the crucial link between the spy adventures and the espionage novels of the twentieth century. Buchan developed a formula that was adopted and given various twists by successive authors. Includes an excellent bibliography and appendices.

Daniell, David. *The Interpreter's House: A Critical Assessment of John Buchan*. London: Nelson, 1975. Concentrates on the tension between Calvinism and Platonism in Buchan's life, identified as the key to appreciating and understanding Buchan and his works. Scholarly and very thorough, the book refutes many of the common myths about Buchan.

Green, Martin. *A Biography of John Buchan and His Sister Anna: The Personal Background of Their Literary Work*. Lewiston: The Edwin Mellen Press, 1990. A useful study of how literary talent is developed. This is a strictly chronological approach, except for the first chapter, "Heroic and Non-Heroic Values." Includes notes and bibliography.

Lownie, Andrew. *John Buchan: The Presbyterian Cavalier*. London: Constable, 1995. As the subtitle indicates, Lownie is concerned with developing the Scottish roots of Buchan's writing. This very helpful biography includes a chronology, family tree, notes, and bibliography.

Smith, Janet Adam. *John Buchan and His World*. New York: Charles Scribner's Sons, 1979. Only 128 pages, this is an updated version of an earlier biography. Makes use of new materials provided by Buchan's family and publisher. Illustrated and well written, the biography concentrates on Buchan's life as both a writer and a public servant.

PEARL S. BUCK

Born: Hillsboro, West Virginia; June 26, 1892
Died: Danby, Vermont; March 6, 1973

PRINCIPAL LONG FICTION
East Wind: West Wind, 1930
The Good Earth, 1931
Sons, 1932
The Mother, 1934
A House Divided, 1935
House of Earth, 1935
This Proud Heart, 1938
The Patriot, 1939
Other Gods: An American Legend, 1940
Dragon Seed, 1942
China Sky, 1942
The Promise, 1943
China Flight, 1945
Portrait of a Marriage, 1945
The Townsman, 1945 (as John Sedges)

Pavilion of Women, 1946
The Angry Wife, 1947 (as Sedges)
Peony, 1948
Kinfolk, 1949
The Long Love, 1949 (as Sedges)
God's Men, 1951
The Hidden Flower, 1952
Bright Procession, 1952 (as Sedges)
Come, My Beloved, 1953
Voices in the House, 1953 (as Sedges)
Imperial Woman, 1956
Letter from Peking, 1957
Command the Morning, 1959
Satan Never Sleeps, 1962
The Living Reed, 1963
Death in the Castle, 1965
The Time Is Noon, 1967
The New Year, 1968
The Three Daughters of Madame Liang, 1969
Mandala, 1970
The Goddess Abides, 1972
All Under Heaven, 1973
The Rainbow, 1974

(The Nobel Foundation)

OTHER LITERARY FORMS

An overwhelmingly prolific writer, Pearl S. Buck
wrote short stories, juvenile fiction and nonfiction,
pamphlets, magazine articles, literary history, biographies, plays (including a musical), educational
works, an Asian cookbook, and a variety of books on
America, democracy, Adolf Hitler and Germany, Japan, China, Russia, the mentally retarded, the sexes,
and the Kennedy women. In addition, she translated
Shui Hu Chuan (1933, *All Men Are Brothers*) and edited a book of Asian fairy tales, several Christmas
books, and a book of Chinese woodcuts.

Besides *The Good Earth*, her finest works are her
biographies of her parents, *The Exile* (1936) and
Fighting Angel: Portrait of a Soul (1936). *The Exile*
portrays the unhappy and frustrating life of her
mother, a missionary wife. *Fighting Angel*, a better
biography because of its greater objectivity, shows
the ruthless missionary zeal of Buck's father. Of her
early articles, "Is There a Case for Foreign Missions?," printed in *Christian Century* in 1933, created

a furor in its charges that missionaries, and churches
themselves, lacked sympathy for the people, worrying more about the numbers of converts than the
needs of the flock.

Buck also delivered several important addresses
which reveal much about her own literary philosophy, including her 1938 Nobel Prize lecture on the
Chinese novel. *Of Men and Women* (first issued in
1941; reissued in 1971 with a new epilogue) is one of
Buck's most important nonfiction works because it
gives her views of Chinese and American family life
and her warnings about "gunpowder" American
women who are educated for work yet lead idle and
meaningless lives at home.

During World War II, Buck delivered many
speeches and published articles, letters, and pamphlets on the Asian view of the war, particularly on
colonial rule and imperialism. Her most famous war

essay is probably "Tinder for Tomorrow." Buck's canon further includes personal works, such as the autobiographical *My Several Worlds: A Personal Record* (1954) and *A Bridge for Passing* (1962). Several of her plays were produced Off-Broadway or in summer stock.

ACHIEVEMENTS

Buck has been enormously successful with popular audiences, more so than with the literati. She is the most widely translated author in all of American literary history. In Denmark, for example, her popularity exceeded that of Ernest Hemingway and John Steinbeck in the 1930's, and in Sweden, ten of her books were translated between 1932 and 1940, more than those of any other American author. *The Good Earth*, her most famous work, has been translated into more than thirty languages (seven different translations into Chinese alone) and made into a play and a motion picture.

Buck's early novels received much acclaim. *The Good Earth* was awarded the Pulitzer Prize; in 1935, she was awarded the William Dean Howells medal by the American Academy of Arts and Letters for the finest work in American fiction from 1930 to 1935, and in 1936, she was elected to membership in the National Institute of Arts and Letters. In 1938, she was awarded the Nobel Prize in Literature, the third American and the fourth woman to receive it, for her "rich and generous epic description of Chinese peasant life and masterpieces of biography." *The Good Earth*, a staple of high school and undergraduate reading, is undoubtedly a masterpiece, and her missionary biographies, *The Exile* and *Fighting Angel*, though currently neglected, have merit in the depth of their analysis. Three other books of the 1930's—*Sons*, *The Mother*, and *The Patriot*—have effective passages. In all her works, Buck evinces a deep humanity, and she did much to further American understanding of Asian culture.

Buck has not fared so well with the literary establishment. Critics of the 1930's disdained her work because she was a woman, because her subjects were not "American," and because they thought she did not deserve the Nobel Prize. Her success in writing best-seller after best-seller and her optimistic faith in progress and humanity have irked later critics. She did, however, achieve success by her own standards. Her books have reached and touched middle-class American women, an enormous body of readers largely ignored by serious writers. Her innate storytelling ability does "please," "amuse," and "entertain" (her three criteria for good writing), but even the kindest of her admirers wish that she had written less, spending more time exploring the minds of her characters and polishing her work.

BIOGRAPHY

Pearl S. Buck was born Pearl Comfort Sydenstricker on June 26, 1892, in the family home at Hillsboro, West Virginia, to Absalom and Caroline (Stulting) Sydenstricker. Her parents were missionaries in China, home on a furlough. After five months she was taken to China. Her parents' marriage was not a particularly happy one because of their disparate natures. Her mother, fun-loving and witty, was torn by her devotion to God; her father, single-minded and zealous, had success with his mission but not with his family. Buck grew up in Chinkiang, an inland city on the Yangtze River. In 1900, during the Boxer Rebellion, her family was forced to flee, and she experienced the horrors of racism. Her education included one year at boarding school in Shanghai and four years at Randolph-Macon Women's College in Virginia.

In 1917, she married John Lossing Buck, an agricultural specialist. They lived in Nanhsuchon in Anhwei Province (the setting of *The Good Earth*). Buck learned much about farming from her husband and from her own observations. After five years, they moved southward to Nanking, where her husband taught agriculture and she taught English at the university. She published her first article in *The Atlantic Monthly* (January, 1923); "In China, Too" described the growing Western influence in China.

Tragedy struck Buck's life with the birth of Carol, her only biological child, who was mentally retarded (she later adopted eight children). She took Carol to the United States for medical treatment in 1925. When her husband took a year's leave of absence,

Buck studied English at Cornell University and received her master's degree. Her first published novel, *East Wind: West Wind*, combined two short stories, one of which was originally published in 1925 in *Asia* magazine. She had written a novel before *East Wind: West Wind*, but the novel was destroyed by soldiers entering her home in the 1926-1927 Nationalist Communist uprising. (During the takeover of Nanking, Buck and her family barely escaped, hiding in a mud hut until relief came.) On March 2, 1931, *The Good Earth* appeared, creating a literary sensation.

Buck's early literary influences included her parents and her old Chinese nurse. Her parents, of course, encouraged her to read the Bible and told her tales of their American homeland, while her nurse told her fantastic Buddhist and Taoist legends of warriors, devils, fairies, and dragons. She learned to speak Chinese before English, but she learned to read and write in English sooner than in Chinese. She read incessantly, Charles Dickens as a child and later Theodore Dreiser. Émile Zola and Sinclair Lewis were also important in her adult life. She paid particular tribute to Dickens: "He opened my eyes to people, he taught me to love all sorts of people." Even as a child, she decided to write: "One longs to make what one loves, and above all I loved to hear stories about people. I was a nuisance of a child, I fear, always curious to know about people and why they were as I found them." Her first writing appeared in the children's section of the *Shanghai Mercury*; in college, she contributed stories to the campus monthly and helped write the class play.

The Bucks were divorced in 1932, and that same year Pearl married her publisher, Richard J. Walsh, president of John Day and editor of *Asia* magazine. Their marriage lasted until his death in 1960. Buck loved both the United States and China throughout her life, serving as an intermediary between the two. In her last years, she was bitterly disappointed when the Chinese Communists would not grant her a visa despite the rapprochement between the United States and China.

Buck's parents instilled in their daughter principles of charity and tolerance. Her love for the needy was also awakened by Miss Jewell, the mistress of her boarding school. Jewell took Buck along as an interpreter on errands of mercy—to visit institutions for slave girls who had fled from their masters and institutions where prostitutes went for help. Buck's own humanitarian efforts began in 1941 with the founding of the East and West Association, which endeavored to increase understanding between diverse cultures. During World War II, Buck actively spoke against racism, against the internment of Japanese Americans, and against the yielding of democratic privileges during wartime.

Her sympathy extended to all, but especially to children and the helpless. In 1949, she and her husband founded Welcome House, an adoption agency for Asian American children. In 1954, her letter of protest to *The New York Times* led to the changing of a policy which put immigrants in federal prisons with criminals. In 1964, she founded the Pearl S. Buck Foundation to care for Asian American children who remained overseas. She also worked for the Training School, a school for the retarded in Vineland, New Jersey. For her many humanitarian efforts, she received the Brotherhood Award of the National Conference of Christians and Jews, the Wesley Award for Distinguished Service to Humanity, and more than a dozen honorary degrees from American colleges and universities.

Along with her extensive humanitarian activities, Buck continued to write. Because her American novels *This Proud Heart* and *Other Gods* were not well received, Buck assumed the pen name "John Sedges" to write with freedom on American subjects. Between 1945 and 1953, five novels were published under this name while she wrote Asian stories under her own name. Unfortunately, as Buck's humanitarian efforts increased, the quality of her fiction declined. Its strident and moralistic tone reflected her growing concern with social issues rather than artistic technique. She continued writing, however, and by the time of her death in 1973 had written more than eighty novels and novellas.

ANALYSIS

Pearl S. Buck's reputation for excellence as a writer of fiction rests primarily on *The Good Earth* and segments of a few of her other novels of the 1930's. The appeal of *The Good Earth* is undeniable and easy to explain: Its universal themes are cloaked in the garments of an unfamiliar and fascinating Chinese culture.

THE GOOD EARTH

Echoing many elements of life, *The Good Earth* speaks of animosity between town and country, love of land, decadent rich and honest poor, marital conflicts, interfering relatives, misunderstandings between generations, the joys of birth and sorrows of old age and death, and the strong bonds of friendship. Added to these universal themes is the cyclical movement of the growth and decay of the crops, the decline of the House of Hwand and the ascent of the House of Wang, the changes of the years, and the birth and death of the people.

Buck fittingly chose to tell her story in language reminiscent of the Bible, with its families and peoples who rise and fall. Her style also owes something to that of the Chinese storytellers, to whom she paid tribute in her Nobel Prize lecture, a style which flows along in short words "with no other technique than occasional bits of description, only enough to give vividness to place or person, and never enough to delay the story." Most of Buck's sentences are long and serpentine, relying on balance, parallelism, and repetition for strength. While the sentences are long, the diction is simple and concrete. She chooses her details carefully: Her descriptions grow out of close observation and are always concise. The simplicity of the diction and the steady, determined flow of the prose fit the sagalike plot. In Chinese folk literature, the self-effacing author, like a clear vessel, transmits but does not color with his or her personality the life which "flows through him." So, also, Buck presents her story objectively. Her authorial presence never intrudes, though her warm feeling for the characters and her own ethical beliefs are always evident.

The strength of the novel also lies in its characterization, particularly that of the two main characters, O-lan and her husband Wang Lung. Whereas characters in Buck's later novels too easily divide into good and bad, the characters of *The Good Earth*, like real people, mix elements of both. Ching, Wang Lung's faithful, doglike friend and later overseer, early in the novel joins a starving mob who ransack Wang Lung's home for food; Ching takes Wang Lung's last handful of beans. The eldest son is a pompous wastrel, but he does make the House of Hwang beautiful with flowering trees and fish ponds, and he does settle into the traditional married life his father has planned for him. Even O-lan, the almost saintly earth mother, seethes with jealousy when Wang Lung takes a second wife, and she feels contempt and bitterness for the House of Hwang in which she was a slave. Her major flaw is her ugliness. Wang Lung delights the reader with his simple wonder at the world and with his perseverance to care for his family and his land, but he, too, has failings. In middle age, he lusts for Lotus, neglecting the much-deserving O-lan, and in old age, he steals Pear Blossom from his youngest son. Rather than confusing the morality of the novel, the intermingling of good and bad increases its reality. Buck acknowledged literary indebtedness to Émile Zola, and the influence of naturalism is evident in *The Good Earth* in its objective, documentary presentation and its emphasis on the influence of environment and heredity. Unlike the naturalists, however, Buck also credits the force of free will.

The Good Earth aroused much fury in some Chinese scholars, who insisted that the novel portrays a China that never was. Younghill Kang criticized the character of Wang Lung. Professor Kiang Kang-Hu said that Buck's details and her knowledge of Chinese history were inaccurate. Buck defended herself by granting that customs differed in the many regions of China. In later novels, she retaliated by harshly portraying Chinese scholars such as Kang and Kiang, who, she believed, distorted the picture of the real China either because of their ignorance of peasant life or because of their desire to aid propagandistic efforts of the Chinese government. Other native Chinese, including Phio Lin Yutang, sprang to Buck's defense, insisting on the accuracy of her portrayal.

THE MOTHER

Like *The Good Earth*, *The Mother* follows the cyclical flow of time: The protagonist, who begins the novel in vigorous work, caring for an elderly parent, ends the novel as an elderly parent himself, cared for by the new generation. *The Mother* is also written in the simple, concrete, and sometimes poetic style of *The Good Earth*. The old mother-in-law, for example, in her early morning hunger, "belched up the evil winds from her inner emptiness." *The Mother*, however, portrays a different side of Chinese peasant life from that seen in *The Good Earth*—a more brutal one. The main character, named only "the mother," is carefully drawn; the other characters are flat and undeveloped, serving only as objects for her attention.

Deserted by her irresponsible, gambling husband, the mother lies about her spouse's absence to protect her family and cover her shame. She proves easy prey for her landlord's agent, by whom she becomes pregnant, later aborting the baby by taking medicine. Her eldest son eventually supports her, but his unfeeling wife will not tolerate having his blind sister underfoot. A husband is found for the blind girl, but when the mother travels to visit her daughter after a year, she discovers that the husband is witless and her daughter, after much mistreatment, has died. Even more sorrow darkens the mother's life. Her younger and most beloved son joins the Communists, is used as their dupe, and finally is arrested and beheaded.

This is not the honest-work-brings-rewards world of Wang Lung, but a world of victims, deformity, hatred, and cruelty. It is a portrait of the life of a woman in China, where girl babies routinely were killed and young girls of poor families were sold as slaves. Only new life—the excitement of birth and spring—balances the misery of the mother's life.

In *The Good Earth* and *The Mother*, Buck provides compelling visions of old age. Her children are mostly silent and inconsequential, her adolescents merely lusty and willful, but her elderly are individuals. The old father in *The Good Earth* cackles with life, drawing strength from his grandchildren-bedfellows. Wang Lung drowses off into a peaceful dream with his Pear Blossom. The mother-in-law basks in the sun and prides herself on wearing out her burial shrouds. The elderly mother in *The Mother* is frustrated because she no longer has the strength to work the land but remains as active as possible, trying to save her blind daughter and her Communist son, finally turning her affections to a new grandchild.

The main flaw in *The Mother* is that the mother seems too distant, too self-contained, for the reader to identify with her, to accept her as the universal mother that Buck intends her to be. The mother's story is interesting, but one does not feel her shame or her misery as one does O-lan's, nor does one feel her delight or her pride as one does Wang Lung's. Also, Buck's feelings about Communism are blatantly evident in the simplistic and oft-repeated phrase that the Communists are a "new kind of robber."

As Buck became more interested in social and political issues and in the media—magazines, film, and radio—her fiction began to deteriorate. She claimed, "The truth is I never write with a sense of mission or to accomplish any purpose whatever except the revelation of human character through a life situation." Her fiction, however, did not demonstrate this belief: More and more it became a forum for her own social and political ideas rather than an exploration of human character and life. Further, Hollywood and women's magazines began to influence her stories: They became drippingly romantic.

DRAGON SEED

Dragon Seed is one of Buck's most popular post-1930's works, with the first half of the novel containing many of the strengths of her earlier work. Her characters are not as fully realized as the mother or Wang Lung, but the story is intriguing. A peasant farming family work the land, much as their ancestors have done for centuries, until the coming of war—flying airships and enemy troops—thrusts them into a world of violence and deprivation. As long as Buck keeps her eye sharp for details, describing the atrocities the people must endure and their struggles to understand what is happening to them, the novel remains interesting.

In the second half of the novel, however, Buck's purposes split. Rather than concentrating on the war story—the people and their experiences—she uses the novel to argue that the Western world is blind and uncaring about the troubles of the Chinese in World War II. In contrast to this didacticism are the Hollywood-style love stories of Lao-Er and Jade and Lao San and Mayli. The dialogue between the happily married Lao-Er and Jade seems straight from a

B-film, and the overly coincidental coming together of Lao San and Mayli is a women's magazine romance of the self-made man and the rich, beautiful woman. Buck tries to portray the strong new woman of China (and the Western world) in Jade and Mayli, but they are *too* strong, *too* clever, almost always posturing with a defiant chin against the sunset. At one point in the novel, Buck even writes that Jade is so skillful in disguising herself that she should have been a film actress. O-lan, in her stoic silence—grudging, jealous, yet loving—is a believable woman; Jade and Mayli are creatures of fantasy.

Buck's power as a novelist derived from her intelligence, her humanity, her interesting stories, and her ability to make Chinese culture real to readers from all over the world. Her weaknesses as a novelist include didacticism, sentimentalism, and an inability to control her energy long enough to explore deeply, revise, and improve. In her later novels, she lost control of her point of view, her language, and her characterization. Her legacy is an enduring masterpiece, *The Good Earth*, and an inestimable contribution to cultural exchange between China and the West.

Ann Willardson Engar

OTHER MAJOR WORKS

SHORT FICTION: *The First Wife and Other Stories*, 1933; *Today and Forever*, 1941; *Twenty-seven Stories*, 1943; *Far and Near, Stories of Japan, China, and America*, 1947; *American Triptych*, 1958; *Hearts Come Home and Other Stories*, 1962; *The Good Deed and Other Stories*, 1969; *Once Upon a Christmas*, 1972; *East and West*, 1975; *Secrets of the Heart*, 1976; *The Lovers and Other Stories*, 1977; *The Woman Who Was Changed and Other Stories*, 1979.

NONFICTION: *East and West and the Novel*, 1932; *The Exile*, 1936; *Fighting Angel: Portrait of a Soul*, 1936; *The Chinese Novel*, 1939; *Of Men and Women*, 1941 (expanded 1971); *American Unity and Asia*, 1942; *What America Means to Me*, 1943; *China in Black and White*, 1945; *Talk About Russia: With Masha Scott*, 1945; *Tell the People: Talks with James Yen About the Mass Education Movement*, 1945; *How It Happens: Talk About the German People, 1914-1933, with Erna von Pustau*, 1947; *American*

Argument: With Eslanda Goods, 1949; *The Child Who Never Grew*, 1950; *My Several Worlds: A Personal Record*, 1954; *Friend to Friend: A Candid Exchange Between Pearl Buck and Carlos F. Romulo*, 1958; *A Bridge for Passing*, 1962; *The Joy of Children*, 1964; *Children for Adoption*, 1965; *The Gifts They Bring: Our Debt to the Mentally Retarded*, 1965; *The People of Japan*, 1966; *To My Daughters with Love*, 1967; *China As I See It*, 1970; *The Kennedy Women: A Personal Appraisal*, 1970; *The Story Bible*, 1971; *Pearl S. Buck's America*, 1971; *China Past and Present*, 1972.

CHILDREN'S LITERATURE: *The Young Revolutionist*, 1932; *Stories for Little Children*, 1940; *One Bright Day and Other Stories for Children*, 1952; *The Man Who Changed China: The Story of Sun Yat-Sen*, 1953; *Johnny Jack and His Beginnings*, 1954; *Fourteen Stories*, 1961; *The Chinese Story Teller*, 1971.

TRANSLATION: *All Men Are Brothers*, 1933 (of Shih Nai-an's novel).

BIBLIOGRAPHY

Cavasco, G. A. "Pearl Buck and the Chinese Novel." *Asian Studies* 5 (1967): 437-450. A laudatory analysis of Buck's Chinese fiction, the study divides her work into three categories. Argues forcefully that these novels, including the Pulitzer Prize-winning *The Good Earth*, remain her best work and will always be popular because they adhere to the structure of Chinese fiction.

Conn, Peter. *Pearl S. Buck: A Cultural Biography*. Cambridge, England: Cambridge University Press, 1996. Attempts to revise the "smug literary consensus" that has relegated Pearl Buck to a "footnote" in literary history. Conn does not rehabilitate Buck as a great author so much as show how her best work broke new ground in subject matter and is still vital to an understanding of American culture. Extensive notes.

Doyle, Paul A. *Pearl S. Buck*. Rev. ed. Boston: Twayne, 1980. Excellent and balanced introduction to Buck the woman and the writer. Neither adulates nor derides Buck but examines her work carefully and concludes that she was an important writer.

Harris, Theodore F. *Pearl S. Buck: A Biography.*
2 vols. New York: John Day, 1969. Harris's
work, written in very close collaboration with
Buck, is an uncritical examination of her life.
The second volume, made up entirely of personal correspondence, reveals Buck's general
philosophy.

Thompson, Dody Weston. "Pearl Buck." In
American Winners of the Nobel Prize, edited
by Warren G. French and Walter E. Kidd.
Norman: University of Oklahoma Press,
1968. Surveys some of Buck's work, reveals
its strengths and limitations, and suggests
that her appeal is limited to students, idealists, and the unsophisticated.

(Library of Congress)

JOHN BUNYAN

Born: Elstow, England; November, 1628
Died: London, England; August 31, 1688

PRINCIPAL LONG FICTION

Grace Abounding to the Chief of Sinners, 1666
*The Pilgrim's Progress from This World to That
    Which Is to Come*, Part I, 1678
The Life and Death of Mr. Badman, 1680
The Holy War, 1682
*The Pilgrim's Progress from This World to That
    Which Is to Come, the Second Part*, 1684

OTHER LITERARY FORMS

Between 1656 and 1688, John Bunyan published
forty-four separate works, including prose narratives
and tracts, sermons, and verse; ten posthumous publications appeared in a folio edition of 1692, which the
author himself had prepared for the press. A nearly
complete edition, in two volumes, was printed between 1736 and 1737, another in 1767 by George
Whitefield, and a six-volume Edinburgh edition in
1784. The best of Bunyan's verse can be found in a
small collection (c. 1664) containing "The Four Last
Things," "Ebal and Gerizim," and "Prison Medita-

tions." In addition, he wrote *A Caution to Stir Up to
Watch Against Sin* (1664), a half-sheet broadside
poem in sixteen stanzas; *A Book for Boys and Girls:
Or, Country Rhymes for Children* (1686); and *Discourse of the Building, Nature, Excellency, and Government of the House of God* (1688), a poem in
twelve parts.

ACHIEVEMENTS

The spirit of seventeenth century Protestant dis-
sent burst into flame within the heart and mind of
Bunyan. He attended only grammar school, served in
the parliamentary army at age sixteen, and returned
to Bedfordshire to undergo religious crisis and conversion. Imprisoned after the Restoration of Charles
II for refusing to obey the laws against religious dis-
sent, he turned to his pen as the only available means
of performing his divinely ordained stewardship. He
wrote his most significant work, the vision of *The
Pilgrim's Progress*, while in jail, and the piece became a companion to the Scriptures among lower-
class English Dissenters. His limited education came
from two sources: the *Actes and Monuments* (1563)

of John Foxe, containing the accounts of the martyrdom of sixteenth century English Protestants; and the Authorized Version of the Bible, the content and style of which he skillfully applied to his own prose.

Bunyan's art grew out of his natural abilities of observation and analysis. He was a Puritan and a product of the Puritan movement, yet, as can be seen clearly from the autobiographical *Grace Abounding to the Chief of Sinners*, he was chiefly interested in actual human experience, not in religious doctrine for its own sake. His allegorical characters—Mr. Timorous, Mr. Talkative, Mrs. Diffidence, Mr. By-ends, Lord Turn-about, Mr. Smooth-man, Mr. Facing-bothways—originated in everyday life. Similarly, the Valley of Humiliation, the Slough of Despond, Vanity Fair, and Fair-speech can be found by all people everywhere, no matter what their culture or religion. In *The Pilgrim's Progress*, Bunyan universalized his Puritanism, depicting every earnest Christian's search for salvation, every upright person's attempt to achieve some degree of faith. He wrote to awaken conscience, to strengthen faith, and to win souls—the last being the true object of his evangelical mission. At the same time, he managed to write tracts and narratives worthy of recognition as *literature*—even, in certain instances, as masterpieces.

BIOGRAPHY

John Bunyan was born in the village of Elstow, in Bedfordshire (one mile south of Bedford) in November, 1628. The parish register of Elstow records his baptism on November 30. His father, Thomas Bunyan, a native of Elstow, married three times between January, 1623, and August, 1644; John Bunyan was the first child of his father's second marriage—on May 23, 1627, to Margaret Bentley, also of Elstow. The boy's father was a "whitesmith," a maker and mender of pots and kettles, although by the time the son adopted the same vocation, the job reference had changed to "tinker." Young Bunyan attended a nearby grammar school (either the one at Bedford or another at Elstow), where he learned to read and write—but little else. In fact, what he did learn he promptly forgot after his father removed him from school to help in the family forge and workshop. When, in 1644, his

mother died and the elder Bunyan promptly remarried, Bunyan lost all interest in his family; he entered the parliamentary army in November, at age sixteen, and remained until the disbanding of that force in 1646. He then returned to Elstow and the family trade.

At the end of 1648 or the beginning of 1649, Bunyan married a pious but otherwise unidentified woman who bore him four children—one of whom, Mary, was born blind. He spent some four years wrestling with his finances and his soul, and in 1653 joined a dissenting sect that met at St. John's Church, Bedford. Shortly after his removal to that city in 1655, his wife died, and two years later he was called upon to preach by the Baptist sect whose church he had joined. In 1659, he married again, to a woman named Elizabeth, who spent considerable time rearing his children, bearing him two more, and trying to secure her husband's release from a series of prison terms.

Bunyan's career as a writer cannot be separated from his difficulties immediately preceding and during the Restoration of Charles II. The period of Cromwell's Commonwealth produced a number of dissenting preachers, both male and female, who achieved their offices through inspiration rather than ordination; they professed to be filled with inner light and the gifts of the Holy Spirit rather than with learning. Charles II had promised to tolerate these preachers, but the established Church, in November, 1660, set about to persecute and to silence them. Thus, Bunyan, who chose imprisonment rather than silence, spent all but a few weeks of the next eleven years in jail in Bedford, where he preached to his fellow prisoners, made tagged laces, and wrote religious books—the most noteworthy being his spiritual autobiography, *Grace Abounding to the Chief of Sinners*. He was freed in September, 1672, when Charles II, through his Declaration of Indulgence, suspended all penal statutes against Nonconformists and papists.

Upon his release from prison, Bunyan returned to his ministerial duties at St. John's Church in Bedford, this time with a license (given to him by royal authority) to preach. By 1675, however, he was again imprisoned in Bedford, the result of refusing to declare formal allegiance to Charles II (against whom he had no real objection) and the Church of England. While serving this particular sentence, Bunyan produced his most significant piece of prose, *The Pilgrim's Progress*. Bunyan's major prose works were written within the last ten years of his life, the period during which he both suffered from intolerance and received honors from the intolerant. In the last year of his life, he served as the unofficial chaplain to Sir John Shorter, the Lord Mayor of London. Indeed, Bunyan endured the entire tide of religious and political trauma of the middle and late seventeenth century: parliamentary acts, ministerial changes, popish plots, the rebellious factions. His work bears testimony to that endurance, to the patience of a nonpolitical yet deeply pious man who lost much of his freedom to the impatience of a supposedly pious but terribly political religious establishment.

Bunyan died on August 31, 1688, at the London house of his friend, John Strudwick, a grocer and chandler. Supposedly, in order to settle a dispute between a father and his son, he rode through heavy rain and caught a severe cold that led to his death. He was buried in Bunhill Fields, the burial ground of London Dissenters.

ANALYSIS

John Bunyan viewed his life as a commitment to Christian stewardship, to be carried on by gospel preaching and instructive writing. Although practically everything that he wrote reflects that commitment, he possessed the ability to create interesting variations on similar themes, keeping in mind the needs of his lower-class audience. Thus, *The Pilgrim's Progress* in an allegory of human life and universal religious experience. In *The Life and Death of Mr. Badman*, Bunyan abandoned allegory and developed a dialogue between Mr. Wiseman and Mr. Attentive through which he publicized the aims and methods of the late seventeenth century bourgeois scoundrel, whose lack of principle and honesty was well known among Bunyan's readers (the victims of Mr. Badman). Finally, his first major work, *Grace Abounding to the Chief of Sinners*, is a "spiritual autobiography" which presents adventures and experi-

ences not unlike those undergone by any human being at any moment in history who must wrestle with the fundamental questions of life. The function of Bunyan's prose in every case was to spread the Word of God and to establish a holy community of humankind in which that Word could be practiced. Once the Word took hold, Bunyan believed, the world would become a veritable garden of peace and order.

GRACE ABOUNDING TO THE CHIEF OF SINNERS

Published in 1666, *Grace Abounding to the Chief of Sinners* remains one of the most significant spiritual autobiographies by an English writer. Bunyan's style is perhaps more formal in this piece than in *The Pilgrim's Progress*, although he did well to balance the heavy phrasing of Scripture (as it appeared in the Authorized Version) with picturesque, colloquial English. A richly emotional work in which such highly charged experiences as the Last Judgment and the tortures of Hell become as clear as the mundane experiences of daily existence, Bunyan's autobiography is a narrative of spiritual adventure set against the backdrop of a real village in Britain. Although he omitted specific names and dates, obviously to universalize the piece, he did not forget to describe what he had seen after his return from the army: the popular game of "cat," with its participants and spectators; the bellringers at the parish church; the poor women sitting, in sunlight, before the door of a village house; the puddles in the road. Woven into this fabric of reality are the experiences of the dreamer; the people of Bedford appear as though in a vision on the sunny side of a high mountain, as the dreamer, shut out by an encompassing wall, shivers in the cold storm. Such interweaving of reality and fantasy was to take place again, with greater force and allegorical complexity, in the first part of *The Pilgrim's Progress*.

Bunyan's intention in *Grace Abounding to the Chief of Sinners* was to point the way by which average Christians, convinced of their own sins, can be led by God's grace to endure the pain of spiritual crisis. He determined to record how, as an obscure Bedfordshire tinker, he had changed his course from sloth and sin to become an eloquent and fearless man of God. Of course, when he wrote the work, he had been in prison for ten years, and (as stated in the preface) he set about to enlighten and assist those from whom he had, for so long a period, been separated.

From the confinement of his prison cell, Bunyan felt the desire to survey his entire life—to grasp his soul in his hands and take account of himself. Thus, *Grace Abounding to the Chief of Sinners* emerged from the heart and the spirit of a man isolated from humankind to become not merely one more testimonial for the instruction of the faithful, but a serious, psychological self-study—one so truthful and so sincere (and also so spontaneous) that it may be the first work of its kind. Bunyan's language is simple and direct, and his constant references to Scripture emphasize the typicality of his experiences as a struggling Christian. His fears, doubts, and moments of comfort are filtered through the encounter between David and Goliath and God's deliverance of the young shepherd, while his lively imagination gathers images from the Psalms and the Proverbs and reshapes them to fit the context of his spiritual experiences.

THE PILGRIM'S PROGRESS

Bunyan's ability to universalize his experience is supremely evident in *The Pilgrim's Progress*, perhaps the most successful allegory in British literature. *The Pilgrim's Progress* has as its basic metaphor the familiar idea of life as a journey. Bunyan confronts his pilgrim, Christian, with homely and commonplace sights: a quagmire, the bypaths and shortcuts through pleasant country meadows, the inn, the steep hill, the town fair on market day, the river to be forded. Such places belong to the everyday experience of every man, woman, and child; on another level, they recall the holy but homely parables of Christ's earthly ministry, and thus assume spiritual significance. Those familiar details serve as an effective background for Bunyan's narrative, a story of adventure intended to hold the reader in suspense. Bunyan grew up among the very people who constituted his audience, and he knew how to balance the romantic and the strange with the familiar. Thus, Christian travels the King's Highway at the same time that he traverses a perilous path to encounter giants, wild beasts, hobgoblins, and the terrible Apollyon, the angel of the bottomless pit with whom the central character must fight. Other travelers are worthy of hu-

morous characterization, as they represent a variety of intellectual and moral attitudes, while Christian himself runs the gamut of universal experience, from the moment he learns of his sins until the account of his meeting with Hopeful in the river.

As always, Bunyan molds his style from the Authorized Version of the Bible. By relying upon concrete, common language, he enables even the simplest of his readers to share experiences with the characters of *The Pilgrim's Progress*. Even the conversations relating to complex and tedious theological issues do not detract from the human and dramatic aspects of the allegory: Evangelist pointing the way; Christian running from his home with his fingers stuck in his ears; the starkness of the place of the Cross in contrast to the activity of Vanity Fair; the humorous but terribly circumstantial trial. It is this homely but vivid realism that accounts for the timeless appeal of Bunyan's allegory. *The Pilgrim's Progress* reveals the truth about humankind—its weakness, its imperfection, its baseness—but also its search for goodness and order.

THE LIFE AND DEATH OF MR. BADMAN

The Life and Death of Mr. Badman represents Bunyan's major attempt at a dialogue, a confrontation between the Christian and the atheist, between the road to Paradise and the route to Hell. Mr. Wiseman, a Christian, tells the story of Mr. Badman to Mr. Attentive, who in turn comments upon it. Badman is an example of the reprobate, one whose sins become evident during childhood. In fact, he is so addicted to lying that his parents cannot distinguish when he is speaking the truth. Bunyan does not place much blame upon the parents, for they indeed bear the burden of their son's actions; they even attempt to counsel him and to redirect his ways. The situation becomes worse, however, as Badman's lying turns to pilfering and then to outright stealing. All of this, naturally, leads to a hatred of Sunday, of the Puritan demands of that day: reading Scripture, attending conferences, repeating sermons, praying to God. Wiseman, the defender of the Puritan Sabbath, maintains that little boys, as a matter of course, must learn to appreciate the Sabbath; those who do not are victims of their own wickedness. Hatred of the Sabbath leads to swearing and cursing, which become as natural to young Badman as eating, drinking, and sleeping.

Badman's adult life is painstakingly drawn out through realistic descriptions, anecdotes, and dialogue. He cheats and steals his way through the world of debauchery and commerce and creates misery for his wife and seven children. Growing in importance, he forms a league with the devil and becomes a wealthy man by taking advantage of others' misfortunes. When the time comes for his end, he cannot be saved—nor does Bunyan try to fabricate an excuse for his redemption and salvation. As Mr. Wiseman states, "As his life was full of sin, so his death was without repentance." Throughout a long sickness, Badman fails to acknowledge his sins, remaining firm in his self-satisfaction. He dies without struggle, "like a chrisom child, quietly and without fear."

The strength of *The Life and Death of Mr. Badman* derives in large part from Bunyan's ability to depict common English life of the mid- and late seventeenth century. The details are so accurate, so minute, that the reader can gain as much history from the piece as morality or practical theology. Bunyan places no demands upon the reader's credulity by providential interpositions, nor does he alter his wicked character's ways for the sake of a happy ending. In portraying Badman's ways, Bunyan concedes nothing, nor does he exaggerate. Badman succeeds, gains wealth and power, and dies at peace with himself. Bunyan creates a monstrous product of sin and places him squarely in the center of English provincial life. The one consolation, the principal lesson, is that Badman travels the direct route to everlasting hellfire. On his way, he partakes of life's pleasures and is gratified by them as only an unrepentant sinner could be. For Bunyan, the harsh specificity of Badman's life is a sufficient lesson through which to promote his version of positive Christianity.

Beneath the veil of seventeenth century British Puritanism, for all its seeming narrowness and sectarian strife, there was something for all persons of all eras—the struggle to know God, to do his will, to find peace. If Bunyan's first major prose work was a spiritual autobiography, then it is fair to state that the principal efforts that followed—*The Pilgrim's Prog-*

ress and *The Life and Death of Mr. Badman*—constituted one of the earliest spiritual histories of all humankind.

Samuel J. Rogal

OTHER MAJOR WORKS

POETRY: *A Caution to Stir Up to Watch Against Sin*, 1664; *A Book for Boys and Girls: Or, Country Rhymes for Children*, 1686; *Discourse of the Building, Nature, Excellency, and Government of the House of God*, 1688.

NONFICTION: *Some Gospel Truths Opened*, 1656; *A Vindication . . . of Some Gospel Truths Opened*, 1657; *A Few Signs from Hell*, 1658; *The Doctrine of the Law and Grace Unfolded*, 1659; *Profitable Meditations Fitted to Man's Different Condition*, 1661; *I Will Pray with the Spirit*, 1663; *A Mapp Shewing the Order and Causes of Salvation and Damnation*, 1664; *One Thing Is Needful*, 1665; *The Holy City: Or, The New Jerusalem*, 1665; *A Confession of My Faith and a Reason for My Practice*, 1671; *A New and Useful Concordance to the Holy Bible*, 1672; *A Defence of the Doctrine of Justification by Faith*, 1672; *The Strait Gate: Or, The Great Difficulty of Going to Heaven*, 1676; *Saved by Grace*, 1676; *A Treatise of the Fear of God*, 1679; *A Holy Life, the Beauty of Christianity*, 1684; *Solomon's Temple Spiritualized: Or, Gospel Light Fecht Out of the Temple at Jerusalem*, 1688; *The Jerusalem Sinner Saved*, 1688.

BIBLIOGRAPHY

Collmer, Robert G. *Bunyan in Our Time*. Kent, Ohio: Kent State University Press, 1989. A collection of distinguished literary criticism and appraisals of Bunyan. Includes essays on his use of language, satire and its biblical sources, and *The Pilgrim's Progress* as allegory. Of particular interest are the essays on Marxist perspectives on Bunyan and a comparison between Bunyan's quest and C. S. Lewis's quest in *The Pilgrim's Regress* (1933).

Harrison, G. B. *John Bunyan: A Study in Personality*. New York: Archon Books, 1967. A short study that traces the mind and personality of Bunyan as shown in his writings. Discusses his conversion, his imprisonment, and his roles as pastor and writer. The close analysis of minor works makes this an important critical source.

Kelman, John. *The Road: A Study of John Bunyan's "Pilgrim's Progress."* 2 vols. Port Washington, N.Y.: Kennikat Press, 1912. These volumes are intended as a commentary or textbook, to be read point by point with *The Pilgrim's Progress.* An evangelical approach to Bunyan, filled with praise for his work. Gives close analysis of the text from a strongly Christian point of view.

Newey, Vincent. *"The Pilgrim's Progress": Critical and Historical Views.* Liverpool, England: Liverpool University Press, 1980. Brings together critical essays on *The Pilgrim's Progress* to provide fresh, detailed, and varied approaches to this work. Discusses the tension between allegory and naturalism and Bunyan's handling of the language and values of the people. Indispensable to the serious scholar of this work.

Sadler, Lynn Veach. *John Bunyan.* Boston: Twayne, 1979. A useful introduction to beginning readers of Bunyan. Discusses his life, his religious milieu, and his works. Places *Grace Abounding to the Chief of Sinners* in the genre of "spiritual autobiography." Most of the literary criticism goes to *The Pilgrim's Progress,* but there is also discussion of *The Life and Death of Mr. Badman* and *The Holy War.* Also includes a selected bibliography.

Spargo, Tamsin. *The Writing of John Bunyan.* Brookfield, Mass.: Ashgate, 1997. A detailed exploration of how Bunyan established his authority as an author. Includes notes and detailed bibliography. Recommended for advanced students and scholars.

Anthony Burgess
John Anthony Burgess Wilson

Born: Manchester, England; February 25, 1917
Died: London, England; November 25, 1993

Principal long fiction

Time for a Tiger, 1956
The Enemy in the Blanket, 1958
Beds in the East, 1959
The Doctor Is Sick, 1960
The Right to an Answer, 1960
Devil of a State, 1961
One Hand Clapping, 1961 (as Joseph Kell)
The Worm and the Ring, 1961
A Clockwork Orange, 1962 (reprinted with final chapter, 1986)
The Wanting Seed, 1962
Honey for the Bears, 1963
Inside Mr. Enderby, 1963 (as Joseph Kell)
The Eve of Saint Venus, 1964
Nothing Like the Sun: A Story of Shakespeare's Love-Life, 1964
The Long Day Wanes, 1965 (includes *Time for a Tiger*, *The Enemy in the Blanket*, and *Beds in the East*)
A Vision of Battlements, 1965
Tremor of Intent, 1966
Enderby, 1968 (includes *Mr. Enderby* and *Enderby Outside*)
Enderby Outside, 1968
MF, 1971
The Clockwork Testament: Or, Enderby's End, 1974
Napoleon Symphony, 1974
Beard's Roman Woman, 1976
Moses: A Narrative, 1976
Abba, Abba, 1977
1985, 1978
Man of Nazareth, 1979
Earthly Powers, 1980
The End of the World News, 1983
Enderby's Dark Lady, 1984
The Kingdom of the Wicked, 1985
The Pianoplayers, 1986
Any Old Iron, 1989
A Dead Man in Deptford, 1993
Byrne, 1995

Other literary forms

In addition to his novels, Anthony Burgess published eight works of literary criticism. He paid tribute to his self-confessed literary mentor, James Joyce, in such works as *Re Joyce* (1965) and *Joysprick: An Introduction to the Language of James Joyce* (1972). His book reviews and essays were collected in *The Novel Now* (1967, revised 1971), *Urgent Copy* (1968), and *But Do Blondes Prefer Gentlemen? Homage to Qwert Yuiop and Other Writings* (1986). His fascination with language and with the lives of writers led to such works as *Language Made Plain* (1964), *Shakespeare* (1970), and *Flame into Being: The Life and Work of D. H. Lawrence* (1985). An autobiographical work, *Little Wilson and Big God*, was published in 1987 (part of which was republished in 1996 as *Childhood*), and a collection of short fiction, *The Devil's Mode*, in 1989. A posthumous volume of his uncollected writings, *One Man's Chorus* (1998), includes a variety of essays divided into secions on travel, contemporary life, literary criticism, and personality sketches.

ACHIEVEMENTS

In his novels, Burgess extended the boundaries of English fiction. His inventive use of language, his use of symphonic forms and motifs, his rewriting of myths and legends, his examination of cultural clashes between the Third World and the West, and his pursuit of various ways to tell a story established him as one of the chief exemplars of postmodernism. His novels are studied in contemporary fiction courses, and he also achieved popular success with such works as *A Clockwork Orange* and *Earthly Powers*, for which he received the Prix du Meilleur Livre Étranger in 1981. Stanley Kubrick's controversial film *A Clockwork Orange* (1971) further established Burgess's popular reputation.

BIOGRAPHY

John Anthony Burgess Wilson was born in Manchester, England, on February 25, 1917. His mother and sister died in the influenza epidemic of 1918. Of Irish background, his mother had performed in the music halls of the period and was known as "the Beautiful Belle Burgess." His father performed as a silent-film pianist and when he remarried, played piano in a pub called "The Golden Eagle," owned by

(Monitor/Archive Photos)

his new wife; Burgess himself began to compose music when he was fourteen. Burgess graduated from the Bishop Bilsborrow School and planned to study music at Manchester University. When he failed a required physics entrance exam there, he changed his focus to literature and graduated from Xaverian College in Manchester; in 1940, he wrote his senior honors thesis on Christopher Marlowe, while Nazi bombs fell overhead.

In October, 1940, Burgess joined the army and was placed in the Army Medical Corps. He was later shifted to the Army Educational Corps—a prophetic move, since he became a teacher for nearly twenty years afterwards. In 1942, Burgess married Llewela Isherwood Jones, a Welsh fellow student. He spent three years, from 1943 to 1946, with the British Army on Gibraltar, during which time he wrote his first novel, *A Vision of Battlements* (which was not published until 1965).

Burgess left the army as a sergeant major and as a training college lecturer in speech and drama in 1946 to become a member of the Central Advisory Council for Adult Education in the armed forces. He lectured at Birmingham University until 1948, when he served as a lecturer in phonetics for the Ministry of Education in Preston, Lancashire. From 1950 until 1954, he taught English literature, phonetics, Spanish, and music at the Banbury grammar school in Oxfordshire.

Throughout these years, Burgess was painfully aware of his Irish heritage and Catholic religion. Though he had renounced Catholicism early, the Irish-Catholic stigma remained with him in rigorously Protestant England. His decision to apply for the job of education officer for the Colonial Service may have had something to do with his desire to leave England and his need to exile himself physically from a homeland that had already exiled him in spirit. From 1954 to 1957, he was the Senior Lecturer in English at the Malayan Teachers Training College in Kahta Baru, Malaya. There, he had more leisure time to write, and he published his first novel, *Time for a Tiger*, in 1956 under his middle names, Anthony Burgess. Members of the Colonial Service were not allowed to publish fiction under their own names.

Burgess continued working for the Colonial Service as an English-language specialist in Brunei, Borneo, from 1957 to 1959 and published two more novels, which, with his first, eventually constituted his Malayan trilogy, *The Long Day Wanes*. The clash between the manners and morals of East and West became the major focus of his early novels.

Apparent tragedy struck in 1959, when Burgess collapsed in his Borneo classroom. After excruciating medical tests, he was diagnosed with an inoperable brain tumor. He was given a year to live and was returned to England. Unable to teach, virtually penniless, Burgess set himself to writing as much as he could in order to provide for his wife. Not only had she already shown signs of the cirrhosis of the liver that was eventually to kill her, but also she had attempted suicide. In the next three years, Burgess wrote and published nine novels, including *A Clockwork Orange* and *Enderby*.

On the first day of spring, March 20, 1968, Llewela Burgess finally died. That October, Burgess married Liliana Macellari, a member of the linguis-

tics department at Cambridge, intensifying the scandal that originally developed when their affair produced a son, Andreas, in 1964. The personal guilt involved with his first wife's death always haunted Burgess and provided one of the major underlying themes of his fiction. "Guilt's a good thing," Burgess once said, "because the morals are just ticking away very nicely." In fact, persistent guilt shadows all of his characters and consistently threatens to overwhelm them completely.

Burgess, Liliana, and Andrew left England in October, 1968; they moved to Malta, to Bracciano in Italy, and eventually settled in Monaco. Burgess's life changed dramatically in 1971, when director Stanley Kubrick filmed *A Clockwork Orange*, making Burgess a celebrity. Regardless of his continuous production of new works in several genres, Burgess lived in the shadow of his 1962 novel. In 1980, he published *Earthly Powers*, a long and ambitious novel on which he had been working for more than ten years. He continued to compose symphonies and write reviews and articles for major newspapers and periodicals. He also became a skilled dramatic writer, with credits that include a version of Edmond Rostand's *Cyrano de Bergerac* (1897), produced on Broadway in 1972, the screenplay for Franco Zeffirelli's 1977 extravaganza *Jesus of Nazareth*, and *A Clockwork Orange 2004*, produced at the Barbizon Theater, London, in 1990. Burgess's production never slackened. In the last decade of his life, he produced six more novels, his last, *A Dead Man in Deptford*, being published just before his death, due to cancer, in 1993.

ANALYSIS

Anthony Burgess shares with many postmodernist writers an almost obsessive awareness of his great modernist predecessors—particularly James Joyce. The vision that Burgess inherited from modernism is informed by the anguish of a sensitive soul lost in a fragmented, shattered world. Each of Burgess's novels reveals one central character virtually "at sea" in a landscape of battered, broken figures and events. Burgess conveys this fragmented worldview by means of many of the literary devices of his modernist predecessors. Often he employs a stream-of-consciousness narration, in which his main characters tell their own stories; he also has used what T. S. Eliot, reviewing Joyce's *Ulysses* (1922), called the "mythic method," in which contemporary chaos is compared with and contrasted to heroic myths, legends, religious ceremonies, and rituals of the past. As Eliot remarked, the mythic method "is simply a way of controlling, of ordering, of giving a shape and significance to the intense panorama of futility and anarchy which is contemporary history."

Like many postmodernists, convinced that most literary forms are serious games devised to stave off approaching chaos and collapse, Burgess delights in the play of language for its own sake. Here again, Joyce is a prime source of inspiration: surprising images, poetic revelations, linguistic twists and turns, and strange evocative words nearly overwhelm the narrative shape of *Ulysses* and certainly overwhelm it in *Finnegans Wake* (1939). Burgess's best novels are those in which language for its own sake plays an important role, as in *Enderby, Nothing Like the Sun, A Clockwork Orange*, and *Napoleon Symphony*.

At the heart of his vision of the world lies Burgess's Manichean sensibility, his belief that there is "a duality that is fixed almost from the beginning of the world and the outcome is in doubt." God and the Devil reign over a supremely divided universe; they are equal in power, and they will battle to the end of the world. In the Manichean tradition—most notably, that of the Gnostics—Burgess sees the world as a materialistic trap, a prison of the spirit and a place devised by the Devil to incarcerate people until their death. Only art can break through the battlelines; only art can save him. The recasting of a religious commitment in aesthetic terms also belongs to the legacy of modernism. Burgess's Manichean vision produces such clashes of opposites as that between East and West, between the self and the state, and between a single character and an alien social environment. These recurring polarities structure Burgess's fiction.

THE RIGHT TO AN ANSWER

This principle of polarity or opposition is evident in the early novel *The Right to an Answer*, in which

J. W. Denham, businessman and exile, returns to his father's house in the suburban British Midlands and finds a provincial, self-satisfied community engaged in wife-swapping, television-viewing, and pub-crawling. He remains a detached observer, longing for a kind of communion he cannot find, and in his telling his own tale, he reveals himself as friendless, disillusioned, and homeless.

The wife-swapping quartet at the Black Swan pub is disturbed by the entrance of Mr. Raj, a Ceylonese gentleman, interested in English sociology and in satisfying his lust for white women. He plays by no rules but his own and espouses a kind of deadly Eastern realism that threatens the suburban sport. Moving in with Denham's father, he unfortunately kills the old man by "currying" him to death with his hot dishes. The upshot of this clash of cultural and social values is that Raj kills Winterbottom, the most innocent member of the *ménage à quatre*, and then kills himself.

Throughout the novel, Burgess explores both Denham's point of view and Raj's within the seedy suburban landscape. Their viewpoints reflect the irreconcilable differences between East and West, between black and white, between sex and love, and between true religion and dead ritual. Denham's stream-of-consciousness narration eventually reveals his own spirit of exile, which he cannot overcome. He remains disconnected from both worlds, from England and the East, and epitomizes the state of lovelessness and isolation that has permeated modern culture. This early novel clearly explores Burgess's main themes and narrative forms.

TREMOR OF INTENT

In the guise of a thriller à la James Bond, *Tremor of Intent* explores a world of "God" and "Not-God," a profoundly Manichaean universe. Soviet spies battle English spies, while the real villains of the novel, the "neutralists," play one camp off against the other purely for personal gain. Burgess derides the whole notion of the spy's realm, but he insists that taking sides is essential in such a world, whether ultimate good or evil is ever really confronted.

Denis Hillier, aging technician and spy, writes his confessional memoirs in the light of his possible redemption. His Catholic sense of original sin never falters for an instant, and he is constantly in need of some higher truth, some ultimate communion and revelation. In the course of the novel, he fights every Manichaean division, drinks "Old Mortality," sees himself as a "fallen Adam," and works his way toward some vision of hope. Finally, he abandons the spy game and becomes a priest, exiling himself to Ireland. From this new perspective, he believes that he can approach the real mysteries of good and evil, of free will and predestination, beyond the limiting and limited categories of the Cold War.

Hillier's opposite in the novel is Edwin Roper, a rationalist who has jettisoned religious belief and who hungers for an ultimately unified universe based on scientific truth and explanation. Such rationalism leads him to the Marxist logic of Soviet ideology, and he defects to the Russian side. Hillier has been sent to rescue him. One section of the novel consists of Roper's autobiographical explanation of his actions; its flat, logical prose reflects his methodical and disbelieving mind, in contrast to Hillier's more religious sensibility.

Within the complicated plot of the novel, self-serving scoundrels such as Mr. Theodorescu and Richard Wriste set out to destroy both Hillier and Roper and gather information to sell to the highest bidder. They fail, owing largely to the actions of Alan and Clara Walters, two children on board the ship that is taking Hillier to meet Roper. The children become initiated into the world of double agents and sexual intrigue, and Theodorescu and Wriste are assassinated.

Burgess displays his love of language for its own sake in exotic descriptions of sex, food, and life aboard a cruise ship. Such language intensifies the Manichaean divisions in the book, the constant battle between the things of this world and the imagined horrors of the next. The very language that Hillier and Roper use to tell their own stories reveals their own distinctly different personalities and visions.

Tremor of Intent insists on the mystery of human will. To choose is to be human; that is good. Thus, to choose evil is both a good and a bad thing, a Manichaean complication that Burgess leaves with

the reader. In allegorical terms the novel presents the problems of free will and its consequences, which underlie all of Burgess's fiction.

NOTHING LIKE THE SUN

Nothing Like the Sun, Burgess's fanciful novel based on the life of Shakespeare, showcases every facet of his vision and technique as a novelist. Shakespeare finds himself caught between his love for a golden man and a black woman. Sex feeds the fires of love and possession, and from these fires grows his art, the passion of language. From these fires also comes syphilis, the dread disease that eventually kills him, the source of the dark vision that surfaces in his apocalyptic tragedies. Shakespeare as a writer and Shakespeare as a man battle it out, and from that dualistic confrontation emerges the perilous equilibrium of his greatest plays.

In part, Burgess's fiction is based on the theories about Shakespeare's life which Stephen Dedalus expounds in *Ulysses*. Dedalus suggests that Shakespeare was cuckolded by his brother Richard, that Shakespeare's vision of a treacherous and tragic world was based on his own intimate experience. To this conjecture, Burgess adds the notion that the Dark Lady of the sonnets was a non-Caucasian and that Shakespeare himself was a victim of syphilis. All of these "myths" concerning Shakespeare serve Burgess's Manichaean vision: Sex and disease, art and personality are ultimately at war with one another and can only be resolved in the actual plays that Shakespeare wrote.

Nothing Like the Sun is written in an exuberant, bawdy, pseudo-Elizabethan style. It is clear that Burgess relished the creation of lists of epithets, curses, and prophecies, filled as they are with puns and his own outrageous coinings. Burgess audaciously attempts to mime the development of Shakespeare's art as he slowly awakens to the possibilities of poetry, trying different styles, moving from the sweet rhymes of "Venus and Adonis" to the "sharp knives and brutal hammers" of the later tragedies.

The book is constructed in the form of a lecture by Burgess himself to his Malayan students. He drinks as he talks and explains his paradoxical theories as he goes along. His passing out from too much drink at the novel's end parallels Shakespeare's death. He puns also with his real last name, Wilson, regarding himself as in fact "Will's son," a poet and author in his own right.

ENDERBY

Enderby is prototypic of Burgess's preoccupation with the duality of forces that influence life: the struggle between society's capacity to do good and the dilemma that human nature inevitably leads to evil. Originally conceived as a whole, *Enderby* was written as two independent novels, *Mr. Enderby* and *Enderby Outside*, for the pragmatic reason that Burgess wanted to tell at least half the tale before he died from his supposed brain tumor. One of Burgess's most popular characters, the flatulent poet F. X. Enderby, was spawned in a men's room when the author thought he saw a man feverishly writing poetry as he purged his bowels. *Enderby* is teeming with opposites, juxtaposing the sublime with the ridiculous. Enderby is catapulted into life-transforming situations as the outside world continually plays on and alters the poet's sensibilities. Burgess, the writer, examines his creation, a writer, whom he happens to admire in spite of his foibles.

Mr. Enderby and *Enderby Outside* depict the difference between transformations that originate within the individual and those that society imposes upon the individual. In the first novel, the very private poet is lured into marriage with Vesta Bainbridge, who leads him into a pop-art world that strips away his integrity and identity. Enderby achieves some success by prostituting his talent, but he is ultimately outraged when a rival poet gains fame and fortune by stealing his ideas, transforming them into a horror film. Enderby escapes from his wife and public life but is despondent and intellectually withered. He is taken to Wapenshaw, a psychologist, who "cures" him by destroying his poetic muse. Enderby is transmuted into Piggy Hogg, a bartender and useful citizen.

Enderby Outside is the mirror image of *Mr. Enderby*, transforming Hogg back into Enderby through a series of parallel experiences. Bainbridge has married a pop singer, Yod Crewsey, whose success is the result of poems stolen from Enderby. When the singer is shot, Enderby is accused of the

murder and flees, confronting the chaos and confusion of the modern world and falling prey to another woman, the sensuous Miranda Boland. During sexual intercourse with Boland, inspiration finally strikes Enderby. In the end, he meets a sibylline girl, Muse, who leads him to his art. Enderby is as he began, alone and free, but a poet.

THE CLOCKWORK TESTAMENT and
ENDERBY'S DARK LADY

In *Enderby*, Burgess shows that the master must come to peace with both his body and society before he can indulge in the intellectual. Shortly after the film version of *A Clockwork Orange* was released, Enderby returned in *The Clockwork Testament: Or, Enderby's End*, which satirized the writer reduced to production assistant by the film industry. Enderby dies of a heart attack when he sees the violent, pornographic film made from his novel. Just as British detective novelist Arthur Conan Doyle was forced to return Sherlock Holmes to life, Burgess resurrects his antihero in *Enderby's Dark Lady*. Enderby travels to Indiana, where he writes the libretto for a ridiculous musical about Shakespeare. Burgess directs his satire at American culture, but his exploration of the poetic muse is sacrificed for the comic adventure.

EARTHLY POWERS

Earthly Powers, Burgess's longest novel, features perhaps his most arresting first sentence: "It was the afternoon of my 81st birthday, and I was in bed with my catamite when Ali announced that the archbishop had come to see me." Thus begin the memoirs of Kenneth Toomey, cynical agnostic and homosexual writer, a character based loosely on Somerset Maugham.

Toomey's memoirs span the twentieth century—its literary intrigues, cultural fashions, and political horrors. Toomey is seduced on June 16, 1904, that Dublin day immortalized by Joyce in *Ulysses*, revels in the Paris of the 1920's, the Hollywood of the 1930's, and the stylish New York of the 1940's and 1950's; his old age is spent in exotic exile in Tangier and Malta in the 1970's. During his long life he writes plays and film scenarios, carries on with a host of male secretary-lovers, and experiences the traumas of Nazism and Communism. He abhors the state-controlled collective soul, which he sees as the ultimate product of the twentieth century.

Burgess's huge, sprawling novel displays a plot crowded with coincidence and bursting with stylistic parodies and re-creations. A priest on his way to becoming pope saves a dying child, only to see him grow up to be the leader of a fanatical religious cult akin to that of Jim Jones in Guyana. An American anthropologist and his wife are butchered during a Catholic mass in Africa: The natives there take the commands of the ceremony all too literally and swallow their visitors.

Toomey believes that evil lies firmly within all people and that his experiences of the twentieth century prove that the world is a murderous place. His Manichean opposite in faith is his brother-in-law, Carlo Campanati, the gambler-gourmet priest who becomes Pope Gregory XVII. Evil remains external to humanity, the pope maintains; humankind is essentially good. In Burgess's jaundiced view of things, such misconceived idealism produces only further evils. Any similarities between Gregory and John XXIII are strictly intentional.

The world of *Earthly Powers* is Toomey's world, a bright place with clipped, swift glimpses of fads and fashion. Librettos, snippets of plays, even a recreation of the Garden of Eden story from a homosexual point of view appear in this modernist memoir. The style itself reflects Burgess's conception of the "brittle yet excruciatingly precise" manner of the homosexual.

Earthly Powers wobbles. More than six hundred pages of bright wit can cloy. Verbal surfaces congeal and trail off into trivial documentation. The pope's spiritual observations impede the novel's progress, encased as they are in lectures, sermons, and tracts. Indeed, Gregory is as thin a character as Toomey is an interesting one.

The book proves that Toomey is right: Things are rotten. No amount of linguistic fun, modernist maneuverings, or Manichaean machinations can change the fact that this is the worst of all possible worlds. Chunks of smart conversation cannot hide that fact; they become stupefying and evasive in the end. The nature of free will, however, and its legacy of unquestionable evil in the twentieth century pervade Burgess's fat book and linger to undermine any "safe" position the reader may hope to find.

A CLOCKWORK ORANGE

Burgess's Manichaean nightmare in *A Clockwork Orange* occupies the center of his most accomplished book. The language of *nadsat* in its harsh, Russian-accented diction, the ongoing battle between the State and Alex the *droog*, the vision of an urban landscape wracked with violence and decay, the mysterious interpenetration of Beethoven and lust, and the unresolved issues of good and evil reflect and parallel one another so completely that the novel emerges as Burgess's masterpiece.

The issue raised is an increasingly timely one: Can the state program the individual to be good? Can it eradicate the individual's right to freedom of choice, especially if in choosing, he or she chooses to commit violent and evil acts? Burgess replies in the negative. No matter how awful Alex's actions become, he should be allowed to choose them.

Since the novel is written from Alex's point of view, the reader sympathizes with him, despite his acts of rape and mayhem. Alex loves Beethoven; he "shines artistic"; he is brighter than his ghoulish friends; he is rejected by his parents. He is in all ways superior to the foul futuristic landscape that surrounds him. When the state brainwashes him, the reader experiences his pain in a personal, forthright manner. The violence in the rest of the book falls upon outsiders and remains distanced by the very language Alex uses to describe his actions.

Burgess's slang creates a strange and distant world. The reader approaches the novel as an outsider to that world and must try diligently to decode it to understand it. Never has Burgess used language so effectively to create the very atmosphere of his fiction. The Russian-influenced slang of the novel is a tour de force of the highest order and yet functions perfectly as a reflection of Alex's state of mind and of the society of which he is a rebellious member.

The world of *A Clockwork Orange* recognizes only power and political force. All talk of free will dissolves before such a harrowing place of behaviorist psychologists and social controllers. Individual freedom in such a world remains a myth, not a reality, a matter of faith, not an ultimate truth. Everyone is in some sense a clockwork orange, a victim of his or her society, compelled to act in a social order that celebrates only power, manipulation, and control.

Even the cyclical form of *A Clockwork Orange* reveals a world trapped within its own inevitable patterns. At first, Alex victimizes those around him. He in turn is victimized by the state. In the third and final part of the novel, he returns to victimize other people once again: "I was cured all right." Victimization remains the only reality here. There are no loopholes, no escape hatches from the vicious pattern. The frightening cityscape at night, the harsh language, the paradoxical personality of Alex, the collaborationist or revolutionary tactics of Alex's "friends," and the very shape of the novel reinforce this recognition of utter entrapment and human decay. "Oh, my brothers," Alex addresses his readers, as Eliot in *The Waste Land* (1922) quoted Charles Baudelaire: *"Hypocrite lecteur, mon semblable, mon frère."*

Despite Burgess's pessimistic vision of contemporary life and the creative soul's place in it, the best of his novels still reveal a commitment to literature as a serious ceremony, as a game which the reader and the writer must continue to play, if only to transcend momentarily the horrors of Western civilization in the twentieth century.

Samuel Coale, updated by Gerald S. Argetsinger

OTHER MAJOR WORKS

SHORT FICTION: *The Devil's Mode*, 1989.

SCREENPLAY: *Jesus of Nazareth*, 1977.

TELEPLAY: *Moses the Lawgiver*, 1976.

NONFICTION: *English Literature: A Survey for Students*, 1958 (as John Burgess Wilson); *The Novel Today*, 1963; *Language Made Plain*, 1964; *Here Comes Everybody: An Introduction to James Joyce for the Ordinary Reader*, 1965 (pb. in U.S. as *Re Joyce*, 1965); *The Novel Now*, 1967, rev. ed. 1971; *Urgent Copy: Literary Studies*, 1968; *Shakespeare*, 1970; *Joysprick: An Introduction to the Language of James Joyce*, 1972; *Ernest Hemingway and His World*, 1978; *On Going to Bed*, 1982; *This Man and Music*, 1983; *Flame into Being: The Life and Work of D. H.*

Lawrence, 1985; *But Do Blondes Prefer Gentlemen? Homage to Qwert Yuiop and Other Writings*, 1986 (also known as *Homage to Qwert Yuiop*, 1985); *Little Wilson and Big God*, 1987 (partly reprinted as *Childhood*, 1996); *You've Had Your Time*, 1990; *A Mouthful of Air: Languages, Languages—Especially English*, 1992; *One Man's Chorus: The Uncollected Writings*, 1998.

CHILDREN'S LITERATURE: *A Long Trip to Teatime*, 1976.

TRANSLATIONS: *The Man Who Robbed Poor-Boxes*, 1965 (of Michel Servin's play); *Cyrano de Bergerac*, 1971 (of Edmond Rostand's play); *Oedipus the King*, 1972 (of Sophocles' play).

MISCELLANEOUS: *On Mozart: A Paean for Wolfgang*, 1991.

BIBLIOGRAPHY

Aggeler, Geoffrey, ed. *Critical Essays on Anthony Burgess*. Boston: G. K. Hall, 1986. A collection of well-regarded criticism on Burgess, with particular attention given to his "linguistic pyrotechnics." Aggeler's introduction presents an overview of Burgess's work and discussion of his novels, followed by a *Paris Review* interview with Burgess.

Bloom, Harold, ed. *Modern Critical Views: Anthony Burgess*. New York: Chelsea House, 1987. A compilation of fine critical essays, including an essay by the eminent critic of James Joyce, Robert Martin Adams, who considers Joyce's influence on Burgess. In the introduction, Bloom presents his views on Burgess's writing, citing *Inside Mr. Enderby* as one of the most underrated English novels of this era.

Boytinck, Paul W. *Anthony Burgess: An Annotated Bibliography and Reference Guide*. New York: Garland, 1985. A checklist of Burgess's works up to 1984, including bibliographical background on Burgess and extracts from reviews, essays, and articles on his work. An excellent and informative resource for both the beginning reader and scholar of Burgess.

Critique: Studies in Modern Fiction 27 (Fall, 1981). This special issue gathers together seven critical essays on Burgess, some of which are appreciative—"Burgess is clearly in command of his material," in reference to *Earthly Powers*—and others which are less favorable—"Burgess' plots have a tendency to twitch and gyrate."

Keen, Suzanne. "Ironies and Inversions: The Art of Anthony Burgess." *Commonweal* 121 (February 11, 1994). This is an examination of the "Catholic quality" in Burgess's fiction and nonfiction. Focuses primarily upon the autobiographies, the literary criticism of Joyce's works, and Burgess's final novel, *A Dead Man in Deptford*.

Mathews, Richard. *The Clockwork Orange Universe of Anthony Burgess*. San Bernardino, Calif.: Borgo Press, 1978. This admiring monograph traces the thematic and temporal concerns that led Burgess to write his futuristic novels, including *A Clockwork Orange*. Mathews discusses ten novels that fit the metaphor of "clockwork universe."

Stinson, John J. *Anthony Burgess Revisited*. Boston: Twayne, 1991. This is particularly valuable for biographical information and critical analysis of the later works. Particular attention is given Burgess's increasing reputation as a public intellectual and the use of language, the importance of moral choice, and the conflict between the Pelagian and Augustinian philosophies in his works.

FANNY BURNEY

Born: King's Lynn, England; June 13, 1752
Died: London, England; January 6, 1840

PRINCIPAL LONG FICTION

Evelina: Or, The History of a Young Lady's
    Entrance into the World, 1778
Cecilia: Or, Memoirs of an Heiress, 1782
Camilla: Or, A Picture of Youth, 1796
The Wanderer: Or, Female Difficulties, 1814

OTHER LITERARY FORMS

In addition to editing the memoirs of her father—the noted organist, composer, and music historian

Dr. Charles Burney (1726-1814)—Fanny Burney wrote an *Early Diary, 1768-1778* (1889) and then a later *Diary and Letters, 1778-1840* (1842-1846). The first work, not published until 1889, contains pleasant sketches of Samuel Johnson, James Boswell, David Garrick, and Richard Brinsley Sheridan. Notable figures from government and the arts march across the pages of the early diary, which scholars have claimed surpasses her fiction in literary quality. The latter diary and correspondence appeared between 1842 and 1846; the seven volumes are notable for the record of the writer's meeting in her garden with the insane George III of England, the account of her glimpse of Napoleon I, and the recollections of her chat with the weary Louis XVIII of France.

Of her eight dramatic productions, three are worthy of mention: *The Witlings* (never published); *Edwy and Elgiva*, written in 1790, performed at Drury Lane on March 21, 1795, and withdrawn after the first night; and *Love and Fashion*, written in 1800, accepted by the manager at Covent Garden, but never performed. Finally, Burney published, in 1793, a political essay entitled *Brief Reflections Relative to the French Emigrant Clergy*, an address to the women of Great Britain in behalf of the French emigrant priests.

ACHIEVEMENTS

Most critics tend to place the reputation of Burney within the shadow of her most immediate successor, Jane Austen. Reasons for this assessment are not immediately clear, especially in the light of responses to the novels from contemporary readers. Burney's problem during the past two centuries, however, has not concerned popularity, subject matter, or even literary style; rather, certain personal circumstances under which she wrote seriously reduced her artistic effectiveness and considerably dulled her reputation. Essentially, Burney produced fiction at a time in history when a lady of means and social standing could not easily write fiction and still be considered a lady. Adding to that inhibition was the aura of her noted and influential father and his circle of even more influential friends: Samuel Johnson, Mrs. Hester Lynch Thrale Piozzi, Oliver Goldsmith, and Sir Joshua Reynolds. Both her father and his friends held literary standards not always easy for a self-educated young woman to attain. She burned her early manuscript efforts, wrote secretly at night, and published anonymously; she labored under the artistic domination of her father and the advice of his friends; she remained cautious, intimidated by and dependent on elderly people who served as guardians of her intellect.

Nevertheless, Burney succeeded as a novelist and achieved significance as a contributor to the history and development of the English novel. She brought to that genre an ability to observe the natural activities and reactions of those about her and to weave those observations through narrative structures and character delineations similar to those employed by her predecessors: Samuel Johnson, Henry Fielding, Samuel Richardson, Tobi2as Smollett, Aphra Behn, Mary De La Riviere Manley, Eliza Heywood, and Clara Reeve. In her preface to *Evelina*, she set forth the criteria that, throughout her fiction, she would develop and maintain. For Burney, the novel would be the means by which to portray realistic persons and to represent the times in which they functioned. In her own concept of the form, those characters had to be real but not necessarily true; they had to be drawn "from nature, though not from life." Further, those same fictional characters had to confront and solve complex human problems—problems that they might avoid for a time but eventually would be forced to encounter.

Although Burney's four novels were published anonymously, the sophisticated readers of the day recognized the woman's point of view and immediately set the works apart from those of their contemporaries. The female readership, especially, both appreciated and praised the woman's view of the contemporary world; on the other hand, the young dandies of the late eighteenth century and the pre-Victorian age scoffed at the novels' heroines as comic sentimentalists, products of blatant amateurism, and characteristic examples of a sex that would continue to be dominated by men.

The real basis on which to place Burney's popularity, however, rests with the ability of the novelist to develop fully the effects of female intelligence upon and within a society dominated by men and to

(Library of Congress)

convince her audience that coexistence between the sexes was far more beneficial than the dominance of one over the other. The essential difference between Fanny Burney and her female predecessors (Aphra Behn is the most obvious example) is the extent to which the issue of feminism was developed and then thrust forward as a major consideration.

As a woman writing about women, Burney could not cling too long to the models that the past century had provided for her. Despite the mild increase in the numbers of female novelists during the last quarter of the eighteenth century, Burney had little guidance in developing the woman's point of view. She had, essentially, to find her own way within the confines of a limited world and even more limited experience. Thus, she determined early to purge her fictional environment of masculine influence. In its place, she would establish the importance of her titled characters as working parts in the machinery of eighteenth century British society. Burney's heroines do not convey appearances of being rebels, radicals, or social freaks; rather, their creator has drawn each one of them with a fine and firm hand. As a group, they are indeed meant to be carbon copies of one another; individually, each portrays a young lady in pursuit of traditional goals: marriage, money, and the discovery of the self.

BIOGRAPHY

Fanny (Frances) Burney, later Madame D'Arblay, the third of six children of Charles Burney and Esther Sleepe Burney, was born on June 13, 1752, at King's Lynn, Norfolk, where her father served as church organist while recuperating from consumption. In 1760, his health completely restored, Burney moved his family to London, where he resumed his professional involvements in teaching, composition, and music history. Upon the death of Esther Burney on September 28, 1761, two of the children (Esther and Susannah) went to school in Paris, while Frances remained at home. Apparently, Dr. Burney feared that his middle daughter's devotion to her grandmother (then living in France) would bring about the child's conversion to Catholicism. He seemed prepared to change that point of view and send Frances to join her sisters, when, in 1766, he married Mrs. Stephen Allen. Thus, the fourteen-year-old girl remained at home in London, left to her own educational aims and directions, since her father had no time to supervise her learning. She had, at about age ten, begun to write drama, poetry, and fiction; on her fifteenth birthday, she supposedly burned her manuscripts because she felt guilty about wasting her time with such trifles.

Still, she could not purge her imagination, and the story of Evelina and her adventures did not die in the flames of her fireplace. Her brother, Charles, offered the first two volumes of *Evelina* to James Dodsley, who declined to consider an anonymous work for publication; Thomas Lowndes, however, asked to see the completed manuscript. After finishing *Evelina* and then securing her father's permission, Burney gave the work to the London publisher, who issued it in January, 1778, and paid the writer thirty pounds and ten bound copies. Its success and popularity owed some debt to Dr. Burney, who passed the novel

on to Mrs. Thrale, a prominent figure in London's literary society. From there, it made its way to the select seat of London's intellectual empire, presided over by Dr. Johnson, Joshua Reynolds, and Edmund Burke. Shortly afterward, Fanny Burney met Mrs. Thrale, who took the new novelist into her home at Streatham (south of London) and introduced her to Johnson, Reynolds, Sheridan, and Arthur Murphy—all of whom pressed her to write drama. The result took the form of *The Whitlings*, a dramatic piece that, principally because of her father's displeasure over the quality of the work, she never published.

Returning to the form that produced her initial success, Burney published *Cecilia* in the summer of 1782, further advancing her literary reputation and social standing. She met Mary Delany, an intimate of the royal family, who helped secure for her an appointment in July, 1786, as second keeper of the Queen's robes, a position worth two hundred pounds per year. Her tenure at court proved to be more of a confinement than a social or political advantage because of the menial tasks, the rigid schedule, and the stiffness of the Queen and her attendants.

The activities and events at court, however, did contribute to the value of Burney's diaries, though her health suffered from the extreme physical demands of her labors. She continued in service until July, 1791, at which time she sought and gained permission to retire on a pension of one hundred pounds per annum. Then followed a period of domestic travel aimed at improving her health, followed by her marriage, on July 31, 1793, to General Alexandre D'Arblay, a comrade of the Marquis de Lafayette and a member of the small French community living at Juniper Hall, near Mickleham (north of Dorking, in Surrey). The couple's entire income rested with Madame D'Arblay's pension, and thus she sought to increase the family's fortunes through her writing. A tragedy, *Edwy and Elgiva*, lasted but a single night at Drury Lane, but a third novel, *Camilla*, generated more than three thousand pounds from subscriptions and additional sales, although the piece failed to achieve the literary merit of *Evelina* or *Cecilia*.

In 1801, General D'Arblay returned to France to seek employment but managed only a pension of fifteen hundred francs. His wife and son, Alexander, joined him the next year, and the family spent the succeeding ten years at Passy, in a state of quasi exile that lasted throughout the Napoleonic Wars. Madame D'Arblay and her son returned to England in 1812, and there, the novelist attended her aged father until his death in April, 1814. Her last novel, begun in France in 1802 and entitled *The Wanderer*, appeared early in 1814. Again, the financial returns far exceeded the literary quality of the piece; there were considerable buyers and subscribers but extremely few readers. After Napoleon's exile, the novelist returned to her husband in Paris; she then went to Brussels after the emperor's return from Elba. General D'Arblay, meanwhile, had been seriously injured by the kick of a horse, which brought about an immediate end to his military career. The family returned to England to spend the remainder of their years: General D'Arblay died on May 3, 1818, and Alexander died on January 19, 1837—less than a year after having been nominated minister of Ely chapel. In November, 1839, Madame D'Arblay suffered a severe illness and died on January 6, 1840, in her eighty-seventh year.

ANALYSIS

Despite the relative brevity of her canon, Fanny Burney's fiction cannot be dismissed with the usual generalizations from literary history: specifically that the author shared the interests of her youthful heroines in good manners. She possessed a quick sense for the comic in character and situation, and those talents distinctly advanced the art of the English novel in the direction of Jane Austen. From one viewpoint, she indeed exists as an important transitional figure between the satiric allegories of the earlier eighteenth century and the instruments that portrayed middle-class manners in full flourish during the first quarter of the nineteenth century.

Burney's contemporaries understood both her method and her purpose. Samuel Johnson thought her a "real wonder," one worth being singled out for her honest sense of modesty and her ability to apply it to fiction, while Edmund Burke seemed amazed by her knowledge of human nature. Three years after

her death, Thomas Babington Macaulay proclaimed that the author of *Evelina* and *Cecilia* had done for the English novel what Jeremy Collier, at the end of the seventeenth century, did for the drama: maintain rigid morality and virgin delicacy. Macaulay proclaimed that Fanny Burney had indeed vindicated the right of woman "to an equal share in a fair and noble promise of letters" and had accomplished her task in clear, natural, and lively "woman's English."

Nevertheless, Fanny Burney contributed more to the English novel than simply the advancement of her sex's cause. Her heroines are mentally tormented and yet emerge as wiser and stronger human beings. The fictional contexts into which she placed her principal characters are those that readers of every time and place could recognize: situations in which the proponents of negative values seem to prosper and the defenders of virtue cling tenaciously to their ground. Burney's women must learn the ways of a difficult world, a society composed of countless snares and endless rules; they must quickly don the accoutrements for survival: modesty, reserve, submission, and (above all else) manners. What makes Burney's depiction of women in society particularly poignant is the knowledge that the author herself had to endure trials of survival. An awareness of the author's accounts of actual struggles for social survival, then, becomes a necessity for understanding and appreciating the problems confronted by her fictional characters.

EVELINA

In Burney's first novel, *Evelina*, the title character brings with her to London and Bristol two qualities most difficult for a young provincial girl to defend: her sense of propriety and her pure innocence—the latter quality not to be confused with ignorance. In London, Evelina stumbles into false, insecure situations because she does not comprehend the rules of the social game. During the course of eighty-five epistles, however, she learns. The learning process is of utmost importance to Burney, for it serves as both plot for her fiction and instruction for her largely female readership. Once in London, life unfolds new meanings for Evelina Anville, as she samples the wares of urbanity: assemblies, amusements, parks and gardens, drawing rooms, operas, and theaters. Accompanying the activities is a corps of sophisticates by whose rules Evelina must play: Lord Orville, the well-bred young man and the jealous lover; Sir Clement Willoughby, the obnoxious admirer of Evelina who tries (through forged letters) to breach the relationship between Orville and Evelina; Macartney, the young poet whom Evelina saves from suicide and against whom Orville exercises his jealous streak; Captain Mirvan, the practical joker who smiles only at the expense of others; Mrs. Beaumont, who would have the heroine believe that good qualities originate from pride rather than from principles; Lady Louisa Larpent, the sullen and distraught (but always arrogant) sister of Lord Orville who tries to separate her brother from Evelina; Mr. Lovel, a demeaning fop who constantly refers to Evelina's simple background; the Watkins sisters, who chide Evelina because they envy her attractiveness to young men.

Despite these obstacles of situation and character, however, Evelina does not lack some protection. The Reverend Arthur Villars, her devoted guardian since the death of her mother, guides and counsels the seventeen-year-old girl from his home in Dorsetshire. Villars receives the major portion of Evelina's letters; in fact, he initally advises her to be wary of Lord Orville but then relents when he learns of his ward's extreme happiness. Since Evelina cannot count on immediate assistance from Villars, she does rely on several people in London. Mrs. Mirvan, the amiable and well-bred wife of the captain, introduces Evelina to a variety of social affairs, while their daughter, Maria, becomes the heroine's only real confidante, sharing mutual happiness and disappointment. Finally, there is the Reverend Villars's neighbor, Mrs. Selwyn, who accompanies Evelina on a visit to Bristol Hot Wells. Unfortunately, the one person closest to Evelina during her London tenure, her maternal grandmother, Madame Duval, proves of little use and even less assistance. A blunt, indelicate, and severe woman, she is bothered by her granddaughter's display of independence and vows that the young lady will not share in her inheritance.

Villars emerges as the supporting character with the most depth, principally because he is ever present in the letters. From the novel's beginning, the heroine reaches out to him for guidance and support, scarcely prepared "to form a wish that has not [his] sanction." The local clergyman, Villars serves as parent for a motherless and socially fatherless young lady who, for the first time, is about to see something of the world. Thus, Villars's caution and anxiety appear natural, for he knows the bitter effects of socially unequal marriages, as in the cases of Evelina's own parents and grandparents. He naturally mistrusts Lord Orville and fears the weakness of the young girl's imagination. Everyone knows that as long as Evelina remains obedient to Villars's will, no union between her and Orville can occur. Once the girl's father, Sir John Belmont, repents for his many years of unkindness to his daughter and then bequeaths her thirty thousand pounds, however, the guardian cleric no longer remains the dominant influence. Lord Orville proceeds to put his own moral house in order and supplants his rivals; the reserve felt by Evelina because of the Reverend Villars's fears and anxieties gradually disintegrates, and the romance proceeds towards its inevitable conclusion.

The process may be inevitable, but it is sufficiently hampered by a series of struggles and conflicts, as is typical of the late eighteenth century novel of manners. Both her grandmother and Mrs. Mirvan provide Evelina with fairly easy access to fashionable society, but the socialites in that society involve the girl in a number of uncomfortable and burdensome situations. For example, Biddy and Polly Branghton and Madam Duval use Evelina's name in requesting the use of Lord Orville's coach. Evelina realizes the impropriety of the request and knows that Orville's benevolence would never permit him to refuse it. Furthermore, Tom Branghton, an admirer of Evelina, solicits business from Orville also by relying on Evelina's name; he does so after damaging the borrowed vehicle. Evelina's innocence forces her to bear the responsibility for her relatives' actions and schemes, although she opposes all that they attempt. Fortunately, the fierce determination with which she advances her innocence and honesty enables her to endure such problems until rescued, in this case, by Lord Orville and Mrs. Selwyn. Vulgarity (Madam Duval), ill breeding (the Branghtons), and impertinence (Sir Clement Willoughby) eventually fall before the steadfastness and the force of Evelina's emerging wisdom and strength. Burney here demonstrates the specific means by which an eighteenth century woman could surmount the perplexities of that era.

Cecilia

If Evelina Anville must defend her innocence and honesty against the social vultures of London and Bristol, Cecilia Beverley, the heroine of *Cecilia*, carries the added burden of retaining a fortune left to her by an eccentric uncle. She must withstand assaults upon her coffers from a variety of attackers. One of her guardians, Mr. Harrel, draws heavily upon Cecilia's funds to repay the moneylenders who underwrite his fashionable existence. At the other extreme, Mr. Briggs, the third legally appointed guardian, manages Cecilia's money during her minority. Although wealthy in his own right, Briggs evidences obvious eccentricity and uncouthness; he is a miser who wants the heroine to live with him to conserve money. In the middle stands another guardian, Compton Delvile, who has priorities other than money; however, he can hardly be recommended as an asset to the development of his ward. Simply, Delvile cares only to preserve the family name, and beneath his pride lie hard layers of meanness. Against such onslaughts upon her morality and her fortune Cecilia must rebel; she is both angry and bewildered at what Burney terms as "acts so detrimental to her own interest."

Unlike Evelina, who has many opportunities to address and receive concerns from a surrogate parent, Cecilia has few people and even less guidance upon which to rely. *Cecilia* revealed to the world not only a trio of impotent guardians but also a number of irritating male characters who devote considerable time to tormenting her. Obviously bent upon revealing the grotesqueness and instability of London life, Burney created a variety of grotesque and unstable supporting players: Harrel, Dr. Lyster, Mrs. Wyers, and Mrs. Hill are some examples. Clearly, Burney's characters in *Cecilia* were total strangers to the mainstream of the late eighteenth century fictional world, even though they truly belonged to reality. While at times creating humorous scenes and incidents, these ugly characters nevertheless produced a disturbing effect upon the novelist's reading audience. Unfortunately, from a social or historical perspective, that audience was not yet ready for significant action to effect social change, which meant that much of the novel's force was lost amid the apathy of its audience.

Camilla

The publication of *Camilla*, eighteen years after *Evelina* and fourteen following *Cecilia*, marked the reappearance of a young lady entering society and enduring shameful experiences. Like her immediate predecessor, Cecilia Beverley, Camilla Tyrold has money problems, only hers involve involuntary indebtedness. Also like *Cecilia*, the novel contains several grotesque minor characters, whose manners and actions play psychological havoc with Camilla's attempts to overcome her distress. Particularly vulgar are Mr. Dubster and the mercenary Mrs. Mittin, aided by the overscholarly Dr. Orkborne and the foppish Sir Sedley Clarendel. A major problem, however, is that these characters are pulled from the earlier novels. On the surface, *Camilla* gives evidence that Burney has matured as a writer and as a commentator on the affairs of women, but that maturity did not broaden her literary experience. If anything, there are signs of regression, for Camilla definitely lacks Evelina's common sense and her instinct toward feminine resourcefulness.

Camilla further suffers from its length; Burney barely holds the plot together through countless episodes, intrigues, misunderstandings, all in front of a backdrop of drollery and absurdity. Stripped of its comic elements, the novel is no more than an overstrained romance. Burney's motive, however, was to draw the exact conditions that brought about Camilla's collection of debts and thus contributed to her highly anxious state of mind. Burney rises to her usual level of excellence in detailing the plight of a woman distracted and deprived by misfortune not of her own doing. For late eighteenth century women, especially, such misfortune carried with it an underlying sense of shame. Thus, Burney gave to English prose fiction a sense of psychological depth not always apparent in the works of her female counterparts or in those fictional efforts written by men but concerned with women.

THE WANDERER

Burney's last novel, *The Wanderer*, appeared in 1814 and became lost in the new sensibility of Jane Austen and Maria Edgeworth. The work, however, reveals Burney's determination that the nineteenth century should not forget its women. Her heroine—known variously as L. S. (or Ellis), Incognita, Miss Ellis, and Juliet—determines that the cause of her suffering points directly to the fact that she was born a woman, which automatically places her on the lowest rung of the social order. The woman's lot contains little beyond the usual taboos, disqualifications, discomforts, and inconveniences; the novelist, through the various predicaments of Juliet Granville, rarely allows her readers to forget the degree to which her heroine must suffer because of society's insensitivity and stupidity. *The Wanderer*, like Burney's previous novels, has a number of supporting characters; some of these, while they do not always understand Juliet's plight, at least try to help her through her difficulties. Others, such as Mrs. Ireton and Miss Arbe, represent the tyranny, frivolity, and insensitivity of the times and thus merely compound Juliet's problems.

The strength of *The Wanderer*, however, lies in its thematic relationship to the three earlier novels. Although Burney tends to repeat herself, particularly through her minor characters—and again the plot hardly deserves the length of the narrative—her ability to depict the misgivings of those who are driven by external circumstances to earn a livelihood through unaccustomed means is powerful. In coming to grips with an obvious and serious problem of her time, she demonstrated how her major fictional characters and she herself, as a character from the real world, could indeed rely successfully upon the resources endowed upon all individuals, female as well as male. If nothing else, the novelist showed her society and the generations that followed not only how well women could function in the real world but also how much they could contribute and take advantage of opportunities offered them. In a sense, Burney's composi-

tions belong to social history as much as to literature, and they serve as some of the earliest examples of a struggle that has yet to be won.

Samuel J. Rogal

OTHER MAJOR WORKS

PLAYS: *Edwy and Elgiva: A Tragedy*, pr. 1795; *Love and Fashion*, pr. 1800; *The Complete Plays of Frances Burney*, pb. 1995 (2 volumes).

NONFICTION: *Brief Reflections Relative to the French Emigrant Clergy*, 1793; *Diary and Letters, 1778-1840*, 1842-1846 (7 volumes; Charlotte Frances Barrett, editor); *The Early Diary of Frances Burney, 1768-1778*, 1889 (Anne Raine Ellis, editor).

EDITED TEXT: *Memoirs of Dr. Charles Burney*, 1832.

BIBLIOGRAPHY

Bloom, Harold, ed. *Fanny Burney's "Evelina": Modern Critical Interpretations*. New York: Chelsea House, 1988. This group of essays, written between 1967 and 1988, focuses on Burney's first novel. Included are essays by Ronald Paulson, Susan Staves, Patricia Meyer Spacks, Judith Lowder Newton, Mary Poovey, Jennifer A. Wagner, and Julia L. Epstein. Bloom's introduction disparages the feminist tendency of recent Burney criticism, even though this volume includes primarily feminist approaches to Burney's work. This collection of focused essays provides an illuminating look at current critical opinion of *Evelina*.

Epstein, Julia L. *The Iron Pen: Frances Burney and the Politics of Women's Writing*. Madison: University of Wisconsin Press, 1989. Takes a feminist approach, focusing primarily on the violence, hostility, and danger in Burney's work. Finds these parts of her novels to be generally controlled, but occasionally bursting forth into rage. This study meshes moments of physical and emotional danger and pain from Burney's life with similar images in her novels. Epstein's interest lies in Burney's construction of a self-image that plays down danger and violence but that she is frequently unable to control. The bibliography and index are excellent and quite helpful.

Simons, Judy. *Fanny Burney.* Totowa, N.J.: Barnes &
Noble Books, 1987. Contains a condensed look at
Burney's life. The introductory biographical essay
places Burney in a tradition of other women writers, such as Elizabeth Inchbald, Mary Wollstonecraft Godwin, and Eliza Haywood, and discusses
these women's views on their roles in society. Includes a chapter on the heroines of Burney's novels; a chapter on each of her four best-known
works, *Evelina, Cecilia, Camilla*, and *The Wanderer*; and one on her journals and plays. The bibliography is short but helpful, especially since it
includes a section on works about women's history in the eighteenth century.

Straub, Kristina. *Divided Fictions: Fanny Burney and
Feminine Strategy.* Lexington: University Press of
Kentucky, 1987. Examines the "ambiguous social
definition of the woman novelist at mid-century,"
specifically as it related to Burney. A feminist approach grounded in eighteenth century cultural
history. Devotes three chapters to *Evelina*, one to
Cecilia, and one to both *Camilla* and *The Wanderer*. Straub's introductory chapter, "Critical
Methods and Historic Contexts," is excellent and
useful, as well as the chapter "The Receptive
Reader and Other Necessary Fictions," which
makes intriguing points about Burney's reaction
to the publicity of being a novelist and part of the
literary circles of her day.

Zonitch, Barbara. *Familiar Violence: Gender and So-
cial Upheaval in the Novels of Frances Burney.*
Newark: University of Delaware Press, 1997.
Chapters on *Evelina, Cecilia, Camilla*, and *The
Wanderer*. See especially Zonitch's introduction,
"Social Transformations: The Crisis of the Aris-
tocracy and the Status of Women." Includes de-
tailed notes and excellent bibliography.

WILLIAM S. BURROUGHS

Born: St. Louis, Missouri; February 5, 1914
Died: Lawrence, Kansas; August 2, 1997

PRINCIPAL LONG FICTION

Junkie, 1953
The Naked Lunch, 1959 (republished as *Naked
Lunch*, 1962)
The Soft Machine, 1961
The Ticket That Exploded, 1962
Dead Fingers Talk, 1963
Nova Express, 1964
The Wild Boys: A Book of the Dead, 1971
Cities of the Red Night, 1981
The Place of Dead Roads, 1983
The Burroughs File, 1984
Queer, 1985
The Western Lands, 1987
My Education: A Book of Dreams, 1995
Ghost of Chance, 1995

OTHER LITERARY FORMS

Because of their experimental techniques, William Burroughs's works are especially difficult to
classify within established literary forms. *Exterminator!* (1973), for example, although published as a
"novel," is actually a collection of previously published poems, short stories, and essays. Other
unclassifiable works are book-length experiments,
often written in collaboration and in the "cut-up,
fold-in" technique pioneered by Burroughs, which
might be considered novels by some. Examples of
such works are *Minutes to Go* (1960), written in collaboration with Sinclair Beiles, Gregory Corso, and
Brion Gysin; *The Exterminator* (1960), written with
Gysin; *Time* (1965), which contains drawings by
Gysin; and *Œuvre Croisée* (1976), written in collaboration with Gysin and reissued as *The Third Mind* in
1978. *White Subway* (1965), *Apomorphine* (1969),
and *The Job: Interviews with William S. Burroughs*
(1970), written in collaboration with Daniel Odier,
are additional short-story and essay collections. *The
Dead Star* (1969) is a journalistic essay that contains
photocollage inserts; *APO-33 Bulletin: A Metabolic
Regulator* (1966) is a pamphlet; and *Electronic Revolution 1970-71* (1971) is an essay that fantasizes bizarre political and business uses for the cut-up, fold-
in technique. Burroughs has also published scores of
essays, stories, and articles in numerous journals, pe-

riodicals, and short-lived magazines. One of Burroughs's most revealing publications, *The Yage Letters* (1963), collects his correspondence with Allen Ginsberg concerning Burroughs's 1952 expedition to South America in search of yage, a legendary hallucinogen. In these letters, Burroughs is Govinda, the master, to Ginsberg's Siddhartha, the disciple.

ACHIEVEMENTS

Although his novel *Naked Lunch* was made notorious by American censorship attempts and consequently became a best-seller, Burroughs wrote primarily for a cult audience. He is essentially a fantasist and satirist, is often misread, and in these respects has accurately been compared to Jonathan Swift. Both writers focus on the faults and evils of humankind and society, employ fantastic satire to ridicule these shortcomings, and hope through this vehicle to effect some positive change in the human condition. Burroughs's works are exceptionally vicious satires, however, "necessarily brutal, obscene and disgusting"—his own description of them— because they must mime the situations from which their recurring images and metaphors (of drug addiction, aberrant sexual practices, and senseless violence) are drawn.

(Archive Photos)

Superficially, Burroughs's satiric attacks are aimed at humanity's "addictions" to pleasure or power in any of the many forms either craving might take. Those who, obeying the dictates of "the algebra of need," will stop at nothing to fulfill their desires have, in the terms of the moral allegory Burroughs creates, "lost their human citizenship" and become nonhuman parasites feeding on the life essences of others. They shamelessly lie, cheat, and manipulate to attain what Burroughs's associative imagery repeatedly equates with perversion, excrement, and death. Burroughs's satire, however, cuts deeper than this. It attacks not only humankind and its addictions but also the structures of the cultures that enable these addictions to flourish and proliferate. It attacks the myths and linguistic formulas that imprison the human race, the stone walls of patriotism and religion. It demands that people first free themselves from these "word and image addictions" before they kick their more obvious habits and regain their humanity, and thus calls for nothing less than a revolution of consciousness.

The Grove Press edition of *Naked Lunch* became a national best-seller and was cleared of obscenity charges in Los Angeles in 1965 and in Massachusetts in 1966. Ginsberg and Norman Mailer, who asserted that Burroughs is "the only American novelist living today who may conceivably be possessed by genius," were among those who testified in the book's defense. While it does detail with exceptional brutality the ugly, revolting, and perverse, *Naked Lunch* is at bottom a strikingly moral but darkly comic work that employs irony and allegory, as well as more unconventional techniques, to satirize much that is false and defective in modern American life in particular and human nature in general. Especially effective as a subliminal argument against heroin abuse, the book's

successful publication in America elevated its heretofore practically unknown author to membership in
the literary elite.

Many reviewers—some seemingly oblivious to
the irony of Burroughs's works—have not been responsive or sympathetic to his themes and techniques, and none of his novels after *Naked Lunch*,
with the exception of *The Wild Boys: A Book of the
Dead*, received comparable critical acclaim. While
Naked Lunch was lauded by Terry Southern, Mary
McCarthy, Karl Shapiro, and Marshall McLuhan, as
well as by Ginsberg and Mailer, the less successfully
realized subsequent novels were considered by some
critics, not totally inaccurately, as "language without
content" and "the world's greatest put-on." Burroughs himself admitted that "*Naked Lunch* demands
silence from the reader. Otherwise he is taking his
own pulse." He warned that his novels do not present
their "content" in the manner the reader ordinarily
anticipates. One of the triumphs of Burroughs's
unique style is that he has created a low-content
form, a narrative near vacuum, upon which the un-
wary reader is tempted to project his own psyche,
personal myths, or forgotten dreams. While they do
have their own message to convey, his works also encourage the reader to develop or invent his or her private fictions and to append them to the skeletal narrative structure provided by the author. Readers are
thus invited to create the work as they read it. In
place of relying on the easily perceived, clearly coherent story the reader might have expected, Burroughs's best work keeps one reading through the
hypnotic fascination of the author's flow of images
and incantatory prose.

BIOGRAPHY

William Seward Burroughs was born on February 5, 1914, in St. Louis, Missouri, to Perry Mortimer
Burroughs, son of the industrialist who invented the
cylinder that made the modern adding machine possible, and Laura Lee, a direct descendant of Robert E.
Lee, Civil War general and commander in chief of
the Confederate army. Dominated by his mother's
obsessive Victorian prudery and haunted by vivid
nightmares and hallucinations, Burroughs led a rest-

less childhood. He was educated in private schools in
St. Louis and Los Alamos, New Mexico, where he
developed seemingly disparate fascinations with literature and crime, and later studied ethnology and
archaeology at Harvard University, where he encountered a set of wealthy homosexuals. He was graduated
with an A.B. in 1936.

Subsequently, Burroughs traveled to Europe,
briefly studied medicine at the University of Vienna,
and returned to the United States and Harvard to resume his anthropological studies, which he soon abandoned because of his conviction that academic life is
little more than a series of intrigues broken by teas.
Although he attempted to use family connections to
obtain a position with the Office of Strategic Services,
Burroughs was rejected after he deliberately cut off
the first joint of one finger in a Vincent van Gogh-
like attempt to impress a friend. Moving to New York
City, he worked as a bartender and in an advertising
agency for a year and underwent psychoanalysis.
Burroughs entered the Army in 1942 as a glider pilot
trainee, engineered his discharge for psychological
reasons six months later, and then moved to Chicago,
where he easily found work as an exterminator and a
private detective, among other odd jobs.

In 1943, Burroughs returned to New York City and
met Joan Vollmer, a student at Columbia University
whom he married on January 17, 1945. She introduced Burroughs to Jack Kerouac, who in turn introduced him to Ginsberg. The Beat generation was born
in Burroughs's 115th Street apartment after Burroughs
acquainted Kerouac and Ginsberg with the writings
of William Blake, Arthur Rimbaud, and others; the
three friends soon emerged as leaders of the movement. Late in 1944, Herbert Huncke, a Times Square
hustler involved in criminal activity to support his
drug habit, introduced Burroughs to the use of morphine and its derivatives. Burroughs was for most of
the next thirteen years a heroin addict who frequently
altered his place of residence to evade the police.

He moved to Waverly, Texas, where he tried farming, in 1946; had a son, William, Jr., in 1947; and
voluntarily entered a drug rehabilitation center at
Lexington, Kentucky, in 1948. Returning to Waverly
and already back on drugs, Burroughs was hounded

by the police until he moved to Algiers, Louisiana, later that same year. To avoid prosecution for illegal possession of drugs and firearms after a 1949 raid on his Algiers farm, Burroughs relocated to Mexico City in 1950, where he began writing *Junkie*. He continued his archaeological studies at Mexico City University, pursuing an interest in the Mayan codices. On September 7, 1951, Burroughs accidentally killed his wife while allegedly attempting to shoot a champagne glass off her head while playing "William Tell." Although Mexican authorities let the matter drop, Burroughs soon left Mexico for the jungles of Colombia.

He returned again to New York City in 1953, the year *Junkie* was published, lived for a while with Ginsberg, and then settled in Tangier, Morocco, where from 1955 to 1958 he was frequently visited by other Beat writers and worked on the manuscript that would develop into his quartet of science-fiction-like novels: *Naked Lunch*, *The Soft Machine*, *Nova Express*, and *The Ticket That Exploded*. In 1957, Burroughs again sought treatment for his heroin addiction. This time he placed himself in the care of John Yerby Dent, an English physician who treated drug addicts with apomorphine—a crystalline alkaloid derivative of morphine—a drug Burroughs praises and mythologizes in his writings. The following year, cured of his addiction, Burroughs moved to Paris, where *The Naked Lunch* was published in 1959.

In 1960, Gysin, who had helped Burroughs select the Paris edition of *The Naked Lunch* from a suitcase full of manuscript pages, introduced his experimental "cut-up" technique to Burroughs and collaborated with him on *The Exterminator* and *Minutes to Go*. Burroughs's literary reputation was firmly established with the American publication of *Naked Lunch* in 1962, and by the mid-1960's Burroughs had settled in London. He returned to St. Louis for a visit in 1965, covered the Democratic National Convention for *Esquire* in 1968, and moved again to New York to teach writing at City College of New York in 1974. In 1975, he embarked on a reading tour of the United States and conducted a writers' workshop in Denver, Colorado. After returning to London briefly, Burroughs settled in New York. In 1983, he was inducted into the American Academy and Institute of Arts and Letters.

Burroughs published a number of novels and collections throughout the 1980's and 1990's, including 1987's *The Western Lands*, the last novel in the trilogy that included *Cities of the Red Night* and *The Place of Dead Roads*. Burroughs moved to rural Kansas shortly after the publication of this novel, where he died in 1997.

ANALYSIS

William Burroughs did not begin writing seriously until 1950, although he had unsuccessfully submitted a story entitled "Twilight's Last Gleaming" to *Esquire* in 1938. His first novelistic effort, *Queer*, which deals with homosexuality, was not published until 1985. Allen Ginsberg finally persuaded Ace Books to publish Burroughs's first novel, *Junkie*, which originally appeared with the pseudonym William Lee, as half of an Ace double paperback. It was bound with Maurice Helbront's *Narcotic Agent*. While strictly conventional in style, *Junkie* is a luridly hyperbolic, quasi-autobiographical first-person account of the horrors of drug addiction. Of little literary merit in itself, this first novel is interesting in that it introduces not only the main character, Lee, but also several of the major motifs that appear in Burroughs's subsequent works: the central metaphor of drug addiction, the related image of man reduced to a subhuman (usually an insectlike creature) by his drug and other lusts, and the suggestion of concomitant and pervasive sexual aberration.

In *Naked Lunch* and its three less celebrated sequels, *The Soft Machine*, *Nova Express*, and *The Ticket That Exploded*, Burroughs weaves an intricate and horrible allegory of human greed, corruption, and debasement. Like Aldous Huxley's *Brave New World* (1932) and George Orwell's *Nineteen Eighty-Four* (1949), these four works seize on the evils or tendencies toward a certain type of evil—which the author sees as particularly malignant in the contemporary world—and project them into a dystopian future, where, magnified, they grow monstrous and take on an exaggerated and fantastic shape. While progressively clarifying and developing Burroughs's thought, these novels share themes, metaphorical images, characters, and stylistic mannerisms. In them, Burroughs utilizes the "cut-up, fold-in" technique which has its closest analog in the cinematic technique of montage. He juxtaposes one scene with another without regard to plot, character, or, in the short view, theme, to promote an association of the reader's negative emotional reaction to the content of certain scenes (sexual perversion, drug abuse, senseless violence) with the implied allegorical content of others (examples of "addictions" to drugs, money, sex, power). The theory is that if such juxtapositions recur often enough, the feeling of revulsion strategically created by the first set of images will form the reader's negative attitude toward the second set of examples.

In these novels, Burroughs develops a science-fiction-like, paranoid fantasy wherein, on a literal level, Earth and its human inhabitants have been taken over by the Nova Mob, an assortment of extraterrestrial, non-three-dimensional entities who live parasitically on the reality of other organisms. Exploitation of Earth has reached such proportions that the intergalactic Nova Police have been alerted. The Nova Police are attempting to thwart the Nova Mob without so alarming them that they will detonate the planet in an attempt to destroy the evidence (and thus escape prosecution in the biologic courts) while trying to make what escape they can. The most direct form of Nova control, control that enables the Nova Mob to carry on its viruslike metaphysical vampirism with impunity, is thought control of the human population through control of the mass communication media. Nova Mob concepts and perspectives attach themselves to and are replicated by the terrestrial host media much as a virus invades and reproduces through a host organism, a thought-control process analogous to the "cut-up, fold-in" technique itself. By the middle of *Nova Express*, the reader is caught up in a war of images in which the weapons are cameras and tape recorders. The Nova Police and the inhabitants of Earth have discovered how to combat the Nova Mob with their own techniques (of which these novels are examples) and are engaged in a guerrilla war with the Nova Criminals, who are desperately trying to cut and run. The ending of *The Ticket That*

Exploded is optimistic for Earth but inconclusive, leaving the reader to wonder if Earth will be rid of the Nova Mob or destroyed by it.

NAKED LUNCH

A vividly and relentlessly tasteless fantasy-satire that portrays humankind's innate greed and lack of compassion in general and contemporary American institutions and values in particular, *Naked Lunch* immerses the reader in the impressions and sensations of William Lee (Burroughs's pseudonym in *Junkie*). Lee is an agent of the Nova Police who has assumed the cover of a homosexual heroin addict because with such a cover he is most likely to encounter Nova Criminals, who are all addicts of one sort or another and thus prefer to operate through human addict collaborators. Nothing of importance seems to occur in the novel, and little of what does happen is explained. Only toward the conclusion does the reader even suspect that Lee is some sort of agent "clawing at a not-yet of Telepathic Bureaucracies, Time Monopolies, Control Drugs, Heavy Fluid Addicts." The "naked lunch" of the title is that reality seen by Lee, that "frozen moment when everyone sees what is on the end of every fork." The random scenes of mutilation and depravity, bleak homosexual encounters, and desperate scrambles for drug connections into which the book plunges yield its two key concepts: the idea of addiction, the central conceit that men become hooked on power, pleasure, illusions, and so on much as a junkie does on heroin, and that of "the algebra of need," which states simply that when an addict is faced with absolute need (as a junkie is) he will do anything to satisfy it.

The Nova Criminals are nonhuman personifications of various addictions. The Uranians, addicted to Heavy Metal Fluid, are types of drug addicts. Dr. Benway, Mr. Bradley Mr. Martin (a single character), and the insect people of Minraud—all control addicts—are types of the human addiction to power. The green boy-girls of Venus, addicted to Venusian sexual practices, are types of the human addiction to sensual pleasure. The Death Dwarf, addicted to concentrated words and images, is the analog of the human addiction to various cultural myths and beliefs; he is perhaps the most pathetic of these depraved creatures. Burroughs explains that "Junk yields a basic formula of 'evil' virus: the face of evil is always the face of total need. A dope fiend is a man in total need of dope. Beyond a certain frequency need knows absolutely no limit or control." As poet and literary critic John Ciardi noted,

> Only after the first shock does one realize that what Burroughs is writing about is not only the destruction of depraved men by their drug lust, but the destruction of all men by their consuming addictions, whether the addiction be drugs or over-righteous propriety or sixteen-year-old girls.

THE SOFT MACHINE

Burroughs sees *The Soft Machine* as "a sequel to *Naked Lunch*, a mathematical extension of the Algebra of Need beyond the Junk virus." Here, the consuming addiction, displayed again in juxtaposition with scenes of drug abuse and sexual perversion, and through a number of shifting narrators, is the addiction to power over others. The central episode is the destruction by a time-traveling agent of the control apparatus of the ancient Mayan theocracy (Burroughs's primary archaeological interest), which exercises its control through the manipulation of myths; this is a clear analog of the present-day struggle between the Nova Police and the Nova Mob that breaks into the open in the subsequent two novels.

The time traveler uses the same technique to prepare himself for time travel as Burroughs does in writing his novels, a type of "cut-up, fold-in" montage: "I started my trip in the morgue with old newspapers, folding in today with yesterday and typing out composites." Since words tie men to time, the time traveler character is given apomorphine (used to cure Burroughs of his heroin addiction) to break this connection.

The "soft machine" is both the "wounded galaxy," the Milky Way seen as a biological organism diseased by the viruslike Nova Mob, and the human body, riddled with parasites and addictions and programmed with the "ticket," obsolete myths and dreams, written on the "soft typewriter" of culture and civilization. Burroughs contends that any addiction dehumanizes its victims. The Mayan priests, for

example, tend to become half-men, half-crab creatures who eventually metamorphosize into giant centipedes and exude an erogenous green slime. Such hideous transformations also strike Lee, a heroin addict, and other homosexuals. Bradley the Buyer, who reappears as Mr. Bradley Mr. Martin, Mr. and Mrs. D., and the Ugly Spirit, has a farcical habit of turning into a bloblike creature who is addicted to and absorbs drug addicts.

NOVA EXPRESS and THE TICKET THAT EXPLODED

Instances of metamorphosis are almost innumerable in *Nova Express* and *The Ticket That Exploded*. These novels most clearly reveal the quartet's plot and explore the Nova Mob's exploitation of media. Here addiction to language is investigated. As Stephen Koch argues,

> Burroughs's ideology . . . is based on an image of consciousness in bondage to the organism: better, of consciousness as an organism, gripped by the tropisms of need. Consciousness is addicted—it is here the drug metaphor enters—to what sustains it and gives it definition: in particular, it is addicted to the word, the structures of language that define meaning and thus reality itself.

Thus, while in *The Soft Machine* the time traveler is sent to Trak News Agency (whose motto is "We don't report the news—we write it") to learn how to defeat the Mayan theocracy by first learning "how this writing the news before it happens is done," in *The Ticket That Exploded* it is axiomatic that "you can run a government without police if your conditioning program is tight enough but you can't run a government without [nonsense and deception]."

Contemporary existence is seen ultimately as a film that is rerun again and again, trapping the human soul like an insect imprisoned in amber, negating any possibility of choice or freedom. In these last two novels, Burroughs issues a call for revolt against humanity's imprisoning addiction to language. In *Nova Express*, he notes that "their garden of delights is a terminal sewer" and demands that everyone heed the last words of Hassan I Sabbah (cribbed out of context from Fyodor Dostoevski's Ivan Karamazov): "Nothing is True—Everything is Permitted." In *The Ticket*

That Exploded, he rages, "Better than the 'real thing'?—There is no real thing—Maya—Maya—It's all show business."

THE WILD BOYS

Burroughs's other notably science-fiction-like novel, *The Wild Boys*, is also composed of scenes linked more by associated images than by any clearly linear narrative framework. Here, the author posits a bizarre alternative to the problematical apocalypse-in-progress depicted in his earlier quartet. In a world wrecked by famine and controlled by police, the wild boys, a homosexual tribe of hashish smokers, have withdrawn themselves from space and time through indifference and have developed into a counterculture complete with its own language, rituals, and economy. The existence of this counterculture poses a threat to those who create the false images upon which the larger, repressive, external society is based; but the wild boys cannot be tamed because their cold indifference to the mass culture entails a savagery that refuses to submit to control. Although Burroughs's thinking clearly becomes more political in *The Wild Boys* and in the book that followed it, *Exterminator!*, a collection of short stories and poems that revolve around the common theme of death through sinister forces, his primary concern for freedom from the controllers and manipulators—chemical, political, sexual, or cultural—has remained constant from the beginning of his literary career.

CITIES OF THE RED NIGHT

Continuing the utopian vision of *The Wild Boys*, but encompassing it into a larger, more anthropological context, Burroughs's next three works form a trilogy to expand his vision of society and its place in the natural order. The first book in the series, *Cities of the Red Night*, continues the twin themes of freedom from control and the power of mythmaking, but does so on a much larger scale. One of Burroughs's longest works, *Cities of the Red Night* is unique in that in it he sustains a rather conventional narrative voice, utilizing conventional popular genre, to achieve a re-creation of history through fantasy and myth.

The novel begins with three distinct plots, which seem at first to be only tenuously related. One plot concerns a retroactive utopia founded by eighteenth-century pirates, which Burroughs uses as a foundation for social criticism. A second plot, from which the title comes, depicts mythical "cities of the red night," which existed in prehistoric time and function as a dystopia through which the reader views present culture. A third plot involves a present-day investigator who traces the mystery of a deadly virus known as B-23 to its historical origins in the "cities of the red night." Each plot employs conventions from one popular genre or another: The story of the utopian pirates' colony reads very much like a boys' adventure story; the story of the advanced prehistoric cities takes its structure from science fiction; and the story of the investigation of the virus lends itself to the conventions of the hard-boiled detective story.

THE PLACE OF DEAD ROADS

In the second book of the trilogy, *The Place of Dead Roads*, Burroughs continues the process of mythmaking. His protagonist is Kim Carsons, a late nineteenth century gunslinger who utilizes a sort of "hole in time," a phenomenon introduced in *Cities of the Red Night*. Through this hole, Carsons becomes a time-traveler, moving precariously across time and space, encountering different cultures and time periods in an effort to forge some sense of the whole, some sense of control over his own destiny. He seeks fulfillment in disparate, almost lonely, homosexual encounters, in drugs, and in the sense of power he feels by manipulating others.

The story begins with a clipping from a Boulder, Colorado, newspaper which tells the reader that William Seward Hall, who writes Western novels under the pen name Kim Carsons, was shot in a gunfight in the year 1899. The story then introduces the character Carsons and, after a disjointed series of adventures and misadventures, returns the reader to that same date when Carsons loses his life, as if to say that destiny will not be averted in the end. The similarity of Carsons's true name to Burroughs's is striking here because, like Hall, Burroughs tends to fictionalize himself as author, as though an author can reach his true potential only through the life of his character—perhaps another way of understanding Burroughs's fascination with somehow circumventing destiny through manipulation.

THE WESTERN LANDS

In the third book of the trilogy, *The Western Lands*, the reader learns that Carsons was not shot by his opponent, Mike Chase, but by a killer from the Land of the Dead named Joe, described as a NO (Natural Outlaw), whose job it is to break natural laws. The Western land itself is a mythical place, a utopian vision of a place beyond one's images of earth and heaven—a land where natural law, religious law, and human law have no meaning. It is a paradise, but a paradise difficult to reach.

The intent of Burroughs's trilogy is first to create a science-fiction myth which explains all of human history; then to reveal the power of fantasy and myth to offer alternative histories; and finally, by realizing these alternative histories, to explore alternative anthropological patterns by which to organize society. The three separate plots interrelate and merge at various points throughout the trilogy, but eventually each is abandoned before completion—a technique that, Burroughs claims, allows the reader to create his or her own stories, to engage his or her own sense of mythmaking. The reader is encouraged to play a kind of "what if" game along with Burroughs: What if the Spanish had not defeated the New World into submission? What if the true foundations of liberty and individual freedom had taken hold in the Third World? What if all of our assumptions, whether religious, historical, or psychological, are wrong? This process of mythmaking in Burroughs is not a means to an end, but rather the object of the struggle—the great creative process of defining and redefining ourselves, which is our ultimate defense against those who would manipulate us.

Although Burroughs's innovative, highly unconventional fictive style and often abrasive thematic preoccupations were not without their detractors, by the end of his career Burroughs had firmly established his place as one of late twentieth century fiction's most significant innovators. In fact, his "cut-up" technique has reached beyond the bounds of obscure cult fiction to influence both mainstream cinema and popular music. Burroughs played a semiautobiographical role as Tom the Priest in Gus Van Sant's 1989 film about drug addiction, *Drugstore Cowboy*; in 1991,

acclaimed director David Cronenberg adapted *Naked Lunch* to the screen. In her introduction to his unprecedented reading on the popular American television show *Saturday Night Live* in 1981, actress Lauren Hutton lauded Burroughs as "America's greatest living writer," while rock music icons Lou Reed and David Bowie have both recognized Burroughs's disjointed and surreal but surprisingly moralistic approach to writing as enormously influential on their own work. "Heavy metal," a genre of rock-and-roll music prominent in the 1980's, borrows its name from a phrase in Burroughs's *Naked Lunch*.

Upon his death in 1997 at age eighty-three, Burroughs was eulogized as everything from the "most dangerous" of Beat writers to the undisputed patriarch of this important movement in twentieth century American writing. Although Burroughs's lifelong penchant for the cutting edge of fiction continues to intimidate some scholars and critics, none can dispute his role as a significant innovator and catalyst for change in twentieth century fiction and popular culture.

Donald Palumbo, updated by Gregory D. Horn

OTHER MAJOR WORKS

NONFICTION: *The Yage Letters*, 1963 (with Allen Ginsberg); *APO-33 Bulletin: A Metabolic Regulator*, 1966; *The Job: Interviews with William S. Burroughs*, 1970 (with Daniel Odier); *Electronic Revolution 1970-71*, 1971; *Letters to Allen Ginsberg: 1953-1957*, 1983; *The Adding Machine: Collected Essays*, 1985; *The Letters of William S. Burroughs: 1945-1959*, 1993; *Last Words: The Final Journals of William S. Burroughs*, 2000.

MISCELLANEOUS: *The Exterminator*, 1960 (with Brion Gysin); *Minutes to Go*, 1960 (with Sinclair Beiles, Gregory Corso, and Gysin); *Time*, 1965 (drawings by Gysin); *White Subway*, 1965; *The Dead Star*, 1969; *Apomorphine*, 1969; *The Last Words of Dutch Schultz*, 1970; *Exterminator!*, 1973; *The Book of Breeething*, 1974; *Œuvre Croisée*, 1976 (with Gysin; also known as *The Third Man*, 1978); *Blade Runner: A Movie*, 1979; *Interzone*, 1989; *Word Virus: The William S. Burroughs Reader*, 1998 (James Grauerholz and Ira Silverberg, editors).

BIBLIOGRAPHY

Caveney, Graham. *Gentleman Junkie: The Life and Legacy of William S. Burroughs.* Boston: Little, Brown, 1998. An unconventional biography of Burroughs with an imaginative visual presentation that superimposes the text on reproductions of photographs, newspaper clippings, and other visual features, all printed on multicolored pages. Caveney considers the myths and legends surrounding Burroughs as well as his life and influence on later generations of musicians, writers, and artists.

Cook, Bruce. *The Beat Generation.* New York: Charles Scribner's Sons, 1971. Cook's survey of the Beat generation emphasizes their social impact rather than their literary importance. He devotes a chapter to Burroughs's work, notably *Naked Lunch*, describing it as primarily self-revelation. He includes a biography of Burroughs and an interview that takes place in London.

Goodman, Michael Barry. *Contemporary Literary Censorship: The Case History of Burroughs's "Naked Lunch."* Metuchen, N.J.: Scarecrow Press, 1981. Michael Goodman offers a narrative history of the writing, publication, critical reception, and subsequent censorship of *Naked Lunch* in the United States, a work he describes as one of the last works to receive such treatment in such a universal way. Provides much previously unpublished Burroughs material.

Lee, Robert A. "William Burroughs and the Sexuality of Power." *Twentieth Century Studies* 2 (November, 1969): 74-88. Lee analyzes the structure and imagery in several of Burroughs's novels, including *Junkie, Naked Lunch, The Soft Machine, The Ticket That Exploded*, and *Nova Express*. Lee argues that Burroughs's theme of the sexuality of power forms a basis for his mythology. He praises Burroughs as a moralist and serious social critic.

Mottram, Eric. *William Burroughs: The Algebra of Need.* London: Marion Boyars, 1977. Mottram sees Burroughs's works as a radical critique of Western power structures and the myths that support them, classifying the writer as an anarchic individualist. Mottram's comparisons of Burroughs with other radical thinkers is insightful and unique.

Skerl, Jennie. *William S. Burroughs.* Boston: Twayne, 1985. Skerl attempts to provide an overview of contemporary thought on Burroughs's art and life for the general reader and literary historian. She also argues, in a rather concise analysis section, that Burroughs's art comes from a worldview that revolves around the "hipsterism" ideas of Norman Mailer.

Tanner, Tony. *City of Words, American Fiction 1950-1970.* New York: Harper & Row, 1971. Tanner's influential survey of the contemporary American novel includes a lengthy chapter on Burroughs. His discussion centers on *Junkie, The Yage Letters, Naked Lunch, The Ticket That Exploded*, and *Nova Express*. Tanner sees Burroughs as giving major emphasis to a central theme in contemporary American literature—namely, the conflict between the dream of freedom and the dread of control.

OCTAVIA E. BUTLER

Born: Pasadena, California; June 22, 1947

PRINCIPAL LONG FICTION

Patternmaster, 1976
Mind of My Mind, 1977
Survivor, 1978
Kindred, 1979
Wild Seed, 1980
Clay's Ark, 1984
Dawn, 1987
Adulthood Rites, 1988
Imago, 1989
Parable of the Sower, 1993
Parable of the Talents, 1998

OTHER LITERARY FORMS

Octavia E. Butler has contributed short stories to various science-fiction collections and periodicals, including *Isaac Asimov's Science Fiction Magazine*, *Future Life*, and *Clarion*. Her story "Speech Sounds" won the Hugo Award in 1984; a short work of fiction, "Bloodchild," was honored with the Hugo and various other prizes in 1985.

ACHIEVEMENTS

Broad and growing popularity among readers of science fiction greeted first Butler's Patternist series of novels and then her Xenogenesis series. She has won multiple prizes for her short fiction as well as critical acceptance for her longer work. Her portrayal of the "loner" of science and adventure fiction is given depth and complexity by the implied treatment of sexual and racial prejudices and the direct treatment of social power structures. Entertaining stories with alien settings, sometimes narrated by alien characters, provide a platform for her contemplative approach to human dynamics. Love and miscegenation, male-female roles, the responsibilities of power, and the urge to survive are among the recurring themes that insistently invite the reader to reexamine long-standing attitudes.

BIOGRAPHY

Octavia E. Butler grew up in a family that reflected some of the hard realities for African Americans. Her father, who died when she was very young, shined shoes; her mother, who had been taken from school at the age of ten, supported herself by working as a maid.

Reared by her mother, grandmother, and other relatives, Butler felt most comfortable in the company of her adult relatives, even while she was uncomfortable with a social system that routinely denied their humanity. She was tall for her age, shy, bookish, and further set off from her peer group by strict Baptist prohibitions against dancing and the use of makeup. Her escape from a less-than-satisfactory everyday life was provided by her ability to write. She began writing when she was about ten years old and began to experiment with science fiction one day at age twelve, when she decided that she could write a better story than the poor science-fiction film she was watching on television.

Her family did not support her decision to write, and her teachers did not support her choice of science fiction as a medium. She attended Pasadena City College and then California State College at Los Angeles, where she was unable to major in creative writing but took a potpourri of other subjects. After attending evening writing classes at the University of California at Los Angeles (UCLA), she found a long-sought entrée into science-fiction writing when she met writer Harlan Ellison through the Writers Guild of America and Ellison brought her to the six-week Clarion Science Fiction Writers Workshop in 1970. She continued her study of science-fiction writing in classes taught by Ellison at UCLA. Although she had sold some of her science fiction as early as 1970, her breakthrough publication came in 1976 with *Patternmaster*, with which she began the Patternist series.

ANALYSIS

Octavia E. Butler presents a version of humanity as a congenitally flawed species, possibly doomed to destroy itself because it is both intelligent and hierarchical. In this sense, her work does not follow the lead of Isaac Asimov's *Foundation* series (1951-1993), Arthur C. Clarke's *2001: A Space Odyssey* (1968), and similar science fiction in offering an optimistic, rational, and agreeable view of humanity. As Butler herself says, she does not believe that imperfect human beings can create a perfect world.

Butler's diverse societies are controlled by Darwinian realities: competition to survive, struggle for power, domination of the weak by the strong, parasitism, and the like. Within this framework, there is room for both pain and hope, for idealism, love, bravery and compassion, for an outsider to challenge the system, defeat the tyrant, and win power. There is, however, no happy ending but a conclusion in which the lead characters have done their best and the world (wherever it is) remains ethically and morally unchanged.

In contemplative but vividly descriptive prose, Butler tells her story from the first- or third-person perspective of someone who is passive or disfranchised and is forced by events or other characters to take significant action. In order to fulfill her destiny, often the protagonist—most often a black woman—must do or experience something not only unprecedented but also alien and even grotesque. What begins as an act of courage usually ends as an act of love, or at least understanding. Through an alien, alienated, or excluded person, a crucial compromise is struck, civilization is preserved in some form, and life goes on.

Butler's fiction reflects and refracts the attempts—and failures—of the twentieth century to deal with ethnic and sexual prejudice. She frequently uses standard images of horror, such as snakelike or insectlike beings, to provoke an aversion that the reader is unable to sustain as the humanity of the alien becomes clear. Being human does not mean being faultless—merely familiar. Therefore, each of her human, nonhuman, and quasi-human societies displays its own form of selfishness and, usually, a very clear power structure. The maturity and independence achieved by the protagonists imply not the advent of universal equality and harmony but merely a pragmatic personal obligation to wield power responsibly. Characters unable to alter or escape the order of things are expected to show a sort of *noblesse oblige.*

KINDRED

Butler's most atypical work in terms of genre is *Kindred*, published in 1979. While the protagonist is shuttled helplessly back and forth between 1824 and 1976 in a kind of time travel, this device is of no intrinsic importance to the message of the story. At one point, the heroine, Edana, asks herself how it can be that she—the as yet unborn black descendant of a nineteenth century slaveholder—can be the instrument of keeping that slaveholder alive until he fulfills his destiny and fathers her ancestor. By asking, she preempts the reader's own curiosity, and when there is no answer, the story simply moves forward.

Kindred uses a black woman of the 1970's and her white husband to probe beneath the surface stereotypes of "happy slave" on the one hand and "Uncle Tom" on the other. When Edana and Kevin are separated by the South of 1824 into slave and master, they each begin unwillingly to imbibe the feelings and at-

titudes of the time from that perspective. The impact of the novel results from Butler's ability to evoke the antebellum South from two points of view: the stubborn, desperate attempts of blacks to lead meaningful lives in a society that disregards family ties and disposes of individuals as marketable animals; and the uncomprehending, sometimes oppressively benevolent ruthlessness of a ruling class that defines slaves in terms of what trouble or pleasure they can give.

THE PATTERNIST SERIES

Butler began her science-fiction novels with the Patternist series, and in this series the reader can observe the beginning of her development from a writer of well-crafted science/adventure fiction to a writer who recalls in her own way the reflectiveness of Ray Bradbury. The internal chronology of the series is reflected in the following ordering: *Wild Seed* (published in 1980), *Clay's Ark* (1984), *Patternmaster* (1976), *Mind of My Mind* (1977), and *Survivor* (1978).

SURVIVOR

First written but third published was *Survivor,* the tale of an orphaned Afro-Asian girl who becomes a "wild human" in order to survive in a harsh environment. She is found and adopted, in an atypical act of reaching out, by two members of the Missionaries—a nouveau-Fundamentalist Christian sect. The Missionaries' escape from a hostile Earth takes them to a planet inhabited by furred bipeds, whom they regard as less than human. These beings are, in fact, a science-fiction version of the noble savage, but the protagonist is alone in recognizing their nobility. Internally untouched by Missionary dogma, she is truly socialized as a captive of the Tehkohn and, in the end, chooses them as her own people. Her survival and success require an understanding of the color classes of fur among the Tehkohn, where blue is the highest color, suggesting a tongue-in-cheek reference to "blue blood." She makes her own way by dint of qualities often found in protagonists of adventure novels: physical agility, courage, and adaptability.

PATTERNMASTER

Patternmaster features an appealing duo, with the younger son of the Patternmaster—the psychic control-central of a society of advanced human beings—confronting and defeating his brutal older brother in an unwanted competition to succeed their father. His helper, mentor, and lover is a bisexual Healer; he trusts her enough to "link" with her in order to pool their psionic power. She teaches him that Healing is, paradoxically, also a deadly knowledge of the body with which he can defeat his brother. Thus, trust and cooperation overcome ambition and brutality. The "mutes" of this novel are nontelepathic human beings whose vulnerability to cruelty or kindness and inability to control their own destinies reflect the earlier status of slaves in America.

Mind of My Mind

Mary, in *Mind of My Mind*, is a "latent" who must undergo a painful transition in order to become a full-fledged telepath. The pain and danger of this passage from adolescence to adulthood are emblematic of the turmoil of coming of age everywhere and of the physical or psychological pain that is required as the price of initiation in many, if not all, societies. The deadened, sometimes crazed, helplessness of latents who cannot become telepaths but must continue to live with the intrusive offal of other people's thoughts is a powerful metaphor for people trapped in poverty, and some of the horrors Butler paints are familiar.

Mary has no choice at first. The founder of her "people," a nontelepathic immortal named Doro, prescribes her actions until she acquires her power. He senses danger only when she reaches out reflexively to control other, powerful telepaths, thus forming the first Pattern. Mary's destruction of the pitiless Doro, like the death of the older brother in *Patternmaster* and of the rival alien chief in *Survivor*, is foreordained and accomplished with a ruthlessness appropriate to the society and to the character of the victim. The incipient change in Butler's style is evident here in the comparative lack of adventure-action sequences and in the greater concentration on psychological adaptation to and responsible use of social power.

Wild Seed

The technique of historical reconstruction is seen again in *Wild Seed*, whose evocation of Ibo West Africa owes something to the work of writers such as Chinua Achebe. *Wild Seed* traces Doro and Anyanwu from their seventeenth century meeting in West Africa to the establishment of Doro's settlements in America. Doro is a centuries-old being who lives by "taking" another man's or woman's body and leaving his previous body behind. Anyanwu, the Emma of *Mind of My Mind*, is a descendant of Doro. She is a "wild seed" because she has unexpectedly developed the power to shape-shift, becoming young or old, an animal, fish, or bird, at will. Their relationship is completely one-sided, since Doro could "take" her any time he chose, although he would not acquire her special abilities. His long life and unremitting efforts to create a special people of his own have left him completely insensitive to the needs and desires of others. Anyanwu finally achieves some balance of power simply by being willing to die and leave Doro without the only companion who could last beyond a mortal lifetime.

Clay's Ark

The last Patternist novel, *Clay's Ark*, introduces the reader to those brutish enemies of both Patternist and "mute" humanity, the Clayarks, so named because the disease that created them was brought back to Earth on a spaceship called "Clay's Ark." The disease culls its victims, killing some and imbuing others with a will to live that overcomes the horror of their new existence. They become faster and stronger, and their children evolve even further, taking on animal shapes and attributes of speed, power, and heightened senses, but retaining human thought and use of their hands. In the guise of a horror story, *Clay's Ark* follows the first Clayarks' attempt to come to terms with their condition and live responsibly, shut off from civilization. Their failed attempt demonstrates that it is not possible to contain cataclysmic natural change, but the story enlists the reader's sympathy for human beings who suffer even as they afflict others.

The Xenogenesis series

With the exception of *Clay's Ark*, where there is much action, the pace of Butler's novels slows progressively; action is increasingly internalized and psychological. Moral judgmentalism and the contest of right versus wrong dwindle to insignificance. The next, and quite logical, development is the Xenogenesis series: *Dawn, Adulthood Rites, Imago*. This series confirmed Butler as a science-fiction writer of sufficient depth to be of significance beyond the genre.

The change from her originally projected title for the series is informative. "Exogenesis" would have implied merely genesis effected from outside humanity. "Xenogenesis" has both text and subtext. Its meaning is the production of an organism altogether and permanently unlike the parent. The subtext is a function of the best-known English word built on the same root: xenophobia, fear and dislike of that which is foreign or alien. Butler makes the series title a statement of the thesis she will address.

Many of the techniques and themes of her earlier, developing style come to fruition here: the alternating use of first- and third-person narrative, the slow pace of a plot laden with psychological development and sensory perceptions, the meticulous foreclosure of value judgments, the concern with hierarchy and responsibility, the objective observation of feelings of revulsion for that which is alien, and those feelings' gradual dissipation as the alien becomes familiar and therefore less threatening. Action in the series is sparse, normally kept to the minimum necessary to maintain the pace of psychological and social observation. In some ways, it is a chilling series of seductions of human beings by an alien, benevolent oppressor not entirely unlike Rufus of *Kindred* in his better moments. In some ways, it is a demonstration of the infinite capacity of humanity to seek satisfaction in the destruction of itself and others.

Words used to describe two of Butler's shorter works in the 1984 and 1987 issues of *The Year's Best Science Fiction* may serve here as a characterization of the Xenogenesis series: "strange, grotesque, disturbing . . . and ultimately moving," a "tale of despair, resignation, and, most painfully, hope." It is apparently to examine the capacity of human beings to adapt, to survive, and perhaps stubbornly to pursue a self-destructive course of action that Butler has created the nightmarish situation that the reader encounters in *Dawn*.

DAWN

In a world devastated by nuclear exchange between East and West, the dying remnants of humanity survive largely in the Southern Hemisphere. The heroine of *Dawn* is an African, Lilith, whose name suggests the demonic goddess of Hebrew tradition, the famous medieval witch who appears in Johann Wolfgang von Goethe's *Faust* (1808, 1833), and the medieval, alternate "first mother" who was put aside in favor of Eve.

Enter the Oankali, a nonviolent race of benevolent parasites and genetic engineers, who exist for the opportunity of combining with other species to acquire new cellular "knowledge" and capabilities. They live for miscegenation. They are trisexual: male, female, and ooloi. The ooloi is the indispensable link between male and female, channeling, altering, or amplifying all genetic material and sexual contact, including transfer of sperm and pleasurable sensations. The ooloi is capable of internal healing; for example, one cures Lilith of a cancer and finds the cancer to be an exciting new biological material with which to work.

The Oankali blend with another species by linking a male and female of that species and a male and female Oankali through an ooloi. Thereafter, independent conception is not possible for those members of that species. The progeny are "constructs," who, at least at first, resemble their direct parents but carry genetic change within them. Lilith's first husband is killed in *Dawn*, but she bears his child posthumously because Nikanj, the ooloi that has chosen her, has preserved his seed. The resultant humanoid male child is the protagonist of *Adulthood Rites*, while a much later child of Lilith with another husband and the same Oankali parents is the protagonist of *Imago*.

Lilith is at first appalled by even the more humanoid Oankali, with their Medusan tentacles and sensory arms. She is gradually acclimated to them, cooperates with them to save humanity, bears children with them, is overwhelmed by the sensory pleasure they can give, and becomes sympathetic to their need to unite with other species, but she is never fully resigned. In *Imago*, Lilith compares the Oankali's description of the "flavors" of human beings to physical cannibalism and implies that the spiritual equivalent is no less predatory.

Lilith's conversion from complete repugnance in *Dawn*, a stylistic tour de force, shapes the following novels, as human beings are ultimately allowed a choice of living with the Oankali, staying behind on a doomed and barren Earth, or living in an experimental, all-human world on Mars. The Oankali, who seem to make decisions as a kind of committee-of-the-whole, foresee that the same old combination of intelligence and hierarchical tendencies (in a rather Darwinian sense) will lead this last outpost of humanity to destroy itself. No one convincingly denies it.

ADULTHOOD RITES and IMAGO

Butler's stylistic virtuosity also extends to narrative person. *Dawn* is a third-person account of Lilith's absorption into the Oankali social structure; *Adulthood Rites* is the third-person narrative of Akin, a male-human construct, who convinces the more rational human beings left on Earth to trust the Oankali, and convinces the Oankali to offer the humans the choice of planetary residences; *Imago* is a first-person account of Jodahs, a child whose transformation to adulthood reveals it to be an ooloi. Use of the first-person narrative to tell the story of an apparent human who becomes wholly alien in both psychology and physiology is risky but rewarding. Through the eyes of a being routinely referred to as "it" in its own society, the reader observes its benevolent stalking and drug-induced brainwashing of human mates and the final planting of a seed that will grow into an organic town and then an organic spaceship, which will carry Jodahs and his people to new worlds for new genetic blendings.

Imago's conclusion serves as a reminder that Butler's imaginary worlds are primarily arenas for hard, necessary decisions in the business of survival. There is compassion as well as bitterness, and love as well as prejudice, but there is no triumph or glory. There is only doing what must be done as responsibly as possible.

PARABLE OF THE SOWER

Parable of the Sower was published in 1993. It is set in California in 2024. The narrator is a fifteen-year-old African American girl who lives with her family in the fictitious town of Robledo, some twenty miles from Los Angeles. At the time of the story, the social order has nearly disintegrated. Society consists of "haves" and "have-nots." The haves live in walled and fortified neighborhoods; the have-nots roam outside the walls along with packs of wild dogs and drug addicts called "Paints," whose addiction imbues them with an orgasmic desire to burn things. Apparently due to the follies of humankind, the climate has been altered, and the entire world is in a state of near-collapse. Disease is rampant, natural disasters are frequent, and though there are stores, some jobs, and even television programming, the social order, at least in California, is almost gone.

Against this backdrop, the heroine, Lauren Olamina, founds a new religion named Earthseed. The novel takes the form of a journal Lauren keeps. Entries are dated and each chapter is prefaced with a passage from the new religion, the essence of which is that everything changes, even God. In fact, God is change.

Butler has said that humankind is not likely to change itself, but that humans will go elsewhere and be forced to change. When the Paints destroy Lauren's neighborhood and most of her family, she treks north toward Canada, and new members join her group, one by one. Most survive and reach their destination, a burned farm in Oregon. The ending is a classic Butler resolution: There is no promised land; people who have not changed generally perish. Lauren has changed nothing in society; she has merely adapted and learned to survive. The structure, style, and plot of *Parable of the Sower* are all deceptively simple. Beneath the surface of the story, the novel deals directly with social power, its use and abuse, and its possible consequences.

James L. Hodge, updated by John T. West III

OTHER MAJOR WORKS

SHORT FICTION: "Crossover," 1971; "Near of Kin," 1979; "Speech Sounds," 1983; "Bloodchild," 1984; "The Evening and the Morning and the Night," 1987.

NONFICTION: "Birth of a Writer," 1989 (later renamed "Positive Obsession"); "Furor Scribendi," 1993.

MISCELLANEOUS: *Bloodchild: And Other Stories*, 1995 (collected short stories and essays).

BIBLIOGRAPHY

Crossley, Robert. Introduction to *Kindred*, by Octavia Butler. Boston: Beacon Press, 1988. One of the more scholarly critical appreciations of *Kindred*. Crossley deals with the political and social content of Butler's writing, noting how few science-fiction writers have been able to treat questions of race and sex without a patronizing attitude.

Foster, Frances Smith. "Octavia Butler's Black Female Future Fiction." *Extrapolation* 23 (Spring, 1982): 37-49. A very early article, published before Butler had completed the *Patternmaster* series. The article outlines the way "Butler consciously explores the impact of race and sex on future society." Unfettered by the pretentious writing common to much later Butler criticism, Foster illuminates the early texts and, with Sandy Govan's articles, remains among the best Butler criticism.

Govan, Sandra Y. "Connections, Links, and Extended Networks: Patterns in Octavia Butler's Science Fiction." *Black American Literature Forum* 18 (1984): 82-87. Demonstrates how Butler uses elements of slave narratives and historical novels to produce a new kind of science fiction, one which "features black characters in major significant roles" and also "features black women as heroic characters, protagonists who either share power with men or who maintain their right to wield power on an equal basis." Govan's clear and convincing demonstration is enlightening and thought provoking.

McCaffery, Larry. "Interview with Octavia E. Butler." In *Across the Wounded Galaxies*. Urbana: University of Illinois Press, 1990. Among the best of numerous Butler interviews.

Peppers, Cathy. "Dialogue Origins and Alien Identities in Butler's *Xenogenesis*." *Science Fiction Studies* 22 (1995): 47-62. Peppers's article carefully lays out the way Butler uses origin stories and the African American story of diaspora and slavery. An illuminating article with too much postmodern and poststructural verbiage.

Shinn, Thelma. "The Wise Witches: Black Woman Mentors in the Fiction of Octavia E. Butler." In *Conjuring: Black Women, Fiction, and Literary Tradition*, edited by Marjorie Pryse and Hortense Spillers. Bloomington: Indiana University Press, 1985. An interesting discussion of some of Butler's early heroines. Shinn draws on Annis Pratt's work, which defines archetypal patterns in women's fiction. She then demonstrates convincingly how Butler employs wise witches in her fiction.

ROBERT OLEN BUTLER

Born: Granite City, Illinois; January 20, 1945

PRINCIPAL LONG FICTION
The Alleys of Eden, 1981
Sun Dogs, 1982
Countrymen of Bones, 1983
On Distant Ground, 1985
Wabash, 1987
The Deuce, 1989
They Whisper, 1994
The Deep Green Sea, 1997
Mr. Spaceman, 2000

OTHER LITERARY FORMS

Although highly praised as a novelist, Robert Olen Butler has received his greatest acclaim for his work as a writer of short stories, especially for his 1992 book, *A Good Scent from a Strange Mountain*, a celebrated collection of short stories about Vietnamese refugees settled in communities in Louisiana.

ACHIEVEMENTS

Before succeeding as an author, Butler wrote several unpublished novels, and his first published work, *The Alleys of Eden*, was rejected by at least twenty publishers before it was finally accepted. In spite of the rejections, Butler persisted, and *The Alleys of Eden* was praised by critics and reviewers. In 1984,

(Gray Little)

Butler sold this first novel to Home Box Office (HBO) to be made into a film for cable television. His work became well-known to the general public, though, only in 1993, when he was awarded the Pulitzer Prize for fiction for *A Good Scent from a Strange Mountain*. That year he also won the Notable Book Award from the American Library Association and the Richard and Hilda Rosenthal Foundation Award from the American Academy of Arts and Letters, was nominated for the PEN/Faulkner award, and was named a Guggenheim fellow. Despite his new fame, Butler continued an impressive level of productivity, publishing three books in three years.

BIOGRAPHY

Robert Olen Butler, Jr., grew up in Granite City, Illinois, a steel town near St. Louis, Missouri. His father, Robert Olen Butler, Sr., was chair of the theater department at St. Louis University. Butler majored in

theater at Northwestern University in Illinois, where he graduated summa cum laude with a B.S. in oral interpretation in 1967. He went on to graduate school in the writing program at the University of Iowa, where he earned a master's degree in playwriting in 1969. While a student in Iowa, he married Carol Supplee, whom he divorced in 1972.

American involvement in the war in Vietnam was at its height when Butler finished graduate school, and, believing he would be drafted, he decided to enlist in the Army instead, hoping that he would have some choice in his assignment. Although he wanted to serve in the United States, he was assigned to military intelligence, was given intensive training in the Vietnamese language, and was sent to Vietnam, where he served until 1972. Butler became fluent in Vietnamese, and the language and culture of Vietnam, together with the experience of war, greatly influenced his thinking and writing.

In July of 1972, he married the poet Marilyn Geller. He worked for a year as an editor and reporter in New York City. When his wife became pregnant with their son, Joshua, the family moved back to Illinois. Butler taught high school in his hometown of Granite City in 1973 and 1974, then became a reporter in Chicago. He moved back to the New York City area in 1975 and took a job as editor-in-chief of *Energy User News*. According to Butler, he wrote much of his first three novels while commuting on the Long Island Railroad to and from his job in Manhattan. Butler left New York in 1985 to take a position teaching writing at McNeese State University, a small college in the southwestern Louisiana city of Lake Charles. Louisiana is home to several Vietnamese communities, and the Louisiana Vietnamese provided Butler with material for his Pulitzer Prize-winning collection of short stories, *A Good Scent from a Strange Mountain*. Divorced from Marilyn Geller, Butler married twice more while living in Lake Charles, to Maureen Donlan and then to the novelist Elizabeth Dewberry.

ANALYSIS

Butler's novels are notable for their depth of psychological insight. All his works depend heavily on presenting the perspectives and shifting emotions of characters, particularly characters caught in crises. His writing attempts to enter and follow the private thoughts of troubled people. Tensions and unresolved conflicts, especially sexual and romantic tensions between men and women, are central to his fiction. These men and women are usually placed in stormy social and historical situations, such as the Vietnam War and its aftermath or the class struggles of the Great Depression, but Butler is always interested more in how events in the world complicate the private relationships of individuals than he is in social problems or questions of ideology.

Butler's characters tend to be lonely people struggling to make contact with one another. Differences in culture complicate these efforts at contact. Many of Butler's Vietnam novels examine emotional and sexual involvements between an American soldier or veteran and a Vietnamese woman. In interviews, Butler has maintained that although the novels are set in Vietnam, the country itself is not the theme of his work, and the romantic entanglements of war are not his main concern. Instead, he sees Vietnam as a metaphor for the human condition, and he sees its tragedy as a specific instance of continual human tragedy. The cultural gaps between Western men and Asian women, similarly, are concrete examples of the distances that exist between all people and of the often unbridgeable gaps between men and women.

Butler's novels are frequently connected to one another in characters and in themes. His first three novels form a loose trilogy, since they deal with the postwar experiences of three men who served in the same intelligence unit in Vietnam. A central character in one of Butler's books will often appear as a minor character in another, so that each narrative seems to be part of a single larger fictional world.

The style of Butler's writing is usually spare and stark, relying on unadorned, simple sentences. He often employs a traditional, invisible, omniscient narrator who relates the thoughts and feelings of the characters as well as the settings of the story; this time-honored fictional strategy may seem a bit old-fashioned and artificial to some readers. Butler also uses the first-person interior monologue, as in *The*

Deep Green Sea, in which the entire story unravels through the thoughts of the two protagonists.

Critics have generally identified a tendency to lapse into melodrama as the greatest weakness in Butler's fiction. His works strive to achieve a high seriousness and a moral and emotional intensity that is sometimes difficult to sustain. Butler's background in theater may be the reason his work seems sometimes excessively staged and self-consciously tragic.

THE ALLEYS OF EDEN

The Alleys of Eden, Butler's first novel, treats the conflict between Vietnamese and American culture and contemplates the destructiveness of the Vietnam War for both of these. Its two main characters are Cliff Wilkes, a deserter from the U.S. Army in Vietnam, and Lanh, a Vietnamese bar girl and Cliff's lover. The novel is, appropriately, divided into two parts. The first part is set in Saigon in the last few days before the city's fall to the Communist forces of the North Vietnamese. The second part takes place in the United States, after Cliff and Lanh manage to flee.

Cliff had been with the Army intelligence, but he deserted after the torture and killing of a Viet Cong captive. Fluent in Vietnamese, he has come to feel himself more Vietnamese than American, but barriers continue to exist between him and his adopted country. He awaits the arrival of the North Vietnamese in a room that he has shared with Lanh for five years, since his desertion. As Cliff's memories move through his past, the scene shifts from images of his time with military intelligence to his failed marriage to his family in Illinois. At the last minute, Cliff decides to flee, and he convinces Lanh to join him. They make it onto one of the last helicopters out of the city.

On a ship heading back to America, the deserter passes himself off as a journalist and then runs away before being fingerprinted in California. Reunited with Lanh, he returns to Illinois. There, the two find that Lanh's struggles to adapt to an unfamiliar world and Cliff's uncertainties about his past and his future place too much strain on their love for each other, and Cliff ultimately leaves alone for Canada.

Told primarily from Cliff's perspective, *The Alleys of Eden* is impressive for its evocation of his collage of memories. The strategy of dividing the novel into a Vietnamese half and an American half is in some respects an effective way of structuring the plot to highlight the troubled love of Cliff and Lanh. However, the second half of the novel is also anticlimactic, after the review of Cliff's troubled past and the sudden flight through the alleys of Saigon, and the part of the story that takes place in America lacks the tension and momentum of the first half.

WABASH

Wabash and *They Whisper* are the only two novels by Butler that do not deal with the Vietnam War. *Wabash* is, however, set in a war of sorts. It takes place in the Depression year of 1932 in a steel town based on Butler's hometown. It tells the story of Jeremy and Deborah Cole, a couple mourning the death of their daughter. Jeremy is a steelworker employed in a mill where his friends and coworkers are being laid off every day. Through a man he meets at work, Jeremy becomes involved with communist radicals. At first he is put off by their rhetoric and by their language of ideology. However, he is angered by the brutality of the mine's management and by the victimization of other men on the job. Eventually, he decides to attempt to kill the politically ambitious owner of the mine.

While Jeremy fights his battles in the masculine world of the steel mill, Deborah struggles with conflicts among the women in her family. Her mother and two of her aunts are close-knit but troubled in their relations with one another and with Deborah. Her grandmother is approaching death; a third aunt has converted to Catholicism and has been rejected by all the other women of the family. Deborah finds the ostracized aunt, Effie, and after the grandmother's death Deborah manages to convince Effie to attend the funeral. Even the death of their mother will not reconcile the other women with Aunt Effie, though, and Deborah fails in her efforts to bring the family together.

Jeremy and Deborah's lives and struggles come together when Deborah stops Jeremy's assassination attempt and the two of them leave Wabash. Though both lose their separate battles, the story reaches a resolution as the two narratives, one of the woman and one of the man, reach a single end.

Wabash is a moving novel that established Butler's ability to deal with topics other than the Vietnam War. It does echo the central themes of the Vietnam novels, though: the importance and difficulty of love between a woman and a man and the private pains of those caught up in social and political crises. If, at times, the characters seem a bit too cinematic and a bit too unbelievable, this may be a consequence of Butler's efforts to reach back in time for the legendary past of his present-day Illinois.

THE DEEP GREEN SEA

As in so many of Butler's fictions, two lovers occupy center stage in *The Deep Green Sea*. Ben Cole, son of Jeremy and Deborah Cole of *Wabash*, is a Vietnam War veteran. Ben is haunted by his memory of the war and world-weary from his failed marriage. Returning to Vietnam, he meets Tien, a tour guide. Tien is the daughter of a Vietnamese bar girl who sold herself to American soldiers, one of whom was Tien's father. Tien is also haunted, by both her mother's desertion and her unknown father.

The novel uses first-person narration, alternating between Ben and Tien, enabling Butler to present their affair through the eyes of each. Butler presents a woman's point of view with an insight possessed by few other male novelists, and the fact that he speaks convincingly with the voice of a Vietnamese woman is a tribute to his versatility. The beginning of the story takes place in Tien's room, where the lovers recall scenes from their pasts. These two sets of thoughts and memories provide rather weak structure for the narrative; the novel does not, at first, seem to be leading anywhere. However, soon the question of Tien's parents emerges and the tragic appeal of the story is made evident.

While serving in the war, Ben had a Vietnamese girlfriend, a bar girl. Because Tien's mother was a bar girl, the apparently faint possibility that Tien's mother and Ben's former girlfriend might be the same person trouble the couple. They leave for the town of Nha Trang, where Tien's mother is known to live, for proof that the only relationship between the two of them is that of lovers. The truth that they find in Nha Trang is ultimately devastating to them both. *The Deep Green Sea* may well be the least complex of Butler's novels in plot and action. However, with its echoes of Oedipal tragedy and its evocation of the many-sided adversities of the Vietnam War, it is a haunting work.

Carl L. Bankston III

OTHER MAJOR WORKS

SHORT FICTION: *A Good Scent from A Strange Mountain*, 1992; *Tabloid Dreams*, 1996.

BIBLIOGRAPHY

Kelsay, Michael. "An Interview with Robert Olen Butler." *Poets and Writers* 24, no. 3 (May/June, 1996). In this interview, Butler talks about the six novels he published before winning the Pulitzer Prize for his 1992 book of short stories. He also discusses how his Vietnam experiences contributed to his writing.

Ryan, Maureen. "Robert Olen Butler's Vietnam Veterans: Strangers in an Alien Home." *The Midwest Quarterly* 38, no. 3 (Spring, 1997). This essay examines Butler's first three novels, arguing that because the chief characters served together in an intelligence unit in Vietnam the three should be regarded as a loose trilogy.

Schulman, Candy. "My First Novel: Good News for Unpublished Novelists." *Writer's Digest* 63 (January, 1983). This article is useful for giving a view of Butler at an early point in his career, prior to achieving recognition. It gives the accounts of eight novelists, including Butler, concerning their struggles to complete and publish their first books.

SAMUEL BUTLER

Born: Langar Rectory, England; December 4, 1835
Died: London, England; June 18, 1902

PRINCIPAL LONG FICTION
  Erewhon, 1872
  The Fair Haven, 1873

(Archive Photos)

  Erewhon Revisited, 1901
  The Way of All Flesh, 1903

OTHER LITERARY FORMS

The Shrewsbury editions of Samuel Butler's works, published between 1923 and 1926, reveal the breadth of his interests. Butler's fiction was perhaps less important to him than his work in other fields, notably his theorizing on religion and evolution. He was also an art critic (*Ex Voto*, 1888; *Alps and Sanctuaries of Piedmont and the Ticino*, 1881); a literary critic (*The Authoress of the "Odyssey,"* 1897; *Shakespeare's Sonnets Reconsidered*, 1899); the biographer of his famous grandfather, Dr. Samuel Butler; a letter-writer; and a poet. An age which produces "specialists" may find Butler to be a talented dabbler or dilettante, but his unifying philosophy gives a center to all his work.

ACHIEVEMENTS

Butler was a figure of controversy during his lifetime, and perhaps his greatest achievement resides in his ability to challenge: He contended with Charles Darwin and Darwinism; he took on the established scholars of William Shakespeare, classical literature, and art; and he was part of the nineteenth century revolt against traditional religion. He approached all of these areas in such a way that his opponents could not ignore him; whether he was right or wrong, any subject benefited by his treatment, which opened it up to new and candid thought.

Of his four works which may be labeled as fiction, by far the greatest is *The Way of All Flesh*. Virginia Woolf, in *Contemporary Writers* (1965), described this novel as a seed from which many others developed—a biological image which would have pleased Butler. In earlier novels, indifferent or cruel families had been portrayed as agents of the hero's youthful unhappiness—witness Charles Dickens's *David Copperfield* (1849-1850)—but only in *The Way of All Flesh* did the oppressiveness and cruelty of family life become a theme in itself, worthy of generation-by-generation treatment.

BIOGRAPHY

Samuel Butler was born in 1835, the son of a clergyman who wished him to go into the Church. After a successful career at Cambridge University, Butler prepared for a career in the Church but found himself unable to face the prospect of that life. Letters between Butler and his father show the young man to be considering a half-dozen plans at once: art, the army, cotton-growing, and bookselling among them. Finally, father and son agreed that the young man should emigrate to New Zealand and try his fortune there, with Butler's father providing capital. Both father and son hoped that the experience would "settle" Butler and build his character.

Butler arrived in New Zealand in January of 1860, remaining there for four years. It was a useful time: He made money, which freed him of his family, at least financially, and he saw an unusual country which gave him a subject and setting for his later writings. New Zealand, however, was too rough a land to be his permanent home. His "hut" there was an island of comfort and civilization, where Butler devoted himself to music and study. His optimistic

letters home became the basis of *A First Year in Canterbury Settlement* (1863), a book assembled and published by Butler's father.

Returning to England in 1864, Butler settled at Clifford's Inn in London, which would be his home for the rest of his life. He began to study art; his paintings had some success. He wished to do something greater, however—something which would express his developing ideas. Out of this desire grew *Erewhon*, a satire which was published anonymously in 1872 at the author's own expense. By that time, Butler was already at work on *The Fair Haven*. This book may or may not be considered fiction; it is a dispute over the validity of Christianity, but the dispute is conducted in a fictional frame.

The following year, 1873, was an important one for Butler. *The Fair Haven* was published, his mother died, he made a risky financial investment, and he began *The Way of All Flesh*. All of these events shaped his later years. *The Fair Haven*, following on the heels of *Erewhon*, marked him as a belligerent enemy of traditional religion. His mother's death caused him some grief, but it spurred him to begin *The Way of All Flesh*, the work for which he is most remembered. That work was slowed, though, by financial troubles. Butler invested his New Zealand fortune in a Canadian venture which soon failed. He salvaged less than a quarter of his investment and had to seek help from his father. Not until 1886, when his father died, was Butler wholly free of financial pressures.

The next several years were occupied by work on evolution and religion. In 1882, Butler returned to *The Way of All Flesh*, completing it the following year. He felt, however, that the book should not be published while anyone who could be hurt by it was still alive; therefore it did not appear until a year after his own death.

In 1883, Butler began to write music. Music and music criticism were to occupy him intermittently for several years, interspersed with art criticism. The last decade of his life was filled with the study of literature, culminating in his publications on Shakespeare's sonnets and his translations of the *Iliad* (1898) and the *Odyssey* (1900). These works were characterized by the combativeness that to some degree sums up Butler's life. He was always the rebellious, contradictory son.

Butler's life was shaped by a number of intense relationships. His relationship with his family was unresolved; the work (*The Way of All Flesh*) which might have laid the ghosts to rest was haunted by another ghost, Butler's lifelong friend Eliza Mary Ann Savage. A fellow art student, she gave the writer friendship, friendly criticism, advice, and approval. Her own understanding of the relationship can never be known, but Butler feared she wished to marry him. His implicit rejection disturbed him deeply after her death. Other friendships were equally ambiguous. Charles Paine Pauli consumed much of Butler's attentions and resources from their first meeting in New Zealand until Pauli's death in 1897, when Butler discovered that Pauli had been supported by two other men. The perhaps sexual ambiguities of this relationship were repeated in Butler's affection for a young Swiss, Hans Faesch, and to a lesser degree in his long-lasting bonds with Henry Festing Jones and Alfred Emery Cathie. Butler's emotional makeup seems similar to that of Henry James. Both men formed passionate attachments to other men; both appreciated women more as memories than as living beings.

ANALYSIS

On his deathbed, Samuel Butler spoke of the "pretty roundness" of his career, beginning with *Erewhon* and ending, thirty years later, with *Erewhon Revisited*.

EREWHON

Erewhon must be understood first of all as a satire rather than as a novel. It is in the tradition of Jonathan Swift's *Gulliver's Travels* (1726) and Samuel Johnson's *Rasselas, Prince of Abyssinia* (1759), works which sacrifice unity and development to a vision of the writer's society in the guise of an imaginary foreign land. Like Rasselas and Gulliver, Higgs of *Erewhon* is a young man, ready for adventure, out to learn about the world. He quickly reveals his image of himself as sharp, cunning, and bold. Before he tells his story, he lets the reader know the things he

will hold back so that no reader will be able to find Erewhon and thus profit financially from Higgs's exploration.

His story begins as he is working on a sheep farm in a colony, the name of which he will not reveal. Intending to find precious metals or at least good sheep-grazing land, he journeys alone inland, over a mountain range. On the other side, he finds a kingdom called Erewhon (Nowhere), which looks very much like England. Higgs's point of reference is England; all aspects of Erewhonian life he measures by that standard.

Many such satires work through the narrator's quick judgment that his new land is either much better or much worse than his native country: The narrator's rather simple view plays against the author's more complex perspective. In *Erewhon*, however, the narrator is not quite so naïve. His own failings, rather than his naïveté, become part of the satire, which thus has a dual focus, much like book 4 of *Gulliver's Travels*. Higgs, like many good Victorian heroes, is out to make money. It is this prospect which motivates him most strongly. Coexisting with his desire for fortune is his religiosity. Here, Butler's satire upon his character is most pronounced and simplistic. Higgs observes the Sabbath, but he seduces Yram (Mary) with no regret. He plans to make his fortune by selling the Erewhonians into slavery, arguing that they would be converted to Christianity in the process; the slaveholders would be lining their pockets and doing good simultaneously. Thus, Butler exposes, to no one's great surprise, the mingled piety and avarice of British colonialists.

Butler satirizes European culture through the Erewhonians more often than through his hero, Higgs, gradually unfolding their lives for the reader to observe. Their lives are, on the surface, peaceful and pleasant; they are a strikingly attractive race. Only through personal experience does Higgs learn the underpinnings of the society: When he is ill, he learns that illness is a crime in Erewhon, while moral lapses are regarded in the same way as illnesses are in England. When his pocket watch is discovered, he learns that all "machines" have been banned from Erewhon. Erewhonian morality is based on reversals:

The morally corrupt receive sympathy, while the ill are imprisoned; a child duped by his guardian is punished for having been ignorant, while the guardian is rewarded; children are responsible for their own birth, while their parents are consoled for having been "wronged" by the unborn. This pattern of reversals is of necessity incomplete, a problem noted by reviewers of *Erewhon* in 1872.

"The Book of the Machines" is the section of the satire which has drawn the most attention, because of its relationship to Darwinian thought. It may well be, as it has often been considered, a *reductio ad absurdum* of Darwinism, but the chapter also takes on reasoning by analogy as a less complex target of satire. "The Book of the Machines" is Higgs's translation of the Erewhonian book which led to the banning of all mechanical devices. Its author claimed that machines had developed—evolved—more rapidly than humankind and thus would soon dominate, leaving humans mere slaves or parasites. He argued that machines were capable of reproduction, using humans in the process as flowers use bees. The arguments proved so convincing that all machines in Erewhon were soon destroyed, leaving the country in the rather primitive state in which Higgs found it.

The purpose of "The Book of the Machines" becomes clearer in the following two chapters, which detail Erewhonian debates on the rights of animals and the rights of vegetables. At one point in the past, insistence on the rights of animals had turned Erewhon into a land of vegetarians, but the philosophers went a step further and decreed that vegetables, too, had rights, based upon their evolving consciousness. Again, Butler plays with argument by analogy, as the philosophers compare the vegetables' intelligence to that of a human embryo.

The Erewhonians who believed in the rights of vegetables were led nearly to starvation by their extremism, and it is this same extremism which causes Higgs to leave Erewhon. Fearful that disfavor is growing against his foreign presence, he plans to escape by balloon, taking with him his beloved Arowhena. The perilous escape takes place, and the hero, married to Arowhena and restored to England, becomes a fairly successful hack writer. His account of Erewhon, he says at the end, constitutes an appeal for subscriptions to finance his scheme to return to Erewhon.

EREWHON REVISITED

The broad, traditional satire of *Erewhon* is abandoned in its sequel. Written years later, *Erewhon Revisited* reflects the maturity of its author, then in his sixties. In the later work, Butler treats Erewhon as a habitation of human beings, not satiric simplifications. *Erewhon Revisited* is thus a novel, not a satire; its focus is on human relationships. Butler had already written (though not published) *The Way of All Flesh*, and the preoccupations of that work are also evident in *Erewhon Revisited*. Both works grew out of Butler's fascination with family relationships, especially those between father and son.

The narrator of *Erewhon Revisited* is John Higgs, the son of George Higgs and Arowhena. He tells of his mother's early death and of his father's desire to return to Erewhon. This time, though, Higgs's desire is sentimental; he has grown past his earlier wish to profit from the Erewhonians. He goes to Erewhon, returns in ill health, tells the story of his adventure to John, and dies. The book in this way becomes John's tribute to his father.

Although *Erewhon Revisited* may be identified as a novel rather than as a satire, it does have a satiric subject as part of its plot. Upon reentering Erewhon, Higgs discovers that his ascent by balloon has become the source of a new religion. The Erewhonians revere his memory and worship him as the "Sun Child." Higgs is horrified to find that there are theologians of Sunchildism fighting heretics. Unfortunately, Sunchildism has not made the Erewhonians a better or kinder people. Here is the heart of Butler's satire: that a religion based upon a supernatural event will divide people, place power in the wrong hands, and humiliate reason.

In *Erewhon*, Higgs was a pious and hypocritical prig, a target of satire himself. In the sequel, he is a genial, loving humanist, appalled by the "evolution" of his frantic escape into the ascent of a god. Much of *Erewhon Revisited* develops his plans to deflate Sunchildism, to reveal himself as the "Sun Child" and tell the truth about his "ascent."

Higgs has a special motive which transcends his disgust with Sunchildism. Upon arriving in Erewhon, he meets a young man whom he soon recognizes as his own son, a son he did not know he had. The young man is the product of Higgs's brief romance with Yram, the jailer's daughter. Higgs keeps his identity from his son (also named George) for a while, but eventually the two are revealed to each other in a touching and intense scene. To earn his newfound son's respect, Higgs determines to deflate Sunchildism. Thus, the process of satire in *Erewhon Revisited* is rooted in its human relationships.

Higgs's son John, the narrator of the novel, feels no jealousy toward his half brother. Instead, he shares the elder Higgs's enthusiasm for young George. Following his father's death, John goes to Erewhon himself to meet George and to deliver a large gift of gold to him. This legacy exemplified one of Butler's tenets about parent-child relations: that the best parents are kind, mostly absent, and very free with money. This theme is repeated throughout *The Way of All Flesh*. In *Erewhon Revisited*, however, it has a simpler expression. The relationship of Higgs and his two sons forms the emotional center of the novel and creates the impetus for some of its plot, but it is distinct from the satire on religion which makes up much of the book.

THE FAIR HAVEN

It is fitting that Butler's last work, *Erewhon Revisited*, should have presented a genial hero determined to strip away what he saw as ridiculous supernatural beliefs. Much of "Sunchildism" is a response to the religious foment of the nineteenth century with which Butler had begun contending early in his career. *The Fair Haven* was his first satire concerned with Christian belief. This work is "fiction" only in a very limited sense: Butler creates a persona, John Pickard Owen, whose arguments in favor of Christianity are in fact the vehicle for Butler's satire against it. *The Fair Haven* begins with a fictional memoir of John Pickard Owen by his brother. The memoir reveals that Owen moved from faith to disbelief to faith, and that his efforts to prove the validity of his religion pushed him to mental exhaustion and, eventually, death.

THE WAY OF ALL FLESH

The characters of *The Fair Haven* are forerunners of the Pontifex family in *The Way of All Flesh*, Butler's fullest and most characteristic work. *The Way of All Flesh* encompasses all of Butler's concerns: family life, money, sexual attitudes, class structure, religion, and art. This novel too is a satire, but in it Butler does not portray an Erewhon; much more disturbingly, he keeps the reader at home.

The Way of All Flesh is Ernest Pontifex's story, but it does not begin with Ernest. Butler the evolutionist shows Ernest as the product of several generations of social changes and personal tensions. The genealogical background, as well as the title and biblical epigraph, "We know that all things work together for good to them that love God," helps to create the ironic treatment of religion which will permeate the novel. What is the way of all flesh? The biblical echo suggests sin and decay; Butler's fiction, however, reminds the reader that the way of all flesh is change, for better or worse.

Ernest is the product of three generations of upward mobility. His great-grandfather is a simple, kind craftsman who sends his only son into the city. The son, George Pontifex, becomes successful as a publisher and even more successful as a bully. He chooses the Church as a career for his second son, Theobald, who revolts briefly, then acquiesces and evolves into the image of his father. Butler is careful to show personalities as products of environment. George's bullying is only that of an egotistical, self-made man; Theobald's is more harsh, the product of his own fear and suppressed anger. The unfortunate object of this anger is Theobald's firstborn son, Ernest Pontifex.

Ernest's childhood is dominated by fear of his father. His mother, Christina, is of little help; Butler portrays her as the product of her own family life and the larger social system, both of which make marriage a necessity for her. Like Theobald, Christina becomes a hypocrite pressed into the service of "what is done." Much later in life, Ernest reflects that the family is a painful anachronism, confined in nature to the lower species. His opinion is shared by Overton, the narrator of the novel, an old family friend who takes an interest in young Ernest and becomes his lifelong friend and adviser. The two of them, in fact, eventually come to constitute a kind of family—an evolved, freely chosen family, not one formed by mere biological ties.

This outcome occurs only after long agony on Ernest's part. As a child, he believes all that is told: that he is, for example, a wicked, ungrateful boy who deserves Theobald's frequent beatings. His young life is lightened, however, by the interest taken in him by his aunt Alethea and by Overton, who has known all of the Pontifexes well and who tells their story with compassion.

Ernest is still an innocent and unformed young man when he goes to Cambridge to prepare for a career in the Church. Near the end of his peaceful, happy years there, he comes under the influence of an Evangelical group which alters his perceptions of what his life as a clergyman ought to be. Instead of stepping into a pleasant rural parish, Ernest becomes a missionary in the slums of London. He falls under the spell of the oily clergyman Nicholas Pryor, who "invests" Ernest's money and eventually absconds with it. Pryor, the Cambridge enthusiasts, and Theobald Pontifex all represent the clerical life; they are radically different kinds of people, and they are all portrayed negatively. Butler took no prisoners in his war on the clergy; his use of the genial Overton as a narrator partially masks this characteristic.

Sexual ignorance, imposed (and shared) by Theobald and his kind, provides Butler with his next target for satire. In despair over his religious life, Ernest seeks a prostitute and approaches the wrong woman, the eponymous Miss Snow. Ernest's ignorance lands him in prison and cuts him off forever from mere gentility. It redeems him, however, from a life circumscribed by his father: Ironically, Theobald's strict control over Ernest liberates Ernest at last. In prison, stripped of all his former identity, Ernest begins to come to terms with what his life has been and may be. A long illness serves to clarify his mind; he rejects traditional religion, society, and his family's condescending offers of help. Overton alone stands by Ernest, and it is at this point in Ernest's development that they become fast friends. Overton takes on the role of the ideal father—fond, genteel, and moneyed.

It is in this last area that Overton's role is most important to the events of the book: He keeps Alethea's substantial bequest in trust for Ernest, allowing him knowledge of it and access to it, according to Alethea's wish, only when he judges that Ernest is prepared to use it wisely. Ernest's ill-advised marriage and his decision to work as a tailor cause Overton to hold the money back. Eventually, Ernest's maturity evolves to a level acceptable to Overton, and the two of them lead a pleasant life of wealth and, on Ernest's side at least, accomplishment: He has become a writer who, like Butler, writes thoughtful, theoretical books.

In his role as a father, Ernest also has evolved. The children of his marriage to Ellen are reared by simple country people and grow up free of the pressures of Ernest's childhood. After four generations, the Pontifexes have returned to the peaceful and happy life of Ernest's great-grandfather.

Liberal amounts of money, however, keep Ernest's son and daughter from any want that ordinary country folk might experience. Ernest's son wants to be a riverboat captain: Ernest buys him riverboats. This scenario is nearly as idealized a version of country life as was Marie Antoinette's. What makes this vision disconcerting is that Ernest's attitudes are clearly shared by Butler. Early in the novel, Ernest the bullied child is the object of the reader's pity. As a student and young cleric, his life creates a sense of pity but also humor. The more fully Ernest evolves, however, the less appealing the reader is likely to find him. The Ernest who finally comes into his aunt's fortune is a rather dull prig, who, upon learning of his wealth, considers how his emotion might be rendered in music. He tells Overton that he regrets nothing— not his parents' brutality, not prison—because everything has contributed to his evolution away from the "swindle" of middle-class expectations. Unfortunately, this self-satisfied view makes his character seem shallow, consisting only of words and affectations.

In spite of this problem, Butler's achievement is considerable. *The Way of All Flesh* is an immensely ambitious book, and much of it succeeds. Butler articulated fully and convincingly the varied stresses of family life, and that aspect alone would make the novel worthwhile. *Erewhon* and *Erewhon Revisited* share some of that evocative power. They also express Butler's optimism. For all his satirical vision and contentiousness, Butler does offer happy endings: Higgs's successful escape from Erewhon with his beloved, the reunion of the brothers in *Erewhon Revisited*, and the pleasant life of Ernest and Overton in *The Way of All Flesh*. Though societies may often be in the wrong, Butler seems to tell the reader, there is hope in freely chosen human relationships.

Deborah Core

OTHER MAJOR WORKS

NONFICTION: *A First Year in Canterbury Settlement*, 1863; *Life and Habit*, 1877; *Evolution, Old and New*, 1879; *God the Known and God the Unknown*, 1879; *Unconscious Memory*, 1880; *Alps and Sanctuaries of Piedmont and the Ticino*, 1881; *A Psalm of Montreal*, 1884; *Luck or Cunning*, 1887; *Ex Voto*, 1888; *The Life and Letters of Dr. Samuel Butler*, 1896; *The Authoress of the "Odyssey,"* 1897; *Shakespeare's Sonnets Reconsidered*, 1899; *The Notebooks*, 1912 (H. Festing Jones, editor).

TRANSLATIONS: *Iliad*, 1898 (Homer); *Odyssey*, 1900 (Homer).

BIBLIOGRAPHY

Bekker, W. G. *An Historical and Critical Review of Samuel Butler's Literary Works*. 1925. Reprint. New York: Russell & Russell, 1964. A full-length study of Butler written by a native of Holland, where *Erewhon* found popularity and immediate acceptance. Bekker argues for the unity in Butler's works.

Cole, G. D. H. *Samuel Butler and "The Way of All Flesh."* London: Home & Van Thal, 1947. An appreciative study of Butler's novel *The Way of All Flesh*. Contains some discussion of his other works, including *Erewhon*. Also includes valuable background material on Butler, such as his upbringing and his relationship to Darwinism.

Holt, Lee E. *Samuel Butler.* Rev. ed. Boston: Twayne, 1989. Updates this introductory study, first published in 1964. Holt takes into account new scholarships and criticism and new editions of Butler's work. There are chapters on Butler's major fiction, a chronology, and an annotated bibliography.

Jones, Joseph. *The Cradle of "Erewhon": Samuel Butler in New Zealand*. Austin: University of Texas Press, 1959. A valuable account of Butler's five years in New Zealand and the origins of his later *Erewhon* books.

Raby, Peter. *Samuel Butler: A Biography.* Iowa City: University of Iowa Press, 1991. A comprehensive scholarly biography, with detailed notes and bibliography.

C

JAMES BRANCH CABELL

Born: Richmond, Virginia; April 14, 1879
Died: Richmond, Virginia; May 5, 1958

PRINCIPAL LONG FICTION

The Eagle's Shadow, 1904
The Cords of Vanity, 1909
The Soul of Melicent, 1913 (republished as
    Domnei, 1920)
The Rivet in Grandfather's Neck, 1915
The Cream of the Jest, 1917
Jurgen, 1919
Figures of Earth: A Comedy of Appearances, 1921
The High Place, 1923
The Silver Stallion, 1926
Something About Eve, 1927
The White Robe, 1928
The Way of Ecben, 1929
Smirt, 1934
Smith, 1935
Smire, 1937
The King Was in His Counting House, 1938
Hamlet Had an Uncle, 1940
The First Gentleman of America, 1942
There Were Two Pirates, 1946
The Devil's Own Dear Son, 1949

OTHER LITERARY FORMS

James Branch Cabell was both prolific and versatile. In addition to his many novels, he produced a volume of poetry entitled From the Hidden Way (1916) and a play, *The Jewel Merchants* (1921). His short stories are collected in *The Line of Love* (1905), *Gallantry* (1907), *Chivalry* (1909), and *The Certain Hour* (1916). Included among his writings are critical volumes on his contemporaries Joseph Hergesheimer and Ellen Glasgow; *Taboo* (1921), a satire dedicated to Cabell's nemesis, John S. Sumner, who initiated

obscenity charges against his novel Jurgen; Some of *Us* (1930), a defense of the individualism of such writers as Elinor Wylie, Sinclair Lewis, and H. L. Mencken; and *The St. Johns* (1943), a history of a Florida river written with A. J. Hanna, for Stephen Vincent Benét's series entitled "The Rivers of America."

Perhaps Cabell's most interesting volumes are those that illuminate his life and literary development. He wrote two epistolary volumes: *Special Delivery* (1933), which presents both his conventional responses to letters he received and the nonconventional replies he would have preferred to send, and *Ladies and Gentlemen* (1934), a collection of addresses to dead historical figures—from Solomon to George Washington, from Pocahontas to Madame de Pompadour—who have inspired myths and legends. He explores the past of his native region and its impact upon his writings in his trilogy "Virginians Are Various," consisting of *Let Me Lie* (1947), *Quiet, Please* (1952), and *As I Remember It* (1955). Providing readers with insight into Cabell's art are *Beyond Life* (1919), which clarifies his values, literary precedents, and thematic concerns; *These Restless Heads* (1932), a discussion of creativity based upon the four seasons of the year; and *Straws and Prayer-Books* (1924), an explanation of his reasons for writing *The Biography of the Life of Manuel* (1927-1930). Two volumes of Cabell's letters have been published: *Between Friends: Letters of James Branch Cabell and Others* (1962), edited by his second wife, Margaret Freeman Cabell, and Padraic Colum; the other, *The Letters of James Branch Cabell* (1975), edited by Edward Wagenknecht. His manuscripts and memorabilia are in the James Branch Cabell Collections at the University of Virginia in Charlottesville.

ACHIEVEMENTS

Cabell's aesthetic individualism—as expressed in his highly artificial style, his loose, episodic structure, and his peculiar synthesis of romance and comedy, idealism and cynicism, mythology and personal experience—has limited both his popular and critical appeal. As Arvin R. Wells observes in *Jesting Moses:*

A Study in Cabellian Comedy (1962), "It seems fair to say that rarely has a serious literary artist had so little luck in finding a responsive, judicious, and articulate audience." The essays, short stories, and books that Cabell published from 1901 to 1919 received only a small readership along with generally negative reviews, although both Mark Twain and Theodore Roosevelt praised his collection of chivalric tales, *The Line of Love*. Most readers, advocates of realism, found his works too romantic, whereas those with a taste for romance complained that Cabell was too abstruse.

In 1920, when obscenity charges were brought against *Jurgen*, Cabell found himself in the public eye, perceived as a valiant iconoclast battling the forces of puritanical repression. Sales of *Jurgen* skyrocketed, and Cabell enjoyed praise from such respected literary figures as Vernon Louis Parrington, Carl Van Doren, H. L. Mencken, and Sinclair Lewis, who, in his Nobel Prize address of 1930, acknowledged Cabell's achievement. Suddenly, in critical studies, literary histories, and anthologies, Cabell was elevated to, as the critic Joe Lee Davis explains, "the rank of a 'classic' and an 'exotic' in the movement of spiritual liberation led by H. L. Mencken, Theodore Dreiser, Eugene O'Neill, and Sinclair Lewis." The public fanfare of the 1920's, however, inspired primarily by the eroticism in Cabell's works, proved to be short-lived—not to the surprise of Cabell, who, in *These Restless Heads*, predicted the decline of his literary generation. In the 1930's and 1940's, Cabell was viewed as a trifling talent, rooted to the 1920's and to his native Virginia. His aestheticism displeased the ethical neohumanists; his escapism annoyed the Marxists. The New Critics and mythic critics paid him scant attention. In the 1950's, three major literary historians—Edward Wagenknecht, Edd Winfield Parks, and Edmund Wilson—called for a reevaluation of Cabell's career, but they did little to change public opinion. Virtually all of Cabell's books are out of print, although a late twentieth century surge of interest in fantasy literature brought some attention to his work, and he is appreciated primarily by a coterie of scholars and graduate students.

BIOGRAPHY

Born on April 14, 1879, in Richmond, Virginia, James Branch Cabell grew up there as a Southern gentleman. His parents—Robert Gamble Cabell II, a physician, and Anne Branch—were both from distinguished Southern families. Cabell's paternal great-grandfather was a governor of Virginia; his paternal grandfather held two claims to fame, having been a schoolmate of Edgar Allan Poe at the English and Classical School in Richmond and later a neighbor and the personal physician of General Robert E. Lee. On his mother's side of the family, Cabell was related through marriage to a number of prominent Virginia families and was cousin to a governor of Maryland. Fostering Cabell's aristocratic pride still further was his "mammy," Mrs. Louisa Nelson, who, in her several decades of service in the Cabell household, doted upon James and encouraged him to consider himself a privileged member of society.

Cabell's outstanding intellect asserted itself early. He performed brilliantly at the College of William

(Library of Congress)

and Mary in Williamsburg, which he attended from 1894 to 1898. His professors suggested that he revise a sophomore paper entitled "The Comedies of William Congreve" for publication, and later asked him to teach courses in French and Greek at the college. The only blemish upon Cabell's academic career was a scandal during his senior year. One of his professors was accused of having homosexual relations with his students; Cabell, because he had been friends with the man, was briefly implicated. The unpleasant episode had positive repercussions, however, for in wandering about Williamsburg alone and troubled, Cabell met Ellen Glasgow, who had come to town to research the background for a novel. She offered him sympathy, and thus began a lifelong friendship. Soon, the charges against Cabell were dropped for lack of evidence, and he was graduated with highest honors.

After his graduation, Cabell pursued writing both as a vocation and an avocation. He served as a copyholder on the *Richmond Times* in 1898, then spent two years working for the *New York Herald*, and in 1901 he worked for the *Richmond News*. For the next decade, he worked as a genealogist, traveling about America, England, Ireland, and France to examine archives. Not only did this occupation result in two volumes of the Branch family history—*Branchiana* (1907), a record of the Branch family in Virginia, and *Branch of Abingdon* (1911), a record of the Branch family in England, but it also prepared Cabell for his future literary endeavors in tracing the lineage of a character through twenty-two subsequent generations. During that same time, Cabell wrote several novels and steadily produced short stories, which he contributed to such periodicals as *The Smart Set, Collier's Weekly, Red Book, Lippincott's,* and *Harper's Monthly*. In 1911, Cabell, disappointed by his lack of acclaim as a writer, took a position in coal-mining operations in West Virginia; in 1913, he abandoned the experiment and returned to Richmond to resume work as a genealogist.

On November 8, 1913, at the age of thirty-four, Cabell gave up what had been a carefree bachelorhood, filled with romantic intrigues, to marry Rebecca Priscilla Bradley Shepard, a widow with five children. Marriage proved mutually satisfying to Cabell and Priscilla. He enjoyed the domesticity of his new lifestyle, including the rearing of their son Ballard Hartwell; she delighted in performing the literary and social duties that came with being his wife. Their thirty-five-year union was marked by undying affection and loyalty.

Literary prominence, or perhaps one should say notoriety, came to Cabell in 1920 when John S. Sumner, the executive secretary of the New York Society for the Suppression of Vice, seized the plates and copies of his novel *Jurgen* and accused the publishing company, McBride, of violating the anti-obscenity statutes of the New York State penal code. Sumner's action proved ill-advised, for it only increased the public's interest in Cabell's writings during the two and a half years before the obscenity trial was finally held. On October 19, 1922, after a three-day trial, the jury acquitted McBride, and Cabell emerged as a celebrity.

During the 1920's, Cabell took a more active role as a literary leader and was instrumental, along with Ellen Glasgow, in making the nation aware of Richmond as a literary center. While writing books with great regularity (during the 1920's, he published seven novels, one play, and several works of short fiction and nonfiction), Cabell also entertained and corresponded with a number of important literary figures, including Sinclair Lewis, Hugh Walpole, and Carl Van Vechten. In addition, he served as a writer and guest editor for *The Reviewer*, Richmond's impressive contribution to the vogue of little magazines. As active as Cabell was on the literary scene, he was still able to continue his career as a genealogist, working for the Virginia Chapter of the Sons of the Revolution and other historical societies, as well as serving as editor of the Virginia War History Commission.

The last decades of Cabell's life were anticlimactic, fraught with physical ailments and an increasing disillusionment with the American reading public. With the advent of the Great Depression, his literary fame seemed to weaken and then die. From 1932 to 1935, Cabell—like Sherwood Anderson, George Jean Nathan, Eugene O'Neill, and Theodore Dreiser—attempted to rekindle the vital skepticism of the 1920's, serving as editor of the *American Spectator*; he soon realized, however, that his efforts to enlighten the public were useless. In the mid-1930's, Cabell suffered from repeated attacks of pneumonia, and Priscilla developed severe arthritis; thus, they frequently sought relief in the warm climate of St. Augustine, Florida. There, Priscilla died of heart failure on March 29, 1949. Her death left Cabell feeling bitter, lost, and angry, but he continued to write steadily. In 1950, he regained some of his former zest for life when he decided to wed Margaret Waller Freeman, a member of the Richmond literati whose acquaintance he had made years earlier while writing for *The Reviewer*. Cabell died of a cerebral hemorrhage on May 5, 1958, in Richmond.

ANALYSIS

James Branch Cabell's art rests upon a paradox. On the one hand, he contends that man is idealistic and must therefore create dreams to sustain himself. On the other, he mocks man's tendency "to play the ape to his dreams"—that is, to seek the unattainable foolishly. Manipulating the polarities of romance and comedy, Cabell responded to the predominant intellectual trend of the early twentieth century—naturalism. From a cosmic perspective, he had no difficulty accepting the premise that man is like a bit of flotsam in a deterministic universe, subject to environmental forces, but unable to control or understand them. From a humanistic point of view, however, he could not tolerate the limitations that naturalism imposed upon man's mind. For Cabell, man does not survive because he adapts to biological, social, or economic forces, but rather because he persists in believing in the products of his own imagination—what he terms "dynamic illusions." These illusions, according to Cabell, emanate from the demiurge, or psyche, yet they are rooted in man's primitive, animal instincts. Their source of energy is the libido. Thus, Cabell's protagonists move between two realms of experience. They are romantic questers after ideal beauty, perfection, and salvation; they are also comic bumblers whose lusts, vanities, and misconceptions entangle them in a web of complexities. Cabell's narratives follow a Hegelian pattern. His thesis is that man desires to escape from the dull, routine world of actuality. His antithesis is that such a desire can never be attained; disillusionment is inevitable. Yet in the synthesis, man achieves a degree of satisfaction. He learns that his ideals are illusions, but also that they should be cherished, for in the realm of the imagination, dreams themselves have a reality.

Cabell's background explains his propensity for blending the romantic and the comic. Quite early, he developed a love for myth and legend. As a child, he delighted in such books as *Old Greek Stories Simply Told, Stories of Old Rome, Book of Bible Stories*, and *Stories of the Days of King Arthur*. Cabell gained a strong sense of aristocratic pride—an appreciation of the Southern characteristics of chivalry and gallantry—yet he was no dreamy-eyed romantic. He saw the ironic underside of life. In growing up, he heard frank gossip, as well as heroic tales, from his elders. In college, Cabell became interested in the Restoration comedy of manners, which heightened his awareness of the hypocrisies and absurdities of human behavior. Such weaknesses became more immediately apparent when, as a bachelor in his twenties and early thirties, he vacationed at the Virginia resort of Rockbridge Alum. There, he witnessed and participated in affairs that assumed the facade of chaste, genteel encounters, but were actually indulgences in lust. From his various experiences, Cabell developed a dichotomous concept of the artist, appropriate to his blending of romance and comedy. The artist assumes an exalted status, painting beautiful visions of life as it ought to be. Ironically, however, because of this detached, godlike perspective, skepticism intrudes. The world that the artist portrays becomes a caricature; it mocks and contradicts his idealistic presentation. For Cabell, the ideal and the real coexist.

THE BIOGRAPHY OF THE LIFE OF MANUEL

Cabell's major literary achievement is his eighteen-volume *The Biography of the Life of Manuel*, which he wished readers to regard as a single book. In 1915, Cabell conceived the idea of bringing together his writings into one vast architectural construct, and for the next fifteen years, he strove to achieve his plan:

revising published works, deciding upon a logical arrangement, and writing new tales and romances to clarify his design. The result was the Storisende Edition of *The Works of James Branch Cabell*, bound in green and gold. Cabell's magnum opus represents an ingenious application of his genealogical talents to the realm of fiction. Spanning seven centuries and moving from the imaginary medieval realm of Poictesme to modern Virginia, it celebrates the life force passed on by Manuel to his descendants.

The design of *The Biography of the Life of Manuel* is best viewed in musical terms. Whether one considers it to be a fugue, as does Louis Untermyer in *James Branch Cabell: The Man and the Masks* (1970), or a sonata, which is the thesis of Warren McNeil in *Cabellian Harmonics* (1928), it revolves upon three themes and their variations. These themes are three philosophies of life: the chivalrous, the gallant, and the poetic. The chivalrous attitude views life as a testing; dominated by the will, it represents an ideal tradition in which men revere first God and then noble women. Quite the opposite, the gallant attitude views life as a toy; its social principle is hedonism. This attitude emphasizes the intelligence and is thus skeptical. Celebrating both chivalry and gallantry, the final attitude, the poetic, views life as raw material out of which it creates something that transcends life. It is controlled by the imagination.

These attitudes of the chivalrous, the gallant, and the poetic determine the structure of Cabell's work. In *Beyond Life*, the prologue to *The Biography of the Life of Manuel*, he defines them. Then, in *Figures of Earth*, Cabell presents the life of Manuel of Poictesme, who at various times is affected by all three codes, and follows it with *The Silver Stallion*, which traces the development of the legend of Manuel the Redeemer. The fourth volume—composed of *Domnei* and *The Music from Behind the Moon*—treats one aspect of the chivalric code: woman worship. Cabell then elaborates upon the subject in his short-story collection entitled *Chivalry*. He next examines the gallant attitude in *Jurgen*; inserts *The Line of Love*, which treats all three attitudes; then returns to gallantry in *The High Place* and the short-story collection *The Certain Hour*. The next four volumes

move to the modern world: *The Cords of Vanity* presents Robert Townsend, a gallant; *From the Hidden Way* offers Townsend's verses; *The Rivet in Grandfather's Neck* portrays a chivalrous character; and *The Eagle's Shadow* examines the poet. Finally, *The Biography of the Life of Manuel* circles back upon itself, as the soul of Felix Kennaston, the protagonist of *The Cream of the Jest*, journeys back to Poictesme through his dreams. Cabell's vast design concludes with an epilogue, *Straws and Prayer-Books*, and *Townsend of Lichfield*, containing notes and addenda.

FIGURES OF EARTH

Figures of Earth, one of Cabell's finest novels, follows its author's typical tripartite pattern of quest, ensuing disillusionment, and final transcendence, as it traces the career of the swineherd Manuel. Subtitled *A Comedy of Appearances*, it is a complex allegorical work peopled with supernatural and preternatural beings who reside in the imaginary medieval land of Poictesme. The tale begins when Miramon Lluagor, the master of dreams, appears to Manuel at the pool of Haranton. There, he convinces Manuel to abandon his job as a swineherd—that is, to rebel against the elemental forces of life—and to pursue knight-errantry in seeking the beautiful yet unattainable Lady Gisele. Eager to make a fine figure in the world, Manuel repudiates his lover Suskind, a mysterious creature who represents the unconscious desires of the libido, and sets forth, unaware that he is being victimized by Horvendile, the diabolical spirit of romance. On his journey, he has a series of encounters with allegorical women. He first meets Niafer, a rather plain kitchen servant, who symbolizes worldly wisdom and domesticity. Dressed as a boy, she accompanies Manuel on his quest until, when faced with his own death unless he gives up Niafer, Manuel decides to sacrifice her to Grandfather Death. His next encounter is with the Princess Alianora, who represents political power, worldly position, and the undercurrent of sexual excitement that accompanies them. Manuel surrenders to lust, but eventually rejects Alianora, discovering the limitations of self-seeking gallantry. His third important encounter is with the supernal Queen Freydis, who symbolizes creative inspiration. Using magic, Manuel persuades her to leave her realm of Audela and enter the ordinary world. She does so out of love for him and animates a set of clay figures that he sculpted as a swineherd. These eventually enter history as major writers.

Manuel soon discovers that Freydis cannot give him fulfillment; only Niafer can, so he submits to thirty years of slavery to The Head of Misery to bring Niafer back from the dead. Then he settles down to a comfortable existence as a husband, father, and the Count of Poictesme. One day, however, while watching his wife and daughter through the window of Ageus (Usage) in his palace study, he discovers to his horror that their figures are only scratched upon the glass—that beyond the window is a chaos containing the images of preexistence, including the disturbing Suskind. Manuel must then choose whether to die himself or to allow his child Melicent to die in his place, while he resumes his relationship with Suskind. Acting decisively, he murders Suskind, bricks up the study window, and departs with Grandfather Death. In the last chapter, Grandfather Death accompanies him to the River Lethe, where he watches the images of his life as they sweep by him. Then the scene blurs, as Cabell moves his readers back to the pool of Haranton where Manuel began his quest. He repeats the dialogue of the first chapter, in which Miramon refers to Count Manuel, who has just died. Thus, Cabell ends with an appropriate reminder of his view of life as a cycle in which one life passes into other lives through heredity.

Manuel is Cabell's man of action, driven by dreams of a better life than that of a swineherd, yet the pursuit of dreams proves frustrating. Even in the mythical realm of Poictesme, Cabell constantly emphasizes through allegory the realities of death, misery, and madness. Life, Manuel learns, is full of obligations: to Alianora, Melicent, and especially to Niafer. Indeed, Cabell underscores this lesson by structuring his episodes into five books entitled "Credit," "Spending," "Cash Accounts," "Surcharge," and "Settlement." Yet it is in confronting his obligations that Manuel finds fulfillment. The romantic quest results in a comic exposure of man's limitations, but the final picture is of human dignity in accepting those limitations. Manuel can never completely obliterate discontent, but he decides that the human possessions of a kingdom, a wife, and a family, even if they are illusions, are better than a return to the primitive unconsciousness. Thus, although he never achieves the object of his initial quest, he does transcend experience through belief in his destined role as the Redeemer of Poictesme and his ultimate rejection of lust for love.

Figures of Earth, because of its confusing cast of characters—some of whom are figures of earth and some unearthly—and the artificialities of Cabell's prose, makes difficult reading. The effort is rewarding, however, for Cabell offers some intriguing insights into man's values: that the demands of the family and the aspirations of the individual often conflict; that the world is duplicitous; and that the search for perfection involves paradoxically the self-realization of imperfection. The work is thought-provoking and timely.

JURGEN

Jurgen follows the same movement as *Figures of Earth*: the pursuit of perfection, the discovery that it does not exist, and then the satisfaction achieved through accepting actuality; it merely views these ideas from a different perspective. The controlling concept is justice, which to Cabell's title character, a poetry-producing pawnbroker, means that in the universe, every idealistic desire should have a means of being fulfilled. Jurgen's problem, however, is that existence is unjust; since man's intellect increases as his physical prowess diminishes, he can never completely realize his potential. Granting Jurgen a temporary respite from his dilemma, Cabell allows his middle-aged poet to retain his youthful body and then lets his reader see the subsequent effects upon his protagonist's values.

Jurgen began as a tale entitled "Some Ladies and Jurgen," which Cabell published in *The Smart Set* in 1918. His novel simply expands upon the narrative of that story. The hero meets a monk, who curses the devil for causing him to trip over a stone. Jurgen, playing the devil's advocate, defends evil. Shortly thereafter, he meets a black gentleman who thanks him for the defense and expresses the hope that his life will be carefree. When Jurgen replies that such a life is impossible, since he is married, the stranger promises to reward him. The reward turns out to be the disappearance of Jurgen's wife, Dame Lisa. When he returns home, she is gone; he later learns that she has been seen near a cave outside town. Feeling an obligation, he goes there, only to encounter the black gentleman—who, he learns, is Koshchei the Deathless, the controller of the universe. Koshchei tempts Jurgen by evoking three women that he feels would be more suitable for a poet: Queen Guenevere, Queen Anaïtis, and Queen Helen—standing respectively for faith, desire, and vision. Jurgen rejects each, however, and asks for Dame Lisa back. She appears, lectures him, and then leaves for home. In response, Jurgen praises her as a source of poetic inspiration more valuable than faith, desire, and vision, and then follows her home.

Expanding his narrative for the novel, Cabell added two fantasy sequences that would explain Jurgen's ultimate attraction to Lisa. In the first, Jurgen visits the Garden between Dawn and Sunrise, where he relives falling in love with Dorothy la Désirée, one of the daughters of Manuel. She destroys his romantic bliss when she marries the wealthy Heitman Michael and then engages in adulterous affairs. Because of Dorothy's behavior, Jurgen marries Lisa. In the second episode, Jurgen, having been granted by Mother Sereda the recovery of a bygone Wednesday, fantasizes about how his relationship with Dorothy might have developed. He imagines himself killing Heitman Michael and claiming her, but as the Wednesday ends, he finds himself embracing the Dorothy of reality, an aged femme fatale.

Cabell also expanded his original tale by depicting Jurgen's adventures in five realms: Glathion, Cocaigne, Leukê, Hell, and Heaven. Throughout these episodes, Jurgen assumes the roles of charlatan and womanizer, as he tests historical systems of values. In Glathion, he examines the medieval tradition of Christian chivalry, but rejects it as being irrational. In Cocaigne, he becomes equally dissatisfied with hedonistic paganism. Leukê, a stronghold of the Hellenic tradition, teaches him the danger of the realm of utilitarian Philistia. In Hell, Jurgen learns of the sin of pride, and in Heaven he encounters selfless love.

Feeling the shadow of worldly wisdom trailing him, Jurgen finally decides to give up his youthful body and return to the domestic comforts that Dame Lisa can provide. He trades the ideal for the actual, yet in so doing bestows romantic value upon his ordinary existence and his ordinary wife.

Although entertaining, *Jurgen* lacks clarity of design. The reader who is steeped in mythology may enjoy Cabell's manipulation of the legends of Faust, Don Juan, King Arthur, Troilus and Cressida, and Ulysses and Penelope, but somehow, the integration of the hero's adventures with the narrative line exploring the feelings between husband and wife is incomplete. The episodic looseness of the novel is distracting. Thus, modern readers, like those titillated readers of the 1920's, may be absorbed by Jurgen's amorous exploits without fully considering Cabell's analysis of the values that make life worth living.

Cabell's great achievement is that he celebrated the illusion-making capacity of the mind while simultaneously exposing man's follies in pursuing dreams. He merged the traditions of humanism and skepticism. Reacting against naturalism, Cabell had the courage to present a transcendent view of life—one that acknowledged not man's impotency, but his potential. A meticulous craftsman, a daring iconoclast, an imaginative thinker, Cabell deserves recognition as a major writer of the twentieth century.

Lynne P. Shackelford

OTHER MAJOR WORKS

SHORT FICTION: *The Line of Love*, 1905; *Gallantry*, 1907; *Chivalry*, 1909; *The Certain Hour*, 1916; *The Music from Behind the Moon*, 1926.

PLAY: *The Jewel Merchants*, pb. 1921.

POETRY: *From the Hidden Way*, 1916.

NONFICTION: *Branchiana*, 1907; *Branch of Abingdon*, 1911; *Beyond Life*, 1919; *The Judging of Jurgen*, 1920; *Taboo*, 1921; *Joseph Hergesheimer*, 1921; *Straws and Prayer-Books*, 1924; *Some of Us*, 1930; *These Restless Heads*, 1932 (contains two short stories and personal reminiscences); *Special Delivery*, 1933; *Ladies and Gentlemen*, 1934; *Of Ellen Glasgow*, 1938; *The St. Johns*, 1943 (with A. J. Hanna); *Let Me Lie*, 1947; *Quiet, Please*, 1952; *As I Remem-*

ber It, 1955; *Between Friends: Letters of James Branch Cabell and Others*, 1962 (Margaret Freeman Cabell and Padraic Colum, editors); *The Letters of James Branch Cabell*, 1975 (Edward Wagenknecht, editor).

MISCELLANEOUS: *The Biography of the Life of Manuel: The Works of James Branch Cabell*, 1927-1930 (18 volumes).

BIBLIOGRAPHY

Duke, Maurice. *James Branch Cabell: A Reference Guide*. Boston: G. K. Hall, 1979. A most useful guide, in a chronological format, to the writings about Cabell; spans reviews to full-length studies.

Himelick, Raymond. *James Branch Cabell and the Modern Temper: Three Essays*. New York: Revisionist Press, 1974. Himelick explores realism and romance, the fact and the dream in Cabell's novels. Sees Cabell as an antiromantic whose novels convey his understanding of life as a "grotesque comedy."

Inge, Thomas M., and Edgar E. MacDonald, eds. *James Branch Cabell: Centennial Essays*. Baton Rouge: Louisiana State University Press, 1983. A compilation of essays that were presented at Virginia Commonwealth University, 1979, in commemoration of the centennial of Cabell's birth. A most useful volume with valuable biographical information and criticism. Also includes a bibliographical essay.

MacDonald, Edgar. *James Branch Cabell and Richmond-in-Virginia*. Jackson: University Press of Mississippi, 1983. A very detailed, authoritative biography that seeks to set Cabell in his period and region. Includes excellent bibliography.

Riemer, James D. *From Satire to Subversion: The Fantasies of James Branch Cabell*. New York: Greenwood Press, 1989. Riemer devotes separate chapters to *The Cream of the Jest, Jurgen, Figures of Earth, The High Place, The Silver Stallion*, and *Something About Eve*. These books encompass Cabell's greatest achievement, Riemer argues. His introduction provides a good overview of the writer's career. Includes a very useful bibliography.

Tarrant, Desmond. *James Branch Cabell: The Dream and the Reality*. Norman: University of Oklahoma Press, 1967. A full-length critical study of Cabell that examines the author as mythmaker. Discusses both Cabell's early and later works, but Tarrant's eulogistic approach weakens his criticism.

Van Doren, Carl, H. L. Mencken, and Hugh Walpole. *James Branch Cabell: Three Essays*. Port Washington, N.Y.: Kennikat Press, 1967. Criticism of a very high standard—both erudite and entertaining—by three eminent authors. Included in the appendix is a sampling of book reviews. A valuable contribution to critical studies on Cabell.

GEORGE WASHINGTON CABLE

Born: New Orleans, Louisiana; October 12, 1844
Died: St. Petersburg, Florida; January 31, 1925

PRINCIPAL LONG FICTION
The Grandissimes, 1880
Dr. Sevier, 1884
Bonaventure, 1888
John March, Southerner, 1894
The Cavalier, 1901
Bylow Hill, 1902
Kincaid's Battery, 1908
Gideon's Band, 1914
Lovers of Louisiana, 1918

OTHER LITERARY FORMS

In addition to nine novels, George Washington Cable published a novella, *Madame Delphine* (1881), and four collections of short stories: *Old Creole Days* (1879); *Strong Hearts* (1899); *Posson Jone' and Père Raphaël* (1909); and *The Flower of the Chapdelaines* (1918). He also wrote a dramatized version of one of his novels, *The Cavalier*. His eight books of nonfiction cover miscellaneous subjects. *The Creoles of Louisiana* (1884) is a collection of history articles, and *Strange True Stories of Louisiana* (1889) is a collection of factual stories; both collections are set in

Cable's native state. *The Silent South* (1885) and *The Negro Question* (1890) are collections of essays on southern problems. *The Busy Man's Bible* (1891) and *The Amateur Garden* (1914) grew out of Cable's hobbies of Bible-teaching and gardening. *A Memory of Roswell Smith* (1892) is a memorial tribute to a friend. *The Cable Story Book: Selections for School Reading* (1899) is a book of factual and fictional material for children. Cable also wrote magazine articles and a newspaper column.

ACHIEVEMENTS

In his study *George W. Cable* (1962), Philip Butcher shows the high position that Cable held in American literature in the last years of the nineteenth century. In 1884, the *Critic* ranked him ahead of fourteenth-place Mark Twain on its list of "Forty Immortals." A cartoon in *Life* (May 27, 1897) depicted Cable among the ten most popular authors of the day. In the American edition of *Literature* in 1899, he was tenth on the list of greatest living American writers.

Popular both with critics and with the reading public in his own time, Cable is little known today. His reputation as a writer of fiction rests on three works: the novel *The Grandissimes*, the novella *Madame Delphine*, and the collection of short stories *Old Creole Days*, later editions of which include *Madame Delphine* as the lead story. Although *Dr. Sevier* and *John March, Southerner* contain serious commentary, the three novels which followed in the first decade of the new century are trivial romances. His last two novels, *Gideon's Band* and *Lovers of Louisiana*, signal only an incomplete return to the artistic level and social worth of his first three books. Because much of his energy went into provocative social essays on southern racial problems, into humanitarian reforms in such areas as prisons and insane asylums, into cultural projects, and, as a major source of income, into platform tours, Cable found insufficient time for the fiction he might otherwise have created. Nevertheless, as late as 1918 he published a collection of short stories and a novel, and up to his death in 1925 he was working on still another novel.

Cable was much admired by his contemporaries. William Dean Howells praised him privately and in

(Library of Congress)

print. Twain took him as a partner on a reading tour, and for four months (1884-1885) the two shared the stage as they read from their respective works. Cable also read on programs that included Hamlin Garland, James Whitcomb Riley, Eugene Field, and other popular writers of the day.

Popular in Great Britain as well, he was invited to England by James S. Barrie for the first of two trips abroad (1898, 1905). For nearly three months in 1898, he traveled and visited in the homes of Barrie, Sir Arthur Conan Doyle, Rudyard Kipling, Henry James, and other well-known figures. He was an interesting conversationalist, an effective speaker, and an entertaining performer. His British friends arranged for him to read his fiction, play a guitar, and sing Creole-black songs in their homes and in public halls. Andrew Carnegie, his host at Skibo Castle, was so impressed with Cable's personality and writing that he later bestowed a lifetime pension on him. Among his honorary degrees was the Doctorate of

Letters given by Yale University in 1901 to Cable, Twain, Howells, Theodore Roosevelt, Woodrow Wilson, and other contemporary notables.

Cable's reputation began to decline before his death and has never recovered. In the 1980's he was considered too important a writer to be omitted from southern literature anthologies and American literature textbooks, but at the end of the twentieth century he had yet to be deemed worthy of widespread revival.

BIOGRAPHY

George Washington Cable was born in New Orleans, Louisiana, on October 12, 1844. Ancestors of his mother, Rebecca Boardman Cable, had lived in New England since the seventeenth century and had moved to Indiana in 1807. The background of his father, the elder George Washington Cable, dates back to pre-Revolutionary times in Virginia. The elder Cable lived in Virginia and Pennsylvania with his parents before moving to Indiana, where he married Rebecca in 1834. The Cable family migrated to New Orleans in 1837, where George, their fifth child, was born.

In the 1840's, the Cables lived a comfortable existence, owning several household slaves until the father's business failed. Through the 1850's, the elder Cable worked at a series of jobs until, weakened in health, he died on February 28, 1859. Because young George's older brother, along with an older sister, had died of scarlet fever, his father's death required him, not yet fourteen, to leave school to support the family. Until the third year of the Civil War, he held his father's former position as a clerk at the customhouse.

Slight in size—only five feet five inches and weighing one hundred pounds—and deceptively youthful in features, Cable enlisted in the Confederate Army on October 9, 1863, three days before his nineteenth birthday. Incurring two slight wounds during his service, he was discharged in 1865.

After the war, Cable worked as errand boy, store clerk, and, until malaria stopped him, as a rodsman with a surveying party on the Red River. In 1868, he became a bookkeeper for two cotton firms in New Orleans. He married Louise Stewart Bartlett on December 7, 1869, and soon fathered the first of a large family of children. At one time, he worked simultaneously for the cotton house of William C. Black and Company, the New Orleans Cotton Exchange, and the National Cotton Exchange.

Newspaper work provided Cable's first opportunity to see his writing in print. While continuing as an accountant, he worked for newspapers as a freelance contributor and then as a full-time reporter. For eighteen months, beginning February 27, 1870, he wrote the column "Drop Shot" weekly, and then daily, for the New Orleans *Picayune*. While working for the *Picayune*, his research into Louisiana history at city hall, the cathedral, and the Cabildo, former seat of colonial government, led him to factual stories later to be shaped into fiction. In addition, his newspaper reports on contemporary local affairs interested him in reform on civic, regional, and national levels.

Appearing in *Scribner's Monthly*, Cable's stories were based on his knowledge of the people and activities of New Orleans and of events in Louisiana history. Six of the stories appearing in *Scribner's Monthly* and a seventh story, "Posson Jone'," which was published in *Appleton's Journal*, were later collected as *Old Creole Days*, published by Scribner's. His first novel, *The Grandissimes*, also based on the people and history of Louisiana, was serialized in *Scribner's Monthly* over a twelve-month period and then published in book form in 1880. Next came the novella *Madame Delphine*, first printed in *Scribner's Monthly* as a three-part serial, and then published in book form in 1881.

In 1881, Cable gave up his position as an accountant, depending for the rest of his life on lectures and public readings of his fiction to supplement his income as a writer. One of his successes was a series of six lectures at The Johns Hopkins University in 1883, and he continued to find himself in demand on platforms in many cities. In 1884, his regional history *The Creoles of Louisiana* appeared, and in the same year his second novel, *Dr. Sevier*, was published. In 1884-1885 he went on a successful reading tour with Mark Twain.

Cable, son of a slaveholding family, was a loyal Confederate soldier during the Civil War and apparently remained unchanged in political stance for some time thereafter. Later, however, he began to express feeling against racial injustice. Although criticism of discrimination is present in his fiction, it was only through the direct statements of his magazine articles and public lectures that fellow southerners became fully aware of his radical stance. The publication of a volume of his essays, *The Silent South* (1885), made his stand clear. Newspaper editorialists who had acclaimed his fiction now began to attack his social and political views.

Cable had two households to support—one including his wife and children, and the other his mother, his sisters, and the children of his widowed sister. His wife, who traced her ancestry back to the Mayflower, was born and reared in New England. Cable believed that a return to the climate of New England would be beneficial for his wife's frail health. In addition, the attraction that a location near his publishers in New York held for him, and a sensitivity to the criticism aimed at him in the South, influenced his decision to leave New Orleans after forty years of residence there. Having previously visited Northampton, Massachusetts, he moved his wife and children to a home there in 1885, and his mother, sisters, and cousins followed soon thereafter.

Despite his desire to write fiction, Cable allowed other interests to take much of his time. In 1885, he championed black rights in an essay read nationwide, "The Freedman's Case in Equity." In 1886, he founded the first of the Home Culture Clubs, in which he would be involved for the next thirty-five years. Through his Open Letter Club (1888-1890), in whose name he lectured, wrote, and published, Cable completed the period identified as his greatest effort for reform in the South. From 1887 to 1889, he undertook an extensive program of religious writing and teaching; he conducted a large Bible class in Northampton each Sunday, traveling to Boston on Saturdays to hold a similar class.

For five years, Cable published a book annually; *Bonaventure, Strange True Stories of Louisiana, The Negro Question, The Busy Man's Bible,* and *A Mem-*

ory of Roswell Smith were all published during this period. At the same time, he was giving readings and lectures from coast to coast. A popular speaker, he was frequently invited to deliver commencement addresses and to give talks on literary subjects, southern problems, and Creole history. Despite his endeavors, however, he remained constantly in debt—receiving advances on royalties from his publishers, obtaining loans, repaying old debts, and incurring new ones.

By this time, Cable had ceased actively campaigning for civil rights, and his writing developed a noncontroversial tone. His third novel, *John March, Southerner,* although concerned with Reconstruction problems, avoided racial issues, as did his collection of short stories *Strong Hearts. The Cable Story Book,* needless to say, offended no one. The following novels, *The Cavalier* and *Bylow Hill,* veered even more sharply from controversy to entertainment, their artistic value diminishing proportionately.

Meanwhile, in 1898, Cable had made a triumphal reading tour in Britain. Philanthropist Andrew Carnegie, with whom Cable became friends while in Scotland, donated money to one of Cable's long-enduring projects. In 1903, Carnegie agreed to give fifty thousand dollars for a building for the Home Culture Clubs on the condition that five thousand dollars a year be guaranteed locally for five years.

Dimming Cable's good fortune, his beloved wife died on February 27, 1904, ending a devoted marriage of nearly thirty-five years. Cable continued to write, although without immediately readying a book for publication. Two years and nine months after Louise's death, he married Eva C. Stevenson. In 1908, he published the novel *Kincaid's Battery,* and in 1909 he put two of his short stories (one of them selected from the *Old Creole Days* collection) into book form, *Posson Jone' and Père Raphaël.* In 1911, Carnegie began sending Cable one thousand dollars a year to support his writing. Three years later, *Gideon's Band* and *The Amateur Garden* were published.

Despite his debts, Cable managed to travel outside the United States even before Carnegie began to subsidize him. When traveling, he often carried with him an unfinished manuscript, working on it when he had time. In later years, no longer dependent on the platform circuit, he began staying in Northampton in the summer, spending the winter in New Orleans, Florida, and Bermuda. In 1918, at the age of seventy-four, he published two books—*The Flower of the Chapdelaines*, a collection of short stories, and *Lovers of Louisiana*.

When Carnegie died in 1919, his will provided Cable with five thousand dollars a year for life, the annuity to be transferred to Eva if she survived her husband. Eva, however, died on June 7, 1923. Six months after her death, Cable married his third wife, Hanna Cowing. A little more than a year later, on January 31, 1925, he died. Among his literary papers was an unfinished novel on which he had been working.

ANALYSIS

Although George Washington Cable's reputation rests primarily on one collection of short stories and two pieces of longer fiction, his total output includes twenty-two books. For an understanding of Cable as a writer of fiction, one should first consider his non-fiction and his reasons for writing it. Cable's interest in history is shown in two books centered on Creole culture, *The Creoles of Louisiana*, a collection of history articles, and *Strange True Stories of Louisiana*, a collection of factual stories about the Creoles. On a juvenile level, *The Cable Story Book* is a combination of factual and fictional material that emphasizes the same Creole subjects as his fiction. *The Silent South* and *The Negro Question*, his best-known works of nonfiction, are collections of essays on controversial southern problems, notably the problem of racial discrimination. Characteristic of Cable's prose is a moral posture and a humanitarian zeal, openly stated in his nonfiction and imaginatively expressed in the most important of his fiction. He worked for the reform of people and institutions and for a reversal in racial attitudes.

THE GRANDISSIMES

Cable's first novel, *The Grandissimes*, is his unqualified masterpiece. Louis D. Rubin, Jr., has called it the first "modern" southern novel, dealing realistically as it does with the role of the black in American

society. Added to the rich portrayal of aristocratic Creole settings and family problems, a panoramic array of characters of Native American, black, and mixed bloods vivify problems of social castes and racial discrimination in Louisiana in 1803, the year of the Louisiana Purchase. Using the historical actuality of racially tangled bloodlines as the theme for dramatic episodes, Cable emphasizes the ramifications of black-white relationships. The free quadroon caste, for example, had its special role in southern society, as shown historically in the New Orleans "quadroon balls." Beautiful young women of one-quarter black blood (quadroons) or, perhaps, one-eighth (octoroons) danced at these balls with white men, were chosen by them as mistresses, and were set up in separate households in the city.

Two principal quadroons interact in *The Grandissimes*. A male quadroon is the identically named half-brother of the aristocratic Creole Honoré Grandissime. The darker Honoré Grandissime flouts the law by refusing to inscribe the letters "f.m.c." (free man of color) after his name. Educated in Paris along with his half-brother and heir to most of their deceased father's wealth, the quadroon nevertheless remains unrecognized as a legitimate member of the Grandissime family. The Creoles' acceptance of an American Indian chieftain as ancestor is introduced to point up their unwonted prejudice against the taint of black blood. The main female quadroon is Palmyre Philosophe, a freed slave who bears a hopeless love for the all-white Honoré Grandissime and, in turn, is loved by his quadroon half-brother. To illustrate the injustices perpetrated against blacks, Cable inserts the episode of the black Bras-Coupé, a historical figure used earlier in Cable's unpublished short story "Bibi." Palmyre hates Agricola Fusclier, her former owner and uncle to Honoré Grandissime, who forced her unconsummated marriage to Bras-Coupé.

The character who serves throughout the novel as spokesman for Cable is Joseph Frowenfeld, a German American newcomer to New Orleans, who observes, participates in, and comments critically on the action. Honoré Grandissime, the leading male character, is a Creole who recognizes the faults of his society and works with moderation to correct them. He provides a liberal Creole viewpoint, supplementary to the rigid moral judgment of Frowenfeld. Agricola Fuselier, in direct contrast to Frowenfeld, represents the proud old Creoles who insist on purity of race.

Action antecedent to the yearlong events of the novel goes back to 1673, the year of the birth of the American Indian girl whose choice of a De Grapion suitor began a feud between two Creole families, the De Grapions and the Grandissimes. Preceding the main plot by eight years comes the tale of Bras-Coupé. Otherwise, the action takes place between September, 1803, and September, 1804.

The leading female character, Aurora Nancanou, daughter of a De Grapion, is the young widow of a man killed by Agricola Fuselier in a duel over a card game. Agricola took Nancanou's estate in payment for the gambling debt, passing the estate on to his nephew, the white Honoré, and leaving Aurora and her daughter Clotilde without land or money. The novel opens at a masked ball in New Orleans where Aurora and Honoré meet, unaware of each other's identity, thus beginning a romantic complication. Paralleling the love triangle of Palmyre and the Grandissime half-brothers, Joseph Frowenfeld falls in love with Clotilde, who, at the same time, is desired by Frowenfeld's friend Dr. Charlie Keene.

Honoré Grandissime, as leader of the Grandissime family and as Cable's symbol of right-thinking Creoles, upsets his relatives on several occasions: Endangering the Grandissime finances, he returns Aurora Nancanou's property to her; in an act socially degrading to the family, he becomes a partner with the quadroon Honoré, under the business title "The Grandissime Brothers"; on an uneasy political level, he cooperates with Claiborne, the newly appointed territorial governor.

Romance, realism, and melodrama are mingled in *The Grandissimes*. In a romantic resolution, the De Grapion-Grandissime feud is ended, and marriage is imminent for two sets of lovers—Aurora and the white Honoré Grandissime, Clotilde and Frowenfeld. On the realistic side—with an admixture of melodramatic incidents—the two leading quadroons of the

story are defeated. After Palmyre's several attempts to get revenge on the object of her hate, Agricola Fuselier, and after he is stabbed by the quadroon Honoré, she is forced to flee for safety to Paris. She is accompanied by her fellow refugee, Honoré Grandissime (f.m.c.), who commits suicide by drowning because of her final rejection of him.

Intentional obscurity is a characteristic of Cable's style in *The Grandissimes*. Lack of direct statement and slow revelation of relationships mark the progress of the plot. Facts are given through hints and implication; full information is withheld in a dense accumulation of incidents. This technique, typical of his early and best works, has been praised for its artistry and criticized for its lack of clarity.

Cable's portrayal of slaveholders, slaves, and the stubbornly held traditions of French Louisiana added a new dimension to southern literature. Succeeding in his aim as a novelist, Cable found that fame brought a painful backlash. His radical views caused this native son to be identified as a traitor to New Orleans and the South.

MADAME DELPHINE

In 1881, Cable published the novella *Madame Delphine*, the third in the three-year sequence of Cable's finest literary works (after the short-story collection *Old Creole Days* and the novel *The Grandissimes*). First published as a three-part novelette in *Scribner's Monthly* from May to July, 1881, *Madame Delphine* was published by Scribner's in book form later that year. In editions of *Old Creole Days* succeeding its initial publication, *Madame Delphine* is included and given lead position in the book.

The story begins with beautiful Olive Delphine returning from France on a ship that is boarded by the Creole pirate Ursin Lemaitre. Confronted by Olive's piety and charm, Lemaitre is struck with repentance for his sinful life and with love for the unidentified stranger. Settling in New Orleans, the reformed Lemaitre changes his name to Vignevielle and turns from piracy to banking. When not in his banker's office, he wanders through the streets, searching for the mysterious young woman.

Eventually, the lovelorn banker and Olive develop a friendship and marriage becomes their intention.

Olive, however, is not legally able to become Lemaitre's wife, for she has black ancestry. Her mother, Madame Delphine, is a quadroon, the mistress to a white man, Olive's father. Madame Delphine, despite the laws against miscegenation, approves of the marriage. Indeed, she has made it clear that she is seeking a white husband for her daughter.

Vignevielle's relatives and friends, knowing that Madame Delphine is a quadroon, attempt to stop the illegal marriage, going so far as to threaten to turn him over to government agents who are searching for him. Madame Delphine meanwhile puts forth the ultimate effort to make the union possible. Producing fabricated evidence, she perjures herself by swearing that she is not the girl's blood mother. After Vignevielle and Olive are married, Madame Delphine goes for confession to the priest Père Jerome, admits her lie, and dies. Père Jerome speaks the closing line: "Lord, lay not this sin to her charge!"

The style of *Madame Delphine* is leisurely. Little mysteries cling to characters and actions, with revelation coming in glimpses, suggestions, and half-expressed statements. Early reviewers compared Cable to Nathaniel Hawthorne in achievement of mood, atmosphere, and ambiguity. Adverse criticism of *Madame Delphine*, however, finds the work excessively obscure; most troubling to critics is the needlessly complicated unfolding of the plot.

Furthermore, the characterization of the lovers is weak. Vignevielle's switch from dashing pirate to banker is inadequately motivated. Olive is a shadowy figure without distinguishable traits. Madame Delphine, despite her maneuvers, approaches the stereotype of the helpless mother. The only strong character is Père Jerome, a compassionate observer and spokesman for Cable. Père Jerome sees that society deserves blame, both for its actions and for its failure to act. Society acquiesces in evil—from its unprotesting profit in Lemaitre's smuggled goods to its deliberate manipulation of the lives of mulattoes.

More significant than the style of *Madame Delphine* is its portrayal of the southern attitude toward miscegenation. Although romanticism embellishes the outwardly happy ending of the story, Cable's recognition of the female mulatto's untenable

position is clear. Looking beyond the temporary bliss of the wedding day, the reader realizes that prospects for Olive in New Orleans are not favorable. Madame Delphine's perjury has made the marriage legally permissible, but in the eyes of Lemaitre's friends, Olive is not and will never be an acceptable member of their aristocratic society.

The developing social consciousness revealed by Cable in *Madame Delphine* gives the work a lasting value. After this novella, though, he confined the most telling of his indictments to essays, disappointing readers who waited for his familiar critical tone in future novels. He was never able to duplicate the blend of artistic craftsmanship, authentic local color, and social commentary which distinguishes *Madame Delphine*, *The Grandissimes*, and *Old Creole Days*.

Bernice Larson Webb

OTHER MAJOR WORKS

SHORT FICTION: *Old Creole Days*, 1879; *Madame Delphine*, 1881; *Strong Hearts*, 1899; *Posson Jone' and Père Raphaël*, 1909; *The Flower of the Chapdelaines*, 1918.

NONFICTION: *The Creoles of Louisiana*, 1884; *The Silent South*, 1885; *Strange True Stories of Louisiana*, 1889; *The Negro Question*, 1890; *The Busy Man's Bible*, 1891; *A Memory of Roswell Smith*, 1892; *The Amateur Garden*, 1914.

MISCELLANEOUS: *The Cable Story Book: Selections for School Reading*, 1899.

BIBLIOGRAPHY

Bikle, Lucy Leffingwell. *George W. Cable: His Life and Letters*. New York: Charles Scribner's Sons, 1928. A valuable intimate portrait by Cable's daughter, Bikle's biography stresses family interests more than literary ones and tends to drop names. The student may be interested in the illustrations of Cable's residence, family, and the people he knew.

Cleman, John. *George Washington Cable Revisited*. New York: Twayne, 1996. Cleman provides a critical introduction to Cable's life and work, focusing on the major works: *Old Creole Days*, *Madame Delphine*, and, in particular, *The Grandissimes*.

Less attention is paid to Cable's other work. Cleman also includes chapters devoted to Cable's advocacy of civil rights for African Americans, his political writing, and his later works of "pure fiction."

Petry, Alice Hall. *A Genius in His Way*. Cranbury, N.J.: Associated University Presses, 1988. A literary study focusing on the short stories from *Old Creole Days*, but opening with a chapter on *Madame Delphine*, this book is rather scholarly, but accessible to an advanced high school student. The bibliography includes only items cited in the text.

Rubin, Louis D., Jr. *George W. Cable: The Life and Times of a Southern Heretic*. New York: Pegasus, 1979. By Rubin's own admission, the biography in this book is dependent on the work of Arlin Turner, but Rubin's comments on the individual stories are insightful and helpful. Has complete chapters on *Old Creole Days, The Grandissimes, Dr. Sevier*, and *John March, Southerner*.

Turner, Arlin. *George W. Cable: A Biography*. Durham, N.C.: Duke University Press, 1957. This award-winning biography by an important critic emphasizes Cable's life but offers helpful insight into his writing as well, with three novels receiving their own chapters. Still the most detailed biography of Cable available.

_____. *Mark Twain and George W. Cable: The Record of a Literary Friendship*. East Lansing: Michigan State University Press, 1960. Drawing almost exclusively on letters between the two writers, this short volume is useful for its personal insights.

James M. Cain

Born: Annapolis, Maryland; July 1, 1892
Died: Hyattsville, Maryland; October 27, 1977

PRINCIPAL LONG FICTION

The Postman Always Rings Twice, 1934
Double Indemnity, 1936
Serenade, 1937
The Embezzler, 1940
Mildred Pierce, 1941
Love's Lovely Counterfeit, 1942
Three of a Kind, 1943 (includes *Career in C Major, Double Indemnity*, and *The Embezzler*)
Past All Dishonor, 1946
The Butterfly, 1947
Sinful Woman, 1947
The Moth, 1948
Three of Hearts, 1949 (inludes *Love's Lovely Counterfeit, Past All Dishonor*, and *The Butterfly*)
Jealous Woman, 1950
The Root of His Evil, 1951
Galatea, 1953
Mignon, 1963
The Magician's Wife, 1965
Cain x 3, 1969 (includes *The Postman Always Rings Twice, Double Indemnity*, and *Mildred Pierce*)
Rainbow's End, 1975
The Institute, 1976
Cloud Nine, 1984
The Enchanted Isle, 1985

OTHER LITERARY FORMS

James M. Cain's career as a novelist began relatively late in life. Cain first wrote professionally as a journalist. Long after he had become famous for his fiction, he would describe himself in *Who's Who in America* as a "newspaperman." Cain used his newspaper work as a springboard to a broader literary career in the 1920's. As a member of the editorial staff of the New York *World* he commented acerbically on contemporary American culture. Cain also authored a number of short stories, which never appeared in hardcover during his lifetime. Following Cain's death, Roy Hoopes edited three collections of his journalistic writing and short fiction, *The Baby in the Icebox and Other Short Fiction* (1981), *Sixty Years of Journalism* (1986), and *Career in C Major and Other Fiction* (1986). Cain long dreamed of becoming a playwright, but success eluded him. An early effort, *Crashing the Gates* (1926), failed before reaching

Broadway. A dramatization of *The Postman Always Rings Twice* (1936) ran for seventy-two performances in New York. Cain spent many years in Hollywood as a screenwriter but only received screen credit for three films, *Algiers* (1938), *Stand up and Fight* (1939), and *Gypsy Wildcat* (1944).

ACHIEVEMENTS

James M. Cain's standing as a novelist has long been the subject of critical controversy. His first novel, *The Postman Always Rings Twice*, became a sensational best-seller. Yet its lurid mix of sex and violence inevitably led to doubts about Cain's literary seriousness. In the years that followed, Cain never strayed from his twin themes of crime and sexual obsession. Critical opinion was divided among those who appreciated Cain as a poet of tabloid murder, such as writer Edmund Wilson, and those who believed that Cain exploited rather than explored the material of his books, such as the novelist James T. Farrell. After his period of greatest notoriety during the Depression and the World War II years, Cain's work was largely ignored by critics and scholars. He never received a literary prize for his novels, though late in life he received a lifetime achievement award from the Mystery Writers of America. Cain himself tended to dismiss critical commentary on his artistry, preferring instead to quote his sales figures. Novels such as *The Postman Always Rings Twice*, *Double Indemnity* (1936), and *Mildred Pierce* (1941) endure as classic examples of the "hard-boiled" or "tough guy" school of writing which flourished in the 1930's and 1940's, and inspired American film noir. Along with such contemporaries as Dashiell Hammett and Raymond Chandler, James M. Cain will be remembered as a writer who illuminated an existential terror lying just beneath the often-glittering surface of American life.

BIOGRAPHY

James Mallahan Cain was the eldest of two sons and three daughters born to James William Cain and Rose Mallahan Cain. His father was a professor of English and a college administrator who became the president of Washington College. His mother was a trained opera coloratura who gave up her professional ambitions to raise a family. Later in life Cain repeatedly expressed a sense of resentment and rivalry regarding his handsome and accomplished father. He revered his mother and imbibed from her an abiding love of the opera. After graduating from Washington College in 1910, Cain attempted to realize his dreams of a career in the opera by studying to be a singer. Unfortunately his voice could not match his aspiration, and he quit after a year of frustration. Between 1910 and 1914, Cain worked at a succession of jobs as he searched for a direction in life. He decided to become a writer, though he always regarded writing as a second choice because of his failure to express himself in music. He moved home and began writing short stories and sketches, none of which he could sell. Cain supported himself by teaching mathematics and English at Washington College and earned a master's degree in drama.

Restless, Cain moved to Baltimore in 1917 and found work as a newspaper reporter. He volunteered for service in World War I and edited the seventy-ninth-division newspaper. Upon demobilization, Cain returned to Baltimore and journalism. He embarked upon a course that made him a successful man of letters in the 1920's. He began publishing essays and stories in journals such as *The Atlantic Monthly*, *The Nation*, and the *Saturday Evening Post*. He became friends with editor H. L. Mencken and contributed a series of satirical dialogues to Mencken's *The American Mercury*, published in *Our Government* in 1930. After a brief stint teaching at St. John's College in Annapolis, Cain moved to New York City in 1924. He joined the editorial staff of the New York *World*. There he wrote witty commentaries on life during the Jazz Age. When the *World* failed in 1931, Cain moved to *The New Yorker* as managing editor. He stayed at *The New Yorker* only nine months. Like many other writers, Cain traveled to Hollywood, taking advantage of a lucrative offer to write screenplays.

Cain never became a great success at screenwriting. By 1933, he was out of a job. Financially pressed, he wrote his first novel that spring and summer. *The Postman Always Rings Twice* appeared in

1934 and was a literary sensation and popular triumph. *The Postman Always Rings Twice* revived Cain's Hollywood career, and he made California the setting of his most powerful works. During the 1930's, Cain produced a string of rough-edged novels which evoked some of the darkest shadows of life in Depression-era America. With the 1940's, however, Cain's inspiration seemed to fade, though he published for another thirty years. In 1946-1947, he attempted to organize an American Authors' Authority, which would have protected the economic rights of writers, but the effort failed. Cain proved a poor husband to three wives, but in 1947 he married successfully for the fourth time, to Florence Macbeth, an opera singer like his mother. In 1948, Cain returned home to Maryland, moving to Hyattsville. He lived there quietly, continuing to write until his death in 1977.

ANALYSIS

James M. Cain's strengths as a novelist are inextricably bound to his weaknesses. He has often been praised for the economy of his style and the speed with which he moves his narrative. Readers experience a delicious sense of surrender to the headlong impetus of his storytelling. Yet, motion in Cain often masks wayward prose and manipulative plotting. Critics have remarked on the cinematic quality of his writing. His protagonists live in his pages with the vibrant immediacy of Hollywood icons on the big screen. Cain's actors flirt with caricature; his characterizations are often so primitive and mechanical that they are ludicrous in retrospect.

Cain explores elemental passions in his novels. Sex, jealousy, and greed drive his characters as they thrust themselves into webs of crime and deceit. The intensity of Cain's evocation of this raw emotionalism imbues certain of his most notorious scenes with a surreal naturalism. Frank and Cora's frenzied love-making next to the body of the man they have killed in *The Postman Always Rings Twice* and Sharp's rape of Juana in a church in *Serenade* transcend and transfigure the more mundane trappings of Cain's stories. Moments like these also open Cain to the charge that he is trafficking in sensationalism, reveling in the

sordid for its own sake. There is a voyeuristic quality to Cain's writing. He exposes his readers to the scabrous underside of the American Dream. Although he occasionally referred to his novels as morality tales, Cain rarely provides any moral alternative to the obsessive dreams of his characters, other than the faceless brutality of authority.

In Cain's universe the only law is chance. His protagonists enjoy no dignity with their various ends. Unlike the heroes of classical tragedy, their destinies do not illuminate the contours of a higher moral order. They are simply victims of an impersonal and blindly malevolent fate. This nihilism gives Cain's writings much of their enduring power. He captured the desperation of people leading blighted lives in a world wracked by the Great Depression. As long as men and women continue to sense their own powerlessness in a modern, mass-produced society, Cain's fables of reckless desire will resonate with readers.

THE POSTMAN ALWAYS RINGS TWICE

Cain's first novel is generally considered his greatest. It adumbrates themes and techniques that characterize his fiction. The novel is cast in the form of a confession, written by Frank Chambers on the eve of his execution. Frank, like many of Cain's protagonists, is doomed by his relationship with a woman. A homeless drifter, Frank wanders into a roadside "bar-b-que" and meets Cora, the frustrated wife of the Greek owner. Immediately drawn together by an overwhelming sexual magnetism, Frank and Cora kill the Greek in a fake auto accident. However, the murder drives the lovers apart, as their passion is clouded by suspicion and fear. Ironically, Cora dies in a real car crash. Frank is then condemned for a murder he did not commit. Cain's grim tale proved very influential. French writer Albert Camus acknowledged *The Postman Always Rings Twice* as an inspiration for *L'Étranger* (1942; *The Stranger*, 1946), his own existential meditation on crime and punishment.

DOUBLE INDEMNITY

Double Indemnity first appeared as a magazine serial. Cain wrote it for money, and he did not regard it very highly. Over time, the novel has come to be regarded as one of Cain's greatest achievements. Like

The Postman Always Rings Twice, it is written in confessional form and tells a story of the fatal consequences of the wrong man meeting the wrong woman. Walter Huff, an insurance salesman, encounters Phyliss Nirdlinger, a beautiful, unhappily married woman. Desire and villainy blossom together as Huff sees an opportunity to win the woman he loves while at the same time beating the system he has long served. Huff and Phyliss kill Mr. Nirdlinger, making it look like an unusual accident, worth a double indemnity on his life insurance. As always in Cain, however, success in crime brings only anxiety and distrust. The lovers' mutual doubts and jealousy culminate in a deadly meeting on a cruise ship.

SERENADE

Serenade provided sensational reading in the 1930's. It is Cain's psychologically outlandish commentary on sex and artistry. The protagonist and narrator, John Sharp, is an opera singer who has retreated to Mexico because of the failure of his voice. Cain's premise is that Sharp cannot sing because of his receptiveness to the homosexual advances of conductor Stephen Hawes. Sharp falls under the spell of Juana, an uneducated earth mother, whose embraces restore his sexual and vocal potency. Sharp returns to California and stardom. His success is challenged when Hawes appears. Juana kills Hawes, almost ritually, during a mock bullfight. Sharp insists on fleeing with Juana and inadvertently causes her death.

MILDRED PIERCE

Mildred Pierce marked a departure for Cain. The book contains no murders; it is told in the third person; its protagonist is a woman. Yet the novel remains true to Cain's dark vision of human relationships. Mildred Pierce is a middle-class housewife who rejects her philandering husband. Forced to support herself, she begins as a waitress and becomes the owner of a chain of restaurants. Mildred's undoing is her extravagant, almost incestuous, love for her daughter Veda, an aspiring opera singer. Mildred mortgages her restaurants to finance Veda's career. Veda responds by leaving, taking with her Mildred's second husband. Mildred lives on, ruined and alone, her career a perverse distortion of America's Horatio Alger myth.

THE BUTTERFLY

Cain's originality and intensity seemed to dissipate with the end of the Depression and the advent of World War II. Some critics think highly of *The Butterfly*, a tale of incest and murder set in the mountains of eastern Kentucky. In this novel Cain ambitiously attempts to delineate the psychology of a delusional and obsessive personality as he traces the agonies of a self-righteous mountaineer sexually drawn to a young woman he believes to be his daughter. Cain's lofty intentions never attain fruition, however, because he allows his mountaineer and supporting characters to dissolve into vulgar and simplistic stereotypes. Flawed as it is, *The Butterfly* is the best of Cain's later writing, which separates into unrealized historical romances and diffident echoes of his earlier work. Cain's reputation as a novelist will always rest upon the bitter existential melodramas he produced in the 1930's.

Daniel P. Murphy

OTHER MAJOR WORKS

SHORT FICTION: *The Baby in the Icebox and Other Short Fiction* (1981, posthumous, Roy Hoopes, editor); *Career in C Major and Other Fiction*, 1986 (Hoopes, editor).

PLAYS: *Crashing the Gates*, pr. 1926; *The Postman Always Rings Twice*, pr. 1936; *7-11*, pr. 1938.

SCREENPLAYS: *Algiers*, 1938; *Stand up and Fight*, 1939; *Gypsy Wildcat*, 1944.

NONFICTION: *Our Government*, 1930; *Sixty Years of Journalism*, 1985 (Hoopes, editor).

BIBLIOGRAPHY

Fine, Richard. *James M. Cain and the American Authors' Authority.* Austin: University of Texas Press, 1992. A solid study of Cain's attempt to create an American Authors' Authority in the mid-1940's. The AAA would have been a national writer's organization with wide-ranging powers to protect its members' property rights. Fine argues that the failure of the AAA contributed to the economic marginalization of American writers.

Hoopes, Roy. *Cain.* New York: Holt, Rinehart and Winston, 1982. An exhaustive and admiring biography of Cain by the editor of several posthumous collections of Cain's writings.

Madden, David. *Cain's Craft*. Metuchen, N.J.: Scarecrow Press, 1985. A collection of essays exploring Cain's literary techniques by one of his earliest academic champions. Madden compares some of Cain's works to novels by other writers and addresses the ways his books have been adapted to the screen.

_____. *James M. Cain*. New York: Twayne, 1970. An early but essential overview of Cain's career and literary contribution. Madden recognizes Cain's artistic limitations but evaluates his work sympathetically, and he sees him as an important member of the "tough-guy" school of American literature.

Marling, William. *The American Roman Noir: Hammett, Cain, and Chandler*. Athens: University of Georgia Press, 1995. An intriguing exercise in literary criticism which links the hard-boiled writing of Dashiell Hammett, James M. Cain, and Raymond Chandler to contemporary economic and technological changes. Marling sees them as pioneers of an aesthetic for the postindustrial age.

Skenazy, Paul. *James M. Cain*. New York: Continuum, 1989. A comprehensive study of Cain's work. Skenazy is more critical of his subject's writing than is Madden but acknowledges Cain's importance and his continuing capacity to attract readers.

ERSKINE CALDWELL

Born: White Oak, Georgia; December 17, 1903
Died: Paradise Valley, Arizona; April 11, 1987

PRINCIPAL LONG FICTION

The Bastard, 1929
Poor Fool, 1930
Tobacco Road, 1932
God's Little Acre, 1933
Journeyman, 1935
Trouble in July, 1940
All Night Long: A Novel of Guerrilla Warfare in Russia, 1942
Tragic Ground, 1944
A House in the Uplands, 1946
The Sure Hand of God, 1947
This Very Earth, 1948
Place Called Estherville, 1949
Episode in Palmetto, 1950
A Lamp for Nightfall, 1952
Love and Money, 1954
Gretta, 1955
Claudelle Inglish, 1958
Jenny by Nature, 1961
Close to Home, 1962
The Last Night of Summer, 1963
Miss Mamma Aimee, 1967
Summertime Island, 1968
The Weather Shelter, 1969
The Earnshaw Neighborhood, 1972
Annette, 1974

OTHER LITERARY FORMS

Erskine Caldwell's first published work was "The Georgia Cracker," a 1926 article. Other pieces were printed in "little" magazines, and then in *Scribner's Magazine*. For several decades, he regularly wrote articles for magazines and newspapers. He produced several nonfiction books, some in collaboration with photojournalist Margaret Bourke-White (at one time his wife): *You Have Seen Their Faces* (1937), *North of the Danube* (1939), *All-Out on the Road to Smolensk* (1942), and *Russia at War* (1942). His collections of short stories include *American Earth* (1931), *We Are the Living: Brief Stories* (1933), *Kneel to the Rising Sun and Other Stories* (1935), *Southways: Stories* (1938), and *Jackpot: The Short Stories of Erskine Caldwell* (1940), which contains all the stories of the first four books in addition to nine new ones.

ACHIEVEMENTS

More than sixty-four million copies of Caldwell's books have been published in thirty-four countries, with 320 editions released in such languages as Croatian, Chinese, Slovene, Turkmenian, Arabic, Danish, Hebrew, Icelandic, Russian, and Turkish. He has been called the best-selling writer in America.

In 1933, Caldwell received the *Yale Review* award for fiction for his short story "Country Full of Swedes." Between 1940 and 1955, he was editor of twenty-five volumes of a regional series, *American Folkways*. His novel *Tobacco Road* was adapted for the stage in 1934 by Jack Kirkland and ran seven and a half years on Broadway, a record run. It was made into a motion picture in 1941. *Claudelle Inglish* became a film in 1961. *God's Little Acre*, possibly his best-known novel, sold more than eight million copies in paperback in the United States alone and became a film in 1959.

BIOGRAPHY

Erskine Caldwell was the son of a preacher, Ira Sylvester Caldwell. His mother was Caroline "Carrie" Preston (Bell) Caldwell of Staunton, Virginia. At the time Erskine was born, on December 17, 1903, the Reverend Caldwell was minister in Newman, Georgia, in Coweta County, forty miles from Atlanta. His wife, active in helping her husband in his ministry, also ran a small school. She taught Caldwell through much of his elementary and secondary education, both in her school and at home. He actually spent only one year in public school and one in high school.

Between 1906 and 1919, the Caldwells moved several times as the ministry dictated. This not-quite-nomadic existence and the straitened circumstances under which the family lived were probably influential in molding Caldwell into early self-reliance and in fostering a wanderlust that persisted throughout his youth and adult life. Caldwell left home at fourteen, roaming about the Deep South, Mexico, and Central America. He did return home, however, to complete his high school education.

In 1920, Caldwell enrolled in Erskine College in Due West, South Carolina. From 1923 to 1924, he attended the University of Virginia on a scholarship; in 1924, he studied for two terms at the University of Pennsylvania. In 1925, he returned to the University of Virginia for an additional term, but he was never graduated.

(CORBIS/Hulton-Deutsch Collection)

While attending the University of Virginia, he married Helen Lannegan, and it was at this time that he decided to write for a living. With his wife and growing family of three children (Erskine Preston, Dabney Withers, and Janet), he lived in Maine between 1925 and 1932 while he wrote and earned a living at odd jobs; seven years of writing elapsed before any of his work was published. In his lifetime, Caldwell had experience as a mill laborer, cook, cabdriver, farmhand, stonemason's helper, soda jerk, professional football player, bodyguard, stagehand at a burlesque theater, and once even a hand on a boat running guns to a Central American country in revolt.

He published his first article in 1926. Soon Maxwell Perkins, the legendary editor at Charles Scribner's Sons, discovered some of his works and was enthusiastic and encouraging about his talent. Subsequently, Perkins published *American Earth* and *Tobacco Road*, which brought Caldwell his first real recognition. When Caldwell and Perkins had a serious disagreement, Caldwell switched his publishing allegiance to The Viking Press.

Divorced from his first wife in 1938, Caldwell married the photojournalist Margaret Bourke-White. They collaborated on several successful books, but the marriage ended in divorce in 1942. The same year, he married June Johnson, with whom he had one son, Jay Erskine. In 1957, after divorcing his third wife, he married Virginia Moffett Fletcher.

During the 1940's, Caldwell traveled to China, Mongolia, Turkestan, and Russia. Because of the powerful, enthusiastic way in which he wrote about Russia and in turn indicated certain aspects of American capitalism, some accused him of being a Communist, a charge he emphatically denied.

Caldwell was a member of the National Institute of Arts and Letters, the Authors League of America, the Phoenix Press Club, and the San Francisco Press Club. Active as a writer and lecturer, Caldwell toured Europe in the 1960's under the auspices of the United States State Department. In the 1970's, he made a series of speeches in Georgia, promoting the paperback reprint of his 1937 book *You Have Seen Their Faces*. He used this opportunity to decry the remaining poverty in the South despite its industrialization.

In 1974, Caldwell underwent surgery for the removal of a growth on his lung; he submitted to similar surgery the following year. He regained enough health to publish two collections of short stories and two nonfiction volumes in the 1980's. Caldwell died in Arizona in 1987.

ANALYSIS

Erskine Caldwell is the chronicler of the poor white. He has told the story of the diversions and disasters of the poor Southerner with more detail and sympathetic attention than any other American writer of his time. In doing so, he has created memorable characters and unforgettable episodes and has provoked scandalized eyebrow-raising at his language, his imagery, and his view of life.

Obscenity charges have been filed against an inordinate number of Caldwell's books, only to be fought down in court: One man's obscenity is another man's earthy realism. The attendant publicity generated more curiosity about his books, and sales soared. The

self-appointed censors who attacked his books in court were only slightly more antagonistic than the reviewers who labeled his works "orgiastic litanies" and "particularly ugly stories" to be read with disgust and "a slight retching."

Charges of obscenity barraged the publication of *God's Little Acre* from New York to Denver. *Tobacco Road* had an arduous struggle to stay on the booksellers' shelves. *Tragic Ground* ran into trouble with Canadian censors. But how obscene are these books? By today's standards even *God's Little Acre* seems only mildly lewd. Under the layer of animalistic sexual behavior and uncouth, uncultured dialogue, qualities of literary merit are readily discernible.

The most prominent and lasting quality of Caldwell's fiction—the one which has made *Tobacco Road* a minor classic and several other of his earlier novels important literary pieces—is comic grotesquerie. Caldwell conveys a kind of ludicrous horror that becomes more horrible when the reader realizes that hyperbole does not negate the truth behind the most ridiculous episodes: The poor people of the South were deprived to the point of depravity. Writing in a naturalistic style, Caldwell allows the reader to observe the day-to-day activities of poor white families whose impoverished condition has created tragicomic eccentricities.

Those impoverished conditions are the key to understanding Caldwell's main thrust in nearly all of his earlier novels. Living in hopeless hunger, illiterate, and essentially cut off from the world of progress, ambition, and culture, Caldwell's characters seem not quite human. The veneer of civilized attitudes and activities has been ground away by the endless struggle to satisfy the daily hunger and to find some hope, in a vast vista of barren prospects, of a better day tomorrow.

Caldwell was deeply concerned that this segment of society he chose to depict in his work had been repressed by ignorance and poverty as an almost direct result of society's indifference. In later works such as *The Weather Shelter* or even *Claudelle Inglish*, he shifted his attention from the thoroughly downtrodden to the merely browbeaten, but he continued to make a statement about society's indifference to the poor and about the survival instinct of the poor that makes them persevere.

Caldwell's earlier books are generally considered his better efforts; his themes and characters were fresh, and he had not yet begun to rework them with regularity. Still, there is a kind of plot formula in his first important novels: The main characters are introduced with a recounting of their day-to-day activities wherein their basic problem is presented; a new character is introduced, bringing what seems to be an opportunity for some degree of betterment; then tragedy strikes, usually resulting in the death of a sympathetic character. There are seldom any "bad guys" in Caldwell's novels, no dastardly villains. The villain is society, which allows abject poverty, ignorance, hunger, and hopelessness to exist without trying to correct the circumstances that caused them. His characters, victims of society, flounder into tragic situations without knowing how to save themselves.

TOBACCO ROAD

In the case of *Tobacco Road*, tragedy strikes as unpredictably as lightning, and the characters accept their lot as though it were a natural, unalterable phenomenon. This book, perhaps his best-known work, is the story of a family of ignorant poor white Georgians who at the outset are at the depths of degradation. They have no food, no prospects, and no apparent opportunity to get either. They have settled into a bleak routine, planning to plant a crop in the vague future and hoping for something to happen to change their lot. Jeeter Lester, the patriarch, has the last trace of a noble love of the land and a strong inherent need to farm his land and produce a crop, yet he cannot or will not do any of the practical things that must be done for serious, lifesaving farming. He has no money and no credit, and he will not leave his farm to find work in the town to get the money for seed and fertilizer. Thus, he drifts from day to day with good intentions but takes no positive action. Survival for him and his family has reached an "every man for himself" level. His mother is treated with less consideration than a dog: When any food is acquired, as when Jeeter steals a bag of turnips from his son-in-law, the old mother is not given any. The others in the family—Jeeter's wife Ada and the

two remaining children, Ellie Mae and Dude—are equally unfeeling.

These people seem to be as far down the scale of humanity as anyone can get, yet the story relates a series of episodes that carries them progressively further to degeneracy and death. The casual attitude toward sex, as shown in the scenes with Dude and his "new" wife Bessie, brings to mind the blasé attitude that farmers show toward the breeding of their farm animals. There is no particularly lewd interest in the family's attempts to spy on the "honeymooning" couple. Rather, their curiosity seems born of boredom or the simple need for distraction. Because Caldwell has narrated these episodes in blunt, realistic language, a puritanical mind might see a moral looseness in them which could be (and was) attributed to an immoral intent on the part of the author. Viewed from the perspective of fifty years, however, the actions of the characters appear not obscene but merely uncivilized.

Another scene involves the accidental killing of an African American in a wagon. Rammed and overturned by the new car acquired by Bessie (as a not-very-subtle enticement to persuade Dude to marry her), the black is crushed by the wagon. The Lesters, having caused the accident, go blithely on their way. Their only concern is the wrecked fender of the car. They philosophize that "niggers will get killed." The killing of another human being is as casually natural to them as the killing of a dog on a highway.

The most inhuman and inhumane episode involves the death of Mother Lester, who is hit by the car in the Lester yard. She is knocked down and run over, "her face mashed on the hard white sand." She lies there, unaided by any of the family, hardly even referred to beyond Ada's comment that "I don't reckon she could stay alive with her face all mashed like that." The old woman struggles a bit, every part of her body in agonizing pain, and manages to turn over. Then she is still. When Jeeter at last decides something must be done with his old mother, he looks down and moves one of her arms with his foot, and says, "She aint stiff yet, but I don't reckon she'll live. You help me tote her out in the field and I'll dig a ditch to put her in."

When Caldwell depicts the indifference of the family members to Mother Lester's slow, painful death, he is really depicting the degeneracy of people whom society has deprived of all "human" feeling. Thus, when in the last chapter the old Lester house catches fire and burns up the sleeping occupants without their ever waking, the reader may well feel that poetic justice has been served: The Lesters have lived a subhuman existence, and their end is fittingly subhuman. Yet, one does not entirely blame the Lesters for their lack of humanity; Caldwell moves his readers to wonder that a rich, progressive country such as the United States could still harbor such primitive conditions.

The comic quality that is so much a part of Caldwell's work saves *Tobacco Road* from utter grimness. Some of the episodes with the car, Jeeter's maneuverings to get money from his new daughter-in-law, the turnip filching—all create a climate that lightens the pervading ugliness. The sexual adventures are irreverent and bawdy; the dialogue is the ridiculous, repetitive gibberish of single-minded illiterates engrossed in their own narrow concerns. There is a particularly comic quality in Jeeter's serious pronouncements, which bespeak a completely unrealistic creature, out of touch with himself and his true condition. The enduring ridiculousness of Jeeter and his family is undercoated with a pathos that is obvious to the thoughtful reader. The condition and ultimate end of Jeeter and Ada are perhaps atypical but are still symptomatic of the condition and ultimate end of the many others like them living in the destitute areas of the South.

GOD'S LITTLE ACRE

Caldwell's *God's Little Acre* was considered by some critics his best work up to that time. A *Forum* review said it was "the first thing [Caldwell] has done which seems . . . to justify in any way the praise the critics have heaped upon him." There are flaws, as some reviewers were quick to point out, including repetitiousness and a too sudden and unexpected transition from a comic atmosphere to violent tragedy, yet it is second in quality only to *Tobacco Road* among Caldwell's novels.

God's Little Acre tells the story of Ty Ty Walden, a Georgia dirt farmer who for fifteen years has been digging enormous holes in his land looking for gold. Ty Ty, who is in most other respects a man with considerable mother wit, has a curious tunnel vision where this quest for gold is concerned. Because of it, he neglects his farming to the point of endangering his livelihood and that of his family. Worse yet, he fails to see the peril in the growing tension among the members of his family living on the farm with him. The inevitable tragedy results from the fact that he has two beautiful daughters and an even more beautiful daughter-in-law, Griselda. Ty Ty himself praises Griselda so much to anyone who will listen that he is largely instrumental in encouraging the fatal allure she has for the other men in the family. When these men—a son, Jim Leslie, and a son-in-law, Will Thompson—make advances toward Griselda, her husband Buck understandably becomes enraged. He is thwarted in his revenge against Will Thompson by another calamity—Will, a mill worker, is killed during a strike action—but Jim Leslie does not escape his brother Buck's wrath, nor does the tragedy stop there, for Buck's action is harshly punished.

The opening episodes of the novel are comic: Pluto Swint, the fat, lazy suitor of the younger daughter, Darling Jill, is clearly a comic character in the mold of the sad clown. The enthusiastic search for the albino Dave, who according to black lore can divine gold lodes, is humorous: The process of finding him, roping him, dragging him away from his home and wife, and keeping him under guard like a prized animal is handled with a matter-of-fact detachment that makes these actions acceptable, predictable, and ridiculous, all at once. Darling Jill's sexual promiscuity and amoral attitude are refreshingly animalistic, even though some readers might disapprove of her untouched conscience.

When Darling Jill steals Pluto's car to go joyriding; when Ty Ty, along with the rest, goes to town to ask the well-off son Jim Leslie for money to help him through the winter because of inadequate crops; when Rosamond finds Will Thompson, her husband, in bed with her sister Darling Jill and chases him, buck-naked, out of the house—these richly comic scenes create a humorously cockeyed view of the Georgia poor white.

The deaths which occur later in the novel, however, are not funny, nor are their reasons; the comic existence Caldwell has depicted turns somber. This shift in tone has been described as a flaw, but such a judgment assumes that *God's Little Acre* is a comic novel gone astray. In fact, it is a serious story about people who in their daily lives do things that seem comic to those who observe them from a distance. Caldwell begins with a feckless existence that gradually becomes tragic; the comical infighting and escapades of Ty Ty's clan assume a grim inevitability.

Ty Ty has set aside one acre of his land for God. His intent is to farm the land, raise a crop, and give the proceeds to God through the church. Ty Ty has been digging for gold all over his farm, however, and there is very little land left that can still be farmed. Because he needs to raise a crop to feed his family and the two black families who tenant-farm for him, Ty Ty must constantly shift the acre for God from place to place. He readily admits that he will not dig for gold on God's little acre because then he would be honorbound to give the gold to the church. He has no compunctions about doing God out of what he has declared is God's due. Later in the story, however, when he learns of Will Thompson's death, he has a sudden need to bring the acre closer to the homestead:

He felt guilty of something—maybe it was sacrilege or desecration—whatever it was, he knew he had not played fair with God. Now he wished to bring God's little acre back to its rightful place beside the house where he could see it all the time. . . . He promised himself to keep it there until he died.

After this decision, however, blood is shed on God's little acre: Buck kills his own brother, Jim Leslie. The bloodletting on God's ground is almost a ceremonial sacrifice wherein Ty Ty, albeit involuntarily, atones for a life spent giving only lip service to God. This ironic justice has the tragicomic grotesquerie characteristic of Caldwell's best work. The fall of his protagonists is both inevitable and absurd, utterly lacking in dignity.

Beginning in 1936, Caldwell produced different work. Perhaps he was aware that he had gone to the well often enough and needed to find new or different subjects. At any rate, traveling about the United States and Europe, with the drama of Adolf Hitler's Germany taking form, he wrote other books on uncustomary subjects: *North of the Danube, You Have Seen Their Faces, Some American People* (1935), *Southways, Jackpot, Say! Is This the U.S.A.?* (1941, with Margaret Bourke-White), *All-Out on the Road to Smolensk, Russia at War*, and more.

The novels that poured from Caldwell's pen on into the 1940's, 1950's, 1960's, and 1970's more or less followed the pattern of his early work. Reviewers observed that Caldwell seemed to have grown lackadaisical, content with repeating himself. He no longer seemed to instruct the reader subtly about the social and economic problems of the South; his work had begun to take on the dullness that results from the same joke and the same protestations repeated too often in the same way. He continued to use the same old formula without the zest and the imagination that made *Tobacco Road* and *God's Little Acre* so memorable.

Of the more than thirty novels Caldwell wrote over more than forty years, it is disappointing to find that two written in the 1930's—*Tobacco Road* and *God's Little Acre*—are the only ones likely to endure. Still, Caldwell is considered to be among the significant twentieth century writers produced by the South. His major contribution was his naturalistic comedic approach to his subjects. His best work depicts, with admirable craftsmanship, the harsh life of the sharecropper and tenant farmer through painful explicitness and comic vigor, juxtaposing social issues with the grotesque.

Jane L. Ball

OTHER MAJOR WORKS

SHORT FICTION: *American Earth*, 1931; *Mama's Little Girl*, 1932; *Message for Genevieve*, 1933; *We Are the Living: Brief Stories*, 1933; *Kneel to the Rising Sun and Other Stories*, 1935; *Southways: Stories*, 1938; *Jackpot: The Short Stories of Erskine Caldwell*, 1940; *Georgia Boy*, 1943; *Stories by Erskine Caldwell: Twenty-four Representative Stories*, 1944; *Jackpot: Collected Short Stories*, 1950; *The Courting of Susie Brown*, 1952; *Complete Stories*,

1953; *Gulf Coast Stories*, 1956; *Certain Women*, 1957; *When You Think of Me*, 1959; *Men and Women: Twenty-two Stories*, 1961; *Stories of Life: North and South*, 1983; *The Black and White Stories of Erskine Caldwell*, 1984.

NONFICTION: *Tenant Farmer*, 1935; *Some American People*, 1935; *You Have Seen Their Faces*, 1937 (with Margaret Bourke-White); *North of the Danube*, 1939 (with Bourke-White); *Say! Is This the U.S.A.?*, 1941 (with Bourke-White); *All-Out on the Road to Smolensk*, 1942 (with Bourke-White; also known as *Moscow Under Fire: A Wartime Diary*, 1941); *Russia at War*, 1942 (with Bourke-White); *The Humorous Side of Erskine Caldwell*, 1951; *Call It Experience: The Years of Learning How to Write*, 1951; *Around About America*, 1964; *In Search of Bisco*, 1965; *In the Shadow of the Steeple*, 1967; *Deep South: Memory and Observation*, 1968; *Writing in America*, 1968; *Afternoons in Mid-America*, 1976; *With All My Might*, 1987; *Conversations with Erskine Caldwell*, 1988.

CHILDREN'S LITERATURE: *Molly Cottontail*, 1958; *The Deer at Our House*, 1966.

MISCELLANEOUS: *The Caldwell Caravan: Novels and Stories*, 1946.

BIBLIOGRAPHY

Cook, Sylvia Jenkins. *Erskine Caldwell and the Fiction of Poverty: The Flesh and the Spirit*. Baton Rouge: Louisiana State University Press, 1991. Contains chapters on Caldwell's apprenticeship years as a writer, his short stories, his novels of the 1930's, 1940's, and later novels dealing with sex, race, and degeneracy. A concluding chapter discusses Caldwell and his critics. Includes bibliography and index.

Devlin, James. *Erskine Caldwell*. Boston: Twayne, 1984. The first book-length study of Caldwell, this volume is the fullest available introduction to his major work. Its biographical treatment of Caldwell is limited, but five of Caldwell's best novels are considered in detail, as well as many short stories. Contains a chronology and a detailed bibliography.

Klevar, Harvey L. *Erskine Caldwell: A Biography*. Knoxville: University of Tennessee Press, 1993. Klevar explores the regional context of Caldwell's life and writing, emphasizing the reason for the popular and critical success of his early fiction and the decline of his later work. The biography is based not only on extensive archival research but also on interviews with Caldwell.

Korges, James. *Erskine Caldwell*. Minneapolis: University of Minnesota Press, 1969. This forty-eight-page monograph is scholarly and rich in literary allusion. Has a tendency to exaggerate Caldwell's achievement on occasion but also condemns his *Summertime Island*. Treats not only early books but also neglected later novels, as well as a number of short stories and nonfiction pieces.

MacDonald, Scott. *Critical Essays on Erskine Caldwell*. Boston: G. K. Hall, 1981. Divided into three sections: The first reprints contemporary "reviews" or reactions to Caldwell's work, the second does the same for the man, and the final section reprints a number of helpful essays by Malcolm Cowley, Sylvia Cook, William Frobock, and others and some of Caldwell's own introductions to his novels. Gathers much hard-to-find material in one place. Also contains a good introductory essay and a fine bibliography.

Pembroke Magazine 11 (1979). This special issue, devoted to Caldwell on the occasion of his seventy-sixth year, contains a large number of articles, many of them characterized by a note of nostalgia. Old friends, scholars, and foreign admirers acknowledge the septuagenarian's realism, politics, and permanent contribution to American fiction.

MORLEY CALLAGHAN

Born: Toronto, Canada; February 22, 1903
Died: Toronto, Canada; August 25, 1990

PRINCIPAL LONG FICTION
Strange Fugitive, 1928
It's Never Over, 1930

No Man's Meat, 1931
A Broken Journey, 1932
Such Is My Beloved, 1934
They Shall Inherit the Earth, 1935
More Joy in Heaven, 1937
The Varsity Story, 1948
The Loved and the Lost, 1951
The Many Coloured Coat, 1960
A Passion in Rome, 1961
A Fine and Private Place, 1975
Season of the Witch, 1976
Close to the Sun Again, 1977
A Time for Judas, 1983
Our Lady of the Snows, 1985
A Wild Old Man on the Road, 1988

(John Martin)

OTHER LITERARY FORMS

Morley Callaghan's early reputation was based primarily on his short stories, many of which appeared in European and American magazines such as *The Transatlantic Review, The Exile, Transition, The New Yorker, Esquire, The Atlantic Monthly*, and *Scribner's Magazine*. Several significant collections of these stories have been published, including *A Native Argosy* (1929), *Now That April's Here and Other Stories* (1936), *Morley Callaghan's Stories* (1959), and *The Lost and Found Stories of Morley Callaghan* (1985). In addition to the novels and stories, Callaghan wrote a few plays and published many articles in *The Toronto Star, New World, Maclean's*, and *Saturday Night*. In 1963, he published *That Summer in Paris: Memories of Tangled Friendships with Hemingway, Fitzgerald, and Some Others*, a memoir of his early years as a writer in the company of Ernest Hemingway, F. Scott Fitzgerald, Robert McAlmon, James Joyce, and Ford Madox Ford.

ACHIEVEMENTS

It seems almost typical of the Canadian literary scene that Callaghan has been more widely praised outside his home country than within it. Many American and European critics have compared Callaghan's work, especially the short stories, to that of the great Russians: Leo Tolstoy, Anton Chekhov, and Ivan Turgenev. Edmund Wilson claimed that Callaghan was probably the most neglected novelist in the English-speaking world. From the beginning of his career in the 1920's, Callaghan attracted the attention of some of the foremost figures in the literary world: F. Scott Fitzgerald, Ernest Hemingway, Sinclair Lewis, James T. Farrell, Ezra Pound, Erskine Caldwell, and Ford Madox Ford, to name but a few. These writers praised his direct, laconic style, which was unencumbered by many of the excesses in language and description prevalent in the fiction of the 1920's and 1930's. American and European editors also found a special quality in Callaghan's work and promoted it in the leading magazines of the day: *The Exile, Transition*, and *The New Yorker*.

In Canada, on the other hand, Callaghan's early critical reception was often less than positive, as if there were some acute embarrassment in having a local author achieve international success. Callaghan himself was particularly sensitive to the vicissitudes of his reputation, and in *A Fine and Private Place*, using the persona of neglected author Eugene Shore, he placed himself at the forefront of Canadian letters. Certainly, much of the international praise of Callaghan has been extravagant, and much Canadian criticism has been parochial, but in the late twentieth century a more incisive and serious approach to this work created a well-deserved and long overdue balance. Callaghan was awarded the Lorne Pierce Medal for Literature by the Royal Society of Canada and Canada's most prestigious literary prize, the Governor General's Award (1951), for his novel *The Loved and the Lost*.

BIOGRAPHY

Edward Morley Callaghan was born in Toronto, Ontario, on February 22, 1903. His parents, both of whom encouraged his literary bent, were Roman Catholics of Irish descent. Callaghan was educated at Riverdale Collegiate and St. Michael's College, University of Toronto, where he excelled in academics and in sports. His college interests are often illustrated in his writing, most prominently in *The Varsity Story*, a novel of university life written on the occasion of a fund-raising campaign, and *That Summer in Paris*, which includes his account of his famous boxing match with Ernest Hemingway. During his university days, Callaghan worked as a reporter on the *Toronto Daily Star*; in 1923, he met Ernest Hemingway, who was the European correspondent for the paper. The two became good friends, and Hemingway not only provided stimulating conversation concerning Callaghan's favorite authors, Sherwood Anderson (Callaghan's "literary father"), James Joyce, Pound, and Fitzgerald, but also encouraged him to continue writing fiction.

Callaghan was graduated with a B.A. from St. Michael's in 1925 and enrolled in Osgoode Law School, from which he was graduated in 1928. From 1926 to 1928, he made numerous trips to New York, where he met many friends of Hemingway who were to help him in his career. Among them were Katherine Anne Porter, William Carlos Williams, Nathan Asch, and Maxwell Perkins of Charles Scribner's Sons. Perkins, after reading Callaghan's material, decided to publish his first novel, *Strange Fugitive*, and a collection of stories, *A Native Argosy*. Following his marriage to Loretto Dee in 1929, Callaghan traveled to Paris, where in a few months he completed a novel, *It's Never Over*, a novella, *No Man's Meat*, and a number of stories.

In 1930, Callaghan returned to Toronto permanently and began to produce his mature work, including *Such Is My Beloved, The Loved and the Lost*, and *Close to the Sun Again*. Although his work has a universal appeal which distinguishes it from much Canadian fiction, it is rooted in his observations of ordinary Canadian life and the particular attitudes of people as they respond to social and institutional forces. Into his eighties, Callaghan continued to write effectively, challenging the moral and social complacency which threatens the individual consciousness. He died in Toronto on August 25, 1990.

ANALYSIS

Much has been made of Morley Callaghan's streamlined style—in his own words, the art of getting the writing down "so directly that it wouldn't feel or look like literature." Callaghan wished to get an effect that was "transparent as glass." Life should be delineated without embellishment and to a large extent without metaphor. The language should be stripped of all artistic and symbolic associations, and objects should be seen as they are, like Paul Cezanne's apples, which are merely apples and yet capture the essence of apples. The central idea of Callaghan's style is that reality must be accepted for what it is, and that it can be conveyed directly and simply. Leon Edel suggests that this method has its origins in Callaghan's journalism, that Callaghan, like Hemingway, transfers the clipped, almost perfunctory prose of the newsroom into the realm of the novel, evading the images and symbols so often used in fiction. In its formative stages, Callaghan's style was perhaps also affected by the naturalism which was popular in the 1920's and 1930's, especially with American writers who wanted a mode of expression to capture the grim realities of the Depression.

Whatever its antecedents, Callaghan's style, especially in the early novels such as *Strange Fugitive* and *It's Never Over*, is handicapped by its programmatic simplicity; the prose is ill equipped to handle complexities of character. Callaghan's novels, even the later ones, are also marked by a structural simplicity, with a limited number of characters, few subplots, and, usually, a single controlling consciousness. They seem to plod on to an inevitably tragic but morally ambiguous conclusion, giving an illusion of time that is almost static, reduced to its elemental character.

Callaghan did not, however, adhere slavishly to the avowed principles of his early fiction. Beginning with *Such Is My Beloved*, the sentences are more complex; the dialogue is richer, less stylized in the Hemingway manner; the prose is more rhythmic; and the structure of the novels is more intricate. Still, all of Callaghan's work is characterized by an unremarkable surface, which at first glance has little aesthetic appeal. A more discriminating appraisal must therefore be made which accounts for the enduring quality of his work. Some critics have noted the parabolic nature of Callaghan's fiction, which limits the need for rounded characterization and necessitates simplicity of structure. Others argue that Christian humanism, especially in *Such Is My Beloved, More Joy in Heaven*, and *A Passion in Rome*, with their obvious biblical titles, informs Callaghan's work, giving it veracity and insight. Finally, some conclude that Callaghan's power derives from the influence of Charles Darwin, Karl Marx, and Sigmund Freud and a particular setting in history.

To a certain extent, all these theories are true, but all are equally unsatisfying as comprehensive theories. Underlying each of the novels is an ironic point of view which defeats easy answers and leaves the reader with both an unsatisfying vision of life with few moral or aesthetic certainties, and a sense of mystery, an awareness of the infinite complexities of human action and thought which make life worthwhile. This deliberate ambiguity is a narrative strategy designed to force the reader into reevaluating his own observations of life and his own moral stance. Callaghan's novels, then, demand an involved sensibility and a questioning attitude; perhaps what is needed is the passionate intensity which Callaghan so frequently hints is the key to self-realization and independence.

Many of Callaghan's novels are animated by the tension between an individual and the institutions which circumscribe his behavior. The Church, the government, and the business community insist on a patterned, prudent existence which gives society stability and order. As such, they serve a useful function in most people's lives, but they are no substitute for a personal, compassionate, and intuitive vision which, in everyday relationships, often subverts the legalistic intentions of the institutions. An individual can be caught betraying society because he refuses to betray his own conscience. Thus, Father Dowling in *Such Is My Beloved* befriends two prostitutes to rescue them, and himself, with the power of love. His seemingly inordinate concern for them strikes a local parishioner and Dowling's bishop as unorthodox, and Dowling is relieved of his position and finally is admitted to a sanatorium. In *The Loved and the Lost*, Jim McAlpine is torn between his ambition to be a respectable columnist on a Montreal newspaper and the love of a mysterious woman who inhabits the seamier region of the city. By losing faith in Peggy at a crucial moment, Jim allows the circumstances which bring about her death and a loss of faith in himself.

In *Close to the Sun Again*, a more complex relationship between private and public values is explored. Ira Groome, former "lord" of the Brazilian Power Company and now chairman of Toronto's police commission, reflects to no avail on why he has become impersonal and detached from the stream of life. After suffering severe injuries in a car accident, he relives his career as a naval commander and realizes that he had tried to escape the pain of human involvement by representing an institutional view of life. In a final epiphany, he accepts the voices in his own heart and dies with the profound self-knowledge that had been lacking in the earlier part of his life. In all of these works, the ultimate irony is that the individual can rarely reconcile the public demands of the world with a passionate, often barbaric, private vision.

SUCH IS MY BELOVED

The dedication to Callaghan's finest early novel, *Such Is My Beloved*, reads, "To Those Times With M.

In The Winter Of 1933"; "M." was Jacques Maritain, the world-renowned philosopher, who came to St. Michael's College Institute for Medieval Studies as a visiting lecturer. Perhaps from his discussions with Maritain, especially concerning the nature of Christian humanism and the role of the saint in the world, Callaghan chose to concentrate on an explicitly religious theme, probing the relationship between the Roman Catholic Church, an agency of worldly prudence, and its priests, who must minister to individuals' needs through the love of Christ. The title suggests the focus of the novel; as Brandon Conron has noted, it is an echo of God's expression of love for His Son on the occasion of Christ's baptism. The epigraph confirms the theme of the nature of love and the consequences of the spiritual attitude of the novel. Taken from the Song of Songs, it reads: "Many waters cannot quench love, neither can the floods drown it: if a man give all the substance of his house for love, it would utterly be contemned."

The story is simple. Father Dowling, the central figure of the novel, befriends two prostitutes, Veronica (Ronnie) Olsen and Catherine (Midge) Bourassa, in order to save them from their degrading way of life. He soon realizes that they need not only love but also material necessities to sustain them through the Depression. Aware that the money he earns from his parish will not be enough, Dowling enlists the help of a wealthy parishioner, James Robison, to provide jobs for them. Robison, however, is not willing to risk the possibility of scandal and reports Dowling to his bishop. The two women are forced to leave the city (ostensibly Toronto), and Dowling, driven by these betrayals to madness, has only momentary periods of lucidity in the sanatorium.

Brandon Conron and Malcolm Ross both have argued that the novel presents at least a superficial allegory, with Dowling as Christ, Robison as Judas, and the bishop as Pontius Pilate, with certain minor characters also serving symbolic roles. The success of the novel, however, resides in Callaghan's ability to draw these characters as vulnerable human beings and not merely as types. Dowling conveys a disturbing naïveté which, despite his powerful love, causes his downfall. He brings Ronnie and Midge presents and

money in an effort to keep them off the streets, but the gifts are ineffective. Dowling exhibits many other traits which seduce the reader into a kind of Conradian belief in him as "one of us." In the confessional, he is so consumed by his thoughts for the girls that he is harsh with others. He is jealous of Father Jolly's room, which Dowling himself covets; he admits to the natural sexual feelings of a young man his age; he hates the owner of the bawdy house, Henry Baer; and he lies about his involvement with the two prostitutes. Ironically, these human weaknesses make his love seem more potent.

The other characters, although not as well portrayed as Dowling, are effective in that the reader's responses to them are never wholly one-sided. Robison, much of the time, is a kind, helpful Christian who is confused by Dowling's love. The bishop, representing the position of the worldly Church, doubts himself and does not seem secure in his opinion of Dowling. Ronnie's pimp, Joe Wilenski, is a brutish man who often takes advantage of her, yet respects her as a person. Ronnie, coming from a broken home in Detroit, and Midge, abandoned by her lover, react with affecting girlishness, especially when Dowling gives them pretty clothes. The ambivalent, realistic natures of these people condition the reader's response to the novel as a whole. One sees human beings with limited control over their circumstances; the Church and society seem to conspire to destroy the idealistic impulse in the individual consciousness.

Professor David Dooley identifies the central moral problem of the novel as the conflict between quixotic idealism and worldly prudence, with no satisfactory conclusion being evinced. Father Dowling tries to love the prostitutes as Christ loved sinners; all people are worthy of love without distinction, despite their failures. Love, he thinks, will overcome worldly considerations, but his faith cannot change the economic conditions which have driven the girls into sin. Dowling also tries to console the Canzanos, a family with twelve children living in abject poverty. Mr. Canzano says that they need money, not faith, and there is nothing left for him but despair. Even Dowling's great love is unconvincing here; he spends so much time with the girls that he can give little to his other parishioners. Although the bishop is satirized by Callaghan for his concern that the scandal will hurt his charity campaign, he is perhaps correct in thinking that the church should play a more material part in helping people such as the Canzanos.

Dowling's best friend, Charlie Stewart, a medical student who is an avowed Marxist, also views the world in terms of economics. Because he is a secular idealist, he believes that the ideal state could transform society and put an end to poverty. For him, there is no religious problem, only an economic one. The church, the business community (represented by Robison and his uncharitable wife), Stewart, and Dowling are all caught up in the same dilemma. The personal qualities of spiritual love and secular compassion are defeated by institutions which must force their representatives to make rational, pragmatic choices. Even though these choices are often hypocritical, they are necessary to sustain order in society.

Such Is My Beloved ends with the two prostitutes forced out of the city by the police, and Dowling, in the sanatorium, is left to think of them as two of the many restless souls who cannot find peace. Dowling has occasional moments of clarity in which he offers his sanity as a sacrifice to God so that He might spare their souls. The priest is content in this offering and, at peace with himself, plans to write a commentary on the Song of Songs. The only positive note in the book is that this powerful love of Dowling's is somehow good, and although it cannot change society, it can transcend it, making even the tragic elements of life worthwhile.

In his next two novels, *They Shall Inherit the Earth* and *More Joy in Heaven*, Callaghan continued to examine the theme of love and its relation to society in explicitly religious terms. Neither novel is as well wrought as *Such Is My Beloved*, but they are nevertheless effective renderings of complex human motives. In the period between 1937 and 1948, his "dark period," Callaghan published no major novels. In 1948, however, his period of "spiritual dryness" over, Callaghan published *Luke Baldwin's Vow* and *The Varsity Story* and began work on *The Loved and the Lost*, which appeared in 1951.

THE LOVED AND THE LOST

Although the religious dimension is understated in *The Loved and the Lost*, the inner opposition between the individual and the dictates of society is again explored. For the most part, the narrative consciousness is that of Jim McAlpine, through whose eyes the reader receives impressions of Montreal's clearly divided social strata. Formerly an associate professor of history at the University of Toronto, Jim is brought to the city by a publisher, Joseph Carver, to write a political column for the Montreal *Sun*. Carver, a professed "liberal," admired Jim's article, "The Independent Man," in *The Atlantic Monthly*. Living on "the mountain," an affluent district in Montreal, Carver and his divorced daughter, Catherine, represent the social status to which Jim has aspired all his life. Through a friend, Jim meets Peggy Sanderson, a seemingly generous and warm-hearted woman. Jim falls in love with her innocence and her compassion, knowing that their relationship, as elusive as it may be, could destroy his ambitions. After a brawl involving Peggy at Café St. Antoine, a black jazz club on the river, Jim feels compelled to protect her and to profess his love for her. When Peggy's need for him is greatest, however, Jim loses faith in her, inadvertently leaving her to be raped and murdered. Unable to choose between the stable values of "the mountain" and the uncertain values of the river, Jim betrays not only Peggy, but also himself.

The novel works in parallels of discrete oppositions between the mountain and the river, with Jim at the center, torn by the attractiveness of each and unable to reconcile the contradictions inherent in both. Carver has wealth and power, which he uses to operate a newspaper dedicated, like *The New York Times* or *Manchester Guardian*, to the principles of independent thinking. His editorial stance, however, is compromised by his personal objection to giving his own writers freedom of thought; he wants supreme loyalty from his staff, and he is disturbed by the possibility that Jim may be an embarrassment to him. His daughter, Catherine, embodies the beauty and social grace of her class, but she is unsure of herself and hides her ardent character. She sees a hockey game with Jim, remarking on the artistic patterns of play. For her, life is a pattern, like her orderly room, which should not be disturbed. When Jim seems to side with the hockey player breaking the pattern by receiving a penalty, she asks why he is not "with us." In the end, however, discovering Jim's complicity in the murder, she empathizes with Peggy, violently slapping Jim for what she thinks is his betrayal.

Evoking similarly complex responses in all those who know her, Peggy Sanderson is an extremely ambiguous character. She has an air of innocence which enchants Jim and makes him want to protect her, but there is also a suggestion of carnality; as a young girl she admired the body of a naked black boy, and there are many comments made on her promiscuity with the blacks at the Café St. Antoine, although they are not verified. In her indiscriminate, but platonic, love for all souls "without distinction" (here she echoes Father Dowling), she is seen as Saint Joan and Christ. This spiritual gift, however, invites fear and resentment, not peace and understanding. Symbolically, she is associated with a carved leopard and a small antique church, both of which she takes Jim to see. The fierce, uncertain jungle violence of the leopard contrasts with the stable religious feeling of the church, but Callaghan never lets the reader know if these are indeed Peggy's responses to these objects. Jim thinks that her innocence is attracted to violence, that in fact her actions are self-destructive. By refusing to compromise her personal vision to social prudence, she is destroyed; the reader is never really sure of the extent to which she is culpable for her own fate.

Much of the novel is controlled by Jim's subjective, ambivalent feelings. He is estranged from the world of status as a child, a boy outside the hedge of the wealthy Havelocks, so his ambition is understandable even if excessively rationalized. Although he is drawn to Catherine and her tidy universe, he feels more comfortable in the "middle world" of the Chalet restaurant. Peggy shatters his balance by showing him a different side of life, where society's rules are broken and ambition becomes mere illusion. At the hockey game, he dismisses the patterns and sees the ice surface as a pit with writhing sacrificial figures. His vision, however, is only refracted, not

significantly altered, and rather than accept Peggy for what she is, he tries to mold her into his possession. Like Peter denying Christ, Jim denies knowing Peggy at Angela Murdoch's party on the mountain, hoping at some later date to bring the two worlds into harmony.

Wolfgast, the owner of the Chalet restaurant, tells Jim the story of a white horse he believed belonged to him although it was owned by his father's landlord. The circumstances of losing the horse impressed upon him the need for some definitive personal possession, In buying the Chalet, he achieved his dream. Peggy becomes Jim's "white horse," and he tries to own her by using her apartment to write his articles. Every day he tidies it up and makes a change which reflects his own personality. Only after her death does he recognize that his sin resided in not accepting Peggy for herself. Ironically, by not abandoning himself completely, by losing faith in Peggy as Orpheus lost faith in Euridice, he loses his own sense of identity as well. Confused about the values of high and low society and the mysterious values embodied by Peggy, Jim is left only with a dream of Peggy being trampled by white horses from the mountain as he draws back. In desperation, he attempts to find Peggy's antique church, hoping that in this symbol of belief Peggy will be with him always. The gesture is futile: Jim does not find the church.

The reader, too, is left without a clear moral resolution. Is Peggy really a virgin, a pure innocent? Is she a saint like Saint Joan, destroyed by an insensitive society? Is there really something primitive in her character which attracts violence? Could Jim cope with Peggy as a human being and not as the ideal he made her out to be? How do the symbols clarify and support meaning? After all, Wolfgast's "white horse," the possession of his restaurant, is something quite different from the possession of a human being. Does the church symbolize religious values or innocence, or is there a more ephemeral quality to it? Does the leopard represent the passionate nature of man or perhaps only independence? Beneath the surface of a straightforward, well-told story, then, there are ambiguities admitting no easy resolutions.

Through the 1950's, 1960's, and early 1970's, Callaghan continued to write many interesting stories; his novels, however, met with mixed reviews. His style became more ambitious, and his ideas remained adventurous, but his plots were clumsy, his dialogue often unrealistic, and his characterizations more stereotyped than ever before. In *A Fine and Private Place*, an entertaining *roman à clef* for Callaghan followers, there is even a strident attack on critics unwilling to accept him as a major novelist. With *Close to the Sun Again*, however, Callaghan returned to some earlier themes with great success. The values of the novel are less ambiguous, and the story is simply but powerfully told in his characteristic clipped style, which suits the material admirably.

CLOSE TO THE SUN AGAIN

The story relates the psychic journey of former naval commander Ira Groome, who quits his job as head of the Brazilian Power Corporation to become chairman of the police commission in a large, metropolitan city, probably Toronto. After the death of his alcoholic wife, Julia, he feels a sense of astonishment which shocks him into the realization that imperceptibly he has lost the passion that makes life real. He has, in fact, become so detached that his wife only felt comfortable calling him "Commander," and his son has rejected him as a father. Voices from within challenge him to break the pattern of impersonality which has characterized his life, but they do not completely penetrate his conscious mind.

As introspective as he was in Brazil, Groome still projects the image of stable authority in Toronto, demanding and getting loyalty from the members of the police commission and starting a casual, uninvolved affair with Mrs. Oscar Finley (Carol) of the prestigious Hunt Club set. Still seeking some "enchantment," however, he begins to drink gin, which softens his disciplined view of life but forces him into the Maplewood rest home every few weeks for a temporary "cure." One night, shocked by some harsh but vaguely familiar words from Carol, he leaves Maplewood for home in an excited state, only to be involved in a serious car accident. In the hospital, holding the hand of his former ship's boatswain, Horler, Groome experiences the enchantment he so

badly desires and drifts into a dream world of memory and heightened perception.

Groome relives an important part of his life in which he is again Lieutenant Groome on a ship in the North Atlantic during the war. Upon realizing that he is alive after being severely wounded in action, he sees people as unique individuals, each inhabiting a wonderful private world, and is then able to respond to his men with a sensitivity rarely shown by officers. Groome's life is changed radically, however, when two survivors of a torpedo raid board his ship. Gina Bixby, trying to reach England to see her father, a boxing promoter, is accompanied by huge, silent Jethroe Chone, her father's bodyguard. They are escaping Marty Rosso, a mobster involved in fixing fights, who wants to use Gina to prevent her father from testifying to the boxing commission. Rosso has already caused the death of Robert Riopelle, a naïve boxer duped into believing in himself: With his hands smashed by Rosso, Riopelle perceived that his whole being was corrupted and committed suicide. During their escape from Rosso, the mysterious Chone raped Gina but feels no remorse for an act which "kills" part of her. Although there still seems to be a perverse bond between them, Gina confesses to Groome that, when they reach London, she will kill Chone for this brutal betrayal.

Groome is disturbed by this world so unlike the well-ordered naval existence; it is a world of violent passions beyond his experience. In her questioning of Groome, however, Gina brings to the surface his fascination for the Mayan religious rituals he had encountered as a young archaeology student on the Yucatán peninsula. This society with its sacrificial violence seems to parallel Gina's world in a strange way. Groome recalls a native girl, Marina, an image of light suffusing his memory, who gave him the ancient piece of wisdom that in a cruel, senseless world, all one can do is create something beautiful from the nightmare.

Before they can reach the safety of London, the ship is torpedoed, leaving Groome, Horler, Gina, a wounded Chone, and a few sailors on a life raft. Defiantly, Chone tells Groome that no one knew or loved Gina more than he did; soon after, Chone rolls himself into the water to die at sea. Yelling for him to come back, in the same words that Carol later spoke to Groome, Gina swims after Chone, her passion overcoming any sense of safety. She is also lost in the water. Groome is horrified at the emotions he feels—the jungle terrors of involvements with people living in intense personal worlds. He rationalizes that getting too close to people, being intoxicated by violent passions, only causes pain and suffering. Groome closes his heart to these sufferings and resists the voices in his own heart. He changes into secure Ira Groome, the Commander, dedicated to a high purpose in life, a world of order unencumbered by the depth of personal relationships.

Remembering all this from his hospital bed, Groome realizes that he has committed treason to his own nature. He finally understands the significance of Chone's life. He sees the brightness from a sunlit jungle clearing into which a white leopard emerges, and finally, Groome understands himself. Recognizing the necessity of leading a life of passion in all respects, bearing the suffering and sacrifice which enrich the individual sensibility, Groome dies, "close to the sun again."

In this novel, Callaghan reiterates the themes of his other works, but makes it clear that passion should not be compromised to suit the values of society. In earlier novels, the conflict between private passions and the imposed, prudent views of society is unresolved, but *Close to the Sun Again* concludes with an epiphany which clearly emphasizes that the individual's responsibility is above all to himself. Throughout his career, Callaghan offered his readers a vision which is thought provoking, humane, and replete with the passions which touch everyone's life. There is little doubt that in the future his reputation as a significant twentieth century novelist will remain secure.

James C. MacDonald

OTHER MAJOR WORKS

SHORT FICTION: *A Native Argosy*, 1929; *Now That April's Here and Other Stories*, 1936; *Morley Callaghan's Stories*, 1959; *The Lost and Found Stories of Morley Callaghan*, 1985.

PLAYS: *Turn Home Again*, pr. 1940 (also known as *Going Home*); *To Tell the Truth*, pr. 1949; *Season of the Witch*, pb. 1976.

NONFICTION: *That Summer in Paris: Memories of Tangled Friendships with Hemingway, Fitzgerald, and Some Others*, 1963.

CHILDREN'S LITERATURE: *Luke Baldwin's Vow*, 1948.

BIBLIOGRAPHY

Boire, Gary. "Rewriting Callaghan." *Essays on Canadian Writing* 41 (Summer, 1990): 16-19. Examines Callahan's last novel, *A Wild Old Man on the Road*, situating it in the context of *That Summer in Paris* and *A Fine and Private Place*.

Conron, Brandon. *Morley Callaghan*. New York: Twayne, 1966. A comprehensive, carefully organized analysis of Callaghan's short fiction and novels up to *A Passion in Rome*. Its straightforward style and format make this book accessible to students. Also includes a useful biographical chronology and a selected bibliography.

Gooch, Bryan N. S. "Callaghan." *Canadian Literature* 126 (Autumn, 1990): 148-149. Discusses *A Wild Old Man on the Road*, comparing it to *Such Is My Beloved* and *They Shall Inherit the Earth*. Praises the novel's compelling quality and suggests that this "short tense" fiction ranks with the best of Callaghan's work.

Hoar, Victor. *Morley Callaghan*. Toronto: Copp Clark, 1969. Discusses the style and thematic concerns in Callaghan's fiction up to 1963 in two sections, "The Technique" and "The Themes." Hoar supports his commentary with numerous quotations from Callaghan's work. A useful bibliography is included.

Kendle, Judith. "Morley Callaghan: An Annotated Bibliography." In *The Annotated Bibliography of Canada's Major Authors*, edited by Robert Lecker and Jack David. Vol. 5. Toronto: ECW Press, 1984. Contains the most exhaustive listing of primary sources and secondary sources for Callaghan's work up to 1984 that a student is likely to need. The categories cover the spectrum from books and articles to interviews to audiovisual material. A helpful "Index to Critics Listed in the Bibliography" is also included.

Stuewe, Paul. "The Case of Morley Callaghan." In *Clearing the Ground: English-Canadian Fiction After "Survival."* Toronto: Proper Tales Press, 1984. In this chapter, Stuewe takes Callaghan to task for sloppy writing and his critics to task for concentrating on Callaghan's thematic concerns to the exclusion of his technical flaws. Stuewe's own writing and tone are lively and incisive.

Woodcock, George. "Possessing the Land: Notes on Canadian Fiction." In *The Canadian Imagination: Dimensions of a Literary Culture*, edited by David Staines. Cambridge, Mass.: Harvard University Press, 1977. Callaghan's fiction is discussed in the context of Woodcock's overview of Canadian fiction and its development and direction since the nineteenth century.

(Jerry Bauer)

ITALO CALVINO

Born: Santiago de las Vegas, Cuba; October 15, 1923
Died: Siena, Italy; September 19, 1985

PRINCIPAL LONG FICTION

Il sentiero dei nidi di ragno, 1947, 1957, 1965 (*The Path to the Nest of Spiders*, 1956)

Il visconte dimezzato, 1952 (novella *The Cloven Viscount*, 1962)

Il barone rampante, 1957 (novella *The Baron in the Trees*, 1959)

Il cavaliere inesistente, 1959 (novella *The Non-Existent Knight*, 1962)

I nostri atenati, 1960 (*Our Ancestors*, 1980; includes *The Cloven Viscount*, *The Non-Existent Knight*, and *The Baron in the Trees*)

Il castello dei destini incrociati, 1969, 1973 (*The Castle of Crossed Destinies*, 1976)

Le città invisibili, 1972 (*Invisible Cities*, 1974)

Se una notte d'inverno un viaggiatore, 1979 (*If on a Winter's Night a Traveler*, 1981)

Palomar, 1983 (*Mr. Palomar*, 1985)

OTHER LITERARY FORMS

Italo Calvino was known to the Italian reading public as a novelist, but internationally he was often associated with his tales and stories. In the comprehensive and critically acclaimed *Fiabe italiane* (1956; partially translated as *Italian Fables*, 1959, and completed as *Italian Folktales*, 1975), he collected and transcribed tales and fables from the various Italian dialects. Influenced by the Russian Formalist Vladimir Propp's *Historical Roots of Russian Fairy Tales* (1946) and by structuralist theory in general, Calvino made it his scholarly objective to represent every morphological type of Italian folktale as well as every region of the country. His academic study of these tales confirmed in theory what he had already discovered in practice: the power of fantasy to signify, to reflect the real world. The work also influenced his subsequent approach to narrative through variable combinations of component forms and archetypes.

Calvino's most widely known short-story collections are the science-fiction fantasies *Le cosmicomiche*

(1965; *Cosmicomics*, 1968) and *Ti con zero* (1967; *T Zero*, 1969). Unlike most science fiction, which tends to be futuristic or antiutopian, these stories envision, in intense and sharp detail, the remote past before the universe of space and time—moving to the present, in *T Zero*—and they project an unusually open and positive view of evolution. Through the narrator, Qfwfq, a sort of protean cosmic consciousness, the prehuman past becomes sentient, familiar-seeming, and thus reassuring about the future, suggesting continuity in transformation and possibility in change.

This "fabulous" Calvino was better known to Americans than the one familiar to Italian readers, the politically and socially engaged author of satires on urban expansion and the advocate of pollution control and birth control well before those causes became popular. In *I racconti* (1958; partially translated as *The Watcher and Other Stories*, 1971) and *Marcovaldo: Ovvero, Le stagioni in città* (1963; *Marcovaldo: Or, The Seasons in the City*, 1983), the city, or the immediate contemporary environment, is often actually the main character. The stories in this neorealistic mode, influenced by Ernest Hemingway as well as by Italian Resistance literature, are documentary in texture but often parabolic enough to be described as Kafkaesque. They reflect the futility felt by many during the postwar years, though that sense of futility was mitigated by a stubborn human persistence that is resistant to tyranny and despair.

In addition to his tales and stories, Calvino wrote a critical study of Elio Vittorini (1968), edited the letters of Cesare Pavese (1966), and published many essays on literary, cultural, and political topics.

ACHIEVEMENTS

If Calvino was often treated as a storyteller or fabulator rather than as a novelist, that reputation is in most respects deserved. Whether classified as *novellini* (novellas) or *racconti* (short stories), his works are essentially stories narrated at some length and often interrelated in a series: in *Cosmicomics* and *T Zero*, as episodes or "strips" out of chronological sequence; in *The Cloven Viscount, The Baron in the Trees*, and *The Non-Existent Knight*, as parts of the trilogy *Our Ancestors*; in *Invisible Cities, The Castle*

of *Crossed Destinies*, and *If on a Winter's Night a Traveler*, as tales spun from a frame story, standing for the oldest of narrative impulses. Calvino's conscious revival and complete mastery of the storyteller's art deserves special acclaim.

Calvino himself called attention to his alternation of two characteristic modes of writing: the one, factual and immersed in present time and space; the other, quite "fantastic"—baroque, witty, removed from the realm of the probable. In the first mode, everyday reality is presented with striking immediacy; the familiar is seen as if for the first time; in the second, the unbelievable is given verisimilitude, is imagined into life, and is realized in such minute detail as to be taken for granted. Critics often distinguish between the neorealistic or "engaged" Calvino and the fabulist or "escapist"; such distinctions fail to hold in the final analysis, however, considering his development of what J. R. Woodhouse has pronounced a new genre in Italian literature, a combination of fairy tale and novel of ideas. In this genre, realism and fantasy are interdependent; both are necessary to a perspective that acknowledges the creative connections between fact and fiction. Calvino's last development was his metafiction, which outshines that of his postmodernist peers in clarity, brilliance, and human interest. Perhaps his finest achievement lies in his ability to give the unimaginable, abstract, or complex a palpable life and, often, popular appeal.

Within this mode, Calvino covers a wide range of techniques, subjects, and themes, all of which contribute to his larger point: the inexhaustible potential of narrative and language. Confirming his success is the popular and critical acclaim accorded him after the publication of his first novel, for which he received the Riccione Prize in 1947. Subsequently he won the Viareggio Prize for *The Baron in the Trees* in 1957, the Bagutta Prize for *I racconti* in 1957, the Salento Prize in 1960 for *Our Ancestors*, the Veillon Prize in 1962 for *The Watcher*, and the Feltrinelli Prize in 1975. In 1968, he again won and then refused the Viareggio Prize, in protest against the literary prize as an outmoded institution. Such making and breaking of patterns characterizes Calvino's stance and contributes to his appeal.

BIOGRAPHY

Italo Calvino was born of Italian parents in Santiago de las Vegas, Cuba, in 1923, but he spent his childhood and youth in San Remo, on the Italian Riviera. In 1943, at the age of twenty, he left the security of his middle-class background to join the partisans of the Italian Resistance against the Fascists and Nazis. Like many European writers of the postwar period, he joined the Communist Party and then left it in disillusionment, in 1958.

After World War II, Calvino finished his thesis on Joseph Conrad and completed his degree at the University of Turin. He subsequently became a member of the editorial staff of the Turin publishing firm Giulio Einaudi, which first published his novels and short stories. He lived in Turin until 1964 and then in Paris with his wife and daughter until 1980, thereafter residing in Rome.

Although he lived in Paris during most of the 1960's and 1970's, much of Calvino's career reflects his involvement in Italian political, cultural, and literary life. His two years in the partisans' resistance were the source material of *The Path to the Nest of Spiders*. He wrote often of local urban problems, using his experience as an election scrutineer to study poverty and alienation in the industrial regions around Turin in the postwar period (as in *The Watcher and Other Stories*). The environments in which he lived—in particular, the Ligurian coast, the Alpine foothills, and the cities of San Remo and Turin—appear over and over in his fiction, which is concerned, as he wrote in a preface to the 1965 edition of *The Path to the Nest of Spiders*, with relations between human events and their contexts. This perspective is reflected in the regional emphasis of *Italian Folktales*, through which Calvino served his country as the Brothers Grimm did Germany. Early and formative influences were the Italian novelists Elio Vittorini and Cesare Pavese, who recognized his talent immediately and encouraged the development of his characteristic style.

Calvino's later fiction reflects an increasingly cosmopolitan outlook, but one that developed naturally out of his involvement with Italian culture. During the 1960's and 1970's, the most obvious literary influences on his work were French, in keeping with the structuralist leanings first revealed in *Italian Folktales:* the New Novel, Roland Barthes and the semiologists, and the poststructuralism of Jacques Derrida. Although Calvino's later works turn increasingly toward fabulation and metafiction, his fiction echoes, variously and lightly, a considerable range: Ludovico Ariosto, Miguel de Cervantes, and Giovanni Boccaccio; Ernest Hemingway, Jean-Paul Sartre, and Albert Camus; Lewis Carroll, Luigi Pirandello, Franz Kafka, and Jorge Luis Borges. Calvino died in Siena, Italy, on September 19, 1985.

ANALYSIS

The anti-Fascist Resistance was the impetus for Italo Calvino's first novel, as it was for a generation of Italian neorealists, who believed that literature should be dedicated, as Calvino asserted in the 1950's, to "political engagement," to "social battle." In a slightly different way, the Resistance shaped the later Calvino. As the postwar period brought on disillusionment with power politics, Resistance writers had to find new directions. "What I did not want to renounce," wrote Calvino in 1960, "was [the] epic adventurous grasp, the combination of physical and moral strength" of the literature that the Resistance inspired. Daily life having failed to provide such "images full of . . . energy," Calvino turned to nonrealistic literary forms such as the fairy tale, the fable, and the philosophical romance (in the trilogy *Our Ancestors*); to science fiction and cartoons (in *Cosmicomics*); to myth and tarot cards (in *The Castle of Crossed Destinies*); and, in general, toward metafiction, or fiction about fiction itself.

Calvino's direction was not, in his view, a retreat from his earlier committed stance; it was, rather, an engagement with the cultural life that inspired the Resistance. In turning to popular sources such as the cartoon or the fairy tale, he intended to evoke the classless culture he found with the partisans in the Resistance, for whom storytelling was recreation and camaraderie. Thus, Calvino's art carries over from his early experience an oral quality, regardless of his subject matter.

If Calvino had a single model, it was Ariosto, as

Calvino himself acknowledged in an article written in 1960 for *Italian Quarterly*, "Main Currents in Italian Fiction Today," In Calvino's view, Ariosto's *Orlando furioso* (1516, 1521, 1532; English translation, 1591) teaches an epistemology, an "up-to-date lesson" in "how the mind lives by fantasy, irony, and formal accuracy." In an age of "electronic brains and space flights," of relativism increasing with change, such an understanding of how one perceives and creates reality is necessary to one's evaluation of it—in order to make ethical decisions. Calvino's shift from epic to meta-epic and literature as game—in *Invisible Cities* and *The Castle of Crossed Destinies*—makes sense in terms of his emphasis throughout on "energy turned toward the future." The emphasis also helps to explain his mixture of fantasy and realism, one that leads the reader to imagine what might be in a world where transformation is the rule.

Typically, Calvino's tales begin with a fantastic premise, often a bizarre image, from which—as in Lewis Carroll's *Alice's Adventures in Wonderland* (1865)—conclusions follow logically and matter-of-factly. His imaginary gardens have Marianne Moore's real toads in them. Because he takes these images from popular associations of ideas or words, they invariably seem apt; they are figures of speech literalized, clichés revitalized in strange new forms of life. The ghost in armor becomes the nonexistent knight, a fully armed identity, without substance, who manages to become a fully realized character. A young idealist elects to live in the trees, where he shapes his destiny between earth and sky. In *Cosmicomics*, the moon is composed of a lactic substance comparable in texture to ricotta cheese. In *If on a Winter's Night a Traveler*, the novelist's convention of characterizing the "dear Reader" is extended as the protagonist becomes "you, the Reader."

As Teresa de Lauretis has pointed out, Calvino's themes are elementary: desire, rivalry, guilt; the need for communication; self-assertion and belonging; the necessity to choose. He combines and varies these elements with a virtuosity that stands for his larger theme—the inexhaustible potential of language and life.

THE PATH TO THE NEST OF SPIDERS

The Path to the Nest of Spiders reflects the neorealistic trend in Italian film and literature fostered by the Italian Resistance and its aftermath. Neither propaganda nor a servile fidelity to fact, neorealism was a spontaneous expression of the times, as Calvino has often remarked. The Resistance fostered realism primarily by opening up "new Italies" through the peripheral voices of authors from regions previously unrepresented in literature. Calvino's Italy was the northern Ligurian coast, with its landscape of contrasts and its balance of natural and human elements. Written in 1946, shortly after the events of the Ligurian Resistance which it depicts, *The Path to the Nest of Spiders* shows a strong regional interest: in its documentation of random details of daily life and local countryside, in its rendition of speech patterns and dialects, and in its primitive subject matter, which is treated in a deliberately rough, antiliterary style. The mood of oral narration carries the book, yet the war itself is vaguely overheard in the distance. Calvino is interested in the repercussions of such events within the contexts in which they take place. It is from this perspective that commitment to social and political struggle shaped the later Calvino's characteristic texture: an intense, almost nearsighted concreteness of surface.

The hero is the orphan Pin, who pimps for his sister and is known by local tavern society for singing bawdy songs and baiting all—Nazis, Fascists, and Communists, men, women, and children—with scurrilous remarks. His bravado masks his loneliness in a disrupted environment, for he scorns and is scorned by adults and children (mostly backstreet urchins) alike. After various altercations that bring him into the middle of the Resistance, he finds a sense of community with a partisan band and finds a comrade in Cousin, who shares his distrust of people, especially women—who, in his view, are all prostitutes and traitors (like his wife).

The treatment of Cousin is typical of Calvino's realism in its total lack of sentimentality about the character and motives of the partisans and an avoidance of the conventional rhetoric of Communism, despite Calvino's committed stance. As the intellectual

Kim, a thinly veiled Calvino, points out, the partisans are colorfully, if notably, ignorant of the reasons behind their behavior—and thus every bit as immature, in a sense, as Pin. For the most part from the fringes of society, physically defective and emotionally unbalanced, they hate and kill the Fascists but do not know why or even what they are fighting. When Mancino, the cook, offers a knowledgeable Marxist interpretation, he is jeered and hooted: His arguments "seem useless, as he talks about enemies they know nothing about, such as capitalists and financiers. It's rather like Mussolini expecting the Italians to hate the British and the Abyssinians, whom none of them had ever seen." As for the causes of the war, Cousin's rationale is typically monomaniacal—the women started it. As Kim suggests, the cause is really the existential "mess," the ignorance and squalor and resentment that have been the lives of partisans and Fascists alike.

The sense of confusion, purposelessness, and impotence reflected in the characters' dialogue is borne out in their actions. Dritto, the commander of the vagabond band, shuns responsibilities, accidently sets fire to their hideout while seducing the cook's wife, and is executed by the Party commissars. Pin's sister is a prostitute who betrays some partisans to the SS, and the book ends as Cousin shoots her with a pistol Pin has stolen.

Besides antiliterary qualities that are meant to convey the color, randomness, crudity, and mixed character of life, *The Path to the Nest of Spiders* is consciously derived from literary sources. One is American naturalism, from which Italian neorealism took a great deal. In an article entitled "Hemingway e noi" which appeared in *Il contemporaneo*, in 1954, Calvino acknowledged that author's strong formative influence on his contemporaries, including Vittorini and himself. The obvious parallels coincide with Calvino's antiliterary stance: the documentary texture, the staccato style, the terse dialogue, and a pervasive, understated, somewhat grim irony, through which Pin's innocence, like that of Hemingway's Nick Adams, flickers. The best example is perhaps the last, in which Calvino imitates Hemingway's ambiguous or offhand treatment of dramatic irony. Like

Nick, Pin is already alienated; his mixture of world weariness and naïveté shows through in some odd remarks about fireflies that follow Cousin's offstage shooting of Pin's sister, which is reported indirectly. Thus ends the book:

> "Filthy creatures, women, Cousin . . ." says Pin.
> "All of them . . ." agrees Cousin. "But they weren't always; now my mother . . ."
> "Can you remember your mother, then?" asks Pin. . . .
> "Yes," says Cousin, "she was nice."
> "Mine was nice too," says Pin.
> "What a lot of fireflies," says Cousin.
> "If you look at them really closely, the fireflies," says Pin, "They're filthy creatures too, reddish."
> "Yes," says Cousin, "I've never seen them looking so beautiful."

This flat dialogue might have come out of Hemingway's "A Clean, Well-Lighted Place" or "The Killers"; it also reveals Calvino's fascination with the private languages created among comrades. Calvino's other major literary source here is quite different from Hemingway: the adventure tales of Robert Louis Stevenson—*Treasure Island* (1881-1882), for example—in which the inexperience of the youthful narrator and his transition from childish make-believe to adult reality shape the unfolding of the action. Thus, the title refers to the symbol of Pin's inner life: The spider's nest is the sanctum of his childhood in an adult world without friends or games. The plot turns on the pistol that Pin steals from a German soldier and hides in the spider's nest, where it becomes a rather Freudian symbol of his unawakened manhood and where he flourishes it, now transformed into a "strange enchanted toy," as part of an elaborate drama: "One who had a real pistol could play marvelous games . . . that no child had ever played."

Regardless of documentary surface, the book is really about Pin's initiation into adulthood through his search for a "real friend" with whom he can share his private world. As for Calvino's later heroes, the real life of the community is only partly satisfactory. His solace is unspoiled nature, which exists to free his imagination, revealing, in contrast to "the squalid ambiguous world of human beings," "all kinds of colored things; yellow and brown mushrooms growing damp in the earth, red spiders on huge invisible nets, hares all legs and ears which appear suddenly on the path then leap zigzagging out of sight."

Pin's commitment to the Resistance movement, like that of most of the other characters, hardly goes beyond a kind of camaraderie, a sharing of fantasies through a common language. An examination of the neorealism of his "Resistance novel" also shows how Calvino imposes on his scrupulously documented materials a literary and intellectual construct—in this case, the boy's adventure tale, with a psychology of the human need for fantasy. Pin's case, representing the mind's "natural" distortion of reality into fiction, becomes Calvino's specific concern in later works. It is really the semantics of commitment that interests him as he rummages through literature and ideas for a medium of engagement with the world outside the self.

After *The Path to the Nest of Spiders*, and with the exception of *The Watcher and Other Stories* and *Marcovaldo: Or, The Seasons in the City*, Calvino's method becomes increasingly parabolic. The best and best known of his realistic short stories, "The Argentine Ant" and "Smog," in *The Watcher and Other Stories*—however immersed in the contemporary urban context—have fablelike qualities. The ants and smog in question have the same function as the rats in Camus's *La Peste* (1947; *The Plague*, 1948), the trials in Kafka's works, or the monsters that are found in Japanese horror films; they become larger than life, inexorable forces of doom that are brought on by man's disruption of the environment.

The trilogy *Our Ancestors* is therefore not the radical departure from realism that many critics have made it seem. It does mark Calvino's growing interest in the potential of the fairy tale and the folktale to reflect popular culture and convey universal truths. In these three intellectual fantasies, or fabulations, Calvino backs up absurd premises with almost documentary verisimilitude and narrates with the wide-eyed matter-of-factness of a child. *Our Ancestors* is pseudohistorical; Calvino uses the legendary past as a distancing device, a means of commenting indirectly on the present and the timeless. Notably, all three fantasies are set against a background of war, and two of them, *The Cloven Viscount* and *The Non-Existent Knight*, are ridden with a hard, glittering violence more like that of children's cartoons than anything else. It is not irrelevant that Red Wolf, the legendary Resistance fighter of *The Path to the Nest of Spiders*, "belongs to the generation brought up on strip cartoons" and takes them quite seriously. So does Calvino, who often defends his departures into fantasy on the basis of its popular appeal and immediacy of communication.

THE CLOVEN VISCOUNT

The Cloven Viscount begins the trilogy in a blackly humorous vein. In this game of "just suppose," Medardo of Terralba, a seventeenth century nobleman, is split from head to crotch by a cannonball in a war against the Turks. He becomes a cartoonlike illustration of the split, or alienated, personality; there are allusions as well to Judeo-Christian dualism. One-half of the Viscount appears to have been lost or destroyed; the doctors on the battlefield save his other half, sending it, the evil or "Bad'un," as it comes to be called, home. Bad Medardo wreaks havoc on the countryside and its inhabitants, even burning down part of his own castle while attempting to dispose of his old nurse, Sebastiana. His terrorism, however, is for the most part more specialized. Driven by an obsession with his own halfness and wishing to imprint his image on a world that has split him, he bifurcates every living thing in his path. "'If only I could halve every whole thing like this,'" he says to his nephew while "stroking the convulsive half of an octopus, 'so that everyone could escape from his obtuse and ignorant wholeness.'" Halfness brings consciousness of one's alienation from the world and the self.

Eventually the Viscount's better half shows up. He is predictably and unbearably good and profoundly boring, although equally obsessed with halfness: "One understands the sorrow of every person and thing in the world at its own incompleteness." When whole, he "did not understand" the tragedy of the human condition, which he attempts to mitigate. The story has a fairy-tale ending through which, after a duel between the two halves over Pamela, a wench beloved of both, the brilliant Doctor Trelawney puts them back together. The narrator marvels in detail at the skill involved in the operation: the doctor's "great care to get all guts and arteries of both parts to correspond, and then a mile of bandages had tied them together. . . ." Once again a whole man, Medardo marries Pamela, and they live wisely, "having had the experience of both halves each on its own. . . ." He has a "happy life, many children and a just rule. Our life too change[s] for the better."

The allusion to Samuel Richardson's *Pamela* (1740-1741) is relevant, for this worthy squire, in living "wholly" ever after, lives above all "dully." The *story* is over. If the real life signified by wholeness is not "marvelous happiness," as the young narrator remarks, it is partly because of his state of mind. The narrator is the Viscount's nephew, on "the threshold of adolescence" by the end of the tale, whereupon he grows discontented "amid all this fervor of wholeness . . . growing sadder and more lacking."

In the introduction to the trilogy, Calvino provides a moral for the story: The Viscount's bifurcation is parabolic of modern alienation and mutilation. Certainly another is the brutality of war, conveyed in a starkly surreal landscape (however misperceived by the as yet uncloven Medardo): plains of "horses' carcasses, some supine with hooves to the sky, others prone with muzzles dug into the earth," and "a few limbs, fingers in particular, scattered over the stubble." (Says Medardo, "Every now and again I see a finger pointing our way. . . . What does that mean?") Yet another interpretation has been suggested by Gore Vidal: *The Cloven Viscount* is a "sendup of Plato and the idea of the whole." Calvino's main point in providing a moral is probably to stress what his tale does mean, but as allegory it spins off in many directions. The narrator's mood suggests that it is finally about the human and modern need for fictions which, like Calvino's disembodied fingers on a battleground, enigmatically point the way. As the tale ends, the narrator is conscious of loss and thus of his own incompleteness, and so remains "deep in the woods telling [himself] stories."

The Baron in the Trees

The intellectual's or artist's alienation is more explicitly the issue of *The Baron in the Trees*, the second novel in the trilogy. The protagonist is the eighteenth century Baron Cosimo Piovasco di Rindó, who, at the age of twelve, on June 15, in the midst of a family quarrel at dinner, defies all present by climbing into the trees, vowing never to come down.

The fantastic premise of the novel only thinly disguises its autobiographical nature; it is a fairy-tale version of Calvino's Resistance experience and bears comparison to *The Path to the Nest of Spiders*. Like Pin and his comrade, Cosimo finds that a certain imaginative aloofness from the world—in this case, the "natural" environment of the trees of Ombrosa, which, although rooted in earth, seem to touch the sky—paradoxically makes an effective commitment to it possible. As Cosimo's brother, meeting Voltaire in Paris, explains, "anyone who wants to see the earth properly must keep himself at a necessary distance from it." Voltaire's reply may well be Calvino's philosophy of life: "Once it was only Nature which produced living phenomena. . . . Now 'tis Reason."

In the revolt from his family, Cosimo rejects a lifestyle of aristocratic decadence. He must transcend both the grasping ambition of his father, who lives to regain the lapsed title of Duke of Ombrosa and thinks only of "genealogies and successions and family rivalries and alliances"—and the sanctified alienation of his sister Battista, "a kind of stay-at-home nun" confined to the pleasure of dismaying her brothers with sadistic cookery—snails' heads artfully arranged in wire mesh, grasshopper claw tarts, rats' liver pâté.

The trees are less an escape from this microcosm of monomaniacs than they are avenues to the world—or, rather, to a newly opened world. For the first time, Cosimo can mix freely with people of all classes, from charcoal burners to robber barons to the noble family next door, with whom he can talk rather than feud, as before. Roving bands of waiflike fruit thieves accept him as a fellow outsider and then as a leader. His distanced perspective allows him to perceive and solve engineering problems and to organize a voluntary fire brigade. Saving Ombrosa from incendiary destruction, Cosimo discovers joy in fighting for a common goal and simultaneously teaches the people to unite in moments of danger. He repels an invasion of wolves from the Alps, fights off Turkish pirates, and reforms the vicious brigand, Gian dei Brughi, by supplying him with novels. As his brother, the narrator, explains, "the more determined [Cosimo] was to hide away in his den of branches, the more he felt the need to create new links with the human race." He therefore founds or joins such "associations and confraternities of trades and professions" as the Conscientious Capmakers, the Enlightened Skin Tanners, and the Masons. Indeed, he becomes quite reconciled with his family, who are better for dealing with his rebellion, and he frequently watches over them from a mulberry branch with a view through his mother's window.

In the trees, Cosimo has more time to read and think than his earthbound fellows and begins a Rousseauistic "Project for the Constitution of an Ideal State in the Trees." For his various accomplishments, he is acknowledged by author Denis Diderot and paid homage by Napoleon. The utopian scheme, however, remains incomplete. Beginning it as "a treatise on laws and governments," he loses his point as his storytelling impulse takes over and out pours "a rough sketch of adventures, duels, and erotic tales, the latter inserted in a chapter on matrimonial rights." It is the texture of Cosimo's life, or his story in its eccentric variety of adventures, enterprises, and love affairs, that counts.

The same childlike ingenuousness which made the first two novels engaging and believable down to the last detail, informs most of *The Baron in the Trees*. Sustained at greater length is the Hemingwayesque fidelity to empirical detail. Cosimo might be Nick Adams preparing to fish—such is the intentness and precision with which Calvino compels the reader to concentrate on the matter at hand, whether it be the fabrication of a suspended sleeping bag or the construction of an irrigation system. Thus, the message of commitment, however obvious, is never obtrusive. What one remembers is the clarity and naturalness of arboreal life and the symbiosis of individual, society, and nature that seems illusory only at the end of the book.

In the last paragraph, the narrator, now perhaps Calvino, succumbs to a radical failure of belief. Looking at a sky left empty by the dying Cosimo and the changing times, he asks himself if Ombrosa ever really existed, if

> that mesh of leaves and twigs of fork and froth, minute and endless, with the sky glimpsed only in sudden specks and splinters . . . was embroidered on nothing, like this thread of ink which I have let run on for page after page . . . until it splutters and bursts into a last senseless cluster of words, ideas, dreams, and so ends.

In an introduction to the 1965 scholastic edition of the book, Calvino asserted that Cosimo is an allegorical figure for the poet. The trees are therefore his medium, providing a language for social and political engagement. *The Baron in the Trees* is more than a portrait of the artist, but it is Calvino's first fiction to examine the semantic possibilities of his subject of engagement, to focus directly on the relations between literature and empirical reality, as Joann Cannon has pointed out. The long Gian dei Brughi episode, a benign parody of eighteenth century critical theory concerning the moral influence of literature, is a case in point. Cosimo lends Alain-René Lesage's *The History of Gil Blas of Santillane* (1715-1735) to the chief of brigands, who becomes hooked on novels and is especially taken with Richardson's *Clarissa* (1747-1748), which brings out "a disposition long latent in him; a yearning for the cozy habits of family life, for relations, for sentiments . . . a sense of virtue . . ." and vice. Unfortunately, the result of his conversion is that he is caught and sentenced; yet, poised to hang, he wishes only to know the ending of Henry Fielding's *Jonathan Wilde* (1743, 1754), which Cosimo sorrowfully tells him. "Thank you. Like me! Goodby!" replies de Brughi as he himself kicks away his support and is strangled. Calvino's charming mixture of irony with good humor both supports and qualifies the eighteenth century dictum: Literature delights and thus instructs, but the real-life result may be imperfect (even if somewhat poetic) justice.

In the more minor key that ends the book are other hints that Calvino questions its premise. In contrast to Pin and the Viscount's nephew, who get no further than puberty by the ends of their stories, Cosimo's brother grows old and dull and, as narrator, begins to question this very role and its sources. As the story progresses and as Cosimo becomes more renowned in rumor and legend, the narrator feels more distant from valid representations. In a French almanac, in a chapter on monsters and between the Hermaphrodite and the Siren, he discovers a figure of his brother "all covered in leaves, with a long beard and . . . tail, eating a locust." Cosimo himself is partly responsible for such distortions, his brother observes: "So many and so incredible were the tales Cosimo told about his activities in the woods during the war" that no one version can be accepted outright. Cosimo at times becomes imbecile with erotic passion, is disturbed by the French Revolution and its aftermath, and grows disconsolate with age. Even *his* imagination fails to keep pace with events.

This theme of the failure of imagination to correspond with external reality has its other side: the view of literature as true empirically in the experience of the people who, in part, create it, as a collective and infinitely variable fantasy—a view that Calvino takes up with gusto in his later works. In the two years between *The Cloven Viscount* and *The Baron in the Trees*, Calvino compiled and edited *Italian Folktales*, a project that deepened his critical interest in the ways tales are generated orally. *The Baron in the Trees* reflects this interest in the way the truth of Cosimo's life is seen to depend on context, on the community in which it flourished; thus, Cosimo and his dream exist only so long and so far as Ombrosa does. The bizarre legends that dismay his brother can thus be seen to affirm the effectiveness of Cosimo's arboreal commitment. This is the case even to the end, when some English aeronauts passing by on an experimental balloon flight are made partly responsible for Cosimo's rather spectacular comic apotheosis. However inadvertently, through some fumbling with and dropping of an anchor, they take the dying idealist with them into the sky. The primitive "poem" on the family tombstone hits the note typical of Calvino at his best on this theme: "'Cosimo Piovasco di Rondò—Lived in Trees—Always loved earth—Went into sky.'"

THE NON-EXISTENT KNIGHT

The Non-Existent Knight takes up where *The Baron in the Trees* ends—with a study of being, nothingness, and semantics. The trees of Ombrosa finally seem no more substantial than words "embroidered on a void"; Agilulf, the nonexistent knight, personifies the metaphysics implied in that imaginary landscape. His complete title, "Agilulf Emo Bertrandin of the Guildivern and of the Others of Corbentraz and Sura, Knight of Selimpia Citeriore and Fez," suggests his need for substantiation, for he is a void, an empty suit of white armor from which echoes a metallic voice standing for essence or identity. He is a sort of walking embodiment of René Descartes's famous dictum, *Cogito, ergo sum* (I think, therefore I am). Agilulf's nonexistence calls to mind just about everything from Platonic forms to Cartesian rationalism, from Miguel de Cervantes' *Don Quixote de la Mancha* (1605, 1615) to T. S. Eliot's "The Hollow Men" (1925) and Jean-Paul Sartre's *L'Être et le néant* (1943; *Being and Nothingness*, 1956). Calvino's touch is light and witty, however, as usual. His tales are novels of ideas in the briefest of senses; for the most part, he drops philosophical connections as he takes them up, generating sparks, flashes, and kaleidoscopically transformed patterns rather than deepening levels of meaning.

In devoted service to Charlemagne, who takes his holy wars far less seriously than does Agilulf, the nonexistent knight is dismayingly perfect. He is thus detested by the other knights—except for Raimbaut, a novice who takes him for a role model. His unpopularity is increased by his absurd attempts to share in the community life. He does not eat, of course, but insists on observing all forms with rigor, sitting interminably at table and slicing his meat into tiny, uniform pieces. Agilulf's passion for perfection makes him obnoxiously unconquerable in war—and love. He is, strangely enough, the perfect ladies' man. Although he cannot love, he more than satisfies the noble widow Priscilla, entering her bed "fully armed from head to foot and stretched out taut as if on a tomb." "Don't you even loosen the sword from its scabbard?" asks Priscilla. "Amorous passion knows no half measures," answers Agilulf. Priscilla shuts her eyes "in ecstasy."

To solve two problems at once, Charlemagne assigns Agilulf a squire named Gurduloo—or Omoboo, or Martinzoo, or "Cheese," depending upon who is addressing him. If Agilulf is pure identity, form, or idea, his Sancho Panza is elemental protean substance or pure existence in a state of continuous transformation. He confuses himself with whatever he touches. When he drinks soup, he becomes soup and is to be drunk in turn, "the world being nothing but a vast shapeless mass of soup in which all things [are] dissolved." Together, the characters Agilulf and Gurduloo bring up a theme that Calvino will pursue later: the confusion of subject and object and the arbitrary nature of names and categories. The vaguely ancient, mythical quality of Charlemagne's era becomes Calvino's excuse to evoke a major dilemma of twentieth century epistemology. In the era when this story took place, writes the narrator, it was common "to find names and thoughts and forms and institutions that corresponded to nothing in existence," yet the world at the same time was "polluted with objects and capacities and persons who lacked any name or distinguishing mark."

Much of the book is a lusty parody of the stuff of Ariosto, whose mode becomes a vehicle for charming takeoffs on ideologies fundamental to Western culture: Judeo-Christian dualism, the cult of virginity and purity in general, the notion of progress, the idealization of war—"the passing of more and more dented objects from hand to hand." A complicated plot replete with fancifully misplaced identities, and through which Agilulf finally ceases to "nonexist," is also reminiscent of Ariosto. Awarded knighthood for having saved the virgin Sophronia from bandits, Agilulf's precarious being depends upon the lady-in-question's immaculate virtue. Torrismond, a competing knight, swears at the crucial time that Sophronia is his mother and, therefore, no virgin. As it turns out several subplots later, Sophronia is really Torrismond's half sister and a virgin after all—until he deflowers her under the impression that she is a nun recently forced into a sultan's harem. The good news comes too late for Agilulf, however, who, thinking that his identity is inauthentic—a long title embroidered on a void—loses the will to exist and vanishes.

This resolution collapses the primary triangle of the plot. The young Raimbaut falls in love with a knight who turns out to be Bradamante, a young woman, who in turn falls in love with the nonexistent knight—until the latter bequeaths his armor to the younger, more authentic man, and Bradamante is thus free to find her true love embodied in it. The most surprising turn of plot, however, occurs in the subtext, which emerges in the fourth chapter and gradually frames the story proper.

The Non-Existent Knight is narrated by an ingenue different from Calvino's previous ones: a Sister Theodora, who had been assigned to tell this story as a penance. Some very funny false notes are sounded when she protests her inadequacy for lack of contact with soldiers. Outside of "religious ceremonies, triduums, novenas, gardening, harvesting, vintaging, whippings, slavery, incest, fires, hangings, invasion, sacking, rape and pestilence, we [nuns] have had no experience." Her comments have to do, predictably enough, with the gap between her words and the external world. Ironically, her "assiduous penance" of "seeking words and . . . meditating on ultimate truths" works like Agilulf's strenuous willing of himself into significant being: It ends in self-consciousness and a consequent failure of will and imagination. Sister Theodora experiences writer's block with symptoms anticipating what John Barth called a postmodernist "literature of exhaustion": "The pen merely grates in dusty ink, and not a drop of life flows, and life is all outside, outside the window, outside oneself."

Fortunately, Sister Theodora is unlike the nonexistent knight in that she has substantial resources on which to draw, an existence apart from words and significations. Pushing the tale precipitously to its conclusion, she confesses that she is really the Amazon Bradamante, yet a Bradamante changed radically by her discipline as convent scribe. She joined the convent out of "desperate love" for the ideal Agilulf but now burns for "the young and passionate Raimbaut"—in all his imperfect but vital reality— and rushes from the convent walls to meet him. Her new aesthetic, which corresponds with her new love (Raimbaut in Agilulf's armor), insists on the interdependence of art and life, if not exactly *littérature engagée:* "A page is good only when we turn it and find life urging along, confusing every page in the book. The pen rushes on, urged by the same joy that makes me course the open road." If—or because—words fail to make present an external reality (and a desperate Sister Theodora resorts at one point to drawing word pictures), they must create exits to new worlds. Lest the conclusion seem a contradiction of *The Baron in the Trees,* Calvino has Theodora/Bradamante admit that "after affrays and affairs and blighted hopes," she will "always return to this cloister" of art, which, after all, was responsible for changing her mind. He thus posits a symbiosis of essence and substance, words and things, self and world.

A combination of fabulation and metafiction, *The Non-Existent Knight* sets the stage for Calvino's later works in at least three ways. One is deliberate anachronism—the allusion to the legendary past in a story with a transparently contemporary outlook—to achieve a timelessness of reference and appeal. A related strategy is the playful and multileveled parody, which extends to the acts of writing and reading, turning literature, whatever the genre, into an epistemological and semantic game. Finally, there is the mixture of literary and popular sources to confuse the borders of high and low culture. In general, the deliberate confusion of times, genres, and cultures expresses Calvino's mature view of the world. However reminiscent of Gurduloo's "vast shapeless mass of soup" in which things continuously dissolve and begin again, *The Non-Existent Knight* is up to date, as Calvino stresses. It is meant to address the future.

COSMICOMICS and T ZERO

Similar concerns inform *Cosmicomics* and its sequel, *T Zero.* Neither short-story collections nor novels (although perhaps a cross between them)—nor even fictions in the sense of representations of the empirical world—these books combine contemporary science and fantasy in a completely new way, to imagine what could not have been and never will be (unlike science fiction, which imagines what might be). At the same time, they domesticate scientific theories that are quoted or summarized before each narrative, much as the earlier Calvino "realized"

fairy-tale premises. "All at One Point" explains Edwin P. Hubble's big bang theory in terms of Mrs. Ph(i)Nk$_0$'s spontaneous desire to make noodles for everyone. This desire, verbalized at a certain moment ("Oh, if I only had some room, how I'd like to make some noodles for you boys!"), causes everyone to think space and time into existence, "the space that her round arms would occupy, moving backward and forward with the rolling pin over the dough," the space for the flour for the dough, the fields for the wheat for the flour, and so on, until a "true outburst of general love" has initiated the concept of space, "space itself, and time, and universal gravitation, and the gravitating universe." In so humanizing science, Calvino makes strange new worlds comfortable and inhabitable—in contrast to much science fiction, which exploits its capacity to estrange and dislocate.

Also in contrast to most science fiction is the treatment of time. *Cosmicomics* and *T Zero* trace the creation of the universe rather than transporting readers into the future. The stories correlate the billions of years covered with natural stages in a human life span, conveying vividly, for example, the sense that Qfwfq, the narrator, was "just a child" in the dark before the sun's condensation. He is quite adolescent as a mollusk in love for the first time. A number of "families" run through the equivalent of several generations.

In another sense, these stories do not trace anything, however, for they are randomly arranged. The randomness exists in part to avoid the teleological perspective of most evolutionary theory. In this universe, there are really no endings or final causes, only present moments erupting into new beginnings. The protean hero Qfwfq exists only to be transformed in an unending process, and the random arrangement of his various formations makes the reader adapt to dislocation with him. Qfwfq's nonchalance makes such jolts quite easy. As he so simply puts it, "I went on my way."

Qfwfq's radical openness to experience marks him as another of Calvino's "children," wide-eyed and matter-of-fact at the same time. He and his family of protean beings are childlike in another way: They are cartoon characters in words, as Calvino implies in the title of *Cosmicomics* and as he shows by "drawing" the story "The Origin of the Birds," in *T Zero*. He has compared Qfwfq to Popeye, the partly domesticated sailor, and certainly Qfwfq is just as "real," experiencing narcissism, desire, and love in "The Spiral," making his mark on the world in "A Sign in Space," confronting competitors in sign making, and betting on future events. Throughout his bewildering transformations, and much like a cartoon character, Qfwfq remains unruffled. As Calvino seems to say, all that is life. His cartoons show what it is like to embody a meson, a dinosaur, a mollusk, a racing car. They educate the imagination by strengthening its capacity and so provide a kind of insurance against future shock.

Throughout *Cosmicomics* and increasingly in *T Zero*, Calvino delights in drawing out abstract concepts in semiotics, reflecting the theories of Roland Barthes and the fictional methods of Jorge Luis Borges. In "A Sign in Space," Qfwfq makes the first sign in the universe. A rival, Kgwgk, erases his sign and replaces it with his own, so that Qfwfq must make a new, competitive sign, and so on, so that language, style, and art are born. Eventually (and reflecting the media blitz), the universe is covered with a meaningless scrawl, obscuring space and making distinctions between sign and sign, and between sign and space, nonexistent.

INVISIBLE CITIES

In three novels written in the 1970's, Calvino continued to explore the relationship between signs and the reality that they are supposed to represent. *Invisible Cities*, the first of these three metafictions, declares its concern with semiology at the outset, erecting a frame tale that stands for Barthes's concept of the world as text. The teller of the body of the narrative is revealed to be Marco Polo, who re-creates or imagines his journeys to countless fabulous cities. The listener is Kublai Khan, now old and confined to his fabled court, who cannot travel to the vast kingdom he possesses except through Marco Polo's tales. As suggested in the title, the outside world cannot live except through the dialogue that composes the book itself. Calvino provides no other characters, no plot, and no adventures other than the brief accounts

of the cities themselves to detract from this metafictional perspective.

Kublai Khan's (and the reader's) part in this dialogue is to search for a pattern in Marco Polo's fifty-five cities, varied according to categories such as "cities and memory," "cities and desire," "thin cities," "cities and eyes," "cities and names," and "continuous cities." Listening or reading is made into a game or puzzle standing for the human need to seek out order and meaning in an otherwise random world. As in *Cosmicomics* and *T Zero*, the possibility of moves, the "catalogue of forms," is "endless: until every shape has found its cities, new cities will continually begin." In *Invisible Cities*, Calvino applies to narrative alternatives his view of life as infinitely transformable. He also attempts to rejuvenate the written medium by portraying the situation and capturing the mood of oral narrative—consciously repeating, establishing rhythm, to the Khan's delight, in tapestries of words and patterns for their own sake.

As Marco Polo and Kublai Khan converse, the Venetian learns the Khan's Tartar language. In the beginning, Marco Polo can recount his journeys only in pantomime—with gestures, cries, and objects he has collected along the way. Although the Khan finds "the connection between them and the places visited . . . uncertain," and must to a great extent create his own story, Marco Polo's mute representations have "the power of emblems." After he learns to speak in the local idiom, communication is more precise but strangely "less happy than in the past." Emblems, however primitive, are more eloquent than conventional language.

THE CASTLE OF CROSSED DESTINIES

The Castle of Crossed Destinies, Calvino's next metafiction, employs tarot cards as an emblematic language more evocative than words. In the frame story, several pilgrims come together at a castle and, trying to tell one another their tales, find that they have been struck dumb. One pilgrim hits on an idea that had come to obsess Calvino: He uses cards, with the aid of grimaces and gestures, to represent himself and his adventures. With the tarot's four suits—coins, cups, clubs, and swords—and the arcana, twenty-one picture cards capable of suggesting multiple interpretations, Calvino again tells a story about telling stories—about the inexhaustible resources of narrative. Two decks are used in two sections: In "Castle," the richly beautiful deck painted by Bonifacio Bembo for the Dukes of Milan in the fifteenth century, and in "Tavern," the popular *ancien tarot de Marseille* from the eighteenth century. The cards are reproduced in the margins of the book. To stress his use of pictorial, popular, and communal art forms, Calvino had hoped to create a third section, called "Motel," to be narrated through fragments of comic strips.

As it is, he almost succeeds in his plan to use every card in the pack—in a sort of pictorial crossword puzzle through which each story is a reading of a vertical or horizontal card sequence, with the card-stories interlocking and permutating *ad infinitum*. *The Castle of Crossed Destinies* comes close to being Calvino's monomyth, his answer to James Joyce's *Finnegans Wake* (1939), cross-referencing tales of Faust, Macbeth, Hamlet, Lear, Oedipus, Helen of Troy, the Marquis de Sade, and Ariosto's Roland in a world animated by the elements of war, love, and magic. In spite of the obvious temptation toward the esoteric and alinear, Calvino carries through with much of his usual simplicity and literalness. Still, these tales lack the concreteness of his previous invisible cities, as Calvino virtually admits in an afterword: He had seen in the cards a perfect "machine for constructing stories" and, after exhausting them and himself in the process, published the book "to be free of" an obsession not far from the nonexistent knight's intricate, empty rituals, the "diabolical idea" of "conjuring up all the stories that could be contained in a tarot deck."

IF ON A WINTER'S NIGHT A TRAVELER

After six years of silence, Calvino emerged from this diabolic/penitential formalism in the mood of Sister Theodora's abrupt revelation: He rushed out, like Bradamante, burning for young and passionate life. *If on a Winter's Night a Traveler* is on one level another tour de force; it is composed entirely of beginnings, with one set inside and precipitating another, as in *The Arabian Nights' Entertainments*. It is also about fiction as a transaction with the reader, and in that sense engaged with the world beyond the

page. *If on a Winter's Night a Traveler* dramatizes, literalizes, and so becomes a kind of love affair with (and among) readers.

It is an active human element, in part—the felt presence of living characters—that Calvino's earlier metafictions fail to communicate. In *Invisible Cities* and *The Castle of Crossed Destinies*, Calvino breaks with his premises, however theoretically perfect their representation—most notably in the use of ancient emblems to create an equivalence between card reading and tale telling, between art and life. *If on a Winter's Night a Traveler* has rough edges, at least partly because it is told almost completely in the present tense, like his first book, and in the second person. From the first word, "you," the Reader, are the hero of "Italo Calvino's new novel," which "you" are beginning to read. "You" are therefore the most living, breathing character ever invented, literalized into your own story—as opposed to the mechanical plots of the mass media: "Tell the others right away, 'No, I don't want to watch TV!'"

Such a premise is so blatant as to seem downright silly, which is what Calvino intends. His usual naïve narrator is now a transparent parody of himself, a myopically concerned but quite real "Calvino" peering out of the page. Certainly, in a sense, this book is his most bookish. The premise is based, after all, on a mere extension of structuralism and semiotics (responsible for the premises of his previous metafictions) toward the reader-response emphasis of poststructuralism. It again presumes Barthes's world as text: Ten novels from countries around the world are telescoped into one. The difference is in the way it directs characterized—and real—readers toward the unwritten world, through an unfolding series of beginnings into realms "somewhere beyond the book, beyond the author, beyond the conventions of writing" toward a voice "from the unsaid, from what the world has not yet said of itself and does not yet have the words to say."

In fact, the dramatic tension of the book comes from its conflict between Calvino's self-confessed obsession with print and his desire to reach whatever lies beyond it. The plot is an editor's nightmare of "pages, lines, words, whirling in a dust storm"; it is engaged with the politics of print—with terrorist organizations, conspiracies, censors, and the like, all militating against the writer. The plot is generated by a scheme by the character Ermes Marana, the brilliant translator and founder of OEPHLW (Organization for the Electronic Production of Homogenized Literary Works), to "flood the world" with a "literature of apocrypha, of false attributions, of imitations and counterfeits and pastiches." Marana, representing the mass media, has paralyzed the world's best-selling author, Silas Flannery, upon whose creativity much of the world's economy, and thus world peace, depends. The fate of civilization hangs on the word, on Flannery's ability (as a fan of Snoopy) to get beyond "It was a dark and stormy night. . . ." Calvino has therefore returned to the battleground of his first novels—transformed, however, into the media blitz of the 1980's. This is the world war as he sees it for the late twentieth century. If the medium is the message, the "fascist machine" is whoever made this chaos in the first place. This is not Marana but Calvino, or his persona's diabolic mania for mechanically contrived order, leading to the cosmic scrawl or entropy of "A Sign in Space."

What redeems the real Calvino is not his contemporary self-awareness, which is the root of the problem, but his ability to lose himself, as in his first fantasies, in the game with the reader taken as far as it can go. Behind his main gimmick is, as usual, a theoretical source, Barthes's *Le Plaisir du texte* (1973; *The Pleasure of the Text*, 1975), which correlates reading with lovemaking. In a search through ten fragmentary novels for the true text of *If on a Winter's Night a Traveler*, Marana's machinations having jumbled and displaced the lot of them, the Reader discovers the Other Reader, Ludmilla, who is searching for the same book—or thing. A love story develops that extends Calvino's romance with the reader into one between readers. The diametrical opposite of her sister Lotaria, whose computer-assisted thesis catalogs Flannery's words as he writes them, Ludmilla is the "common," or naïve, reader, for whom reading is a creation and a search. The "circuits of her mind" transform the "current" of reading into "what in her is most personal and incommunicable."

In present-tense moments between the pseudo-novels, "you," as Reader, are allowed by your (however passive) rival "Calvino" to "read" the furniture of her apartment, her kitchen utensils, her body, and so on, until she "skims" your "index," and so on. Hence, the real reader is to learn how common, how true to life, and how vital reading is.

According to the narrator, the crucial resemblance between reading and lovemaking is that "within both of them times and spaces open, different from measurable time and space." It is in these open passages, Calvino shows, that transactions between solitary readers take place. He extends a concept of reading as an act of becoming by showing how the shared activity of reading brings individuals together. As early as the thirty-second page, reading has become a dialogue. Hoping that the book has become "an instrument, a channel of communication, a rendezvous," "Calvino" asks, "What is more natural than [that] a solidarity, a complicity, a bond should be established between Reader and Reader, thanks to the book?" The book ends in "your" (plural) marriage, a commitment to the common activity and cause of reading. In the final chapter, a "great double bed" receives "your parallel readings."

The marriage stands for the existence of a larger context, a community of individual, parallel readers "out there" or underground, resisting, in their passive, private way, formulation and system—the tyranny of plots, codes, propaganda, Marana's literature of "bad faith." Thus, Calvino is back where he started in *The Path to the Nest of Spiders*, with a unique form of *littérature engagée*: The partisans' movement has become a "reading resistance." Even the government censor goes home every night, as he says, "to abandon myself to reading, like that distant unknown woman," Ludmilla, the common reader, and Marana himself has to admit that when he is reading, "something happens over which I have no power." This happening, as the censor explains, "is the limit that even the most omnipotent police force cannot broach."

If on a Winter's Night a Traveler admirably sums up Calvino's career: His was a search for a "true text," a medium of engagement, and he seems to have found it. Throughout his various transformations, he made the reader's experience his primary concern, his secondary one being language's power to change the mind—by charming imagination into a life of its own.

Linda C. Badley

OTHER MAJOR WORKS

SHORT FICTION: *Ultimo viene il corvo*, 1949 (partial trans. *Adam, One Afternoon, and Other Stories*, 1957); *La formica Argentina*, 1952 (*The Argentine Ant*, 1957); *L'entrata in guerra*, 1954; *La nuvola di smog*, 1958 (*Smog*, 1971); *I racconti*, 1958; *La giornata d'uno scrutatore*, 1963 (*The Watcher and Other Stories*, 1971); *Marcovaldo: Ovvero, Le Stagioni in città*, 1963 (*Marcovaldo: Or, The Seasons in the City*, 1983); *Le cosmicomiche*, 1965 (*Cosmicomics*, 1968); *Ti con zero*, 1967 (*T Zero*, 1969); *Gli amore difficili*, 1970 (*Difficult Loves*, 1984); *Sotto il sole giaguaro*, 1986 (*Under the Jaguar Sun*, 1988).

NONFICTION: *Una pietra sopra: Discorsi di letteratura e societa*, 1980 (*The Uses of Literature*, 1986); *Collezione di sabbia*, 1984; *The Literature Machine: Essays*, 1986; *Sulla fiaba*, 1988 (*Six Memos for the Next Millennium*, 1988); *Perché leggere i classici*, 1991 (*Why Read the Classics?*, 1999).

EDITED TEXTS: *La letteratura americana e altri saggi*, 1951; *Fiabe italiane: Raccolte della tradizione popolare durante gli ultimi cento anni e transcritte in lingua dai vari dialetti*, 1956 (*Italian Fables*, 1959); *Cesare Pavese: Lettere, 1926-1950*, 1966; *L'Uccel Belverde e altre fiabe italiane*, 1972 (*Italian Folk Tales*, 1975).

BIBLIOGRAPHY

Adler, Sara Maria. *Calvino: The Writer as Fablemaker*. Potomac, Md.: Jose Porua Turanzas, 1979. Chapters on Calvino's war experiences, career as a literary adventurer, war stories, fantasy fiction, basic themes in his work, and handling of point of view, images, and fables. Includes bibliography, index, and critical approaches to his work.

Cannon, JoAnn. *Italo Calvino: Writer and Critic*. Ravenna, Italy: Longo Editore, 1981. A good introduction, with chapters on Calvino's longer fiction and a bibliography.

Carter, Albert Howard, III. *Italo Calvino: Metamor-phoses of Fantasy*. Ann Arbor, Mich.: UMI Research Press, 1987. Chapters on Calvino's biography and his major novels and stories. With notes, bibliography, and index.

Gabriele, Tommasina. *Italo Calvino: Eros and Language*. Madison, N.J.: Fairleigh Dickinson University Press, 1994. Explores Calvino's language of love and his treatment of sex, language, and laughter. Includes notes and bibliography.

Hume, Kathryn. *Calvino's Fictions: Cogito and Cosmos*. Oxford, England: Clarendon Press, 1992. Explores Calvino's treatment of the cosmos and of cosmogony, with separate chapters on *The Path to the Nest of Spiders* and *Marcovaldo*, *The Castle of Crossed Destinies* and *If on a Winter's Night a Traveler*, and *Invisible Cities* and *Mr. Palomar*. Includes notes and bibliography.

McLaughlin, Martin. *Italo Calvino*. Edinburgh, Scotland: Edinburgh University Press, 1998. A very detailed study of Calvino's fiction, beginning with his early stories and his development of a neorealistic style. Includes a chronology of Calvino's fictions and a bibliography.

Olken, I. T. *With Pleated Eye and Garnet Wing: Symmetries of Italo Calvino*. Ann Arbor: University of Michigan Press, 1984. A formal study of Calvino's fiction, exploring his use of various symmetries (natural, thematic, structural). Includes notes and bibliography.

BEBE MOORE CAMPBELL

Born: Philadelphia, Pennsylvania; 1950

PRINCIPAL LONG FICTION

Your Blues Ain't Like Mine, 1992
Brothers and Sisters, 1994
Singing in the Comeback Choir, 1998

OTHER LITERARY FORMS

Bebe Campbell's early works were primarily nonfiction. Her first book, *Successful Women, Angry*

Men: Backlash in the Two-Career Marriage (1986), delves into the effect of the feminist movement on family structure, most notably the shifting gender roles that result when women, either of necessity or in quest of self-actualization, seek work outside the home, sometimes upsetting the balance within. Her second work, *Sweet Summer: Growing Up with and Without My Dad* (1989), is her memoir as a child of divorce having to spend the school year with her mother in Philadelphia and summer with her father in North Carolina. The book was hailed for showing loving relationships in the black community and for stressing the importance of men or male figures in young girls' lives. Poet Nikki Giovanni praised it for providing "a corrective to some of the destructive images of black men that are prevalent in our society" and doing so with great vitality and clarity. Campbell has produced nonfiction articles for a wide range of publications, including *Essence*, *The New York Times*, *The Washington Post*, the *Los Angeles Times*, *Black Enterprise*, *Working Mother*, *Adweek*, *Ms.*, and *Glamour*; she was a contributing editor for *Essence*, *Black Enterprise*, and *Savvy*. In the late 1990's she was a regular commentator on National Public Radio's *Morning Edition*.

ACHIEVEMENTS

Campbell has been called one of the most important African American authors of the twentieth century, and she has received numerous awards and grants and earned national attention and praise. She won the Body of Work Award from the National Association of Negro Business and Professional Women in 1978, received a National Endowment for the Arts Literature Grant in 1980, was awarded the Mayor's Certificate of Appreciation from Los Angeles Mayor Tom Bradley, and won the National Association for the Advancement of Colored People (NAACP) Award for fiction in 1994. She has had two radio dramas produced by the Midwestern Radio Theater, earning first place in one of its Workshop Competitions.

BIOGRAPHY

Though not growing up in a traditional two-parent family, Bebe Moore Campbell never felt an absence of love and understanding from either her mother or father. Her school months in Philadelphia were slightly constrained because of the close supervision of her mother, grandmother, and aunt, who oversaw her every move. They instructed her in proper speech, manners, and behavior. Summers with her father and his mother in North Carolina were much more carefree. There she felt total love and acceptance.

When she was in third grade, a teacher recognized her potential, placing her in a special creative-writing class. She began sending letters to her father that were intended to intrigue him—installments of stories—all of them calling for a response. She wanted to keep his interest alive all year long. Her idealization of her father ended abruptly when, at fourteen, she learned that his speeding had caused the crash that resulted in his paralysis and lifelong need for a wheelchair and that he was responsible for another accident in which a young boy had been killed. Her initial anger abated, but the relationship suffered.

Campbell earned a B.S. degree in elementary education at the University of Pittsburgh, later teaching elementary school for ten years in Pittsburgh, Atlanta, and Washington, D.C. An early marriage ended in divorce. Campbell, as her mother had, assumed the responsibilities of a single parent. Her writing career began when the editor of *Essence* gave a lecture at Howard University. Campbell hurriedly handed her young daughter, Maia, to a friend for care so that she could chase the woman to the ladies room and tell her of her writing aspirations. The woman, impressed, helped Campbell enter the publishing world. Campbell moved to Los Angeles in the early 1980's. There she married a banker, Ellis Gordon, Jr., who also had a child, a son named Ellis Gordon III.

ANALYSIS

Bebe Moore Campbell's fiction is based largely on her own experiences as a female member of a racial minority in a white, male-dominated culture. Her works are sociopolitical, generally dealing with matters of race, class, and gender. They cover such issues as sexism and sexual harassment in the workplace, racism—black to black, white to black, and black to white—and issues of racial solidarity versus gender solidarity. Her works have received widespread approval, with only minor criticisms for a tendency to create somewhat one-dimensional characters and, at times, to present slightly unflattering pictures of women. She is considered a serious writer, who, while popular, never popularizes by resorting to superhuman characters in glamorous sexual situations. Her white characters, as well as her black ones, ring true. Some have questioned how she could enter the minds of people of a different race. In response, she has explained that she socializes with people of all races and classes and has close white friends who help her gain the perspective she needs.

YOUR BLUES AIN'T LIKE MINE

Your Blues Ain't Like Mine appeared on best-seller lists and was chosen by *The New York Times* as one of the most notable books of 1992. It is based on the actual 1955 Mississippi murder of Emmett Till, a black teenager who dared to speak to a white woman. Campbell's fictionalized account has a black northern boy, Armstrong Todd, staying with his southern grandmother while his divorced mother attempts to pull her life together in Chicago. Unfamiliar with the deep-seated racism in this part of the country, he teasingly recites some harmless French phrases to a bored, obviously bemused, white woman as she stands in a barroom door waiting for her husband. The woman, despite being ordered to stay in the truck by her abusive husband, had ventured toward the sounds of laughter and gaiety, so sadly lacking in her own life.

Her husband, Floyd Cox, himself a victim of constant verbal abuse from his father and brother (the favored son), sees obtaining retribution for this slight as a way of gaining his family's respect. He hunts down Armstrong because he wants to please his father. For a short while in the truck, drinking and laughing after they had just terrorized, beaten, and shot to death the frightened black fifteen-year-old, Floyd seems to have gained his father's acceptance. The sense of closeness is fleeting, however, since, upon his arrest, his father and brother all but abandon him.

Southern justice being what it was in the 1950's, Floyd Cox's punishment is minimal, and he is soon released from jail. The subsequent ruination of his family strongly interests Campbell. She wants to show their suffering as well as the suffering of the victim and his family. Campbell's point is that racism hurts the racist as well as the victim. She said that she chose to present both sides of the story because she firmly believes that until people understand the ramifications of racism, they cannot begin to deal with it. Through seeing and feeling the pain of others, even of unsympathetic characters, people will recognize that bias is hateful and ultimately harmful to all.

Campbell also explores the efforts of the murdered boy's family to make some sense out of what is left of their lives. The mother determines to have another son, one who will have a chance to experience a full life. However, this boy yields to the lure of the streets and soon has gang affiliations; his chances of survival are slim. Hopelessness and despair have turned black men against one another and each man against himself. The future seems bleak, with only a hint of promise when the son responds slightly to his father's initiative of friendship.

BROTHERS AND SISTERS

Brothers and Sisters takes place in Los Angeles, in the aftermath of the Rodney King verdict riots. It is a novel of relationships, most notably that between a black bank manager, Esther Jackson, and Mallory Post, a white loan officer. Mallory holds a position coveted by Esther but denied her because of racism. These two women are cautious friends, neither completely comfortable with the other race—one filled with underlying anger, the other always fearful of appearing racially insensitive. Esther is the sort of woman who will not date "down": She is insistent on running a kind of financial background check on her suitors. Mallory urges Esther to relax her demand for upward mobility and to date the mail-truck driver because he is nice and will treat her well. Campbell notes that Mallory, as a middle-class white woman, has "the freedom to exercise these choices because she's not so clutched about trying to get to the next rung on the ladder and thinking she's got to be with the proper partner to get there."

Campbell hoped that the novel would "serve as a kind of blueprint, to help people foster racial understanding." She says that "our strengths lie in saluting our differences and getting along." While she is aware that many of the problems in the black community have to do with institutionalized racism, she also feels that "African-Americans need to begin to look really closely and make some movement toward changing the problems" and to recognize that some of them are the result of choices they have made. The response to *Brothers and Sisters* was uncommon, in that hundreds of discussion groups formed to come to terms with its issues. In Prince George's County, Maryland, an area with a heavy black population as well as a relatively stable white one, the book became the basis of a community project: People studied the impact of bias and sought ways to deal effectively with communication breakdowns between races.

Campbell laments the abandonment of the old neighborhoods, feeling that integration should not entail embracing white communities at the expense of black ones. She urges middle-class blacks to stay in touch with those less fortunate, to mentor the young. She feels that men, in particular, must take steps toward regaining control of their children and of the streets. In an interview with Martha Satz published in the *Southwest Review* (Spring, 1996), she observed that the Million Man March, with its resultant reawakening of moral, ethical, familial, and racial responsibilities, may have been responsible for the dramatically lower number of arson incidents in Detroit on Halloween of that year.

SINGING IN THE COMEBACK CHOIR

Singing in the Comeback Choir is the story of Malindy Walker, a once-famous entertainer who has fallen ungracefully into old age, with its sometimes attendant sense of the pointlessness of the battle. Her life consists mainly of stealthily smoking and drinking, despite admonitions from her doctor. Based loosely on Alberta Hunter, jazz legend of the 1940's and 1950's, Malindy is a fiercely independent soul who has no intention of bowing to her granddaughter's wish to have her cared for (and closely supervised) in a senior citizen compound. The old neighborhood in which she lives has fallen into ruin, but Malindy's friends are there; memories of her great triumphs, of her sequined gowns and the applause, seem to sustain her. Her underlying sadness is over her diminished singing ability. She sees herself as

finished, so she partakes of the fleeting pleasures of alcohol and nicotine.

Her granddaughter, Maxine Lott McCoy, a highly successful television producer with a relatively good marriage and a child on the way, is a professional who bears some resemblance to Campbell herself. She comes to the rescue of her grandmother, only to find that she herself is the one who needs to be rescued—from the high-powered yet insular and protected world in which she has lost touch with her origins. Therein lies the point of the novel. The old neighborhoods are dying because they have been abandoned by those who could give them life, the ones who are capable of regeneration. Maxine is saddened by what is left of her grandmother's street and by the dead eyes of the neighborhood boy she once knew; now grown and playing at being a man, he curses her and makes sexually threatening gestures. She confronts him but sees that he is the wave of the future unless others can intervene and help.

Part of Campbell's intent in the novel was "to talk about the work that needs to be done" in order to salvage and rebuild the decaying neighborhoods and despairing lives. She has noted that she wants "black folks to do the hard work that we've done in the past that we haven't been doing as much in the years following the civil rights movement."

Gay Annette Zieger

OTHER MAJOR WORKS

NONFICTION: *Successful Women, Angry Men: Backlash in the Two-Career Marriage*, 1986; *Sweet Summer: Growing Up with and Without My Dad*, 1989.

BIBLIOGRAPHY

Chambers, Veronica. "Which Counts More, Gender or Race?" *The New York Times Magazine*, December 25, 1994, 16-19. Chambers moderates a conversation between Bebe Moore Campbell and Joyce Carol Oates dealing with Black English, interracial dating, liberal white guilt, and the historic importance of the black church.

Edgerton, Clyde. "Medicine for Broken Souls." *The New York Times Book Review*, September 20,

1992, 13. Edgerton offers an interesting re- view of Campbell's *Your Blues Ain't Like Mine.*

Olendorf, Donna, ed. *Contemporary Authors.* Vol. 139. Detroit, Mich.: Gale Research, 1993. A brief biographical entry on Campbell appears on pages 76-77.

Powers, Retha. "A Tale of Two Women." *Ms.,* September/October, 1994, 78. A review of *Brothers and Sisters.*

Satz, Martha. "I Hope I Can Teach a Little Bit: An Interview with Bebe Moore Campbell." *Southwest Review* 81 (Spring, 1996): 195-213 An in-depth discussion (which occurred in November, 1995) of Campbell's views on the need for African Americans to stay in touch with the old neighborhoods, particularly with the children who are still there and need mentoring.

See, Lisa. "Bebe Moore Campbell." *Publishers Weekly,* June 30, 1989, 82-83. Includes a dis- cussion of "Sweet Summer: Growing Up with and Without My Dad" and an interview with Campbell.

Winter, Kari J. "Brothers and Sisters, by B. M. Campbell." *African American Review* 31, no. 2 (Summer, 1997): 369-372. A comparative re- view of Bebe Moore Campbell's *Brothers and Sisters* and Gita Brown's *Be I Whole* in which Brown fares better. Campbell is charged with "rep- licating many of the objectifying, spiritually bank- rupt attitudes of American capitalism" and using "cliché-ridden prose."

ALBERT CAMUS

Born: Mondovi, Algeria; November 7, 1913
Died: Near Villeblevin, France; January 4, 1960

PRINCIPAL LONG FICTION

L'Étranger, 1942 (*The Stranger,* 1946)
La Peste, 1947 (*The Plague,* 1948)

(The Nobel Foundation)

La Chute, 1956 (*The Fall,* 1957)
La Mort heureuse, 1971 (wr. 1936-1938; *A Happy Death,* 1972)
Le Premier homme, 1994 (*The First Man,* 1995)

OTHER LITERARY FORMS

Albert Camus considered his vocation to be that of novelist, but the artist in him was always at the ser- vice of his dominant passion, moral philosophy. As a result, Camus was led to cultivate several other liter- ary forms which could express his central concerns as a moralist: the short story, drama, and nonfiction forms such as the philosophical essay and political journalism, all of which he practiced with enough distinction to be influential among his contemporar- ies. Moreover, these works were generally written side by side with his novels; it was Camus's customary procedure, throughout his brief writing career, always to be working on two or more compositions simultaneously, each expressing a different facet of the same philosophical issue. Thus, within a year of the publication of his most celebrated novel, *The Stranger*, there appeared a long essay entitled *Le Mythe de Sisyphe* (1942; *The Myth of Sisyphus*, 1955), a meditation on the meaning of life in an irrational universe that begins with the assertion that the only serious question confronting modern man is the question of suicide and concludes with a daring argument that finds in the legend of Sisyphus a strangely comforting allegory of the human condition. Sisyphus, who becomes in Camus's hands an exemplary existentialist, spent his days in the endlessly futile task of pushing a boulder to the top of a hill from which it always rolled down again. Every human life is expended as meaninglessly as that of Sisyphus, Camus argues, yet one must conceive of Sisyphus as happy, because he was totally absorbed by his assigned task and found sufficient satisfaction in its daily accomplishment, without requiring that it also have some enduring significance. There are close links between such reasoning and the ideas that inform *The Stranger*, but it is erroneous to argue, as some have, that *The Myth of Sisyphus* is an "explanation" of *The Stranger*. The former work is, rather, a discussion of similar themes in a different form and from a different perspective, in accordance with Camus's unique way of working as a writer.

That unique way of working produced another long philosophical essay, *L'Homme révolté* (1951; *The Rebel*, 1953), which has affinities with the novel *The Plague* as well as with four plays written and produced in the 1940's: *Caligula* (pb. 1944; English translation, 1948); *Le Malentendu* (1944; *The Misunderstanding*, 1948); *L'État de siège* (1948; *State of Siege*, 1958), and *Les Justes* (1949; *The Just Assassins*, 1958)—each of which is related by certain thematic elements to the two novels that Camus published in the same period. His earliest political journalism, written before 1940 and dealing with the problems of his native Algeria, attracted little attention, but his work for the underground newspaper

Combat, during and after World War II, achieved considerable celebrity, and the best articles were later collected in a volume widely read and admired. During the civil war in Algeria, in the 1950's, Camus again entered the lists as a political journalist, and because he was by then indisputably Algeria's most famous man of letters, his articles were of major importance at the time, though highly controversial and much less widely approved than the wartime pieces from *Combat*. Camus produced only one collection of short stories, *L'Exil et le royaume* (1957; *Exile and the Kingdom*, 1958), composed during the same years as the novel *The Fall*, but those stories have been very popular and are regarded by many as among the finest short stories published in France in the twentieth century. The volume is particularly noteworthy because it offers the only examples Camus ever published of fiction composed in the third-person mode of the omniscient narrator. The first three of his published novels are variations of the limited-perspective first-person narrative.

Deeply involved in the theater throughout his career, both as writer and director, Camus adapted for the French stage the work of foreign novelists Fyodor Dostoevski and William Faulkner, and of playwrights of Spain's Golden Age, including Pedro Calderón de la Barca and Lope de Vega Carpio. These adaptations have all been published and form part of Camus's contribution to the theater.

ACHIEVEMENTS

To the immediate postwar public, not only in France but also throughout Europe, Albert Camus seemed a writer of unassailable stature. Although Camus himself repudiated the designation, he was regarded worldwide as one of the two principal exponents of existentialism (the other was Jean-Paul Sartre), the single most influential philosophical movement of the twentieth century. Indeed, the existentialist worldview—according to which the individual human being "must assume ultimate responsibility for his acts of free will without any certain knowledge of what is right or wrong or good or bad"—has profoundly shaped the values of countless people who have never read Camus or Sartre.

In the 1950's, Camus was widely admired not only as a writer but also as a hero of the war against fascism, a spokesman for the younger generation, and a guardian of the moral conscience of Europe. That reputation was consecrated in 1957 with the award to Camus of the Nobel Prize in Literature, at the remarkably young age of forty-four. Yet, as has happened to many other recipients of the Nobel Prize, the award seemed almost a signal of the rapid deflation of his renown. He suddenly came under severe criticism for his stand on the Algerian Civil War, was attacked as self-righteous and artistically sterile, and was finally denounced as irrelevant by the new literary generation then coming to prominence, who were weary of moral issues and more concerned with aesthetic questions of form and language. Camus's fame and influence appeared to many to have suffered an irreversible decline by the end of the decade, at least in France. (In America, the case was different: Made more accessible by the "paperback revolution," Camus's works were enormously influential among American college students in the 1960's.) There were those who suggested that the automobile accident that took his life in January of 1960 was a disguised blessing, sparing him the pain of having to witness the collapse of his own career.

It is true that, in the late twentieth century, generations after the height of Camus's fame, French writers and intellectuals showed no influence of Camus in their writings and scant critical interest in his works. Still, his works have enjoyed steady sales among the French public, and outside France, especially in America, interest in Camus has remained strong. There has been an inevitable sifting of values, a crystallization of what it is, in Camus's work, that still has the power to survive and what no longer speaks to successive generations. It has become clear, for example, that his philosophical essays are too closely tied to the special circumstances that occasioned them; in spite of a few brilliant passages, those essays now seem rambling and poorly argued as well as irrelevant to the concerns of modern readers. Camus's theater, too, has held up poorly, being too abstract and inhuman to engage the emotions of an audience. While his plays have continued to be performed on both sides of the Atlantic, interest in them has steadily declined over the years. It is his fiction that still seems most alive, both in characters and ideas, and that still presents to the reader endlessly fascinating engimas which delight the imagination and invite repeated readings.

Although the total number of his fictional works is small, those works are, in both form and content, among the most brilliantly original contributions to the art of fiction produced anywhere in the twentieth century. In particular, Camus expressed through fiction, more powerfully and more memorably than anyone else in his time, the painful moral and spiritual dilemmas of modern man: evil, alienation, meaninglessness, and death. He invented techniques and created characters by which he was able to make manifest, in unforgettable terms, the eternal struggle of Everyman for some shred of dignity and happiness. His stories have accordingly taken on some of the haunting quality, and the prestige, of myths. For that reason, it seems safe to predict that it is Camus's fiction which represents his greatest achievement—an achievement that will endure long after his philosophical musings and political arguments have been forgotten.

BIOGRAPHY

Though born in the interior village of Mondovi, near Constantine, Algeria, Albert Camus was actually brought up in the big city, in a working-class suburb of Algiers. His widowed mother, who was from Algiers, took her two sons back there to live after her husband was killed, early in World War I. Albert, the younger of the two sons, was not yet a year old when his father was killed, and he was to grow up with a need for relationships with older men, apparently to replace the father he never had. It was important to Camus that his father's forebears had immigrated *by choice* to Algeria from France in the nineteenth century, since it made him feel that his roots were authentically both French and Algerian. Because his mother was of Spanish extraction, Camus felt himself to be even more authentically Algerian, for Spanish blood gave him his share of that passionate Mediterranean temperament which he felt made French Algeria distinctive and unique. It comes as no surprise, therefore, that the great bulk of Camus's writing is set in Algeria or relates directly to that country. Being Algerian was the central fact of Camus's consciousness.

In his early twenties, he began to write essays for a leftist political journal published in Algiers; his subject was the political and economic plight of Algeria in its role as a colony of France. During those same years, he helped to found a theater group, for which he acted, directed, and did some writing, and he was a candidate for an advanced degree in philosophy at the University of Algiers. At times, he had to interrupt his studies because of ill health; he had contracted tuberculosis in 1930, at the age of seventeen, and was subject to periodic attacks from it for the rest of his life. When only twenty-one, he made a rather impulsive marriage that ended in separation within a year and eventual divorce. He worked at a number of odd jobs before becoming a full-time journalist, and he was active enough in politics in the 1930's to have become, for a few months, a member of the Algerian Communist Party. Altogether, his Algerian youth had been a difficult and turbulent experience, yet it had also been a time of growth and self-discovery, and he looked back on those years, ever after, with a special nostalgia for the sun, sand, sea, and simplicity of life which he felt had formed him and made him what he had become.

Early in 1940, with a war in progress and the newspaper for which he worked closed down, Camus found himself forced to leave Algeria in order to make a living. He went to Paris to work for a Paris newspaper—a job procured for him by his older friend Pascal Pia, with whom he had worked on the Algiers newspaper before it folded. Within a year, the Paris job ended, and Camus, who had married again, returned to Algeria with his wife. They lived in Oran, his wife's hometown, and while she worked as a teacher, Camus worked at his writing projects, completing both the novel *The Stranger* and the essay *The Myth of Sisyphus* and arranging for their publication in Paris by Gallimard. By late 1942, Camus was so ill with tuberculosis that his wife persuaded him to seek a more favorable climate in the mountainous area of central France, which was then unoccupied territory. He went there alone, to continue writing, and found himself cut off from all contact with his family when the Allies invaded North Africa and the Germans occupied the rest of France as a defensive measure. During this period of isolation, Camus began to sketch out his next novel, *The Plague*. He also began to make frequent trips to Paris to see literary friends. His publisher, Gallimard, not only sent him royalties for *The Stranger*, which sold quite well, but also helped Camus by putting him on the Gallimard payroll as a reader—a position he enjoyed so much that he continued to fulfill it for the rest of his life. Late in 1943, Camus moved to Paris to be where the literary action was, increasingly associating with those friends who were in the Resistance movement, with which Camus was strongly sympathetic. Before long, Camus joined the Resistance and was assigned the task of writing for the Resistance newspaper, *Combat*. After the liberation of Paris, in 1944, *Combat* went aboveground as a daily newspaper, and Camus was for a time its editor. He had become part of the Paris literary world, had met the best-known figures—Sartre, André Malraux, and many others—and had achieved a certain fame. By that time, it was clear that he would never go back to Algeria to live. As soon as it was possible for her to do so, Camus's wife joined him in Paris, their marriage resumed, and in September of 1945 she gave birth to twins, a boy and a girl. By war's end, Camus was not only a confirmed Parisian but also a domesticated one, with a family to support.

In the postwar years, Camus's fame quickly began to spread outside France—*The Stranger* appeared in English translation in 1946 and was an immediate sensation—and Camus took up the life of a lionized man of letters, dropping all employment except for his work with Gallimard and making lecture tours to foreign countries, including the United States. The publication of *The Plague* in 1947 was hailed by critics as the fulfillment of his great promise as a writer, and that book became one of the best-sellers of the postwar era, making Camus economically secure for the first time. Success and fame seemed to make him artistically insecure, however—there were suddenly too many demands from admirers, too many intrusions into his privacy and working time, and above all, too much self-doubt about his own powers for him to be able to live up to his public's expectations of him. Camus soon began to experience a crisis of literary sterility. It took him until 1951 to complete the essay *The Rebel*, begun nearly ten years earlier, and throughout the first half of the decade of the 1950's, he published nothing and was rumored to have a permanent case of writer's block. The outbreak of violence in Algeria and the campaign for independence, which began in 1952, added severely to Camus's troubled state, and the controversial articles he wrote in that period on the Algerian question certainly lost him many friends and much support. His unhappy attempt to be the voice of reason and conciliation at a time in the dispute when opinions had already become hopelessly polarized ("if you are not with us, you are against us") is poignantly described in the powerful tale "The Guest," one of the best stories in the collection *Exile and the Kingdom*.

Camus emerged from this period of intense personal suffering and frustration by venting his feelings in the short, bitterly satiric novel *The Fall*, published in 1956—his first work of fiction in nearly ten years, as his detractors were quick to point out. Nevertheless, the comic verve of the work attracted many readers, even though its intended meanings often seemed obscure to them. The book sold well, and Camus's reputation rebounded somewhat, especially outside France. The publication of the volume of short stories *Exile and the Kingdom*, the following year, earned for him additional respect as a writer who still had something to say. Internationally, his reputation peaked with the award of the Nobel Prize later that same year. Reinvigorated by the successes of 1956 and 1957, Camus was, as the decade ended, once again confidently and productively at work, with the usual three or four projects going simultaneously, one of which was an autobiographical novel about his youth in Algeria, to be called "Le Premier Homme" (the first man). His "block" seemed to be definitively overcome, and friends and family who spent Christmas of 1959 with him at the country retreat he had purchased in southern France recalled

that he was in a generally optimistic frame of mind about his career. Fate, however, abruptly shattered that optimism. Camus's career came to a premature— and, he would have said, absurd—end only a few days after that happy Christmas. On January 4, 1960, Michel Gallimard, nephew of Camus's publisher, lost control of his car, in which Camus was riding as a passenger, just outside the tiny village of Villeblevin, and crashed into a tree, killing Camus instantly. Camus had passed his forty-sixth birthday only two months before. The evolution of his work strongly suggests that a banal motor accident cut him off when he seemed, finally, to have mastered his craft and to be entering upon his prime creative years.

ANALYSIS

Two persistent themes animate all of Albert Camus's writing and underlie his artistic vision: One is the enigma of the universe, which is breathtakingly beautiful yet indifferent to life; the other is the enigma of man, whose craving for happiness and meaning in life remains unextinguished by his full awareness of his own mortality and of the sovereign indifference of his environment. At the root of every novel, every play, every essay, even every entry in his notebooks can be found Camus's incessant need to probe and puzzle over the ironic double bind that he perceived to be the essence of the human condition: Man is endowed with the imagination to conceive an ideal existence, but neither his circumstances nor his own powers permit its attainment. The perception of this hopeless double bind made inescapable for Camus the obligation to face up to an overriding moral issue for man: Given man's circumscribed condition, are there honorable terms on which his life can be lived?

A HAPPY DEATH

In his earliest attempt at casting these themes in fictional form, Camus made use of the traditional novel of personal development, or *Bildungsroman*, to describe one young man's encounters with life, love, and death. The result was an episodic novel, obviously based on his own experiences, but composed in the third person and so lacking in unity and coherence as to betray the central idea on which he wished to focus: the problem of accepting death. He called the novel *A Happy Death* and showed his hero resolutely fixing his consciousness on the inanimate world around him, striving to become one with the stones and achieve a happy death by blending gently and painlessly into the silent harmony of the universe, while retaining his lucidity until his last breath. The book's last sentence strives to convince the reader by rhetoric that the hero has indeed achieved the happy death he sought: "And stone among the stones, he returned in the joy of his heart to the truth of motionless worlds." Camus seems to have sensed, however, that the rhetoric was unconvincing and that the ideal of a happy death was an illusion. Perhaps he even recognized that his hero's struggle to remain conscious of life until his last breath was, in reality, a protest against death and a contradiction of his desire to make the transition to death serene and imperceptible. It was doubtless some such sense of the book's failure that convinced Camus not to publish this work, composed when he was not yet twenty-five. Its posthumous publication has given scholars the opportunity to see Camus's first halting steps in trying to formulate the subtle and complex themes of the novels that were to make him great.

THE STRANGER

The Stranger, Camus's second attempt at writing a novel, includes a number of the scenes, characters, and situations found in *A Happy Death* (Mersault, the hero of *A Happy Death*, becomes Meursault in *The Stranger*). A detailed comparison of the two novels, however, makes it clear that *The Stranger*, which appeared in 1942, four years and many events after Camus abandoned *A Happy Death*, is a wholly different work in both conception and theme. No longer preoccupied with happiness in death, Camus turned his attention in *The Stranger* to the problem of happiness in life, to man's irrational and desperate need to find meaning in existence. His protagonist, Meursault, is not the frail, sophisticated, death-haunted figure of the earlier novel, but rather a robust primitive who seems eerily devoid of the normal attitudes, values, and culturally induced feelings of his

society, as though he had been brought up on some other planet—a "stranger" in the fullest sense of the word. Moreover, Camus hit upon the device of first-person narration as the most effective and dramatic means of confronting his readers with his disturbing protagonist, so alien to his environment. The famous opening words shock the reader into an awareness of the disquieting strangeness of the narrator:

"Mama died today. Or perhaps yesterday, I don't know. I received a telegram from the home: 'Mother passed away. Funeral tomorrow. Yours truly.' That doesn't mean anything. Perhaps it was yesterday."

Shrewdly focusing on a mother's death as a revealing touchstone of humankind's most deeply ingrained social attitudes, these words achieve a double effect: They tell the reader that the son of the deceased mother can speak of her death without any of the expected symptoms of grief, but at the same time, they remind the reader that the rest of society, having no familial ties with the deceased, habitually masks its indifference under empty rhetorical formulas such as the telegraphic announcement. This dual perspective is fully developed in subsequent chapters as the basic theme of the book: While Meursault shows by his own forthright account of his life that he does not share his society's conventional notions about death, religion, family, friendship, love, marriage, and ambition, he also manages to reveal—often without realizing it—that those conventional notions are often shallow, hypocritical, or delusory and constitute the pathetic inventions of a society desperate to invest its existence with a meaning it does not have. Thus, when Meursault, asked by his boss whether he would be interested in an assignment to establish a Paris office for his boss's business, says that he has no interest in living in Paris, the reader recognizes that Meursault simply does not believe that material surroundings can make his life any different. At the same time, the boss's dismayed reaction to Meursault's indifference to opportunity subtly disturbs the reader with the suspicion that, after all, the boss may have a touching but misplaced faith in the value of ambition. A similar moment occurs when Meursault and his girlfriend Marie discuss love and marriage. The reader is surely made uncomfortable by Meursault's casualness in saying that he does not know what love is, but that he is willing to marry Marie if she wants it. It is, however, a different order of discomfort that overcomes the reader when Marie insists that marriage is a very serious matter and Meursault calmly replies that it is not. All of part 2 of the novel, devoted to Meursault's trial after he has killed an Arab, brings additional and even more disturbing changes on the same dual perspective, with Meursault showing no awareness or acceptance of conventional beliefs about justice, murder, legal procedures, and the nature of evidence, while all the "normal" people involved show unexamined or self-deceiving convictions about all such matters. The ironic meaning that emerges from the novel is that while Meursault was guilty of taking a life, society sentenced him to death not for his crime, with which it seemed incapable of dealing, but for his refusal to live by society's values, for not "playing the game." As Camus himself laconically remarked, his novel means that any man who does not weep at his mother's funeral risks being condemned to death.

Critics have regularly protested that, in *The Stranger*, Camus manipulates his readers' emotions, inducing sympathy for Meursault even though he is a moral monster and ridiculing everyone else as representative of a society afraid to face reality, hence threatened by Meursault's clear-eyed and unsentimental acceptance of the world. Such protests are justified, however, only if one assumes that Camus intended *The Stranger* to be a realistic representation of the world, holding the mirror up to nature. In fact, Meursault is not a believable human figure, the events of the novel are but dimly evoked and unconvincingly motivated, and the very existence of the text itself, as Meursault's first-person account of events, is never explained. In *The Stranger*, Camus makes almost no concessions to the conventional procedures of realism, constructing instead a kind of mythic tale of philosophic intent to dramatize an imaginary confrontation between man's basic nature as a simple, sensual being and his grandly narcissistic self-image as an intelligent being whose every gesture has transcendent significance. Read as a kind of

poetic allegory rather than as an exemplary tale of human conduct, *The Stranger* will be seen as a powerful depiction of man's painfully divided soul, at once joyous for the gift of life and miserable at the absence of any discernible purpose in that life and at the indifference of the surrounding universe. Viewed that way, *The Stranger* deserves its reputation as one of the great works of art of the first half of the twentieth century.

THE PLAGUE

The allegorical mode is given a much more detailed and realistically human foundation in Camus's next novel, *The Plague*, regarded by many critics as his masterpiece. This time, there is a concerted effort by Camus to create a strong sense of place in a real setting and to depict fully rounded and believable characters. With the vividness of concrete details and actual place-names, Camus takes the reader to the city of Oran, in Algeria—a city of which he had intimate personal knowledge, having lived there for an extended period—and describes the impact on that real place of an imaginary outbreak of bubonic plague. The reader shares the first frightening discovery of rats dying in the streets and apartment house hallways and experiences the spread of terror and panic as the first human victims of the plague appear in random locations around the city. Soon, the city is ordered closed, quarantined from the rest of the world, and the authorities try to mobilize the trapped population and lay down strict sanitation rules to try to limit the impact of a disease they know they cannot cure. The heart of the novel is the depiction of the various ways in which individuals react to the fear and isolation imposed by this sudden state of siege, in which the invading army is invisible. To convey the variety of responses to such an extreme and concentrated crisis in human affairs, Camus deliberately eschews the convenient device of the omniscient narrator, making the depiction of every event and scene an eyewitness account in some form: the spoken words of reports or dialogues, the written words of letters or private diaries, and, as the main device, the written record of the daily observations of the novel's main character, Dr. Rieux. Whereas, in *The Stranger*, first-person narration was primarily a device of characterization, used to portray an alien figure's disconcertingly remote and hollow personality, in *The Plague* it is a device of narrative realism, used to reduce devastatingly incomprehensible events to a human, hence believable, scale, by portraying the way these events are seen by a representative group of ordinary citizens.

The Plague differs from its predecessor not only technically but also thematically. Camus's inspiration for *The Plague* was no philosophical abstraction but a specific event of his own life: the frustration and despair he experienced during the war, when the aftermath of the Allied invasion of North Africa trapped his wife in Oran (while he was in the Resistance organization in the Massif Central) and cut off all communication between them. That experience started the fictional idea germinating in his mind, and a literary model—Daniel Defoe's *A Journal of the Plague Year* (1722)—gave the idea more concrete form. Central to the idea of *The Plague*, certainly, is the theme of man's encounter with death rather than the theme of man's interpretation of life, which dominates *The Stranger*. Indeed, with *The Plague*, Camus was returning to the preoccupation of his earliest work of fiction, *A Happy Death*, but with a major new emphasis. *The Plague* concerns not an individual's quest in relation to death but a collectivity's involuntary confrontation with it. In *The Plague*, death is depicted as a chance outgrowth of an indifferent nature which suddenly, and for no apparent reason, becomes an evil threat to man. Death in the form of a plague is unexpected, irrational—a manifestation of that absurdity, that radical absence of meaning in life which is a major underlying theme of *The Stranger*. In *The Plague*, however, Camus proposes the paradox that, when death is a manifestation of the absurd, it galvanizes something in man's spirit which enables him to join with others to fight against death and thus give meaning and purpose to his life. From evil may come happiness, this novel seems to suggest: It is a painful irony of the human condition that man often discovers his own capacity for courage and for fraternal affection—that is, for happiness—only if he is forced by the threat of evil to make the discovery. The hint of optimism in this paradoxical theme—

happiness is, after all, possible for some if the circumstances are dire enough—is, however, insufficient to offset the fundamental pessimism of *The Plague*. A glance at the fate of the main characters will make the basic bleakness of this work manifest.

At the center of the action is Bernard Rieux, a doctor who risks his life every day to lead the fight against the plague and who, more than anyone else in the novel, experiences the satisfaction and the joy of finding himself equal to a heroic task and feeling with others a fraternal bond engendered by their common struggle. Yet his satisfaction is brief and his joys few. He knows that he cannot cure victims of the plague and must suppress his sympathy for them if he is to be effective in palliating their suffering and in keeping them from infecting others. The result of this bind is that Rieux strikes his patients and their families as cold and indifferent; he ends up being hated by those he is trying to help. The fraternal bond with others who are trying to help develops in only a few instances, since most of his fellow citizens are too frightened or egocentric to join him in the effort. Moreover, where the bond does develop, it proves too tenuous to penetrate his natural isolation.

The limits of the fraternal bond are most graphically expressed by the moment in the novel when Rieux and Jean Tarrou (a traveler through whose journal part of the novel is related), seeing the first signs that the plague is receding, decide to go for a swim together, in celebration. The point is carefully made that, while each feels a sense of fraternity with the other as they swim in the same water, each is also conscious of being ultimately quite alone in the joy and freedom of moving serenely through the water and forgetting the plague for a short while. In spite of the shared emotion that unites them, each feels the swim to be predominantly a solitary experience. Finally, when the plague does end, Rieux finds himself strangely empty and alienated from the joyous crowds now once more filling the streets of Oran; the urgency of his task no longer exists to summon forth his courage. Indeed, because he has lost those dearest to him—his wife and Tarrou—he feels more alone than ever after the plague has gone. The other important characters fare no better than Rieux: Tarrou is killed by the plague; Joseph Grand suffers from it but recovers and resumes his self-imposed task of writing a novel, of which he has yet to complete the first sentence, because he has endlessly revised and recast it in a fruitless search for perfection; Rembart, a journalist who is trapped in Oran by the plague, leaves when it is over, but without having written anything about it, having found his profession inadequate to such an awesome task; and Cottard, who engages in black-market profiteering during the plague, goes crazy when the plague ends, shooting citizens at random until he is caught and killed by the police. There is little in this novel to nourish an optimistic outlook, except for the hesitant and tentative statement of Rieux, at the end of his chronicle, that amid the ravages of pestilence, one learns that "there are, in men, more things to admire than to despise."

The Plague is the longest, the most realistic, and artistically the most impressive of Camus's novels, offering a richly varied cast of characters and a coherent and riveting plot, bringing an integrated world memorably to life while stimulating the reader's capacity for moral reflection. In spite of its vivid realism, *The Plague* is no less mythical and allegorical in its impact than is *The Stranger*. When first published, *The Plague* was widely interpreted as a novel about the German Occupation and the French Resistance, with the plague symbolizing the evil presence of the Nazis. Since the 1940's, however, more universal themes and symbols have been discovered in the book, including the frighteningly random nature of evil and the perception that man's conquest of evil is never more than provisional, that the struggle will always have to be renewed. It has also been widely recognized that *The Plague* is, in significant degree, a profound meditation on the frustrating limits of human language both as a means of communication and as a means of representing the truth about human existence. The discovery of that theme has made *The Plague* the most modern of Camus's novels, the one with the most to say to future generations of Camus's readers.

For nearly a decade after the publication of *The Plague*, impeded by the consequences of fame, Camus struggled to find enough time and privacy to compose a new work of fiction and to complete philosophical and theatrical writings begun before he wrote *The Plague*. In the mid-1950's, he began to compose a group of short stories with the common theme of the condition of the exile, and it was one of those stories which he was suddenly inspired to expand into a short novel written in the form of a monologue and published in 1956 as *The Fall*.

THE FALL

The product of a troubled time in Camus's life, *The Fall* is a troubling work, full of brilliant invention, dazzling wordplay, and devastating satire, but so profoundly ironic and marked by so many abrupt shifts in tone as to leave the reader constantly off-balance and uncertain of the author's viewpoint or purpose. This difficulty in discerning the book's meaning is inherent in its basic premise, for the work records a stream of talk—actually one side of a dialogue—by a French man who haunts a sleazy bar in the harbor district of Amsterdam and who does not trouble to hide the fact that most of what he says, including his name, is invented. Because he is worldly and cultivated, his talk is fascinating and seizes the attention of his implied interlocutor (who is also, of course, the reader) with the same riveting force as Samuel Taylor Coleridge's Ancient Mariner. The name he gives himself is Jean-Baptiste Clamence, a name that evokes the biblical figure of the prophet John the Baptist as the voice crying in the wilderness (*vox clamantis in deserto*) and that coincides neatly with the occupation he claims to follow, also of his own invention: judge-penitent. When Clamence remarks to his interlocutor, near the end of his five-day monologue, "I know what you are thinking: it is very difficult to distinguish the true from the false in what I am telling you. I confess that you are right," the reader feels that Camus has suddenly made a personal intervention into the novel in order to warn the reader that he has been deliberately manipulated by Clamence's playacting and that he has every right to feel bewildered. Camus thus signals to the reader that the book's troubling impact has been calculated and deliberate from the start. Only in the closing pages of the novel does he clarify the purpose of Clamence's invented narrative and the meaning of his invented calling, but the explanation comes too late—deliberately so, for the reader can never rid himself of the doubts that Clamence's entire performance has been designed to raise questions concerning what is true and what is false, what is good and what is evil.

Clamence's "explanation" is, in fact, the most unsettling element in the book. He pointedly admits to his interlocutor that he has been penitently "confessing" his own sins to him in a carefully controlled pattern, only in order to induce his interlocutor to "confess" in his turn, thus enabling Clamence to play the role of judge. Clamence begins his "confession" by describing his successful career in Paris as a much-admired lawyer known for his defense of "widows and orphans"—that is, the helpless and disadvantaged of society. He had every reason to see himself as a man of virtue, he says, until he began to "hear" a woman's mocking laughter whenever he looked at himself in the mirror with those feelings of self-satisfaction. The mocking laughter reminded him that his lawyerly altruism was only a mask for selfishness and forced him to recall an incident he had tried to forget: Crossing a bridge over the Seine one night, he had seen a young woman throw herself into the water and had made no effort to rescue her or to get help, instead walking hurriedly away without looking back. The mocking laughter was thus his conscience taunting him with the suppressed memory of his guilt: The admired man of virtue was in reality a fraud, a sinner like everyone else.

Clamence goes on to explain that thereafter he had found it increasingly difficult to continue his career in Paris and live with his guilt. At the same time, he could not give up his need to feel morally superior to others. His solution to this private inner conflict, he then declares, was his brilliant invention of a new career for himself as a judge-penitent. He closed his Paris office and moved to the harbor section of Amsterdam—which, he notes, is in the center of the concentric circles of Amsterdam's canals, like the ninth circle of Dante's *Inferno*, and is, moreover, "the site of one of the greatest crimes of modern history," meaning the Nazi destruction of the entire Jewish community of Amsterdam. In these new surround-

ings, he not only could assuage his guilt by the feeling that he was in the ninth circle of Hell, where he belonged, but also could have access to the endless succession of tourists who gravitated to that spot, whom he could "help," in such propitious surroundings, to recognize their own guilt as well. His "help" consisted of a recital of his own sins, so arranged as to emphasize their universality, thus subtly prompting his listener to confess the same sins in turn. In this way, Clamence uses his perfected performance as a penitent in order to put himself in the deeply satisfying position of judge, hearing his listener's confession while basking in the warm glow of his own moral superiority. Because everyone, without exception, is a guilty sinner, says Clamence, he has solved the dilemma of how to live happily with his nagging guilt. The essential secret, he says, is to accuse oneself first—and of all seven cardinal sins—thereby earning the right to accuse everyone else.

Clamence's "solution," which concludes *The Fall*, is a burlesque of moral reasoning, underscoring the bitterness of the satire which is at the heart of this novel. Like Camus's other novels, *The Fall* is an exploration of man's moral nature and his passionate search for happiness in a world that is indifferent to such spiritual values, but unlike any of his other works of fiction, *The Fall* is both unrelievedly pessimistic and irreducibly ambiguous. In Clamence's confession, is Camus's intention to castigate himself for having taken his own fame too seriously and thus expiate his personal sin of pride? There were many critics who read the book that way when it appeared in 1956. Or is he using Clamence, rather, to avenge himself on his enemies, whom he thought too quick to adopt a tone of moral superiority in judging his position on the Algerian Civil War? Many other critics saw *The Fall* that way. Generations later, it seems reasonable to suggest that both interpretations have validity. *The Fall* is a comic masterpiece, remarkably parallel in its tone, its themes, and its ambiguity to the short story "Jonas," written about the same time—a story in which, everyone agrees, Camus attempted to come to terms with his artistic sterility and with the conflict he felt between public obligation and the need for privacy.

Camus's short story "Jonas" ends with a celebrated verbal ambiguity: The painter-hero of the story, after long meditation, translates his thought to canvas by means of a single word, but it is impossible to discern whether that word is "solitary" or "solidary." It is tempting to conclude, using that short story as analogue, that the ambiguity of *The Fall* is also deliberate and that Camus meant his work both as private confession and as public condemnation. Those two meanings, the one private and the other public, are surely intended to combine retrospectively in the reader's mind to form Camus's universal condemnation of man's moral bankruptcy. As the title is meant to suggest, *The Fall* is a modern parable about Original Sin and the Fall of Man.

There is reason to believe that the unrelenting pessimism of *The Fall* was not Camus's final word on humanity but was rather the expression of a temporary discouragement which he had almost succeeded in dispelling at the time of his death. In 1959, he was at work on a new novel, to be called "Le Premier Homme," the theme of which was to be a celebration of the formative experience of his Algerian youth. It seems clear that it would have turned out to offer another perspective, perhaps a less bleakly pessimistic one, on the one subject that, at bottom, always animated Camus's fiction: the enigma of man's struggle against the indifference of creation and his unquenchable thirst for moral significance in his life. Camus's unforgettable contribution to the ongoing dialogue inspired by that vast subject is embodied in the three great novels he managed to complete before his untimely death.

Murray Sachs

OTHER MAJOR WORKS

SHORT FICTION: *L'Exil et le royaume*, 1957 (*Exile and the Kingdom*, 1958).

PLAYS: *Caligula*, wr. 1938-1939, pb. 1944 (English translation, 1948); *Le Malentendu*, pr., pb. 1944 (*The Misunderstanding*, 1948); *L'État de siège*, pr., pb. 1948 (*State of Siege*, 1958); *Les Justes*, pr. 1949 (*The Just Assassins*, 1958); *Caligula and Three Other Plays*, 1958.

NONFICTION: *L'Envers et l'endroit*, 1937 ("The Wrong Side and the Right Side"); *Noces*, 1938 ("Nuptials"); *Le Mythe de Sisyphe*, 1942 (*The Myth of Sisyphus*, 1955); *L'Homme révolté*, 1951 (*The Rebel*, 1953); *L'Été*, 1954 ("Summer"); *Carnets: Mai 1935-février 1942*, 1962 (*Notebooks*, 1965); *Carnets: Janvier 1942-mars 1951*, 1964 (*Notebooks*, 1963); *Lyrical and Critical Essays*, 1968 (includes "The Wrong Side and the Right Side," "Nuptials," and "Summer").

BIBLIOGRAPHY

Bloom, Harold, ed. *Albert Camus*. New York: Chelsea House, 1989. Essays on *The Stranger*, *The Plague*, *The Fall*, the plays, and Camus's literary and political relationships. Includes introduction, chronology, and bibliography.

Brée, Germaine, ed. *Camus: A Collection of Critical Essays*. Englewood Cliffs, N.J.: Prentice Hall, 1962. Covers the whole range of Camus's life and work, with an excellent introduction, chronology, and bibliography.

Fitch, Brian T. *The Fall: A Matter of Guilt*. New York: Twayne, 1995. Divided into sections on literary and historical context and interpretations. A meticulous study of the novel's themes and characters, with detailed notes, chronology, and bibliography.

Kellman, Steven G., ed. *Approaches to Teaching Camus's "The Plague."* New York: The Modern Language Association of America, 1985. Part 1 concentrates on the history and background, and part 2 on different approaches to interpreting the novel. Biographical, critical, psychological, and philosophical readings are explored.

_____. *"The Plague": Fiction and Resistance.* New York: Twayne, 1993. Separated into sections on literary and historical context and on different readings of the novel. Separate chapters are devoted to major characters as well as to the mysterious narrator.

King, Adele, ed. *Camus's "L'Étranger": Fifty Years On*. New York: St. Martin's Press, 1992. Addresses the contexts and influences of the novel, its reception and influence on other writers, textual studies, and comparative studies. Contains a useful introduction but no bibliography.

Lottman, Herbert. *Albert Camus: A Life.* Garden City, N.Y.: Doubleday, 1979. A very detailed biography by one of the most important biographers of French literary figures.

McCarthy, Patrick. *Camus: A Critical Study of His Life and Work.* London: Hamish Hamilton, 1982. A meticulous attempt to reconstruct Camus through his childhood and early influences. McCarthy also covers every major phase of the life and work. Includes notes and short bibliography.

Rhein, Phillip. *Albert Camus.* New York: Twayne, 1969. Chapters on Camus's childhood, his understanding of the absurd, his career in the theater, his view of man and rebellion. Includes notes and bibliography. Still a useful, short introduction to the life and work.

Sprintzen, David. *Camus: A Critical Examination.* Philadelphia: Temple University Press, 1988. An early chapter delves into the biographical experience that informs Camus's work. Chapters on *The Stranger*, Camus's drama, his interpretation of social dislocation, society and rebellion, revolt and history, metaphysical rebellion, confrontations with modernity, and the search for a style of life. Includes notes and bibliography.

ELIAS CANETTI

Born: Ruse, Bulgaria; July 25, 1905
Died: Zurich, Switzerland; August 13, 1994

PRINCIPAL LONG FICTION

Die Blendung, 1935 (*Auto-da-Fé*, 1946; also known as *The Tower of Babel*)

OTHER LITERARY FORMS

Although he published only one work of fiction, Elias Canetti wrote a great deal of prose. His *magnum opus*, the product of decades of work, is *Masse und Macht* (1960; *Crowds and Power*, 1962), an ex-

tended essay in social psychology which is as unorthodox and provocative as it is brilliant. In an effort to present a sort of taxonomic typology of the mass mind, Canetti casts a wide net over all of human history. Historical, political, psychological, anthropological, philosophical, sociological, and cultural elements and insights are enlisted in an occasionally idiosyncratic search for the wellsprings of human behavior in general and the root causes of fascism in particular.

A much lighter work is *Der Ohrenzeuge* (1974; *Earwitness*, 1979), subtitled "Fifty Characters," a series of mordant characterizations of eccentric figures that exemplify the quirks and extremes inherent in the human personality. This collection includes thumbnail sketches of such specimens as "Der Papiersäufer" ("The Paper Drunkard"), "Der Demutsahne" ("The Humility-forebear"), "Die Verblümte" ("The Allusive Woman"), "Der Heroszupfer" ("The Hero-tugger"), "Der Maestroso" ("The Maestroso"), "Der Nimmermust" ("The Never-must"), "Der Tränenwärmer" ("The Tearwarmer"), "Die Tischtuchtolle" ("The Tablecloth-lunatic"), "Der Fehlredner" ("The Misspeaker"), "Der Tückenfänger" ("The Wilecatcher"), and "Die Archäokratin" ("The Archeocrat").

Canetti's aphoristic jottings from 1942 to 1972 have been collected in a volume entitled *Die Provinz des Menschen* (1973; *The Human Province*, 1978). *Die Stimmen von Marrakesch* (1968; *The Voices of Marrakesh*, 1978) is a profound travel book subtitled "A Record of a Visit." *Das Gewissen der Worte* (1975; *The Conscience of Words*, 1979) brings together Canetti's essays on philosophy, art, and literature. The perceptive literary critic is shown to good advantage in *Der andere Prozess: Kafkas Briefe an Felice* (1969; *Kafka's Other Trial*, 1974).

As a young man, Canetti came under the spell of the great Viennese satirist Karl Kraus, many of whose spellbinding readings he attended, and his dramatic works exemplify the Krausian concept of "acoustical masks," as he unsparingly sketches the linguistic (and, in a sense, moral) physiognomy of his characters on the basis of each person's individual, unmistakable speech pattern. *Hochzeit* (1932; *The Wedding*, 1984) presents a *danse macabre* of petit-bourgeois Viennese society motivated by cupidity and hypocrisy, with the collapse of a house coveted by those attending a wedding party, symbolizing the breakdown of this corrupt society. *Komödie der Eitelkeit* (1950; *Comedy of Vanity*, 1983) explores the genesis of a mass psychosis. A totalitarian government, having proscribed vanity, has all the mirrors, photos, and films burned. As vanity goes underground, distrust, dehumanization, and disaster ensue. *Die Befristeten* (1956; *The Numbered*, 1964; also known as *Life-Terms*) is, as it were, a primer of death. People carry their predetermined dates of death in capsules around their necks, to be opened eventually only by the "Capsulan." One man, Fünfzig (Mr. Fifty), finally rebels against this knowledge and breaks the taboo. The discovery that the capsules are empty replaces presumed security with fear of death.

Canetti also achieved considerable prominence as an autobiographer. The first volume of his memoirs, *Die gerettete Zunge: Geschichte einer Jugend* (*The Tongue Set Free: Remembrance of a European Childhood*, 1979), appeared in 1977. The title of the second volume, *Die Fackel im Ohr* (1980; *The Torch in My Ear*, 1982), reflects Canetti's indebtedness to Karl Kraus and his celebrated journal.

(The Nobel Foundation)

ACHIEVEMENTS

The award of the 1981 Nobel Prize to Elias Canetti for his multifaceted literary oeuvre caught the world by surprise and focused international attention on a seminal writer and thinker who had lived and worked in relative obscurity for decades. Canetti then became increasingly recognized as a representative of a distinguished Austrian literary tradition. The misleading statement of the *The New York Times* that Canetti was "the first Bulgarian writer" to achieve the distinction of a Nobel Prize was refuted by Canetti himself when he said that "like Karl Kraus and Nestroy, I am a Viennese writer." Even more suggestive is Canetti's statement that "the language of my mind will remain German—because I am a Jew."

BIOGRAPHY

Born July 25, 1905, in a Danube port city in northern Bulgaria as the oldest son of Mathilde and

Jacques Canetti, Elias Canetti had a polyglot and multicultural upbringing. As he details in the first volume of his autobiography, German was the fourth language he acquired—after Ladino (an archaic Spanish dialect spoken by Sephardic Jews that is also known as Spaniolic and Judezmo), Bulgarian, and English. In June, 1911, he was taken to England and enrolled in a Manchester school. Following the sudden death of his father, the family (consisting of his high-minded, strong-willed, and rather overbearing mother as well as his two younger brothers) settled in Vienna, but they spent some of the war years in Switzerland. After attending secondary school in Zurich and Frankfurt am Main, Canetti returned to Vienna and studied chemistry at the university from 1924 to 1929, taking a doctorate of philosophy. For a time, he lived in Berlin and worked as a freelance writer, translating books by Upton Sinclair. In February, 1934, Canetti married Veza Taubner-Calderón. His mother died in Paris in June, 1937, and that is where Canetti and his wife immigrated in November of the following year, later settling in London in January, 1939. While working on *Crowds and Power* and other writings, Canetti eked out a living as a freelance journalist and language teacher. After the death of his wife in May, 1963, Canetti spent some time with his brother Georges in Paris. In 1971, he married Hera Buschor and became the father of a daughter, Johanna, the following year. They settled in Zurich, with Canetti making periodic trips to London. He died in Zurich in 1994.

ANALYSIS

Elias Canetti's *Auto-da-Fé*, completed in 1931, is as impressive a first novel as was written in the twentieth century. It was originally intended to be the first of an eight-volume *comédie* (or *tragicomédie*) *humaine* of modern times, peopled by madmen of the type that were confined in the Steinhof, the insane asylum that Canetti could see from the window of his room while he was writing. It was to be an enormous fictional typology of the madness of the age, with each novel intended to present a different kind of monomaniac—among others, a religious fanatic, a truth fanatic, a technological maniac, a wastrel, an obsessive collector, and a bibliomaniac. Through such exemplary figures, Canetti wanted to turn a glaring spotlight on the contemporary world. It is thought that only one other novel in the projected series has been completed, a novel entitled "Der Todfeind" (not in the usual sense of "mortal enemy" but meaning "the enemy of death," which is a fair description of Canetti himself). Sketches may exist for other works of fiction, but after expressing his own alienation and frustration in his first book, Canetti apparently found the novel form wanting for his purposes and became increasingly interested in presenting his thoughts in nonfictional form, particularly in *Crowds and Power*.

AUTO-DA-FÉ

Canetti's working title for his novel was "Kant fängt Feuer" (Kant catches fire), but the author soon chose not to use the name of the famous German philosopher for his protagonist. He also rejected the name Brand as too obvious an evocation of the Holocaust motif, though he finally settled on the scarcely less evocative name Kien, which means "pinewood." Rembrandt's painting *The Blinding of Samson* appears to have suggested the somewhat ambiguous title of the novel (*Die Blendung* means "the blinding," with suggestions also of "dazzlement" and "deception").

The ascetic Peter Kien describes himself as a "library owner"; as reclusive as he is erudite, this renowned philologist and sinologist represents a "head without a world." He allows himself to get into the clutches of his scheming housekeeper, Therese, whose favorite item of apparel is a starched blue skirt (a garment worn by Canetti's far more humane real-life landlady). When Kien marries this mindless, avaricious, lustful, and generally evil creature, he ostensibly does so for the sake of his beloved books (and on the advice of Confucius, one of the savants with whom he communes).

Following his traumatic expulsion from the paradise of his enormous library, Kien embarks on a peculiar odyssey and descends to the lower depths of society, a "world without a head." Therese's work of degradation is continued and completed by the predatory chess-playing hunchback, Fischerle, and the philistine janitor, Benedikt Pfaff. Their cruelly exploitative stratagems, including the pawning of some of Kien's books at the Theresianum (a disguised version of the actual Dorotheum, Vienna's state-owned pawnshop and auction house), serve as a grotesque counterpoint to Kien's *idées fixes* and the progressive unhinging of his mind. Peter Kien's final act is an apocalyptic self-immolation amid his books to his own uncontrollable laughter—a "wedge driven into our consciousness."

Canetti's novel seems to have been written in the white heat of rage and hate. To that extent, it reflects the influence of his mentor, Kraus, who wrote: "Hatred must make a person productive; otherwise one might as well love." *Auto-da-Fé* may be read as a subtle political and social satire, an allegorical portrayal of a sick society, and a chilling adumbration of the crushing of the vulnerable "pure" intellect by the brutish "practical" forces of our time. Aside from the narrator, the only sane person in the book is a sweet child who appears at the very beginning. Even Kien's brother Georges, a Paris psychiatrist who comes to his demented brother's aid and seems to represent an oasis of rationality, finds insanity more interesting and worthwhile than sanity and may, paradoxically, abet the forces that push Kien over the edge. Despite the banal viciousness of the characters and the prevalence of violence in the book, *Auto-da-Fé* may be read as a great comic novel with many genuinely funny scenes and situations that give rise to that "thoughtful laughter" which George Meredith identified as the index of the comic spirit. In this typology of madness, however, any laughter is bound to be the sardonic rather than the liberating kind. Bertha Keveson-Hertz has properly identified "Swiftean satire, Dickensian humor, Proustian insulation, Joycean interiorization, and Poe's maelstrom nightmares" in Canetti's novel.

Claudio Magris has observed that

> the narrative of *Die Blendung* points ardently and yearningly to the missing life, to undiscoverable and suffocated love. It is the most total and shattering tragedy of the destruction of the self, the tragedy of individuality which, shortly before entering the dimensions of the crowd, exaggerates its particularity to the point of caricature and robs its existence of every passion, of every sensation. The most powerful and impressive motif of *Die Blendung* is the total, icy absence of all passions, pulsations, and stimuli; paranoia has removed any power of attraction from objects and does not know how to project the slightest libido onto them.

In his depictions of the range of elementary human instincts, Canetti somehow neglects the erotic sphere, but he does suggest that the urge to merge with the crowd implies a kind of sexual energy and interest.

Through Canetti's craftsmanship, the reader is drawn into the oppressive atmosphere of the book with a growing sense of discomfort. The *erlebte Rede*, or interior monologue, is an effective device by means of which the storyteller lets the reader get into the mind of each character. The narrative ambience contains many surreal touches, yet these grotesque elements somehow seem natural.

It is possible to read *Auto-da-Fé* as a sort of inversion of Dante's *The Divine Comedy:* Peter Kien's library is the Paradise; the city (of Vienna) is the Purgatory; the fire is the Inferno. Everything in the book moves in a magic circle of aberration; yet Canetti separates reality and absurdity, the real world and the hallucinatory world more consistently than does Kafka, in whose writings these spheres tend to blend into a "purer" entity. The author identifies with the limitations of his characters, and unlike many other novelists he makes no attempt to act as an omniscient narrator who restores order and sits in judgment. Canetti ascribes a peculiar role to madness: The aberrant becomes the rule and normality the exception as contrasts are leveled and personal qualities are impoverished. The blessing of originality has a price, and it is loneliness. The language of lunatics ought to unite them; instead, it creates a gulf between them, and soliloquy replaces discourse. At the Ideal Heaven café, frequented by Fischerle and other shady characters, there is a "geschlossene Masse," a closed company; the other characters live outside the crowd. Brother Georges judges the masses positively, whereas Peter Kien hates the masses as an incarnation of the primitive and the barbaric. The hypnotic attraction to fire is seen as one of the characteristics of the crowd, and in this regard (as in others, though not in political, historical, and other topical matters), Canetti drew on his real-life experiences. In July of 1927, he had witnessed the burning of the building of the Ministry of Justice on Vienna's Ringstrasse by a mob enraged by a jury's acquittal of some killers; the ensuing police riot claimed many innocent victims.

The disturbing figure of the scheming pimp and pander, Siegfried Fischer, known as Fischerle, has come in for some critical speculation. Might Canetti intend this petty criminal to represent the assimilated Jew in Austrian society, and is the cutting off of his hump (by a beggar) a symbolic adumbration of the bloody end of assimilation for Austrian Jewry? It is difficult, however, to accept such an interpretation of a character who is depicted as an anti-Semite's stereotype; in any case, the drama of Fischerle's life begins when he abandons the crowd and desires to become a chess champion in America, where his hunchback will somehow disappear. As for the vicious building superintendent, Pfaff—with huge fists and powerful feet—he is a recognizable Viennese type who was to see his day of fascist glory in Hitler's Austria. Georges seems to be a paragon of strength, worldliness, empathy, and sanity. He attempts to straighten out his brother's life and to act as a *deus ex machina*, but he fails to recognize Peter's true state of mind. The doctor finds the insane more interesting than the sane; for example, the patient called the "Gorilla" has access to levels of experience not available to the sane. Is insanity, Georges wonders, perhaps a higher form of existence? In his inner complexity, Georges may actually represent only a more sublime form of moral aberration, a metaphysical type of madness.

Kien may be regarded as a modern Don Quixote. Both characters may be pictured as middle-aged, tall, emaciated, storklike, sexless, and virtually disembodied in their unworldliness and rejection of bodily needs and functions. Therese, Pfaff, and Fischerle are the satellites that correspond to Sancho Panza. In both cases, there is an obsession with books, a consultation with them in times of need, and a readiness to do battle with their enemies. In Miguel de Cervantes, the absoluteness of literature is stressed; in Canetti, the absoluteness of scholarship has pride of place. Don Quixote reads the world in confirmation of books; Kien finds bliss in them and distress in the reality surrounding him. Don Quixote misinterprets reality; Kien negates it. Don Quixote has a catharsis and regains his good judgment before his idyllic or lyric death; Kien is vouchsafed no such grace: He piles his books into a mighty fortress before torching them, perishing with the treasures he has tried so hard to preserve. His flight into the flames is his only escape from his own isolation; death by fire is his deliverance, his expiation, and also an act of nemesis. In *Don Quixote de la Mancha* (1605, 1615), there is some real dialogue, but Kien's conversations, with the possible exception of some of those with his brother, create no human contacts. Certainly the split between the hero (or antihero) and the world has been a recurrent theme in world literature since Cervantes. In his only published work of fiction, Canetti

handled it with consummate skill, with awful prescience, and with soul-searing impact.

Harry Zohn

OTHER MAJOR WORKS

PLAYS: *Hochzeit*, pb. 1932 (*The Wedding*, 1984); *Komödie der Eitelkeit*, pb. 1950 (*Comedy of Vanity*, 1983); *Die Befristeten*, pb. 1956 (*The Numbered*, 1964; also known as *Life-Terms*); *Dramen*, pb. 1964 (collection of plays).

NONFICTION: *Fritz Wotruba*, 1955 (English translation, 1955); *Masse und Macht*, 1960 (*Crowds and Power*, 1962); *Aufzeichnungen 1942-1948*, 1965; *Die Stimmen von Marrakesch: Aufzeichnungen nach einer Reise*, 1967 (*The Voices of Marrakesh: A Record of a Visit*, 1978); *Der andere Prozess: Kafkas Briefe an Felice*, 1969 (*Kafka's Other Trial*, 1974); *Alle vergeudete Verehrung: Aufzeichnungen 1949-1960*, 1970; *Die gespaltene Zukunft*, 1972; *Macht und Überleben*, 1972; *Die Provinz des Menschen: Aufzeichnungen 1942-1972*, 1973 (*The Human Province*, 1978); *Der Ohrenzeuge: Fünfzig Charaktere*, 1974 (character sketches; *Earwitness: Fifty Characters*, 1979); *Das Gewissen der Worte*, 1975 (*The Conscience of Words*, 1979); *Der Beruf des Dichters*, 1976; *Die gerettete Zunge: Geschichte einer Jugend*, 1977 (*The Tongue Set Free: Remembrance of a European Childhood*, 1979); *Die Fackel im Ohr: Lebensgeschichte 1921-1931*, 1980 (*The Torch in My Ear*, 1982); *Das Augenspiel: Lebensgeschichte 1931-1937*, 1985 (*The Play of the Eyes*, 1986); *Das Geheimherz der Uhr: Aufzeichnungen 1973-1985*, 1987 (*The Secret Heart of the Clock: Notes, Aphorisms, Fragments 1973-1985*, 1989); *Die Fliegenpein: Aufzeichnungen*, 1992 (*The Agony of Flies: Notes and Notations*, 1994).

BIBLIOGRAPHY

Berman, Russell A., ed. *The Rise of the Modern German Novel: Crisis and Charisma*. Cambridge, Mass.: Harvard University Press, 1986. Situates Canetti's novel in the context of fiction contemporary with his time.

Daviau, Donald. *Major Figures of Contemporary Austrian Literature*. New York: Peter Lang, 1987.

Contains a very thorough study of Canetti's career by a seasoned scholar.

_____, ed. *Modern Austrian Literature* 16 (1983). This special Elias Canetti issue features several essays on *Auto-da-Fé*, some in English, some in German.

Falk, Thomas W. *Elias Canetti*. New York: Twayne, 1993. Contains a separate chapter on Canetti's novel as well as chapters on all his important book-length works. A chronology, notes, and annotated bibliography make this a very useful introductory study.

Hulse, Michael, ed. *Essays in Honor of Elias Canetti*. New York: Farrar, Straus & Giroux, 1987. Contains several essays on *Auto-da-Fé* and Canetti's other books. The lack of notes, introduction, or bibliography makes this work less useful than Falk's. Recommended for advanced students of Canetti.

Lawson, Richard A. *Understanding Elias Canetti*. Columbia: University of South Carolina Press, 1991. A short, succinct, introductory study, the best place to begin a study of Canetti's work.

Powe, B. W. *The Solitary Outlaw*. Toronto: Lester & Orpen Dennys, 1987. Explores Canetti's handling of language and of writing. Recommended for advanced students and scholars.

Sontag, Susan. *Under the Sign of Saturn*. New York: Farrar, Straus & Giroux, 1980. Contains what is still perhaps the best single essay in English on the range of Canetti's work.

KAREL ČAPEK

Born: Malé Svatoňovice, Bohemia, Austro-Hungarian Empire (now Czech Republic); January 9, 1890

Died: Prague, Czechoslovakia (now Czech Republic); December 25, 1938

PRINCIPAL LONG FICTION

Továrna na absolutno, 1922 (*The Absolute at Large*, 1927)

Krakatit, 1924 (English translation, 1925)
Hordubal, 1933 (English translation, 1934)
Povětroň, 1934 (*Meteor*, 1935)
Obyčejný život, 1934 (*An Ordinary Life*, 1936)
Válka s mloky, 1936 (*The War with the Newts*, 1937)
První parta, 1937 (*The First Rescue Party*, 1939)
Život a dílo skladatele Foltýna, 1939 (*The Cheat*, 1941)

OTHER LITERARY FORMS

Apart from long fiction, Karel Čapek authored many stories, travelogues, and plays. An important journalist, he published many of his *feuilletons*, as well as his conversations with T. G. Masaryk, then President of Czechoslovakia. He also published a book on philosophy, *Pragmatismus* (1918), and a book of literary criticism, *Kritika slov* (1920).

Čapek's collections of short stories include *Zářivé hlubiny* (1916; with Josef Čapek); *Boží muka* (1917); *Krakonošova zahrada* (1918); *Trapné povídky* (1921; *Money and Other Stories*, 1929); *Povídky z jedné kapsy and Povídky z druhé kapsy* (1929; *Tales from Two Pockets*, 1932); *Devatero pohádek* (1931; *Fairy Tales*, 1933); and *Kniha apokryfů* (1946; *Apocryphal Stories*, 1949). Among his most important plays are *R.U.R.* (1921; with Josef Čapek; English translation, 1923); *Ze života hmyzu* (1920; with Josef Čapek; *The Insect Play*, 1923); *Věc Makropulos*, 1920 (*The Macropulos Secret*, 1925); *Bílá nemoc* (1937; *Power and Glory*, 1938); and *Matka*, 1938 (*The Mother*, 1939).

ACHIEVEMENTS

Čapek is among the best-known modern Czech writers. He became prominent between the two world wars and was recognized by and acquainted with such eminent figures as George Bernard Shaw, H. G. Wells, G. K. Chesterton, and Jules Romains. Čapek's international reputation earned for him the presidency of the Czechoslovak P.E.N. Club, and he was suggested for the post of the president of the International P.E.N. Club, an honor which he declined. Though he was equally versatile in fiction and drama, his fame abroad rests mostly on his science-fiction play *R.U.R.*, written in collaboration with his brother

Josef, which introduced into the world vocabulary the Czech word *robot*, a neologism derived from the Czech *robota*, meaning forced labor.

Despite Čapek's lifelong interest in science and its destructive potential, examined in such novels as *The Absolute at Large* and *Krakatit*, and despite the worldwide fame that such science fantasies brought him, he is remembered in Czechoslovakia as a dedicated humanist, a spokesman for the tolerance, pragmatism, and pluralism best manifested in the philosophy of relativism which his works so creatively demonstrate. He was one of the strongest voices of his time against totalitarianism, be it fascist or communist.

Čapek's work is deeply philosophical, but in a manner that is accessible to a wide readership. He managed to achieve this with the help of a chatty, almost pedestrian style informed by a genuine belief in the reasonable man, a man open to a rational argu-

(Archive Photos)

ment when all else fails. Hence Čapek's humanism; hence, also, his disappointment when, after the infamous appeasement of 1938, he had to acknowledge that the very paragons of the democratic ideal and of Western culture, England and France, had sold out his country to the Nazis.

Such concerns of Čapek as the conflict between man's scientific achievements and the very survival of the human race—a conflict illustrated by the fight between the robots and human beings in *R.U.R.*—are not merely alive today but have become more and more pressing as the world is becoming increasingly aware of the threat of nuclear holocaust. Čapek was among the first to see the dangerous potential of man's creative ability, not because he was particularly gifted in science, but because he was quite realistic, approaching the tendencies of his time with the far-seeing and far-reaching attitude of one whose relativism was tempered by pessimism derived from his awareness of the past, the tradition from which the imperfect-but-perfectible man departed.

An urbane wit, a certain intimacy with the reader, deft characterization, and concise expression are the hallmarks of Čapek's style, heightening the impact of his fictional treatment of profound issues.

BIOGRAPHY

The youngest child of a country doctor, Karel Čapek was born in 1890 in Bohemia, then still a part of the Austro-Hungarian Empire. A weak and sickly boy, Čapek was pampered by his mother and protected by his older brother, Josef; they, together with his maternal grandmother, inspired him with a love for literature. Čapek and his brother Josef prepared themselves for a literary vocation by their prodigious reading in many foreign literatures; among Čapek's juvenilia are some verses influenced by Symbolism and the Decadents—French and Czech. Josef was to collaborate with Karel on some of his most celebrated successes, including *R.U.R.*, but he was primarily a gifted artist, illustrator, and designer who gradually established himself as such, leaving Čapek to write alone, though never really drifting spiritually, or even physically, far away.

A brilliant student, Čapek enrolled at Charles

University in Prague, though two stints took him to the University of Berlin and the University of Paris. In 1915, Čapek took his doctorate, having defended his dissertation on objective methods in aesthetics. The next year saw the publication of the short-story collection *Zářivé hlubiny*, written with Josef. This genre was particularly suited to Čapek's talents, and throughout his life he continued to write short stories: philosophical, mystical, detective, and apocryphal. Parody and satire, down to the political lampoon, are not rare among them; they seem to flow naturally from the day-to-day concerns of a journalist sharply reacting to the crises and momentous events of his time.

The first such event was the establishment of the Czechoslovak Republic in 1918, at which time Čapek worked for a National Democrat paper, switching in 1921 to the more liberal *Lindové noviny*, where he stayed to the end of his life. Čapek's youth and his middle age parallel the youth and growing pains of his country's first Republic, right down to its (and his) death in 1938. Thus, Čapek is the literary embodiment of the principles of this Republic, led by a philosopher-president, Masaryk; among these principles were a distrust of radical solutions, an accent on the small work on a human scale, and a faith in the goodwill of people. In this respect, one can consider Čapek an unofficial cultural ambassador to the world at large.

Čapek was not indifferent to the world: A cosmopolitan spirit, he was drawn toward England in particular, and he traveled widely, reporting on his travels in books on England, Holland, Italy, Spain, and Scandinavia. Indeed, he was a quintessential European, protesting the deteriorating situation in Europe before the war which he did not live to witness but the coming of which he foresaw only too clearly. This prescience is particularly evident in his novel *The War with the Newts*, a thinly disguised presentiment of the Orwellian battle of totalitarian superpowers that left Eastern Europe, after years of Nazi occupation, in the stranglehold of the Soviet Union.

Oddly enough, the fact that a Czech writer became known throughout the world did not result in adulation of Čapek by Czech readers and critics. On the contrary, it inspired jealous critical comments to the effect that Čapek in his unusual works was pandering to foreign tastes. In retrospect, this charge seems particularly unfair. Another oddity is the fact that Čapek abandoned the theater after the worldwide success of *R.U.R.* and *The Insect Play*, chiefly producing short stories until his greatest triumph, the trilogy of philosophical novels *Hordubal, Meteor,* and *An Ordinary Life*. When, in 1937, he returned to the theater with *Power and Glory*, followed in 1938 by *The Mother*, it was to appeal to the conscience of the world with two timely plays concerned with the catastrophe prepared by Nazism. The plays were designed to counter the spirit of pacifism and appeasement then sweeping Europe; Čapek hoped to salvage Czechoslovakia, destined to be given to the Nazis as a peace offering.

Čapek's last work of great importance was *The Cheat*, written after the tragedy of Munich. Čapek mourned the death of his Republic and yet inspired his compatriots not to despair. *The Cheat* breaks with the relativist philosophy common to all of his works: The cheat is a cheat, a fake, a swindler and not a composer, and the novel's many vantage points only underscore this judgment. Death overtook Čapek while he was writing the conclusion of the novel, on Christmas Day, 1938; for political reasons, his grateful readers were not permitted to say good-bye to him in a public ceremony. He was survived by Olga Scheinpflugová, an actress and writer, his companion and wife.

Though Čapek's life was comfortable in material terms, he was afflicted with calcification of the spine, a painful condition that made full enjoyment of those comforts impossible; it also postponed his marriage to only a few years before his death. This physical suffering was accompanied by a spiritual search. For years, as the testimony of his literary works shows, he was content with pragmatism and relativism, though he was not an ethical relativist. Only toward the end of his life, as witness his last novel, did he embrace the idea that, often, people are what they seem, definitely and irrevocably: They are fully responsible for their actions.

Never does Čapek complain or rant against destiny: There is a sunny and humorous side to his work that balances the dark visions. Perhaps his excellence in life and art is explained by his personal heroism in alchemizing his suffering into a quest for a meaningful life.

ANALYSIS

Karel Čapek was a philosophical writer *par excellence*, regardless of the genre that he employed in a given work, but the form of long fiction in particular afforded him the amplitude to express complicated philosophical ideas. Thus, his greatest achievement is the trilogy consisting of *Hordubal, Meteor*, and *An Ordinary Life*. These three novels preserve the fruit of Čapek's life's work: the searchings and findings of his many short stories, plays, and newspaper columns, as well as his lifelong preoccupation with the philosophy of pragmatism and relativism.

While the trilogy is a complex and at the same time harmonious statement of Čapek's philosophy, his last novel, *The Cheat*, though shorter than either of the three novels of the trilogy, is important for representing a sharp and shocking departure from the trilogy's philosophy. It represents a further development of Čapek's philosophical search.

HORDUBAL

Hordubal is based on a newspaper story of a crime that took place in the most backward region of prewar Czechoslovakia, the Transcarpathian Ukraine. Juraj Hordubal, an unsophisticated but very sensitive and even saintly peasant, returns from the United States, where he worked and made some money, to his wife Polana and daughter Hafia. He is unaware that in his absence, Polana has fallen in love with Stefan Manya, a Hungarian hired hand. To disguise this affair, Polana forces Manya to become engaged to the eleven-year-old Hafia. When this ruse does not work, the lovers kill Hordubal with a long needle. An investigation uncovers the crime and identifies the criminals, who are caught and punished.

Appropriating the bare facts of the newspaper report with minimal modifications, Čapek invests this simple tale of passion with philosophical depth, first by making Juraj Hordubal a rather sensitive man who

is aware of the changed circumstances upon his return home. The reader is painfully aware of this when the author lets us follow Hordubal's thoughts in beautifully stylized, lyric passages of almost saintly insight and renunciation of violence, leading to the acceptance of his death. The tension develops on several levels simultaneously.

The first level is the *crime passionnelle*, the road which introduces us to the contrasting figures of Hordubal and Manya. A deeper level is attained when the reader perceives the cultural-ethnic contrast: Hordubal, the sedentary agricultural type, is opposed to the Hungarian Manya, the nomadic, violent type. Finally, there is the level on which the tension is between subjective reality, the reality of a given character who sees the world his own way, and objective reality. The conclusion, however, undercuts any confident faith in the existence of objective reality. Hordubal is seriously ill when he is murdered, so that a question arises whether the needle of the killer entered his heart before or after his death; if after, there was no murder.

The problem of the interpretation of even simple phenomena is brought to a head in the confrontation between two irreconcilable types of criminal investigations, based on different sets of assumptions and interpretations of events. In the conflict between the young policeman and his seasoned colleague, the deceptively simple case grows more and more complicated. In a plot twist that stresses the evanescent nature of man's certainties, the key evidence, Juraj Hordubal's heart, is lost in transport, condemning those involved in the investigation to eternal incertitude. The novel shakes the certitudes established in the mystery genre, suggesting that mutually exclusive interpretations are not only possible but also inevitable. More to the point, with the death of Hordubal, the protagonist's internal monologue ceases; the reader no longer sees Hordubal from inside. What the others think about Hordubal is widely off the mark.

METEOR

If the truth is relative and hopelessly compromised by the very fact that it is being approached by different people, the second novel of the trilogy reverses the procedure and asks if different people might not discover the truth on the basis of sharing with one another the human condition and thus having very much in common: first the difference, then the commonality. The second novel, *Meteor*, approaches this further elaboration of Čapek's philosophical quest in an original manner.

Čapek uses three narrators who speculate about the identity of a man fatally wounded in a plane crash and brought to a hospital as "patient X." The three narrators, including a Sister of Mercy, a clairvoyant, and a writer, try to reconstruct his life and the reason for his flight.

The first narrator, the Sister, sees X as a young man who runs away from home unaware of the real meaning of love and responsibility. After some peregrinations, he decides to return home, only to crash and die in the process.

The clairvoyant sees X as a talented chemist who discovered important new formulas but lacked the patience to see his experiments through and develop them commercially. When he finds that his experiments were founded on a sound basis, he decides to return and claim the discoveries as his own.

The writer sees the patient as a victim of amnesia who falls in love with a Cuban girl but is unable to live without memory. When his suffering triggers the recovery of his past, the man flies home to lay claim to his position.

All three accounts differ from one another in approach and in substance, yet each of them identifies an important facet of the victim and provides an insight into the character of the individual narrator. Čapek thus raises the question of self-discovery, the perennial identity problem: What happens when X and the observer are one and the same person? The third novel of the trilogy, *An Ordinary Life*, provides the answer.

An Ordinary Life

A retired bureaucrat, a self-confessed "ordinary man," decides to write the story of his own life. Looking back, he concludes that he lived an ordinary life governed only by habit and chance; it seems repetitious and predictable to him. There are, however, a few incidents that do not fit this summary generalization of his life, and the more he thinks about them, the more fully he understands that right within his ordinary life, there is a multitude of lives: He as a person is not an individuality but a plurality. He, like a microcosm, mirrors the macrocosm of society. Does he have a stable point of view, or does it too change with each different personality as he comes to adopt it? This is not a case of a pathological disorder; the protagonist is a normal official who, before he settled down to his ways, explored radically different lifestyles. Like all people, he bears within him the potential for many selves, never fully realized.

Thus, the tension between subjective and objective reality that animates *Hordubal* collapses in *An Ordinary Life*, which proposes that even that which is considered a subjective reality (the only accessible one, since the objective escapes forever) is itself a plurality.

As an experiment, as individual novels, and as a philosophical trilogy, these three novels are brilliant. What is difficult to communicate beyond the pale outlines and philosophical underpinnings of these works is their distinctive tone, their often lyric air. This atmosphere of numinous twilight, so difficult to communicate, bathes the novels in an unearthly light and adds to them a certain air of beauty. It comes as a surprise, then, that Čapek's last work, *The Cheat*, makes a departure from the finished whole of the trilogy on philosophical grounds.

The Cheat

The trilogy was the culmination of Čapek's work; the relativist philosophy enshrined within it is the summation of findings and beliefs that, for better or worse, animated Čapek's entire oeuvre. *The Cheat* continues with the insights gained in the trilogy—for example, the method of multiple narration is preserved. The several narratives, nine in all, gradually fill out the picture of the fake artist Foltýn, the would-be composer. These multiple narratives, however, do not yield a relativistic perspective: The individual accounts never contradict one another; rather, they gradually illuminate Foltýn and answer some of the questions that the various narrators have raised. The collective finding is damning, and yet there is something admirable in Foltýn: His obsessive love of art saves him from utter condemnation. In his attempt to express the impossible, Foltýn is like every artist; every artist has a little Foltýn in him. It is only fitting, given Čapek's sense of balance, that, after providing in his trilogy examples of the power of art to do good, to express the truth, he should point to the capacity of art to profess evil. Thus, he embraced the totality of the world that his suffering enabled him to know intimately.

Peter Petro

OTHER MAJOR WORKS

SHORT FICTION: *Zářivé hlubiny*, 1916 (with Josef Čapek); *Boží muka*, 1917; *Krakonošova zahrada*, 1918; *Trapné povídky*, 1921 (*Money and Other Stories*, 1929); *Povídky z jedné kapsy* and *Povídky z druhé kapsy*, 1929 (*Tales from Two Pockets*, 1932); *Devatero pohádek*, 1931 (*Fairy Tales*, 1933); *Kniha apokryfů*, 1946 (*Apocryphal Stories*, 1949).

DRAMA: *Lásky hra osudná*, wr. 1910, pr. 1930 (with Josef Čapek); *Loupezník*, pr. 1920 (*The Robber*, 1931); *Ze života hmyzu*, pb. 1920 (with Josef Čapek; *The Insect Play*, 1923); *Věc Makropulos*, pb. 1920 (*The Macropulos Secret*, 1925); *R.U.R.: Rossum's Universal Robots*, pr. 1921 (with Josef Čapek; English translation, 1923); *Adam Stvořitel*, pb. 1927 (with Josef Čapek; *Adam the Creator*, 1929); *Bílá nemoc*, pr. 1937 (*Power and Glory*, 1938); *Matka*, pr. 1938 (*The Mother*, 1939).

NONFICTION: *Pragmatismus*, 1918; *Kritika slov*, 1920; *O nejbližších vecech*, 1920 (*Intimate Things*, 1935); *Musaion*, 1920-1921; *Italské listy*, 1923 (*Letters from Italy*, 1929); *Anglické listy*, 1924 (*Letters from England*, 1925); *Hovory s T. G. Masarykem*, 1928-1935 (3 volumes; *President Masaryk Tells His Story*, 1934; also as *Masaryk on Thought and Life*, 1938); *Zahradníkův rok*, 1929 (*The Gardener's Year*, 1931); *Výlet do Španěl*, 1930 (*Letters from Spain*, 1931); *Marsyas*, 1931 (*In Praise of Newspapers*, 1951); *O věcech obecných: Čili, Zóon politikon*, 1932; *Obrázky z Holandska*, 1932 (*Letters from Holland*, 1933); *Dášeňka*, 1933 (*Dashenka*, 1940); *Cesta na sever*, 1936 (*Travels in the North*, 1939); *Měl jsem psa a kočku*, 1939 (*I Had a Dog and a Cat*, 1940);

Obrázky z domova, 1953; *Veci kolemnás*, 1954; *Poznámky o tvorbě*, 1959; *Viktor Dyk-S. K. Neumannbratří Č.: Korespondence z let 1905-1918*, 1962.

TRANSLATION: *Francouzská poesie nové doby*, 1920 (of French poetry).

BIBLIOGRAPHY

Bradbrook, Bohuslava R. *Karel Čapek: In Pursuit of Truth, Tolerance, and Trust*. Portland, Oreg.: Sussex Academic Press, 1998. Chapters on Čapek's biography, early writings, career as dramatist, novels, short stories, fairy tales, essays, biographies, and journalism. The detailed notes and bibliography make this a comprehensive guide to Čapek's life and career.

Dolezel, Lubomir. *Narrative Modes in Czech Literature*. Toronto: University of Toronto Press, 1973. Advanced students should consult "Karel Čapek and Vladislav Vančura: An Essay in Comparative Stylistics." Includes a bibliography.

Kussi, Peter, ed. *Toward the Radical Center: A Karel Čapek Reader*. Highland Park, Mich.: Catbird Press, 1990. Kussi's introduction provides an excellent short overview of Čapek's career. There is also a chronology and helpful list of English translations.

Makin, Michael, and Jindrich Toman, eds. *On Karel Čapek*. Ann Arbor: Michigan Slavic Publications, 1992. Essays on Čapek as a modern storyteller, on his versions of dystopia, his early work, his short stories, and his reception in America. No bibliography or introduction, making this a less-than-ideal work for beginning students.

Schubert, Peter Z. *The Narratives of Čapek and Cexov: A Typological Comparison of the Authors' World Views*. Bethesda, Md.: International Scholars Publications, 1997. Although this is a somewhat difficult work for beginning students, it proves valuable with its discussion of the themes of freedom, lack of communication, justice, and truth. There is also a separate section discussing critical views of Čapek and of his worldview. The comprehensive bibliography alone makes this a volume well worth consulting.